# RELIGIOUS FREEDOM AND THE SUPREME COURT

# Religious Freedom and the Supreme Court

## Ronald B. Flowers

John F. Weatherly Emeritus Professor of Religion
Texas Christian University

## Melissa Rogers

Visiting Professor of Religion and Public Policy and
Director, Center for Religion and Public Affairs
Wake Forest University Divinity School

## Steven K. Green

Professor of Law and Director,
Center for Religion, Law and Democracy
Willamette University

BAYLOR UNIVERSITY PRESS

*Book Design* by Ellen Condict
*Cover Design* by Blue Farm Graphic Design


Library of Congress Cataloging-in-Publication Data

Flowers, Ronald B. (Ronald Bruce), 1935-
Religious freedom and the Supreme Court / Ronald B. Flowers, Melissa Rogers, Steven K. Green. -- 1st ed.
p. cm.
Includes bibliographical references and index.
ISBN 978-1-60258-160-9 (pbk. : alk. paper)
1. Freedom of religion--United States. 2. United States. Supreme Court.
I. Rogers, Melissa. II. Green, Steven K. (Steven Keith), 1955- III. Title.

KF4783.F598 2008
342.7308'52--dc22
2008025618

THE AUTHORS DEDICATE THIS BOOK TO THE
LIFE AND MEMORY OF ROBERT T. MILLER,
CONSTITUTIONAL SCHOLAR, MASTER TEACHER,
AND BAPTIST LEADER.

# TABLE OF CONTENTS

## APPENDICES

# PART I

# INTRODUCTION

## CHAPTER I

# THE IMPACT OF THE U.S. SUPREME COURT ON AMERICAN RELIGIOUS FREEDOM

Why study the development of religious freedom in America through the medium of the United States Supreme Court? Surely, there are many approaches to understanding the forces that have contributed to religious liberty, plurality and equality in the United States. Religious freedom can be studied from a theological perspective, by taking a historical, political, or sociological approach, or by even applying an economic model. All of these various approaches have merit; however, when people commonly speak about issues of religious liberty and the appropriate relationship between religious and governmental institutions, the discussion usually leads to a legal question: what has the Supreme Court said about the matter?

No other institution in America, governmental or private sector, has had greater impact on the development of religious freedom and the relationship between the church and the state than the U.S. Supreme Court. The Supreme Court, as the highest judicial authority in the nation and final arbiter of the meaning of the United States Constitution, defines our legal rights, including those touching on religious matters. As Justice Robert Jackson said of the United States Supreme Court in 1953: "We are not final because we are infallible, but we are infallible only because we are final."[1] The Court is the ultimate decision-maker, for example, on what it means to have freedom of speech, association and religion, to be free from cruel and unusual punishment and what is required of the government in order to ensure that each citizen has equal protection of the laws.

Religion is expressly mentioned in two places in the Constitution: the Establishment and Free Exercise Clauses of the First Amendment;[2] and the "no religious test for public office-holding" clause contained in Article VI, clause 3.[3] The Court's decisions interpreting these clauses, even though directed at resolving legal conflicts between the litigants in the specific cases before it, often produce results that affect the lives of all Americans.

At times, the Court's decisions have aligned with or reflected dominant cultural attitudes. For example, the Court's approval of congressional efforts to eradicate Mormon polygamy during the nineteenth century echoed popular disdain for that religiously based practice. In other instances, the high court has through its decisions led American law and culture in seemingly new directions. Consider the reaction both in Congress and the general public to the 1962 and 1963 decisions outlawing school-sponsored prayer and Bible reading in the nation's public schools. Critics severely chastised the high court and introduced legislation to amend the Constitution to permit the reintroduction of such religious exercises in the public schools. As with school desegregation in the 1950s and abortion rights in the 1970s, the Court's decisions regarding church and state—whether it has been to strike the posting of the Ten Commandments in public school classrooms or to uphold the right to animal sacrifices—have often been controversial. But the Court's holdings have done more than resolve legal disputes or produce headlines and interesting dinner conversation; they have directly impacted the way people express themselves religiously on a daily basis and shaped our understanding of what it means to live in a democracy with substantial religious diversity.

Because federal judges, including Supreme Court justices, are not elected for limited terms but appointed for lifetime tenure (assuming good behavior), they are less subject to pressures from the popular majority. This insulation from the will of the majority and independence from the political process serve a particularly important function in the Court's consideration of rights enumerated in the Bill of Rights. The Bill of Rights is a counter-majoritarian document, meaning it protects certain individual rights from challenge by any political majority. As Justice Jackson said in the 1943 case of *West Virginia St. Bd. of Ed. v. Barnette*:

> The very purpose of a Bill of Rights was to withdraw certain subjects from the vicissitudes of political controversy, to place them beyond the reach of majorities and officials and to establish them as legal principles to be applied by the courts. One's right to life, liberty, and property, to free speech, a free press, freedom of worship and assembly, and other fundamental rights may not be submitted to vote; they depend on the outcome of no elections.[4]

As that branch of the government most insulated from the will of the majority, the judicial branch, most prominently the Supreme Court, is well-suited to protect these rights. Of course, justices are not immune from political pressures—they are appointed by elected officials and confirmed by them; they are concerned about the way in which their decisions are received by the public; and they have personal political opinions. But their comparative insulation from political pressures makes it more likely that they will be able to take politically unpopular stands if they believe the Constitution or other law requires them to do so. As mentioned, the Court's desegregation ruling in the *Brown v. Board of Education* decision was met with strong popular disapproval, as were its decisions involving school-sponsored prayer and Bible readings. These decisions would not have been made by elected officials at the time they were handed down by the Court. Over time, however, the principles that these rulings represent have gained significant popular approval.

Thus the Supreme Court has been a (or the) leading catalyst in the development of religious freedom in America. Before that contribution can be explored or understood, however, it is important to consider the role of the Supreme Court in our constitutional system and in society.

### Understanding the Supreme Court

To appreciate the impact the Supreme Court has had on religious freedom in America, it is important to understand the organization, structure, and role of the high court in our legal system. As its name suggests, the Supreme Court is the highest court in the federal judicial system. The Court serves as the apex of the third branch of our system of divided government that the framers purposefully designed to disburse power, ensure account-ability, and protect liberty. Similar to the executive branch, with the president at its head and the various federal departments and agencies serving under its authority, the Supreme Court hears appeals from lower federal appellate and trial courts, the latter called district courts. Currently, the nation is divided into 94 judicial districts and 11 appellate circuits. Each intermediate appeals court hears cases from the district courts within its circuit, while a 12th Federal Circuit Court hears appeals from specialty courts, such as the Court of Claims. In most instances, the courts of appeals are the final stages of review for contro-versies arising in federal court—the Supreme Court hears very few cases.

Moreover, the Court has near absolute discretion over what appeals it will hear. As a result, it is generally inaccurate to say that cases are "appealed" to the Supreme Court (in actuality, very few matters can be appealed to the Court as a matter of right); instead, the Court chooses what cases to hear under a discretionary procedure called a "writ of certiorari." (For the purposes of this discussion, we will use the term "appeal" in its generic sense.) In its own rules, the Supreme Court states, "[a] petition for a writ of certiorari will be granted only for compelling reasons."[5] As Justice Ruth Bader Ginsburg has put it, "[o]ur principal job, as we see it, is to keep federal law fairly uniform—to resolve splits that arise among federal or state tribunals over the meaning of a federal legislative, executive or constitutional prescription."[6] Indeed, about 70 percent of the cases that the Court accepts involve splits of authority among federal appellate courts or the highest state courts of vari-ous states.[7] Because the Supreme Court can hear only a limited number of controversies every year and denies review in the vast majority of cases, it is inaccurate to assign any meaning to a "denial of cert." In particular, it is incorrect to say that the Court has affirmed the ruling of the court below when it has only refused to hear the case.

Interestingly, only the Supreme Court is specifically provided for in the Constitu-tion. Article III authorizes Congress to create "inferior" courts and to determine many of the controversies the federal courts hear (called "subject-matter" jurisdiction). As a result, Congress could try—as some members did unsuccessfully in the 1980s—to remove the Court's authority to hear particular controversies over issues such as school prayer. The removal of an entire constitutional subject from federal judicial review—such as the au-thority to adjudicate school prayer cases—would raise serious separation of powers issues because it is ultimately up to the courts to determine the meaning of the Constitution.[8] Congress also determines the number and composition of the lower federal courts and even the number of justices on the Supreme Court (which has varied from 3 to 10 justices throughout American history).

The Supreme Court also may hear cases that have originated in the various state court systems. As with the federal system, state judiciaries are usually divided into levels of trial and appellate courts. Most state judiciaries are more extensive than the federal system— a state may have dozens of state trial courts but only one federal district court sitting within its boundaries—a fact that reflects the design of our national-state system of dual sovereignty under which states exercise plenary authority over most legal matters. Each state has its own constitution, all of which contain one or more provisions similar to the First Amendment. In fact, state constitutional provisions regarding religious liberty are commonly more extensive than the First Amendment's religion clauses. For example, the Washington state constitution contains four provisions affecting religious interests: Article

I, section 11; Article IX, sections 2 and 4; and Article XXVI. The primary provision, Article I, section 11 provides in pertinent part:

> Absolute freedom of conscience in all matters of religious sentiment, belief and worship, shall be guaranteed to every individual, and no one shall be molested or disturbed in person or property on account of religion; but the liberty of conscience hereby secured shall not be so construed as to excuse acts of licentiousness or justify practices inconsistent with the peace and safety of the state. No public money or property shall be appropriated for or applied to any religious worship, exercise or instruction, or the support of any religious establishment. . . .

As is evident, this state provision is much more detailed than the simple language of the First Amendment which directs that "Congress shall make no law respecting an establishment of religion, or prohibiting the free exercise thereof; . . ." The Washington Constitution is not unique, as a majority of state constitutions contain similarly broad language.

Given these differences between the federal constitution and various state constitutions, two related questions arise: do these more extensive state constitutional provisions provide additional protections or rights beyond those afforded under the First Amendment and, if so, who has the ultimate say on the meaning of such language, the federal or state courts? The short answer is that state constitutions may provide greater—but not lesser—protection than is guaranteed under the federal constitution and that state supreme courts have the final say on interpreting their respective constitutional provisions. For example, in 1986 the U.S. Supreme Court ruled unanimously that the federal Establishment Clause would not be violated if a college student used his Washington state scholarship to attend a religious college (see *Witters v. Washington Department of Services for the Blind*, in chapter 12). After so ruling, the Court remanded the case back to the Washington courts to determine whether the scholarship would violate Article I, section 11 of the Washington Constitution. In 1989, the Washington Supreme Court ruled that it would, effectively barring the scholarship based on the state constitution's stricter "no-aid" provision which provides greater protection from religious establishments (for a fuller discussion, see the materials accompanying *Locke v. Davey* and the controversy over state Blaine Amendments contained in chapter 12). The U.S. Supreme Court declined to review that latter holding, even though it had earlier held that such aid would be permissible under the federal Establishment Clause. In essence, unless an interpretation of a state constitutional provision conflicts with a right guaranteed under the U.S. Constitution, the U.S. Supreme Court cannot review the decisions of state supreme courts interpreting their own religious liberty provisions.

How then do holdings from state courts make their way to the U.S. Supreme Court? Originally, the federal and state constitutions were viewed as distinct instruments, with the former governing actions of the national government and the latter controlling matters at the state levels. In fact, it is widely accepted that the federal Bill of Rights was enacted to alleviate fears of the state governments that the U.S. Constitution would give the national government authority to invade state powers and infringe individual rights. State constitutions were generally viewed as the guardians of individual liberties (although state bills of rights were rarely enforced rigorously). Early in the nineteenth century, the U.S. Supreme Court ruled that the provisions (and protections) of the federal Bill of Rights did not restrict actions of state officials.[9] In essence, the First Amendment only governed actions of

the national government. Following the Civil War, however, Congress enacted the Fourteenth Amendment to the Constitution, which prohibits *states* from denying a person
liberty without due process of law or equal protection under the law. Although some
members of Congress in 1868 may have intended the notion of due process to include
those interests contained in the Bill of Rights, the Supreme Court in 1873 again ruled
that the Bill of Rights does not apply to actions of state officials, the Fourteenth Amendment notwithstanding.[10] In the early twentieth century, however, several members of the
Supreme Court became attracted to the idea that select provisions of the Bill of Rights
were "incorporated" through the Fourteenth Amendment's due process clause, such that
those rights provided a basis for claims against state officials and laws. In 1925, in an
appeal from a state criminal prosecution of a socialist who advocated the overthrow of
the government, the Court stated that it would "assume that freedom of speech and of the
press—which are protected by the First Amendment from abridgement by Congress—are
among the fundamental personal rights and 'liberties' protected by the due process clause
of the Fourteenth Amendment from impairment by the States."[11] Later, in 1940, the
Court held that First Amendment religion clauses were incorporated into the due process
clause and governed actions of state officials and agencies.[12] Thus, despite its long journey,
the provisions of the religion clauses now apply to all federal and state laws and regulations
and control the actions of federal, state, and local officials and agencies.

Not only can a person bring a lawsuit against a state official or local entity for violating the federal religion clauses, she may also file that suit in state courts. The U.S. Constitution authorizes state courts to uphold its provisions, meaning that state courts also may
rule whether an official action violates the First Amendment. A great number of the cases
contained in this book originated, like *Witters*, in state courts and were appealed to the
U.S. Supreme Court. They involved state courts ruling on whether a particular state action
infringed on a person's rights afforded under the First Amendment.

As mentioned above, the Court can hear only a limited number of cases each year,
so it must select the most important legal controversies to adjudicate. The justices fully
appreciate that through their church-state holdings they are not only resolving a particular legal dispute, they also are announcing a rule that will be relied on by legislators and
other governmental officials when they make a variety of policy decisions. Through the
Court's ability to select those cases it will adjudicate, it often hears cases with great legal
and political significance. This points to a key reason for the strong public interest in the
judicial nomination and confirmation processes. Presidents nominate judges and justices
that they believe will reflect their own philosophical or ideological perspective; in that way,
presidents attempt to extend their influence far beyond their limited terms of public office.
Justices decide cases based primarily on the interpretation of statutes and prior relevant
holdings (called "precedent"), but their interpretation of the legal issues is influenced by
their judicial philosophy and, as some argue, their ideological beliefs. As you will see,
the Court's church-state holdings have often been closely divided, reflecting the different
perspectives of the justices. Not unlike other controversial legal issues such as abortion or
homosexual rights, church-state cases frequently result in "five-to-four" or "six-to-three"
decisions.

At the same time, justices of the Supreme Court have always been keenly aware that
they are an unelected body in a representative democracy. Public policy, where it does not
have a strong connection to constitutional or legal principles, is for the elected branches
to decide. This self-awareness has resulted in a practice of "judicial restraint." Despite

recurring claims of "judicial activism," the vast majority of Court decisions have been quite constrained, with the justices deciding only the issue before them.

An example may help explain this practice of judicial restraint. In 1973 the Supreme Court ruled that state tuition payments to parochial schools violated the Establishment Clause.[13] Supporters of religious school funding then seized on the concept of "vouchers," by which state funds would be paid to parents rather than directly to the parochial schools; however, many others questioned whether this "indirect" funding mechanism was constitutional. Between 1983 and 2002, the Court decided a half-dozen funding cases that raised issues similar to those that would be present under a voucher program. During that same time, a handful of states instituted voucher programs, all of which were challenged on federal or state establishment grounds. Even though the Court could have used any of those funding cases to opine on the constitutionality of vouchers—and settle much uncertainty for state education officials, let alone save thousands of dollars in legal expenses—the Court declined to so rule until it had a true voucher case before it in 2002.[14] In essence, the Court will not rule on the constitutionality of a particular legal controversy until a case with the exact issue has worked its way through the legal system.

In addition, the Court may decline to hear cases that it is otherwise qualified to hear based on its awareness of its limited judicial role. On one hand, the Constitution states that the Court shall hear "cases" and "controversies," which the Court has interpreted as requiring that it rule only on actual controversies between litigants who have a true stake in the lawsuit. In essence, the Court will not render advisory opinions on abstract legal or political questions. The Court has extended this textual limitation on its jurisdiction to create prudential rules of judicial restraint. The Court will not hear cases that raise "political questions" better left to the elected branches (such as whether the President's action appointing an ambassador to the Vatican violates the Establishment Clause), cases where the parties to the suit have not been injured or lack a stake in the outcome (called "standing to sue"), or where the legal issues are not fully developed (called "ripeness") or the controversy between the parties is now over or "moot." As an example of this last principle, one of this book's authors helped litigate a school prayer case on behalf of an eighth-grade junior high school student that took several years to work its way through the federal court system. While the petition for certiorari was pending at the Supreme Court, the student graduated, thereby canceling out the controversy between the student and the public school. The petition was rejected because the controversy had become moot.

The doctrine of "standing to sue" also has restricted judicial review of some church-state controversies. In the 1990s, an Alabama state trial judge placed a representation of the Ten Commandments in his courtroom. Although several people complained that the display violated the Establishment Clause by indicating governmental favoritism for religion, a federal court dismissed a lawsuit because the out-of-town plaintiffs lacked standing—in essence, they were not "injured" by having to see the display on a regular basis (as would a local attorney or court employee, who were unlikely to file suit against the county's only judge). Mere status as a citizen is insufficient to raise a constitutional claim; one must have a particularized injury brought about by the government's action.

Standing also has been a recurring issue in challenges to government financial aid to religious schools and other religious institutions. Most such lawsuits are brought by taxpayers who object to government funding of religious education or activities. In the 1920s, however, the Supreme Court ruled generally that taxpayers were not individually injured by congressional expenditures that might be unconstitutional—that any increase in an individual tax burden as a result of the purported unconstitutional appropriation would be minimal.[15] The theory for barring taxpayer lawsuits was that courts would become clogged if citizens could sue over any and every legislative appropriation with which they disagreed. In 1968, however, the Court created an exception from this general rule against taxpayer standing to allow Establishment Clause challenges. In *Flast v. Cohen*, the Court ruled that taxpayers could challenge a federal education appropriation that included services for students attending parochial schools, provided they could show the appropriation arose out of Congress' taxing and spending power under Article I, § 8 of the Constitution. The Establishment Clause provided an exception to the general standing rule requiring personalized injury, the Court said, because "one of the specific evils feared by those who drafted [it] and fought for its adoption was that the taxing and spending power would be used to favor one religion over another or to support religion in general."[16] Several years later, the Court declined to expand on the *Flast* exception by denying a public interest organization standing to challenge an administrative transfer of government property to a religious college, reaffirming that standing must be based on a Congressional appropriation pursuant to Article I, § 8 and not, as in that case, based on a decision by an administrative agency pursuant to other constitutional authority.[17] Absent this congressional spending-power connection, Justice Rehnquist wrote, "the Establishment Clause does not provide a special license to roam the country in search of governmental wrongdoing and to reveal their discoveries in federal court."[18] A fuller consideration of the Court's standing cases is contained in chapter 5.

While this book gives most attention to the opinions of the Court majorities, the concurring and dissenting opinions are often as important for understanding the complexity of the legal issues at stake and the various perspectives on religious liberty and separation of church and state. Concurring and dissenting opinions are also important as they provide opportunities for justices to propose new ideas or approaches to the legal issues; justices also feel freer to express themselves in a concurring or dissenting opinion because they are not constrained by the need to forge a majority. Sometimes concurring and dissenting opinions serve as the basis for future majority opinions. Conversely, majority opinions are often the product of compromise and are less revealing of the author's true feelings about an issue. For example, if you read closely, you will notice that former Chief Justice Rehnquist—generally a critic of the separationist-leaning *Lemon v. Kurtzman* test—sometimes relied on that standard when he needed to form a majority with more moderate justices. While the majority opinions are controlling as to the law, the concurring and dissenting opinions are frequently important to understanding the various issues in a case. Finally, while this book omits most of the footnotes contained in the opinions, it retains some that are significant. Again, the justices sometimes use footnotes (like concurring and dissenting opinions) to flesh out their arguments, distinguish facts or closely related precedent, or respond to critics.

## Understanding the Protection of "Rights" and "Liberties"

The previous discussion of standing to sue provides a nice transition to a brief overview of the nature of constitutionally protected rights. As the standing discussion indicates, a person is not normally entitled to bring a lawsuit unless she has been directly impacted by some government action and is thus "injured," to use the legal term. But how does one know or establish that her constitutional rights have been infringed or that the Constitution has been violated? Not all offense at a government action results in a constitutional violation. For example, a religious pacifist may object to all military spending based on sincerely held religious beliefs. Does the fact that the government spends a portion of each citizen's taxes on the military constitute a violation of the Free Exercise Clause? Or assume someone shouts a religious epithet at another person, insulting his or her faith. Has the Constitution or some other law been violated? And finally, suppose Congress or a state legislature enacts a law prohibiting employers from discriminating on the basis of religion in their hiring practices. How is such a law related to the First Amendment?

First, some history. During the Revolutionary period, the concept of "rights" was still developing. The Framers, steeped in Enlightenment and Whig theories from writers such as John Locke, Francois Voltaire, Baron Montesquieu, George Berkeley, and Thomas Gordon believed in a set of inalienable rights based on natural law—rights that were not granted by, or could not legally be trampled upon, by the sovereign. Natural law, according to the Roman philosopher Cicero, preexisted organized society and was eternal, unchangeable, and binding at all times and on all peoples. Some viewed natural law rights as originating in divine law or God's law, but by the end of the Enlightenment natural law had been separated from its theological basis. The Dutch political philosopher Hugo Grotius wrote that these rights were "self evident" and inherent in all people. The Framers absorbed these legal theories as they were developing their complaints against Parliament. The Framers also found the basis of rights in the British common law and bill of rights, the latter as it had developed since the Glorious Revolution of 1688–1689. Writers like Edward Coke (who predated the Glorious Revolution), Locke, Algernon Sidney, James Harrington, John Trenchard, and Gordon all spoke of the common law rights of Englishmen that could not be contravened by either Parliament or the Crown.[19]

With the development of the revolutionary state constitutions—and later with the federal constitution—a debate ensued whether these compacts should expressly provide for the protection of these natural, inalienable rights. Most anti-federalists, who advocated a decentralized government with most authority residing at the state or local levels, preferred an enumerated declaration or bill of rights to serve as a check on government tyranny and oppression, which led to their creation in most state constitutions. Other Framers, such as James Madison and Alexander Hamilton, the primary authors of the *Federalist Papers*, believed that a declaration of rights in the proposed federal constitution would imply that natural rights were limited to those that were enumerated, giving credence to the argument that the federal constitution had some authority over individual and political rights in the first instance. Hamilton wrote in Federalist 84 that a bill of rights would "not only be unnecessary in the proposed Constitution, but would even be dangerous. They would contain various exceptions to powers which are not granted [under the Constitution]; and, on this very account, would afford a colorable pretext to claim more than were granted." In the end, the federalists yielded to the anti-federalists' demands for a bill of rights as a condition for ratification of the Constitution by several of the states. One of the first orders of business for the new Congress was to draft a Bill of Rights, the first ten amendments to the Constitution, for ratification by the states.

For the purposes of the First Amendment, it is important to note that drafters were likely less concerned about the precise language of the religion clauses than they were about the underlying concepts. After all, they were not "creating" individual and political rights that people could assert against the government but merely affirming the inviolability of inalienable rights by government oppression. As discussed in more detail in the next chapter, early drafts of the religion clauses used the term "rights of conscience," which most of the drafters viewed as synonymous with freedom of religious belief and practice. The final omission of the term "rights of conscience" in the First Amendment probably had more to do with economy of language than with any attempt to narrowly define the free exercise right.

In addition, the drafters were primarily concerned with protecting political rights—those rights that dealt with citizenship (such as freedom of press and speech)—as opposed to individual rights (such as freedom from certain economic or behavioral regulations). The concept of rights was not viewed as expansively as it is today. In the late eighteenth century, the primary roles of government were to regulate foreign trade, provide for a common defense, operate post offices, and establish roads; government did not generally regulate commercial activities or provide the public services and benefits as developed later in the twentieth century. As a result, the opportunities for government infringement on a person's rights were minimal, particularly with respect to the new federal government. In addition, rights were viewed primarily in negative sense—as a check on government oppression—not affirmatively as something the government was obligated to protect. To be sure, many Americans in the founding era assumed that by agreeing to submit to the authority of a popular government (and thus surrendering some of their liberty), the government was legally obligated to protect their natural rights in return. Therefore, there may be greater enjoyment of liberty and natural rights under a government than in a state of nature. But that was different from presuming that government must protect or facilitate the exercise of rights, as that idea developed in the twentieth century.

For the purposes of the religion clauses, this raises an interesting question: Is the government only obligated not to infringe on religious liberty or must it take the next step and affirmatively protect that liberty? At the risk of gross oversimplification, one common view is that the religion clauses act as negative checks on actions of legislatures and government officials. When it comes to providing affirmative protection of rights, that obligation frequently falls on the political branches to accommodate religious practice in venues such as workplaces, prisons, and public schools through legislation, executive orders, and regulations.

Consequently, the Constitution deals with what the Court has called "fundamental rights"—vague notions of individual and political liberty. Many more specific "rights" (e.g., not to be discriminated against in employment based on one's religious affiliation) are created by legislatures and are called "statutory" rights, even though they draw meaning from the Constitution.

As discussed earlier, state constitutions can also be a source of religious liberty rights. Many state constitutions contain religion clauses that are more detailed in their language and sometimes more expansive in their coverage. While the basic notion of religious exercise is fairly uniform across federal and state constitutions, state constitutions may provide greater protection by applying different standards of judicial review (i.e., requiring the state government to justify its infringement on religious practice by a compelling interest) or providing for protection in a greater number of circumstances.

Importantly, the rights contained in the First Amendment, and the protections they afford, apply only against actions of the government and its officials (called "state action"). Said differently, the Bill of Rights does not apply to private individuals and organizations, save for the rare instances in which such entities are deemed to be "state actors." Thus, a nongovernmental employer may fire an employee over disagreement with his political or religious views without violating the Constitution, even though a government employer would be constitutionally prohibited from doing the same. In most instances, it is clear when a state actor is involved in a controversy (e.g., a public school principal prohibits a teacher from leading prayers in the classroom). But with the growing privatization of government services and the increase in public-private collaborations, those lines are becoming increasingly hazy.

Even though the Constitution's protections apply only against the action of the government, Congress and state legislatures have enacted several laws to extend similar rights of religious protection against nongovernmental actors. Thus in the example in the previous paragraph, nongovernmental employers with fifteen or more employees cannot discriminate against employees on the basis of their religion, lest they violate the 1964 Civil Rights Act. Federal, state, and local law also may provide protection against religious discrimination by private landlords or educational institutions. The authority for such legislation at the federal level rests under the power of Congress to regulate commercial activities or attach conditions to the receipt of federal funds. Congress also can enact specific legislation to remediate express constitutional violations by government officials. Importantly, however, Congress cannot expand on the understanding of what constitutes a violation of the First Amendment. As Chief Justice Marshall said more than 200 years ago, it is the province of the Court to define what is a constitutional violation. This principle is discussed in the 1997 case of *City of Boerne v. Flores* case in chapter 8.

As a result, it is important to distinguish between the sources or types of rights that affect religious liberty. The majority of Supreme Court church-state holdings have involved controversies concerning constitutional rights arising under the Free Exercise and Establishment Clauses. However, several notable cases contained in this book involved Court interpretations of statutory rights (e.g., *National Labor Relations Board v. Catholic Bishop of Chicago*[20]). These latter cases are nonetheless important because the decisions often have a "constitutional ring" to them and are revealing of the Court's attitude toward religious freedom generally.

## Chapter 2

# The Historical Background to the First Amendment Religion Clauses

It is commonly said that our Pilgrim and Puritan[1] ancestors came to the new world for religious freedom. The statement is ordinarily made to show the contrast between the church-state history of Europe and the American system of church-state separation and its corollary, religious freedom, and to praise the latter. The problem is that the assertion is only partly true; it lacks historical accuracy. To understand and support that statement, some background is necessary.

Christianity essentially became the established church of the Roman Empire in the fourth century. Prior to that time, the Christian religion had been an outlaw religion in the empire and had been, from time to time, actively persecuted by various Roman Emperors. During those days, it was a political liability and sometimes extremely dangerous to be a Christian. That began to change in the fourth century, in the time of Emperor Constantine. There is some debate as to whether Constantine acted from Christian conviction or political expediency (he seems to have believed that Christianity could be a unifying influence in the empire) or perhaps both, but in 313 C.E. he decreed that Christianity would no longer be an unacceptable religion, that it be at least equal with the traditional Roman religions. During his reign, Constantine gave considerable support to Christianity and it began to gain more political and social favor. It gained even more in the reigns of subsequent emperors. By the end of the fourth century, during the reign of Theodosius I, Christianity became the established religion of the empire.

What did that mean? Its meaning can be largely determined from a definition of "establishment," a word used throughout this book. *An establishment is a formal, official relationship between religion and civil authority.* The idea was that this symbiotic relationship between church and state was good for both institutions. The church could rely on the police power of the state to compel adherence to church doctrine and regular attendance at worship. In turn, the state received legitimacy as a government sanctioned by God (or the particular deities). The state also could rely on the teaching of the official religion to provide moral standards for citizens to live by, resulting in a moral, stable society. Establishments typically meant that the official religion received political and financial favors from the state and, later, that political and civil rights—such as the privilege of voting and holding public office—were dependent on adherence to the official religion. Finally, establishments usually meant that the state interjected itself into the internal operations of the recognized church by having a say in the formulation of religious doctrine and the appointment of ecclesiastical officials.

Christianity was the official religion of the successive governments in the western world for approximately the next 1,000 years. The relation between church and state was not always tranquil. There were fierce battles, sometimes real battles of warfare, over who would predominate in the relationship, religious authorities or civil authorities. But the political battles, or battlefield combat, were always for advantage in the relationship, "jockeying for position," rather than over disagreement about the concept. Hardly anyone disagreed with the necessity of an establishment for a holy and stable society.

The Protestant Reformation brought about significant societal changes, but not the end of established religion. Even those with only a basic knowledge of the Reformation know it was essentially a schism prompted by disagreement about Roman Catholic theology and political power. Beginning with Martin Luther in Germany in 1517[2] and continuing later with Huldreich Zwingli, the Anabaptists, and John Calvin in Switzerland and Henry VIII in England, resulting in the Church of England, various groups separated from the Catholic church. One might think that when these various movements disavowed Catholic thought, they also would have disagreed with the Catholic belief about state religion. But, with one exception, they did not. Christians had become so immersed, over a thousand years, in the philosophy of the desirability of state-established religion that they did not depart from it when they left Catholicism and started their own movements.

The one exception to that generalization was the Anabaptists, a religious community that formed in Zurich, Switzerland about 1522. The Anabaptists believed that civil authorities should have nothing to do with matters of conscience. The principal matter of conscience for them was religion. The state, they insisted, had no business being involved with religion. Thus, this group believed in separation of church and state, although they did not use that term, and religious freedom. What happened to the Anabaptists, in fact, proves the generalization that other Christian groups believed in the concept of a state church. Among other reasons, Protestants and Catholics alike persecuted the Anabaptists *because* they believed established religion was wrong. For Catholics and Protestants—who insisted that established religion was necessary for a moral and stable society—Anabaptists were political subversives and anarchists, and they persecuted the Anabaptists, often to death, for their beliefs.

As a result of the Reformation, Western Christendom became fragmented. Furthermore, virtually every group believed in the necessity of a union between church and state. In such a situation the question naturally arose about who would run the establishment, that is, what religion would unite with the state to be the official religion of the realm. Wars were fought over the issue. Finally, in 1555 a treaty was signed, the Peace of Augsburg, which set forth, for Germany, the principle of *cujus regio, ejus religio,* "whose the rule, his the religion." The actual phrase was not used until 1648, in the treaty called the Peace of Westphalia, which expanded the principle to apply to all of Europe. Under this principle, the ruler of a territory had the right to determine the religion of that territory. The theory of *cujus regio, ejus religio* was used in the settlement of the colonies in America, to which we now turn.

The United States traces its cultural and legal origins to the British settlers of the new world, who founded the Virginia colony in 1607. These settlers came primarily for secular reasons: for adventure, land, and raw materials to send back to England for manufacture. But they also believed that God wanted Christian civilization planted in the new world, so they brought with them clergy and the intent to create churches in their colony. Because these settlers had been allied with the Church of England or Anglican Church in the old country, it was only natural they should make the Anglican Church the religion of Virginia. Anglicanism was also the established religion of North and South Carolina, Georgia, and, after a few years when Roman Catholics ruled, Maryland.

These Anglican colonies illustrate why the generalization "Our ancestors came to this country for religious freedom" is not completely true. The Anglican Church was the established church in England after 1534 (with the exception of the reign of Queen Mary, a Catholic). Because Anglicans were of the established church, they were not persecuted. To be sure, many Anglicans who settled first in Virginia were Puritan Anglicans, that is, they believed that the church could and should be purified of some of its carry-overs from Catholicism. Consequently, their relations with the Anglican authorities in England were sometimes tense and prickly, but they were still Anglicans and thus not persecuted as dissenters. It cannot be said that they came to the new world to escape persecution or to gain religious freedom. Whatever their secular motivations for coming, their religious goal was to make the colonies they controlled outposts of the religion of the homeland. They were not rebels or people seeking freedom from an oppressive (to them) religious regime of the old country. They did not come seeking religious freedom but to create religious "business as usual" in the new world.

That religious business consisted principally of enforcing the Anglican way in the colonies where it was established. Virginia serves as the best example. As early as 1610 "Dale's laws" (named for a governor of the colony) were passed. Their effect was to impose Anglican worship and theology on Virginia. Only Anglican clergy could minister in the colony. People, Anglican or not, were required to attend Anglican worship when it was held. The laws prohibited blasphemy or criticism of the doctrines of Christianity or the Anglican understanding of them. There were penalties for violation of these kinds of laws. By the middle of the seventeenth century Anglicanism was firmly entrenched as the established church of the colony of Virginia. As time progressed, the rules were relaxed. But, as we shall see, the Anglican establishment was still an issue in the 1770s and 1780s.

The other Anglican establishments in the southern colonies were not quite as strict as that in Virginia, but required or attempted to require some measure of religious uniformity in their colonies, as well.

Puritans created the New England colonies of Plymouth, Massachusetts Bay, and Connecticut, also. But unlike their southern brethren, they believed that a major part of the purification of the Anglican Church was to depart from the episcopal, hierarchical government of the church and to adopt a congregational form of church structure. That is, each congregation should be self-governing, autonomous, rather than under the supervision of a bishop or any other church authority. Although the congregations were self-governing, the "Congregationalists" shared some common assumptions about religion that enabled the church to be established where it was dominant. They believed that the colonies they occupied should be run on biblical principles; they sometimes called themselves a "Bible commonwealth." In 1648, the Massachusetts Bay General Court adopted the first comprehensive legal code in the American colonies, the *Lawes and Libertyes*, which relied extensively on Biblical scripture for authority. Criminal laws in particular were drawn from the Pentateuch and cited scripture as authority for the punishment. One such offense provided that if "any man after legall conviction shall have or worship any other god, but the lord god, he shall be put to death," and cited Deuteronomy 13:6 and 10 and Exodus 22:20 as authority. (The *Lawes and Libertyes* were abandoned in the 1690s following the Glorious Revolution and the enactment of the Toleration Acts.) Such laws and practices indicate that the Puritans believed that their colonies ought to be as religiously homogeneous as possible (although that was impossible to achieve virtually from the beginning of their time in the New World; 1620 for the Plymouth colony and 1628–1630 for the Massachusetts Bay colony). They believed that although clergy ought not hold public office, they should have enormous moral influence on those who did. This was made easier by the fact that only those who were church members could hold public office. The clergy had great influence and even power over church members. This is illustrated by the action of the General Court in Boston expelling Roger Williams in 1635 and Anne Hutchinson in 1638 from the colony because of their deviation from the expected theological principles of the colony.

Maryland, founded in 1634, was first a Roman Catholic colony, but not a Catholic establishment. Cecil Calvert, the Catholic proprietor of Maryland declared that Protestants as well as Catholics should be able to worship there. This policy was designed to hold anti-Catholicism at bay, and it worked for a while. But, in 1692 the Anglicans gained political control of Maryland and any sort of toleration was subsumed under the Anglican establishment.

In New Amsterdam, a colony begun by the West India Company of Holland in 1626, the Dutch Reformed Church was theoretically established. However, the governor, Peter Stuyvesant, was exceedingly upset that the colony was populated by people of many different religious beliefs. He set about to purify the colony, to bring it in line with Dutch Reform belief and practice. But the Company, concerned about alienating customers and trading partners, instructed Stuyvesant to be more accepting of diversity in his colony. In 1664 the English took control of New Amsterdam, renamed it New York, and made Anglicanism the established religion. However, due to its religious diversity and tradition of toleration, the Anglican establishment in New York was perpetually weak.

There were notable exceptions to the general pattern so far described. As mentioned above, Roger Williams was expelled from the Massachusetts Bay colony for expressing beliefs inconsistent with the prevailing establishment. A chief point of disagreement concerned the legitimacy of religious establishments themselves. Williams was a dedicated Christian who believed that the state should have nothing to do with matters of salvation or of the worship of the sovereign God. One of his more famous lines was: "forced worship stinks in God's nostrils." So, when he left Massachusetts Bay, he went south, bought some land from the Indians, and started Providence, also called Rhode Island, based on the principle of religious freedom. As scholars Edwin S. Gaustad and Leigh E. Schmidt have noted:

> Williams, concerned about his own religious liberty, was equally dedicated to the religious liberty of all others. His colony would be a haven for all dissenters, for people of all shades of religious opinion or of no religious opinion at all. Whoever wished might come. And come they did, in considerable number and variety.[3]

Another colony with a similar outlook on the relation of religion and civil authority was Pennsylvania. Founded in 1682 by William Penn, a Quaker, Pennsylvania was based on Quaker principles. Lest that sound like one more establishment, Quakers had believed for a long time in religious freedom, in the freedom of conscience. So, in Penn's "Holy Experiment," religious freedom was extended to anyone who acknowledged God to be the creator (thus making the freedom somewhat narrower than that in Rhode Island).

This brief survey of the church-state arrangements in the colonial period illustrates the assertion made earlier, that the post-Reformation European concept of *cujus regio, ejus religio*, "whose the rule, his the religion," was largely transferred to the New World. Whether a colony was Anglican, Congregationalist, Dutch Reform, or granted religious freedom, it was because of the policy of the power that administered the territory. In the majority of the colonies, some form of establishment ruled.

During the late seventeenth and early eighteenth centuries, therefore, a religious establishment meant several things. First and foremost, it signified the financial support of recognized ministers and their churches by the government. This support came from assessments (taxes) and land grants that the churches could then lease for income. Second, many political rights (such as the ability to hold public office, take legal oaths or serve on juries) depended on one's membership in the established church. And, under religious establishments, public officials enforced religiously based codes of conduct, including laws enforcing Sabbath attendance and prohibiting blasphemy. But more than anything, a religious establishment meant an interdependency of sacred and profane institutions, whereby both the church and the state reinforced and legitimized each other. While these factors varied in each colony and over time, all of the colonial establishments shared some common attributes.

A religious establishment could be "exclusive," meaning that the state had an official relationship with one faith, or "multiple," meaning that the state had an official relationship with more than one faith. Under the multiple-establishment model, the state sometimes allowed taxpayers to direct their tax money to a church of their choosing, provided that church was of the Protestant faith.

Yet, in the late eighteenth century, the founders of the United States wrote into the Constitution a principle prohibiting the federal government from establishing religion and from preventing its free exercise. What are some of the factors that explain this development?

As discussed in more detail below, it is important to note that the framers of the First Amendment intended to restrain only the federal government, not state governments. This was part of the larger scheme of the Bill of Rights, which was directed at limiting only the power of the federal government. The founders' focus on the federal government simplified the debate and cleared the way for greater unanimity—it respected the widespread desire to ensure that the states retained a good deal of power under the Constitution, and it mostly avoided debate over the variety of approaches to religion then practiced in the states.

It is equally important to note, however, that religious establishments within the various states were on the wane at this time. Between the American Revolution and the drafting of the Bill of Rights, four states—New Jersey, New York, North Carolina, and Virginia—joined Delaware, Pennsylvania, and Rhode Island in prohibiting any religious establishment. The religious establishments in Georgia, Maryland, and South

Carolina fell quickly thereafter. The growing disenchantment with the concept of religious establishments not only undermined (and eventually led to the complete abolition of) established religion in the states, it also helped generate support for religious freedom at the federal level.

The traditional argument for establishment had included the idea that establishment was necessary to maintain a stable political order. Without the "glue" that an establishment and its moral ideas provided, the state would disintegrate or, barring that apocalyptic outcome, at least be characterized by moral and political chaos. But Rhode Island and Pennsylvania had existed with no establishment, offering political and intellectual haven to all sorts of theological ne'er-do-wells. People in the other colonies regarded Rhode Island and Pennsylvania as outposts for all sorts of zany and/or heretical theology, cesspools for the waste who could not fit in elsewhere. Supporters of establishments insisted that such systems could not survive. But Rhode Island and Pennsylvania did not disintegrate in theological polemic or sectarian strife. They continued as durable political entities. Some people began to think that these laboratory schools of religious freedom illustrated that establishment was not necessary for a stable political order.

One of the presuppositions for an effective establishment is religious homogeneity. It is simply much easier to maintain an establishment if all or most all the people living in the country or colony are of the official religion. In the late seventeenth and throughout the eighteenth centuries the religious populations of the colonies became increasingly diverse. More and more people came, not only from England, but from western European countries. Many of them were not religious or not followers of the official religion of the colony. As described below, many of them even had philosophical and/or theological objections to establishment. This pluralism caused many to think that it was just not practical to try to maintain an official religion by government power.

In the late 1730s and most of the 1740s a phenomenon church historians have labeled the "Great Awakening" happened in the colonies, all up and down the eastern seaboard. The Great Awakening was a religious revival movement that arose in response to a half-century of spiritual malaise that many have referred to as the "Big Sleep." A revival movement, by definition, is the attempt to arouse people from religious lethargy. Many clergy in the various colonies believed that the people in their churches had been deadened to spiritual vitality by the struggle to make a living in difficult surroundings, or, alternatively, had been caught up in the commerce, and the profits to be made, that had emerged between England and the colonies. In either case, struggling with poverty or with wealth tended to divert people's attention from spiritual matters.

Truth be told, many of the clergy themselves contributed to spiritual listlessness. The common preaching style was to deliver long, tightly-reasoned intellectual, theological dissertations. While that had been accepted and appreciated in the early seventeenth century, late seventeenth and early eighteenth people found such preaching less challenging and more stupefying. Worship had become wooden. For whatever reasons, many clergy believed their congregations were "going through the motions" of religion, that they were in need of revival.

Although the revival began with the attempt of Theodore J. Frelinghuysen to wake up his congregation of the Dutch Reform Church in New Jersey, the two principal personalities of the Great Awakening are George Whitefield (pronounced "Whitfield") and Jonathan Edwards. Although Edwards was the theoretician or theologian of the revival, Whitefield, "the Grand Itinerant," was its principal practitioner. He traveled up and down the eastern seaboard preaching to large crowds, both in church buildings and outside. Whitefield and other revival preachers made many converts; church attendance grew. The point of revivalism for the history of religious freedom is that those people who responded to the revival preachers did so *voluntarily*. A traditional argument for establishment had been that the police power of the state, or at least the threat of it, was necessary to get people to go to church. But in the Great Awakening the persuasive power of the preachers caused people to voluntarily go to church.[4] Some people began to think that an establishment was irrelevant to religious vitality (or perhaps even detrimental).

Related to revivalism is the fact that many Protestant Christians began to construct theological arguments against establishment. The experience of salvation, a right and correct relationship with God, was a gift of God. Many Christians believed that God anointed Jesus to provide salvation to all who would respond. The proper response was to believe that the gift of salvation was true. Once one made that response, he was "born again," was a "new creation," and had a new relationship with God. It began to dawn on people that this experience was not dependent upon the state. No matter how much the state tried to control religion and guarantee orthodoxy, ultimately the experience of salvation was between God and the believer. So, why involve the state in the religious experience? Some began to think that this was a sufficient reason to bypass the state, to argue for disestablishment.

A different intellectual impulse also contributed to the rise of disestablishment and religious freedom. It was rationalism, the principal characteristic of the Enlightenment of the eighteenth century. Simply put, rationalism was/is the view that reason is the sole authority for knowledge or behavior. All knowledge can be ascertained by human reason, the ability to think and draw conclusions based on those thoughts. Likewise, reason was the source of action, i.e., one could decide what was acceptable and unacceptable behavior on the basis of reason. In the area of religion, some rationalists decided that human reason was so all-sufficient that there was no need for a belief in or dependence on God. Other rationalists did not go that far but believed that a Designer was behind the complex and ordered universe and that his rules (or "laws of nature") could be discovered through reason. Many rationalists were Deists, in that they believed in the existence of God, the life of virtue, and even immortality (it was reasonable to expect that there should be rewards or punishments in the next life for virtuous or bad behavior in this). Some of the authors of the Constitution were Deists; most, if not all, were schooled in Enlightenment thought. Still, the Deists were religious men, although not orthodox Christians.[5] The point is that, as students of history, they knew of the persecutions, heresy trials, and inquisitions of earlier times when the state and the church collaborated to enforce orthodoxy. They knew what suffering this alliance had produced. They wanted to avoid such evils in the new nation they were creating. As rationalists who believed in the power of the free reign of reason, they couched the issue like this: they were opposed to any institution(s) that shackled people's minds. The established church of medieval times had been such an institution. Consequently, they believed that established religion was a bad idea, something to be avoided in the new America.

Practical disestablishments, religious pluralism, revivalism/voluntary religion, evangelical Christian arguments and rationalist arguments for disestablishment—in the late eighteenth century all these coalesced into an intellectual mixture that ultimately produced bold action. That bold action was for the founders of the nation to write into its charter, its basic law, the twin principles of no establishment and free exercise. Americans rightly speak of the Revolutionary War that obtained the independence of the colonies from England. What was equally revolutionary was that the founders, for the first time in Western history, made separation of church and state and religious freedom the law of the land.

But there was another scene in the drama that ultimately led to the founders' bold action. As mentioned, many of the new states, whose first constitutions predated the federal charter, wrote provisions for separation and religious freedom into their constitutions. The process in Virginia is especially noteworthy, both because the process is well documented and because it involved several individuals who were prominent on the national stage. The experience in Virginia functioned as a kind of precursor laboratory school for the later episodes in Philadelphia.

Toward the end of the eighteenth century, the Anglican establishment in Virginia was considerably weaker than it had been in its early years. This was because of the increasing religious pluralism in the state and because the Anglican church had never sent a bishop to America to provide oversight to the church. (Fear of the appointment of an Anglican bishop in America helped fuel the growing colonial distain for religious establishments.) Following the Revolutionary War, the Anglican church sought to retain its privileged status in Virginia or at least maintain the financial support from the state. Public resistance to the former led to the introduction of a bill in the Virginia legislature to support the Christian religion generally. The proposed law, entitled a "Bill Establishing a Provision for Teachers of the Christian Religion," provided that each taxpayer could designate the religious body that should receive his taxes, so long as it was Christian. Tax assessments of Jews or those with no religious affiliation would go to support education in Virginia. The tax was collected by civil law officers and there was a penalty for tax evasion.

Many were convinced the tax was necessary to give support for the moral welfare of the state. The bill's most visible supporter was Patrick Henry. The bill was opposed by some religious groups, principally the Baptists and Presbyterians, although, if the bill had passed, their positions would have improved considerably over the time when they had lived under an Anglican establishment. Their objection was principally the theological one mentioned above; the relation between God and persons is individual. It cannot be mediated by the state and the state ought not try.

The principal opponent was not a group, but an individual, James Madison. Madison was already an influential political figure. In the summer of 1776 he served as a delegate to the Virginia Convention, where he was instrumental in guiding the language of the Virginia Declaration of Rights in favor of religious freedom for Virginians. Between 1777 and 1779 he was a member of Virginia's Council of State, advising governors of the state. In 1780–1783 he served as a delegate in the Continental Congress. And, at the time the bill for the support of Christianity was introduced, he was a member of the Virginia House of Delegates. In that capacity he had high visibility to lead opposition to the tax bill. He composed a document of fifteen reasons why the proposed bill was unacceptable, the *Memorial and Remonstrance Against Religious Assessments*. It consisted principally of rationalistic and historical arguments against the taxation bill and, indeed, against establishments generally, but it also included a number of religious references and appeals. It was in the form of a petition that circulated through the state. People who agreed with its argument were to sign and return it to the state legislature. It is a classic in American history and in the history of church-state relations. The preamble ended with the phrase "We remonstrate against the said Bill." Then each of the fifteen substantive paragraphs began with "Because." Some of the more famous arguments are samples of the thrust of the entire document.

1. Because we hold it for a fundamental and undeniable truth, "that Religion or the duty which we owe our Creator and the manner of discharging it, can be directed only by reason and conviction, not by force or violence."[6] The Religion then of every man must be left to the conviction and conscience of every man; and it is the right of every man to exercise it as these may dictate. This right is in its nature an unalienable right. . . . It is the duty of every man to render to the Creator such homage and such only as he believes to be acceptable to him. This duty is precedent, both in order of time and in degree of obligation, to the claims of Civil Society. . . . We maintain therefore that in matters of Religion, no man's right is abridged by the institution of Civil Society and that Religion is wholly exempt from its cognizance. . . .

2. Because if Religion be exempt from the authority of Society at large, still less can it be subject to that of the Legislative Body. The latter are but the creatures and viceregents of the former. . . .

3. Because it is proper to take alarm at the first experiment on our liberties. . . . Who does not see that the same authority which can establish Christianity, in exclusion of all other Religions, may establish with the same ease any particular sect of Christians, in exclusion of all other Sects? that the same authority which can force a citizen to contribute three pence only of his property for the support of any one establishment, may force him to conform to any other establishment in all cases whatsoever? . . .

6. Because the establishment proposed by the Bill is not requisite for the support of the Christian Religion. To say it is, is a contradiction to the Christian Religion itself, for every page of it disavows a dependence on the powers of this world: it is a contradiction to fact; for it is known that this Religion both existed and flourished, not only without the support of human laws, but in spite of every opposition from them, and not only during the period of miraculous aid, but long after it had been left to its own evidence and the ordinary power of Providence. Nay, it is a contradiction in terms; for a Religion not invented by human policy, must have pre-existed and been supported, before it was established by human policy. It is moreover to weaken in those who profess this Religion a pious confidence in its innate excellence and the patronage of its Author; and to foster in those who still reject it, a suspicion that its friends are too conscious of its fallacies to trust it to its own merits. . . .[7]

The *Memorial and Remonstrance* gained enough signatures such that Madison was able to defeat the Bill for a General Assessment in the Virginia Legislature. Madison then was able to fill that void by reintroducing a bill for religious freedom that the legislature had tabled for some years. In 1779 Thomas Jefferson had introduced a bill for religious freedom in Virginia. The legislature had not been ready for that, so it tabled the bill in 1779 and in subsequent sessions until 1785. In that year Madison, after the defeat for the general assessment bill, brought Jefferson's bill off the table again (Jefferson was serving as ambassador to France), thinking that now the time was ripe for its adoption. He was right. The bill was passed and became law in January 1786.

The official title of Jefferson's bill was "A Bill for Establishing Religious Freedom." The language of the philosophical or rationale section is hard to follow; it is all one sentence, given that Jefferson in this instance showed an affection for the semicolon. But the effort to read it is rewarding, for it expresses some profound truths about religion and civil authority.

relationships. The bill against which he wrote the *Memorial and Remonstrance* was one which gave government support to Christianity in all its then-existing permutations. But his document shows that he roundly rejected the "multiple establishment" approach. That shall become important in the discussion of "nonpreferentialism" in chapter 3, the chapter on principles of interpretation of the First Amendment.

The Constitutional Convention convened in Philadelphia on 25 May 1787. Its delegates ultimately produced what George Washington described as "little short of a miracle."[10] Verbatim notes of the debates of the delegates about the various provisions of the Constitution, comparable to today's *Congressional Record*, do not exist. We do not know as much as we would like about the process or who said what. Apparently there was little discussion of religion. What we do know, however, is that in the final text of the document there is no mention of God, Jesus Christ, or Christianity. For this reason, Isaac Kramnick and Laurence Moore have called it a "Godless Constitution."[11] Indeed, even the word "religion" appears in only one place. That is in the last clause of the last sentence in Article VI: "[N]o religious Test shall ever be required as a Qualification to any Office or public Trust under the United States." One's qualification for public office is independent of one's religious beliefs. The founders wrote this to reverse the common colonial practice of disqualifying non-Christians (and in some instances, non-Protestants) from public office holding. It was consistent with one of the provisions of Jefferson's bill in Virginia.

Although pathbreaking, the "no religious test" clause passed the Constitutional Convention with little debate. During ratification, however, criticism of the no religious test rule mounted, and the matter became a subject of fierce debate in several state conventions. Some railed against it because they believed the nation should be ruled by Christian people. (Some believed that governing should be restricted to Protestants). Some also were alarmed that the provision, along with the lack of any other religious language, signified that the Constitution was a secular document, that it created a secular state. Consequently, some argued that the Constitution should not be ratified. Not all opposed the no religious test feature, however, and some of those were clergy. They recognized that the authors had advanced human rights by recognizing that one's rights in a nation should not depend on one's religion.[12] In fact, opposition to the no religious test clause forced its supporters to articulate arguments on behalf of religious liberty—support for freedom of conscience and religious equality—that would lay the groundwork for the First Amendment. As future Supreme Court Justice James Iredell of North Carolina argued:

> I consider this clause under consideration as one of the strongest proofs that could be adduced, that it was the intention of those who formed this system to establish general religious liberty in America. * * * [H]ow is it possible to exclude any sect of men [from rights of citizenship] without taking away that principle of religious freedom which we ourselves so warmly contend for?[13]

What seems to have been a much greater concern of the general population was the Constitution's lack of any explicit language prohibiting the federal government from infringing on the political and civil rights of citizens. During the ratification process, numerous state conventions demanded that the document include a list of rights due the citizens of the nation. One might say they held the Constitution hostage, refusing to ratify it unless the authors agreed to produce a bill of particulars about civil rights. Upon assurances that the first Congress would address the matter, the Constitution was ratified 21 June 1788.

True to their word, the first Congress, primarily through the leadership of James Madison, who had been elected to the House of Representatives, presented a list of amendments to the Constitution on 8 June 1789. There was no unanimous agreement over the language of what was to become the religion clauses of the First Amendment. Again, the record is sketchy, but we do have the various proposals that were made as Congress tried to come to agreement on this matter. These various proposals were spread out over time (from 8 June 1789 until 25 September 1789) and were introduced by various members of the House of Representatives and the Senate. The last, and finally agreed upon, language was the result of the work of a conference committee.[14] Without going into detail about who introduced what, the proposals were:

### House drafts

1. The civil rights of none shall be abridged on account of religious belief, nor shall any national religion be established, nor shall the full and equal rights of conscience in any manner or in any respect be infringed.
2. No religion shall be established by law, nor shall the equal rights of conscience be infringed.
3. Congress shall make no laws touching religion, or infringing the rights of conscience.
4. Congress shall make no law establishing religion, or to prevent the free exercise thereof, or to infringe the rights of conscience.
5. Congress shall make no law establishing religion, or prohibiting the free exercise thereof, nor shall the rights of conscience be infringed.

### Senate drafts

6. Congress shall make no law establishing one religious sect or society in preference to others, nor shall the rights of conscience be infringed.
7. Congress shall not make any law, infringing the rights of conscience, or establishing any Religious Sect or Society.
8. Congress shall make no law establishing any particular denomination of religion in preference to another, or prohibiting free exercise thereof, nor shall the rights of conscience be infringed.
9. Congress shall make no law establishing religion, or prohibiting the free exercise thereof.
10. Congress shall make no law establishing articles of faith or a mode of worship, or prohibiting the free exercise of religion.

Finally, a House-Senate conference committee met and submitted to the bodies a joint resolution which was approved by both houses and became the approved wording of the Religion Clauses of the First Amendment:

11. Congress shall make no law respecting an establishment of religion, or prohibiting the free exercise thereof.[15]

What can be taken from the various proposals for a religious liberty amendment and accompanying debate? How do they help us understand the principles underlying the establishment and free exercise clauses? First, the framers appeared to have consciously rejected efforts to adopt a narrow prohibition on religious establishments. Some people, including some current Supreme Court justices, argue that the purpose of the

civil authority; in many instances they have been seen upholding the thrones of political tyranny; in no instance have they been seen as the guardians of the liberties of
the people.[32]

Finally, disestablishment was necessary to ensure equal treatment of all religious faiths.
"[A]ll men are to be considered as entering into society on equal conditions" Madison
wrote. "Above all, are they to be considered as retaining an '*equal* title to the free exercise
of religion according to the dictates of conscience.'"[33]

The Establishment Clause therefore reflects broad substantive values upon which a
majority of early Americans could agree. While those who drafted and ratified the Establishment Clause may have disagreed over the precise meaning of "nonestablishment" and
its day to day application to issues such as days of Thanksgiving or Sabbath laws—in the
same way that modern observers diverge over issues such as vouchers and the government
posting of the Ten Commandments—they shared common, broad ideals that found their
way into the language of the First Amendment: freedom of conscience; no compelled support of religion; no delegation of government authority to religious institutions; and equal
treatment of all sects. Thomas Curry has summed up those shared concerns:

> [T]he people of almost every state that ratified the First Amendment believed that
> religion should be maintained and supported voluntarily. They saw government at-
> tempts to organize and regulate such support as a usurpation of power and a violation
> of liberty of conscience and free exercise of religion, and as falling within the scope of
> what they termed an establishment of religion.[34]

With respect to understandings of religious exercise, the framers conceived of religious
freedom broadly. Free exercise, by its language, implied more than a freedom to believe
without government punishment or constraint, but also the ability to *exercise* or practice
one's beliefs. It would have been a hollow freedom for the government to have said: "You
can believe whatever you want, so long as you do not do anything about it." Nothing
should be drawn from the fact that earlier drafts of the religion clauses used the more inclusive term "rights of conscience," a phrase that did not make it into the final language of
the First Amendment. It appears that most framers viewed the terms "rights of conscience"
and "free exercise of religion" interchangeably. The ultimate decision on language likely
had more to do with efforts to economize on language than to suggest that only those with
conventional religious beliefs were to be protected under the First Amendment.

For that reason, it is not surprising that the framers did not define what constitutes
"religion" under the Free Exercise and Establishment Clauses. For free exercise purposes,
various speeches and writings indicate that they considered protected belief to encompass
degrees of heterodoxy and disbelief.

Conversely, most of the leaders of the new nation likely held conventional views
of what was covered by the Free Exercise and Establishment Clauses. Absent a few forward thinkers like Jefferson, Madison, and George Mason, most contemporaries would
likely have considered the protections and proscriptions of the religion clauses to apply to
Christian faiths, or more accurately to Protestant denominations. In a new nation with
few Catholics and Jews, and likely no admitted Muslims or Buddhists, the average citizen
believed America would always be a Protestant or Christian country. Thus for most Americans, the purposes of the religion clauses were to guarantee freedom of belief ranging from
Protestant orthodoxy to Deistic rationalism and to prevent preferential treatment of one
Protestant faith over others. At the time, America was likely the most religiously diverse

nation in the world, but that diversity was limited primarily to Protestant sects. Most early Americans would have had a difficult time believing that the religion clauses would ever be applied to religions other than Christianity and Judaism. It was the rare thinker like Jefferson, Madison, and later John Adams who conceived that the religion clause protections would (and should) extend to non-Judeo-Christian faiths. But the language of the religion clauses has proved broad enough to extend their vision to encompass the dizzying array of religions in twenty-first century America.

The framers of the American republic thus perceived the principles informing the religion clauses in broad terms. Religious liberty had been an unfolding idea, and notions of religious equality, rights of conscience, and church-state separation were dynamic and developing. In the words of Justice Felix Frankfurter, the principle of religious liberty has been viewed as a "spacious conception," one that "unfold[s] as appeal is made to the principle from case to case." Historian Michael Kamen summed up the prevailing contemporary attitude toward the Constitution and the rights it protected, by saying that the framers considered it was "a machine that would go of itself." So it has been with the concepts of free exercise and no establishment.[35]

---

### NOTES AND QUESTIONS

1. Describe the concept of *cujus regio, ejus religio* and its effect on church-state relations in the colonial period in America.

2. How was it possible for late eighteenth century Christian evangelicals and rationalists, who had radically different theologies or philosophies, to unite in a common objective to promote religious freedom?

3. Describe James Madison's role in the development of separation of church and state and religious freedom in this country.

4. Thomas Jefferson argued that it is wrong for a government to compel a person to support a religion in which he disbelieves. He also objected to compulsory support of a religion in which one does believe. What was the nature of Jefferson's objection to these practices?

5. Was it inconsistent for Jefferson to argue for strict separation and yet to allow government to interfere with religious conduct in certain circumstances? What were those circumstances?

6. What conclusions may be drawn about the intended meaning of the First Amendment from the evidence we have about the drafting process? What are some of the risks inherent in the historical interpretation of these materials?

7. Is it possible to argue that the authors of the Constitution and Bill of Rights wrote a secular document and yet were sympathetic to the role of religion in American life?

At a conference sponsored by the Pew Forum on Religion and Public Life on religion and the death penalty, Supreme Court Justice Antonin Scalia, an originalist,[3] elaborated on this approach as it relates to judging the constitutionality of the death penalty:

> The Constitution that I interpret and apply is not living, but dead; or as I prefer to call it, enduring. It means today not what current society, much less the Court, thinks it ought to mean, but what it meant when it was adopted. For me, therefore, the constitutionality of the death penalty is not a difficult, soul-wrenching question. It was clearly permitted when the Eighth Amendment was adopted—not merely for murder, by the way, but for all felonies, including, for example, horse thieving, as anyone can verify by watching a western movie. And so it is clearly permitted today as far as the Constitution is concerned.

Consistent with this approach, Justice Scalia has argued that certain government-sponsored religious expressions were part of the original meaning of the Constitution, and thus, should be constitutionally permissible today. In the 2005 case of *McCreary v. ACLU*, for example, where the Court majority struck down the posting of the Ten Commandments in county courthouses, Justice Scalia pointed to official acknowledgments of God during the founding era as evidence of the original understanding of the nonestablishment prohibition. "The Establishment Clause . . . *was* enshrined in the Constitution's text, and these official actions show *what it meant*. . . . What is more probative of the meaning of the Establishment Clause than the actions of the very Congress that proposed it, and of the first President charged with observing it?"[4]

A competing approach to originalism is one that values the history that undergirds the adoption of various constitutional provisions (to the extent it can be divined), but rejects attempts to limit constitutional interpretation to original understandings of these provisions. Professor Kent Greenawalt expressed this approach succinctly: "I do not think that the original understanding, either of those who enacted the constitutional provisions or of those who then read the provisions, should be the final determinant in constitutional adjudication. Nevertheless, I agree that original understanding, in some form, should be an important consideration in Supreme Court decisions."[5] While there is great variation in this school of thinking, this view generally holds that we should allow current reasoning and understanding to influence contemporary interpretation of the Constitution.

In a book published in 2005, sitting U.S. Supreme Court Justice Stephen Breyer places himself in this camp. His book is entitled *Active Liberty: Interpreting Our Democratic Constitution*. Justice Breyer notes that American liberty "means not only freedom from government coercion but also the freedom to participate in the government itself,"[6] and he argues that "courts should take greater account of the Constitution's democratic nature when they interpret constitutional and statutory texts."[7] Breyer believes that consideration of the consequences of a potential judicial decision is a valid part of judicial decision-making, something originalists say they reject. Justice Breyer says that "[t]he judge must examine the consequences [of a proposed decision] through the lens of the relevant constitutional value or purpose."[8]

For example, in a case involving a school voucher program that included religious schools as well as other nongovernmental schools, Breyer considered whether upholding the program would create division along religious lines because he believes the Establishment Clause seeks to avoid such divisions.[9] In that case, Breyer's analysis of this factor and others (including relevant Supreme Court precedent) caused him to vote against the constitutionality of the voucher program. (See chapter 12.) Justice Breyer also considered the potential for social divisiveness in a case involving a Ten Commandments monument that had stood for forty years on the grounds of the Texas state capitol without any legal complaints being filed.[10] In that case, Breyer said he was concerned that the removal of the monument, and others like it, would cause great unrest in surrounding communities. For this and other reasons, he voted to uphold this Ten Commandments monument.[11] (See chapter 20.)

Originalists, Breyer says, have concerns about this kind of reasoning. They "fear that, once judges become accustomed to justifying legal conclusions through appeal to real-world consequences, they will too often act subjectively and undemocratically, substituting an elite's view of good policy for sound law."[12] Justice Breyer argues, however, that under his philosophy of constitutional interpretation, "important safeguards of objectivity remain,"[13] such as "legal precedents, rules, standards, practices, and institutional understanding . . . ."[14] Indeed, Breyer argues that his approach actually better guards against judicial subjectivity because it is more transparent. Breyer explains: "I believe that when a judge candidly acknowledges that, in addition to text, history, and precedent, consequences also guide his decision-making, he is more likely to be disciplined in emphasizing, for example, constitutionally relevant consequences rather than allowing his own subjectively held values to be outcome determinative."[15] And Justice Breyer adds:

> Significantly, an effort to answer [questions about how to decide which of the competing linguistic characteristics, history, and traditions are determinative in a given case] can produce a decision that is not only subjective but also *unclear*, lacking transparency about the factors that the judge considers truly significant. A decision that directly addresses consequences, purposes, and values is no more subjective, at worst, and has the added value of exposing underlying judicial motivations, specifying the points of doubt for all to read. This is particularly important because transparency of rationale permits informed public criticism of opinions; and that criticism, in a democracy, plays an important role in checking abuse of judicial power.[16]

Breyer also argues that it is a mistake to assume that the originalist approach involves no subjectivity. "The [originalist's] tools—language and structure, history and tradition—often fail to provide objective guidance in those truly difficult cases about which I have spoken,"[17] Breyer says. That means that the originalist approach itself "possess[es] inherently subjective elements."[18] In this same vein, Professor Sunstein cautions against what he calls "false" originalism—"hiding behind the Constitution to impose judges' own political values."[19] Sunstein concludes: "[Originalists] get a lot of rhetorical mileage out of the claim that their approach is neutral while other approaches are simply a matter of 'politics.' But there is nothing neutral in [originalism.] It is a political choice, which must be defended on political grounds."[20]

Justice Breyer says that another reason his approach is preferable to originalism is that originalism may "produce seriously harmful consequences—outweighing whatever risks of subjectivity or uncertainty are inherent in other approaches."[21] For example, if the Constitution were to be viewed today as it was by those who ratified its provisions, "discrimination by states on the basis of sex would be entirely acceptable,"[22] and "[t]he national government would be permitted to discriminate on the basis of race,"[23] some scholars say. Moreover, some scholars believe that an originalist approach would "[a]lmost certainly [allow] states [to] establish official churches. . . ."[24] In the minds of some, consequences like these weigh heavily against the originalist approach.

At the same time, Justice Breyer counsels in favor of what he and others call "judicial modesty," meaning that "[t]he judge, compared to the legislator, lacks relevant expertise" to make certain decisions.[25] He usually favors pragmatic, incremental steps, citing Judge Learned Hand's admonition: "The spirit of liberty is the spirit which is not too sure that it is right."[26]

Another wing of judicial thought also criticizes originalism but is less concerned about the values of judicial minimalism and modesty. That is the approach that views the Constitution as a living document, one that is flexible enough to absorb and reflect evolving senses of morality. As Professor Sunstein explains, judges who take this approach "believe that the continuing judicial task is to make the document as good as it can be by interpreting its broad terms in a way that casts its ideals in the best possible light."[27]

The late Justice William Brennan is probably the best known proponent of this approach. Justice Brennan said:

> We current Justices read the Constitution in the only way that we can: as Twentieth-Century Americans. We look to the history of the time of framing and to the intervening history of interpretation. But the ultimate question must be, what do the words of the text mean in our time? For the genius of the Constitution rests not in any static meaning it might have had in a world that is dead and gone, but in the adaptability of its great principles to cope with current problems and current needs. What the constitutional fundamentals meant to the wisdom of other times cannot be their measure to the vision of our time. Similarly, what those fundamentals mean for us, our descendants will learn, cannot be the measure to the vision of their time.[28]

A good example of the application of this approach is found in Justice Brennan's concurring opinion in the 1963 school prayer decision, *Abington Township v. Schempp*, where he cautioned that a "too literal quest for the advice of the Founding Fathers upon the issues of these cases seems to me futile and misdirected."

> First, on our precise problem the historical record is at best ambiguous, and statements can readily be found to support either side of the proposition. The ambiguity of history is understandable if we recall the nature of the problems uppermost in the thinking of the statesmen who fashioned the religious guarantees; they were concerned with far more flagrant intrusions of government into the realm of religion than any that our century has witnessed. While it is clear to me that the Framers meant the Establishment Clause to prohibit more than the creation of an established federal church such as existed in England, I have no doubt that, in their preoccupation with the imminent question of established churches, they gave no distinct consideration to the particular question whether the clause also forbade devotional exercises in public institutions.
>
> Second, the structure of American education has greatly changed since the First Amendment was adopted. In the context of our modern emphasis upon public education available to all citizens, any views of the eighteenth century as to whether the exercises at bar are an "establishment" offer little aid to decision. Education, as the Framers knew it, was in the main confined to private schools more often than not under strictly sectarian supervision. Only gradually did control of education pass largely to public officials. It would, therefore, hardly be significant if the fact was that the nearly universal devotional exercises in the schools of the young Republic did not provoke criticism. . . .
>
> Third, our religious composition makes us a vastly more diverse people than were our forefathers. They knew differences chiefly among Protestant sects. Today the

Nation is far more heterogeneous religiously, including as it does substantial minorities not only of Catholics and Jews but as well of those who worship according to no version of the Bible and those who worship no God at all. See *Torcaso v. Watkins,* 367 U.S. 488, 495. In the face of such profound changes, practices which may have been objectionable to no one in the time of Jefferson and Madison may today be highly offensive to many persons, the deeply devout and the nonbelievers alike.

Whatever Jefferson or Madison would have thought of Bible reading or the recital of the Lord's Prayer in what few public schools existed in their day, our use of the history of their time must limit itself to broad purposes, not specific practices. . . .

Fourth, the American experiment in free public education available to all children has been guided in large measure by the dramatic evolution of the religious diversity among the population which our public schools serve. The interaction of these two important forces in our national life has placed in bold relief certain positive values in the consistent application to public institutions generally, and public schools particularly, of the constitutional decree against official involvements of religion which might produce the evils the Framers meant the Establishment Clause to forestall. . . .[29]

As has already been suggested, this approach to constitutional interpretation has many critics as well. Critics charge that it leads to judging that is idiosyncratic and to a judiciary that is unaccountable. For example, former Judge Robert Bork has charged:

> There is no way of deciding these matters other than by reference to some system of moral or ethical values that has no objective or intrinsic validity of its own and about which men can and do differ. Where the Constitution does not embody the moral or ethical choice, the judge has no basis other than his own values upon which to set aside the community judgment embodied in the statute.[30]

Critics of this approach argue that it is the legislative and executive branches that should have the latitude to ensure that the law reflects current morality and philosophies, not judges. In contrast to appointed judges, these critics say, political leaders may be held accountable by the electorate for their decisions.

It is not only originalists who criticize approaches like that of Justice Brennan. Professor Sunstein, a critic of originalism, says that "[a] big problem with [this approach] is that it gives the judges enormous power to pick and choose—to select the values they deem crucial to democracy, or dignity, and to understand the Constitution so as to promote those values."[31]

Finally, it should be noted that others reject the terms of the debate over originalism. For example, Professor Jack Balkin argues that "the choice between originalism and living constitutionalism is a false one," saying he regards himself "both as an originalist and as a living constitutionalist."[32] Balkin explains:

> [My perspective] may seem strange to some readers, who have grown accustomed to thinking that living constitutionalism is just a form of non-originalism. However what we call "non-originalism" depends on what we think originalism entails. Given any particular version of originalism, non-originalism means only that we reject the originalist's view of what fidelity to the Constitution requires. Now I argue that fidelity to the Constitution means fidelity to the original meaning of the Constitution's text and to the principles that underlie the text. From my perspective, then, a non-originalist is a person who argues that we do not have to be faithful to the original meaning of the Constitution's text or to its underlying principles. But living

constitutionalists need not be non-originalists of that sort, and, in my view, they should not be.[33]

As Professor Balkin demonstrates, some scholars find the traditional distinctions between originalism and nonorginalism unsastisfactory.

In these and other ways, the debate over originalism continues to evolve. Awareness of this overarching debate aids in understanding the more specific disagreements over the meaning of the religion clauses.

## "Nonpreferentialism" and Governmental Financial Aid for Religion

As noted above, judges and scholars on all sides of the debate about originalism agree that we should explore the complex history that undergirds the First Amendment and try to understand it as accurately as possible. As Judge Michael McConnell has said: "Even opponents of originalism generally agree that the historical understanding [of the First Amendment] is relevant, even if not dispositive."[34] Furthermore, even advocates who are some of the most ardent critics of originalism recognize that historical arguments have strategic value—they can help fold originalist judges into a working Court majority. History appears to be particularly relevant in interpreting the religion clauses, or so the justices seem to believe. Justice Wiley B. Rutledge summed up the feeling when he wrote: "No provision of the Constitution is more closely tied to or given content by its generating history than the religion clause of the First Amendment."[35]

One of the most prominent debates about the historical record of the religion clauses has been the debate about what the founders intended to accomplish when they framed the Establishment Clause of the First Amendment. For example, William Rehnquist and some scholars[36] have argued that the original intent of the Establishment Clause was to bar the establishment of a national church, but not to prohibit the federal government from providing aid to religions generally. In a dissenting opinion in the 1986 case of *Wallace v. Jaffree*, then-Justice Rehnquist reviewed some historical evidence surrounding the adoption of the First Amendment. Based on this evidence, he argued:

> It would seem from this evidence that the Establishment Clause of the First Amendment had acquired a well-accepted meaning: it forbade establishment of a national religion, and forbade preference among religious sects or denominations. Indeed, the first American dictionary defined the word "establishment" as "the act of establishing, founding, ratifying or ordaining," such as in "[the] episcopal form of religion, so called, in England." 1 N. Webster, *American Dictionary of the English Language* (1st ed. 1828). The Establishment Clause did not require government neutrality between religion and irreligion nor did it prohibit the Federal Government from providing nondiscriminatory aid to religion.[37]

In the wake of Rehnquist's dissenting opinion in the *Wallace* case, Professor Douglas Laycock wrote an influential rejoinder to this argument. Professor Laycock's article, which was published in 1986, is entitled "'Nonpreferential' Aid to Religion: A False Claim About Original Intent."[38] Laycock uses the term "nonpreferential aid" to refer to government aid that flows to all religions in contrast to funds the state directs to a preferred church or group of churches. In his article, Professor Laycock wrote:

> There are several versions of the nonpreferential aid argument, but all reach substantially the same conclusion. The claim is that the framers of the religion clauses

intended . . . [that] government may not prefer one religion over others, but it may aid all religions evenhandedly. Under this view, the Supreme Court's more expansive interpretation is a usurpation that remains illegitimate no matter how long the Court adheres to it.

This claim is false. The framers of the religion clauses certainly did not consciously intend to permit nonpreferential aid, and those of them who thought about the question probably intended to forbid it. In fact, substantial evidence suggests that the Framers expressly considered the question and that they believed that nonpreferential aid would establish religion. To assert the opposite as historical fact, and to charge the Supreme Court with usurpation without acknowledging the substantial evidence that supports the Court's position, is to mislead the American people.

The fact is that the First Congress repeatedly rejected versions of the establishment clause that would have permitted nonpreferential aid, and nothing in the sparse legislative history gives much support to the view that the Framers intended to permit nonpreferential aid. Proposals for nonpreferential financial aid were squarely rejected in Maryland and Virginia in 1785 and 1786, amidst much public debate. No state offered nonpreferential aid to churches, and only Maryland and Virginia seriously proposed such aid. Some of the New England states provided financial aid to more than one church, but these systems were preferential in practice and were the source of bitter religious strife. There is no evidence that those schemes were the model for the establishment clause.

The Framers also had a second, less considered intention. Both the states and the federal government openly endorsed Protestantism and provided a variety of preferential, nonfinancial aid to Protestants. This aid was wholly noncontroversial, because the nation was so uniformly Protestant and hostile to other faiths. The early preference for Protestantism is not a precedent for nonpreferential aid, and it is not an attractive model for establishment clause interpretation. The Framers' generation thought about establishment clause issues in the context of financial aid; they did not think about those issues in connection with nonfinancial aid. We can make better sense of the establishment clause if we follow what the Framers did when they were thinking about establishment. Thus, to the extent that the Framers' intent is thought to matter, the relevant intent is their analysis of financial aid to churches.[39]

It is important to note that Professor Laycock was not arguing that this history precludes the government from providing aid to religious as well as other nongovernmental groups for secular activities. Instead, he argued that the founders considered and rejected the notion that the government could provide aid to a variety of religious institutions for their religious activities.[40] (See section below entitled, "No-Aid Separation" v. "Evenhanded Neutrality").

Professor Laycock's article basically had the effect of ending this particular debate within the Court and academic circles and shifting the focus to other historical and doctrinal debates.

## INCORPORATION OF THE ESTABLISHMENT CLAUSE

Another locus of historical debate concerns the doctrine of incorporation and the Establishment Clause. A bit of background regarding the incorporation doctrine is necessary before describing this debate.

When the Bill of Rights was ratified in 1791, the First Amendment ban on laws respecting a religious establishment applied only to actions of the federal government. The text states that "*Congress* shall make no law. . . ," referring to the United States Congress. In other words, state and local governments were not bound by the restrictions of the First Amendment, but only by state constitutions and laws. This had the effect of leaving the states free to maintain their laws regarding religion, whether those laws preferred one religion or a group of religions over others, or provided for equal rights for religious freedom for all faiths or fell somewhere in between.

With the conclusion of the Civil War, however, several constitutional amendments were adopted that changed the understanding of individual liberty in the United States— the Thirteenth, Fourteenth and Fifteenth Amendments. The amendments were intended to ensure that former slaves enjoyed the full benefit of citizenship and individual liberties guaranteed by the Constitution. The Fourteenth Amendment states in part: "No State shall make or enforce any law which shall abridge the privileges or immunities of citizens of the United States; nor shall any State deprive any person of life, liberty, or property, without due process of law; nor deny to any person within its jurisdiction the equal protection of the laws."[41]

The Supreme Court eventually ruled that this amendment had the effect of applying the First Amendment (as well as other portions of the Bill of Rights) to state and local law. In 1940, the Court applied the Free Exercise Clause to a local ordinance for the first time, stating:

> The fundamental concept of liberty embodied in that Amendment embraces the liberties guaranteed by the First Amendment. The First Amendment declares that Congress shall make no law respecting an establishment of religion or prohibiting the free exercise thereof. The Fourteenth Amendment has rendered the legislatures of the states as incompetent as Congress to enact such laws.[42]

In 1947, the Court held that the Establishment Clause also applied to the states through the provisions of the Fourteenth Amendment. The Court stated:

> The meaning and scope of the First Amendment, preventing establishment of religion or prohibiting the free exercise thereof, in the light of its history and the evils it was designed forever to suppress, have been several times elaborated by the decisions of this Court prior to the application of the First Amendment to the states by the Fourteenth. The broad meaning given the Amendment by these earlier cases has been accepted by this Court in its decisions concerning an individual's religious freedom rendered since the Fourteenth Amendment was interpreted to make the prohibitions of the First applicable to state action abridging religious freedom. There is every reason to give the same application and broad interpretation to the "establishment of religion" clause.[43]

Historian John Witte notes that, "[v]iewed in isolation, the development might seem to be a rather remarkable attack on the basic principles of federalism built into the text of the First Amendment ('*Congress* shall make no law. . .')." But, Witte says, "this development was of a piece with other movements of the day—the growing federalization of society and the economy through the New Deal legislation and case law, the pressing need for national solidarity in the face of World War II and in the Cold War to follow, the grim lessons about religious and cultural bigotry learned through the Holocaust and the gulag."[44]

The application of the Free Exercise Clause to the states has been almost universally accepted. But, as Professor Steven Green has noted, however, "ever since the Court incorporated the Establishment Clause in 1947, critics have charged that freedom from religious establishments does not constitute an individual liberty interest protected by the due process clause of the Fourteenth Amendment."[45] Green traces the early history of this argument on the Court and within academic circles:

> In the second school prayer case, a dissenting Justice Stewart half-heartedly asserted: "the Establishment Clause was primarily an attempt to insure that Congress not only would be powerless to establish a national church but would also be unable to interfere with existing state establishments." But by then, Stewart stood alone in his belief, with Justice Brennan replying that the argument was coming too late in the day and had been rendered irrelevant by the passage of the Fourteenth Amendment. Still, the argument lingered throughout the 1960s and 1970s. In a 1978 monograph popular in conservative circles, Michael Malbin reviewed the various proposals for the Establishment Clause and concluded that the final language selected—"a law respecting an establishment of religion"—was designed to prohibit Congress from passing law that would affect the religious establishments in the states.[46]

Justice Thomas picked up this line of argument in 2004 in the case of *Elk Grove Unified School District v. Newdow*. Thomas wrote a concurring opinion in which he concluded that "it makes little sense" to apply the Establishment Clause to the states:

> I accept that the Free Exercise Clause, which clearly protects an individual right, applies against the States through the Fourteenth Amendment. But the Establishment Clause is another matter. The text and history of the Establishment Clause strongly suggest that it is a federalism provision intended to prevent Congress from interfering with state establishments. Thus, unlike the Free Exercise Clause, which does protect an individual right, it makes little sense to incorporate the Establishment Clause. . . .
>
> As a textual matter, this Clause probably prohibits Congress from establishing a national religion. But . . . nothing in the text of the Clause suggests that it reaches any further. The Establishment Clause does not purport to protect individual rights. By contrast, the Free Exercise Clause plainly protects individuals against congressional interference with the right to exercise their religion, and the remaining Clauses within the First Amendment expressly disable Congress from "abridging [particular] *freedom[s]*." . . .
>
> Quite simply, the Establishment Clause is best understood as a federalism provision—it protects state establishments from federal interference but does not protect any individual right. These two features independently make incorporation of the Clause difficult to understand. The best argument in favor of incorporation would be that, by disabling Congress from establishing a national religion, the Clause protected an individual right, enforceable against the Federal Government, to be free from coercive federal establishments. . . .
>
> But even assuming that the Establishment Clause precludes the Federal Government from establishing a national religion, it does not follow that the Clause created or protects any individual right. For the reasons discussed above, it is more likely that States and only States were the direct beneficiaries. . . .
>
> I would welcome the opportunity to consider more fully the difficult questions whether and how the Establishment Clause applies against the States. One observation suffices for now: As strange as it sounds, an incorporated Establishment Clause prohibits exactly what the Establishment Clause protected—state practices that pertain to "an establishment of religion." At the very least, the burden of persuasion rests with anyone who claims that the term took on a different meaning upon incorporation.[47]

It is important to note that Justice Thomas not only believes that the Establishment Clause should not bind the states; he also argues that the Establishment Clause creates no individual rights. Justice Thomas spoke only for himself in this opinion, but this issue is likely to continue to be prominent in future debates on the Court. If a future Court ever adopted Justice Thomas' view, there would be a sea change in our understanding of the relationship between religion and government. States presumably could choose to prefer one or more faiths through their laws and policies, as long as such laws did not violate state law or the federal Free Exercise Clause. And, presumably many of the Supreme Court's decisions would be undone under this view, including the Court's decisions prohibiting school-sponsored prayer and Bible readings.

In response to Thomas' argument, Professor Steven Green has argued that, while "the ultimate phrasing of the Establishment Clause may indicate the presence of federalism concerns, such was not the primary or overriding impetus behind the call for or drafting of the First Amendment. Rather, the Establishment Clause reflects broad substantive values upon which a majority of early Americans could agree."[48] Further, Professor Kurt Lash has argued that it is appropriate to focus the historical analysis of incorporated rights on the time of the adoption of the civil war amendments rather than at the time of our nation's founding.[49] According to Professor Lash's research, there is ample evidence that the framers of the Fourteenth Amendment believed that the interests embodied in both the Establishment and Free Exercise Clauses were liberties that should not be abridged by the states.

## The "Distinctiveness" of Religion

A significant—and ongoing—issue in religion clause jurisprudence has been the extent to which the First Amendment requires the government—and courts through their application of the clauses—to treat religious activities and institutions distinctively from similarly situated actions and institutions. By identifying the word "religion," the language of the First Amendment suggests, in some instances, that religion should be singled out for special protection ("free exercise"), but that in other instances, religious institutions may be disabled from receiving certain government benefits ("nonestablishment"). According to Professors Ira Lupu and Robert Tuttle,

> The founders' experiment took form in provisions that assumed the distinctiveness of religious beliefs and institutions. Provisions like the Nonestablishment Clause of the First Amendment single out religious institutions for special treatment, originally limiting the support that the federal government may provide them when compared with their secular counterparts, and insulating state establishments from federal interference. Guarantees of religious liberty, such as the Free Exercise Clause of the First Amendment, seem to empower religious institutions, creating immunities against state regulation that other entities may not share.[50]

This approach was perhaps best represented on the modern Court by Justice William Brennan, who championed a robust interpretation of the Free Exercise Clause while advocating a rigorous application of nonestablishment principles. The alternative approach— one that argues that government should treat religion the same as non-religion—has been prominently advanced by Professor Philip B. Kurland. Kurland argued that the religion clauses mean "that government cannot utilize religion as a standard for action or inaction because these clauses, read together as they should be, prohibit classification in terms of religion either to confer a benefit or to impose a burden."[51] At a minimum, this latter approach, by eliminating any constitutional mandate for the distinctive treatment of religion, has the virtue of simplicity: it diffuses perceived tension between the two clauses while it precludes the specter of government officials evaluating the religiosity of any motivation or institution.

This fundamental issue of religious distinctiveness—and how judges perceive the appropriate balance—underlies much of the Court's jurisprudence. In the free exercise context, the Court in 1990 departed from an almost thirty year practice of viewing free exercise claims as distinctive, choosing instead to treat religion basically the same as non-religion in this context.[52] On the Establishment Clause side, the question of whether, and in what contexts, the government should be able to "take religion into account" through its policies and practices, remains undecided.[53] Several members of the current Court believe, however, that the evenhanded treatment of religious motivations and institutions and their secular counterparts should be the default rule.

## "No-Aid Separation" v. "Evenhanded Neutrality"

One such recurring theme in the interpretation of the Establishment Clause includes the struggle between what is often called a "no-aid separationist" approach to church-state issues, an approach that generally prohibits government funding for religious activities, and a competing approach, sometimes known as "evenhanded neutrality," that generally insists that the government should treat religion the same as non-religion in terms of access to government funds.

In the Court's first interpretation and application of the Establishment Clause in the 1947 *Everson v. Board of Education* case, Justice Hugo Black wrote: "No tax in any amount, large or small, can be levied to support any religious activities or institutions, whatever they may be called, or whatever form they may adopt to teach or practice religion."[54] Despite this ringing, "no-aid separation" rhetoric, the Court actually narrowly approved the specific aid at issue in the *Everson* case—the provision of state-subsidized bus rides for the students of religious as well as public schools. Thus, as Professor Douglas Laycock has explained, the themes of "no-aid separation" and evenhanded neutrality were present in the *Everson* case and "[t]he tension between these two approaches has continued ever since."[55]

While some support for the evenhanded neutrality theory can be detected in Supreme Court case law handed down in the period between the 1940s to the mid-1980s, the dominant approach during that time was "no-aid separation." During this era, any government aid that flowed to religious institutions was carefully scrutinized to ensure that the aid would not be used to support religious activities. One of the Court's responses to this concern was to adopt the "pervasively sectarian" test. This test basically presumes that some religious institutions are ineligible for government funding because they are so pervaded with religion that one of two unconstitutional things would occur if aid flowed to them: either the aid would support religion or the aid would have to be so closely regulated and monitored to ensure that it does not to flow to religion, it would result in excessive church-state entanglement.

As noted above, it must be emphasized that the "no-aid" approach did not mean that the Court did not allow any government aid to flow to religious institutions. The Court recognized a class of religious institutions as falling outside the category of "pervasively sectarian," most prominently religiously affiliated institutions of higher education and some religiously affiliated social service providers. These entities were permitted to receive direct government aid so long as that aid subsidized only secular rather than religious activities. And, even during the high water mark of the Court's "separationist" approach to these issues, it still allowed certain forms of aid ultimately to reach "pervasively sectarian" religious schools under various legal theories, but the aid was relatively minimal and it was subjected to exacting scrutiny. (See chapter 11.)

However, certain changes in Court personnel that occurred during the late 1980s and early 1990s had a profound affect on this issue. In the 1990s, support for the "evenhanded neutrality" approach began to grow. Whereas the baseline for the separationist approach is to treat some religious institutions differently from nonreligious institutions and religious activities differently from nonreligious activities, the "evenhanded neutrality" approach basically rejects the notion that religious institutions must be treated differently in terms of their ability to access government funding and tends to lift most regulations that are placed on religious but not nonreligious activities.

A plurality opinion written by Justice Thomas in 2000 in the case of *Mitchell v. Helms* describes this approach in greater detail. Thomas wrote:

> If the religious, irreligious, and areligious are all alike eligible for governmental aid, no one would conclude that any indoctrination that any particular recipient conducts has been done at the behest of the government. For attribution of indoctrination is a relative question. If the government is offering assistance to recipients who provide, so to speak, a broad range of indoctrination, the government itself is not thought responsible for any particular indoctrination.[56]

In his dissenting opinion in that case, Justice David Souter profoundly objected to the plurality's attempt to compress the Establishment Clause analysis in this way. He argued that a government program did not pass constitutional muster simply because it gave religious groups no preferential access to government funds over nongovernmental groups. Souter explained:

> [I]f we looked no further than evenhandedness, and failed to ask what activities the aid might support, or in fact did support, religious schools could be blessed with government funding as massive as expenditures made for the benefit of their public school counterparts, and religious missions would thrive on public money. This is why the consideration of less than universal neutrality has never been recognized as dispositive and has always been teamed with attention to other facts bearing on the substantive prohibition of support for a school's religious objective.[57]

In this same plurality opinion in the *Mitchell* case, Justice Thomas and the three justices who joined him (Chief Justice Rehnquist and Justices Scalia and Kennedy) also vigorously objected to the "pervasively sectarian" test. Among his many objections to the test, Thomas argued that it was based in anti-Catholic bigotry.[58] Justice Souter and his fellow dissenters vigorously objected to this argument as well, stating: "The relevance of [whether the institution is pervasively religious] is simply a matter of common sense: where religious indoctrination pervades school activities of children and adolescents, it takes great care to be able to aid the school without supporting the doctrinal effort." Souter concluded:

> My concern with [the plurality's] arguments [on the pervasively sectarian test] goes not so much to their details as it does to the fact that the plurality's choice to employ imputations of bigotry and irreligion as terms in the Court's debate makes one point

clear: that in rejecting the principle of no aid to a school's religious mission the plurality is attacking the most fundamental assumption underlying the Establishment Clause, that government can in fact operate with neutrality in its relation to religion. I believe that it can, and so respectfully dissent.[59]

The year 2002 marked a clear victory for the evenhanded neutrality approach in the context of indirect government aid. In that year the Court held that the federal Establishment Clause does not bar the inclusion of religious, as well as other non-private, schools in certain publicly funded voucher programs.[60] The justices continue to be more deeply divided, however, when the aid involved is direct (e.g., government grants or contracts) rather than indirect (e.g., government vouchers or certificates), making the outcome on these issues much less certain. In short, while it seems clear that the Court is in the midst of some sort of paradigm shift, it is not yet clear how extensive the shift will be.

### Use of Speech Principles in Religion Clause Jurisprudence

An additional approach in modern religion clause jurisprudence has been the Court's borrowing from free speech analysis to resolve religion clause conflicts. This application of free speech concepts has been most noticeable in the free exercise context, as religious expression is also considered a subset of protected free speech and assembly. But as will be seen in several of the Court's Establishment Clause cases, free speech paradigms are often juxtaposed against claims that providing access or financial benefits to religious groups violates the Establishment Clause. Significantly, it is in its free speech jurisprudence that the Court first began to apply an evenhanded neutrality approach to religion clause conflicts.

In a nutshell, the Free Speech Clause places severe restrictions on the ability of the government to regulate nongovernmental expression on the basis of its content or subject matter. For example, a government entity could not enact a law allowing commercial billboards but prohibiting billboards endorsing political candidates. As the Court has frequently reaffirmed, "above all else, the First Amendment means that government has no power to restrict expression because of [disfavor with] its message, its ideas, its subject matter or its content."[61] As Justice Anthony Kennedy has observed:

> [It] is through speech that our convictions and beliefs are influenced, expressed, and tested. It is through speech that we bring those beliefs to bear on Government and on society. It is through speech that our personalities are formed and expressed. The citizen is entitled to seek out or reject certain ideas or influences without Government interference or control.[62]

Relatedly, the Court has held that government regulations that turn on the *viewpoint* of any particular expression are equally invalid, if not more so. In essence, the government could not permit billboards endorsing Democratic candidates for public office but forbid billboards that endorsed Republican candidates for public office. The theory, again, is that the government should not disfavor the expression of certain topics, ideas, or perspectives by private individuals. (In contrast, the Court has been more deferential to government regulations that do not turn on subject matter or viewpoint but place neutral restrictions on the time, place, or manner of expression, such as a sound ordinance in public parks after dark.)

Beginning in the 1980s, the Court began applying these free speech concepts in the religion clause context, sometimes relying on the Free Speech Clause to resolve religious expression claims rather than applying the Free Exercise Clause. (In actuality, many of the cases involving government restrictions on the proselytizing activities of Jehovah's Witnesses in the 1930s and 1940s were resolved by applying other free speech concepts, such as prohibitions on prior restraints.) Thus, in *Widmar v. Vincent*, the Court held that a public university could not prohibit a student religious group from using its classrooms and student center for meetings when it had a policy permitting similar access to nonreligious student groups. Despite the university's claim that providing such access to the religious group would violate the Establishment Clause (i.e., by using government property for worship activities), the Court found that the university had impermissibly discriminated against the group based on the religious content of its speech.[63]

Twelve years later the Court extended its *Widmar* analysis to strike a more limited access policy of a school district that barred a religious group from using a public school facility to show a film series in the evenings. The Court found that because the school district permitted access for discussions about family and child rearing issues from a secular perspective, it could not prohibit access for similar discussions from a religious perspective. "The film series involved here no doubt dealt with a subject otherwise permissible," the Court wrote, "and its exhibition was denied solely because the series dealt with the subject from a religious standpoint. The principle that has emerged from our cases 'is that the First Amendment forbids the government to regulate speech in ways that favor some viewpoints or ideas at the expense of others.'"[64]

In subsequent cases, the high court has applied free expression principles to reaffirm the distinction between government expression and expression of nongovernment groups that takes place on government property. In *Board of Education v. Mergens* (1990), involving the constitutionality of student-led Bible clubs in public secondary schools, the Court wrote that "there is a crucial difference between government[al] speech endorsing religion, which the Establishment Clause forbids, and [nongovernmental] speech endorsing religion, which the Free Speech and Free Exercise Clauses protect."

The Court's application of free speech standards in the religion clause context has not been without controversy, particularly from those who argue that religion represents more than a mere viewpoint to be counterbalanced against nonreligious perspectives. As Justice Kennedy acknowledged in *Rosenberger v. Rector of the University of Virginia*,

> [it] is, in a sense, something of an understatement to speak of religious thought and discussion as just a viewpoint, as distinct from a comprehensive body of thought. . . . Religion may be a vast area of inquiry, but it also provides . . . a specific premise, a perspective, a standpoint from which a variety of subjects may be discussed and considered.[65]

Even more controversial has been the movement to apply rules against viewpoint distinctions to other religion clause contexts, such as with government funding programs, which frequently impose restrictions on using public monies for religious purposes. Some have argued that because the framers intended to create a secular state, the government can prefer nonreligious perspectives in its own programs without disparaging religion, provided it is not funding or facilitating nongovernmental expression. Others disagree, claiming that even in government-run programs, the government must afford similar treatment of religious and nonreligious values. Finally, the application of content and viewpoint analysis in religion clause cases is also indicative of the general trend toward treating religiously motivated conduct and religious institutions the same as their secular counterparts.

## Accommodation of Religion

When the government accommodates religion, it tailors its laws and policies in ways that provide citizens greater freedom to practice their faith. Scholars have enumerated three types of accommodation: accommodations that are mandatory under the Constitution, ones that the Constitution permits and ones the Constitution forbids. Mandatory accommodations are those that are required under the Free Exercise Clause. Before 1990, the Supreme Court used a legal standard that was quite favorable to religious accommodations. The basic rule was that the government had to accommodate religious exercise if the exercise was substantially burdened by the government and the government had no narrowly tailored compelling interest to justify such a burden. Thus, the government could prevail under this standard, but it had to have an interest of the highest order, such as health and safety, to justify the substantial burdens that it placed on religious practices, regardless of whether religion was intentionally targeted by the government for such burdensome treatment or whether such treatment was purely unintentional. Under this standard, the Court held that Amish schoolchildren must be excused from mandatory schooling requirements after the eighth grade if they seek such accommodation.[66] The Court also required a state unemployment compensation board to pay unemployment benefits to a woman who had been fired from her job because she would not work on her Sabbath and could find no other job that would not require her to work on this day.[67]

But, in 1990, the Supreme Court ruled in *Employment Division of Oregon v. Smith* that the state need not accommodate religious exercise in cases where the law was neutral and generally applicable—meaning laws that did not single out religion for adverse treatment, but merely treated religion exercise the same as nonreligious activities.[68] Under this new rule, the government no longer had any constitutional duty to accommodate religious exercise in most circumstances. (See chapter 8.)

The *Smith* decision left open the door, however, for permissive accommodations, ones that the legislature or other governmental bodies are not required to make under the Constitution, but may chose to make in order to provide greater protection for religious freedom. The government had often made such accommodations even before the *Smith* decision was handed down. For example, states and localities have long exempted property held by religious or other charitable and educational groups from taxation. The Court upheld such an exemption in 1970 in *Walz v. Tax Commission.*[69] The Court did not find that this exemption was mandated by the Free Exercise Clause, but that the Establishment Clause did not prohibit the state from granting religious and other entities such an exemption.

The Court also upheld accommodations that excused only religious bodies from particular burdens. For example, the 1964 Civil Rights Act prohibits religious discrimination (as well as other forms of discrimination) in employment, but it allows religious organizations to discriminate on the basis of religion when hiring staff and in other employment matters. When the Act originally passed in 1964, it only exempted jobs within religious organizations that performed religious activities, but this exemption was broadened in 1972 to extend to all employment positions within religious groups. The Court upheld this exemption in 1987, saying it did not violate the Establishment Clause because it lifted a burden on religious exercise. The burden was that, without this exemption, religious organizations would be forced to guess which job positions a court would consider religious and which positions it would not consider religious, and this could inhibit the mission of a religious organization. The Court noted:

This Court has long recognized that the government may (and sometimes must) accommodate religious practices and that it may do so without violating the Establishment Clause. It is well established, too, that "the limits of permissible state accommodation to religion are by no means co-extensive with the noninterference mandated by the Free Exercise Clause." There is ample room under the Establishment Clause for "benevolent neutrality which will permit religious exercise to exist without sponsorship and without interference." At some point, accommodation may devolve into "an unlawful fostering of religion," but these are not such cases, in our view. . . .

We find unpersuasive the District Court's reliance on the fact that [the Act] singles out religious entities for a benefit. Although the Court has given weight to this consideration in its past decisions, it has never indicated that statutes that give special consideration to religious groups are *per se* invalid. That would run contrary to the teaching of our cases that there is ample room for accommodation of religion under the Establishment Clause. Where, as here, government acts with the proper purpose of lifting a regulation that burdens the exercise of religion, we see no reason to require that the exemption come packaged with benefits to secular entities.[70]

Once the *Smith* decision was handed down in 1990, these permissive accommodations became even more important—they generally were the only way for a religious observer to be exempted from a legal obligation that conflicted with his or her faith. Among other legislative action, this led to the enactment of the Religious Freedom Restoration Act (RFRA) in 1993 and the Religious Land Use and Institutionalized Persons Act (RLUIPA) in 2000. (See chapter 8.)

In 2005, the Court further solidified its position in support of permissive accommodations, including ones that single out religion for special treatment.[71] The case was *Cutter v. Wilkinson*, which involved a challenge to the constitutionality of RLUIPA. In that case, the Court explained that the institutionalized persons provisions of the Act, which singled out religious exercise for special treatment, "alleviate[d] exceptional government-created burdens on private religious exercise" and thus did not violate the Establishment Clause. The Court further noted that

the Act on its face does not founder on shoals our prior decisions have identified: Properly applying RLUIPA, courts must take adequate account of the burdens a requested accommodation may impose on nonbeneficiaries, see *Estate of Thornton v. Caldor, Inc.*, (1985); and they must be satisfied that the Act's prescriptions are and will be administered neutrally among different faiths, see *Board of Education of Kiryas Joel School District. v. Grumet*, (1994).[72]

The *Cutter* Court's efforts to distinguish the cases of *Thornton v. Caldor* and *Kiryas Joel School District v. Grumet* help to clarify some important limits on the state's ability to accommodate religion. In *Thornton*, the Court considered a state law that guaranteed every employee the right not to work on whatever day he or she considered to be the Sabbath. In the Court's words, "[t]he State has thus decreed that those who observe a Sabbath any day of the week as a matter of religious conviction must be relieved of the duty to work on that day, no matter what burden or inconvenience this imposes on the employer or fellow workers."[73] The Court found that the absolute nature of this right violated the Establishment Clause. The fact that it placed burdens on nongovernmental actors (private employers and non-Sabbath observing employees) also appears to have been viewed as significant by the Court.

In the *Kiryas Joel* case, the Court "invalidated a state law that carved out a separate school district to serve exclusively a community of highly religious Jews, the Satmar Hasidim . . . in part because it 'singled out a particular religious sect for special treatment.'"[74] In contrast, the Court stated in *Cutter*, "RLUIPA presents no such defect[;] [i]t confers no privileged status on any particular religious sect, and singles out no bona fide faith for disadvantageous treatment." Thus, the Court emphasized that an accommodation runs afoul of the Constitution when it prefers some faiths over others. Indeed, as the Court has long recognized, "[t]he clearest command of the Establishment Clause is that one religious denomination cannot be officially preferred over another."[75]

This helps to underscore the point that proper accommodations fulfill objectives embodied not only by the Free Exercise Clause, but also by the Establishment Clause. When an accommodation ensures that all religions are treated the same, equal rights to religious freedom are furthered. Moreover, when the government lifts regulatory burdens from the practice of faith, it can be said that the government is leaving religion where it belongs—in the hands of religious individuals and groups rather than the government. As the Court said in the *Amos* case: "A law is not unconstitutional simply because it *allows* churches to advance religion, which is their very purpose. For a law to have forbidden 'effects' under *Lemon*, it must be fair to say that the *government itself* has advanced religion through its own activities and influence."[76]

## "Play in the Joints"

A constitutional principle that is closely related to the accommodation notion is the idea that "there is room for play in the joints" between the religion clauses of the First Amendment. Permissive accommodations, such as the ones embodied in the institutionalized persons provisions of RLUIPA, are one example of governmental laws and policies that exist within this space. As the Court stated in *Cutter*: "Our decisions recognize that 'there is room for play in the joints' between the Clauses, some space for legislative action neither compelled by the Free Exercise Clause nor prohibited by the Establishment Clause."[77]

Another type of governmental action that exists within this space between dictates of the two religion clauses is one that forbids certain interaction between religion and government that, while not prohibited by the federal Establishment Clause, is also not required by the federal Free Exercise Clause. In the 2004 case of *Locke v. Davey*, the Court considered a Washington state scholarship program designed to assist students of high achievement with their postsecondary educational expenses.[78] In light of the Washington constitution's stringent prohibition on the use of government funds for religious purposes (a provision that is interpreted in ways that places tighter limits on government aid for religious institutions and activities than does the federal Constitution), the program prohibited students from using state scholarship money at any school where they were pursuing a degree in devotional theology. Washington viewed the use of state money to pay for such degrees as violating its important interest in refraining from becoming involved in the training of clergy.

The Court rejected the argument that the state's refusal to subsidize degrees in devotional theology as part of this scholarship program violated the Free Exercise Clause. Writing for the Court majority in *Locke*, Chief Justice Rehnquist stated: "The State's interest in not funding the pursuit of devotional degrees is substantial and the exclusion of such funding places a relatively minor burden on Promise Scholars. If any room exists between the two Religion Clauses, it must be here."[79]

With the *Locke* and *Cutter* decisions, it is clear that governmental bodies will be permitted a significant amount of latitude to shape policies that do not violate either religion clause, but draw on the values of one or both of them. The further definition of this space between the clauses will be an important area to watch in the future.

## "Complementary Values, Conflicting Pressures"

In the 2005 *Cutter* decision, the Court stated:

> The Religion Clauses of the First Amendment provide: "Congress shall make no law respecting an establishment of religion, or prohibiting the free exercise thereof." The first of the two Clauses, commonly called the Establishment Clause, commands a separation of church and state. The second, the Free Exercise Clause, requires government respect for, and noninterference with, the religious beliefs and practices of our Nation's people. While the two Clauses express complementary values, they often exert conflicting pressures. See *Walz*, 397 U.S., 668-669 ("The Court has struggled to find a neutral course between the two Religion Clauses, both of which are cast in absolute terms, and either of which, if expanded to a logical extreme, would tend to clash with the other.")[80]

Without doubt, there is some tension between the requirements of the two religion clauses. As the Court recognized in the *Cutter* case, when the state strives to protect free exercise, it must steer clear of governmental actions that have the primary effect of promoting religion. A law that requires the absolute accommodation of religious practice, regardless of other factors, is one example of the ways in which such efforts may run afoul of the Establishment Clause. Conversely, when the government takes steps to ensure that it does not itself promote religion, it must leave ample room for citizens and religious groups to do so on their own behalf. For example, while the government itself is prohibited from promoting religion, the government generally must permit religious speakers the same access to its property that other nongovernmental groups enjoy.

The tension between the clauses sometimes is viewed in a negative light because it can create legal issues that are difficult to resolve. But this tension also should be regarded as a positive quality—it helps to ensure that the nation does not go astray by placing government sanction on religion on the one hand, or running roughshod over personal religious practice on the other. That "tension" may exist does not mean that the values represented in the two religion clauses are in conflict. Indeed, Supreme Court jurisprudence may be viewed as an ongoing effort to harmonize the two clauses in service of the elusive and important goal of religious freedom for all.

# CHAPTER 4

# WHAT IS RELIGION?

Earlier chapters have described the Constitution's provisions on religion and the history of their writing and interpretation. They provide the background and context for the rest of the book's explanation of themes of church-state relationships that have emerged from the courts' interpretation of the Constitution. But a fundamental question remains. What is religion? How has the Supreme Court understood the nature of religion as it has decided First Amendment cases?

In the approximately one hundred cases it has decided involving the religion clauses, the Supreme Court has never developed a definitive definition of religion for the purposes of the First Amendment. Why?

On the one hand, courts must develop ways of deciding whether an activity or belief is religious, otherwise they will not be able to carry out their constitutional mandate to protect the free exercise of religion and to prohibit actions respecting governmental establishments of faith. The First Amendment singles out religion for distinctive treatment. Therefore, there must be some understanding of what serves as "religion" in order for courts to interpret the religion clauses. On the other hand, attempts to define and describe religion may undermine the very values the religion clauses seek to protect. After all, to define a right is to place limitations on understandings of that interest. Defining "religion," in particular, may raise risks that the courts or the government have defined what activity qualifies as "religious" either too broadly or too narrowly.

For example, if the courts were to rely on a theistic definition of religion, one that includes only those faiths that believe in a god, that would leave the exercise of nontheistic faiths such as Theravda[1] Buddhism or Taoism unprotected. However, if courts were to rely on a definition of religion that had no real boundaries, it would make it impossible to give religion the kind of special treatment commanded by the religion clauses. Moreover, if the courts were to attempt to evaluate the truthfulness of a particular religion, they would cross a constitutional line, because the Establishment Clause forbids the government from declaring what is true and what is false in matters of faith.

The Court saw less complexity in these issues in its early years. In one of the Mormon polygamy cases decided in 1890, *Davis v. Beason* (chapter 6), the Court described religion in theistic terms: "The term 'religion' has reference to one's views of his relations to his Creator, and to the obligations they impose of reverence for his being and character, and of obedience to his will."[2] Similarly, in a 1931 case, *United States v. Macintosh* (chapter 6), in which the Court denied a selective conscientious objector alien the right to American citizenship because of his attitude toward fighting in war, Chief Justice Charles Evans Hughes wrote in dissent: "The essence of religion is belief in a relation to God involving duties superior to those arising from any human relation."[3]

Subsequent circumstances caused the Court to think about religion more broadly. *Torcaso v. Watkins* (chapter 22) presented a challenge to a Maryland constitutional provision that required one to affirm a belief in God as a condition to holding public office. In finding for the plaintiff, Justice Hugo Black wrote:

> We repeat and again reaffirm that neither a State nor the Federal Government can constitutionally force a person "to profess a belief or disbelief in any religion." Neither can constitutionally pass laws or impose requirements which aid all religions as against non-believers, and neither can aid those religions based on a belief in the existence of God as against those religions founded on different beliefs. . . .[4]

To emphasize the last point, Justice Black said in what has become one of the more controversial footnotes in the church-state corpus: "Among religions in this country which do not teach would generally be considered a belief in the existence of God are Buddhism, Taoism, Ethical Culture, Secular Humanism, and others."[5] Thus, the 1961 case of *Torcaso* indicated that the Court now understood religion as a concept that included certain non-theistic as well as theistic beliefs.[6]

In 1965 the Court accepted a case that required it to squarely confront the question of the nature of religion, *United States v. Seeger*.[7] Because *Seeger* is about the interpretation of Selective Service law—in particular, what qualifies as a religious conscientious objection to war—some background is in order.

In the Draft Act of 1917, enacted in conjunction with America's involvement in World War I, Congress exempted from bearing arms those who were members of historic "peace churches": groups such as the Quakers, the Mennonites, and the Church of the Brethren. The exact language was:

> Nothing in this Act contained shall be construed to require or compel any person to serve in any of the forces herein provided for who is found to be a member of any well-recognized religious sect or organization at present organized and existing and whose existing creed or principles forbid its members to participate in war in any form and whose religious convictions are against war or participation therein in accordance with the creed or principles of said religious organization.[8]

Notice there was no definition of what religions or creeds qualified for the exemption, but only language deferential to those groups which could demonstrate a traditional belief against bearing arms.

In 1940, the statutory language was shortened to read:

> Nothing contained in this Act shall be construed to require any person to be subject to combatant training and service in the land or naval forces of the United States who, by reason religious training or belief, is conscientiously opposed to participation in war in any form.[9]

At the same time, the exemption was broadened in that it was no longer necessary to belong to a peace church, so long as one's objection to war was based on "religious training or belief," which was not defined.

Apparently Congress was not comfortable with "religious training or belief" being undefined, however, for in 1948 it changed the language of the statute yet again.

> Nothing contained in this title shall be construed to require any person to be subject to combatant training and service in the armed forces of the United States who, by reason of religious training or belief, is conscientiously opposed to participating in war in any form. Religious training or belief in this connection means an individual's belief in a relation to a Supreme Being involving duties superior to those arising from any human relation, but does not include essentially political, sociological, or philosophical view or a merely personal moral code.[10]

Note that the definition of "religious training and belief" in this last enactment was a theistic one (i.e., "Supreme Being"), but was not as specific in its reference to the deity as in the earlier Court definitions described above. This definition made a significant difference in the *Seeger* case when the Supreme Court had to tackle the eligibility for conscientious objector status of several applicants with unconventional beliefs. *Seeger* is widely described as the case in which the Supreme Court came closest to articulating a definition of religion. Although the Court merely defined a term in the conscientious objector statute, and was not considering a free exercise challenge to the law, the Court's discussion of religion has a constitutional ring to it.

*Seeger* was the consolidation of petitions for conscientious objector status from three individuals, all with unconventional "religious" beliefs. None of the three applicants thought of himself as religious in any sectarian or even traditional theological sense. One applicant (Seeger) was unwilling to state whether he believed in God, "except in the remotest sense." His moral aversion to war was based on philosophical study and his "belief in and devotion to goodness and virtue for their own sakes, and a religious faith in a purely ethical creed." Another applicant stated he believed in "'Godness' which was 'the Ultimate Cause for the fact of the Being of the Universe.'" His unwillingness to bear arms was based on his belief that the "'most important religious law' was that 'no man ought ever to wilfully sacrifice another man's life as a means to any other end.'" The third applicant defined religion as "'the supreme expression of human nature; it is man thinking his highest, feeling his deepest, and living his best.'" This last applicant stated that he supposed "'you could call that a belief in the Supreme Being or God. These just do not happen to be the words I use.'"[11]

In the *Seeger* case, the Court faced the task of deciding whether these expressions of objection to participating in war fit the statutory requirement of "religious training or belief" defined as "an individual's belief in a relation to a Supreme Being." In an opinion written by Justice Tom Clark, the Court decided that the applicants' beliefs did fit. Highly significant for the Court was that the "Supreme Being" clause in the 1948 statute virtually replicated the definition of religion in Chief Justice Charles Evans Hughes' dissent in *United States v. Macintosh*, quoted above. But whereas Hughes had used the term "God," Congress had used the phrase "Supreme Being." In Justice Clark's mind, that was the key to deciding *Seeger*.

> In spite of the elusive nature of the inquiry, we are not without certain guidelines. In amending the 1940 Act, Congress adopted almost intact the language of Chief

Justice Hughes in *United States v. Macintosh*: "The essence of religion is belief in a relation to *God* involving duties superior to those arising from any human relation."

By comparing the statutory definition with those words, however, it becomes readily apparent that the Congress deliberately broadened them by substituting the phrase "Supreme Being" for the appellation "God." And in so doing it is also significant that Congress did not elaborate on the form or nature of this higher authority which it chose to designate as "Supreme Being."[12]

After noting the elastic nature of the statutory language, the Court applied it to the conscientious objection applicants at bar. It did so by formulating a new test to define religion.

Under the 1940 Act it was necessary only to have a conviction based on religious training and belief; we believe that is all that is required here. Within that phrase would come all sincere religious beliefs which are based upon a power or being, or upon a faith, to which all else is subordinate or upon which all else is ultimately dependent. The test might be stated in these words: A sincere and meaningful belief which occupies in the life of its possessor a place parallel to that filled by the God of those admittedly qualifying for the exemption comes within the statutory definition. This construction avoids imputing to Congress an intent to classify different religious beliefs, exempting some and excluding others, and is in accord with the well-established congressional policy of equal treatment for those whose opposition to service is grounded in their religious tenets. . . . While the applicant's words may differ, the test is simple of application. It is essentially an objective one, namely, does the claimed belief occupy the same place in the life of the objector as an orthodox belief in God holds in the life of one clearly qualified for exemption?[13]

As noted above, the Court found that the applicants' beliefs met this test. In part, the Court relied on the applicants' own characterization of their beliefs. The Court said:

The records in these cases . . . show that at no time did any one of the applicants suggest that his objection was based on a "merely personal moral code." Indeed at the outset each of them claimed in his application that his objection was based on a religious belief. We have construed the statutory definition broadly and it follows that any exception to it must be interpreted narrowly. The use by Congress of the words "merely personal" seems to us to restrict the exception to a moral code which is not only personal but which is the sole basis for the registrant's belief and is in no way related to a Supreme Being.[14]

Along the way toward formulating this test, the Court cited its concern to ensure that its concept of religion "embrace[d] the ever-broadening understanding of the modern religious community." In other words, traditional religious beliefs and practices clearly qualified as religion under the law, but the Court wanted to articulate a definition of religion that also would protect less orthodox or less familiar religious beliefs and practices. To define some of these less orthodox religious beliefs, it looked to several contemporary theologians. One was Protestant theologian Paul Tillich, who defined religion as "ultimate concern" and described God as "the ground of our very being," as "the seriousness of that doubt in which meaning within meaningless is affirmed." People may perceive this meaning within meaninglessness even when they cannot profess the God of traditional theism, Tillich said.

The Court also quoted the Second Vatican Council of the Roman Catholic Church, which was in progress when *Seeger* was decided. The Court said the Council had articulated "a most significant declaration on religion."

> Ever since primordial days, numerous peoples have had a certain perception of that hidden power which hovers over the course of things and over the events that make up the lives of men; some have even come to know of a Supreme Being and Father. . . . The Church regards with sincere reverence those ways of action and of life, precepts and teachings which, although they differ from the ones she sets forth, reflect nonetheless a ray of that Truth which enlightens all men.[15]

Accordingly, the Court concluded:

> These are but a few of the views that comprise the broad spectrum of religious beliefs found among us. But they demonstrate very clearly the diverse manners in which beliefs, equally paramount in the lives of their possessors, may be articulated. They further reveal the difficulties inherent in placing too narrow a construction on the provisions of the [conscientious objector statute] and thereby lend conclusive support to the construction which we find today that Congress intended.[16]

The Court's construction of the statute was not explicitly theistic. It was broad enough to encompass those who were not able or willing to use traditional God-language in their articulation of their ultimate commitments. But, as a practical matter, how were draft boards or courts to determine whether people with such nebulous religious expression actually met the statutory requirements for conscientious objector status? The authority making the judgment on an applicant's qualification evaluated the applicant's sincerity and compared the applicant's beliefs with that of a person (real or hypothetical) of conventional belief who clearly did qualify. If the unconventional applicant's views were sincere and occupied the same place in the person's life as the religious commitments of a conventional believer, he qualified. As quoted above, the Court said the test was "simple" and "objective." But the Court was being highly optimistic. One can hardly think of a more difficult, and subjective, task than determining another person's sincerity, much less trying to gauge one person's sincerity in comparison with another person's, and then evaluating the depth of that conviction. The "bottom line" of *Seeger* is that it formulated an extremely broad, and pliable, concept of religion.

The *Seeger* Court also emphasized that while the sincerity of the applicants' beliefs were fair game for evaluation, the validity of their beliefs were not.

> The validity of what he believes cannot be questioned. Some theologians, and indeed some examiners, might be tempted to question the existence of the registrant's "Supreme Being" or the truth of his concepts. But these are inquiries foreclosed to Government. . . . Local boards and courts in this sense are not free to reject beliefs because they consider them to be "incomprehensible." Their task is to decide whether the beliefs professed by a registrant are sincerely held and whether they are, in his own scheme of things, religious.
>
> But we hasten to emphasize that while the "truth" of a belief is not open to question, there remains the significant question whether it is "truly held." This is the threshold question of sincerity which must be resolved in every case.[17]

In 1967 Congress responded to the *Seeger* decision by rewriting the conscientious objection statute and removing the "Supreme Being" language:

> Nothing contained in this title shall be construed to require any person to be subject to combatant training and service in the armed forces of the United States who, by reason of religious training and belief, is conscientiously opposed to war in any form. As used in this subsection, the term "religious training and belief" does not include essentially political, sociological or philosophical views, or a merely personal moral code.[18]

"Religious training and belief" was defined in terms of what it was not. That it was not political, sociological, philosophical, or an obviously personal moral standard implied that it had to have a transcendent dimension, but not necessarily an explicit or even an attenuated belief in a Supreme Being.

In 1970 the Supreme Court heard another conscientious objection case, *Welsh v. United States*.[19] Because Welsh had been denied conscientious status in 1966, the case was heard under the version of the law that contained the "Supreme Being" clause.

If Seeger and his coplaintiffs were unconventional in their "religious" beliefs, Welsh was even more so. On his application Welsh had struck out "religious training and" and had disavowed a belief in a Supreme Being. He said his conscientious objection to war was formed "by reading in the fields of history and sociology." But, despite insisting that his objection was not religiously based, the Court found that Welsh's beliefs qualified as religious ones for purposes of the statute. The Court explained its conclusion:

> The Court of Appeals found that Welsh had "denied that his objection to war was premised on religious belief" and concluded that "[t]he Appeal Board was entitled to take him at his word." We think this attempt to distinguish *Seeger* fails for the reason that it places undue emphasis on the registrant's interpretation of his own beliefs. The Court's statement in *Seeger* that a registrant's characterization of his own belief as "religious" should carry great weight, does not imply that his declaration that his views are nonreligious should be treated similarly. When a registrant states that his objections to war are "religious," that information is highly relevant to the question of the function his beliefs have in his life. But very few registrants are fully aware of the broad scope of the word "religious" as used in § 6(j), and accordingly a registrant's statement that his beliefs are nonreligious is a highly unreliable guide for those charged with administering the exemption.[20]

But the statute explicitly denied conscientious objector status to those whose objection to war was based on philosophical or purely moral grounds. In order to get around that provision the Court interpreted that language in an extremely narrow fashion.

> What is necessary under *Seeger* for a registrant's conscientious objection to all war to be "religious" within the meaning of § 6(j) is that this opposition to war stem from the registrant's moral, ethical, or religious beliefs about what is right and wrong and that these beliefs be held with the strength of traditional religious convictions. Most of the great religions of today and of the past have embodied the idea of a Supreme Being or a Supreme Reality—a God—who communicates to man in some way a consciousness of what is right and should be done, of what is wrong and therefore should be shunned. If an individual deeply and sincerely holds beliefs that are purely ethical or moral in source and content but that nevertheless impose upon him a duty of conscience to refrain from participating in any war at any time, those beliefs

certainly occupy in the life of that individual "a place parallel to that filled by . . . God" in traditionally religious persons. Because his beliefs function as a religion in his life, such an individual is as much entitled to a "religious" conscientious objector exemption under § 6(j) as is someone who derives his conscientious opposition to war from traditional religious convictions.[21]

The Court continued:

> We certainly do not think that § 6(j)'s exclusion of those persons with "essentially political, sociological, or philosophical views or a merely personal moral code" should be read to exclude those who hold strong beliefs about our domestic and foreign affairs or even those whose conscientious objection to participation in all wars is founded to a substantial extent upon considerations of foreign policy. The two groups of registrants that obviously do fall within these exclusions from the exemption are those whose beliefs are not deeply held and those whose objection to war does not rest at all upon moral, ethical, or religious principles but instead rests solely upon considerations of policy, pragmatism, or expediency. . . . [W]e think Welsh was clearly entitled to a conscientious objector exemption. Section 6(j) requires no more. That section exempts from military service all those whose consciences, spurred by deeply held moral, ethical, or religious beliefs, would give them no rest or peace if they allowed themselves to become a part of an instrument of war.[22]

The Draft Cases represent the Supreme Court's most definitive statements on how it would view the term "religion." Again, those cases involved the Court's interpretation of statutory terms and did not require the justices to rule on the definition of religion for free exercise or establishment purposes.

Yet the Court has emphasized similar themes in several Free Exercise Cases. For example, the Court has said it is constitutionally inappropriate for the government to say that some beliefs were too nonsensical to qualify as religious convictions. In *United States v. Ballard*[23] (chapter 9), the Court heard an appeal by defendants who were convicted of mail fraud for soliciting contributions for a nonmainstream religion with rather unorthodox claims about personal revelation and healing of physical ailments. The Court wrote:

> Heresy trials are foreign to our Constitution. Men may believe what they cannot prove. They may not be put to the proof of their religious doctrines or beliefs. Religious experiences which are as real as life to some may be incomprehensible to others. Yet the fact that they may be beyond the ken of mortals does not mean that they can be made suspect before the law. . . . The Fathers of the Constitution were not unaware of the varied and extreme views of religious sects, of the violence of disagreement among them, and of the lack of any one religious creed on which all men would agree. They fashioned a charter of government which envisaged the widest possible toleration of conflicting views. Man's relation to his God was made no concern of the state. He was granted the right to worship as he pleased and to answer to no man for the verity of his religious views. The religious views espoused by respondents might seem incredible, if not preposterous, to most people. But if those doctrines are subject to trial before a jury charged with finding their truth or falsity, then the same can be done with the religious beliefs of any sect.[24]

In 1981 in the case of *Thomas v. Review Board of Indiana Employment Security Division*[25] (chapter 7), the Court approached this issue again, once more from the practical perspective of judicial restraint. Thomas was a Jehovah's Witness employed in a steel mill.

When the mill began to manufacture military tank turrets, he quit his job because of his religiously based conscientious objection against war. He applied for unemployment compensation, which was denied because he had voluntarily terminated his employment. Also, other Witness employees had agreed to work on the tank turrets.

The Court ruled in Thomas' favor. In the process, Chief Justice Warren Burger addressed the question of defining or describing religion. He began by saying that a Free Exercise Clause appeal such as Thomas' clearly had to have a religious dimension.

> Only beliefs rooted in religion are protected by the Free Exercise Clause, which, by its terms, gives special protection to the exercise of religion. The determination of what is a "religious" belief or practice is more often than not a difficult and delicate task. . . . However, the resolution of that question is not to turn upon a judicial perception of the particular belief or practice in question; religious beliefs need not be acceptable, logical, consistent, or comprehensible to others to merit First Amendment protection.[26]

In his application for unemployment compensation, Thomas had admitted that he was struggling with his beliefs on making military armaments and had not articulated his position in an elegant manner. Indiana had considered those factors in denying benefits, assuming that Thomas' action was not really based on his religion. The Court disagreed. "Courts should not undertake to dissect religious beliefs because the believer admits that he is "struggling" with his position or because his beliefs are not articulated with the clarity and precision that a more sophisticated person might employ."[27]

That another Witness was willing to work in the turret factory led Indiana to conclude that Thomas' position was not characteristic of Jehovah's Witness theology, thus disqualifying him for unemployment benefits. Chief Justice Burger rejected that conclusion, as well.

> One can, of course, imagine an asserted claim so bizarre, so clearly nonreligious in motivation, as not to be entitled to protection under the Free Exercise Clause; but that is not the case here, and the guarantee of free exercise is not limited to beliefs which are shared by all of the members of a religious sect. Particularly in this sensitive area, it is not within the judicial function and judicial competence to inquire whether the petitioner or his fellow worker more correctly perceived the commands of their common faith. Courts are not the arbiters of scriptural interpretation.[28]

At the same time, the Court has said that merely philosophical beliefs do not count as religious beliefs under the First Amendment. The Court made this clear in a passage of a case in which it held that Amish children could be exempted from compulsory school attendance laws after the eighth grade. Accommodating their free exercise was the justification was the reason for such an exemption. In this case, *Wisconsin v. Yoder*[29] (chapter 7), the Court said:

> A way of life, however virtuous and admirable, may not be interposed as a barrier to reasonable state regulation of education if it is based on purely secular considerations; to have the protection of the Religion Clauses, the claims must be rooted in religious belief. Although a determination of what is a "religious" belief or practice entitled to constitutional protection may present a most delicate question, the very concept of ordered liberty precludes allowing every person to make his own standards on matters of conduct in which society as a whole has important interests. Thus, if

the Amish asserted their claims because of their subjective evaluation and rejection of the contemporary secular values accepted by the majority, much as Thoreau rejected the social values of his time and isolated himself at Walden Pond, their claims would not rest on a religious basis. Thoreau's choice was philosophical and personal rather than religious, and such belief does not rise to the demands of the Religion Clauses.

Giving no weight to such secular considerations, however, we see that the record in this case abundantly supports the claim that the traditional way of life of the Amish is not merely a matter of personal preference, but one of deep religious conviction, shared by an organized group, and intimately related to daily living.[30]

As noted above, the *Ballard, Thomas* and *Yoder* cases deal with the nature of religious beliefs and practices in the Free Exercise context. Judges also have heard Establishment Clause cases in which they had to decide whether certain activities were religious. A leading decision in this area is a 1979 case heard by Court of Appeals for the Third Circuit. The case, *Malnak v. Yogi*,[31] concerned whether the Establishment Clause would permit New Jersey public high schools to teach the Science of Creative Intelligence/Transcendental Meditation, supported with both state and federal funds. The district court said "no." Because SCI/TM was a religion, the district court held, it violated the no-establishment principle for the material to be taught in public schools funded with government money.

The Court of Appeals affirmed that opinion in relatively short order. It explained that this elective course was taught by teachers "specially trained by the World Plan Executive Council United States, an organization whose objective is to disseminate the teachings of SCI/TM throughout the United States," and that "the textbook used was developed by Maharishi Mahesh Yogi, the founder of the Science of Creative Intelligence." SCI "teaches that 'pure creative intelligence' is the basis of life, and that through the process of Transcendental Meditation students can perceive the full potential of their lives." Students who signed up for the course were given "mantras" (a sound aid used while meditating) at a mandatory ceremony called a "puja." This ceremony was conducted off school premises on a Sunday. The student was required to bring some offerings to this ceremony "for a deified 'Guru Dev,'" which was described as a "personification of 'kindness' and of 'the creative impulse of cosmic life,' and the personification of 'the essence of creation,' . . . ." For these and other reasons, the trial and appellate courts concluded that the SCI/TM course was religious.

In this appellate case, Judge Arlin M. Adams wrote a long, thoughtful, concurring opinion that explored the issue of "what is religion?" for purposes of Establishment Clause law. It can be only summarized here, but it is worth reading in its entirety by anyone interested in this issue.[32]

Judge Adams said he was convinced that the case presented "a novel and important question that may not be disposed of simply on the basis of past precedent." Instead, Judge Adams said, "the result reached today is largely based upon a newer, more expansive reading of 'religion' that has been developed in the last two decades in the context of free exercise and selective service cases but not, until today, applied by an appellate court to invalidate a government program under the [E]stablishment [C]lause." Judge Adams summarized the history and contours of the discussion much as this chapter has done so far, and then offered his own analysis of these cases. Judge Adams wrote:

> It seems unavoidable, from *Seeger, Welsh,* and *Torcaso,* that the Theistic formulation presumed to be applicable in the late nineteenth century cases is no longer sustainable.

Under the modern view, "religion" is not confined to the relationship of man with his Creator, either as a matter of law or as a matter of theology. . . . Such movement, when coupled with the growth in the United States, of many Eastern and non-traditional beliefs systems, suggest that the older, limited definition would deny "religious" identification to faiths now adhered to by millions of Americans. . . .

If the old definition has been repudiated, however, the new definition remains not yet fully formed. It would appear to be properly described as a definition by analogy. The *Seeger* court advertently declined to distinguish beliefs holding "parallel positions in the lives of their respective holders." Presumably beliefs holding the same important position for members of one of the new religions as the traditional faith holds for more orthodox believers are entitled to the same treatment as the traditional beliefs. . . . The modern approach thus looks to the familiar religions as models in order to ascertain, by comparison, whether the new set of ideas or beliefs is confronting the same concerns, or serving the same purposes, as unquestioned and accepted "religions."

But it is one thing to conclude "by analogy" that a particular group or cluster of ideas is religious; it is quite another to explain exactly what indicia are to be looked to in making such an analogy and justifying it. There appear to be three useful indicia that are basic to our traditional religions and that are themselves related to the values that undergird the first amendment [*sic*].

The first and most important of these indicia is the nature of the ideas in question. This means that a court must, at least to a degree, examine the content of the supposed religion, not to determine its truth or falsity, or whether it is schismatic or orthodox, but to determine whether the subject matter it comprehends is consistent with the assertion that it is, or is not, a religion. . . .[33]

Judge Adams then described the "subject matter" that "is consistent with the assertion that it is . . . a religion" primarily in terms suggested by the theologian Paul Tillich. Tillich said that religion is a person's "ultimate concern," by which he meant concepts that are of the utmost depth and importance in the life of an individual. That is, they address the fundamental questions of life and death. "Who am I?" "What is the meaning of my life, if any? Or, differently, is there a moral code and how do I respond to it? Am I a moral or immoral person?" "Is there any meaning to history and, if so, how do I fit into it; how can I contribute positively to it?" "What is the nature and meaning of death? More importantly, what will it mean for me to die?" Judge Adams continued:

Thus, the "ultimate" nature of the ideas presented is the most important and convincing evidence that they should be treated as religious. Certain isolated answers to "ultimate" questions, however, are not necessarily "religious" answers, because they lack the element of comprehensiveness, the second of the three indicia. A religion is not generally confined to one question or one moral teaching; it has a broader scope. It lays claim to an ultimate and comprehensive "truth." . . . [M]oral or patriotic views are not by themselves "religious," but if they are pressed as divine law or a part of a comprehensive belief-system that presents them as "truth," they might well rise to the religious level. . . .

A third element to consider in ascertaining whether a set of ideas should be classified as a religion is any formal, external, or surface signs that may be analogized to accepted religions. Such signs might include formal services, ceremonial functions, the existence of clergy, structure and organization, efforts at propagation, observation of holidays and other similar manifestations associated with the traditional religions. Of course, a religion may exist without any of these signs, so they are not determinative, at least by their absence, in resolving a question of definition. But they can be helpful in supporting a conclusion of religious status given the important role such ceremonies play in religious life. . . . Thus, even if it is true that a religion can exist without rituals and structure, they may nonetheless be useful signs that a group or a belief system is religious.

Although these indicia will be helpful, they should not be thought of as a final "test" for religion. Defining religion is a sensitive and important legal duty. Flexibility and careful consideration of each belief system are needed. Still, it is important to have some objective guidelines in order to avoid *Ad hoc* justice.[34]

Thus, Judge Adams said, when considering what is and what is not a religion, a "definition by analogy" is the best approach. In an article published in 1984, Professor Kent Greenawalt agreed and helpfully expounded on this idea.[35] Greenawalt proposed "that in both free exercise and establishment cases, courts should decide whether something is religious by comparison with what is indisputably religious, in light of the particular legal problem involved. No single characteristic should be regarded as essential to religiousness." Greenawalt further argued that this "definition by analogy" approach is far superior to a "dictionary definition" approach:

> Religion is a highly complex concept. As courts have occasionally noted, dictionary definitions of religion vary widely, and agreement upon a settled account of what makes something religious has been elusive.
>
> The very assumption that some kind of "dictionary" approach will suffice may constitute a significant stumbling block. By a dictionary approach, I mean the identification of a single element or a conjunction of two or more central elements that are taken to be essential for the application of a concept. Thus, if religion is constituted by "belief in a Supreme Being," one would decide whether a doubtful instance involves religion by determining whether such belief is present. Under this approach, religion would be characterized by a condition that is both necessary and sufficient. A decision about the presence or absence of that condition would determine whether something was religious. Some other major suggestions about defining religion share with the Supreme Being standard a focus on one central feature, such as "ultimate concern" or "belief in extratemporal consequences." However, a single central element is not an inevitable feature of the dictionary approach in my sense. One might believe that two or three, or more, crucial features are all present in every genuine instance of religion.
>
> Nevertheless, any dictionary approach oversimplifies the concept of religion, and the very phrase "definition of religion" is potentially misleading. No specification of essential conditions will capture all and only the beliefs, practices, and organizations that are regarded as religious in modern culture and should be treated as such under the Constitution.
>
> A more fruitful approach to understanding and employing the concept of religion is to identify instances to which the concept indisputably applies, and to ask in more doubtful instances how close the analogy is between these and the indisputable instances. Such an approach can yield applications of the concept to instances that share no common feature, a result that the dictionary approach precludes. . . .
>
> The thrust of this Article is not a proposal of a new approach to the elucidation of concepts, but rather the application of a widely accepted idea to the constitutional concept of religion. Even this more focused claim is hardly novel; it corresponds closely with what many courts have done and what one court has explicitly said, it has been proposed by at least one scholar, and it may be implicit in other scholarly discussions that decline to set out required conditions of religion.[36]

## Defining Religion

In the *Malnak* case, Judge Adams also considered the issue of whether religion should be defined in one way when evaluating free exercise claims and another way when evaluating Establishment Clause claims. Adams rejected this notion for the following reasons:

> There has been considerable speculation whether the broader definition of religion developed in the free exercise cases should be applied under the establishment clause. Professor Tribe of Harvard has advanced the argument that the free exercise clause should be read broadly to include anything "arguably religious," but that the establishment clause should not be construed to encompass anything "arguably non-religious." In so doing, he has summarized the position of those favoring a dual definition:
>
> > "Clearly, the notion of religion in the free exercise clause must be expanded beyond the closely bounded limits of theism to account for the multiplying forms of recognizably legitimate religious exercise. It is equally clear, however, that in the age of the affirmative and increasingly pervasive state, a less expansive notion of religion was required for establishment clause purposes lest all "humane" programs of government be deemed constitutionally suspect. Such a twofold definition of religion expansive for the free exercise clause, less so for the establishment clause may be necessary to avoid confronting the state with increasingly difficult choices that the theory of permissible accommodation . . . could not indefinitely resolve."*
>
> This view is not without other academic and some judicial support, and appellants here urge upon us a modified version of it.
>
> Despite the distinguished scholars who advocate this approach, a stronger argument can be made for a unitary definition to prevail for both clauses. This would seem to be the preferable choice for several reasons. First, it is virtually required by the language of the first amendment. As Justice Rutledge put it over thirty years ago:
>
> > "'Religion' appears only once in the Amendment. But the word governs two prohibitions and governs them alike. It does not have two meanings, one narrow to forbid "an establishment" and another, much broader, for securing "the free exercise thereof." "Thereof" brings down "religion" with its entire and exact content, no more and no less, from the first into the second guaranty, so that Congress and now the states are as broadly restricted concerning the one as they are regarding the other."
>
> Although the Constitution has often been subject to a broad construction, it remains a written document. It is difficult to justify a reading of the first amendment so as to support a dual definition of religion, nor has our attention been drawn to any support for such a view in the conventional sources that have been thought to reveal the intention of the framers. Moreover, the policy reasons put forward by the supporters of a dual definition, in my view at least, are unpersuasive.
>
> The advocates of a dual definition appear to be motivated primarily by an anxiety that too extensive a definition under the establishment clause will lead to "wholesale invalidation" of government programs. Behind this fear lurks, I believe, too broad a reading of the teachings of *Seeger*, *Welsh*, and *Torcaso*. The selective service case did not hold that Seeger, Welsh and the other conscientious objectors were advancing views sufficient to qualify as a religion or religions, only that their views were based on religious

In another lower court Establishment Clause case, *Smith v. Board of School Commissioners* (1987),[37] religiously conservative parents in Mobile, Alabama, contended that textbooks used in their children's public schools violated the Establishment Clause because the books promoted the religion of secular humanism. (Recall that in *Torcaso v. Watkins* the Court suggested in a footnote that Secular Humanism might be considered a nontheistic religion entitled to free exercise protection.) According to the plaintiffs in the *Smith* case, the textbooks advanced the religion of secular humanism in two ways. One was by ignoring the role of theistic religions in history. The books were essentially silent on the role that Christianity, Judaism, and other religions played in the history of Western civilization, including the United States, for example. The other way the books allegedly advanced the religion of secular humanism was by articulating a morality of relativism. In the words of the district court:

> The books teach that the student must determine right and wrong based only on his own experience, feelings, and "values." These "values" are described as originating from within. . . . The books require the student to accept that the validity of a moral choice is only to be decided by the student. The requirement is not stated explicitly. Instead, the books repeat, over and over, that the decision is "yours alone," or is "purely personal" or that "only you can decide." . . . This highly relativistic and individualistic approach constitutes the promotion of a fundamental faith claim opposed to other religious faiths.[38]

*continued from page 58*

belief. Were a school, or government agency, to advance the cause of peace, or opposition to war, such an official position would not qualify as a "religion" even though some citizens might come to adopt that very view because of their own religious beliefs. All programs or positions that entangle the government with issues and problems that might be classified as "ultimate concerns" do not, because of that, become "religious" programs or positions. Only if the government favors a comprehensive belief system and advances its teachings does it establish a religion. It does not do so by endorsing isolated moral precepts or by enacting humanitarian economic programs.

In this regard it should be noted that the modern definition of religion does not extend so far as to include those who hold beliefs however passionately regarding the utility of Keynesian economics, Social Democracy or, for that matter, Sociobiology. These ideas may in some instances touch on "ultimate concerns," but they are less analogous to religious views than they are to the political or sociological ideas that they are. Thus *Torcaso* does not stand for the proposition that "humanism" is a religion, although an organized group of "Secular Humanists" may be. An undefined belief in humanitarianism, or good intentions, is still far removed from a comprehensive belief system laying a claim to ultimate truth and supported by a formal group with religious trappings.

Moreover, the [E]stablishment [C]lause does not forbid government activity encouraged by the supporters of even the most orthodox of religions if that activity is itself not unconstitutional. The Biblical and clerical endorsement of laws against stealing and murder do not make such laws establishments of religion. Similarly, agitation for social welfare programs by progressive churchmen, even if motivated by the most orthodox of theological reasons, does not make those programs religious. The Constitution has not been interpreted to forbid those inspired by religious principle or conscience from participation in this nation's political, social and economic life.

*continued from page 59*

Finally, in addition to these doubts whether "doctrinal chaos" would in fact result from resort to the new definition in the establishment clause context, the practical result of a dual definition is itself troubling. Such an approach would create a three-tiered system of ideas: those that are unquestionably religious and thus both free from government interference and barred from receiving government support; those that are unquestionably non-religious and thus subject to government regulation and eligible to receive government support; and those that are only religious under the newer approach and thus free from governmental regulation but open to receipt of government support. That belief systems classified in the third grouping are the most advantageously positioned is obvious. No reason has been advanced, however, for favoring the newer belief systems over the older ones. If a Roman Catholic is barred from receiving aid from the government, so too should be a Transcendental Meditator or a Scientologist if those two are to enjoy the preferred position guaranteed to them by the free exercise clause. It may be, of course, that they are not entitled to such a preferred position, but they are clearly not entitled to the advantages given by the first amendment while avoiding the apparent disadvantages. The rose cannot be had without the thorn.

For these reasons, then, I think it is correct to read religion broadly in both clauses and agree that the precedents developed in the free exercise context are properly relied upon here.

While this view is not without its critics, it is generally supported by courts and commentators.

* Professor Tribe once supported this approach, but his views have since changed. Compare L. Tribe, American Constitutional Law Section 14-6 at 828-829 (1st ed. 1978) with L. Tribe, American Constitutional Law Section 14-6 at 1186-1188 (2d ed. 1988). Professor Tom Berg has argued that "[s]ome of the practical advantages of [Professor Laurence] Tribe's proposal [of defining religion differently for free exercise and establishment purposes] might be achieved by a slightly different route, without taking the textually questionable step of defining religion differently under the two clauses. One might say that whether a belief involves the free exercise of religion depends largely on how the individual believer views its rule in his life, but that whether a belief is a religious one being established by the government depends much more on how society understands it." Thomas C. Berg, *The State and Religion*, 272 (1998).

The plaintiffs asserted that the books' failure to acknowledge traditional religious influences and their advocacy of relativistic morality were consistent with secular humanism. But for the plaintiffs to make their case, they had to show that secular humanism was a religion. Secular humanism was described as a world view that denies the existence of God or any transcendent power operative in the world. Furthermore, it asserts that humans should not rely on traditional (theistic) religion for wisdom and ethical guidelines, but rather should live by an ethic based on naturalism and physical science. But is it a religion? The plaintiffs chose a functional definition to argue that it was. The trial court described the functional approach as such:

> The functional approach defines religion according to what it does. For the individual, religion provides a sense of order, a sense of place in life and in the cosmos, a sense of direction and meaning in life. It also provides moral coordinates by which

individuals can live everyday life, a means by which they can know right from wrong, correct from incorrect, appropriate from inappropriate and so on. It also provides an explanation for such things as death.[39]

Based on this approach, the trial court held that nontheistic "meaning systems" such as secular humanism were religions. Further, the plaintiffs argued that secular humanism had other characteristics one finds in definitions of religion, including an organized body of belief, an ethical dimension, and proselytizing activity. The trial court agreed with the plaintiffs' arguments and ruled the Mobile public schools violated the Establishment Clause by promoting the religion of secular humanism in its textbooks. The court ordered that the books be removed from the schools.[40]

The Court of Appeals for the Eleventh Circuit rejected both the analysis and the conclusion of the district court.[41] The court declined to be drawn into the issue of defining religion, much less whether secular humanism fit such a definition. The court said:

> The Supreme Court has never established a comprehensive test for determining the "delicate question" of what constitutes a religious belief for purposes of the [F]irst [A]mendment, and we need not attempt to do so in this case, for we find that, even assuming that secular humanism is a religion for purposes of the [E]stablishment [C]lause, [the plaintiffs] have failed to prove a violation of the [E]stablishment [C]lause through the use in the Alabama public schools of the textbooks at issue in this case.

The court concluded that school officials did not choose books either because they endorsed or disapproved of either traditional religion or secular humanism. The books might be deficient in their treatment of religion in human history, but poor scholarship did not raise a constitutional problem unless it could be shown that there was some intent to discredit or advance some religion or religion in general. That intent had not been demonstrated, the court said. On the issue of moral relativism, the court acknowledged that the home economics books contained some material that was consistent with secular humanism, but it also noted that they contained some material consistent with theistic religion as well.[42]

Despite this general hesitancy of courts to define religion, governmental entities sometimes need a working definition of religion or religious entities for reasons other than deciding First Amendment issues.[43] For example, the Internal Revenue Service uses a list of criteria to determine whether a group is a church for tax purposes. If an organization is a church under the IRS definition, it qualifies for a certain tax-exempt status and associated legal protections. In order to qualify as a church for income tax purposes, an organization must satisfy some, but not all, of the following criteria:

1. a distinct legal existence
2. a recognized creed and form of worship
3. a definite and distinct ecclesiastical government
4. a formal code of doctrine and discipline
5. a distinct religious history
6. a membership not associated with any other church or denomination
7. an organization of ordained ministers
8. ordained ministers selected after completing prescribed studies
9. a literature of its own

10. established places of worship
11. regular congregations
12. regular religious services
13. Sunday schools for religious instruction of the young
14. schools for the preparation of its ministers.[44]

Notice that these criteria do not evaluate the truth or falsity of theology; indeed, they do not even inquire into the content of doctrine or belief. They try to ascertain whether a group has some theology, doctrine, worship, and history as a religion, but they do not make judgments about the validity of those things.

As Professor John Witte, Jr. has said:

[T]he term "religion" must be assigned some consistent boundaries to be useful, at least for a constitutional rights regime. . . . Fairness commands as broad a legal defini- tion of religion as possible, so that no legitimate religious claim is excluded. Prudence commends a narrower definition, so that not every claim becomes religious (and thus no claim becomes deserving of special religious rights protection). To define "religion" too closely is to place too much trust in the capacity of the lexicon or the legislature. To leave the term undefined is to place too much faith in the self-declarations of the claimant or the discernment of local judges and administrators.[45]

As this discussion demonstrates, courts and other governmental bodies have tried to strike an appropriate balance among these competing concerns. The most promising ap- proach may be the one Judge Adams articulated in his concurring opinion in the *Malnak* case and Professor Greenawalt expounded upon. It recognizes that decisions in this area must be made, but it eschews narrow and wooden definitions that might do violence to the precious rights of religious freedom.

## NOTES AND QUESTIONS

1. Does it make sense that the Free Exercise and Establishment clauses might prohibit the government, including the courts, from devising a formal defini- tion of religion? If so, does Judge Adams' formula violate the Constitution?

2. Conversely, how are courts to protect free exercise rights or prohibit the gov- ernment from advancing religion if they are unable to determine what con- stitutes "religion?" It has sometimes been proposed that courts simply ought to accept a person's statement that his or her beliefs or activities are religious in nature. Can you think of some difficulties that would result if courts were to take such an approach?

3. Do you think the Court should have awarded conscientious objector status to *Seeger* and the others with "unconventional" understandings of religion? Did the Court stretch the definition of religion beyond what religion really is? Why or why not? Do you think the fact that *Seeger* and *Welsh* were decided during the Vietnam War era affected the Court's rulings in these cases?

4. In the *Seeger* case, the Court quoted a number of liberal theologians regard- ing their understanding of religion. In addition to embracing Paul Tillich's notion of "ultimate concern," the Court cited John A. T. Robinson, author of the (then) best-selling book, *Honest to God* (1963). The Court quoted Robinson's argument that the traditional (Biblical) view of God as Lord of

the "three-decker universe," heaven above the earth and the underworld below the earth, needed to be discarded as the scientific view of the universe becomes our world view. Additionally, the Supreme Court quoted David Saville Muzzey, a leader in the Ethical Culture Movement, who wrote that "the 'God' that we love is not the figure on the great white throne, but the perfect pattern, envisioned by faith, of humanity as it should be, purged of the evil elements which retard its progress toward the knowledge, love and practice of the right."

Does the Court's reliance on these theologians indicate that it was saying that these views are more correct religious views than more orthodox religious views? In essence, by siding with liberal theologians who advocated a more expansive view of religion, was the Court doing exactly what it disclaims—taking sides in a theological dispute?

5. Professor Kent Greenawalt has written a critique of the notion of "ultimate concern" as the criteria for defining religion:

> Ultimate concern is fundamentally flawed as a single criterion for religiousness. . . . As a proposed standard for legal categorization, ultimate concern retains deep ambiguity and vagueness. Plainly, it involves the relevance of something for one's life, not just the grandness of the questions answered by a system of belief. Beyond this solid ground, we reach the ambiguities, which can best be introduced by a series of questions: Does everyone have an ultimate concern? Does anyone have more than one? Is a person's ultimate concern determined by his cognitive beliefs or his psychological attitudes? How does ultimate concern relate to absolute moral prohibitions? To one's deepest desires? For a claim to qualify as based on ultimate concern, what must be the connection between the act involved and that which constitutes the ultimate concern? [46]

Do you agree with this assessment? Is Professor Greenawalt arguing that evaluation of whether a person's beliefs or activities are bound up in matters of ultimate concern is an improper concern altogether, or is he making a narrower argument?

CHAPTER 5

# THE CONCEPT OF STANDING

Over the years, the Supreme Court has developed rules of "justiciability" that govern the ability of federal courts to hear certain legal controversies. Justiciability—as distinguished from a court's jurisdiction (i.e., inherent authority) to rule on a particular controversy—concerns matters of judicial restraint. Federal judges are ever mindful of their nonelected status and that their legitimacy and ultimate authority depend on the willingness of the people and the political branches to accede to their interpretations of the Constitution and legislative statutes. As a result, the Court has held that both the Constitution's grant of judicial authority over "cases" and "controversies," as well as nonbinding prudential rules, instruct that the federal courts decline to hear some cases that they otherwise may have the authority to adjudicate. According to Chief Justice Earl Warren in *Flast v. Cohen*, 392 U.S. 88 (1968), justiciability

> limit[s] the business of federal courts to questions presented in an adversary context and in a form historically viewed as capable of resolution through the judicial process. [Justiciability] define[s] the role assigned to the judiciary [to] assure that the federal courts will not intrude into areas committed to the other branches of government. . . . Federal judicial power is limited to those disputes which confine federal courts to a role consistent with a system of separate powers and which are traditionally thought to be capable of resolution through the judicial process.

One of the more important justiciability rules is often referred to as "standing to sue." Courts are supposed to address real cases and controversies,[1] not abstract philosophical or political questions or render advisory opinions about interesting intellectual or policy questions. Included in this idea is the notion that cases are supposed to be between at least two parties that have an actual stake in the outcome of the case. In essence, standing is concerned with whether one legitimately is in court, whether one is best suited to bring a legal challenge, and whether there is a true legal dispute between the parties, rather than some disagreement over policy or politics. It is not enough that one should disagree with the content of a law or the way it is being applied; to have standing, one has to demonstrate that a genuine legal conflict exists, that he has a personal stake in the outcome of the suit, that it will have a material effect on him (or it, in the case of a group) rather than being a "generalized grievance." If one has no personal stake in the outcome, the issue becomes an abstract question, the answering of which is not a proper function for courts.

The classic example of this is taxpayer lawsuits. People whose only relation to a controversy is that they are taxpayers usually do not have the right to challenge government programs in federal courts. The case that established this rule was *Frothingham v. Mellon.*[2] The case involved federal grants made under the Maternity Act of 1921 to state programs to reduce maternal and infant mortality. Mrs. Frothingham argued that the Act usurped the power of the states. She alleged that this federal action would increase her tax liability and thereby deprive her of property without due process of law. She sued in her status as a taxpayer and asked that the grants be discontinued.

The Supreme Court denied her the standing to sue. Mrs. Frothingham did not have a personal stake in the outcome of the case, the Court said. The federal budget is huge, the Court emphasized. Only an extremely small portion of the federal budget was expended on the program Mrs. Frothingham was protesting. In addition, Mrs. Frothingham's tax payments contributed only a minuscule amount to the overall federal budget. Consequently, it was obvious that only a nanoportion of her taxes, if that, actually supported the program to which she objected.

The Court said:

> Mrs. Frothingham as a taxpayer has an abstract interest in the way the public revenues are appropriated. But there are many million taxpayers (seven millions alone paying an income tax), and as the enforcement of every law presumably requires some expenditure of money by the Federal Government, it cannot be that every taxpayer has a right to challenge a law as unconstitutional because its enforcement requires the expenditure of public moneys and these are in part raised by taxation.
>
> This tribunal is a court and not a council of revision, and as a court it requires that the litigant who invokes its judgment must have some direct, tangible, and practical interest in the question litigated.

In short, the Court determined that Mrs. Frothingham had no personal stake in the outcome. The rule that emerged from *Frothingham* is that simply being a taxpayer is not enough to create standing in federal court.

The Supreme Court applied this prohibition on taxpayer standing in a church-state context in the 1952 case of *Doremus v. Board of Education*, 342 U.S. 429. There, a taxpayer and a taxpayer-parent sued a public school district over its practice of reading from the Bible at the opening of each school day. The parent did not allege that her daughter felt coerced by the Bible reading, merely that she disagreed with the practice. The Supreme Court dismissed the suit on the ground the plaintiffs were asserting only a "taxpayer grievance" and lacked standing to sue. Justice Robert Jackson wrote that "[t]here is no allegation that this activity is supported by any separate tax or paid from any particular appropriation or that it adds any sum whatever to the cost of conducting the school . . . [neither is there an] averment that the Bible reading increases any tax they do pay or that as taxpayers they are, will, or possibly can be out of pocket because of it." The Court reaffirmed *Frothingham* that "the interests of a taxpayer in the moneys of the federal treasury are too indeterminate, remote, uncertain and indirect to furnish a basis for an appeal to the preventative powers of the Court over their manner of expenditure."[3]

It is interesting to note, however, that some states do not have the same rule, that is, they will allow taxpayer suits in their state systems. And occasionally the Supreme Court will accept a taxpayer case that has a federal question from a state court. In the church-state corpus of cases, the classic example is the 1947 case of *Everson v. Board of Education*. As a taxpayer in New Jersey, Mr. Everson filed suit against a community for using government money to reimburse the expenses of parents who sent their children to religious schools on public buses. He claimed the program was a violation of the Establishment Clause, thus providing a federal question to his suit. He filed suit in a New Jersey state court, which allowed taxpayer suits. When the Supreme Court accepted *Everson*, it essentially winked at the *Frothingham* rule. *Everson* was a backdoor taxpayer suit in the Supreme Court.

The Supreme Court revisited these issues in a 1968 church-state case, *Flast v. Cohen*. The federal Elementary and Secondary Education Act of 1965 (ESEA) authorized federal money to be paid to schools, including church-related schools. Mrs. Flast, in her capacity as a federal taxpayer, filed suit, claiming the parochial school portion of ESEA violated the Establishment Clause. The case went to the Supreme Court. The Court did not consider the constitutionality of ESEA, but it did consider the issue of whether Mrs. Flast had standing.

In an opinion written by Chief Justice Warren, the Court decided that she did. It said taxpayers must prove two things in order to have standing in federal courts. The plaintiff must show that the program involved in the case (1) was financed under the taxing and spending clause of the Constitution[4] and (2) violated a *constitutional* prohibition against the expenditure of government money. If the taxpayer could demonstrate these two things, then he or she had standing. The *Flast* decision did not overturn *Frothingham*, but it substituted a more complex inquiry for the evaluation of these issues. As you read *Flast*, see if you can identify the rationale supporting an exception from the standing rules for Establishment Clause challenges.

---

## FLAST v. COHEN
### 392 U.S. 83 (1968)

MR. CHIEF JUSTICE WARREN delivered the opinion of the Court.

In *Frothingham v. Mellon*, this Court ruled that a federal taxpayer is without standing to challenge the constitutionality of a federal statute. That ruling has stood for 45 years as an impenetrable barrier to suits against Acts of Congress brought by individuals who can assert only the interest of federal taxpayers. In this case, we must decide whether the *Frothingham* barrier should be lowered when a taxpayer attacks a federal statute on the ground that it violates the Establishment and Free Exercise Clauses of the First Amendment. . . .

The fundamental aspect of standing is that it focuses on the party seeking to get his complaint before a federal court and not on the issues he wishes to have adjudicated. The "gist of the question of standing" is whether the party seeking relief has "alleged such a personal stake in the outcome of the controversy as to assure that concrete adverseness which sharpens the presentation of issues upon which the court so largely depends for illumination of difficult constitutional questions." In other words, when standing is placed in issue in a case, the question is whether the person whose standing is challenged is a proper party to request an adjudication of a particular issue and not whether the issue itself is justiciable. Thus, a party may have standing in a particular

taxpayers against increases in tax liability, and the taxpayer in *Frothingham* failed to make any additional claim that the harm she alleged resulted from a breach by Congress of the specific constitutional limitations imposed upon an exercise of the taxing and spending power.

We have noted that the Establishment Clause of the First Amendment does specifically limit the taxing and spending power conferred by Art. I, § 8. Whether the Constitution contains other specific limitations can be determined only in the context of future cases. However, whenever such specific limitations are found, we believe a taxpayer will have a clear stake as a taxpayer in assuring that they are not breached by Congress. Consequently, we hold that a taxpayer will have standing consistent with Article III to invoke federal judicial power when he alleges that congressional action under the taxing and spending clause is in derogation of those constitutional provisions which operate to restrict the exercise of the taxing and spending power. The taxpayer's allegation in such cases would be that his tax money is being extracted and spent in violation of specific constitutional protections against such abuses of legislative power. Such an injury is appropriate for judicial redress, and the taxpayer has established the necessary nexus between his status and the nature of the allegedly unconstitutional action to support his claim of standing to secure judicial review. Under such circumstances, we feel confident that the questions will be framed with the necessary specificity, that the issues will be contested with the necessary adverseness and that the litigation will be pursued with the necessary vigor to assure that the constitutional challenge will be made in a form traditionally thought to be capable of judicial resolution. We lack that confidence in cases such as *Frothingham* where a taxpayer seeks to employ a federal court as a forum in which to air his generalized grievances about the conduct of government or the allocation of power in the Federal System.

While we express no view at all on the merits of appellants' claims in this case, their complaint contains sufficient allegations under the criteria we have outlined to give them standing to invoke a federal court's jurisdiction for an adjudication on the merits.

*Reversed. . . .*

### MR. JUSTICE HARLAN, dissenting.

The problems presented by this case are narrow and relatively abstract, but the principles by which they must be resolved involve nothing less than the proper functioning of the federal courts, and so run to the roots of our constitutional system. The nub of my view is that the end result of *Frothingham v. Mellon*, was correct, even though, like others, I do not subscribe to all of its reasoning and premises. Although I therefore agree with certain of the conclusions reached today by the Court, I cannot accept the standing doctrine that it substitutes for *Frothingham*, for it seems to me that this new doctrine rests on premises that do not withstand analysis. Accordingly, I respectfully dissent. . . .

The Court's analysis consists principally of the observation that the requirements of standing are met if a taxpayer has the "requisite personal stake in the outcome" of his suit. This does not, of course, resolve the standing problem; it merely restates it. The Court implements this standard with the declaration that taxpayers will be "deemed" to have the necessary personal interest if their suits satisfy two criteria: *first*, the challenged expenditure must form part of a federal spending program, and not merely be "incidental" to a regulatory program; and *second*, the constitutional provision under which the plaintiff claims must be a "specific limitation" upon Congress' spending powers. The difficulties with these criteria are many and severe, but it is enough for the moment to emphasize that they are not in any sense a measurement of any plaintiff's interest in the outcome of any suit. As even a cursory examination of the criteria will show, the Court's standard for the determination of standing and its criteria for the satisfaction of that standard are entirely unrelated.

It is surely clear that a plaintiff's interest in the outcome of a suit in which he challenges the constitutionality of a federal expenditure is not made greater or smaller by the unconnected fact that the expenditure is, or is not, "incidental" to an "essentially regulatory" program. An example will illustrate the point. Assume that two independent federal programs are authorized by Congress, that the first is designed to encourage a specified religious group by the provision to it of direct grants-in-aid, and that the second is designed to discourage all other religious groups by the imposition of various forms of discriminatory regulation. Equal amounts are appropriated by Congress for the two programs. If a taxpayer challenges their constitutionality in separate suits, are we to suppose, as evidently does the Court, that his "personal stake" in the suit involving the second is necessarily smaller than it is in the suit involving the first, and that he should therefore have standing in one but not the other?

Presumably the Court does not believe that regulatory programs are necessarily less destructive of First Amendment rights, or that regulatory programs are necessarily less prodigal of public funds than are grants-in-aid, for both these general propositions are demonstrably false. The Court's disregard of regulatory expenditures is not even a logical consequence of its apparent assumption that taxpayer-plaintiffs assert essentially monetary interests, for it surely cannot matter to a taxpayer *qua* taxpayer whether an unconstitutional expenditure is used to hire the services of regulatory personnel or is distributed among private and local governmental agencies as grants-in-aid. His interest as taxpayer arises, if at all, from the fact of an unlawful expenditure, and not as a consequence of the expenditure's form. Apparently the Court has repudiated the emphasis in *Frothingham* upon the amount of the plaintiff's tax bill, only to substitute an equally irrelevant emphasis upon the form of the challenged expenditure.

The Court's second criterion is similarly unrelated to its standard for the determination of standing. The intensity of a plaintiff's interest in a suit is not measured, even obliquely, by the fact that the constitutional provision under which he claims is, or is not, a "specific limitation" upon Congress' spending powers. Thus, among the claims in *Frothingham* was the assertion that the Maternity Act deprived the petitioner of property without due process of law. The Court has evidently concluded that this claim did not confer standing because the Due Process Clause of the Fifth Amendment is not a specific limitation upon the spending powers. Disregarding for the moment the formidable obscurity of the Court's categories, how can it be said that Mrs. Frothingham's interests in her suit were, as a consequence of her choice of a constitutional claim, necessarily less intense than those, for example, of the present appellants? I am quite unable to understand how, if a taxpayer believes that a given public expenditure is unconstitutional, and if he seeks to vindicate that belief in a federal court, his interest in the suit can be said necessarily to vary according to the constitutional provision under which he states his claim.

The absence of any connection between the Court's standard for the determination of standing and its criteria for the satisfaction of that standard is not merely a logical ellipsis. Instead, it follows quite relentlessly from the fact that, despite the Court's apparent belief, the plaintiffs in this and similar suits are [not personal and proprietary], and it is very nearly impossible to measure sensibly any differences in the intensity of their personal interests in their suits. The Court has thus been compelled simply to postulate situations in which such taxpayer-plaintiffs will be "deemed" to have the requisite "personal stake and interest." The logical inadequacies of the Court's criteria are thus a reflection of the deficiencies of its entire position. These deficiencies will, however, appear more plainly from an examination of the Court's treatment of the Establishment Clause.

Although the Court does not altogether explain its position, the essence of its reasoning is evidently that a taxpayer's claim under the Establishment Clause is "not merely one of *ultra vires*," but one which instead asserts "an abridgment of individual religious liberty" and a "governmental infringement of individual rights protected by the Constitution." It must first be emphasized that this is apparently not founded upon any "preferred" position for the First Amendment, or upon any asserted unavailability of other plaintiffs. The Court's position is instead that, because of the Establishment Clause's historical purposes, taxpayers retain rights under it quite different from those held by them under other constitutional provisions.

The difficulties with this position are several. First, we have recently been reminded that the historical purposes of the religious clauses of the First Amendment are significantly more obscure and complex than this Court has heretofore acknowledged. Careful students of the history of the Establishment Clause have found that "it is impossible to give a dogmatic interpretation of the First Amendment, and to state with any accuracy the intention of the men who framed it. . . ." Above all, the evidence seems clear that the First Amendment was not intended simply to enact the terms of Madison's Memorial and Remonstrance against Religious Assessments. I do not suggest that history is without relevance to these questions, or that the use of federal funds for religious purposes was not a form of establishment that many in the 18th century would have found objectionable. I say simply that, given the ultimate obscurity of the Establishment Clause's historical purposes, it is inappropriate for this Court to draw fundamental distinctions among the several constitutional commands upon the supposed authority of isolated dicta extracted from the clause's complex history. In particular, I have not found, and the opinion of the Court has not adduced, historical evidence that properly permits the Court to distinguish, as it has here, among the Establishment Clause, the Tenth Amendment, and the Due Process Clause of the Fifth Amendment as limitations upon Congress' taxing and spending powers.

The Court's position is equally precarious if it is assumed that its premise is that the Establishment Clause is in some uncertain fashion a more "specific" limitation upon Congress' powers than are the various other constitutional commands. It is obvious, first, that only in some Pickwickian sense are any of the provisions with which the Court is concerned "specific[ally]" limitations upon spending, for they contain nothing that is expressly directed at the expenditure of public funds. The specificity to which the Court repeatedly refers must therefore arise, not from the provisions' language, but from something implicit in their purposes. But this Court has often emphasized that Congress' powers to spend are coterminous with the purposes for which, and methods by which, it may act, and that the various constitutional commands applicable to the central government, including those implicit both in the Tenth Amendment and in the General Welfare Clause, thus operate as limitations upon spending. I can attach no constitutional significance to the various degrees of specificity with which these limitations appear in the terms or history of the Constitution. If the Court accepts the proposition, as I do, that the number and scope of public actions should be restricted, there are, as I shall show, methods more appropriate, and more nearly permanent, than the creation of an amorphous category of constitutional provisions that the Court has deemed, without adequate foundation, "specific limitations" upon Congress' spending powers.

Even if it is assumed that such distinctions may properly be drawn, it does not follow that federal taxpayers hold any "personal constitutional right" such that they may each contest the validity under the Establishment Clause of all federal expenditures. The difficulty, with which the Court never comes to grips, is that taxpayers' suits under the Establishment Clause are not in these circumstances meaningfully different from other public actions. If this case involved a tax specifically designed for the support of religion, as was the Virginia tax opposed by Madison in his Memorial and Remonstrance, I would agree that taxpayers have rights under the religious clauses of the First Amendment that would permit them standing to challenge the tax's validity in the federal courts. But this is not such a case, and appellants challenge an expenditure, not a tax. Where no such tax is involved, a taxpayer's complaint can consist only of an allegation that public funds have been, or shortly will be, expended for purposes inconsistent with the Constitution. The taxpayer cannot ask the return of any portion of his previous tax payments, cannot prevent the collection of any existing tax debt, and cannot demand an adjudication of the propriety of any particular level of taxation. His tax payments are received for the general purposes of the United States, and are, upon proper receipt, lost in the general revenues. The interests he represents, and the rights he espouses, are, as they are in all public actions, those held in common by all citizens. To describe those rights and interests as personal, and to intimate that they are in some unspecified fashion to be differentiated from those of the general public, reduces constitutional standing to a word game played by secret rules. . . .

## III

It seems to me clear that public actions, whatever the constitutional provisions on which they are premised, may involve important hazards for the continued effectiveness of the federal judiciary. Although I believe such actions to be within the jurisdiction conferred upon the federal courts by Article III of the Constitution, there surely can be little doubt that they strain the judicial function and press to the limit judicial authority. There is every reason to fear that unrestricted public actions might well alter the allocation of authority among the three branches of the Federal Government. It is not, I submit, enough to say that the present members of the Court would not seize these opportunities for abuse, for such actions would, even without conscious abuse, go far toward the final transformation of this Court into the Council of Revision which, despite Madison's support, was rejected by the Constitutional Convention. I do not doubt that there must be "some effectual power in the government to restrain or correct the infractions" of the Constitution's several commands, but neither can I suppose that such power resides only in the federal courts. We must as judges recall that, as Mr. Justice Holmes wisely observed, the other branches of the Government "are ultimate guardians of the liberties and welfare of the people in quite as great a degree as the courts." *Missouri, Kansas & Texas R. Co. v. May*, 194 U.S. 267, 270.The powers of the federal judiciary will be adequate for the great burdens placed upon them only if they are employed prudently, with recognition of the strengths as well as the hazards that go with our kind of representative government.

Presumably the Court recognizes at least certain of these hazards, else it would not have troubled to impose limitations upon the situations in which, and purposes for which, such suits may be brought. Nonetheless, the limitations adopted by the Court are, as I have endeavored to indicate, wholly untenable. This is the more unfortunate because there is available a resolution of this problem that entirely satisfies the demands of the principle of separation of powers. This Court has previously held that individual litigants have standing to represent the public interest, despite their lack of economic or other personal interests, if Congress has appropriately authorized such suits. I would adhere to that principle. Any hazards to the proper allocation of authority among the three branches of the Government would be substantially diminished if public actions had been pertinently authorized by Congress and the President. I appreciate that this Court does not ordinarily await the mandate of other branches of the Government, but it seems to me that the extraordinary character of public actions, and of the mischievous, if not dangerous, consequences they involve for the proper functioning of our constitutional system, and in particular of the federal courts, makes such judicial forbearance the part of wisdom. It must be emphasized that the implications of these questions of judicial policy are of fundamental significance for the other branches of the Federal Government. . . .

This does not mean that we would, under such a rule, be enabled to avoid our constitutional responsibilities, or that we would confine to limbo the First Amendment or any other constitutional command. The question here is not, despite the Court's unarticulated premise, whether the religious clauses of the First Amendment are hereafter to be enforced by the federal courts; the issue is simply whether plaintiffs of an *additional* category, heretofore excluded from those courts, are to be permitted to maintain suits. The recent history of this Court is replete with illustrations, including even one announced today that questions involving the religious clauses will not, if federal taxpayers are prevented from contesting federal expenditures, be left "unacknowledged, unresolved, and undecided."

Accordingly, for the reasons contained in this opinion, I would affirm the judgment of the District Court.

## NOTES AND QUESTIONS

1. Why do courts observe rules of standing? In your opinion, do these rules protect important interests or unfairly deny people access to the legal system?

2. What are the rationales the Court discusses in *Flast* that justify creating an exception to the *Frothingham* rule? Do the distinctions the *Flast* majority draws between the two cases make sense? Is there something unique or special about the Establishment Clause—or at least the founders' concerns about religious

establishments—that necessitates a relaxation or a different understanding of the standing rules in such cases?

3.  In his dissenting opinion in *Flast v. Cohen*, Justice Harlan says there is a better resolution to the issue of standing presented in that case. What is his proposal? What are some of the proposal's strengths and weaknesses?

*Flast* is an important case in the church-state arena because it opened the door to many of the Establishment Clause suits in this book, especially those pertaining to government aid to church-related schools.

The Court also addressed the issue of standing in the church-state arena in the 1982 case of *Valley Forge Christian College v. Americans United for Separation of Church and State*. Here the federal government gave a parcel of land, with buildings, to a church-related college. This transfer occurred under the authority of the Federal Property and Administrative Services Act of 1949, which allows the government to give surplus property (property no longer of use to the government) to nongovernmental entities at little or no charge.

The transaction was challenged by Americans United for Separation of Church and State, an advocacy and litigation group in the District of Columbia. Co-plaintiffs were four employees of Americans United. They complained that the land transfer to a religious college violated the Establishment Clause. They sued as federal taxpayers and as citizens who had a strong interest that the Establishment Clause should not be violated.

The Court, in an opinion by Justice William Rehnquist, ruled against Americans United, not on the merits of the case, but because it found that the group lacked standing. The Court recognized the precedent of *Flast* and did not overrule it. Rather, it decided that plaintiffs in this case did not make the kind of showing *Flast* requires.

*Flast* insists that challenge must be made to an act of Congress under the taxing and spending clause of Article I, section 8, clause 1. But here the government's action was pursuant to a decision of the Department of Health, Education and Welfare under the authority of the Property Clause of the Constitution. Consequently, the allegation of the plaintiffs in *Valley Forge* did not fit the requirements of *Flast*, and they did not have standing. Further, Justice Rehnquist asserted that Americans United suffered no personal injury by the government's action in this case. The case excerpt below includes the Court's reasoning on that issue.

## VALLEY FORGE COLLEGE v. AMERICANS UNITED FOR SEPARATION OF CHURCH AND STATE
### 454 U.S. 464 (1982)

▨ JUSTICE REHNQUIST delivered the opinion of the Court.

The Court again visited the problem of taxpayer standing in *Flast v. Cohen*. . . . The Court developed a two-part test to determine whether the plaintiffs had standing to sue. First, because a taxpayer alleges injury only by virtue of his liability for taxes, the Court held that "a taxpayer will be a proper party to allege the unconstitutionality only of exercises of congressional power under the taxing and spending clause of Art. I, § 8, of the Constitution." Second, the Court required the taxpayer to "show that the challenged enactment exceeds specific constitutional limitations upon the exercise of the taxing and spending power and not simply that the enactment is generally beyond the powers delegated to Congress by Art. I, § 8.". . .

Thus, the Court reaffirmed that the "case or controversy" aspect of standing is unsatisfied "where a taxpayer seeks to employ a federal court as a forum in which to air his generalized grievances about the conduct of government or the allocation of power in the Federal System."

Unlike the plaintiffs in *Flast*, respondents fail the first prong of the test for taxpayer standing. Their claim is deficient in two respects. First, the source of their complaint is not a congressional action, but a decision by HEW to transfer a parcel of federal property. *Flast* limited taxpayer standing to challenges directed "only [at] exercises of congressional power.". . .

Second, and perhaps redundantly, the property transfer about which respondents complain was not an exercise of authority conferred by the Taxing and Spending Clause of Art. I, § 8. The authorizing legislation, the Federal Property and Administrative Services Act of 1949, was an evident exercise of Congress' power under the Property Clause, Art. IV, § 3, cl. 2. Respondents do not dispute this conclusion, and it is decisive of any claim of taxpayer standing under the *Flast* precedent. . . .

Respondents, therefore, are plainly without standing to sue as taxpayers. The Court of Appeals apparently reached the same conclusion. . . .

Although respondents claim that the Constitution has been violated, they claim nothing else. They fail to identify any personal injury suffered by them as a consequence of the alleged constitutional error, other than the psychological consequence presumably produced by observation of conduct with which one disagrees. That is not an injury sufficient to confer standing under Art. III, even though the disagreement is phrased in constitutional terms. It is evident that respondents are firmly committed to the constitutional principle of separation of church and State, but standing is not measured by the intensity of the litigant's interest or the fervor of his advocacy. . . .

We simply cannot see that respondents have alleged an *injury* of *any* kind, economic or otherwise, sufficient to confer standing. Respondents complain of a transfer of property located in Chester County, Pa. The named plaintiffs reside in Maryland and Virginia; their organizational headquarters are located in Washington, D.C. They learned of the transfer through a news release. Their claim that the Government has violated the Establishment Clause does not provide a special license to roam the country in search of governmental wrongdoing and to reveal their discoveries in federal court. The federal courts were simply not constituted as ombudsmen of the general welfare. . . .

---

### NOTES AND QUESTIONS

1. What is the difference between the holdings in *Flast* and *Valley Forge*? Were the litigants in *Valley Forge* less able or willing aggressively to pursue the lawsuit, or was it that they lacked no real injury other than a psychic injury shared by all concerned taxpayers? Was the "injury" to the plaintiffs in *Flast* any different?

> 2. How broadly or narrowly should courts read the taxpayer exception in
> *Flast*—in essence, is the existence of an Article I, § 8 funding authorization
> essential for standing, or did that fact in *Flast* simply assure the Court that the
> plaintiffs could prove the constitutional wrong (i.e., spending on behalf of re-
> ligion) and that a government entity had authorized the wrongful action? Are
> the evils of an establishment mentioned in *Flast* any less problematic when
> they are accomplished by a property transfer rather than through a direct
> congressional appropriation? Consider this last question when you read the
> following case.

*Hein v. Freedom From Religion Foundation* involved an Establishment Clause challenge by
the Freedom From Religion Foundation (FFRF) to actions by the White House Office
of Faith Based and Community Initiatives (OFBCI) that promoted President George
W. Bush's Faith-Based Initiative (see chapter 14). Specifically, FFRF claimed that the
White House-sponsored conferences, and expended funds in the process, in which officials engaged in religious speech and promoted religious groups over secular groups. In
order to bring the challenge, FFRF relied on taxpayer standing as established in 1968 in
*Flast v. Cohen*.

In a 5-4 decision (more accurately, a 3-2-4 decision), the Supreme Court ruled that
FFRF lacked standing under *Flast* because it was challenging an expenditure by the Executive that lacked an "express congressional mandate and a specific congressional appropriation" as required by the *Flast* exception to the standing rules. Because FFRF could not
identify a specific congressional authorization establishing or funding the OFBCI (there
was none), it failed to satisfy the *Flast* requirement that litigants establish a link between
a congressional action pursuant to the tax and spend power and the alleged constitutional
violation. As you read the opinions in the case, ask which of the various opinions is closest
to the letter and spirit of *Flast*.

## HEIN v. FREEDOM FROM RELIGION FOUNDATION
### 551 U.S. (2007)

JUSTICE ALITO announced the judgment of the Court and delivered an
opinion in which THE CHIEF JUSTICE and JUSTICE KENNEDY join.

I
A

In 2001, the President issued an executive order creating the White House
Office of Faith-Based and Community Initiatives within the Executive Office
of the President. The purpose of this new office was to ensure that "private
and charitable community groups, including religious ones . . . have the fullest opportunity permitted by law to compete on a level playing field, so long
as they achieve valid public purposes" and adhere to "the bedrock principles
of pluralism, nondiscrimination, evenhandedness, and neutrality." The office

was specifically charged with the task of eliminating unnecessary bureaucratic, legislative, and regulatory barriers that could impede such organizations' effectiveness and ability to compete equally for federal assistance.

By separate executive orders, the President also created Executive Department Centers for Faith-Based and Community Initiatives within several federal agencies and departments. These centers were given the job of ensuring that faith-based community groups would be eligible to compete for federal financial support without impairing their independence or autonomy, as long as they did "not use direct Federal financial assistance to support any inherently religious activities, such as worship, religious instruction, or proselytization." . . .

No congressional legislation specifically authorized the creation of the White House Office or the Executive Department Centers. Rather, they were "created entirely within the executive branch . . . by Presidential executive order." Nor has Congress enacted any law specifically appropriating money for these entities' activities. Instead, their activities are funded through general Executive Branch appropriations. . . .

B

The respondents are Freedom from Religion Foundation, Inc., a nonstock corporation "opposed to government endorsement of religion," and three of its members. Respondents brought suit . . . alleging that petitioners violated the Establishment Clause by organizing conferences at which faith-based organizations allegedly "are singled out as being particularly worthy of federal funding . . . , and the belief in God is extolled as distinguishing the claimed effectiveness of faith-based social services." Respondents further alleged that the content of these conferences sent a message to religious believers "that they are insiders and favored members of the political community" and that the conferences sent the message to nonbelievers "that they are outsiders" and "not full members of the political community." In short, respondents alleged that the conferences were designed to promote, and had the effect of promoting, religious community groups over secular ones.

The only asserted basis for standing was that the individual respondents are federal taxpayers who are "opposed to the use of Congressional taxpayer appropriations to advance and promote religion." In their capacity as federal taxpayers, respondents sought to challenge Executive Branch expenditures for these conferences, which, they contended, violated the Establishment Clause. . . .

II . . .
B

As a general matter, the interest of a federal taxpayer in seeing that Treasury funds are spent in accordance with the Constitution does not give rise to the kind of redressable "personal injury" required for Article III standing. Of course, a taxpayer has standing to challenge the *collection* of a specific tax assessment as unconstitutional; being forced to pay such a tax causes a real and immediate economic injury to the individual taxpayer. See, e.g., *Follett v. Town of McCormick*, 321 U.S. 573 (1944) (invalidating tax on preaching on First Amendment grounds). But that is not the interest on which respondents assert standing here. Rather, their claim is that, having paid lawfully collected taxes into the Federal Treasury at some point, they have a continuing, legally cognizable interest in ensuring that those funds are not *used* by the Government in a way that violates the Constitution.

We have consistently held that this type of interest is too generalized and attenuated to support Article III standing. . . .

Because the interests of the taxpayer are, in essence, the interests of the public-at-large, deciding a constitutional claim based solely on taxpayer standing "would be[,] not to decide a judicial controversy, but to assume a position of authority over the governmental acts of another and co-equal department, an authority which plainly we do not possess." . . .

In *Flast [v. Cohen]*, the Court carved out a narrow exception to the general constitutional prohibition against taxpayer standing. . . . The Court set out a two-part test for determining whether a federal taxpayer has standing to challenge an allegedly unconstitutional expenditure:

First, the taxpayer must establish a logical link between that status and the type of legislative enactment attacked. Thus, a taxpayer will be a proper party to allege the unconstitutionality only of exercises of congressional power under the taxing and spending clause of Art. I, § 8, of the Constitution. It will not be sufficient to allege an incidental expenditure of tax funds in the administration of an essentially regulatory statute. . . . Secondly, the taxpayer must establish a nexus between that status and the precise nature of the constitutional infringement alleged. Under this requirement, the taxpayer must show that the challenged enactment exceeds specific constitutional limitations imposed upon the exercise of the congressional taxing and spending power and not simply that the enactment is generally beyond the powers delegated to Congress by Art. I, § 8. . . .

### III

### A

Respondents argue that this case falls within the *Flast* exception, which they read to cover any "expenditure of government funds in violation of the Establishment Clause." But this broad reading fails to observe "the rigor with which the *Flast* exception to the *Frothingham* principle ought to be applied." *Valley Forge*, 454 U.S., 481.

The expenditures challenged in *Flast* . . . were funded by a specific congressional appropriation and were disbursed to private schools (including religiously affiliated schools) pursuant to a direct and unambiguous congressional mandate. Indeed, the *Flast* taxpayer-plaintiff's constitutional claim was premised on the contention that if the Government's actions were "'within the authority and intent of the Act, the Act is to that extent unconstitutional and void.'" And the judgment reviewed by this Court in *Flast* solely concerned the question whether "if [the challenged] expenditures are authorized by the Act the statute constitutes a 'law respecting an establishment of religion' and law 'prohibiting the free exercise thereof'" under the First Amendment.

Given that the alleged Establishment Clause violation in *Flast* was funded by a specific congressional appropriation and was undertaken pursuant to an express congressional mandate, the Court concluded that the taxpayer-plaintiffs had established the requisite "logical link between [their taxpayer] status and the type of legislative enactment attacked." In the Court's words, "[t]heir constitutional challenge [was] made to an exercise by Congress of its power under Art. I, § 8, to spend for the general welfare." But as this Court later noted, *Flast* "limited taxpayer standing to challenges directed 'only [at] exercises of congressional power'" under the Taxing and Spending Clause. *Valley Forge*, 454 U.S., 479.

B

The link between congressional action and constitutional violation that supported taxpayer standing in *Flast* is missing here. Respondents do not challenge any specific congressional action or appropriation; nor do they ask the Court to invalidate any congressional enactment or legislatively created program as unconstitutional. That is because the expenditures at issue here were not made pursuant to any Act of Congress. Rather, Congress provided general appropriations to the Executive Branch to fund its day-to-day activities. These appropriations did not expressly authorize, direct, or even mention the expenditures of which respondents complain. Those expenditures resulted from executive discretion, not congressional action.

We have never found taxpayer standing under such circumstances. . . .

*Bowen v. Kendrick*, 487 U.S. 589 (1988), on which respondents rely heavily, is not to the contrary. In that case, we held that the taxpayer-plaintiffs had standing to mount an as-applied challenge to the Adolescent Family Life Act (AFLA), which authorized federal grants to private community service groups including religious organizations. The Court found "a sufficient nexus between the taxpayer's standing as a taxpayer and the congressional exercise of taxing and spending power," notwithstanding the fact that the "the funding authorized by Congress had flowed through and been administered" by an Executive Branch official.

But the key to that conclusion was the Court's recognition that AFLA was "at heart a program of disbursement of funds pursuant to Congress' taxing and spending powers," and that the plaintiffs' claims "call[ed] into question how the funds authorized by Congress [were] being disbursed *pursuant to the AFLA's statutory mandate.*" AFLA not only expressly authorized and appropriated specific funds for grant-making, it also expressly contemplated that some of those moneys might go to projects involving religious groups. Unlike this case, *Kendrick* involved a "program of disbursement of funds pursuant to Congress' taxing and spending powers" that "Congress had created," "authorized," and "mandated." . . .

Respondents attempt to paint their lawsuit as a *Kendrick*-style as-applied challenge, but this effort is unavailing for the simple reason that they can cite no statute whose application they challenge. The best they can do is to point to unspecified, lump-sum "Congressional budget appropriations" for the general use of the Executive Branch—the allocation of which "is a[n] administrative decision traditionally regarded as committed to agency discretion."[7]

In short, this case falls outside the "the narrow exception" that *Flast* "created to the general rule against taxpayer standing established in *Frothingham*." Because the expenditures that respondents challenge were not expressly authorized or mandated by any specific congressional enactment, respondents'

---

[7] Nor is it relevant that Congress may have informally "earmarked" portions of its general Executive Branch appropriations to fund the offices and centers whose expenditures are at issue here. "[A] fundamental principle of appropriations law is that where 'Congress merely appropriates lump-sum amounts without statutorily restricting what can be done with those funds, a clear inference arises that it does not intend to impose legally binding restrictions, and indicia in committee reports and other legislative history as to how the funds should or are expected to be spent do not establish any legal requirements on' the agency." . . .

lawsuit is not directed at an exercise of congressional power, and thus lacks the requisite "logical nexus" between taxpayer status "and the type of legislative enactment attacked."

IV

A

1

Respondents argue that it is "arbitrary" to distinguish between money spent pursuant to congressional mandate and expenditures made in the course of executive discretion, because "the injury to taxpayers in both situations is the very injury targeted by the Establishment Clause and *Flast*—the expenditure for the support of religion of funds exacted from taxpayers." The panel majority below agreed, based on its observation that "there is so much that executive officials could do to promote religion in ways forbidden by the establishment clause."

But *Flast* focused on congressional action, and we must decline this invitation to extend its holding to encompass discretionary Executive Branch expenditures. *Flast* itself distinguished the "incidental expenditure of tax funds in the administration of an essentially regulatory statute," and we have subsequently rejected the view that taxpayer standing "extends to 'the Government as a whole, regardless of which branch is at work in a particular instance.'" . . .

2

While respondents argue that Executive Branch expenditures in support of religion are no different from legislative extractions, *Flast* itself rejected this equivalence: "It will not be sufficient to allege an incidental expenditure of tax funds in the administration of an essentially regulatory statute."

Because almost all Executive Branch activity is ultimately funded by some congressional appropriation, extending the *Flast* exception to purely executive expenditures would effectively subject every federal action—be it a conference, proclamation or speech—to Establishment Clause challenge by any taxpayer in federal court. To see the wide swathe of activity that respondents' proposed rule would cover, one need look no further than the amended complaint in this action, which focuses largely on speeches and presentations made by Executive Branch officials. . . .

B

Respondents set out a parade of horribles that they claim could occur if *Flast* is not extended to discretionary Executive Branch expenditures. For example, they say, a federal agency could use its discretionary funds to build a house of worship or to hire clergy of one denomination and send them out to spread their faith. Or an agency could use its funds to make bulk purchases of Stars of David, crucifixes, or depictions of the star and crescent for use in its offices or for distribution to the employees or the general public. Of course, none of these things has happened, even though *Flast* has not previously been expanded in the way that respondents urge. In the unlikely event that any of these executive actions did take place, Congress could quickly step in. And respondents make no effort to show that these improbable abuses could not be challenged in federal court by plaintiffs who would possess standing based on grounds other than taxpayer standing.

## C

Over the years, *Flast* has been defended by some and criticized by others. But the present case does not require us to reconsider that precedent. The Court of Appeals did not apply *Flast*; it extended *Flast*. It is a necessary concomitant of the doctrine of *stare decisis* that a precedent is not always expanded to the limit of its logic. That was the approach that then-Justice Rehnquist took in his opinion for the Court in *Valley Forge,* and it is the approach we take here. We do not extend *Flast*, but we also do not overrule it. We leave *Flast* as we found it.

For these reasons, the judgment of the Court of Appeals for the Seventh Circuit is reversed.

▓ JUSTICE KENNEDY, concurring. . . .

*Flast* established a "narrow exception" to the rule against taxpayer standing. To find standing in the circumstances of this case would make the narrow exception boundless. The public events and public speeches respondents seek to call in question are part of the open discussion essential to democratic self-government. The Executive Branch should be free, as a general matter, to discover new ideas, to understand pressing public demands, and to find creative responses to address governmental concerns. The exchange of ideas between and among the State and Federal Governments and their manifold, diverse constituencies sustains a free society. Permitting any and all taxpayers to challenge the content of these prototypical executive operations and dialogues would lead to judicial intervention so far exceeding traditional boundaries on the Judiciary that there would arise a real danger of judicial oversight of executive duties. The burden of discovery to ascertain if relief is justified in these potentially innumerable cases would risk altering the free exchange of ideas and information. And were this constant supervision to take place the courts would soon assume the role of speech editors for communications issued by executive officials and event planners for meetings they hold. . . .

It must be remembered that, even where parties have no standing to sue, members of the Legislative and Executive Branches are not excused from making constitutional determinations in the regular course of their duties. Government officials must make a conscious decision to obey the Constitution whether or not their acts can be challenged in a court of law and then must conform their actions to these principled determinations.

▓ JUSTICE SCALIA, with whom JUSTICE THOMAS joins, concurring in the judgment.

Today's opinion is, in one significant respect, entirely consistent with our previous cases addressing taxpayer standing to raise Establishment Clause challenges to government expenditures. Unfortunately, the consistency lies in the creation of utterly meaningless distinctions which separate the case at hand from the precedents that have come out differently, but which cannot possibly be (in any sane world) the reason it comes out differently. If this Court is to decide cases by rule of law rather than show of hands, we must surrender to logic and choose sides: Either *Flast v. Cohen,* should be applied to (at a minimum) all challenges to the governmental expenditure of general tax revenues in a manner alleged to violate a constitutional provision specifically limiting the taxing and spending power, or *Flast* should be repudiated. For me, the choice is easy. *Flast* is wholly irreconcilable with the Article III restrictions on federal-court jurisdiction that this Court has repeatedly confirmed are embodied in the doctrine of standing. . . .

## II

### A

The plurality today . . . offers no explanation of why the factual differences between this case and *Flast* are *material*. It virtually admits that express congressional allocation *vel non* has nothing to do with whether the plaintiffs have alleged an injury in fact that is fairly traceable and likely to be redressed. As the dissent correctly contends and I shall not belabor, *Flast* is *indistinguishable* from this case for purposes of Article III. Whether the challenged government expenditure is expressly allocated by a specific congressional enactment *has absolutely no relevance* to the Article III criteria of injury in fact, traceability, and redressability. . . .

Because the express-allocation line has no mooring to our tripartite test for Article III standing, it invites demonstrably absurd results. For example, the plurality would deny standing to a taxpayer challenging the President's disbursement to a religious organization of a discrete appropriation that Congress had not explicitly allocated to that purpose, even if everyone knew that Congress and the President had informally negotiated that the entire sum would be spent in that precise manner. And taxpayers should lack standing to bring Establishment Clause challenges to the Executive Branch's use of appropriated funds when those expenditures have the *added vice* of violating congressional restrictions. If, for example, Congress instructs the President to disburse grants to hospitals that he deems worthy, and the President instead gives all of the money to the Catholic Church, "[t]he link between congressional action and constitutional violation that supported taxpayer standing in *Flast* [would be] missing." Indeed, taking the plurality at its word, Congress could insulate the President from *all Flast*-based suits by codifying the truism that no appropriation can be spent by the Executive Branch in a manner that violates the Establishment Clause. . . .

I thus share the dissent's bewilderment as to why the plurality fixates on the amount of *additional* discretion the Executive Branch enjoys under the law beyond the only discretion relevant to the Establishment Clause issue: whether to spend taxpayer funds for a purpose that is unconstitutional.

### B

While I have been critical of the Members of the plurality, I by no means wish to give the impression that respondents' legal position is any more coherent. . . .

The logical consequence of respondents' position finds no support in this Court's precedents or our Nation's history. Any taxpayer would be able to sue whenever tax funds were used in alleged violation of the Establishment Clause. So, for example, any taxpayer could challenge the fact that the Marshal of our Court is paid, in part, to call the courtroom to order by proclaiming "God Save the United States and this Honorable Court." As much as respondents wish to deny that this is what *Flast* logically entails, it blinks reality to conclude otherwise. If respondents are to prevail, they must endorse a future in which ideologically motivated taxpayers could "roam the country in search of governmental wrongdoing and . . . reveal their discoveries in federal court," transforming those courts into "ombudsmen of the general welfare" with respect to Establishment Clause issues. . . .

The rule of law is ill served by forcing lawyers and judges to make arguments that deaden the soul of the law, which is logic and reason. Either *Flast* was correct, and must be accorded the wide application that it logically dictates, or it was not, and must be abandoned in its entirety. I turn, finally, to that question.

## III

Is a taxpayer's purely psychological displeasure that his funds are being spent in an allegedly unlawful manner ever sufficiently concrete and particularized to support Article III standing? The answer is plainly no. . . .

The fact that it is the alleged violation of a specific constitutional limit on the taxing and spending power that produces the taxpayer's mental angst does not change the fundamental flaw. It remains the case that the taxpayer seeks "relief that no more directly and tangibly benefits him than it does the public at large." And it is of no conceivable relevance to this issue whether the Establishment Clause was originally conceived of as a specific limitation on the taxing and spending power. Madison's Remonstrance has nothing whatever to say on the question whether suits alleging violations of that limitation are anything other than the generalized grievances that federal courts had always been barred from considering before *Flast*. *Flast* was forced to rely on the slim reed of the Remonstrance since there was no better support for its novel conclusion, in 1968, that violation of the Establishment Clause, unique among the provisions of our law, had always inflicted a personalized Psychic Injury upon all taxpayers that federal courts had the power to remedy. . . .

My call for the imposition of logic and order upon this chaotic set of precedents will perhaps be met with the snappy epigram that "[t]he life of the law has not been logic: it has been experience." But what experience has shown is that *Flast's* lack of a logical theoretical underpinning has rendered our taxpayer-standing doctrine . . . a jurisprudential disaster. . . . I can think of few cases less warranting of *stare decisis* respect. It is time—it is past time—to call an end. *Flast* should be overruled.

▨ JUSTICE SOUTER, with whom JUSTICE STEVENS, JUSTICE GINSBURG, and JUSTICE BREYER join, dissenting.

*Flast v. Cohen* held that plaintiffs with an Establishment Clause claim could "demonstrate the necessary stake as taxpayers in the outcome of the litigation to satisfy Article III requirements." Here, the controlling, plurality opinion declares that *Flast* does not apply, but a search of that opinion for a suggestion that these taxpayers have any less stake in the outcome than the taxpayers in *Flast* will come up empty: the plurality makes no such finding, nor could it. Instead, the controlling opinion closes the door on these taxpayers because the Executive Branch, and not the Legislative Branch, caused their injury. I see no basis for this distinction in either logic or precedent, and respectfully dissent.

## I

We held in *Flast*, and repeated just last Term, that the injury alleged in Establishment Clause challenges to federal spending is "the very 'extract[ion] and spen[ding]' of 'tax money' in aid of religion." As the Court said in *Flast*, the importance of that type of injury has deep historical roots going back to the ideal of religious liberty in James Madison's Memorial and Remonstrance Against Religious Assessments, that the government in a free society may not "force a citizen to contribute three pence only of his property for the support of any one establishment" of religion. Madison thus translated into practical terms the right of conscience described when he wrote that "[t]he Religion . . . of every man must be left to the conviction and conscience of every man; and it is the right of every man to exercise it as these may dictate." . . .

The right of conscience and the expenditure of an identifiable three pence raised by taxes for the support of a religious cause are therefore not to be split off from one another. The three pence implicates the conscience, and the injury from Government expenditures on religion is not accurately classified with the "Psychic Injury" that results whenever a congressional appropriation or executive expenditure raises hackles of disagreement with the policy supported. JUSTICE STEWART recognized this in his concurring opinion in *Flast*, when he said that "every taxpayer can claim a personal constitutional right not to be taxed for the support of a religious institution," and thus distinguished the case from one in which a taxpayer sought only to air a generalized grievance in federal court.

Here, there is no dispute that taxpayer money in identifiable amounts is funding conferences, and these are alleged to have the purpose of promoting religion. . . .When executive agencies spend identifiable sums of tax money for religious purposes, no less than when Congress authorizes the same thing, taxpayers suffer injury. . . .

The plurality points to the separation of powers to explain its distinction between legislative and executive spending decisions, but there is no difference on that point of view between a Judicial Branch review of an executive decision and a judicial evaluation of a congressional one. We owe respect to each of the other branches, no more to the former than to the latter, and no one has suggested that the Establishment Clause lacks applicability to executive uses of money. It would surely violate the Establishment Clause for the Department of Health and Human Services to draw on a general appropriation to build a chapel for weekly church services (no less than if a statute required it), and for good reason: if the Executive could accomplish through the exercise of discretion exactly what Congress cannot do through legislation, Establishment Clause protection would melt away. . . .

Thus, *Flast* speaks for this Court's recognition (shared by a majority of the Court today) that when the Government spends money for religious purposes a taxpayer's injury is serious and concrete enough to be "judicially cognizable." The judgment of sufficient injury takes account of the Madisonian relationship of tax money and conscience, but it equally reflects the Founders' pragmatic "conviction that individual religious liberty could be achieved best under a government which was stripped of all power to tax, to support, or otherwise to assist any or all religions," and the realization continuing to the modern day that favoritism for religion "'sends the . . . message to . . . nonadherents "that they are outsiders, not full members of the political community.'" . . .

Because the taxpayers in this case have alleged the type of injury this Court has seen as sufficient for standing, I would affirm.

## NOTES AND QUESTIONS

1. Is *Hein* consistent with both *Flast* and *Valley Forge*? Does the plurality opinion uphold *Flast* or undercut it? Or, does it do some of both? How does Justice Kennedy's concurring opinion distinguish itself from the plurality opinion in terms of its perspective on the *Flast* decision? Finally, does *Hein* present a stronger case for denying taxpayer standing than *Valley Forge*, or is it a closer case?

2. What are the differences and similarities between the criticisms that Justice Scalia and Justice Souter make of the rationale articulated by Justice Alito in this case?

3. In his opinion concurring in the judgment, Justice Scalia attacks the notion of judicial minimalism. His criticisms are directed at the plurality's approach in this case and, more generally, the judicial philosophy articulated by Chief Justice John Roberts, among others. Chief Justice Roberts has said: "If it is not necessary to decide more to dispose of a case, in my view it is necessary not to decide more."[5]

   What are the advantages and disadvantages of this kind of judicial minimalism, both in this case and more broadly? For contrasting views on this matter, see Cass Sunstein, "The Minimalist," *Los Angeles Times* (May 25, 2006) and Geoffrey R. Stone, "A Narrow View of the Law," *Chicago Tribune* (February 6, 2007).

4. One *amicus* brief in support of the FFRF argued that, based on the Founders' experience with the British crown, they would not have viewed the actions of an Executive as less threatening to religious liberty or less likely to create an establishment than similar actions by a legislative body. Is the majority opinion response to this argument too legalistic? If so, how do you explain the language of the First Amendment: "*Congress* shall make no law respecting an establishment of religion . . . ." Does not this language suggest that Congress intended to limit the prohibitions of the Establishment Clause to *legislatively* authorized actions?

5. What are the implications of *Hein*? Are the religious actions of the President effectively immune from legal challenge provided he acts without congressional authorization or does not rely on an express congressional appropriation? Could a federal agency, for example, use some funds that are drawn from general Congressional appropriations to build a church? Or are the examples offered in Justice Souter's dissenting opinion unlikely to occur? In a related vein, does the majority opinion subtly suggest that many Establishment Clause controversies involve both political and legal considerations, such that some are better resolved in the political arena rather than in the courts? How might changing the decisionmaker (shifting from the judicial to the political branches) change the decision in these cases?

6. Of course, taxpayer lawsuits are only one form of standing to sue. A plaintiff may demonstrate the requisite injury in other ways (see chapter 20). But, in certain cases, if a plaintiff cannot bring a taxpayer lawsuit, it is possible that

some aspects of the Establishment Clause may never be enforced because no one else has a sufficient injury and inclination to bring another kind of lawsuit. Professors Ira Lupu and Bob Tuttle expound on this point:

> In some of the cases that have been brought to challenge grants made under the [faith-based initiative], taxpayers are the only conceivable plaintiffs, because typically no one is injured by a decision to fund a particular grantee. In such cases, a lack of taxpayer standing may mean that no private citizens can sue to enforce the Establishment Clause against government funding agencies. Other government agencies, such as a state Attorney General, might be able to take action to enforce the Clause, but that sort of action is rare.
>
> In other situations, however, potential plaintiffs other than taxpayers might be available. For example, a disappointed competitor for a grant may complain that the grant was unlawfully awarded, but these cases too are extremely rare. Such rivals typically do not want to alienate the granting agency with accusations of unconstitutional spending. And in cases where the rival is a religious organization, the only claim that will be raised is one of discrimination among faiths, not a challenge to the promotion of religion with government funds.
>
> Another example of an alternative plaintiff arises in cases in which there are allegations of religious coercion. Some cases about faith-based programs in prison have raised such claims, as does the recent lawsuit against North Dakota for funding the Dakota Boys and Girls Ranch, which the complaint alleges is coercing teenagers placed there into religious observance. A teenager placed against his or her will in such a facility would unquestionably have standing to complain about such coercion, but the same teenager would not have standing to complain about government funding of voluntary religious experience at the Ranch, because uncoerced religious experience would not cause such a plaintiff any injury. So non-taxpayer plaintiffs may be available in some cases, but they may be limited in the kinds of claims they can present to those connected to the particular injury they have suffered.
>
> How does the availability of non-taxpayer plaintiffs affect the scope of taxpayer standing? As a formal matter, the availability of other plaintiffs should make no difference with respect to taxpayer-plaintiffs. Courts often say that no one's standing should be denied just because there might be a better plaintiff somewhere. And courts also frequently say that they should not grant standing to a particular plaintiff simply because no other plaintiff would have standing. But we can nevertheless imagine, in the hard cases, that some lower court judges will be influenced by the potential magnitude of the violation and the question of availability of non-taxpayer plaintiffs. Where the violation seems egregious, and no one other than a taxpayer is a potential plaintiff, some judges may resolve the close calls in favor of recognizing taxpayer standing.

Ira C. Lupu and Bob W. Tuttle, "Analysis of the *Hein v. Freedom From Religion Foundation* Decision," *The Roundtable on Religion and Social Welfare Policy* (July 2, 2007). The analysis may be found at http://www.religionandsocialpolicy.org/legal/legal_update_display.cfm?id=60.

7. Might the Court's ruling in *Hein* on taxpayer standing open the door to changes in doctrine regarding other types of standing to sue? An opinion written by a federal appellate judge after the *Hein* decision was handed down provides some food for thought on this issue. The opinion is a concurring opinion written by Judge DeMoss, and it addresses the constitutionality of prayer before school board meetings. After discussing the *Hein* case, Judge DeMoss wrote:

> To me, the critical issue is whether each of [the plantiffs] has proved that he individually sustained an injury in fact as a result of the school board's practice of permitting citizens of the school district to freely exercise their own rights of religion and free speech under the *First Amendment* by offering a prayer or invocation at the beginning of school board meetings. On the basis of the stipulations before us in this case, I would find these facts helpful in evaluating injury in fact: this prayer practice has existed for more than thirty years, the school board does not specify or approve the contents of any prayer or invocation in advance, and in giving the prayer or invocation, the speaker does not purport to speak for, or on behalf of, the school board. In my view, the fact that the Does "take offense" to this prayer practice should not constitute an injury in fact for standing purposes.

*Doe v. Tangipahoa Parish School Board*, 2007 U.S. App. LEXIS 17810 (5th Cir. 2007) (DeMoss, J., concurring). If Judge DeMoss's opinion were to be embraced by the Supreme Court, how would it change the ability of a plaintiff to bring a lawsuit in cases involving religious expression? How could this affect the enforcement of the Establishment Clause?

---

The standing rules can be used not only to limit a litigant's access to the federal courts; they also can be a handy tool for courts seeking to avoid ruling on controversial subjects. Consider the following case, *Elk Grove Unified School District v. Newdow*, involving one of the more contentious issues in the early 2000s: whether a school district's policy of requiring the Pledge of Allegiance with the phrase "under God" to be said at the beginning of each school day violates the Establishment Clause as an impermissible endorsement of religion (see the discussions in chapters 17 and 18). In *Newdow*, the Ninth Circuit Court of Appeals ruled in June 2002 that the school district's policy violated the Establishment Clause.

The holding created a maelstrom of criticism, and most observers believed the Supreme Court would be unable to avoid ruling on the issue. Most commentators believed the Court would uphold the phrase "under God," and some feared that such a holding would open the door to many forms of government-sponsored religion. But a majority of the justices found a way to side-step the merits of the case, ruling that the plaintiff's father lacked "prudential" standing to bring the case.

## ELK GROVE UNIFIED SCHOOL DISTRICT v. MICHAEL A. NEWDOW

## 542 U.S. 1 (2004)

▓ JUSTICE STEVENS delivered the opinion of the Court.

Each day elementary school teachers in the Elk Grove Unified School District (School District) lead their classes in a group recitation of the Pledge of Allegiance. Respondent, Michael A. Newdow, is an atheist whose daughter participates in that daily exercise. Because the Pledge contains the words "under God," he views the School District's policy as a religious indoctrination of his child that violates the First Amendment. A divided panel of the Court of Appeals for the Ninth Circuit agreed with Newdow. In light of the obvious importance of that decision, we granted certiorari to review the First Amendment issue and, preliminarily, the question whether Newdow has standing to invoke the jurisdiction of the federal courts. We conclude that Newdow lacks standing and therefore reverse the Court of Appeals' decision. . . .

II

Under California law, "every public elementary school" must begin each day with "appropriate patriotic exercises." The statute provides that "[t]he giving of the Pledge of Allegiance to the Flag of the United States of America shall satisfy" this requirement. The Elk Grove Unified School District has implemented the state law by requiring that "[e]ach elementary school class recite the pledge of allegiance to the flag once each day." Consistent with our case law, the School District permits students who object on religious grounds to abstain from the recitation. See *West Virginia Bd. of Ed. v. Barnette*, 319 U.S. 624 (1943).

In March 2000, Newdow filed suit in the United States District Court for the Eastern District of California against the United States Congress, the President of the United States, the State of California, and the Elk Grove Unified School District and its superintendent. . . .

The case was referred to a Magistrate Judge, whose brief findings and recommendation concluded, "the Pledge does not violate the Establishment Clause." The District Court adopted that recommendation and dismissed the complaint on July 21, 2000. The Court of Appeals reversed and issued three separate decisions discussing the merits and Newdow's standing.

In its first opinion the appeals court unanimously held that Newdow has standing "as a parent to challenge a practice that interferes with his right to direct the religious education of his daughter." . . . On the merits, over the dissent of one judge, the court held that both the 1954 Act and the School District's policy violate the Establishment Clause of the First Amendment.

After the Court of Appeals' initial opinion was announced, Sandra Banning, the mother of Newdow's daughter, filed a motion for leave to intervene, or alternatively to dismiss the complaint. She declared that although she and Newdow shared "physical custody" of their daughter, a state-court order granted her "exclusive legal custody" of the child, "including the sole right to represent [the daughter's] legal interests and make all decision[s] about her education" and welfare. Banning further stated that her daughter is a Christian who believes in God and has no objection either to reciting or hearing others recite the Pledge of Allegiance, or to its reference to God. Banning expressed the belief that her daughter would be harmed if the litigation were permitted to proceed, because others might incorrectly perceive the child as sharing her father's atheist views. Banning accordingly concluded, as her daughter's sole legal custodian, that it was not in the child's interest to be a party to Newdow's lawsuit. On September 25, 2002, the California Superior Court entered an order enjoining Newdow from including his daughter as an unnamed party or suing as her "next friend." That order did not purport to answer the question of Newdow's Article III standing.

In a second published opinion, the Court of Appeals reconsidered Newdow's standing in light of Banning's motion. The court noted that Newdow no longer claimed to represent his daughter, but unanimously concluded that "the grant of sole legal custody to Banning" did not deprive Newdow, "as a noncustodial parent, of Article III standing to object to unconstitutional government action affecting his child." The court held that under California law Newdow retains the right to expose his child to his particular religious views even if those views contradict the mother's, and that Banning's objections as sole legal custodian do not defeat Newdow's right to seek redress for an alleged injury to his own parental interests.

On February 28, 2003, the Court of Appeals issued an order amending its first opinion and denying rehearing en banc. The amended opinion omitted the initial opinion's discussion of Newdow's standing to challenge the 1954 Act and declined to determine whether Newdow was entitled to declaratory relief regarding the constitutionality of that Act. . . .

## III

In every federal case, the party bringing the suit must establish standing to prosecute the action. "In essence the question of standing is whether the litigant is entitled to have the court decide the merits of the dispute or of particular issues." *Warth v. Selden*, 422 U.S. 490, 498 (1975) The standing requirement is born partly of "'an idea, which is more than an intuition but less than a rigorous and explicit theory, about the constitutional and prudential limits to the powers of an unelected, unrepresentative judiciary in our kind of government.'" *Allen v. Wright*, 468 U.S. 737, 750 (1984). . . .

Even in cases concededly within our jurisdiction under Article III, we abide by "a series of rules under which [we have] avoided passing upon a large part of all the constitutional questions pressed upon [us] for decision." *Ashwander v. TVA*, 297 U.S. 288, 346 (1936) Always we must balance "the heavy obligation to exercise jurisdiction," against the "deeply rooted" commitment "not to pass on questions of constitutionality" unless adjudication of the constitutional issue is necessary. . . .

Consistent with these principles, our standing jurisprudence contains two strands: Article III standing, which enforces the Constitution's case or controversy requirement, and prudential standing, which embodies "judicially self-imposed limits on the exercise of federal jurisdiction.". . . Although we have not exhaustively defined the prudential dimensions of the standing doctrine, we have explained that prudential standing encompasses "the general prohibition on a litigant's raising another person's legal rights, the rule barring adjudication of generalized grievances more appropriately addressed in the representative branches, and the requirement that a plaintiff's complaint fall within the zone of interests protected by the law invoked." *Allen v. Wright*, 468 U.S. 737, 751. . . .

One of the principal areas in which this Court has customarily declined to intervene is the realm of domestic relations. . . . So strong is our deference to state law in this area that we have recognized a "domestic relations exception" that "divests the federal courts of power to issue divorce, alimony, and child custody decrees." We have also acknowledged that it might be appropriate for the federal courts to decline to hear a case involving "elements of the domestic relationship," even when divorce, alimony, or child custody is not strictly at issue. . . . *Ankenbrandt v. Richards*, 504 U.S. 689, 703, 705 (1992)

As explained briefly above, the extent of the standing problem raised by the domestic relations issues in this case was not apparent until August 5, 2002, when Banning filed her motion for leave to intervene or dismiss the complaint following the Court of Appeals' initial decision. At that time, the child's custody was governed by a February 6, 2002, order of the California Superior Court. That order provided that Banning had "'*sole* legal custody as to the rights and responsibilities to make decisions relating to the health, education and welfare of'" her daughter. . . .

That family court order was the controlling document at the time of the Court of Appeals' standing decision. After the Court of Appeals ruled, however, the Superior Court announced [after a new hearing] . . . that the parents have "joint legal custody," but that Banning "makes the final decisions if the two . . . disagree."

Newdow contends that despite Banning's final authority, he retains "an unrestricted right to inculcate in his daughter—free from governmental interference—the atheistic beliefs he finds persuasive." The difficulty with that argument is that Newdow's rights, as in many cases touching upon family relations, cannot be viewed in isolation. This case concerns not merely Newdow's interest in inculcating his child with his views on religion, but also the rights of the child's mother as a parent generally and under the Superior Court orders specifically. And most important, it implicates the interests of a young child who finds herself at the center of a highly public debate over her custody, the propriety of a widespread national ritual, and the meaning of our Constitution. . . .

Newdow's standing derives entirely from his relationship with his daughter, but he lacks the right to litigate as her next friend. . . .

Newdow's parental status is defined by California's domestic relations law. . . .

Nothing that either Banning or the School Board has done, however, impairs Newdow's right to instruct his daughter in his religious views. Instead, Newdow requests relief that is more ambitious. . . . He wishes to forestall his daughter's exposure to religious ideas that her mother, who wields a form of veto power, endorses, and to use his parental status to challenge the influences to which his daughter may be exposed in school when he and Banning disagree. The California cases simply do not stand for the proposition that Newdow has a right to dictate to others what they may and may not say to his child respecting religion. . . .

In our view, it is improper for the federal courts to entertain a claim by a plaintiff whose standing to sue is founded on family law rights that are in dispute when prosecution of the lawsuit may have an adverse effect on the person who is the source of the plaintiff's claimed standing. When hard questions of domestic relations are sure to affect the outcome, the prudent course is for the federal court to stay its hand rather than reach out to resolve a weighty question of federal constitutional law. . . . We conclude that, having been deprived under California law of the right to sue as next friend, Newdow lacks prudential standing to bring this suit in federal court.

> The judgment of the Court of Appeals is reversed. . . .

CHIEF JUSTICE REHNQUIST, . . . concurring in the judgment. . . .

The domestic relations exception is not a prudential limitation on our federal jurisdiction. It is a limiting construction of the statute defining federal diversity jurisdiction, which "divests the federal courts of power to issue divorce, alimony, and child custody decrees," *Ankenbrandt*, 504 U.S., 703. This case does not involve diversity jurisdiction, and respondent does not ask this Court to issue a divorce, alimony, or child custody decree. Instead it involves a substantial federal question about the constitutionality of the School District's conducting the pledge ceremony, which is the source of our jurisdiction. Therefore, the domestic relations exception to diversity jurisdiction forms no basis for denying standing to respondent. . . .

---

## NOTES AND QUESTIONS

1. In *Newdow*, the Court acknowledges that it has constitutional authority to hear the case (Article III jurisdiction) but claims it is ill-suited to rule on Newdow's custody rights. However, could it be argued that the majority does exactly that? Does the majority effectively rule on the substance of Dr. Newdow's claims by not ruling on them?

2. Was Chief Justice Rehnquist correct when he argued that the *Newdow* case presented a substantial federal question that should be resolved?

3. After the Court rendered its decision in *Newdow*, Dr. Newdow quickly refiled his claim along with some other atheist parents, making it likely that the Supreme Court will eventually hear the case again. Does that information change your answer to the previous question?

# Part II

# The Free Exercise Clause

CHAPTER 6

# BASIC CONCEPTS AND DEVELOPMENT OF FREE EXERCISE DOCTRINE

One of the Founders' chief priorities in creating a new democratic society was to secure religious freedom by guaranteeing its "free exercise." Even before the Philadelphia Constitutional Convention of 1787, all of the states that had drafted constitutions during the revolutionary period (Connecticut and Rhode Island continued to operate under their colonial charters) included provisions in their respective declarations of rights that recognized the importance of religious exercise. Though the exact language varied from state to state, the documents reinforced commonly shared principles. Georgia's 1777 Constitution chose simple language: "All persons whatever shall have the free exercise of their religion; provided it be not repugnant to the peace and safety of the State." New Hampshire's 1783 constitution was more elaborate and expressive about what the right entailed:

> Every individual has a natural and unalienable right to worship GOD according to the dictates of his own conscience, and reason; and no subject shall be hurt, molested, or restrained in his person, liberty or estate for worshipping GOD in the manner and season most agreeable to the dictates of his own conscience, or for his religious profession, sentiments or persuasion; provided he doth not disturb the public peace, or disturb others in their religious worship.[1]

As a result, when the First Congress convened in New York in 1789 to undertake the drafting of a free exercise provision for the Bill of Rights, they were not writing on a clean slate. They were mindful of the religious favoritism and persecution that had existed under the colonial religious establishments and the subsequent efforts of the new state legislatures to rectify those wrongs. In drafting both state and federal religion provisions, it is likely that the Founders took an expansive view of the concept of religious "free exercise" to include "freedom of belief" (or the freedom to disbelieve or hold heterodoxical religious beliefs). A majority of state constitutions used the more inclusive terms "conscience" or "rights of conscience," sometimes in conjunction with the word "religion" and other times as encompassing that latter concept but not necessarily limited by it. As discussed in the second chapter, early drafts of the First Amendment also included the word "conscience." Its exclusion from the final language should not be interpreted as representing a narrow view on religious exercise but simply that the Founders viewed the terms interchangeably when expressing notions about protected rights of belief.

At tension with this broad concept of freedom of conscience and belief is the likely narrow view among the Founders of what constituted religious conduct worthy of protection. Not only did a majority of the Founders hold a limited, eighteenth century understanding of "religion" (assigning that designation to Protestantism, Catholicism, and possibly Judaism, for example, but not to Muslim or Native American beliefs), they also likely took a limited view over what satisfied as religious conduct that justified protection (e.g., prayer, church worship, liturgy, sacraments). Thomas Jefferson was an exception when he wrote about extending equal treatment to "the Jew, the Mohometan, and the Hindoo," and he elicited outrage when he wrote "it does me no injury for my neighbor to say there are twenty gods, or no God. It neither picks my pocket nor breaks my leg."[2] Even to this day, judges and government officials struggle with determining whether certain beliefs or conduct are rooted in "religion" and then are therefore religiously motivated. (See chapter 4, "What Is Religion?"). The history of the development of free exercise doctrine has been one of an expansion of the concept of what is religious and what constitutes religiously motivated conduct deserving of protection. For example, underlying the Mormon cases discussed in the first part of this chapter were issues over whether public officials and judges were willing to recognize Mormonism as a religion, and then polygamy as religiously motivated conduct.

An understanding of terms tells us little about how the Founders saw the Free Exercise Clause working in a practical way. What does it mean to afford or guarantee the right to freely practice or exercise one's religion? Does this mean that the government, in its various capacities, is obligated to assist people to engage in religious worship and expression? Must the government create conditions that facilitate religious belief and practice or is it sufficient for constitutional purposes that the government merely not unduly burden one's ability to practice her religion? Thus one initial question may be whether the free exercise right contains a "positive" quality that imposes obligations on the government to enhance religious belief and practice, or is free exercise simply a "negative right" that serves as a check on government action. Most scholars would agree with the assessment of Professor Carl Esbeck: "As with all freedoms guaranteed by the Bill of Rights, the Free Exercise and Establishment Clauses protect 'negative' rights. That is, the Religion Clauses tell the government what it may not do."[3] Thus the free exercise right may mean that I can freely engage in religiously motivated conduct up to the point that my conduct (e.g., animal sacrifice) faces some limitation through a government regulation (e.g., an animal protection law). And further, the right may mean that I can raise my free exercise claim as a defense to prosecution or regulation under that law. This is what is meant when we think of rights as imposing "negative checks" on government regulation. However, as discussed in the next chapter, the Supreme Court has at times ruled that that free exercise "check" on government regulation may sometimes require the government to accommodate a person's religious practice by taking the affirmative step of exempting that person from the requirements of a particular law. Thus while the Free Exercise Clause does not generally require affirmative actions by the government, where a government law or policy substantially burdens religious practice the government may be required to act.

The right to free exercise clearly is not absolute. Even in the heady days of the *Sherbert v. Verner* era (1963–1990) when the Court provided the greatest protection for religious practice from the application of general laws and regulations, the Court always balanced the government's interest against that of the free exercise claimant. (See chapter 9.)

Concerns about public order, health, and safety have frequently outweighed a person's right to exercise his religion. Note the two state constitutional provisions quoted above, both of which contained limitations on the free exercise right when it came to matters of public peace and safety. Such qualifying language was common in early state constitutions and these notions continue to serve as limiting constraints on free exercise. This, of course, raises issues of how broadly a legislative body can define such interests and the extent to which courts can and should second-guess those legislative judgments. Certainly, we can all agree on those cases at the extreme margins—laws prohibiting human sacrifice, for example. But what about an ordinance that protects a person's "peace" at dinnertime by prohibiting Jehovah's Witnesses from ringing his or her front door bell?

The "public peace and safety" language can be read two different ways, at least with respect to the issue of what the Founders may have intended. On one hand, the provisions could mean that although the Founders did not consider free exercise rights to be absolute, religious practice should be protected and allowed, even as against a religiously neutral law that would otherwise prohibit that conduct (e.g., an ordinance prohibiting door-to-door solicitations after 6 p.m.) *unless* the religious conduct violated public peace and safety. The presumption or default is that religious conduct should be exempted from general laws if possible. A contrary reading views such provisions (and the principle they established) more broadly as indicating that the Founders did not consider the free exercise right to include exemptions from neutral laws to which people had religious objections. Here, the peace and safety provisions are representative of religiously neutral laws generally, which must prevail over religiously motivated conduct. For more on this debate among historians and law professors, compare Michael W. McConnell, "The Origins and Historical Understanding of Free Exercise of Religion," *Harvard Law Review* 103 (1990): 1409, with Philip A. Hamburger, "A Constitutional Right of Religious Exemption: An Historical Perspective," *George Washington Law Review* 60 (1992): 915.

When considering manifestations of the free exercise interest, readers need to think of the right in both a macro and micro sense. Free exercise affords certain protection to individuals to engage in religious worship and expression. But in what sense does free exercise also protect the right of individuals to worship together and engage in other forms of corporate religious expression and conduct? If the free exercise interest contains a corporate quality—and the Court has said that it does—is that right merely the aggregate manifestation of the individual rights of the believers? Or do religious organizations, denominations, and houses of worship possess religious liberty interests that are unique to them as religious bodies and are distinct from the rights of their individual members? The following chapters 8 and 9 will discuss the development of free exercise doctrine generally, but primarily as it has affected individuals. Chapters 10 and 11 will consider how free exercise protection manifests itself when the asserted government burden falls on corporate religion: denominations, religious organizations, and houses of worship. As you will see, even though the notions of individual and corporate free exercise are interrelated, the Court has at times viewed the interests as distinct and taken different approaches to addressing the free exercise claims at stake.

## THE "BELIEF-ACTION" DICHOTOMY

The United States Supreme Court first interpreted the Free Exercise Clause in *Reynolds v. United States.*[4] *Reynolds* involved a challenge to anti-polygamy legislation passed by

Congress in 1862 in response to public outrage over the practice of polygamy conducted by the Church of Jesus Christ of Latter-day Saints, also known as the Mormon Church.

In order to appreciate the free exercise issue at stake in *Reynolds*, it is helpful to understand the theological basis for polygamy as practiced by the Mormon Church. Joseph Smith Jr. founded the Mormon Church in 1830 after having received a revelation from an angel named Moroni several years earlier. The Mormon Church, arising at a time of an explosion of new religious movements in America, taught the imminent second coming of Jesus Christ, which required its adherents to return to many of the early biblical practices. One such practice, derived from the Old Testament, was polygamy or plural marriages, as was practiced by several of the early biblical patriarchs. Mormon theology taught that polygamy was tied to "celestial marriage," the highest form of marriage which could endure after death and would affect the rewards one received in heaven. As one commentator has described the centrality of polygamy to early Mormon theology: "Perhaps the most radical doctrinal tenet of Mormonism is that mankind can achieve godhead and God himself was once mere mortal. The Prophet Joseph Smith explicitly taught that a man would progress through eternity in proportion to the magnitude of his posterity on earth and that polygamy as a central part of the pursuit of godhead. More wives ensured both increased progeny and greater future glory."[5]

Polygamy was never practiced by many Mormons,[6] but that it was taught and practiced by some highly visible church leaders elicited enormous public criticism. It was widely rumored that Joseph Smith had practiced polygamy as early as the 1830s and secretly taught the practice of plural marriage as a major doctrine of the church. Smith's successor, Brigham Young, beginning in 1852, openly taught polygamy as a theological tenet of the church and practiced it himself.

Most Americans believed polygamy was harmful to the idea of a monogamous family as a bulwark of a stable society; that it was immoral and indecent. Congress responded to this public outrage by passing the Morrill Act in 1862,[7] which made plural marriages illegal. Remember that until the implementation of the concept of incorporation in the 1940s, the religion clauses of the First Amendment did not apply to the states. But, at the time of *Reynolds*, Utah was a federal territory and thus subject to federal law. Consequently, because the case involved a federal law and was brought in federal court, the Free Exercise Clause applied.

The case arose when George Reynolds, secretary to Brigham Young, was prosecuted and convicted under the anti-polygamy statute. Reynolds invoked the Free Exercise Clause as his defense. He argued that because polygamy was a theological tenet of his church and because the free exercise principle protected the acting out of theological beliefs, he could not legitimately be convicted of plural marriage. That contention failed in a territorial court, so he asked the Supreme Court to render a judgment. It did, adversely to Reynolds. In the process, it articulated some general principles for interpreting the Free Exercise Clause.

---

## REYNOLDS v. UNITED STATES
98 U.S. 145 (1879)

▓ MR. CHIEF JUSTICE WAITE delivered the opinion of the court.

Upon this charge and refusal to charge the question is raised, whether religious belief can be accepted as a justification of an overt act made criminal by the law of the land. The inquiry is not as to the power of Congress to prescribe criminal laws for the Territories, but as to the guilt of one who knowingly violates a law which has been properly enacted, if he entertains a religious belief that the law is wrong.

Congress cannot pass a law for the government of the Territories which shall prohibit the free exercise of religion. The first amendment to the Constitution expressly forbids such legislation. Religious freedom is guaranteed everywhere throughout the United States, so far as congressional interference is concerned. The question to be determined is, whether the law now under consideration comes within this prohibition. . . .

Congress was deprived of all legislative power over mere opinion, but was left free to reach actions which were in violation of social duties or subversive of good order.

Polygamy has always been odious among the Northern and Western Nations of Europe and, until the establishment of the Mormon Church, was almost exclusively a feature of the life of Asiatic and African people. At common law, the second marriage was always void, and from the earliest history of England polygamy has been treated as an offence against society. . . .

In fact, according as monogamous or polygamous marriages are allowed, do we find the principles on which the government of the people, to a greater or lesser extent, rests. Professor Lieber says, polygamy leads to the patriarchal principle, and which, when applied to large communities, fetters the people in stationary despotism, while that principle cannot long exist in connection with monogamy.

In our opinion the statute immediately under consideration is within the legislative power of Congress. It is constitutional and valid as prescribing a rule of action for all those residing in the Territories, and in places over which the United States shall have exclusive control. This being so, the only question which remains is, whether those who make polygamy a part of their religion are excepted from the operation of the statute. . . . Laws are made for the government of actions, and while they cannot interfere with mere religious belief and opinions, they may with practices. Suppose one believed that human sacrifices were a necessary part of religious worship, would it be seriously contended that the civil government under which he lived could not interfere to prevent a sacrifice? . . .

So here, as a law of the organization of society under the exclusive dominion of the United States, it is provided that plural marriages shall not be allowed. Can a man excuse his practices to the contrary because of his religious belief? To permit this would be to make the professed doctrines of religious belief superior to the law of the land, and in effect to permit every citizen to become a law unto himself. Government could exist only in name under such circumstances.

---

*Reynolds* established the notion of a "belief/action dichotomy." Under the First Amendment, one can believe what one wants without government interference. But one cannot act on those beliefs if the government determines that such action is harmful or potentially harmful to individuals (including the actor), groups, or the community as a whole, the

Court said. In other words, the free exercise principle does not protect religiously motivated behavior that is contrary to the common good. It found polygamy had always been regarded as harmful to marriage. Also, the Court said that the mentality created by polygamous relationships was antithetical to the spirit of democracy at the heart of American government; it had strong negative political implications. Although the *Reynolds* Court did not go so far as to declare that the free exercise principle would never require an exemption for religiously motivated conduct, its dualistic approach in *Reynolds* made it easier for legislatures and public officials to regulate religious practice while giving lip-service to the First Amendment.

Polygamy endured judicial scrutiny again in *Davis v. Beason*.[8] Here the issue was not its practice, but its advocacy. The territory of Idaho passed a law requiring an oath to be able to vote. One was required to swear he was not a bigamist and that he belonged to no organization that believed in or advocated plural marriage. Davis, a nonpolygamist Mormon, took the oath. He was charged with swearing falsely, given that he belonged to an organization that advocated polygamy. The result of the case was consistent with *Reynolds*.

## DAVIS v. BEASON
133 U.S. 333 (1890)

MR. JUSTICE FIELD delivered the opinion of the court. . . .

Bigamy and polygamy are crimes by the laws of the civilized and Christian countries. They are crimes by the laws of the United States, and they are crimes by the laws of Idaho. They tend to destroy the purity of the marriage relation, to disturb the peace of families, to degrade woman and debase man. Few crimes are more pernicious to the best interests of society and receive more general or more deserved punishment. To extend exemption from punishment for such crimes would be to shock the moral judgment of the community. To call their advocacy a tenet of religion is to offend the common sense of mankind. . . . The term "religion" has reference to one's views of his relations to his Creator, and to the obligations they impose on reverence for his being and character, and of obedience to his will. It is often confounded with the *cultus* or form of worship of a particular sect, but is distinguishable from the latter. The first amendment to the constitution, in declaring that congress shall make no law respecting the establishment of religion or forbidding the free exercise thereof, was intended to allow every one under the jurisdiction of the United States to entertain such notions respecting his relations to his Maker and the duties they impose as may be approved by his judgment and conscience, and to exhibit his sentiments in such form of worship as he may think proper, not injurious to the equal rights of others, and to prohibit legislation for the support of any religious tenets, or the modes of worship of any sect. . .

It was never intended or supposed that the [First] Amendment could be invoked as a protection against legislation for the punishment of acts inimical to the peace, good order and morals of society. With man's relations to his Maker and the obligations he may think they impose, and the manner in which an expression shall be made by him of his belief on those subjects, no interference can be permitted, provided always the laws of society, designated

to secure its peace and prosperity, and the morals of its people, are not interfered with. However free the exercise of religion may be, it must be subordinate
to the criminal laws of the country, passed with reference to actions regarded
by general consent as properly the subjects of punitive legislation. . . . Probably
never before in the history of this country has it been seriously contended that
the whole punitive power of the government for acts, recognized by the general
consent of the Christian world in modern times as proper matters for prohibi-
tory legislation, must be suspended in order that the tenets of a religious sect
encouraging crime may be carried out without hindrance . . . .

   Crime is not the less odious because sanctioned by what any particular
sect may designate as religion.

---

## NOTES AND QUESTIONS

1. As in *Reynolds*, the "belief/action" distinction was utilized and government
   officials were given wide discretion to determine what kinds of religious behavior were contrary to the public good. But what was fatal to Davis' claim?
   Was it that his "advocacy" of the practice of polygamy was not a *religious*
   practice as defined by the Court? Did it lack aspects of religiosity, so as to
   render it nonreligious? In essence, was it Davis' crime that he merely swore
   falsely, conduct which on its own was not religious? Or was the Court speaking more generally about polygamy, that it lacked a theological quality?

2. Does the belief/action distinction apply as readily here as in *Reynolds*? Unlike
   Reynolds who *practiced* polygamy, was Davis prosecuted only for his *beliefs*?
   Should Davis have won? Or finally, is the holding in *Davis* that irrespective
   of the religious quality of particular conduct, certain acts contravene societal
   norms and will always lose in the balancing of interests? If so, does this mean
   that the freedom to engage in religious conduct extends no further than
   whatever the current political majority considers to be criminal or immoral?

3. The regulation of polygamy remains a controversial issue. Polygamy is still
   openly practiced by some Mormon Fundamentalists, and critics have charged
   that local officials often turn a blind eye to enforcement of anti-polygamy
   laws. Assume that a local sheriff charges a Mormon Fundamentalist with
   violating a state anti-polygamy statute and the defendant raises a free exercise
   defense to the charge. Also assume that polygamy is a central theological
   tenet and is practiced only by sincere believers. On what grounds should
   enforcement of the statute be upheld—that the practice is harmful to women
   and children, that it violates moral and cultural norms held by the majority,
   that the practice is not sufficiently religious, or that the defendant can still
   believe in the practice, but just not partake in it? Or should the Mormon
   Fundamentalist win?

---

*Postscript.* The political disenfranchisement and prosecution of Mormon polygamists and
their allies continued throughout the 1870s to 1890s. The theological practice of polygamy also brought about legal controversies over issues of divorce, inheritance, and property ownership. In the same year as *Davis*, the Supreme Court decided *Late Corporation*

*of the Church of Jesus Christ of Latter-day Saints v. Untied States*, 136 U.S. 1 (1890),
upholding the federal Edmunds-Tucker Act of 1887 which authorized the dissolution
of the church and confiscation of its property for its failure to abandon polygamy. The
Church attorneys, appreciating the likely hostile reaction to the Church's free exercise
claims, argued that the federal law interfered with its contractual rights to create a charitable corporation. The Court rejected the Church's argument, holding that Congress had
authority to revoke the charter. As a chief ground authorizing that Congressional revocation, the Court wrote that:

> the religious and charitable uses intended to be subserved and promoted are the in-
> culcation and spread of the doctrines and usages of the Mormon Church . . . one of
> the distinguishing features of which is the practice of polygamy—a crime against the
> law, and abhorrent to the sentiments and feelings of the civilized world. . . .The orga-
> nization of a community for the spread and practice of polygamy is, in a measure, a
> return to barbarism. It is contrary to the spirit of Christianity and of the civilization
> which Christianity has produced in the Western World. . . .
>
> One pretence for this obstinate course is, that their belief in the practice of po-
> lygamy, or in the right to indulge in it, is a religious belief, and therefore under the
> protection of the constitutional guaranty of religious freedom. This is altogether a
> sophistical plea. No doubt the Thugs of India imagined that their belief in the right
> of assassination was a religious belief; but their thinking so did not make it so. The
> practice of suttee by the Hindu widow may have sprung from a supposed religious
> conviction. The offering of human sacrifices by our own ancestors in Britain was no
> doubt sanctioned by an equally conscientious impulse. But no one, on that account,
> would hesitate to brand these practices, now, as crimes against society, and obnoxious
> to condemnation and punishment by civil authority.
>
> The state has a perfect right to prohibit polygamy, and all other open offenses
> against the enlightened sentiment of mankind, notwithstanding the pretense of reli-
> gious conviction by which they may be advocated and practiced. . . . 136 U.S., 49-50.

Following the *Davis* and *Late Corporation* decisions, and facing continuing pressure
from Congress for the Church to repudiate the practice of polygamy as a condition for
Utah statehood, Mormon President Wilford Woodruff issued a Manifesto on October
6, 1890, announcing that the LDS Church had officially abandoned the practice of polygamy. For more on this episode, see Edwin Brown Firmage and Richard Collin Mangrum, *Zion in the Courts: A Legal History of the Church of Jesus Christ of Latter-day Saints,
1830-1900* (Urbana: University of Illinois Press, 1988), and Sarah Barringer Gordon, *The
Mormon Question: Polygamy and Constitutional Conflict in Nineteenth Century America*,
(Chapel Hill: University of North Carolina Press, 2002).

### RELIGIOUS LIBERTY AS DUE PROCESS LIBERTY

Free exercise doctrine developed not solely in response to legal conflicts involving home-
grown religious movements like the Mormons. Challenges to World War I legislation that
reflected jingoism and anti-immigrant attitudes had a freedom-of-religion dimension, as
well. Although opposition to immigration had been prevalent in America since the mid-
nineteenth century, resistance to "aliens" intensified during and after the war. Many believed that extraordinary efforts should be exerted to assimilate immigrants into American
society. Various state legislatures passed laws to try to minimize cultural difference and
promote Americanization of immigrants. For example, in 1919 Nebraska passed a law

prohibiting the teaching of a modern foreign language in any school until the student had completed the eighth grade. Thus, linguistic differences between children would be eliminated because schools could not teach in a way that would perpetuate foreign language. But, the Supreme Court, in *Meyer v. Nebraska*[9] held such laws violated the Due Process Clause of the Fourteenth Amendment in that they denied teachers the liberty to make a living by teaching.

Oregon's legislature, in 1922, passed a more far-reaching law. It required all children, unless they had special educational needs, to attend public schools. Public schools were perceived as a great homogenizing influence in society. This law requiring public school attendance of all able-bodied and teachable children would mitigate the foreignness of immigrant children and make them as uniform as possible. The law was challenged by a private military academy and a school operated by the Society of the Sisters of the Holy Names of Jesus and Mary. They contended the law endangered their right to do business, indeed, their right to exist. The case was argued on Fourteenth Amendment grounds, that is, the law threatened to deprive the schools of their property without due process of law. The Court, citing the precedent of *Meyer*, agreed with the schools. In the process, it also addressed the rights of parents to direct the education of their children.

---

## PIERCE v. SOCIETY OF THE SISTERS OF THE HOLY NAMES OF JESUS AND MARY
### 268 U.S. 510 (1925)

MR. JUSTICE McREYNOLDS delivered the opinion of the court. . . .

No question is raised concerning the power of the state reasonably to regulate all schools, to inspect, supervise, and examine them, their teachers and pupils; to require that all children of proper age attend some school, that teachers shall be of good moral character and patriotic disposition, that certain studies plainly essential to good citizenship must be taught, and that nothing be taught which is manifestly inimical to the public welfare.

The inevitable practical result of enforcing the act under consideration would be destruction of appellees' primary schools, and perhaps all other private primary schools for normal children within the state of Oregon. . . .

Under the doctrine of *Meyer v. Nebraska* we think it entirely plain that the Act of 1922 unreasonably interferes with the liberty of parents and guardians to direct the upbringing and education of children under their control. . . . The fundamental theory of liberty upon which all governments in this Union repose excludes any general power of the state to standardize its children by forcing them to accept instruction from public teachers only. The child is not the mere creature of the state; those who nurture him and direct his destiny have the right, coupled with the high duty, to recognize and prepare him for additional obligations.

---

*Pierce*, while not a free exercise of religion case, contributed to the development of free exercise doctrine. It expressed, at least in *dicta*, that parents have the right to choose the form of the education of their children, based on the liberty provision contained in the Due Process Clause of the Fourteenth Amendment. This was an important legal development: while the Court initially spoke of "liberty" generically in a way that could encompass various interests, this milestone would lead the Court in the 1930s and 1940s to identify specific manifestations of liberty—speech and religion, among others—borrowed from the First Amendment. By first identifying due process liberty as a way of protecting religious interests, among others, the Court laid the groundwork for establishing a free-standing free exercise right. But *Pierce* was a cautious holding, with the Court taking only a baby step, albeit an important one. The holding also asserted that the state has the right to insist on curricular and safety standards of schools and on teacher competence. Most immediately, however, it held that private and religious schools had the right to exist. *Pierce* has frequently been called the "Magna Carta" of the parochial school movement.

In the following section, dealing with conscientious objectors, the courts also considered the litigants' religious claims as raising due process liberty claims.

## Conscientious Objector Cases

Beginning in 1929 the Court heard some cases on whether noncitizens applying for citizenship could be naturalized if they were conscientious objectors to war. The answer was "no." These were not free exercise cases, but rested on the interpretation of naturalization law. The Naturalization Act of 1906 specified: "He [the applicant] shall, before he is admitted to citizenship, declare on oath in open court . . . That he will support and defend the Constitution and laws of the United States against all enemies, foreign and domestic, and bear true faith and allegiance to the same. It shall be made to appear to the satisfaction of the court . . . that he . . . [is] attached to the principles of the Constitution of the United States, and well disposed to the good order and happiness of the same."[10] Naturalization officials believed anyone not willing to promise to bear arms in defense of the country was not "well disposed" to the Constitution and should not become a citizen. The Supreme Court agreed. In *United States v. Schwimmer*[11] it denied citizenship to Rosika Schwimmer, a well-known feminist, suffragette, and pacifist, although Justice Oliver Wendell Holmes wrote a strong dissent.

---

### UNITED STATES v. SCHWIMMER
### 279 U.S. 644 (1929)

■ MR. JUSTICE BUTLER delivered the opinion of the court. . . .

That it is the duty of citizens by force of arms to defend our government against all enemies whenever necessity arises is a fundamental principle of the Constitution. . . .

The influence of conscientious objectors against the use of military force in defense of the principles of our government is apt to be more detrimental than their mere refusal to bear arms. The fact that, by reason of sex, age or other cause, they may be unfit to serve, does not lessen their purpose or power to influence others. . . .

The fact that she is an uncompromising pacifist with no sense of national-ism but only a cosmic sense of belonging to the human family justifies belief that she may be opposed to the use of military force as contemplated by our Constitution and laws. And her testimony clearly suggests that she is disposed to exert her power to influence others to such opposition. . . .

▓ MR. JUSTICE HOLMES, dissenting. . . .

So far as the adequacy of her oath is concerned, I hardly can see how that is affected by the statement [of facts], inasmuch as she is a woman over fifty years of age, and would not be allowed to bear arms if she wanted to. . . .

Some of her answers might excite popular prejudice, but if there is any principle of the Constitution that more imperatively calls for attachment than any other it is the principle of free thought—not free thought for those who agree with us but freedom for the thought we hate. . . .

Rosika Schwimmer was a philosophical conscientious objector; her beliefs were not based on religion. Two subsequent cases derived from religious objection to war. Marie Averil Bland, an Episcopalian war nurse, and Douglas Clyde Macintosh, an American Baptist and professor of theology at Yale Divinity School, had religious objections to bearing arms. But, on the precedent of *Schwimmer*, the Supreme Court denied both of them citizenship, *United States v. Bland*[12] and *United States v. Macintosh*.[13] To the extent that these cases had free exercise of religion dimensions, it was clear that the Court was not willing to extend that freedom over the obvious public welfare need for national defense. It should be noted, however, that in 1946 the Court closed out this line of cases about conscientious objections to bearing arms by noncitizens by reversing itself in *Girouard v. United States*.[14] James Louis Girouard, a Seventh-day Adventist, was willing to serve in the military, but only as a noncombatant. The Court ruled that the oath of naturalization was not significantly different from the oath required of all government office holders, yet the latter oath did not bar conscientious objectors. Given that circumstance, alien conscientious objectors should not be prohibited from taking the oath, either. There are many ways to defend the country other than actual bearing of arms.

## GIROUARD v. UNITED STATES
### 328 U.S. 61 (1946)

▓ MR. JUSTICE DOUGLAS delivered the opinion of the Court. . . .

The bearing of arms, as important as it is, is not the only way in which our institutions may be supported and defended, even in times of great peril. Total war in its modern form dramatizes as never before the great cooperative effort necessary for victory. The nuclear physicists who developed the atomic bomb, the worker at his lathe, the seaman on cargo vessels, construction bat-talions, nurses, engineers, litter bearers, doctors, chaplains—these, too, made

essential contributions. . . . Refusal to bear arms is not necessarily a sign of dis-
loyalty or a lack of attachment to our institutions. One may serve his country
faithfully and devotedly, though his religious scruples make it impossible for
him to shoulder a rifle. Devotion to one's country can be as real and as enduring among non-combatants as among combatants. One may adhere to what he
deems to be his obligations to God and yet assume all military risks to secure
victory. The effort of war is indivisible; and those whose religious scruples
prevent them from killing are no less patriots than those whose special traits
or handicaps result in their assignment to duties far behind the fighting front.
. . .

Petitioner's religious scruples would not disqualify him from becoming a
member of Congress or holding other public offices. While Article 6, Clause
3 of the Constitution provides that such officials, both of the United States
and the several States, "shall be bound by Oath or Affirmation, to support this
Constitution," it significantly adds that "no religious Test shall ever be required
as a Qualification to any Office or public Trust under the United States." The
oath required is in no material respect different from that prescribed for aliens
under the Nationality Act. . . .

There is not the slightest suggestion that Congress set a stricter standard
for aliens seeking admission to citizenship than it did for officials who make
and enforce the laws of the nation and administer its affairs. It is hard to believe that one need forsake his religious scruples to become a citizen but not
to sit in the high councils of state. . . .

The struggle for religious liberty has through the centuries been an effort
to accommodate the demands of the State to the conscience of the individual.
The victory of freedom of thought recorded in our Bill of Rights recognizes
that in the domain of conscience there is a moral power higher than the State.
. . . The test oath is abhorrent to our tradition. . . .

We conclude that the *Schwimmer*, *Macintosh*, and *Bland* cases do not state
the correct rule of law.

A conscientious objector case of a different sort came before the Court in 1934, *Hamilton
v. Regents of the University of California*.[15] Several students, members of the Methodist church, wanted to attend the university without participating in the Reserve Officer
Training Corps, as required by university regulation. The students were convinced that
training for participation in war was contrary to the teaching of Jesus Christ. They were
supported in this by their church. In 1931, the Southern California Conference of the
Methodist Episcopal Church asked the General Conference of the church to petition the
United States to exempt from military service all members of the Methodist Episcopal
Church who had conscientious objections to war. The General Conference did this in
1932. However, it also petitioned the government to exempt Methodist conscientious
objectors from military training in all educational institutions that required such training.
The Southern California Conference, in its 1933 convention, specifically petitioned California state universities to exempt Methodist conscientious objectors from ROTC training. The students at bar, when they enrolled in the University of California, requested
to be exempt from ROTC. Their petition was denied. They then proceeded to attend all
their other classes except the military classes. At that point they were suspended from the

university, with the welcome to apply again when they had changed their minds about military service.

The students based their litigation on the privileges and immunities and due process clauses of the Fourteenth Amendment. They claimed that not being exempted from military training abridged their privileges and immunities as citizens and deprived them of their liberty interests. They also asserted that they could not afford to go to schools other than state-supported ones. The Court rejected those arguments, holding that States could formulate plans to instruct men in military service and that ROTC programs at state universities were a reasonable way to do that. Students were not required to go to state schools. If they chose to go to those schools, they were not entitled to exemptions to military training. The requirement violated no constitutional rights.

The case was decided on Fourteenth Amendment grounds, but it had free exercise implications. The students were free to believe what they would, but given the reasonable nature of the programs and the voluntary nature of university attendance, they were not free not to participate in military training, the Court said. The nation obviously had the responsibility to defend itself and to devise ways of training people to do that. That overrode the implicit free exercise petition of the students, according to the Court. Interestingly, in a concurring opinion, Justice Benjamin Cardozo explicitly raised the free exercise of religion issue. In the process, he also mentioned what the Court had not yet done, incorporate the Free Exercise Clause into the Due Process Clause of the Fourteenth Amendment and apply it to state law.

---

## HAMILTON v. REGENTS OF THE UNIVERSITY OF CALIFORNIA
## 293 U.S 245 (1934)

MR. JUSTICE BUTLER delivered the opinion of the court. . . .

Appellants assert—unquestionably in good faith—that all war, preparation for war and the training required by the university are repugnant to the tenets and discipline of their church, to their religion and to their consciences. The "privilege" of attending the university as a student comes not from federal sources but is given by the State. It is not within the asserted protection. The only "immunity" claimed by these students is freedom from obligation to comply with the rule prescribing military training. But that "immunity" cannot be regarded as not within, or as distinguishable from, the "liberty" of which they claim to have been deprived by the enforcement of the regents' order. If the regents' order is not repugnant to the due process clause, then it does not violate the privileges and immunities clause. Therefore we need only decide whether by state action the "liberty" of these students has been infringed. . . .

The fact that they are able to pay their way in this university but not in any other institution in California is without significance upon any constitutional or other question here involved. California has not drafted or called them to attend the university. They are seeking education offered by the State and at the same time insisting that they be excluded from the prescribed course solely upon grounds of their religious beliefs and conscientious objection to war, preparation for war and military education. . . . [A]ppellants' contentions amount to no more than an assertion that the due process clause of the Fourteenth Amendment as a safeguard of "liberty" confers the right to be students in the state university free from obligation to take military training as one of the conditions of attendance.

Viewed in the light of our decisions [*United States v. Schwimmer* and *United States v. Macintosh*] that proposition must at once be put aside as untenable.

Government, federal and state, each in its own sphere owes a duty to the people within its jurisdiction to preserve itself in adequate strength to maintain peace and order and to assure the just enforcement of law. And every citizen owes the reciprocal duty, according to his capacity, to support and defend government against all enemies. . . .

### ▨ MR. JUSTICE CARDOZO:

Concurring in the opinion I wish to say an extra word.

I assume for present purposes that the religious liberty protected by the First Amendment against invasion by the nation is protected by the Fourteenth Amendment against invasion by the states.

Accepting that premise, I cannot find in the respondents' ordinance an obstruction by the state to "the free exercise" of religion as the phrase was understood by the founders of the nation, and by the generations that have followed. . . .

Instruction in military science is not instruction in the practice or tenets of a religion. Neither directly nor indirectly is government establishing a state religion when it insists upon such training. Instruction in military science, unaccompanied here by any pledge of military service, is not an interference by the state with the free exercise of religion when the liberties of the Constitution are read in the light of a century and a half of history during days of peace and war.

———————————— ·•·•·•· ————————————

## Embracing Free Exercise as a Right

Following the cases referenced above, which were decided on Fourteenth Amendment due process liberty grounds but had free exercise implications, came a group of cases that were decided by interpretation of the Free Exercise Clause itself. Many of these cases were brought by the Jehovah's Witnesses. Historians of church-state relations readily acknowledge that the Jehovah's Witness made an enormously positive contribution to religious liberty in the United States through the litigation they initiated in the 1930s and 1940s.

Seldom, if ever, in the past, has one individual group been able to shape the course, over a period of time, of any phase of our vast body of constitutional law. But it *can* happen, and it *has* happened, here. The group is Jehovah's Witnesses. Through almost constant litigation this organization has made possible an ever-increasing list of precedents concerning the application of the Fourteenth Amendment to freedom of speech and religion.[16]

The Jehovah's Witnesses believe we are living in the last days of human existence, that God will soon bring the end of time as we know it. When the end comes, only those who are among God's true believers will be saved. The rest will suffer eternal damnation. Consequently, Witnesses believe they have a divine commission to take the message of salvation to all they can. Evangelism is the top priority for all members of God's people. Consequently, because every baptized Witness is considered a minister, Witnesses historically have aggressively taken their message to the unsaved. Many of the cases they took to the Supreme Court were about their proselytizing on streets and in neighborhoods where city ordinances prohibited such activity, under the guise of wanting to preserve public peace and tranquility.

That was the situation in the landmark case *Cantwell v. Connecticut*.[17] Newton Cantwell and his two sons, Jesse and Russell, were preaching on the streets of New Haven, Connecticut. State law required them to apply to a government official for a permit to distribute their materials or proclaim their message on the street. The official was to determine if the applicant's cause was a bona fide religion or charitable cause. If so, the permit would be issued; if not, it would not be issued. The Cantwells did not seek the permit because they were only talking with persons and distributing books and pamphlets, not trying to make a profit. Furthermore, they believed because they were doing the work of God, they did not need to get the government's permission to do it.

A second dimension of the case emerged from the Cantwells' proselytizing activity. In the 1930s the Jehovah's Witnesses vigorously opposed Catholicism. Although they believed that all religions other than their own, were "a snare and a racket" (one of their favorite slogans), they were particularly ill-disposed toward the Catholic Church. Indeed, the leader of the Jehovah's Witnesses, Joseph Franklin "Judge" Rutherford, wrote a book about religion, entitled *Enemies*, in which the Catholics received the bulk of his disdain.

In their proselytizing work, Witnesses carried spring-driven phonographs and short records containing their messages. When the Cantwells went to New Haven, Connecticut to proclaim God's message as the Witnesses understood it, they carried the record "Enemies," a condensation of Rutherford's anti-Catholic book. New Haven was predominantly Catholic, so it was hardly surprising when Jesse Cantwell approached two men to deliver his message, they were Catholic. Cantwell asked if he could play a record for the men. They agreed. But when the message attacked their religion, they became outraged and demanded that Cantwell pack up his records and pamphlets and leave. He did; he went down the street without any rejoinders or smart-aleck words to the men. In spite of Cantwell's peaceful demeanor, the men summoned the police and had him arrested. He was charged with "disturbing the peace" and "incitement to riot." Obviously, when their case went to trial for not obtaining the permit and unlawful behavior on the street, the Cantwells defended themselves on the basis of the constitutional guarantee of freedom of religion.

When the Supreme Court decided this case, it was extremely important not only to the Jehovah's Witnesses, who won, but to the development of Free Exercise Clause jurisprudence. This was the first case in which the clause was applied to the states through the Due Process Clause of the Fourteenth Amendment (in other words, the Court held that the Free Exercise Clause now placed limitations on actions of state and local officials through the "liberty" provision of the Due Process Clause). Another significant aspect of the case is that the Court held that the law requiring permission of a government official before religious people could proclaim their message on the streets and sidewalks of a city was a "prior restraint" on speech protected by the First Amendment. (Historically, prior restraints had been considered particularly onerous because they allowed public officials to censor speech before it occurred, regardless of whether the resulting speech would have been protected or not). Justice Owen Roberts, for a unanimous Court, noted that no one could commit fraud against the public in the name of religion. But the free exercise principle would not permit government, in the attempt to prevent fraud, to determine what was a valid religion and then condition the right to publicly proclaim the religion on the decision. Third, the Court used a new standard for interpreting the Free Exercise Clause, the "clear and present danger" test. This test, first articulated in a free speech case, *Schenck v. United States*,[18] was now applied to freedom of religion. Before *Cantwell*, the test was the "belief/action" distinction of *Reynolds v. United States*, under which government officials had wide discretion to interfere with religious behavior. Now government had to demonstrate that religious action presented a clear and present danger (the Court also used the phrase "immediate threat") to individuals or society before it could curtail or prevent religious activity. The Court found in favor of the Cantwells and against Connecticut. Because Jesse Cantwell asked permission to play his records and because he withdrew peacefully when his departure was demanded, it was obvious that his behavior posed no clear and present danger to his auditors or to the community.

## CANTWELL v. STATE OF CONNECTICUT
## 310 U.S. 296 (1940)

MR. JUSTICE ROBERTS, delivered the opinion of the Court.

Newton Cantwell and his two sons, Jesse and Russell, members of a group known as Jehovah's Witnesses, and claiming to be ordained ministers, were arrested in New Haven, Connecticut, and each was charged by information in five counts, with statutory and common law offenses. After trial in the Court of Common Pleas of New Haven County each of them was convicted on the third count, which charged a violation of § 6294 of the General Statutes of Connecticut, and on the fifth count, which charged commission of the common law offense of inciting a breach of the peace. . . .

The facts adduced to sustain the convictions on the third count follow. On the day of their arrest the appellants were engaged in going singly from house to house on Cassius Street in New Haven. They were individually equipped with a bag containing books and pamphlets on religious subjects, a portable phonograph and a set of records, each of which, when played, introduced, and was a description of, one of the books. Each appellant asked the person who responded to his call for permission to play one of the records. If permission was granted he asked the person to buy the book described and, upon refusal, he solicited such contribution towards the publication of the pamphlets as the listener was willing to make. If a contribution was received a pamphlet was delivered upon condition that it would be read.

Cassius Street is in a thickly populated neighborhood, where about ninety per cent of the residents are Roman Catholics. A phonograph record, describing a book entitled "Enemies," included an attack on the Catholic religion. None of the persons interviewed were members of Jehovah's Witnesses.

The statute under which the appellants were charged provides:

No person shall solicit money, services, subscriptions or any valuable thing for any alleged religious, charitable or philanthropic cause, from other than a member of the organization for whose benefit such person is soliciting or within the county in which such person or organization is located unless such cause shall have been approved by the secretary of the public welfare council. Upon application of any person in behalf of such cause, the secretary shall determine whether such cause is a religious one or is a bona fide object of charity or philanthropy and conforms to reasonable standards of efficiency and integrity, and, if he shall so find, shall approve the same and issue to the authority in charge a certificate to that effect. Such certificate may be revoked at any time. Any person violating any provision of this section shall be fined not more than one hundred dollars or imprisoned not more than thirty days or both. . . .

The facts which were held to support the conviction of Jesse Cantwell on the fifth count were that he stopped two men in the street, asked, and received, permission to play a phonograph record, and played the record "Enemies," which attacked the religion and church of the two men, who were Catholics. Both were incensed by the contents of the record and were tempted to strike Cantwell unless he went away. On being told to be on his way he left their presence. There was no evidence that he was personally offensive or entered into any argument with those he interviewed. . . .

*First.* We hold that the statute, as construed and applied to the appellants, deprives them of their liberty without due process of law in contravention of the Fourteenth Amendment. The fundamental concept of liberty embodied in that Amendment embraces the liberties guaranteed by the First Amendment. The First Amendment declares that Congress shall make no law respecting an establishment of religion or prohibiting the free exercise thereof. The Fourteenth Amendment has rendered the legislatures of the states as incompetent as Congress to enact such laws. The constitutional inhibition of legislation on the subject of religion has a double aspect. On the one hand, it forestalls compulsion by law of the acceptance of any creed or the practice of any form of worship. Freedom of conscience and freedom to adhere to such religious organization or form of worship as the individual may choose cannot be restricted by law. On the other hand, it safeguards the free exercise of the chosen form of religion. Thus the Amendment embraces two concepts—freedom to believe and freedom to act. The first is absolute but, in the nature of things, the second cannot be. Conduct remains subject to regulation for the protection of society. The freedom to act must have appropriate definition to preserve the enforcement of that protection. In every case the power to regulate must be so exercised as not, in attaining a permissible end, unduly to infringe the protected freedom. No one would contest the proposition that a state may not, by statute, wholly deny the right to preach or to disseminate religious views. Plainly such a previous and absolute restraint would violate the terms of the guarantee. It is equally clear that a state may by general and non-discriminatory legislation regulate the times, the places, and the manner of soliciting upon its streets, and of holding meetings thereon; and may in other respects safeguard the peace, good order and comfort of the community, without unconstitutionally invading the liberties protected by the Fourteenth Amendment. The appellants are right in their insistence that the Act in question is not such a regulation. If a certificate is procured, solicitation is permitted without restraint but, in the absence of a certificate, solicitation is altogether prohibited.

The appellants urge that to require them to obtain a certificate as a condition of soliciting support for their views amounts to a prior restraint on the exercise of their religion within the meaning of the Constitution. The State insists that the Act, as construed by the Supreme Court of Connecticut, imposes no previous restraint upon the dissemination of religious views or teaching but merely safeguards against the perpetration of frauds under the cloak of religion. Conceding that this is so, the question remains whether the method adopted by Connecticut to that end transgresses the liberty safeguarded by the Constitution.

The general regulation, in the public interest, of solicitation, which does not involve any religious test and does not unreasonably obstruct or delay the collection of funds, is not open to any constitutional objection, even though the collection be for a religious purpose. Such regulation would not constitute a prohibited previous restraint on the free exercise of religion or interpose an inadmissible obstacle to its exercise.

It will be noted, however, that the Act requires an application to the secretary of the public welfare council of the State; that he is empowered to determine whether the cause is a religious one, and that the issue of a certificate depends upon his affirmative action. If he finds that the cause is not that of religion, to solicit for it becomes a crime. He is not to issue a certificate as a matter of course. His decision to issue or refuse it involves appraisal of facts, the exercise of judgment, and the formation of an opinion. He is authorized to withhold his approval if he determines that the cause is not a religious one. Such a censorship of religion as the means of determining its right to survive is a denial of liberty protected by the First Amendment and included in the liberty which is within the protection of the Fourteenth. . . .

Nothing we have said is intended even remotely to imply that, under the cloak of religion, persons may, with impunity, commit frauds upon the public. Certainly penal laws are available to punish such conduct. Even the exercise of religion may be at some slight inconvenience in order that the state may protect its citizens from injury. Without doubt a state may protect its citizens from fraudulent solicitation by requiring a stranger in the community, before permitting him publicly to solicit funds for any purpose, to establish his identity and his authority to act for the cause which he purports to represent. The state is likewise free to regulate the time and manner of solicitation generally, in the interest of public safety, peace, comfort or convenience. But to condition the solicitation of aid for the perpetuation of religious views or systems upon a license, the grant of which rests in the exercise of a determination by state authority as to what is a religious cause, is to lay a forbidden burden upon the exercise of liberty protected by the Constitution.

*Second.* We hold that, in the circumstances disclosed, the conviction of Jesse Cantwell on the fifth count must be set aside. Decision as to the lawfulness of the conviction demands the weighing of two conflicting interests. The fundamental law declares the interest of the United States that the free exercise of religion be not prohibited and that freedom to communicate information and opinion be not abridged. The state of Connecticut has an obvious interest in the preservation and protection of peace and good order within her borders. We must determine whether the alleged protection of the State's interest, means to which end would, in the absence of limitation by the federal Constitution, lie wholly within the State's discretion, has been pressed, in this instance, to a point where it has come into fatal collision with the overriding interest protected by the federal compact. . . .

The offense known as breach of the peace embraces a great variety of conduct destroying or menacing public order and tranquility. It includes not only violent acts but acts and words likely to produce violence in others. No one would have the hardihood to suggest that the principle of freedom of speech sanctions incitement to riot or that religious liberty connotes the privilege to exhort others to physical attack upon those belonging to another sect. When clear and present danger of riot, disorder, interference with traffic upon the public streets, or other immediate threat to public safety, peace, or order, appears, the power of the state to prevent or punish is obvious. Equally obvious is it that a state may not unduly suppress free communication of views, religious or other, under the guise of conserving desirable conditions. Here we have a situation analogous to a conviction under a statute sweeping in a great variety of conduct under a general and indefinite characterization, and leaving to the executive and judicial branches too wide a discretion in its application.

Having these considerations in mind, we note that Jesse Cantwell, on April 26, 1938, was upon a public street, where he had a right to be, and where he had a right peacefully to impart his views to others. There is no showing that his deportment was noisy, truculent, overbearing or offensive. He requested of two pedestrians permission to play to them a phonograph record. The permission was granted. It is not claimed that he intended to insult or affront the hearers by playing the record. It is plain that he wished only to interest them in his propaganda. The sound of the phonograph is not shown to have disturbed residents of the street, to have drawn a crowd, or to have impeded traffic. Thus far he had invaded no right or interest of the public or of the men accosted.

The record played by Cantwell embodies a general attack on all organized religious systems as instruments of Satan and injurious to man; it then singles out the Roman Catholic Church for strictures couched in terms which naturally would offend not only persons of that persuasion, but all others who respect the honestly held religious faith of their fellows. The hearers were in fact highly offended. One of them said he felt like hitting Cantwell and the other that he was tempted to throw Cantwell off the street. The one who testified he felt like hitting Cantwell said, in answer to the question "Did you do anything else or have any other reaction?" "No, sir, because he said he would take the victrola and he went." The other witness testified that he told Cantwell he had better get off the street before something happened to him and that was the end of the matter as Cantwell picked up his books and walked up the street.

Cantwell's conduct, in the view of the court below, considered apart from the effect of his communication upon his hearers, did not amount to a breach of the peace. One may, however, be guilty of the offense if he commit acts or make statements likely to provoke violence and disturbance of good order, even though no such eventuality be intended. Decisions to this effect are many, but examination discloses that, in practically all, the provocative language which was held to amount to a breach of the peace consisted of profane, indecent, or abusive remarks directed to the person of the hearer. Resort to epithets or personal abuse is not in any proper sense communication of information or opinion safeguarded by the Constitution, and its punishment as a criminal act would raise no question under that instrument.

We find in the instant case no assault or threatening of bodily harm, no truculent bearing, no intentional discourtesy, no personal abuse. On the contrary, we find only an effort to persuade a willing listener to buy a book or to contribute money in the interest of what Cantwell, however misguided others may think him, conceived to be true religion.

In the realm of religious faith, and in that of political belief, sharp differences arise. In both fields the tenets of one man may seem the rankest error to his neighbor. To persuade others to his own point of view, the pleader, as we know, at times, resorts to exaggeration, to vilification of men who have been, or are, prominent in church or state, and even to false statement. But the people of this nation have ordained in the light of history, that, in spite of the probability of excesses and abuses, these liberties are, in the long view, essential to enlightened opinion and right conduct on the part of the citizens of a democracy.

The essential characteristic of these liberties is, that under their shield many types of life, character, opinion and belief can develop unmolested and unobstructed. Nowhere is this shield more necessary than in our own country for a people composed of many races and of many creeds. There are limits to the exercise of these liberties. The danger in these times from the coercive activities of those who in the delusion of racial or religious conceit would incite violence and breaches of the peace in order to deprive others of their equal right to the exercise of their liberties, is emphasized by events familiar to all. These and other transgressions of those limits the states appropriately may punish. Although the contents of the record not unnaturally aroused animosity, we think that, in the absence of a statute narrowly drawn to define and punish specific conduct as constituting a clear and present danger to a substantial interest of the State, the petitioner's communication, considered in the light of the constitutional guarantees, raised no such clear and present menace to public peace and order as to render him liable to conviction of the common law offense in question.

The judgment affirming the convictions on the third and fifth counts is reversed and the cause is remanded for further proceedings not inconsistent with this opinion. So ordered.

*Reversed and remanded.*

Hard on the heels of *Cantwell*, the Court decided *Minersville School District v. Gobitis*,[19] another Jehovah's Witness case. The Witnesses object to saluting or pledging allegiance to the flag of any country. It is not that they are not patriotic, but they believe that God is the only sovereign worthy of the allegiance of humans. To salute a flag is to recognize the sovereignty of a state rather than of God. Jehovah's Witnesses also believe that saluting or pledging allegiance to a country's flag violates the First and Second Commandments, which say "You shall have no other gods before me" and "You shall not make yourself a graven image, or any likeness of anything that is in heaven above, or that is in the earth beneath, or that is in the water under the earth; you shall not bow down to them or serve them; . . ."[20] Some Christians interpret these verses to prohibit them from saluting a national flag.

When the public schools in Minersville, Pennsylvania required teachers and students to recite the flag salute, the children of a Jehovah's Witness family named Gobitis refused. They were expelled from school. They sued to be reinstated, claiming that the salute requirement denied them their free exercise of religion. The Court ruled against the Witnesses, saying that the state-imposed flag salute was a legitimate effort by the state to promote patriotism and national unity.

[I]n safeguarding conscience we are dealing with interests so subtle and dear, every possible leeway should be given to the claims of religious faith. . . . The mere possession of religious convictions which contradict the relevant concerns of a political society does not relieve the citizen from the discharge of political responsibilities. . . .

We are dealing with an interest inferior to none in the hierarchy of legal values. National unity is the basis of national security. *Minersville School District v. Gobitis* 310 U.S. 586, 594, 595.

*Gobitis* was followed by an outbreak of persecution of Jehovah's Witnesses across the country. Many lost their homes, their jobs, their physical safety (some were castrated), and a few lost their lives. More school districts passed laws requiring all students to say the pledge. All this was a manifestation of dislike of the Witnesses and the rise of patriotism because of the beginning of World War II. More cases challenging the requirements were initiated. In 1943 the Supreme Court decided one of those, *West Virginia Board of Education v. Barnette*.[21] Why did the justices take up another flag salute case so soon after it had rendered a decision on the issue? They could not help but be aware of the raging persecution of the Witnesses after *Gobitis*. A year earlier, three justices in the majority in *Gobitis* took the unusual step of publicly announcing that they had come to believe it was wrongly decided.[22] Finally, two *Gobitis* justices, Harlan F. Stone and James C. McReynolds, had been replaced by Robert H. Jackson and Wiley B. Rutledge.

West Virginia passed a law patterned on *Gobitis*, requiring students and teachers to salute the American flag, with the proviso "that refusal to salute the Flag be regarded as an Act of insubordination, and shall be dealt with accordingly." Refusal was "dealt with" by expelling the students and prosecuting their parents because children were delinquent. Children could not be readmitted until they promised to salute. Parents were subject to a monetary fine and jail time.

*Barnette* is remarkable because it was decided while World War II was raging and patriotism was at a fever pitch.[23] It should be noted also that the dissenting opinion of Justice Felix Frankfurter contains most of the themes of the majority opinion in *Gobitis*, of which he was the author. Its motif, that a law of general applicability, so long as it does not target religious behavior, will prevail over the free exercise of religion foreshadows the principal argument of an extremely important Free Exercise Clause case 47 years later, *Employment Division of Oregon v. Smith*,[24] described in chapter 9.

## WEST VIRGINIA STATE BOARD OF EDUCATION v. BARNETTE
### 319 U.S. 624 (1943)

MR. JUSTICE JACKSON delivered the opinion of the court.

Following the decision by this Court on June 3, 1940, in *Minersville School District v. Gobitis*, the West Virginia legislature amended its statutes to require all schools therein to conduct courses of instruction in history, civics, and in the Constitutions of the United States and of the State "for the purpose of teaching, fostering and perpetuating the ideals, principles and spirit of Americanism, and increasing the knowledge of the organization and machinery of the government." Appellant Board of Education was directed, with advice of the State Superintendent of Schools, to "prescribe the courses of study covering these subjects" for public schools. The Act made it the duty of private, parochial and denominational schools to prescribe courses of study "similar to those required for the public schools."

The Board of Education on January 9, 1942, adopted a resolution containing recitals taken largely from the Court's *Gobitis* opinion and ordering that the salute to the flag become "a regular part of the program of activities in the public schools," that all teachers and pupils "shall be required to participate in the salute honoring the Nation represented by the Flag; provided, however, that refusal to salute the Flag be regarded as an Act of insubordination, and shall be dealt with accordingly."[2] The resolution originally required the "commonly accepted salute to the Flag" which it defined. Objections to the salute as "being too much like Hitler's" were raised by the Parent and Teachers Association, the Boy and Girl Scouts, the Red Cross, and the Federation of Women's Clubs. Some modification appears to have been made in deference to these objections, but no concession was made to Jehovah's Witnesses. What is now

---

[2] The text is as follows:

"WHEREAS, The West Virginia State Board of Education holds in highest regard those rights and privileges guaranteed by the Bill of Rights in the Constitution of the United States of America and in the Constitution of West Virginia, specifically, the first amendment to the Constitution of the United States as restated in the fourteenth amendment to the same document and in the guarantee of religious freedom in Article III of the Constitution of this State, and

"WHEREAS, The West Virginia State Board of Education honors the broad principle that one's convictions about the ultimate mystery of the universe and man's relation to it is placed beyond the reach of law; that the propagation of belief is protected whether in church or chapel, mosque or synagogue, tabernacle or meeting house; that the Constitutions of the United States and of the State of West Virginia assure generous immunity to the individual from imposition of penalty for offending, in the course of his own religious activities, the religious views of others, be they a minority or those who are dominant in the government, but

"WHEREAS, The West Virginia State Board of Education recognizes that the manifold character of man's relations may bring his conception of religious duty into conflict with the secular interests of his fellowman; that conscientious scruples have not in the course of the long struggle for religious toleration relieved the individual from obedience to the general law not aimed at the promotion or restriction of the religious beliefs; that the mere possession of convictions which contradict the relevant concerns of political society does not relieve the citizen from the discharge of political responsibility, and

"WHEREAS, The West Virginia State Board of Education holds that national unity is the basis of national security; that the flag of our Nation is the symbol of our National Unity transcending all internal differences, however large within the framework of the Constitution; that the Flag is the symbol of the Nation's power; that emblem of freedom in its truest, best sense; that it signifies government resting on the consent of the governed, liberty regulated by law, protection of the weak against the strong, security against the exercise of arbitrary power, and absolute safety for free institutions against foreign aggression, and

"WHEREAS, The West Virginia State Board of Education maintains that the public schools, established by the legislature of the State of West Virginia under the authority of the Constitution of the State of West Virginia and supported by taxes imposed by legally constituted measures, are dealing with the formative period in the development in citizenship that the Flag is an allowable portion of the program of schools thus publicly supported.

"Therefore, be it RESOLVED, That the West Virginia Board of Education does hereby recognize and order that the commonly accepted salute to the Flag of the United States—the right hand is placed upon the breast and the following pledge repeated in unison: 'I pledge allegiance to the Flag of the United States of America and to the Republic for which it stands; one Nation, indivisible, with liberty and justice for all'—now becomes a regular part of the program of activities in the public schools, supported in whole or in part by public funds, and that all teachers as defined by law in West Virginia and pupils in such schools shall be required to participate in the salute honoring the Nation represented by the Flag; provided, however, that refusal to salute the Flag be regarded as an act of insubordination, and shall be dealt with accordingly.

required is the "stiff-arm" salute, the saluter to keep the right hand raised with palm turned up while the following is repeated: "I pledge allegiance to the Flag of the United States of America and to the Republic for which it stands; one Nation, indivisible, with liberty and justice for all."

Failure to conform is "insubordination" dealt with by expulsion. Readmission is denied by statute until compliance. Meanwhile the expelled child is "unlawfully absent" and may be proceeded against as a delinquent. His parents or guardians are liable to prosecution, and if convicted are subject to fine not exceeding $50 and jail term not exceeding thirty days.

Appellees, citizens of the United States and of West Virginia, brought suit in the United States District Court for themselves and others similarly situated asking its injunction to restrain enforcement of these laws and regulations against Jehovah's Witnesses. The Witnesses are an unincorporated body teaching that the obligation imposed by law of God is superior to that of laws enacted by temporal government. Their religious beliefs include a literal version of Exodus, hapter 20, verses 4 and 5, which says: "Thou shalt not make unto thee any graven image, or any likeness of anything that is in heaven above, or that is in the earth beneath, or that is in the water under the earth; thou shalt not bow down thyself to them nor serve them." They consider that the flag is an "image" within this command. For this reason they refuse to salute it. Children of this faith have been expelled from school and are threatened with exclusion for no other cause. Officials threaten to send them to reformatories maintained for criminally inclined juveniles. Parents of such children have been prosecuted and are threatened with prosecutions for causing delinquency. . . .

This case calls upon us to reconsider a precedent decision, as the Court throughout its history often has been required to do. Before turning to the *Gobitis* case, however, it is desirable to notice certain characteristics by which this controversy is distinguished.

The freedom asserted by these appellees does not bring them into collision with rights asserted by any other individual. It is such conflicts which most frequently require intervention of the State to determine where the rights of one end and those of another begin. But the refusal of these persons to participate in the ceremony does not interfere with or deny rights of others to do so. Nor is there any question in this case that their behavior is peaceable and orderly. The sole conflict is between authority and rights of the individual. The State asserts power to condition access to public education on making a prescribed sign and profession and at the same time to coerce attendance by punishing both parent and child. The latter stand on a right of self-determination in matters that touch individual opinion and personal attitude.

As the present Chief Justice said in dissent in the *Gobitis* case, the State may "require teaching by instruction and study of all in our history and in the structure and organization of our government, including the guaranties of civil liberty which tend to inspire patriotism and love of country." 310 U.S. at 604. Here, however, we are dealing with a compulsion of students to declare a belief. They are not merely made acquainted with the flag salute so that they may be informed as to what it is or even what it means. The issue here is whether this slow and easily neglected route to aroused loyalties constitutionally may be short-cut by substituting a compulsory salute and slogan. This issue is not prejudiced by the Court's previous holding that where a State, without compelling attendance, extends college facilities to pupils who voluntarily enroll, it may prescribe military training as part of the course without offense to the Constitution. It was held that those who take advantage of its opportunities may not on ground of conscience refuse compliance with such conditions. *Hamilton v. Regents.* In the present case attendance is not optional. That case is also to be distinguished from the present one because, independently of college privileges or requirements, the State has power to raise militia and impose the duties of service therein upon its citizens.

There is no doubt that, in connection with the pledges, the flag salute is a form of utterance. Symbolism is a primitive but effective way of communicating ideas. The use of an emblem or flag to symbolize some system, idea, institution, or personality, is a short cut from mind to mind. Causes and nations, political parties, lodges and ecclesiastical groups seek to knit the loyalty of their followings to a flag or banner, a color or design. The State announces rank, function, and authority through crowns and maces, uniforms and black robes; the church speaks through the Cross, the Crucifix, the altar and shrine, and clerical raiment. Symbols of State often convey political ideas just as religious symbols come to convey theological ones. Associated with many of these symbols are appropriate gestures of acceptance or respect: a salute, a bowed or bared head, a bended knee. A person gets from a symbol the meaning he puts into it, and what is one man's comfort and inspiration is another's jest and scorn.

Over a decade ago Chief Justice Hughes led this Court in holding that the display of a red flag as a symbol of opposition by peaceful and legal means to organized government was protected by the free speech guaranties of the Constitution. *Stromberg v. California*, 283 U.S. 359. Here it is the State that employs a flag as a symbol of adherence to government as presently organized. It requires the individual to communicate by word and sign his acceptance of the political ideas it thus bespeaks. Objection to this form of communication when coerced is an old one, well known to the framers of the Bill of Rights.

It is also to be noted that the compulsory flag salute and pledge requires affirmation of a belief and an attitude of mind. It is not clear whether the regulation contemplates that pupils forego any contrary convictions of their own and become unwilling converts to the prescribed ceremony or whether it will be acceptable if they simulate assent by words without belief and by a gesture barren of meaning. It is now a commonplace that censorship or suppression of expression of opinion is tolerated by our Constitution only when the expression presents a clear and present danger of action of a kind the State is empowered to prevent and punish. It would seem that involuntary affirmation could be commanded only on even more immediate and urgent grounds than silence. But here the power of compulsion is invoked without any allegation that remaining passive during a flag salute ritual creates a clear and present danger that would justify an effort even to muffle expression. To sustain the compulsory flag salute we are required to say that a Bill of Rights which guards the individual's right to speak his own mind, left it open to public authorities to compel him to utter what is not in his mind.

Whether the First Amendment to the Constitution will permit officials to order observance of ritual of this nature does not depend upon whether as a voluntary exercise we would think it to be good, bad or merely innocuous. Any credo of nationalism is likely to include what some disapprove or to omit what others think essential, and to give off different overtones as it takes on different accents or interpretations. If official power exists to coerce acceptance of any patriotic creed, what it shall contain cannot be decided by courts, but must be largely discretionary with the ordaining authority, whose power to prescribe would no doubt include power to amend. Hence validity of the asserted power to force an American citizen publicly to profess any statement of belief or to engage in any ceremony of assent to one presents questions of power that must be considered independently of any idea we may have as to the utility of the ceremony in question.

Nor does the issue as we see it turn on one's possession of particular religious views or the sincerity with which they are held. While religion supplies appellees' motive for enduring the discomforts of making the issue in this case, many citizens who do not share these religious views hold such a compulsory rite to infringe constitutional liberty of the individual. It is not necessary to inquire whether non-conformist beliefs will exempt from the duty to salute unless we first find power to make the salute a legal duty.

The *Gobitis* decision, however, assumed, as did the argument in that case and in this, that power exists in the State to impose the flag salute discipline upon school children in general. The Court only examined and rejected a claim based on religious beliefs of immunity from an unquestioned general rule. The question which underlies the flag salute controversy is whether such a ceremony so touching matters of opinion and political attitude may be imposed upon the individual by official authority under powers committed to any political organization under our Constitution. We examine rather than assume existence of this power and, against this broader definition of issues in this case, re-examine specific grounds assigned for the *Gobitis* decision.

1. It was said that the flag-salute controversy confronted the Court with "the problem which Lincoln cast in memorable dilemma: 'Must a government of necessity be too *strong* for the liberties of its people, or too weak to maintain its own existence?'" and that the answer must be in favor of strength. *Minersville School District v. Gobitis*, 310 U.S., 596.

We think these issues may be examined free of pressure or restraint growing out of such considerations.

It may be doubted whether Mr. Lincoln would have thought that the strength of government to maintain itself would be impressively vindicated by our confirming power of the State to expel a handful of children from school. Such oversimplification, so handy in political debate, often lacks the precision necessary to postulates of judicial reasoning. If validly applied to this problem, the utterance cited would resolve every issue of power in favor of those in authority and would require us to override every liberty thought to weaken or delay execution of their policies.

Government of limited power need not be anemic government. Assurance that rights are secure tends to diminish fear and jealousy of strong government, and by making us feel safe to live under it makes for its better support. Without promise of a limiting Bill of Rights it is doubtful if our Constitution could have mustered enough strength to enable its ratification. To enforce those rights today is not to choose weak government over strong government. It is only to adhere as a means of strength to individual freedom of mind in preference to officially disciplined uniformity for which history indicates a disappointing and disastrous end.

The subject now before us exemplifies this principle. Free public education, if faithful to the ideal of secular instruction and political neutrality, will not be partisan or enemy of any class, creed, party, or faction. If it is to impose any ideological discipline, however, each party or denomination must seek to control, or failing that, to weaken the influence of the educational system. Observance of the limitations of the Constitution will not weaken government in the field appropriate for its exercise.

2. It was also considered in the *Gobitis* case that functions of educational officers in states, counties and school districts were such that to interfere with their authority "would in effect make us the school board for the country." *Id.*, 310 U.S., 598.

The Fourteenth Amendment, as now applied to the States, protects the citizen against the State itself and all of its creatures—Boards of Education not excepted. These have, of course, important, delicate, and highly discretionary functions, but none that they may not perform within the limits of the Bill of Rights. That they are educating the young for citizenship is reason for scrupulous protection of Constitutional freedoms of the individual, if we are not to strangle the free mind at its source and teach youth to discount important principles of our government as mere platitudes.

Such Boards are numerous and their territorial jurisdiction often small. But small and local authority may feel less sense of responsibility to the Constitution, and agencies of publicity may be less vigilant in calling it to account. The action of Congress in making flag observance voluntary and respecting the conscience of the objector in a matter so vital as raising the Army contrasts sharply with these local regulations in matters relatively trivial to the welfare of the nation. There are village tyrants as well as village Hampdens, but none who acts under color of law is beyond reach of the Constitution.

3. The *Gobitis* opinion reasoned that this is a field "where courts possess no marked and certainly no controlling competence," that it is committed to the legislatures as well as the courts to guard cherished liberties and that it is constitutionally appropriate to "fight out the wise use of legislative authority in the forum of public opinion and before legislative assemblies rather than to transfer such a contest to the judicial arena," since all the "effective means of inducing political changes are left free." *Id.*, 310 U.S., 597, 598, 600.

The very purpose of a Bill of Rights was to withdraw certain subjects from the vicissitudes of political controversy, to place them beyond the reach of majorities and officials and to establish them as legal principles to be applied by the courts. One's right to life, liberty, and property, to free speech, a free press, freedom of worship and assembly, and other fundamental rights may not be submitted to vote; they depend on the outcome of no elections. In weighing arguments of the parties it is important to distinguish between the due process clause of the Fourteenth Amendment as an instrument for transmitting the principles of the First Amendment and those cases in which it is applied for its own sake. The test of legislation which collides with the Fourteenth Amendment, because it also collides with the principles of the First, is much more definite than the test when only the Fourteenth is involved. Much of the vagueness of the due process clause disappears when the specific prohibitions of the First become its standard. The right of a State to regulate, for example, a public utility may well include, so far as the due process test is concerned, power to impose all of the restrictions which a legislature may have a "rational basis" for adopting. But freedoms of speech and of press, of assembly, and of worship may not be infringed on such slender grounds. They are susceptible of restriction only to prevent grave and immediate danger to interests which the state may lawfully protect. It is important to note that while it is the Fourteenth Amendment which bears directly upon the State it is the more specific limiting principles of the First Amendment that finally govern this case. . . .

4. Lastly, and this is the very heart of the *Gobitis* opinion, it reasons that "National unity is the basis of national security," that the authorities have "the right to select appropriate means for its attainment," and hence reaches the conclusion that such compulsory measures toward "national unity" are constitutional. *Id.*, 310 U.S., 595. Upon the verity of this assumption depends our answer in this case.

National unity as an end which officials may foster by persuasion and example is not in question. The problem is whether under our Constitution compulsion as here employed is a permissible means for its achievement.

Struggles to coerce uniformity of sentiment in support of some end thought essential to their time and country have been waged by many good as well as by evil men. Nationalism is a relatively recent phenomenon but at other times and places the ends have been racial or territorial security, support of a dynasty or regime, and particular plans for saving souls. As first and moderate methods to attain unity have failed, those bent on its accomplishment must resort to an ever-increasing severity. As governmental pressure toward unity becomes greater, so strife becomes more bitter as to whose unity it shall be. Probably no deeper division of our people could proceed from any provocation than from finding it necessary to choose what doctrine and whose program public educational officials shall compel youth to unite in embracing. Ultimate futility of such attempts to compel coherence is the lesson of every such effort from the Roman drive to stamp out Christianity as a disturber of its pagan unity, the Inquisition, as a means to religious and dynastic unity, the Siberian exiles as a means to Russian unity, down to the fast failing efforts of our present totalitarian enemies. Those who begin coercive elimination of dissent soon find themselves exterminating dissenters. Compulsory unification of opinion achieves only the unanimity of the graveyard.

It seems trite but necessary to say that the First Amendment to our Constitution was designed to avoid these ends by avoiding these beginnings. There is no mysticism in the American concept of the State or of the nature or origin of its authority. We set up government by consent of the governed, and the Bill of Rights denies those in power any legal opportunity to coerce that consent. Authority here is to be controlled by public opinion, not public opinion by authority.

The case is made difficult not because the principles of its decision are obscure but because the flag involved is our own. Nevertheless, we apply the limitations of the Constitution with no fear that freedom to be intellectually and spiritually diverse or even contrary will disintegrate the social organization. To believe that patriotism will not flourish if patriotic ceremonies are voluntary and spontaneous instead of a compulsory routine is to make an unflattering estimate of the appeal of our institutions to free minds. We can have intellectual individualism and the rich cultural diversities that we owe to exceptional minds only at the price of occasional eccentricity and abnormal attitudes. When they are so harmless to others or to the State as those we deal with here, the price is not too great. But freedom to differ is not limited to things that do not matter much. That would be a mere shadow of freedom. The test of its substance is the right to differ as to things that touch the heart of the existing order.

If there is any fixed star in our constitutional constellation, it is that no official, high or petty, can prescribe what shall be orthodox in politics, nationalism, religion, or other matters of opinion or force citizens to confess by word or act their faith therein. If there are any circumstances which permit an exception, they do not now occur to us.

We think the action of the local authorities in compelling the flag salute and pledge transcends constitutional limitations on their power and invades the sphere of intellect and spirit which it is the purpose of the First Amendment to our Constitution to reserve from all official control.

The decision of this Court in *Minersville School District v. Gobitis* and the holdings of those few *per curiam* decisions which preceded and foreshadowed it are overruled, and the judgment enjoining enforcement of the West Virginia Regulation is affirmed.

*Affirmed.*

⊞ MR. JUSTICE ROBERTS and MR. JUSTICE REED adhere to the views expressed by the Court in *Minersville School District v. Gobitis*, and are of the opinion that the judgment below should be reversed.

⊞ MR. JUSTICE BLACK and MR. JUSTICE DOUGLAS, concurring.

We are substantially in agreement with the opinion just read, but since we originally joined with the Court in the *Gobitis* case, it is appropriate that we make a brief statement of reasons for our change of view.

Reluctance to make the Federal Constitution a rigid bar against state regulation of conduct thought inimical to the public welfare was the controlling influence which moved us to consent to the *Gobitis* decision. Long reflection convinced us that although the principle is sound, its application in the particular case was wrong. *Jones v. Opelika,* 316 U.S. 584, 623. We believe that the statute before us fails to accord full scope to the freedom of religion secured to the appellees by the First and Fourteenth Amendments.

The statute requires the appellees to participate in a ceremony aimed at inculcating respect for the flag and for this country. The Jehovah's Witnesses, without any desire to show disrespect for either the flag or the country, interpret the Bible as commanding, at the risk of God's displeasure, that they not go through the form of a pledge of allegiance to any flag. The devoutness of their belief is evidenced by their willingness to suffer persecution and punishment, rather than make the pledge.

No well-ordered society can leave to the individuals an absolute right to make final decisions, unassailable by the State, as to everything they will or will not do. The First Amendment does not go so far. Religious faiths, honestly held, do not free individuals from responsibility to conduct themselves obediently to laws which are either imperatively necessary to protect society as a whole from grave and pressingly imminent dangers or which, without any general prohibition, merely regulate time, place or manner of religious activity. Decision as to the constitutionality of particular laws which strike at the substance of religious tenets and practices must be made by this Court. The duty is a solemn one, and in meeting it we cannot say that a failure, because of religious scruples, to assume a particular physical position and to repeat the words of a patriotic formula creates a grave danger to the nation. Such a statutory exaction is a form of test oath, and the test oath has always been abhorrent in the United States.

Words uttered under coercion are proof of loyalty to nothing but self-interest. Love of country must spring from willing hearts and free minds, inspired by a fair administration of wise laws enacted by the people's elected representatives within the bounds of express constitutional prohibitions. These laws must, to be consistent with the First Amendment, permit the widest toleration of conflicting viewpoints consistent with a society of free men.

Neither our domestic tranquility in peace nor our martial effort in war depend on compelling little children to participate in a ceremony which ends in nothing for them but a fear of spiritual condemnation. If, as we think, their fears are groundless, time and reason are the proper antidotes for their errors. The ceremonial, when enforced against conscientious objectors, more likely to defeat than to serve its high purpose, is a handy implement for disguised religious persecution. As such, it is inconsistent with our Constitution's plan and purpose.

▦ MR. JUSTICE MURPHY, concurring.

I agree with the opinion of the Court and join in it. . . .

A reluctance to interfere with considered state action, the fact that the end sought is a desirable one, the emotion aroused by the flag as a symbol for which we have fought and are now fighting again—all of these are understandable. But there is before us the right of freedom to believe, freedom to worship one's Maker according to the dictates of one's conscience, a right which the Constitution specifically shelters. Reflection has convinced me that as a judge I have no loftier duty or responsibility than to uphold that spiritual freedom to its farthest reaches.

The right of freedom of thought and of religion as guaranteed by the Constitution against State action includes both the right to speak freely and the right to refrain from speaking at all, except in so far as essential operations of government may require it for the preservation of an orderly society—as in the case of compulsion to give evidence in court. Without wishing to disparage the purposes and intentions of those who hope to inculcate sentiments of loyalty and patriotism by requiring a declaration of allegiance as a feature of public education, or unduly belittle the benefits that may accrue therefrom, I am impelled to conclude that such a requirement is not essential to the maintenance of effective government and orderly society. To many it is deeply distasteful to join in a public chorus of affirmation of private belief. By some, including the members of this sect, it is apparently regarded as incompatible with a primary religious obligation and therefore a restriction on religious freedom. Official compulsion to affirm what is contrary to one's religious beliefs is the antithesis of freedom of worship which, it is well to recall, was achieved in this country only after what Jefferson characterized as the "severest contests in which I have ever been engaged," *Autobiography*, vol. 1, pp. 53-59.

I am unable to agree that the benefits that may accrue to society from the compulsory flag salute are sufficiently definite and tangible to justify the invasion of freedom and privacy that it entailed or to compensate for a restraint on the freedom of the individual to be vocal or silent according to his conscience or personal inclination. The trenchant words in the preamble to the Virginia Statute for Religious Freedom remain unanswerable: ". . . all attempts to influence (the mind) by temporal punishment, or burthens, or by civil incapacitations, tend only to beget habits of hypocrisy and meanness, . . . ." Code Va. 1919, 34. Any spark of love for country which may be generated in a child or his associates by forcing him to make what is to him an empty gesture and recite words wrung from him contrary to his religious beliefs is overshadowed by the desirability of preserving freedom of conscience to the full. It is in that freedom and the example of persuasion, not in force and compulsion, that the real unity of America lies.

▧ MR. JUSTICE FRANKFURTER, dissenting.

One who belongs to the most vilified and persecuted minority in history is not likely to be insensible to the freedoms guaranteed by our Constitution. Were my purely personal attitude relevant I should whole-heartedly associate myself with the general libertarian views in the Court's opinion, representing as they do the thought and action of a lifetime. But as judges we are neither Jew nor Gentile, neither Catholic nor agnostic. We owe equal attachment to the Constitution and are equally bound by our judicial obligations whether we derive our citizenship from the earliest or the latest immigrants to these shores. As a member of this Court I am not justified in writing my private notions of policy into the Constitution, no matter how deeply I may cherish them or how mischievous I may deem their disregard. The duty of a judge who must decide which of two claims before the Court shall prevail, that of a State to enact and enforce laws within its general competence or that of an individual to refuse obedience because of the demands of his conscience, is not that of the ordinary person. It can never be emphasized too much that one's own opinion about the wisdom or evil of a law should be excluded altogether when one is doing one's duty on the bench. The only opinion of our own even looking in that direction that is material is our opinion whether legislators could in reason have enacted such a law. In the light of all the circumstances, including the history of this question in this Court, it would require more daring than I possess to deny that reasonable legislators could have taken the action which is before us for review. Most unwillingly, therefore, I must differ from my brethren with regard to legislation like this. I cannot bring my mind to believe that the "liberty" secured by the Due Process Clause gives this Court authority to deny to the State of West Virginia the attainment of that which we all recognize as a legitimate legislative end, namely, the promotion of good citizenship, by employment of the means here chosen. . . .

The admonition that judicial self-restraint alone limits arbitrary exercise of our authority is relevant every time we are asked to nullify legislation. The Constitution does not give us greater veto power when dealing with one phase of "liberty" than with another, or when dealing with grade school regulations than with college regulations that offend conscience, as was the case in *Hamilton v. Regents*. In neither situation is our function comparable to that of a legislature or are we free to act as though we were a superlegislature. Judicial self-restraint is equally necessary whenever an exercise of political or legislative power is challenged. There is no warrant in the constitutional basis of this Court's authority for attributing different roles to it depending upon the nature of the challenge to the legislation. Our power does not vary according to the particular provision of the Bill of Rights which is invoked. The right not to have property taken without just compensation has, so far as the scope of judicial power is concerned, the same constitutional dignity as the right to be protected against unreasonable searches and seizures, and the latter has no less claim than freedom of the press or freedom of speech or religious freedom. In no instance is this Court the primary protector of the particular liberty that is invoked. This Court has recognized, what hardly could be denied, that all the provisions of the first ten Amendments are "specific" prohibitions, *United States v. Carolene Products Co.* 304 U.S. 144, 152, note 4. But each specific Amendment, in so far as embraced within the Fourteenth Amendment, must be equally respected, and the function of this Court does not differ in passing on the constitutionality of legislation challenged under different Amendments. . . .

The framers of the federal Constitution might have chosen to assign an active share in the process of legislation to this Court. . . . But the framers of the Constitution denied such legislative powers to the federal judiciary. They chose instead to insulate the judiciary from the legislative function. They did not grant to this Court supervision over legislation.

The reason why from the beginning even the narrow judicial authority to nullify legislation has been viewed with a jealous eye is that it serves to prevent the full play of the democratic process. The fact that it may be an undemocratic aspect of our scheme of government does not call for its rejection or its disuse. But it is the best of reasons, as this Court has frequently recognized, for the greatest caution in its use.

The precise scope of the question before us defines the limits of the constitutional power that is in issue. The State of West Virginia requires all pupils to share in the salute to the flag as part of school training in citizenship. The present action is one to enjoin the enforcement of this requirement by those in school attendance. We have not before us any attempt by the State to punish disobedient children or visit penal consequences on their parents. All that is in question is the right of the state to compel participation in this exercise by those who choose to attend the public schools.

We are not reviewing merely the action of a local school board. The flag salute requirement in this case comes before us with the full authority of the State of West Virginia. We are in fact passing judgment on "the power of the State as a whole." *Rippey v. Texas*, 193 U.S. 504, 509. Practically we are passing upon the political power of each of the forty-eight states. Moreover, since the First Amendment has been read into the Fourteenth, our problem is precisely the same is it would be if we had before us an Act of Congress for the District of Columbia. To suggest that we are here concerned with the heedless action of some village tyrants is to distort the augustness of the constitutional issue and the reach of the consequences of our decision.

Under our constitutional system the legislature is charged solely with civil concerns of society. If the avowed or intrinsic legislative purpose is either to promote or to discourage some religious community or creed, it is clearly within the constitutional restrictions imposed on legislatures and cannot stand. But it by no means follows that legislative power is wanting whenever a general non-discriminatory civil regulation in fact touches conscientious scruples or religious beliefs of an individual or a group. Regard for such scruples or beliefs undoubtedly presents one of the most reasonable claims for the exertion of legislative accommodation. It is, of course, beyond our power to rewrite the state's requirement, by providing exemptions for those who do not wish to participate in the flag salute or by making some other accommodations to meet their scruples. That wisdom might suggest the making of such accommodations and that school administration would not find it too difficult to make them and yet maintain the ceremony for those not refusing to conform, is outside our province to suggest. Tact, respect, and generosity toward variant views will always commend themselves to those charged with the duties of legislation so as to achieve a maximum of good will and to require a minimum of unwilling submission to a general law. But the real question is, who is to make such accommodations, the courts or the legislature?

This is no dry, technical matter. It cuts deep into one's conception of the democratic process—it concerns no less the practical differences between the means for making these accommodations that are open to courts and to legislatures. A court can only strike down. It can only say "This or that law is void." It cannot modify or qualify, it cannot make exceptions to a general requirement. And it strikes down not merely for a day. At least the finding of unconstitutionality ought not to have ephemeral significance unless the Constitution is to be reduced to the fugitive importance of mere legislation. When we are dealing with the Constitution of the United States, and more particularly with the great safeguards of the Bill of Rights, we are dealing with principles of liberty and justice "so rooted in the traditions and conscience of our people as to be ranked as fundamental"—something without which "a fair and enlightened system of justice would be impossible." *Palko v. Connecticut*, 302 U.S. 319, 325. If the function of this Court is to be essentially no different from that of a legislature, if the considerations governing constitutional construction are to be substantially those that underlie legislation, then indeed judges should not have life tenure and they should be made directly responsible to the electorate. There have been many but unsuccessful proposals in the last sixty years to amend the Constitution to that end.

Conscientious scruples, all would admit, cannot stand against every legislative compulsion to do positive acts in conflict with such scruples. We have been told that such compulsions override religious scruples only as to major concerns of the state. But the determination of what is major and what is minor itself raises questions of policy. For the way in which men equally guided by reason appraise importance goes to the very heart of policy. Judges should be very diffident in setting their judgment against that of a state in determining what is and what is not a major concern, what means are appropriate to proper ends, and what is the total social cost in striking the balance of imponderables.

What one can say with assurance is that the history out of which grew constitutional provisions for religious equality and the writings of the great exponents of religious freedom—Jefferson, Madison, John Adams, Benjamin Franklin—are totally wanting in justification for a claim by dissidents of exceptional immunity from civic measures of general applicability, measures not in fact disguised assaults upon such dissident views. The great leaders of the American Revolution were determined to remove political support from every religious establishment. They put on an equality the different religious sects—Episcopalians, Presbyterians, Catholics, Baptists, Methodists, Quakers, Huguenots—which, as dissenters, had been under the heel of the various orthodoxies that prevailed in different colonies. So far as the state was concerned, there was to be neither orthodoxy nor heterodoxy. And so Jefferson and those who followed him wrote guaranties of religious freedom into our constitutions. Religious minorities as well as religious majorities were to be equal in the eyes of the political state. But Jefferson and the others also knew that minorities may disrupt society. It never would have occurred to them to write into the Constitution the subordination of the general civil authority of the state to sectarian scruples.

The constitutional protection of religious freedom terminated disabilities, it did not create new privileges. It gave religious equality, not civil immunity.

Its essence is freedom from conformity to religious dogma, not freedom from conformity to law because of religious dogma. Religious loyalties may be exercised without hindrance from the state, not the state may not exercise that which except by leave of religious loyalties is within the domain of temporal power. Otherwise each individual could set up his own censor against obedience to laws conscientiously deemed for the public good by those whose business it is to make laws.

The prohibition against any religious establishment by the government placed denominations on an equal footing—it assured freedom from support by the government to any mode of worship and the freedom of individuals to support any mode of worship. Any person may therefore believe or disbelieve what he pleases. He may practice what he will in his own house of worship or publicly within the limits of public order. But the lawmaking authority is not circumscribed by the variety of religious beliefs, otherwise the constitutional guaranty would be not a protection of the free exercise of religion but a denial of the exercise of legislation.

The essence of the religious freedom guaranteed by our Constitution is therefore this: no religion shall either receive the state's support or incur its hostility. Religion is outside the sphere of political government. This does not mean that all matters on which religious organizations or beliefs may pronounce are outside the sphere of government. Were this so, instead of the separation of church and state, there would be the subordination of the state on any matter deemed within the sovereignty of the religious conscience. Much that is the concern of temporal authority affects the spiritual interests of men. But it is not enough to strike down a non-discriminatory law that it may hurt or offend some dissident view. It would be too easy to cite numerous prohibitions and injunctions to which laws run counter if the variant interpretations of the Bible were made the tests of obedience to law. The validity of secular laws cannot be measured by their conformity to religious doctrines. It is only in a theocratic state that ecclesiastical doctrines measure legal right or wrong.

An act compelling profession of allegiance to a religion, no matter how subtly or tenuously promoted, is bad. But an act promoting good citizenship and national allegiance is within the domain of governmental authority and is therefore to be judged by the same considerations of power and of constitutionality as those involved in the many claims of immunity from civil obedience because of religious scruples.

That claims are pressed on behalf of sincere religious convictions does not of itself establish their constitutional validity. Nor does waving the banner of religious freedom relieve us from examining into the power we are asked to deny the states. Otherwise the doctrine of separation of church and state, so cardinal in the history of this nation and for the liberty of our people, would mean not the disestablishment of a state church but the establishment of all churches and of all religious groups. . . .

Law is concerned with external behavior and not with the inner life of man. It rests in large measure upon compulsion. Socrates lives in history partly because he gave his life for the conviction that duty of obedience to secular law does not presuppose consent to its enactment or belief in its virtue. The consent upon which free government rests is the consent that comes from sharing in the process of making and unmaking laws. The state is not shut out from a domain because the individual conscience may deny the state's claim. The individual conscience may profess what faith it chooses. It may affirm and promote that faith—in the language of the Constitution, it may "exercise" it freely—but it cannot thereby restrict community action through political organs in matters of community concern, so long as the action is not asserted in a discriminatory way either openly or by stealth. One may have the right to practice one's religion and at the same time owe the duty of formal obedience to laws that run counter to one's beliefs. Compelling belief implies denial of opportunity to combat it and to assert dissident views. Such compulsion is one thing. Quite another matter is submission to conformity of action while denying its wisdom or virtue and with ample opportunity for seeking its change or abrogation. . . .

When dealing with religious scruples we are dealing with an almost numberless variety of doctrines and beliefs entertained with equal sincerity by the particular groups for which they satisfy man's needs in his relation to the mysteries of the universe. There are in the United States more than 250 distinctive established religious denominations. In the state of Pennsylvania there are 120 of these, and in West Virginia as many as 65. But if religious scruples afford immunity from civic obedience to laws, they may be invoked by the religious beliefs of any individual even though he holds no membership in any sect or organized denomination. Certainly this Court cannot be called upon to determine what claims of conscience should be recognized and what should be rejected as satisfying the "religion" which the Constitution protects. That would indeed resurrect the very discriminatory treatment of religion which the Constitution sought forever to forbid. . . .

We are told that a flag salute is a doubtful substitute for adequate understanding of our institutions. The states that require such a school exercise do not have to justify it as the only means for promoting good citizenship in children, but merely as one of diverse means for accomplishing a worthy end. We may deem it a foolish measure, but the point is that this Court is not the organ of government to resolve doubts as to whether it will fulfill its purpose. Only if there be no doubt that any reasonable mind could entertain can we deny to the states the right to resolve doubts their way and not ours.

That which to the majority may seem essential for the welfare of the state may offend the consciences of a minority. But, so long as no inroads are made upon the actual exercise of religion by the minority, to deny the political power of the majority to enact laws concerned with civil matters, simply because they may offend the consciences of a minority, really means that the consciences of a minority are more sacred and more enshrined in the Constitution than the consciences of a majority.

We are told that symbolism is a dramatic but primitive way of communicating ideas. Symbolism is inescapable. Even the most sophisticated live by symbols. But it is not for this Court to make psychological judgments as to the effectiveness of a particular symbol in inculcating concededly indispensable feelings, particularly if the state happens to see fit to utilize the symbol that represents our heritage and our hopes. And surely only flippancy could be responsible for the suggestion that constitutional validity of a requirement to salute our flag implies equal validity of a requirement to salute a dictator. The significance of a symbol lies in what it represents. To reject the swastika does not imply rejection of the Cross. And so it bears repetition to say that it mocks reason and denies our whole history to find in the allowance of a requirement to salute our flag on fitting occasions the seeds of sanction for obeisance to a leader. To deny the power to employ educational symbols is to say that the state's educational system may not stimulate the imagination because this may lead to unwise stimulation.

The right of West Virginia to utilize the flag salute as part of its educational process is denied because, so it is argued, it cannot be justified as a means of meeting a "clear and present danger" to national unity. In passing it deserves to be noted that the four cases which unanimously sustained the power of states to utilize such an educational measure arose and were all decided before the present World War. But to measure the state's power to make such regulations as are here resisted by the imminence of national danger is wholly to misconceive the origin and purpose of the concept of "clear and present danger." To apply such a test is for the Court to assume, however unwittingly, a legislative responsibility that does not belong to it. To talk about "clear and present danger" as the touchstone of allowable educational policy by the states whenever school curricula may impinge upon the boundaries of individual conscience, is to take a felicitous phrase out of the context of the particular situation where it arose and for which it was adapted. *Mr. Justice HOLMES* used the phrase "clear and present danger" in a case involving mere speech as a means by which alone to accomplish sedition in time of war. By that phrase he meant merely to indicate that, in view of the protection given to utterance by the First Amendment, in order that mere utterance may not be proscribed, "the words used are used in such circumstances and are of such a nature as to create a clear and present danger that they will bring about the substantive evils that Congress has a right to prevent." *Schenck v. United States*, 249 U.S. 47, 52. The "substantive evils" about which he was speaking were inducement of insubordination in the military and naval forces of the United States and obstruction of enlistment while the country was at war. He was not enunciating a formal rule that there can be no restriction upon speech and, still less, no compulsion where conscience balks, unless imminent danger would thereby be wrought "to our institutions or our government."

The flag salute exercise has no kinship whatever to the oath tests so odious in history. For the oath test was one of the instruments for suppressing heretical beliefs. Saluting the flag suppresses no belief nor curbs it. Children and their parents may believe what they please, avow their belief and practice it. It is not even remotely suggested that the requirement for saluting the flag involves the slightest restriction against the fullest opportunity on the part both of the children and of their parents to disavow as publicly as they choose to do so the meaning that others attach to the gesture of salute. All channels of affirmative free expression are open to both children and parents. Had we before us any act of the state putting the slightest curbs upon such free expression, I should not lag behind any member of this Court in striking down such an invasion of the right to freedom of thought and freedom of speech protected by the Constitution. . . .

The uncontrollable power wielded by this Court brings it very close to the most sensitive areas of public affairs. As appeal from legislation to adjudication becomes more frequent, and its consequences more far-reaching, judicial self-restraint becomes more and not less important, lest we unwarrantably enter social and political domains wholly outside our concern. I think I appreciate fully the objections to the law before us. But to deny that it presents a question upon which men might reasonably differ appears to me to be intolerance. And since men may so reasonably differ, I deem it beyond my constitutional power to assert my view of the wisdom of this law against the view of the State of West Virginia. . . .

Of course patriotism cannot be enforced by the flag salute. But neither can the liberal spirit be enforced by judicial invalidation of illiberal legislation. Our constant preoccupation with the constitutionality of legislation rather than with its wisdom tends to preoccupation of the American mind with a false value. The tendency of focusing attention on constitutionality is to make constitutionality synonymous with wisdom, to regard a law as all right if it is constitutional. Such an attitude is a great enemy of liberalism. Particularly in legislation affecting freedom of thought and freedom of speech much which should offend a free-spirited society is constitutional. Reliance for the most precious interests of civilization, therefore, must be found outside of their vindication in courts of law. Only a persistent positive translation of the faith of a free society into the convictions and habits and actions of a community is the ultimate reliance against unabated temptations to fetter the human spirit.

## Notes and Questions

1. *Cantwell v. Connecticut* has three parts to it, the prior restraint rule, the concept of incorporation, and the clear and present danger rule. How would you explain each of these to a newcomer to this subject and tell how they relate to the Free Exercise Clause?

2. How does the holding in *Cantwell* modify the belief/action distinction? Does the Court hold that all religiously motivated action, in addition to religious belief, is now protected against government infringement by the First Amendment? If not, how would you describe the limitations that the *Cantwell* Court still allows on religiously motivated conduct?

3. In *Minersville School District v. Gobitis* the Court allowed public schools to require students to recite the pledge of allegiance to the flag under the concept that "National unity is the basis of national security. . . . The flag is the symbol of our national unity. . . ." Three years later, in *West Virginia Board of Education v. Barnette* the Court reversed itself under the concept that "To sustain the compulsory flag salute we are required to say that a Bill of Rights which guards the individual's right to speak his own mind, left it open to public authorities to compel him to utter what is not in his mind." With which decision do you agree, and why?

4. How does reciting an obligatory oath or salute burden one's religious liberty? Is it that one has to swear allegiance to or associate themselves with a principle to which they conscientiously disagree? How far does this free exercise principle extend—can I cut out the words "in God We Trust" from my dollar bills because I disagree with the concept on religious grounds? Back to *Barnette*, would it matter if the public school still conducted the Pledge but allowed those students with religious objections not to participate by remaining seated? Does the Free Exercise Clause protect children from taking compulsory oaths but not from the derision they may receive if they refuse to participate in the ceremony?

5. In 2000, Michael Newdow, an avowed atheist, brought suit against his daughter's public school district challenging the practice of having students recite the Pledge of Allegiance with the words "under God," as was incorporated into the Pledge in 1954. (See *Elk Grove Unified School District v. Newdow*, in chapter 5.) Even though the school officials allowed objecting students to opt-out of reciting the Pledge, Newdow raised a combination of free speech, free exercise, and establishment clause arguments (the latter being that the district was promoting religion by having students acknowledge "one nation under God", which he argued was effectively a religious exercise). The free exercise argument went something like this: first, his daughter was likely to be coerced into participating in a religious exercise by peer pressure and the coercive school environment (i.e., the opt-out was ineffective); second, that he had a right not to have his daughter exposed to religious ideas in the compulsory school environment that conflicted with his own belief system (i.e., atheism). The Supreme Court dismissed Newdow's suit without addressing his claims by finding that he lacked standing to sue. Assume standing exists, how would you resolve Newdow's free exercise claims using the authority of *Barnette*?

6. In *Barnette*, Justice Jackson wrote: "One's right to life, liberty, and property, to free speech, a free press, freedom to worship and assembly, and other fundamental rights may not be submitted to vote; they depend on the outcome of no elections." What does this statement say about the role of the Bill of Rights in a popular democracy? Is it consistent with the idea of majority rule?

---

Soon the Court confronted a case that involved the application of the Free Exercise Clause to children, *Prince v. Massachusetts*.[25] Again, the issue was proselytizing in public places. Sarah Prince was the aunt and custodian of Betty Simmons, nine years old. Prince regularly took her two sons and Betty onto the streets of her community to distribute Jehovah's Witnesses literature and testify to their faith. She was warned regularly by the truant officer that allowing Betty to do this violated the state's child labor laws. Those laws forbade a parent or guardian from supplying materials for sale to girls under 18 years old or allowing them to distribute such materials in public places. When the officer compelled Prince and Betty to stop their witnessing, Prince said: "This child is exercising her God-given right and her constitutional right to preach the gospel, and no creature has a right to interfere with God's commands."[26] Prince sued the state on free exercise and due process grounds. The Supreme Court decided against her on the reasoning that the state has a greater interest in the welfare of children than it does for adults. The Court decided the case under the common law concept *parens patriae*, which means the state may assume the authority of a parent to ensure the physical and emotional welfare of children. In this case, the *parens patriae* authority superseded the free exercise right of Prince and Betty to exercise their religion. In other words, this form of religious exercise put children in harm's way, according to the Court, and thus the state was justified in its actions.

## PRINCE v. MASSACHUSETTS
## 321 U.S. 158 (1944)

▦ MR. JUSTICE RUTLEDGE delivered the opinion of the court. . . .

Appellant does not stand on freedom of the press. . . . Hence, she rests squarely on freedom of religion under the First Amendment, applied by the Fourteenth to the states. She buttresses this foundation, however, with a claim of parental right as secured by the due process clause of the latter Amendment. . . . Thus, two claimed liberties are at stake. One is the parent's, to bring up the child in the way he should go, which for appellant means to teach him the tenets and the practices of their faith. The other freedom is the child's, to observe these; and among them is "to preach the gospel . . . by public distribution" of "Watchtower" and "Consolation," in conformity with the scripture: "A little child shall lead them." . . .

To make accommodation between these freedoms and an exercise of state authority always is delicate. It hardly could be more so than in such a clash as this case presents. On one side is the obviously earnest claim for freedom of conscience and religious practice. With it is allied the parent's claim to authority in her own household and in the rearing of her children. . . . Against these sacred private interests, basic in a democracy, stand the interests of society to protect the welfare of children, and the state's assertion of authority to that end, made here in a manner conceded valid if only secular things were involved. . . . It is the interest of youth itself, and of the whole community, that children be both safeguarded from abuses and given opportunities for growth into free and independent well-developed men and citizens. . . .

It is cardinal with us that the custody, care and nurture of the child reside first in the parents, whose primary function and freedom include preparation for obligations the state can neither supply nor hinder. . . .

But the family itself is not beyond regulation in the public interest, as against a claim of religious liberty. And neither rights of religion nor rights of parenthood are beyond limitation. Acting to guard the general interest in youth's well being, the state as *parens patriae* may restrict the parent's control by requiring school attendance, regulating or prohibiting the child's labor, and in many other ways. Its authority is not nullified merely because the parent grounds his claim to control the child's course of conduct on religion or conscience. . . . [T]he state has a wide range of power for limiting parental freedom and authority in things affecting the child's welfare; and that this includes, to some extent, matters of conscience and religious conviction. . . .

The state's authority over children's activities is broader than over like actions of adults. This is peculiarly true of public activities and in matters of employment. A democratic society rests, for its continuance, upon the healthy, well-rounded growth of young people into full maturity as citizens, with all that implies. . . . Among evils most appropriate for such action are the crippling effects of child employment, more especially in public places, and the possible harms arising from other activities subject to all the diverse influences of the street. It is too late now to doubt that legislation appropriately designed to reach such evils is within the state's police power, whether against the parent's claim to control of the child or one that religious scruples dictate contrary action. . . .

What may be wholly permissible for adults therefore may not be so for children, either with or without their parents' presence.

Street preaching, whether oral or by handing out literature, is not the primary use of the highway, even for adults. While for them it cannot be wholly prohibited, it can be regulated within reasonable limits in accommodation to the primary and other incidental uses. But, for obvious reasons, notwithstanding appellant's contrary view, the validity of such a prohibition applied to children not accompanied by an older person hardly would seem open to question. The case reduces itself therefore to the question whether the presence of the child's guardian puts a limit to the state's power. That fact may lessen the likelihood that some evils the legislation seeks to avert will occur. But it cannot forestall all of them. . . . Parents may be free to become martyrs themselves. But it does not follow they are free, in identical circumstances, to make martyrs of their children before they have reached the age of full and legal discretion when they can make that choice for themselves. . . . We think that with reference to the public proclaiming of religion, upon the streets and in other similar public places, the power of the state to control the conduct of children reaches beyond the scope of its authority over adults, as is true in the case of other freedoms, and the rightful boundary of its power has not been crossed in this case.

In so ruling we dispose also of appellant's argument founded upon denial of equal protection. . . . Shortly, the contention is that the street, for Jehovah's Witnesses and their children, is their church, since their conviction makes it so; and to deny them access to it for religious purposes as was done here has the same effect as excluding altar boys, youthful choristers, and other children from the edifices in which they practice their religious beliefs and worship. . . . However Jehovah's Witnesses may conceive them, the public highways have not become their religious property merely by their assertion. And there is no denial of equal protection in excluding their children from doing there what no other children may do.

## Notes and Questions

1. Jehovah's Witnesses have theological objections to receiving blood transfusions. They believe God, in Genesis 9:3-4, Leviticus 17:10-11 and Acts 15:28-29, among others, prohibits humans from ingesting blood because blood is the source of life and it is a sin to eat life. In modern times, with technological methods of ingesting blood, it is still prohibited. Courts have ruled that Witnesses may be compelled to give their dangerously ill children blood transfusions, in spite of their or their parents' religious beliefs. The precedent for that is *Prince v. Massachusetts*, although it has nothing to do with blood transfusions. The idea of *parens patriae* and the ruling that the state must be more solicitous of the welfare of children than of adults makes the case the authority in these most difficult of family issues. See *Jehovah's Witnesses v. King County Hospital.*[27]

2. Suppose that, based on sincere religious convictions, parents refuse to vaccinate their children for tetanus as required for admittance to the local public

schools. Alternatively, assume that Christian Science parents refuse to obtain medical treatment for their sick, though not terminal, child, preferring
to rely on prayer. In both situations health officials seek judicial authority to
override the parents' wishes so as to administer the vaccination or medical
treatment, respectively. How would you approach these cases? Is the preferable approach that the potential court order and government action be seen
as a burden only on the parents' religiously motivated practices but not on
their beliefs, and thus the burden is not problematic? Or should the burden
be viewed as one that affects only the children's religious beliefs and practices,
not those of the parents? Alternatively, should a court take the view that the
government has a sufficiently important interest in protecting the health of
the children that overrides any religious burden? Or should the parents' religious interests override those of the state?

## EARLY FREE EXERCISE ON GOVERNMENT PROPERTY

Several of the cases discussed above (*Cantwell, Prince*) involved people preaching or engaging in religious expression on public streets, sidewalks, and parks. Importantly, not all
property owned by the government is open to expression by private individuals, whether
that expression is religious, political, or merely celebratory as during Mardi Gras. The
*Cantwell* Court was concerned that government officials might use their authority to determine what was an appropriate religion and then, whether their speech was appropriate
before it occurred (a prior restraint). The Court appeared to assume that the Cantwells
could otherwise use the streets and sidewalks of New Haven for walking or engaging in
other expression. Thus the city could not exclude access to the streets and sidewalks because their speech was religious. But the Court did not hold that the Cantwells had a free
exercise right to preach on any public property at any time of their choosing. Assume instead that the Cantwells had been prosecuted from playing their records at an exceedingly
loud volume in the middle of the night. They may have claimed that God told them that
time was of the essence and that the loud record playing was necessary for their religious
message to reach as many people as possible. Would this prosecution similarly have violated the Cantwell's free exercise rights?

Welcome to the complex and occasionally confusing world of "public forum" doctrine, a part of free speech jurisprudence. In a nutshell, the Supreme Court has determined
that the level of nongovernmental expression—and correspondingly, the ability of the
government to restrict that expression—will vary depending on the history or characteristics of the government property in question. The Court has declared that some government property—streets, parks, sidewalks, in particular—have pedigrees as places for
robust, nongovernmental expression. These "traditional" or "quintessential public forums"
are places that have "immemorially been held in trust for the use of the public and, time
out of mind, have been used for purposes of assembly, communicating thoughts between
citizens, and discussing public questions." See *Hague v. CIO*, 307 U.S. 496 (1939). In
such places, government restrictions on access and expression are to be minimal, although
the government may impose "time, place, and manner" restrictions on the property's use

that are reasonable and not based on the subject matter of the expression (such as, political versus religious speech). Governments may also designate other less traditional places for public expression, such as a community room in a public library, referred to as "designated public forums." Finally, other government property may have less of a history of being available for nongovernmental expression or its functions are inconsistent with robust expression (think of the remainder of the library, a public hospital, or a military base). These are called "nonpublic forums" and the government has more discretion to exclude speakers and their speech based on their identity and the content of their speech. (Ironically, the Supreme Court has held that the front plaza of the Supreme Court building in Washington, D.C. is a nonpublic forum, thus requiring demonstrators to remain on the public sidewalks). Because of the close overlap of free exercise and free speech claims, throughout this book you will encounter issues about the character or designation of the "forum" within which the religious expression took place. Determining the character of a public forum will normally set the level of regulation the government may impose on public property, and will go a long way to deciding whether the religious expression in question will be allowed or prohibited.

A late nineteenth century case that prefigured some of the Jehovah's Witnesses and public forum analysis cases discussed below was *Davis v. Massachusetts*.[28] All we know about Davis is that he believed the Fourteenth Amendment of the Constitution gave him the right to preach in the Boston Common, which had existed as a place of public discourse (and cattle grazing) since the seventeenth century. But the Boston city council had passed a law prohibiting public speeches on the Common without a permit from the Mayor. Davis had lost in courts below, including a decision written by Judge Oliver Wendell Holmes of the Massachusetts Supreme Judicial Court. Holmes wrote: "For the legislature [to] forbid public speaking in a highway or public park is no more an infringement of the rights of a member of the public than for the owner of a private house to forbid it in his house."[29] The high court also found against Davis.

---

## DAVIS v. COMMONWEALTH OF MASSACHUSETTS
### 167 U.S. 43 (1897)

⊞ MR. JUSTICE WHITE . . . delivered the opinion of the court. . . .

It is argued that:

"Boston Common is the property of the inhabitants of the city of Boston, and dedicated to the use of the people of that city and the public in many ways; and the preaching of the gospel there has been, from time immemorial to a recent period, one of these ways. For the making of this ordinance in 1862, and its enforcement against preaching since 1885, no reason whatever has been or can be shown."

The record, however, contains no evidence showing the manner in which the ordinance in question had been previously enforced, nor does it include any proof whatever as to the nature of the ownership in the common from which it can be deduced that the plaintiff in error had any particular right to use the common apart from the general enjoyment, which he was entitled, as a citizen, to avail himself of along with others, and to the extent only which the law permitted. On the contrary, the legislative act and the ordinance passed in pursuance thereof, . . . show an assumption by the state of control over the common in question. Indeed, the supreme judicial court, in affirming the conviction, placed its conclusion upon the express ground that the common was absolutely under the control of the legislature, which, in the exercise of its discretion, could limit the use to the extent deemed by it advisable, and could and did delegate to the municipality the power to assert such authority.

It is therefore conclusively determined there was no right in the plaintiff in error to use the common except in such mode and subject to such regulations as the legislature, in its wisdom, may have deemed proper to prescribe. The fourteenth amendment to the constitution of the United States does not destroy the power of the states to enact police regulations as to the subjects within their control and does not have the effect of creating a particular and personal right in the citizen to use public property in defiance of the constitution and laws of the state.

The right to absolutely exclude all right to use necessarily includes the authority to determine under what circumstances such use may be availed of, as the greater power contains the lesser. The finding of the court of last resort of the state of Massachusetts, being that no particular right was possessed by the plaintiff in error to the use of the common, is in reason, therefore, conclusive of the controversy which the record presents, entirely aside from the fact that the power conferred upon the chief executive officer of the city of Boston by the ordinance in question may be fairly claimed to be a mere administrative function vested in the mayor in order to effectuate the purpose for which the common was maintained and by which its use was regulated. The plaintiff in error cannot avail himself of the right granted by the state, and yet obtain exemption from the lawful regulations to which this right on his part was subjected by law.

---

As discussed, the free exercise of religion and the right of free speech, also guaranteed by the First Amendment, frequently coalesce in one case. Such was *Murdock v. Pennsylvania*,[30] another Jehovah's Witness case. As we saw in *Cantwell* and *Prince*, Witnesses were active and persistent in evangelizing. That was because of their belief that every baptized member is an ordained minister and because they believe that the world needs to hear their understanding of God's word. *Murdock* posed the question of whether the Free Exercise and Free Speech Clauses allowed a city to impose a tax or licensing fee on Witnesses for permission to preach in that city. In *Cantwell* the Court had ruled a city could not impose a prior restraint on evangelizing by insisting on obtaining permission from a government official. *Murdock* was different because money changed hands; the city charged a fee for the permission. Part of the issue was that Witnesses solicited money for the religious literature they distributed. The City of Jeannette claimed its tax was a license to transact business in the community. The Witnesses claimed they were not a commercial enterprise, that the money they asked of listeners was a "contribution" to the religion. They sometimes gave the literature away even when one did not make a contribution.

The Court found in favor of the Witnesses and, in the process, affirmed language from some previous cases that both freedom of religion and of speech are "preferred freedoms," that is, among the most important freedoms Americans enjoy. Although the "preferred freedom" concept of free exercise of religion disappeared in the late 1980s, *Murdock* remains good law and foreshadowed a decision favorable to the Witnesses in a similar case in 2002, *Watchtower Bible and Tract Society v. Stratton*.[31]

## MURDOCK v. PENNSYLVANIA
### 319 U.S. 105 (1943)

▦ MR. JUSTICE DOUGLAS delivered the opinion of the Court. . . .

The First Amendment, which the Fourteenth makes applicable to the states, declares that "Congress shall make no law respecting an establishment of religion, or prohibiting the free exercise thereof; or abridging the freedom of speech, or of the press. . . ." It could hardly be denied that a tax laid specifically on the exercise of those freedoms would be unconstitutional. Yet the license tax imposed by this ordinance is, in substance, just that. . . .

The hand distribution of religious tracts is an age-old form of missionary evangelism—as old as the history of printing presses. . . . It is more than preaching; it is more than distribution of religious literature. It is a combination of both. Its purpose is as evangelical as the revival meeting. This form of religious activity occupies the same high estate under the First Amendment as do worship in the churches and preaching from the pulpits. It has the same claim to protection as the more orthodox and conventional exercises of religion. It also has the same claim as the others to the guarantees of freedom of speech and freedom of the press. . . .

We only hold that spreading one's religious beliefs or preaching the Gospel through distribution of religious literature and through personal visitations is an age-old type of evangelism with as high a claim to constitutional protection as the more orthodox types. The manner in which it is practiced at times gives rise to special problems with which the police power of the states is competent to deal. But that merely illustrates that the rights with which we are dealing are not absolutes. . . . The cases present a single issue—the constitutionality of an ordinance which as construed and applied requires religious colporteurs to pay a license tax as a condition to the pursuit of their activities. . . .

[T]he mere fact that the religious literature is "sold" by itinerant preachers rather than "donated" does not transform evangelism into a commercial enterprise. If it did, then the passing of the collection plate in church would make the church service a commercial project. The constitutional rights of those spreading their religious beliefs through the spoken and printed word are not to be gauged by standards governing retailers or wholesalers of books. . . . Freedom of speech, freedom of the press, freedom of religion are available to all, not merely to those who can pay their own way. As we have said, the problem of drawing the line between a purely commercial activity and a religious one will at times be difficult. On this record it plainly cannot be said that petitioners were engaged in a commercial rather than a religious venture. It is a distortion of the facts of record to describe their activities as the occupation of selling books and pamphlets. . . .

We do not mean to say that religious groups and the press are free from all financial burdens of government. We have here something quite different, for example, from a tax on the income of one who engages in religious activities or a tax on property used or employed in connection with those activities. It is one thing to impose a tax on the income or property of a preacher. It is quite another thing to exact a tax from him for the privilege of delivering a sermon. The tax imposed by the City of Jeannette is a flat license tax, the payment of which is a condition of the exercise of these constitutional privileges. The power to tax the exercise of a privilege is the power to control or suppress its enjoyment. Those who can tax the exercise of this religious practice can make its exercise so costly as to deprive it of the resources necessary for its maintenance. Those who can tax the privilege of engaging in this form of missionary evangelism can close its doors to all those who do not have a full purse. Spreading religious beliefs in this ancient and honorable manner would thus be denied the needy. . . .

A state may not impose a charge for the enjoyment of a right granted by the Federal Constitution. . . . The power to impose a license tax on the exercise of these freedoms is indeed as potent as the power of censorship which this Court has repeatedly struck down. . . .

The fact that the ordinance is "nondiscriminatory" is immaterial. The protection afforded by the First Amendment is not so restricted. A license tax certainly does not acquire constitutional validity because it classifies the privileges protected by the First Amendment along with the wares and merchandise of hucksters and peddlers and treats them all alike. Such equality in treatment does not save the ordinance. Freedom of press, freedom of speech, freedom of religion are in a preferred position. . . .

▨ MR. JUSTICE REED, dissenting. . . .

But whether we give content to the literal words of the First Amendment or to principles of the liberty of the press and the church, we conclude that cities or states may levy reasonable, non-discriminatory taxes on such activities as occurred in these cases. . . .

It is urged that such a tax as this may be used readily to restrict the dissemination of ideas. This must be conceded but the possibility of misuse does not make a tax unconstitutional. No abuse is claimed here. . . . If the tax is used oppressively, the law will protect the victims of such action.

This decision forces a tax subsidy notwithstanding our accepted belief in the separation of church and state. Instead of all bearing equally the burdens of government, this Court now fastens upon the communities the entire cost of policing the sales of religious literature. . . . The distributors of religious literature, possibly of all informatory publications, become today privileged to carry on their occupations without contributing their share to the support of the government which provides the opportunity for the exercise of their liberties.

Nor do we think it can be said, properly, that these sales of religious books are religious exercises. . . .

And even if the distribution of religious books was a religious practice protected from regulation by the First Amendment, certainly the affixation of a price for the articles would destroy the sacred character of the transaction. The evangelist becomes also a book agent.

The rites which are protected by the First Amendment are in essence spiritual—prayer, mass, sermons, sacrament—not sales of religious goods. . . .

◼ MR. JUSTICE FRANKFURTER, dissenting. . . .

It is altogether incorrect to say that the question here is whether a state can limit the free exercise of religion by imposing burdensome taxes. . . .

It is only fair that he also who preaches the word of God should share in the costs of the benefits provided by government to him as well as to the other members of the community. And so, no one would suggest that a clergyman who uses an automobile or the telephone in connection with his work thereby gains a constitutional exemption from taxes levied upon the use of automobiles or upon telephone calls. Equally alien is it to our constitutional system to suggest that the Constitution of the United States exempts church-held lands from state taxation. Plainly, a tax measure is not invalid under the federal Constitution merely because it falls upon persons engaged in activities of a religious nature. . . .

A tax upon newspaper publishing is not invalid simply because it falls upon the exercise of a constitutional right. Such a tax might be invalid if it invidiously singled out newspaper publishing for bearing the burdens of taxation or imposed upon them in such ways as to encroach on the essential scope of a free press. If the Court could justifiably hold that the tax measures in these cases were vulnerable on that ground, I would unreservedly agree. But the Court has not done so, and indeed could not. . . .

The fact that a power can be perverted does not mean that every exercise of the power is a perversion of the power. Thus, if a tax indirectly suppresses or controls the enjoyment of a constitutional privilege which a legislature cannot directly suppress or control, of course it is bad. But it is irrelevant that a tax can suppress or control if it does not.

---

Although the *Murdock* Court held government may not impose prior restraint on religious groups from evangelizing in public, either through permission of an official or imposition of a licensing tax, it never held religious groups were exempt from all restrictions. In the interest of public safety, order and crowd control, communities are permitted to impose "time, place, and manner" restrictions on even permissible activities. See the Jehovah's Witness case *Cox v. New Hampshire*.[32] Sometimes such restrictions have been imposed in a way to disadvantage unpopular groups, as the Witnesses cases illustrate. This was true in the 1980s and beyond, when the country was convulsed with concern about "cults." An example is a case involving the International Society for Krishna Consciousness (ISKCON), commonly known as "Hare Krishna."

ISKCON has a doctrine, *sankirtan*, which requires members to go to public places to distribute or sell literature and solicit donations for the maintenance of the Krishna religion. At times, this practice has run up against time, place, and manner rules that regulate expressive activities in airports, shopping malls, and other places with dense populations in ways unfavorable to Hare Krishnas.

Such a circumstance resulted in *Heffron v. International Society for Krishna Consciousness*.[33] The Minnesota State Fair had required any group that wanted to sell, exhibit, or distribute materials do so from a booth assigned by fair officials on a first-come, first-served basis. The universality of the rule and the fact that booths were assigned upon application enabled fair officials to contend the rule was nondiscriminatory and equitable to all groups.

Because *sankirtan* was essential to their religion, the Hare Krishnas argued, on the basis of religious freedom and free speech, that they should not be confined to booths, but should be able to distribute literature and solicit contributions anywhere on the fair grounds. The Minnesota Supreme Court agreed. But the U.S. Supreme Court reversed, primarily on free speech grounds, holding the fair's restrictions reasonable and appropriate.

---

## HEFFRON v. INTERNATIONAL SOCIETY FOR KRISHNA CONSCIOUSNESS
### 452 U.S. 640 (1981)

▦ JUSTICE WHITE delivered the opinion of the Court. . . .

The State does not dispute that the oral and written dissemination of the Krishnas' religious views and doctrines is protected by the First Amendment. Nor does it claim that this protection is lost because the written materials sought to be distributed are sold rather than given away or because contributions or gifts are solicited in the course of propagating the faith. . . .

It is also common ground, however, that the First Amendment does not guarantee the right to communicate one's views at all times and places or in any manner that may be desired. . . . The issue here, . . . is whether Rule 6.05 is a permissible restriction on the place and manner of communicating the views of the Krishna religion, more specifically, whether the [State Fair] Society may require the members of ISKCON who desire to practice Sankirtan at the State Fair to confine their distribution, sales, and solicitation activities to a fixed location.

A major criterion for a valid time, place, and manner restriction is that the restriction "may not be based upon either the content or subject matter of speech." *Consolidated Edison Co. v. Public Service Comm'n,* 447 U.S. 530, 536. Rule 6.05 qualifies in this respect, since, . . . the Rule applies evenhandedly to all who wish to distribute and sell written materials or to solicit funds. . . .

A valid time, place, and manner regulation must also "serve a significant governmental interest." *Virginia Pharmacy Board v. Virginia Citizens Consumer Council,* 425 U.S. 748, 771. Here, the principal justification asserted by the State in support of Rule 6.05 is the need to maintain the orderly movement of the crowd given the large number of exhibitors and persons attending the Fair. . . .

As a general matter, it is clear that a State's interest in protecting the "safety and convenience" of persons using a public forum is a valid governmental objective. Furthermore, consideration of a forum's special attributes is relevant to the constitutionality of a regulation since the significance of the governmental interest must be assessed in light of the characteristic nature and function of the particular forum involved. This observation bears particular import in the present case since respondents make a number of analogies between the fairgrounds and city streets, which have "immemorially been held in trust for the use of the public and . . . have been used for purposes of assembly, communicating thoughts between citizens, and discussing public questions." *Hague v. CIO,* 307 U.S. 496, 515. But it is clear that there are significant differences between a street and the fairgrounds. A street is continually open, often uncongested, and constitutes not only a necessary conduit in the daily affairs of a locality's citizens, but also a place where people may enjoy the open air or the company of friends and neighbors in a relaxed environment. The Minnesota Fair, as described above, is a temporary event attracting great numbers of visitors who come to the event for a short period to see and experience the host of exhibits and attractions at the Fair. The flow of the crowd and demands of safety are more pressing in the context of the Fair. As such, any comparisons to public streets are necessarily inexact. . . .

The justification for the Rule should not be measured by the disorder that would result from granting an exemption solely to ISKCON. That organization and its ritual of Sankirtan have no special claim to First Amendment protection as compared to that of other religions who also distribute literature and solicit funds. None of our cases suggest that the inclusion of peripatetic solicitation as part of a church ritual entitles church members to solicitation rights in a public forum superior to those of members of other religious groups that raise money but do not purport to ritualize the process. Nor for present purposes do religious organizations enjoy rights to communicate, distribute, and solicit on the fairgrounds superior to those of other organizations having social, political, or other ideological messages to proselytize. . . .

Indeed, the court below agreed that without Rule 6.05 there would be widespread disorder at the fairgrounds. The court also recognized that some disorder would inevitably result from exempting the Krishnas from the Rule. Obviously, there would be a much larger threat to the State's interest in crowd control if all other religious, nonreligious, and noncommercial organizations could likewise move freely about the fairgrounds distributing and selling literature and soliciting funds at will.

Given these considerations, we hold that the State's interest in confining distribution, selling, and fund solicitation activities to fixed locations is sufficient to satisfy the requirement that a place or manner restriction must serve a substantial state interest. . . . In our view, the Society may apply its Rule and confine the type of transactions at issue to designated locations without violating the First Amendment. . . .

For Rule 6.05 to be valid as a place and manner restriction, it must also be sufficiently clear that alternative forums for the expression of respondents' protected speech exist despite the effects of the Rule. Rule 6.05 is not vulnerable on this ground. First, the Rule does not prevent ISKCON from practicing Sankirtan anywhere outside the fairgrounds. More importantly, the Rule has not been shown to deny access within the forum in question. . . .

---

A later case, *International Society for Krishna Consciousness v. Lee*,[34] examined the question whether airport regulations forbidding solicitations of money or distribution of literature violated the Hare Krishnas' religious freedom. Rather than decide the issue on free exercise principles, the Court used "public forum analysis" solely. As discussed above, there are three types of public fora: traditional; designated; and non-public fora. The Court in *Heffron* determined that the Minnesota State Fair grounds was a designated public forum, open for public expression, but only of a particular sort. Because the restriction on the Hare Krishnas expressive activity did not turn on the subject manner of their speech, but only on its manner, the Court found it to be constitutional. In *ISKCON v. Lee*, the Court found that the third type of fora existed in airport terminals: a nonpublic forum. As mentioned, the nonpublic forum designation encompasses most government property. Speech in a nonpublic forum is considerably less protected by the First Amendment: regulations need only be reasonable and not aimed at suppressing an unpopular point of view. Thus, in applying this less restrictive standard, the Court upheld limits on the Hare Krishnas' religious expression without even mentioning the Free Exercise Clause.

---

## INTERNATIONAL SOCIETY FOR KRISHNA CONSCIOUSNESS v. LEE
### 505 U.S. 672 (1992)

▦ CHIEF JUSTICE REHNQUIST delivered the opinion of the Court. . . .

It is uncontested that the solicitation at issue in this case is a form of speech protected under the First Amendment. But it is also well settled that the government need not permit all forms of speech on property that it owns and controls. Where the government is acting as a proprietor, managing its internal operations, rather than acting as lawmaker with the power to regulate or license, its action will not be subjected to the heightened review to which its actions as a lawmaker may be subject. Thus, we have upheld a ban on political advertisements in city-operated transit vehicles, *Lehman v. Shaker Heights*, 418 U.S. 298 (1974), even though the city permitted other types of advertising on those vehicles. Similarly, we have permitted a school district to limit access to an internal mail system used to communicate with teachers employed by the district. *Perry Ed. Assn. v. Perry Local Educators' Assn.* 460 U.S. 37 (1983).

These cases reflect, either implicitly or explicitly, a "forum based" approach for assessing restrictions that the government seeks to place on the use of its property. Under this approach, regulation of speech on government property that has traditionally been available for public expression is subject to the highest scrutiny. Such regulations survive only if they are narrowly drawn to achieve a compelling state interest. The second category of public property is the designated public forum, whether of a limited or unlimited character—property that the State has opened for expressive activity by part or all of the public. Regulation of such property is subject to the same limitations as that governing a traditional public forum. Finally, there is all remaining public property. Limitations on expressive activity conducted on this last category of property must survive only a much more limited review. The challenged regulation need only be reasonable, as long as the regulation is not an effort to suppress the speaker's activity due to disagreement with the speaker's view. . . .

In *Cornelius v. NAACP Legal Defense Ed. Fund, Inc.*, 473 U.S. 788 (1985), we noted that a traditional public forum is property that has as "a principal purpose . . . the free exchange of ideas." 473 U.S., 800. Moreover, consistent with the notion that the government—like other property owners—"has power to preserve the property under its control for the use to which it is lawfully dedicated," *Greer v. Spock* 424 U.S., 836, the government does not create a public forum by inaction. Nor is a public forum created "whenever members of the public are permitted freely to visit a place owned or operated by the Government." Ibid. The decision to create a public forum must instead be made "by intentionally opening a nontraditional forum for public discourse." *Cornelius,* 802. Finally, we have recognized that the location of property also has bearing, because separation from acknowledged public areas may serve to indicate that the separated property is a special enclave, subject to greater restriction. *United States v. Grace,* 461 U.S. 171, 179-180 (1983).

These precedents foreclose the conclusion that airport terminals are public fora. . . . Thus, the tradition of airport activity does not demonstrate that airports have historically been made available for speech activity. Nor can we say that these particular terminals, or airport terminals generally, have been intentionally opened by their operators to such activity; the frequent and continuing litigation evidencing the operators' objections belies any such claim. In short, there can be no argument that society's time-tested judgment, expressed through acquiescence in a continuing practice, has resolved the issue in petitioner's favor. . . .

[A]irports are commercial establishments funded by users fees and designed to make a regulated profit, and where nearly all who visit do so for some travel related purpose. As commercial enterprises, airports must provide services attractive to the marketplace. In light of this, it cannot fairly be said that an airport terminal has as a principal purpose promoting "the free exchange of ideas." *Cornelius* 473 U.S. 788, 800. To the contrary, the record demonstrates that Port Authority management considers the purpose of the terminals to be the facilitation of passenger air travel, not the promotion of expression. . . .

Thus, we think that neither by tradition nor purpose can the terminals be described as satisfying the standards we have previously set out for identifying a public forum.

The restrictions here challenged, therefore, need only satisfy a requirement of reasonableness. . . . We have no doubt that, under this standard, the prohibition on solicitation passes muster. . . .

The Port Authority has concluded that its interest in monitoring the activities can best be accomplished by limiting solicitation and distribution to the sidewalk areas outside the terminals. This sidewalk area is frequented by an overwhelming percentage of airport users, . . . Thus the resulting access of those who would solicit the general public is quite complete. . . .

[I]f ISKCON is given access, so too must other groups. . . . As a result, we conclude that the solicitation ban is reasonable.

---

### Notes and Questions

1. Provide a rationale why the free exercise interest should protect religious expression outside one's house of worship, home, or other nongovernmental property. In essence, why should a free exercise right extend to religious activities engaged in on government property? Is it because people can engage in other, nonreligious expression on government property, such that to exclude religious expression would be discriminatory? Suppose a local governmental body prohibits all nongovernmental expression on government property, religious and otherwise (understandably, this would be impossible to police). Is there still a free exercise violation?

2. Do you think it is proper for "public forum criteria" to override free exercise of religion concerns, as in *Heffron* and *ISCKON v. Lee*? Why or why not?

CHAPTER 7

# RISE AND FALL OF FREE EXERCISE EXEMPTIONS:
## FROM *SHERBERT* TO *SMITH*

We have seen the Court establish the principle that the government may interfere with religious behavior if the conduct is perceived to be harmful to personal or public good. In *Reynolds v. United States* the Court gave broad discretion to legislatures to decide what was contrary to the public welfare. But in *Cantwell v. Connecticut*, the Court used a balancing test, weighing the right of free religious expression against the state's right to preserve public peace and order, thus raising the bar for the government. And, beginning in the 1960s, the Court began to apply a more complex method of interpreting the Free Exercise Clause, a method that required the government to take even greater care before interfering with religious practices.

Initially, in 1961 the Court confronted several "Sunday closing law" cases, one of which had a free exercise dimension. Sunday closing laws or "Sabbath laws" had existed since the early colonial period, commonly prohibiting all "worldly activity" and requiring church attendance on Sundays. Early Sabbath laws had an indisputable Biblical basis and sought to protect the peace and sanctity of Sundays by imposing religious conformity. Sunday laws were unevenly enforced and evolved over time; by the mid-twentieth century the laws were limited to prohibiting certain commercial activities on Sunday. In *McGowan v. Maryland* the Court said that the Sunday closing laws at issue in that case did not violate the Establishment Clause because the laws had lost the religious character that distinguished them at the time of their adoption. Instead, as the Court said, "[t]he present purpose and effect of most of [these laws] is to provide a uniform day of rest for all citizens." (See chapter 23.) But in the companion case of *Braunfeld v. Brown*, some Orthodox Jews claimed Sunday closing laws put them at an economic disadvantage because of their religion. Their religion demanded that they close their businesses on Saturday, while their competitors remained open. The Sunday closing laws required them, along with their competitors, to close their businesses on Sunday as well. So, they could be open only five days a week, while their competitors could be open on six. The Jewish merchants claimed this economic inequity violated their free exercise of religion.

In an opinion written by Chief Justice Earl Warren, the Court found no free exercise violation. The law did not prevent the plaintiffs from practicing their religion, the

Court said—the state was not interfering with their right to go to synagogue. The Court acknowledged that "[c]ompulsion by law of the acceptance of any creed or the practice of any form of worship is strictly forbidden." But, the Court continued, "the statute at bar does not make unlawful any religious practices of appellants; the Sunday law simply regulates a secular activity and, as applied to appellants, operates so as to make the practice of their religious beliefs more expensive."[1] Thus the only effect of the law was to make their religious practice more costly to their economic well-being. Justice Potter Stewart wrote a short dissent that both starkly described the issue of the case and the flaw, in his opinion, in the majority's approach: "Pennsylvania has passed a law which compels an Orthodox Jew to choose between his religious faith and his economic survival," Stewart wrote. "That is a cruel choice. It is a choice which I think no State can constitutionally demand."[2] So even though the Court acknowledged that the law with its Christian origins impacted the Jewish merchants differently from other merchants, it held that it did not "impede the observance of one or all religions or . . . discriminate between religions." In so doing, many believed the Court had departed from its own pronouncements and exhibited insensitivity to the Jews' religious freedom.

## THE RISE OF JUDICIALLY MANDATED FREE EXERCISE EXEMPTIONS

In 1963, the Court announced a revised standard for interpreting the Free Exercise Clause that was somewhat stricter than previous tests. Indeed, the standard is commonly called "strict scrutiny." The case was *Sherbert v. Verner*, involving Adell Sherbert, a Seventh-day Adventist. Seventh-day Adventists are Christians who believe the proper day of worship is the seventh day, sundown Friday until sundown Saturday, rather than Sunday, the day of worship for most Christians. The Sabbath is to be observed by cessation from work and by worship.

Ms. Sherbert was employed by a textile mill in South Carolina. When her employer went to a six-day work week, she informed her supervisor she could not work on Saturday for religious reasons. When no accommodation could be worked out, she was fired by her employer. Sherbert then filed for unemployment compensation from the state. She was denied benefits because she had failed to accept work offered to her. She filed suit, claiming her free exercise of religion had been infringed because the state had denied her benefits when she refused work because of religious principles.

The Supreme Court ruled in Sherbert's favor and, in the process, articulated a new test for interpreting the Free Exercise Clause. Sometimes called the "*Sherbert* test" or "compelling state interest test," it acknowledges the state may interfere with religious behavior if it is contrary to public welfare, yet raises the bar for government intervention even higher than the tests used by the Court to evaluate earlier free exercise claims. The operation and effect of the "compelling interest test" can best be expressed in a series of questions:

1.  In the case before the court, has the government imposed a substantial burden on the free exercise of the plaintiff's religion? If the answer to this inquiry is negative, the case is over and the plaintiff has lost. If the answer is affirmative, the consideration must go on to the second major question.
2.  Does a compelling state interest justify the burden placed on the exercise of religion? The state's interest must be of the greatest importance to take precedence over the free exercise of an individual's religion. If the answer to this question is negative, the plaintiff has won the case. If the answer is affirmative, the inquiry goes to the third question.

3.  Does the state have an alternative way of achieving its goals that puts less of a burden on the free exercise of the individual's religion? If the answer is negative, the state has won its case. If the answer is affirmative, the state must adopt the alternative method and cease its assault on the plaintiff's religious exercise; the plaintiff has won the case.

In *Sherbert*, the inquiry never reached the third question because the Court found the state did not have a sufficiently compelling interest to overbalance the weighty interest in protecting the free exercise of religion.

---

## SHERBERT v. VERNER
## 374 U.S. 398 (1963)

▓ MR. JUSTICE BRENNAN delivered the opinion of the Court.

Appellant, a member of the Seventh-day Adventist Church, was discharged by her South Carolina employer because she would not work on Saturday, the Sabbath Day of her faith. When she was unable to obtain other employment because from conscientious scruples she would not take Saturday work, she filed a claim for unemployment compensation benefits under the South Carolina Unemployment Compensation Act. That law provides that, to be eligible for benefits, a claimant must be "able to work and . . . available for work"; and, further, that a claimant is ineligible for benefits "[i]f. . . he has failed, without good cause . . . to accept available suitable work when offered him by the employment office or the employer . . . ." The appellee Employment Security Commission, in administrative proceedings under the statute, found that appellant's restriction upon her availability for Saturday work brought her within the provision disqualifying for benefits insured workers who fail, without good cause, to accept "suitable work when offered. . . by the employment office or the employer . . ."

### I

The door of the Free Exercise Clause stands tightly closed against any governmental regulation of religious beliefs as such, *Cantwell v. Connecticut*, 310 U.S. 296, 303. Government may neither compel affirmation of a repugnant belief, *Torcaso v. Watkins*, 367 U.S. 488; nor penalize or discriminate against individuals or groups because they hold religious views abhorrent to the authorities, *Fowler v. Rhode Island*, 345 U.S. 67; nor employ the taxing power to inhibit the dissemination of particular religious views, *Murdock v. Pennsylvania*, 319 U.S. 105. . . . On the other hand, the Court has rejected challenges under the Free Exercise Clause to governmental regulation of certain overt acts prompted by religious beliefs or principles, for "even when the action is in accord with one's religious convictions, [it] is not totally free from legislative restrictions." *Braunfeld v. Brown*, 366 U.S. 599, 603. The conduct or actions so regulated have invariably posed some substantial threat to public safety, peace or order. . . .

Plainly enough, appellant's conscientious objection to Saturday work constitutes no conduct prompted by religious principles of a kind within the reach of state legislation. If, therefore, the decision of the South Carolina Supreme Court is to withstand appellant's constitutional challenge, it must be either because her disqualification as a beneficiary represents no infringement by the State of her constitutional rights of free exercise, or because any incidental burden on the free exercise of appellant's religion may be justified by a "compelling state interest in the regulation of a subject within the State's constitutional power to regulate . . . ." *NAACP v. Button*, 371 U.S. 415, 438.

## II

We turn first to the question whether the disqualification for benefits imposes any burden on the free exercise of appellant's religion. We think it is clear that it does. In a sense the consequences of such a disqualification to religious principles and practices may be only an indirect result of welfare legislation within the State's general competence to enact; it is true that no criminal sanctions directly compel appellant to work a six-day week. But this is only the beginning, not the end, of our inquiry. For "[i]f the purpose or effect of a law is to impede the observance of one or all religions or is to discriminate invidiously between religions, that law is constitutionally invalid even though the burden may be characterized as being only indirect." *Braunfeld v. Brown* at 607. Here not only is it apparent that appellant's declared ineligibility for benefits derives solely from the practice of her religion, but the pressure upon her to forego that practice is unmistakable. The ruling forces her to choose between following the precepts of her religion and forfeiting benefits, on the one hand, and abandoning one of the precepts of her religion in order to accept work, on the other hand. Governmental imposition of such a choice puts the same kind of burden upon the free exercise of religion as would a fine imposed against appellant for her Saturday worship.

Nor may the South Carolina court's construction of the statute be saved from constitutional infirmity on the ground that unemployment compensation benefits are not appellant's "right" but merely a "privilege." It is too late in the day to doubt that the liberties of religion and expression may be infringed by the denial of or placing of conditions upon a benefit or privilege. . . . [T]o condition the availability of benefits upon this appellant's willingness to violate a cardinal principle of her religious faith effectively penalizes the free exercise of her constitutional liberties.

Significantly South Carolina expressly saves the Sunday worshipper from having to make the kind of choice which we here hold infringes the Sabbatarian's religious liberty. When in times of "national emergency" the textile plants are authorized by the State Commissioner of Labor to operate on Sunday, "no employee shall be required to work on Sunday . . . who is conscientiously opposed to Sunday work; and if any employee should refuse to work on Sunday on account of conscientious . . . objections he or she shall not jeopardize his or her seniority by such refusal or be discriminated against in any other manner." No question of the disqualification of a Sunday worshipper for benefits is likely to arise, since we cannot suppose that an employer will discharge him in violation of this statute. The unconstitutionality of the disqualification of the Sabbatarian is thus compounded by the religious discrimination which South Carolina's general statutory scheme necessarily effects.

## III

We must next consider whether some compelling state interest enforced in the eligibility provisions of the South Carolina statute justifies the substantial infringement of appellant's First Amendment right. It is basic that no showing merely of a rational relationship to some colorable state interest would suffice; in this highly sensitive constitutional area, "[o]nly the gravest abuses, endangering paramount interests, give occasion for permissible limitation," *Thomas v. Collins*, 323 U.S. 516, 530. No such abuse or danger has been advanced in the present case. The appellees suggest no more than a possibility that the filing of fraudulent claims by unscrupulous claimants feigning religious objections to Saturday work might not only dilute the unemployment compensation fund but also hinder the scheduling by employers of necessary Saturday work. But that possibility is not apposite here because no such objection appears to have been made before the South Carolina Supreme Court, and we are unwilling to assess the importance of an asserted state interest without the views of the state court. Nor, if the contention had been made below, would the record appear to sustain it; there is no proof whatever to warrant such fears of malingering or deceit as those which the respondents now advance. Even if consideration of such evidence is not foreclosed by the prohibition against judicial inquiry into the truth or falsity of religious beliefs—a question as to which we intimate no view since it is not before us—it is highly doubtful whether such evidence would be sufficient to warrant a substantial infringement of religious liberties. For even if the possibility of spurious claims did threaten to dilute the fund and disrupt the scheduling of work, it would plainly be incumbent upon the appellees to demonstrate that no alternative forms of regulation would combat such abuses without infringing First Amendment rights.[7]

In these respects, then, the state interest asserted in the present case is wholly dissimilar to the interests which were found to justify the less direct burden upon religious practices in *Braunfeld v. Brown*. The Court recognized that the Sunday closing law which that decision sustained undoubtedly served "to make the practice of [the Orthodox Jewish merchants'] . . . religious beliefs more expensive," 366 U.S., 605. But the statute was nevertheless saved by a countervailing factor which finds no equivalent in the instant case—a strong state interest in providing one uniform day of rest for all workers. That secular objective could be achieved, the Court found, only by declaring Sunday to be that day of rest. Requiring exemptions for Sabbatarians, while theoretically possible, appeared to present an administrative problem of such magnitude, or to afford the exempted class so great a competitive advantage, that such a requirement would have rendered the entire statutory scheme unworkable. In

---

[7] We note that before the instant decision, state supreme courts had, without exception, granted benefits to persons who were physically available for work but unable to find suitable employment solely because of a religious prohibition against Saturday work. . . . One author has observed, "the law was settled that conscientious objections to work on the Sabbath made such work unsuitable and that such objectors were nevertheless available for work. . . . A contrary opinion would make the unemployment compensation law unconstitutional, as a violation of freedom of religion. Religious convictions, strongly held, are so impelling as to constitute good cause for refusal. Since availability refers to suitable work, religious observers were not unavailable because they excluded Sabbath work." Altman, *Availability for Work: A Study in Unemployment Compensation* (1950), 187. . . . Of the 47 States which have eligibility provisions similar to those of the South Carolina statute, only 28 appear to have given administrative rulings concerning the eligibility of persons whose religious convictions prevented them from accepting available work. Twenty-two of those States have held such persons entitled to benefits, although apparently only one such decision rests exclusively upon the federal constitutional ground which constitutes the basis of our decision. . . .

the present case no such justifications underlie the determination of the state court that appellant's religion makes her ineligible to receive benefits.

## IV

In holding as we do, plainly we are not fostering the "establishment" of the Seventh-day Adventist religion in South Carolina, for the extension of unemployment benefits to Sabbatarians in common with Sunday worshippers reflects nothing more than the governmental obligation of neutrality in the face of religious differences, and does not represent that involvement of religious with secular institutions which it is the object of the Establishment Clause to forestall. Nor does the recognition of the appellant's right to unemployment benefits under the state statute serve to abridge any other person's religious liberties. Nor do we, by our decision today, declare the existence of a constitutional right to unemployment benefits on the part of all persons whose religious convictions are the cause of their unemployment. This is not a case in which an employee's religious convictions serve to make him a nonproductive member of society. Finally, nothing we say today constrains the States to adopt any particular form or scheme of unemployment compensation. Our holding today is only that South Carolina may not constitutionally apply the eligibility provisions so as to constrain a worker to abandon his religious convictions respecting the day of rest. This holding but reaffirms a principle that we announced a decade and a half ago, namely that no State may "exclude individual Catholics, Lutherans, Mohammedans, Baptists, Jews, Methodists, Non-believers, Presbyterians, or the members of any other faith, because of their faith, or lack of it, from receiving the benefits of public welfare legislation." *Everson v. Board of Education*, 330 U.S. 1, 16.

The judgment of the South Carolina Supreme Court is reversed and the case is remanded for further proceedings not inconsistent with this opinion.

*It is so ordered.*

### ▦ MR. JUSTICE DOUGLAS, concurring.

The case we have for decision seems to me to be of small dimensions, though profoundly important. The question is whether the South Carolina law which denies unemployment compensation to a Seventh-day Adventist, who, because of her religion, has declined to work on her Sabbath, is a law "prohibiting the free exercise" of religion as those words are used in the First Amendment. It seems obvious to me that this law does run afoul of that clause.

Religious scruples of Moslems require them to attend a mosque on Friday and to pray five times daily. Religious scruples of a Sikh require him to carry a regular or a symbolic sword. . . . Religious scruples of a Jehovah's Witness teach him to be a colporteur, going from door to door, from town to town, distributing his religious pamphlets. . . . Religious scruples of a Quaker compel him to refrain from swearing and to affirm instead. . . . Religious scruples of a Buddhist may require him to refrain from partaking of any flesh, even of fish.

The examples could be multiplied, including those of the Seventh-day Adventist whose Sabbath is Saturday and who is advised not to eat some meats.

These suffice, however, to show that many people hold beliefs alien to the majority of our society—beliefs that are protected by the First Amendment but which could easily be trod upon under the guise of "police" or "health" regulations reflecting the majority's views.

Some have thought that a majority of a community can, through state action, compel a minority to observe their particular religious scruples so long as the majority's rule can be said to perform some valid secular function. That was the essence of the Court's decision in the Sunday Blue Law Cases, . . . a ruling from which I then dissented (*McGowan v. Maryland* 366 U.S. 420, 575-576) and still dissent. . . .

That ruling of the Court travels part of the distance that South Carolina asks us to go now. She asks us to hold that when it comes to a day of rest a Sabbatarian must conform with the scruples of the majority in order to obtain unemployment benefits.

The result turns not on the degree of injury, which may indeed be nonexistent by ordinary standards. The harm is the interference with the individual's scruples or conscience—an important area of privacy which the First Amendment fences off from government. The interference here is as plain as it is in Soviet Russia, where a churchgoer is given a second-class citizenship, resulting in harm though perhaps not in measurable damages.

This case is resolvable not in terms of what an individual can demand of government, but solely in terms of what government may not do to an individual in violation of his religious scruples. The fact that government cannot exact from me a surrender of one iota of my religious scruples does not, of course, mean that I can demand of government a sum of money, the better to exercise them. For the Free Exercise Clause is written in terms of what the government cannot do to the individual, not in terms of what the individual can exact from the government.

Those considerations, however, are not relevant here. If appellant is otherwise qualified for unemployment benefits, payments will be made to her not as a Seventh-day Adventist, but as an unemployed worker. Conceivably these payments will indirectly benefit her church, but no more so than does the salary of any public employee. Thus, this case does not involve the problems of direct or indirect state assistance to a religious organization—matters relevant to the Establishment Clause, not in issue here.

## ▓ MR. JUSTICE STEWART, concurring in the result.

Although fully agreeing with the result which the Court reaches in this case, I cannot join the Court's opinion. This case presents a double-barreled dilemma, which in all candor I think the Court's opinion has not succeeded in papering over. The dilemma ought to be resolved.

### I . . .

I am convinced that no liberty is more essential to the continued vitality of the free society which our Constitution guarantees than is the religious liberty protected by the Free Exercise Clause explicit in the First Amendment and imbedded in the Fourteenth. And I regret that on occasion, and specifically in *Braunfeld v. Brown*, the Court has shown what has seemed to me a distressing insensitivity to the appropriate demands of this constitutional guarantee. By contrast I think that the Court's approach to the Establishment Clause has on occasion, and specifically in *Engel, Schempp* and *Murray*, been not only insensitive, but positively wooden, and that the Court has accorded to the Establishment Clause a meaning which neither the words, the history, nor the intention of the authors of that specific constitutional provision even remotely suggests.

But my views as to the correctness of the Court's decisions in these cases are beside the point here. The point is that the decisions are on the books. And the result is that there are many situations where legitimate claims under the Free Exercise Clause will run into head-on collision with the Court's insensitive and sterile construction of the Establishment Clause. The controversy now before us is clearly such a case.

Because the appellant refuses to accept available jobs which would require her to work on Saturdays, South Carolina has declined to pay unemployment compensation benefits to her. Her refusal to work on Saturdays is based on the tenets of her religious faith. The Court says that South Carolina cannot under these circumstances declare her to be not "available for work" within the meaning of its statute because to do so would violate her constitutional right to the free exercise of her religion.

Yet what this Court has said about the Establishment Clause must inevitably lead to a diametrically opposite result. If the appellant's refusal to work on Saturdays were based on indolence, or on a compulsive desire to watch the Saturday television programs, no one would say that South Carolina could not hold that she was not "available for work" within the meaning of its statute. That being so, the Establishment Clause as construed by this Court not only permits but affirmatively requires South Carolina equally to deny the appellant's claim for unemployment compensation when her refusal to work on Saturdays is based upon her religious creed. For, as said in *Everson v. Board of Education* 330 U.S. 1, 11, the Establishment Clause bespeaks "a government . . . stripped of all power . . . to support, or otherwise to assist any or all religions . . .," and no State "can pass laws which aid one religion . . . ." *Id.*, 15. In Mr. Justice Rutledge's words, adopted by the Court today in *Schempp*, the Establishment Clause forbids "every form of public aid or support for religion," 330 U.S., 32. In the words of the Court in *Engel v. Vitale,* 370 U.S., 431, reaffirmed today in the *Schempp* case, the Establishment Clause forbids the "financial support of government" to be "placed behind a particular religious belief."

To require South Carolina to so administer its laws as to pay public money to the appellant under the circumstances of this case is thus clearly to require the State to violate the Establishment Clause as construed by this Court. This poses no problem for me, because I think the Court's mechanistic concept of the Establishment Clause is historically unsound and constitutionally wrong. I think the process of constitutional decision in the area of the relationships between government and religion demands considerably more than the invocation of broadbrushed rhetoric of the kind I have quoted. And I think that the guarantee of religious liberty embodied in the Free Exercise Clause affirmatively requires government to create an atmosphere of hospitality and accommodation to individual belief or disbelief. In short, I think our Constitution commands the positive protection by government of religious freedom—not only for a minority, however small—not only for the majority, however large—but for each of us.

South Carolina would deny unemployment benefits to a mother unavailable for work on Saturdays because she was unable to get a babysitter. Thus, we do not have before us a situation where a State provides unemployment compensation generally, and singles out for disqualification only those persons who are unavailable for work on religious grounds. This is not, in short, a scheme which operates so as to discriminate against religion as such. But the Court nevertheless holds that the State must prefer a religious over a secular ground for being unavailable for work—that state financial support of the appellant's religion is constitutionally required to carry out "the governmental obligation of neutrality in the face of religious differences. . . ."

Yet in cases decided under the Establishment Clause the Court has decreed otherwise. It has decreed that government must blind itself to the differing religious beliefs and traditions of the people. With all respect, I think it is the Court's duty to face up to the dilemma posed by the conflict between the Free Exercise Clause of the Constitution and the Establishment Clause as interpreted by the Court. It is a duty, I submit, which we owe to the people, the States, and the Nation, and a duty which we owe to ourselves. For so long as the resounding but fallacious fundamentalist rhetoric of some of our Establishment Clause opinions remains on our books, to be disregarded at will as in the present case, or to be undiscriminatingly invoked as in the *Schempp* case, so long will the possibility of consistent and perceptive decision in this most difficult and delicate area of constitutional law be impeded and impaired. And so long, I fear, will the guarantee of true religious freedom in our pluralistic society be uncertain and insecure.

II

My second difference with the Court's opinion is that I cannot agree that today's decision can stand consistently with *Braunfeld v. Brown*. The Court says that there was a "less direct burden upon religious practices" in that case than in this. With all respect, I think the Court is mistaken, simply as a matter of fact. The *Braunfeld* case involved a state *criminal* statute. The undisputed effect of that statute, as pointed out by MR. JUSTICE BRENNAN in his dissenting opinion in that case, was that "'Plaintiff, Abraham Braunfeld, will be unable to continue in his business if he may not stay open on Sunday and he will thereby lose his capital investment.' In other words, the issue in this case—and we do not understand either appellees or the Court to contend otherwise—is whether a State may put an individual to a choice between his business and his religion." 366 U.S., 611.

The impact upon the appellant's religious freedom in the present case is considerably less onerous. We deal here not with a criminal statute, but with the particularized administration of South Carolina's Unemployment Compensation Act. Even upon the unlikely assumption that the appellant could not find suitable non-Saturday employment, the appellant at the worst would be denied a maximum of 22 weeks of compensation payments. I agree with the Court that the possibility of that denial is enough to infringe upon the appellant's constitutional right to the free exercise of her religion. But it is clear to me that in order to reach this conclusion the Court must explicitly reject the reasoning of *Braunfeld v. Brown*. I think the *Braunfeld* case was wrongly decided and should be overruled, and accordingly I concur in the result reached by the Court in the case before us.

⌗ MR. JUSTICE HARLAN, whom MR. JUSTICE WHITE joins, dissenting.

Today's decision is disturbing both in its rejection of existing precedent and in its implications for the future. The significance of the decision can best be understood after an examination of the state law applied in this case.

South Carolina's Unemployment Compensation Law was enacted in 1936 in response to the grave social and economic problems that arose during the depression of that period. As stated in the statute itself:

Economic insecurity due to unemployment is a serious menace to health, morals and welfare of the people of this State; *involuntary unemployment* is therefore a subject of general interest and concern . . .; the achievement of social security requires protection against this greatest hazard of our economic life; this can be provided by encouraging the employers *to provide more stable employment and by the systematic accumulation of funds during periods of employment to provide benefits for periods of unemployment*, thus maintaining purchasing power and limiting the serious social consequences of poor relief assistance. § 68-38. (Emphasis added.)

Thus the purpose of the legislature was to tide people over, and to avoid social and economic chaos, during periods when *work was unavailable*. But at the same time there was clearly no intent to provide relief for those who for purely personal reasons were or became *unavailable for work*. In accordance with this design, the legislature provided, in § 68-113, that "[a]n unemployed insured worker shall be eligible to receive benefits with respect to any week *only* if the Commission finds that . . . [h]e is able to work and is available for work . . . ." (Emphasis added.)

The South Carolina Supreme Court has uniformly applied this law in conformity with its clearly expressed purpose. It has consistently held that one is not "available for work" if his unemployment has resulted not from the inability of industry to provide a job but rather from personal circumstances, no matter how compelling. The reference to "involuntary unemployment" in the legislative statement of policy, whatever a sociologist, philosopher, or theologian might say, has been interpreted not to embrace such personal circumstances. See, e.g., *Judson Mills v. South Carolina Unemployment Compensation Comm'n* 28 S. E. 2d 535 (claimant was "unavailable for work" when she became unable to work the third shift, and limited her availability to the other two, because of the need to care for her four children).

In the present case all that the state court has done is to apply these accepted principles. Since virtually all of the mills in the Spartanburg area were operating on a six-day week, the appellant was "unavailable for work," and thus ineligible for benefits, when personal considerations prevented her from accepting employment on a fulltime basis in the industry and locality in which she had worked. The fact that these personal considerations sprang from her religious convictions was wholly without relevance to the state court's application of the law. Thus in no proper sense can it be said that the State discriminated against the appellant on the basis of her religious beliefs or that she was denied benefits because she was a Seventh-day Adventist. She was denied benefits just as any other claimant would be denied benefits who was not "available for work" for personal reasons.

With this background, this Court's decision comes into clearer focus. What the Court is holding is that if the State chooses to condition unemployment compensation on the applicant's availability for work, it is constitutionally compelled to carve out an exception—and to provide benefits—for those whose unavailability is due to their religious convictions. Such a holding has particular significance in two respects.

*First*, despite the Court's protestations to the contrary, the decision necessarily overrules *Braunfeld v. Brown*, which held that it did not offend the "Free Exercise" Clause of the Constitution for a State to forbid a Sabbatarian to do business on Sunday. The secular purpose of the statute before us today is even clearer than that involved in *Braunfeld*. And just as in *Braunfeld*—where exceptions to the Sunday closing laws for Sabbatarians would have been inconsistent with the purpose to achieve a uniform day of rest and would have required case-by-case inquiry into religious beliefs—so here, an exception to the rules of eligibility based on religious convictions would necessitate judicial examination of those convictions and would be at odds with the limited purpose of the statute to smooth out the economy during periods of industrial instability. Finally, the indirect financial burden of the present law is far less than that involved in *Braunfeld*. Forcing a store owner to close his business on Sunday may well have the effect of depriving him of a satisfactory livelihood if his religious convictions require him to close on Saturday as well. Here we are dealing only with temporary benefits, amounting to a fraction of regular weekly wages and running for not more than 22 weeks. Clearly, any difference between this case and *Braunfeld* cut against the present appellant.

*Second*, the implications of the present decision are far more troublesome than its apparently narrow dimensions would indicate at first glance. The meaning of today's holding, as already noted, is that the State must furnish unemployment benefits to one who is unavailable for work if the unavailability stems from the exercise of religious convictions. The State, in other words, must single out for financial assistance those whose behavior is religiously motivated, even though it denies such assistance to others whose identical behavior (in this case, inability to work on Saturdays) is not religiously motivated.

It has been suggested that such singling out of religious conduct for special treatment may violate the constitutional limitations on state action. . . . My own view, however, is that at least under the circumstances of this case it would be a permissible accommodation of religion for the State, if it chose to do so, to create an exception to its eligibility requirements for persons like the appellant. The constitutional obligation of "neutrality," see *School District of Abington Township v. Schempp*, is not so narrow a channel that the slightest deviation from an absolutely straight course leads to condemnation. There are too many instances in which no such course can be charted, too many areas in which the pervasive activities of the State justify some special provision for religion to prevent it from being submerged by an all-embracing secularism. The State violates its obligation of neutrality when, for example, it mandates a daily religious exercise in its public schools, with all the attendant pressures on the school children that such an exercise entails. . . . But there is, I believe, enough flexibility in the Constitution to permit a legislative judgment accommodating an unemployment compensation law to the exercise of religious beliefs such as appellant's.

For very much the same reasons, however, I cannot subscribe to the conclusion that the State is constitutionally compelled to carve out an exception to its general rule of eligibility in the present case. Those situations in which the Constitution may require special treatment on account of religion are, in my view, few and far between, and this view is amply supported by the course of constitutional litigation in this area. . . . Such compulsion in the present case is particularly inappropriate in light of the indirect, remote, and insubstantial effect of the decision below on the exercise of appellant's religion and in light of the direct financial assistance to religion that today's decision requires.

For these reasons I respectfully dissent from the opinion and judgment of the Court.

1.  How did the Court majority distinguish the burden on Ms. Sherbert's faith from the one imposed by the Sunday closing law in *Braunfeld*? Weren't both burdens of an economic nature (i.e., the loss of income)? Or did Sherbert's burden more directly impact her religious practice? Or is Justice Stewart correct that the holdings in *Braunfeld* and *Sherbert* are irreconcilable?

2.  How do you distinguish the respective government interests represented through the laws in *Braunfeld* and *Sherbert*? Why is not the prevention of fraud at least as compelling as a uniform day of rest, which is at best aspirational? Or was the state's interest in preventing fraud dismissed because it was simply too speculative or ill-founded in *Sherbert*? Alternatively, did the Court simply apply different levels of deference to the governments' stated rationales for their rules?

3.  Why did the *Sherbert* majority write that to exempt Ms. Sherbert from the unemployment requirements would not violate the Establishment Clause? Looking ahead, does an exemption for religiously motivated conduct—but not for comparable secular-motivated conduct—give preferential and unconstitutional treatment to religion as the dissents assert? As you think about your answer to that question, bear in mind that the government is permitted to sponsor or endorse secular messages but is prohibited from sponsoring or endorsing religious messages, pursuant to the Establishment Clause (see chapter 17). Are these kinds of different treatment for religion justifiable, either separately or collectively?

Church-state scholars agree that one of the best illustrations of the use and impact of the "*Sherbert* test" is the case of *Wisconsin v. Yoder*. The case involved the refusal of Old Order Amish to have their children receive formal education after they have reached the eighth grade. Descendants of the sixteenth century Anabaptists, the Amish, like their forebears, believe that "the world" is evil. Consequently, every true Christian should be separate from the world in order to not be corrupted by it. So the Amish famously wear distinctive clothing, avoid the use of modern conveniences, and do not participate in government, including military service. An expression of their attempt to avoid the corroding influences of modernity is their refusal to send their children to school past the eighth grade. They are not anti-intellectual. Rather, they believe in educating their children in reading, writing, and arithmetic so they can read the Bible and otherwise function in the essentials of Amish society. But, according to these religious believers, any formal schooling beyond the eighth grade will expose their children to the evils of "the world." So they withdraw their children from school at that age and continue their education at home in the practical skills required to live in the Amish community.

The various states, however, have compulsory attendance laws that require children to attend school through the ninth grade or a particular age, usually sixteen or seventeen. Wisconsin had such a law and prosecuted Amish parents for not complying with it. The Amish, however, claimed that the Free Exercise Clause protected their decision to withdraw their children from school before the age allowed by law. Because their belief about school attendance was grounded in their theology, it was a religious issue and thus covered by the free exercise guarantee.

The Court found in favor of the Amish, with Chief Justice Warren Burger writing for the majority. He applied the "compelling state interest test." Chief Justice Burger acknowledged that creating an educated citizenry was of great importance to Wisconsin, as it was to any state. But even weightier in the balance scale was the constitutional freedom of religion. The state's interest was not compelling enough to prevail over that freedom. It would have been an entirely different matter if the Amish objected to any education for their children. But because only one year of formal education was at stake in the case, plus the fact that the Amish continued the informal education of their children after school attendance was over (education specifically suited to prepare them to life in the Amish community), Wisconsin's interest was not sufficiently compelling to defeat the Amish's free exercise claim.

------

## WISCONSIN v. YODER
## 406 U.S. 205 (1972)

MR. CHIEF JUSTICE BURGER delivered the opinion of the Court.

On petition of the State of Wisconsin, we granted the writ of certiorari in this case to review a decision of the Wisconsin Supreme Court holding that respondents' convictions of violating the State's compulsory school-attendance law were invalid under the Free Exercise Clause of the First Amendment to the United States Constitution made applicable to the States by the Fourteenth Amendment. For the reasons hereafter stated we affirm the judgment of the Supreme Court of Wisconsin.

Respondents Jonas Yoder and Wallace Miller are members of the Old Order Amish religion, and respondent Adin Yutzy is a member of the Conservative Amish Mennonite Church. They and their families are residents of Green County, Wisconsin. Wisconsin's compulsory school-attendance law required them to cause their children to attend public or private school until reaching age 16 but the respondents declined to send their children, ages 14 and 15, to public school after they completed the eighth grade. The children were not enrolled in any private school, or within any recognized exception to the compulsory-attendance law, and they are conceded to be subject to the Wisconsin statute.

On complaint of the school district administrator for the public schools, respondents were charged, tried, and convicted of violating the compulsory-attendance law in Green Country Court and were fined the sum of $5 each. Respondents defended on the ground that the application of the compulsory-attendance law violated their rights under the First and Fourteenth Amendments. The trial testimony showed that respondents believed, in accordance with the tenets of Old Order Amish communities generally, that their children's attendance at high school, public or private, was contrary to the Amish religion and way of life. They believed that by sending their children to high school, they would not only expose themselves to the danger of the censure of the church community, but, as found by the county court, also endanger their own salvation and that of their children. The State stipulated that respondents' religious beliefs were sincere.

In support of their position, respondents presented as expert witnesses scholars on religion and education whose testimony is uncontradicted. They expressed their opinions on the relationship of the Amish belief concerning school attendance to the more general tenets of their religion, and described the impact that compulsory high school attendance could have on the continued survival of Amish communities as they exist in the United States today. The history of the Amish sect was given in some detail, beginning with the Swiss Anabaptists of the 16th century who rejected institutionalized churches and sought to return to the early, simple, Christian life de-emphasizing material success, rejecting the competitive spirit, and seeking to insulate themselves from the modern world. As a result of their common heritage, Old Order Amish communities today are characterized by a fundamental belief that salvation requires life in a church community separate and apart from the world and worldly influence. This concept of life aloof from the world and its values is central to their faith.

A related feature of Old Order Amish communities is their devotion to a life in harmony with nature and the soil, as exemplified by the simple life of the early Christian era that continued in America during much of our early national life. Amish beliefs require members of the community to make their living by farming or closely related activities. Broadly speaking, the Old Order Amish religion pervades and determines the entire mode of life of its adherents. Their conduct is regulated in great detail by the *Ordnung*, or rules, of the church community. Adult baptism, which occurs in late adolescence, is the time at which Amish young people voluntarily undertake heavy obligations, not unlike the Bar Mitzvah of the Jews, to abide by the rules of the church community.

Amish objection to formal education beyond the eighth grade is firmly grounded in these central religious concepts. They object to the high school, and higher education generally, because the values they teach are in marked variance with Amish values and the Amish way of life; they view secondary school education as an impermissible exposure of their children to a "worldly" influence in conflict with their beliefs. The high school tends to emphasize intellectual and scientific accomplishments, self-distinction, competitiveness, worldly success, and social life with other students. Amish society emphasizes informal learning-through-doing; a life of "goodness," rather than a life of intellect; wisdom, rather than technical knowledge; community welfare, rather than competition; and separation from, rather than integration with, contemporary worldly society.

Formal high school education beyond the eighth grade is contrary to Amish beliefs, not only because it places Amish children in an environment hostile to Amish beliefs with increasing emphasis on competition in class work and sports and with pressure to conform to the styles, manners, and ways of the peer group, but also because it takes them away from their community, physically and emotionally, during the crucial and formative adolescent period of life. During this period, the children must acquire Amish attitudes favoring manual work and self-reliance and the specific skills needed to perform the adult role of an Amish farmer or housewife. They must learn to enjoy physical labor. Once a child has learned basic reading, writing, and elementary mathematics, these traits, skills, and attitudes admittedly fall within the category of those best learned through example and "doing" rather than in a classroom. And, at this time in life, the Amish child must also grow in his faith and his relationship to the Amish community if he is to be prepared to accept the heavy obligations imposed by adult baptism. In short, high school attendance with teachers who are not of the Amish faith—and may even be hostile to it—interposes a serious barrier to the integration of the Amish child into the Amish religious community. Dr. John Hostetler, one of the experts on Amish society, testified that the modern high school is not equipped, in curriculum or social environment, to impart the values promoted by Amish society.

The Amish do not object to elementary education through the first eight grades as a general proposition because they agree that their children must have basic skills in the "three R's" in order to read the Bible, to be good farmers and citizens, and to be able to deal with non-Amish people when necessary in the course of daily affairs. They view such a basic education as acceptable because it does not significantly expose their children to worldly values or interfere with their development in the Amish community during the crucial adolescent period. While Amish accept compulsory elementary education generally, wherever possible they have established their own elementary schools in many respects like the small local schools of the past. In the Amish belief higher learning tends to develop values they reject as influences that alienate man from God.

On the basis of such considerations, Dr. Hostetler testified that compulsory high school attendance could not only result in great psychological harm to Amish children, because of the conflicts it would produce, but would also, in his opinion, ultimately result in the destruction of the Old Order Amish church community as it exists in the United States today. The testimony of Dr. Donald A. Erickson, an expert witness on education, also showed that the Amish succeed in preparing their high school age children to be productive members of the Amish community. He described their system of learning through doing the skills directly relevant to their adult roles in the Amish community as "ideal" and perhaps superior to ordinary high school education. The evidence also showed that the Amish have an excellent record as law-abiding and generally self-sufficient members of society.

Although the trial court in its careful findings determined that the Wisconsin compulsory school-attendance law "does interfere with the freedom of the Defendants to act in accordance with their sincere religious belief" it also concluded that the requirement of high school attendance until age 16 was a "reasonable and constitutional" exercise of governmental power, and therefore denied the motion to dismiss the charges. The Wisconsin Circuit Court affirmed the convictions. The Wisconsin Supreme Court, however, sustained respondents' claim under the Free Exercise Clause of the First Amendment and reversed the convictions. A majority of the court was of the opinion that the State had failed to make an adequate showing that its interest in "establishing and maintaining an educational system overrides the defendants' right to the free exercise of their religion." 182 N. W. 2d 539, 547 (1971).

I

There is no doubt as to the power of a State, having a high responsibility for education of its citizens, to impose reasonable regulations for the control and duration of basic education. Providing public schools ranks at the very apex of the function of a State. Yet even this paramount responsibility was, in

*Pierce v. Society of Sisters*, made to yield to the right of parents to provide an equivalent education in a privately operated system. There the Court held that Oregon's statute compelling attendance in a public school from age eight to age 16 unreasonably interfered with the interest of parents in directing the rearing of their offspring, including their education in church-operated schools. As that case suggests, the values of parental direction of the religious upbringing and education of their children in their early and formative years have a high place in our society. . . . Thus, a State's interest in universal education, however highly we rank it, is not totally free from a balancing process when it impinges on fundamental rights and interests, such as those specifically protected by the Free Exercise Clause of the First Amendment, and the traditional interest of parents with respect to the religious upbringing of their children so long as they, in the words of *Pierce*, "prepare [them] for additional obligations." 268 U.S., 535.

It follows that in order for Wisconsin to compel school attendance beyond the eighth grade against a claim that such attendance interferes with the practice of a legitimate religious belief, it must appear either that the State does not deny the free exercise of religious belief by its requirement, or that there is a state interest of sufficient magnitude to override the interest claiming protection under the Free Exercise Clause. Long before there was general acknowledgment of the need for universal formal education, the Religion Clauses had specifically and firmly fixed the right to free exercise of religious beliefs, and buttressing this fundamental right was an equally firm, even if less explicit, prohibition against the establishment of any religion by government. The values underlying these two provisions relating to religion have been zealously protected, sometimes even at the expense of other interests of admittedly high social importance. The invalidation of financial aid to parochial schools by government grants for a salary subsidy for teachers is but one example of the extent to which courts have gone in this regard, notwithstanding that such aid programs were legislatively determined to be in the public interest and the service of sound educational policy by States and by Congress. *Lemon v. Kurtzman,* 403 U.S. 602 (1971). . . .

The essence of all that has been said and written on the subject is that only those interests of the highest order and those not otherwise served can overbalance legitimate claims to the free exercise of religion. We can accept it as settled, therefore, that, however strong the State's interest in universal compulsory education, it is by no means absolute to the exclusion or subordination of all other interests.

## II

We come then to the quality of the claims of the respondents concerning the alleged encroachment of Wisconsin's compulsory school-attendance statute on their rights and the rights of their children to the free exercise of the religious beliefs they and their forebears have adhered to for almost three centuries. In evaluating those claims we must be careful to determine whether the Amish religious faith and their mode of life are, as they claim, inseparable and interdependent. A way of life, however virtuous and admirable, may not be interposed as a barrier to reasonable state regulation of education if it is based on purely secular considerations; to have the protection of the Religion Clauses, the claims must be rooted in religious belief. Although a determination of what is a "religious" belief or practice entitled to constitutional protection may present a most delicate question, the very concept of ordered liberty precludes allowing every person to make his own standards on matters of conduct in which society as a whole has important interests. Thus, if the Amish asserted their claims because of their subjective evaluation and rejection of the contemporary secular values accepted by the majority, much as Thoreau rejected the social values of his time and isolated himself at Walden Pond, their claims would not rest on a religious basis. Thoreau's choice was philosophical and personal rather than religious, and such belief does not rise to the demands of the Religion Clauses.

Giving no weight to such secular considerations, however, we see that the record in this case abundantly supports the claim that the traditional way of life of the Amish is not merely a matter of personal preference, but one of deep religious conviction, shared by an organized group, and intimately related to daily living. That the Old Order Amish daily life and religious practice stem from their faith is shown by the fact that it is in response to their literal interpretation of the Biblical injunction from the Epistle of Paul to the Romans, "be not conformed to this world . . . ." This command is fundamental to the Amish faith. Moreover, for the Old Order Amish, religion is not simply a matter of theocratic belief. As the expert witnesses explained, the Old Order Amish religion pervades and determines virtually their entire way of life, regulating it with the detail of the Talmudic diet through the strictly enforced rules of the church community.

The record shows that the respondents' religious beliefs and attitude toward life, family, and home have remained constant—perhaps some would say static—in a period of unparalleled progress in human knowledge generally and great changes in education. The respondents freely concede, and indeed assert as an article of faith, that their religious beliefs and what we would today call "life style" have not altered in fundamentals for centuries. Their way of life in a church-oriented community, separated from the outside world and "worldly" influences, their attachment to nature and the soil, is a way inherently simple and uncomplicated, albeit difficult to preserve against the pressure to conform. Their rejection of telephones, automobiles, radios, and television, their mode of dress, of speech, their habits of manual work do indeed set them apart from much of contemporary society; these customs are both symbolic and practical.

As the society around the Amish has become more populous, urban, industrialized, and complex, particularly in this century, government regulation of human affairs has correspondingly become more detailed and pervasive. The Amish mode of life has thus come into conflict increasingly with requirements of contemporary society exerting a hydraulic insistence on conformity to majoritarian standards. So long as compulsory education laws were confined to eight grades of elementary basic education imparted in a nearby rural schoolhouse, with a large proportion of students of the Amish faith, the Old Order Amish had little basis to fear that school attendance would expose their children to the worldly influence they reject. But modern compulsory secondary education in rural areas is now largely carried on in a consolidated school, often remote from the student's home and alien to his daily home life. As the record so strongly shows, the values and programs of the modern secondary school are in sharp conflict with the fundamental mode of life mandated by the Amish religion; modern laws requiring compulsory secondary education have accordingly engendered great concern and conflict. The conclusion is inescapable that secondary schooling, by exposing Amish children to worldly influences in terms of attitudes, goals, and values contrary to beliefs, and by substantially interfering with the religious development of the Amish child and his integration into the way of life of the Amish faith community at the crucial adolescent stage of development, contravenes the basic religious tenets and practice of the Amish faith, both as to the parent and the child.

The impact of the compulsory-attendance law on respondents' practice of the Amish religion is not only severe, but inescapable, for the Wisconsin law affirmatively compels them, under threat of criminal sanction, to perform acts undeniably at odds with fundamental tenets of their religious beliefs. . . . Nor is the impact of the compulsory-attendance law confined to grave interference with important Amish religious tenets from a subjective point of view. It carries with it precisely the kind of objective danger to the free exercise of religion that the First Amendment was designed to prevent. As the record shows, compulsory school attendance to age 16 for Amish children carries with it a very real threat of undermining the Amish community and religious practice as they exist today; they must either abandon belief and be assimilated into society at large, or be forced to migrate to some other and more tolerant region.[9]

In sum, the unchallenged testimony of acknowledged experts in education and religious history, almost 300 years of consistent practice, and strong evidence of a sustained faith pervading and regulating respondents' entire mode of life support the claim that enforcement of the State's requirement of compulsory formal education after the eighth grade would gravely endanger if not destroy the free exercise of respondents' religious beliefs.

### III

Neither the findings of the trial court nor the Amish claims as to the nature of their faith are challenged in this Court by the State of Wisconsin. Its position is that the State's interest in universal compulsory formal secondary education to age 16 is so great that it is paramount to the undisputed claims of respondents that their mode of preparing their youth for Amish life, after the traditional elementary education, is an essential part of their religious belief and practice. Nor does the State undertake to meet the claim that the Amish mode of life and education is inseparable from and a part of the basic tenets of their religion—indeed, as much a part of their religious belief and practices as baptism, the confessional, or a sabbath may be for others.

Wisconsin concedes that under the Religion Clauses religious beliefs are absolutely free from the State's control, but it argues that "actions," even though religiously grounded, are outside the protection of the First Amendment. But our decisions have rejected the idea that religiously grounded conduct is always outside the protection of the Free Exercise Clause. It is true that activities of individuals, even when religiously based, are often subject to regulation by the States in the exercise of their undoubted power to promote the health,

---

[9] Some States have developed working arrangements with the Amish regarding high school attendance. However, the danger to the continued existence of an ancient religious faith cannot be ignored simply because of the assumption that its adherents will continue to be able, at considerable sacrifice, to relocate in some more tolerant State or country or work out accommodations under threat of criminal prosecution. Forced migration of religious minorities was an evil that lay at the heart of the Religion Clauses. . . .

safety, and general welfare, or the Federal Government in the exercise of its delegated powers. . . . But to agree that religiously grounded conduct must often be subject to the broad police power of the State is not to deny that there are areas of conduct protected by the Free Exercise Clause of the First Amendment and thus beyond the power of the State to control, even under regulations of general applicability. . . . This case, therefore, does not become easier because respondents were convicted for their "actions" in refusing to send their children to the public high school; in this context belief and action cannot be neatly confined in logic-tight compartments.

Nor can this case be disposed of on the grounds that Wisconsin's require- ment for school attendance to age 16 applies uniformly to all citizens of the State and does not, on its face, discriminate against religions or a particular religion, or that it is motivated by legitimate secular concerns. A regulation neutral on its face may, in its application, nonetheless offend the constitutional requirement for governmental neutrality if it unduly burdens the free exercise of religion. . . . The Court must not ignore the danger that an exception from a general obligation of citizenship on religious grounds may run afoul of the Establishment Clause, but that danger cannot be allowed to prevent any ex- ception no matter how vital it may be to the protection of values promoted by the right of free exercise. By preserving doctrinal flexibility and recognizing the need for a sensible and realistic application of the Religion Clauses "we have been able to chart a course that preserved the autonomy and freedom of religious bodies while avoiding any semblance of established religion. This is a 'tight rope' and one we have successfully traversed." *Walz v. Tax Commission* 397 U.S. 664, 672.

We turn, then, to the State's broader contention that its interest in its system of compulsory education is so compelling that even the established religious practices of the Amish must give way. Where fundamental claims of religious freedom are at stake, however, we cannot accept such a sweeping claim; despite its admitted validity in the generality of cases, we must search- ingly examine the interests that the State seeks to promote by its requirement for compulsory education to age 16, and the impediment to those objectives that would flow from recognizing the claimed Amish exemption. . . .

The State advances two primary arguments in support of its system of compulsory education. It notes, as Thomas Jefferson pointed out early in our history, that some degree of education is necessary to prepare citizens to par- ticipate effectively and intelligently in our open political system if we are to preserve freedom and independence. Further, education prepares individuals to be self-reliant and self-sufficient participants in society. We accept these propositions.

However, the evidence adduced by the Amish in this case is persuasively to the effect that an additional one or two years of formal high school for Amish children in place of their long-established program of informal voca- tional education would do little to serve those interests. Respondents' experts testified at trial, without challenge, that the value of all education must be assessed in terms of its capacity to prepare the child for life. It is one thing to say that compulsory education for a year or two beyond the eighth grade may be necessary when its goal is the preparation of the child for life in modern society as the majority live, but it is quite another if the goal of education be viewed as the preparation of the child for life in the separated agrarian com- munity that is the keystone of the Amish faith.

The State attacks respondents' position as one fostering "ignorance" from which the child must be protected by the State. No one can question the State's duty to protect children from ignorance but this argument does not square with the facts disclosed in the record. Whatever their idiosyncrasies as seen by the majority, this record strongly shows that the Amish community has been a highly successful social unit within our society, even if apart from the conventional "mainstream." Its members are productive and very law-abiding members of society; they reject public welfare in any of its usual modern forms. The Congress itself recognized their self-sufficiency by authorizing exemption of such groups as the Amish from the obligation to pay social security taxes. 26 U.S.C. § 1402(h).

It is neither fair nor correct to suggest that the Amish are opposed to education beyond the eighth grade level. What this record shows is that they are opposed to conventional formal education of the type provided by a certified high school because it comes at the child's crucial adolescent period of religious development. Dr. Donald Erickson, for example, testified that their system of learning-by-doing was an "ideal system" of education in terms of preparing Amish children for life as adults in the Amish community, and that "I would be inclined to say they do a better job in this than most of the rest of us do." As he put it, "These people aren't purporting to be learned people, and it seems to me the self-sufficiency of the community is the best evidence I can point to—whatever is being done seems to function well."

We must not forget that in the Middle Ages important values of the civilization of the Western World were preserved by members of religious orders who isolated themselves from all worldly influences against great obstacles. There can be no assumption that today's majority is "right" and the Amish and others like them are "wrong." A way of life that is odd or even erratic but interferes with no rights or interests of others is not to be condemned because it is different.

The State, however, supports its interest in providing an additional one or two years of compulsory high school education to Amish children because of the possibility that some such children will choose to leave the Amish community, and that if this occurs they will be ill-equipped for life. The State argues that if Amish children leave their church they should not be in the position of making their way in the world without the education available in the one or two additional years the State requires. However, on this record, that argument is highly speculative. There is no specific evidence of the loss of Amish adherents by attrition, nor is there any showing that upon leaving the Amish community Amish children, with their practical agricultural training and habits of industry and self-reliance, would become burdens on society because of educational short-comings. Indeed, this argument of the State appears to rest primarily on the State's mistaken assumption, already noted, that the Amish do not provide any education for their children beyond the eighth grade, but allow them to grow in "ignorance." To the contrary, not only do the Amish accept the necessity for formal schooling through the eighth grade level, but continue to provide what has been characterized by the undisputed testimony of expert educators as an "ideal" vocational education for their children in the adolescent years.

There is nothing in this record to suggest that the Amish qualities of reliability, self-reliance, and dedication to work would fail to find ready markets in today's society. Absent some contrary evidence supporting the State's position, we are unwilling to assume that persons possessing such valuable vocational skills and habits are doomed to become burdens on society should they determine to leave the Amish faith, nor is there any basis in the record to warrant a finding that an additional one or two years of formal school education beyond the eighth grade would serve to eliminate any such problem that might exist.

Insofar as the State's claim rests on the view that a brief additional period of formal education is imperative to enable the Amish to participate effectively and intelligently in our democratic process, it must fall. The Amish alternative to formal secondary school education has enabled them to function effectively in their day-to-day life under self-imposed limitations on relations with the world, and to survive and prosper in contemporary society as a separate, sharply identifiable and highly self-sufficient community for more than 200 years in this country. In itself this is strong evidence that they are capable of fulfilling the social and political responsibilities of citizenship without compelled attendance beyond the eighth grade at the price of jeopardizing their free exercise of religious belief. . . .

The requirement for compulsory education beyond the eighth grade is a relatively recent development in our history. Less than 60 years ago, the educational requirements of almost all of the States were satisfied by completion of the elementary grades, at least where the child was regularly and lawfully employed. The independence and successful social functioning of the Amish community for a period approaching almost three centuries and more than 200 years in this country are strong evidence that there is at best a speculative gain, in terms of meeting the duties of citizenship, from an additional one or two years of compulsory formal education. Against this background it would require a more particularized showing from the State on this point to justify the severe interference with religious freedom such additional compulsory attendance would entail.

We should also note that compulsory education and child labor laws find their historical origin in common humanitarian instincts, and that the age limits of both laws have been coordinated to achieve their related objectives. . . .

The requirement of compulsory schooling to age 16 must be viewed as aimed not merely at providing educational opportunities for children, but as an alternative to the equally undesirable consequence of unhealthful child labor displacing adult workers, or, on the other hand, forced idleness. The two kinds of statutes—compulsory school attendance and child labor laws—tend to keep children of certain ages off the labor market and in school; this regimen in turn provides opportunity to prepare for a livelihood of a higher order than that which children could pursue without education and protects their health in adolescence.

In these terms, Wisconsin's interest in compelling the school attendance of Amish children to age 16 emerges as somewhat less substantial than requiring such attendance for children generally. For, while agricultural employment is not totally outside the legitimate concerns of the child labor laws, employment of children under parental guidance and on the family farm from age 14 to age 16 is an ancient tradition that lies at the periphery of the objectives of such laws. There is no intimation that the Amish employment of their children on family farms is in any way deleterious to their health or that Amish parents exploit children at tender years. Any such inference would be contrary to the record before us. Moreover, employment of Amish children on the family farm does not present the undesirable economic aspects of eliminating jobs that might otherwise be held by adults.

IV

Finally, the State, on authority of *Prince v. Massachusetts*, argues that a decision exempting Amish children from the State's requirement fails to recognize the substantive right of the Amish child to a secondary education, and fails to give due regard to the power of the State as *parens patriae* to extend the benefit of secondary education to children regardless of the wishes of their parents. Taken at its broadest sweep, the Court's language in *Prince*, might be read to give support to the State's position. However, the Court was not confronted in *Prince* with a situation comparable to that of the Amish as revealed in this record; this is shown by the Court's severe characterization of the evils that it thought the legislature could legitimately associate with child labor, even when performed in the company of an adult. 321 U.S., 169-170. The Court later took great care to confine *Prince* to a narrow scope in *Sherbert v. Verner*, when it stated:

> On the other hand, the Court has rejected challenges under the Free Exercise Clause to governmental regulation of certain overt acts prompted by religious beliefs or principles, for "even when the action is in accord with one's religious convictions, [it] is not totally free from legislative restrictions." *Braunfeld v. Brown* 366 U.S. 599, 603. The conduct or actions so regulated have invariably posed some substantial threat to public safety, peace or order. . . . 374 U.S., 402-403.

This case, of course, is not one in which any harm to the physical or mental health of the child or to the public safety, peace, order, or welfare has been demonstrated or may be properly inferred. The record is to the contrary, and any reliance on that theory would find no support in the evidence.

Contrary to the suggestion of the dissenting opinion of MR. JUSTICE DOUGLAS, our holding today in no degree depends on the assertion of the religious interest of the child as contrasted with that of the parents. It is the parents who are subject to prosecution here for failing to cause their children to attend school, and it is their right of free exercise, not that of their children, that must determine Wisconsin's power to impose criminal penalties on the parent. The dissent argues that a child who expresses a desire to attend public high school in conflict with the wishes of his parents should not be prevented from doing so. There is no reason for the Court to consider that point since it is not an issue in the case. The children are not parties to this litigation. The State has at no point tried this case on the theory that respondents were preventing their children from attending school against their expressed desires, and indeed the record is to the contrary. The State's position from the outset has been that it is empowered to apply its compulsory-attendance law to Amish parents in the same manner as to other parents—that is, without regard to the wishes of the child. That is the claim we reject today.

Our holding in no way determines the proper resolution of possible competing interests of parents, children, and the State in an appropriate state court proceeding in which the power of the State is asserted on the theory that Amish parents are preventing their minor children from attending high school despite their expressed desires to the contrary. Recognition of the claim of the State in such a proceeding would, of course, call into question traditional concepts of parental control over the religious up-bringing and education of their minor children recognized in this Court's past decisions. It is clear that such an intrusion by a State into family decisions in the area of religious training would give rise to grave questions of religious freedom comparable to those raised here and those presented in *Pierce v. Society of Sisters*, 268 U.S. 510 (1925). On this record we neither reach nor decide those issues. . . .

Indeed it seems clear that if the State is empowered, as *parens patriae*, to "save" a child from himself or his Amish parents by requiring an additional two years of compulsory formal high school education, the State will in large measure influence, if not determine, the religious future of the child. Even more markedly than in *Prince*, therefore, this case involves the fundamental interest of parents, as contrasted with that of the State, to guide the religious future and education of their children. The history and culture of Western civilization reflect a strong tradition of parental concern for the nurture and upbringing of their children. This primary role of the parents in the upbringing of their children is now established beyond debate as an enduring American tradition. If not the first, perhaps the most significant statements of the Court in this area are found in *Pierce v. Society of Sisters*, in which the Court observed:

> Under the doctrine of *Meyer v. Nebraska*, 262 U.S. 390, we think it entirely plain that the Act of 1922 unreasonably interferes with the liberty of parents and guardians to direct the upbringing and education of children under their control. As often heretofore pointed out, rights guaranteed by the Constitution may not be abridged by legislation which has no reasonable relation to some purpose within the competency of the State. The fundamental theory of liberty upon which all governments in this Union repose excludes any general power of the State to standardize its children by forcing them to accept instruction from public teachers only. The child is not the mere creature of the State; those who nurture him and direct his destiny have the right, coupled with the high duty, to recognize and prepare him for additional obligations. 268 U.S., 534-535.

The duty to prepare the child for "additional obligations," referred to by the Court, must be read to include the inculcation of moral standards, religious beliefs, and elements of good citizenship. *Pierce*, of course, recognized that where nothing more than the general interest of the parent in the nurture and education of his children is involved, it is beyond dispute that the State acts "reasonably" and constitutionally in requiring education to age 16 in some public or private school meeting the standards prescribed by the State.

However read, the Court's holding in *Pierce* stands as a charter of the rights of parents to direct the religious up-bringing of their children. And, when the interests of parenthood are combined with a free exercise claim of the nature revealed by this record, more than merely a "reasonable relation to some purpose within the competency of the State" is required to sustain the validity of the State's requirement under the First Amendment. To be sure, the power of the parent, even when linked to a free exercise claim, may be subject to limitation under *Prince* if it appears that parental decisions will jeopardize the health or safety of the child, or have a potential for significant social burdens. But in this case, the Amish have introduced persuasive evidence undermining the arguments the State has advanced to support its claims in terms of the welfare of the child and society as a whole. The record strongly indicates that accommodating the religious objections of the Amish by forgoing one, or at most two, additional years of compulsory education will not impair the physical or mental health of the child, or result in an inability to be self-supporting or to discharge the duties and responsibilities of citizenship, or in any other way materially detract from the welfare of society.

In the face of our consistent emphasis on the central values underlying the Religion Clauses in our constitutional scheme of government, we cannot accept a *parens patriae* claim of such all-encompassing scope and with such sweeping potential for broad and unforeseeable application as that urged by the State.

V

For the reasons stated we hold, with the Supreme Court of Wisconsin, that the First and Fourteenth Amendments prevent the State from compelling respondents to cause their children to attend formal high school to age 16.[22] Our disposition of this case, however, in no way alters our recognition of the obvious fact that courts are not school boards or legislatures, and are ill-equipped to determine the "necessity" of discrete aspects of a State's program of compulsory education. This should suggest that courts must move with great circumspection in performing the sensitive and delicate task of weighing a State's legitimate social concern when faced with religious claims for exemption from generally applicable educational requirements. It cannot be over-emphasized that we are not dealing with a way of life and mode of education by a group claiming to have recently discovered some "progressive" or more enlightened process for rearing children for modern life.

Aided by a history of three centuries as an identifiable religious sect and a long history as a successful and self-sufficient segment of American society, the Amish in this case have convincingly demonstrated the sincerity of their religious beliefs, the interrelationship of belief with their mode of life, the vital role that belief and daily conduct play in the continued survival of Old Order Amish communities and their religious organization, and the hazards presented by the State's enforcement of a statute generally valid as to others. Beyond this, they have carried the even more difficult burden of demonstrating the adequacy of their alternative mode of continuing informal vocational education in terms of precisely those overall interests that the State advances in support of its program of compulsory high school education. In light of this convincing showing, one that probably few other religious groups or sects could make, and weighing the minimal difference between what the State would require and what the Amish already accept, it was incumbent on the State to show with more particularity how its admittedly strong interest in

---

[22] What we have said should meet the suggestion that the decision of the Wisconsin Supreme Court recognizing an exemption for the Amish from the State's system of compulsory education constituted an impermissible establishment of religion. In *Walz v. Tax Commission*, the Court saw the three main concerns against which the Establishment Clause sought to protect as "sponsorship, financial support, and active involvement of the sovereign in religious activity." 397 U.S. 664, 668 (1970). Accommodating the religious beliefs of the Amish can hardly be characterized as sponsorship or active involvement. The purpose and effect of such an exemption are not to support, favor, advance, or assist the Amish, but to allow their centuries-old religious society, here long before the advent of any compulsory education, to survive free from the heavy impediment compliance with the Wisconsin compulsory-education law would impose. Such an accommodation "reflects nothing more than the governmental obligation of neutrality in the face of religious differences, and does not represent that involvement of religious with secular institutions which it is the object of the Establishment Clause to forestall." *Sherber v. Verner*, 374 U.S. 398, 409 (1963).

compulsory education would be adversely affected by granting an exemption to the Amish.

Nothing we hold is intended to undermine the general applicability of the State's compulsory school-attendance statutes or to limit the power of the State to promulgate reasonable standards that, while not impairing the free exercise of religion, provide for continuing agricultural vocational education under parental and church guidance by the Old Order Amish or others similarly situated. The States have had a long history of amicable and effective relationships with church-sponsored schools, and there is no basis for assuming that, in this related context, reasonable standards cannot be established concerning the content of the continuing vocational education of Amish children under parental guidance, provided always that state regulations are not inconsistent with what we have said in this opinion.

*Affirmed.*

⬛ MR. JUSTICE POWELL and MR. JUSTICE REHNQUIST took no part in the consideration or decision of this case.

⬛ MR. JUSTICE STEWART, with whom MR. JUSTICE BRENNAN joins, concurring.

This case involves the constitutionality of imposing criminal punishment upon Amish parents for their religiously based refusal to compel their children to attend public high schools. Wisconsin has sought to brand these parents as criminals for following their religious beliefs, and the Court today rightly holds that Wisconsin cannot constitutionally do so.

This case in no way involves any questions regarding the right of the children of Amish parents to attend public high schools, or any other institutions of learning, if they wish to do so. As the Court points out, there is no suggestion whatever in the record that the religious beliefs of the children here concerned differ in any way from those of their parents. . . .

It is clear to me, therefore, that this record simply does not present the interesting and important issue discussed in Part II of the dissenting opinion of MR. JUSTICE DOUGLAS. With this observation, I join the opinion and the judgment of the Court.

⬛ MR. JUSTICE WHITE, with whom MR. JUSTICE BRENNAN and MR. JUSTICE STEWART join, concurring.

Cases such as this one inevitably call for a delicate balancing of important but conflicting interests. I join the opinion and judgment of the Court because I cannot say that the State's interest in requiring two more years of compulsory education in the ninth and tenth grades outweighs the importance of the concededly sincere Amish religious practice to the survival of that sect.

This would be a very different case for me if respondent's claim were that their religion forbade their children from attending any school at any time and from complying in any way with the educational standards set by the State. Since the Amish children are permitted to acquire the basic tools of literacy to survive in modern society by attending grades one through eight and since the deviation from the State's compulsory-education law is relatively slight, I conclude that respondents' claim must prevail, largely because "religious

freedom—the freedom to believe and to practice strange and, it may be, foreign creeds—has classically been one of the highest values of our society."
*Braunfeld v. Brown* 366 U.S. 599, 612 (1961) (BRENNAN, J., concurring and
dissenting).

The importance of the state interest asserted here cannot be denigrated,
however:

> Today, education is perhaps the most important function of state and local
> governments. Compulsory school attendance laws and the great expendi-
> tures for education both demonstrate our recognition of the importance
> of education to our democratic society. It is required in the performance
> of our most basic public responsibilities, even service in the armed forces.
> It is the very foundation of good citizenship. Today it is a principal in-
> strument in awakening the child to cultural values, in preparing him for
> later professional training, and in helping him to adjust normally to his
> environment. *Brown v. Board of Education,* 347 U.S. 483, 493 (1954).

As recently as last Term, the Court re-emphasized the legitimacy of the
State's concern for enforcing minimal educational standards, *Lemon v. Kurtzman* 403 U.S. 602, 613 (1971). *Pierce v. Society of Sisters* 268 U.S. 510 (1925),
lends no support to the contention that parents may replace state educational
requirements with their own idiosyncratic views of what knowledge a child
needs to be a productive and happy member of society; in *Pierce*, both the
parochial and military schools were in compliance with all the educational
standards that the State had set, and the Court held simply that while a State
may posit such standards, it may not pre-empt the educational process by
requiring children to attend public schools. In the present case, the State is
not concerned with the maintenance of an educational system as an end in
itself, it is rather attempting to nurture and develop the human potential of its
children, whether Amish or non-Amish: to expand their knowledge, broaden
their sensibilities, kindle their imagination, foster a spirit of free inquiry, and
increase their human understanding and tolerance. It is possible that most
Amish children will wish to continue living the rural life of their parents, in
which case their training at home will adequately equip them for their future
role. Others, however, may wish to become nuclear physicists, ballet dancers,
computer programmers, or historians, and for these occupations, formal training will be necessary. There is evidence in the record that many children desert
the Amish faith when they come of age. A State has a legitimate interest not
only in seeking to develop the latent talents of its children but also in seeking
to prepare them for the life style that they may later choose, or at least to provide them with an option other than the life they have led in the past. In the
circumstances of this case, although the question is close, I am unable to say
that the State has demonstrated that Amish children who leave school in the
eighth grade will be intellectually stultified or unable to acquire new academic
skills later. The statutory minimum school attendance age set by the State is,
after all, only 16.

Decision in cases such as this and the administration of an exemption for
Old Order Amish from the State's compulsory school-attendance laws will
inevitably involve the kind of close and perhaps repeated scrutiny of religious
practices, as is exemplified in today's opinion, which the Court has heretofore
been anxious to avoid. But such entanglement does not create a forbidden

establishment of religion where it is essential to implement free exercise values threatened by an otherwise neutral program instituted to foster some permissible, nonreligious state objective. I join the Court because the sincerity of the Amish religious policy here is uncontested, because the potentially adverse impact of the state requirement is great, and because the State's valid interest in education has already been largely satisfied by the eight years the children have already spent in school.

⊞ MR. JUSTICE DOUGLAS, dissenting in part.

### I

I agree with the Court that the religious scruples of the Amish are opposed to the education of their children beyond the grade schools, yet I disagree with the Court's conclusion that the matter is within the dispensation of parents alone. The Court's analysis assumes that the only interests at stake in the case are those of the Amish parents on the one hand, and those of the State on the other. The difficulty with this approach is that, despite the Court's claim, the parents are seeking to vindicate not only their own free exercise claims, but also those of their high-school-age children.

It is argued that the right of the Amish children to religious freedom is not presented by the facts of the case, as the issue before the Court involves only the Amish parents' religious freedom to defy a state criminal statute imposing upon them an affirmative duty to cause their children to attend high school.

First, respondents' motion to dismiss in the trial court expressly asserts, not only the religious liberty of the adults, but also that of the children, as a defense to the prosecutions. It is, of course, beyond question that the parents have standing as defendants in a criminal prosecution to assert the religious interests of their children as a defense. Although the lower courts and a majority of this Court assume an identity of interest between parent and child, it is clear that they have treated the religious interest of the child as a factor in the analysis.

Second, it is essential to reach the question to decide the case, not only because the question was squarely raised in the motion to dismiss, but also because no analysis of religious-liberty claims can take place in a vacuum. If the parents in this case are allowed a religious exemption, the inevitable effect is to impose the parents' notions of religious duty upon their children. Where the child is mature enough to express potentially conflicting desires, it would be an invasion of the child's rights to permit such an imposition without canvassing his views. As in *Prince v. Massachusetts*, it is an imposition resulting from this very litigation. As the child has no other effective forum, it is in this litigation that his rights should be considered. And, if an Amish child desires to attend high school, and is mature enough to have that desire respected, the State may well be able to override the parents' religiously motivated objections. . . .

### II . . .

On this important and vital matter of education, I think the children should be entitled to be heard. While the parents, absent dissent, normally speak for the entire family, the education of the child is a matter on which the child will often have decided views. He may want to be a pianist or an astronaut or an oceanographer. To do so he will have to break from the Amish tradition.

It is the future of the student, not the future of the parents, that is imperiled by today's decision. If a parent keeps his child out of school beyond the grade school, then the child will be forever barred from entry into the new and amazing world of diversity that we have today. The child may decide that that is the preferred course, or he may rebel. It is the student's judgment, not his parents', that is essential if we are to give full meaning to what we have said about the Bill of Rights and of the right of students to be masters of their own destiny. . . .

### III

I think the emphasis of the Court on the "law and order" record of this Amish group of people is quite irrelevant. A religion is a religion irrespective of what the misdemeanor or felony records of its members might be. I am not at all sure how the Catholics, Episcopalians, the Baptists, Jehovah's Witnesses, the Unitarians, and my own Presbyterians would make out if subjected to such a test. . . .

The Court rightly rejects the notion that actions, even though religiously grounded, are always outside the protection of the Free Exercise Clause of the First Amendment. In so ruling, the Court departs from the teaching of *Reynolds v. United States* 98 U.S. 145, 164, where it was said concerning the reach of the Free Exercise Clause of the First Amendment, "Congress was deprived of all legislative power over mere opinion, but was left free to reach actions which were in violation of social duties or subversive of good order." In that case it was conceded that polygamy was a part of the religion of the Mormons. Yet the Court said, "It matters not that his belief [in polygamy] was a part of his professed religion: it was still belief, and belief only." *Id.* at 167.

Action, which the Court deemed to be antisocial, could be punished even though it was grounded on deeply held and sincere religious convictions. What we do today, at least in this respect, opens the way to give organized religion a broader base than it has ever enjoyed; and it even promises that in time *Reynolds* will be overruled. . . .

---

### NOTES AND QUESTIONS

1. The state of Wisconsin offered a number of arguments in support of its claim that the state's uniform requirement for school attendance to age 16 must apply uniformly to all citizens. What were those arguments? How did the Court respond to them? Was it enough, for example, that the state asserted a broad interest in its system of compulsory education?

2. The *Yoder* majority distinguished the case from the facts in *Prince v. Massachusetts* (upholding a ban on children distributing religious literature) (discussed in chapter 5) on the grounds that the state had a greater interest in child protection in that case. Even though the majority characterized *Prince* as involving "child labor"—a loaded term that overstates the facts in *Prince*—aren't the state's *parens patriae* interests in education equally as compelling? What other facts exist in *Yoder* that tip the balance in favor of the Amish parents? Consider whether the *Yoder* Court could alternatively have decided the case based on the third step in the *Sherbert* test.

3. Is the *Yoder* holding unique and limited to its particular facts, as several commentators have argued, or does it have wider application for other free exercise claims? Would this case have turned out differently if the Amish had objected to mandatory formal education of any kind for their children? Would the case have turned out differently if the expected impact of requiring compliance with this general law was less severe for the Amish community? Would the case have turned out differently if it had involved a religious group that did not place any value on learning past the age of 16? If you answered "yes" to any of these questions, what does *Yoder* tell us about how to apply the compelling interest test in free exercise cases?

4. The Court states that its decision "in no way determines the proper resolution of possible competing interests of parents, children, and the State in an appropriate state court proceeding in which the power of the State is asserted on the theory that Amish parents are preventing their minor children from attending high school despite their expressed desires to the contrary." How does Justice Douglas respond to this statement in his opinion? Who do you think is more persuasive on this point?

## REFINING THE *SHERBERT* TEST

Neither of the laws involved in *Sherbert* and *Yoder* singled out religion or religiously motivated conduct for disparate treatment (i.e., purposeful discrimination against religion). Rather, both laws were religiously neutral—meaning that they regulated all related conduct regardless of the motives of the actor. Still, the Court found that even neutral laws of generally applicability can impose burdens on religious practice, thus possibly requiring the government to provide a weighty justification for its regulation and/or provide an exemption from its enforcement. But by identifying the compelling interest test as the appropriate standard in free exercise challenges to neutral laws, the Court invited other questions. What constitutes a burden on religion, and how significant must that burden be (and how is that significance measured, objectively or subjectively)? How central must the regulated practice be to one's theological system or to recognized church doctrine, if at all? What if one's beliefs change, such that a religious objection to a regulation grows over time? And under what circumstances is a government's interest sufficiently compelling so as to outweigh the burden on religion?

A different kind of Amish case came before the Court in 1982. The Amish believe in taking care of their own aged and sick members rather than relying on government assistance. Furthermore, as part of their separation from government, they do not want to pay any Social Security or welfare taxes or receive any benefits. Given the Amish's attitude and self-sufficiency, Congress exempted self-employed Amish from paying Social Security taxes, 26 U.S.C. 1402(g). In *United States v. Lee*, an Amish employer tried to extend that exemption by not withholding Social Security taxes on his Amish employees or paying the employer's share of those taxes. The government claimed Lee violated the law and charged him back taxes for the years he had not paid. Lee sued, claiming statutory and free exercise exemption from paying the Social Security taxes.

The Supreme Court decided in favor of the government. The law exempted self-employed Amish from paying the taxes, not Amish employers, even when their employees were Amish. The Congress had carved out a very narrow exemption, and the Court was not willing to go beyond it. The Court also accepted the government's compelling interest argument: the government could not allow randomly requested exemptions from paying taxes. It would seriously impair the effective administration of the Social Security program.

## UNITED STATES v. LEE
### 455 U.S. 252 (1982)

CHIEF JUSTICE BURGER delivered the opinion of the Court. . . .

### II

The exemption [from the requirement of withholding Social Security taxes] provided by § 1402(g) is available only to self-employed individuals and does not apply to employers or employees. Consequently, appellee and his employees are not within the express provisions of § 1402(g). . . .

Not all burdens on religion are unconstitutional. . . . The state may justify a limitation on religious liberty by showing that it is essential to accomplish an overriding governmental interest. . . .

The tax system could not function if denominations were allowed to challenge the tax system because tax payments were spent in a manner that violates their religious belief. . . . Because the broad public interest in maintaining a sound tax system is of such a high order, religious belief in conflict with the payment of taxes affords no basis for resisting the tax.

### III

Congress has accommodated, to the extent compatible with a comprehensive national program, the practices of those who believe it a violation of their faith to participate in the social security system. In § 1402(g) Congress granted an exemption, on religious grounds, to self-employed Amish and others. Confining the § 1402(g) exemption to the self-employed provided for a narrow category which was readily identifiable. Self-employed persons in a religious community having its own "welfare" system are distinguishable from the generality of wage earners employed by others. . . .

Granting an exemption from social security taxes to an employer operates to impose the employer's religious faith on the employees. Congress drew a line in § 1402(g), exempting the self-employed Amish but not all persons working for an Amish employer. The tax imposed on employers to support the social security system must be uniformly applicable to all, except as Congress provides explicitly otherwise. . . .

---

### NOTES AND QUESTIONS

1. A major reason for denying the tax relief claimed by the employer in *United States v. Lee* was the efficient administration of the tax system. Do you think that is a sufficient reason to outweigh a free exercise claim? Why or why not?

2. How is *Lee* distinguishable from *Sherbert* and *Yoder*? Is the burden on religion less in *Lee*, or is the government interest greater? Or is the Court troubled by the potential breadth of such an exemption in *Lee*, a concern diffused by the relatively unique situation presented in *Yoder*? Why is the Court willing in *Lee* to consider that a religious accommodation may result in a burden on third persons, but in *Yoder* was unwilling to consider the impact of the exemption on Amish children? To what extent should potential burdens on third persons be a factor in allowing a religious exemption from a law?

---

Other unemployment compensation cases came before the Court. They were all free exercise cases and decided by using the "*Sherbert* test." In *Thomas v. Review Board of Indiana Employment Security Division,* a Jehovah's Witness objected to being assigned to make military armaments. He worked in a steel mill and was satisfied with his job until he was transferred to a department that made turrets for military tanks. He cited religious objections to such work and, when his employer would not relieve him of it, he quit his job. As in *Sherbert*, he was denied unemployment compensation because he had quit his job even though work was available for him.

An interesting feature of this case is that other Jehovah's Witnesses working in the foundry had no objections to the making of armaments. The Indiana Employment Commission used this to argue that such labor was not against Jehovah's Witnesses' theology and this was another reason Thomas should be denied benefits. Still, the Court ruled in favor of Thomas.

---

## THOMAS v. REVIEW BOARD
### 450 U.S. 707 (1981)

CHIEF JUSTICE BURGER delivered the opinion of the Court. . . .

II

Only beliefs rooted in religion are protected by the Free Exercise Clause, which, by its terms, gives special protection to the exercise of religion. . . . The determination of what is a "religious" belief or practice is more often than not a difficult and delicate task, as the division in the Indiana Supreme Court attests. However, the resolution of that question is not to turn upon a judicial perception of the particular belief or practice in question; religious beliefs need not be acceptable, logical, consistent, or comprehensible to others in order to merit First Amendment protection. . . .

Courts should not undertake to dissect religious beliefs because the believer admits that he is "struggling" with his position or because his beliefs are not articulated with the clarity and precision that a more sophisticated person might employ.

The Indiana court also appears to have given significant weight to the fact that another Jehovah's Witness had no scruples about working on tank turrets; for that other Witness, at least, such work was "scripturally" acceptable. Intrafaith differences of that kind are not uncommon among followers of a particular creed, and the judicial process is singularly ill equipped to resolve such differences in relation to the Religion Clauses. One can, of course, imagine an asserted claim so bizarre, so clearly nonreligious in motivation, as not to be entitled to protection under the Free Exercise Clause; but that is not the case here, and the guarantee of free exercise is not limited to beliefs which are shared by all of the members of a religious sect. Particularly in this sensitive area, it is not within the judicial function and judicial competence to inquire whether the petitioner or his fellow worker more correctly perceived the commands of their common faith. Courts are not arbiters of scriptural interpretation. . . .

### III . . .

It is true that, as in *Sherbert*, the Indiana law does not compel a violation of conscience. But, "this is only the beginning, not the end, of our inquiry." 374 U.S., 403-404. In a variety of ways we have said that "[a] regulation neutral on its face may, in its application, nonetheless offend the constitutional requirement for governmental neutrality if it unduly burdens the free exercise of religion." *Wisconsin v. Yoder* 406 U.S., 220.

Here, as in *Sherbert*, the employee was put to a choice between fidelity to religious belief or cessation of work; the coercive impact on Thomas is indistinguishable from *Sherbert*, . . .

Where the state conditions receipt of an important benefit upon conduct proscribed by a religious faith, or where it denies such a benefit because of conduct mandated by religious belief, thereby putting substantial pressure on an adherent to modify his behavior and to violate his beliefs, a burden upon religion exists. While the compulsion may be indirect, the infringement upon free exercise is nonetheless substantial. . . .

When the focus of the inquiry is properly narrowed, however, we must conclude that the interests advanced by the State do not justify the burden placed on free exercise of religion.

▦ JUSTICE REHNQUIST, dissenting. . . .

[T]he Court today reads the Free Exercise Clause more broadly than is warranted. As to the proper interpretation of the Free Exercise Clause, I would accept the decision of *Braunfeld v. Brown* and the dissent in *Sherbert*. . . . Likewise in this case, it cannot be said that the State discriminated against Thomas on the basis of his religious beliefs or that he was denied benefits because he was a Jehovah's Witness. Where, as here, a State has enacted a general statute, the purpose and effect of which is to advance the State's secular goals, the Free Exercise Clause does not in my view require the State to conform that statute to the dictates of religious conscience of any group. . . . I believe that although a State could choose to grant exemptions to religious persons from state unemployment regulations, a State is not constitutionally compelled to do so.

The case of *Hobbie v. Unemployment Appeals Commission* was much like *Sherbert v. Verner*. A Seventh-day Adventist woman experienced a conflict with her work schedule due to her religious beliefs and practices. But whereas it was the employer's change of schedule that gave rise to the conflict in Ms. Sherbert's case, Ms. Hobbie's work schedule did not change. Instead, Hobbie's religious beliefs changed. In other words, Hobbie was content with her work schedule until she converted to the Adventist religion. Hobbie's employer then dismissed her because she could not work on Saturday. Consequently, Florida denied her unemployment compensation because she was "the agent of change." Citing *Sherbert* as precedent, the Court dismissed Florida's action and argument.

## HOBBIE v. UNEMPLOYMENT APPEALS COMMISSION OF FLORIDA
### 480 U.S. 136 (1987)

JUSTICE BRENNAN delivered the opinion of the Court. . . .

The Appeals Commission [that handled Hobbie's claim] . . . attempts to distinguish this case by arguing that, unlike the employees in *Sherbert* and *Thomas*, Hobbie was the "agent of change" and is therefore responsible for the consequences of the conflict between her job and her religious beliefs. . . .

In effect, the Appeals Commission asks us to single out the religious convert for different, less favorable treatment than that given an individual whose adherence to his or her faith precedes employment. We decline to do so. The First Amendment protects the free exercise rights of employees who adopt religious beliefs or convert from one faith to another after they are hired. The timing of Hobbie's conversion is immaterial to our determination that her free exercise rights have been burdened; the salient inquiry under the Free Exercise Clause is the burden involved. In *Sherbert*, *Thomas*, and the present case, the employee was forced to choose between fidelity to religious belief and continued employment; the forfeiture of unemployment benefits for choosing the former over the latter brings unlawful coercion to bear on the employee's choice.

Finally, we reject the Appeals Commission's argument that the awarding to benefits to Hobbie would violate the Establishment Clause. This Court has long recognized that the government may (and sometimes must) accommodate religious practices and that it may do so without violating the Establishment Clause. . . .

We conclude that Florida's refusal to award unemployment compensation benefits to appellant violated the Free Exercise Clause of the First Amendment. Here, as in *Sherbert* and *Thomas*, the State may not force an employee "to choose between following the precepts of her religion and forfeiting benefits, . . . and abandoning one of the precepts of her religion in order to accept work." *Sherbert*, 374 U.S., 404. . . .

———— •—•—• ————

Finally, *Frazee v. Illinois Department of Employment Security* involved a plaintiff who refused on religious grounds to work on Sunday. The state denied him unemployment compensation because he did not belong to a religious organization with a doctrine about
abstaining from work on Sunday. Justice Byron White acknowledged that in *Sherbert*,
*Thomas*, and *Hobbie* the plaintiffs belonged to denominations that taught the behavior
followed by those plaintiffs. But Justice White, writing for a unanimous Court, declared
that fact irrelevant in order for a claimant to receive free exercise protection.

———— •—•—• ————

## FRAZEE v. ILLINOIS EMPLOYMENT SECURITY DEPARTMENT
### 489 U.S. 829 (1989)

▓ Justice WHITE delivered the opinion of the Court . . .

We have had more than one occasion before today to consider denials of
unemployment compensation benefits to those who have refused work on the
basis of their religious beliefs. . . . In each of th[o]se cases, the appellant was
"forced to choose between fidelity to religious belief and . . . employment,"
and we found "the forfeiture of unemployment benefits for choosing the former over the latter brings unlawful coercion to bear on the employee's choice."
[*Hobbie*, 480 U.S., at 144]. . . .

Our judgments in those cases rested on the fact that each of the claimants
had a sincere belief that religion required him or her to refrain from the work
in question. Never did we suggest that unless a claimant belongs to a sect that
forbids what his job requires, his belief, however sincere, must be deemed a
purely personal preference rather than a religious belief. . . .

There is no doubt that "[o]nly beliefs rooted in religion are protected by
the Free Exercise Clause," *Thomas*, 450 U.S., at 713. Purely secular views do
not suffice. . . . We do not face problems about sincerity or about the religious
nature of Frazee's convictions, however. . . .

Frazee asserted that he was a Christian, but did not claim to be a member
of a particular Christian sect. It is also true that there are assorted Christian
denominations that do not profess to be compelled by their religion to refuse
Sunday work, but this does not diminish Frazee's protection flowing from the
Free Exercise Clause. . . .[W]e reject the notion that to claim the protection of
the Free Exercise Clause, one must be responding to the commands of a particular religious organization. Here, Frazee's refusal was based on a sincerely
held religious belief. Under our cases, he was entitled to invoke First Amendment protection. . . .

## NOTES AND QUESTIONS

1. In these unemployment compensation cases, can you generalize about why the Court consistently found in favor of the plaintiffs? Even though the facts of the cases are different, is there a common theme that runs through the cases that caused the Court to decide the way it did?

2. Some have argued that the "*Sherbert* test" requires that the plaintiff be an adherent of a religion that demands the behavior in question. Does the *Frazee* case nullify that requirement? If so, how are government agencies to ensure that the motivation in question is religious, so as to satisfy the Court's statement from *Thomas* that "Only beliefs rooted in religion are protected by the Free Exercise Clause"?

3. Can you make an argument that *Hobbie* and *Frazee* are the logical extensions of the *Sherbert* rule but, at the same time, placed the rule in jeopardy? Is a government equipped to anticipate and accommodate religious claims that are increasingly individualistic and idiosyncratic? Do the government's interests in uniformity and efficiency (as discussed in *Lee*) increase as claims become more idiosyncratic, or are these the very claims most in need of protection under the Free Exercise Clause?

---

### FREE EXERCISE IN TRANSITION

The Court was confronted with other kinds of Free Exercise Clause issues than just unemployment compensation cases in the 1980s. In many of these cases the Court was not as expansive in its interpretation of the free exercise principle as it had been in *Sherbert* and its progeny. Indeed, scholars debate whether the Court abandoned the *Sherbert* compelling state interest test in these cases. Justice Scalia, in his opinion in the important case of *Employment Division of Oregon v. Smith*, discussed below, explicitly argued that the Court did not employ *Sherbert* in the line of cases just ahead. Others believe that it is implicit in these cases.

*Bowen v. Roy* was a Native American case. Roy, of the Abenaki Tribe, protested when the Pennsylvania Department of Public Welfare and the federal government assigned his young daughter, Little Bird of the Snow, a Social Security number as necessary for her to receive welfare services. He claimed his tribal religion believed that her having such an individual identification number would "rob her of her spirit," a matter of considerable importance in Native American religion. He invoked the Free Exercise Clause to say his family's religious beliefs and practices should be honored; his daughter should not have a Social Security number. When it was discovered, late in the trial, that Little Bird of the Snow already had a Social Security number, Roy then argued that it should not be used; its use would deprive her of her spiritual nature.

In an opinion written by Chief Justice Warren Burger, the Court ruled against Roy. He held the government cannot be compelled to alter its programs and procedures to accommodate individual's or groups' religious beliefs and practices.

---

## BOWEN v. ROY
### 476 U.S. 693 (1986)

※ CHIEF JUSTICE BURGER announced the judgment of the Court. . . .

Never to our knowledge has the Court interpreted the First Amendment to require the Government *itself* to behave in ways that the individual believes will further his or her spiritual development or that of his or her family. The Free Exercise Clause simply cannot be understood to require the Government to conduct its own internal affairs in ways that comport with the religious beliefs of particular citizens. . . . "[T]he Free Exercise Clause is written in terms of what the government cannot do to the individual, not in terms of what the individual can extract from the government." *Sherbert v. Verner*, 374 U.S. 398, 412 (1963) (Douglas, J., concurring).

As a result, Roy may no more prevail on his religious objection to the Government's use of a Social Security number for his daughter than he could on a sincere religious objection to the size or color of the Government's filing cabinets. The Free Exercise Clause affords an individual protection from certain forms of governmental compulsion; it does not afford an individual a right to dictate the conduct of the Government's internal procedures. . . .

### III (Plurality)

The First Amendment's guarantee that "Congress shall make no law . . . prohibiting the free exercise" of religion holds an important place in our scheme of ordered liberty, but the Court has steadfastly maintained that claims of religious conviction do not automatically entitle a person to fix unilaterally the conditions and terms of dealings with the Government. Not all burdens on religion are unconstitutional. . . .

The statutory requirement that applicants provide a Social Security number is wholly neutral in religious terms and uniformly applicable. There is no claim that there is any attempt by Congress to discriminate invidiously or any covert suppression of particular religious beliefs. . . .

We conclude then that government regulation that indirectly and incidentally calls for a choice between securing a government benefit and adherence to religious beliefs is wholly different from governmental action or legislation that criminalizes inspired activity or inescapably compels that some find objectionable for religious reasons. Although the denial of government benefits over religious objection can raise serious Free Exercise problems, these two very different forms of government action are not governed by the same constitutional standard. . . .

[A] policy decision by a government that it wishes to treat all applicants alike and that it does not wish to become involved in case-by-case inquiries into the genuineness of each religious objection to such condition or restrictions is entitled to substantial deference. Moreover, legitimate interests are implicated in the need to avoid any appearance of favoring religious over nonreligious applicants.

The test applied in cases like *Wisconsin v. Yoder*, 406 U.S. 205 (1972), is not appropriate in this setting. In the enforcement of a facially neutral and uniformly applicable requirement for the administration of welfare programs reaching many millions of people, the Government is entitled to wide latitude. The Government should not be put to the strict test applied by the District Court; that standard required the Government to justify enforcement of the use of Social Security number requirement as the least restrictive means of accomplishing a compelling state interest. Absent proof of an intent to discriminate against particular religious beliefs or against religion in general, the Government meets its burden when it demonstrates that a challenged requirement for governmental benefits, neutral and uniform in its application, is a reasonable means of promoting a legitimate public interest. . . .

Here there is nothing whatever suggesting antagonism by Congress towards religion generally or towards any particular religious beliefs. The requirement that applicants provide a Social Security number is facially neutral and applies to all applicants for the benefits involved. Congress has made no provision for individual exemptions to the requirement in the two statutes in question. . . .

The Social Security number requirement clearly promotes a legitimate and important public interest. No one can doubt that preventing fraud in these benefits programs is an important goal. . . .

We also think it plain that the Social Security number requirement is a reasonable means of promoting that goal. The programs at issue are of truly staggering magnitude. . . .

[W]e know of no case obligating the Government to tolerate a slight risk of "one or perhaps a few individuals" fraudulently obtaining benefits in order to satisfy a religious objection to a requirement designed to combat that very risk. Appellees may not use the Free Exercise Clause to demand Government benefits, but only on their own terms, particularly where that insistence works a demonstrable disadvantage to the Government in the administration of the programs. . . .

We conclude that the Congress' refusal to grant appellees a special exemption does not violate the Free Exercise Clause. . . .

⊞ JUSTICE O'CONNOR, with whom JUSTICE BRENNAN and JUSTICE MARSHALL join, concurring in part and dissenting in part.

. . . Given that a majority of the Court believes that the Government may use and disseminate information already in its possession . . . there is probably less remaining in this case than meets the eye. The interest asserted by the Government before the District Court could be wholly served after accommodating appellees' sincere religious beliefs . . . .

The Government has identified its goal as preventing fraud and abuse in the welfare system, a goal that is both laudable and compelling. The District Court, however, soundly rejected the Government's assertion that provision of the Social Security number was necessary to prevent such fraud and abuse. . . . The District Court's generalized evaluation of the asserted indispensability of the Social Security number similarly undermines the Government's claim here: "*The government's interest* in preventing Little Bird of the Snow from fraudulently receiving welfare benefits *can be satisfied without requiring a social security number* for Little Bird of the Snow." (Emphasis added.)

Faced with these facts, however, THE CHIEF JUSTICE not only believes appellees themselves must provide a Social Security number to the Government before receiving benefits, but he also finds it necessary to invoke a new standard to be applied to test the validity of Government regulations under the Free Exercise Clause. He would uphold any facially neutral and uniformly applicable governmental requirement if the Government shows its rule to be "a reasonable means of promoting a legitimate public interest." Such a test has no basis in precedent and relegates a serious First Amendment value to the barest level of minimal scrutiny that the Equal Protection Clause already provides. I would apply our long line of precedents to hold that the Government must accommodate a legitimate free exercise claim unless pursuing an especially important interest by narrowly tailored means. . . .

Granting an exemption to Little Bird of the Snow, and to the handful of others who can be expected to make a similar religious objection to providing the Social Security number in conjunction with the receipt of welfare benefits, will not demonstrably diminish the Government's ability to combat welfare fraud. The District Court found that the governmental appellants had hardly shown that a significant number of other individuals were likely to make a claim similar to that at issue here:

"There have been four reported cases involving challenges to the social security number requirement for welfare benefits based upon the contention that the number violates sincerely held religious beliefs of the welfare recipient." 590 F. Supp., at 607. . . .

This Court's opinions have never turned on so slender a reed as whether the challenged requirement is merely a "reasonable means of promoting a legitimate public interest." (opinion of BURGER, C. J.). THE CHIEF JUSTICE appears to believe that the added inconvenience to the State of administering a selective exemption overbalances any burden on individual religious exercise. But this Court has held that administrative inconvenience is not alone sufficient to justify a burden on free exercise unless it creates problems of substantial magnitude. See *Sherbert v. Verner*, 374 U.S., at 408-409. And as Part II of THE CHIEF JUSTICE's opinion makes clear, there is essentially no administrative burden imposed on the Government in this case.

Appellants have rested their case on vague allegations of administrative inconvenience and harm to the public fisc that are wholly unsubstantiated by the record and the findings of the District Court. The Court simply cannot, consistent with its precedents, distinguish this case from the wide variety of factual situations in which the Free Exercise Clause indisputably imposes significant constraints upon government. Indeed, five Members of the Court agree that *Sherbert* and *Thomas*, in which the government was required to accommodate sincere religious beliefs, control the outcome of this case to the extent it is not moot.

THE CHIEF JUSTICE's distinction between this case and the Court's previous decisions on free exercise claims—that here "it is appellees who seek benefits from the Government and who assert that . . . they should be excused from compliance with a condition that is binding on all other persons who seek the same benefits from the Government"—has been directly rejected. The fact that the underlying dispute involves an award of benefits rather than an exaction of penalties does not grant the Government license to apply a different version of the Constitution. . . .

Our precedents have long required the Government to show that a compelling state interest is served by its refusal to grant a religious exemption. The

Government here has clearly and easily met its burden of showing that the prevention of welfare fraud is a compelling governmental goal. If the Government could meet its compelling needs only by refusing to grant a religious exemption, and chose a narrowly tailored means to do so, then the Government would prevail. But the Government has failed to show that granting a religious exemption to those who legitimately object to providing a Social Security number will do any harm to its compelling interest in preventing welfare fraud.

## NOTES AND QUESTIONS

1. The plurality writes that choosing between acquiring a government benefit and adhering to a religious belief is quite different from legislation that criminalized religious activity. But wasn't the former the exact situation in *Sherbert* where the Court found for the claimant? Has the Court's notion of an actionable religious burden changed?

2. Note that in *Bowen* the Court deferred to the government's rationale for imposing its rule: the prevention of fraud and the efficient administration of the Social Security system. As you remember, in *Sherbert*, prevention of fraud (as a reason not to recognize the religious claim) failed as a compelling interest, but in *Bowen*, the fraud-prevention rationale prevailed. What explains the difference?

   Did the standard for judging free exercise burdens change in *Bowen*, or were the fraud concerns with respect to the Social Security system more significant? Or was there some difference between the exemptions sought in *Sherbert* and *Bowen*, that in the latter case the government would have had to do more than merely exempt the claimant from its internal rule, but also change its internal operating procedures?

3. In her opinion, Justice O'Connor argues that the plurality has indefensibly departed from the proper constitutional standard for the evaluation of free exercise claims. Is she correct? Or was the plurality justified in using a different analysis in *Bowen* than the Court did in cases such as *Sherbert* and *Yoder*?

In *Bowen v. Roy*, the Court wrote that the government's use of the Social Security number "does not itself in any degree impair Roy's freedom to believe, express and exercise his religion." Compare the burden on religious practice in *Bowen* with that of the claimants in the following case.

In *Lyng v. Northwest Indian Cemetery Protective Association*, a tract of land in California that had long served Indians as sacred land, that is, a place for meditation and communing with the spirit world, had become federal property. The government allowed logging operations on the land. To facilitate logging, a road was built through the area. However, the tribal associations had gained an injunction to prevent the completion of the road. The government was determined, however, so this suit was brought by the Indians to permanently stop the completion of the road. They claimed the government's action would violate their free exercise of religion.

The Court, with Justice Sandra Day O'Connor writing for the majority, ruled against the Indians, using *Bowen v. Roy* as precedent. Although she acknowledged the action would be devastating to Indian religious practices, she said the government did not have to modify its procedures to accommodate them.

---

## LYNG v. NORTHWEST INDIAN CEMETERY PROTECTION ASSOCIATION
### 485 U.S. 439 (1988)

▓ JUSTICE O'CONNOR delivered the opinion of the Court.

This case requires us to consider whether the First Amendment's Free Exercise Clause prohibits the Government from permitting timber harvesting in, or constructing a road through, a portion of a National Forest that has traditionally been used for religious purposes by members of three American Indian tribes in northwestern California. We conclude that it does not. . . .

III

A

The Free Exercise Clause of the First Amendment provides that "Congress shall make no law . . . prohibiting the free exercise [of religion]." It is undisputed that the Indian respondents' beliefs are sincere and that the Government's proposed actions will have severe adverse effects on the practice of their religion. Those respondents contend that the burden on their religious practices is heavy enough to violate the Free Exercise Clause unless the Government can demonstrate a compelling need to complete the G[asquet]-O[rleans] road or to engage in timber harvesting in the Chimney Rock area. We disagree.

In *Bowen v. Roy*, we considered a challenge to a federal statute that required the States to use Social Security numbers in administering certain welfare programs. Two applicants for benefits under these programs contended that their religious beliefs prevented them from acceding to the use of a Social Security number for their 2-year-old daughter because the use of a numerical identifier would "'rob the spirit' of [their] daughter and prevent her from attaining greater spiritual power." *Id*. 476 U.S. 693, 696. Similarly, in this case, it is said that disruption of the natural environment caused by the G-O road will diminish the sacredness of the area in question and create distractions that will interfere with "training and ongoing religious experience of individuals using [sites within] the area for personal medicine and growth . . . and as integrated parts of a system of religious belief and practice which correlates ascending degrees of personal power with a geographic hierarchy of power." The Court rejected this kind of challenge in *Roy*:

> The Free Exercise Clause simply cannot be understood to require the Government to conduct its own internal affairs in ways that comport with the religious beliefs of particular citizens. Just as the Government may not insist that [the Roys] engage in any set form of religious observance, so [they] may not demand that the Government join in their chosen religious practices by refraining from using a number to identify their daughter. . . .

. . . The Free Exercise Clause affords an individual protection from certain forms of governmental compulsion; it does not afford an individual a right to dictate the conduct of the Government's internal procedures. 476 U.S., 699 -700.

The building of a road or the harvesting of timber on publicly owned land cannot meaningfully be distinguished from the use of a Social Security number in *Roy*. In both cases, the challenged Government action would interfere significantly with private persons' ability to pursue spiritual fulfillment according to their own religious beliefs. In neither case, however, would the affected individuals be coerced by the Government's action into violating their religious beliefs; nor would either governmental action penalize religious activity by denying any person an equal share of the rights, benefits, and privileges enjoyed by other citizens.

We are asked to distinguish this case from *Roy* on the ground that the infringement on religious liberty here is "significantly greater," or on the ground that the Government practice in *Roy* was "purely mechanical" whereas this case involves "a case-by-case substantive determination as to how a particular unit of land will be managed." Similarly, we are told that this case can be distinguished from *Roy* because "the government action is not at some physically removed location where it places no restriction on what a practitioner may do." The State suggests that the Social Security number in *Roy* "could be characterized as interfering with Roy's religious tenets from a subjective point of view, where the government's conduct of 'its own internal affairs' was known to him only secondhand and did not interfere with his ability to practice his religion." In this case, however, it is said that the proposed road will "physically destro[y] the environmental conditions and the privacy without which the [religious] practices cannot be conducted." *Ibid.*

These efforts to distinguish *Roy* are unavailing. This Court cannot determine the truth of the underlying beliefs that led to the religious objections here or in *Roy*, . . . and accordingly cannot weigh the adverse effects on the appellees in *Roy* and compare them with the adverse effects on the Indian respondents. Without the ability to make such comparisons, we cannot say that the one form of incidental interference with an individual's spiritual activities should be subjected to a different constitutional analysis than the other.

Respondents insist, nonetheless, that the courts below properly relied on a factual inquiry into the degree to which the Indians' spiritual practices would become ineffectual if the G-O road were built. They rely on several cases in which this Court has sustained free exercise challenges to government programs that interfered with individuals' ability to practice their religion. See *Wisconsin v. Yoder* (compulsory school-attendance law); *Sherbert v. Verner* (denial of unemployment benefits to applicant who refused to accept work requiring her to violate the Sabbath); *Thomas v. Review Board, Indiana Employment Security Div.* (denial of unemployment benefits to applicant whose religion forbade him to fabricate weapons); *Hobbie* (denial of unemployment benefits to religious convert who resigned position that required her to work on the Sabbath).

Even apart from the inconsistency between *Roy* and respondents' reading of these cases, their interpretation will not withstand analysis. It is true that this Court has repeatedly held that indirect coercion or penalties on the free exercise of religion, not just outright prohibitions, are subject to scrutiny under the First Amendment. Thus, for example, ineligibility for unemployment benefits, based solely on a refusal to violate the Sabbath, has been analogized to a fine imposed on Sabbath worship. *Sherbert*, 379 U.S., 404. This does not and cannot imply that incidental effects of government programs, which may make it more difficult to practice certain religions but which have no tendency to coerce individuals into acting contrary to their religious beliefs, require government to bring forward a compelling justification for its otherwise lawful actions. The crucial word in the constitutional text is "prohibit": "For the Free Exercise Clause is written in terms of what the government cannot do to the individual, not in terms of what the individual can exact from the government." *Sherbert*, 412 (Douglas, J., concurring).

Whatever may be the exact line between unconstitutional prohibitions on the free exercise of religion and the legitimate conduct by government of its own affairs, the location of the line cannot depend on measuring the effects of a governmental action on a religious objector's spiritual development. The Government does not dispute, and we have no reason to doubt, that the logging and road-building projects at issue in this case could have devastating effects on traditional Indian religious practices. Those practices are intimately and inextricably bound up with the unique features of the Chimney Rock area, which is known to the Indians as the "high country." Individual practitioners use this area for personal spiritual development; some of their activities are believed to be critically important in advancing the welfare of the Tribe, and indeed, of mankind itself. The Indians use this area, as they have used it for a very long time, to conduct a wide variety of specific rituals that aim to accomplish their religious goals. According to their beliefs, the rituals would not be efficacious if conducted at other sites than the ones traditionally used, and too much disturbance of the area's natural state would clearly render any meaningful continuation of traditional practices impossible. To be sure, the Indians themselves were far from unanimous in opposing the G-O road, and it seems less than certain that construction of the road will be so disruptive that it will doom their religion. Nevertheless, we can assume that the threat to the efficacy of at least some religious practices is extremely grave.

Even if we assume that we should accept the Ninth Circuit's prediction, according to which the G-O road will "virtually destroy the . . . Indians' ability to practice their religion," 795 F.2d, 693, the Constitution simply does not provide a principle that could justify upholding respondents' legal claims. However much we might wish that it were otherwise, government simply could not operate if it were required to satisfy every citizen's religious needs and desires. A broad range of government activities—from social welfare programs to foreign aid to conservation projects—will always be considered essential to the spiritual well-being of some citizens, often on the basis of sincerely held religious beliefs. Others will find the very same activities deeply offensive, and perhaps incompatible with their own search for spiritual fulfillment and with the tenets of their religion. The First Amendment must apply to all citizens alike, and it can give to none of them a veto over public programs that do not prohibit the free exercise of religion. The Constitution does not, and courts cannot, offer to reconcile the various competing demands on government, many of them rooted in sincere religious belief, that inevitably arise in so diverse a society as ours. That task, to the extent that it is feasible, is for the legislatures and other institutions.

One need not look far beyond the present case to see why the analysis in *Roy*, but not respondents' proposed extension of *Sherbert* and its progeny, offers a sound reading of the Constitution. Respondents attempt to stress the limits of the religious servitude that they are now seeking to impose on the Chimney Rock area of the Six Rivers National Forest. While defending an injunction against logging operations and the construction of a road, they apparently do not at present object to the area's being used by recreational visitors, other Indians, or forest rangers. Nothing in the principle for which they contend, however, would distinguish this case from another lawsuit in which they (or similarly situated religious objectors) might seek to exclude all human activity but their own from sacred areas of the public lands. The Indian respondents insist that "[p]rivacy during the power quests is required for the practitioners to maintain the purity needed for a successful journey." Similarly: "The practices conducted in the high country entail intense meditation and require the practitioner to achieve a profound awareness of the natural environment. Prayer seats are oriented so there is an unobstructed view, and the practitioner must be surrounded by *undisturbed* naturalness." No disrespect for these practices is implied when one notes that such beliefs could easily require *de facto* beneficial ownership of some rather spacious tracts of public property. Even without anticipating future cases, the diminution of the Government's property rights, and the concomitant subsidy of the Indian religion, would in this case be far from trivial: the District Court's order permanently forbade commercial timber harvesting, or the construction of a two-lane road, anywhere within an area covering a full 27 sections (i.e., more than 17,000 acres) of public land.

The Constitution does not permit government to discriminate against religions that treat particular physical sites as sacred, and a law prohibiting the Indian respondents from visiting the Chimney Rock area would raise a different set of constitutional questions. Whatever rights the Indians may have to the use of the area, however, those rights do not divest the Government of its right to use what is, after all, *its* land. . . .

B

Nothing in our opinion should be read to encourage governmental insensitivity to the religious needs of any citizen. The Government's rights to the use of its own land, for example, need not and should not discourage it from accommodating religious practices like those engaged in by the Indian respondents. It is worth emphasizing, therefore, that the Government has taken numerous steps in this very case to minimize the impact that construction of the G-O road will have on the Indians' religious activities. . . .

Except for abandoning its project entirely, and thereby leaving the two existing segments of road to dead-end in the middle of a National Forest, it is difficult to see how the Government could have been more solicitous. Such solicitude accords with "the policy of the United States to protect and preserve for American Indians their inherent right of freedom to believe, express, and exercise the traditional religions of the American Indian . . . including but not limited to access to sites, use and possession of sacred objects, and the freedom to worship through ceremonials and traditional rites." American Indian Religious Freedom Act (AIRFA), 92 Stat. 469, 42 U.S.C. 1996.

Respondents, however, suggest that AIRFA goes further and in effect enacts their interpretation of the First Amendment into statutory law. Although this contention was rejected by the District Court, they seek to defend the judgment below by arguing that AIRFA authorizes the injunction against completion of the G-O road. This argument is without merit. After reciting several legislative findings, AIRFA "resolves" upon the policy quoted above. A second section of the statute, 92 Stat. 470, required an evaluation of federal policies and procedures, in consultation with native religious leaders, of changes necessary to protect and preserve the rights and practices in question. The required report dealing with this evaluation was completed and released in 1979. . . . Nowhere in the law is there so much as a hint of any intent to create a cause of action or any judicially enforceable individual rights.

What is obvious from the face of the statute is confirmed by numerous indications in the legislative history. The sponsor of the bill that became AIRFA, Representative Udall, called it "a sense of Congress joint resolution," aimed at ensuring that "the basic right of the Indian people to exercise their traditional religious practices is not infringed without a clear decision on the part of the Congress or the administrators that such religious practices must yield to some higher consideration." 124 Cong. Rec. 21444 (1978). Representative Udall emphasized that the bill would not "confer special religious rights on Indians," would "not change any existing State or Federal law," and in fact "has no teeth in it." *Id.*, 21444-21445. . . .

*It is so ordered.*

JUSTICE KENNEDY took no part in the consideration or decision of this case.

JUSTICE BRENNAN, with whom JUSTICE MARSHALL and JUSTICE BLACKMUN join, dissenting.

"'[T]he Free Exercise Clause,'" the Court explains today, "'is written in terms of what the government cannot do to the individual, not in terms of what the individual can exact from the government.'" (quoting *Sherbert v. Verner* 374 U.S. 398, 412 (1963) (Douglas, J., concurring)). Pledging fidelity to this unremarkable constitutional principle, the Court nevertheless concludes that even where the Government uses federal land in a manner that threatens the very existence of a Native American religion, the Government is simply not "doing" anything to the practitioners of that faith. Instead, the Court believes that Native Americans who request that the Government refrain from destroying their religion effectively seek to exact from the Government de facto beneficial ownership of federal property. These two astonishing conclusions follow naturally from the Court's determination that federal land-use decisions that render the practice of a given religion impossible do not burden that religion in a manner cognizable under the Free Exercise Clause, because such decisions neither coerce conduct inconsistent with religious belief nor penalize religious activity. The constitutional guarantee we interpret today, however, draws no such fine distinctions between types of restraints on religious exercise, but rather is directed against any form of governmental action that frustrates or inhibits religious practice. Because the Court today refuses even to acknowledge the constitutional injury respondents will suffer, and because this refusal essentially leaves Native Americans with absolutely no constitutional protection against perhaps the gravest threat to their religious practices, I dissent.

I . . .

In marked contrast to traditional Western religions, the belief systems of Native Americans do not rely on doctrines, creeds, or dogmas. Established or universal truths—the mainstay of Western religions—play no part in Indian faith. Ceremonies are communal efforts undertaken for specific purposes in accordance with instructions handed down from generation to generation. Commentaries on or interpretations of the rituals themselves are deemed absolute violations of the ceremonies, whose value lies not in their ability to explain the natural world or to enlighten individual believers but in their efficacy as protectors and enhancers of tribal existence. Where dogma lies at the heart of Western religions, Native American faith is inextricably bound to the use of land. The site-specific nature of Indian religious practice derives from the Native American perception that land is itself a sacred, living being. . . . Rituals are performed in prescribed locations not merely as a matter of traditional orthodoxy, but because land, like all other living things, is unique, and specific sites possess different spiritual properties and significance. Within this belief system, therefore, land is not fungible; indeed, at the time of the Spanish colonization of the American Southwest, "all . . . Indians held in some form a belief in a sacred and indissoluble bond between themselves and the land in which their settlements were located." . . .

For respondent Indians, the most sacred of lands is the high country where, they believe, prehuman spirits moved with the coming of humans to the Earth. Because these spirits are seen as the source of religious power, or "medicine," many of the tribes' rituals and practices require frequent journeys to the area. Thus, for example, religious leaders preparing for the complex of ceremonies that underlie the Tribes' World Renewal efforts must travel to specific sites in the high country in order to attain the medicine necessary for successful renewal. Similarly, individual tribe members may seek curative powers for the healing of the sick, or personal medicine for particular purposes such as good luck in singing, hunting, or love. A period of preparation generally precedes such visits, and individuals must select trails in the sacred area according to the medicine they seek and their abilities, gradually moving to increasingly more powerful sites, which are typically located at higher altitudes. Among the most powerful of sites are Chimney Rock, Doctor Rock, and Peak 8, all of which are elevated rock outcroppings.

According to the Theodoratus Report, the qualities "of silence, the aesthetic perspective, and the physical attributes, are an extension of the sacredness of [each] particular site." The act of medicine making is akin to meditation: the individual must integrate physical, mental, and vocal actions in order to communicate with the prehuman spirits. As a result, "successful use of the high country is dependent upon and facilitated by certain qualities of the physical environment, the most important of which are privacy, silence, and an undisturbed natural setting." Although few Tribe members actually make medicine at the most powerful sites, the entire Tribe's welfare hinges on the success of the individual practitioners. . . .

## II

The Court does not for a moment suggest that the interests served by the G-O road are in any way compelling, or that they outweigh the destructive effect construction of the road will have on respondents' religious practices. Instead, the Court embraces the Government's contention that its prerogative as landowner should always take precedence over a claim that a particular use of federal property infringes religious practices. Attempting to justify this rule, the Court argues that the First Amendment bars only outright prohibitions, indirect coercion, and penalties on the free exercise of religion. All other "incidental effects of government programs," it concludes, even those "which may make it more difficult to practice certain religions but which have no tendency to coerce individuals into acting contrary to their religious beliefs," simply do not give rise to constitutional concerns. Since our recognition nearly half a century ago that restraints on religious conduct implicate the concerns of the Free Exercise Clause, see *Prince v. Massachusetts*, we have never suggested that the protections of the guarantee are limited to so narrow a range of governmental burdens. The land-use decision challenged here will restrain respondents from practicing their religion as surely and as completely as any of the governmental actions we have struck down in the past, and the Court's efforts simply to define away respondents' injury as nonconstitutional are both unjustified and ultimately unpersuasive.

## A

The Court ostensibly finds support for its narrow formulation of religious burdens in our decisions in *Hobbie v. Unemployment Appeals Comm'n of Fla.*, *Thomas v. Review Bd., Indiana Employment Security Division*, and *Sherbert v. Verner*. In those cases, the laws at issue forced individuals to choose between adhering to specific religious tenets and forfeiting unemployment benefits on the one hand, and accepting work repugnant to their religious beliefs on the other. The religions involved, therefore, lent themselves to the coercion analysis the Court espouses today, for they proscribed certain conduct such as munitions work (*Thomas*) or working on Saturdays (*Sherbert*, *Hobbie*) that the unemployment benefits laws effectively compelled. In sustaining the challenges to these laws, however, we nowhere suggested that such coercive compulsion exhausted the range of religious burdens recognized under the Free Exercise Clause. . . .

I . . . cannot accept the Court's premise that the form of the government's restraint on religious practice, rather than its effect, controls our constitutional analysis. Respondents here have demonstrated that construction of the G-O road will completely frustrate the practice of their religion, for as the lower courts found, the proposed logging and construction activities will virtually destroy respondents' religion, and will therefore necessarily force them into abandoning those practices altogether. Indeed, the Government's proposed activities will restrain religious practice to a far greater degree here than in any of the cases cited by the Court today. None of the religious adherents in *Hobbie*, *Thomas*, and *Sherbert*, for example, claimed or could have claimed that the denial of unemployment benefits rendered the practice of their religions impossible; at most, the challenged laws made those practices more expensive. Here, in stark contrast, respondents have claimed—and proved—that the desecration of the high country will prevent religious leaders from attaining the religious power or medicine indispensable to the success of virtually all their rituals and ceremonies. Similarly, in *Yoder* the compulsory school law threatened to "undermin[e] the Amish community and religious practice," and thus to force adherents to "abandon belief . . . or . . . to migrate to some other and more tolerant region." 406 U.S., 218. Here the threat posed by the desecration of sacred lands that are indisputably essential to respondents' religious practices is both more direct and more substantial than that raised by a compulsory school law that simply exposed Amish children to an alien value system. And of course respondents here do not even have the option, however unattractive it might be, of migrating to more hospitable locales; the site-specific nature of their belief system renders it nontransportable.

Ultimately, the Court's coercion test turns on a distinction between governmental actions that compel affirmative conduct inconsistent with religious belief, and those governmental actions that prevent conduct consistent with religious belief. In my view, such a distinction is without constitutional significance. The crucial word in the constitutional text, as the Court itself acknowledges, is "prohibit," a comprehensive term that in no way suggests that the intended protection is aimed only at governmental actions that coerce affirmative conduct. Nor does the Court's distinction comport with the principles animating the constitutional guarantee: religious freedom is threatened no less by governmental action that makes the practice of one's chosen faith impossible than by governmental programs that pressure one to engage in conduct inconsistent with religious beliefs. The Court attempts to explain the line it draws by arguing that the protections of the Free Exercise Clause "cannot depend on measuring the effects of a governmental action on a religious objector's spiritual development," for in a society as diverse as ours, the Government cannot help but offend the "religious needs and desires" of some citizens. While I agree that governmental action that simply offends religious sensibilities may not be challenged under the Clause, we have recognized that laws that affect spiritual development by impeding the integration of children into the religious community or by increasing the expense of adherence to religious principles—in short, laws that frustrate or inhibit religious practice—trigger the protections of the constitutional guarantee. Both common sense and our prior cases teach us, therefore, that governmental action that makes the practice of a given faith more difficult necessarily penalizes that practice and thereby tends to prevent adherence to religious belief. The harm to the practitioners is the same regardless of the manner in which the government restrains their religious expression, and the Court's fear that an "effects" test will permit religious adherents to challenge governmental actions they merely find "offensive" in no way justifies its refusal to recognize the constitutional injury citizens suffer when governmental action not only offends but actually restrains their religious practices. Here, respondents have demonstrated that the Government's proposed activities will completely prevent them from practicing their religion, and such a showing, no less than those made out in *Hobbie, Thomas, Sherbert*, and *Yoder*, entitles them to the protections of the Free Exercise Clause.

## B

Nor can I agree with the Court's assertion that respondents' constitutional claim is foreclosed by our decision in *Bowen v. Roy*. There, applicants for certain welfare benefits objected to the use of a Social Security number in connection with the administration of their 2-year-old daughter's application for benefits, contending that such use would "rob the [child's] spirit" and thus interfere with her spiritual development. In rejecting that challenge, we stated that "[t]he Free Exercise Clause simply cannot be understood to require the Government to conduct its own *internal affairs* in ways that comport with the religious beliefs of particular citizens." 476 U.S. 693, 699 (emphasis added). Accordingly, we explained that Roy could

> no more prevail on his religious objection to the Government's use of a Social Security number for his daughter than he could on a sincere religious objection to the size or color of the Government's filing cabinets. The Free Exercise Clause affords an individual protection from certain

forms of governmental compulsion; it does not afford an individual a right to dictate the conduct of the Government's *internal procedures. Id.*, 700 (emphasis added).

Today the Court professes an inability to differentiate *Roy* from the present case, suggesting that "[t]he building of a road or the harvesting of timber on publicly owned land cannot meaningfully be distinguished from the use of a Social Security number." I find this inability altogether remarkable. In *Roy*, we repeatedly stressed the "internal" nature of the Government practice at issue: noting that Roy objected to "the widespread use of the social security number by the federal or state governments *in their computer systems*," 476 U.S., 697 (emphasis added), we likened the use of such recordkeeping numbers to decisions concerning the purchase of office equipment. When the Government processes information, of course, it acts in a purely internal manner, and any free exercise challenge to such internal recordkeeping in effect seeks to dictate how the Government conducts its own affairs.

Federal land-use decisions, by contrast, are likely to have substantial external effects that government decisions concerning office furniture and information storage obviously will not, and they are correspondingly subject to public scrutiny and public challenge in a host of ways that office equipment purchases are not. Indeed, in the American Indian Religious Freedom Act (AIRFA), 42 U.S.C. 1996, Congress expressly recognized the adverse impact land-use decisions and other governmental actions frequently have on the site-specific religious practices of Native Americans, and the Act accordingly directs agencies to consult with Native American religious leaders before taking actions that might impair those practices. Although I agree that the Act does not create any judicially enforceable rights, the absence of any private right of action in no way undermines the statute's significance as an express congressional determination that federal land management decisions are not "internal" Government "procedures," but are instead governmental actions that can and indeed are likely to burden Native American religious practices. That such decisions should be subject to constitutional challenge, and potential constitutional limitations, should hardly come as a surprise.

The Court today, however, ignores *Roy's* emphasis on the internal nature of the Government practice at issue there, and instead construes that case as further support for the proposition that governmental action that does not coerce conduct inconsistent with religious faith simply does not implicate the concerns of the Free Exercise Clause. That such a reading is wholly untenable, however, is demonstrated by the cruelly surreal result it produces here: governmental action that will virtually destroy a religion is nevertheless deemed not to "burden" that religion. Moreover, in AIRFA Congress explicitly acknowledged that federal "policies and regulations" could and often did "intrud[e] upon [and] interfer[e] with" site-specific Native American religious ceremonies, 92 Stat. 469, and in *Roy* we recognized that this Act—"with its emphasis on protecting the freedom to believe, express, and exercise a religion—accurately identifies the mission of the Free Exercise Clause itself." Ultimately, in *Roy* we concluded that, however much the Government's recordkeeping system may have offended Roy's sincere religious sensibilities, he could not challenge that system under the Free Exercise Clause because the Government's practice did not "in any degree impair Roy's 'freedom to believe, express, and *exercise'* his religion." That determination distinguishes the injury at issue here, which the Court finds so "remarkably similar" to Roy's, for respondents have made an uncontroverted showing that the proposed construction and logging activities will impair their freedom to exercise their religion in the greatest degree imaginable, and Congress has "accurately identifie[d]" such injuries as falling within the scope of the Free Exercise Clause. The Court's reading of *Roy*, therefore, simply cannot be squared with our endorsement—in that very same case—of this congressional determination. More important, it lends no support to the Court's efforts to narrow both the reach and promise of the Free Exercise Clause itself.

C

In the final analysis, the Court's refusal to recognize the constitutional dimension of respondents' injuries stems from its concern that acceptance of respondents' claim could potentially strip the Government of its ability to manage and use vast tracts of federal property. In addition, the nature of respondents' site-specific religious practices raises the specter of future suits in which Native Americans seek to exclude all human activity from such areas. These concededly legitimate concerns lie at the very heart of this case, which represents yet another stress point in the longstanding conflict between two disparate cultures—the dominant Western culture, which views land in terms of ownership and use, and that of Native Americans, in which concepts of private property are not only alien, but contrary to a belief system that holds land sacred. Rather than address this conflict in any meaningful fashion, however, the Court disclaims all responsibility for balancing these competing and potentially irreconcilable interests, choosing instead to turn this difficult task over to the Federal Legislature. Such an abdication is more than merely indefensible as an institutional matter: by defining respondents' injury as "nonconstitutional," the Court has effectively bestowed on one party to this conflict the unilateral authority to resolve all future disputes in its favor, subject only to the Court's toothless exhortation to be "sensitive" to affected religions. In my view, however, Native Americans deserve—and the Constitution demands—more than this. . . .

I believe it appropriate, therefore, to require some showing of "centrality" before the Government can be required either to come forward with a compelling justification for its proposed use of federal land or to forgo that use altogether. "Centrality," however, should not be equated with the survival or extinction of the religion itself. In *Yoder*, for example, we treated the objection to the compulsory school attendance of adolescents as "central" to the Amish faith even though such attendance did not prevent or otherwise render the practice of that religion impossible, and instead simply threatened to "undermine" that faith. Because of their perceptions of and relationship with the natural world, Native Americans consider all land sacred. Nevertheless, the Theodoratus Report reveals that respondents here deemed certain lands more powerful and more directly related to their religious practices than others. Thus, in my view, while Native Americans need not demonstrate, as respondents did here, that the Government's land-use decision will assuredly eradicate their faith, I do not think it is enough to allege simply that the land in question is held sacred. Rather, adherents challenging a proposed use of federal land should be required to show that the decision poses a substantial and realistic threat of frustrating their religious practices. Once such a showing is made, the burden should shift to the Government to come forward with a compelling state interest sufficient to justify the infringement of those practices.

The Court today suggests that such an approach would place courts in the untenable position of deciding which practices and beliefs are "central" to a given faith and which are not, and invites the prospect of judges advising some religious adherents that they "misunderstand their own religious beliefs." In fact, however, courts need not undertake any such inquiries: like all other religious adherents, Native Americans would be the arbiters of which practices are central to their faith, subject only to the normal requirement that their claims be genuine and sincere. The question for the courts, then, is not whether the Native American claimants understand their own religion, but rather whether they have discharged their burden of demonstrating, as the Amish did with respect to the compulsory school law in *Yoder*, that the land-use decision poses a substantial and realistic threat of undermining or frustrating their religious practices. Ironically, the Court's apparent solicitude for the integrity of religious belief and its desire to forestall the possibility that courts might second-guess the claims of religious adherents leads to far greater inequities than those the Court postulates: today's ruling sacrifices a religion at least as old as the Nation itself, along with the spiritual well-being of its approximately 5,000 adherents, so that the Forest Service can build a 6-mile segment of road that two lower courts found had only the most marginal and speculative utility, both to the Government itself and to the private lumber interests that might conceivably use it.

Similarly, the Court's concern that the claims of Native Americans will place "religious servitudes" upon vast tracts of federal property cannot justify its refusal to recognize the constitutional injury respondents will suffer here. It is true, as the Court notes, that respondents' religious use of the high country requires privacy and solitude. The fact remains, however, that respondents have never asked the Forest Service to exclude others from the area. Should respondents or any other group seek to force the Government to protect their religious practices from the interference of private parties, such a demand would implicate not only the concerns of the Free Exercise Clause, but also those of the Establishment Clause as well. That case, however, is most assuredly not before us today, and in any event cannot justify the Court's refusal to acknowledge that the injuries respondents will suffer as a result of the Government's proposed activities are sufficient to state a constitutional cause of action.

### III

Today, the Court holds that a federal land-use decision that promises to destroy an entire religion does not burden the practice of that faith in a manner recognized by the Free Exercise Clause. Having thus stripped respondents and all other Native Americans of any constitutional protection against perhaps the most serious threat to their age-old religious practices, and indeed to their entire way of life, the Court assures us that nothing in its decision "should be read to encourage governmental insensitivity to the religious needs of any citizen." I find it difficult, however, to imagine conduct more insensitive to religious needs than the Government's determination to build a marginally useful road in the face of uncontradicted evidence that the road will render the practice of respondents' religion impossible. Nor do I believe that respondents will derive any solace from the knowledge that although the practice of their religion will become "more difficult" as a result of the Government's actions, they remain free to maintain their religious beliefs. Given today's ruling, that freedom amounts to nothing more than the right to believe that their religion will be destroyed. The safeguarding of such a hollow freedom not only makes a mockery of the "'policy of the United States to protect and preserve for American Indians their inherent right of freedom to believe, express, and exercise the[ir] traditional religions,'" it fails utterly to accord with the dictates of the First Amendment.

I dissent.

---

## Notes and Questions

1. In *Lyng*, which opinion—the majority or the dissent—makes the more compelling argument for the significance of *Bowen v. Roy*? Are the burdens on the claimants and the government similar in *Bowen* and *Lyng*, or can they be distinguished?

2. The dissent argues for a "centrality" test for such cases. What does the dissent mean? What are the pros and cons of courts utilizing such a standard in Free Exercise cases?

3. How significant for the *Lyng* holding was the government's underlying concern—that recognition of the natives' claim would invite a host of similar, religiously based claims that would constrain the ability of the government to administer its programs and manage its resources? Who is correct—is the issue in *Lyng* (and *Bowen*) about placing demands on government-run programs or, in an era of massive government regulation, is the issue correctly characterized as a government-imposed constraint on religiously motivated conduct? If you sympathize with the Native American claimants, how far should the accommodation principle go?

4. Is it possible to reconcile Justice O'Connor's opinion concurring in part and dissenting in part in *Bowen v. Roy* with the opinion she wrote for the Court in *Lyng*? If so, how?

5. Some critics have charged that the rulings in *Bowen* and *Lyng* are not surprising, given the long and sad treatment of Native Americans at the hands of the government. In fact, during the nineteenth century, the federal government had an official policy of suppressing Indian religious practices and converting Indians to Christianity.[3] Can *Bowen* and *Lyng* be explained in part as evincing cultural insensitivity to Native American religious traditions, or would the result have been the same if the cases had involved Presbyterian claimants? To what extent (if any) should the Free Exercise Clause be "extra" sensitive when the claim involves a nontraditional faith claim by a group that has historically been politically powerless?

---

During the 1980s the Court also decided some free exercise cases about persons in specialized environments. In these cases, too, it retreated from the expansive interpretation of the Free Exercise Clause it articulated in *Sherbert v. Verner*. One of those specialized environments was the military. In *Goldman v. Weinberger*, the plaintiff was an Orthodox Jewish officer (also a rabbi) in the Air Force. A Ph.D. psychologist, his duty was to be a clinical psychologist in a base mental health clinic. He believed his religion required him to wear a head covering (yarmulke) all the time, even though Air Force regulations forbade wearing headgear indoors. When Goldman's commanding officer explicitly prohibited him from wearing his yarmulke, he sued the Secretary of Defense.

The Court ruled in favor of the government. The military is a special environment and its commanders know best how to efficiently maintain the environment, the Court said. The dress code was part of that maintenance. Consequently, the Court deferred to military leadership, pointedly noting that persons in the military do not enjoy the same scope of civil liberties as civilians.

---

## GOLDMAN v. WEINBERGER
475 U.S. 503 (1986)

JUSTICE REHNQUIST delivered the opinion of the Court. . . .

Petitioner argues that AFR 35-10 [Air Force regulation on headgear], as applied to him, prohibits religiously motivated conduct and should therefore be analyzed under the standard enunciated in *Sherbert v. Verner*. . . . But we have repeatedly held that "the military is, by necessity, a specialized society separate from civilian society." *Parker v. Levy* 417 U.S. 733, 743 (1974). . . . "[T]he military must insist upon a respect for duty and a discipline without counterpart in civilian life," in order to prepare for and perform its vital role. . . .

Our review of military regulations challenged on First Amendment grounds is far more deferential than constitutional review of similar laws or regulations designed for civilian society. The military need not encourage debate or tolerate protest to the extent that such tolerance is required of the civilian state by the First Amendment; to accomplish its mission the military must foster instinctive obedience, unity, commitment, and esprit de corps. . . . The essence of military service "is the subordination of the desires and interests of the individual to the needs of the service."

These aspects of military life do not, of course, render entirely nugatory in the military context the guarantees of the First Amendment. . . . But "within the military community there is simply not the same [individual] autonomy as there is in the larger civilian community." In the context of the present case, when evaluating whether military needs justify a particular restriction on religiously motivated conduct, courts must give great deference to the professional judgment of military authorities concerning the relative importance of a particular military interest. . . . Not only are courts "'ill-equipped to determine the impact upon discipline that any particular intrusion upon military authority might have,'" . . . but the military authorities have been charged by the Executive and Legislative Branches with carrying out our Nation's military policy. "[J]udicial deference . . . is at its apogee when legislative action under the congressional authority to raise and support armies and make rules and regulations for their governance is challenged."

JUSTICE STEVENS, with whom JUSTICE WHITE and JUSTICE POWELL join, concurring.

. . . . The very strength of Captain Goldman's claim creates the danger that a similar claim on behalf of a Sikh or a Rastafarian might readily be dismissed as "so extreme, so unusual, or so faddish an image that public confidence in his ability to perform his duties will be destroyed." If exceptions from dress code regulations are to be granted on the basis of a multifactored test such as that proposed by JUSTICE BRENNAN, inevitably the decisionmaker's evaluation of the character and the sincerity of the requester's faith—as well as the probable reaction of the majority to the favored treatment of a member of that faith—will play a critical part in the decision. For the difference between a turban or a dreadlock on the one hand, and a yarmulke on the other, is not merely a difference in "appearance"—it is also the difference between a Sikh or a Rastafarian, on the one hand, and an Orthodox Jew on the other. The Air Force has no business drawing distinctions between such persons when it is enforcing commands of universal application.

As the Court demonstrates, the rule that is challenged in this case is based on a neutral, completely objective standard—visibility. It was not motivated by hostility against, or any special respect for, any religious faith. An exception for yarmulkes would represent a fundamental departure from the true principle of uniformity that supports that rule. For that reason, I join the Court's opinion and its judgment.

⬛ JUSTICE BRENNAN, with whom JUSTICE MARSHALL joins, dissenting.

Today the Court eschews its constitutionally mandated role. It adopts for review of military decisions affecting First Amendment rights a subrational-basis standard—absolute, uncritical "deference to the professional judgment of military authorities." If a branch of the military declares one of its rules sufficiently important to outweigh a service person's constitutional rights, it seems that the Court will accept that conclusion, no matter how absurd or unsupported it may be.

A deferential standard of review, however, need not, and should not, mean that the Court must credit arguments that defy common sense. When a military service burdens the free exercise rights of its members in the name of necessity, it must provide, as an initial matter and at a minimum, a credible explanation of how the contested practice is likely to interfere with the proffered military interest.[2] Unabashed *ipse dixit* cannot outweigh a constitutional right.

---

[2] I continue to believe that Government restraints on First Amendment rights, including limitations placed on military personnel, may be justified only upon showing a compelling state interest which is precisely furthered by a narrowly tailored regulation. I think that any special needs of the military can be accommodated in the compelling-interest prong of the test. My point here is simply that even under a more deferential test Dr. Goldman should prevail. . . .

The contention that the discipline of the Armed Forces will be subverted if Ortho-dox Jews are allowed to wear yarmulkes with their uniforms surpasses belief. It lacks support in the record of this case, and the Air Force offers no basis for it as a general proposition. While the perilous slope permits the services arbitrarily to refuse exceptions requested to satisfy mere personal preferences, before the Air Force may burden free exercise rights it must advance, at the very least, a rational reason for doing so. . . .

The Government dangles before the Court a classic parade of horribles, the specter of a brightly-colored, "rag-tag band of soldiers." Although turbans, saffron robes, and dreadlocks are not before us in this case and must each be evaluated against the reasons a service branch offers for prohibiting personnel from wearing them while in uniform, a reviewing court could

Ironically for Captain Goldman, in 1988, Congress enacted a statute that had the effect of reversing the outcome in the *Goldman* case. It provided that "a member of the armed forces may wear an item of religious apparel while wearing the uniform of the member's armed force." However, that could be prevented in an individual case if the religious apparel would interfere with one's duties or was not "neat and conservative." See 10 U.S.C. § 774.

The other specialized environment case was *O'Lone v. Estate of Shabazz*, having to do with free exercise in the context of prisons. Muslim minimum security prisoners, working

---

legitimately give deference to dress and grooming rules that have a reasoned basis in, for example, functional utility, health and safety considerations, and the goal of a polished, professional appearance. It is the lack of any reasoned basis for prohibiting yarmulkes that is so striking here.

Furthermore, contrary to its intimations, the Air Force has available to it a familiar standard for determining whether a particular style of yarmulke is consistent with a polished, professional military appearance—the "neat and conservative" standard by which the service judges jewelry. No rational reason exists why yarmulkes cannot be judged by the same criterion. Indeed, at argument Dr. Goldman declared himself willing to wear whatever style and color yarmulke the Air Force believes best comports with its uniform.

Department of Defense Directive 1300.17 (June 18, 1985) grants commanding officers the discretion to permit service personnel to wear religious items and apparel that are not visible with the uniform, such as crosses, temple garments, and scapulars. JUSTICE STEVENS favors this "visibility test" because he believes that it does not involve the Air Force in drawing distinctions among faiths. He rejects functional utility, health, and safety considerations, and similar grounds as criteria for religious exceptions to the dress code, because he fears that these standards will allow some servicepersons to satisfy their religious dress and grooming obligations, while preventing others from fulfilling theirs. But, the visible/not visible standard has that same effect. Furthermore, it restricts the free exercise rights of a larger number of servicepersons. The visibility test permits only individuals whose outer garments and grooming are indistinguishable from those of mainstream Christians to fulfill their religious duties. In my view, the Constitution requires the selection of criteria that permit the greatest possible number of persons to practice their faiths freely.

Implicit in JUSTICE STEVENS' concurrence, and in the Government's arguments, is what might be characterized as a fairness concern. It would be unfair to allow Orthodox Jews to wear yarmulkes, while prohibiting members of other minority faiths with visible dress and grooming requirements from wearing their saffron robes, dreadlocks, turbans, and so forth. While I appreciate and share this concern for the feelings and the free exercise rights of members of these other faiths, I am baffled by this formulation of the problem. What puzzles me is the implication that a neutral standard that could result in the disparate treatment of Orthodox Jews and, for example, Sikhs is more troublesome or unfair than the existing neutral standard that does result in the different treatment of Christians, on the one hand, and Orthodox Jews and Sikhs on the other. Both standards are constitutionally suspect; before either can be sustained, it must be shown to be a narrowly tailored means of promoting important military interests.

. . . . Burdens placed on the free exercise rights of members of one faith must be justified independently of burdens placed on the rights of members of another religion. It is not enough to say that Jews cannot wear yarmulkes simply because Rastafarians might not be able to wear dreadlocks.

Unless the visible/not visible standard for evaluating requests for religious exceptions to the dress code promotes a significant military interest, it is constitutionally impermissible. JUSTICE STEVENS believes that this standard advances an interest in the "uniform treatment" of all religions. As I have shown, that uniformity is illusory, unless uniformity means uniformly accommodating majority religious practices and uniformly rejecting distinctive minority practices. But, more directly, Government agencies are not free to define their own interests in uniform treatment of different faiths. That function has been assigned to the First

outside the prison, wanted to return to the prison for Friday noon prayers, "Jumu'ah." Previously, prison officials had allowed some Muslim prisoners to remain on site on Fridays so they could attend Jumu'ah. The officials subsequently changed the policy, citing concerns about security risks and additional administrative burdens on the prison staff. The Supreme Court responded to their suit in the same way it did in the *Goldman* case, deferring to prison authorities' expertise on how to run a prison, with its concern for security. The Court acknowledged that the prisoners' "sincerely held religious beliefs compelled attendance at Jumu'ah" and that policy burdened that practice. Even so, the Court made it clear that prisoners have less protection for their rights than regular civilians. Chief Justice Rehnquist wrote for the Court.

---

## O'LONE v. ESTATE OF SHABAZZ
482 U.S. 342 (1987)

▦ CHIEF JUSTICE REHNQUIST delivered the opinion of the Court.

To ensure that courts afford appropriate deference to prison officials, we have determined that prison regulations alleged to infringe constitutional rights are judged under a "reasonableness" test less restrictive than that ordinarily applied to alleged infringement of fundamental constitutional rights. We recently restated the proper standard: "[W]hen a prison regulation impinges on inmates' constitutional rights, the regulation is valid if it is reasonably related to legitimate penological interests." *Turner v. Safley*, 482 U.S. 78, 89. . . .

---

Amendment. The First Amendment requires that burdens on free exercise rights be justified by independent and important interests that promote the function of the agency. The only independent military interest furthered by the visibility standard is uniformity of dress. And, that interest, as I [have] demonstrated, does not support a prohibition against yarmulkes.

The Air Force has failed utterly to furnish a credible explanation why an exception to the dress code permitting Orthodox Jews to wear neat and conservative yarmulkes while in uniform is likely to interfere with its interest in discipline and uniformity. . . .

It is not the province of the federal courts to second-guess the professional judgments of the military services, but we are bound by the Constitution to assure ourselves that there exists a rational foundation for assertions of military necessity when they interfere with the free exercise of religion. . . . [I]n pluralistic societies such as ours, institutions dominated by a majority are inevitably, if inadvertently, insensitive to the needs and values of minorities when these needs and values differ from those of the majority. The military, with its strong ethic of conformity and unquestioning obedience, may be particularly impervious to minority needs and values. A critical function of the Religion Clauses of the First Amendment is to protect the rights of members of minority religions against quiet erosion by majoritarian social institutions that dismiss minority beliefs and practices as unimportant, because unfamiliar. It is the constitutional role of this Court to ensure that this purpose of the First Amendment be realized.

The Court and the military services have presented patriotic Orthodox Jews with a painful dilemma—the choice between fulfilling a religious obligation and serving their country. Should the draft be reinstated, compulsion will replace choice. Although the pain the services inflict on Orthodox Jewish servicemen is clearly the result of insensitivity rather than design, it is unworthy of our military because it is unnecessary. The Court and the military have refused these servicemen their constitutional rights; we must hope that Congress will correct this wrong.

Our decision in *Turner* also found it relevant that "alternative means of exercising the right . . . remain open to prison inmates." There are, of course, no alternative means of attending Jumu'ah; respondents' religious beliefs insist that it occur at a particular time. But the very stringent requirements as to the time at which Jumu'ah may be held may make it extraordinarily difficult for prison officials to assure that every Muslim prisoner is able to attend that service. While we in no way minimize the central importance of Jumu'ah to respondents, we are unwilling to hold that prison officials are required by the Constitution to sacrifice legitimate penological objectives to that end. . . . Here . . . we think it appropriate to see whether under these regulations respondents retain the ability to participate in other Muslim religious ceremonies. The record establishes that respondents are not deprived of all forms of religious exercise, but instead freely observe a number of their religious obligations. . . .

We take this opportunity to reaffirm our refusal, even where claims are made under the First Amendment, to "substitute our judgment on . . . difficult and sensitive matters of institutional administration," for the determinations of those charged with the formidable task of running a prison. . . .

JUSTICE BRENNAN, with whom JUSTICE MARSHALL, JUSTICE BLACK-MUN, and JUSTICE STEVENS join, dissenting.

The religious ceremony that these respondents seek to attend is not presumptively dangerous, and the prison has completely foreclosed respondents' participation in it. I therefore would require prison officials to demonstrate that the restrictions they have imposed are necessary to further an important government interest, and that these restrictions are no greater than necessary to achieve prison objectives. As a result, I would affirm the Court of Appeals' order to remand the case to the District Court, and would require prison officials to make this showing. Even were I to accept the Court's standard of review, however, I would remand the case to the District Court, since that court has not had the opportunity to review respondents' claim under the new standard established by this Court in *Turner*. As the record now stands, the reasonableness of foreclosing respondents' participation in Jumu'ah has not been established. . . .

## NOTES AND QUESTIONS

1. What distinguishes the environments in *Goldman* and *O'Lone* that supports applying a less rigorous standard of review of government regulation of religious conduct? Is this standard of deference justifiable in each case?

2. Note the significance of the Court's use of a more deferential standard. First, are the military's and prison's justifications for their restrictions on religious practice—i.e., uniformity and security/administrative convenience, respectively—"legitimate" concerns (rather than "compelling")? If so, consider the fact that the government was not required to show that the religious conduct at issue necessarily threatened those interests. Does that undermine the finding that those interests are legitimate? In any case, should the government have been required to make such a showing in these cases?

3. The *O'Lone* Court places weight on the fact that Muslim prisoners could take part in other Muslim religious ceremonies. In a part of his dissent that is not

reproduced here, Justice Brennan describes how Jumu'ah is "the central religious ceremony of Muslims" and that the "ability to engage in other religious activities cannot obscure the fact that the denial at issue in this case is absolute." Considering the special nature of the prison environment, who has the stronger argument? Certainly, the confined and restricted nature of prisons means that all inmate religious requests cannot be accommodated. Is there a danger to the right to religious free exercise, however, if the government can point to the availability of one mode of religious expression as a justification for restricting other modes of expression (e.g., "because we allowed you to be baptized, you have no ground to complain when we do not allow the Eucharist")?

But see *Cruz v. Beto*, 405 U.S. 319 (1972), where Buddhist inmates in the Texas prison system were denied the opportunity to hold Buddhist worship services or meet with Buddhist spiritual advisors, with Cruz being placed in solitary confinement on a diet of bread and water for two weeks because he shared Buddhist materials with fellow inmates. In contrast, Protestant, Catholic, and Jewish inmates were able to engage in religious services and meet with their respective spiritual advisors. The district court denied Cruz relief, writing that: "Valid disciplinary and security reasons not known to this court may prevent the 'equality' of exercise of religious practices in prison." The Supreme Court reversed: "If Cruz was a Buddhist and if he was denied a reasonable opportunity of pursuing his faith comparable to the opportunity afforded fellow prisoners who adhere to conventional religious precepts, then there was palpable discrimination by the State against the Buddhist religion [in violation of the First Amendment]." *Id.*, 322. However, the Court included a significant footnote that reaffirmed that prison officials were still to be afforded discretion with respect to accommodating inmates' religious needs:

> We do not suggest, of course, that every religious sect or group within a prison—however few in number—must have identical facilities or personnel. A special chapel or place of worship need not be provided for every faith regardless of size; nor must a chaplain, priest, or minister be provided without regard to the extent of the demand. But reasonable opportunities must be afforded to all prisoners to exercise the religious freedom guaranteed by the First and Fourteenth Amendment without fear of penalty. *Id.*, 322, n. 2.

4. In a part of his dissenting opinion in *O'Lone* that is not reproduced here, Justice Brennan wrote: "When prisoners themselves present alternatives [that would allow them to practice their faith and meet prison objectives,] and when they fairly call into question official claims that these alternatives are infeasible, we must demand at least some evidence beyond mere assertion that the religious practice at issue cannot be accommodated." Brennan found that an "[e]xamination of the alternatives proposed in this case indicates that prison officials have not provided such substantiation." The following is one of the alternatives proposed by the prisoners:

> [The prisoners] suggested that gang minimum inmates be assigned to Saturday or Sunday work details, which would allow them to make up any time lost by attending Jumu'ah on Friday. While prison officials admitted the

existence of weekend work details, they stated that "since prison personnel are needed for other programs on weekends, the creation of additional weekend details would be a drain on scarce human resources." The record provides no indication, however, of the number of Muslims that would seek such a work detail, the current number of weekend details, or why it would be infeasible simply to reassign current Saturday or Sunday workers to Friday, rather than create additional details. The prison is able to arrange work schedules so that Jewish inmates may attend services on Saturday and Christian inmates may attend services on Sunday. Despite the fact that virtually all inmates are housed in the main building over the weekend, so that the demand on the facility is greater than at any other time, the prison is able to provide sufficient staff coverage to permit Jewish and Christian inmates to participate in their central religious ceremonies. Given the prison's duty to provide Muslims a "reasonable opportunity of pursuing [their] faith comparable to the opportunity afforded fellow prisoners who adhere to conventional religious precepts," *Cruz v. Beto*, 405 U.S. 319, 322 (1972), prison officials should be required to provide more than mere assertions of the infeasibility of weekend details for Muslim inmates.

Should it have mattered to the Court that the prison appears to have regularly accommodated the needs of Christian and Jewish inmates to attend their religious services?

5. In late 2007, newspapers reported that the federal Bureau of Prisons had conducted a purge of many religious books from prison libraries nationwide. The bureau asserted that concerns about terrorism prompted it to develop a list of "approved" religious texts and to purge all "non-approved" books from prison libraries. In other words, it feared that some religious texts were encouraging terrorism and needed to be removed from prisons; but instead of removing only those texts, the bureau removed all religious texts that did not appear on an agency-generated list.

   Critics of this action complained that the list of approved religious texts was arbitrary in many ways and that the Bureau of Prisons had seriously overreacted by purging such a large number of books, many of which did not in any way counsel or advocate terrorism. Did the Bureau of Prisons violate the free exercise rights of inmates with this purge?

---

Finally, issues of taxation of religious organizations and religiously motivated conduct have bedeviled courts. Historically, religious organizations have enjoyed exemptions from paying taxes, and ministers benefit from tax breaks that others do not enjoy. As is discussed in chapter 20, the Supreme Court has upheld the constitutionality of tax exemptions for religious organizations under the Establishment Clause. See *Walz v. Tax Commission* (1970) (upholding a property tax exemption for churches and other charitable organizations). But see *Texas Monthly v. Bullock* (1989) (tax exemption for religious publications only held unconstitutional). But such tax exemptions are usually accommodations of religion that are granted by the legislature. In the absence of legislative action, does the imposition of a tax on religion burden its practice in violation of free exercise principles? Clearly, a tax on religious conduct or expression only would be unconstitutional. But is there something inherent in government taxation of religion and religious conduct that makes it a per se violation of free exercise values?

In 1989, the Court heard a claim involving a provision of the Internal Revenue Code (26 U.S.C. § 170) that allows a taxpayer to deduct from gross income the amount of a charitable contribution. As the Court noted, the Code defines the term "charitable contribution" as a "contribution or gift" to certain eligible entities, including bodies organized and operated exclusively for religious purposes. The Court agreed to hear the case in order to determine whether taxpayers may deduct payments made to the Church of Scientology for services known as "auditing" and "training." The Court held that taxpayers could not deduct such payments because they were made in response to the church's fee schedule; they were not charitable contributions.

In this case, *Hernandez v. Commissioner of Internal Revenue*, one argument asserted by the taxpayers was that a refusal to allow them to deduct such payments violated their free exercise rights. In an opinion written by Justice Thurgood Marshall, the Court rejected that argument. The following excerpt from the decision provides the Court's analysis of that argument.

## HERNANDEZ v. COMMISSIONER OF INTERNAL REVENUE
## 490 U.S. 680 (1989)

JUSTICE MARSHALL delivered the opinion of the Court. . . .

The Tax Court . . . observed first that the term "charitable contribution" in § 170 is synonymous with the word "gift," which case law had defined "as a *voluntary transfer* of property by the owner to another *without consideration* therefore." It then determined that petitioners had received consideration for their payments, namely, "the benefit of various religious services provided by the Church of Scientology." 83 T.C. 575, 580. . . .

In ascertaining whether a given payment was made with "the expectation of a quid pro quo," the Internal Revenue Service (IRS) has customarily examined the external features of the transaction in question . . . "[t]he *sine qua non* of a charitable contribution is a transfer of money or property *without adequate compensation.*"

In light of this understanding of § 170, it is readily apparent that petitioners' payments to the Church do not qualify as "contribution[s] or gift[s]." As the Tax Court found, these payments were part of a quintessential quid pro quo exchange: in return for their money, petitioners received an identifiable benefit, namely, auditing and training sessions. The Church established fixed price schedules for auditing and training sessions in each branch church; it calibrated particular prices to auditing or training sessions of particular lengths and levels of sophistication; it returned a refund if auditing and training services went unperformed; it distributed "account cards" on which persons who had paid money to the Church could monitor what prepaid services they had not yet claimed; and it categorically barred provision of auditing or training sessions for free. Each of these practices reveals the inherently reciprocal nature of the exchange. . . .

Petitioners contend that disallowance of their § 170 deductions violates their right to the free exercise of religion by "plac[ing] a heavy burden on the central practice of Scientology." The precise nature of this claimed burden is unclear, but it appears to operate in two ways. First, the deduction disallowance is said to deter adherents from engaging in auditing and training sessions. Second, the deduction disallowance is said to interfere with observance of the doctrine of exchange, which mandates equality of an adherent's "outflow" and "inflow."

The free exercise inquiry asks whether government has placed a substantial burden on the observation of a central religious belief or practice and, if so, whether a compelling governmental interest justifies the burden. It is not within the judicial ken to question the centrality of particular beliefs or practices to a faith, or the validity of particular litigants' interpretations of those creeds. We do, however, have doubts whether the alleged burden imposed by the deduction disallowance on the Scientologists' practices is a substantial one. Neither the payment nor the receipt of taxes is forbidden by the Scientology faith generally, and Scientology does not proscribe the payment of taxes in connection with auditing or training sessions specifically. Any burden imposed on auditing or training therefore derives solely from the fact that, as a result of the deduction denial, adherents have less money available to gain access to such sessions. This burden is no different from that imposed by any public tax or fee; indeed, the burden imposed by the denial of the "contribution or gift" deduction would seem to pale by comparison to the overall federal income tax burden on an adherent. Likewise, it is unclear why the doctrine of exchange would be violated by a deduction disallowance so long as an adherent is free to equalize "outflow" with "inflow" by paying for as many auditing and training sessions as he wishes.

In any event, we need not decide whether the burden of disallowing the § 170 deduction is a substantial one, for our decision in *Lee* establishes that even a substantial burden would be justified by the "broad public interest in maintaining a sound tax system," free of "myriad exceptions flowing from a wide variety of religious beliefs." 455 U.S., 260. In *Lee*, we rejected an Amish taxpayer's claim that the Free Exercise Clause commanded his exemption from Social Security tax obligations, noting that "[t]he tax system could not function if denominations were allowed to challenge the tax system" on the ground that it operated "in a manner that violates their religious belief." That these cases involve federal income taxes, not the Social Security system, is of no consequence. The fact that Congress has already crafted some deductions and exemptions in the Code also is of no consequence, for the guiding principle is that a tax "must be uniformly applicable to all, except as *Congress* provides explicitly otherwise." *Id.*, 261. Indeed, in one respect, the Government's interest in avoiding an exemption is more powerful here than in *Lee*; the claimed exemption in *Lee* stemmed from a specific doctrinal obligation not to pay taxes, whereas petitioners' claimed exemption stems from the contention that an incrementally larger tax burden interferes with their religious activities. This argument knows no limitation. We accordingly hold that petitioners' free exercise challenge is without merit.

## JIMMY SWAGGART MINISTRIES v. BOARD OF EQUALIZATION
493 U.S. 378 (1990)

◼ JUSTICE O'CONNOR delivered the opinion of the Court.

This case presents the question whether the Religion Clauses of the First Amendment prohibit a State from imposing a generally applicable sales and use tax on the distribution of religious materials by a religious organization.

I . . .

[Editors' summary: Between 1974 and 1981, Jimmy Swaggart Ministries (Ministries), a nonprofit evangelical organization based in Louisiana, held 23 crusades in California—each lasting 1 to 3 days, with one crusade lasting 6 days—for a total of 52 days. At the crusades, Ministries conducted religious services that included preaching and singing. Some of these services were recorded for later sale or broadcast. Ministries also sold Bibles, religious books, tapes, records, and other religious and nonreligious merchandise at the crusades. Ministries also offered its items for sale through a monthly magazine, *The Evangelist*, . . . and on radio, television, and cable television broadcasts, including broadcasts through local California stations.

In 1980, the California Board of Equalization informed Ministries that religious materials were not exempt from the state sales and use tax, the latter reaching out-of-state purchases by residents of the state. The Board determined (and Ministries conceded), that during the time period in question, the latter had $1,702,942.00 in mail order sales from California residents and $240,560.00 for crusade merchandise sales conducted in California. These figures represented the sales and use in California of merchandise with specific religious content—Bibles, Bible study manuals, printed sermons and collections of sermons, audiocassette tapes of sermons, religious books and pamphlets, and religious music in the form of songbooks, tapes, and records. Based on the sales figures for Ministries' religious materials, the Board determined that it owed sales and use taxes of $118,294.54, plus interest of $36,021.11, and a penalty of $11,829.45, for a total amount due of $166,145.10. Ministries did not contest the Board's assessment of tax liability for the sale and use of certain nonreligious merchandise but asserted at an administrative hearing that the tax on religious materials violated the First Amendment. The Board denied Ministries' claim, and on appeal, California courts affirmed the Board's assessment of the tax.]

II

Appellant's central contention is that the State's imposition of sales and use tax liability on its sale of religious materials contravenes . . . both the Free Exercise and Establishment Clauses. . . .

Appellant relies almost exclusively on our decisions in *Murdock v. Pennsylvania*, 319 U.S. 105 (1943) and *Follett v. McCormick*, 321 U.S. 573 (1944), for the proposition that a State may not impose a sales or use tax on the evangelical distribution of religious material by a religious organization. Appellant contends that the State's imposition of use and sales tax liability on it burdens its evangelical distribution of religious materials in a manner identical to the manner in which the evangelists in *Murdock* and *Follett* were burdened. . . .

Our decisions in these cases, however, resulted from the particular nature of the challenged taxes—flat license taxes that operated as a prior restraint on the exercise of religious liberty. In *Murdock,* for instance, we emphasized that the tax at issue was "a license tax—a flat tax imposed on the exercise of a privilege granted by the Bill of Rights," 319 U.S., 113, and cautioned that "[w]e do not mean to say that religious groups and the press are free from all financial burdens of government. . . . We have here something quite different, for example, from a tax on the income of one who engages in religious activities or a tax on property used or employed in connection with those activities." *Id.,* 112. . . . In *Follett,* we reiterated that a preacher is not "free from all financial burdens of government, including taxes on income or property" and, "like other citizens, may be subject to *general* taxation." 321 U.S., 578 (emphasis added). . . .

Thus, although *Murdock* and *Follett* establish that appellant's form of religious exercise has "as high a claim to constitutional protection as the more orthodox types," those cases are of no further help to appellant. Our concern in *Murdock* and *Follett*—that a flat license tax would act as a *precondition* to the free exercise of religious beliefs—is simply not present where a tax applies to all sales and uses of tangible personal property in the State. . . .

As such, *Murdock* and *Follett* plainly do not support appellant's free exercise claim. California's generally applicable sales and use tax is not a flat tax, represents only a small fraction of any retail sale, and applies neutrally to all retail sales of tangible personal property made in California. California imposes its sales and use tax even if the seller or the purchaser is charitable, religious, nonprofit, or state or local governmental in nature. Thus, the sales and use tax is not a tax on the right to disseminate religious information, ideas, or beliefs *per se;* rather, it is a tax on the privilege of making retail sales of tangible personal property and on the storage, use, or other consumption of tangible personal property in California. For example, California treats the sale of a Bible by a religious organization just as it would treat the sale of a Bible by a bookstore; as long as both are in-state retail sales of tangible personal property, they are both subject to the tax regardless of the motivation for the sale or the purchase. There is no danger that appellant's religious activity is being singled out for special and burdensome treatment.

Moreover, our concern in *Murdock* and *Follett* that flat license taxes operate as a precondition to the exercise of evangelistic activity is not present in this case, because the registration requirement, and the tax itself do not act as prior restraints—no fee is charged for registering, the tax is due regardless of preregistration, and the tax is not imposed as a precondition of disseminating the message. . . .

There is no evidence in this case that collection and payment of the tax violates appellant's sincere religious beliefs. California's nondiscriminatory Sales and Use Tax Law requires only that appellant collect the tax from its California purchasers and remit the tax money to the State. The only burden on appellant is the claimed reduction in income resulting from the presumably lower demand for appellant's wares (caused by the marginally higher price) and from the costs associated with administering the tax. As the Court made clear in *Hernandez,* however, to the extent that imposition of a generally applicable tax merely decreases the amount of money appellant has to spend on its religious activities, any such burden is not constitutionally significant. . . .

We therefore conclude that the collection and payment of the generally applicable tax in this case imposes no constitutionally significant burden on appellant's religious practices or beliefs. The Free Exercise Clause accordingly does not *require* the State to grant appellant an exemption from its generally applicable sales and use tax. Although it is of course possible to imagine that a more onerous tax rate, even if generally applicable, might effectively choke off an adherent's religious practices, we face no such situation in this case. Accordingly, we intimate no views as to whether such a generally applicable tax might violate the Free Exercise Clause.

B

Appellant also contends that application of the sales and use tax to its sale of religious materials violates the Establishment Clause because it fosters "an excessive government entanglement with religion." . . . Appellant alleges, for example, that the present controversy has featured on-site inspections of appellant's evangelistic crusades, lengthy on-site audits, examinations of appellant's books and records, threats of criminal prosecution, and layers of administrative and judicial proceedings. . . .

[W]e hold that California's imposition of sales and use tax liability on appellant threatens no excessive entanglement between church and state. First, we note that the evidence of administrative entanglement in this case is thin. Appellant alleges that collection and payment of the sales and use tax impose severe accounting burdens on it. The Court of Appeal, however, expressly found that the record did not support appellant's factual assertions, noting that appellant "had a sophisticated accounting staff and had recently computerized its accounting and that [appellant] in its own books and for purposes of obtaining a federal income tax exemption segregated 'retail sales' and 'donations.'"

Second, even assuming that the tax imposes substantial administrative burdens on appellant, such administrative and recordkeeping burdens do not rise to a constitutionally significant level. Collection and payment of the tax will of course require some contact between appellant and the State, but we have held that generally applicable administrative and recordkeeping regulations may be imposed on religious organization without running afoul of the Establishment Clause. See *Hernandez*, 490 U.S., 696-697 ("[R]outine regulatory interaction [such as application of neutral tax laws] which involves no inquiries into religious doctrine, . . . no delegation of state power to a religious body, . . . and no 'detailed monitoring and close administrative contact' between secular and religious bodies, . . . does not of itself violate the nonentanglement command"). . . .

Most significantly, the imposition of the sales and use tax without an exemption for appellant does not require the State to inquire into the religious content of the items sold or the religious motivation for selling or purchasing the items, because the materials are subject to the tax regardless of content or motive. From the State's point of view, the critical question is not whether the materials are religious, but whether there is a sale or a use, a question which involves only a secular determination. Thus, this case stands on firmer ground than *Hernandez*, because appellant offers the items at a stated price, thereby relieving the State of the need to place a monetary value on appellant's religious items. . . . Ironically, appellant's theory, under which government may not tax "religious core" activities but may tax "nonreligious" activities, would require government to do precisely what appellant asserts the Religion Clauses prohibit: "determine which expenditures are religious and which are secular." . . .

*Affirmed.*

---

### NOTES AND QUESTIONS

1. As one ground for finding no free exercise violation in *Jimmy Swaggart Ministries*, a unanimous Court writes that "[t]he only burden on appellant is the claimed reduction in income resulting from the presumably lower demand for appellant's wares." This quote is reminiscent of language found in *Braunfeld*. But wasn't that latter holding modified by *Sherbert*? What explains the difference here?

2. "A tax on Bibles?!" The *Swaggart Ministries* Court distinguishes *Murdock v. Pennsylvania* and *Follett v. McCormick* on the ground that those laws were "flat license taxes" that operated as a "prior restraint" on engaging in religious expression. But in striking the tax in *Follett*, the Court there noted that it was being imposed on the sale of a "religious book," and "that its publication and distribution [by Follett] c[a]me within the words, 'exercise of religion', as they are used in the Constitution." Is there something special about the Bible and other sacred texts that should render them immune from government regulation including taxation? If so, where does one draw the line? Most likely, a requirement that clergy pay income taxes necessitates churches to allocate a greater share of their income for salary in order to off-set the tax, resulting in less money to be spent on religious ministry. Does this inhibit the free exercise of religion?

3. Does California's uniform and religiously neutral tax system not violate the Free Exercise Clause because there is no cognizable burden on religious practice, or is there no cognizable burden on religious practice because California's tax system is uniform and religiously neutral? How does the Court see it? Why is this distinction significant?

4. The *Swaggart Ministries* Court states that California's tax system produces less entanglement between government and religion than a system that provides an exemption for the sale of religious items. What factors would support or refute this assertion? If the Court is correct, would not this issue arise in all situations involving mandated exemptions of religious conduct? Or can it be argued that there is something fundamentally different about a person citing his or her religious beliefs and activities and asking for an exemption from certain laws and tasking the government with identifying and separating religious from nonreligious expenditures in cases like this one?

## CHAPTER 8

# RISE AND FALL OF FREE EXERCISE EXEMPTIONS: *SMITH* AND BEYOND

In 1990 the rather uncertain course of the Free Exercise Clause, traced in the last chapter, was dramatically clarified, much to the detriment of Americans' freedom of religion, in the minds of many. The case was *Employment Division of Oregon v. Smith*. It combined issues of Native American religion, unemployment compensation, criminal law, and a new way of interpreting the Free Exercise Clause.

This chapter begins with an examination of the *Smith* case. It then considers a subsequent decision by the Court that helped to illuminate the limits of the *Smith* holding, the case of *Church of the Lukumi Babalu Aye v. City of Hialeah*. The final section of this chapter discusses two pieces of federal legislation that were enacted to provide a higher level of protection for the right to practice one's faith in the wake of the Court's shrinking interpretation of the Free Exercise Clause. The names of these pieces of legislation are the Religious Freedom Restoration Act (RFRA) of 1993 and the Religious Land Use and Institutionalized Persons Act (RLUIPA) of 2000. This final section of the chapter also includes two Supreme Court cases that address aspects of the constitutionality of these federal statutes. Thus, this chapter provides a window on some of the ways in which the political and judicial branches of government view their respective roles in protecting free exercise rights.

## THE FALL OF JUDICIALLY MANDATED FREE EXERCISE EXEMPTIONS

The plaintiffs in *Employment Division of Oregon v. Smith*, Alfred Smith and Galen Black, were employed at an organization devoted to helping people overcome chemical dependency. They had agreed, as a condition of employment, not to use or ingest any substance on Oregon's list of dangerous drugs. As members of the Native American Church, however, they used peyote in worship. Peyote is a mild hallucinogenic drug derived from the mescaline cactus. It had been used by the Native American Church for decades as an integral part of worship, designed to alter participants' consciousness and enhance their awareness of God or the spiritual realm. Peyote was on Oregon's list of prohibited drugs. When their employer discovered their use of peyote, Smith and Black were dismissed from their jobs. When they applied for state unemployment compensation, they were denied on grounds that they were guilty of misconduct in the workplace.

The Court, in an opinion by Justice Antonin Scalia, ruled against Smith and Black. That was not terribly surprising. In spite of the precedents of *Sherbert*, *Thomas*, and *Hobbie*, Smith and Black had violated a criminal law, i.e., peyote was a prohibited drug, and they had disobeyed a condition of their employment. What was unexpected was that the Court explicitly abandoned the "compelling state interest test" and narrowed its reading of the Free Exercise Clause, even though neither side in the dispute had briefed the Court on the idea or raised it in oral argument. The Court held the state did not need to have a compelling interest to interfere with religious behavior, provided the law did not single out religious conduct for regulation but was "generally applicable." In essence, a law of general application, so long as it did not target religious behavior, would prevail over a free exercise claim, no matter how much it burdened religious conduct. By so doing, the Court significantly reinterpreted the understanding of the requisites of the Free Exercise Clause.

Justice Scalia, in his *Smith* opinion and subsequently, has disagreed with the characterization that the *Smith* holding was inconsistent with Free Exercise jurisprudence. In the opinion, he argued that the "compelling state interest test" had not been uniformly used after its articulation in *Sherbert v. Verner*. The Court had used that standard in *Yoder* and in the unemployment compensation cases but, Scalia insisted, had not applied it in *Goldman v. Weinberger*, *O'Lone v. Estate of Shabazz*, *Bowen v. Roy*, and *Lyng v. Northwest Indian Cemetery Protection Association*. Scalia also argued there was strong precedent for his position in *Minersville School District v. Gobitis*, though he failed to mention that that case had been reversed in *West Virginia Board of Education v. Barnette*.

Whether Justice Scalia is correct or not about the precedent, it is uncontested that in the *Smith* decision the Court pulled back from a broader understanding of the Free Exercise Clause. The opinion suggests that a tension exists between the efficient functioning of modern democratic government and a robust free exercise interest. This narrower view of free exercise is also seen in the Court's statement that heightened scrutiny should be used only in cases where a free exercise right as well as some other constitutional right are infringed—such as freedom of the press, free speech, or freedom of assembly—that these rights should prevail over a law of general application. These are sometimes referred to as cases involving "hybrid rights." The opinion also states that the proper forum for the protection of religious practices that are burdened by neutral laws of general applicability rests with elected legislative majorities rather than with the courts. While there may or may not be merit to each of the Court's claims, they certainly represent a shift in the Court's philosophical approach to free exercise matters.

Justice O'Connor concurred in the judgment. She would have reached the same decision by using the "compelling state interest test." She believed Oregon had a strong interest in preserving obedience to its prohibited drug laws. But she criticized the Court severely for its new approach to free exercise disputes, claiming it was not consistent with either the First Amendment or the precedents of the Court.

Justices Blackmun, Brennan, and Marshall joined Justice O'Connor in her criticism of the Court's abandoning the *Sherbert* test. But they also argued that the case had been wrongly decided, that Smith and Black should have been awarded unemployment compensation. They argued that on the basis of the Native American Church's rules about the controlled use of peyote and the fact that many states and the federal government had made exceptions for the use of peyote in worship.

---

## EMPLOYMENT DIVISION v. SMITH
### 494 U.S. 872 (1990)

☒ JUSTICE SCALIA delivered the opinion of the Court.

This case requires us to decide whether the Free Exercise Clause of the First Amendment permits the State of Oregon to include religiously inspired peyote use within the reach of its general criminal prohibition on use of that drug, and thus permits the State to deny unemployment benefits to persons dismissed from their jobs because of such religiously inspired use.

### I

Oregon law prohibits the knowing or intentional possession of a "controlled substance" unless the substance has been prescribed by a medical practitioner. The law defines "controlled substance" as a drug classified in Schedules I through V of the Federal Controlled Substances Act, as modified by the State Board of Pharmacy. Persons who violate this provision by possessing a controlled substance listed on Schedule I are "guilty of a Class B felony." As compiled by the State Board of Pharmacy under its statutory authority, Schedule I contains the drug peyote, a hallucinogen derived from the plant *Lophophora williamsii Lemaire.*

Respondents Alfred Smith and Galen Black (hereinafter respondents) were fired from their jobs with a private drug rehabilitation organization because they ingested peyote for sacramental purposes at a ceremony of the Native American Church, of which both are members. When respondents applied to petitioner Employment Division (hereinafter petitioner) for unemployment compensation, they were determined to be ineligible for benefits because they had been discharged for work-related "misconduct." . . .

Before this Court in 1987, petitioner continued to maintain that the illegality of respondents'. peyote consumption was relevant to their constitutional claim. We agreed, concluding that "if a State has prohibited through its criminal laws certain kinds of religiously motivated conduct without violating the First Amendment, it certainly follows that it may impose the lesser burden of denying unemployment compensation benefits to persons who engage in that conduct." *Employment Div., Dept. of Human Resources of Oregon v. Smith,* 485 U.S. 660, 670 (1988) (*Smith I*). We noted, however, that the Oregon Supreme Court had not decided whether respondents' sacramental use of peyote was in fact proscribed by Oregon's controlled substance law, and that this issue was a matter of dispute between the parties. Being "uncertain about the legality of the religious use of peyote in Oregon," we determined that it would not be "appropriate for us to decide whether the practice is protected by the Federal Constitution." *Id.*, 673. Accordingly, we vacated the judgment of the Oregon Supreme Court and remanded for further proceedings. *Id.*, 674.

On remand, the Oregon Supreme Court held that respondents' religiously inspired use of peyote fell within the prohibition of the Oregon statute, which "makes no exception for the sacramental use" of the drug. 763 P.2d 146, 148 (1988). It then considered whether that prohibition was valid under the Free Exercise Clause, and concluded that it was not. The court therefore reaffirmed its previous ruling that the State could not deny unemployment benefits to respondents for having engaged in that practice.

We again granted certiorari.

## II

Respondents' claim for relief rests on our decisions in *Sherbert v. Verner*, *Thomas v. Review Bd. of Indiana Employment Security Div.*, and *Hobbie v. Unemployment Appeals Comm'n of Florida*, in which we held that a State could not condition the availability of unemployment insurance on an individual's willingness to forgo conduct required by his religion. As we observed in *Smith I*, however, the conduct at issue in those cases was not prohibited by law. We held that distinction to be critical, for "if Oregon does prohibit the religious use of peyote, and if that prohibition is consistent with the Federal Constitution, there is no federal right to engage in that conduct in Oregon," and "the State is free to withhold unemployment compensation from respondents for engaging in work-related misconduct, despite its religious motivation." 485 U.S., 672 . Now that the Oregon Supreme Court has confirmed that Oregon does prohibit the religious use of peyote, we proceed to consider whether that prohibition is permissible under the Free Exercise Clause.

## A

The Free Exercise Clause of the First Amendment, which has been made applicable to the States by incorporation into the Fourteenth Amendment, provides that "Congress shall make no law respecting an establishment of religion, or *prohibiting the free exercise thereof* . . . ." (emphasis added). The free exercise of religion means, first and foremost, the right to believe and profess whatever religious doctrine one desires. Thus, the First Amendment obviously excludes all "governmental regulation of religious beliefs as such." *Sherbert v. Verner*, 374 U.S. 398, 402. The government may not compel affirmation of religious belief, see *Torcaso v. Watkins*, punish the expression of religious doctrines it believes to be false, *United States v. Ballard*, impose special disabilities on the basis of religious views or religious status, see *McDaniel v. Paty*, or lend its power to one or the other side in controversies over religious authority or dogma, see *Presbyterian Church in U.S. v. Mary Elizabeth Blue Hull Memorial Presbyterian Church.* . . .

But the "exercise of religion" often involves not only belief and profession but the performance of (or abstention from) physical acts: assembling with others for a worship service, participating in sacramental use of bread and wine, proselytizing, abstaining from certain foods or certain modes of transportation. It would be true, we think (though no case of ours has involved the point), that a State would be "prohibiting the free exercise [of religion]" if it sought to ban such acts or abstentions only when they are engaged in for religious reasons, or only because of the religious belief that they display. It would doubtless be unconstitutional, for example, to ban the casting of "statues that are to be used for worship purposes," or to prohibit bowing down before a golden calf.

Respondents in the present case, however, seek to carry the meaning of "prohibiting the free exercise [of religion]" one large step further. They contend that their religious motivation for using peyote places them beyond the reach of a criminal law that is not specifically directed at their religious practice, and that is concededly constitutional as applied to those who use the drug for other reasons. They assert, in other words, that "prohibiting the free exercise [of religion]" includes requiring any individual to observe a generally applicable law that requires (or forbids) the performance of an act that his religious belief forbids (or requires). As a textual matter, we do not think the words must be given that meaning. It is no more necessary to regard the collection of a general tax, for example, as "prohibiting the free exercise [of religion]" by those citizens who believe support of organized government to be sinful, than it is to regard the same tax as "abridging the freedom . . . of the press" of those publishing companies that must pay the tax as a condition of staying in business. It is a permissible reading of the text, in the one case as in the other, to say that if prohibiting the exercise of religion (or burdening the activity of printing) is not the object of the tax but merely the incidental effect of a generally applicable and otherwise valid provision, the First Amendment has not been offended. . . .

Our decisions reveal that the latter reading is the correct one. We have never held that an individual's religious beliefs excuse him from compliance with an otherwise valid law prohibiting conduct that the State is free to regulate. On the contrary, the record of more than a century of our free exercise jurisprudence contradicts that proposition. As described succinctly by Justice Frankfurter in *Minersville School Dist. Bd. of Ed. v. Gobitis,* 310 U.S. 586, 594-595 (1940): "Conscientious scruples have not, in the course of the long struggle for religious toleration, relieved the individual from obedience to a general law not aimed at the promotion or restriction of religious beliefs. The mere possession of religious convictions which contradict the relevant concerns of a political society does not relieve the citizen from the discharge of political responsibilities (footnote omitted)." We first had occasion to assert that principle in *Reynolds v. United States,* where we rejected the claim that criminal laws against polygamy could not be constitutionally applied to those whose religion commanded the practice. "Laws," we said, "are made for the government of actions, and while they cannot interfere with mere religious belief and opinions, they may with practices. . . . Can a man excuse his practices to the contrary because of his religious belief? To permit this would be to make the professed doctrines of religious belief superior to the law of the land, and in effect to permit every citizen to become a law unto himself." *Id.,* 166-167.

Subsequent decisions have consistently held that the right of free exercise does not relieve an individual of the obligation to comply with a "valid and neutral law of general applicability on the ground that the law proscribes (or prescribes) conduct that his religion prescribes (or proscribes)." *United States v. Lee,* 455 U.S. 252, 263, n. 3 (1982) (STEVENS, J., concurring in judgment). . . . In *Prince v. Massachusetts,* we held that a mother could be prosecuted under the child labor laws for using her children to dispense literature in the streets, her religious motivation notwithstanding. We found no constitutional infirmity in "excluding [these children] from doing there what no other children may do." 321 U.S. 158, 171. In *Braunfeld v. Brown,* we upheld Sunday-closing laws against the claim that they burdened the religious practices of persons whose religions compelled them to refrain from work on other days. In *Gillette v. United States,* we sustained the military Selective Service System against the claim that it violated free exercise by conscripting persons who opposed a particular war on religious grounds.

Our most recent decision involving a neutral, generally applicable regulatory law that compelled activity forbidden by an individual's religion was *United States v. Lee*. There, an Amish employer, on behalf of himself and his employees, sought exemption from collection and payment of Social Security taxes on the ground that the Amish faith prohibited participation in governmental support programs. We rejected the claim that an exemption was constitutionally required. There would be no way, we observed, to distinguish the Amish believer's objection to Social Security taxes from the religious objections that others might have to the collection or use of other taxes.

> If, for example, a religious adherent believes war is a sin, and if a certain percentage of the federal budget can be identified as devoted to war-related activities, such individuals would have a similarly valid claim to be exempt from paying that percentage of the income tax. The tax system could not function if denominations were allowed to challenge the tax system because tax payments were spent in a manner that violates their religious belief. 455 U.S. 252, 260.

The only decisions in which we have held that the First Amendment bars application of a neutral, generally applicable law to religiously motivated action have involved not the Free Exercise Clause alone, but the Free Exercise Clause in conjunction with other constitutional protections, such as freedom of speech and of the press, see *Cantwell v. Connecticut* 310 U.S., 304-307 (invalidating a licensing system for religious and charitable solicitations under which the administrator had discretion to deny a license to any cause he deemed nonreligious); *Murdock v. Pennsylvania* (invalidating a flat tax on solicitation as applied to the dissemination of religious ideas); *Follett v. McCormick* (same); or the right of parents, acknowledged in *Pierce v. Society of Sisters*, to direct the education of their children. Some of our cases prohibiting compelled expression, decided exclusively upon free speech grounds, have also involved freedom of religion, cf. *Wooley v. Maynard* (invalidating compelled display of a license plate slogan that offended individual religious beliefs); *West Virginia Bd. of Education v. Barnette* (invalidating compulsory flag salute statute challenged by religious objectors). And it is easy to envision a case in which a challenge on freedom of association grounds would likewise be reinforced by Free Exercise Clause concerns. Cf. *Roberts v. United States Jaycees*, 468 U.S. 609, 622 (1984) ("An individual's freedom to speak, to worship, and to petition the government for the redress of grievances could not be vigorously protected from interference by the State [if] a correlative freedom to engage in group effort toward those ends were not also guaranteed").

The present case does not present such a hybrid situation, but a free exercise claim unconnected with any communicative activity or parental right. Respondents urge us to hold, quite simply, that when otherwise prohibitable conduct is accompanied by religious convictions, not only the convictions but the conduct itself must be free from governmental regulation. We have never held that, and decline to do so now. There being no contention that Oregon's drug law represents an attempt to regulate religious beliefs, the communication of religious beliefs, or the raising of one's children in those beliefs, the rule to which we have adhered ever since *Reynolds* plainly controls. "Our cases do not at their farthest reach support the proposition that a stance of conscientious opposition relieves an objector from any colliding duty fixed by a democratic government." *Gillette v. United States*, 401 U.S. 437, 461.

B

Respondents argue that even though exemption from generally applicable criminal laws need not automatically be extended to religiously motivated actors, at least the claim for a religious exemption must be evaluated under the balancing test set forth in *Sherbert v. Verner*. Under the *Sherbert* test, governmental actions that substantially burden a religious practice must be justified by a compelling governmental interest. . . . Applying that test we have, on three occasions, invalidated state unemployment compensation rules that conditioned the availability of benefits upon an applicant's willingness to work under conditions forbidden by his religion. See *Sherbert v. Verner*; *Thomas v. Review Bd. of Indiana Employment Security Div.*; *Hobbie v. Unemployment Appeals Comm'n of Florida*. We have never invalidated any governmental action on the basis of the *Sherbert* test except the denial of unemployment compensation. Although we have sometimes purported to apply the *Sherbert* test in contexts other than that, we have always found the test satisfied, see *United States v. Lee*; *Gillette v. United States*. In recent years we have abstained from applying the *Sherbert* test (outside the unemployment compensation field) at all. In *Bowen v. Roy*, we declined to apply *Sherbert* analysis to a federal statutory scheme that required benefit applicants and recipients to provide their Social Security numbers. The plaintiffs in that case asserted that it would violate their religious beliefs to obtain and provide a Social Security number for their daughter. We held the statute's application to the plaintiffs valid regardless of whether it was necessary to effectuate a compelling interest. . . . In *Lyng v. Northwest Indian Cemetery Protective Assn.*, we declined to apply *Sherbert* analysis to the Government's logging and road construction activities on lands used for religious purposes by several Native American Tribes, even though it was undisputed that the activities "could have devastating effects on traditional Indian religious practices," 485 U.S., 451. In *Goldman v. Weinberger*, we rejected application of the *Sherbert* test to military dress regulations that forbade the wearing of yarmulkes. In *O'Lone v. Estate of Shabazz*, we sustained, without mentioning the *Sherbert* test, a prison's refusal to excuse inmates from work requirements to attend worship services.

Even if we were inclined to breathe into *Sherbert* some life beyond the unemployment compensation field, we would not apply it to require exemptions from a generally applicable criminal law. The *Sherbert* test, it must be recalled, was developed in a context that lent itself to individualized governmental assessment of the reasons for the relevant conduct. As a plurality of the Court noted in *Roy*, a distinctive feature of unemployment compensation programs is that their eligibility criteria invite consideration of the particular circumstances behind an applicant's unemployment: "The statutory conditions [in *Sherbert* and *Thomas*] provided that a person was not eligible for unemployment compensation benefits if, 'without good cause,' he had quit work or refused available work. The 'good cause' standard created a mechanism for individualized exemptions." *Bowen v. Roy*, 476 U.S., at 708 (opinion of *Burger*, C. J., joined by *Powell* and REHNQUIST, JJ.). See also *Sherbert*, 374 U.S., at 401, n. 4 (reading state unemployment compensation law as allowing benefits for unemployment caused by at least some "personal reasons"). As the plurality pointed out in *Roy*, our decisions in the unemployment cases stand for the proposition that where the State has in place a system of individual exemptions, it may not refuse to extend that system to cases of "religious hardship" without compelling reason. *Bowen v. Roy*, 476 U.S., at 708.

Whether or not the decisions are that limited, they at least have nothing to do with an across-the-board criminal prohibition on a particular form of conduct. Although, as noted earlier, we have sometimes used the *Sherbert* test to analyze free exercise challenges to such laws, see *United States v. Lee*, 257-260; *Gillette v. United States*, 462, we have never applied the test to invalidate one. We conclude today that the sounder approach, and the approach in accord with the vast majority of our precedents, is to hold the test inapplicable to such challenges. The government's ability to enforce generally applicable prohibitions of socially harmful conduct, like its ability to carry out other aspects of public policy, "cannot depend on measuring the effects of a governmental action on a religious objector's spiritual development." *Lyng*, 451. To make an individual's obligation to obey such a law contingent upon the law's coincidence with his religious beliefs, except where the State's interest is "compelling"—permitting him, by virtue of his beliefs, "to become a law unto himself," *Reynolds v. United States* 98 U.S., 167—contradicts both constitutional tradition and common sense.

The "compelling government interest" requirement seems benign, because it is familiar from other fields. But using it as the standard that must be met before the government may accord different treatment on the basis of race or before the government may regulate the content of speech is not remotely comparable to using it for the purpose asserted here. What it produces in those other fields—equality of treatment and an unrestricted flow of contending speech—are constitutional norms; what it would produce here—a private right to ignore generally applicable laws—is a constitutional anomaly.

Nor is it possible to limit the impact of respondents' proposal by requiring a "compelling state interest" only when the conduct prohibited is "central" to the individual's religion. . . . It is no more appropriate for judges to determine the "centrality" of religious beliefs before applying a "compelling interest" test in the free exercise field, than it would be for them to determine the "importance" of ideas before applying the "compelling interest" test in the free speech field. What principle of law or logic can be brought to bear to contradict a believer's assertion that a particular act is "central" to his personal faith? Judging the centrality of different religious practices is akin to the unacceptable "business of evaluating the relative merits of differing religious claims." *United States v. Lee*, 455 U.S., 263 n. 2 (STEVENS, J., concurring). As we reaffirmed only last Term, "[i]t is not within the judicial ken to question the centrality of particular beliefs or practices to a faith, or the validity of particular litigants' interpretations of those creeds." *Hernandez v. Commissioner*, 490 U.S., 699. Repeatedly and in many different contexts, we have warned that courts must not presume to determine the place of a particular belief in a religion or the plausibility of a religious claim. See, e.g., *Thomas v. Review Bd. of Indiana Employment Security Div.*; *Presbyterian Church in U.S. v. Mary Elizabeth Blue Hull Memorial Presbyterian Church*; *Jones v. Wolf*; *United States v. Ballard*.

If the "compelling interest" test is to be applied at all, then, it must be applied across the board, to all actions thought to be religiously commanded. Moreover, if "compelling interest" really means what it says (and watering it down here would subvert its rigor in the other fields where it is applied), many laws will not meet the test. Any society adopting such a system would be courting anarchy, but that danger increases in direct proportion to the society's diversity of religious beliefs, and its determination to coerce or suppress none of them. Precisely because "we are a cosmopolitan nation made up of people of almost every conceivable religious preference," *Braunfeld v. Brown* 366 U.S., 606, and precisely because we value and protect that religious divergence, we cannot afford the luxury of deeming presumptively invalid, as applied to the religious objector, every regulation of conduct that does not protect an interest of the highest order. The rule respondents favor would open the prospect of constitutionally required religious exemptions from civic obligations of almost every conceivable kind—ranging from compulsory military service, see, e.g., *Gillette v. United States*, to the payment of taxes, see, e.g., *United States v. Lee*; to health and safety regulation such as manslaughter and child neglect laws, see, e.g., *Funkhouser v. State* 763 P.2d 695 (Okla. Crim. App. 1988), compulsory vaccination laws, see, e.g., *Cude v. State* 377 S. W. 2d 816 (1964), drug laws, see, e.g., *Olsen v. Drug Enforcement Administration* 878 F.2d 1458 (1989), and traffic laws, see *Cox v. New Hampshire*; to social welfare legislation such as minimum wage laws, see *Tony and Susan Alamo Foundation v. Secretary of Labor*, child labor laws, see *Prince v. Massachusetts*, animal cruelty laws, see, e.g., *Church of the Lukumi Babalu Aye Inc. v. City of Hialeah*, 723 F. Supp. 1467 (SD Fla. 1989), environmental protection laws, see *United States v. Little* 638 F. Supp. 337 (Mont. 1986), and laws providing for equality of opportunity for the races, see, e.g., *Bob Jones University v. United States*. The First Amendment's protection of religious liberty does not require this. Values that are protected against government interference through enshrinement in the Bill of Rights are not thereby banished from the political process. Just as a society that believes in the negative protection accorded to the press by the First Amendment is likely to enact laws that affirmatively foster the dissemination of the printed word, so also a society that believes in the negative protection accorded to religious belief can be expected to be solicitous of that value in its legislation as well. It is therefore not surprising that a number of States have made an exception to their drug laws for sacramental peyote use. See, e.g., Ariz. Rev. Stat. Ann. 13-3402(B)(1)-(3) (1989); Colo. Rev. Stat. 12-22-317(3) (1985); N. M. Stat. Ann. 30-31-6(D) (Supp. 1989). But to say that a nondiscriminatory religious-practice exemption is permitted, or even that it is desirable, is not to say that it is constitutionally required, and that the appropriate occasions for its creation can be discerned by the courts. It may fairly be said that leaving accommodation to the political process will place at a relative disadvantage those religious practices that are not widely engaged in; but that unavoidable consequence of democratic government must be preferred to a system in which each conscience is a law unto itself or in which judges weigh the social importance of all laws against the centrality of all religious beliefs.

\*\*\*\*

Because respondents' ingestion of peyote was prohibited under Oregon law, and because that prohibition is constitutional, Oregon may, consistent with the Free Exercise Clause, deny respondents unemployment compensation when their dismissal results from use of the drug. The decision of the Oregon Supreme Court is accordingly reversed.

*It is so ordered.*

JUSTICE O'CONNOR, with whom JUSTICE BRENNAN, JUSTICE MARSHALL, and JUSTICE BLACKMUN join as to Parts I and II, concurring in the judgment. (Although JUSTICE BRENNAN, JUSTICE MARSHALL, and

JUSTICE BLACKMUN join Parts I and II of this opinion, they do not concur in the judgment.)

Although I agree with the result the Court reaches in this case, I cannot join its opinion. In my view, today's holding dramatically departs from well-settled First Amendment jurisprudence, appears unnecessary to resolve the question presented, and is incompatible with our Nation's fundamental commitment to individual religious liberty.

I . . .
II

The Court today extracts from our long history of free exercise precedents the single categorical rule that "if prohibiting the exercise of religion . . . is . . . merely the incidental effect of a generally applicable and otherwise valid provision, the First Amendment has not been offended." Indeed, the Court holds that where the law is a generally applicable criminal prohibition, our usual free exercise jurisprudence does not even apply. To reach this sweeping result, however, the Court must not only give a strained reading of the First Amendment but must also disregard our consistent application of free exercise doctrine to cases involving generally applicable regulations that burden religious conduct.

A

The Free Exercise Clause of the First Amendment commands that "Congress shall make no law . . . prohibiting the free exercise [of religion]." In *Cantwell v. Connecticut*, we held that this prohibition applies to the States by incorporation into the Fourteenth Amendment and that it categorically forbids government regulation of religious beliefs. As the Court recognizes, however, the "free exercise" of religion often, if not invariably, requires the performance of (or abstention from) certain acts. Cf. 3 *A New English Dictionary on Historical Principles* 401-402 (J. Murray ed. 1897) (defining "exercise" to include "[t]he practice and performance of rites and ceremonies, worship, etc.; the right or permission to celebrate the observances (of a religion)" and religious observances such as acts of public and private worship, preaching, and prophesying). "[B]elief and action cannot be neatly confined in logic-tight compartments." *Wisconsin v. Yoder* 406 U.S. 205, 220 (1972). Because the First Amendment does not distinguish between religious belief and religious conduct, conduct motivated by sincere religious belief, like the belief itself, must be at least presumptively protected by the Free Exercise Clause.

The Court today, however, interprets the Clause to permit the government to prohibit, without justification, conduct mandated by an individual's religious beliefs, so long as that prohibition is generally applicable. But a law that prohibits certain conduct—conduct that happens to be an act of worship for someone—manifestly does prohibit that person's free exercise of his religion. A person who is barred from engaging in religiously motivated conduct is barred from freely exercising his religion. Moreover, that person is barred from freely exercising his religion regardless of whether the law prohibits the conduct only when engaged in for religious reasons, only by members of that religion, or by all persons. It is difficult to deny that a law that prohibits religiously motivated conduct, even if the law is generally applicable, does not at least implicate First Amendment concerns.

The Court responds that generally applicable laws are "one large step" removed from laws aimed at specific religious practices. The First Amendment, however, does not distinguish between laws that are generally applicable and laws that target particular religious practices. Indeed, few States would be so naive as to enact a law directly prohibiting or burdening a religious practice as such. Our free exercise cases have all concerned generally applicable laws that had the effect of significantly burdening a religious practice. If the First Amendment is to have any vitality, it ought not be construed to cover only the extreme and hypothetical situation in which a State directly targets a religious practice. As we have noted in a slightly different context, "'[s]uch a test has no basis in precedent and relegates a serious First Amendment value to the barest level of minimum scrutiny that the Equal Protection Clause already provides.'" *Hobbie v. Unemployment Appeals Comm'n of Florida* 480 U.S. 136, 141-142 (1987) (quoting *Bowen v. Roy* 476 U.S. 693, 727 (1986) (O'CONNOR, J., concurring in part and dissenting in part)).

To say that a person's right to free exercise has been burdened, of course, does not mean that he has an absolute right to engage in the conduct. Under our established First Amendment jurisprudence, we have recognized that the freedom to act, unlike the freedom to believe, cannot be absolute. . . . Instead, we have respected both the First Amendment's express textual mandate and the governmental interest in regulation of conduct by requiring the government to justify any substantial burden on religiously motivated conduct by a compelling state interest and by means narrowly tailored to achieve that interest. . . . The compelling interest test effectuates the First Amendment's command that religious liberty is an independent liberty, that it occupies a preferred position, and that the Court will not permit encroachments upon this liberty, whether direct or indirect, unless required by clear and compelling governmental interests "of the highest order," *Yoder*, 215. "Only an especially important governmental interest pursued by narrowly tailored means can justify exacting a sacrifice of First Amendment freedoms as the price for an equal share of the rights, benefits, and privileges enjoyed by other citizens." *Roy*, 728 (opinion concurring in part and dissenting in part).

The Court attempts to support its narrow reading of the Clause by claiming that "[w]e have never held that an individual's religious beliefs excuse him from compliance with an otherwise valid law prohibiting conduct that the State is free to regulate." But as the Court later notes, as it must, in cases such as *Cantwell* and *Yoder* we have in fact interpreted the Free Exercise Clause to forbid application of a generally applicable prohibition to religiously motivated conduct. See *Cantwell*, 304-307; *Yoder* 406 U.S., 214-234. Indeed, in *Yoder* we expressly rejected the interpretation the Court now adopts:

> [O]ur decisions have rejected the idea that religiously grounded conduct is always outside the protection of the Free Exercise Clause. It is true that activities of individuals, even when religiously based, are often subject to regulation by the States in the exercise of their undoubted power to promote the health, safety, and general welfare, or the Federal Government in the exercise of its delegated powers. But to agree that religiously grounded conduct must often be subject to the broad police power of the State is not to deny that there are areas of conduct protected by the Free Exercise Clause of the First Amendment and thus beyond the power of the State to control, *even under regulations of general applicability*. . . .

... A regulation neutral on its face may, in its application, nonetheless offend the constitutional requirement for government neutrality if
it unduly burdens the free exercise of religion. *Id.*, 219-220 (emphasis
added; citations omitted).

The Court endeavors to escape from our decisions in *Cantwell* and *Yoder*
by labeling them "hybrid" decisions, but there is no denying that both cases
expressly relied on the Free Exercise Clause, see *Cantwell* 310 U.S., 303-307;
*Yoder*, 219-229, and that we have consistently regarded those cases as part of
the mainstream of our free exercise jurisprudence. Moreover, in each of the
other cases cited by the Court to support its categorical rule, we rejected the
particular constitutional claims before us only after carefully weighing the
competing interests. See *Prince v. Massachusetts* 321 U.S. 158, 168-170 (1944)
(state interest in regulating children's activities justifies denial of religious exemption from child labor laws); *Braunfeld v. Brown* 366 U.S. 599, 608-609
(1961) (plurality opinion) (state interest in uniform day of rest justifies denial
of religious exemption from Sunday closing law); *Gillette*, 462 (state interest in
military affairs justifies denial of religious exemption from conscription laws);
*Lee*, 258-259 (state interest in comprehensive Social Security system justifies denial of religious exemption from mandatory participation requirement).
That we rejected the free exercise claims in those cases hardly calls into question the applicability of First Amendment doctrine in the first place. Indeed,
it is surely unusual to judge the vitality of a constitutional doctrine by looking
to the win-loss record of the plaintiffs who happen to come before us.

B

Respondents, of course, do not contend that their conduct is automatically immune from all governmental regulation simply because it is motivated
by their sincere religious beliefs. The Court's rejection of that argument might
therefore be regarded as merely harmless dictum. Rather, respondents invoke
our traditional compelling interest test to argue that the Free Exercise Clause
requires the State to grant them a limited exemption from its general criminal
prohibition against the possession of peyote. The Court today, however, denies them even the opportunity to make that argument, concluding that "the
sounder approach, and the approach in accord with the vast majority of our
precedents, is to hold the [compelling interest] test inapplicable to" challenges
to general criminal prohibitions.

In my view, however, the essence of a free exercise claim is relief from a
burden imposed by government on religious practices or beliefs, whether the
burden is imposed directly through laws that prohibit or compel specific religious practices, or indirectly through laws that, in effect, make abandonment
of one's own religion or conformity to the religious beliefs of others the price
of an equal place in the civil community. As we explained in *Thomas*:

"Where the state conditions receipt of an important benefit upon conduct
proscribed by a religious faith, or where it denies such a benefit because of
conduct mandated by religious belief, thereby putting substantial pressure on
an adherent to modify his behavior and to violate his beliefs, a burden upon
religion exists." 450 U.S., 717-718.

... A State that makes criminal an individual's religiously motivated conduct burdens that individual's free exercise of religion in the severest manner
possible, for it "results in the choice to the individual of either abandoning

his religious principle or facing criminal prosecution." *Braunfeld*, 605. I would have thought it beyond argument that such laws implicate free exercise concerns.

Indeed, we have never distinguished between cases in which a State conditions receipt of a benefit on conduct prohibited by religious beliefs and cases in which a State affirmatively prohibits such conduct. The *Sherbert* compelling interest test applies in both kinds of cases. . . . As I noted in *Bowen v. Roy*:

> The fact that the underlying dispute involves an award of benefits rather than an exaction of penalties does not grant the Government license to apply a different version of the Constitution. . . .
>
> . . . The fact that appellees seek exemption from a precondition that the Government attaches to an award of benefits does not, therefore, generate a meaningful distinction between this case and one where appellees seek an exemption from the Government's imposition of penalties upon them. 476 U.S., 731-732 (opinion concurring in part and dissenting in part).

I would reaffirm that principle today: A neutral criminal law prohibiting conduct that a State may legitimately regulate is, if anything, more burdensome than a neutral civil statute placing legitimate conditions on the award of a State benefit.

Legislatures, of course, have always been "left free to reach actions which were in violation of social duties or subversive of good order." *Reynolds* 98 U.S., 164; see also *Yoder*, 219-220; *Braunfeld* 366 U.S., 603-604. Yet because of the close relationship between conduct and religious belief, "[i]n every case the power to regulate must be so exercised as not, in attaining a permissible end, unduly to infringe the protected freedom." *Cantwell* 310 U.S., 304. Once it has been shown that a government regulation or criminal prohibition burdens the free exercise of religion, we have consistently asked the government to demonstrate that unbending application of its regulation to the religious objector "is essential to accomplish an overriding governmental interest," *Lee*, 257-258, or represents "the least restrictive means of achieving some compelling state interest," *Thomas*, 718. . . . To me, the sounder approach—the approach more consistent with our role as judges to decide each case on its individual merits—is to apply this test in each case to determine whether the burden on the specific plaintiffs before us is constitutionally significant and whether the particular criminal interest asserted by the State before us is compelling. Even if, as an empirical matter, a government's criminal laws might usually serve a compelling interest in health, safety, or public order, the First Amendment at least requires a case-by-case determination of the question, sensitive to the facts of each particular claim. . . . Given the range of conduct that a State might legitimately make criminal, we cannot assume, merely because a law carries criminal sanctions and is generally applicable, that the First Amendment never requires the State to grant a limited exemption for religiously motivated conduct.

Moreover, we have not "rejected" or "declined to apply" the compelling interest test in our recent cases. Recent cases have instead affirmed that test as a fundamental part of our First Amendment doctrine. See, e.g., *Hernandez* 490 U.S., 699; *Hobbie*, 141-142 (rejecting Chief Justice Burger's suggestion in *Roy*, 707-708, that free exercise claims be assessed under a less rigorous "reasonable means" standard). The cases cited by the Court signal no retreat from our consistent adherence to the compelling interest test. In both *Bowen v. Roy* and *Lyng v. Northwest Indian Cemetery Protective Assn.*, for example, we expressly distinguished *Sherbert* on the ground that the First Amendment does not "require the Government itself to behave in ways that the individual believes will further his or her spiritual development. . . . The Free Exercise Clause simply cannot be understood to require the Government to conduct its own internal affairs in ways that comport with the religious beliefs of particular citizens." *Roy*, 699. . . . This distinction makes sense because "the Free Exercise Clause is written in terms of what the government cannot do to the individual, not in terms of what the individual can exact from the government." *Sherbert*, 412 (DOUGLAS, J., concurring). Because the case *sub judice*, like the other cases in which we have applied *Sherbert*, plainly falls into the former category, I would apply those established precedents to the facts of this case.

Similarly, the other cases cited by the Court for the proposition that we have rejected application of the *Sherbert* test outside the unemployment compensation field, are distinguishable because they arose in the narrow, specialized contexts in which we have not traditionally required the government to justify a burden on religious conduct by articulating a compelling interest. See *Goldman v. Weinberger* 475 U.S. 503, 507 (1986) ("Our review of military regulations challenged on First Amendment grounds is far more deferential than constitutional review of similar laws or regulations designed for civilian society"); *O'Lone v. Estate of Shabazz* 482 U.S. 342, 349 (1987) ("[P]rison regulations alleged to infringe constitutional rights are judged under a 'reasonableness' test less restrictive than that ordinarily applied to alleged infringements of fundamental constitutional rights") (citation omitted). That we did not apply the compelling interest test in these cases says nothing about whether the test should continue to apply in paradigm free exercise cases such as the one presented here.

The Court today gives no convincing reason to depart from settled First Amendment jurisprudence. There is nothing talismanic about neutral laws of general applicability or general criminal prohibitions, for laws neutral toward religion can coerce a person to violate his religious conscience or intrude upon his religious duties just as effectively as laws aimed at religion. Although the Court suggests that the compelling interest test, as applied to generally applicable laws, would result in a "constitutional anomaly," the First Amendment unequivocally makes freedom of religion, like freedom from race discrimination and freedom of speech, a "constitutional nor[m]," not an "anomaly." Nor would application of our established free exercise doctrine to this case necessarily be incompatible with our equal protection cases. We have in any event recognized that the Free Exercise Clause protects values distinct from those protected by the Equal Protection Clause. See *Hobbie* 480 U.S., 141-142. As the language of the Clause itself makes clear, an individual's free exercise of religion is a preferred constitutional activity. See, e.g., McConnell, Accommodation of Religion, *1985 S. Ct. Rev.* 1, 9 ("[T]he text of the First Amendment itself 'singles out' religion for special protections"); P. Kauper, *Religion and the Constitution* 17 (1964). A law that makes criminal such an activity therefore triggers constitutional concern—and heightened judicial scrutiny—even if it does not target the particular religious conduct at issue. Our free speech cases similarly recognize that neutral regulations that affect free speech values are subject to a balancing, rather than categorical, approach. See, e.g., *United States v. O'Brien* 391 U.S. 367, 377 (1968); *Renton v. Playtime Theatres, Inc.* 475 U.S. 41, 46-47

(1986); cf. *Anderson v. Celebrezze* 460 U.S. 780, 792-794 (1983) (generally applicable laws may impinge on free association concerns). The Court's parade of horribles, not only fails as a reason for discarding the compelling interest test, it instead demonstrates just the opposite: that courts have been quite capable of applying our free exercise jurisprudence to strike sensible balances between religious liberty and competing state interests.

Finally, the Court today suggests that the disfavoring of minority religions is an "unavoidable consequence" under our system of government and that accommodation of such religions must be left to the political process. In my view, however, the First Amendment was enacted precisely to protect the rights of those whose religious practices are not shared by the majority and may be viewed with hostility. The history of our free exercise doctrine amply demonstrates the harsh impact majoritarian rule has had on unpopular or emerging religious groups such as the Jehovah's Witnesses and the Amish. Indeed, the words of Justice Jackson in *West Virginia State Bd. of Ed. v. Barnette* (overruling *Minersville School Dist. v. Gobitis*) are apt:

> The very purpose of a Bill of Rights was to withdraw certain subjects from the vicissitudes of political controversy, to place them beyond the reach of majorities and officials and to establish them as legal principles to be applied by the courts. One's right to life, liberty, and property, to free speech, a free press, freedom of worship and assembly, and other fundamental rights may not be submitted to vote; they depend on the outcome of no elections. 319 U.S., 638.

See also *United States v. Ballard* 322 U.S. 78, 87 (1944) ("The Fathers of the Constitution were not unaware of the varied and extreme views of religious sects, of the violence of disagreement among them, and of the lack of any one religious creed on which all men would agree. They fashioned a charter of government which envisaged the widest possible toleration of conflicting views"). The compelling interest test reflects the First Amendment's mandate of preserving religious liberty to the fullest extent possible in a pluralistic society. For the Court to deem this command a "luxury," is to denigrate "[t]he very purpose of a Bill of Rights."

### III

The Court's holding today not only misreads settled First Amendment precedent; it appears to be unnecessary to this case. I would reach the same result applying our established free exercise jurisprudence.

### A

There is no dispute that Oregon's criminal prohibition of peyote places a severe burden on the ability of respondents to freely exercise their religion. Peyote is a sacrament of the Native American Church and is regarded as vital to respondents' ability to practice their religion. . . . As we noted in *Smith I*, the Oregon Supreme Court concluded that "the Native American Church is a recognized religion, that peyote is a sacrament of that church, and that respondent's beliefs were sincerely held." 485 U.S., 667. Under Oregon law, as construed by that State's highest court, members of the Native American Church must choose between carrying out the ritual embodying their religious beliefs and avoidance of criminal prosecution. That choice is, in my view, more than sufficient to trigger First Amendment scrutiny.

There is also no dispute that Oregon has a significant interest in enforcing laws that control the possession and use of controlled substances by its citizens. See, e.g., *Sherbert* 374 U.S., 403 (religiously motivated conduct may be regulated where such conduct "pose[s] some substantial threat to public safety, peace or order"); *Yoder* 406 U.S., 220 ("[A]ctivities of individuals, even when religiously based, are often subject to regulation by the States in the exercise of their undoubted power to promote the health, safety, and general welfare"). As we recently noted, drug abuse is "one of the greatest problems affecting the health and welfare of our population" and thus "one of the most serious problems confronting our society today." *Treasury Employees v. Von Raab* 489 U.S. 656, 668, 674 (1989). Indeed, under federal law (incorporated by Oregon law in relevant part), peyote is specifically regulated as a Schedule I controlled substance, which means that Congress has found that it has a high potential for abuse, that there is no currently accepted medical use, and that there is a lack of accepted safety for use of the drug under medical supervision. . . . In light of our recent decisions holding that the governmental interests in the collection of income tax, *Hernandez* 490 U.S., 699-700, a comprehensive Social Security system, see *Lee* 455 U.S., 258-259, and military conscription, see *Gillette* 401 U.S., 460, are compelling, respondents do not seriously dispute that Oregon has a compelling interest in prohibiting the possession of peyote by its citizens.

B

Thus, the critical question in this case is whether exempting respondents from the State's general criminal prohibition "will unduly interfere with fulfillment of the governmental interest." *Lee*, 259; see also *Roy* 476 U.S., 727 ("[T]he Government must accommodate a legitimate free exercise claim unless pursuing an especially important interest by narrowly tailored means"); *Yoder*, 221. . . . Although the question is close, I would conclude that uniform application of Oregon's criminal prohibition is "essential to accomplish," *Lee*, 257, its overriding interest in preventing the physical harm caused by the use of a Schedule I controlled substance. Oregon's criminal prohibition represents that State's judgment that the possession and use of controlled substances, even by only one person, is inherently harmful and dangerous. Because the health effects caused by the use of controlled substances exist regardless of the motivation of the user, the use of such substances, even for religious purposes, violates the very purpose of the laws that prohibit them. . . . Moreover, in view of the societal interest in preventing trafficking in controlled substances, uniform application of the criminal prohibition at issue is essential to the effectiveness of Oregon's stated interest in preventing any possession of peyote. . . .

For these reasons, I believe that granting a selective exemption in this case would seriously impair Oregon's compelling interest in prohibiting possession of peyote by its citizens. Under such circumstances, the Free Exercise Clause does not require the State to accommodate respondents' religiously motivated conduct. . . . Unlike in *Yoder*, where we noted that "[t]he record strongly indicates that accommodating the religious objections of the Amish by forgoing one, or at most two, additional years of compulsory education will not impair the physical or mental health of the child, or result in an inability to be self-supporting or to discharge the duties and responsibilities of citizenship, or in any other way materially detract from the welfare of society," 406 U.S., 234; . . . a religious exemption in this case would be incompatible with the State's interest in controlling use and possession of illegal drugs.

Respondents contend that any incompatibility is belied by the fact that the Federal Government and several States provide exemptions for the religious use of peyote,. But other governments may surely choose to grant an exemption without Oregon, with its specific asserted interest in uniform application of its drug laws, being required to do so by the First Amendment. Respondents also note that the sacramental use of peyote is central to the tenets of the Native American Church, but I agree with the Court, that because "'[i]t is not within the judicial ken to question the centrality of particular beliefs or practices to a faith,'" quoting *Hernandez*, 699, our determination of the constitutionality of Oregon's general criminal prohibition cannot, and should not, turn on the centrality of the particular religious practice at issue. This does not mean, of course, that courts may not make factual findings as to whether a claimant holds a sincerely held religious belief that conflicts with, and thus is burdened by, the challenged law. The distinction between questions of centrality and questions of sincerity and burden is admittedly fine, but it is one that is an established part of our free exercise doctrine, . . . and one that courts are capable of making. . . .

I would therefore adhere to our established free exercise jurisprudence and hold that the State in this case has a compelling interest in regulating peyote use by its citizens and that accommodating respondents' religiously motivated conduct "will unduly interfere with fulfillment of the governmental interest." *Lee*, 259. Accordingly, I concur in the judgment of the Court.

JUSTICE BLACKMUN, with whom JUSTICE BRENNAN and JUSTICE MARSHALL join, dissenting.

This Court over the years painstakingly has developed a consistent and exacting standard to test the constitutionality of a state statute that burdens the free exercise of religion. Such a statute may stand only if the law in general, and the State's refusal to allow a religious exemption in particular, are justified by a compelling interest that cannot be served by less restrictive means.

Until today, I thought this was a settled and inviolate principle of this Court's First Amendment jurisprudence. The majority, however, perfunctorily dismisses it as a "constitutional anomaly." As carefully detailed in JUSTICE O'CONNOR's concurring opinion, the majority is able to arrive at this view only by mischaracterizing this Court's precedents. The Court discards leading free exercise cases such as *Cantwell v. Connecticut* and *Wisconsin v. Yoder*, as "hybrid." The Court views traditional free exercise analysis as somehow inapplicable to criminal prohibitions (as opposed to conditions on the receipt of benefits), and to state laws of general applicability (as opposed, presumably, to laws that expressly single out religious practices). The Court cites cases in which, due to various exceptional circumstances, we found strict scrutiny inapposite, to hint that the Court has repudiated that standard altogether. In short, it effectuates a wholesale overturning of settled law concerning the Religion Clauses of our Constitution. One hopes that the Court is aware of the consequences, and that its result is not a product of overreaction to the serious problems the country's drug crisis has generated.

This distorted view of our precedents leads the majority to conclude that strict scrutiny of a state law burdening the free exercise of religion is a "luxury" that a well-ordered society cannot afford, and that the repression of minority religions is an "unavoidable consequence of democratic government." I do not believe the Founders thought their dearly bought freedom from religious persecution a "luxury," but an essential element of liberty—and they could not have thought religious intolerance "unavoidable," for they drafted the Religion Clauses precisely in order to avoid that intolerance.

For these reasons, I agree with JUSTICE O'CONNOR's analysis of the applicable free exercise doctrine, and I join parts I and II of her opinion. As she points out, "the critical question in this case is whether exempting respondents from the State's general criminal prohibition 'will unduly interfere with fulfillment of the governmental interest,'" quoting *United States v. Lee* 455 U.S. 252, 259 (1982). I do disagree, however, with her specific answer to that question.

I

In weighing the clear interest of respondents Smith and Black (hereinafter respondents) in the free exercise of their religion against Oregon's asserted interest in enforcing its drug laws, it is important to articulate in precise terms the state interest involved. It is not the State's broad interest in fighting the critical "war on drugs" that must be weighed against respondents' claim, but the State's narrow interest in refusing to make an exception for the religious, ceremonial use of peyote. See *Bowen v. Roy* 476 U.S. 693, 728 (1986) (O'CONNOR, J., concurring in part and dissenting in part) ("This Court has consistently asked the Government to demonstrate that unbending application of its regulation to the religious objector 'is essential to accomplish an overriding governmental interest,'" quoting *Lee*, 455 U.S., 257-258); *Thomas v. Review Bd. of Indiana Employment Security Div.* 450 U.S. 707, 719 (1981) ("focus of the inquiry" concerning State's asserted interest must be "properly narrowed"); *Yoder* 406 U.S., 221 ("Where fundamental claims of religious freedom are at stake," the Court will not accept a State's "sweeping claim" that its interest in compulsory education is compelling; despite the validity of this interest "in the generality of cases, we must searchingly examine the interests that the State seeks to promote . . . and the impediment to those objectives that would flow from recognizing the claimed Amish exemption"). Failure to reduce the competing interests to the same plane of generality tends to distort the weighing process in the State's favor. . . .

The State's interest in enforcing its prohibition, in order to be sufficiently compelling to outweigh a free exercise claim, cannot be merely abstract or symbolic. The State cannot plausibly assert that unbending application of a criminal prohibition is essential to fulfill any compelling interest, if it does not, in fact, attempt to enforce that prohibition. In this case, the State actually has not evinced any concrete interest in enforcing its drug laws against religious users of peyote. Oregon has never sought to prosecute respondents, and does not claim that it has made significant enforcement efforts against other religious users of peyote. The State's asserted interest thus amounts only to the symbolic preservation of an unenforced prohibition. But a government interest in "symbolism, even symbolism for so worthy a cause as the abolition of unlawful drugs," *Treasury Employees v. Von Raab* 489 U.S. 656, 687 (1989) (SCALIA, J., dissenting), cannot suffice to abrogate the constitutional rights of individuals.

Similarly, this Court's prior decisions have not allowed a government to rely on mere speculation about potential harms, but have demanded evidentiary support for a refusal to allow a religious exception. See *Thomas* 450 U.S., 719 (rejecting State's reasons for refusing religious exemption, for lack of "evidence in the record"); *Yoder* 406 U.S., 224-229 (rejecting State's argument concerning the dangers of a religious exemption as speculative, and unsupported by the record); *Sherbert v. Verner* 374 U.S. 398, 407 (1963) ("[T]here is no proof whatever to warrant such fears . . . as those which the [State] now advance[s]"). In this case, the State's justification for refusing to recognize an exception to its criminal laws for religious peyote use is entirely speculative.

The State proclaims an interest in protecting the health and safety of its citizens from the dangers of unlawful drugs. It offers, however, no evidence that the religious use of peyote has ever harmed anyone. The factual findings of other courts cast doubt on the State's assumption that religious use of peyote is harmful. See *State v. Whittingham* 504 P.2d 950, 953 (1973) ("[T]he State failed to prove that the quantities of peyote used in the sacraments of the Native American Church are sufficiently harmful to the health and welfare of the participants so as to permit a legitimate intrusion under the State's police power"); *People v. Woody* 394 P.2d 813, 818 (1964) ("[A]s the Attorney General . . . admits, . . . the opinion of scientists and other experts is 'that peyote . . . works no permanent deleterious injury to the Indian'").

The fact that peyote is classified as a Schedule I controlled substance does not, by itself, show that any and all uses of peyote, in any circumstance, are inherently harmful and dangerous. The Federal Government, which created the classifications of unlawful drugs from which Oregon's drug laws are derived, apparently does not find peyote so dangerous as to preclude an exemption for religious use. Moreover, other Schedule I drugs have lawful uses. . . .

The carefully circumscribed ritual context in which respondents used peyote is far removed from the irresponsible and unrestricted recreational use of unlawful drugs. The Native American Church's internal restrictions on, and supervision of, its members' use of peyote substantially obviate the State's health and safety concerns. . . .

Moreover, just as in *Yoder*, the values and interests of those seeking a religious exemption in this case are congruent, to a great degree, with those the State seeks to promote through its drug laws. See *Yoder* 406 U.S., 224, 228-229 (since the Amish accept formal schooling up to 8th grade, and then provide "ideal" vocational education, State's interest in enforcing its law against the Amish is "less substantial than . . . for children generally"); *id.*, 238 (WHITE, J., concurring). Not only does the church's doctrine forbid nonreligious use of peyote; it also generally advocates self-reliance, familial responsibility, and abstinence from alcohol. . . . There is considerable evidence that the spiritual and social support provided by the church has been effective in combating the tragic effects of alcoholism on the Native American population. Two noted experts on peyotism, Dr. Omer C. Stewart and Dr. Robert Bergman, testified by affidavit to this effect on behalf of respondent Smith before the Employment Appeal Board. Far from promoting the lawless and irresponsible use of drugs, Native American Church members' spiritual code exemplifies values that Oregon's drug laws are presumably intended to foster.

The State also seeks to support its refusal to make an exception for religious use of peyote by invoking its interest in abolishing drug trafficking. There is, however, practically no illegal traffic in peyote. . . . Also, the availability of peyote for religious use, even if Oregon were to allow an exemption from its criminal laws, would still be strictly controlled by federal regulations, see 21 U.S.C. §§ 821-823 (registration requirements for distribution of controlled substances); 21 CFR § 1307.31 (1989) (distribution of peyote to

Native American Church subject to registration requirements), and by the State of Texas, the only State in which peyote grows in significant quantities. . . . Peyote simply is not a popular drug; its distribution for use in religious rituals has nothing to do with the vast and violent traffic in illegal narcotics that plagues this country.

Finally, the State argues that granting an exception for religious peyote use would erode its interest in the uniform, fair, and certain enforcement of its drug laws. The State fears that, if it grants an exemption for religious peyote use, a flood of other claims to religious exemptions will follow. It would then be placed in a dilemma, it says, between allowing a patchwork of exemptions that would hinder its law enforcement efforts, and risking a violation of the Establishment Clause by arbitrarily limiting its religious exemptions. This argument, however, could be made in almost any free exercise case. . . . This Court, however, consistently has rejected similar arguments in past free exercise cases, and it should do so here as well. See *Frazee v. Illinois Dept. of Employment Security* 489 U.S. 829, 835 (1989) (rejecting State's speculation concerning cumulative effect of many similar claims); *Thomas* 450 U.S., 719 (same); *Sherbert* 374 U.S., 407.

The State's apprehension of a flood of other religious claims is purely speculative. Almost half the States, and the Federal Government, have maintained an exemption for religious peyote use for many years, and apparently have not found themselves overwhelmed by claims to other religious exemptions. Allowing an exemption for religious peyote use would not necessarily oblige the State to grant a similar exemption to other religious groups. The unusual circumstances that make the religious use of peyote compatible with the State's interests in health and safety and in preventing drug trafficking would not apply to other religious claims. Some religions, for example, might not restrict drug use to a limited ceremonial context, as does the Native American Church. . . . Some religious claims involve drugs such as marijuana and heroin, in which there is significant illegal traffic, with its attendant greed and violence, so that it would be difficult to grant a religious exemption without seriously compromising law enforcement efforts. That the State might grant an exemption for religious peyote use, but deny other religious claims arising in different circumstances, would not violate the Establishment Clause. Though the State must treat all religions equally, and not favor one over another, this obligation is fulfilled by the uniform application of the "compelling interest" test to all free exercise claims, not by reaching uniform results as to all claims. A showing that religious peyote use does not unduly interfere with the State's interests is "one that probably few other religious groups or sects could make," *Yoder* 406 U.S., 236; this does not mean that an exemption limited to peyote use is tantamount to an establishment of religion. See *Hobbie v. Unemployment Appeals Comm'n of Fla.* 480 U.S. 136, 144-145 (1987) ("[T]he government may (and sometimes must) accommodate religious practices and . . . may do so without violating the Establishment Clause"); *Yoder* 406 U.S., 220-221 ("Court must not ignore the danger that an exception from a general [law] . . . may run afoul of the Establishment Clause, but that danger cannot be allowed to prevent any exception no matter how vital it may be to the protection of values promoted by the right of free exercise"); *id.*, 234, n. 22.

## II

Finally, although I agree with JUSTICE O'CONNOR that courts should refrain from delving into questions whether, as a matter of religious doctrine, a particular practice is "central" to the religion, I do not think this means that the courts must turn a blind eye to the severe impact of a State's restrictions on the adherents of a minority religion. Cf. *Yoder* 406 U.S., 219 (since "education is inseparable from and a part of the basic tenets of their religion . . . [, just as] baptism, the confessional, or a sabbath may be for others," enforcement of State's compulsory education law would "gravely endanger if not destroy the free exercise of respondents' religious beliefs").

Respondents believe, and their sincerity has never been at issue, that the peyote plant embodies their deity, and eating it is an act of worship and communion. Without peyote, they could not enact the essential ritual of their religion. See Brief for Association on American Indian Affairs et al. as *Amici Curiae* 5-6 ("To the members, peyote is consecrated with powers to heal body, mind and spirit. It is a teacher; it teaches the way to spiritual life through living in harmony and balance with the forces of the Creation. The rituals are an integral part of the life process. They embody a form of worship in which the sacrament Peyote is the means for communicating with the Great Spirit"). . . .

If Oregon can constitutionally prosecute them for this act of worship, they, like the Amish, may be "forced to migrate to some other and more tolerant region." *Yoder* 406 U.S., 218. This potentially devastating impact must be viewed in light of the federal policy—reached in reaction to many years of religious persecution and intolerance—of protecting the religious freedom of Native Americans. See American Indian Religious Freedom Act, 92 Stat. 469, 42 U.S.C. 1996 (1982 ed.) ("[I]t shall be the policy of the United States to protect and preserve for American Indians their inherent right of freedom to believe, express, and exercise the traditional religions . . . including but not limited to access to sites, use and possession of sacred objects, and the freedom to worship through ceremonials and traditional rites"). Congress recognized that certain substances, such as peyote, "have religious significance because they are sacred, they have power, they heal, they are necessary to the exercise of the rites of the religion, they are necessary to the cultural integrity of the tribe, and, therefore, religious survival." H. R. Rep. No. 95-1308, p. 2 (1978).

The American Indian Religious Freedom Act, in itself, may not create rights enforceable against government action restricting religious freedom, but this Court must scrupulously apply its free exercise analysis to the religious claims of Native Americans, however unorthodox they may be. Otherwise, both the First Amendment and the stated policy of Congress will offer to Native Americans merely an unfulfilled and hollow promise.

### III

For these reasons, I conclude that Oregon's interest in enforcing its drug laws against religious use of peyote is not sufficiently compelling to outweigh respondents' right to the free exercise of their religion. Since the State could not constitutionally enforce its criminal prohibition against respondents, the interests underlying the State's drug laws cannot justify its denial of unemployment benefits. Absent such justification, the State's regulatory interest in denying benefits for religiously motivated "misconduct," is indistinguishable from the state interests this Court has rejected in *Frazee, Hobbie, Thomas,* and *Sherbert*. The State of Oregon cannot, consistently with the Free Exercise Clause, deny respondents unemployment benefits.

I dissent.

## NOTES AND QUESTIONS

1. In *Employment Division of Oregon v. Smith*, Justices Scalia and O'Connor present two very different ways of interpreting and applying the Free Exercise Clause. What are those two different ways?

2. Thinking of the different approaches to free exercise issues by Justices Scalia and O'Connor, by whom were you persuaded? As you think about this, consider these other questions: Which better uses precedent? Which seems to be most faithful to the history and language of the Free Exercise Clause itself? Which best maximizes freedom of religion for individuals and groups? Which approach best balances the needs of government administrators and those of free exercise claimants?

3. How does Justice O'Connor distinguish the previous Court decisions that have not applied the "compelling interest" test? Are her arguments persuasive?

4. Few modern decisions of the Court have been more highly criticized than Scalia's *Smith* opinion, as to its use of precedent, its ultimate holding and its general attitude toward the importance of free exercise values. But does the holding have some merit? For example, can it not be argued that the greatest threat to free exercise values come from laws and government actions that purposefully discriminate against religion, not from generally applicable neutral laws that place unintended burdens on the religious practices of some? Under Equal Protection analysis, by comparison, laws that do not purposefully discriminate on the basis of race or gender (either in the language of the statutes or through their application) are reviewed by a deferential rational basis standard, similar to what *Smith* announces. This lower standard applies even though a person can show that they are disproportionately impacted by the neutral law. Only intentional discrimination is judged by a higher standard under the Equal Protection Clause. In addition to the appeal of legal consistency—that hobgoblin of small minds—the *Smith* opinion makes a passionate case for the social disutility of requiring the government to assert a rigorous justification for all laws that substantially burden free exercise rights or provide an exemption for the religious claimant. Is Justice Scalia correct that modern society with its ubiquitous regulatory apparatus cannot operate—or at least cannot operate efficiently—if religious objectors may seek exemptions for any governmental action?

   Or is the *Smith* holding still troubling because it sanctions serious—if unintended—interference with free exercise rights, rights central to human dignity? And would it ultimately be even more disruptive for the government to routinely reject claims that would require exemptions from "neutral, generally applicable" laws, given the backlash that could result? What about the fact that neutral laws disproportionately burden nontraditional religious practices in part because legislators are often less familiar with, and sometimes less sympathetic to, minority religious groups? Further, could it be argued that maintaining the *Sherbert* standard for decades had not opened the litigation floodgates and would not have done so had *Smith* been differently decided?

   Finally, consider Judge (then professor) Michael McConnell's response to the argument made above regarding possible parallels between free exercise and race-based equal protection claims. McConnell defended a wider application of the "compelling interest" test in the free-exercise arena, arguing that "the difference in doctrinal analysis is rooted in the nature of the underlying constitutional principles." He explained:

> At the risk of oversimplification, it can be said that the ideal of racial nondiscrimination is that individuals are fundamentally equal and must be treated as such; differences based on race are irrelevant and must be overcome. The ideal of free exercise of religion, by contrast, is that people of different religious convictions are different and that those differences are precious and must not be disturbed. The ideal of racial justice is assimilationist and integrationist. The ideal of free exercise is counter-assimilationist; it strives to allow individuals of different religious faiths to maintain their differences in the face of powerful pressures to conform.

Michael McConnell, "Free Exercise Revisionism and the *Smith* Decision," *University of Chicago Law Review* 57 (1990): 1109, 1139 (footnote omitted). Does McConnell make a persuasive argument for thinking about and treating free exercise claims differently than we do racial nondiscrimination claims?

Like it or not, the *Smith* opinion asks an important question facing many different societies: how does one accommodate free exercise rights while advancing the common good?

## THE FREE EXERCISE CLAUSE BEYOND SMITH

In 1993 the Court agreed to hear *Church of the Lukumi Babalu Aye v. City of Hialeah*, dealing with the animal sacrifice practices of a religion called Santeria, "the way of the saints." Santeria emerged from the dark history of slavery in the Caribbean. Slaves were brought from eastern Africa to Cuba. Their Cuban masters imposed their Roman Catholic religion on them. The slaves reconstructed their religious identity by syncretizing their traditions with the Catholicism forced on them by their captors. They continued to worship their Yoruba gods, but gave them the names of the Catholic saints. Santeria flourished in Cuba for hundreds of years, although usually underground. Santeria came to the United States during the migration of Cubans trying to escape the communist regime of Fidel Castro.

Santerias believe in *orishas*, spiritual beings who can impact human life. Consequently, it is necessary for humans to maintain a personal and benign relationship with the *orishas*. This is done principally through the sacrifice of small animals. It was the practice of animal sacrifice that caused the confrontation between the city of Hialeah, Florida, and a group of Santeria worshipers. The city government, expressing concern about the morality of the practice and also about health hazards, passed ordinances forbidding the animal sacrifices. The Church of the Lukumi Babalu Aye responded, claiming a denial of free exercise of religion.

When the Court took the case, many who believed that *Employment Division of Oregon v. Smith* was wrongly decided hoped the justices would use *Babalu Aye* to announce a *mea culpa* and correct what it had done in the earlier case. It did not. In an opinion written by Justice Anthony Kennedy, the Court ruled against Hialeah by applying *Smith*. *Smith* said a law of general applicability would prevail over a free exercise claim. But a law that targeted religious practice would be unconstitutional under the Free Exercise Clause. In reading the decision, see if you can identify how the Court determined that the Hialeah ordinance was not religiously neutral and how its analysis might open doors to challenging other governmental action with similar defects.

---

## CHURCH OF LUKUMI BABALU AYE v. CITY OF HIALEAH
### 508 U.S. 520 (1993)

▨ JUSTICE KENNEDY delivered the opinion of the Court, except as to Part II-A-2. (THE CHIEF JUSTICE, JUSTICE SCALIA, and JUSTICE THOMAS join all but Part II-A-2 of this opinion. JUSTICE WHITE joins all but Part II-A of this opinion. JUSTICE SOUTER joins only Parts 1, III, and IV of this opinion.)

The principle that government may not enact laws that suppress religious belief or practice is so well understood that few violations are recorded in our opinions. Cf. *McDaniel v. Paty* 435 U.S. 618 (1978); *Fowler v. Rhode Island* 345 U.S. 67 (1953). Concerned that this fundamental nonpersecution principle of the First Amendment was implicated here, however, we granted certiorari.

Our review confirms that the laws in question were enacted by officials who did not understand, failed to perceive, or chose to ignore the fact that their official actions violated the Nation's essential commitment to religious freedom. The challenged laws had an impermissible object; and in all events, the principle of general applicability was violated because the secular ends asserted in defense of the laws were pursued only with respect to conduct motivated by religious beliefs. We invalidate the challenged enactments, and reverse the judgment of the Court of Appeals.

I

A

This case involves practices of the Santeria religion, which originated in the 19th century. When hundreds of thousands of members of the Yoruba people were brought as slaves from western Africa to Cuba, their traditional African religion absorbed significant elements of Roman Catholicism. The resulting syncretion, or fusion, is Santeria, "the way of the saints." The Cuban Yoruba express their devotion to spirits, called *orishas*, through the iconography of Catholic saints, Catholic symbols are often present at Santeria rites, and Santeria devotees attend the Catholic sacraments. . . .

The Santeria faith teaches that every individual has a destiny from God, a destiny fulfilled with the aid and energy of the *orishas*. The basis of the Santeria religion is the nurture of a personal relation with the *orishas*, and one of the principal forms of devotion is an animal sacrifice. The sacrifice of animals as part of religious rituals has ancient roots, and it played an important role in the practice of Judaism before destruction of the second Temple in Jerusalem. In modern Islam, there is an annual sacrifice commemorating Abraham's sacrifice of a ram in the stead of his son.

According to Santeria teaching, the *orishas* are powerful, but not immortal. They depend for survival on the sacrifice. Sacrifices are performed at birth, marriage, and death rites, for the cure of the sick, for the initiation of new members and priests, and during an annual celebration. Animals sacrificed in Santeria rituals include chickens, pigeons, doves, ducks, guinea pigs, goats, sheep, and turtles. The animals are killed by the cutting of the carotid arteries in the neck. The sacrificed animal is cooked and eaten, except after healing and death rituals.

Santeria adherents faced widespread persecution in Cuba, so the religion and its rituals were practiced in secret. The open practice of Santeria and its rites remains infrequent. . . . The religion was brought to this Nation most often by exiles from the Cuban revolution. The District Court estimated that there are at least 50,000 practitioners in South Florida today.

B

Petitioner Church of the Lukumi Babalu Aye, Inc. (Church), is a not-for-profit corporation organized under Florida law in 1973. The Church and its congregants practice the Santeria religion. The president of the Church is petitioner Ernesto Pichardo, who is also the Church's priest and holds the religious title of *Italero*, the second highest in the Santeria faith. In April, 1987, the Church leased land in the city of Hialeah, Florida, and announced plans to establish a house of worship as well as a school, cultural center, and museum. Pichardo indicated that the Church's goal was to bring the practice of the Santeria faith, including its ritual of animal sacrifice, into the open. The Church began the process of obtaining utility service and receiving the necessary licensing, inspection, and zoning approvals. Although the Church's efforts at obtaining the necessary licenses and permits were far from smooth, . . . it appears that it received all needed approvals by early August 1987.

The prospect of a Santeria church in their midst was distressing to many members of the Hialeah community, and the announcement of the plans to open a Santeria church in Hialeah prompted the city council to hold an emergency public session on June 9, 1987. . . .

A summary suffices here, beginning with the enactments passed at the June 9 meeting. First, the city council adopted Resolution 87-66, which noted the "concern" expressed by residents of the city "that certain religions may propose to engage in practices which are inconsistent with public morals, peace or safety," and declared that "[t]he City reiterates its commitment to a prohibition against any and all acts of any and all religious groups which are inconsistent with public morals, peace or safety." Next, the council approved an emergency ordinance, Ordinance 87-40, which incorporated in full, except as to penalty, Florida's animal cruelty laws. Among other things, the incorporated state law subjected to criminal punishment "[w]hoever . . . unnecessarily or cruelly . . . kills any animal."

The city council desired to undertake further legislative action, but Florida law prohibited a municipality from enacting legislation relating to animal cruelty that conflicted with state law. To obtain clarification, Hialeah's city attorney requested an opinion from the attorney general of Florida as to whether 828.12 prohibited "a religious group from sacrificing an animal in a religious ritual or practice," and whether the city could enact ordinances "making religious animal sacrifice unlawful." The attorney general responded in mid-July. He concluded that the "ritual sacrifice of animals for purposes other than food consumption" was not a "necessary" killing, and so was prohibited by [Florida law.] The attorney general appeared to define "unnecessary" as "done without any useful motive, in a spirit of wanton cruelty or for the mere pleasure of destruction without being in any sense beneficial or useful to the person killing the animal." He advised that religious animal sacrifice was against state law, so that a city ordinance prohibiting it would not be in conflict.

The city council responded at first with a hortatory enactment that noted its residents' "great concern regarding the possibility of public ritualistic animal sacrifices" and the state-law prohibition. The resolution declared the city policy "to oppose the ritual sacrifices of animals" within Hialeah, and announced that any person or organization practicing animal sacrifice "will be prosecuted."

In September 1987, the city council adopted three substantive ordinances addressing the issue of religious animal sacrifice. Ordinance 87-52 defined "sacrifice" as "to unnecessarily kill, torment, torture, or mutilate an animal in a public or private ritual or ceremony not for the primary purpose of food consumption," and prohibited owning or possessing an animal "intending to use such animal for food purposes." It restricted application of this prohibition, however, to any individual or group that "kills, slaughters or sacrifices animals for any type of ritual, regardless of whether or not the flesh or blood of the animal is to be consumed." The ordinance contained an exemption for slaughtering by "licensed establishment[s]" of animals "specifically raised for food purposes." Declaring, moreover, that the city council "has determined that the sacrificing of animals within the city limits is contrary to the public health, safety, welfare and morals of the community," the city council adopted Ordinance 87-71. That ordinance defined sacrifice as had Ordinance 87-52, and then provided that "[i]t shall be unlawful for any person, persons, corporations or associations to sacrifice any animal within the corporate limits of the City of Hialeah, Florida." The final Ordinance, 87-72, defined "slaughter" as "the killing of animals for food," and prohibited slaughter outside of areas zoned for slaughterhouse use. The ordinance provided an exemption, however, for the slaughter or processing for sale of "small numbers of hogs and/or cattle per week in accordance with an exemption provided by state law." All ordinances and resolutions passed the city council by unanimous vote. Violations of each of the four ordinances were punishable by fines not exceeding $500 or imprisonment not exceeding 60 days, or both.

Following enactment of these ordinances, the Church and Pichardo filed this action pursuant to 42 U.S.C. 1983 in the United States District Court for the Southern District of Florida. . . . Alleging violations of petitioners rights under, *inter alia*, the Free Exercise Clause, the complaint sought a declaratory judgment and injunctive and monetary relief. . . .

II

The Free Exercise Clause of the First Amendment, which has been applied to the States through the Fourteenth Amendment, provides that "Congress shall make no law respecting an establishment of religion, or *prohibiting the free exercise thereof*. . . ." (Emphasis added.) The city does not argue that Santeria is not a "religion" within the meaning of the First Amendment. Nor could it. Although the practice of animal sacrifice may seem abhorrent to some, "religious beliefs need not be acceptable, logical, consistent, or comprehensible to others in order to merit First Amendment protection." *Thomas v. Review Bd. of Indiana*

*Employment Security Div.* 450 U.S. 707, 714 (1981). Given the historical association between animal sacrifice and religious worship, petitioners' assertion that animal sacrifice is an integral part of their religion "cannot be deemed bizarre or incredible." *Frazee v. Illinois Dept. of Employment Security* 489 U.S. 829, 834, n. 2 (1989). Neither the city nor the courts below, moreover, have questioned the sincerity of petitioners' professed desire to conduct animal sacrifices for religious reasons. We must consider petitioners' First Amendment claim.

In addressing the constitutional protection for free exercise of religion, our cases establish the general proposition that a law that is neutral and of general applicability need not be justified by a compelling governmental interest even if the law has the incidental effect of burdening a particular religious practice. *Employment Div.. v. Smith.* Neutrality and general applicability are interrelated, and, as becomes apparent in this case, failure to satisfy one requirement is a likely indication that the other has not been satisfied. A law failing to satisfy these requirements must be justified by a compelling governmental interest, and must be narrowly tailored to advance that interest. These ordinances fail to satisfy the *Smith* requirements. We begin by discussing neutrality.

## A

In our Establishment Clause cases, we have often stated the principle that the First Amendment forbids an official purpose to disapprove of a particular religion or of religion in general. . . . These cases, however, for the most part, have addressed governmental efforts to benefit religion or particular religions, and so have dealt with a question different, at least in its formulation and emphasis, from the issue here. Petitioners allege an attempt to disfavor their religion because of the religious ceremonies it commands, and the Free Exercise Clause is dispositive in our analysis.

At a minimum, the protections of the Free Exercise Clause pertain if the law at issue discriminates against some or all religious beliefs or regulates or prohibits conduct because it is undertaken for religious reasons. . . . Indeed, it was "historical instances of religious persecution and intolerance that gave concern to those who drafted the Free Exercise Clause." *Bowen v. Roy* 476 U.S. 693, 703 (1986) (opinion of BURGER, C.J.). . . . These principles, though not often at issue in our Free Exercise Clause cases, have played a role in some. In *McDaniel v. Paty*, for example, we invalidated a state law that disqualified members of the clergy from holding certain public offices, because it "impose[d] special disabilities on the basis of . . . religious status," *Employment Div. v. Smith,* 494 U.S., 877. On the same principle, in *Fowler v. Rhode Island,* 345 U.S. 67 (1953), we found that a municipal ordinance was applied in an unconstitutional manner when interpreted to prohibit preaching in a public park by a Jehovah's Witness, but to permit preaching during the course of a Catholic mass or Protestant church service. . . .

## 1

Although a law targeting religious beliefs as such is never permissible, . . . if the object of a law is to infringe upon or restrict practices because of their religious motivation, the law is not neutral, and it is invalid unless it is justified by a compelling interest and is narrowly tailored to advance that interest. There are, of course, many ways of demonstrating that the object or purpose of a law is the suppression of religion or religious conduct. To determine the object of a law, we must begin with its text, for the minimum requirement of neutrality is that a law not discriminate on its face. A law lacks facial neutrality if it refers to a religious practice without a secular meaning discernable from the language or context. Petitioners contend that three of the ordinances fail this test of facial neutrality because they use the words "sacrifice" and "ritual," words with strong religious connotations. . . . We agree that these words are consistent with the claim of facial discrimination, but the argument is not conclusive. The words "sacrifice" and "ritual" have a religious origin, but current use admits also of secular meanings. See *Webster's Third New International Dictionary* 1961, 1996 (1971). See also 12 *Encyclopedia of Religion*, 556 ("[T]he word sacrifice ultimately became very much a secular term in common usage"). The ordinances, furthermore, define "sacrifice" in secular terms, without referring to religious practices.

We reject the contention advanced by the city, . . . that our inquiry must end with the text of the laws at issue. Facial neutrality is not determinative. The Free Exercise Clause, like the Establishment Clause, extends beyond facial discrimination. The Clause "forbids subtle departures from neutrality," *Gillette v. United States* 401 U.S. 437, 452 (1971), and "covert suppression of particular religious beliefs," *Bowen v. Roy*, 703 (opinion of BURGER, C.J.). Official action that targets religious conduct for distinctive treatment cannot be shielded by mere compliance with the requirement of facial neutrality. The Free Exercise Clause protects against governmental hostility which is masked as well as overt. "The Court must survey meticulously the circumstances of governmental categories to eliminate, as it were, religious gerrymanders." *Walz v. Tax Comm'n of New York City* 397 U.S. 664, 696 (1970) (HARLAN, J., concurring).

The record in this case compels the conclusion that suppression of the central element of the Santeria worship service was the object of the ordinances. First, though use of the words "sacrifice" and "ritual" does not compel a finding of improper targeting of the Santeria religion, the choice of these words is support for our conclusion. There are further respects in which the text of the city council's enactments discloses the improper attempt to target Santeria. Resolution 87-66, adopted June 9, 1987, recited that "residents and citizens of the City of Hialeah have expressed their concern that certain religions may propose to engage in practices which are inconsistent with public morals, peace or safety," and "reiterate[d]" the city's commitment to prohibit "any and all [such] acts of any and all religious groups." No one suggests, and, on this record, it cannot be maintained, that city officials had in mind a religion other than Santeria.

It becomes evident that these ordinances target Santeria sacrifice when the ordinances' operation is considered. Apart from the text, the effect of a law in its real operation is strong evidence of its object. To be sure, adverse impact will not always lead to a finding of impermissible targeting. For example, a social harm may have been a legitimate concern of government for reasons quite apart from discrimination. . . . The subject at hand does implicate, of course, multiple concerns unrelated to religious animosity, for example, the suffering or mistreatment visited upon the sacrificed animals and health hazards from improper disposal. But the ordinances, when considered together, disclose an object remote from these legitimate concerns. The design of these laws accomplishes, instead, a "religious gerrymander," *Walz v. Tax Comm'n of New York City*, 696 (HARLAN, J., concurring), an impermissible attempt to target petitioners and their religious practices.

It is a necessary conclusion that almost the only conduct subject to Ordinances 87-40, 87-52, and 87-71 is the religious exercise of Santeria church members. The texts show that they were drafted in tandem to achieve this result. We begin with Ordinance 87-71. It prohibits the sacrifice of animals, but defines sacrifice as "to unnecessarily kill . . . an animal in a public or private ritual or ceremony not for the primary purpose of food consumption." The definition excludes almost all killings of animals except for religious sacrifice, and the primary purpose requirement narrows the proscribed category even further, in particular by exempting kosher slaughter. We need not discuss whether this differential treatment of two religions is, itself, an independent constitutional violation. . . . It suffices to recite this feature of the law as support for our conclusion that Santeria alone was the exclusive legislative concern. The net result of the gerrymander is that few, if any, killings of animals are prohibited other than Santeria sacrifice, which is proscribed because it occurs during a ritual or ceremony and its primary purpose is to make an offering to the *orishas*, not food consumption. Indeed, careful drafting ensured that, although Santeria sacrifice is prohibited, killings that are no more necessary or humane in almost all other circumstances are unpunished.

Operating in similar fashion is Ordinance 87-52, which prohibits the "possess[ion], sacrifice, or slaughter" of an animal with the "inten[t] to use such animal for food purposes." This prohibition, extending to the keeping of an animal, as well as the killing itself, applies if the animal is killed in "any type of ritual" and there is an intent to use the animal for food, whether or not it is in fact consumed for food. The ordinance exempts, however, "any licensed [food] establishment" with regard to "any animals which are specifically raised for food purposes," if the activity is permitted by zoning and other laws. This exception, too, seems intended to cover Kosher slaughter. Again, the burden of the ordinance, in practical terms, falls on Santeria adherents, but almost no others: if the killing is—unlike most Santeria sacrifices—unaccompanied by the intent to use the animal for food, then it is not prohibited by Ordinance 87-52; if the killing is specifically for food, but does not occur during the course of "any type of ritual," it again falls outside the prohibition; and if the killing is for food and occurs during the course of a ritual, it is still exempted if it occurs in a properly zoned and licensed establishment and involves animals "specifically raised for food purposes." A pattern of exemptions parallels the pattern of narrow prohibitions. Each contributes to the gerrymander.

Ordinance 87-40 incorporates the Florida animal cruelty statute, Fla.Stat. 828.12 (1987). Its prohibition is broad on its face, punishing "[w]hoever . . . unnecessarily . . . kills any animal." The city claims that this ordinance is the epitome of a neutral prohibition. . . . The problem, however, is the interpretation given to the ordinance by respondent and the Florida attorney general. Killings for religious reasons are deemed unnecessary, whereas most other killings fall outside the prohibition. The city, on what seems to be a *per se* basis, deems hunting, slaughter of animals for food, eradication of insects and pests, and euthanasia as necessary. There is no indication in the record that respondent has concluded that hunting or fishing for sport is unnecessary. Indeed, one of the few reported Florida cases decided under 828.12 concludes that the use of live rabbits to train greyhounds is not unnecessary. Further, because it requires an evaluation of the particular justification for the killing, this ordinance represents a system of "individualized governmental assessment of the reasons for the relevant conduct," *Employment Div. v. Smith,* 494 U.S., 884. As we noted in *Smith*, in circumstances in which individualized exemptions from a general requirement are available, the government "may not refuse to extend that system to cases of 'religious hardship' without compelling reason." *Ibid.* quoting *Bowen v. Roy* 476 U.S., 708 (opinion of BURGER, C.J.). Respondent's application of the ordinance's test of necessity devalues religious reasons for killing by judging them to be of lesser import than nonreligious reasons. Thus, religious practice is being singled out for discriminatory treatment.

We also find significant evidence of the ordinances' improper targeting of Santeria sacrifice in the fact that they proscribe more religious conduct than is necessary to achieve their stated ends. It is not unreasonable to infer, at least when there are no persuasive indications to the contrary, that a law which visits "gratuitous restrictions" on religious conduct, *McGowan v. Maryland* 366 U.S., 520 (opinion of FRANKFURTER, J.), seeks not to effectuate the stated governmental interests, but to suppress the conduct because of its religious motivation.

The legitimate governmental interests in protecting the public health and preventing cruelty to animals could be addressed by restrictions stopping far short of a flat prohibition of all Santeria sacrificial practice. If improper disposal, not the sacrifice itself, is the harm to be prevented, the city could have imposed a general regulation on the disposal of organic garbage. It did not do so. Indeed, counsel for the city conceded at oral argument that, under the ordinances, Santeria sacrifices would be illegal even if they occurred in licensed, inspected, and zoned slaughterhouses. . . . Thus, these broad ordinances prohibit Santeria sacrifice even when it does not threaten the city's interest in the public health. The District Court accepted the argument that narrower regulation would be unenforceable because of the secrecy in the Santeria rituals and the lack of any central religious authority to require compliance with secular disposal regulations. It is difficult to understand, however, how a prohibition of the sacrifices themselves, which occur in private, is enforceable if a ban on improper disposal, which occurs in public, is not. The neutrality of a law is suspect if First Amendment freedoms are curtailed to prevent isolated collateral harms not themselves prohibited by direct regulation.

Under similar analysis, narrower regulation would achieve the city's interest in preventing cruelty to animals. With regard to the city's interest in ensuring the adequate care of animals, regulation of conditions and treatment, regardless of why an animal is kept, is the logical response to the city's concern, not a prohibition on possession for the purpose of sacrifice. The same is true for the city's interest in prohibiting cruel methods of killing. Under federal and Florida law and Ordinance 87-40, which incorporates Florida law in this regard, killing an animal by the "simultaneous and instantaneous severance of the carotid arteries with a sharp instrument"—the method used in kosher slaughter—is approved as humane. The District Court found that, though Santeria sacrifice also results in severance of the carotid arteries, the method used during sacrifice is less reliable, and therefore not humane. If the city has a real concern that other methods are less humane, however, the subject of the regulation should be the method of slaughter itself, not a religious classification that is said to bear some general relation to it.

Ordinance 87-72—unlike the three other ordinances—does appear to apply to substantial nonreligious conduct, and not to be overbroad. For our purposes here, however, the four substantive ordinances may be treated as a group for neutrality purposes. Ordinance 87-72 was passed the same day

as Ordinance 87-71, and was enacted, as were the three others, in direct response to the opening of the Church. It would be implausible to suggest that
the three other ordinances, but not Ordinance 87-72, had as their object the
suppression of religion. We need not decide whether the Ordinance 87-72
could survive constitutional scrutiny if it existed separately; it must be invalidated because it functions, with the rest of the enactments in question, to
suppress Santeria religious worship.

2

In determining if the object of a law is a neutral one under the Free Exercise Clause, we can also find guidance in our equal protection cases. As Justice
HARLAN noted in the related context of the Establishment Clause, "[n]eutral-
ity in its application requires an equal protection mode of analysis." *Walz v.
Tax Comm'n of New York City* 397 U.S. at 696 (concurring opinion). Here, as in
equal protection cases, we may determine the city council's object from both
direct and circumstantial evidence. . . . Relevant evidence includes, among
other things, the historical background of the decision under challenge, the
specific series of events leading to the enactment or official policy in question, and the legislative or administrative history, including contemporaneous
statements made by members of the decision-making body. . . .These objective
factors bear on the question of discriminatory object. . . .

That the ordinances were enacted "'because of,' not merely 'in spite of,'"
their suppression of Santeria religious practice, is revealed by the events preceding enactment of the ordinances. Although respondent claimed at oral argument that it had experienced significant problems resulting from the sacrifice
of animals within the city before the announced opening of the Church, . . .
the city council made no attempt to address the supposed problem before its
meeting in June 1987, just weeks after the Church announced plans to open.
The minutes and taped excerpts of the June 9 session, both of which are in the
record, evidence significant hostility exhibited by residents, members of the
city council, and other city officials toward the Santeria religion and its practice of animal sacrifice. The public crowd that attended the June 9 meetings
interrupted statements by council members critical of Santeria with cheers and
the brief comments of Pichardo with taunts. When Councilman Martinez, a
supporter of the ordinances, stated that, in prerevolution Cuba, "people were
put in jail for practicing this religion," the audience applauded. . . .

Other statements by members of the city council were in a similar vein.
For example, Councilman Martinez, after noting his belief that Santeria was
outlawed in Cuba, questioned: "If we could not practice this [religion] in our
homeland [Cuba], why bring it to this country?" Councilman Cardoso said
that Santeria devotees at the Church "are in violation of everything this country stands for." Councilman Mejides indicated that he was "totally against the
sacrificing of animals," and distinguished kosher slaughter because it had a
"real purpose." The "Bible says we are allowed to sacrifice an animal for consumption," he continued, "but for any other purposes, I don't believe that the
Bible allows that." The president of the city council, Councilman Echevarria,
asked: "What can we do to prevent the Church from opening?"

Various Hialeah city officials made comparable comments. The chaplain
of the Hialeah Police Department told the city council that Santeria was a sin,
"foolishness," "an abomination to the Lord," and the worship of "demons."
He advised the city council: "We need to be helping people and sharing with

them the truth that is found in Jesus Christ." He concluded: "I would exhort you . . . not to permit this Church to exist." The city attorney commented that Resolution 87-66 indicated: "This community will not tolerate religious practices which are abhorrent to its citizens. . . ." Similar comments were made by the deputy city attorney. This history discloses the object of the ordinances to target animal sacrifice by Santeria worshippers because of its religious motivation.

### 3

In sum, the neutrality inquiry leads to one conclusion: the ordinances had as their object the suppression of religion. The pattern we have recited discloses animosity to Santeria adherents and their religious practices; the ordinances, by their own terms, target this religious exercise; the texts of the ordinances were gerrymandered with care to proscribe religious killings of animals but to exclude almost all secular killings; and the ordinances suppress much more religious conduct than is necessary in order to achieve the legitimate ends asserted in their defense. These ordinances are not neutral, and the court below committed clear error in failing to reach this conclusion.

### B

We turn next to a second requirement of the Free Exercise Clause, the rule that laws burdening religious practice must be of general applicability. . . . All laws are selective to some extent, but categories of selection are of paramount concern when a law has the incidental effect of burdening religious practice. The Free Exercise Clause "protect[s] religious observers against unequal treatment," *Hobbie v. Unemployment Appeals Comm'n of Fla.* 480 U.S. 136, 148 (1987) (STEVENS, J., concurring in judgment), and inequality results when a legislature decides that the governmental interests it seeks to advance are worthy of being pursued only against conduct with a religious motivation.

The principle that government, in pursuit of legitimate interests, cannot in a selective manner impose burdens only on conduct motivated by religious belief is essential to the protection of the rights guaranteed by the Free Exercise Clause. The principle underlying the general applicability requirement has parallels in our First Amendment jurisprudence. . . . In this case, we need not define with precision the standard used to evaluate whether a prohibition is of general application, for these ordinances fall well below the minimum standard necessary to protect First Amendment rights.

Respondent claims that Ordinances 87-40, 87-52, and 87-71 advance two interests: protecting the public health and preventing cruelty to animals. The ordinances are underinclusive for those ends. They fail to prohibit nonreligious conduct that endangers these interests in a similar or greater degree than Santeria sacrifice does. The underinclusion is substantial, not inconsequential. Despite the city's proffered interest in preventing cruelty to animals, the ordinances are drafted with care to forbid few killings but those occasioned by religious sacrifice. Many types of animal deaths or kills for nonreligious reasons are either not prohibited or approved by express provision. For example, fishing—which occurs in Hialeah . . .—is legal. Extermination of mice and rats within a home is also permitted. Florida law incorporated by Ordinance 87-40 sanctions euthanasia of "stray, neglected, abandoned, or unwanted animals,"; destruction of animals judicially removed from their owners "for humanitarian reasons" or when the animal "is of no commercial value"; the infliction of pain or suffering "in the interest of medical science"; the placing of poison in one's yard or enclosure; and the use of a live animal "to pursue or take wildlife or to participate in any hunting," and "to hunt wild hogs."

The city concedes that "neither the State of Florida nor the City has enacted a generally applicable ban on the killing of animals.". . . It asserts, however, that animal sacrifice is "different" from the animal killings that are permitted by law. According to the city, it is "self-evident" that killing animals for food is "important"; the eradication of insects and pests is "obviously justified"; and the euthanasia of excess animals "makes sense." . . . These *ipse dixits* do not explain why religion alone must bear the burden of the ordinances, when many of these secular killings fall within the city's interest in preventing the cruel treatment of animals.

The ordinances are also underinclusive with regard to the city's interest in public health, which is threatened by the disposal of animal carcasses in open public places and the consumption of uninspected meat. . . . Neither interest is pursued by respondent with regard to conduct that is not motivated by religious conviction. The health risks posed by the improper disposal of animal carcasses are the same whether Santeria sacrifice or some nonreligious killing preceded it. The city does not, however, prohibit hunters from bringing their kill to their houses, nor does it regulate disposal after their activity. Despite substantial testimony at trial that the same public health hazards result from improper disposal of garbage by restaurants, . . . restaurants are outside the scope of the ordinances. Improper disposal is a general problem that causes substantial health risks, . . . but which respondent addresses only when it results from religious exercise.

The ordinances are underinclusive as well with regard to the health risk posed by consumption of uninspected meat. Under the city's ordinances, hunters may eat their kill and fishermen may eat their catch without undergoing governmental inspection. Likewise, state law requires inspection of meat that is sold, but exempts meat from animals raised for the use of the owner and "members of his household and nonpaying guests and employees." The asserted interest in inspected meat is not pursued in contexts similar to that of religious animal sacrifice.

Ordinance 87-72, which prohibits the slaughter of animals outside of areas zoned for slaughterhouses, is underinclusive on its face. The ordinance includes an exemption for "any person, group, or organization" that "slaughters or processes for sale, small numbers of hogs and/or cattle per week in accordance with an exemption provided by state law." Respondent has not explained why commercial operations that slaughter "small numbers" of hogs and cattle do not implicate its professed desire to prevent cruelty to animals and preserve the public health. Although the city has classified Santeria sacrifice as slaughter, subjecting it to this ordinance, it does not regulate other killings for food in like manner.

We conclude, in sum, that each of Hialeah's ordinances pursues the city's governmental interests only against conduct motivated by religious belief. The ordinances "ha[ve] every appearance of a prohibition that society is prepared to impose upon [Santeria worshippers], but not upon itself." This precise evil is what the requirement of general applicability is designed to prevent.

### III

A law burdening religious practice that is not neutral or not of general application must undergo the most rigorous of scrutiny. To satisfy the commands of the First Amendment, a law restrictive of religious practice must advance "'interests of the highest order,'" and must be narrowly tailored in pursuit of those interests. *McDaniel v. Paty* 435 U.S., 628, quoting *Wisconsin v. Yoder* 406 U.S. 205, 215 (1972). The compelling interest standard that we apply once a law fails to meet the *Smith* requirements is not "water[ed] . . . down" but "really means what it says." *Employment Div. v. Smith*, 494 U.S., 888. A law that targets religious conduct for distinctive treatment or advances legitimate governmental interests only against conduct with a religious motivation will survive strict scrutiny only in rare cases. It follows from what we have already said that these ordinances cannot withstand this scrutiny.

First, even were the governmental interests compelling, the ordinances are not drawn in narrow terms to accomplish those interests. As we have discussed, . . . all four ordinances are overbroad or underinclusive in substantial respects. The proffered objectives are not pursued with respect to analogous nonreligious conduct, and those interests could be achieved by narrower ordinances that burdened religion to a far lesser degree. The absence of narrow tailoring suffices to establish the invalidity of the ordinances. . . .

Respondent has not demonstrated, moreover, that, in the context of these ordinances, its governmental interests are compelling. Where government restricts only conduct protected by the First Amendment and fails to enact feasible measures to restrict other conduct producing substantial harm or alleged harm of the same sort, the interest given in justification of the restriction is not compelling. It is established in our strict scrutiny jurisprudence that "a law cannot be regarded as protecting an interest 'of the highest order' . . . when it leaves appreciable damage to that supposedly vital interest unprohibited." . . . As we show above, . . . the ordinances are underinclusive to a substantial extent with respect to each of the interests that respondent has asserted, and it is only conduct motivated by religious conviction that bears the weight of the governmental restrictions. There can be no serious claim that those interests justify the ordinances.

## IV

The Free Exercise Clause commits government itself to religious tolerance, and upon even slight suspicion that proposals for state intervention stem from animosity to religion or distrust of its practices, all officials must pause to remember their own high duty to the Constitution and to the rights it secures. Those in office must be resolute in resisting importunate demands and must ensure that the sole reasons for imposing the burdens of law and regulation are secular. Legislators may not devise mechanisms, overt or disguised, designed to persecute or oppress a religion or its practices. The laws here in question were enacted contrary to these constitutional principles, and they are void.

*Reversed.*

JUSTICE SCALIA, with whom THE CHIEF JUSTICE joins, concurring in part and concurring in the judgment.

The Court analyzes the "neutrality" and the "general applicability" of the Hialeah ordinances in separate sections (Parts II-A and II-B, respectively), and allocates various invalidating factors to one or the other of those sections. If it were necessary to make a clear distinction between the two terms, I would draw a line somewhat different from the Court's. But I think it is not necessary, and would frankly acknowledge that the terms are not only "interrelated," but substantially overlap.

The terms "neutrality" and "general applicability" are not to be found within the First Amendment itself, of course, but are used in *Employment Div. v. Smith* 494 U.S. 872 (1990), and earlier cases to describe those characteristics which cause a law that prohibits an activity a particular individual wishes to engage in for religious reasons nonetheless not to constitute a "law . . . prohibiting the free exercise" of religion within the meaning of the First Amendment. In my view, the defect of lack of neutrality applies primarily to those laws that by their terms impose disabilities on the basis of religion (e.g., a law excluding members of a certain sect from public benefits, cf. *McDaniel v. Paty* 435 U.S. 618 [1978]), . . . whereas the defect of lack of general applicability applies primarily to those laws which, though neutral in their terms, through their design, construction, or enforcement target the practices of a particular religion for discriminatory treatment. . . . But certainly a law that is not of general applicability (in the sense I have described) can be considered "nonneutral"; and certainly no law that is nonneutral (in the relevant sense) can be thought to be of general applicability. Because I agree with most of the invalidating factors set forth in Part II of the Court's opinion, and because it seems to me a matter of no consequence under which rubric ("neutrality," Part II-A, or "general applicability," Part II-B) each invalidating factor is discussed, I join the judgment of the Court and all of its opinion except section 2 of Part II-A.

I do not join that section, because it departs from the opinion's general focus on the object of the laws at issue to consider the subjective motivation of the *lawmakers*, i.e., whether the Hialeah City Council actually intended to disfavor the religion of Santeria. As I have noted elsewhere, it is virtually impossible to determine the singular "motive" of a collective legislative body, see, e.g., *Edwards v. Aguillard* 482 U.S. 578, 636-639 (1987) (dissenting opinion), and this Court has a long tradition of refraining from such inquiries, . . .

Perhaps there are contexts in which determination of legislative motive must be undertaken. . . . But I do not think that is true of analysis under the First Amendment (or the Fourteenth, to the extent it incorporates the First). . . . The First Amendment does not refer to the purposes for which legislators enact laws, but to the effects of the laws enacted: "Congress shall make no law . . . prohibiting the free exercise [of religion]. . . ." This does not put us in the business of invalidating laws by reason of the evil motives of their authors. Had the Hialeah City Council set out resolutely to suppress the practices of Santeria, but ineptly adopted ordinances that failed to do so, I do not see how those laws could be said to "prohibi[t] the free exercise" of religion. Nor, in my view, does it matter that a legislature consists entirely of the purehearted, if the law it enacts in fact singles out a religious practice for special burdens. Had the ordinances here been passed with no motive on the part of any councilman except the ardent desire to prevent cruelty to animals (as might in fact have been the case), they would nonetheless be invalid.

▦ JUSTICE SOUTER, concurring in part and concurring in the judgment.

This case turns on a principle about which there is no disagreement, that the Free Exercise Clause bars government action aimed at suppressing religious belief or practice. The Court holds that Hialeah's animal sacrifice laws violate that principle, and I concur in that holding without reservation.

Because prohibiting religious exercise is the object of the laws at hand, this case does not present the more difficult issue addressed in our last free exercise case, *Employment Div. v. Smith*, which announced the rule that a "neutral, generally applicable" law does not run afoul of the Free Exercise Clause even when it prohibits religious exercise in effect. The Court today refers to that rule in dicta, and, despite my general agreement with the Court's opinion, I do not join Part II, where the dicta appear, for I have doubts about whether the *Smith* rule merits adherence. I write separately to explain why the *Smith* rule is not germane to this case, and to express my view that, in a case presenting the issue, the Court should reexamine the rule *Smith* declared.

I

According to *Smith*, if prohibiting the exercise of religion results from enforcing a "neutral, generally applicable" law, the Free Exercise Clause has not been offended. . . . I call this the *Smith* rule to distinguish it from the noncontroversial principle, also expressed in *Smith*, though established long before, that the Free Exercise Clause is offended when prohibiting religious exercise results from a law that is not neutral or generally applicable. It is this noncontroversial principle, that the Free Exercise Clause requires neutrality and general applicability, that is at issue here. But before turning to the relationship of *Smith* to this case, it will help to get the terms in order, for the significance of the *Smith* rule is not only in its statement that the Free Exercise Clause requires no more than "neutrality" and "general applicability," but also in its adoption of a particular, narrow conception of free exercise neutrality.

That the Free Exercise Clause contains a "requirement for governmental neutrality," *Wisconsin v. Yoder* 406 U.S. 205, 220 (1972), is hardly a novel proposition; though the term does not appear in the First Amendment, our cases have used it as shorthand to describe, at least in part, what the Clause commands. . . . Nor is there anything unusual about the notion that the Free Exercise Clause requires general applicability, though the Court, until today, has not used exactly that term in stating a reason for invalidation. . . .

While general applicability is, for the most part, self-explanatory, free exercise neutrality is not self-revealing. . . . A law that is religion neutral on its face or in its purpose may lack neutrality in its effect by forbidding something that religion requires or requiring something that religion forbids. . . . A secular law, applicable to all, that prohibits consumption of alcohol, for example, will affect members of religions that require the use of wine differently from members of other religions and nonbelievers, disproportionately burdening the practice of, say, Catholicism or Judaism. Without an exemption for sacramental wine, Prohibition may fail the test of religion neutrality.

It does not necessarily follow from that observation, of course, that the First Amendment requires an exemption from Prohibition; that depends on the meaning of neutrality as the Free Exercise Clause embraces it. The point here is the unremarkable one that our common notion of neutrality is broad enough to cover not merely what might be called formal neutrality, which, as a free exercise requirement, would only bar laws with an object to discriminate against religion, but also what might be called substantive neutrality, which, in addition to demanding a secular object, would generally require government to accommodate religious differences by exempting religious practices from formally neutral laws. . . . If the Free Exercise Clause secures only protection against deliberate discrimination, a formal requirement will exhaust the Clause's neutrality command; if the Free Exercise Clause, rather, safeguards a right to engage in religious activity free from unnecessary governmental interference, the Clause requires substantive, as well as formal, neutrality.

Though *Smith* used the term "neutrality" without a modifier, the rule it announced plainly assumes that free exercise neutrality is of the formal sort. Distinguishing between laws whose "object" is to prohibit religious exercise and those that prohibit religious exercise as an "incidental effect," *Smith* placed only the former within the reaches of the Free Exercise Clause; the latter, laws that satisfy formal neutrality, *Smith* would subject to no free exercise scrutiny at all, even when they prohibit religious exercise in application. 494 U.S., 878. The four Justices who rejected the *Smith* rule, by contrast, read the Free Exercise Clause as embracing what I have termed substantive neutrality. The enforcement of a law "neutral on its face," they said, may "nonetheless offend [the Free Exercise Clause's] requirement for government neutrality if it unduly burdens the free exercise of religion." *Id.*, 896 (opinion of O'CONNOR, J., joined by BRENNAN, MARSHALL, and BLACKMUN, JJ.) (internal quotation marks and citations omitted). The rule these Justices saw as flowing from free exercise neutrality, in contrast to the *Smith* rule, "requir[es] the government to justify *any* substantial burden on religiously motivated conduct by a compelling state interest and by means narrowly tailored to achieve that interest." *Id.*, 894 (emphasis added).

The proposition for which the *Smith* rule stands, then, is that formal neutrality, along with general applicability, are sufficient conditions for constitutionality under the Free Exercise Clause. That proposition is not at issue in this case, however, for Hialeah's animal sacrifice ordinances are not neutral under any definition, any more than they are generally applicable. This case, rather, involves the noncontroversial principle, repeated in *Smith*, that formal neutrality and general applicability are necessary conditions for free exercise constitutionality. It is only "this fundamental nonpersecution principle of the First Amendment [that is] implicated here,". . . and it is to that principle that the Court adverts when it holds that Hialeah's ordinances "fail to satisfy the *Smith* requirements." . . . In applying that principle, the Court does not tread on troublesome ground.

In considering, for example, whether Hialeah's animal sacrifice laws violate free exercise neutrality, the Court rightly observes that, "[a]t a minimum, the protections of the Free Exercise Clause pertain if the law at issue discriminates against some or all religious beliefs or regulates or prohibits conduct because it is undertaken for religious reasons," and correctly finds Hialeah's laws to fail those standards. The question whether the protections of the Free Exercise Clause also pertain if the law at issue, though nondiscriminatory in its object, has the effect nonetheless of placing a burden on religious exercise is not before the Court today, and the Court's intimations on the matter are therefore dicta.

The Court also rightly finds Hialeah's laws to fail the test of general applicability, and as the Court "need not define with precision the standard used to evaluate whether a prohibition is of general application, for these ordinances fall well below the minimum standard necessary to protect First Amendment rights," . . . it need not discuss the rules that apply to prohibitions found to be generally applicable. The question whether "there are areas of conduct protected by the Free Exercise Clause of the First Amendment and thus beyond the power of the State to control, even under regulations of general applicability," *Yoder* 406 U.S., 220+, is not before the Court in this case, and, again, suggestions on that score are dicta.

## II

In being so readily susceptible to resolution by applying the Free Exercise Clause's "fundamental nonpersecution principle," . . . . this is far from a representative free-exercise case. While, as the Court observes, the Hialeah City Council has provided a rare example of a law actually aimed at suppressing religious exercise, *Smith* was typical of our free exercise cases, involving as it did a formally neutral, generally applicable law. The rule *Smith* announced, however, was decidedly untypical of the cases involving the same type of law. Because *Smith* left those prior cases standing, we are left with a free-exercise jurisprudence in tension with itself, a tension that should be addressed, and that may legitimately be addressed, by reexamining the *Smith* rule in the next case that would turn upon its application.

### A

In developing standards to judge the enforceability of formally neutral, generally applicable laws against the mandates of the Free Exercise Clause, the Court has addressed the concepts of neutrality and general applicability by indicating, in language hard to read as not foreclosing the *Smith* rule, that the Free Exercise Clause embraces more than mere formal neutrality, and that formal neutrality and general applicability are not sufficient conditions for free exercise constitutionality:

> In a variety of ways, we have said that "[a] regulation neutral on its face may, in its application, nonetheless offend the constitutional requirement for governmental neutrality if it unduly burdens the free exercise of religion." *Thomas* 450 U.S., 717 (quoting *Yoder* 406 U.S., 220).
>
> [T]o agree that religiously grounded conduct must often be subject to the broad police power of the State is not to deny that there are areas of conduct protected by the Free Exercise Clause of the First Amendment, and thus beyond the power of the State to control, even under regulations of general applicability. *Ibid.*

Not long before the *Smith* decision, indeed, the Court specifically rejected the argument that "neutral and uniform" requirements for governmental benefits need satisfy only a reasonableness standard, in part because "[s]uch a test has no basis in precedent." *Hobbie v. Unemployment Appeals Comm'n of Florida* 480 U.S. 136, 141 (1987) (internal quotation marks and citations omitted). Rather, we have said, "[o]ur cases have established that '[t]he free exercise inquiry asks whether government has placed a substantial burden on the observation of a central religious belief or practice and, if so, whether a compelling governmental interest justifies the burden.'" *Swaggart Ministries* 493 U.S., 384-385 (quoting *Hernandez v. Commissioner* 490 U.S. 680, 699 [1989]).

Thus, we have applied the same rigorous scrutiny to burdens on religious exercise resulting from the enforcement of formally neutral, generally applicable laws as we have applied to burdens caused by laws that single out religious exercise: "'only those interests of the highest order and those not otherwise served can overbalance legitimate claims to the free exercise of religion.'" *McDaniel v. Paty* 435 U.S., 628 (plurality opinion) (quoting *Yoder*, 215). Compare *McDaniel*, 628-629 (plurality opinion) (applying that test to a law aimed at religious conduct) with *Yoder*, 215-229 (applying that test to a formally neutral, general law). Other cases in which the Court has applied heightened scrutiny to the enforcement of formally neutral, generally applicable laws that burden religious exercise include *Hernandez v. Commissioner*, 699; *Frazee v. Illinois Dept. of Employment Security* 489 U.S. 829, 835 (1989); *Hobbie v. Unemployment Appeals Comm'n*, 141; *Bob Jones Univ. v. United States* 461 U.S. 574, 604 (1983); *United States v. Lee* 455 U.S. 252, 257-258 (1982); *Thomas*, 718; *Sherbert v. Verner* 374 U.S. 398, 403 (1963); and *Cantwell v. Connecticut* 310 U.S. 296, 304-307 (1940).

Though *Smith* sought to distinguish the free-exercise cases in which the Court mandated exemptions from secular laws of general application, . . . I am not persuaded. *Wisconsin v. Yoder* and *Cantwell v. Connecticut*, according to *Smith*, were not true free-exercise cases, but "hybrid[s]" involving "the Free Exercise Clause in conjunction with other constitutional protections, such as freedom of speech and of the press, or the right of parents . . . to direct the education of their children." *Smith*, 881, 882. Neither opinion, however, leaves any doubt that "fundamental claims of religious freedom [were] at stake." *Yoder*, 221. See also *Cantwell*, 303-307. And the distinction *Smith* draws strikes me as ultimately untenable. If a hybrid claim is simply one in which another constitutional right is implicated, then the hybrid exception would probably be so vast as to swallow the *Smith* rule, and, indeed, the hybrid exception would cover the situation exemplified by *Smith*, since free speech and associational rights are certainly implicated in the peyote ritual. But if a hybrid claim is one in which a litigant would actually obtain an exemption from a formally neutral, generally applicable law under another constitutional provision, then there would have been no reason for the Court in what *Smith* calls the hybrid cases to have mentioned the Free Exercise Clause at all.

*Smith* sought to confine the remaining free exercise exemption victories, which involved unemployment compensation systems, . . . as "stand[ing] for the proposition that where the State has in place a system of individual exemptions, it may not refuse to extend that system to cases of "religious hardship" without compelling reason." 494 U.S., 884. But prior to *Smith*, the Court had already refused to accept that explanation of the unemployment compensation cases. . . . And, again, the distinction fails to exclude *Smith*: "If *Smith* is viewed as a hypothetical criminal prosecution for peyote use, there would be an individual governmental assessment of the defendants' motives and actions in the form of a criminal trial." McConnell, Free Exercise Revisionism and the Smith Decision, 57 U.Chi.L.Rev. 1109 1124 (1990). *Smith* also distinguished the unemployment compensation cases on the ground that they did not involve "an across-the-board criminal prohibition on a particular form of conduct." 494 U.S., 884. But even Chief Justice Burger's plurality opinion in *Bowen v. Roy*, on which *Smith* drew for its analysis of the unemployment compensation cases, would have applied its reasonableness test only to "denial of government benefits" and not to "governmental action or legislation that criminalizes religiously inspired activity or inescapably compels conduct that some find objectionable for religious reasons," *Bowen v. Roy*, 706 (opinion of BURGER, C.J., joined by POWELL and REHNQUIST, JJ.); to the latter category of governmental action, it would have applied the test employed in *Yoder*, which involved an across-the-board criminal prohibition and which Chief Justice Burger's opinion treated as an ordinary free-exercise case. . . .

As for the cases on which *Smith* primarily relied as establishing the rule it embraced, *Reynolds v. United States* and *Minersville School Dist. v. Gobitis*, see *Smith*, 879, their subsequent treatment by the Court would seem to require rejection of the *Smith* rule. *Reynolds*, which, in upholding the polygamy conviction of a Mormon, stressed the evils it saw as associated with polygamy, see 98 U.S., 166 ("polygamy leads to the patriarchal principle, and . . . fetters the people in stationary despotism"); *id.*, 165, 168, has been read as consistent with the principle that religious conduct may be regulated by general or targeting law only if the conduct "pose[s] some substantial threat to public safety, peace or order." *Sherbert v. Verner* 374 U.S., 403; . . . And *Gobitis*, after three Justices who originally joined the opinion renounced it for disregarding the government's constitutional obligation "to accommodate itself to the religious views of minorities," *Jones v. Opelika* 316 U.S. 584, 624 (1942) (opinion of BLACK, DOUGLAS, and MURPHY, JJ.), was explicitly overruled in *West Virginia Bd. of Ed. v. Barnette* 319 U.S. 624, 642 (1943); . . .

Since holding in 1940 that the Free Exercise Clause applies to the States, . . . the Court repeatedly has stated that the Clause sets strict limits on the government's power to burden religious exercise, whether it is a law's object to do so or its unanticipated effect. *Smith* responded to these statements by suggesting that the Court did not really mean what it said, detecting in at least the most recent opinions a lack of commitment to the compelling interest test in the context of formally neutral laws. *Smith*, 884–885. But even if the Court's commitment were that palid, it would argue only for moderating the language of the test, not for eliminating constitutional scrutiny altogether. In any event, I would have trouble concluding that the Court has not meant what it has said in more than a dozen cases over several decades, particularly when, in the same period, it repeatedly applied the compelling-interest test to require exemptions, even in a case decided the year before *Smith*. See *Frazee v. Illinois Dept. of Employment Security* 489 U.S. 829 (1989). In sum, it seems to me difficult to escape the conclusion that, whatever *Smith's* virtues, they do not include a comfortable fit with settled law.

B

The *Smith* rule, in my view, may be reexamined consistently with principles of *stare decisis*. To begin with, the *Smith* rule was not subject to "full-dress argument" prior to its announcement. The State of Oregon, in *Smith*, contended that its refusal to exempt religious peyote use survived the strict scrutiny required by "settled free exercise principles," inasmuch as the State had "a compelling interest in regulating" the practice of peyote use and could not "accommodate the religious practice without compromising its interest." . . . Respondents joined issue on the outcome of strict scrutiny on the facts before the Court, . . . and neither party squarely addressed the proposition the Court was to embrace, that the Free Exercise Clause was irrelevant to the dispute. Sound judicial decision-making requires "both a vigorous prosecution and a vigorous defense" of the issues in dispute, and a constitutional rule announced *sua sponte* is entitled to less deference than one addressed on full briefing and argument.

The *Smith* rule's vitality as precedent is limited further by the seeming want of any need of it in resolving the question presented in that case. JUSTICE O'CONNOR reached the same result as the majority by applying, as the parties had requested, "our established free exercise jurisprudence," 494 U.S., 903, and the majority never determined that the case could not be resolved on the narrower ground, going instead straight to the broader constitutional rule. But the Court's better practice, one supported by the same principles of restraint that underlie the rule of *stare decisis*, is not to "'formulate a rule of constitutional law broader than is required by the precise facts to which it is to be applied.'" While I am not suggesting that the *Smith* Court lacked the power to announce its rule, I think a rule of law unnecessary to the outcome of a case, especially one not put into play by the parties, approaches without more the sort of "dicta . . . which may be followed if sufficiently persuasive but which are not controlling." . . .

The considerations of full briefing, necessity, and novelty thus do not exhaust the legitimate reasons for reexamining prior decisions, or even for reexamining the *Smith* rule. One important further consideration warrants mention here, however, because it demands the reexamination I have in mind. *Smith* presents not the usual question of whether to follow a constitutional rule, but the question of which constitutional rule to follow, for *Smith* refrained from overruling prior free exercise cases that contain a free exercise rule fundamentally at odds with the rule *Smith* declared. *Smith*, indeed, announced its rule by relying squarely upon the precedent of prior cases. See 494 U.S., 878 ("Our decisions reveal that the . . . reading" of the Free Exercise Clause contained in the *Smith* rule "is the correct one"). Since that precedent is nonetheless at odds with the *Smith* rule, as I have discussed above, the result is an intolerable tension in free exercise law which may be resolved, consistently with principles of *stare decisis*, in a case in which the tension is presented and its resolution pivotal.

While the tension on which I rely exists within the body of our extant case law, a rereading of that case law will not, of course, mark the limits of any enquiry directed to reexamining the *Smith* rule, which should be reviewed in light not only of the precedent on which it was rested, but also of the text of the Free Exercise Clause and its origins. As for text, *Smith* did not assert that the plain language of the Free Exercise Clause compelled its rule, but only that the rule was "a permissible reading" of the Clause. Suffice it to say that a respectable argument may be made that the pre-*Smith* law comes closer to fulfilling the language of the Free Exercise Clause than the rule *Smith* announced. "[T]he Free Exercise Clause . . ., by its terms, gives special protection to the exercise of religion," *Thomas* 450 U.S., 713, specifying an activity and then flatly protecting it against government prohibition. The Clause draws no distinction between laws whose object is to prohibit religious exercise and laws with that effect, on its face seemingly applying to both.

Nor did *Smith* consider the original meaning of the Free Exercise Clause, though overlooking the opportunity was no unique transgression. Save in a handful of passing remarks, the Court has not explored the history of the Clause since its early attempts in 1879 and 1890, see *Reynolds v. United States* 98 U.S., 162-166, and *Davis v. Beason* 133 U.S. 333, 342 (1890), attempts that recent scholarship makes clear were incomplete. The curious absence of history from our free exercise decisions creates a stark contrast with our cases under the Establishment Clause, where historical analysis has been so prominent.

This is not the place to explore the history that a century of free exercise opinions have overlooked, and it is enough to note that, when the opportunity to reexamine *Smith* presents itself, we may consider recent scholarship raising serious questions about the *Smith* rule's consonance with the original understanding and purpose of the Free Exercise Clause. . . . There appears to be a strong argument from the Clause's development in the First Congress, from its origins in the post-Revolution state constitutions and pre-Revolution colonial charters, and from the philosophy of rights to which the Framers adhered, that the Clause was originally understood to preserve a right to engage in activities necessary to fulfill one's duty to one's God, unless those activities threatened the rights of others or the serious needs of the State. If, as this scholarship suggests, the Free Exercise Clause's original "purpose [was] to secure religious liberty in the individual by prohibiting any invasions thereof by civil authority," *School Dist. of Abington v. Schempp* 374 U.S., 223, then there would be powerful reason to interpret the Clause to accord with its natural reading, as applying to all laws prohibiting religious exercise in fact, not just those aimed at its prohibition, and to hold the neutrality needed to implement such a purpose to be the substantive neutrality of our pre-*Smith* cases, not the formal neutrality sufficient for constitutionality under *Smith*.

The scholarship on the original understanding of the Free Exercise Clause is, to be sure, not uniform. And there are differences of opinion as to the weight appropriately accorded original meaning. But whether or not one considers the original designs of the Clause binding, the interpretive significance of those designs surely ranks in the hierarchy of issues to be explored in resolving the tension inherent in free exercise law as it stands today.

III

The extent to which the Free Exercise Clause requires government to refrain from impeding religious exercise defines nothing less than the respective relationships in our constitutional democracy of the individual to government and to God. "Neutral, generally applicable" laws, drafted as they are from the perspective of the nonadherent, have the unavoidable potential of putting the believer to a choice between God and government. Our cases now present competing answers to the question when government, while pursuing secular ends, may compel disobedience to what one believes religion commands. The case before us is rightly decided without resolving the existing tension, which remains for another day when it may be squarely faced.

▓ JUSTICE BLACKMUN, with whom JUSTICE O'CONNOR joins, concurring in the judgment.

The Court holds today that the city of Hialeah violated the First and Fourteenth Amendments when it passed a set of restrictive ordinances explicitly directed at petitioners' religious practice. With this holding, I agree. I write separately to emphasize that the First Amendment's protection of religion extends beyond those rare occasions on which the government explicitly targets religion (or a particular religion) for disfavored treatment, as is done in this case. In my view, a statute that burdens the free exercise of religion "may stand only if the law in general, and the State's refusal to allow a religious exemption in particular, are justified by a compelling interest that cannot be served by less restrictive means." *Employment Div. v. Smith* 494 U.S. 872, 907 (1990) (dissenting opinion). The Court, however, applies a different test. It applies the test announced in *Smith*, under which "a law that is neutral and of general applicability need not be justified by a compelling governmental interest even if the law has the incidental effect of burdening a particular religious practice." I continue to believe that *Smith* was wrongly decided, because it ignored the value of religious freedom as an affirmative individual liberty, and treated the Free Exercise Clause as no more than an antidiscrimination principle. See 494

U.S., 908-909. Thus, while I agree with the result the Court reaches in this case, I arrive at that result by a different route.

When the State enacts legislation that intentionally or unintentionally places a burden upon religiously motivated practice, it must justify that burden by "showing that it is the least restrictive means of achieving some compelling state interest." *Thomas v. Review Bd. of Indiana Employment Security Div.* 450 U.S. 707, 718 (1981). . . . A State may no more create an underinclusive statute, one that fails truly to promote its purported compelling interest, than it may create an overinclusive statute, one that encompasses more protected conduct than necessary to achieve its goal. In the latter circumstance, the broad scope of the statute is unnecessary to serve the interest, and the statute fails for that reason. In the former situation, the fact that allegedly harmful conduct falls outside the statute's scope belies a governmental assertion that it has genuinely pursued an interest "of the highest order." *Ibid.* If the State's goal is important enough to prohibit religiously motivated activity, it will not and must not stop at religiously motivated activity. . . .

In this case, the ordinances at issue are both overinclusive and underinclusive in relation to the state interests they purportedly serve. They are overinclusive, as the majority correctly explains, because the "legitimate governmental interests in protecting the public health and preventing cruelty to animals could be addressed by restrictions stopping far short of a flat prohibition of all Santeria sacrificial practice." They are underinclusive as well, because, "[d]espite the city's proffered interest in preventing cruelty to animals, the ordinances are drafted with care to forbid few killings but those occasioned by religious sacrifice." Moreover, the "ordinances are also underinclusive with regard to the city's interest in public health. . . ."

When a law discriminates against religion as such, as do the ordinances in this case, it automatically will fail strict scrutiny under *Sherbert v. Verner* 374 U.S. 398, 402-403, 407 (1963) (holding that governmental regulation that imposes a burden upon religious practice must be narrowly tailored to advance a compelling state interest). This is true because a law that targets religious practice for disfavored treatment both burdens the free exercise of religion and, by definition, is not precisely tailored to a compelling governmental interest.

Thus, unlike the majority, I do not believe that "[a] law burdening religious practice that is not neutral or not of general application must undergo the most rigorous of scrutiny." In my view, regulation that targets religion in this way, *ipso facto*, fails strict scrutiny. It is for this reason that a statute that explicitly restricts religious practices violates the First Amendment. Otherwise, however, "[t]he First Amendment . . . does not distinguish between laws that are generally applicable and laws that target particular religious practices." *Smith* 494 U.S., 894 (opinion concurring in judgment).

It is only in the rare case that a state or local legislature will enact a law directly burdening religious practice as such. Because respondent here does single out religion in this way, the present case is an easy one to decide.

A harder case would be presented if petitioners were requesting an exemption from a generally applicable anticruelty law. The result in the case before the Court today, and the fact that every Member of the Court concurs in that result, does not necessarily reflect this Court's views of the strength of a State's interest in prohibiting cruelty to animals. This case does not present, and I therefore decline to reach, the question whether the Free Exercise Clause would require a religious exemption from a law that sincerely pursued the goal of protecting animals from cruel treatment. The number of organizations that have filed amicus briefs on behalf of this interest, however, demonstrates that it is not a concern to be treated lightly.

---

### NOTES AND QUESTIONS

1. What test did the Court apply to *Church of the Lukumi Babalu Aye v. Hialeah*? Was it consistent with the Court majority's reasoning in the *Smith case*?

2. Did the Court look only at the text of the ordinances when it evaluated their constitutionality? What kinds of evidence did the Court use to arrive at its conclusion that the ordinances were neither neutral nor generally applicable?

3. Suppose that following reversal, the Hialeah city council enacts a new ordinance that outlaws all killings of large animals except in licensed slaughterhouses. The new ordinance omits all biased language (e.g., "sacrifice," "ritual"), applies equally to all religious groups, and there is no evidence that the councilors were motivated by animus toward any religious group. The impact on Santerias' religious practice is the same as before, however. Is the new ordinance constitutional under the *Smith* standard? If so, what constituted the free exercise infringement before, the way the law was written or the impact on the Santerias' religion?

4. According to *Hialeah*, what is problematic about a law—that it targets a religious practice or that the law targets a religious practice for the wrong reason (i.e., with animus)? Suppose, based on an increase in infection-related illnesses, a state legislature amends an existing law prohibiting circumcision by non-medically certified individuals by removing an exemption from the law that permits Jewish rabbis to conduct circumcisions of male infants in *a b'rit mila*, commonly called a *bris*. The legislative history expressly refers to the medical need to prohibit this Jewish religious ceremony. The amended law now prohibits all non-medical circumcisions, religious or otherwise. Is the new law neutral? Does it engage in impermissible targeting?

5. According to Justice Blackmun, what should the Court do if it finds that a practice was targeted by the government for bad treatment precisely because it was motivated by religious commitments? How does his analysis differ from the approach set forth in Justice Kennedy's opinion? Which approach is more persuasive, in your view?

6. In their opinions, Justices Blackmun and Souter argue for reversing the *Smith* holding and reestablishing the *Sherbert* standard for free exercise challenges involving neutral laws. Justice Souter argues that a reconsideration of the *Smith* rule would be consistent with the principle of *stare decisis*. What are Souter's arguments on this point? Do Souter and Blackmun make a persuasive case that *Smith* should be revisited and overruled?

7. Justice Souter makes the point that the *Smith* Court did not consider the original meaning of the Free Exercise Clause when making its decision in that case. Given that some who call themselves originalists were part of the *Smith* majority, how does one explain that fact?

## Congress Stands in the Gap: RFRA and RLUIPA

As described above, the United States Supreme Court's decision in the case of *Employ-ment Division v. Smith* triggered negative reactions from a wide range of religious leaders, including Christians, Jews, Muslims, Sikhs and Buddhists, as well as a number of civil rights activists and legal experts from across the political spectrum. When the Supreme Court declined requests to hear the case again, these leaders formed an unusually broad coalition to urge lawmakers on Capitol Hill to consider crafting a legislative response to the *Smith* decision.

Congress convened a series of hearings to examine this issue. In that context, it con-sidered some evidence of the early impact of the *Smith* ruling. For example, the *Smith* decision forced a recall of a ruling in favor of a Laotian Hmong family that had objected for religious reasons to a government autopsy of their son.[1] (The son had died during his sleep.) In the recall of its prior decision, the court said it continued to believe that the Hmongs' religious freedom was seriously damaged by the performance of the autopsy against the family's religious objections. However, because the state law governing au-topsies met the new *Smith* standard—it was generally applicable and neutral—that harm was no longer constitutionally significant, the court said. Congress also heard about the impact of the *Smith* decision on a 1989 decision in favor of Amish plaintiffs.[2] In the 1989 case, a court found that the federal constitution required a state government to exempt the Amish from a public safety law that required slow-moving vehicles to display a bright orange triangle. The Amish considered the orange triangle to be a "worldly," and thus religiously objectionable, symbol, but they were willing to use silver reflector tape on their horse-drawn buggies instead. The court said that the state had not established that the use of this silver tape would be less effective in furthering the compelling governmental inter-est of public safety, and thus it ruled in favor of the Amish under the Free Exercise Clause of the First Amendment. Post-*Smith*, however, the Supreme Court asked the lower court to reconsider its decision in this case. When the court did so, it noted that the public safety law was a law of general application and, as such, its application to the Amish no longer merited strict scrutiny under the Free Exercise Clause.[3] While the court said that *Smith's* exception for "hybrid rights" might have some application to this case, it relied on a state constitutional provision to shore up its 1989 ruling.

In the wake of cases like these, Congress sought to ensure that state action of this na-ture was subjected to exacting scrutiny as a matter of federal law. It drafted the Religious Freedom Restoration Act (RFRA) to respond to claims that such neutral and generally applicable laws infringed on religious liberty. Under RFRA, people who claimed that laws or other governmental action substantially burdened their religious practice could sue the government, regardless of whether the governmental action targeted religious exercise for poor treatment. Similar to the pre-*Smith* standard, the government would have to dem-onstrate that its actions served a compelling interest and that there were no less restrictive ways to accomplish its goals. If the government could not make such a showing, it would be found to have violated RFRA. As drafted by Congress, RFRA applied to the actions of the government, whether local, state, or federal.

Perhaps the most controversial aspect of RFRA within Congress was its application to prisoners' free exercise claims. There was some attempt to exempt prisoners from the provisions of RFRA. However, once Congress specifically noted that the Act applies to the claims of prisoners in a way that respects the need of prison administrators to preserve security and order, this challenge to the legislation was resolved. Congress passed RFRA with little opposition and President Clinton signed the bill into law in 1993.

Other aspects of the RFRA were controversial at the time of its passage and thereafter. To apply RFRA to the states, Congress relied on its power under Section Five of the Fourteenth Amendment to the Constitution to ensure that state and local governments do not interfere with the right to exercise one's religion guaranteed by the First Amendment. Congress had relied on this power in the past to enact many important civil rights laws, but RFRA drew special attention because it responded to a Supreme Court decision, *Employment Division v. Smith*. Some state and local governments argued that RFRA was unconstitutional because it exceeded Congress' authority under the Fourteenth Amendment, in that Congress was not merely enforcing an existing constitutional right (as defined by the Supreme Court) but was expanding that right. RFRA supporters acknowledged that RFRA extended beyond the limited free exercise protection the Constitution provided after *Smith*, but they insisted that Congress had broad powers under the Fourteenth Amendment to protect individual liberties from state interference as RFRA did.

Critics of RFRA also argued that it went well beyond the constitutional rule abandoned by the Supreme Court in the *Smith* case. RFRA provided that whenever the government substantially burdened religious practice, it must prove that the governmental action served a compelling interest and that there was no other way to accomplish its goal. The Supreme Court had applied this kind of test in a few free exercise cases prior to the *Smith* decision, but it often found some reason to refrain from applying the test and, in most free exercise cases, the religious claimant lost. Also, the pre-*Smith* Court had been unclear whether the government method of accomplishing its compelling goal had to be the least restrictive means possible, or merely that the chosen means was tailored toward achieving that goal. RFRA supporters emphasized that, while the compelling interest test was a tough standard, it did require the claimant to prove a substantial burden on their faith and allowed the courts to weigh governmental interests against the needs of religious people.

Another argument made against RFRA was that religious people should not be exempted from general laws that applied to everyone else. Some charged to exempt

---

THE RELIGIOUS FREEDOM RESTORATION ACT

The Religious Freedom Restoration Act provides in part:

(a) In general. Government shall not substantially burden a person's exercise of religion even if the burden results from a rule of general applicability, except as provided in subsection (b).

(b) Exception. Government may substantially burden a person's exercise of religion only if it demonstrates that application of the burden to the person — (1) is in furtherance of a compelling governmental interest; and (2) is the least restrictive means of furthering that compelling governmental interest.

(c) Judicial relief. A person whose religious exercise has been burdened in violation of this section may assert that violation as a claim or defense in a judicial proceeding and obtain appropriate relief against a government. . . .

—42 U.S.C. § 2000bb-1(a)-(c)

religiously motivated conduct from general laws, but not similar conduct based on secular motivations, violated the Establishment Clause by preferring religion over non-religion. Supporters of RFRA responded that the ability to practice one's faith was a fundamental human right that deserved this kind of special protection. They also emphasized that the law required people of faith to establish that their religious practice had been substantially burdened before the state was required to justify that burden with a compelling interest. Referencing cases such as those mentioned above, RFRA's supporters argued that state and local governments often ignore the interests of religious minorities. Under RFRA, however, states would have to take a second look at such issues.

Once RFRA became law, claimants began using it to obtain religious exemptions from general laws that infringed on religious practice. In response, government bodies charged that RFRA was unconstitutional, either that it exceeded Congress' lawmaking authority or that it violated the Establishment Clause or both. The Supreme Court eventually agreed to hear one of these cases, *City of Boerne v. Flores.* In 1997, the Supreme Court held that RFRA exceeded Congress' power under the Fourteenth Amendment and thus did not apply to state and local governments. The Court recognized that Congress had some authority to prevent and remedy constitutional violations by prohibiting state action that did not technically violate constitutional requirements, but the Court held that RFRA went beyond Congress' limited power in this area.

---

## CITY OF BOERNE v. ARCHBISHOP FLORES
### 521 U.S. 507 (1997)

JUSTICE KENNEDY delivered the opinion of the Court.

A decision by local zoning authorities to deny a church a building permit was challenged under the Religious Freedom Restoration Act of 1993 (RFRA), 42 U.S.C. § 2000bb *et seq.* The case calls into question the authority of Congress to enact RFRA. We conclude the statute exceeds Congress' power. . . .

Legislation which deters or remedies constitutional violations can fall within the sweep of Congress' enforcement power even if in the process it prohibits conduct which is not itself unconstitutional and intrudes into "legislative spheres of autonomy previously reserved to the States." *Fitzpatrick v. Bitzer,* 427 U.S. 445, 455 (1976). For example, the Court upheld a suspension of literacy tests and similar voting requirements under Congress' parallel power to enforce the provisions of the Fifteenth Amendment as a measure to combat racial discrimination in voting, *South Carolina v. Katzenbach,* 383 U.S. 301, 308 (1966), despite the facial constitutionality of the tests under *Lassiter v. Northampton County Bd. of Elections,* 360 U.S. 45 (1959). We have also concluded that other measures protecting voting rights are within Congress' power to enforce the Fourteenth and Fifteenth Amendments, despite the burdens those measures placed on the States. . . .

It is also true, however, that "as broad as the congressional enforcement power is, it is not unlimited." In assessing the breadth of § 5's enforcement power, we begin with its text. Congress has been given the power "to enforce" the "provisions of this article." We agree with respondent, of course, that Congress can enact legislation under § 5 enforcing the constitutional right to the free exercise of religion. The "provisions of this article," to which § 5 refers, include the Due Process Clause of the Fourteenth Amendment. Congress' power to enforce the Free Exercise Clause follows from our holding in *Cantwell v. Connecticut*, 310 U.S. 296, 303 (1940), that the "fundamental concept of liberty embodied in [the Fourteenth Amendment's Due Process Clause] embraces the liberties guaranteed by the First Amendment."....

Congress' power under § 5, however, extends only to "enforcing" the provisions of the Fourteenth Amendment. The Court has described this power as "remedial." The design of the Amendment and the text of § 5 are inconsistent with the suggestion that Congress has the power to decree the substance of the Fourteenth Amendment's restrictions on the States. Legislation which alters the meaning of the Free Exercise Clause cannot be said to be enforcing the Clause. Congress does not enforce a constitutional right by changing what the right is. It has been given the power "to enforce," not the power to determine what constitutes a constitutional violation. Were it not so, what Congress would be enforcing would no longer be, in any meaningful sense, the "provisions of [the Fourteenth Amendment]."

While the line between measures that remedy or prevent unconstitutional actions and measures that make a substantive change in the governing law is not easy to discern, Congress must have wide latitude in determining where it lies, the distinction exists and must be observed. There must be a congruence and proportionality between the injury to be prevented or remedied and the means adopted to that end. Lacking such a connection, legislation may become substantive in operation and effect. History and our case law support drawing the distinction, one apparent from the text of the Amendment...

Respondent contends that RFRA is a proper exercise of Congress' remedial or preventive power. The Act, it is said, is a reasonable means of protecting the free exercise of religion as defined by *Smith*. It prevents and remedies laws which are enacted with the unconstitutional object of targeting religious beliefs and practices. See *Church of the Lukumi Babalu Aye, Inc. v. Hialeah*, 508 U.S. 520, 533 (1993) ("[A] law targeting religious beliefs as such is never permissible"). To avoid the difficulty of proving such violations, it is said, Congress can simply invalidate any law which imposes a substantial burden on a religious practice unless it is justified by a compelling interest and is the least restrictive means of accomplishing that interest. If Congress can prohibit laws with discriminatory effects in order to prevent racial discrimination in violation of the Equal Protection Clause, then it can do the same, respondent argues, to promote religious liberty.

While preventive rules are sometimes appropriate remedial measures, there must be a congruence between the means used and the ends to be achieved. The appropriateness of remedial measures must be considered in light of the evil presented. Strong measures appropriate to address one harm may be an unwarranted response to another, lesser one.

A comparison between RFRA and the Voting Rights Act is instructive. In contrast to the record which confronted Congress and the judiciary in the voting rights cases, RFRA's legislative record lacks examples of modern instances of generally applicable laws passed because of religious bigotry. The history of persecution in this country detailed in the hearings mentions no episodes occurring in the past 40 years. . . . This lack of support in the legislative record, however, is not RFRA's most serious shortcoming. Judicial deference, in most cases, is based not on the state of the legislative record Congress compiles but "on due regard for the decision of the body constitutionally appointed to decide." As a general matter, it is for Congress to determine the method by which it will reach a decision.

Regardless of the state of the legislative record, RFRA cannot be considered remedial, preventive legislation, if those terms are to have any meaning. RFRA is so out of proportion to a supposed remedial or preventive object that it cannot be understood as responsive to, or designed to prevent, unconstitutional behavior. It appears, instead, to attempt a substantive change in constitutional protections. Preventive measures prohibiting certain types of laws may be appropriate when there is reason to believe that many of the laws affected by the congressional enactment have a significant likelihood of being unconstitutional. . . .

RFRA is not so confined. Sweeping coverage ensures its intrusion at every level of government, displacing laws and prohibiting official actions of almost every description and regardless of subject matter. RFRA's restrictions apply to every agency and official of the Federal, State, and local governments. RFRA applies to all federal and state law, statutory or otherwise, whether adopted before or after its enactment. RFRA has no termination date or termination mechanism. Any law is subject to challenge at any time by any individual who alleges a substantial burden on his or her free exercise of religion.

The reach and scope of RFRA distinguish it from other measures passed under Congress' enforcement power, even in the area of voting rights. In *South Carolina v. Katzenbach*, the challenged provisions were confined to those regions of the country where voting discrimination had been most flagrant, and affected a discrete class of state laws, i.e., state voting laws. Furthermore, to ensure that the reach of the Voting Rights Act was limited to those cases in which constitutional violations were most likely (in order to reduce the possibility of overbreadth), the coverage under the Act would terminate "at the behest of States and political subdivisions in which the danger of substantial voting discrimination has not materialized during the preceding five years." The provisions restricting and banning literacy tests, upheld in *Katzenbach v. Morgan*, 384 U.S. 641 (1966), and *Oregon v. Mitchell*, 400 U.S. 112, attacked a particular type of voting qualification, one with a long history as a "notorious means to deny and abridge voting rights on racial grounds." . . .

The stringent test RFRA demands of state laws reflects a lack of proportionality or congruence between the means adopted and the legitimate end to be achieved. If an objector can show a substantial burden on his free exercise, the State must demonstrate a compelling governmental interest and show that the law is the least restrictive means of furthering its interest. Claims that a law substantially burdens someone's exercise of religion will often be difficult to contest. . . . Requiring a State to demonstrate a compelling interest and show that it has adopted the least restrictive means of achieving that interest is the most demanding test known to constitutional law. If "'compelling interest' really means what it says . . . many laws will not meet the test. . . . [The test] would open the prospect of constitutionally required religious exemptions from civic obligations of almost every conceivable kind." Laws valid under *Smith* would fall under RFRA without regard to whether they had the object of stifling or punishing free exercise. We make these observations not to reargue the position of the majority in *Smith* but to illustrate the substantive alteration of its holding attempted by RFRA. Even assuming RFRA would be interpreted in effect to mandate some lesser test, say one equivalent to intermediate scrutiny, the statute nevertheless would require searching judicial scrutiny of state law with the attendant likelihood of invalidation. This is a considerable congressional intrusion into the States' traditional prerogatives and general authority to regulate for the health and welfare of their citizens.

The substantial costs RFRA exacts, both in practical terms of imposing a heavy litigation burden on the States and in terms of curtailing their traditional general regulatory power, far exceed any pattern or practice of unconstitutional conduct under the Free Exercise Clause as interpreted in *Smith*. Simply put, RFRA is not designed to identify and counteract state laws likely to be unconstitutional because of their treatment of religion. In most cases, the state laws to which RFRA applies are not ones which will have been motivated by religious bigotry. If a state law disproportionately burdened a particular class of religious observers, this circumstance might be evidence of an impermissible legislative motive. RFRA's substantial burden test, however, is not even a discriminatory effects or disparate impact test. It is a reality of the modern regulatory state that numerous state laws, such as the zoning regulations at issue here, impose a substantial burden on a large class of individuals. When the exercise of religion has been burdened in an incidental way by a law of general application, it does not follow that the persons affected have been burdened any more than other citizens, let alone burdened because of their religious beliefs. In addition, the Act imposes in every case a least restrictive means requirement—a requirement that was not used in the pre-*Smith* jurisprudence RFRA purported to codify—which also indicates that the legislation is broader than is appropriate if the goal is to prevent and remedy constitutional violations. . . .

Our national experience teaches that the Constitution is preserved best when each part of the government respects both the Constitution and the proper actions and determinations of the other branches. When the Court has interpreted the Constitution, it has acted within the province of the Judicial Branch, which embraces the duty to say what the law is. When the political branches of the Government act against the background of a judicial interpretation of the Constitution already issued, it must be understood that in later cases and controversies the Court will treat its precedents with the respect due them under settled principles, including *stare decisis*, and contrary expectations must be disappointed. RFRA was designed to control cases and controversies, such as the one before us; but as the provisions of the federal statute here invoked are beyond congressional authority, it is this Court's precedent, not RFRA, which must control.

---

It is for Congress in the first instance to "determine whether and what legislation is needed to secure the guarantees of the Fourteenth Amendment," and its conclusions are entitled to much deference. Congress' discretion is not unlimited, however, and the courts retain the power, as they have since *Marbury v. Madison*, to determine if Congress has exceeded its authority under the Constitution. Broad as the power of Congress is under the Enforcement Clause of the Fourteenth Amendment, RFRA contradicts vital principles necessary to maintain separation of powers and the federal balance. The judgment of the Court of Appeals sustaining the Act's constitutionality is reversed.

*It is so ordered.*

▦ JUSTICE STEVENS, concurring.

In my opinion, the Religious Freedom Restoration Act of 1993 (RFRA) is a "law respecting an establishment of religion" that violates the First Amendment to the Constitution.

If the historic landmark on the hill in Boerne happened to be a museum or an art gallery owned by an atheist, it would not be eligible for an exemption from the city ordinances that forbid an enlargement of the structure. Because the landmark is owned by the Catholic Church, it is claimed that RFRA gives its owner a federal statutory entitlement to an exemption from a generally applicable, neutral civil law. Whether the Church would actually prevail under the statute or not, the statute has provided the Church with a legal weapon that no atheist or agnostic can obtain. This governmental preference for religion, as opposed to irreligion, is forbidden by the First Amendment. *Wallace v. Jaffree*, 472 U.S. 38, 52-55 (1985).

▦ JUSTICE SCALIA, with whom JUSTICE STEVENS joins, concurring in part.

I write to respond briefly to the claim of JUSTICE O'CONNOR's dissent (hereinafter "the dissent") that historical materials support a result contrary to the one reached in *Employment Div. v. Smith*, 494 U.S. 872 (1990). We held in *Smith* that the Constitution's Free Exercise Clause "does not relieve an individual of the obligation to comply with a 'valid and neutral law of general applicability on the ground that the law proscribes (or prescribes) conduct that his religion prescribes (or proscribes).'" 494 U.S., 879 (quoting *United States v. Lee*, 455 U.S. 252, 263, n. 3 (1982) (STEVENS, J., concurring in judgment)). The material that the dissent claims is at odds with *Smith* either has little to say about the issue or is in fact more consistent with *Smith* than with the dissent's interpretation of the Free Exercise Clause. The dissent's extravagant claim that the historical record shows *Smith* to have been wrong should be compared with the assessment of the most prominent scholarly critic of *Smith*, who, after an extensive review of the historical record, was willing to venture no more than that "constitutionally compelled exemptions [from generally applicable laws regulating conduct] were *within the contemplation* of the framers and ratifiers as a *possible interpretation* of the free exercise clause." McConnell, The Origins and Historical Understanding of Free Exercise of Religion, 103 Harv. L. Rev. 1409, 1415 (1990) (emphasis added); see also Hamburger, A Constitutional Right of Religious Exemption: An Historical Perspective, 60 Geo. Wash. Law Rev. 915 (1992) (arguing that historical evidence supports *Smith's* interpretation of free exercise).

The dissent first claims that *Smith's* interpretation of the Free Exercise Clause departs from the understanding reflected in various statutory and constitutional protections of religion enacted by Colonies, States, and Territories in the period leading up to the ratification of the Bill of Rights. But the protections afforded by those enactments are in fact more consistent with *Smith's* interpretation of free exercise than with the dissent's understanding of it. The Free Exercise Clause, the dissent claims, "is best understood as an affirmative guarantee of the right to participate in religious practices and conduct without impermissible governmental interference, even when such conduct conflicts with a neutral, generally applicable law"; thus, even neutral laws of general application may be invalid if they burden religiously motivated conduct. However, the early "free exercise" enactments cited by the dissent protect only against action that is taken "for" or "in respect of" religion, (Maryland Act Concerning Religion of 1649, Rhode Island Charter of 1663, and New Hampshire Constitution); or action taken "on account of" religion, (Maryland Declaration of Rights of 1776 and Northwest Ordinance of 1787); or "discriminatory" action, (New York Constitution); or, finally (and unhelpfully for purposes of interpreting "free exercise" in the Federal Constitution), action that interferes with the "free exercise" of religion, (Maryland Act Concerning Religion of 1649 and Georgia Constitution). It is eminently arguable that application of neutral, generally applicable laws of the sort the dissent refers to—such as zoning laws—would not constitute action taken "for," "in respect of," or "on account of" one's religion, or "discriminatory" action.

Assuming, however, that the affirmative protection of religion accorded by the early "free exercise" enactments sweeps as broadly as the dissent's theory would require, those enactments do not support the dissent's view, since they contain "provisos" that significantly qualify the affirmative protection they grant. According to the dissent, the "provisos" support *its* view because they would have been "superfluous" if "the Court was correct in *Smith* that generally applicable laws are enforceable regardless of religious conscience." I disagree. In fact, the most plausible reading of the "free exercise" enactments (if their affirmative provisions are read broadly, as the dissent's view requires) is a virtual restatement of *Smith*: Religious exercise shall be permitted *so long as it does not violate general laws governing conduct.* The "provisos" in the enactments negate a license to act in a manner "unfaithful to the Lord Proprietary" (Maryland Act Concerning Religion of 1649), or "behave" in other than a "peaceable and quiet" manner (Rhode Island Charter of 1663), or "disturb the public peace" (New Hampshire Constitution), or interfere with the "peace [and] safety of the State" (New York, Maryland, and Georgia Constitutions), or "demean" oneself in other than a "peaceable and orderly manner" (Northwest Ordinance of 1787). At the time these provisos were enacted, keeping "peace" and "order" seems to have meant, precisely, obeying the laws. "Every breach of law is against the peace." *Queen v. Lane,* 6 Mod. 128, 87 Eng. Rep. 884, 885 (Q. B. 1704). Even as late as 1828, when Noah Webster published his *American Dictionary of the English Language*, he gave as one of the meanings of "peace": "8. Public tranquility; that quiet, order and security which is guaranteed by the laws; as, to keep the *peace;* to break the *peace.*" 2 *An American Dictionary of the English Language* 31 (1828). This limitation upon the scope of religious exercise would have been in accord with the background political philosophy of the age (associated most prominently with John Locke), which regarded freedom as the right "to do only what was not lawfully prohibited," West, The Case Against a Right to Religion-Based Exemptions, 4 Notre Dame J. of Law, Ethics & Public Policy 591, 624 (1990). "Thus, the disturb-the-peace caveats apparently permitted government to deny religious freedom, not merely in the event of violence or force, but, more generally, upon the occurrence of illegal actions." Hamburger, 918-919. And while, under this interpretation, these early "free exercise" enactments support the Court's judgment in *Smith,* I see no sensible interpretation that could cause them to support what I understand to be the position of JUSTICE O'CONNOR, or any of *Smith*'s other critics. No one in that camp, to my knowledge, contends that their favored "compelling state interest" test conforms to any possible interpretation of "breach of peace and order"—i.e., that *only* violence or force, or any other category of action (more limited than "violation of law") which can possibly be conveyed by the phrase "peace and order," justifies state prohibition of religiously motivated conduct.

Apart from the early "free exercise" enactments of Colonies, States, and Territories, the dissent calls attention to those bodies', and the Continental Congress', legislative accommodation of religious practices prior to ratification of the Bill of Rights. This accommodation—which took place both before and after enactment of the state constitutional protections of religious liberty—suggests (according to the dissent) that "the drafters and ratifiers of the First Amendment . . . assumed courts would apply the Free Exercise Clause similarly." But that legislatures sometimes (though not always) found it "appropriate," to accommodate religious practices does not establish that accommodation was understood to be constitutionally *mandated* by the Free Exercise Clause. As we explained in *Smith*, "To say that a nondiscriminatory religious-practice exemption is permitted, or even that it is desirable, is not to say that it is constitutionally required." 494 U.S., 890. "Values that are protected against government interference through enshrinement in the Bill of Rights are not thereby banished from the political process." *Ibid.*

The dissent's final source of claimed historical support consists of statements of certain of the Framers in the context of debates about proposed legislative enactments or debates over general principles (not in connection with the drafting of State or Federal Constitutions). Those statements are subject to the same objection as was the evidence about legislative accommodation: There is no reason to think they were meant to describe what was constitutionally required (and judicially enforceable), as opposed to what was thought to be legislatively or even morally desirable. Thus, for example, the pamphlet written by James Madison opposing Virginia's proposed general assessment for support of religion, does not argue that the assessment would violate the "free exercise" provision in the Virginia Declaration of Rights, although that provision had been enacted into law only eight years earlier; rather the pamphlet argues that the assessment wrongly placed civil society ahead of personal religious belief and, thus, should not be approved by the legislators. Likewise, the letter from George Washington to the Quakers, by its own terms refers to Washington's "wish and desire" that religion be accommodated, not his belief that existing constitutional provisions required accommodation. These and other examples offered by the dissent reflect the speakers' views of the "proper" relationship between government and religion, but not their views (at least insofar as the content or context of the material suggests) of the constitutionally required relationship. The one exception is the statement by Thomas Jefferson that he considered "the government of the United States as interdicted by the Constitution from intermeddling with religious institutions, their doctrines, discipline, or exercises," (internal quotation marks omitted); but it is quite clear that Jefferson did not in fact espouse the broad principle of affirmative accommodation advocated by the dissent, see McConnell, 103 Harv. L. Rev., 1449-1452.

It seems to me that the most telling point made by the dissent is to be found, not in what it says, but in what it fails to say. Had the understanding in the period surrounding the ratification of the Bill of Rights been that the various forms of accommodation discussed by the dissent were constitutionally required (either by State Constitutions or by the Federal Constitution), it would be surprising not to find a single state or federal case refusing to enforce a generally applicable statute because of its failure to make accommodation. Yet the dissent cites none—and to my knowledge, and to the knowledge of the academic defenders of the dissent's position, none exists. . . .

The dissent's approach has, of course, great popular attraction. Who can possibly be against the abstract proposition that government should not, even in its general, nondiscriminatory laws, place unreasonable burdens upon religious practice? Unfortunately, however, that abstract proposition must ultimately be reduced to concrete cases. The issue presented by *Smith* is, quite simply, whether the people, through their elected representatives, or rather this Court, shall control the outcome of those concrete cases. For example, shall it be the determination of this Court, or rather of the people, whether church construction will be exempt from zoning laws? The historical evidence put forward by the dissent does nothing to undermine the conclusion we reached in *Smith*: It shall be the people.

⊞ JUSTICE O'CONNOR, with whom JUSTICE BREYER joins except as to a portion of Part I, dissenting.

I dissent from the Court's disposition of this case. I agree with the Court that the issue before us is whether the Religious Freedom Restoration Act (RFRA) is a proper exercise of Congress' power to enforce § 5 of the Fourteenth Amendment. But as a yardstick for measuring the constitutionality of RFRA, the Court uses its holding in *Employment Div. v. Smith*, 494 U.S. 872 (1990), the decision that prompted Congress to enact RFRA as a means of more rigorously enforcing the Free Exercise Clause. I remain of the view that *Smith* was wrongly decided, and I would use this case to reexamine the Court's holding there. Therefore, I would direct the parties to brief the question whether *Smith* represents the correct understanding of the Free Exercise Clause and set the case for reargument. If the Court were to correct the misinterpretation of the Free Exercise Clause set forth in *Smith*, it would simultaneously put our First Amendment jurisprudence back on course and allay the legitimate concerns of a majority in Congress who believed that *Smith* improperly restricted religious liberty. We would then be in a position to review RFRA in light of a proper interpretation of the Free Exercise Clause. . . .

## I

I agree with much of the reasoning set forth in Part III-A of the Court's opinion. Indeed, if I agreed with the Court's standard in *Smith*, I would join the opinion. . . .

## II

I shall not restate what has been said in other opinions, which have demonstrated that *Smith* is gravely at odds with our earlier free exercise precedents. Rather, I examine here the early American tradition of religious free exercise to gain insight into the original understanding of the Free Exercise Clause—an inquiry the Court in *Smith* did not undertake. We have previously recognized the importance of interpreting the Religion Clauses in light of their history. *Lynch v. Donnelly*, 465 U.S. 668, 673 (1984) ("The Court's interpretation of the Establishment Clause has comported with what history reveals was the contemporaneous understanding of its guarantees"); *School Dist. of Abington Township v. Schempp*, 374 U.S. 203, 212-214, (1963).

The historical evidence casts doubt on the Court's current interpretation of the Free Exercise Clause. The record instead reveals that its drafters and ratifiers more likely viewed the Free Exercise Clause as a guarantee that government may not unnecessarily hinder believers from freely practicing their religion, a position consistent with our pre-*Smith* jurisprudence.

A . . .

It would be disingenuous to say that the Framers neglected to define precisely the scope of the Free Exercise Clause because the words "free exercise" had a precise meaning. L. Levy, Essays on American Constitutional History 173 (1972). As is the case for a number of the terms used in the Bill of Rights, it is not exactly clear what the Framers thought the phrase signified. *Ibid.* ("It is astonishing to discover that the debate on a Bill of Rights was conducted on a level of abstraction so vague as to convey the impression that Americans of 1787-1788 had only the most nebulous conception of the meanings of the particular rights they sought to insure"). But a variety of sources supplement the legislative history and shed light on the original understanding of the Free Exercise Clause. These materials suggest that—contrary to *Smith*—the Framers did not intend simply to prevent the Government from adopting laws that discriminated against religion. Although the Framers may not have asked precisely the questions about religious liberty that we do today, the historical record indicates that they believed that the Constitution affirmatively protects religious free exercise and that it limits the government's ability to intrude on religious practice.

B

The principle of religious "free exercise" and the notion that religious liberty deserved legal protection were by no means new concepts in 1791, when the Bill of Rights was ratified. To the contrary, these principles were first articulated in this country in the colonies of Maryland, Rhode Island, Pennsylvania, Delaware, and Carolina, in the mid-1600's. These colonies, though established as sanctuaries for particular groups of religious dissenters, extended freedom of religion to groups—although often limited to Christian groups—beyond their own. Thus, they encountered early on the conflicts that may arise in a society made up of a plurality of faiths.

The term "free exercise" appeared in an American legal document as early as 1648, when Lord Baltimore extracted from the new Protestant governor of Maryland and his councilors a promise not to disturb Christians, particularly Roman Catholics, in the "free exercise" of their religion. McConnell, The Origins and Historical Understanding of Free Exercise of Religion, 103 Harv. L. Rev. 1409, 1425 (1990) (hereinafter Origins of Free Exercise). Soon after, in 1649, the Maryland Assembly enacted the first free exercise clause by passing the Act Concerning Religion: "Noe person . . . professing to believe in Jesus Christ, shall from henceforth bee any waies troubled, Molested or discountenanced for or in respect of his or her religion nor in the free exercise thereof . . . nor any way [be] compelled to the believe or exercise of any other Religion against his or her consent, soe as they be not unfaithful to the Lord Proprietary, or molest or conspire against the civil Governemt [sic]." Act Concerning Religion of 1649, reprinted in 5 The Founders' Constitution 49, 50 (P. Kurland & R. Lerner eds. 1987) (hereinafter Founders' Constitution). Rhode Island's Charter of 1663 used the analogous term "liberty of conscience." It protected residents from being "in any ways molested, punished, disquieted, or called into question, for any differences in opinion, in matters of religion, and do not actually disturb the civil peace of our said colony." The Charter further provided that residents may "freely, and fully have and enjoy his and their own judgments, and conscience in matters of religious concernments . . . ; they behaving themselves peaceably and quietly and not using this liberty to licentiousness and profaneness; nor to the civil injury, or outward disturbance of others." Charter of Rhode Island and Providence Plantations, 1663, in 8 W. Swindler, Sources and Documents of United States Constitutions 363 (1979). Various agreements between prospective settlers and the proprietors of Carolina, New York, and New Jersey similarly guaranteed religious freedom, using language that paralleled that of the Rhode Island Charter of 1663. See New York Act Declaring Rights & Priviledges (1691); Concession and Agreement of the Lords Proprietors of the Province of New Caesarea, or New-Jersey (1664); Laws of West New-Jersey, Art. X (1681); Fundamental Constitutions for East New-Jersey, Art. XVI (1683); First Charter of Carolina, Art. XVIII (1663). N. Cogan, The Complete Bill of Rights 23-27 (Galley 1997).

These documents suggest that, early in our country's history, several colonies acknowledged that freedom to pursue one's chosen religious beliefs was an essential liberty. Moreover, these colonies appeared to recognize that government should interfere in religious matters only when necessary to protect the civil peace or to prevent "licentiousness." In other words, when religious beliefs conflicted with civil law, religion prevailed unless important state interests militated otherwise. Such notions parallel the ideas expressed in our pre-*Smith* cases—that government may not hinder believers from freely exercising their religion, unless necessary to further a significant state interest.

C

The principles expounded in these early charters re-emerged over a century later in state constitutions that were adopted in the flurry of constitution-drafting that followed the American Revolution. By 1789, every State but Connecticut had incorporated some version of a free exercise clause into its constitution. Origins of Free Exercise 1455. These state provisions, which were typically longer and more detailed than the federal Free Exercise Clause, are perhaps the best evidence of the original understanding of the Constitution's protection of religious liberty. After all, it is reasonable to think that the States that ratified the First Amendment assumed that the meaning of the federal free exercise provision corresponded to that of their existing state clauses. The precise language of these state precursors to the Free Exercise Clause varied, but most guaranteed free exercise of religion or liberty of conscience, limited by particular, defined state interests. For example, the New York Constitution of 1777 provided:

> The free exercise and enjoyment of religious profession and worship, without discrimination or preference, shall forever hereafter be allowed, within this State, to all mankind: *Provided,* That the liberty of conscience, hereby granted, *shall not be so construed as to excuse acts of licentiousness, or justify practices inconsistent with the peace or safety of this State.* N.Y. Const., Art. XXXVIII (1777), in 7 Swindler, 178 (emphasis added).

Similarly, the New Hampshire Constitution of 1784 declared:

> Every individual has a natural and unalienable right to worship GOD according to the dictates of his own conscience, and reason; and no sub-

ject shall be hurt, molested, or restrained in his person, liberty or estate for worshipping GOD, in the manner and season most agreeable to the dictates of his own conscience, . . . *provided he doth not disturb the public peace, or disturb others,* in their religious worship. N.H. Const., Art. I, § 5 (1784), in 6 Swindler, 345 (emphasis added).

The Maryland Declaration of Rights of 1776 read:

No person ought by any law to be molested in his person or estate on account of his religious persuasion or profession, or for his religious practice; unless, under colour of religion, *any man shall disturb the good order, peace or safety of the State, or shall infringe the laws of morality, or injure others,* in their natural, civil, or religious rights. Md. Const., Declaration of Rights, Art. XXXIII in 4 Swindler, 374 (emphasis added).

The religious liberty clause of the Georgia Constitution of 1777 stated:

All persons whatever shall have the free exercise of their religion; provided *it be not repugnant to the peace and safety of the State.* Ga. Const., Art. LVI (1777), in 2 Swindler, 449 (emphasis added).

In addition to these state provisions, the Northwest Ordinance of 1787—which was enacted contemporaneously with the drafting of the Constitution and re-enacted by the First Congress—established a bill of rights for a territory that included what is now Ohio, Indiana, Michigan, Wisconsin, and part of Minnesota. Article I of the Ordinance declared: "No person, *demeaning himself in a peaceable and orderly manner,* shall ever be molested on account of his mode of worship or religious sentiments, in the said territory." Northwest Territory Ordinance of 1787, Art. I, 1 Stat. 52 (emphasis added).

The language used in these state constitutional provisions and the Northwest Ordinance strongly suggests that, around the time of the drafting of the Bill of Rights, it was generally accepted that the right to "free exercise" required, where possible, accommodation of religious practice. If not—and if the Court was correct in *Smith* that generally applicable laws are enforceable regardless of religious conscience—there would have been no need for these documents to specify, as the New York Constitution did, that rights of conscience should not be "construed as to excuse acts of licentiousness, or justify practices inconsistent with the peace or safety of [the] State." Such a proviso would have been superfluous. Instead, these documents make sense only if the right to free exercise was viewed as generally superior to ordinary legislation, to be overridden only when necessary to secure important government purposes.

The Virginia Legislature may have debated the issue most fully. In May 1776, the Virginia Constitutional Convention wrote a constitution containing a Declaration of Rights with a clause on religious liberty. The initial drafter of the clause, George Mason, proposed the following:

That religion, or the duty which we owe to our CREATOR, and the manner of discharging it, can be (directed) only by reason and conviction, not by force or violence; and therefore, *that all men should enjoy the fullest toleration in the exercise of religion,* according to the dictates of conscience, unpunished and unrestrained by the magistrate, *unless, under colour of religion, any man disturb the peace, the happiness, or safety of society.* And that it is the mutual duty of all to practice Christian forbearance, love, and charity towards each other. Committee Draft of the Virginia Declaration of Rights, 1 Papers of George Mason 284-285 (R. Rutland ed. 1970) (emphasis added).

Mason's proposal did not go far enough for a 26-year-old James Madison, who had recently completed his studies at the Presbyterian College of Princeton. He objected first to Mason's use of the term "toleration," contending that the word implied that the right to practice one's religion was a governmental favor, rather than an inalienable liberty. Second, Madison thought Mason's proposal countenanced too much state interference in religious matters, since the "exercise of religion" would have yielded whenever it was deemed inimical to "the peace, happiness, or safety of society." Madison suggested the provision read instead:

> "That religion, or the duty we owe our Creator, and the manner of discharging it, being under the direction of reason and conviction only, not of violence or compulsion, *all men are equally entitled to the full and free exercise of it, according to the dictates of conscience;* and therefore that no man or class of men ought on account of religion to be invested with peculiar emoluments or privileges, nor subjected to any penalties or disabilities, *unless under color of religion the preservation of equal liberty, and the existence of the State be manifestly endangered.*" G. Hunt, James Madison and Religious Liberty, 1 Annual Report of the American Historical Association 163, 166-167 (1901) (emphasis added).

Thus, Madison wished to shift Mason's language of "toleration" to the language of rights. See S. Cobb, The Rise of Religious Liberty in America 492 (1902) (reprint 1970) (noting that Madison objected to the word "toleration" as belonging to "a system where was an established Church, and where a certain liberty of worship was granted, not of right, but of grace"). Additionally, under Madison's proposal, the State could interfere in a believer's religious exercise only if the State would otherwise "be manifestly endangered." In the end, neither Mason's nor Madison's language regarding the extent to which state interests could limit religious exercise made it into the Virginia Constitution's religious liberty clause. Like the federal Free Exercise Clause, the Virginia religious liberty clause was simply silent on the subject, providing only that "all men are equally entitled to the free exercise of religion, according to the dictates of conscience." Virginia Declaration of Rights, Art. XVI (1776), in 10 Swindler, Sources and Documents of United States Constitutions, at 50. For our purposes, however, it is telling that *both* Mason's and Madison's formulations envisioned that, when there was a conflict, a person's interest in freely practicing his religion was to be balanced against state interests. Although Madison endorsed a more limited state interest exception than did Mason, the debate would have been irrelevant if either had thought the right to free exercise did not include a right to be exempt from certain generally applicable laws. Presumably, the Virginia Legislature intended the scope of its free exercise provision to strike some middle ground between Mason's narrower and Madison's broader notions of the right to religious freedom.

D

The practice of the colonies and early States bears out the conclusion that, at the time the Bill of Rights was ratified, it was accepted that government should, when possible, accommodate religious practice. Unsurprisingly, of course, even in the American colonies inhabited by people of religious per-suasions, religious conscience and civil law rarely conflicted. Most 17th and 18th century Americans belonged to denominations of Protestant Christian-ity whose religious practices were generally harmonious with colonial law. Curry, The First Freedoms, at 219 ("The vast majority of Americans assumed that theirs was a Christian, i.e. Protestant, country, and they automatically expected that government would uphold the commonly agreed on Protestant ethos and morality"). Moreover, governments then were far smaller and less intrusive than they are today, which made conflict between civil law and reli-gion unusual.

Nevertheless, tension between religious conscience and generally applica-ble laws, though rare, was not unknown in pre-Constitutional America. Most commonly, such conflicts arose from oath requirements, military conscription, and religious assessments. Origins of Free Exercise 1466. The ways in which these conflicts were resolved suggest that Americans in the colonies and early States thought that, if an individual's religious scruples prevented him from complying with a generally applicable law, the government should, if possible, excuse the person from the law's coverage. For example, Quakers and certain other Protestant sects refused on Biblical grounds to subscribe to oaths or "swear" allegiance to civil authority. A. Adams & C. Emmerich, A Nation Dedi-cated to Religious Liberty: The Constitutional Heritage of the Religion Clauses 14 (1990) (hereinafter Adams & Emmerich). Without accommodation, their beliefs would have prevented them from participating in civic activities involv-ing oaths, including testifying in court. Colonial governments created alter-natives to the oath requirement for these individuals. In early decisions, for example, the Carolina proprietors applied the religious liberty provision of the Carolina Charter of 1665 to permit Quakers to enter pledges in a book. Curry, The First Freedoms, 56. Similarly, in 1691, New York enacted a law allowing Quakers to testify by affirmation, and in 1734, it permitted Quakers to qualify to vote by affirmation. *Id.*, 64. By 1789, virtually all of the States had enacted oath exemptions. See Adams & Emmerich 62.

Early conflicts between religious beliefs and generally applicable laws also occurred because of military conscription requirements. Quakers and Men-nonites, as well as a few smaller denominations, refused on religious grounds to carry arms. Members of these denominations asserted that liberty of con-science should exempt them from military conscription. Obviously, excusing such objectors from military service had a high public cost, given the impor-tance of the military to the defense of society. Nevertheless, Rhode Island, North Carolina, and Maryland exempted Quakers from military service in the late 1600's. New York, Massachusetts, Virginia, and New Hampshire followed suit in the mid-1700's. Origins of Free Exercise 1468. The Continental Con-gress likewise granted exemption from conscription:

> "As there are some people, who, from religious principles, cannot bear arms in any case, this Congress intend no violence to their consciences, but earnestly recommend it to them, to contribute liberally in this time of universal calamity, to the relief of their distressed brethren in the sev-eral colonies, and to do all other services to their oppressed Country, which they can consistently with their religious principles." Resolution of July 18, 1775, reprinted in 2 Journals of the Continental Congress, 1774-1789, pp. 187, 189 (W. Ford ed. 1905).

Again, this practice of excusing religious pacifists from military service demonstrates that, long before the First Amendment was ratified, legislative accommodations were a common response to conflicts between religious practice and civil obligation. Notably, the Continental Congress exempted objectors from conscription to avoid "violence to their consciences," explicitly recognizing that civil laws must sometimes give way to freedom of conscience. Origins of Free Exercise 1468.

States and colonies with established churches encountered a further religious accommodation problem. Typically, these governments required citizens to pay tithes to support either the government-established church or the church to which the tithepayer belonged. But Baptists and Quakers, as well as others, opposed all government-compelled tithes on religious grounds. Id., 1469. Massachusetts, Connecticut, New Hampshire, and Virginia responded by exempting such objectors from religious assessments. Ibid. There are additional examples of early conflicts between civil laws and religious practice that were similarly settled through accommodation of religious exercise. Both North Carolina and Maryland excused Quakers from the requirement of removing their hats in court; Rhode Island exempted Jews from the requirements of the state marriage laws; and Georgia allowed groups of European immigrants to organize whole towns according to their own faith. Id., 1471.

To be sure, legislatures, not courts, granted these early accommodations. But these were the days before there was a Constitution to protect civil liberties—judicial review did not yet exist. These legislatures apparently believed that the appropriate response to conflicts between civil law and religious scruples was, where possible, accommodation of religious conduct. It is reasonable to presume that the drafters and ratifiers of the First Amendment—many of whom served in state legislatures—assumed courts would apply the Free Exercise Clause similarly, so that religious liberty was safeguarded.

E

The writings of the early leaders who helped to shape our Nation provide a final source of insight into the original understanding of the Free Exercise Clause. The thoughts of James Madison—one of the principal architects of the Bill of Rights—as revealed by the controversy surrounding Virginia's General Assessment Bill of 1784, are particularly illuminating. Virginia's debate over religious issues did not end with its adoption of a constitutional free exercise provision. Although Virginia had disestablished the Church of England in 1776, it left open the question whether religion might be supported on a nonpreferential basis by a so-called "general assessment." Levy, Essays on American Constitutional History, 200. In the years between 1776 and 1784, the issue how to support religion in Virginia—either by general assessment or voluntarily—was widely debated. Curry, The First Freedoms, 136.

By 1784, supporters of a general assessment, led by Patrick Henry, had gained a slight majority in the Virginia Assembly. M. Malbin, Religion and Politics: The Intentions of the Authors of the First Amendment 23 (1978); Levy, 200. They introduced "A Bill Establishing a Provision for the Teachers of the Christian Religion," which proposed that citizens be taxed in order to support the Christian denomination of their choice, with those taxes not designated for any specific denomination to go to a public fund to aid seminaries. Levy, 200-201; Curry, 140-141; Malbin, 23. Madison viewed religious assessment as a dangerous infringement of religious liberty and led the opposition to the bill. He took the case against religious assessment to the people of Virginia in his now-famous "Memorial and Remonstrance Against Religious Assessments." Levy, 201. This pamphlet led thousands of Virginians to oppose the bill and to submit petitions expressing their views to the legislature. Malbin, 24. The bill eventually died in committee, and Virginia instead enacted a Bill for Establishing Religious Freedom, which Thomas Jefferson had drafted in 1779. Malbin, 24.

The "Memorial and Remonstrance" begins with the recognition that "the Religion . . . of every man must be left to the conviction and conscience of every man; and it is the right of every man to exercise it as these may dictate." 2 Writings of James Madison 184 (G. Hunt ed. 1901). By its very nature, Madison wrote, the right to free exercise is "unalienable," both because a person's opinion "cannot follow the dictates of others," and because it entails "a duty toward the Creator." *Ibid.* Madison continued:

> "This duty [owed the Creator] is precedent both in order of time and degree of obligation, to the claims of Civil Society. . . . Every man who becomes a member of any Civil Society, [must] do it with a saving of his allegiance to the Universal Sovereign. We maintain therefore that in matters of Religion, no man's right is abridged by the institution of Civil Society, and that Religion is wholly exempt from its cognizance." *Id.,* at 184-185.

To Madison, then, duties to God were superior to duties to civil authorities—the ultimate loyalty was owed to God above all. Madison did not say that duties to the Creator are precedent only to those laws specifically directed at religion, nor did he strive simply to prevent deliberate acts of persecution or discrimination. The idea that civil obligations are subordinate to religious duty is consonant with the notion that government must accommodate, where possible, those religious practices that conflict with civil law.

Other early leaders expressed similar views regarding religious liberty. Thomas Jefferson, the drafter of Virginia's Bill for Establishing Religious Freedom, wrote in that document that civil government could interfere in religious exercise only "when principles break out into overt acts against peace and good order." In 1808, he indicated that he considered "'the government of the United States as interdicted by the Constitution from intermeddling with religious institutions, their doctrines, discipline, or exercises.'" 11 The Writings of Thomas Jefferson 428-429 (A. Lipscomb ed. 1904). Moreover, Jefferson believed that "'every religious society has a right to determine for itself the time of these exercises, and the objects proper for them, according to their own particular tenets; and this right can never be safer than in their own hands, where the Constitution has deposited it.'" *Ibid.*

George Washington expressly stated that he believed that government should do its utmost to accommodate religious scruples, writing in a letter to a group of Quakers:

> "In my opinion the conscientious scruples of all men should be treated with great delicacy and tenderness; and it is my wish and desire, that the laws may always be as extensively accommodated to them, as a due regard to the protection and essential interests of the nation may justify and permit." Letter from George Washington to the Religious Society Called Quakers (Oct. 1789), in George Washington on Religious Liberty and Mutual Understanding 11 (E. Humphrey ed. 1932).

Oliver Ellsworth, a Framer of the First Amendment and later Chief Justice of the United States, expressed the similar view that government could interfere in religious matters only when necessary "to prohibit and punish gross immoralities and impieties; because the open practice of these is of evil example and detriment." Oliver Ellsworth, Landholder, No. 7 (Dec. 17, 1787), reprinted in 4 Founders' Constitution, 640. Isaac Backus, a Baptist minister who was a delegate to the Massachusetts ratifying convention of 1788, declared that "'every person has an unalienable right to act in all religious affairs according to the full persuasion of his own mind, where others are not injured thereby.'" Backus, A Declaration of Rights, of the Inhabitants of the State of Massachusetts-Bay, in Isaac Backus on Church, State, and Calvinism 487 (W. McLoughlin ed. 1968).

These are but a few examples of various perspectives regarding the proper relationship between church and government that existed during the time the First Amendment was drafted and ratified. Obviously, since these thinkers approached the issue of religious freedom somewhat differently, see Adams & Emmerich, 21-31, it is not possible to distill their thoughts into one tidy formula. Nevertheless, a few general principles may be discerned. Foremost, these early leaders accorded religious exercise a special constitutional status. The right to free exercise was a substantive guarantee of individual liberty, no less important than the right to free speech or the right to just compensation for the taking of property. See P. Kauper, Religion and the Constitution 17 (1964) ("Our whole constitutional history . . . supports the conclusion that religious liberty is an independent liberty, that its recognition may either require or permit preferential treatment on religious grounds in some instances . . . "). As Madison put it in the concluding argument of his "Memorial and Remonstrance": "'The equal right of every citizen to the free exercise of his Religion according to the dictates of [his] conscience' is held by the same tenure with all our other rights. . . . It is equally the gift of nature; . . . it cannot be less dear to us; . . . it is enumerated with equal solemnity, or rather studied emphasis." 2 Writings of James Madison, 191.

Second, all agreed that government interference in religious practice was not to be lightly countenanced. Adams & Emmerich, 31. Finally, all shared the conviction that "'true religion and good morals are the only solid foundation of public liberty and happiness.'" Curry, The First Freedoms, 219 (quoting Continental Congress); see Adams & Emmerich, 72 ("The Founders . . . acknowledged that the republic rested largely on moral principles derived from religion"). To give meaning to these ideas—particularly in a society characterized by religious pluralism and pervasive regulation—there will be times when the Constitution requires government to accommodate the needs of those citizens whose religious practices conflict with generally applicable law.

## III

The Religion Clauses of the Constitution represent a profound commitment to religious liberty. Our Nation's Founders conceived of a Republic receptive to voluntary religious expression, not of a secular society in which religious expression is tolerated only when it does not conflict with a generally applicable law. As the historical sources discussed above show, the Free Exercise Clause is properly understood as an affirmative guarantee of the right to participate in religious activities without impermissible governmental interference, even where a believer's conduct is in tension with a law of general application. Certainly, it is in no way anomalous to accord heightened protection to a right identified in the text of the First Amendment. For example, it has long been the Court's position that freedom of speech—a right enumerated only a few words after the right to free exercise—has special constitutional status. Given the centrality of freedom of speech and religion to the American concept of personal liberty, it is altogether reasonable to conclude that both should be treated with the highest degree of respect.

Although it may provide a bright line, the rule the Court declared in *Smith* does not faithfully serve the purpose of the Constitution. Accordingly, I believe that it is essential for the Court to reconsider its holding in *Smith*—and to do so in this very case. I would therefore direct the parties to brief this issue and set the case for reargument.

I respectfully dissent from the Court's disposition of this case.

### JUSTICE SOUTER, dissenting.

To decide whether the Fourteenth Amendment gives Congress sufficient power to enact the Religious Freedom Restoration Act, the Court measures the legislation against the free-exercise standard of *Employment Div. v. Smith*. For the reasons stated in my opinion in *Church of Lukumi Babalu Aye, Inc. v. Hialeah*, (opinion concurring in part and concurring in judgment), I have serious doubts about the precedential value of the *Smith* rule and its entitlement to adherence. These doubts are intensified today by the historical arguments going to the original understanding of the Free Exercise Clause presented in JUSTICE O'CONNOR's opinion, which raises very substantial issues about the soundness of the *Smith* rule. See also JUSTICE SCALIA, concurring (addressing historical arguments). But without briefing and argument on the merits of that rule (which this Court has never had in any case, including *Smith* itself), I am not now prepared to join JUSTICE O'CONNOR in rejecting it or the majority in assuming it to be correct. In order to provide full adversarial consideration, this case should be set down for reargument permitting plenary reexamination of the issue. Since the Court declines to follow that course, our free-exercise law remains marked by an "intolerable tension," *Lukumi*, 508 U.S., 574, and the constitutionality of the Act of Congress to enforce the free-exercise right cannot now be soundly decided. I would therefore dismiss the writ of certiorari as improvidently granted, and I accordingly dissent from the Court's disposition of this case.

### JUSTICE BREYER, dissenting.

I agree with JUSTICE O'CONNOR that the Court should direct the parties to brief the question whether *Employment Div. v. Smith*, was correctly decided, and set this case for reargument. I do not, however, find it necessary to consider the question whether, assuming *Smith* is correct, § 5 of the Fourteenth Amendment would authorize Congress to enact the legislation before us. Thus, while I agree with some of the views expressed in the first paragraph of Part I of JUSTICE O'CONNOR's dissent, I do not necessarily agree with all of them. I therefore join JUSTICE O'CONNOR's dissent, with the exception of the first paragraph of Part I.

NOTES AND QUESTIONS

1. Explain how the rule established by the Religious Freedom Restoration Act (RFRA) differs from the rule the Court announced in the *Employment Division v. Smith* case.

2. The *Boerne* Court says: "Congress does not enforce a constitutional right by changing what the right is." What is the Court's point here? Is it persuasive?

3. According to the majority opinion in the *Boerne* case, what kind of demonstration must be made by Congress in order for a law to constitute an appropriate exercise of Congress' "remedial" power under Section 5 of the Fourteenth Amendment? In what ways did RFRA fail to meet this test? What reasons does the Court give for interpreting the Fourteenth Amendment to require this kind of proof?

4. Writing for the Court majority in the *Boerne* case, Justice Kennedy states: "When the exercise of religion has been burdened in an incidental way by a law of general application, it does not follow that the persons affected have been burdened any more than other citizens, let alone burdened because of their religious beliefs." Do you agree?

5. Justice Stevens argues that RFRA violates the Establishment Clause. Describe his argument. If RFRA is an unconstitutional preference for religion, consider the constitutionality of a law that allows the government to directly fund secular social services but prohibits direct funding of social services that are explicitly religious in nature. Is such a law an unconstitutional disapproval of religion by government? What would Justice Stevens say? What would Justice O'Connor say?

6. How would Justice Sandra Day O'Connor have handled the *Boerne* case? Do Justice O'Connor or any of the other justices vote in favor of finding RFRA constitutional? Why did Justice Souter decline to join Justice O'Connor's opinion?

7. Describe Justice O'Connor's historical arguments and Justice Scalia's critique of those arguments. Who is more convincing on these points? Is it somewhat strange that Justice Scalia, who often makes originalist arguments, only addresses the historical evidence in the free exercise arena when other justices, who do not claim to be originalists (Justices Souter and O'Connor), raise it?

   When lawyers present historical evidence in cases, it is sometimes pejoratively called "law office history," meaning that it is skewed so as to help the lawyer win the case. Could a similar critique be made of the history presented in this case by the justices, or does the presentation of historical evidence here seem more balanced, honest, and careful?

8. Does the Court's decision in this case strike down RFRA entirely, or does it only invalidate its application to state and local governments? If you are unsure, consult the discussion of the next case in this chapter.

Courts have interpreted the *City of Boerne v. Flores* decision as striking down the Religious Freedom Restoration Act (RFRA) in terms of its application to state and local governments but leaving RFRA intact in terms of its application to laws and actions of the federal government. Thus, lower courts and the Supreme Court have continued to wrestle with the ways in which RFRA should be applied to the actions of the federal government.

In 2006, the Supreme Court considered such a case, *Gonzales v. O Centro Espirita Beneficente Uniao Do Vegetal.* This case involved the religious practices of a small American branch of a religious group known as O Centro Espirita Beneficente Uniao Do Vegetal (UDV), which has its origins in the Amazon Rainforest. An important practice of the UDV's faith is receiving communion through *hoasca* (pronounced "wass-ca"), a tea made from plants from the Amazon region.

In 1999, United States customs inspectors intercepted a shipment to the American UDV containing three drums of *hoasca. Hoasca* contains a hallucinogen that is regulated under the Controlled Substances Act. When the customs inspectors threatened UDV with prosecution, the UDV filed a lawsuit, alleging that the application of the Controlled Substances Act to its sacramental use of *hoasca* violated RFRA.

The Supreme Court ultimately agreed to review the case. When it did so, it did not interpret the First Amendment's religion clauses. Instead, it interpreted certain provisions of RFRA, a federal statute. Among other things, this case required the Court to decide what kind of showing the government had to make in order to demonstrate that it had a "compelling state interest" for burdening religious exercise.

This was the first decision touching on church-state issues that was decided after Chief Justice John Roberts took his place on the Supreme Court. Note that he wrote the opinion for a unanimous Court in this case.

## GONZALES v. O CENTRO ESPIRITA BENEFICENTE UNIAO DO VEGETAL
### 546 U.S. 418 (2006)

CHIEF JUSTICE ROBERTS delivered the opinion of the Court.

A religious sect with origins in the Amazon Rainforest receives communion by drinking a sacramental tea, brewed from plants unique to the region, that contains a hallucinogen regulated under the Controlled Substances Act by the Federal Government. The Government concedes that this practice is a sincere exercise of religion, but nonetheless sought to prohibit the small American branch of the sect from engaging in the practice, on the ground that the Controlled Substances Act bars all use of the hallucinogen. The sect sued to block enforcement against it of the ban on the sacramental tea, and moved for a preliminary injunction.

It relied on the Religious Freedom Restoration Act of 1993, which prohibits the Federal Government from substantially burdening a person's exercise of religion, unless the Government "demonstrates that application of the burden to the person" represents the least restrictive means of advancing a compelling interest. . . . Before this Court, the Government's central submission is that it has a compelling interest in the *uniform* application of the Controlled Substances Act, such that no exception to the ban on use of the hallucinogen can be made to accommodate the sect's sincere religious practice. We conclude that the Government has not carried the burden expressly placed on it by Congress in the Religious Freedom Restoration Act, and affirm the grant of the preliminary injunction.

I

In *Employment Div., Dept. of Human Resources of Ore. v. Smith,* this Court held that the Free Exercise Clause of the First Amendment does not prohibit governments from burdening religious practices through generally applicable laws. In *Smith,* we rejected a challenge to an Oregon statute that denied unemployment benefits to drug users, including Native Americans engaged in the sacramental use of peyote. In so doing, we rejected the interpretation of the Free Exercise Clause announced in *Sherbert v. Verner,* 374 U.S. 398 (1963), and, in accord with earlier cases, held that the Constitution does not require judges to engage in a case-by-case assessment of the religious burdens imposed by facially constitutional laws.

Congress responded by enacting the Religious Freedom Restoration Act of 1993 (RFRA), which adopts a statutory rule comparable to the constitutional rule rejected in *Smith.* Under RFRA, the Federal Government may not, as a statutory matter, substantially burden a person's exercise of religion, "even if the burden results from a rule of general applicability." The only exception recognized by the statute requires the Government to satisfy the compelling interest test—to "demonstrate that application of the burden to the person—(1) is in furtherance of a compelling government interest; and (2) is the least restrictive means of furthering that compelling governmental interest." A person whose religious practices are burdened in violation of RFRA "may assert that violation as a claim or defense in a judicial proceeding and obtain appropriate relief."[1]

The Controlled Substances Act, 84 Stat. 1242, as amended, 21 U.S.C. § 801 *et seq.* (2000 ed. and Supp. I), regulates the importation, manufacture, distribution, and use of psychotropic substances. The Act classifies substances into five schedules based on their potential for abuse, the extent to which they have an accepted medical use, and their safety. Substances listed in Schedule I of the Act are subject to the most comprehensive restrictions, including an outright ban on all importation and use, except pursuant to strictly regulated research projects. The Act authorizes the imposition of a criminal sentence for simple possession of Schedule I substances, and mandates the imposition of a criminal sentence for possession "with intent to manufacture, distribute, or dispense" such substances.

O Centro Espirita Beneficente Uniao do Vegetal (UDV) is a Christian Spiritist sect based in Brazil, with an American branch of approximately 130

---

[1] As originally enacted, RFRA applied to States as well as the Federal Government. In *City of Boerne v. Flores* 521 U.S. 507 (1997) we held the application to States to be beyond Congress' legislative authority under § 5 of the 14th Amendment.

individuals. Central to the UDV's faith is receiving communion through *hoasca* (pronounced "wass-ca"), a sacramental tea made from two plants unique to the Amazon region. One of the plants, *psychotria viridis*, contains dimethyl-tryptamine (DMT), a hallucinogen whose effects are enhanced by alkaloids from the other plant, *banisteriopsis caapi*. DMT, as well as "any material, compound, mixture, or preparation, which contains any quantity of [DMT]," is listed in Schedule I of the Controlled Substances Act.

In 1999, United States Customs inspectors intercepted a shipment to the American UDV containing three drums of *hoasca*. A subsequent investigation revealed that the UDV had received 14 prior shipments of *hoasca*. The inspectors seized the intercepted shipment and threatened the UDV with prosecution.

The UDV filed suit against the Attorney General and other federal law enforcement officials, seeking declaratory and injunctive relief. The complaint alleged, *inter alia,* that applying the Controlled Substances Act to the UDV's sacramental use of *hoasca* violates RFRA. Prior to trial, the UDV moved for a preliminary injunction, so that it could continue to practice its faith pending trial on the merits.

At a hearing on the preliminary injunction, the Government conceded that the challenged application of the Controlled Substances Act would substantially burden a sincere exercise of religion by the UDV. The Government argued, however, that this burden did not violate RFRA, because applying the Controlled Substances Act in this case was the least restrictive means of advancing three compelling governmental interests: protecting the health and safety of UDV members, preventing the diversion of *hoasca* from the church to recreational users, and complying with the 1971 United Nations Convention on Psychotropic Substances, a treaty signed by the United States and implemented by the Act.

The District Court heard evidence from both parties on the health risks of *hoasca* and the potential for diversion from the church. The Government presented evidence to the effect that use of *hoasca*, or DMT more generally, can cause psychotic reactions, cardiac irregularities, and adverse drug interactions. The UDV countered by citing studies documenting the safety of its sacramental use of *hoasca* and presenting evidence that minimized the likelihood of the health risks raised by the Government. With respect to diversion, the Government pointed to a general rise in the illicit use of hallucinogens, and cited interest in the illegal use of DMT and *hoasca* in particular; the UDV emphasized the thinness of any market for *hoasca*, the relatively small amounts of the substance imported by the church, and the absence of any diversion problem in the past.

The District Court concluded that the evidence on health risks was "in equipoise," and similarly that the evidence on diversion was "virtually balanced." In the face of such an even showing, the court reasoned that the Government had failed to demonstrate a compelling interest justifying what it acknowledged was a substantial burden on the UDV's sincere religious exercise. The court also rejected the asserted interest in complying with the 1971 Convention on Psychotropic Substances, holding that the Convention does not apply to *hoasca*.

The court entered a preliminary injunction prohibiting the Government from enforcing the Controlled Substances Act with respect to the UDV's importation and use of *hoasca*. The injunction requires the church to import the tea pursuant to federal permits, to restrict control over the tea to persons of church authority, and to warn particularly susceptible UDV members of the dangers of *hoasca*. The injunction also provides that "if [the Government] believes that evidence exists that *hoasca* has negatively affected the health of UDV members," or "that a shipment of *hoasca* contains particularly dangerous levels of DMT, [the Government] may apply to the Court for an expedited determination of whether the evidence warrants suspension or revocation of [the UDV's authority to use *hoasca*]."

The Government appealed the preliminary injunction and a panel of the Court of Appeals for the Tenth Circuit affirmed, as did a majority of the Circuit sitting en banc. We granted certiorari.

III . . .

The Government contends that the [Controlled Substances] Act's description of Schedule I substances as having "a high potential for abuse," "no currently accepted medical use in treatment in the United States," and "a lack of accepted safety for use . . . under medical supervision," by itself precludes any consideration of individualized exceptions such as that sought by the UDV. The Government goes on to argue that the regulatory regime established by the Act—a "closed" system that prohibits all use of controlled substances except as authorized by the Act itself—"cannot function with its necessary rigor and comprehensiveness if subjected to judicial exemptions." According to the Government, there would be no way to cabin religious exceptions once recognized, and "the public will misread" such exceptions as signaling that the substance at issue is not harmful after all. Under the Government's view, there is no need to assess the particulars of the UDV's use or weigh the impact of an exemption for that specific use, because the Controlled Substances Act serves a compelling purpose and simply admits of no exceptions.

A

RFRA, and the strict scrutiny test it adopted, contemplate an inquiry more focused than the Government's categorical approach. RFRA requires the Government to demonstrate that the compelling interest test is satisfied through application of the challenged law "to the person"—the particular claimant whose sincere exercise of religion is being substantially burdened. RFRA expressly adopted the compelling interest test "as set forth in *Sherbert v. Verner*, 374 U.S. 398, and *Wisconsin v. Yoder*, 406 U.S. 205 (1972)." 42 U.S.C. § 2000bb(b)(1). In each of those cases, this Court looked beyond broadly formulated interests justifying the general applicability of government mandates and scrutinized the asserted harm of granting specific exemptions to particular religious claimants. In *Yoder*, for example, we permitted an exemption for Amish children from a compulsory school attendance law. We recognized that the State had a "paramount" interest in education, but held that "despite its admitted validity in the generality of cases, we must searchingly examine the interests that the State seeks to promote . . . and the impediment to those objectives that would flow from recognizing *the claimed Amish exemption*." 406 U.S., 213, 221 (emphasis added). The Court explained that the State needed "to show with more particularity how its admittedly strong interest . . . would be adversely affected by granting an exemption *to the Amish*." *Id.*, 236 (emphasis added).

In *Sherbert,* the Court upheld a particular claim to a religious exemption from a state law denying unemployment benefits to those who would not work on Saturdays, but explained that it was not announcing a constitutional right to unemployment benefits for "*all* persons whose religious convictions are the cause of their unemployment." 374 U.S., 410 (emphasis added). The Court distinguished the case "in which an employee's religious convictions serve to make him a nonproductive member of society." *Ibid.* Outside the Free Exercise area as well, the Court has noted that "context matters" in applying the compelling interest test, and has emphasized that "strict scrutiny *does* take 'relevant differences' into account—indeed, that is its fundamental purpose," *Adarand Constructors, Inc. v. Pena,* 515 U.S. 200, 228 (1995).

B

Under the more focused inquiry required by RFRA and the compelling interest test, the Government's mere invocation of the general characteristics of Schedule I substances, as set forth in the Controlled Substances Act, cannot carry the day. It is true, of course, that Schedule I substances such as DMT are exceptionally dangerous. Nevertheless, there is no indication that Congress, in classifying DMT, considered the harms posed by the particular use at issue here—the circumscribed, sacramental use of *hoasca* by the UDV. The question of the harms from the sacramental use of *hoasca* by the UDV *was* litigated below. Before the District Court found that the Government had not carried its burden of showing a compelling interest in preventing such harms, the court noted that it could not "ignore that the legislative branch of the government elected to place materials containing DMT on Schedule I of the [Act], reflecting findings that substances containing DMT have 'a high potential for abuse,' and 'no currently accepted medical use in treatment in the United States,' and that 'there is a lack of accepted safety for use of [DMT] under medical supervision.'" But Congress' determination that DMT should be listed under Schedule I simply does not provide a categorical answer that relieves the Government of the obligation to shoulder its burden under RFRA.

This conclusion is reinforced by the Controlled Substances Act itself. The Act contains a provision authorizing the Attorney General to "waive the requirement for registration of certain manufacturers, distributors, or dispensers if he finds it consistent with the public health and safety." The fact that the Act itself contemplates that exempting certain people from its requirements would be "consistent with the public health and safety" indicates that congressional findings with respect to Schedule I substances should not carry the determinative weight, for RFRA purposes, that the Government would ascribe to them.

And in fact an exception has been made to the Schedule I ban for religious use. For the past 35 years, there has been a regulatory exemption for use of peyote—a Schedule I substance—by the Native American Church. In 1994, Congress extended that exemption to all members of every recognized Indian Tribe. Everything the Government says about the DMT in *hoasca*—that, as a Schedule I substance, Congress has determined that it "has a high potential for abuse," "has no currently accepted medical use," and has "a lack of accepted safety for use . . . under medical supervision"—applies in equal measure to the mescaline in peyote, yet both the Executive and Congress itself have decreed an exception from the Controlled Substances Act for Native American religious use of peyote. If such use is permitted in the face of the congressional findings in § 812(b)(1) for hundreds of thousands of Native Americans practicing their faith, it is difficult to see how those same findings alone can preclude any consideration of a similar exception for the 130 or so American members of the UDV who want to practice theirs. . . .

The Government responds that there is a "unique relationship" between the United States and the Tribes, but never explains what about that "unique" relationship justifies overriding the same congressional findings on which the Government relies in resisting any exception for the UDV's religious use of *hoasca*. In other words, if any Schedule I substance is in fact *always* highly dangerous in any amount no matter how used, what about the unique relationship with the Tribes justifies allowing their use of peyote? Nothing about the unique political status of the Tribes makes their members immune from the health risks the Government asserts accompany any use of a Schedule I substance, nor insulates the Schedule I substance the Tribes use in religious exercise from the alleged risk of diversion.

The Government argues that the existence of a *congressional* exemption for peyote does not indicate that the Controlled Substances Act is amenable to *judicially crafted* exceptions. RFRA, however, plainly contemplates that *courts* would recognize exceptions—that is how the law works. . . . Congress' role in the peyote exemption—and the Executive's—confirms that the findings in the Controlled Substances Act do not preclude exceptions altogether; RFRA makes clear that it is the obligation of the courts to consider whether exceptions are required under the test set forth by Congress.

## C

The well-established peyote exception also fatally undermines the Government's broader contention that the Controlled Substances Act establishes a closed regulatory system that admits of no exceptions under RFRA. The Government argues that the effectiveness of the Controlled Substances Act will be "necessarily . . . undercut" if the Act is not uniformly applied, without regard to burdens on religious exercise. The peyote exception, however, has been in place since the outset of the Controlled Substances Act, and there is no evidence that it has "undercut" the Government's ability to enforce the ban on peyote use by non-Indians.

The Government points to some pre-*Smith* cases relying on a need for uniformity in rejecting claims for religious exemptions under the Free Exercise Clause, but those cases strike us as quite different from the present one. Those cases did not embrace the notion that a general interest in uniformity justified a substantial burden on religious exercise; they instead scrutinized the asserted need and explained why the denied exemptions could not be accommodated. In *United States* v. *Lee,* 455 U.S. 252 (1982), for example, the Court rejected a claimed exception to the obligation to pay Social Security taxes, noting that "mandatory participation is indispensable to the fiscal vitality of the social security system" and that the "tax system could not function if denominations were allowed to challenge the tax system because tax payments were spent in a manner that violates their religious belief." In *Braunfeld* v. *Brown,* 366 U.S. 599 (1961) the Court denied a claimed exception to Sunday closing laws, in part because allowing such exceptions "might well provide [the claimants] with an economic advantage over their competitors who must remain closed on that day." *Id.,* 608-609. The whole point of a "uniform day of rest for all workers" would have been defeated by exceptions. These cases show that the

Government can demonstrate a compelling interest in uniform application of a particular program by offering evidence that granting the requested religious accommodations would seriously compromise its ability to administer the program.

Here the Government's argument for uniformity is different; it rests not so much on the particular statutory program at issue as on slippery-slope concerns that could be invoked in response to any RFRA claim for an exception to a generally applicable law. The Government's argument echoes the classic rejoinder of bureaucrats throughout history: If I make an exception for you, I'll have to make one for everybody, so no exceptions. But RFRA operates by mandating consideration, under the compelling interest test, of exceptions to "rules of general applicability." Congress determined that the legislated test "is a workable test for striking sensible balances between religious liberty and competing prior governmental interests." This determination finds support in our cases; in *Sherbert*, for example, we rejected a slippery-slope argument similar to the one offered in this case, dismissing as "no more than a possibility" the State's speculation "that the filing of fraudulent claims by unscrupulous claimants feigning religious objections to Saturday work" would drain the unemployment benefits fund. 374 U.S., 407.

We reaffirmed just last Term the feasibility of case-by-case consideration of religious exemptions to generally applicable rules. In *Cutter v. Wilkinson*, 544 U.S. 709 (2005), we held that the Religious Land Use and Institutionalized Persons Act of 2000, which allows federal and state prisoners to seek religious accommodations pursuant to the same standard as set forth in RFRA, does not violate the Establishment Clause. We had "no cause to believe" that the compelling interest test "would not be applied in an appropriately balanced way" to specific claims for exemptions as they arose. Nothing in our opinion suggested that courts were not up to the task.

We do not doubt that there may be instances in which a need for uniformity precludes the recognition of exceptions to generally applicable laws under RFRA. But it would have been surprising to find that this was such a case, given the longstanding exemption from the Controlled Substances Act for religious use of peyote, and the fact that the very reason Congress enacted RFRA was to respond to a decision denying a claimed right to sacramental use of a controlled substance. And in fact the Government has not offered evidence demonstrating that granting the UDV an exemption would cause the kind of administrative harm recognized as a compelling interest in *Lee*, *Hernandez*, and *Braunfeld*. The Government failed to convince the District Court at the preliminary injunction hearing that health or diversion concerns provide a compelling interest in banning the UDV's sacramental use of *hoasca*. It cannot compensate for that failure now with the bold argument that there can be no RFRA exceptions at all to the Controlled Substances Act. See Tr. of Oral Arg. 17 (Deputy Solicitor General statement that exception could not be made even for "rigorously policed" use of "one drop" of substance "once a year").

IV

Before the District Court, the Government also asserted an interest in compliance with the 1971 United Nations Convention on Psychotropic Substances. The Convention, signed by the United States and implemented by the Controlled Substances Act, calls on signatories to prohibit the use of hallucinogens, including DMT. The Government argues that it has a compelling interest in meeting its international obligations by complying with the Convention. . . .

The fact that *hoasca* is covered by the Convention, however, does not automatically mean that the Government has demonstrated a compelling interest in applying the Controlled Substances Act, which implements the Convention, to the UDV's sacramental use of the tea. At the present stage, it suffices to observe that the Government did not even *submit* evidence addressing the international consequences of granting an exemption for the UDV. The Government simply submitted two affidavits by State Department officials attesting to the general importance of honoring international obligations and of maintaining the leadership position of the United States in the international war on drugs. We do not doubt the validity of these interests, any more than we doubt the general interest in promoting public health and safety by enforcing the Controlled Substances Act, but under RFRA invocation of such general interests, standing alone, is not enough.

The Government repeatedly invokes Congress' findings and purposes underlying the Controlled Substances Act, but Congress had a reason for enacting RFRA, too. Congress recognized that "laws 'neutral' toward religion may burden religious exercise as surely as laws intended to interfere with religious exercise," and legislated "the compelling interest test" as the means for the courts to "strike sensible balances between religious liberty and competing prior governmental interests."

We have no cause to pretend that the task assigned by Congress to the courts under RFRA is an easy one. Indeed, the very sort of difficulties highlighted by the Government here were cited by this Court in deciding that the approach later mandated by Congress under RFRA was not required as a matter of constitutional law under the Free Exercise Clause. But Congress has determined that courts should strike sensible balances, pursuant to a compelling interest test that requires the Government to address the particular practice at issue. Applying that test, we conclude that the courts below did not err in determining that the Government failed to demonstrate, at the preliminary injunction stage, a compelling interest in barring the UDV's sacramental use of *hoasca*.

The judgment of the United States Court of Appeals for the Tenth Circuit is affirmed, and the case is remanded for further proceedings consistent with this opinion.

*It is so ordered.*

▓ JUSTICE ALITO took no part in the consideration or decision of this case.

---

## NOTES AND QUESTIONS

1. The Court says: "RFRA requires the Government to demonstrate that the compelling interest test is satisfied through application of the challenged law 'to the person'—the particular claimant whose sincere exercise of religion is being substantially burdened." Why is this aspect of the statutory language so important in this case?

2. How does the judicial branch demonstrate deference to the legislative branch in this opinion? Is such deference well-advised in this case?

3. Describe the "peyote exception" the Court references. Why does the Court discuss the peyote exception in this case? How did the government try to argue that the peyote exception is different from an exception for *hoasca*? Did you find the government's arguments on this score persuasive? Did the Court?

4. How does the Court distinguish this case from earlier cases in which it found the government's interest in uniformity was compelling enough to defeat an assertion of a burden on free exercise interests?

5. Assume that this case had involved a religious group that claimed it uses marijuana as a sacrament. Do you think the result would have been the same? What about a case in which a religious group claimed it uses cocaine or heroin as a sacrament?

6. Along with their other colleagues, Justices Scalia, Kennedy, and Stevens joined the Court's opinion in this case. You will recall that Justice Scalia wrote the majority opinion in the *Employment Division v. Smith* case. Justices Kennedy and Stevens joined Scalia's opinion in the *Smith* case. Does the unanimous Court decision in the UDV case represent a change of heart for these justices in this area? Why or why not?

---

After the *City of Boerne v. Archbishop Flores* case, a ruling striking down parts of the Religious Freedom Restoration Act (RFRA), the coalition that had urged the U.S. Congress to pass RFRA urged it to pass the Religious Liberty Protection Act (RLPA). With RLPA, Congress attempted once again to protect religion by enforcing the compelling interest standard against the actions of state and local as well as federal government. RLPA relied principally on the government's power to regulate interstate commerce and impose conditions on federal spending to reach governmental conduct that substantially burdened religious exercise. The House of Representatives passed RLPA, but the Senate declined to take up the legislation. The main reason for the demise of the legislation was the fact that gay rights and civil rights groups feared that RLPA would be interpreted to require governments to grant exemptions for religious individuals and groups from state and local laws prohibiting discrimination on the basis of sexual orientation.

The failure of RLPA ultimately led to the enactment of more limited legislation, the Religious Land Use and Institutionalized Persons Act of 2000 ("RLUIPA"). RLUIPA provides increased protection for religious practices from state and local zoning and landmarking laws. It also provides special protection for prisoners and others in governmental institutions who wish to exercise their faith.

RLUIPA relies on three Congressional powers. Congress relied on its power to attach conditions to the funds it provides to state and local governments and to regulate activities that affect interstate commerce. Thus, Congress asserted its authority to regulate local and state prisons by virtue of the fact that the Congress usually provides federal funding for these institutions. Congress also noted that zoning and land-marking matters frequently involve building materials that move through interstate commerce and that the denial of building permits may affect interstate commerce, thus giving Congress the power to assert its jurisdiction over these types of transactions. Finally, Congress relied on its power to protect religious freedom from state interference under Section 5 of the Fourteenth Amendment, albeit in a much more narrow way than it did when it drafted RFRA.

In these contexts, RLUIPA requires the government to demonstrate that any substantial burden it places on religious practice must be supported by a compelling interest and that there is no less restrictive way of advancing that interest. The Act also prohibits the government from implementing a land use regulation that treats religious assemblies or institutions less favorably than non-religious assemblies or institutions. For example, under RLUIPA, a city may not allow non-religious neighborhood club meetings and deny religious people the right to hold similar-sized neighborhood Bible studies. RLUIPA also bars land use regulations that discriminate against religion or discriminate in favor of some religions over others. Finally, RLUIPA specifically prohibits municipalities from totally excluding religious assemblies from a jurisdiction.

---

THE RELIGIOUS LAND USE AND INSTITUTIONALIZED PERSONS ACT, 42 U.S.C. § 2000CC *ET SEQ.*, PROVIDES IN PART:

SEC. 2. PROTECTION OF LAND USE AS RELIGIOUS EXERCISE.
  (a) SUBSTANTIAL BURDENS—
    (1) GENERAL RULE—No government shall impose or implement a land use regulation in a manner that imposes a substantial burden on the religious exercise of a person, including a religious assembly or institution, unless the government demonstrates that imposition of the burden on that person, assembly, or institution—
      (A) is in furtherance of a compelling governmental interest; and
      (B) is the least restrictive means of furthering that compelling governmental interest.
    (2) SCOPE OF APPLICATION—This subsection applies in any case in which—
      (A) the substantial burden is imposed in a program or activity that receives Federal financial assistance, even if the burden results from a rule of general applicability;
      (B) the substantial burden affects, or removal of that substantial burden would affect, commerce with foreign nations, among the several States, or with Indian tribes, even if the burden results from a rule of general applicability; or
      (C) the substantial burden is imposed in the implementation of a land use regulation or system of land use regulations, under which a government makes, or has in place formal or informal procedures or practices that permit the government to make, individualized assessments of the proposed uses for the property involved.
  (b) DISCRIMINATION AND EXCLUSION—
    (1) EQUAL TERMS—No government shall impose or implement a land use regulation in a manner that treats a religious assembly or institution on less than equal terms with a nonreligious assembly or institution.

(2) NONDISCRIMINATION—No government shall impose or implement a land use regulation that discriminates against any assembly or institution on the basis of religion or religious de nomination.

(3) EXCLUSIONS AND LIMITS—No government shall impose or implement a land use regulation that—

(A) totally excludes religious assemblies from a jurisdiction; or

(B) unreasonably limits religious assemblies, institutions, or structures within a jurisdiction.

SEC. 3. PROTECTION OF RELIGIOUS EXERCISE OF INSTITUTIONALIZED PERSONS.

(a) GENERAL RULE—No government shall impose a substantial burden on the religious exercise of a person residing in or confined to an institution, as defined in section 2 of the Civil Rights of Institutionalized Persons Act (42 U.S.C. § 1997), even if the burden results from a rule of general applicability, unless the government demonstrates that imposition of the burden on that person—

(1) is in furtherance of a compelling governmental interest; and

(2) is the least restrictive means of furthering that compelling governmental interest.

(b) SCOPE OF APPLICATION—This section applies in any case in which—

(1) the substantial burden is imposed in a program or activity that receives Federal financial assistance; or

(2) the substantial burden affects, or removal of that substantial burden would affect, commerce with foreign nations, among the several States, or with Indian tribes.

RLUIPA's constitutionality also has been challenged in the courts. In 2005, the U.S. Supreme Court ruled on one of these issues in a case entitled *Cutter v. Wilkinson*.

## CUTTER v. WILKINSON
### 544 U.S. 709 (2005)

JUSTICE GINSBURG delivered the opinion of the Court.

Section 3 of the Religious Land Use and Institutionalized Persons Act of 2000 (RLUIPA), provides in part: "No government shall impose a substantial burden on the religious exercise of a person residing in or confined to an institution," unless the burden furthers "a compelling governmental interest," and does so by "the least restrictive means." Plaintiffs below, petitioners here, are current and former inmates of institutions operated by the Ohio Department of Rehabilitation and Correction and assert that they are adherents of "nonmainstream" religions: the Satanist, Wicca, and Asatru religions, and the Church of Jesus Christ Christian. They complain that Ohio prison officials (respondents here), in violation of RLUIPA, have failed to accommodate their religious exercise "in a variety of different ways, including retaliating and discriminating against them for exercising their nontraditional faiths, denying them access to religious literature, denying them the same opportunities for group worship that are granted to adherents of mainstream religions, forbidding them to adhere to the dress and appearance mandates of their religions, withholding religious ceremonial items that are substantially identical to those that the adherents of mainstream religions are permitted, and failing to provide a chaplain trained in their faith."

For purposes of this litigation at its current stage, respondents have stipulated that petitioners are members of bona fide religions and that they are sincere in their beliefs.

In response to petitioners' complaints, respondent prison officials have mounted a facial challenge to the institutionalized-persons provision of RLUIPA; respondents contend, *inter alia*, that the Act improperly advances religion in violation of the First Amendment's Establishment Clause. The District Court denied respondents' motion to dismiss petitioners' complaints, but the Court of Appeals reversed that determination. The appeals court held, as the prison officials urged, that the portion of RLUIPA applicable to institutionalized persons, 42 U.S.C. § 2000cc-1, violates the Establishment Clause. We reverse the Court of Appeals' judgment.

"This Court has long recognized that the government may . . . accommodate religious practices . . . without violating the Establishment Clause." *Hobbie v. Unemployment Appeals Comm'n of Fla.*, 480 U.S. 136, 144-145 (1987). Just last Term, in *Locke v. Davey*, 540 U.S. 712, (2004), the Court reaffirmed that "there is room for play in the joints between" the Free Exercise and Establishment Clauses, allowing the government to accommodate religion beyond free exercise requirements, without offense to the Establishment Clause. "At some point, accommodation may devolve into 'an unlawful fostering of religion.'" *Corporation of Presiding Bishop of Church of Jesus Christ of Latter-day Saints v. Amos*, 483 U.S. 327, 334-335 1987. But § 3 of RLUIPA, we hold, does not, on its face, exceed the limits of permissible government accommodation of religious practices.

I

A

RLUIPA is the latest of long-running congressional efforts to accord religious exercise heightened protection from government-imposed burdens, consistent with this Court's precedents. Ten years before RLUIPA's enactment, the Court held, in *Employment Div. v. Smith*, 494 U.S. 872, 878-882 (1990), that the First Amendment's Free Exercise Clause does not inhibit enforcement of otherwise valid laws of general application that incidentally burden religious conduct. In particular, we ruled that the Free Exercise Clause did not bar Oregon from enforcing its blanket ban on peyote possession with no allowance for sacramental use of the drug. Accordingly, the State could deny unemployment benefits to persons dismissed from their jobs because of their religiously inspired peyote use. The Court recognized, however, that the political branches could shield religious exercise through legislative accommodation, for example, by making an exception to proscriptive drug laws for sacramental peyote use.

Responding to *Smith*, Congress enacted the Religious Freedom Restoration Act of 1993 (RFRA). RFRA "prohibits 'government' from 'substantially burdening' a person's exercise of religion even if the burden results from a rule of general applicability unless the government can demonstrate the burden

'(1) is in furtherance of a compelling governmental interest; and (2) is the least restrictive means of furthering that compelling governmental interest.'" *City of Boerne v. Flores,* 521 U.S. 507, 515-516. "Universal" in its coverage, RFRA "applied to all Federal and State law," but notably lacked a Commerce Clause underpinning or a Spending Clause limitation to recipients of federal funds. In *City of Boerne*, this Court invalidated RFRA as applied to States and their subdivisions, holding that the Act exceeded Congress' remedial powers under the Fourteenth Amendment.[2]

Congress again responded, this time by enacting RLUIPA. Less sweeping than RFRA, and invoking federal authority under the Spending and Commerce Clauses, RLUIPA targets two areas: Section 2 of the Act concerns land-use regulation;[3] § 3 relates to religious exercise by institutionalized persons. Section 3, at issue here, provides that "no [state or local] government shall impose a substantial burden on the religious exercise of a person residing in or confined to an institution," unless the government shows that the burden furthers "a compelling governmental interest" and does so by "the least restrictive means." The Act defines "religious exercise" to include "any exercise of religion, whether or not compelled by, or central to, a system of religious belief." Section 3 applies when "the substantial burden [on religious exercise] is imposed in a program or activity that receives Federal financial assistance,"[4] or "the substantial burden affects, or removal of that substantial burden would affect, commerce with foreign nations, among the several States, or with Indian tribes." "A person may assert a violation of [RLUIPA] as a claim or defense in a judicial proceeding and obtain appropriate relief against a government."

Before enacting § 3, Congress documented, in hearings spanning three years, that "frivolous or arbitrary" barriers impeded institutionalized persons' religious exercise. . . .[5] To secure redress for inmates who encountered undue barriers to their religious observances, Congress carried over from RFRA the "compelling governmental interest"/"least restrictive means" standard. Lawmakers anticipated, however, that courts entertaining complaints under § 3 would accord "due deference to the experience and expertise of prison and jail administrators."

---

[2] RFRA, Courts of Appeals have held, remains operative as to the Federal Government and federal territories and possessions. See *O'Bryan v. Bureau of Prisons,* 349 F.3d 399, 400-401 (CA7 2003); *Guam v. Guerrero,* 290 F.3d 1210, 1220-1222 (CA9 2002); *Kikumura v. Hurley,* 242 F.3d 950, 958-960 (CA10 2001); *In re Young,* 141 F.3d 854, 858-863 (CA8 1998). This Court, however, has not had occasion to rule on the matter.

[3] Section 2 of RLUIPA is not at issue here. We therefore express no view on the validity of that part of the Act.

[4] Every State, including Ohio, accepts federal funding for its prisons.

[5] The hearings held by Congress revealed, for a typical example, that "[a] state prison in Ohio refused to provide Moslems with Hallal food, even though it provided Kosher food. . . . Across the country, Jewish inmates complained that prison officials refused to provide sack lunches, which would enable inmates to break their fasts after nightfall. . . . The "Michigan Department of Corrections . . . prohibited the lighting of Chanukah candles at all state prisons" even though "smoking" and "votive candles" were permitted. A priest responsible for communications between Roman Catholic dioceses and corrections facilities in Oklahoma stated that there "was [a] nearly yearly battle over the Catholic use of Sacramental Wine . . . for the celebration of the Mass," and that prisoners' religious possessions, "such as the Bible, the Koran, the Talmud or items needed by Native Americans[,] . . . were frequently treated with contempt and were confiscated, damaged or discarded" by prison officials. . . .

B . . .

We granted certiorari to resolve the conflict among Courts of Appeals on the question whether RLUIPA's institutionalized-persons provision, § 3 of the Act, is consistent with the Establishment Clause of the First Amendment.[7] We now reverse the judgment of the Court of Appeals for the Sixth Circuit.

II

A

The Religion Clauses of the First Amendment provide: "Congress shall make no law respecting an establishment of religion, or prohibiting the free exercise thereof." The first of the two Clauses, commonly called the Establishment Clause, commands a separation of church and state. The second, the Free Exercise Clause, requires government respect for, and noninterference with, the religious beliefs and practices of our Nation's people. While the two Clauses express complementary values, they often exert conflicting pressures. . . .

Our decisions recognize that "there is room for play in the joints" between the Clauses, some space for legislative action neither compelled by the Free Exercise Clause nor prohibited by the Establishment Clause. . . . In accord with the majority of Courts of Appeals that have ruled on the question, we hold that § 3 of RLUIPA fits within the corridor between the Religion Clauses: On its face, the Act qualifies as a permissible legislative accommodation of religion that is not barred by the Establishment Clause.

Foremost, we find RLUIPA's institutionalized-persons provision compatible with the Establishment Clause because it alleviates exceptional government-created burdens on private religious exercise. . . . Furthermore, the Act on its face does not founder on shoals our prior decisions have identified: Properly applying RLUIPA, courts must take adequate account of the burdens a requested accommodation may impose on nonbeneficiaries, and they must be satisfied that the Act's prescriptions are and will be administered neutrally among different faiths.[8]

"The 'exercise of religion' often involves not only belief and profession but the performance of . . . physical acts [such as] assembling with others for a worship service [or] participating in sacramental use of bread and wine . . . ." *Smith*, 494 U.S., 877. Section 3 covers state-run institutions—mental hospitals, prisons, and the like—in which the government exerts a degree of control unparalleled in civilian society and severely disabling to private religious exercise. RLUIPA thus protects institutionalized persons who are unable freely

---

[7] Respondents argued below that RLUIPA exceeds Congress' legislative powers under the Spending and Commerce Clauses and violates the Tenth Amendment. The District Court rejected respondents' challenges under the Spending Clause and the Tenth Amendment, and declined to reach the Commerce Clause question. The Sixth Circuit, having determined that RLUIPA violates the Establishment Clause, did not rule on respondents' further arguments. Respondents renew those arguments in this Court. They also augment their federalism-based or residual-powers contentions by asserting that, in the space between the Free Exercise and Establishment Clauses, the States' choices are not subject to congressional oversight. Because these defensive pleas were not addressed by the Court of Appeals, and mindful that we are a court of review, not of first view, we do not consider them here. . . .

[8] Directed at obstructions institutional arrangements place on religious observances, RLUIPA does not require a State to pay for an inmate's devotional accessories. . . .

to attend to their religious needs and are therefore dependent on the government's permission and accommodation for exercise of their religion.[10]

We note in this regard the Federal Government's accommodation of religious practice by members of the military. In *Goldman v. Weinberger,* 475 U.S. 503 (1986), we held that the Free Exercise Clause did not require the Air Force to exempt an Orthodox Jewish officer from uniform dress regulations so that he could wear a yarmulke indoors. In a military community, the Court observed, "there is simply not the same [individual] autonomy as there is in the larger civilian community." Congress responded to *Goldman* by prescribing that "a member of the armed forces may wear an item of religious apparel while wearing the uniform," unless "the wearing of the item would interfere with the performance [of] military duties [or] the item of apparel is not neat and conservative." 10 U.S.C. § 774(a)-(b).

We do not read RLUIPA to elevate accommodation of religious observances over an institution's need to maintain order and safety. Our decisions indicate that an accommodation must be measured so that it does not override other significant interests. In *Caldor,* the Court struck down a Connecticut law that "armed Sabbath observers with an absolute and unqualified right not to work on whatever day they designated as their Sabbath." 472 U.S., 709. We held the law invalid under the Establishment Clause because it "unyieldingly weighted" the interests of Sabbatarians "over all other interests."

We have no cause to believe that RLUIPA would not be applied in an appropriately balanced way, with particular sensitivity to security concerns. While the Act adopts a "compelling governmental interest" standard, "context matters" in the application of that standard.[11] Lawmakers supporting RLUIPA were mindful of the urgency of discipline, order, safety, and security in penal institutions. They anticipated that courts would apply the Act's standard with "due deference to the experience and expertise of prison and jail administrators in establishing necessary regulations and procedures to maintain good order, security and discipline, consistent with consideration of costs and limited resources."

---

[10] Respondents argue, in line with the Sixth Circuit, that RLUIPA goes beyond permissible reduction of impediments to free exercise. The Act, they project, advances religion by encouraging prisoners to "get religion," and thereby gain accommodations afforded under RLUIPA. While some accommodations of religious observance, notably the opportunity to assemble in worship services, might attract joiners seeking a break in their closely guarded day, we doubt that all accommodations would be perceived as "benefits." For example, congressional hearings on RLUIPA revealed that one state corrections system served as its kosher diet "a fruit, a vegetable, a granola bar, and a liquid nutritional supplement—each and every meal."

The argument, in any event, founders on the fact that Ohio already facilitates religious services for mainstream faiths. The State provides chaplains, allows inmates to possess religious items, and permits assembly for worship. . . .

[11] The Sixth Circuit posited that an irreligious prisoner and member of the Aryan Nation who challenges prison officials' confiscation of his white supremacist literature as a violation of his free association and expression rights would have his claims evaluated under the deferential rational-relationship standard described in *Turner v. Safley*, 482 U.S. 78. A member of the Church of Jesus Christ Christian challenging a similar withholding, the Sixth Circuit assumed, would have a stronger prospect of success because a court would review his claim under RLUIPA's compelling-interest standard. Courts, however, may be expected to recognize the government's countervailing compelling interest in not facilitating inflammatory racist activity that could imperil prison security and order. . . .

Finally, RLUIPA does not differentiate among bona fide faiths. In *Kiryas Joel*, we invalidated a state law that carved out a separate school district to serve exclusively a community of highly religious Jews, the Satmar Hasidim. We held that the law violated the Establishment Clause, in part because it "singled out a particular religious sect for special treatment." RLUIPA presents no such defect. It confers no privileged status on any particular religious sect, and singles out no bona fide faith for disadvantageous treatment.

B

The Sixth Circuit misread our precedents to require invalidation of RLUIPA as "impermissibly advancing religion by giving greater protection to religious rights than to other constitutionally protected rights." Our decision in *Amos* counsels otherwise. There, we upheld against an Establishment Clause challenge a provision exempting "religious organizations from Title VII's prohibition against discrimination in employment on the basis of religion." 483 U.S., 329. The District Court in *Amos*, reasoning in part that the exemption improperly "singled out religious entities for a benefit," had "declared the statute unconstitutional as applied to secular activity." Religious accommodations, we held, need not "come packaged with benefits to secular entities."

Were the Court of Appeals' view the correct reading of our decisions, all manner of religious accommodations would fall. Congressional permission for members of the military to wear religious apparel while in uniform would fail, as would accommodations Ohio itself makes. Ohio could not, as it now does, accommodate "traditionally recognized" religions: The State provides inmates with chaplains "but not with publicists or political consultants," and allows "prisoners to assemble for worship, but not for political rallies."

In upholding RLUIPA's institutionalized-persons provision, we emphasize that respondents "have raised a facial challenge to [the Act's] constitutionality, and have not contended that under the facts of any of [petitioners'] specific cases . . . [that] applying RLUIPA would produce unconstitutional results. The District Court, noting the underdeveloped state of the record, concluded: A finding "that it is *factually impossible* to provide the kind of accommodations that RLUIPA will require without significantly compromising prison security or the levels of service provided to other inmates" cannot be made at this juncture.[13] We agree.

"For more than a decade, the federal Bureau of Prisons has managed the largest correctional system in the Nation under the same heightened scrutiny standard as RLUIPA without compromising prison security, public safety, or the constitutional rights of other prisoners." Brief for United States, 24. The Congress that enacted RLUIPA was aware of the Bureau's experience. . . . We see no reason to anticipate that abusive prisoner litigation will overburden the operations of state and local institutions. The procedures mandated by

---

[13] Respondents argue that prison gangs use religious activity to cloak their illicit and often violent conduct. The instant case was considered below on a motion to dismiss. Thus, the parties' conflicting assertions on this matter are not before us. It bears repetition, however, that prison security is a compelling state interest, and that deference is due to institutional officials' expertise in this area. Further, prison officials may appropriately question whether a prisoner's religiosity, asserted as the basis for a requested accommodation, is authentic. Although RLUIPA bars inquiry into whether a particular belief or practice is "central" to a prisoner's religion, the Act does not preclude inquiry into the sincerity of a prisoner's professed religiosity. . . .

the Prison Litigation Reform Act of 1995, we note, are designed to inhibit frivolous filings.

Should inmate requests for religious accommodations become excessive, impose unjustified burdens on other institutionalized persons, or jeopardize the effective functioning of an institution, the facility would be free to resist the imposition. In that event, adjudication in as-applied challenges would be in order.

---

For the reasons stated, the judgment of the United States Court of Appeals for the Sixth Circuit is reversed, and the case is remanded for further proceedings consistent with this opinion.

*It is so ordered.*

JUSTICE THOMAS, concurring.

I join the opinion of the Court. I agree with the Court that the Religious Land Use and Institutionalized Persons Act of 2000 (RLUIPA) is constitutional under our modern Establishment Clause case law. I write to explain why a proper historical understanding of the Clause as a federalism provision leads to the same conclusion.[2]

I

The Establishment Clause provides that "Congress shall make no law respecting an establishment of religion." As I have explained, an important function of the Clause was to "make clear that Congress could not interfere with state establishments." *Elk Grove Unified School Dist. v. Newdow*, 542 U.S. 1, 50. The Clause, then, "is best understood as a federalism provision" that "protects state establishments from federal interference." Ohio contends that this federalism understanding of the Clause prevents federal oversight of state choices within the "'play in the joints'" between the Free Exercise and Establishment Clauses. In other words, Ohio asserts that the Clause protects the States from federal interference with otherwise constitutionally permissible choices regarding religious policy. In Ohio's view, RLUIPA intrudes on such state policy choices and hence violates the Clause.

Ohio's vision of the range of protected state authority overreads the Clause. Ohio and its *amici* contend that, even though "States can no longer establish preferred churches" because the Clause has been incorporated against the States through the Fourteenth Amendment, "Congress is as unable as ever to contravene constitutionally permissible *State choices regarding*

---

[2] The Court dismisses the parties' arguments about the federalism aspect of the Clause with the brief observation that the Court of Appeals did not address the issue. The parties' contentions on this point, however, are fairly included in the question presented, which asks "whether Congress violated the Establishment Clause by enacting [RLUIPA]." Further, both parties have briefed the federalism understanding of the Clause, and neither suggests that a remand on it would be useful or that the record in this Court lacks relevant facts.

Also, though RLUIPA is entirely consonant with the Establishment Clause, it may well exceed Congress' authority under either the Spending Clause or the Commerce Clause. . . . The Court, however, properly declines to reach those issues, since they are outside the question presented and were not addressed by the Court of Appeals.

*religious policy.*" That is not what the Clause says. The Clause prohibits Congress from enacting legislation "respecting an *establishment* of religion" (emphasis added); it does not prohibit Congress from enacting legislation "respecting religion" or "taking cognizance of religion." At the founding, establishment involved "'coercion of religious orthodoxy and of financial support *by force of law and threat of penalty*,'" *Newdow*, 52. . . . In other words, establishment at the founding involved, for example, mandatory observance or mandatory payment of taxes supporting ministers. . . . To proscribe Congress from making laws "respecting an establishment of religion," therefore, was to forbid legislation respecting coercive state establishments, not to preclude Congress from legislating on religion generally.

History, at least that presented by Ohio, does not show that the Clause hermetically seals the Federal Government out of the field of religion. Ohio points to, among other things, the words of James Madison in defense of the Constitution at the Virginia Ratifying Convention: "There is not a shadow of right in the general government to intermeddle with religion. Its least interference with it would be a most flagrant usurpation." Ohio also relies on James Iredell's statement discussing the Religious Test Clause at the North Carolina Ratifying Convention:

> [Congress] certainly [has] no authority to interfere in the establishment of any religion whatsoever. . . . Is there any power given to Congress in matters of religion? Can they pass a single act to impair our religious liberties? If they could, it would be a just cause of alarm. . . . If any future Congress should pass an act concerning the religion of the country, it would be an act which they are not authorized to pass, by the Constitution, and which the people would not obey. Debate in North Carolina Ratifying Convention (June 30, 1788), in 5 Founders' Constitution 90 (P. Kurland & R. Lerner eds. 1987).

These quotations do not establish the Framers' beliefs about the scope of the Establishment Clause. Instead, they demonstrate only that some of the Framers may have believed that the National Government had no authority to legislate concerning religion, because no enumerated power gave it that authority. Ohio's Spending Clause and Commerce Clause challenges, therefore, may well have merit.

In any event, Ohio has not shown that the Establishment Clause codified Madison's or Iredell's view that the Federal Government could not legislate regarding religion. An *unenacted* version of the Clause, proposed in the House of Representatives, demonstrates the opposite. It provided that "Congress shall make no laws touching religion, or infringing the rights of conscience." The words ultimately adopted, "Congress shall make no law respecting an establishment of religion," "identified a position from which [Madison] had once sought to distinguish his own." Whatever he thought of those words, "he clearly did not mind language less severe than that which he had [previously] used." The version of the Clause finally adopted is narrower than Ohio claims.

Nor does the other historical evidence on which Ohio relies—Joseph Story's Commentaries on the Constitution—prove its theory. Leaving aside the problems with relying on this source as an indicator of the original understanding, it is unpersuasive in its own right. Justice Story did say that "the whole power over the subject of religion is left exclusively to the state governments, to be acted upon according to their own sense of justice, and the state constitutions." In context, however, his statement concerned only Congress' inability to legislate with respect to religious *establishment*. . . .

In short, the view that the Establishment Clause precludes Congress from legislating respecting religion lacks historical provenance, at least based on the history of which I am aware. Even when enacting laws that bind the States pursuant to valid exercises of its enumerated powers, Congress need not observe strict separation between church and state, or steer clear of the subject of religion. It need only refrain from making laws "respecting an establishment of religion"; it must not interfere with a state establishment of religion. For example, Congress presumably could not require a State to establish a religion any more than it could preclude a State from establishing a religion.

II

On its face—the relevant inquiry, as this is a facial challenge—RLUIPA is not a law "respecting an establishment of religion." . . . [RLUIPA] does not prohibit or interfere with state establishments, since no State has established (or constitutionally could establish, given an incorporated Clause) a religion. Nor does the provision require a State to establish a religion: It does not force a State to coerce religious observance or payment of taxes supporting clergy, or require a State to prefer one religious sect over another. It is a law respecting religion, but not one respecting an establishment of religion.

In addition, RLUIPA's text applies to all laws passed by state and local governments, including "rules of general applicability," whether or not they concern an establishment of religion. State and local governments obviously have many laws that have nothing to do with religion, let alone establishments thereof. Numerous applications of RLUIPA therefore do not contravene the Establishment Clause, and a facial challenge based on the Clause must fail.

It also bears noting that Congress, pursuant to its Spending Clause authority, conditioned the States' receipt of federal funds on their compliance with RLUIPA. As noted above, RLUIPA may well exceed the spending power. Nonetheless, while Congress' condition stands, the States subject themselves to that condition by voluntarily accepting federal funds. The States' voluntary acceptance of Congress' condition undercuts Ohio's argument that Congress is encroaching on its turf.

## NOTES AND QUESTIONS

1. According to the Court, what are the factors demonstrating that the Religious Land Use and Institutionalized Persons Act (RLUIPA) is a permissible accommodation of religion? What earlier decisions does the Court rely upon in its enumeration of these factors?

2. The Court says RLUIPA "alleviates exceptional government-created burdens on private religious exercise." What does the modifier "exceptional" mean?

3. Remember the discussion of *O'Lone* above, also involving a prisoner's religious claim. Does the *Cutter* decision reflect an appropriate balance of competing interests or does it tip the scales too far in favor of the prisoner or the prison? Would the *O'Lone* case come out differently if the RLUIPA standard was applied?

4. If an inmate says he needs to have candles for use in his religious worship, is the prison obligated to purchase the candles and provide them to the inmate under the *Cutter* decision? If the prisoner requests kosher food, is the prison obligated to purchase such food? If the prisoner says a certain wine is required for his communion observance and that wine is quite expensive, is the prison obligated to purchase the wine?

5. Under RLUIPA, can a prison deny a prisoner access to racist literature even if such literature is supposedly religious?

6. According to the Court majority, how did the lower court misread Supreme Court precedent? If the Court had upheld the lower court's opinion, what affect would that decision have had on existing religious accommodations?

7. The Court emphasizes that it has only rejected a facial challenge to the statute under the Establishment Clause. What kind of litigation would you expect to ensue in *Cutter's* wake?

8. Does RLUIPA permit the government to inquire into whether a particular belief or practice is "central" to a person's belief? Does it permit the government to inquire into whether a particular religious belief is sincere?

9. According to Justice Thomas, what was "an important function" of the Establishment Clause when it was framed? How does his view of this matter affect the way in which he would interpret that Clause today?

10. Respondents argue that actions by the state that fall within the space between the federal Free Exercise and Establishment Clauses are not subject to Congressional oversight. What are Justice Thomas' reasons for rejecting that argument? How does the rest of the Court respond to this argument?

11. In Justice Thomas' opinion, is RLUIPA vulnerable to constitutional attack under the Spending or Commerce Clauses? Why? How does the rest of the Court respond to these arguments?

---

Even before the Supreme Court's decision in *City of Boerne v. Flores*, some states had begun to adopt their own laws to provide heightened protection for free exercise rights. These laws are known as "state RFRAs." In the wake of the *Boerne* decision, more states passed these kinds of laws.

According to a 2004 article by University of Texas Law Professor Douglas Laycock, twelve state legislatures have passed state RFRAs: Arizona, Connecticut, Florida, Idaho, Illinois, Missouri, New Mexico, Oklahoma, Pennsylvania, Rhode Island, South Carolina and Texas.[4] As Laycock notes, Alabama included a similar provision in its state constitution.[5]

Moreover, some state constitutions are read to require the government to meet the compelling interest test when it burdens religious practices. According to Professor Laycock's research, when these states are added to the number of states that have adopted state RFRAs, "more than half the states appear to have adopted some version of the [compelling interest] test." Thus, even in the wake of the *Smith* decision, the right to freely exercise one's faith currently receives a high level of protection in some situations due to a patch-work of federal and state statutes as well as through the interpretation of certain state constitutional provisions.

The flurry of efforts (both on and off the Court) to get the U.S. Supreme Court to revisit its 1990 ruling in *Employment Division v. Smith* have subsided. For the time being, the opponents of *Smith* seem to have grudgingly accepted the fact that there are not five votes on the Court to reconsider this issue. The result is that *Smith* is becoming increas-ingly embedded in the law. Still, there may come a day when a future Court sees things differently. In other words, a future Court may find the dissenting opinions in *Smith* more persuasive than the opinion of the Court majority in that case. It is that prospect upon which *Smith* critics must now pin their hopes.

# CHAPTER 9

# CHURCHES AND THE CIVIL JUSTICE SYSTEM

This chapter considers a separate but significant strain of free exercise jurisprudence: the extent to which religious organizations and houses of worship (we will use the term "churches" for the sake of simplicity) and their internal procedures should be exempt from the oversight of civil courts. One should not expect that the internal operation of churches and religious organizations will be conflict free. Churches are large social organizations with many members and employees. Disputes frequently arise over theology, leadership, finances, property interests, and employee relations. In fact, the history of Western Christianity, particularly since the Reformation, has been one of intra-church conflicts that have frequently led to schisms and the founding of new religious movements and denominations. Finally, conflicts have also arisen between church officials and lay members over alleged inappropriate conduct of clergy. In all of these disputes, wronged parties have often sought to vindicate their interests in the civil courts. This raises the specter of churches and church officials being sued, deposed, and forced to testify about internal church operations and decision making, many of which may involve theological considerations. Civil law suits may also force churches to disclose financial information, pay monetary damages, or even file for bankruptcy. This too raises the specter of judicial authorities or court-appointed trustees evaluating internal church practices and procedures, which are often rooted in theological matters.

These controversies thus raise an important religious freedom question: to what extent can churches be subject to civil judicial authority without infringing on the free exercise rights of churches to define their religious missions and operate free from government oversight? How are free exercise interests associated with religious autonomy different from the ones discussed in the previous chapters? As discussed earlier, courts have accepted the principle, with little dispute, that free exercise protections extend beyond individuals to cover groups of people who have chosen to associate for worship and other religious activity. While this latter free exercise interest may be viewed as the aggregate of the individual rights, the courts have not so limited the interest. Courts have historically recognized that churches possess distinct free exercise interests that are unique to a corporate body of worshipers. As you read this and the following chapter on religious institutions as employers, see if you can identify these additional interests and the different ways civil courts have approached this expression of the free exercise value.

This chapter considers these issues within two contexts: church autonomy cases often involving intra-church disputes over property and leadership; and church susceptibility to suit for tortious conduct (i.e., personal injury law suits).

## Church Autonomy/Schisms

May the state intervene in a dispute between warring factions of a religious body? More specifically, how should a court respond if, in a dispute between two factions of a religious entity, one faction sues the other? May the civil court hear the case and render a decision, or does the fact that the dispute is intra-religious render the civil court incompetent? Should a civil court's jurisdiction to adjudicate an intra-church dispute depend on the issues at stake (e.g., an interpretation of church doctrine or polity versus the application of secular contract or property law principles) or should the First Amendment bar civil courts from hearing all intra-church disputes?

Intra-religious controversies with the attendant involvement of civil courts raise both free exercise and nonestablishment concerns. If a decision favors one faction's interpretation of religious doctrine, it would impact the other faction's religious liberty. And the very act of judicial review could excessively entangle the state in religious matters.

A line of cases, the first of which came up shortly after the Civil War, thrust the Supreme Court in the middle of these kinds of questions. The Court, in deciding these cases, articulated some principles that answered the immediate questions and created some lasting precedents.

Many Christian denominations split over the issue of slavery before and during the Civil War. That is, churches that were large enough to have congregations in both the north and the south frequently disagreed over the theological, ethical, and legal permissibility of slavery. Some Christians found biblical justification for slavery while others found the pro-slavery position to be flatly contrary to the gospel. An example of such a split was the one that occurred among American Baptists. Slavery split Baptists into the Southern Baptist Convention (it still goes by that name) and Northern Baptist churches (now called the American Baptist Churches USA). Another example of a church that experienced schism during this time was the Presbyterian church, which is what the first of our cases is about.

*Watson v. Jones* involved not the entire Presbyterian denomination, but one of its congregations that represented the church controversy in microcosm. During the war, some Presbyterian congregations in border states contained both pro-Union and pro-Confederacy members. That was the situation in the Walnut Street Presbyterian church in Louisville, Kentucky. In 1866 the General Assembly of the Presbyterian Church declared that those persons during the war who supported slavery and the Confederacy could not be readmitted as valid members of their local congregations and to the national church until they had repented of their sin and reapplied for membership. The formerly pro-slavery members of the Walnut Street church resented the declaration of the national church and chose not to comply. They believed they were *bona fide* Presbyterians and, furthermore, ought to have possession of the local church in Louisville. The anti-slavery faction of the church believed the same about themselves. Thus, two parties claimed to be the owners and rightful users of the church property. When they could not resolve their differences, the formerly pro-slavery party sued in civil court to gain possession of the church. The case ultimately arrived in the Supreme Court.

The Court, in a decision by Justice Samuel F. Miller, decided not to decide. This was not because it refused to hear the case or used some other mechanism to avoid the issue, but because it articulated a constitutional prohibition on civil courts deciding such issues.

In order to understand Justice Miller's decision, it is necessary to touch on some of the principles of church government in the Christian tradition. There are essentially three patterns of church government, the *episcopal*, the *presbyterian*, and the *congregational*. The *episcopal* is church government from the top down, the most hierarchical form of church government. In this form, authority flows from the top official(s) through intermediary officials ultimately to the laypeople of the church. The earliest and most classic example is the Roman Catholic church, in which authority flows from the Bishop of Rome (known as the Pope), through the bishops, the priests, and finally to the laypeople.

The *presbyterian* form is more complicated, for authority flows from the bottom to the top and then back down. Each local congregation elects members to its "session," the body that governs the local church. Each local "session" elects representatives to a regional "presbytery." "Presbyteries" from a larger region elect representatives to serve on the "synod," a governing body that encompasses several presbyteries. Finally, the several "synods" of the nation elect representatives to the "general assembly," which serves as the national governing body. The "general assembly" legislates for all the bodies below it, down to the local congregations, which have agreed to be governed by its rulings. The best analogy is the structure of the United States government. The people elect members of the House of Representatives and the Senate, with the understanding that these bodies will pass laws that, if signed by the President, will be binding on the people. Authority flows from the bottom to the top and back down.

The *congregational* form of church government locates authority in local congregations. Each congregation governs itself, sometimes by electing a board which has the responsibility of leading the congregation. There are national congregational denominations, such as the Southern Baptist Convention, but the theory is that whatever bodies exist above the local congregation have advisory authority only. They can advise and make recommendations to local congregations. But ultimately the local congregations can accept *or reject* those pronouncements as they choose.

In *Watson v. Jones*, the Supreme Court was not working with a blank slate. Leading authority, based on an 1817 English case, *Attorney General v. Pearson*, held that in a dispute over church property, civil courts could determine which faction adhered closest to the traditional doctrines of the church (and was thus entitled to ownership of the disputed property). The "*Pearson*" or "departure from doctrine" rule thus required civil courts to engage in detailed examinations of church doctrines and procedures to determine which faction was in error. Although several state appellate courts had rejected the *Pearson* rule as violating rights of conscience and separation of church and state, it was not uncommon for American courts to rule for that faction that could establish closer fealty to traditional church doctrines or procedures. In *Watson*, the Supreme Court decided generally that civil courts cannot adjudicate disputes between members of church congregations over the ownership and use of church property. This is especially true when the dispute involves the interpretation of church doctrine or theology. Civil courts are not competent to decide issues of theology; those questions must be left to the church bodies involved. In reaching this conclusion, Justice Miller wrote of three categories of church property disputes. In each case, he laid down rules that civil courts, including the Supreme Court, must follow.

In reading *Watson* and the subsequent cases, see if you can identify the religious liberty issues at stake and ask yourself whether the Court has adequately addressed the concerns in its holdings. [Note: The *Watson* ruling is based on an interpretation of federal common law rather than on First Amendment grounds; however, the rationale has a distinct constitutional ring to it.]

---

## WATSON v. JONES
### 13 Wallace 679 (80 U.S. 679) (1872)

▒ MR. JUSTICE MILLER delivered the opinion of the Court. . . .

The questions which have come before the civil courts concerning the rights to property held by ecclesiastical bodies, may, so far as we have been able to examine them, be profitably classified under three general heads, which of course do not include cases governed by considerations applicable to a church established and supported by law as the religion of the state.

1. The first of these is when the property which is the subject of controversy has been, by the deed or will of the donor, or other instrument by which the property is held, by the express terms of the instrument devoted to the teaching support, or spread of some specific form of religious doctrine or belief.

2. The second is when the property is held by a religious congregation which, by the nature of its organization, is strictly independent of other ecclesiastical associations, and so far as church government is concerned, owes no fealty or obligation to any higher authority.

3. The third is where the religious congregation or ecclesiastical body holding the property is but a subordinate member of some general church organization in which there are superior ecclesiastical tribunals with a general and ultimate power of control more or less complete, in some supreme judicatory over the whole membership of that general organization.

In regard to the first of these classes it seems hardly to admit of a rational doubt that an individual or an association of individuals may dedicate property by way of trust to the purpose of sustaining, supporting, and propagating definite religious doctrines or principles, provided that in doing so they violate no law of morality, and give to the instrument by which their purpose is evidenced, the formalities which the laws require. And it would seem also to be the obvious duty of the court, in a case properly made, to see that the property so dedicated is not diverted from the trust which is thus attached to its use. So long as there are persons qualified within the meaning of the original dedication, and who are also willing to teach the doctrines or principles prescribed in the act of dedication, and so long as there is any one so interested in the execution of the trust as to have a standing in court, it must be that they can prevent the diversion of the property or fund to other and different uses. This is the general doctrine of courts of equity as to charities, and it seems equally applicable to ecclesiastical matters.

In such case, if the trust is confided to a religious congregation of the independent or congregational form of church government, it is not in the power of the majority of that congregation, however preponderant, by reason of a change of views on religious subjects, to carry the property so confided to them to the support of new and conflicting doctrine. . . . Nor is the principle varied when the organization to which the trust is confided is of the second or associated form of church government. The protection which the law throws around the trust is the same. And though the task may be a delicate one and a difficult one, it will be the duty of the court in such cases, when the doctrine to be taught or the form of worship to be used is definitely and clearly laid down, to inquire whether the party accused of violating the trust is holding or teaching a different doctrine, or using a form of worship which is so far variant as to defeat the declared objects of the trust. . . .

The second class of cases which we have described has reference to the case of a church of a strictly congregational or independent organization, governed solely within itself, either by a majority of its members or by such other local organism as it may have instituted for the purpose of ecclesiastical government; and to property held by such a church, either by way of purchase or donation, with no other specific trust attached to it in the hands of the church than that it is for the use of that congregation as a religious society.

In such cases where there is a schism which leads to a separation into distinct and conflicting bodies, the rights of such bodies to the use of the property must be determined by the ordinary principles which govern voluntary associations. If the principle of government in such cases is that the majority rules, then the numerical majority of members must control the right to the use of the property. If there be within the congregation officers in whom are vested the powers of such control, then those who adhere to the acknowledged organism by which the body is governed are entitled to the use of the property. The minority in choosing to separate themselves into a distinct body, and refusing to recognize the authority of the governing body, can claim no rights in the property from the fact that they had once been members of the church or congregation. This ruling admits of no inquiry into the existing religious opinions of those who comprise the legal or regular organization; for, if such was permitted, a very small minority, without any officers of the church among them, might be found to be the only faithful supporters of the religious dogmas of the founders of the church. There being no such trust imposed upon the property when purchased or given, the court will not imply one for the purpose of expelling from its use those who by regular succession and order constitute the church, because they may have changed in some respect their views of religious truth. . . .

But the third of these classes of cases is the one which is oftenest found in the courts, and which, with reference to the number and difficulty of the questions involved, and to other considerations, is every way the most important.

It is the case of property acquired in any of the usual modes for the general use of a religious congregation which is itself part of a large and general organization of some religious denomination, with which it is more or less intimately connected by religious views and ecclesiastical government.

The case before us is one of this class, growing out of a schism which has divided the congregation and its officers, and the presbytery and synod, and which appeals to the courts to determine the right to the use of the property so acquired. Here is no case of property devoted forever by the instrument which conveyed it, or by any specific declaration of its owner, to the support of any special religious dogmas, or any peculiar form of worship, but of property purchased for the use of a religious congregation, and so long as any existing religious congregation can be ascertained to be that congregation, or its regular and legitimate successor, it is entitled to the use of the property. In the case of an independent congregation we have pointed out how this identity, or succession, is to be ascertained, but in cases of this character we are bound to look at the fact that the local congregation is itself but a member of a much larger and more important religious organization, and is under its government and control, and is bound by its orders and judgments. There are in the Presbyterian system of ecclesiastical government, in regular succession, the presbytery over the session or local church, the synod over the presbytery, and the General Assembly over all. There are called, in the language of the church organs, "judicatories," and they entertain appeals from the decisions of those below, and prescribe corrective measures in other cases.

In this class of cases we think the rule of action which should govern the civil courts, founded in a broad and sound view of the relations of church and state under our system of laws, and supported by a preponderating weight of judicial authority is, that, whenever the questions of discipline, or of faith, or ecclesiastical rule, custom, or law have been decided by the highest of these church judicatories to which the matter has been carried, the legal tribunals must accept such decisions as final, and as binding on them, in their application to the case before them.

We concede at the outset that the doctrine of the English courts is otherwise. In the case of the *Attorney-General v. Pearson*, cited before, the proposition is laid down by Lord Eldon, and sustained by the peers, that it is the duty of the court in such cases to inquire and decide for itself, not only what was the nature and power of these church judicatories, but what is the true standard of faith in the church organization, and which of the contending parties before the court holds to this standard. . .

[However,] in this country the full and free right to entertain any religious belief, to practice any religious principle and to teach any religious doctrine which does not violate the laws of morality and property, and which does not infringe personal rights, is conceded to all. The law knows no heresy, and is committed to the support of no dogma, the establishment of no sect. The right to organize voluntary religious associations to assist in the expression and dissemination of any religious doctrine, and to create tribunals for the decision of controverted questions of faith within the association, and for the ecclesiastical government of all the individual members, congregations, and officers within the general association, is unquestioned. All who unite themselves to such a body do so with an implied consent to this government, and are bound to submit to it. But it would be a vain consent and would lead to the total subversion of such religious bodies, if any one aggrieved by one of their decisions could appeal to the secular courts and have them reversed. It is of the essence of these religious unions, and of their right to establish tribunals for the decision of questions arising among themselves, that those decisions should be binding in all cases of ecclesiastical cognizance, subject only to such appeals as the organism itself provides for.

Nor do we see that justice would be likely to be promoted by submitting those decisions to review in the ordinary judicial tribunals. Each of these large and influential bodies (to mention no others, let reference be had to the Protestant Episcopal, the Methodist Episcopal, and the Presbyterian churches), has a body of constitutional and ecclesiastical law of its own, to be found in their written organic laws, their books of discipline, in their collections of precedents, in their usage and customs, which as to each constitute a system of ecclesiastical law and religious faith that tasks the ablest minds to become familiar with. It is not to be supposed that the judges of the civil courts can be as competent in the ecclesiastical law and religious faith of all these bodies as the ablest men in each are in reference to their own. It would therefore be an appeal from the more learned tribunal in the law which should decide the case, to one which is less so. . . .

There is, perhaps, no word in legal terminology so frequently used as the word jurisdiction, so capable of use in a general and vague sense, and which is used so often by men learned in the law without a due regard to precision in its application. As regards its use in the matters we have been discussing it may very well be conceded that if the General Assembly of the Presbyterian Church should undertake to try one of its members for murder, and punish him with death or imprisonment, its sentence would be of no validity in a civil court or anywhere else. Or if it should at the instance of one of its members entertain jurisdiction as between him and another member as to their individual right to property, real or personal, the right in no sense depending on ecclesiastical questions, its decision would be utterly disregarded by any civil court where it might be set up. And it might be said in a certain general sense very justly, that it was because the General Assembly had no jurisdiction of the case. . . .

But it is a very different thing where a subject-matter of dispute, strictly and purely ecclesiastical in its character—a matter over which the civil courts exercise no jurisdiction—a matter which concerns theological controversy, church discipline, ecclesiastical government, or the conformity of the members of the church to the standard of morals required of them—becomes the subject of its action. It may be said here, also, that no jurisdiction has been conferred on the tribunal to try the particular case before it, or that, in its judgment, it exceeds the powers conferred upon it, or that the laws of the church do not authorize the particular form of proceeding adopted; and, in a sense often used in the courts, all of those may be said to be questions of jurisdiction. But it is easy to see that if the civil courts are to inquire into all these matters, the whole subject of the doctrinal theology, the usages and customs, the written laws, and fundamental organization of every religious denomination may, and must, be examined into with minuteness and care, for they would become, in almost every case, the criteria by which the validity of the ecclesiastical decree would be determined in the civil court. This principle would deprive these bodies of the right of construing their own church laws, would open the way to all the evils which we have depicted as attendant upon the doctrine of Lord Eldon, and would, in effect, transfer to the civil courts where property rights were concerned the decision of all ecclesiastical questions. . . .

---

The *Watson v. Jones* principle of deference to ecclesiastical tribunals was slightly modified in 1929, in *Gonzalez v. Archbishop*. There a person challenged the Catholic Archbishop of the Philippines for not appointing him to a chaplaincy and to be the recipient of the income associated with the chaplaincy. (At that time, the Philippines was a territory of the United States, conferring jurisdiction in the U.S. Supreme Court.) Justice Louis Brandeis, writing for the Supreme Court, purported to follow *Watson*, stating that civil courts must defer to church authorities when faced with an ecclesiastical controversy—the only exception being when the issues involve evidence of "fraud, collusion, or arbitrariness." However, see if you can identify any other differences between the approaches of the *Watson* and *Gonzalez* Courts, specifically over the issue of whether civil courts exercise any initial jurisdiction in church disputes.

---

## GONZALEZ v. ROMAN CATHOLIC ARCHBISHOP OF MANILA
### 280 U.S. 1 (1929)

▓ MR. JUSTICE BRANDEIS delivered the opinion of the Court. . . .

The chaplaincy was founded in 1820, under the will of Dona Petronila de Guzman. By it, she requested "the Father chaplain to celebrate sixty masses annually" in behalf of the souls of her parents, brothers, sisters and herself. The deed of foundation, which was executed by the testamentary executor of Dona Petronila, provided that "said property is segregated from temporal properties and transferred to the spiritual properties of this Archbishopric, without its being possible to alienate or convert the property as such into any other estate for any cause, even though it be of a more pious character, . . . so that by virtue of this Deed of Foundation canonical collation may be conferred on the said appointed chaplain." . . .

The will provided that the foundation should effect the immediate appointment as chaplain of D. Esteban de Guzman, the great-grandson of the testatrix; and "in his default, the nearest relative, . . .

From time to time thereafter four other descendants of the testatrix were successively appointed. The latest of these renounced the chaplaincy in December, 1910; married soon thereafter; and in 1912 became the father of the petitioner, Raul Rogerio Gonzalez, who is a legitimate son of the fifth chaplain and claims to be the nearest relative in descent from the first chaplain and the foundress.

Raul was presented to the Archbishop for appointment in 1922. The Archbishop refused to appoint him, on the ground that he did not then have "the qualifications required for chaplain of the said chaplaincy." He added: "The grounds of my conclusion are the very canons of the new Code of Canon Law." . . .

The new Codex Juris Canonici, which was adopted in Rome in 1917 and was promulgated by the Church to become effective in 1918, provides that no one shall be appointed to a collative chaplaincy who is not a cleric, Can. 1442. It requires students for the priesthood to attend a seminary; and prescribes their studies. . . .

Raul's contention, in effect, is that the nearest male relative in descent from the foundress and the first chaplain, willing to be appointed chaplain, is entitled to enjoy the revenues of the foundation, subject only to the duty of saying himself the sixty masses in each year, if he is qualified so to do, or of causing them to be said by a qualified priest and paying the customary charge therefore out of the income. He claims that the provisions of the new Codex are not applicable and that his rights are to be determined by the Canon Law in force at the time the chaplaincy was founded. . . .

The trial court rested its judgment for Raul largely on the ground that he possessed, at the time of its entry, the qualifications required by the Canon Law in force when the chaplaincy was founded; and that, hence, he was entitled both to be appointed chaplain and to recover the income accrued during the vacancy, even though he did not possess the qualifications prescribed by the new Codex then otherwise in force. . . .

The Archbishop interposes here, as he did below, an objection to the jurisdiction of the Philippine courts. He insists that, since the chaplaincy is confessedly a collative one, its property became spiritual property of a perpetual character subject to the jurisdiction of the ecclesiastical forum; and that thereby every controversy concerning either the right to appointment or the right to the income was removed from the jurisdiction of secular courts. The objection is not sound. The courts have jurisdiction of the parties. For the Archbishop is a juristic person amenable to the Philippine courts for the enforcement of any legal right; and the petitioner asserts such a right. There is jurisdiction of the subject matter. For the petitioner's claim is, in substance, that he is entitled to the relief sought as the beneficiary of a trust.

The fact that the property of the chaplaincy was transferred to the spiritual properties of the Archbishopric affects not the jurisdiction of the court, but the terms of the trust. *Watson v. Jones.*

The Archbishop's claim in this respect is that by an implied term of the gift, the property, which was to be held by the church, should be administered in such manner and by such persons as may be prescribed by the church from time to time. Among the church's laws which are thus claimed to be applicable are those creating tribunals for the determination of ecclesiastical controversies. Because the appointment is a canonical act, it is the function of the church authorities to determine what the essential qualifications of a chaplain are and whether the candidate possesses them. In the absence of fraud, collusion, or arbitrariness, the decisions of the proper church tribunals on matters purely ecclesiastical, although affecting civil rights, are accepted in litigation before the secular courts as conclusive, because the parties in interest made them so by contract or otherwise. . . .

*Affirmed.*

## Notes and Questions

Although *Watson* and *Gonzalez* reached the same conclusion, that civil courts are unqualified to adjudicate ecclesiastical controversies, they arrived at that point by slightly different routes. *Watson* declared that civil courts lack all jurisdiction over intra-church controversies, apparently directing civil courts to dismiss the law suit once the defendant demonstrates in an initial filing that the subject of the controversy is of an ecclesiastical nature. *Gonzalez*, in contrast, appears to grant civil courts initial jurisdiction to ensure the claim is of an ecclesiastical nature (e.g., not fraud or some other civil matter). Only then must the court defer to the ecclesiastical authority. Is this a distinction with a difference for purposes of the First Amendment? Does it suggest that civil courts may adjudicate some intra-church disputes? Keep this distinction in mind as you read further.

In 1952 the Court confronted a different kind of church autonomy case, this one involving the Russian Orthodox Church in New York City. An underlying theme was America's fear of communism and the "red scare" of the late 1940s and 1950s.

The Russian Orthodox Church dates its beginning from 988, when tradition says Prince Vladimir of Kiev, along with most of his subjects, were baptized. Given that the church had its beginning with the baptism of a ruler, the church has been identified with the state since that time. That changed with the Communist revolution of 1917, when the anti-religious Communist government severed the relations between state and church and began aggressively persecuting the church. However, the embattled church continued to exist and to be the governing body for Russian Orthodox churches outside Russia. In 1924 the church in America created a governing body in this country to oversee Russian Orthodox churches here until the Russian government would become friendlier to the churches. The Moscow Patriarchate attempted to reassert its authority over the American churches, particularly St. Nicholas Cathedral in New York City, the seat of the Russian Church. The New York legislature passed a law recognizing the authority of the Russian Church in America to govern the church and to possess and use St. Nicholas Cathedral. Representatives of that faction, consistent with the New York law, filed suit to wrest leadership of the Church and possession of St. Nicholas Cathedral from the Moscow faction.

The Supreme Court, in *Kedroff v. St. Nicholas Cathedral*, Justice Stanley Reed for the majority, held that the New York legislature had improperly intervened in this internal dispute about who was to govern the church and have control of St. Nicholas Cathedral. In essence, it reasserted the principle of *Watson v. Jones*.

There were three differences between *Kedroff* and *Watson*. First was that a state legislature was involved. It was not just two factions arguing over the possession of church property, as in *Watson*, but there was the fact that a state legislature had affirmed the position of one of those factions over the other. Second, in the time since *Watson*, both Religion Clauses of the First Amendment had been incorporated into the Fourteenth Amendment and applied to the states. So, this decision could be decided on constitutional grounds, and not just the law of trust, as in *Watson*. An expression of that heightened prohibition is:

> Legislation that regulates church administration, the operation of the churches, the appointment of clergy, by requiring conformity to church statutes "adopted at a general convention (sobor) held in the City of New York on or about or between October fifth to eighth, nineteen hundred thirty-seven, and any amendments thereto," prohibits the free exercise of religion. 344 U.S. 94, 107-108.

Third, although *Watson* was different from this case, the Court clearly wanted to apply its principles to the case at bar and to reiterate the point made just above. So, it said of *Watson*:

> The opinion radiates, however, a spirit of freedom for religious organizations, an independence from secular control or manipulation—in short, power to decide for themselves, free from state interference, matters of church government as well as those of faith and doctrine. Freedom to select the clergy, where no improper methods of choice are proven, we think, must now be said to have federal constitutional protection as a part of the free exercise of religion against state interference. 344 U.S. 94, 116.

Consequently, the Court held the church itself must decide which faction ruled the Russian Orthodox Church in America and its mother church. The state had no business intervening.

---

## KEDROFF v. ST. NICHOLAS CATHEDRAL
## 344 U.S. 94 (1952)

⊞ MR. JUSTICE REED delivered the opinion of the Court.

The right to the use and occupancy of a church in the city of New York is in dispute. . . .

Determination of the right to use and occupy Saint Nicholas depends upon whether the appointment of Benjamin by the Patriarch or the election of the Archbishop for North America by the convention of the American churches validly selects the ruling hierarch for the American churches. The Court of Appeals of New York, reversing the lower court, determined that the prelate appointed by the Moscow ecclesiastical authorities was not entitled to the Cathedral and directed the entry of a judgment that appellee corporation be reinvested with the possession and administration of the temporalities of St. Nicholas Cathedral. This determination was made on the authority of Article 5-C of the Religious Corporations Law of New York. . . .

Article 5-C was added to the Religious Corporations Law of New York in 1945 and provided both for the incorporation and administration of Russian Orthodox churches. Clarifying amendments were added in 1948. The purpose of the article was to bring all the New York churches, formerly subject to the administrative jurisdiction of the Most Sacred Governing Synod in Moscow or the Patriarch of Moscow, into an administratively autonomous metropolitan district. That district was North American in area, created pursuant to resolutions adopted at a sobor held at Detroit in 1924.[2] This declared autonomy was made effective by a further legislative requirement that all the churches formerly administratively subject to the Moscow synod and patriarchate should for the future be governed by the ecclesiastical body and hierarchy of the American metropolitan district. . . .

Article 5-C is challenged as invalid under the constitutional prohibition against interference with the exercise of religion. The appellants' contention, of course, is based on the theory that the principles of the First Amendment are made applicable to the states by the Fourteenth. . . .

The upheaval [of the Russian Revolution of 1917] caused repercussions in the North American Diocese. That Diocese at the time of the Soviet Revolution recognized the spiritual and administrative control of Moscow. White Russians, both lay and clerical, found asylum in America from the revolutionary conflicts, strengthening the feeling of abhorrence of the secular attitude of the new Russian Government. The church members already here, immigrants and native-born, while habituated to look to Moscow for religious direction, were accustomed to our theory of separation between church and state. . . .

---

[2] A sobor is a convention of bishops, clergymen and laymen with superior powers, with the assistance of which the church officials rule their dioceses or districts. . . .

Naturally the growing number of American-born members of the Russian Church did not cling to a hierarchy identified with their country of remote origin with the same national feeling that moved their immigrant ancestors. These facts and forces generated in America a separatist movement.

That movement brought about the arrangements at the Detroit Sobor of 1924 for a temporary American administration of the church on account of the disturbances in Russia. This was followed by the declarations of autonomy of the successive sobors since that date, a spate of litigation concerning control of the various churches and occupancy of ecclesiastical positions, the New York legislation (known as Article 5-C), and this controversy. . . .

From those circumstances it seems clear that the Russian Orthodox Church was, until the Russian Revolution, an hierarchical church with unquestioned paramount jurisdiction in the governing body in Russia over the American Metropolitanate. Nothing indicates that [the Moscow Patriarchy] relinquished that authority or recognized the autonomy of the American church. The Court of Appeals decision proceeds, we understand, upon the same assumption. . . .

We conclude that Article 5-C undertook by its terms to transfer the control of the New York churches of the Russian Orthodox religion from the central governing hierarchy of the Russian Orthodox Church, the Patriarch of Moscow and the Holy Synod, to the governing authorities of the Russian Church in America, a church organization limited to the diocese of North America and the Aleutian Islands. This transfer takes place by virtue of the statute. Such a law violates the Fourteenth Amendment. It prohibits in this country the free exercise of religion. Legislation that regulates church administration, the operation of the churches, the appointment of clergy, by requiring conformity to church statutes "adopted at a general convention (sobor) held in the City of New York on or about or between October fifth to eighth, nineteen hundred thirty-seven, and any amendments thereto," prohibits the free exercise of religion. Although this statute requires the New York churches to "in all other respects conform to, maintain and follow the faith, doctrine, ritual, communion, discipline, canon law, traditions and usages of the Eastern Confession (Eastern Orthodox or Greek Catholic Church)," their conformity is by legislative fiat and subject to legislative will. Should the state assert power to change the statute requiring conformity to ancient faith and doctrine to one establishing a different doctrine, the invalidity would be unmistakable. . . .

This legislation, Art. 5-C, in the view of the Court of Appeals, gave the use of the churches to the Russian Church in America on the theory that this church would most faithfully carry out the purposes of the religious trust. Thus dangers of political use of church pulpits would be minimized. Legislative power to punish subversive action cannot be doubted. If such action should be actually attempted by a cleric, neither his robe nor his pulpit would be a defense. But in this case no problem of punishment for the violation of law arises. There is no charge of subversive or hostile action by any ecclesiastic. Here there is a transfer by statute of control over churches. This violates our rule of separation between church and state. . . .

This controversy concerning the right to use St. Nicholas Cathedral is strictly a matter of ecclesiastical government, the power of the Supreme Church Authority of the Russian Orthodox Church to appoint the ruling hierarch of the archdiocese of North America. No one disputes that such power did lie in that Authority prior to the Russian Revolution.

*Watson v. Jones*, although it contains a reference to the relations of church and state under our system of laws, was decided without depending upon prohibition of state interference with the free exercise of religion. It was decided in 1871, before judicial recognition of the coercive power of the Fourteenth Amendment to protect the limitations of the First Amendment against state action. . . . The opinion radiates a spirit of freedom for religious organizations, an independence from secular control or manipulation—in short, power to decide for themselves, free from state interference, matters of church government as well as those of faith and doctrine. Freedom to select the clergy, where no improper methods of choice are proven, we think, must now be said to have federal constitutional protection as a part of the free exercise of religion against state interference. . . .

In upholding the validity of Article 5-C, the New York Court of Appeals apparently assumes Article 5-C does nothing more than permit the trustees of the Cathedral to use it for services consistent with the desires of the members of the Russian Church in America. Its reach goes far beyond that point. By fiat it displaces one church administrator with another. It passes the control of matters strictly ecclesiastical from one church authority to another. It thus intrudes for the benefit of one segment of a church the power of the state into the forbidden area of religious freedom contrary to the principles of the First Amendment. . . . New York's Article 5-C directly prohibits the free exercise of an ecclesiastical right, the Church's choice of its hierarchy. . . .

The record before us shows no schism over faith or doctrine between the Russian Church in America and the Russian Orthodox Church. It shows administrative control of the North American Diocese by the Supreme Church Authority of the Russian Orthodox Church, including the appointment of the ruling hierarch in North America from the foundation of the diocese until the Russian Revolution. We find nothing that indicates a relinquishment of this power by the Russian Orthodox Church.

Ours is a government which by the "law of its being" allows no statute, state or national, that prohibits the free exercise of religion. There are occasions when civil courts must draw lines between the responsibilities of church and state for the disposition or use of property. Even in those cases when the property right follows as an incident from decisions of the church custom or law on ecclesiastical issues, the church rule controls. This under our Constitution necessarily follows in order that there may be free exercise of religion. . . .

[*Reversed.*]

MR. JUSTICE FRANKFURTER, concurring. . . .

[T]his proceeding rests on a claim which cannot be determined without intervention by the State in a religious conflict. St. Nicholas Cathedral is not just a piece of real estate. It is no more that than is St. Patrick's Cathedral or the Cathedral of St. John the Divine. A cathedral is the seat and center of ecclesiastical authority. St. Nicholas Cathedral is an archiepiscopal see of one of the great religious organizations. What is at stake here is the power to exercise religious authority. That is the essence of this controversy. It is that even though the religious authority becomes manifest and is exerted through authority over the Cathedral as the outward symbol of a religious faith.

The judiciary has heeded, naturally enough, the menace to a society like ours of attempting to settle such religious struggles by state action. And so, when courts are called upon to adjudicate disputes which, though generated by conflicts of faith, may fairly be isolated as controversies over property and therefore within judicial competence, the authority of courts is in strict subordination to the ecclesiastical law of a particular church prior to a schism. This very limited right of resort to courts for determination of claims, civil in their nature, between rival parties among the communicants of a religious faith is merely one aspect of the duty of courts to enforce the rights of members in an association, temporal or religious, according to the laws of that association.

Legislatures have no such obligation to adjudicate and no such power. Assuredly they have none to settle conflicts of religious authority and none to define religious obedience. The New York legislature decreed that one party to the dispute and not the other should control the common center of devotion. In doing so the legislature effectively authorized one party to give religious direction not only to its adherents but also to its opponents. . . .

MR. JUSTICE JACKSON, dissenting.

New York courts have decided an ordinary ejectment action involving possession of New York real estate in favor of the plaintiff, a corporation organized under the Religious Corporations Law of New York under the name "Saint Nicholas Cathedral of the Russian Orthodox Church in North America." Admittedly, it holds, and since 1925 has held, legal title to the Cathedral property. The New York Court of Appeals decided that it also has the legal right to its possession and control. . . .

I greatly oversimplify the history of this controversy to indicate its nature rather than to prove its merits. This Cathedral was incorporated and built in the era of the Czar, under the regime of a state-ridden church in a church-ridden state. The Bolshevik Revolution may have freed the state from the grip of the church, but it did not free the church from the grip of the state. It only brought to the top a new master for a captive and submissive ecclesiastical establishment. By 1945, the Moscow patriarchy had been reformed and manned under the Soviet regime and it sought to re-establish in other countries its prerevolutionary control of church property and its sway over the minds of the religious. As the Court's opinion points out, it demanded of the Russian Church in America, among other things, that it abstain "from political activities against the U.S.S.R." The American Cathedral group, along with others, refused submission to the representative of the Moscow Patriarch, whom it regarded as an arm of the Soviet Government. Thus, we have an ostensible religious schism with decided political overtones.

If the Fourteenth Amendment is to be interpreted to leave anything to the courts of a state to decide without our interference, I should suppose it would be claims to ownership or possession of real estate within its borders and the vexing technical questions pertaining to the creation, interpretation, termination, and enforcement of uses and trusts, even though they are for religious and charitable purposes. . . .

What has been done here, as I see it, is to exercise this reserved power which permits the State to alter corporate controls in response to the lessons of experience. Of course, the power is not unlimited and could be so exercised as to deprive one of property without due process of law. But, I do not think we can say that a legislative application of a principle so well established in our common law as the *cy-pres* doctrine is beyond the powers reserved by the New York Constitution. . . .

It is important to observe what New York has not done in this case. It has not held that Benjamin may not act as Archbishop or be revered as such by all who will follow him. It has not held that he may not have a Cathedral. Indeed, I think New York would agree that no one is more in need of spiritual guidance than the Soviet faction. It has only held that this cleric may not have a particular Cathedral which, under New York law, belongs to others. It has not interfered with his or anyone's exercise of his religion. New York has not outlawed the Soviet-controlled sect nor forbidden it to exercise its authority or teach its dogma in any place whatsoever except on this piece of property owned and rightfully possessed by the Cathedral Corporation.

The fact that property is dedicated to a religious use cannot, in my opinion, justify the Court in sublimating an issue over property rights into one of deprivation of religious liberty which alone would bring in the religious guaranties of the First Amendment. I assume no one would pretend that the State cannot decide a claim of trespass, larceny, conversion, bailment or contract, where the property involved is that of a religious corporation or is put to religious use, without invading the principle of religious liberty.

Of course, possession of the property will help either side that obtains it to maintain its prestige and to continue or extend its sway over the minds and souls of the devout. So would possession of a bank account, an income-producing office building, or any other valuable property. But if both claimants are religious corporations or personalities, can not the State decide the issues that arise over ownership and possession without invading the religious freedom of one or the other of the parties? . . .

I have supposed that a State of this Union was entirely free to make its own law, independently of any foreign-made law, except as the Full Faith and Credit Clause of the Constitution might require deference to the law of a sister state or the Supremacy Clause require submission to federal law. I do not see how one can spell out of the principles of separation of church and state a doctrine that a state submit property rights to settlement by canon law. . . .

---

### NOTES AND QUESTIONS

1. In his dissent, Justice Robert Jackson, a strong defender of religious liberty (see *Barnette*), asserts that *Kedroff* involves only a controversy over property and does not implicate questions of an ecclesiastical nature. Is he correct that the state could determine rules of property ownership in this manner without violating the Free Exercise Clause? If he is correct, how do you distinguish *Kedroff* from *Watson*, which also involved a property dispute?

2. In 1960 the Court revisited the issue of St. Nicholas Cathedral in *Kreshik v. St. Nicholas Cathedral*, 363 U.S. 190. Whereas in *Kedroff* the Court held that a state legislature could not determine which faction in an ecclesiastical dispute should govern a church and possess its mother church, in *Kreshik* it held that the judiciary could not do that, either.

In 1969 the Court decided *Presbyterian Church in the United States v. Mary Elizabeth Blue Hull Memorial Presbyterian Church*, a case similar to *Watson v. Jones*, except for two features. Unlike *Watson*, in which two factions of a single congregation were battling for its control, in this case two congregations in Savannah, Georgia voted to withdraw from the parent denomination. The national church took over the two congregations until non-dissident leadership could be appointed. At that point, the two congregations sued in civil court. They contended the parent denomination had become too liberal and had thus abandoned traditional Presbyterian faith. Because the national church was no longer truly Presbyterian, the congregations said, they were entitled to secede from the parent denomination and retain ownership and control of the church property.

This contention highlights the other way this case is different from *Watson*. Georgia had a "departure from doctrine" law that allowed civil courts to settle church property disputes if the plaintiffs could show the defendants had departed from traditional church doctrine. Georgia courts had made such a decision and the national church claimed before the Supreme Court that such a law was unconstitutional.

The Court, in a unanimous opinion by Justice William Brennan, generally reasserted the principle of *Watson v. Jones*. If it were necessary for a civil court to render a judgment in a church property dispute by evaluating the theology of the competing sides, it could not do that. The First Amendment prohibits courts from being arbiters of theology. Consequently, a "departure from doctrine" law like Georgia's is contrary to the principles of the First Amendment. However, the Court did say that it is possible for civil courts to decide church property disputes on the basis of "neutral principles of law." That is, if deeds or agreements of ownership could be written in such a way that the dispute could be settled without involving theological reasoning but rather legal analysis, then civil courts could be involved.

## PRESBYTERIAN CHURCH v. HULL MEMORIAL PRESBYTERIAN CHURCH
### 393 U.S. 440 (1969)

▦ MR. JUSTICE BRENNAN delivered the opinion of the Court.

This is a church property dispute which arose when two local churches withdrew from a hierarchical general church organization. Under Georgia law the right to the property previously used by the local churches was made to turn on a civil court jury decision as to whether the general church abandoned or departed from the tenets of faith and practice it held at the time the local churches affiliated with it. The question presented is whether the restraints of the First Amendment, as applied to the States through the Fourteenth Amendment, permit a civil court to award church property on the basis of the interpretation and significance the civil court assigns to aspects of church doctrine. . . .

It is of course true that the State has a legitimate interest in resolving property disputes, and that a civil court is a proper forum for that resolution.

Special problems arise, however, when these disputes implicate controversies over church doctrine and practice. The approach of this Court in such cases was originally developed in *Watson v. Jones*, . . . There, as here, civil courts were asked to resolve a property dispute between a national Presbyterian organization and local churches of that organization. There, as here, the disputes arose out of a controversy over church doctrine. There, as here, the Court was asked to decree the termination of an implied trust because of departures from doctrine by the national organization. The *Watson* Court refused, pointing out that it was wholly inconsistent with the American concept of the relationship between church and state to permit civil courts to determine ecclesiastical questions. . . . The logic of this language leaves the civil courts no role in determining ecclesiastical questions in the process of resolving property disputes. . . .

In *Kedroff v. St. Nicholas Cathedral*, the Court converted the principle of *Watson* as qualified by *Gonzalez* into a constitutional rule. . . .

Thus, the First Amendment severely circumscribes the role that civil courts may play in resolving church property disputes. It is obvious, however, that not every civil court decision as to property claimed by a religious organization jeopardizes values protected by the First Amendment. Civil courts do not inhibit free exercise of religion merely by opening their doors to disputes involving church property. And there are neutral principles of law, developed for use in all property disputes, which can be applied without "establishing" churches to which property is awarded. But First Amendment values are plainly jeopardized when church property litigation is made to turn on the resolution by civil courts of controversies over religious doctrine and practice. If civil courts undertake to resolve such controversies in order to adjudicate the property dispute, the hazards are ever present of inhibiting the free development of religious doctrine and of implicating secular interests in matters of purely ecclesiastical concern. Because of these hazards, the First Amendment enjoins the employment of organs of government for essentially religious purposes, . . . the Amendment therefore commands civil courts to decide church property disputes without resolving underlying controversies over religious doctrine. Hence, States, religious organizations, and individuals must structure relationships involving church property so as not to require the civil courts to resolve ecclesiastical questions.

The Georgia courts have violated the command of the First Amendment. The departure-from-doctrine element of the implied trust theory which they applied requires the civil judiciary to determine whether actions of the general church constitute such a "substantial departure" from the tenets of faith and practice existing at the time of the local churches' affiliation that the trust in favor of the general church must be declared to have terminated. This determination has two parts. The civil court must first decide whether the challenged actions of the general church depart substantially from prior doctrine. In reaching such a decision, the court must of necessity make its own interpretation of the meaning of church doctrines. If the court should decide that a substantial departure has occurred, it must then go on to determine whether the issue on which the general church has departed holds a place of such importance in the traditional theology as to require that the trust be terminated. A civil court can make this determination only after assessing the relative significance to the religion of the tenets from which departure was found. Thus, the departure-from-doctrine element of the Georgia implied trust theory requires the civil court to determine matters at the very core of a religion—the inter-pretation of particular church doctrines and the importance of those doctrines to the religion. Plainly, the First Amendment forbids civil courts from playing such a role.

Since the Georgia courts on remand may undertake to determine whether petitioner is entitled to relief on its cross-claims, we find it appropriate to remark that the departure-from-doctrine element of Georgia's implied trust theory can play *no* role in any future judicial proceedings. . . . The First Amendment prohibits a State from employing religious organizations as an arm of the civil judiciary to perform the function of interpreting and apply-ing state standards. Thus, a civil court may no more review a church deci-sion applying a state departure-from-doctrine standard than it may apply that standard itself.

The judgment of the Supreme Court of Georgia is reversed, and the case is remanded for further proceedings not inconsistent with this opinion.

*It is so ordered.*

MR. JUSTICE HARLAN, concurring.

I am in entire agreement with the Court's rejection of the "departure-from-doctrine" approach taken by the Georgia courts, as that approach necessar-ily requires the civilian courts to weigh the significance and the meaning of disputed religious doctrine. I do not, however, read the Court's opinion to go further to hold that the Fourteenth Amendment forbids civilian courts from enforcing a deed or will which expressly and clearly lays down conditions limiting a religious organization's use of the property which is granted. If, for example, the donor expressly gives his church some money on the condition that the church never ordain a woman as a minister or elder, or never amend certain specified articles of the Confession of Faith, he is entitled to his money back if the condition is not fulfilled. In such a case, the church should not be permitted to keep the property simply because church authorities have deter-mined that the doctrinal innovation is justified by the faith's basic principles.

---

We have seen that in *Gonzalez v. Archbishop* the Court held that minimal review of church property disputes could be done by civil courts if evidence of "fraud, collusion, or arbi-trariness" was detected. In 1976 the Court was asked to revisit its view of the appropriate-ness of civil court review in the instance of evidence of arbitrariness. The case was *Serbian Eastern Orthodox Diocese v. Milivojevich.*

The Serbian Orthodox Church, a hierarchical church with an episcopal-type govern-ment, was administered ultimately by a Holy Synod of Bishops in Yugoslavia. At one point the Holy Synod had appointed Dionisije Milivojevich as Bishop of the Diocese of the United States and Canada. Later the Synod divided the Diocese into three geo-graphical divisions and restricted Milivojevich's authority to only one of them. When Milivojevich protested that action, the Synod removed him from power and divested him of his episcopal and monastic status, essentially defrocking him. Milivojevich then filed suit in an Illinois court, claiming that in both reorganizing the Diocese and in disciplining him for not agreeing, the Holy Synod had not followed its own procedures and had acted arbitrarily. The Illinois Supreme Court agreed. The Diocese petitioned the Supreme Court for a writ of certiorari.

The Court, in an opinion by Justice William Brennan, overturned the Illinois Supreme Court on the grounds that it never should have rendered a decision on a matter of internal dispute in a church that involved interpretation of doctrine. It reasserted the *Watson v. Jones* principle and rejected the arbitrariness exception of *Gonzalez*.

---

## SERBIAN ORTHODOX DIOCESE v. MILIVOJEVICH
### 426 U.S. 696 (1976)

▓ MR. JUSTICE BRENNAN delivered the opinion of the Court. . . .

The fallacy fatal to the judgment of the Illinois Supreme Court is that it rests upon an impermissible rejection of the decisions of the highest ecclesiastical tribunals of this hierarchical church upon the issues in dispute, and impermissibly substitutes its own inquiry into church polity and resolutions based thereon of those disputes. . . . [W]here resolution of the disputes cannot be made without extensive inquiry by civil courts into religious law and polity, the First and Fourteenth Amendments mandate that civil courts shall not disturb the decisions of the highest ecclesiastical tribunal within a church of hierarchical polity, but must accept such decisions as binding on them, in their application to the religious issues of doctrine or polity before them. . . .

[N]o "arbitrariness" exception—in the sense of an inquiry whether the decisions of the highest ecclesiastical tribunal of a hierarchical church complied with church laws and regulations—is consistent with the constitutional mandate that civil courts are bound to accept the decisions of the highest judicatories of a religious organization of hierarchical polity on matters of discipline, faith, internal organization, or ecclesiastical rule, custom, or law. For civil courts to analyze whether the ecclesiastical actions of a church judicatory are in that sense "arbitrary" must inherently entail inquiry into the procedures that canon or ecclesiastical law supposedly requires the church judicatory to follow, or else into the substantive criteria by which they are supposedly to decide the ecclesiastical question. But this is exactly the inquiry that the First Amendment prohibits; recognition of such an exception would undermine the general rule that religious controversies are not the proper subject of civil court inquiry, and that a civil court must accept the ecclesiastical decisions of church tribunals as it finds them. . . .

In short, the First and Fourteenth Amendments permit hierarchical religious organizations to establish their own rules and regulations for internal discipline and government, and to create tribunals for adjudicating disputes over these matters. When this choice is exercised and ecclesiastical tribunals are created to decide disputes over the government and direction of subordinate bodies, the Constitution requires that civil courts accept their decisions as binding upon them.

*Reversed.*

Finally, in *Jones v. Wolf*, the Court revisited the applicability of the "neutral principles of law" approach to solving church property disputes, first suggested in *Hull Memorial Presbyterian Church*. Again, the dispute was between two factions of a congregation of the Presbyterian Church in Macon, Georgia. A majority of the congregation voted to separate from the national church, a minority voted not to secede. The minority sued in federal court to retain possession of the church.

The Supreme Court, in an opinion written by Justice Harry Blackmun, asserted strongly that civil courts could adjudicate church property schisms if they did so on neutral principles of law. While not rejecting the caution that courts may not settle disputes that require the interpretation of doctrine, it endorsed much more strongly than before the neutral principles of law approach. In a sense, the decision is a kind of "how to manual" for congregations and hierarchical denominations for structuring their property relationships so that only neutral principles of law would be involved in cases of dispute. A vigorous dissent by Justice Lewis Powell, joined by three others, argued that the Court's approach was much too intrusive into the internal affairs of ecclesiastical organizations. The dissent stressed again the wisdom and constitutional appropriateness of *Watson v. Jones*.

## JONES v. WOLF
### 443 U.S. 595 (1979)

MR. JUSTICE BLACKMUN delivered the opinion of the Court.

This case involves a dispute over the ownership of church property following a schism in a local church affiliated with a hierarchical church organization. The question for decision is whether civil courts, consistent with the First and Fourteenth Amendments to the Constitution, may resolve the dispute on the basis of "neutral principles of law," or whether they must defer to the resolution of an authoritative tribunal of the hierarchical church.

I

The Vineville Presbyterian Church of Macon, Ga., was organized in 1904, and first incorporated in 1915. Its corporate charter lapsed in 1935, but was revived and renewed in 1939, and continues in effect at the present time.

The property at issue and on which the church is located was acquired in three transactions, and is evidenced by conveyances to the "Trustees of [or 'for'] Vineville Presbyterian Church and their successors in office," or simply to the "Vineville Presbyterian Church." The funds used to acquire the property were contributed entirely by local church members. Pursuant to resolutions adopted by the congregation, the church repeatedly has borrowed money on the property. This indebtedness is evidenced by security deeds variously issued in the name of the "Trustees of the Vineville Presbyterian Church," or, again, simply the "Vineville Presbyterian Church."

In the same year it was organized, the Vineville church was established as a member church of the Augusta-Macon Presbytery of the Presbyterian Church in the United States (PCUS). The PCUS has a generally hierarchical or connectional form of government, as contrasted with a congregational form. Under the polity of the PCUS, the government of the local church is committed to its Session in the first instance, but the actions of this assembly or "court" are subject to the review and control of the higher church courts, the Presbytery, Synod, and General Assembly, respectively. The powers and duties of each level of the hierarchy are set forth in the constitution of the PCUS, the Book of Church Order, which is part of the record in the present case.

On May 27, 1973, at a congregational meeting of the Vineville church attended by a quorum of its duly enrolled members, 164 of them, including the pastor, voted to separate from the PCUS. Ninety-four members opposed the resolution. The majority immediately informed the PCUS of the action, and then united with another denomination, the Presbyterian Church in America. Although the minority remained on the church rolls for three years, they ceased to participate in the affairs of the Vineville church and conducted their religious activities elsewhere.

In response to the schism within the Vineville congregation, the Augusta-Macon Presbytery appointed a commission to investigate the dispute and, if possible, to resolve it. The commission eventually issued a written ruling declaring that the minority faction constituted "the true congregation of Vineville Presbyterian Church," and withdrawing from the majority faction "all authority to exercise office derived from the [PCUS]." The majority took no part in the commission's inquiry, and did not appeal its ruling to a higher PCUS tribunal.

Representatives of the minority faction sought relief in federal court, but their complaint was dismissed for want of jurisdiction. They then brought this class action in state court, seeking declaratory and injunctive orders establishing their right to exclusive possession and use of the Vineville church property as a member congregation of the PCUS. The trial court, purporting to apply Georgia's "neutral principles of law" approach to church property disputes, granted judgment for the majority. The Supreme Court of Georgia, holding that the trial court had correctly stated and applied Georgia law, and rejecting the minority's challenge based on the First and Fourteenth Amendments, affirmed. 243 S. E. 2d 860 (1978). We granted certiorari.

## II

Georgia's approach to church property litigation has evolved in response to *Presbyterian Church v. Hull Church*, 393 U.S. 440 (1969). That case was a property dispute between the PCUS and two local Georgia churches that had withdrawn from the PCUS. The Georgia Supreme Court resolved the controversy by applying a theory of implied trust, whereby the property of a local church affiliated with a hierarchical church organization was deemed to be held in trust for the general church, provided the general church had not "substantially abandoned" the tenets of faith and practice as they existed at the time of affiliation. This Court reversed, holding that Georgia would have to find some other way of resolving church property disputes that did not draw the state courts into religious controversies. The Court did not specify what that method should be, although it noted in passing that "there are neutral principles of law, developed for use in all property disputes, which can be applied without 'establishing' churches to which property is awarded." 393 U.S., 449.

On remand, the Georgia Supreme Court concluded that, without the departure-from-doctrine element, the implied trust theory would have to be abandoned in its entirety. (*Presbyterian Church II*). In its place, the court

The dissent would require the States to abandon the neutral-principles method, and instead would insist as a matter of constitutional law that whenever a dispute arises over the ownership of church property, civil courts must defer to the "authoritative resolution of the dispute within the church itself." It would require, first, that civil courts review ecclesiastical doctrine and polity to determine where the church has "placed ultimate authority over the use of the church property." After answering this question, the courts would be required to "determine whether the dispute has been resolved within that structure of government and, if so, what decision has been made." They would then be required to enforce that decision. We cannot agree, however, that the First Amendment requires the States to adopt a rule of compulsory deference to religious authority in resolving church property disputes, even where no issue of doctrinal controversy is involved.

The dissent suggests that a rule of compulsory deference would somehow involve less entanglement of civil courts in matters of religious doctrine, practice, and administration. Under its approach, however, civil courts would always be required to examine the polity and administration of a church to determine which unit of government has ultimate control over church property. In some cases, this task would not prove to be difficult. But in others, the locus of control would be ambiguous, and "[a] careful examination of the constitutions of the general and local church, as well as other relevant documents, [would] be necessary to ascertain the form of governance adopted by the members of the religious association." In such cases, the suggested rule would appear to require "a searching and therefore impermissible inquiry into church polity." The neutral-principles approach, in contrast, obviates entirely the need for an analysis or examination of ecclesiastical polity or doctrine in settling church property disputes.

The dissent also argues that a rule of compulsory deference is necessary in order to protect the free exercise rights "of those who have formed the association and submitted themselves to its authority." This argument assumes that the neutral-principles method would somehow frustrate the free-exercise rights of the members of a religious association. Nothing could be further from the truth. The neutral-principles approach cannot be said to "inhibit" the free exercise of religion, any more than do other neutral provisions of state law governing the manner in which churches own property, hire employees, or purchase goods. Under the neutral-principles approach, the outcome of a church property dispute is not foreordained. At any time before the dispute erupts, the parties can ensure, if they so desire, that the faction loyal to the hierarchical church will retain the church property. They can modify the deeds or the corporate charter to include a right of reversion or trust in favor of the general church. Alternatively, the constitution of the general church can be made to recite an express trust in favor of the denominational church. The burden involved in taking such steps will be minimal. And the civil courts will be bound to give effect to the result indicated by the parties, provided it is embodied in some legally cognizable form.

IV

It remains to be determined whether the Georgia neutral-principles analysis was constitutionally applied on the facts of this case. Although both the trial court and the Supreme Court of Georgia viewed the case as involving nothing more than an application of the principles developed in *Presbyterian Church II* and in *Carnes*, the present case contains a significant complicating factor absent in each of those earlier cases. *Presbyterian Church II* and *Carnes* each involved a church property dispute between the general church and the entire local congregation. Here, the local congregation was itself divided between a majority of 164 members who sought to withdraw from the PCUS, and a minority of 94 members who wished to maintain the affiliation. Neither of the state courts alluded to this problem, however; each concluded without discussion or analysis that the title to the property was in the local church and that the local church was represented by the majority rather than the minority.

Petitioners earnestly submit that the question of which faction is the true representative of the Vineville church is an ecclesiastical question that cannot be answered by a civil court. At least, it is said, it cannot be answered by a civil court in a case involving a hierarchical church, like the PCUS, where a duly appointed church commission has determined which of the two factions represents the "true congregation." Respondents, in opposition, argue in effect that the Georgia courts did no more than apply the ordinary presumption that, absent some indication to the contrary, a voluntary religious association is represented by a majority of its members.

If in fact Georgia has adopted a presumptive rule of majority representation, defeasible upon a showing that the identity of the local church is to be determined by some other means, we think this would be consistent with both the neutral-principles analysis and the First Amendment. Majority rule is generally employed in the governance of religious societies. Furthermore, the majority faction generally can be identified without resolving any question of religious doctrine or polity. Certainly, there was no dispute in the present case about the identity of the duly enrolled members of the Vineville church when the dispute arose, or about the fact that a quorum was present, or about the final vote. Most importantly, any rule of majority representation can always be overcome, under the neutral-principles approach, either by providing, in the corporate charter or the constitution of the general church, that the identity of the local church is to be established in some other way, or by providing that the church property is held in trust for the general church and those who remain loyal to it. Indeed, the State may adopt any method of overcoming the majoritarian presumption, so long as the use of that method does not impair free exercise rights or entangle the civil courts in matters of religious controversy.

Neither the trial court nor the Supreme Court of Georgia, however, explicitly stated that it was adopting a presumptive rule of majority representation. Moreover, there are at least some indications that under Georgia law the process of identifying the faction that represents the Vineville church involves considerations of religious doctrine and polity. Georgia law requires that "church property be held according to the terms of the church government," and provides that a local church affiliated with a hierarchical religious association "is part of the whole body of the general church and is subject to the higher authority of the organization and its laws and regulations." All this may suggest that the identity of the "Vineville Presbyterian Church" named in the deeds must be determined according to terms of the Book of Church Order, which sets out the laws and regulations of churches affiliated with the PCUS. Such a determination, however, would appear to require a civil court to pass on questions of religious doctrine, and to usurp the function of the commission appointed by the Presbytery, which already has determined that petitioners represent the "true congregation" of the Vineville church. Therefore, if Georgia law provides that the identity of the Vineville church is to be determined according to the "laws and regulations" of the PCUS, then the First Amendment requires that the Georgia courts give deference to the presbyterial commission's determination of that church's identity.

This Court, of course, does not declare what the law of Georgia is. Since the grounds for the decision that respondents represent the Vineville church remain unarticulated, the judgment of the Supreme Court of Georgia is vacated, and the case is remanded for further proceedings not inconsistent with this opinion.

*It is so ordered.*

▓ MR. JUSTICE POWELL, with whom THE CHIEF JUSTICE, MR. JUSTICE STEWART, and MR. JUSTICE WHITE join, dissenting.

This case presents again a dispute among church members over the control of a local church's property. Although the Court appears to accept established principles that I have thought would resolve this case, it superimposes on these principles a new structure of rules that will make the decision of these cases by civil courts more difficult. The new analysis also is more likely to invite intrusion into church polity forbidden by the First Amendment.

I

The Court begins by stating that "[t]his case involves a dispute over the ownership of church property," suggesting that the concern is with legal or equitable ownership in the real property sense. But the ownership of the property of the Vineville church is not at issue. The deeds place title in the Vineville Presbyterian Church, or in trustees of that church, and none of the parties has questioned the validity of those deeds. The question actually presented is which of the factions within the local congregation has the right to control the actions of the titleholder, and thereby to control the use of the property, as the Court later acknowledges.

Since 1872, disputes over control of church property usually have been resolved under principles established by *Watson v. Jones*. Under the new and complex, two-stage analysis approved today, a court instead first must apply newly defined "neutral principles of law" to determine whether property titled to the local church is held in trust for the general church organization with which the local church is affiliated. If it is, then the court will grant control of the property to the councils of the general church. If not, then control by the local congregation will be recognized. In the latter situation, if there is a schism in the local congregation, as in this case, the second stage of the new analysis becomes applicable. Again, the Court fragments the analysis into two substeps for the purpose of determining which of the factions should control the property.

As this new approach inevitably will increase the involvement of civil courts in church controversies, and as it departs from long-established precedents, I dissent.

A

The first stage in the "neutral principles of law" approach operates as a restrictive rule of evidence. A court is required to examine the deeds to the church property, the charter of the local church (if there is one), the book of order or discipline of the general church organization, and the state statutes governing the holding of church property. The object of the inquiry, where the title to the property is in the local church, is "to determine whether there [is] any basis for a trust in favor of the general church." The court's investigation is to be "completely secular," "rel[ying] exclusively on objective, well-established concepts of trust and property law familiar to lawyers and judges." Thus, where religious documents such as church constitutions or books of order must be examined "for language of trust in favor of the general church," "a civil court must take special care to scrutinize the document in purely secular terms, and not to rely on religious precepts in determining whether the document indicates that the parties have intended to create a trust." It follows that the civil courts using this analysis may consider the form of religious government adopted by the church members for the resolution of intrachurch disputes only if that polity has been stated, in express relation to church property, in the language of trust and property law.

One effect of the Court's evidentiary rule is to deny to the courts relevant evidence as to the religious polity—that is, the form of governance—adopted by the church members. The constitutional documents of churches tend to be drawn in terms of religious precepts. Attempting to read them "in purely secular terms" is more likely to promote confusion than understanding. Moreover, whenever religious polity has not been expressed in specific statements referring to the property of a church, there will be no evidence of that polity cognizable under the neutral-principles rule. Lacking such evidence, presumably a court will impose some rule of church government derived from state law. In the present case, for example, the general and unqualified authority of the Presbytery over the actions of the Vineville church had not been expressed in secular terms of control of its property. As a consequence, the Georgia courts could find no acceptable evidence of this authoritative relationship, and they imposed instead a congregational form of government determined from state law.

This limiting of the evidence relative to religious government cannot be justified on the ground that it "free[s] civil courts completely from entanglement in questions of religious doctrine, polity, and practice." For unless the body identified as authoritative under state law resolves the underlying dispute in accord with the decision of the church's own authority, the state court effectively will have reversed the decisions of doctrine and practice made in accordance with church law. The schism in the Vineville church, for example, resulted from disagreements among the church members over questions of doctrine and practice. Under the Book of Church Order, these questions were resolved authoritatively by the higher church courts, which then gave control of the local church to the faction loyal to that resolution. The Georgia courts, as a matter of state law, granted control to the schismatic faction, and thereby effectively reversed the doctrinal decision of the church courts. This indirect interference by the civil courts with the resolution of religious disputes within the church is no less proscribed by the First Amendment than is the direct decision of questions of doctrine and practice.[2]

---

[2] The neutral-principles approach appears to assume that the requirements of the Constitution will be satisfied if civil courts are forbidden to consider certain types of evidence. The First Amendment's Religion Clauses, however, are meant to protect churches and their members from civil law interference, not to protect the courts from having to decide difficult evidentiary questions. Thus, the evidentiary rules to be applied in cases involving

When civil courts step in to resolve intrachurch disputes over control of church property, they will either support or overturn the authoritative resolution of the dispute within the church itself. The new analysis, under the attractive banner of "neutral principles," actually invites the civil courts to do the latter. The proper rule of decision, that I thought had been settled until today, requires a court to give effect in all cases to the decisions of the church government agreed upon by the members before the dispute arose.

B

The Court's basic neutral-principles approach, as a means of isolating decisions concerning church property from other decisions made within the church, relies on the concept of a trust of local church property in favor of the general church. Because of this central premise, the neutral-principles rule suffices to settle only disputes between the central councils of a church organization and a unanimous local congregation. Where, as here, the neutral-principles inquiry reveals no trust in favor of the general church, and the local congregation is split into factions, the basic question remains unresolved: which faction should have control of the local church?

The Court acknowledges that the church law of the Presbyterian Church in the United States (PCUS), of which the Vineville church is a part, provides for the authoritative resolution of this question by the Presbytery. Indeed, the Court indicates that Georgia, consistently with the First Amendment, may adopt the *Watson v. Jones* rule of adherence to the resolution of the dispute according to church law—a rule that would necessitate reversal of the judgment for the respondents. But instead of requiring the state courts to take this approach, the Court approves as well an alternative rule of state law: the Georgia courts are said to be free to "adop[t] a presumptive rule of majority representation, defeasible upon a showing that the identity of the local church is to be determined by some other means." This showing may be made by proving that the church has "provid[ed], in the corporate charter or the constitution of the general church, that the identity of the local church is to be established in some other way."

On its face, this rebuttable presumption also requires reversal of the state court's judgment in favor of the schismatic faction. The polity of the PCUS commits to the Presbytery the resolution of the dispute within the local church. Having shown this structure of church government for the determination of the identity of the local congregation, the petitioners have rebutted any presumption that this question has been left to a majority vote of the local congregation.

---

intrachurch disputes over church property should be fashioned to avoid interference with the resolution of the dispute within the accepted church government. The neutral-principles approach consists instead of a rule of evidence that ensures that in some cases the courts will impose a form of church government and a doctrinal resolution at odds with that reached by the church's own authority.

The neutral-principles approach creates other difficulties. It imposes on the organization of churches additional legal requirements which in some cases might inhibit their formation by forcing the organizers to confront issues that otherwise might never arise. It also could precipitate church property disputes, for existing churches may deem it necessary, in light of today's decision, to revise their constitutional documents, charters, and deeds to include a specific statement of church polity in the language of property and trust law.

The Court nevertheless declines to order reversal. Rather than decide the case here in accordance with established First Amendment principles, the Court leaves open the possibility that the state courts might adopt some restrictive evidentiary rule that would render the petitioners' evidence inadequate to overcome the presumption of majority control. But, aside from a passing reference to the use of the neutral-principles approach developed earlier in its opinion, the Court affords no guidance as to the constitutional limitations on such an evidentiary rule; the state courts, it says, are free to adopt any rule that is constitutional.

"Indeed, the state may adopt any method of overcoming the majoritarian presumption, so long as the use of that method does not impair free-exercise rights or entangle the civil courts in matters of religious controversy."

In essence, the Court's instructions on remand therefore allow the state courts the choice of following the long-settled rule of *Watson v. Jones* or of adopting some other rule—unspecified by the Court—that the state courts view as consistent with the First Amendment. Not only questions of state law but also important issues of federal constitutional law thus are left to the state courts for their decision, and, if they depart from *Watson v. Jones*, they will travel a course left totally uncharted by this Court.

## II

Disputes among church members over the control of church property arise almost invariably out of disagreements regarding doctrine and practice. Because of the religious nature of these disputes, civil courts should decide them according to principles that do not interfere with the free exercise of religion in accordance with church polity and doctrine. . . . The only course that achieves this constitutional requirement is acceptance by civil courts of the decisions reached within the polity chosen by the church members themselves. The classic statement of this view is found in *Watson v. Jones*:

> The right to organize voluntary religious associations to assist in the expression and dissemination of any religious doctrine, and to create tribunals for the decision of controverted questions of faith within the association, and for the ecclesiastical government of all the individual members, congregations, and officers within the general association, is unquestioned. All who unite themselves to such a body do so with an implied consent to this government, and are bound to submit to it. But it would be a vain consent and would lead to the total subversion of such religious bodies, if any one aggrieved by one of their decisions could appeal to the secular courts and have them reversed. It is of the essence of these religious unions, and of their right to establish tribunals for the decision of questions arising among themselves, that those decisions should be binding in all cases of ecclesiastical cognizance, subject only to such appeals as the organism itself provides for.

Accordingly, in each case involving an intrachurch dispute—including disputes over church property—the civil court must focus directly on ascertaining, and then following, the decision made within the structure of church governance. By doing so, the court avoids two equally unacceptable departures from the genuine neutrality mandated by the First Amendment. First, it refrains from direct review and revision of decisions of the church on matters of religious doctrine and practice that underlie the church's determination of intrachurch controversies, including those that relate to control of church property. Equally important, by recognizing the authoritative resolution reached within the religious association, the civil court avoids interfering indirectly with the religious governance of those who have formed the association and submitted themselves to its authority.

## III

Until today, and under the foregoing authorities, the first question presented in a case involving an intrachurch dispute over church property was where within the religious association the rules of polity, accepted by its members before the schism, had placed ultimate authority over the use of the church property, The courts, in answering this question have recognized two broad categories of church government. One is congregational, in which authority over questions of church doctrine, practice, and administration rests entirely in the local congregation or some body within it. In disputes over the control and use of the property of such a church, the civil courts enforce the authoritative resolution of the controversy within the local church itself. The second is hierarchical, in which the local church is but an integral and subordinate part of a larger church and is under the authority of the general church. Since the decisions of the local congregation are subject to review by the tribunals of the church hierarchy, this Court has held that the civil courts must give effect to the duly made decisions of the highest body within the hierarchy that has considered the dispute. As we stated in *Serbian Orthodox Diocese v. Milivojevich*:

> [T]he First and Fourteenth Amendments permit hierarchical religious organizations to establish their own rules and regulations for internal discipline and government, and to create tribunals for adjudicating disputes over these matters. When this choice is exercised and ecclesiastical tribunals are created to decide disputes over the government and direction of subordinate bodies, the Constitution *requires* that civil courts accept their decisions as binding upon them.

A careful examination of the constitutions of the general and local church, as well as other relevant documents, may be necessary to ascertain the form of governance adopted by the members of the religious association. But there is no reason to restrict the courts to statements of polity related directly to church property. For the constitutionally necessary limitations are imposed not on the evidence to be considered but instead on the object of the inquiry, which is both limited and clear: the civil court must determine whether the local church remains autonomous, so that its members have unreviewable authority to withdraw it (and its property) from the general church, or whether the local church is inseparably integrated into and subordinate to the general church.

## IV

The principles developed in prior decisions thus afford clear guidance in the case before us. The Vineville church is Presbyterian, a part of the PCUS. The presbyterian form of church government, adopted by the PCUS, is

> a hierarchical structure of tribunals which consists of, in ascending order,
> (1) the Church Session, composed of the elders of the local church;
> (2) the Presbytery, composed of several churches in a geographical area;
> (3) the Synod, generally composed of all Presbyteries within a State; and
> (4) the General Assembly, the highest governing body.

*Presbyterian Church v. Hull Church*. The Book of Church Order subjects the Session to "review and control" by the Presbytery in all matters, even authorizing the Presbytery to replace the leadership of the local congregation, to winnow its membership, and to take control of it. No provision of the Book of Church Order gives the Session the authority to withdraw the local church from the PCUS; similarly, no section exempts such a decision by the local church from review by the Presbytery.

Thus, while many matters, including the management of the church property, are committed in the first instance to the Session and congregation of the local church, their actions are subject to review by the Presbytery. Here, the Presbytery exercised its authority over the local church, removing the dissidents from church office, asserting direct control over the government of the church, and recognizing the petitioners as the legitimate congregation and Session of the Church. It is undisputed that under the established government of the Presbyterian Church—accepted by the members of the church before the schism—the use and control of the church property have been determined authoritatively to be in the petitioners. Accordingly, under the principles I have thought were settled, there is no occasion for the further examination of the law of Georgia that the Court directs. On remand, the Georgia courts should be directed to enter judgment for the petitioners.

## NOTES AND QUESTIONS

1. As scholar William Ross has observed:

   During the years following the *Wolf* decision, a number of states have formally adopted the neutral principles approach. In several other states, however, courts have refused to use the neutral principles method and have continued to adhere to the so-called polity theory, in which the courts defer to the decisions of the church's own internal system of governance. Other states have handed down decisions that have not required a definitive selection of one theory or the other. The *Wolf* decision has encouraged religious denominations to draft constitutions, charters, and other legal instruments in a manner that clearly provides for the disposition of property in the event of a congregational schism.[1]

2. What is the "departure from doctrine" rule and what kinds of constitutional problems does it raise?

3. In the *Kedroff* decision, did the Court specify whether it was relying on the Free Exercise or Establishment Clause for its conclusion in that case? Is one clause better suited for resolving such disputes than the other, or do both clauses offer complementary values that affirm the importance of church autonomy?

4. What is the "neutral principles of law" approach to deciding cases? In the case of *Jones v. Wolf*, the Court majority argues that this approach actually creates fewer constitutional difficulties than the approach that requires "compulsory deference to religious authority in resolving church property disputes. . . ." What are some of the Court majority's arguments on this point? Do you find those arguments persuasive?

5. Is greater involvement by civil courts in interpreting religious doctrine the only First Amendment concern in this area? When neutral principles for adjudicating the controversy exist, can deference to a religious authority raise Establishment Clause concerns?

## RELIGIOUS TORTS

While the Court was hearing the line of cases just described, it also confronted some cases involving what are sometimes called "religious torts," i.e., alleged wrong actions in the name of religion that were subject to civil court action. At least one of these cases raised the question again about the possibility of the government, through the courts, evaluating the veracity of theology or even believers themselves (albeit in a criminal context rather than involving a civil tort). The other cases discussed here, involving alleged malpractice of religious practitioners, are well-known lower court cases.

The case about testing the veracity and/or sincerity of belief was *United States v. Ballard*, a very difficult case because of poorly expressed jury instructions and because, at the lower court levels, judges and lawyers could not agree on what they were trying to do. In 1930, Guy W. Ballard, a man who had been interested in the metaphysical for some time, said he had an experience of the presence of Saint Germain. Saint Germain was a spiritual being, one of many "ascended masters." Saint Germain revealed to Ballard many spiritual truths, which Ballard then shared with his wife and son, Edna and Donald. These spiritual insights became the basis of a movement, the "I AM" movement, which claimed, at the time of Ballard's death in 1939, over 1,000,000 students.

During the 1930s Ballard wrote a number of books and pamphlets, created the St. Germain Press, and established "I AM" centers around the country. Among the beliefs of "I AM" were that the Ballards were spokespersons for the ascended masters, that the spiritual wisdom they taught could make people's lives better, and that they could heal people with physical diseases. These pronouncements were mailed to members and prospective members all over the country. That caused the U.S. Postal Service to charge the Ballards with mail fraud. The Ballards acted fraudulently because, according to the government, their message was not true and they knew it was not true. Consequently, the government took the Ballards to court because after Guy Ballard's death, Edna and Donald continued the movement and continued to solicit contributions, based on their message, through the mails.

The trial court told the jury that it could not render a decision on the truthfulness of the Ballards' beliefs, but could decide whether they held them "honestly and in good faith," i.e., it could decide on their sincerity. The Ballards were convicted of mail fraud because they did not sincerely believe what they said they believed. The Ninth Circuit decided that the trial court had erred in restricting the jury to sincerity. It said the jury should have been able to consider whether their "representations were false or true."

The Supreme Court, with Justice William O. Douglas writing for the majority, disagreed. In memorable language, he argued that the truth or falsity of people's faith or theology is not the business of the government; it is forbidden territory for civil courts. Interestingly, he did not discuss whether the trial court was right in allowing the jury to judge the sincerity of the Ballards' beliefs.

## UNITED STATES v. BALLARD
### 322 U.S. 78 (1944)

■ MR. JUSTICE DOUGLAS delivered the opinion of the Court. . . .

[W]e do not agree that the truth or verity of respondents' religious doctrines or beliefs should have been submitted to the jury. Whatever this particular indictment might require, the First Amendment precludes such a course, as the United States seems to concede. "The law knows no heresy, and is committed to the support of no dogma, the establishment of no sect." *Watson v. Jones*. The First Amendment has a dual aspect. It not only "forestalls compulsion by law of the acceptance of any creed or the practice of any form of worship" but also "safeguards the free exercise of the chosen form of religion." *Cantwell v. State of Connecticut*. "Thus the Amendment embraces two concepts—freedom to believe and freedom to act. The first is absolute but, in the nature of things, the second cannot be." *Id.* Freedom of thought, which includes freedom of religious belief, is basic in a society of free men. *West Virginia State Board of Education v. Barnette*. It embraces the right to maintain theories of life and of death and of the hereafter which are rank heresy to followers of the orthodox faiths. Heresy trials are foreign to our Constitution. Men may believe what they cannot prove. They may not be put to the proof of their religious doctrines or beliefs. Religious experiences which are as real as life to some may be incomprehensible to others. Yet the fact that they may be beyond the ken of mortals does not mean that they can be made suspect before the law. Many take their gospel from the New Testament. But it would hardly be supposed that they could be tried before a jury charged with the duty of determining whether those teachings contained false representations. The miracles of the New Testament, the Divinity of Christ, life after death, the power of prayer are deep in the religious convictions of many. If one could be sent to jail because a jury in a hostile environment found those teachings false, little indeed would be left of religious freedom. The Fathers of the Constitution were not unaware of the varied and extreme views of religious sects, of the violence of disagreement among them, and of the lack of any one religious creed on which all men would agree. They fashioned a charter of government which envisaged the widest possible toleration of conflicting views. Man's relation to his God was made no concern of the state. He was granted the right to worship as he pleased and to answer to no man for the verity of his religious views. The religious views espoused by respondents might seem incredible, if not preposterous, to most people. But if those doctrines are subject to trial before a jury charged with finding their truth or falsity, then the same can be done with the religious beliefs of any sect. When the triers of fact undertake that task, they enter a forbidden domain. The First Amendment does not select any one group or any one type of religion for preferred treatment. It puts them all in that position. . . .

■ MR. JUSTICE JACKSON, dissenting.

I should say the defendants have done just that for which they are indicted. If I might agree to their conviction without creating a precedent, I cheerfully would do so. I can see in their teachings nothing but humbug, untainted by any trace of truth. But that does not dispose of the constitutional question whether misrepresentation of religious experience or belief is prosecutable; it rather emphasizes the danger of such prosecutions. . . .

In the first place, as a matter of either practice or philosophy I do not see how we can separate an issue as to what is believed from considerations as to what is believable. The most convincing proof that one believes his statements is to show that they have been true in his experience. Likewise, that one knowingly falsified is best proved by showing that what he said happened never did happen. How can the Government prove these persons knew something to be false which it cannot prove to be false? If we try religious sincerity severed from religious verity, we isolate the dispute from the very considerations which in common experience provide its most reliable answer. . . .

I do not know what degree of skepticism or disbelief in a religious representation amounts to actionable fraud. . . . Belief in what one may demonstrate to the senses is not faith. All schools of religious thought make enormous assumptions, generally on the basis of revelations authenticated by some sign or miracle. The appeal in such matters is to a very different plane of credulity than is invoked by representations of secular fact in commerce. . . . It is hard in matters so mystical to say how literally one is bound to believe the doctrine he teaches and even more difficult to say how far it is reliance upon a teacher's literal belief which induces followers to give him money.

There appear to be persons—let us hope not many—who find refreshment and courage in the teachings of the "I Am" cult. If the members of the sect get comfort from the celestial guidance of their "Saint Germain," however doubtful it seems to me, it is hard to say that they do not get what they pay for. Scores of sects flourish in this country by teaching what to me are queer notions. It is plain that there is wide variety in American religious taste. The Ballards are not alone in catering to it with a pretty dubious product.

The chief wrong which false prophets do to their following is not financial. The collections aggregate a tempting total, but individual payments are not ruinous. I doubt if the vigilance of the law is equal to making money stick by over-credulous people. But the real harm is on the mental and spiritual plane. There are those who hunger and thirst after higher values which they feel wanting in their humdrum lives. They live in mental confusion or moral anarchy and seek vaguely for truth and beauty and moral support. When they are deluded and then disillusioned, cynicism and confusion follow. The wrong of these things, as I see it, is not in the money the victims part with half so much as in the mental and spiritual poison they get. But that is precisely the thing the Constitution put beyond the reach of the prosecutor, for the price of freedom of religion or of speech or of the press is that we must put up with, and even pay for, a good deal of rubbish. . . .

I would dismiss the indictment and have done with this business of judicially examining other people's faiths.

---

## Notes and Questions

1. In his dissent, Justice Jackson argued that the courts should not have taken the case in the first place. Why so? Jackson also took on the question Justice Douglas ignored, whether the courts can rule on the sincerity of people's beliefs. Why did Justice Jackson believe this question must be addressed?

2. In 1988, federal authorities brought charges of mail fraud and conspiracy, among others, against Jim Bakker, a well-known television evangelist based in Charlotte, North Carolina. Bakker and his then-wife, Tammy Faye, established the PTL ("Praise the Lord" or "People that Love") ministries in 1974 and built it into one of the more successful and profitable television ministries, with the Bakkers reputedly living a lavish lifestyle. Buoyed with success, Jim Bakker built a Christian-theme amusement park and retreat center with housing outside Charlotte, financing the projects by selling interests to supporters, also known as "lifetime partners." The problem was that Bakker told his lifetime partner investors that he was selling only a limited number of interests, in order to secure the value of their investments, when in actuality Bakker sold substantially more interests than were available. Bakker also secretly diverted the investments to pay for operating expenses of PTL and his lifestyle. Bakker denied any intent to defraud and claimed that he was merely seeking to do God's work. Could a jury determine the sincerity of Bakker's actions without delving into considerations of theology?

A jury convicted Bakker of 24 counts of fraud and conspiracy with the judge sentencing him to serve 45 years in prison (later reduced to 18 years). During sentencing, the judge remarked of Bakker: "He had no thought whatever about his victims, and those of us who do have a religion are ridiculed as being saps from money-grubbing preachers or priests." Did this remark cross the line from expressing a view of Bakker's sincerity to opining about the legitimacy of his religion? On appeal, the Court of Appeals vacated the original sentence of 45 years, expressing concern when a judge takes his own religious beliefs into account in sentencing:

> Our Constitution, of course, does not require a person to surrender his or her religious beliefs upon the assumption of judicial office. Courts, however, cannot sanction sentencing procedures that create the perception of the bench as a pulpit from which judges announce their personal sense of religiosity and simultaneously punish defendants for offending it. Whether or not the trial judge has a religion is irrelevant for purposes of sentencing. Regrettably, we are left with the apprehension that the imposition of a lengthy prison term here may have reflected the fact that the court's own sense of religious propriety had somehow been betrayed. See *United States v. Bakker*, 925 F.2d 728, 740-741 (4th Cir. 1991).

Was the sentencing judge expressing disapproval of Bakker's religious beliefs by comparing them to his own, or was he merely expressing disgust with what the court characterized as deception and massive fraud, albeit occurring within a religious context? How are judges or juries able to put aside their own religious beliefs and separate these considerations?

In 1988 the California Supreme Court decided a case that got the attention of religious practitioners around the country. The case was *Nally v. Grace Community Church*, a "clergy malpractice" case. The action was brought against the clergy staff of Grace Community Church by the parents of Kenneth Nally, who committed suicide in 1979. During the approximately five years prior to the suicide, Nally engaged the services of several physicians, a psychologist, a psychiatrist, and three of the ministerial staff of Grace Community Church.

The ministers offered pastoral counseling based on their understanding of the Bible and theology. The trial record established that during the time they were counseling with Nally, they were aware that he was seeing medical doctors and a psychiatrist. They did not refer Nally to a psychologist or a psychiatrist, but they did not discourage him from seeking medical and psychiatric help; indeed they encouraged him to continue seeing those professionals. That was important to the case, for the parents brought legal action against the clergy for malpractice, in the form of a wrongful death allegation because they did not refer Nally to a psychiatrist while he was seeing them. Nally's parents accused the ministers of negligence and outrageous conduct in failing to prevent their son's suicide by not referring him to mental health professionals.

The California Supreme Court found in favor of the clergy at Grace Community Church. The Court recognized that the clergy staff had encouraged Nally to continue to see the medial and psychiatric personnel. That showed they were not hostile to medical and mental health professionals. The fact they knew and approved of that treatment parallel to the counseling they were providing also illustrated that they believed they did not need to refer Nally to anyone else.

Furthermore, the nature of a tort played a role in reaching the decision. A tort involves a violation of a legal duty owed by the defendant to the person injured. Negligence means that the defendant had such a legal duty which he/she did not fulfill, consequently resulting in injury. In a relationship, if that legal duty is not present, one is under no obligation to protect the other from harm. The plaintiffs in the suit claimed that the clergy counselors had a duty when they learned their son was suicidal to refer him to mental health professionals. The fact they did not fulfill that duty made them negligent under the law, the parents alleged. The Court responded that the legal duty to refer applied only to licensed therapists and medical personnel, not to nonlicensed counselors such as clergy. Consequently, the clergy at Grace Community Church could not be said to have had a legal duty to refer Nally to mental health professionals. They were not guilty of negligence. Furthermore, it would likely be unconstitutional under the Establishment Clause for the legislature to impose a duty of care on those who do counseling from a theological perspective. In essence, how does a legislature or court establish standards of conduct for theological counseling and then determine whether a minister has breached those standards so as to commit malpractice? As in previous cases in this section, the message was the government needed to stay out of the realm of theology.

## NALLY v. GRACE COMMUNITY CHURCH
763 P.2d 948 (1988), cert. denied 490 U.S. 1007 (1989)

CHIEF JUSTICE LUCAS wrote for the court.

On April 1, 1979, 24-year-old Kenneth Nally (hereafter Nally) committed suicide by shooting himself in the head with a shotgun. His parents (hereafter plaintiffs) filed a wrongful death action against Grace Community Church of the Valley (hereafter Church), a Protestant Christian congregation located in Sun Valley, California, and four Church pastors: MacArthur, Thomson, Cory and Rea (hereafter collectively referred to as defendants), alleging "clergyman malpractice," i.e., negligence and outrageous conduct in failing to prevent the suicide. Nally, a member of the Church since 1974, had participated in defendants' pastoral counseling programs prior to his death. . . .

"A tort, whether intentional or negligent, involves a violation of a *legal duty*, imposed by statute, contract or otherwise, owed by the defendant to the person injured. Without such a duty, any injury is 'damnum absque injuria'— injury without wrong." Thus, in order to prove facts sufficient to support a finding of negligence, a plaintiff must show that defendant had a duty to use due care, that he breached that duty, and that the breach was the proximate or legal cause of the resulting injury.

Under traditional tort law principles, one is ordinarily not liable for the actions of another and is under no duty to protect another from harm, in the absence of a special relationship of custody or control. . .

The closeness of connection between defendants conduct and Nally's suicide was tenuous at best.[7] As defendants observe, Nally was examined by five physicians and a psychiatrist during the weeks following his suicide attempt. Defendants correctly assert that they "arranged or encouraged many of these visits and encouraged Nally to continue to cooperate with all doctors." In addition, as stated above, following Nally's overdose attempt Dr. Evelyn warned plaintiffs that Nally remained suicidal and that they should encourage him to see a psychiatrist on his release from the hospital. Plaintiffs also rejected both Dr. Hall's and Dr. Parker's suggestion that Nally be institutionalized because, according to plaintiffs, their son was "not crazy." . . .

We also note that the Legislature has exempted the clergy from the licensing requirements applicable to marriage, family, child and domestic counselors and from the operation of statutes regulating psychologists. In so doing, the Legislature has recognized that access to the clergy for counseling should be free from state imposed counseling standards, and that "the secular state is not equipped to ascertain the competence of counseling when performed by those affiliated with religious organizations." . . .

Even assuming that workable standards of care could be established in the present case, an additional difficulty arises in attempting to identify with precision those to whom the duty should apply. Because of the differing theological views espoused by the myriad of religions in our state and practiced by church members, it would certainly be impractical, and quite possibly unconstitutional, to impose a duty of care on pastoral counselors. Such a duty would necessarily be intertwined with the religious philosophy of the particular denomination or ecclesiastical teachings of the religious entity. We have previously refused to impose a duty when to do so would involve complex policy decisions, and we are unpersuaded by plaintiffs that we should depart from this policy in the present case. . . .

---

[7] Generally, there is a real question about the closeness of the causal connection between a nontherapist counselor's failure to refer to professional help and the suicide of a particular suicidal person. By their very definition, nontherapist counselors are not professional medical experts on suicide. Their activities are undertaken pursuant to doctrines explicitly left unregulated by the state.

1. What constitutional difficulties are inherent in a court finding that a legal duty is owed from a church or a member of the clergy to a church member? On the other hand, what kinds of interests may be sacrificed if a court does not find such a duty?

2. Over the years, standards of pastoral counseling have been developed by professional groups such as the American Pastoral Counseling Association. Many seminaries also require their students to take courses in pastoral counseling. This being the case, could a court use such "objective" professional standards or seminary course requirements as recognized legal standards of care, such that the failure of a minister to follow them would constitute malpractice? Would this solve the dilemma of courts delving into the theological practices of a particular church? If courts adopted this approach, what would they do in situations where the minister had not attended seminary or had any formal psychological training—impose a lesser standard of care? Would this result in a double standard, with seminary trained clergy held to a higher duty of care?

3. How far should the *Nally* rule extend? Suppose First XYZ Church establishes a "Christian Counseling Center," that relies solely on bibilical principles for its counseling techniques. The Christian Counseling Center takes out advertisements in the Yellow Pages and on television encouraging people to avail themselves of its services, for a fee. The advertisements clearly state that the Center uses a "Bible-centered approach" to address all levels of personal crisis: "No problem is too great for the Lord." A non-church member, who is severely depressed, taking prescribed antidepressant drugs and has previously attempted suicide, seeks counseling at the Center. After describing his medical history to a Center counselor, the man is encouraged to stop taking his medication and rely solely on prayer and religious counseling. The man follows the recommendation but becomes more depressed, eventually committing suicide. Does this hypothetical present any factors different from those in *Nally* such that a court should find the Center failed a legal duty of care? If so, what standard would you apply? Suppose additionally that the Center states that it follows the standards of the American Pastoral Counseling Association. Are you now comfortable with a court weighing the conduct of the Center counselor against these standards to see if a duty has been breached? What if those standards are based on or reflect theological notions and bibilical principles?

Beginning in the late 1960s and continuing until the present, a concern for the existence and impact of "cults" has bothered a considerable portion of the population. Neither knowing nor caring about the academic study of alternative religions or the scholarly definition of "cult," the population and most of the media just knows they do not like them. [A short, and oversimplified, definition is that a cult is a group that teaches new truth, i.e., it deviates from the classical theology of the religion from which it springs. As such, a cult is neither inherently good nor evil, just different.] The general perception is that cult leaders are fanatics who want to attract as many people as possible into their groups, usually by deceptive recruiting, and emotionally, if not physically, imprisoning their members so they will not leave. Cult leaders are depicted as greedy manipulators of their members, siphoning off members' personal possessions and compelling them to work long hours for the benefit of the group. In general, cults are thought of as groups with weird, if not heretical, theological ideas that are destructive of families. It is often claimed that cults "brainwash" their devotees into virtual zombies. Unfortunately, there are enough examples of this kind of behavior to make the generalization believable to most of the population.

Because cults are regarded so negatively, at various times groups have organized and procedures have been devised to rescue young people from the cults. The most notorious method of getting people out of cults is "deprogramming," which is usually preceded by forceful removal of cult members from their group, often by deception and kidnapping. Deprogramming is a kind of "reverse brainwashing," in which anti-cult persons bombard the apprehended (and often forcibly detained) cult member with ridicule of the leader of the cult and arguments to show that the theology of the cult is untrue and not consistent with the young person's traditional faith. Deprogramming is based on the premise that cult members had not joined voluntarily but were rather inducted by deceptive mind control procedures. Given that, dramatic measures were necessary, and justified, to bring them back to their "right minds." However, many civil libertarians are critical of both the theory of brainwashing and the procedure of deprogramming, claiming that cult members became so voluntarily and that deprogramming denied the cult adherents their constitutional religious liberty.

One of the most famous cases to test these theories was *Molko v. Holy Spirit Association*. The Holy Spirit Association for the Unification of World Christianity was started by Rev. Sun Myung Moon and was typically called The Unification Church or "the Moonies." David Molko (27 years old) and Tracy Leal (19) were independently recruited into the Unification Church. Later, they were separately apprehended from a public street and deprogrammed. After that experience they sued the church for fraud and deceit, intentional infliction of emotional distress, and false imprisonment. The church denied that it was guilty of such things.

Although Molko and Leal were recruited independently of each other, they described the procedures that brought them into the church in virtually identical terms. In short, they were approached by persons who invited them to a free dinner sponsored by the "Creative Community Project," an international group of persons who met for dinner periodically to discuss how they could help humanity. At the dinner each heard a lecture on social problems and was given considerable personal attention. They also saw a slide show about the group's retreat center and were invited to go there for more extensive orientation of the social program of the group. Impressed by the zeal and hospitality of the group, each agreed to go that very evening. Far from being a relaxed time in the country, the program at the retreat center was intense. They were denied any private time at all. Only after several days of this intense activity did anyone mention that the group was really the Unification Church, even though both Molko and Leal had asked repeatedly from the time of the first contact if there was a religious dimension to the group. At the end of ten to twelve days at the retreat center, each was encouraged to go to another place for "advanced training." Their resistance lowered by this time, they agreed. That training lasted five to seven weeks. During that time, each became a formal church member. They were finally taken back to their home cities, where they worked for the church there. They remained members until they were deprogrammed.

On the issue of fraudulent and deceitful recruiting, the California Supreme Court ruled that Molko and Leal had a legitimate cause of action. They were not challenging the content of the church's beliefs; indeed, they conceded that church members were sincere in their beliefs. Rather they were challenging the impact of the church's actions on them. The court ruled that this was state regulation of the church's actions, permissible under the Free Exercise Clause. Applying the "compelling state interest" test, the court concluded that the law against fraud was compelling enough to allow the suit to go forward. Also, there was no less restrictive means for the state to protect its citizens from deceptive religious recruitment than to allow them to bring private legal actions against churches allegedly practicing such fraud.

Once Molko and Leal were in the church, they were taught that it was the true church and if one left it, God would punish them through divine retribution. That teaching was part of plaintiffs' complaint of infliction of emotional distress. The teaching that they would be punished if they left the church produced extreme anxiety. The other part of the emotional distress claim was the same as their deceptive practices claim; that the church did not reveal who and what it was until late in the recruitment process. When they found out they had been lied to and that they were in the Unification Church, they were distressed both by the deception and the situation in which they found themselves.

The court held the church's statements on divine retribution were protected. That was part of its theology, its belief system, which civil courts could not evaluate. The message may have caused Molko and Leal emotional distress, but the church was still free to believe it and to tell its members about it. On the claim that the concealed identity and deceptive recruitment practices contributed to emotional distress, the court left that for a jury to decide. That is, given that deception had already been held actionable as a dimension of the church's action, rather than belief, it would be inconsistent to now hold that it could not be challenged as a cause of emotional distress.

Tracy Leal raised the issue of false imprisonment. She acknowledged she was physically free to leave at any time, that she was not *physically* imprisoned. She claimed the dread she felt about the possibility of divine retribution on her and her family if she left the church rendered her emotionally unable to leave the church. She was *psychically* imprisoned.

The court disagreed. Her claim once more asked the court to make a judgment about the church's beliefs. That it was unable to do because of the principle that civil courts are not arbiters of the veracity of theological concepts.

The lessons from this case are familiar. Although the state may investigate the actions of a religious body, there are some firm limits on its ability to inquire into theological matters or to make such matters legal issues suitable for judicial resolution.

---

## DAVID MOLKO v. HOLY SPIRIT ASSOCIATION
762 P.2d 46 (1988)

▨ JUDGE MOSK wrote the opinion of the court. . . .

We turn first to the question whether tort liability for fraudulent recruiting practices imposes any burden on the free exercise of the Unification Church's religion. We think it does. While such liability does not impair the Church's right to believe in recruiting through deception, its very purpose is to discourage the Church from putting such belief into practice by subjecting the Church to possible monetary loss for doing so. Further, liability presumably impairs the Church's ability to convert nonbelievers because some potential members who would have been recruited by deception will choose not to associate with the Church when they are told its true identity.

Yet these burdens, while real, are not substantial. Being subject to liability for fraud does not in any way or degree prevent or inhibit Church members from operating their religious communities, worshipping as they see fit, freely associating with one another, selling or distributing literature, proselytizing on the street, soliciting funds, or generally spreading Reverend Moon's message among the population. It certainly does not, like the educational requirement in *Yoder*, compel Church members to perform acts "at odds with fundamental tenets of their religious beliefs." At most, it potentially closes one questionable avenue for bringing new members into the Church.

We must next consider whether a compelling state interest justifies the marginal burden such liability imposes on the Church's free exercise rights. We have no difficulty in finding such an interest in the "substantial threat to public safety, peace or order" the Church's allegedly fraudulent conduct poses. For it is one thing when a person knowingly and voluntarily submits to a process involving coercive influence, as a novice does on entering a monastery or a seminary. But it is quite another when a person is subjected to coercive persuasion without his knowledge or consent. While some individuals who experience coercive persuasion emerge unscathed, many others develop serious and sometimes irreversible physical and psychiatric disorders, up to and including schizophrenia, self-mutilation, and suicide. The state clearly has a compelling interest in preventing its citizens from being deceived into submitting unknowingly to such a potentially dangerous process.

The state has an equally compelling interest in protecting the family institution. . . .

We conclude, therefore, that although liability for deceptive recruitment practices imposes a marginal burden on the Church's free exercise of religion, the burden is justified by the compelling state interest in protecting individuals and families from the substantial threat to public safety, peace and order posed by the fraudulent induction of unconsenting individuals into an atmosphere of coercive persuasion.

Our analysis cannot end here, however. A government action burdening free exercise, even though justified by a compelling state interest, is impermissible if any action imposing a lesser burden on religion would satisfy that interest. After careful consideration, we perceive no such less restrictive alternative available. . . . In short, it appears that to allow injured parties to bring private actions for fraud is the least restrictive means available for advancing the state's interest in protecting individuals and families from the harmful effects of fraudulent recruitment.

Finally, even though the state action is justified by a compelling state interest and imposes the minimum burden required to satisfy that interest, it can be upheld only if it (1) has the purpose and effect of advancing the state's secular goals and (2) does not discriminate between religions, or between religion and nonreligion. We find that judicial sanctioning of traditional tort liability for fraudulent recruitment satisfies these standards. . . .

We conclude that neither the federal nor state Constitution bars Molko and Leal from bringing traditional fraud actions against the Church for allegedly inducing them, by misrepresentation and concealment of its identity, into unknowingly entering an atmosphere in which they were then subjected to coercive persuasion. . . .

The Court of Appeal found in part that threats of divine retribution, of which Molko and Leal complained, were protected religious speech and could not form the basis of a claim of intentional infliction of emotional distress. We agree with this view. To the extent the claims are based merely on threats of divine retribution if Molko and Leal left the church, they cannot stand.

However, the claims do not rest solely or even primarily on threats of divine retribution. Molko and Leal essentially contend the same conduct that supports their fraud actions—i.e., misrepresentation and concealment of the Church's identity for the purpose of inducing them to submit unknowingly to coercive persuasion—also gives rise to an action for intentional infliction of emotional distress. . . .

The Church offers two arguments why its conduct was not, as a matter of law, extreme and outrageous. First it contends its actions amounted to nothing more than "intensive religious practice," and therefore were different only in degree, not in kind, from those of many other religious groups. We find this claim unconvincing. Although fasting, poverty, silence or cloistered living may constitute intensive religious practice, we have already determined that fraud, even though purported to be religiously motivated, is actionable conduct under the circumstances presented here.

Second, as mentioned above, the Church argues that Leal's long hours of work were "self-inflicted." It contends its encouragement for her to sell flowers and solicit money does not constitute outrageous conduct. But since the conduct that the Church relies on occurred after Leal had formally joined the Church, the argument has no bearing on whether its original fraudulent inducement into an atmosphere of coercive persuasion—the conduct at issue—is extreme and outrageous.

Viewed in the light most favorable to plaintiffs, the Church's continued deceptions might well be seen as conduct breaching plaintiffs' trust in the integrity of those who were promising to make their lives more meaningful. So viewed, the Church's actions might well constitute an abuse of "a relation or position which gives [the Church] power to damage the plaintiff's interest." (*Cole v. Fair Oaks Fire Protection Dist.*, 43 Cal.3d, 155, fn. 7.)

"'Where reasonable men may differ, it is for the jury, subject to the control of the court, to determine whether, in the particular case, the conduct has been sufficiently extreme and outrageous to result in liability.'" (*Alcorn v. Anbro Engineering, Inc.* 468 P.2d 216 [1970].) Since reasonable persons could differ here, a question of fact remains as to whether the Church's conduct was outrageous for purposes of this action. It follows that the Court of Appeal erred in affirming the summary judgment for the Church as to plaintiffs' actions for intentional infliction of emotional distress. . . .

Leal contends she was falsely imprisoned by the Church at Boonville, at Camp K, at Boulder, at Los Angeles, and at various locations in San Francisco. She admits she was theoretically free to depart at any time; she was not physically restrained, subjected to threats of physical force, or subjectively afraid of physical force. She insists, however, that her "imprisonment arose from the harm she came to believe would result if she left the community." That harm, specifically, was that her family "would be damned in Hell forever and they would forever feel sorry for having blown their one chance to unite with the Messiah and make it to Heaven."

The claim cannot survive constitutional scrutiny. Although Leal correctly asserts that false imprisonment may be "effected by . . . fraud or deceit" (Pen. Code, § 237), her theory implicates the Church's beliefs: it plainly seeks to make the Church liable for threatening divine retribution. As we stated earlier, such threats are protected religious and cannot provide the basis for tort liability. Accordingly, we hold the Court of Appeal correctly affirmed the summary judgment for the Church as to Leal's action for false imprisonment. . . .

Another area of considerable litigation has involved claims that hierarchical churches have failed to supervise and/or remove clergy accused of engaging in sexual misconduct with parishioners. In recent years, victims of sexual abuse have sued authorities in hierarchical churches for their failure to respond to information corroborating clergy sexual misconduct, resulting in claims in the hundreds of millions of dollars. One such case was *Moses v. Diocese of Colorado*, decided by the Colorado Supreme Court. It involves sordid behavior by an Episcopal priest.

A married woman, Mary Moses (although the Court consistently called her by her maiden name, Tenantry), had been sexually abused as a child. Even as an adult she suffered from psychological distress resulting from that early abuse. As a way of trying to deal with her demons, she went for counseling to the assistant pastor of her church. Father Robinson always ended the counseling sessions with a prayer and a hug. Eventually the hugs became more intense and the priest and his counselee engaged in oral sexual activity, over a period of some time. Eventually Moses told her sister what was happening and the sister told the senior minister of the church. The supervising minister scolded Moses' sister for telling him about Father Robinson's indiscretions. He said Father Robinson was going places in the church, he was "bishop material," and they should be ashamed for trying to damage his career.

Eventually Moses told the bishop of the diocese, Bishop Frey, about the sexual activity between herself and Father Robinson that had grown out of the counseling sessions she believed would be beneficial to her, given that Robinson was her pastor. The Bishop essentially said to Father Robinson, "Shame on you." He gave him a book entitled *Affair Prevention* and told him to get some counseling. He also appointed him as pastor of the Colorado Springs church.

Then Moses sued the diocese and Bishop Frey in state court for breach of fiduciary duty, negligent hiring, and vicarious liability for Father Robinson's unacceptable behavior. The Colorado Supreme Court held that it could decide the issues without making judgments about theology, which civil courts are forbidden to do.

A fiduciary duty exists between two persons when one has a duty to act for or give advice to the other. This is particularly true when one is superior to the other in the relationship, as a counselor to counselee, or, as in this case, the bishop of the diocese to the person allegedly wronged. A principal duty of the superior party is to deal with good faith and for the benefit of the dependent party. Furthermore, in this case the diocese was responsible for the hiring and the conduct of Father Robinson, the court ruled. However, it

## CHAPTER 10

# RELIGIOUS ORGANIZATIONS AS EMPLOYERS

Government regulation of the employment practices of religious organizations, including houses of worship, represents one of the more complex and intractable church-state conflicts. On the one hand, the extension of government regulations that set fair wages and working conditions and prohibit discrimination in hiring, retention, and firing impact directly on the free exercise and religious autonomy concerns discussed in previous chapters. Can a federal or state agency require a church to pay its janitor a statutory minimum wage or prohibit the same church from firing its minister because she acknowledges she is homosexual? What impact would such regulations have on the ability of the church to define and carry out its religious mission, not to mention the religious associational rights of the church members? Even assuming the regulatory burden on those religiously based rights is substantial, should the nation's commitment to fair labor practices and nondiscrimination in employment outweigh a religious organization's interests?

On the other hand, must the government, pursuant to the Free Exercise Clause, accommodate such interests by providing an exemption from the law? If instead the government *chooses* to accommodate the unique interests of a religious organization by exempting it from complying with neutral employment laws (e.g., exempting a church from paying unemployment compensation tax or allowing it to hire only co-religionists for all of its jobs), does that action give preferential treatment to religion and impermissibly advance it in violation of the Establishment Clause? Or does such treatment simply recognize that the government must steer clear of involvement in religious matters, whether to promote religion or to interfere with the exercise of faith?

These issues have become more salient in the twenty-first century as federal, state and local governments have dramatically increased their regulatory authority over nongovernmental employers, including nonprofit organizations, secular and religious alike. By way of background, federal and state regulation of nongovernmental employer-employee relations began in the nineteenth century through early laws addressing working conditions, prohibiting child labor, and authorizing the unionization of workers. Federal power rested on the constitutional authority of Congress to regulate interstate commerce, while states exercised plenary authority under their inherent police powers. Early on, federal courts struck down many attempts at regulating employment relations within nongovernmental bodies, at times holding that such laws interfered with the "sanctity of contracts." With the Great Depression of the 1930s, the New Deal, and new-found judicial deference to congressional authority to regulate the national economy came several landmark laws affecting employment relations: the National Labor Relations Act (NLRA), establishing the National Labor Relations Board to govern collective bargaining of unions; the Fair Labor Standards Act (FLSA) requiring the payment of minimum wages and overtime pay and the keeping of employment records; and the Unemployment Compensation Insurance Act.

Later, during the civil rights era, Congress and state legislatures turned their attention to employment discrimination based on race, national origin, gender, disability, age, and religion. The seminal law remains Title VII of the Civil Rights Act of 1964, prohibiting employers with more than fifteen employees from discriminating on the basis of race, national origin, gender, and religion. Other significant federal laws include the Age Discrimination Act of 1967, the Rehabilitation Act of 1973, and the Americans with Disabilities Act of 1990. Many other federal laws that govern the operations of closely regulated industries and entities—such as the Federal Communications Act—also prohibit discrimination on the basis of religion, among other grounds. Finally, many states and locales have enacted more sweeping nondiscrimination laws, sometimes covering all nongovernmental employers irrespective of the number of employees and extending protection against employment discrimination on the basis of marital status, sexual orientation, or appearance (i.e., extending protection to transvestites and cross-dressers).

Many local, state, and federal nondiscrimination laws apply to religious organizations and houses of worship, although such laws commonly provide limited exemptions for religious employers. For example, in *King's Garden Inc. v. FCC*, 498 F.2d 51 (D.C. Cir.), cert. denied, 419 U.S. 996 (1974), the court of appeals upheld the extension of the Federal Communications Act rule against religious discrimination to a Christian organization licensed to operate two radio stations, notwithstanding the organization's free exercise claim that the regulation burdened its religious practice. While the court acknowledged an implied exemption allowing religious discrimination for employment "connected with the espousal of the licensee's religious views," the court held that a broader exemption extending to all employees would likely be unconstitutional under the Establishment Clause.[1]

Significantly, this increase in government regulation of employment practices has come at a time when religious organizations are expanding their roles as employers. Quite clearly, the definition of a religious organization is not limited to churches, synagogues, mosques, and other houses of worship. Religious organizations run hospitals, nursing homes, orphanages, elementary and secondary schools, colleges, publishing houses, and social service agencies such as Catholic Charities and the United Jewish Appeal. Some religiously owned enterprises are all but indistinguishable from their secular counterparts, at least to nonreligious observers. As can be seen in the *Amos* case, below, the controversy arose over the employment practices at a gymnasium operated by the Church of Jesus Christ of Latter-day Saints (the "Mormon Church"). Arguably, religious organizations nationwide employ millions of workers, many of whom (such as physicians, nurses, and social workers) are engaged in functions and occupations that do not involve explicit religious content or activities.

On one level, the expansion of services and functions provided by religious organizations raises questions about which entities qualify as religious organizations and how the government is to undertake such an inquiry without entangling itself in the internal affairs of putative religious organizations. You may be surprised to learn that many laws and regulations define what is a religious organization. For example, in 1982 a federal district court ruled that a children's home "founded by" and maintaining "close ties with the Methodist Church" did not qualify as a "religious corporation" entitled to an exemption under Title VII.[2] Similarly, another court ruled that a corporation that manufactured mining equipment, but was operated by its owners as "a Christian, faith-operated business," was secular rather than religious.[3] On a different level, the whole-scale exemption of religious employers from wage and hour rules and nondiscrimination provisions would affect the working rights and interests of many Americans who view their employment primarily as a paying job. This concern becomes particularly acute when one considers that many charitable religious organizations and religiously affiliated hospitals receive millions of dollars in government funds for the delivery of nonreligious social services. The ability of religious organizations to receive government grants and contracts for human services but still rely on their ability to discriminate in employment on religious grounds is one of the leading issues at the forefront of Charitable Choice or the Faith-Based Initiative, discussed in chapter 19.

## GOVERNMENT OVERSIGHT OF EMPLOYMENT PRACTICES

### NATIONAL LABOR RELATIONS BOARD v. THE CATHOLIC BISHOP OF CHICAGO
440 U.S. 490 (1979)

MR. CHIEF JUSTICE BURGER delivered the opinion of the Court.

This case arises out of the National Labor Relations Board's exercise of jurisdiction over lay faculty members at two groups of Catholic high schools. We granted certiorari to consider two questions: (a) Whether teachers in schools operated by a church to teach both religious and secular subjects are within the jurisdiction granted by the National Labor Relations Act; and (b) if the Act authorizes such jurisdiction, does its exercise violate the guarantees of the Religion Clauses of the First Amendment?

I

[The schools in the first group, operated by the Catholic Bishop of Chicago, were termed "minor seminaries" because of their role in educating high school students who may become priests. In 1970, the requirement that students manifest a desire to become priests was changed to allow the admission of students who merely had the potential for the priesthood or for Christian leadership. However, the schools continued to provide special religious instruction not offered in other Catholic secondary schools. The schools also offered essentially the same college-preparatory curriculum as public secondary schools, with students participating in a variety of extracurricular activities which included secular as well as religious events.

The second group of schools were five high schools operated by the Diocese of Fort Wayne-South Bend. Although not operated for the purpose

employer's action. But at this stage of our consideration we are not compelled to determine whether the entanglement is excessive as we would were we considering the constitutional issue. Rather, we make a narrow inquiry whether the exercise of the Board's jurisdiction presents a significant risk that the First Amendment will be infringed.

Moreover, it is already clear that the Board's actions will go beyond resolving factual issues. The Court of Appeals' opinion refers to charges of unfair labor practices filed against religious schools. The court observed that in those cases the schools had responded that their challenged actions were mandated by their religious creeds. The resolution of such charges by the Board, in many instances, will necessarily involve inquiry into the good faith of the position asserted by the clergy-administrators and its relationship to the school's religious mission. It is not only the conclusions that may be reached by the Board which may impinge on rights guaranteed by the Religion Clauses, but also the very process of inquiry leading to findings and conclusions. . . .

The Board's exercise of jurisdiction will have at least one other impact on church-operated schools. The Board will be called upon to decide what are "terms and conditions of employment" and therefore mandatory subjects of bargaining. See 29 U.S.C § 158 (d). Although the Board has not interpreted that phrase as it relates to educational institutions, similar state provisions provide insight into the effect of mandatory bargaining. The Oregon Court of Appeals noted that "nearly everything that goes on in the schools affects teachers and is therefore arguably a 'condition of employment.'" . . .

Inevitably the Board's inquiry will implicate sensitive issues that open the door to conflicts between clergy-administrators and the Board, or conflicts with negotiators for unions. What we said in *Lemon* applies as well here: [Parochial] schools involve substantial religious activity and purpose. The substantial religious character of these church-related schools gives rise to entangling church-state relationships of the kind the Religion Clauses sought to avoid." (Footnote omitted.)

Mr. Justice Douglas emphasized this in his concurring opinion in *Lemon*, noting "the admitted and obvious fact that the *raison d'être* of parochial schools is the propagation of a religious faith."

The church-teacher relationship in a church-operated school differs from the employment relationship in a public or other nonreligious school. We see no escape from conflicts flowing from the Board's exercise of jurisdiction over teachers in church-operated schools and the consequent serious First Amendment questions that would follow. We therefore turn to an examination of the National Labor Relations Act to decide whether it must be read to confer jurisdiction that would in turn require a decision on the constitutional claims raised by respondents.

## VI

There is no clear expression of an affirmative intention of Congress that teachers in church-operated schools should be covered by the Act. Admittedly, Congress defined the Board's jurisdiction in very broad terms; . . . [However, o]ur examination of the statute and its legislative history indicates that Congress simply gave no consideration to church-operated schools. It is not without significance, however, that the Senate Committee on Education and Labor chose a college professor's dispute with the college as an example of employer-employee relations *not* covered by the Act. . . .

The most recent significant amendment to the Act was passed in 1974, removing the exemption of nonprofit hospitals. 88 Stat. 395. The Board relies upon that amendment as showing that Congress approved the Board's exercise of jurisdiction over church-operated schools. A close examination of that legislative history, however, reveals nothing to indicate an affirmative intention that such schools be within the Board's jurisdiction. Since the Board did not assert jurisdiction over teachers in a church-operated school until after the 1974 amendment, nothing in the history of the amendment can be read as reflecting Congress' tacit approval of the Board's action. . . .

The Board relies heavily upon *Associated Press v. NLRB*. There the Court held that the First Amendment was no bar to the application of the Act to the Associated Press, an organization engaged in collecting information and news throughout the world and distributing it to its members. Perceiving nothing to suggest that application of the Act would infringe First Amendment guarantees of press freedoms, the Court sustained Board jurisdiction. Here, on the contrary, the record affords abundant evidence that the Board's exercise of jurisdiction over teachers in church-operated schools would implicate the guarantees of the Religion Clauses.

Accordingly, in the absence of a clear expression of Congress' intent to bring teachers in church-operated schools within the jurisdiction of the Board, we decline to construe the Act in a manner that could in turn call upon the Court to resolve difficult and sensitive questions arising out of the guarantees of the First Amendment Religion Clauses.

*Affirmed.*

▦ MR. JUSTICE BRENNAN, with whom MR. JUSTICE WHITE, MR. JUSTICE MARSHALL, and MR. JUSTICE BLACKMUN join, dissenting. . . .

The Court requires that there be a "clear expression of an affirmative intention of Congress" before it will bring within the coverage of a broadly worded regulatory statute certain persons whose coverage might raise constitutional questions. But those familiar with the legislative process know that explicit expressions of congressional intent in such broadly inclusive statutes are not commonplace. . . .

The pertinent legislative history of the NLRA begins with the Wagner Act of 1935, 49 Stat. 449. Section 2(2) of that Act, identical in all relevant respects to the current section, excluded from its coverage neither church-operated schools nor any other private nonprofit organization. Accordingly, in applying that Act, the National Labor Relations Board did not recognize an exception for nonprofit employers, even when religiously associated. An argument for an implied nonprofit exemption was rejected because the design of the Act was as clear then as it is now: "[N]either charitable institutions nor their employees are exempted from operation of the Act by its terms, although certain other employers and employees are exempted." . . .

[In 1947, Congress enacted an exception from the NLRA for nonprofit hospitals, including religious hospitals.]

Even that limited exemption was ultimately repealed in 1974. 88 Stat. 395. In doing so, Congress confirmed the view of the Act expressed here: that it was intended to cover all employers—including nonprofit employers—unless expressly excluded, and that the 1947 amendment excluded only nonprofit hospitals. . . . Moreover, it is significant that in considering the 1974 amendments, the Senate expressly rejected an amendment proposed by Senator Ervin that was analogous to the one the Court today creates—an amendment to exempt nonprofit hospitals operated by religious groups. Senator Cranston, floor manager of the Senate Committee bill and primary opponent of the proposed religious exception, explained: . . .

> [S]uch an exception for religiously affiliated hospitals would seriously erode *the existing national policy which holds religiously affiliated institutions generally such as* proprietary nursing homes, residential communities, and *educational facilities to the same standards as their nonsectarian counterparts*. . . .

Thus, the available authority indicates that Congress intended to include—not exclude—lay teachers of church-operated schools. The Court does not counter this with evidence that Congress *did* intend an exception it never stated. Instead, despite the legislative history to the contrary, it construes the Act as excluding lay teachers only because Congress did not state explicitly that they were covered. In Mr. Justice Cardozo's words, this presses "avoidance of a difficulty . . . to the point of disingenuous evasion." . . .

## NOTES AND QUESTIONS

1. In *NLRB v. Catholic Bishop*, the Court interpreted the National Labor Relations Act not to apply to labor relations affecting lay faculty in church-operated schools so as to avoid what it perceived would otherwise be a constitutional conflict. Does the *Catholic Bishop* case therefore set down a constitutional rule? What religion clause values were implicated in the case? If the ruling has a "constitutional ring" to it, how far does that principle extend? What factors determine whether a generally applicable labor or employment regulation encroaches on religion clause principles? In *Catholic Bishop*, what factors were crucial—that the schools' purpose and functions were pervasively religious or that some of the schools trained future clergy for the Catholic Church (thus justifying greater deference to church officials in control over employees), or some other factor?

2. Suppose that one concern of the Court in this area is that of entanglement: that by deciding when and how to apply a regulation, government officials may determine whether a particular job or function is more central to the operation of the religious organization than other jobs or functions. It is often said that the specter of civil officials weighing the importance of certain religious activities or duties strikes near the heart of the Religion Clause principles. Many have argued that such power in the state would severely hamper the ability of religious organizations to define and carry out their religious missions. On the other hand, religious organizations employ people in various capacities and for a host of functions, some of which are arguably only tangentially related to the organizations' religious ministries. Should the government be able to distinguish between some of these capacities and functions, so as to ensure that the important purposes behind labor and employment laws are effectuated? How should courts weigh the importance of the interest in religious liberty against the importance of these other interests?

3. In *Catholic Bishop*, the Court determined that NLRB jurisdiction would risk oversight of church decision-making, citing the fact that the schools were pervasively sectarian and that teachers played a "key role" in furthering the religious mission of the Catholic Church. Lower courts have emphasized this factor in subsequent decisions. In the vast majority of NLRB cases involving religiously affiliated entities other than elementary and secondary schools, courts have upheld application of the Act, notwithstanding entanglement arguments. Accordingly, courts have applied the NLRA to religiously-run children's and nursing homes and religiously affiliated social service agencies and hospitals, relying on what they believe to be the nonreligious nature of many of the services performed by covered employees.[4] According to these courts, this approach allows them to find that Board review of employment practices would not intrude into religious decision-making. Even if specific job functions cannot be easily categorized, courts have held that Board review of employment decisions places minimal burdens on religious practices. In essence, the mere fact that a regulation imposes reporting and compliance requirements on a religious entity does not mean that it substantially burdens or inhibits religious practice, these courts say. Does this kind of interpretation of the *Catholic Bishop* decision seem correct, or does it read the decision too narrowly?

4. Recall that this decision was handed down at a time when the Court observed strict constitutional limits on the flow of government funds to "pervasively sectarian" instutitions such as religious elementary and secondary schools. But, as noted in chapter 12, the Court's approach in the area of government funding and religious groups has changed somewhat. Generally speaking, the Court has relaxed some of the restrictions on government funding and religious institutions, including institutions that were previously considered "pervasively sectarian." Is it appropriate for the rules regarding government regulation of religious entities to change as the rules about government funding and religion are liberalized? Or should the rather strict analysis of government regulation of religious entities endure, at least to the extent that a religious entity does not receive government funds?

Consider the competing issues discussed above in the following case. In *Tony and Susan Alamo Foundation v. Secretary of Labor*, the former—a nonprofit religious organization (pronounced "a-lamo")—operated several commercial businesses as part of its evangelical ministry to the poor and needy. Alamo Foundation "hired" people to work in its businesses as part of its overall rehabilitation program. The question became whether these workers were subject to the federal minimum wage and overtime requirements established under the Fair Labor Standards Act, or whether the imposition of such regulations interfered with the ability of Alamo Foundation to carry out its religious ministry, as protected by the Free Exercise and Establishment Clauses.

religion. The Establishment Clause does not exempt religious organizations from such secular governmental activity as fire inspections and building and zoning regulations, and the recordkeeping requirements of the Fair Labor Standards Act, while perhaps more burdensome in terms of paperwork, are not significantly more intrusive into religious affairs.

## IV

The Foundation's commercial activities, undertaken with a "common business purpose," are not beyond the reach of the Fair Labor Standards Act because of the Foundation's religious character, and its associates are "employees" within the meaning of the Act because they work in contemplation of compensation. Like other employees covered by the Act, the associates are entitled to its full protection. Furthermore, application of the Act to the Foundation's commercial activities is fully consistent with the requirements of the First Amendment. The judgment below is accordingly

*Affirmed.*

### NOTES AND QUESTIONS

1. The Court decided *Catholic Bishop* on the basis of statutory construction (i.e., that Congress had not intended the NLRA to apply to parochial schools), but the holding has a clear constitutional ring. Considering the subsequent holding in *Alamo*, would the Court now likely find the NLRA unconstitutional, or are there significant factual differences between the two cases?

2. What were the bases for finding no constitutional violation in applying the FLSA to Alamo Foundation? The Court holds that there is no significant burden on the religious rights of the "associates" and, by inference, on Alamo Foundation's religious ministry by adhering to the minimum wage, overtime and recordkeeping requirements. Are these the only religious burdens, or do the regulations affect the ability of Alamo Foundation to define and carry out its religious mission? How should the government (and courts) draw the line with respect to religious burdens (i.e., how significant or intrusive must the burden be before the Free Exercise Clause is triggered)?

3. How significant are the "religious" activities for the respective holdings? In essence, *Catholic Bishop* involved the administration of religious elementary and secondary schools (a function that is widely accepted as religious in nature) while *Alamo Foundation* involved quasi-commercial business enterprises. Should Congress' definitions of commercial versus religious activities be revised? What should be the public policy with respect to applying labor and employment protections to employees of religious enterprises? The best discussion of the competing issues raised in labor regulation of religious enterprises is still Douglas Laycock, "Toward a General Theory of the Religion Clauses: The Case of Church Labor Relations and the Right to Church Autonomy," *Columbia Law Review* 81 (November, 1981): 1373.

4. In *Alamo Foundation*, the Supreme Court interpreted the FLSA as apply-ing only to the organization's commercial activities, such that it would not impact the organization's evangelism. Does this interpretation therefore bar the Act's application to noncommercial activities of religious organizations? Apparently not. The Court's distinction between commercial and noncom-mercial activities was somewhat misleading, as the Act more broadly refers to "enterprises" which by definition include nonprofit activities and entities.[5] Also, even though the Alamo Foundation insisted that its religious and com-mercial functions were intertwined, the Court held that "routine and factual inquiries . . . bear no resemblance to the kind of government surveillance the Court has previously held to pose an intolerable risk of government entangle-ment with religion." Subsequent lower court decisions have clarified that the FLSA applies to nonprofit religious enterprises including religious schools.[6] So even within the context of elementary and secondary religious schools, courts have held that enforcement of the Act's wage and reporting require-ments places a limited burden on religious practice and results in minimal entanglement through potential surveillance and oversight. Does that seem like the correct result to you?

## EMPLOYMENT ACTIONS BY RELIGIOUS ORGANIZATIONS

An additional important law governing employment relations is Title VII of the Civil Rights Act of 1964. Title VII prohibits employers with fifteen or more employees from discriminating in their employment practices (e.g., hiring, retention and promotion, ter-mination) on the basis of an employee's race, color, national origin, gender, and religion. As per Congress's express intention, Title VII applies to religious organizations that oth-erwise qualify under the law; however, the law expressly exempts religious organizations from the prohibition against discrimination on the basis of religion. In *Corporation of Presiding Bishop v. Amos*, the courts considered the claims of dismissed employees of sev-eral nonprofit enterprises operated by the Church of Jesus Christ of Latter-day Saints (the Mormon Church). The former employees claimed that their various job duties had been secular in nature, such that to allow the Mormon Church to discriminate against them based on their religion would violate the Establishment Clause. The lower court agreed with the plaintiff-employees, but the Supreme Court reversed. In reading the following case consider the competing claims of the employees and the Mormon Church and of how the Court views the significance of the 1972 amendment to Title VII.

## CORPORATION OF THE PRESIDING BISHOP OF THE CHURCH OF JESUS CHRIST OF LATTER-DAY SAINTS v. AMOS
483 U.S. 327 (1987)

JUSTICE WHITE delivered the opinion of the Court.

Section 702 of the Civil Rights Act of 1964, 78 Stat. 255, as amended, 42 U.S.C. § 2000e-1, exempts religious organizations from Title VII's prohibition

never been so interpreted. Rather, *Lemon's* "purpose" requirement aims at preventing the relevant governmental decisionmaker—in this case, Congress—
from abandoning neutrality and acting with the intent of promoting a particular point of view in religious matters.

Under the *Lemon* analysis, it is a permissible legislative purpose to alleviate significant governmental interference with the ability of religious organizations to define and carry out their religious missions. Appellees argue that
there is no such purpose here because § 702 provided adequate protection
for religious employers prior to the 1972 amendment, when it exempted only
the religious activities of such employers from the statutory ban on religious
discrimination. We may assume for the sake of argument that the pre-1972
exemption was adequate in the sense that the Free Exercise Clause required
no more. Nonetheless, it is a significant burden on a religious organization
to require it, on pain of substantial liability, to predict which of its activities
a secular court will consider religious. The line is hardly a bright one, and
an organization might understandably be concerned that a judge would not
understand its religious tenets and sense of mission. Fear of potential liability
might affect the way an organization carried out what it understood to be its
religious mission.

After a detailed examination of the legislative history of the 1972 amendment, the District Court concluded that Congress' purpose was to minimize
governmental "interfer[ence] with the decision-making process in religions."
We agree with the District Court that this purpose does not violate the Establishment Clause.

The second requirement under *Lemon* is that the law in question have "a
principal or primary effect . . . that neither advances nor inhibits religion."
Undoubtedly, religious organizations are better able now to advance their purposes than they were prior to the 1972 amendment to § 702. But religious
groups have been better able to advance their purposes on account of many
laws that have passed constitutional muster: for example, the property tax exemption at issue in *Walz v. Tax Comm'n,* or the loans of schoolbooks to schoolchildren, including parochial school students, upheld in *Board of Education v.
Allen,* 392 U.S. 236 (1968). A law is not unconstitutional simply because it
*allows* churches to advance religion, which is their very purpose. For a law to
have forbidden "effects" under *Lemon,* it must be fair to say that the *government
itself* has advanced religion through its own activities and influence. . . .

The District Court appeared to fear that sustaining the exemption would
permit churches with financial resources impermissibly to extend their influence and propagate their faith by entering the commercial, profit-making
world. The cases before us, however, involve a nonprofit activity instituted
over 75 years ago in the hope that "all who assemble here, and who come
for the benefit of their health, and for physical blessings, [may] feel that they
are in a house dedicated to the Lord." Dedicatory Prayer for the Gymnasium,
quoted, 594 F. Supp., 800-801, n. 15. These cases therefore do not implicate
the apparent concerns of the District Court. Moreover, we find no persuasive
evidence in the record before us that the Church's ability to propagate its religious doctrine through the Gymnasium is any greater now than it was prior to
the passage of the Civil Rights Act in 1964. In such circumstances, we do not
see how any advancement of religion achieved by the Gymnasium can be fairly
attributed to the Government, as opposed to the Church.[15]

We find unpersuasive the District Court's reliance on the fact that § 702 singles out religious entities for a benefit. Although the Court has given weight to this consideration in its past decisions, it has never indicated that statutes that give special consideration to religious groups are *per se* invalid. That would run contrary to the teaching of our cases that there is ample room for accommodation of religion under the Establishment Clause. Where, as here, government acts with the proper purpose of lifting a regulation that burdens the exercise of religion, we see no reason to require that the exemption comes packaged with benefits to secular entities. . . .

Appellees argue that § 702 offends equal protection principles by giving less protection to the employees of religious employers than to the employees of secular employers. Appellees rely on *Larson v. Valente,* 456 U.S. 228, 246 (1982) for the proposition that a law drawing distinctions on religious grounds must be strictly scrutinized. But *Larson* indicates that laws discriminating *among* religions are subject to strict scrutiny, *ibid.,* and that laws "affording a uniform benefit to *all* religions" should be analyzed under *Lemon,* 456 U.S. 252. In cases such as these, where a statute is neutral on its face and motivated by a permissible purpose of limiting governmental interference with the exercise of religion, we see no justification for applying strict scrutiny to a statute that passes the *Lemon* test. The proper inquiry is whether Congress has chosen a rational classification to further a legitimate end. We have already indicated that Congress acted with a legitimate purpose in expanding the § 702 exemption to cover all activities of religious employers. To dispose of appellees' equal protection argument, it suffices to hold—as we now do—that as applied to the nonprofit activities of religious employers, § 702 is rationally related to the legitimate purpose of alleviating significant governmental interference with the ability of religious organizations to define and carry out their religious missions.

It cannot be seriously contended that § 702 impermissibly entangles church and state; the statute effectuates a more complete separation of the two and avoids the kind of intrusive inquiry into religious belief that the District Court engaged in in this case. The statute easily passes muster under the third part of the *Lemon* test.[17] . . .

The judgment of the District Court is reversed, and the cases are remanded for further proceedings consistent with this opinion.

*It is so ordered.*

---

[15] Undoubtedly, Mayson's freedom of choice in religious matters was impinged upon, but it was the Church (through the COP and the CPB), and not the Government, who put him to the choice of changing his religious practices or losing his job. This is a very different case than Estate of *Thornton v. Caldor,* 472 U.S. 703 (1985). In *Caldor,* the Court struck down a Connecticut statute prohibiting an employer from requiring an employee to work on a day designated by the employee as his Sabbath. In effect, Connecticut had given the force of law to the employee's designation of a Sabbath day and required accommodation by the employer regardless of the burden which that constituted for the employer or other employees. In the present cases, appellee Mayson was not legally obligated to take the steps necessary to qualify for a temple recommend, and his discharge was not required by statute. We find no merit in appellees' contention that § 702 "impermissibly delegates governmental power to religious employees and conveys a message of governmental endorsement of religious discrimination."

[17] We have no occasion to pass on the argument of the COP and the CPB that the exemption to which they are entitled under § 702 is required by the Free Exercise Clause.

⬛ JUSTICE BRENNAN, with whom JUSTICE MARSHALL joins, concurring in the judgment.

I write separately to emphasize that my concurrence in the judgment rests on the fact that these cases involve a challenge to the application of § 702's categorical exemption to the activities of a *nonprofit* organization. I believe that the particular character of nonprofit activity makes inappropriate a case-by-case determination whether its nature is religious or secular.

These cases present a confrontation between the rights of religious organizations and those of individuals. Any exemption from Title VII's proscription on religious discrimination necessarily has the effect of burdening the religious liberty of prospective and current employees. An exemption says that a person may be put to the choice of either conforming to certain religious tenets or losing a job opportunity, a promotion, or, as in these cases, employment itself.[1] The potential for coercion created by such a provision is in serious tension with our commitment to individual freedom of conscience in matters of religious belief.

At the same time, religious organizations have an interest in autonomy in ordering their internal affairs, so that they may be free to: "select their own leaders, define their own doctrines, resolve their own disputes, and run their own institutions. Religion includes important communal elements for most believers. They exercise their religion through religious organizations, and these organizations must be protected by the [Free Exercise] Clause." . . . Determining that certain activities are in furtherance of an organization's religious mission, and that only those committed to that mission should conduct them, is thus a means by which a religious community defines itself. Solicitude for a church's ability to do so reflects the idea that furtherance of the autonomy of religious organizations often furthers individual religious freedom as well.

The authority to engage in this process of self-definition inevitably involves what we normally regard as infringement on free exercise rights, since a religious organization is able to condition employment in certain activities on subscription to particular religious tenets. We are willing to countenance the imposition of such a condition because we deem it vital that, if certain activities constitute part of a religious community's practice, then a religious organization should be able to require that only members of its community perform those activities.

This rationale suggests that, ideally, religious organizations should be able to discriminate on the basis of religion *only* with respect to religious activities, so that a determination should be made in each case whether an activity is religious or secular. This is because the infringement on religious liberty that results from conditioning performance of *secular* activity upon religious belief cannot be defended as necessary for the community's self-definition. Furthermore, the authorization of discrimination in such circumstances is not an accommodation that simply enables a church to gain members by the normal means of prescribing the terms of membership for those who seek to

---

[1] The fact that a religious organization is permitted, rather than required, to impose this burden is irrelevant; what is significant is that the burden is the *effect* of the exemption. An exemption by its nature merely permits certain behavior, but that has never stopped this Court from examining the effect of exemptions that would free religion from regulations placed on others. . . .

participate in furthering the mission of the community. Rather, it puts at the disposal of religion the added advantages of economic leverage in the secular realm. As a result, the authorization of religious discrimination with respect to nonreligious activities goes beyond reasonable accommodation, and has the effect of furthering religion in violation of the Establishment Clause.

What makes the application of a religious-secular distinction difficult is that the character of an activity is not self-evident. As a result, determining whether an activity is religious or secular requires a searching case-by-case analysis. This results in considerable ongoing government entanglement in religious affairs. Furthermore, this prospect of government intrusion raises concern that a religious organization may be chilled in its free exercise activity. While a church may regard the conduct of certain functions as integral to its mission, a court may disagree. A religious organization therefore would have an incentive to characterize as religious only those activities about which there likely would be no dispute, even if it genuinely believed that religious commitment was important in performing other tasks as well. As a result, the community's process of self-definition would be shaped in part by the prospects of litigation. A case-by-case analysis for all activities therefore would both produce excessive government entanglement with religion and create the danger of chilling religious activity.

The risk of chilling religious organizations is most likely to arise with respect to *nonprofit* activities. The fact that an operation is not organized as a profit-making commercial enterprise makes colorable a claim that it is not purely secular in orientation. . . .

Nonprofit activities therefore are most likely to present cases in which characterization of the activity as religious or secular will be a close question. If there is a danger that a religious organization will be deterred from classifying as religious those activities it actually regards as religious, it is likely to be in this domain. This substantial potential for chilling religious activity makes inappropriate a case-by-case determination of the character of a nonprofit organization, and justifies a categorical exemption for nonprofit activities. Such an exemption demarcates a sphere of deference with respect to those activities most likely to be religious. It permits infringement on employee free exercise rights in those instances in which discrimination is most likely to reflect a religious community's self-definition. While not every nonprofit activity may be operated for religious purposes, the likelihood that many are makes a categorical rule a suitable means to avoid chilling the exercise of religion.

Sensitivity to individual religious freedom dictates that religious discrimination be permitted only with respect to employment in religious activities. Concern for the autonomy of religious organizations demands that we avoid the entanglement and the chill on religious expression that a case-by-case determination would produce. We cannot escape the fact that these aims are in tension. Because of the nature of nonprofit activities, I believe that a categorical exemption for such enterprises appropriately balances these competing concerns. . . .

■ JUSTICE O'CONNOR, concurring in the judgment.

Although I agree with the judgment of the Court, I write separately to note that this action once again illustrates certain difficulties inherent in the Court's use of the test articulated in *Lemon v. Kurtzman*. . . . As a result of this problematic analysis, while the holding of the opinion for the Court extends only to nonprofit organizations, its reasoning fails to acknowledge that the amended § 702, 42 U.S.C. § 2000e-1, raises different questions as it is applied to profit and nonprofit organizations. . . .

While acknowledging that "[u]ndoubtedly, religious organizations are better able now to advance their purposes than they were prior to the 1972 amendment to § 702," the Court seems to suggest that the "effects" prong of the *Lemon* test is not at all implicated as long as the government action can be characterized as "allowing" religious organizations to advance religion, in contrast to government action directly advancing religion. This distinction seems to me to obscure far more than to enlighten. Almost any government benefit to religion could be recharacterized as simply "allowing" a religion to better advance itself, unless perhaps it involved actual proselytization by government agents. In nearly every case of a government benefit to religion, the religious mission would not be advanced if the religion did not take advantage of the benefit; even a direct financial subsidy to a religious organization would not advance religion if for some reason the organization failed to make any use of the funds. It is for this same reason that there is little significance to the Court's observation that it was the Church rather than the Government that penalized Mayson's refusal to adhere to Church doctrine. The Church had the power to put Mayson to a choice of qualifying for a temple recommend or losing his job because *the Government* had lifted from religious organizations the general regulatory burden imposed by § 702.

The necessary first step in evaluating an Establishment Clause challenge to a government action lifting from religious organizations a generally applicable regulatory burden is to recognize that such government action *does* have the effect of advancing religion. The necessary second step is to separate those benefits to religion that constitutionally accommodate the free exercise of religion from those that provide unjustifiable awards of assistance to religious organizations. As I have suggested in earlier opinions, the inquiry framed by the *Lemon* test should be "whether government's purpose is to endorse religion and whether the statute actually conveys a message of endorsement." To ascertain whether the statute conveys a message of endorsement, the relevant issue is how it would be perceived by an objective observer, acquainted with the text, legislative history, and implementation of the statute. Of course, in order to perceive the government action as a permissible accommodation of religion, there must in fact be an identifiable burden *on the exercise of religion* that can be said to be lifted by the government action. The determination whether the objective observer will perceive an endorsement of religion "is not a question of simple historical fact. Although evidentiary submissions may help answer it, the question is, like the question whether racial or sex-based classifications communicate an invidious message, in large part a legal question to be answered on the basis of judicial interpretation of social facts."

The above framework, I believe, helps clarify why the amended § 702 raises different questions as it is applied to nonprofit and for-profit organizations. . . . These cases involve a Government decision to lift from a nonprofit activity of a religious organization the burden of demonstrating that the particular nonprofit activity is religious as well as the burden of refraining from discriminating on the basis of religion. Because there is a probability that a nonprofit activity of a religious organization will itself be involved in the organization's religious mission, in my view the objective observer should perceive the Government action as an accommodation of the exercise of religion rather than as a Government endorsement of religion.

It is not clear, however, that activities conducted by religious organizations solely as profit-making enterprises will be as likely to be directly involved in the religious mission of the organization. While I express no opinion on the issue, I emphasize that under the holding of the Court, and under my view of the appropriate Establishment Clause analysis, the question of the constitutionality of the § 702 exemption as applied to for-profit activities of religious organizations remains open.

## NOTES AND QUESTIONS

1. A crucial issue underlying *Amos* is discussed mostly in passing in the majority opinion (and in footnote 9). As originally enacted by Congress in 1964, the section 702 exemption for religious employers applied only for employees engaged in *religious* functions or activities. In 1972, with little study on the need for a broader exemption, Congress expanded section 702 to apply to all employees of religious organizations, regardless of whether their duties involve explicit religious functions. There was no Congressional testimony or findings that the original version of section 702 provided insufficient protection for religious decision making, although some congressional leaders argued on the floor that such expanded protection was needed (see pages 371-372 in the next section of this chapter for some discussion of those arguments and the larger context of the debate). The *Amos* Court deferred to what it describes as Congress' purpose "to minimize governmental 'interfer[ence] with the decision-making process in religions.'" The Court said:

   > Under the *Lemon* analysis, it is a permissible legislative purpose to alleviate significant governmental interference with the ability of religious organizations to define and carry out their religious missions. Appellees argue that there is no such purpose here because § 702 provided adequate protection for religious employers prior to the 1972 amendment, when it exempted only the religious activities of such employers from the statutory ban on religious discrimination. We may assume for the sake of argument that the pre-1972 exemption was adequate in the sense that the Free Exercise Clause required no more. Nonetheless, it is a significant burden on a religious organization to require it, on pain of substantial liability, to predict which of its activities a secular court will consider religious. The line is hardly a bright one, and an organization might understandably be concerned that a judge would not understand its religious tenets and sense of mission. Fear of potential liability might affect the way an organization carried out what it understood to be its religious mission.

   At the same time, however, the Court majority did not decide the issue of whether the expanded exemption was required by the Free Exercise Clause.

   Should the Court have subjected Congress' stated purpose to greater scrutiny considering Establishment Clause and Equal Protection claims? One of this book's authors has argued that the legislative history behind the 1972 amendment provides little support for the assumption upon which the Court's opinion rests. See Steven K. Green, "Religious Discrimination, Public Funding, and Constitutional Values," *Hastings Constitutional Law Quarterly* 30 (Fall 2002): 1. Another author of the book has written an article arguing that the section 702 exemption is sound public policy but that the state should not permit religious groups to discriminate on the basis of religion with regard to jobs subsidized with direct government aid. See Melissa Rogers, "Federal Funding and Religion-based Employment Decisions," in *Sanctioning Religion? Politics, Law, and Faith-based Public Services*, ed. David K. Ryden and Jeffrey Polet (Boulder, Colo.: Lynne Reinner Publishers, 2005).

2.  In her concurring opinion, Justice O'Connor identifies what she claims is an inherent conflict in applying the *Lemon* test to legislation that is designed to accommodate religious practices. The majority, however, seems to disagree with O'Connor's view of a conflict. Can you identify that apparent conflict and explain why it is of no concern for the majority of the Court? How, in the majority's mind, does the *Lemon* test account for purposeful accommodations of religion?

3.  With respect to the issue of the burden placed on Mr. Mayson in losing his job, Justice White remarks that any burden is attributable to the Church, and not the government. Justices Brennan and O'Connor view the matter differently. Who has the better argument, and why should this issue matter?

4.  How important to the Court's holding is the fact that businesses in issue run by the Mormon Church were not-for-profit? The concurring opinions of Justices Brennan and O'Connor emphasize that they read the Court's holding as being limited to nonprofit activities of religious organizations. The majority opinion, however, is somewhat vague on the legal significance of this point, noting only in its equal protection discussion that its decision relates to "the nonprofit activities of religious employers." Can the majority opinion be read more broadly to afford coverage under section 702 to the *for-profit* activities of a religious organization? What arguments can you make pro or con for an expanded reading of the majority opinion?

5.  To what extent does the holding in *Amos* apply to religious organizations that receive government grants and contracts? Putting aside the question of whether it violates the Establishment Clause to fund a religious organization that engages in religious discrimination, should religious organizations that receive government contracts be able to discriminate on the basis of religion as a matter of policy? Contrast "Protecting the Civil Rights of Religious Liberty of Faith-Based Organizations," *White House Office of Faith-Based and Community Initiatives*, with Green, "Religious Discrimination, Public Funding, and Constitutional Values," *Hastings Constitutional Law Quarterly* 30 (Fall 2002): 1, and Rogers, "Federal Funding and Religion-based Employment Decisions," *Sanctioning Religion? Politics, Law, and Faith-based Public Services,* ed. David K. Ryden and Jeffrey Polet. Does your answer depend on

whether the government monies fund the actual job position in question? Consider that many church-related colleges receive considerable sums in government funding for nonreligious projects but wish to staff their religious studies or theology departments with coreligionists.

How far-reaching is the ability of religious employers to discriminate under Title VII? Should the same concerns about non-interference with decision making based on religion apply to employment actions based on grounds such as race, gender, or, as some state and local regulations provide, sexual orientation? The Supreme Court has not addressed this issue, although it has been actively litigated in the lower federal courts. The various federal circuits that have considered this issue agree that the other restrictions in Title VII still apply to religious employers, such that employment decisions based on an employee's race, national origin, or gender are forbidden. As the Fourth Circuit stated in *Rayburn v. General Conference of Seventh-day Adventists*, 772 F.2d 1164, 1166-1167 (4th Cir. 1985), cert. denied, 478 U.S. 1020 (1986):

> Title VII does not confer upon religious organizations a license to make [hiring] decisions on the basis of race, sex, or national origin. . . . The statutory exemption applies to one particular reason for employment decision—that based on religious preference. It was open to Congress to exempt from Title VII the religious employer, not simply one basis of employment, and Congress plainly did not.

Such holdings have not prevented religious organizations from raising both constitutional and statutory arguments against the application of Title VII's provisions to their employment practices. Consider the following early case involving a claim of gender discrimination by a religious organization.

## EQUAL EMPLOYMENT OPPORTUNITY COMMISSION v. PACIFIC PRESS PUBLISHING ASSOCIATION
676 F.2d 1272 (9th Cir. 1982)

TRASK, Circuit Judge:

I

This is an appeal from the district court's holding that Pacific Press Publishing Association ("Press"), a nonprofit religious publishing house, violated section 703(a) of Title VII of the Civil Rights Act of 1964, 42 U.S.C. 2000e-2(a) (1976) by denying Lorna Tobler monetary allowances paid to similarly situated male employees. Press also was held in violation of section 704(a) of Title VII, 42 U.S.C. 2000e-3(a) (1976) for terminating Tobler's employment in retaliation for her filing charges and participating in proceedings under the Act. Because

Congress clearly intended to protect employees of religious institutions under Title VII, and because the enforcement of Title VII does not infringe religious freedom under the facts of the present case, we affirm the judgment of the district court.

Press, a nonprofit corporation incorporated under California law, is affiliated with the Seventh-Day Adventist Church and engages in the business of publishing, printing, advertising and selling religiously oriented material. All Press employees are required to be members of the church in good standing. Lorna Tobler worked at Press from 1960 until 1975. Her title throughout was "editorial secretary."

Until 1973, Press paid its employees in accordance with written wage scales under which married men received a higher rental allowance than single men, who in turn, received more than female employees regardless of their marital status. As a married woman, Tobler did not receive an annual utility allowance received by married men, nor was she paid automobile allowances paid to married male, single male and single female employees.

Tobler initiated charges of discrimination with the Equal Employment Opportunity Commission (EEOC) in 1972. [After the Press became aware of Tobler's actions, it reassigned her duties, giving her more menial tasks, actions that led to her retaliation claim.] . . . During her employment at Press and throughout this litigation, Tobler has remained a member in good standing of the [Seventh-Day Adventist Church]. . . .

II

Before reaching Press' constitutional arguments, this court must determine whether the dispute may be resolved on statutory grounds. The nature of our inquiry is established by *NLRB v. Catholic Bishop*. We must first determine whether the proposed application of the statute "would give rise to serious constitutional questions." If so, we cannot find the statute applicable unless there is an "'affirmative intention of Congress clearly expressed'" to apply it.

We conclude that the application of Title VII in the circumstances of this case presents serious constitutional questions. . . . We also conclude that Congress clearly expressed the intention that Title VII apply in the present circumstances. . . .

Section 702 of Title VII provides the limited exception available to religious employers:

> This subchapter shall not apply . . . to a religious corporation, association, educational institution or society with respect to the employment of individuals of a particular religion to perform work connected with the carrying on by such corporation, association, educational institution or society of its activities. . . .

The legislative history of this exemption shows that although Congress permitted religious organizations to discriminate in favor of members of their faith, religious employers are not immune from liability for discrimination based on race, sex, national origin, or for retaliatory actions against employees who exercise their rights under the statute.

Every court that has considered Title VII's applicability to religious employers has concluded that Congress intended to prohibit religious organizations from discriminating among their employees on the basis of race, sex or national origin. . . . We recognize that Tobler's position initially included discretionary and administrative responsibilities, and that the wage discrimination took place while she was discharging such responsibilities. But we hold that even when her job duties did include these responsibilities, she was not exempt from EEOC coverage. We reject the argument that the exemption provided by section 702 applies to all actions taken by an employer with respect to an employee whose work is connected with the organization's "religious activities."

IV

## Press' Constitutional Arguments

Pacific Press argues that any legislation affirmatively intended to apply to religious activity is always and necessarily unconstitutional. Because the publishing company is "pervasively sectarian" and "everything Pacific Press does is part of religion," Press contends that EEOC regulations violate the First Amendment to the extent they reach any Press activities. . . .

### A. The Free Exercise Clause

Although the free exercise clause prohibits legislation of religious beliefs, Press incorrectly argues that Congress lacks authority to legislate with respect to any religious activity or conduct. Statutes are not invalid simply because they affect the operation of a religious organization. See *Thomas v. Review Board*, 450 U.S. 707 (1981). . . .

We find that requiring Press to refrain from discriminating against Tobler, as required by Title VII, does not infringe Press' free exercise of its religious beliefs. Preventing discrimination can have no significant impact upon the exercise of Adventist beliefs because the Church proclaims that it does not believe in discriminating against women or minority groups, and that its policy is to pay wages without discrimination on the basis of race, religion, sex, age, or national origin. Thus, enforcement of Title VII's equal pay provision does not and could not conflict with Adventist religious doctrines, nor does it prohibit an activity "rooted in religious belief." *Wisconsin v. Yoder*, 374 U.S., 215. Because the impact on religious belief is minimal and the federal interest in equal employment opportunities is high, the balance weighs heavily in favor of upholding Press' liability under Title VII for its use of sexually discriminatory wage scales. . . .

The retaliatory action taken against Tobler for her participation in EEOC proceedings presents a more serious conflict between Adventist religious beliefs and EEOC jurisdiction. Press justifies Tobler's dismissal on religious grounds, citing her violation of church doctrines which prohibit lawsuits by members against the church. . . . Unlike the wage discrimination issue, there is a substantial impact on the exercise of religious beliefs because EEOC's jurisdiction to prosecute the retaliatory action taken against Tobler potentially will impose liability on Press for disciplinary actions based on religious doctrine. We find, however, that the government's compelling interest in assuring equal employment opportunities justifies this burden. By enacting Title VII, Congress clearly targeted the elimination of all forms of discrimination as a "highest priority." . . . To permit the various Adventist institutions to retaliate against employees who challenge discrimination through EEOC procedures would defeat Congress' intention to protect employees of religious employers. The effect would be to withdraw Title VII's protections from employees at the hundreds of diverse organizations affiliated with the Adventist Church, including businesses which process food, sell insurance, invest in stocks and bonds, and run schools, hospitals, laboratories, rest homes and sanitariums. . . .

## C. Press' Establishment Clause Arguments

Press also contends that Title VII violates the establishment clause because it creates impermissible EEOC entanglement with religion. . . .

The present case is distinguishable from *NLRB v. Catholic Bishop* because neither the judgment in this suit nor Title VII's enforcement mechanisms result in any ongoing scrutiny of Press' operations. The potential for ongoing entanglement or continuous supervision of church affairs by the government's regulations is the critical entanglement issue which deserves the most emphasis. In *Catholic Bishop*, the court found a serious risk of excessive entanglement because the enforcement of the National Labor Relations Act's mandatory collective bargaining provisions at a sectarian school would have empowered the NLRB to judge the good faith beliefs of clergy-administrators, to assess the validity of positions central to the school's religious mission and to issue cease and desist orders. EEOC cannot issue coercive orders and lacks independent authority to initiate actions to enforce Title VII. As discussed earlier, EEOC actions must be initiated by an employee filing charges with the Commission. Although the district court's award of monetary damages to Tobler may inhibit Press from discharging employees who participate in Title VII proceedings, this remedy does not amount to continuous supervision of the kind the Supreme Court sought to avoid in *Catholic Bishop*.

*Affirmed.*

---

### Notes and Questions

1. Do you agree with the *Pacific Press* court that enforcement of Title VII's prohibition on gender discrimination outweighs the First Amendment concerns? Suppose the Seventh-day Adventist Church had a doctrine that taught the inferiority of women, such that the equal pay of men and women for similar work violated its understanding of scripture. Could (should) Title VII still be applied to its religious publishing house?

2. Despite Congress' intent to hold religious organizations subject to its prohibitions on nonreligious discrimination, it is not always easy to determine whether the basis for an employment action is "religious," and thus allowable under section 702, or is based on an unlawful rationale. Consider the case of *Cline v. Catholic Diocese of Toledo*, 206 F.3d 651 (6th Cir. 2000), where an unmarried lay teacher in a Catholic private school was dismissed after school authorities discovered she was pregnant. Had the religious school engaged in unlawful discrimination based on her pregnancy or taken a permissible action based on the teacher's moral transgression of having sexual relations outside of marriage, which is inconsistent with Catholic doctrine? The court acknowledged the conundrum:

   > Because discrimination based on pregnancy is a clear form of discrimination based on sex, religious schools cannot discriminate based on pregnancy. . . . [However,] if the school's purported "discrimination" is based on a policy of preventing nonmarital sexual activity which emanates from the religious and moral precepts of the school, and if that policy is applied equally to its male and female employees, then the school has not discriminated based on pregnancy in violation of Title VII.

The *Cline* court held that the teacher had presented sufficient evidence to raise a genuine factual dispute, such that the case should proceed to trial.

3. Assuming that a religious organization has not based its employment action on a prohibited rationale, such as gender, what does it mean for a decision to be based on "religion?" In essence, is the section 702 exemption limited to allowing religious organizations to discriminate only against people of other faiths, such as a Methodist-run home for children refusing to hire a Jewish social worker? Or does the exemption extend to any religiously based employment decision? Remember in *Amos* that Mr. Mason was a member of the Mormon Church, albeit without a "Temple recommend." The *Amos* Court assumes that section 702 exemption includes actions among people of the same faith in addition to actions between people of different faiths. Similarly, in *Cline*, the dismissed teacher was a practicing Catholic, so if the school's action was to be allowed, it had to be based on her failure to adhere to Church doctrine, not because she was a member of a different faith.

This area of the law has been litigated rather actively, with outcomes turning on the particular facts and whether the asserted religious defense is a proxy for some other form of discrimination. Compare *Cline*, 206 F.3d 651 (6th Cir. 2000) (finding sex discrimination in the termination of a pregnant employee), with *Boyd v. Harding Academy*, 88 F.3d 410 (6th Cir. 1996) (upholding the right of a religiously affiliated preschool to dismiss a pregnant teacher on the grounds she violated the prohibition against premarital sex). But provided the religious justification for the employment action is not a proxy for other forms of discrimination, courts have generally been generous in defining what is a religious action. In *Little v. Wuerl*, 929 F.2d 944 (3rd Cir. 1991), involving a Catholic school's refusal to renew the contract of a teacher who became remarried, the court articulated the concerns:

> The difficulty in determining whether [Title VII's] exceptions apply to the Parish's decision not to rehire Little lies in determining what it means for someone to be "of a particular religion." Little can plausibly claim that she is, and always has been, a Protestant and that because her religious affiliation never changed, the Parish's decision not to rehire her cannot have been based upon whether she was "of a particular religion." The Parish can respond that being "of a particular religion" involves more than denominational affiliation, that it includes conduct considered by the employer or the employee to have religious significance.
>
> Section 701(j) of Title VII, which applies to both exemptions, defines religion broadly: The term "religion" includes all aspects of religious observance and practice, as well as belief . . . .
>
> [T]aken as a whole, the definition seems intended to broaden the prohibition against discrimination—so that religious practice as well as religious belief and affiliation would be protected. There appears to be no legislative history to indicate that Congress considered the effect of this definition on the scope of the exemptions for religious organizations. Although the legislative history never directly addresses the question of whether being "of a particular religion" applies to conduct as well as formal

affiliation, it suggests that the sponsors of the broadened exception were solicitous of religious organizations' desire to create communities faithful to their religious principles. One sponsor claimed that:

> the establishment of church-related educational institutions is the embodiment of the free exercise of religion. This form of religious activity has always been recognized to occupy the same high estate under the first amendment as worshipping in the churches and preaching from the pulpits.118 Cong. Rec. 1994 (1972) (Senator Allen). Another sponsor made it clear that the exception was intended to remove religious employers from government scrutiny: [Question]: Does the Senator's amendment limit itself to the opportunity of a religious organization to have the right to hire people of its own faith? Is that the limitation of the amendment? Senator Ervin: I would allow the religious corporation to do what it pleased. That is what my amendment would allow it to do. It would allow it liberty. It would take it out from under the control of the EEOC entirely. 118 Cong. Rec. 1982 (1972).

The broadening of the exception to cover all employees rather than only those engaged in "religious activities" was done at the same time Congress eliminated a general exception from Title VII for all educational establishments. It is generally acknowledged that "the sponsors of the 1972 exemption were chiefly concerned to preserve the statutory power of sectarian schools and colleges to discriminate on religious grounds in the hiring of all their employees." *King's Garden, Inc. v. Federal Communications Comm'n*, 162 U.S. App. D.C. 100, 498 F.2d 51, 54 (D.C. Cir.), *cert. denied*, 419 U.S. 996, 95 S. Ct. 309, 42 L. Ed. 2d 269 (1974); . . .

We recognize that Congress intended Title VII to free individual workers from religious prejudice. But we are also persuaded that Congress intended the explicit exemptions to Title VII to enable religious organizations to create and maintain communities composed solely of individuals faithful to their doctrinal practices, whether or not every individual plays a direct role in the organization's "religious activities." Against this background and with sensitivity to the constitutional concerns that would be raised by a contrary interpretation, we read the exemption broadly. We conclude that the permission to employ persons "of a particular religion" includes permission to employ only persons whose beliefs and conduct are consistent with the employer's religious precepts. Thus, it does not violate Title VII's prohibition of religious discrimination for a parochial school to discharge a Catholic or a non-Catholic teacher who has publicly engaged in conduct regarded by the school as inconsistent with its religious principles. We therefore hold that the exemptions to Title VII cover the Parish's decision not to rehire Little because of her remarriage.

---

A final area of controversy involving employment decisions by religious organizations has concerned issues of ministers. Do the general prohibitions against nonreligious discrimination contained in Title VII apply when the religious organization takes an action against a minister? Are especial free exercise and religious autonomy concerns raised in this context? If so, how deferential should courts be to a religious organization's own determination of who qualifies as a "minister," taking into consideration that a broad exemption may conflict with Congress' "highest priority" to eliminate discrimination in the workplace? And finally, what if a religious body does not have ordained ministers?

Several of the federal circuits have carved out a constitutionally compelled "ministerial exception" from Title VII that allows religious institutions to discriminate *on any basis*—race, gender, national origin—for employment decisions involving ministers.[7] The exception, first recognized by the Fifth Circuit in *McClure v. Salvation Army*, 460 F.2d 553 (5th Cir. 1972), and later adopted by most of the circuits, removes entirely all aspects of the employment relationship between a church and its ministers from Title VII scrutiny. *McClure* concluded that "matters touching the relationship between a church and its ministers, determinations of salary, and assignment of duties and location, are matters of church administration and government and thus purely of ecclesiastical cognizance."[8] Recognizing that the church-minister relationship lies at the core of religious autonomy concerns, courts have dismissed discrimination claims brought by ministers, even when those claims allege the employment action was racially or gender motivated. As one court has stated, "[a] church's selection of its own clergy is one such core matter of ecclesiastical self-governance with which the state may not constitutionally interfere."[9] Again, the Supreme Court has not ruled on the constitutionality of this exemption. Consider the following case.

## GELLINGTON v. CHRISTIAN METHODIST EPISCOPAL CHURCH, INC.
### 203 F.3d 1299 (11th Cir. 2000)

BLACK, Circuit Judge:

Appellant Lee Otis Gellington brought this action against his former employer, Appellee Christian Methodist Episcopal Church, Inc., alleging he was retaliated against and constructively discharged in violation of Title VII of the Civil Rights Act of 1964. The district court granted summary judgment in favor of Appellee after concluding that the ministerial exception barred Appellant from bringing suit under Title VII against Appellee. . . .

I

Appellant is an ordained minister of the Christian Methodist Episcopal (CME) Church. CME Church is divided into ten Episcopal districts. Beginning in 1995, Appellant served as a minister in a church located in Mobile, Alabama, which is part of the Fifth Episcopal district. One of Appellant's co-workers at the Mobile church was Veronica Little, who also was employed as a minister. On more than one occasion, Little confided in Appellant that her immediate supervisor had made sexual advances toward her, and she asked Appellant for guidance on how to handle this situation. Appellant advised and aided Little in preparing an official complaint to the church elders. Shortly after he aided Little in her complaint, Appellant was reassigned to a church over 800 miles away from his home at a substantial reduction in salary.

Appellant states that he could not comply with this reassignment and consequently was forced to resign.

Appellant brought this action, alleging Appellee retaliated against him and
constructively discharged him for aiding Little in her sexual harassment complaint. . . .

## II

There is no question that the district court's grant of summary judgment
would have been correct prior to 1990. *McClure v. Salvation Army,* 460 F.2d
553 (5th Cir. 1972), established that Title VII is not applicable to the employment relationship between a church and its ministers. In *McClure,* a minister of
the Salvation Army sued the church under Title VII, alleging she was discriminated against on the basis of sex and discharged because of her complaints
regarding this alleged discrimination. After noting that the First Amendment
has built a "wall of separation" between church and state, and that there is a
long history of allowing churches to be free from state interference in matters of church governance, the Fifth Circuit held that it would not apply Title
VII to the minister-church employment relationship. The court reasoned that
applying Title VII to this relationship "would result in an encroachment by
the State into an area of religious freedom which it is forbidden to enter by the
principles of the free exercise clause of the First Amendment." *Id.,* 560. The
court concluded that matters such as "the determination of a minister's salary,
his place of assignment, and the duty he is to perform in furtherance of the
religious mission of the church" were all functions with which the state could
not interfere. *Id.,* 559.

Since *McClure,* many other Circuits also have adopted the ministerial exception to Title VII. . . .

Appellant argues that although *McClure* was the law of this Circuit prior
to 1990, the ministerial exception to Title VII created in *McClure* cannot exist
subsequent to the Supreme Court's decision in *Employment Division v. Smith,*
494 U.S. 872 (1990). . . . Appellant argues that because *Smith* held that religious beliefs do not excuse compliance with a generally applicable law, Appellee cannot evade the legal obligations imposed by Title VII simply because it is
a religious organization. Appellant contends that because Title VII is a neutral
law of general applicability, the First Amendment does not bar the application
of Title VII to Appellee even if its application would burden the free exercise
of religion.

Two Circuits have concluded the ministerial exception survives *Smith.* The
D.C. Circuit first considered this question in *EEOC v. Catholic University of
America,* 83 F.3d 455 (D.C. Cir. 1996). A Catholic nun brought a Title VII
sex discrimination suit against the University after she was denied tenure. In
addressing the plaintiff's claim, the court noted that the "Supreme Court has
recognized that government action may burden the free exercise of religion"
in two ways: "by interfering with a believer's ability to observe the commands
or practices of his faith, and by encroaching on the ability of a church to
manage its internal affairs." *Id,* 460. The court then noted that the ministerial exception was developed, in part, to protect churches from the second
type of government interference. The court reasoned, however, that *Smith* focused exclusively on the first prong of the free exercise clause, the individual's
ability to observe the practices of his or her religion. Concluding that *Smith*
therefore was not applicable to the ministerial exception, the court stated "the
burden on free exercise that is addressed by the ministerial exception is of a

fundamentally different character from that at issue in *Smith* and in the cases cited by the Court in support of its holding. . . . [T]he ministerial exception does not present the dangers warned of in *Smith*." *Id.*, 462.

The D.C. Circuit also concluded the Supreme Court's rejection in *Smith* of the compelling interest test did not affect the continuing existence of the ministerial exception. The court noted that although some of the cases applying the ministerial exception cited the compelling interest test, the exception was not based on this test, but rather on a "long line of Supreme Court cases that affirm the fundamental right of churches to 'decide for themselves, free from state interference, matters of church government as well as those of faith and doctrine.' " *Id.*, 462 (quoting *Kedroff*). Consequently, the D.C. Circuit held that the rejection of the compelling interest test did not alter this "century-old affirmation of a church's sovereignty over its own affairs." *Id.*, 463.

The Fifth Circuit has also held that the ministerial exception to Title VII survives *Smith*. In *Combs v. Central Texas Annual Conference of United Methodist Church*, 173 F.3d 343 (5th Cir. 1999), the court considered a Title VII sex discrimination claim brought by a female clergy member against her church. In concluding that the suit was barred by the ministerial exception, the court agreed with both the reasoning and the conclusion of the D.C. Circuit, noting

> *Smith*'s language is clearly directed at the first strand of free exercise law, where an individual contends that, because of his religious beliefs, he should not be required to conform with generally applicable laws. The concerns raised in *Smith* are quite different from the concerns raised by Reverend Comb's case, which pertains to interference in internal church management. *Id.*, 349.

The court reasoned that the constitutional protection of religious freedom afforded to churches in employment actions involving clergy exists even when such actions are not based on issues of church doctrine or ecclesiastical law. The court also concluded that this "fundamental right of churches to be free from government interference in their internal management and administration" had not been affected by the *Smith* Court's refusal to apply the compelling interest test. *Id.*, 350.

We agree with the Fifth and D.C. Circuits and hold that the ministerial exception created in *McClure* has not been overruled by the Supreme Court's decision in *Smith*. The *Smith* decision focused on the first type of government infringement on the right of free exercise of religion—infringement on an individual's ability to observe the practices of his or her religion. The second type of government infringement—interference with a church's ability to select and manage its own clergy—was not at issue in *Smith*. The Court's concern in *Smith* was that if an individual's legal obligations were contingent upon religious beliefs, those beliefs would allow each individual "'to become a law unto himself.'" *Smith*, 494 U.S., 885. The ministerial exception does not subvert this concern; it was not developed to provide protection to individuals who wish to observe a religious practice that contravenes a generally applicable law. Rather, the exception only continues a long-standing tradition that churches are to be free from government interference in matters of church governance and administration. See, e.g., *Kedroff* ("Legislation that regulates church administration, the operation of the churches, [or] the appointment clergy . . . prohibits the free exercise of religion"). Also, because the ministerial exception is based on this tradition and not on strict scrutiny, the Court's rejection in

of sexual harassment against the Jesuit order. Simply stated, the ministerial exception insulates a religious organization's employment decisions regarding its ministers from judicial scrutiny under Title VII. The Free Exercise and Establishment Clauses of the First Amendment compel this exception to the otherwise fully applicable commands of Title VII when the disputed employment practices involve a church's freedom to choose its ministers or to practice its beliefs. . . .

The ministerial exception to Title VII "precludes civil courts from adjudicating employment discrimination suits by ministers against the church or religious institution employing them." . . . The source of the ministerial exception is the Constitution rather than the statute. Insofar as race, sex, and national origin are concerned, the text of Title VII treats an employment dispute between a minister and his or her church like any other employment dispute. The statute does provide two exemptions from its non-discrimination mandate for religious groups. One permits a religious entity to restrict employment "connected with the carrying on . . . of its activities" to members of its own faith, the other permits parochial schools to do the same. But neither of these statutory exceptions removes race, sex, or national origin as an impermissible basis of discrimination against employees of religious institutions. Nor do they single out ministerial employees for lesser protections than those enjoyed by other church employees.

Despite the lack of a statutory basis for the ministerial exception, and despite Congress' apparent intent to apply Title VII to religious organizations as to any other employer, courts have uniformly concluded that the Free Exercise and Establishment Clauses of the First Amendment require a narrowing construction of Title VII in order to insulate the relationship between a religious organization and its ministers from constitutionally impermissible interference by the government. These First Amendment restrictions on Title VII provide important protections to churches that seek to choose their representatives free from government interference and according to the dictates of faith and conscience. . . .

We cannot conceive how the federal judiciary could determine whether an employment decision concerning a minister was based on legitimate or illegitimate grounds without inserting ourselves into a realm where the Constitution forbids us to tread, the internal management of a church.

Because the plain language of Title VII purports to reach a church's employment decisions regarding its ministers, courts have had to carve a ministerial exception out of Title VII in order to reconcile the statute with the Constitution. But the scope of the ministerial exception to Title VII is limited to what is necessary to comply with the First Amendment. For example, it does not apply to lay employees of a religious institution if they are not serving the function of ministers. . . .

In this case, as in the case of lay employees, the Free Exercise rationales supporting an exception to Title VII are missing. The Jesuits do not offer a religious justification for the harassment Bollard alleges; indeed, they condemn it as inconsistent with their values and beliefs. There is thus no danger that, by allowing this suit to proceed, we will thrust the secular courts into the constitutionally untenable position of passing judgment on questions of religious faith or doctrine. The Jesuits' disavowal of the harassment also reassures us that application of Title VII in this context will have no significant impact on their religious beliefs or doctrines. . . .

Moreover, this is not a case about the Jesuit order's choice of representative, a decision to which we would simply defer without further inquiry. Bollard does not complain that the Jesuits refused to ordain him or engaged in any other adverse personnel action. . . .

The only relevant decision that we can reasonably attribute to the Jesuits on the facts alleged here is the decision not to intervene to stop or curtail the sexual harassment Bollard reported. But, in our view, it strays too far from the rationale of the Free Exercise Clause to extend constitutional protection to this sort of disciplinary inaction simply because a minister is the target as well as the agent of the harassing activity. That Bollard has sued under an employment discrimination statute does not mean that the aspect of the church-minister employment relationship that warrants heightened constitutional protection—a church's freedom to choose its representatives—is present. The Free Exercise Clause rationale for protecting a church's personnel decisions concerning its ministers is the necessity of allowing the church to choose its representatives using whatever criteria it deems relevant. That rationale does not apply here, for the Jesuits most certainly do not claim that allowing harassment to continue unrectified is a method of choosing their clergy. Because there is no protected-choice rationale at issue, we intrude no further on church autonomy in allowing this case to proceed than we do, for example, in allowing parishioners' civil suits against a church for the negligent supervision of ministers who have subjected them to inappropriate sexual behavior.

Thus, we believe that we must apply the *Sherbert* balancing test in roughly the same manner as in cases involving lay employees in order to determine whether the application of Title VII in this case would violate the Free Exercise Clause. We conclude that it would not. Because the Jesuit order doctrinally disavows the harassment, the danger that the application of Title VII in this case will interfere with its religious faith or doctrine is particularly low. And while we recognize that applying any laws to religious institutions necessarily interferes with the unfettered autonomy churches would otherwise enjoy, this sort of generalized and diffuse concern for church autonomy, without more, does not exempt them from the operation of secular laws. Otherwise, churches would be free from all of the secular legal obligations that currently and routinely apply to them. For these reasons, we do not think that applying Title VII in the circumstances of this case will have an unconstitutional impact on the free exercise of the Jesuits' religious beliefs. At the same time, the strength of the government's interest, expressed in the text of Title VII, in protecting employees against sexual harassment is difficult to overstate. As we have said previously, it is a matter of the "highest priority." Further, we know from the text of Title VII that Congress intended it to apply to churches. Where the church provides no doctrinal nor protected-choice based rationale for its alleged actions, and indeed expressly disapproves of the alleged actions, a balancing of interests strongly favors application of the statute. We therefore conclude that Bollard's sexual harassment claim does not run afoul of the Free Exercise Clause.

## B. The Establishment Clause

The Establishment Clause serves as a separate constitutional basis for the ministerial exception to Title VII. . . . The only open question is whether applying Title VII in the circumstances of this case would foster an impermissible government entanglement with religion.

Entanglement has both substantive and procedural dimensions. On a substantive level, applying the statute to the clergy-church employment relationship creates a constitutionally impermissible entanglement with religion if the church's freedom to choose its ministers is at stake. A religious organization's decision to employ or to terminate employment of a minister is at the heart of its religious mission. The "determination of 'whose voice speaks for the church' is *per se* a religious matter. . . . We cannot imagine an area of inquiry less suited to a temporal court for decision; evaluation of the 'gifts and graces' of a minister must be left to ecclesiastical institutions." But as we have explained above in discussing the Free Exercise Clause, such substantive concerns are absent from this case.

As a procedural matter, "entanglement might also result from a protracted legal process pitting church and state as adversaries . . . ." As the Fourth Circuit explained in *Rayburn*,

> A Title VII action is potentially a lengthy proceeding, involving state agencies and commissions, the EEOC, the federal trial courts and courts of appeal. Church personnel and records would inevitably become subject to subpoena, discovery, cross-examination, the full panoply of legal process designed to probe the mind of the church in the selection of its ministers. The remedies that a district court may impose, may be far-reaching in their impact upon religious organizations. Even after entry of judgment, questions of compliance may result in continued court surveillance of the church's policies and decisions. 772 F.2d at 1171.

In a Title VII case, the dangers of procedural entanglement are most acute where there is also a substantive entanglement at issue. Where such a concern is absent, procedural entanglement considerations are reduced to the constitutional propriety of subjecting a church to the expense and indignity of the civil legal process. In this case, we believe that the entanglement between church and state that would result if Bollard pursued his sexual harassment claim is not sufficiently significant to violate the Establishment Clause. . . .

Nothing in the character of this defense will require a jury to evaluate religious doctrine or the "reasonableness" of the religious practices followed within the Jesuit order. Instead, the jury must make secular judgments about the nature and severity of the harassment and what measures, if any, were taken by the Jesuits to prevent or correct it. The limited nature of the inquiry, combined with the ability of the district court to control discovery, can prevent a wide-ranging intrusion into sensitive religious matters. . . .

Taken as a whole, we conclude that the procedural entanglement between church and state that will result from allowing Bollard to pursue his claim is no greater than that attendant on any other civil suit a private litigant might pursue against a church. Accordingly, we fail to see an Establishment Clause violation in applying the commands of Title VII to this case. . . .

---

In 2000, the Catholic institutions that lost the *Bollard* case asked the three-judge panel to rehear it. The panel denied their request. The Catholic institutions then filed what is known as a "petition for rehearing en banc." This is a request that all the judges that sit on a particular court—many more than three—rehear the case. When such a request is made, all of these judges cast their vote on whether the case should be reheard en banc. It is rare for a court to grant such a rehearing, and the required majority of the court did not do so here. Nevetheless, four judges on the Ninth Circuit chose to write a dissent from the majority's refusal to rehear the case en banc. An edited version of that dissent is reproduced in the space below.

---

WARDLAW, Circuit Judge, with whom KOZINSKI, O'SCANNLAIN, and KLEINFELD, Circuit Judges, join, dissenting from denial of rehearing en banc:

At stake in this case is whether the First Amendment continues to protect the Free Exercise and Establishment Clause rights of religious institutions in their church administration, operation, and selection of clergy in the form of the ministerial exception to Title VII. The panel opinion narrows the ministerial exception nearly to the point of extinction by allowing Bollard, a Jesuit novice studying for ordination into the Catholic priesthood, to maintain his Title VII claim of alleged sexual harassment against the Society of Jesus. In so doing, the panel opinion undermines over a century of Supreme Court jurisprudence, runs contrary to every other United States Court of Appeals that has had occasion to visit the issue, and further evidences the confusion among lower courts over the nature of the fundamental religious freedoms protected by the First Amendment.

The panel opinion employs a flawed analysis of the nature of Bollard's allegations and damage claims, the necessary intrusion into church affairs litigation of those claims will entail, and the ministerial exception itself. Bollard does not claim that he was constructively discharged from employment by the Jesuits as a high school teacher, counselor, or youth advisor. Bollard's complaint is that the Jesuits prevented him from becoming a *Jesuit priest* by failing to address his alleged sexual harassment. Thus, Bollard's future in the priesthood is at the heart of his claim. This directly implicates the minister-church relationship, an undisputed matter of core ecclesiastical concern. . . . The judiciary must now evaluate Bollard's claim that the Jesuit Order deprived him of a livelihood as a priest and that he is therefore entitled to compensation for the loss of a lifetime career in the Jesuit Order. This is precisely what the Constitution forbids.

For over a century, the Supreme Court has restricted the government from interfering in the governance, discipline, or doctrine of religious organizations. Resolution of Bollard's sexual harassment claims will require the judicial branch to delve into religious matters outside the judiciary's province, such as conditions of his association with the Jesuits; disciplinary and supervisory decisions they made; whether Bollard would have otherwise been ordained into the priesthood; and the "extent to which [he] would be 'made whole' from loss of a life of spiritual service or the proper compensation for the 'emotional pain' one suffers from this deprivation." Every other circuit that has addressed the scope of the ministerial exception agrees that such an inquiry is barred by the Religion Clauses. See *Gellington v. Christian Methodist Episcopal Church, Inc.*, 203 F.3d 1299, 1304 (11th Cir. 2000) ("Investigation . . . into a church's employment of its clergy would almost always entail excessive government entanglement into the internal management of the church."); *Combs v. Central Texas Annual Conf. of United Methodist Church*, 173 F.3d 343, 350 (5th Cir. 1999) (holding that Title VII claims by ministers against their church necessarily require "secular authorities [to] intrude into church governance in a manner that would be inherently coercive, even if the alleged [misconduct] were purely nondoctrinal"); *EEOC v. Catholic Univ. of Am.*, 317 U.S. App. D.C. 343, 83 F.3d 455, 467 (D.C. Cir. 1996) (holding that Religion Clauses bar nun's Title VII claim for denial of university tenure); *Young v. Northern Ill. Conf. of United Methodist Church*, 21 F.3d 184, 187-88 (7th Cir. 1994) (holding that Free Exercise Clause precluded Title VII sex and race discrimination claim for denial of promotion and discontinuance of minister status); *Scharon v. St. Luke's Episcopal Presbyterian Hosps.*, 929 F.2d 360, 363 (8th Cir. 1991) [**8] ("To allow Scharon's case to continue would necessarily lead to the kind of inquiry into religious matters that the First Amendment forbids."); *Rayburn v. General Conf. of Seventh-Day Adventists*, 772 F.2d 1164, 1171 (4th Cir. 1985) (holding that Religion Clauses barred Title VII sex and race discrimination claims for denial of pastoral position).

As the district court wrote, "the ministerial exception is a well-established compromise between two extremely important interests—the interest in eradicating discrimination in employment and the right of a church to manage its religious affairs free from governmental interference." The panel opinion deviates from that well-established compromise, counter to Supreme Court authority and that of our sister circuits. Because the panel's decision portends serious consequences for one of the bedrock principles of our country's formation—religious freedom—it is undeniably an issue of exceptional importance.

I therefore respectfully dissent from the denial of the petition for rehearing en banc.

---

### NOTES AND QUESTIONS

1. How does Bollard's claim differ from that raised in *Gellington*? Notwithstanding the specific allegation of sexual harassment, does the suit still require courts to examine the church's procedures governing the training and selection of clergy, or can the harassment claims be addressed without courts engaging in such searching inquiries? Are there policy reasons for extending the clergy exemption to cases such as *Bollard*, or are the stronger policy arguments in favor of the *Bollard* holding?

2. Remember the *Moses* case from the previous chapter (involving a parishioner's claim of sexual misconduct by a minister). Is the *Bollard* case closer to *Moses*, or does Bollard's status as a seminarian change the level of inquiry that courts will be required to undertake to address the claims?

# Part III

# The Establishment Clause I

CHAPTER 11

# GOVERNMENT FUNDING OF RELIGIOUS SCHOOLS: THE RISE AND APPLICATION OF THE "NO-AID" PRINCIPLE

No issue has had a greater impact on the development of Establishment Clause jurisprudence than that concerning the government funding of private religious schooling. Government aid to religious and parochial schools has long been one of the more intractable church-state conflicts, and it is within this issue that the Supreme Court has delivered some of its more important, and controversial, rulings.

Questions about state funding of private religious schooling are as old as the nation's public education movement itself—in fact, local religious and church-sponsored schools predated "public" schools in many parts of the new nation. Ministers, particularly in those towns with church establishments, frequently served as the school teachers in what were effectively early public-private partnerships. Government-funded "common" schools often emerged out of (and replaced) these pre-existing relationships. In the nineteenth century, a rule developed that government funds would pay only for public schooling, and not for private religious schooling. The development of America's public schools was also intimately intertwined with the rise of Catholic parochial schooling and the much larger issues of cultural hegemony and the assimilation of immigrant children into the American democratic experiment.

The early funding issue—or the "School Question" or "School Controversy" as it was called during the nineteenth century—was inseparable from issues concerning the religious character of American public schooling. Should public schools teach universal religious tenets and values, in addition to teaching secular subjects? Many early Founders such as Benjamin Rush and Samuel Morse thought so, with Rush writing that "the only foundation for a useful education in a republic is to be laid in RELIGION."[1] In contrast, Thomas Jefferson, in proposing a plan in 1779 for public schools in Virginia, wrote that "[i]nstead . . . of putting the Bible and Testament into the hands of the children at an age when their judgements are not sufficiently matured for religious inquiries, their memories may here be stored with the most useful facts from Grecian, Roman, European and American history."[2]

Jefferson was an anomaly, however. Most early leaders of American public education sincerely believed that they could identify, distill, and teach those essential principles of morality and religion without reverting to sectarian instruction. They viewed their "common schools" as religiously inclusive and open to children of all faiths, as compared to the religiously exclusive denominational schools that existed in many cities.[3] Still, these early educators were, by and large, devoutly religious men, primarily Protestant New Englanders raised in Congregational, Presbyterian, Methodist, and Unitarian traditions, so their conception of nonsectarian education had a distinctly Protestant flavor. This undeniable fact (although many educators at the time denied that their nonsectarian approach was offensive to non-Protestants), along with efforts by public school officials to assimilate Catholic immigrant children into their Protestant vision of America, alienated Catholic leaders and led them to found a system of parochial schools in the mid-nineteenth century. Catholic leaders then petitioned school boards and state legislatures for a pro rata share of the school fund for their parochial schools. Although Catholic leaders were successful with their funding requests in some cities with large immigrant populations, by and large, their requests fell on deaf ears. Public officials, including public school officials, argued that: (1) the public funding of sectarian education violated notions of church-state separation; (2) that public funds should support only those "common" schools open to all children; and (3) that funding of parochial schools would threaten the financial security of the nation's nascent public schools while leading to the balkanization of American schooling which, in turn, would undermine efforts to inculcate common democratic values. Although the School Controversy raged throughout the nineteenth century, the dye had been cast by the middle of that century. Whether by state constitutional amendment, state statute, or court decision, government funding was reserved for public schools only.

Despite this long history, it was not until 1947 that the U.S. Supreme Court first considered the First Amendment implications of public financial assistance to religious education. In *Everson v. Board of Education*,[4] Justice Hugo Black wrote for the Court that "[n]either a state nor the Federal Government can . . . pass laws which aid one religion, aid all religions, or prefer one religion over another. . . . No tax in any amount, large or small, can be levied to support any religious activities or institutions, whatever they may be called, or whatever form they may adopt to teach or practice religion."[5] Justice Black traced this prohibition on funding religious education to the Jeffersonian impulse that "to compel a man to furnish contributions of money for the propagation of opinions which he disbelieves and abhors, is sinful and tyrannical" and that "even forcing him to support . . . that teacher of his own religious persuasion is depriving him of the comfortable liberty of giving his contributions to the particular pastor whose morals he would make his pattern."[6] Although *Everson* announced what later would be called the "no-aid" rule, the holding itself upheld giving a limited financial benefit to religious schools, thus reflecting the complexities surrounding this issue.

The nineteenth century school funding controversy also had an ugly side. Protestant nativists used the "School Question" in their battles against Catholic and foreign immigration. In fact, several infamous conflicts between nativists and immigrants erupted over school funding incidents; for example, in 1844, Protestant nativists and Catholic immigrants battled each other in the streets of Philadelphia for several days, resulting in the loss of lives and the burning of churches, convents, and parochial schools. Later, the nativist Know-Nothing party rose to power as strong advocates of public schooling and church-state separation. As a result of this sordid history, some modern critics of the Court's funding decisions have sought to tar the no-aid principle with the taint of anti-Catholicism. In *Mitchell v. Helms*, for example, Justice Clarence Thomas wrote that the nonsectarian principle was "born of bigotry, and should be buried now."[7] More recently, the legitimacy of state prohibitions on funding religious education was called into question in *Locke v. Davey*.[8] To be sure, some who opposed funding of religious schooling were motivated by animus against Catholics and other immigrants. But the no-funding principle predates the rise of Catholic parochial schooling in America and many who opposed religious school funding did so out of fealty to Mr. Jefferson's command, not animosity toward any religious faith. The controversy still rages, however. Those interested in this issue are invited to read the amicus briefs in *Locke v. Davey* and the papers from a symposium published in the *First Amendment Law Review* in 2004.[9]

Probably more than with any other area of church-state law, the Court's school funding decisions represent a microcosm of the developments and fluctuations in Establishment Clause jurisprudence. Compare the Court's near absolute-sounding language in *Everson* and its struggle to identify a workable analytical standard in *Lemon v. Kurtzman*[10] to later manifestations in *Grand Rapids School District v. Ball*[11] and then in *Agostini v. Felton*.[12] Within this section, you will observe the "high water mark" of no-aid separationism (*Meek v. Pittenger*[13]). The subsequent chapter will trace the gradual development of the alternative theories of "even-handed neutrality" and "private choice." In those cases, beginning with *Committee for Public Education and Religious Liberty v. Nyquist*,[14] the Court struggled with whether forms of "indirect aid" such as tax deductions and vouchers are consistent with Establishment Clause principles. Consider whether in today's modern welfare-state with the myriad public aid and grant programs the no-aid rule remains a viable part of the nonestablishment principle or is now an anachronism.

## DEVELOPING PRINCIPLES

*Cochran v. Louisiana State Board of Education*[15] involved a challenge to a Louisiana law authorizing the state to purchase and distribute free textbooks to schoolchildren, including those attending religious schools. The law was challenged under the Fourteenth Amendment Due Process Clause, rather than the First Amendment Establishment Clause, alleging that the state was "taking private [taxes] for a private purpose." In an opinion written by Chief Justice Charles Evans Hughes, the Court rejected the challenge, finding that the "appropriations were made for the specific purpose of purchasing school books for the use of the school children of the state, free of cost to them. It was for their benefit and the resulting benefit to the state that the appropriations were made."[16]

Although acknowledging that some of the children attended private religious schools, the Court stated that the schools "are not the beneficiaries of these appropriations. They obtain nothing from them, nor are they relieved of a single obligation, because of them. The school children and the state alone are the beneficiaries. It is also true that the sectarian schools, which some of the children attend, instruct their pupils in religion, and books are used for that purpose, but one may search diligently the acts, though without result, in an effort to find anything to the effect that it is the purpose of the state to furnish religious books for the use of such children." This language, along with the result the Court reached, has caused some to say *Cochran* was the originator of the "child benefit theory." That is, if one can show that government benefits are directed at children alone, and not any religious institution, the assistance is constitutional. Also significant for the Court was the fact that the law "does not segregate private schools, or their pupils, as its beneficiaries or attempt to interfere with any matters of exclusively private concern. Its interest is education."

Importantly, however, the Court noted that none of the books provided "was adapted to religious instruction."[17]

Seventeen years later, the Supreme Court issued its landmark ruling in *Everson v. Board of Education*. *Everson* is truly a seminal religion clause case for several reasons. First, it is the modern Supreme Court's initial interpretation of the Establishment Clause. That fact on its own makes the case significant, for it immediately legitimized reliance on certain types of authority and reintroduced an entire generation to writings of James Madison and Thomas Jefferson. Also, because the case dealt with a provision of New Jersey law, the Court had to determine whether the Establishment Clause applied to state as well as federal law. Seven years earlier in *Cantwell v. Connecticut*[18] the Court had found that the Free Exercise Clause applied to state law in addition to federal law. In the *Everson* decision, the Court held that the Due Process Clause of the Fourteenth Amendment also "incorporated" the principles enshrined in the Establishment Clause. Thus, the Establishment Clause applied to official actions and laws of the states and local governments. *Everson* also is significant for announcing two leading theories of church-state analysis: no-aid separationism; and neutrality. More than sixty years later, members of the Court are still battling over the meaning and relevance of these concepts for church-state adjudication. In other words, William Shakespeare's admonition applies here: "The past is prologue."[19]

## EVERSON v. BOARD OF EDUCATION OF EWING TOWNSHIP
## 330 U.S. 1 (1947)

JUSTICE BLACK delivered the opinion of the Court.

A New Jersey statute authorizes its local school districts to make rules and contracts for the transportation of children to and from schools. The appellee, a township board of education, acting pursuant to this statute authorized reimbursement to parents of money expended by them for the bus transportation of their children on regular busses operated by the public transportation system. Part of this money was for the payment of transportation of some children in the community to Catholic parochial schools. These church schools give their students, in addition to secular education, regular religious instruction conforming to the religious tenets and modes of worship of the Catholic Faith. . . .

The appellant, in his capacity as a district taxpayer, filed suit in a state court challenging the right of the Board to reimburse parents of parochial school students. He contended that the statute and the resolution passed pursuant to it violated both the State and the Federal Constitutions. . . . The New Jersey Court of Errors and Appeals [held] that neither the statute nor the resolution passed pursuant to it was in conflict with the State constitution or the provisions of the Federal Constitution. . . .

The contention here is that the state statute and the resolution, in so far as they authorized reimbursement to parents of children attending parochial schools, . . . forced inhabitants to pay taxes to help support and maintain schools which are dedicated to, and which regularly teach, the Catholic Faith. This is alleged to be a use of State power to support church schools contrary to the prohibition of the First Amendment which the Fourteenth Amendment made applicable to the states. . . .

First. . . . It is much too late to argue that legislation intended to facilitate the opportunity of children to get a secular education serves no public purpose. The same thing is no less true of legislation to reimburse needy parents, or all parents, for payment of the fares of their children so that they can ride in public busses to and from schools rather than run the risk of traffic and other hazards incident to walking or "hitchhiking." . . .

Second. The New Jersey statute is challenged as a "law respecting an establishment of religion." The First Amendment, as made applicable to the states by the Fourteenth, *Murdock v. Commonwealth of Pennsylvania*, 319 U.S. 105, commands that a state "shall make no law respecting an establishment of religion, or prohibiting the free exercise thereof." These words of the First Amendment reflected in the minds of early Americans a vivid mental picture of conditions and practices which they fervently wished to stamp out in order to preserve liberty for themselves and for their posterity. Doubtless their goal has not been entirely reached; but so far has the Nation moved toward it that the expression "law respecting an establishment of religion," probably does not so vividly remind present-day Americans of the evils, fears, and political problems that caused that expression to be written into our Bill of Rights. Whether this New Jersey law is one respecting the "establishment of religion" requires an understanding of the meaning of that language, particularly with respect to the imposition of taxes. . . .

A large proportion of the early settlers of this country came here from Europe to escape the bondage of laws which compelled them to support and attend government favored churches. The centuries immediately before and contemporaneous with the colonization of America had been filled with turmoil, civil strife, and persecutions, generated in large part by established sects determined to maintain their absolute political and religious supremacy. With the power of government supporting them, at various times and places, Catholics had persecuted Protestants, Protestants had persecuted Catholics, Protestant sects had persecuted other Protestant sects, Catholics of one shade of belief had persecuted Catholics of another shade of belief, and all of these had from time to time persecuted Jews. In efforts to force loyalty to whatever religious group happened to be on top and in league with the government of a particular time and place, men and women had been fined, cast in jail, cruelly tortured, and killed. Among the offenses for which these punishments had been inflicted were such things as speaking disrespectfully of the views of ministers of government-established churches, non-attendance at those churches, expressions of non-belief in their doctrines, and failure to pay taxes and tithes to support them.

These practices of the old world were transplanted to and began to thrive in the soil of the new America. The very charters granted by the English Crown to the individuals and companies designated to make the laws which would control the destinies of the colonials authorized these individuals and companies to erect religious establishments which all, whether believers or non-believers, would be required to support and attend. An exercise of this authority was accompanied by a repetition of many of the old world practices and persecutions. Catholics found themselves hounded and proscribed because of their faith; Quakers who followed their conscience went to jail; Baptists were peculiarly obnoxious to certain dominant Protestant sects; men and women of varied faiths who happened to be in a minority in a particular locality were persecuted because they steadfastly persisted in worshipping God only as their own consciences dictated. And all of these dissenters were compelled to pay tithes and taxes to support government-sponsored churches whose ministers preached inflammatory sermons designed to strengthen and consolidate the established faith by generating a burning hatred against dissenters.

These practices became so commonplace as to shock the freedom-loving colonials into a feeling of abhorrence. The imposition of taxes to pay ministers' salaries and to build and maintain churches and church property aroused their indignation. It was these feelings which found expression in the First Amendment. No one locality and no one group throughout the Colonies can rightly be given entire credit for having aroused the sentiment that culminated in adoption of the Bill of Rights' provisions embracing religious liberty. But Virginia, where the established church had achieved a dominant influence in political affairs and where many excesses attracted wide public attention, provided a great stimulus and able leadership for the movement. The people there, as elsewhere, reached the conviction that individual religious liberty could be achieved best under a government which was stripped of all power to tax, to support, or otherwise to assist any or all religions, or to interfere with the beliefs of any religious individual or group.

The movement toward this end reached its dramatic climax in Virginia in 1785-86 when the Virginia legislative body was about to renew Virginia's tax levy for the support of the established church. Thomas Jefferson and James Madison led the fight against this tax. Madison wrote his great Memorial and Remonstrance against the law. In it, he eloquently argued that a true religion did not need the support of law; that no person, either believer or non-believer, should be taxed to support a religious institution of any kind; that the best interest of a society required that the minds of men always be wholly free; and that cruel persecutions were the inevitable result of government-established religions. Madison's Remonstrance received strong support throughout Virginia, and the Assembly postponed consideration of the proposed tax measure until its next session. When the proposal came up for consideration at that session, it not only died in committee, but the Assembly enacted the famous "Virginia Bill for Religious Liberty" originally written by Thomas Jefferson. The preamble to that Bill stated among other things that:

> Almighty God hath created the mind free; that all attempts to influence it by temporal punishments, or burthens, or by civil incapacitations, tend only to beget habits of hypocrisy and meanness, and are a departure from the plan of the Holy author of our religion who being Lord both of body and mind, yet chose not to propagate it by coercions on either . . . ; that to compel a man to furnish contributions of money for the propagation of opinions which he disbelieves, is sinful and tyrannical; that even the forcing him to support this or that teacher of his own religious persuasion, is depriving him of the comfortable liberty of giving his contributions to the particular pastor, whose morals he would make his pattern. . . .

And the statute itself enacted

> That no man shall be compelled to frequent or support any religious worship, place, or ministry whatsoever, nor shall be enforced, restrained, molested, or burthened, in his body or goods, nor shall otherwise suffer on account of his religious opinions or belief. . .

This Court has previously recognized that the provisions of the First Amendment, in the drafting and adoption of which Madison and Jefferson played such leading roles, had the same objective and were intended to provide the same protection against governmental intrusion on religious liberty as the Virginia statute. *Reynolds v. United States*, 98 U.S., 164; *Watson v. Jones*, 13 Wall. 679; *Davis v. Beason*, 133 U.S. 333, 342. Prior to the adoption of the Fourteenth Amendment, the First Amendment did not apply as a restraint against the states. Most of them did soon provide similar constitutional protections for religious liberty. But some states persisted for about half a century in imposing restraints upon the free exercise of religion and in discriminating against particular religious groups. In recent years, so far as the provision against the establishment of a religion is concerned, the question has most frequently arisen in connection with proposed state aid to church schools and efforts to carry on religious teachings in the public schools in accordance with the tenets of a particular sect. Some churches have either sought or accepted state financial support for their schools. Here again the efforts to obtain state aid or acceptance of it have not been limited to any one particular faith. The state courts, in the main, have remained faithful to the language of their own constitutional provisions designed to protect religious freedom and to separate religious and governments. Their decisions, however, show the difficulty in drawing the line between tax legislation which provides funds for the welfare of the general public and that which is designed to support institutions which teach religion.

The meaning and scope of the First Amendment, preventing establishment of religion or prohibiting the free exercise thereof, in the light of its history and the evils it was designed forever to suppress, have been several times elaborated by the decisions of this Court prior to the application of the First Amendment to the states by the Fourteenth. The broad meaning given the Amendment by these earlier cases has been accepted by this Court in its decisions concerning an individual's religious freedom rendered since the Fourteenth Amendment was interpreted to make the prohibitions of the First applicable to state action abridging religious freedom. There is every reason to give the same application and broad interpretation to the "establishment of religion" clause. The interrelation of these complementary clauses was well summarized in a statement quoted in *Watson v. Jones*, 13 Wall. 679, 730: "The structure of our government has, for the preservation of civil liberty, rescued the temporal institutions from religious interference. On the other hand, it has secured religious liberty from the invasions of the civil authority."

The "establishment of religion" clause of the First Amendment means at least this: Neither a state nor the Federal Government can set up a church. Neither can pass laws which aid one religion, aid all religions, or prefer one religion over another. Neither can force nor influence a person to go to or to remain away from church against his will or force him to profess a belief or disbelief in any religion. No person can be punished for entertaining or professing religious beliefs or disbeliefs, for church attendance or non-attendance. No tax in any amount, large or small, can be levied to support any religious activities or institutions, whatever they may be called, or whatever form they may adopt to teach or practice religion. Neither a state nor the Federal Government can, openly or secretly, participate in the affairs of any religious organizations or groups and vice versa. In the words of Jefferson, the clause against establishment of religion by law was intended to erect "a wall of separation between Church and State." *Reynolds v. United States*, 98 U.S., 164.

experience in many ages and many lands and with all sorts and conditions of men, takes what, from the viewpoint of its own progress and the success of its mission, is a wise estimate of the importance of education to religion. It does not leave the individual to pick up religion by chance. It relies on early and indelible indoctrination in the faith and order of the Church by the word and example of persons consecrated to the task.

Our public school, if not a product of Protestantism, at least is more consistent with it than with the Catholic culture and scheme of values. It is a relatively recent development dating from about 1840. It is organized on the premise that secular education can be isolated from all religious teaching so that the school can inculcate all needed temporal knowledge and also maintain a strict and lofty neutrality as to religion. The assumption is that after the individual has been instructed in worldly wisdom he will be better fitted to choose his religion. Whether such a disjunction is possible, and if possible whether it is wise, are questions I need not try to answer.

I should be surprised if any Catholic would deny that the parochial school is a vital, if not the most vital, part of the Roman Catholic Church. If put to the choice, that venerable institution, I should expect, would forego its whole service for mature persons before it would give up education of the young, and it would be a wise choice. Its growth and cohesion, discipline and loyalty, spring from its schools. Catholic education is the rock on which the whole structure rests, and to render tax aid to its Church school is indistinguishable to me from rendering the same aid to the Church itself.

### III

It is of no importance in this situation whether the beneficiary of this expenditure of tax-raised funds is primarily the parochial school and incidentally the pupil, or whether the aid is directly bestowed on the pupil with indirect benefits to the school. The state cannot maintain a Church and it can no more tax its citizens to furnish free carriage to those who attend a Church. The prohibition against establishment of religion cannot be circumvented by a subsidy, bonus or reimbursement of expense to individuals for receiving religious instruction and indoctrination.

The Court, however, compares this to other subsidies and loans to individuals. . . . Of course, the state may pay out tax-raised funds to relieve pauperism, but it may not under our Constitution do so to induce or reward piety.
. . .

It seems to me that the basic fallacy in the Court's reasoning, which accounts for its failure to apply the principles it avows, is in ignoring the essentially religious test by which beneficiaries of this expenditure are selected. A policeman protects a Catholic, of course—but not because he is a Catholic; it is because he is a man and a member of our society. The fireman protects the Church school—but not because it is a Church school; it is because it is property, part of the assets of our society. Neither the fireman nor the policeman has to ask before he renders aid "Is this man or building identified with the Catholic Church." . . . That there is no parallel between police and fire protection and this plan of reimbursement is apparent from the incongruity of the limitation of this Act if applied to police and fire service. Could we sustain an Act that said police shall protect pupils on the way to or from public schools and Catholic schools but not while going to and coming from other schools, and firemen shall extinguish a blaze in public or Catholic school buildings but shall not put out a blaze in Protestant Church schools or private schools operated for profit? That is the true analogy to the case we have before us and I should think it pretty plain that such a scheme would not be valid.

The Court's holding is that this taxpayer has no grievance because the state has decided to make the reimbursement a public purpose and therefore we are bound to regard it as such. I agree that this Court has left, and always should leave to each state, great latitude in deciding for itself, in the light of its own conditions, what shall be public purposes in its scheme of things. It may socialize utilities and economic enterprises and make taxpayers' business out of what conventionally had been private business. It may make public business of individual welfare, health, education, entertainment or security. But it cannot make public business of religious worship or instruction, or of attendance at religious institutions of any character. There is no answer to the proposition more fully expounded by MR. JUSTICE RUTLEDGE that the effect of the religious freedom Amendment to our Constitution was to take every form of propagation of religion out of the realm of things which could directly or indirectly be made public business and thereby be supported in whole or in part at taxpayers' expense. That is a difference which the Constitution sets up between religion and almost every other subject matter of legislation, a difference which goes to the very root of religious freedom and which the Court is overlooking today. This freedom was first in the Bill of Rights because it was first in the forefathers' minds; it was set forth in absolute terms, and its strength is its rigidity. It was intended not only to keep the states' hands out of religion, but to keep religion's hands off the state, and above all, to keep bitter religious controversy out of public life by denying to every denomination any advantage from getting control of public policy or the public purse. Those great ends I cannot but think are immeasurably compromised by today's decision.

This policy of our Federal Constitution has never been wholly pleasing to most religious groups. They all are quick to invoke its protections; they all are irked when they feel its restraints. . . .

But we cannot have it both ways. Religious teaching cannot be a private affair when the state seeks to impose regulations which infringe on it indirectly, and a public affair when it comes to taxing citizens of one faith to aid another, or those of no faith to aid all. If these principles seem harsh in prohibiting aid to Catholic education, it must not be forgotten that it is the same Constitution that alone assures Catholics the right to maintain these schools at all when predominant local sentiment would forbid them. *Pierce v. Society of Sisters*, 268 U.S. 510. Nor should I think that those who have done so well without this aid would want to see this separation between Church and State broken down. If the state may aid these religious schools, it may therefore regulate them. Many groups have sought aid from tax funds only to find that it carried political controls with it. Indeed this Court has declared that "It is hardly lack of due process for the Government to regulate that which it subsidizes." . . .

▓ JUSTICE FRANKFURTER joins in this opinion.

▓ JUSTICE RUTLEDGE, with whom JUSTICE FRANKFURTER, JUSTICE JACKSON and JUSTICE BURTON agree, dissenting.

"Congress shall make no law respecting an establishment of religion, or prohibiting the free exercise thereof. . . ." U.S. Const. Amend. I.

"Well aware that Almighty God hath created the mind free; . . . that to compel a man to furnish contributions of money for the propagation of opinions which he disbelieves, is sinful and tyrannical; . . ."

"*We, the General Assembly, do enact,* That no man shall be compelled to frequent or support any religious worship, place, or ministry whatsoever, nor shall be enforced, restrained, molested, or burthened in his body or goods, nor shall otherwise suffer on account of his religious opinions or belief. . . ."[1]

I cannot believe that the great author of those words, or the men who made them law, could have joined in this decision. Neither so high nor so impregnable today as yesterday is the wall raised between church and state by Virginia's great statute of religious freedom and the First Amendment, now made applicable to all the states by the Fourteenth. New Jersey's statute sustained is the first, if indeed it is not the second breach to be made by this Court's action. That a third, and a fourth, and still others will be attempted, we may be sure. For just as *Cochran v. Louisiana State Board of Education,* 281 U.S. 370, has opened the way by oblique ruling for this decision, so will the two make wider the breach for a third. Thus with time the most solid freedom steadily gives way before continuing corrosive decision.

This case forces us to determine squarely for the first time what was "an establishment of religion" in the First Amendment's conception; and by that measure to decide whether New Jersey's action violates its command. . . .

I

Not simply an established church, but any law respecting an establishment of religion is forbidden. The Amendment was broadly but not loosely phrased. It is the compact and exact summation of its author's views formed during his long struggle for religious freedom. In Madison's own words characterizing Jefferson's Bill for Establishing Religious Freedom, the guaranty he put in our national charter, like the bill he piloted through the Virginia Assembly, was "a Model of technical precision, and perspicuous brevity." Madison could not have confused "church" and "religion," or "an established church" and "an establishment of religion."

The Amendment's purpose was not to strike merely at the official establishment of a single sect, creed or religion, outlawing only a formal relation such as had prevailed in England and some of the colonies. Necessarily it was to uproot all such relationships. But the object was broader than separating church and state in this narrow sense. It was to create a complete and permanent separation of the spheres of religious activity and civil authority by comprehensively forbidding every form of public aid or support for religion. In proof the Amendment's wording and history unite with this Court's consistent utterances whenever attention has been fixed directly upon the question.

"Religion" appears only once in the Amendment. But the word governs two prohibitions and governs them alike. It does not have two meanings, one narrow to forbid "an establishment" and another, much broader, for securing "the free exercise thereof." "Thereof" brings down "religion" with its entire and exact content, no more and no less, from the first into the second guaranty, so that Congress and now the states are as broadly restricted concerning the one as they are regarding the other.

---

[1] "A Bill for Establishing Religious Freedom," enacted by the General Assembly of Virginia, January 19, 1786. . . .

No one would claim today that the Amendment is constricted, in "prohib-iting the free exercise" of religion, to securing the free exercise of some formal or creedal observance, of one sect or of many. It secures all forms of religious expression, creedal, sectarian or nonsectarian wherever and however taking place, except conduct which trenches upon the like freedoms of others or clearly and presently endangers the community's good order and security. . . .

"Religion" has the same broad significance in the twin prohibition con-cerning "an establishment." The Amendment was not duplicitous. "Religion" and "establishment" were not used in any formal or technical sense. The prohi-bition broadly forbids state support, financial or other, of religion in any guise, form or degree. It outlaws all use of public funds for religious purposes.

## II

No provision of the Constitution is more closely tied to or given content by its generating history than the religious clause of the First Amendment. It is at once the refined product and the terse summation of that history. The history includes not only Madison's authorship and the proceedings before the First Congress, but also the long and intensive struggle for religious freedom in America, more especially in Virginia, of which the Amendment was the di-rect culmination. In the documents of the times, particularly of Madison, who was leader in the Virginia struggle before he became the Amendment's spon-sor, but also in the writings of Jefferson and others and in the issues which engendered them is to be found irrefutable confirmation of the Amendment's sweeping content.

For Madison, as also for Jefferson, religious freedom was the crux of the struggle for freedom in general. Remonstrance, Par. 15. Madison was coau-thor with George Mason of the religious clause in Virginia's great Declaration of Rights of 1776. He is credited with changing it from a mere statement of the principle of tolerance to the first official legislative pronouncement that freedom of conscience and religion are inherent rights of the individual. He sought also to have the Declaration expressly condemn the existing Virginia establishment. But the forces supporting it were then too strong. . . .

The climax came in the legislative struggle of 1784–1785 over the As-sessment Bill. This was nothing more nor less than a taxing measure for the support of religion, designed to revive the payment of tithes suspended since 1777. So long as it singled out a particular sect for preference it incurred the active and general hostility of dissentient groups. It was broadened to include them, with the result that some subsided temporarily in their opposition. As altered, the bill gave to each taxpayer the privilege of designating which church should receive his share of the tax. In default of designation the legislature ap-plied it to pious uses. But what is of the utmost significance here, "in its final form the bill left the taxpayer the option of giving his tax to education."

Madison was unyielding at all times, opposing with all his vigor the gen-eral and nondiscriminatory as he had the earlier particular and discriminatory assessments proposed. . . . [B]efore the Assembly reconvened in the fall [of 1785] he issued his historic Memorial and Remonstrance.

This is Madison's complete, though not his only, interpretation of relig-ious liberty. It is a broadside attack upon all forms of "establishment" of religion, both general and particular, nondiscriminatory or selective. Reflect-ing not only the many legislative conflicts over the Assessment Bill and the Bill for Establishing Religious Freedom but also, for example, the struggles for religious incorporations and the continued maintenance of the glebes, the

Remonstrance is at once the most concise and the most accurate statement of the views of the First Amendment's author concerning what is "an establishment of religion." . . .

The Remonstrance, stirring up a storm of popular protest, killed the Assessment Bill. It collapsed in committee shortly before Christmas, 1785. With this, the way was cleared at last for enactment of Jefferson's Bill for Establishing Religious Freedom. Madison promptly drove it through in January of 1786, seven years from the time it was first introduced. This dual victory substantially ended the fight over establishments, settling the issue against them.

The next year Madison became a member of the Constitutional Convention. Its work done, he fought valiantly to secure the ratification of its great product in Virginia as elsewhere, and nowhere else more effectively. Madison was certain in his own mind that under the Constitution "there is not a shadow of right in the general government to intermeddle with religion" and that "this subject is, for the honor of America, perfectly free and unshackled. The Government has no jurisdiction over it. . . ." Nevertheless he pledged that he would work for a Bill of Rights, including a specific guaranty of religious freedom, and Virginia, with other states, ratified the Constitution on this assurance.

Ratification thus accomplished, Madison was sent to the first Congress. There he went at once about performing his pledge to establish freedom for the nation as he had done in Virginia. Within a little more than three years from his legislative victory at home he had proposed and secured the submission and ratification of the First Amendment as the first article of our Bill of Rights.

All the great instruments of the Virginia struggle for religious liberty thus became warp and woof of our constitutional tradition, not simply by the course of history, but by the common unifying force of Madison's life, thought and sponsorship. He epitomized the whole of that tradition in the Amendment's compact, but nonetheless comprehensive, phrasing.

As the Remonstrance discloses throughout, Madison opposed every form and degree of official relation between religion and civil authority. For him religion was a wholly private matter beyond the scope of civil power either to restrain or to support. Denial or abridgment of religious freedom was a violation of rights both of conscience and of natural equality. State aid was no less obnoxious or destructive to freedom and to religion itself than other forms of state interference. "Establishment" and "free exercise" were correlative and coextensive ideas, representing only different facets of the single great and fundamental freedom. The Remonstrance, following the Virginia statute's example, referred to the history of religious conflicts and the effects of all sorts of establishments, current and historical, to suppress religion's free exercise. With Jefferson, Madison believed that to tolerate any fragment of establishment would be by so much to perpetuate restraint upon that freedom. Hence he sought to tear out the institution not partially but root and branch, and to bar its return forever.

In no phase was he more unrelentingly absolute than in opposing state support or aid by taxation. Not even "three pence" contribution was thus to be exacted from any citizen for such a purpose. Remonstrance, Par. 3 Tithes had been the life blood of establishment before and after other compulsions disappeared. Madison and his coworkers made no exceptions or abridgments to the complete separation they created. Their objection was not to small tithes.

It was to any tithes whatsoever. "If it were lawful to impose a small tax for religion the admission would pave the way for oppressive levies." Not the amount but "the principle of assessment was wrong." And the principle was as much to prevent "the interference of law in religion" as to restrain religious intervention in political matters. In this field the authors of our freedom would not tolerate "the first experiment on our liberties" or "wait till usurped power had strengthened itself by exercise, and entangled the question in precedents." Remonstrance, Par. 3. Nor should we.

In view of this history no further proof is needed that the Amendment forbids any appropriation, large or small, from public funds to aid or support any and all religious exercises. . . .

## III . . .

Does New Jersey's action furnish support for religion by use of the taxing power? Certainly it does, if the test remains undiluted as Jefferson and Madison made it, that money taken by taxation from one is not to be used or given to support another's religious training or belief, or indeed one's own. Today as then the furnishing of "contributions of money for the propagation of opinions which he disbelieves" is the forbidden exaction; and the prohibition is absolute for whatever measure brings that consequence and whatever mount may be sought or given to that end. . . .

Believers of all faiths, and others who do not express their feeling toward ultimate issues of existence in any creedal form, pay the New Jersey tax. When the money so raised is used to pay for transportation to religious schools, the Catholic taxpayer to the extent of his proportionate share pays for the transportation of Lutheran, Jewish and otherwise religiously affiliated children to receive their non-Catholic religious instruction. Their parents likewise pay proportionately for the transportation of Catholic children to receive Catholic instruction. Each thus contributes to "the propagation of opinions which he disbelieves" in so far as their religions differ, as do others who accept no creed without regard to those differences. Each thus pays taxes also to support the teaching of his own religion, an exaction equally forbidden since it denies "the comfortable liberty" of giving one's contribution to the particular agency of instruction he approves.

New Jersey's action therefore exactly fits the type of exaction and the kind of evil at which Madison and Jefferson struck. Under the test they framed it cannot be said that the cost of transportation is no part of the cost of education or of the religious instruction given. That it is a substantial and a necessary element is shown most plainly by the continuing and increasing demand for the state to assume it. Nor is there pretense that it relates only to the secular instruction given in religious schools or that any attempt is or could be made toward allocating proportional shares as between the secular and the religious instruction. It is precisely because the instruction is religious and relates to a particular faith, whether one or another, that parents send their children to religious schools under the *Pierce* doctrine. And the very purpose of the state's contribution is to defray the cost of conveying the pupil to the place where he will receive not simply secular, but also and primarily religious, teaching and guidance.

Indeed the view is sincerely avowed by many of various faiths, that the basic purpose of all education is or should be religious, that the secular cannot be and should not be separated from the religious phase and emphasis. Hence,

the inadequacy of public or secular education and the necessity for sending the child to a school where religion is taught. But whatever may be the philosophy or its justification, there is undeniably an admixture of religious with secular teaching in all such institutions. That is the very reason for their being.
. . .

Yet this very admixture is what was disestablished when the First Amendment forbade "an establishment of religion." Commingling the religious with the secular teaching does not divest the whole of its religious permeation and emphasis or make them of minor part, if proportion were material. Indeed, on any other view, the constitutional prohibition always could be brought to naught by adding a modicum of the secular. . . .

Finally, transportation, where it is needed, is as essential to education as any other element. Its cost is as much a part of the total expense, except at times in amount, as the cost of textbooks, of school lunches, of athletic equipment, of writing and other materials; indeed of all other items composing the total burden. Now as always the core of the educational process is the teacher-pupil relationship. Without this the richest equipment and facilities would go for naught. . . .

Payment of transportation is no more, nor is it any the less essential to education, whether religious or secular, than payment for tuitions, for teachers' salaries, for buildings, equipment and necessary materials. Nor is it any the less directly related, in a school giving religious instruction, to the primary religious objective all those essential items of cost are intended to achieve. No rational line can be drawn between payment for such larger, but not more necessary, items and payment for transportation. . . .

IV

But we are told that the New Jersey statute is valid in its present application because the appropriation is for a public, not a private purpose, namely, the promotion of education, and the majority accept this idea in the conclusion that all we have here is "public welfare legislation." If that is true and the Amendment's force can be thus destroyed, what has been said becomes all the more pertinent. For then there could be no possible objection to more extensive support of religious education by New Jersey.

If the fact alone be determinative that religious schools are engaged in education, thus promoting the general and individual welfare, together with the legislature's decision that the payment of public moneys for their aid makes their work a public function, then I can see no possible basis, except one of dubious legislative policy, for the state's refusal to make full appropriation for support of private, religious schools, just as is done for public instruction. There could not be, on that basis, valid constitutional objection. . . .

In truth this view contradicts the whole purpose and effect of the First Amendment as heretofore conceived. The "public function"—"public welfare"—"social legislation" argument seeks in Madison's words, to "employ Religion (that is, here, religious education) as an engine of Civil policy." Remonstrance, Par. 5. It is of one piece with the Assessment Bill's preamble, although with the vital difference that it wholly ignores what that preamble explicitly states.

Our constitutional policy is exactly the opposite. It does not deny the value or the necessity for religious training, teaching or observance. Rather it secures their free exercise. But to that end it does deny that the state can undertake or sustain them in any form or degree. For this reason the sphere of religious activity, as distinguished from the secular intellectual liberties, has been given the twofold protection and, as the state cannot forbid, neither can it perform or aid in performing the religious function. The dual prohibition makes that function altogether private. It cannot be made a public one by legislative act. This was the very heart of Madison's Remonstrance, as it is of the Amendment itself.

It is not because religious teaching does not promote the public or the individual's welfare, but because neither is furthered when the state promotes religious education, that the Constitution forbids it to do so. Both legislatures and courts are bound by that distinction. In failure to observe it lies the fallacy of the "public function"—"social legislation" argument, a fallacy facilitated by easy transference of the argument's basing from due process unrelated to any religious aspect to the First Amendment. . . .

The reasons underlying the Amendment's policy have not vanished with time or diminished in force. Now as when it was adopted the price of religious freedom is double. It is that the church and religion shall live both within and upon that freedom. There cannot be freedom of religion, safeguarded by the state, and intervention by the church or its agencies in the state's domain or dependency on its largesse. Madison's Remonstrance, Par. 6, 8. The great condition of religious liberty is that it be maintained free from sustenance, as also from other interferences, by the state. For when it comes to rest upon that secular foundation it vanishes with the resting. *Id.*, Par. 7, 8. Public money devoted to payment of religious costs, educational or other, brings the quest for more. It brings too the struggle of sect against sect for the larger share or for any. Here one by numbers alone will benefit most, there another. That is precisely the history of societies which have had an established religion and dissident groups. *Id.*, Par. 8, 11. It is the very thing Jefferson and Madison experienced and sought to guard against, whether in its blunt or in its more screened forms. *Ibid.* The end of such strife cannot be other than to destroy the cherished liberty. The dominating group will achieve the dominant benefit; or all will embroil the state in their dissensions. *Id.*, Par. 11. . . .

In these conflicts wherever success has been obtained it has been upon the contention that by providing the transportation the general cause of education, the general welfare, and the welfare of the individual will be forwarded; hence that the matter lies within the realm of public function, for legislative determination. State courts have divided upon the issue, some taking the view that only the individual, others that the institution receives the benefit. A few have recognized that this dichotomy is false, that both in fact are aided.

The majority here does not accept in terms any of those views. But neither does it deny that the individual or the school, or indeed both, are benefitted directly and substantially. To do so would cut the ground from under the public function–social legislation thesis. On the contrary, the opinion concedes that the children are aided by being helped to get to the religious schooling. By converse necessary implication as well as by the absence of express denial, it must be taken to concede also that the school is helped to reach the child with its religious teaching. The religious enterprise is common to both, as is the interest in having transportation for its religious purposes provided. . . .

This is not therefore just a little case over bus fares. In paraphrase of Madison, distant as it may be in its present form from a complete establishment of religion, it differs from it only in degree; and is the first step in that direction.

*Id.*, Par. 9. Today as in his time "the same authority which can force a citizen to contribute three pence only . . . for the support of any one [religious] establishment, may force him" to pay more; or "to conform to any other establishment in all cases whatsoever." And now, as then, "either . . . we must say, that the will of the Legislature is the only measure of their authority; and that in the plenitude of this authority, they may sweep away all our fundamental rights; or, that they are bound to leave this particular right untouched and sacred." Remonstrance, Par. 15.

The realm of religious training and belief remains, as the Amendment made it, the kingdom of the individual man and his God. It should be kept inviolately private, not "entangled . . . in precedents" or confounded with what legislatures legitimately may take over into the public domain.

V

No one conscious of religious values can be unsympathetic toward the burden which our constitutional separation puts on parents who desire religious instruction mixed with secular for their children. They pay taxes for others' children's education, at the same time the added cost of instruction for their own. Nor can one happily see benefits denied to children which others receive, because in conscience they or their parents for them desire a different kind of training others do not demand.

But if those feelings should prevail, there would be an end to our historic constitutional policy and command. No more unjust or discriminatory in fact is it to deny attendants at religious schools the cost of their transportation than it is to deny them tuitions, sustenance for their teachers, or any other educational expense which others receive at public cost. Hardship in fact there is which none can blink. But, for assuring to those who undergo it the greater, the most comprehensive freedom, it is one written by design and firm intent into our basic law.

Of course discrimination in the legal sense does not exist. The child attending the religious school has the same right as any other to attend the public school. But he forgoes exercising it because the same guaranty which assures this freedom forbids the public school or any agency of the state to give or aid him in securing the religious instruction he seeks.

Were he to accept the common school, he would be the first to protest the teaching there of any creed or faith not his own. And it is precisely for the reason that their atmosphere is wholly secular that children are not sent to public schools under the *Pierce* doctrine. But that is a constitutional necessity, because we have staked the very existence of our country on the faith that complete separation between the state and religion is best for the state and best for religion. Remonstrance, Par. 8, 12.

That policy necessarily entails hardship upon persons who forego the right to educational advantages the state can supply in order to secure others it is precluded from giving. Indeed this may hamper the parent and the child forced by conscience to that choice. But it does not make the state unneutral to withhold what the Constitution forbids it to give. On the contrary it is only by observing the prohibition rigidly that the state can maintain its neutrality and avoid partisanship in the dissensions inevitable when sect opposes sect over demands for public moneys to further religious education, teaching or training in any form or degree, directly or indirectly. Like St. Paul's freedom, religious liberty with a great price must be bought. And for those who exercise it most fully, by insisting upon religious education for their children mixed with secular, by the terms of our Constitution the price is greater than for others.

The problem then cannot be cast in terms of legal discrimination or its absence. This would be true, even though the state in giving aid should treat all religious instruction alike. Thus, if the present statute and its application were shown to apply equally to all religious schools of whatever faith, yet in the light of our tradition it could not stand. For then the adherent of one creed still would pay for the support of another, the childless taxpayer with others more fortunate. Then too there would seem to be no bar to making appropriations for transportation and other expenses of children attending public or other secular schools, after hours in separate places and classes for their exclusively religious instruction. The person who embraces no creed also would be forced to pay for teaching what he does not believe. Again, it was the furnishing of "contributions of money for the propagation of opinions which he disbelieves" that the fathers outlawed. That consequence and effect are not removed by multiplying to all-inclusiveness the sects for which support is exacted. The Constitution requires, not comprehensive identification of state with religion, but complete separation.

VI . . .

Two great drives are constantly in motion to abridge, in the name of education, the complete division of religion and civil authority which our forefathers made. One is to introduce religious education and observances into the public schools. The other, to obtain public funds for the aid and support of various private religious schools. In my opinion both avenues were closed by the Constitution. Neither should be opened by this Court. The matter is not one of quantity, to be measured by the amount of money expended. Now as in Madison's day it is one of principle, to keep separate the separate spheres as the First Amendment drew them; to prevent the first experiment upon our liberties; and to keep the question from becoming entangled in corrosive precedents. We should not be less strict to keep strong and untarnished the one side of the shield of religious freedom than we have been of the other.

The judgment should be reversed.

## NOTES AND QUESTIONS

1. Justice Black argues that the aid in this case is analogous to situations in which police officers protect children from traffic as they go to and from church schools and to cases in which fire fighters protect church buildings as well as other buildings. In his dissenting opinion, Justice Jackson argues that these analogies are not persuasive. Describe these arguments and offer your own assessment of the ways in which these situations are similar and dissimilar.

2. The Court majority relies partly on the fact that the state sends no government funds directly to the church-related schools. What is the legal significance of this factor? Is there a practical significance?

3. The majority suggests that, were the Court to have prevented the state from reimbursing parents of children who attend Catholic schools the costs of their children's transportation, it would have hampered the free exercise of

religion by depriving certain citizens of the benefits of public welfare based on their religious beliefs. Looking back to the chapters describing free exercise burdens, what are the arguments for and against this characterization?

4.  According to Justice Black, the provisions of the First Amendment "had the same objective and were intended to provide the same protection against governmental intrusion on religious liberty as the Virginia statute [of religious freedom.]" Justice Rutledge makes a similar argument in his dissenting opinion. What proof do the justices offer to support this proposition? How does their conviction on this point inform their interpretations of the First Amendment?

5.  Justice Jackson states: "Our public school, if not a product of Protestantism, at least is more consistent with it than with the Catholic culture and scheme of values." What is the significance of this statement in Jackson's opinion and in what way does it affect his ultimate argument?

6.  In his dissenting opinion, Justice Rutledge writes:

    Payment of transportation is no more, nor is it any the less essential to education, whether religious or secular, than payment for tuitions, for teachers' salaries, for buildings, equipment and necessary materials . . . . No rational line can be drawn between payment for such larger, but not more necessary, items and payment for transportation.

    What line does the Court majority attempt to draw in this case? Do you believe that line is a rational one? Can you think of other rational constitutional distinctions among these various other types of aid?

7.  Justice Rutledge states: "New Jersey's action [ ] exactly fits the type of exaction and the kind of evil at which Madison and Jefferson struck." What reasons does he offer to support this argument? Do you agree or disagree?

8.  According to Justice Rutledge, why is the prohibition on governmental establishment of religion good for religion? Do you find his argument persuasive? Suppose a religious entity is willing to assume the risks associated with government funding. Should Rutledge's rationale still serve as a bar against the receipt of government assistance?

9.  According to Justice Rutledge's dissenting opinion, what is the intended purpose of the Establishment Clause? How does he rebut the claim that this clause was only intended to prevent the establishment of one religion over others?

10. What does Justice Rutledge mean when he says that the religion clauses of the Constitution make religion's "function altogether private"? Are there any implications for the adoption of such a position?

*Board of Education v. Allen*[20] considered the constitutionality of a New York law requiring "local public school authorities to lend textbooks free of charge to all students [enrolled] in grades seven through 12, [including] students attending private [religious] schools."

Initially, in a decision written by Justice Byron White, the Court noted that "*Everson* and later cases have shown that the line between state neutrality to religion and state support of religion is not easy to locate. 'The constitutional standard is the separation of Church and State. The problem, like many problems in constitutional law, is one of degree.' *Zorach v. Clauson*, 343 U.S. 306, 314."[21]

The Court applied the test enunciated in *Abington Township School District v. Schempp* (1963), which considered "what are the purpose and primary effect of the enactment."[22]

The Court analogized the textbook loan to the transportation reimbursement upheld in *Everson*:

> The statute upheld in *Everson* would be considered a law having "a secular legislative purpose and a primary effect that neither advances nor inhibits religion." We reach the same result with respect to the New York law requiring school books to be loaned free of charge to all students in specified grades. The express purpose of § 701 was stated by the New York Legislature to be furtherance of the educational opportunities available to the young. . . . [Also,] [t]he law merely makes available to all children the benefits of a general program to lend school books free of charge. Books are furnished at the request of the pupil and ownership remains, at least technically, in the State. Thus no funds or books are furnished to parochial schools, and the financial benefit is to parents and children, not to schools. Perhaps free books make it more likely that some children choose to attend a sectarian school, but that was true of the state-paid bus fares in *Everson* and does not alone demonstrate an unconstitutional degree of support for a religious institution.[23]

The Court acknowledged the inherent difference between transportation and textbooks:

> Of course books are different from buses. Most bus rides have no inherent religious significance, while religious books are common. However, the language of § 701 does not authorize the loan of religious books, and the State claims no right to distribute religious literature. Although the books loaned are those required by the parochial school for use in specific courses, each book loaned must be approved by the public school authorities; only secular books may receive approval. . . . Absent evidence, we cannot assume that school authorities, who constantly face the same problem in selecting textbooks for use in the public schools, are unable to distinguish between secular and religious books or that they will not honestly discharge their duties under the law. In judging the validity of the statute on this record we must proceed on the assumption that books loaned to students are books that are not unsuitable for use in the public schools because of religious content.
>
> The major reason offered by appellants for distinguishing free textbooks from free bus fares is that books, but not buses, are critical to the teaching process, and in a sectarian school that process is employed to teach religion. However this Court has long recognized that religious schools pursue two goals, religious instruction and secular education. . . . A premise of [*Pierce*] was the view that the State's interest in education would be served sufficiently by reliance on the secular teaching that accompanied religious training in the schools maintained by the Society of Sisters. Since *Pierce*, a substantial body of case law has confirmed the power of the States to insist that attendance at private schools, if it is to satisfy state compulsory-attendance laws, be at institutions which provide minimum hours of instruction, employ teachers of specified training, and cover prescribed subjects of instruction. Indeed, the State's interest in assuring that these standards are being met has been considered a

sufficient reason for refusing to accept instruction at home as compliance with compulsory education statutes. These cases were a sensible corollary of *Pierce v. Society of Sisters*: if the State must satisfy its interest in secular education through the instrument of private schools, it has a proper interest in the manner in which those schools perform their secular educational function. . . .

Underlying these cases, and underlying also the legislative judgments that have preceded the court decisions, has been a recognition that private education has played and is playing a significant and valuable role in raising national levels of knowledge, competence, and experience. Americans . . . have considered high quality education to be an indispensable ingredient for achieving the kind of nation, and the kind of citizenry, that they have desired to create. Considering this attitude, the continued willingness to rely on private school systems, including parochial systems, strongly suggests that a wide segment of informed opinion, legislative and otherwise, has found that those schools do an acceptable job of providing secular education to their students. This judgment is further evidence that parochial schools are performing, in addition to their sectarian function, the task of secular education.

Against this background, we cannot agree with appellants either that all teaching in a sectarian school is religious or that the processes of secular and religious training are so intertwined that secular textbooks furnished to students by the public are in fact instrumental in the teaching of religion. This case comes to us after summary judgment entered on the pleadings. Nothing in this record supports the proposition that all textbooks, whether they deal with mathematics, physics, foreign languages, history, or literature, are used by the parochial schools to teach religion. No evidence has been offered about particular schools, particular courses, particular teachers, or particular books. We are unable to hold, based solely on judicial notice, that this statute results in unconstitutional involvement of the State with religious instruction or that § 701, for this or the other reasons urged, is a law respecting the establishment of religion within the meaning of the First Amendment.[24]

Justice Harlan concurred:

The attitude of government toward religion must, as this Court has frequently observed, be one of neutrality. Neutrality is, however, a coat of many colors. It requires that "government neither engage in nor compel religious practices, that it effect no favoritism among sects or between religion and nonreligion, and that it work deterrence of no religious belief." *Abington School District v. Schempp*, 374 U.S. 203, 305, (concurring opinion of GOLDBERG, J.). Realization of these objectives entails "no simple and clear measure," *id.*, 306, by which this or any case may readily be decided, but these objectives do suggest the principles which I believe to be applicable in the present circumstances. I would hold that where the contested governmental activity is calculated to achieve nonreligious purposes otherwise within the competence of the State, and where the activity does not involve the State "so significantly and directly in the realm of the sectarian as to give rise to . . . divisive influences and inhibitions of freedom," *id.*, 307, it is not forbidden by the religious clauses of the First Amendment.[25]

Justice Hugo Black, the author of *Everson*, and Justice William O. Douglas dissented separately, emphasizing the differences between transportation reimbursements and textbooks that could be used in religious instruction, with Douglas arguing that because

The textbook goes to the very heart of education in a parochial school . . . [and] is the chief, although not solitary, instrumentality for propagating a particular religious creed or faith . . . "there is no reliable standard by which secular and religious text-books can be distinguished from each other." . . . Even where the treatment given to a particular topic in a school textbook is not blatantly sectarian, it will necessarily have certain shadings that will lead a parochial school to prefer one text over another.[26]

Justice Black took a broader view:

The First Amendment's bar to establishment of religion must preclude a State from us-ing funds levied from all of its citizens to purchase books for use by sectarian schools, which, although "secular," realistically will in some way inevitably tend to propagate the religious views of the favored sect. Books are the most essential tool of educa-tion since they contain the resources of knowledge which the educational process is designed to exploit. In this sense it is not difficult to distinguish books, which are the heart of any school, from bus fares, which provide a convenient and helpful gen-eral public transportation service. With respect to the former, state financial support actively and directly assists the teaching and propagation of sectarian religious view-points in clear conflict with the First Amendment's establishment bar; with respect to the latter, the State merely provides a general and nondiscriminatory transportation service in no way related to substantive religious views and beliefs. . . .

It requires no prophet to foresee that on the argument used to support this law others could be upheld providing for state or federal government funds to buy prop-erty on which to erect religious school buildings or to erect the buildings themselves, to pay the salaries of the religious school teachers, and finally to have the sectarian re-ligious groups cease to rely on voluntary contributions of members of their sects while waiting for the Government to pick up all the bills for the religious schools. . . .

The First Amendment's prohibition against governmental establishment of re-ligion was written on the assumption that state aid to religion and religious schools generates discord, disharmony, hatred, and strife among our people, and that any government that supplies such aids is to that extent a tyranny. And I still believe that the only way to protect minority religious groups from majority groups in this country is to keep the wall of separation between church and state high and impregnable.[27]

Justice Abe Fortas also dissented:

This case is not within the principle of *Everson v. Board of Education*. Apart from the differences between textbooks and bus rides, the present statute does not call for extending to children attending sectarian schools the same service or facility extended to children in public schools. This statute calls for furnishing special, separate, and particular books, specially, separately, and particularly chosen by religious sects or their representatives for use in their sectarian schools. This is the infirmity, in my opinion. This is the feature that makes it impossible, in my view, to reach any conclu-sion other than that this statute is an unconstitutional use of public funds to support an establishment of religion. . . .

I would reverse the judgment below.[28]

---

### NOTES AND QUESTIONS

1. In *Allen*, the Court majority claims that its decision is consistent with *Ever-son*, but Justice Black—*Everson's* author—disagrees. Are the cases consistent or, if not, what distinguishes the two at a constitutional level? Is the basis of

Establishment Clause was intended to afford protection: "sponsorship, financial support, and active involvement of the sovereign in religious activity." *Walz v. Tax Commission*, 397 U.S. 664, 668.

Every analysis in this area must begin with consideration of the cumulative criteria developed by the Court over many years. Three such tests may be gleaned from our cases. First, the statute must have a secular legislative purpose; second, its principal or primary effect must be one that neither advances nor inhibits religion, *Board of Education v. Allen*, 392 U.S. 236, 243 (1968); finally, the statute must not foster "an excessive government entanglement with religion." *Walz*, 674.

Inquiry into the legislative purposes of the Pennsylvania and Rhode Island statutes affords no basis for a conclusion that the legislative intent was to advance religion. On the contrary, the statutes themselves clearly state that they are intended to enhance the quality of the secular education in all schools covered by the compulsory attendance laws. A State always has a legitimate concern for maintaining minimum standards in all schools it allows to operate. As in *Allen*, we find nothing here that undermines the stated legislative intent; it must therefore be accorded appropriate deference.

In *Allen* the Court acknowledged that secular and religious teachings were not necessarily so intertwined that secular textbooks furnished to students by the State were in fact instrumental in the teaching of religion. 392 U.S., 248. The legislatures of Rhode Island and Pennsylvania have concluded that secular and religious education are identifiable and separable. In the abstract we have no quarrel with this conclusion.

The two legislatures, however, have also recognized that church-related elementary and secondary schools have a significant religious mission and that a substantial portion of their activities is religiously oriented. They have therefore sought to create statutory restrictions designed to guarantee the separation between secular and religious educational functions and to ensure that State financial aid supports only the former. All these provisions are precautions taken in candid recognition that these programs approached, even if they did not intrude upon, the forbidden areas under the Religion Clauses. We need not decide whether these legislative precautions restrict the principal or primary effect of the programs to the point where they do not offend the Religion Clauses, for we conclude that the cumulative impact of the entire relationship arising under the statutes in each State involves excessive entanglement between government and religion.

### III

In *Walz v. Tax Commission*, the Court upheld state tax exemptions for real property owned by religious organizations and used for religious worship. That holding, however, tended to confine rather than enlarge the area of permissible state involvement with religious institutions by calling for close scrutiny of the degree of entanglement involved in the relationship. The objective is to prevent, as far as possible, the intrusion of either into the precincts of the other.

Our prior holdings do not call for total separation between church and state; total separation is not possible in an absolute sense. Some relationship between government and religious organizations is inevitable. *Zorach v. Clauson*, 343 U.S. 306; *Sherbert v. Verner*, 374 U.S. 398, 422 (HARLAN, J., dissenting). Fire inspections, building and zoning regulations, and state requirements under compulsory school-attendance laws are examples of necessary and permissible contacts. . . . Judicial caveats against entanglement must recognize that the line of separation, far from being a "wall," is a blurred, indistinct, and variable barrier depending on all the circumstances of a particular relationship.

This is not to suggest, however, that we are to engage in a legalistic minuet in which precise rules and forms must govern. . . .

In order to determine whether the government entanglement with religion is excessive, we must examine the character and purposes of the institutions that are benefitted, the nature of the aid that the State provides, and the resulting relationship between the government and the religious authority. Mr. Justice Harlan, in a separate opinion in *Walz*, echoed the classic warning as to "programs, whose very nature is apt to entangle the state in details of administration. . . ." *Id.*, 695. Here we find that both statutes foster an impermissible degree of entanglement.

### (a) Rhode Island program

The District Court made extensive findings on the grave potential for excessive entanglement that inheres in the religious character and purpose of the Roman Catholic elementary schools of Rhode Island, to date the sole beneficiaries of the Rhode Island Salary Supplement Act. . . .

[T]he District Court concluded that the parochial schools constituted "an integral part of the religious mission of the Catholic Church." The various characteristics of the schools make them "a powerful vehicle for transmitting the Catholic faith to the next generation." This process of inculcating religious doctrine is, of course, enhanced by the impressionable age of the pupils, in primary schools particularly. In short, parochial schools involve substantial religious activity and purpose.

The substantial religious character of these church-related schools gives rise to entangling church-state relationships of the kind the Religion Clauses sought to avoid. Although the District Court found that concern for religious values did not inevitably or necessarily intrude into the content of secular subjects, the considerable religious activities of these schools led the legislature to provide for careful governmental controls and surveillance by state authorities in order to ensure that state aid supports only secular education.

The dangers and corresponding entanglements are enhanced by the particular form of aid that the Rhode Island Act provides. Our decisions from *Everson* to *Allen* have permitted the States to provide church-related schools with secular, neutral, or nonideological services, facilities, or materials. Bus transportation, school lunches, public health services, and secular textbooks supplied in common to all students were not thought to offend the Establishment Clause. We note that the dissenters in *Allen* seemed chiefly concerned with the pragmatic difficulties involved in ensuring the truly secular content of the textbooks provided at state expense. . . .

We cannot, however, refuse here to recognize that teachers have a substantially different ideological character from books. In terms of potential for involving some aspect of faith or morals in secular subjects, a textbook's content is ascertainable, but a teacher's handling of a subject is not. We cannot ignore the danger that a teacher under religious control and discipline poses to the separation of the religious from the purely secular aspects of precollege education. . . .

The schools are governed by the standards set forth in a "Handbook of School Regulations," which has the force of synodal law in the diocese. It emphasizes the role and importance of the teacher in parochial schools: "The prime factor for the success or the failure of the school is the spirit and personality, as well as the professional competency, of the teacher. . . ." The Handbook also states that: "Religious formation is not confined to formal courses; nor is it restricted to a single subject area." Finally, the Handbook advises teachers to stimulate interest in religious vocations and missionary work. Given the mission of the church school, these instructions are consistent and logical.

Several teachers testified, however, that they did not inject religion into their secular classes. And the District Court found that religious values did not necessarily affect the content of the secular instruction. But what has been recounted suggests the potential if not actual hazards of this form of state aid. The teacher is employed by a religious organization, subject to the direction and discipline of religious authorities, and works in a system dedicated to rearing children in a particular faith. These controls are not lessened by the fact that most of the lay teachers are of the Catholic faith. Inevitably some of a teacher's responsibilities hover on the border between secular and religious orientation.

We need not and do not assume that teachers in parochial schools will be guilty of bad faith or any conscious design to evade the limitations imposed by the statute and the First Amendment. We simply recognize that a dedicated religious person, teaching in a school affiliated with his or her faith and operated to inculcate its tenets, will inevitably experience great difficulty in remaining religiously neutral. With the best of intentions such a teacher would find it hard to make a total separation between secular teaching and religious doctrine. What would appear to some to be essential to good citizenship might well for others border on or constitute instruction in religion. . . .

We do not assume, however, that parochial school teachers will be unsuccessful in their attempts to segregate their religious beliefs from their secular educational responsibilities. But the potential for impermissible fostering of religion is present. . . . The State must be certain, given the Religion Clauses, that subsidized teachers do not inculcate religion—indeed the State here has undertaken to do so. To ensure that no trespass occurs, the State has therefore carefully conditioned its aid with pervasive restrictions. An eligible recipient must teach only those courses that are offered in the public schools and use only those texts and materials that are found in the public schools. In addition the teacher must not engage in teaching any course in religion.

A comprehensive, discriminating, and continuing state surveillance will inevitably be required to ensure that these restrictions are obeyed and the First Amendment otherwise respected. Unlike a book, a teacher cannot be inspected once so as to determine the extent and intent of his or her personal beliefs and subjective acceptance of the limitations imposed by the First Amendment. These prophylactic contacts will involve excessive and enduring entanglement between state and church. . . .

[Entanglement also exists because] [t]he statute excludes teachers employed by nonpublic schools whose average per-pupil expenditures on secular education equal or exceed the comparable figures for public schools. . . . [T]he program requires the government to examine the school's records in order to determine how much of the total expenditures is attributable to secular education and how much to religious activity. This kind of state inspection and evaluation of the religious content of a religious organization is fraught with the sort of entanglement that the Constitution forbids. It is a relationship pregnant with dangers of excessive government direction of church schools and hence of churches. . . .

### (b) Pennsylvania program . . .

The Pennsylvania statute has the further defect of providing state financial aid directly to the church-related school. This factor distinguishes both *Everson* and *Allen*, for in both those cases the Court was careful to point out that state aid was provided to the student and his parents—not to the church-related school. . . .

The history of government grants of a continuing cash subsidy indicates that such programs have almost always been accompanied by varying measures of control and surveillance. The government cash grants before us now provide no basis for predicting that comprehensive measures of surveillance and controls will not follow. In particular the government's post-audit power to inspect and evaluate a church-related school's financial records and to determine which expenditures are religious and which are secular creates an intimate and continuing relationship between church and state.

### IV

A broader base of entanglement of yet a different character is presented by the divisive political potential of these state programs. In a community where such a large number of pupils are served by church-related schools, it can be assumed that state assistance will entail considerable political activity. Partisans of parochial schools, understandably concerned with rising costs and sincerely dedicated to both the religious and secular educational missions of their schools, will inevitably champion this cause and promote political action to achieve their goals. Those who oppose state aid, whether for constitutional, religious, or fiscal reasons, will inevitably respond and employ all of the usual political campaign techniques to prevail. Candidates will be forced to declare and voters to choose. It would be unrealistic to ignore the fact that many people confronted with issues of this kind will find their votes aligned with their faith.

Ordinarily political debate and division, however vigorous or even partisan, are normal and healthy manifestations of our democratic system of government, but political division along religious lines was one of the principal evils against which the First Amendment was intended to protect. . . .

Of course, as the Court noted in *Walz*, "(a)dherents of particular faiths and individual churches frequently take strong positions on public issues." *Walz v. Tax Commission*, 397 U.S., 670. We could not expect otherwise, for religious values pervade the fabric of our national life. But . . . [h]ere we are confronted with successive and very likely permanent annual appropriations that benefit relatively few religious groups. Political fragmentation and divisiveness on religious lines are thus likely to be intensified. . . .

### V . . .

Finally, nothing we have said can be construed to disparage the role of church-related elementary and secondary schools in our national life. Their contribution has been and is enormous. Nor do we ignore their economic plight in a period of rising costs and expanding need. Taxpayers generally have been spared vast sums by the maintenance of these educational institutions by religious organizations, largely by the gifts of faithful adherents.

The merit and benefits of these schools, however, are not the issue before us in these cases. The sole question is whether state aid to these schools can be squared with the dictates of the Religion Clauses. Under our system the choice has been made that government is to be entirely excluded from the area of religious instruction and churches excluded from the affairs of government. The Constitution decrees that religion must be a private matter for the individual, the family, and the institutions of private choice, and that while some involvement and entanglement are inevitable, lines must be drawn. . . .

▩ JUSTICE BRENNAN (concurring). . . .

The common feature of all three statutes before us is the provision of a direct subsidy from public funds for activities carried on by sectarian educational institutions. We have sustained the reimbursement of parents for bus fares of students *Everson v. Bd. of Ed.*, 330 U.S. 1. . . [and] the loan of textbooks in secular subjects to students of both public and nonpublic schools, *Board of Education of v. Allen*, 392 U.S. 236.

The statutory schemes before us, however, have features not present in either the *Everson* or *Allen* schemes. For example, the reimbursement or the loan of books ended government involvement in *Everson* and *Allen*. In contrast each of the schemes here exacts a promise in some form that the subsidy will not be used to finance courses in religious subjects—promises that must be and are policed to assure compliance. . . .

[F]or more than a century, the consensus, enforced by legislatures and courts with substantial consistency, has been that public subsidy of sectarian schools constitutes an impermissible involvement of secular with religious institutions. . . . These are involvements that threaten "dangers—as much to church as to state—which the Framers feared would subvert religious liberty and the strength of a system of secular government." *Schempp*, 374 U.S., 295 (BRENNAN, J., concurring).

> (G)overnment and religion have discrete interests which are mutually best served when each avoids too close a proximity to the other. It is not only the nonbeliever who fears the injection of sectarian doctrines and controversies into the civil polity, but in as high degree it is the devout believer who fears the secularization of a creed which becomes too deeply involved with and dependent upon the government. *Id.*, 259 (Brennan, J., concurring).

All three of these statutes require "too close a proximity" of government to the subsidized sectarian institutions and in my view create real dangers of "the secularization of a creed." . . .

II . . .

Both the Rhode Island and Pennsylvania statutes prescribe extensive standardization of the content of secular courses, and of the teaching materials and textbooks to be used in teaching the courses. And the regulations to implement those requirements necessarily require policing of instruction in the schools. The picture of state inspectors prowling the halls of parochial schools and auditing classroom instruction surely raises more than an imagined specter of governmental "secularization of a creed." . . .

Policing the content of courses, the specific textbooks used, and indeed the words of teachers is far different from the legitimate policing carried on under state compulsory attendance laws or laws regulating minimum levels of educational achievement. Government's legitimate interest in ensuring certain minimum skill levels and the acquisition of certain knowledge does not carry with it power to prescribe what shall not be taught, or what methods of instruction shall be used, or what opinions the teacher may offer in the course of teaching.

Moreover, when a sectarian institution accepts state financial aid it becomes obligated under the Equal Protection Clause of the Fourteenth Amendment not to discriminate in admissions policies and faculty selection. . . .

III . . .

Pennsylvania, Rhode Island, and the Federal Government argue strenuously that the government monies in all these cases are not "(g)eneral subsidies of religious activities" because they are paid specifically and solely for the secular education that the sectarian institutions provide. . . .

But I do not read *Pierce* or *Allen* as supporting the proposition that public subsidy of a sectarian institution's secular training is permissible state involvement. I read them as supporting the proposition that as an identifiable set of skills and an identifiable quantum of knowledge, secular education may be effectively provided either in the religious context of parochial schools, or outside the context of religion in public schools. . . .

*Allen*, in my view, simply sustained a statute in which the State was "neutral in its relations with groups of religious believers and non-believers." The only context in which the Court in *Allen* employed the distinction between secular and religious in a parochial school was to reach its conclusion that the textbooks that the State was providing could and would be secular. The present cases, however, involve direct subsidies of tax monies to the schools themselves and we cannot blink the fact that the secular education those schools provide goes hand in hand with the religious mission that "is the only reason for the schools'" existence. Within the institution, the two are inextricably intertwined. . . .

The common ingredient of the three prongs of the test set forth at the outset of this opinion is whether the statutes involve government in the "essentially religious activities" of religious institutions. My analysis of the operation, purposes, and effects of these statutes leads me inescapably to the conclusion that they do impermissibly involve the States and the Federal Government with the "essentially religious activities" of sectarian educational institutions. More specifically, for the reasons stated, I think each government uses "essentially religious means to serve governmental ends, where secular means would suffice." This Nation long ago committed itself to primary reliance upon publicly supported public education to serve its important goals in secular education. Our religious diversity gave strong impetus to that commitment. . . .

I conclude that, in using sectarian institutions to further goals in secular education, the statutes do violence to the principle that "government may not employ religious means to serve secular interests, however legitimate they may be, at least without the clearest demonstration that nonreligious means will not suffice." *Schempp*, 374 U.S., 265 (BRENNAN, J., concurring). . . .

JUSTICE WHITE, dissenting. . . .

No one in these cases questions the constitutional right of parents to satisfy their state-imposed obligation to educate their children by sending them to private schools, sectarian or otherwise, as long as those schools meet minimum standards established for secular instruction. The States are not only permitted, but required by the Constitution, to free students attending private schools from any public school attendance obligation. . . .

Our prior cases have recognized the dual role of parochial schools in American society: they perform both religious and secular functions. Our cases also recognize that legislation having a secular purpose and extending governmental assistance to sectarian schools in the performance of their secular functions does not constitute "law(s) respecting an establishment of religion" forbidden by the First Amendment merely because a secular program may incidentally benefit a church in fulfilling its religious mission. That religion may indirectly benefit from governmental aid to the secular activities of churches does not convert that aid into an impermissible establishment of religion. . . .

It is enough for me that the States and the Federal Government are financing a separable secular function of overriding importance in order to sustain the legislation here challenged. That religion and private interests other than education may substantially benefit does not convert these laws into impermissible establishments of religion. . . .

The Court . . . creates an insoluble paradox for the State and the parochial schools. The State cannot finance secular instruction if it permits religion to be taught in the same classroom; but if it exacts a promise that religion not be so taught—a promise the school and its teachers are quite willing and on this record able to give—and enforces it, it is then entangled in the "no entanglement" aspect of the Court's Establishment Clause jurisprudence. . . .

The critical allegations, as paraphrased by the Court, are that "the church-related elementary and secondary schools are controlled by religious organizations, have the purpose of propagating and promoting a particular religious faith, and conduct their operations to fulfill that purpose." From these allegations the Court concludes that forbidden entanglements would follow from enforcing compliance with the secular purpose for which the state money is being paid.

I disagree. There is no specific allegation in the complaint that sectarian teaching does or would invade secular classes supported by state funds. That the schools are operated to promote a particular religion is quite consistent with the view that secular teaching devoid of religious instruction can successfully be maintained. . . . I would no more here than in the Rhode Island case substitute presumption for proof that religion is or would be taught in state-financed secular courses or assume that enforcement measures would be so extensive as to border on a free exercise violation. . . . I cannot hold that the First Amendment forbids an agreement between the school and the State that the state funds would be used only to teach secular subjects.

## Notes and Questions

1. According to the Court majority, the programs at issue in this case run afoul of which prong of the three-prong *Lemon* test? What are the other two prongs of the *Lemon* test? Based on the Court's description of the test, would the Pennsylvania and Rhode Island programs violate either of the other prongs?

2. Describe the three factors the Court says it must examine in order to determine whether government entanglement with religion is excessive. How does the Court apply and evaluate these factors in this case? Why is government entanglement with religion an Establishment Clause concern? How is it related to other religion clause values? Suppose that a religious institution is willing to sign a waiver in order to receive government funding, promising not to complain about any government regulation or oversight. Would that solve the entanglement concern? Should it?

3. For what reasons does the Court believe that state financial aid given directly to church-related schools would be more constitutionally problematic than aid that arrives at the school in an indirect fashion? How would an indirect funding system ameliorate Establishment Clause concerns? Was the system in *Allen*, involving the loan of textbooks to students, direct or indirect, or is this distinction merely one of formalism?

4. In his concurring opinion, what additional arguments does Justice Brennan make against these state programs?

5. In his dissent, Justice White argues:

> It is enough for me that the States and the Federal Government are financing a separable secular function of overriding importance in order to sustain the legislation here challenged. That religion and private interests other than education may substantially benefit does not convert these laws into impermissible establishments of religion.

Similarly, Justice White says that the majority's arguments regarding the constitutional dangers presented by the Rhode Island policy are unconvincing. Do you agree with the majority or the dissent on these issues?

---

*Committee for Public Education and Religious Liberty v. Nyquist* involved a facial challenge to a New York law providing three forms of financial assistance to nonpublic elementary and secondary schools. The first section of the challenged law provided direct money grants to qualifying nonpublic schools to be used for maintenance and repair of school facilities and equipment "to ensure the health, welfare and safety of enrolled pupils." The law defined maintenance and repair to include "the provision of heat, light, water, ventilation and sanitary facilities; cleaning and janitorial and custodial services, snow removal; [and] necessary upkeep and renovation of buildings, grounds and equipment."

The second section provided a tuition reimbursement to lower-income parents of children attending nonpublic schools. The New York legislature justified the reimbursement on the ground that the "right to select among alternative educational systems is diminished or even denied to children of lower-income families," while also noting that the "precipitous decline in the number of nonpublic school pupils would cause a massive increase in public school enrollment and costs, an increase that would aggravate an already serious fiscal crisis in public education." The final challenged section provided for a graduated tax credit for tuition expenses for those parents of children attending nonpublic schools who did not qualify for the tuition reimbursement. Consider how the Court applies the *Lemon* test in this case and what religion clause values it believes are at stake in the funding program.

———————————

## COMMITTEE FOR PUBLIC EDUCATION AND RELIGIOUS LIBERTY v. NYQUIST
### 413 U.S. 756 (1973)

■ JUSTICE POWELL delivered the Opinion for the Court. . . .

### II

The history of the Establishment Clause has been recounted frequently and need not be repeated here. It is enough to note that it is now firmly established that a law may be one "respecting an establishment of religion" even though its consequence is not to promote a "state religion," *Lemon v. Kurtzman*, 403 U.S. 602, 612, and even though it does not aid one religion more than another but merely benefits all religions alike. *Everson v. Board of Education*, 330 U.S. 1, 15. It is equally well established, however, that not every law that confers an "indirect," "remote," or "incidental" benefit upon religious institutions is, for that reason alone, constitutionally invalid. *Everson*. What our cases require is careful examination of any law challenged on establishment grounds with a view to ascertaining whether it furthers any of the evils against which that Clause protects. Primary among those evils have been "sponsorship, financial support, and active involvement of the sovereign in religious activity." *Walz v. Tax Comm'n*, 397 U.S., 668; *Lemon v. Kurtzman*, 403 U.S., 612.

Most of the cases coming to this Court raising Establishment Clause questions have involved the relationship between religion and education. . . . [T]he now well-defined three-part test that has emerged from our decisions is a product of considerations derived from the full sweep of the Establishment Clause cases. Taken together, these decisions dictate that to pass muster under the Establishment Clause the law in question first must reflect a clearly secular legislative purpose, e.g., *Epperson v. Arkansas*, 393 U.S. 97, second, must have a primary effect that neither advances nor inhibits religion, e.g., *McGowan v. Maryland*; *School District of Abington Township v. Schempp*, 374 U.S. 203, and, third, must avoid excessive government entanglement with religion, e.g., *Walz v. Tax Comm'n*, 397 U.S. 644. . . .

We do not question the propriety, and fully secular content, of New York's interest in preserving a healthy and safe educational environment for all of its schoolchildren. And we do not doubt—indeed, we fully recognize—the validity of the State's interest in promoting pluralism and diversity among its public and nonpublic schools. Nor do we hesitate to acknowledge the reality of its concern for an already overburdened public school system that might suffer in the event that a significant percentage of children presently attending nonpublic schools should abandon those schools in favor of the public schools.

But the propriety of a legislature's purposes may not immunize from further scrutiny a law which either has a primary effect that advances religion, or which fosters excessive entanglements between Church and State. Accordingly, we must weigh each of the three aid provisions challenged here against these criteria of effect and entanglement.

## A

The "maintenance and repair" provisions of § 1 authorize direct payments to nonpublic schools, virtually all of which are Roman Catholic schools in low-income areas. The grants, totaling $30 or $40 per pupil depending on the age of the institution, are given largely without restriction on usage. So long as expenditures do not exceed 50% of comparable expenses in the public school system, it is possible for a sectarian elementary or secondary school to finance its entire "maintenance and repair" budget from state tax-raised funds. No attempt is made to restrict payments to those expenditures related to the upkeep of facilities used exclusively for secular purposes, nor do we think it possible within the context of these religion-oriented institutions to impose such restrictions. Nothing in the statute, for instance, bars a qualifying school from paying out of state funds the salaries of employees who maintain the school chapel, or the cost of renovating classrooms in which religion is taught, or the cost of heating and lighting those same facilities. Absent appropriate restrictions on expenditures for these and similar purposes, it simply cannot be denied that this section has a primary effect that advances religion in that it subsidizes directly the religious activities of sectarian elementary and secondary schools.

The state officials nevertheless argue that these expenditures for "maintenance and repair" are similar to other financial expenditures approved by this Court. . . .

[However, *Everson* and *Allen*] simply recognize that sectarian schools perform secular, educational functions as well as religious functions, and that some forms of aid may be channeled to the secular without providing direct aid to the sectarian. But the channel is a narrow one, as the above cases illustrate. Of course, it is true in each case that the provision of such neutral, nonideological aid, assisting only the secular functions of sectarian schools, served indirectly and incidentally to promote the religious function by rendering it more likely that children would attend sectarian schools and by freeing the budgets of those schools for use in other nonsecular areas. But an indirect and incidental effect beneficial to religious institutions has never been thought a sufficient defect to warrant the invalidation of a state law. . . .

*Tilton* [v. *Richardson*] draws the line most clearly. While a bare majority was there persuaded, for the reasons stated in the plurality opinion and in MR. JUSTICE WHITE'S concurrence, that carefully limited construction grants to colleges and universities could be sustained, the Court was unanimous in its rejection of one clause of the federal statute . . . [that allowed] at the end of 20 years, the facilities would thereafter be available for use by the institution for any sectarian purpose. . . . If tax-raised funds may not be granted to institutions of higher learning where the possibility exists that those funds will be used to construct a facility utilized for sectarian activities 20 years hence, *a fortiori* they may not be distributed to elementary and secondary sectarian schools for the maintenance and repair of facilities without any limitations on their use. If the State may not erect buildings in which religious activities are to take place, it may not maintain such buildings or renovate them when they fall into disrepair.

It might be argued, however, that while the New York "maintenance and repair" grants lack specifically articulated secular restrictions, the statute does provide a sort of statistical guarantee of separation by limiting grants to 50% of the amount expended for comparable services in the public schools. The legislature's supposition might have been that at least 50% of the ordinary public school maintenance and repair budget would be devoted to purely secular facility upkeep in sectarian schools. The shortest answer to this argument is that the statute itself allows, as a ceiling, grants satisfying the entire "amount of expenditures for maintenance and repair of such school" providing only that it is neither more than $30 or $40 per pupil nor more than 50% of the comparable public school expenditures. Quite apart from the language of the statute, our cases make clear that a mere statistical judgment will not suffice as a guarantee that state funds will not be used to finance religious education. . . .

B

New York's tuition reimbursement program also fails the "effect" test, for much the same reasons that govern its maintenance and repair grants. The state program is designed to allow direct, unrestricted grants of $50 to $100 per child (but no more than 50% of tuition actually paid) as reimbursement to parents in low-income brackets who send their children to nonpublic schools, the bulk of which is concededly sectarian in orientation. To qualify, a parent must have earned less than $5,000 in taxable income and must present a receipted tuition bill from a nonpublic school.

There can be no question that these grants could not, consistently with the Establishment Clause, be given directly to sectarian schools, since they would suffer from the same deficiency that renders invalid the grants for maintenance and repair. In the absence of an effective means of guaranteeing that the state aid derived from public funds will be used exclusively for secular, neutral, and nonideological purposes, it is clear from our cases that direct aid in whatever form is invalid. . . .

The controlling question here, then, is whether the fact that the grants are delivered to parents rather than schools is of such significance as to compel a contrary result. The State and intervenor-appellees rely on *Everson* and *Allen* for their claim that grants to parents, unlike grants to institutions, respect the "wall of separation" required by the Constitution.[37] It is true that in those cases the Court upheld laws that provided benefits to children attending religious schools and to their parents. But those decisions make clear that, far from providing a *per se* immunity from examination of the substance of the State's program, the fact that aid is disbursed to parents rather than to the schools is only one among many factors to be considered.

---

[37] In addition to *Everson* and *Allen*, THE CHIEF JUSTICE in his dissenting opinion relies on *Quick Bear v. Leupp*, 210 U.S. 50 (1908), for the proposition that "government aid to individuals generally stands on an entirely different footing from direct aid to religious institutions." 413 U.S., 801. *Quick Bear*, however, did not involve the expenditure of tax-raised moneys to support sectarian schools. The funds that were utilized by the Indians to provide sectarian education were treaty and trust funds which the Court emphasized belonged to the Indians as payment for the cession of Indian land and other rights. 210 U.S., 80-81. It was their money, and the Court held that for Congress to have prohibited them from expending their own money to acquire a religious education would have constituted a prohibition of the free exercise of religion. *Id.*, 82. The present litigation is quite unlike *Quick Bear* since that case did not involve the distribution of public funds, directly or indirectly, to compensate parents who send their children to religious schools.

In *Everson*, the Court found the bus fare program analogous to the provision of services such as police and fire protection, sewage disposal, highways, and sidewalks for parochial schools. 330 U.S., 17-18. Such services, provided in common to all citizens, are "so separate and so indisputably marked off from the religious function," *id.*, 18, that they may fairly be viewed as reflections of a neutral posture toward religious institutions. *Allen* is founded upon a similar principle. The Court there repeatedly emphasized that upon the record in that case there was no indication that textbooks would be provided for anything other than purely secular courses.

> Of course books are different from buses. Most bus rides have no inherent religious significance, while religious books are common. However, the language of (the law under consideration) does not authorize the loan of religious books, and the State claims no right to distribute religious literature. . . . Absent evidence, we cannot assume that school authorities . . . are unable to distinguish between secular and religious books or that they will not honestly discharge their duties under the law. 392 U.S., 244-245.[38]

The tuition grants here are subject to no such restrictions. There has been no endeavor "to guarantee the separation between secular and religious educational functions and to ensure the State financial aid supports only the former." *Lemon v. Kurtzman*, 403 U.S., 613. Indeed, it is precisely the function of New York's law to provide assistance to private schools, the great majority of which are sectarian. By reimbursing parents for a portion of their tuition bill, the State seeks to relieve their financial burdens sufficiently to assure that they continue to have the option to send their children to religion-oriented schools. And while the other purposes for that aid—to perpetuate a pluralistic

---

[38] *Allen* and *Everson* differ from the present litigation in a second important respect. In both cases the class of beneficiaries included all schoolchildren, those in public as well as those in private schools. See also *Tilton v. Richardson*, in which federal aid was made available to all institutions of higher learning, and *Walz v. Tax Comm'n*, in which tax exemptions were accorded to all educational and charitable nonprofit institutions. We do not agree with the suggestion in the dissent of THE CHIEF JUSTICE that tuition grants are an analogous endeavor to provide comparable benefits to all parents of schoolchildren whether enrolled in public or nonpublic schools. 413 U.S., 801-803. The grants to parents of private schoolchildren are given in addition to the right that they have to send their children to public schools "totally at state expense." And in any event, the argument proves too much, for it would also provide a basis for approving through tuition grants the complete subsidization of all religious schools on the ground that such action is necessary if the State is fully to equalize the position of parents who elect such schools—a result wholly at variance with the Establishment Clause.

Because of the manner in which we have resolved the tuition grant issue, we need not decide whether the significantly religious character of the statute's beneficiaries might differentiate the present cases from a case involving some form of public assistance (e.g., scholarships) made available generally without regard to the sectarian-nonsectarian, or public-nonpublic nature of the institution benefitted. See *Wolman v. Essex*, 342 F. Supp. 399, 412-413 (SD Ohio), aff'd, 409 U.S. 808 (1972). Thus, our decision today does not compel, as appellees have contended, the conclusion that the educational assistance provisions of the "G. I. Bill," 38 U.S.C. § 1651, impermissibly advance religion in violation of the Establishment Clause.

educational environment and to protect the fiscal integrity of overburdened public schools—are certainly unexceptionable, the effect of the aid is unmistakably to provide desired financial support for nonpublic, sectarian institutions. . . .

Although we think it clear, for the reasons above stated, that New York's tuition grant program fares no better under the "effect" test than its maintenance and repair program, in view of the novelty of the question we will address briefly the subsidiary arguments made by the state officials and intervenors in its defense.

First, it has been suggested that it is of controlling significance that New York's program calls for reimbursement for tuition already paid rather than for direct contributions which are merely routed through the parents to the schools, in advance of or in lieu of payment by the parents. The parent is not a mere conduit, we are told, but is absolutely free to spend the money he receives in any manner he wishes. There is no element of coercion attached to the reimbursement, and no assurance that the money will eventually end up in the hands of religious schools. The absence of any element of coercion, however, is irrelevant to questions arising under the Establishment Clause. . . .

A similar inquiry governs here: if the grants are offered as an incentive to parents to send their children to sectarian schools by making unrestricted cash payments to them, the Establishment Clause is violated whether or not the actual dollars given eventually find their way into the sectarian institutions. Whether the grant is labeled a reimbursement, a reward, or a subsidy, its substantive impact is still the same. . . .

Second, . . . the State argues that it is significant here that the tuition reimbursement grants pay only a portion of the tuition bill, and an even smaller portion of the religious school's total expenses. The New York statute limits reimbursement to 50% of any parent's actual outlay. Additionally, intervenor estimates that only 30% of the total cost of nonpublic education is covered by tuition payments, with the remaining coming from "voluntary contributions, endowments and the like." On the basis of these two statistics, appellees reason that the "maximum tuition reimbursement by the State is thus only 15% of educational costs in the nonpublic schools." And, "since the compulsory education laws of the State, by necessity require significantly more than 15% of school time to be devoted to teaching secular courses," the New York statute provides "a statistical guarantee of neutrality." It should readily be seen that this is simply another variant of the argument we have rejected as to maintenance and repair costs, and it can fare no better here. Obviously, if accepted, this argument would provide the foundation for massive, direct subsidization of sectarian elementary and secondary schools. Our cases, however, have long since foreclosed the notion that mere statistical assurances will suffice to sail between the Scylla and Charybodis of "effect" and "entanglement."

Finally, the State argues that its program of tuition grants should survive scrutiny because it is designed to promote the free exercise of religion. The State notes that only "low-income parents" are aided by this law, and without state assistance their right to have their children educated in a religious environment "is diminished or even denied." It is true, of course, that this Court has long recognized and maintained the right to choose nonpublic over public education. *Pierce v. Society of Sisters*, 268 U.S. 510. It is also true that a state law interfering with a parent's right to have his child educated in a sectarian school would run afoul of the Free Exercise Clause. But this Court repeatedly has recognized that tension inevitably exists between the Free Exercise and the Establishment Clauses, e.g., *Everson v. Board of Education*; *Walz v. Tax Comm'n*, and that it may often not be possible to promote the former without offending the latter. As a result of this tension, our cases require the State to maintain an attitude of "neutrality," neither "advancing" nor "inhibiting" religion. In its attempt to enhance the opportunities of the poor to choose between public and nonpublic education, the State has taken a step which can only be regarded as one "advancing" religion. . . .

C

Sections 3, 4, and 5 establish a system for providing income tax benefits to parents of children attending New York's nonpublic schools. In this Court, the parties have engaged in a considerable debate over what label best fits the New York law. . . . It is, at least in its form, a tax deduction since it is an amount subtracted from adjusted gross income, prior to computation of the tax due. Its effect, as the District Court concluded, is more like that of a tax credit since the deduction is not related to the amount actually spent for tuition and is apparently designed to yield a predetermined amount of tax "forgiveness" in exchange for performing a specific act which the State desires to encourage—the usual attribute of a tax credit. We see no reason to select one label over another, as the constitutionality of this hybrid benefit does not turn in any event on the label we accord it. As MR. CHIEF JUSTICE BURGER'S opinion for the Court in *Lemon v. Kurtzman*, 403 U.S., 614, notes, constitutional analysis is not a "legalistic minuet in which precise rules and forms must govern." Instead we must "examine the form of the relationship for the light that it casts on the substance."

These sections allow parents of children attending nonpublic elementary and secondary schools to subtract from adjusted gross income a specified amount if they do not receive a tuition reimbursement under § 2, and if they have an adjusted gross income of less than $25,000. The amount of the deduction is unrelated to the amount of money actually expended by any parent on tuition, but is calculated on the basis of a formula contained in the statute. The formula is apparently the product of a legislative attempt to assure that each family would receive a carefully estimated net benefit, and that the tax benefit would be comparable to, and compatible with, the tuition grant for lower income families. . . .

In practical terms there would appear to be little difference, for purposes of determining whether such aid has the effect of advancing religion, between the tax benefit allowed here and the tuition grant allowed under § 2. The qualifying parent under either program receives the same form of encouragement and reward for sending his children to nonpublic schools. The only difference is that one parent receives an actual cash payment while the other is allowed to reduce by an arbitrary amount the sum he would otherwise be obliged to pay over to the State. We see no answer to Judge Hays' dissenting statement below that "(i)n both instances the money involved represents a charge made upon the state for the purpose of religious education." 350 F. Supp., 675.

Appellees defend the tax portion of New York's legislative package on two grounds. First, they contend that it is of controlling significance that the grants or credits are directed to the parents rather than to the schools. This is the same argument made in support of the tuition reimbursements. . . . Second, appellees place their strongest reliance on *Walz v. Tax Comm'n*, in which

New York's property tax exemption for religious organizations was upheld. We think that *Walz* provides no support for appellees' position. Indeed, its rationale plainly compels the conclusion that New York's tax package violates the Establishment Clause.

Tax exemptions for church property enjoyed an apparently universal approval in this country both before and after the adoption of the First Amendment. The Court in *Walz* surveyed the history of tax exemptions and found that each of the 50 States has long provided for tax exemptions for places of worship, [and] that Congress has exempted religious organizations from taxation for over three-quarters of a century. . . . We know of no historical precedent for New York's recently promulgated tax relief program. Indeed, it seems clear that tax benefits for parents whose children attend parochial schools are a recent innovation, occasioned by the growing financial plight of such non-public institutions and designed, albeit unsuccessfully, to tailor state aid in a manner not incompatible with the recent decisions of this Court. See *Kosydar v. Wolman*, 353 F. Supp. 744 (SD Ohio 1972), aff'd *sub nom. Grit v. Wolman*, 413 U.S. 901.

But historical acceptance without more would not alone have sufficed, as "no one acquires a vested or protected right in violation of the Constitution by long use." *Walz v. Tax Comm'n* 397 U.S., 678. . . . A proper respect for both the Free Exercise and the Establishment Clauses compels the State to pursue a course of "neutrality" toward religion. . . . Special tax benefits, however, cannot be squared with the principle of neutrality established by the decisions of this Court. To the contrary, insofar as such benefits render assistance to parents who send their children to sectarian schools, their purpose and inevitable effect are to aid and advance those religious institutions. . . .

One further difference between tax exemption for church property and tax benefits for parents should be noted. The exemption challenged in *Walz* was not restricted to a class composed exclusively or even predominantly of religious institutions. Instead, the exemption covered all property devoted to religious, educational, or charitable purposes. As the parties here must concede, tax reductions authorized by this law flow primarily to the parents of children attending sectarian, nonpublic schools. Without intimating whether this factor alone might have controlling significance in another context in some future case, it should be apparent that in terms of the potential divisiveness of any legislative measure the narrowness of the benefitted class would be an important factor.

In conclusion, we find the *Walz* analogy unpersuasive, and in light of the practical similarity between New York's tax and tuition reimbursement programs, we hold that neither form of aid is sufficiently restricted to assure that it will not have the impermissible effect of advancing the sectarian activities of religious schools. . . .

The Court concluded by holding that the programs were also unconstitutional in that they "carrie[d] [a] grave potential for entanglement in the broader sense of continuing political strife over aid to religion." The Court noted that "aid programs of any kind tend to become entrenched, to escalate in cost, and to generate their own aggressive constituencies." Quoting from Justice Harlan's concurring opinion in *Walz*, the Court reiterated that one goal of the Establishment Clause is "preventing that kind and degree of government involvement in religious life that, as history teaches us, is apt to lead to strife and frequently strain a political system to the breaking point."

Justice William Rehnquist, in a dissent joined by Chief Justice Warren Burger and Justice Byron White, argued that, on the authority of *Walz,* "tax deductions and exemptions, even when directed to religious institutions, occupy quite a different constitutional status under the Religion Clauses of the First Amendment than do outright grants to such institutions." The dissenters also argued that: "The reimbursement and tax benefit plans today struck down, no less than the plans in *Everson* and *Allen,* are consistent with the principle of neutrality. New York has recognized that parents who are sending their children to nonpublic schools are rendering the State a service by decreasing the costs of public education and by physically relieving an already overburdened public school system. Such parents are nonetheless compelled to support public school services unused by them and to pay for their own children's education. Rather than offering 'an incentive to parents to send their children to sectarian schools,' New York is effectuating the secular purpose of the equalization of the costs of educating New York children that are borne by parents who send their children to nonpublic schools. . . .'"

---

## NOTES AND QUESTIONS

1. According to the Court majority, which prong of the three-prong *Lemon* test do these programs violate?

2. Are the "maintenance and repair" grants in this case restricted to nonreligious uses? What role does this factor play in the Court's evaluation of this aid?

3. How does the Court majority distinguish the tuition reimbursement grants at issue in this case from other state aid that the Court has approved in earlier cases? Do you find the Court's reasoning on this issue persuasive?

4. In the Court majority's estimation, how important is the fact that the tuition reimbursement aid is distributed to the parents rather than to the schools? Why does the Court not see this factor as determinative?

5. How does the majority distinguish between the tax exemption for church property that was at issue in the *Walz* case and the tax benefits at issue in this case? Is this a rational place to draw the line? If not, where would you recommend making a distinction?

6. How does the Court majority use the term "neutrality"? How do the dissenters use that term?

7. The dissenters state: "Rather than offering 'an incentive to parents to send their children to sectarian schools' as the majority suggests, New York is effectuating the secular purpose of the equalization of the costs of educating New York children that are borne by parents who send their children to nonpublic schools." Which side do you believe has the better view of the case? Is "equalization of tax burden" a persuasive policy argument for extending financial aid to parents with children in religious schools? If so, should that policy argument inform our understanding of the constitutional rules?

In a companion case to *Nyquist*, the Court in *Sloan v. Lemon*[29] struck down a Pennsylvania program that reimbursed parents for a portion of tuition expenses incurred in sending their children to nonpublic schools. Like the program at issue in *Nyquist*, the Pennsylvania program "imposed no restrictions or limitations on the uses to which the reimbursement allotments [could] be put by the qualifying parent." The Court found the program had the impermissible effect of advancing religion, notwithstanding the fact the reimbursement was provided to the parents rather than directly to the religious school: "Whether [the] benefit be viewed as a simple tuition subsidy, as an incentive to parents to send their children to sectarian schools, or as a reward for having done so, at bottom its intended consequences is to preserve and support religion-oriented institutions."

Two years later, in *Meek v. Pittenger*,[30] the Court struck down (7-2) a Pennsylvania law loaning instructional material and equipment to nonpublic elementary and secondary schools and providing "auxiliary services" (counseling, testing, psychological services, speech and hearing therapy, and instruction for exceptional and remedial students) on religious school campuses. (A majority of justices upheld an additional provision loaning textbooks to public and private school students on the authority of *Board of Education v. Allen*.)

Initially, the Court agreed that the purpose of the law was secular and constitutional, noting that the law "extend[s] the benefits of free educational aids to every schoolchild in the Commonwealth, including nonpublic school students who constitute approximately one quarter of [Pennsylvania] schoolchildren."[31] However, the loan of the instructional material and equipment had the "unconstitutional primary effect of advancing religion because of the predominately religious character of the schools [benefitted]." The Court acknowledged that the materials and equipment—maps, charts, and laboratory equipment—like the textbooks in *Allen*, were "self-polic[ing], in that starting as secular, nonideological and neutral, they will not change in use." But because the law authorized "substantial amounts" of direct aid to the religious schools, the Court declared that it would "simply ignore reality to attempt to separate secular functions from the predominately religious role performed" by the religious schools.[32] Embracing the pervasively sectarian formula discussed in *Allen* and *Lemon* and finally applied in *Hunt v. McNair*, 413 U.S. 734 (1973), the Court noted that

> [t]he very purpose of many [parochial] schools is to provide an integrated and secular and religious education; the teaching process is, to a large extent, devoted to the inculcation of religious values and belief. *Lemon*. Substantial aid to the educational function of such schools, accordingly, necessarily results in aid to the sectarian school enterprise as a whole. "[T]he secular education those schools provide goes hand in hand with the religious mission that is the only reason for the schools' existence. Within the institution, the two are inextricably intertwined."

Consequently, the Court held that even though the material and equipment were earmarked for secular purposes, "'when [aid] flows to an institution in which religion is so pervasive that a substantial portion of its functions are subsumed in the religious mission, state aid has the impermissible primary effect of advancing religion.'"[33]

As for the auxiliary services, the Court held that having public school personnel conduct services on religious school premises would result in excessive government entanglement with religion. The Court noted that the teachers were performing educational services in schools in which "education is an integral part of the dominant sectarian mission and in which an atmosphere dedicated to the advancement of religious belief is constantly maintained.". . . "Whether the subject is 'remedial reading,' 'advanced reading,' or simply 'reading,' a teacher remains a teacher, and the danger that religious doctrine will become intertwined with the secular instruction persists. . . . To be certain that auxiliary teachers remain religiously neutral . . . the State would have to impose limitations on the activities of auxiliary personnel and then engage in some form of continuing surveillance to ensure that those restrictions were being followed."[34]

Justices Brennan, Douglas, and Thurgood Marshall concurred and dissented, arguing that the textbook provision was also unconstitutional.

Justices Rehnquist and White dissented and concurred, urging the constitutionality of all of the law's provisions.

---

In *Wolman v. Walter*,[35] a sharply divided Court followed the plurality's holding in *Meek* in upholding and striking a laundry list of assistance and services to private and religious schools in Ohio. As in *Meek*, the Court found that the religious schools in question (accounting for 96% of the nonpublic school enrollment, with 92% of the students attending Catholic schools) were "pervasively sectarian," in that the schools "provide an integrated secular and religious education [and] the teaching process is, to a large extent, devoted to the inculcation of religious values and belief." Nonetheless, the Court (only Justices Blackmun and Stewart agreeing on all points) upheld the loan of textbooks to nonpublic school children and reimbursements to the schools for administering and scoring state standardized tests. The Court also upheld state employees conducting speech/hearing and psychological diagnostic services on religious school premises and therapeutic services at neutral sites off premises. Diagnostic services, Justice Blackmun noted, "unlike teaching or counseling, have little or no educational content and are not closely associated with the educational mission of the nonpublic school."[36] In contrast, whereas therapeutic services allowed for greater interaction between state-paid teachers and parochial school students, thus inviting entanglement concerns, providing the services off religious school premises did not "provoke the same concerns that troubled the Court in *Meek*."[37]

As in *Meek*, however, the Court held that the loan of instructional materials and equipment had the impermissible effect of advancing religion. Because of the schools' pervasively sectarian character, and "the impossibility of separating the secular education function from the sectarian, the state aid inevitably flows in part in support of the religious role of the schools." The Court rejected the argument that the aid was constitutional because it flowed to the student, and not to the religious schools, stating that "it would exalt form over substance if this distinction were found to justify a result different from that in *Meek*."[38] Finally, the Court also struck down reimbursements to religious schools for expenses associated with school field trips, noting that the trips were related to the curriculum and, nevertheless, would necessitate close supervision leading to excessive government entanglement with religion.[39]

Chief Justice Burger and Justices White and Rehnquist voted to uphold all of the programs.

Justice Brennan voted to strike down all of the programs.

Justice Marshall voted to strike down all of the programs except for the diagnostic services.

Justice Powell agreed with the plurality except in voting to uphold the expenditures for field trips.

Justice Stevens agreed with the plurality except in voting to strike down the expenditures for textbooks and testing and scoring.

---

### NOTES AND QUESTIONS

1. In *Agostini v. Felton*, 521 U.S. 203 (1997) (see below at p. 456), the Court overruled *Aguilar v. Felton*, 473 U.S. 402 (1985) and, by implication, portions of *Meek* and *Wolman*, and upheld the constitutionality of state-paid teachers providing remedial and enrichment instruction on religious school premises. Also, in *Mitchell v. Helms*, 530 U.S. 793 (2000) (see below at p. 467), upholding the loan of educational materials and equipment to religious schools, the Court overruled those remaining portions of the *Meek* and *Wolman* holdings to the contrary.

2. Considering *Meek* and *Wolman*, on what basis does the Court distinguish the various forms of aid upheld and struck down? Is it that the aid is not identifiably secular, that it may be diverted for religious uses, that it supplements religious schooling too much, or that it supplants the core functions of religious schooling instead of merely assisting at the periphery? Are all of these alternative rationales of equal constitutional concern, or do some present a greater or lesser threat to Establishment Clause values? If the answer to the above question is the last alternative (i.e., supplants educational roles), how can one distinguish providing textbooks to religious schools, which obviously are used in a core educational function?

3. As one basis for denying the aid, the Court in *Meek* says that aid to "pervasively sectarian institutions (here, parochial schools) is impermissible . . . ." From where did the Court derive this characterization and the accompanying rule? How is such a rule consistent with *Allen*, both as to its rationale and ultimate holding? Is the pervasively sectarian presumption an accurate characterization of most religious schools? Many have argued that the character of many Catholic schools has evolved since the 1960s, such that religious doctrine no longer permeates all aspects of the curriculum, although others point out that the hyper-religious characterization is accurate for many Protestant private schools which have arisen since the 1960s. If the characterization is still accurate, wouldn't any government aid advance the schools' religious missions? To be true to principle, should *Meek* and *Wolman* have struck down all of the aid programs, including the textbook program?

---

In *Committee for Public Education and Religious Liberty v. Regan*, the Court considered yet another state program to assist private religious schools in operating their educational programs. In this instance, the state of New York sought to reimburse private schools for costs associated with administering state mandated testing of children. Only seven years before the Court had held unconstitutional an earlier New York program that had reimbursed private schools for the costs of giving similar tests prepared by the schools' teachers. See *Levitt v. Committee for Public Education and Religious Liberty*, 413 U.S. 472 (1973) (discussed below). In *Regan*, however, the outcome was different. In reading *Regan*, see if you can identify what was significant for the Court. Were the factual differences in the two programs sufficient, or does *Regan* represent a shift in the Court's approach to funding cases?

## COMMITTEE FOR PUBLIC EDUCATION AND RELIGIOUS LIBERTY v. REGAN
### 444 U.S. 646 (1980)

JUSTICE WHITE delivered the opinion of the Court. . . .

### I

In 1970, the New York Legislature appropriated public funds to reimburse both church-sponsored and secular nonpublic schools for the "administration, grading and the compiling and reporting of the results of tests and examinations." 1970 N.Y.Laws, ch. 138, § 2. Covered tests included both state-prepared examinations and the more common and traditional teacher-prepared tests. Although the legislature stipulated that "[n]othing contained in this act shall be construed to authorize the making of any payment under this act for religious worship or instruction," § 8, the statute did not provide for any state audit of school financial records that would ensure that public funds were used only for secular purposes.

In *Levitt v. Committee for Public Education*, 413 U.S. 472 (1973) (*Levitt I*), the Court struck down this enactment as violative of the Establishment Clause. . . . The Court was troubled that, "despite the obviously integral role of such testing in the total teaching process, no attempt is made under the statute, and no means are available, to assure that internally prepared tests are free of religious instruction." . . .

Almost immediately the New York Legislature attempted to eliminate these defects from its statutory scheme. . . .

Of signal interest and importance in light of *Levitt I*, the new scheme does not reimburse nonpublic schools for the preparation, administration, or grading of teacher-prepared tests. Further, the 1974 statute, unlike the 1970 version struck down in *Levitt I*, provides a means by which payments of state funds are audited, thus ensuring that only the actual costs incurred in providing the covered secular services are reimbursed out of state funds. § 7. . . .

### II

Under the precedents of this Court a legislative enactment does not contravene the Establishment Clause if it has a secular legislative purpose, if its principal or primary effect neither advances nor inhibits religion, and if it does not foster an excessive government entanglement with religion.

In *Wolman v. Walter*, this Court reviewed and sustained in relevant part an Ohio statutory scheme that authorized, *inter alia*, the expenditure of state funds "[t]o supply for use by pupils attending nonpublic schools within the district such standardized tests and scoring services as are in use in the public schools of the state." Ohio Rev.Code Ann. § 3317.06(J) (Supp. 1976). . . .

### III

We agree with the District Court that *Wolman v. Walter* controls this case. Addressing first the testing provisions, we note that here, as in *Wolman*, there is clearly a secular purpose behind the legislative enactment: "[T]o provide educational opportunity of a quality which will prepare [New York] citizens for the challenges of American life in the last decades of the twentieth century." 1974 N.Y.Laws, ch. 507, § 1. Also like the Ohio statute, the New York plan calls for tests that are prepared by the State and administered on the premises by nonpublic school personnel. The nonpublic school thus has no control whatsoever over the content of the tests. The Ohio tests, however, were graded by the State; here there are three types of tests involved, one graded by the State and the other two by nonpublic school personnel, with the costs of the grading service, as well as the cost of administering all three tests, being reimbursed by the State. In view of the nature of the tests, the District Court found that the grading of the examinations by nonpublic school employees afforded no control to the school over the outcome of any of the tests. . . .

We see no reason to differ with the factual or legal characterization of the testing procedure arrived at by the District Court. As in *Wolman v. Walter*, 433 U.S., 240, "[t]he nonpublic school does not control the content of the test or its result"; and here, as in *Wolman*, this factor "serves to prevent the use of the test as a part of religious teaching," *ibid.*, thus avoiding the kind of direct aid forbidden by the Court's prior cases. The District Court was correct in concluding that there was no substantial risk that the examinations could be used for religious educational purposes. . . .

### IV

The New York statute, unlike the Ohio statute at issue in *Wolman*, provides for direct cash reimbursement to the nonpublic school for administering the state-prescribed examinations and for grading two of them. We agree with the District Court that such reimbursement does not invalidate the New York statute. If the State furnished state-prepared tests, thereby relieving the nonpublic schools of the expense of preparing their own examinations, but left the grading of the tests to the schools, and if the grading procedures could be used to further the religious mission of the school, serious Establishment Clause problems would be posed under the Court's cases, for by furnishing the tests it might be concluded that the State was directly aiding religious education. But as we have already concluded, grading the secular tests furnished by the State in this case is a function that has a secular purpose and primarily a secular effect. This conclusion is not changed simply because the State pays the school for performing the grading function. . . .

A contrary view would insist on drawing a constitutional distinction between paying the nonpublic school to do the grading and paying state employees or some independent service to perform that task, even though the grading function is the same regardless of who performs it and would not have the primary effect of aiding religion whether or not performed by nonpublic

not to believe) free of any coercive pressures from the State, while at the same time tainting the resulting religious beliefs with a corrosive secularism.

In *Meek v. Pittenger,* 421 U.S. 349, the Court invalidated a statute providing for the loan of state-paid professional staff—including teachers—to nonpublic schools to provide remedial and accelerated instruction, guidance counseling and testing, and other services on the premises of the nonpublic schools. Such a program, if not subjected to a "comprehensive, discriminating, and continuing state surveillance," *Lemon v. Kurtzman,* 403 U.S., 619, would entail an unacceptable risk that the state-sponsored instructional personnel would "advance the religious mission of the church-related schools in which they serve." *Meek,* 421 U.S., 370. . . . The program in *Meek,* if not sufficiently monitored, would simply have entailed too great a risk of state-sponsored indoctrination.

The programs before us today share the defect that we identified in *Meek.* With respect to the Community Education program, the District Court found that "virtually every Community Education course conducted on facilities leased from nonpublic schools has an instructor otherwise employed full time by the same nonpublic school." 546 F. Supp., 1079. These instructors, many of whom no doubt teach in the religious schools precisely because they are adherents of the controlling denomination and want to serve their religious community zealously, are expected during the regular schoolday to inculcate their students with the tenets and beliefs of their particular religious faiths. Yet the premise of the program is that those instructors can put aside their religious convictions and engage in entirely secular Community Education instruction as soon as the schoolday is over. Moreover, they are expected to do so before the same religious school students and in the same religious school classrooms that they employed to advance religious purposes during the "official" schoolday. . . .

We do not question that the dedicated and professional religious school-teachers employed by the Community Education program will attempt in good faith to perform their secular mission conscientiously. Nonetheless, there is a substantial risk that, overtly or subtly, the religious message they are expected to convey during the regular schoolday will infuse the supposedly secular classes they teach after school. . . .

The Shared Time program, though structured somewhat differently, nonetheless also poses a substantial risk of state-sponsored indoctrination. The most important difference between the programs is that most of the instructors in the Shared Time program are full-time teachers hired by the public schools. Moreover, although "virtually every" Community Education instructor is a full-time religious schoolteacher, 546 F. Supp., 1079, only "[a] significant portion" of the Shared Time instructors previously worked in the religious schools. *Id.,* 1078. Nonetheless, as with the Community Education program, no attempt is made to monitor the Shared Time courses for religious content.

Thus, despite these differences between the two programs, our holding in *Meek* controls the inquiry with respect to Shared Time, as well as Community Education. Shared Time instructors are teaching academic subjects in religious schools in courses virtually indistinguishable from the other courses offered during the regular religious schoolday. The teachers in this program, even more than their Community Education colleagues, are "performing important educational services in schools in which education is an integral part of the dominant sectarian mission and in which an atmosphere dedicated to the advancement of religious belief is constantly maintained." *Meek v. Pittenger,* 421 U.S., 371. Teachers in such an atmosphere may well subtly (or overtly) conform their instruction to the environment in which they teach, while students will perceive the instruction provided in the context of the dominantly religious message of the institution, thus reinforcing the indoctrinating effect. . . . Unlike types of aid that the Court has upheld, such as state-created standardized tests, *Committee for Public Education & Religious Liberty v. Regan,* 444 U.S. 646, or diagnostic services, *Wolman v. Walter,* 433 U.S., 241-244, there is a "substantial risk" that programs operating in this environment would "be used for religious educational purposes." *Committee for Public Education & Religious Liberty v. Regan,* 444 U.S., 656. . . .

(2)

Our cases have recognized that the Establishment Clause guards against more than direct, state-funded efforts to indoctrinate youngsters in specific religious beliefs. Government promotes religion as effectively when it fosters a close identification of its powers and responsibilities with those of any—or all—religious denominations as when it attempts to inculcate specific religious doctrines. If this identification conveys a message of government endorsement or disapproval of religion, a core purpose of the Establishment Clause is violated. As we stated in *Larkin v. Grendel's Den,* 459 U.S. 116, 125-126: "[T]he mere appearance of a joint exercise of legislative authority by Church and State provides a significant symbolic benefit to religion in the minds of some by reason of the power conferred."

It follows that an important concern of the effects test is whether the symbolic union of church and state effected by the challenged governmental action is sufficiently likely to be perceived by adherents of the controlling denominations as an endorsement, and by the nonadherents as a disapproval, of their individual religious choices. The inquiry into this kind of effect must be conducted with particular care when many of the citizens perceiving the governmental message are children in their formative years. . . .

In the programs challenged in this case, the religious school students spend their typical schoolday moving between religious school and "public school" classes. Both types of classes take place in the same religious school building and both are largely composed of students who are adherents of the same denomination. In this environment, the students would be unlikely to discern the crucial difference between the religious school classes and the "public school" classes, even if the latter were successfully kept free of religious indoctrination. . . .

This effect—the symbolic union of government and religion in one sectarian enterprise—is an impermissible effect under the Establishment Clause.

(3)

In *Everson v. Board of Education,* 330 U.S. 1, the Court stated that "[n]o tax in any amount, large or small, can be levied to support any religious activities or institutions, whatever they may be called, or whatever form they may adopt to teach or practice religion." *Id.,* 16. With but one exception, our subsequent cases have struck down attempts by States to make payments out of public tax dollars directly to primary or secondary religious educational institutions. . . .

Aside from cash payments, the Court has distinguished between two categories of programs in which public funds are used to finance secular activities that religious schools would otherwise fund from their own resources. In the first category, the Court has noted that it is "well established . . . that not every law that confers an 'indirect,' 'remote,' or 'incidental' benefit upon religious institutions is, for that reason alone, constitutionally invalid." *Committee for Public Education & Religious Liberty v. Nyquist,* 413 U.S., 771. In such "indirect" aid cases, the government has used primarily secular means to accomplish a primarily secular end, and no "primary effect" of advancing religion has thus been found. On this rationale, the Court has upheld programs providing for loans of secular textbooks to nonpublic school students, *Board of Education v. Allen,* 392 U.S. 236; see also *Wolman v. Walter,* 433 U.S., 236-238; *Meek v. Pittenger,* 421 U.S., 359-362, and programs providing bus transportation for nonpublic schoolchildren, *Everson v. Board of Education.*

In the second category of cases, the Court has relied on the Establishment Clause prohibition of forms of aid that provide "direct and substantial advancement of the sectarian enterprise." *Wolman v. Walter,* 433 U.S., 250. . . . Under this rationale, the Court has struck down state schemes providing for tuition grants and tax benefits for parents whose children attend religious school, see *Sloan v. Lemon,* 413 U.S. 825; *Committee for Public Education & Religious Liberty v. Nyquist,* 413 U.S., 780-794, and programs providing for "loan" of instructional materials to be used in religious schools, see *Wolman v. Walter,* 433 U.S., 248-251; *Meek v. Pittenger,* 421 U.S., 365. In *Sloan* and *Nyquist,* the aid was formally given to parents and not directly to the religious schools, while in *Wolman* and *Meek,* the aid was in-kind assistance rather than the direct contribution of public funds. Nonetheless, these differences in form were insufficient to save programs whose effect was indistinguishable from that of a direct subsidy to the religious school.

Thus, the Court has never accepted the mere possibility of subsidization, as the above cases demonstrate, as sufficient to invalidate an aid program. On the other hand, this effect is not wholly unimportant for Establishment Clause purposes. If it were, the public schools could gradually take on themselves the entire responsibility for teaching secular subjects on religious school premises. The question in each case must be whether the effect of the proffered aid is "direct and substantial," *Committee for Public Education & Religious Liberty v. Nyquist,* 413 U.S., 784-785, n. 39, or indirect and incidental. "The problem, like many problems in constitutional law, is one of degree." *Zorach v. Clauson,* 343 U.S., 314. . . .

The programs challenged here, which provide teachers in addition to the instructional equipment and materials, have a similar—and forbidden—effect of advancing religion. This kind of direct aid to the educational function of the religious school is indistinguishable from the provision of a direct cash subsidy to the religious school that is most clearly prohibited under the Establishment Clause.

Petitioners claim that the aid here, like the textbooks in *Allen,* flows primarily to the students, not to the religious schools.[13] Of course, all aid to religious schools ultimately "flows to" the students, and petitioners' argument

---

[13] Petitioners also cite *Mueller v. Allen,* 463 U.S. 388, which upheld a general tax deduction available to parents of all schoolchildren for school expenses, including tuition to religious schools. *Mueller,* however, is quite unlike the instant case. Unlike *Mueller,* the aid provided here is unmediated by the tax code and the "numerous, private choices of individual parents of school-age children." *Id.,* 399.

if accepted would validate all forms of nonideological aid to religious schools, including those explicitly rejected in our prior cases. Yet in *Meek,* we held unconstitutional the loan of instructional materials to religious schools and in *Wolman,* we rejected the fiction that a similar program could be saved by masking it as aid to individual students. . . . Where, as here, no meaningful distinction can be made between aid to the student and aid to the school, "the concept of a loan to individuals is a transparent fiction." *Wolman v. Walter,* 264, (opinion of POWELL, J.).

Petitioners also argue that this "subsidy" effect is not significant in this case, because the Community Education and Shared Time programs supplemented the curriculum with courses not previously offered in the religious schools. . . . As in *Meek,* we do not find that this feature of the program is controlling. First, there is no way of knowing whether the religious schools would have offered some or all of these courses if the public school system had not offered them first. The distinction between courses that "supplement" and those that "supplant" the regular curriculum is therefore not nearly as clear as petitioners allege. Second, although the precise courses offered in these programs may have been new to the participating religious schools, their general subject matter—reading, mathematics, etc.—was surely a part of the curriculum in the past, and the concerns of the Establishment Clause may thus be triggered despite the "supplemental" nature of the courses. Cf. *Meek v. Pittenger,* 421 U.S., 370-371. Third, and most important, petitioners' argument would permit the public schools gradually to take over the entire secular curriculum of the religious school, for the latter could surely discontinue existing courses so that they might be replaced a year or two later by a Community Education or Shared Time course with the same content. . . . [T]here is no principled basis on which this Court can impose a limit on the percentage of the religious schoolday that can be subsidized by the public school. To let the genie out of the bottle in this case would be to permit ever larger segments of the religious school curriculum to be turned over to the public school system, thus violating the cardinal principle that the State may not in effect become the prime supporter of the religious school system. See *Lemon v. Kurtzman,* 403 U.S., 624-625.

## III

We conclude that the challenged programs have the effect of promoting religion in three ways. The state-paid instructors, influenced by the pervasively sectarian nature of the religious schools in which they work, may subtly or overtly indoctrinate the students in particular religious tenets at public expense. The symbolic union of church and state inherent in the provision of secular, state-provided instruction in the religious school buildings threatens to convey a message of state support for religion to students and to the general public. Finally, the programs in effect subsidize the religious functions of the parochial schools by taking over a substantial portion of their responsibility for teaching secular subjects. For these reasons, the conclusion is inescapable that the Community Education and Shared Time programs have the "primary or principal" effect of advancing religion, and therefore violate the dictates of the Establishment Clause of the First Amendment. . . .

*It is so ordered.*

▓ JUSTICE O'CONNOR, concurring in the judgment in part and dissenting in part. . . .

I dissent from the Court's holding that the Grand Rapids Shared Time program impermissibly advances religion. Like the New York Title I program, the Grand Rapids Shared Time program employs full-time public school teachers who offer supplemental instruction to parochial school children on the premises of religious schools. Nothing in the record indicates that Shared Time instructors have attempted to proselytize their students. . . .

I agree with the Court, however, that the Community Education program violates the Establishment Clause. The record indicates that Community Education courses in the parochial schools are overwhelmingly taught by instructors who are current full-time employees of the parochial school. The teachers offer secular subjects to the same parochial school students who attend their regular parochial school classes. In addition, the supervisors of the Community Education program in the parochial schools are by and large the principals of the very schools where the classes are offered. When full-time parochial school teachers receive public funds to teach secular courses to their parochial school students under parochial school supervision, I agree that the program has the perceived and actual effect of advancing the religious aims of the church-related schools. This is particularly the case where, as here, religion pervades the curriculum and the teachers are accustomed to bring religion to play in everything they teach. I concur in the judgment of the Court that the Community Education program violates the Establishment Clause. . . .

▓ CHIEF JUSTICE BURGER concurred in the judgment in part and dissented in part.

▓ JUSTICES WHITE and REHNQUIST filed dissenting opinions.

## NOTES AND QUESTIONS

1. In the *Meek* and *Wolman* cases, how does the Court decide whether the particular types of financial aid are constitutionally permissible or impermissible? What parts of the *Lemon* test are implicated?

2. What kind of aid did the Court find permissible in the *Regan* case? For what reasons? How did the aid differ from that struck down in *Nyquist, Sloan, Meek* and *Wolman*? Are the differences primarily factual or normative?

3. Generally describe the Court's "pervasively sectarian" formula. According to the Court, what constitutional values does this test advance? How does the *Ball* Court define the term "pervasively sectarian"? Why does it focus on the nature of the schools involved at the outset of its majority opinion?

4. How does the Shared Time program at issue in *Ball* differ from the Community Education program? In what ways do the *Ball* programs violate the Constitution, according to the Court majority?

5. According to the *Ball* Court, what is one of the absolute prohibitions of the Establishment Clause?

6. The *Ball* Court states: "With but one exception, our subsequent cases have struck down attempts by States to make payments out of public tax dollars directly to primary or secondary religious educational institutions." What is that one exception?

7. According to the *Ball* Court, what is the main question that should guide the evaluation of government aid other than "cash payments"?

8. The *Ball* Court says that aid cannot be justified simply because it ultimately flows to the students. What other considerations does the Court view as important?

9. At this point, has the Court developed clear, consistent, and defensible rules for determining when government aid for religious schools will be constitutional and when it will not?

CHAPTER 12

# GOVERNMENT FUNDING OF RELIGIOUS SCHOOLS: THE RISE OF EVEN-HANDED NEUTRALITY AND PRIVATE CHOICE

The previous chapter dealt with government funding programs where the private religious schools were the direct beneficiaries of the aid. In essence, in *Lemon*, *Meek* and *Wolman*, for example, the type of state financial assistance—salary supplements, instructional materials, grants for building maintenance and repair—accrued to the schools and thus supplemented the costs associated with running their educational programs. Applying various theories—that the programs subsidized religion too much or lacked sufficient safeguards to ensure the assistance could not be used for religious purposes—the Court struck down the programs as providing direct assistance to the religious schools' educational mission.

One of the programs at issue in *Nyquist* provided financial assistance in a different format. Rather than sending funds or materials directly to the religious schools for them to use for purportedly secular educational purposes, one of the aid programs in *Nyquist* provided partial tuition reimbursements and tax credits to parents of students attending parochial and other nonpublic schools. There, the state of New York argued that those programs survived constitutional scrutiny because the primary beneficiaries in those instances were the children (via their parents), and not the religious schools.

The Court rejected that theory, holding that the effect of the aid was equivalent to direct aid to the religious schools. However, the Court dropped an oblique footnote in its discussion that raised questions as to the firmness of its holding on the tuition reimbursement issue. The footnote stated that "[b]ecause of the manner in which we have resolved the tuition grant issue, we need not decide whether the significantly religious character of the statute's beneficiaries might differentiate the present cases from a case involving some form of public assistance (e.g., scholarships) made available generally without regard to the sectarian-nonsectarian, or public-nonpublic nature of the institution benefitted." As a result, the *Nyquist* holding did little to quash the idea of providing financial assistance to parents of religious school children rather than providing the aid directly to the schools themselves.

This concept—that indirect aid might be constitutional in ways that direct aid was not—had been around since the Court's articulation of the "child benefit" theory in *Cochran* in 1930. But the idea of what came to be known as "private choice" did not become popular until the Court began striking down educational assistance programs in the 1970s. Building on the works of Nobel laureate economist Milton Friedman and later scholars such as John Chubb and Terry Moe, advocates began to construct arguments that *indirect* financial aid in the form of tuition tax deductions, tax credits, and vouchers would survive Establishment Clause review.[1] In reading the following cases, see if you can identify the factors that various Court members see as important in order for an indirect funding program to be constitutional.

---

### MUELLER v. ALLEN
### 463 U.S. 388 (1983)

⊞ JUSTICE REHNQUIST delivered the opinion of the Court.

Minnesota, by a law originally enacted in 1955 and revised in 1978, permits state taxpayers to claim a deduction from gross income for certain expenses incurred in educating their children. The deduction is limited to actual expenses incurred for the "tuition, textbooks and transportation" of dependents attending elementary or secondary schools. A deduction may not exceed $500 per dependent in grades K through six and $700 per dependent in grades seven through twelve. Minn.Stat. § 290.09.[2] . . .

---

[2] Both lower courts found that the statute permits deduction of a range of educational expenses. The District Court found that deductible expenses included:

    1. Tuition in the ordinary sense.
    2. Tuition to public school students who attend public schools outside their residence school districts.
    3. Certain summer school tuition.
    4. Tuition charged by a school for slow learner private tutoring services.
    5. Tuition for instruction provided by an elementary or secondary school to students who are physically unable to attend classes at such school.
    6. Tuition charged by a private tutor or by a school that is not an elementary or secondary school if the instruction is acceptable for credit in an elementary or secondary school.
    7. Montessori School tuition for grades K through 12.
    8. Tuition for driver education when it is part of the school curriculum. 514 F. Supp., at 1000.
    The Court of Appeals concurred in this finding.
    In addition, the District Court found that the statutory deduction for "textbooks" included not only "secular textbooks" but also:
    1. Cost of tennis shoes and sweatsuits for physical education.
    2. Camera rental fees paid to the school for photography classes.
    3. Ice skates rental fee paid to the school.
    4. Rental fee paid to the school for calculators for mathematics classes.
    5. Costs of home economics materials needed to meet minimum requirements.
    6. Costs of special metal or wood needed to meet minimum requirements of shop classes.
    7. Costs of supplies needed to meet minimum requirements of art classes.
    8. Rental fees paid to the school for musical instruments.
    9. Cost of pencils and special notebooks required for class. *Ibid.*
    The Court of Appeals accepted this finding.

Today's case is no exception to our oft-repeated statement that the Establishment Clause presents especially difficult questions of interpretation and application. . . .

One fixed principle in this field is our consistent rejection of the argument that "any program which in some manner aids an institution with a religious affiliation" violates the Establishment Clause. *Hunt v. McNair,* 413 U.S. 734, 742. . . .

Notwithstanding the repeated approval given programs such as those in *Allen* and *Everson,* our decisions also have struck down arrangements resembling, in many respects, these forms of assistance. In this case we are asked to decide whether Minnesota's tax deduction bears greater resemblance to those types of assistance to parochial schools we have approved, or to those we have struck down. Petitioners place particular reliance on our decision in *Committee for Public Education v. Nyquist,* where we held invalid a New York statute providing public funds for the maintenance and repair of the physical facilities of private schools and granting thinly disguised "tax benefits," actually amounting to tuition grants, to the parents of children attending private schools. As explained below, we conclude that § 290.09(22) bears less resemblance to the arrangement struck down in *Nyquist* than it does to assistance programs upheld in our prior decisions and those discussed with approval in *Nyquist.* . . .

This reflects, at least in part, our reluctance to attribute unconstitutional motives to the states, particularly when a plausible secular purpose for the state's program may be discerned from the face of the statute.

A state's decision to defray the cost of educational expenses incurred by parents—regardless of the type of schools their children attend—evidences a purpose that is both secular and understandable. . . . Similarly, Minnesota, like other states, could conclude that there is a strong public interest in assuring the continued financial health of private schools, both sectarian and non-sectarian. By educating a substantial number of students such schools relieve public schools of a correspondingly great burden—to the benefit of all taxpayers. . . .

We turn therefore to the more difficult but related question whether the Minnesota statute has "the primary effect of advancing the sectarian aims of the nonpublic schools." *Committee for Public Education v. Regan,* 444 U.S. 646, 662. In concluding that it does not, we find several features of the Minnesota tax deduction particularly significant. First, an essential feature of Minnesota's arrangement is the fact that § 290.09(22) is only one among many deductions—such as those for medical expenses, Minn. Stat. § 290.09(10) and charitable contributions, Minn. Stat. § 290.21—available under the Minnesota tax laws.[5] Our decisions consistently have recognized that traditionally "[l]egislatures have especially broad latitude in creating classifications and distinctions in tax statutes," *Regan v. Taxation with Representation,* 461 U.S. 540, in part because the "familiarity with local conditions" enjoyed by legislators especially enables them to "achieve an equitable distribution of the tax burden." *Madden*

---

[5] Deductions for charitable contributions, allowed by Minnesota law, Minn. Stat. § 290.21, include contributions to religious institutions, and exemptions from property tax for property used for charitable purposes under Minnesota law include property used for wholly religious purposes, Minn. Stat. § 272.02. In each case, it may be that religious institutions benefit very substantially from the allowance of such deductions. . . .

*v. Kentucky,* 309 U.S. 83, 87 (1940). Under our prior decisions, the Minnesota legislature's judgment that a deduction for educational expenses fairly equalizes the tax burden of its citizens and encourages desirable expenditures for educational purposes is entitled to substantial deference.[6]

Other characteristics of § 290.09(22) argue equally strongly for the provision's constitutionality. Most importantly, the deduction is available for educational expenses incurred by *all* parents, including those whose children attend public schools and those whose children attend non-sectarian private schools or sectarian private schools. . . .

We also agree with the Court of Appeals that, by channeling whatever assistance it may provide to parochial schools through individual parents, Minnesota has reduced the Establishment Clause objections to which its action is subject. It is true, of course, that financial assistance provided to parents ultimately has an economic effect comparable to that of aid given directly to the schools attended by their children. It is also true, however, that under Minnesota's arrangement public funds become available only as a result of numerous, private choices of individual parents of school-age children. For these reasons, we recognized in *Nyquist* that the means by which state assistance flows to private schools is of some importance: we said that "the fact that aid is disbursed to parents rather than to . . . school" is a material consideration in Establishment Clause analysis, albeit "only one among many to be considered." *Nyquist,* 781. It is noteworthy that all but one of our recent cases invalidating state aid to parochial schools have involved the direct transmission of assistance from the state to the schools themselves. The exception, of course, was *Nyquist,* which, as discussed previously, is distinguishable from this case on other grounds. Where, as here, aid to parochial schools is available only as a result of decisions of individual parents no "imprimatur of state approval," *Widmar,* 274, can be deemed to have been conferred on any particular religion, or on religion generally.

We find it useful, in the light of the foregoing characteristics of § 290.09(22), to compare the attenuated financial benefits flowing to parochial schools from the section to the evils against which the Establishment Clause was designed to protect. These dangers are well-described by our statement that "what is at stake as a matter of policy [in Establishment Clause cases] is preventing that kind and degree of government involvement in religious life that, as history teaches us, is apt to lead to strife and frequently strain a political system to the breaking point." . . .

We do not think, however, that its prohibition extends to the type of tax deduction established by Minnesota. The historic purposes of the Clause

---

[6] Our decision in *Nyquist* is not to the contrary on this point. We expressed considerable doubt there that the "tax benefits" provided by New York law properly could be regarded as parts of a genuine system of tax laws. Plainly, the outright grants to low-income parents did not take the form of ordinary tax benefits. . . .

Indeed, the question whether a program having the elements of a "genuine tax deduction" would be constitutionally acceptable was expressly reserved in *Nyquist,* 413 U.S., 790, n. 49. While the economic consequences of the program in *Nyquist* and that in this case may be difficult to distinguish, we have recognized on other occasions that "the form of the [state's assistance to parochial schools must be examined] for the light that it casts on the substance." *Lemon v. Kurtzman,* 403 U.S., 614. The fact that the Minnesota plan embodies a "genuine tax deduction" is thus of some relevance, especially given the traditional rule of deference accorded legislative classifications in tax statutes.

simply do not encompass the sort of attenuated financial benefit, ultimately controlled by the private choices of individual parents, that eventually flows to parochial schools from the neutrally available tax benefit at issue in this case.

Petitioners argue that, notwithstanding the facial neutrality of § 290.09(22), in application the statute primarily benefits religious institutions. Petitioners rely, as they did below, on a statistical analysis of the type of persons claiming the tax deduction. They contend that most parents of public school children incur no tuition expenses, see Minn. Stat. § 120.06, and that other expenses deductible under § 290.09(22) are negligible in value; moreover, they claim that 96% of the children in private schools in 1978-1979 attended religiously-affiliated institutions. Because of all this, they reason, the bulk of deductions taken under § 290.09(22) will be claimed by parents of children in sectarian schools. . . .

We need not consider these contentions in detail. We would be loath to adopt a rule grounding the constitutionality of a facially neutral law on annual reports reciting the extent to which various classes of private citizens claimed benefits under the law. Such an approach would scarcely provide the certainty that this field stands in need of, nor can we perceive principled standards by which such statistical evidence might be evaluated. Moreover, the fact that private persons fail in a particular year to claim the tax relief to which they are entitled—under a facially neutral statute—should be of little importance in determining the constitutionality of the statute permitting such relief. . . .

Finally, the Court had "no difficulty" in concluding that the Minnesota statute did not result in "comprehensive, discriminating, and continuing state surveillance" in violation of the entanglement prong. While acknowledging that state officials were required to determine whether deductions for textbooks did not include "instructional books and materials used in the teaching of religious tenets, doctrines, or worship," the Court found such determinations were no more entangling than those similar decisions that took place in *Allen*.

▓ JUSTICE MARSHALL, writing a dissenting opinion joined by JUSTICES BRENNAN, BLACKMUN, and STEVENS, insisted that the Minnesota deduction was indistinguishable from the tax benefit struck down in *Nyquist*: . . .

That parents receive a reduction of their tax liability, rather than a direct reimbursement, is of no greater significance here than it was in *Nyquist*. "[F]or purposes of determining whether such aid has the effect of advancing religion," it makes no difference whether the qualifying "parent receives an actual cash payment [or] is allowed to reduce . . . the sum he would otherwise be obliged to pay over to the State." *Id.*, 790-791. . . . What is of controlling significance is not the form but the "substantive impact" of the financial aid. . . .

That the Minnesota statute makes some small benefit available to all parents cannot alter the fact that the most substantial benefit provided by the statute is available only to those parents who send their children to schools that charge tuition. It is simply undeniable that the single largest expense that may be deducted under the Minnesota statute is tuition. The statute is little more than a subsidy of tuition masquerading as a subsidy of general educational expenses. The other deductible expenses are *de minimis* in comparison to tuition expenses. . . .

In this case, it is undisputed that well over 90% of the children attending tuition-charging schools in Minnesota are enrolled in sectarian schools.

History and experience likewise instruct us that any generally available financial assistance for elementary and secondary school tuition expenses mainly will further religious education because the majority of the schools which charge tuition are sectarian. Cf. *Nyquist,* 785; *Lemon v. Kurztman,* 403 U.S 628-630 (DOUGLAS, J., concurring). Because Minnesota, like every other State, is committed to providing free public education, tax assistance for tuition payments inevitably redounds to the benefit of nonpublic, sectarian schools and parents who send their children to those schools. . . .

In my view, Minnesota's tax deduction for the cost of textbooks and other instructional materials is also constitutionally infirm. The majority is simply mistaken in concluding that a tax deduction, unlike a tax credit or a direct grant to parents, promotes religious education in a manner that is only "attenuated." A tax deduction has a primary effect that advances religion if it is provided to offset expenditures which are not restricted to the secular activities of parochial schools. . . .

In my view, the lines drawn in *Nyquist* were drawn on a reasoned basis with appropriate regard for the principles of neutrality embodied by the Establishment Clause. I do not believe that the same can be said of the lines drawn by the majority today. For the first time, the Court has upheld financial support for religious schools without any reason at all to assume that the support will be restricted to the secular functions of those schools and will not be used to support religious instruction. This result is flatly at odds with the fundamental principle that a State may provide no financial support whatsoever to promote religion. . . .

I dissent.

---

## Notes and Questions

1. Describe the features of the Minnesota tax deduction that the Court believed saved it from constitutional error. What feature does the Court claim is the "most important" among these features?

2. How does the Court majority distinguish the *Nyquist* case? What factors justify the different result in this case?

3. Why is the indirect path by which state assistance flows to private schools constitutionally significant? What is the appropriate focus: the purported beneficiary of the funding (school children); the ultimate beneficiary of the funding (children? the religious school?); or the formal path the funds take to arrive at their ultimate destination, irrespective of who benefits? How much emphasis should the Court place on the indirect funding pattern? Should it be determinative or "one of several factors" in the constitutional formula?

4. The majority argues that tax deductions should be viewed as constitutionally different matters than tax credits, while the dissent argues that "[t]his is a distinction without a difference." What are the arguments that support these different points of view?

5. The Court states: "We would be loath to adopt a rule grounding the constitutionality of a facially neutral law on annual reports reciting the extent to which various classes of private citizens claimed benefits under the law." What is the argument to the contrary, and why does the Court majority

> reject it? How does Justice Marshall respond to this argument in his dissent-
> ing opinion?
>
> 6. Justice Marshall concludes his dissenting opinion in the following way:
>
>> For the first time, the Court has upheld financial support for religious schools
>> without any reason at all to assume that the support will be restricted to the
>> secular functions of those schools and will not be used to support religious
>> instruction. This result is flatly at odds with the fundamental principle that a
>> State may provide no financial support whatsoever to promote religion.
>
> Is this characterization of the case correct?

*Mueller* invoked principles of indirect private choice within the context of a tax deduction for educational expenses, including tuition costs for private schooling. Although the Court majority embraced the concept of private choice, many argued that the financial assistance there was minimal: a passive tax deduction that did not involve an appropriation of public money and which benefited the religious schools only in the most indirect manner. The *Mueller* holding raised questions, however, whether the concept of indirect private choice was applicable to more substantial forms of assistance, such as actual cash grants in the form of educational scholarships or "vouchers."

That issue quickly came before the Court in a case involving government assistance at the college level. In *Witters v. Washington Department of Services for the Blind* the petitioner applied to the Washington Commission for the Blind for vocational rehabilitation aid to provide for "special education and/or training in the professions, businesses or trades" for "visually handicapped persons." At the time, Larry Witters was attending Inland Empire School of the Bible studying the Bible, ethics, speech, and church administration in order to equip him for a career as a pastor, missionary, or youth director. The Commission denied Petitioner aid based on a reading of the Washington State Constitution, Art. I, sec. 11, and Art. IX, sec. 4, that forbids the use of government funds to assist an individual in the pursuit of a career or degree in theology. State courts affirmed the administrative decision, with the Washington Supreme Court reserving judgment on the state constitutional issue but basing its ruling on the Establishment Clause of the First Amendment.

## WITTERS v. WASHINGTON DEPARTMENT OF SERVICES FOR THE BLIND
### 474 U.S. 481 (1986)

JUSTICE MARSHALL delivered an opinion for the Court in which CHIEF JUSTICE BURGER and JUSTICES BRENNAN, WHITE, BLACKMUN, POWELL, REHNQUIST, and STEVENS joined, and in which JUSTICE O'CONNOR joined as to Parts I and III. . . .

II . . .

We are guided, as was the court below, by the three-part test set out by this Court in *Lemon*. See *Grand Rapids School District v. Ball,* 473 U.S. 373, 382-383. Our analysis relating to the first prong of that test is simple: all parties concede the unmistakably secular purpose of the Washington program. That program was designed to promote the well-being of the visually handicapped through the provision of vocational rehabilitation services, and no more than a minuscule amount of the aid awarded under the program is likely to flow to religious education. No party suggests that the State's "actual purpose" in creating the program was to endorse religion, *Wallace v. Jaffree,* 472 U.S. 38, 74, quoting *Lynch v. Donnelly,* 465 U.S. 668, 690 (O'CONNOR, J., concurring), or that the secular purpose articulated by the legislature is merely "sham." *Wallace,* 472 U.S., 64, (POWELL, J., concurring).

The answer to the question posed by the second prong of the *Lemon* test is more difficult. We conclude, however, that extension of aid to petitioner is not barred on that ground either. It is well settled that the Establishment Clause is not violated every time money previously in the possession of a State is conveyed to a religious institution. For example, a State may issue a paycheck to one of its employees, who may then donate all or part of that paycheck to a religious institution, all without constitutional barrier; and the State may do so even knowing that the employee so intends to dispose of his salary. It is equally well-settled, on the other hand, that the State may not grant aid to a religious school, whether cash or in kind, where the effect of the aid is "that of a direct subsidy to the religious school" from the State. *Grand Rapids School District v. Ball,* 473 U.S., 394. Aid may have that effect even though it takes the form of aid to students or parents. *Ibid.* The question presented is whether, on the facts as they appear in the record before us, extension of aid to petitioner and the use of that aid by petitioner to support his religious education is a permissible transfer similar to the hypothetical salary donation described above, or is an impermissible "direct subsidy."

Certain aspects of Washington's program are central to our inquiry. As far as the record shows, vocational assistance provided under the Washington program is paid directly to the student, who transmits it to the educational institution of his or her choice. Any aid provided under Washington's program that ultimately flows to religious institutions does so only as a result of the genuinely independent and private choices of aid recipients. Washington's program is "made available generally without regard to the sectarian-nonsectarian, or public-nonpublic nature of the institution benefitted," *Committee for Public Education and Religious Liberty v. Nyquist,* 413 U.S., 782-783, n. 38, and is in no way skewed towards religion. It is not one of "the ingenious plans for channeling state aid to sectarian schools that periodically reach this Court," *id.,* 785. It creates no financial incentive for students to undertake sectarian education, see *id.,* 785-786. It does not tend to provide greater or broader benefits for recipients who apply their aid to religious education, nor are the full benefits of the program limited, in large part or in whole, to students at sectarian institutions. On the contrary, aid recipients have full opportunity to expend vocational rehabilitation aid on wholly secular education, and as a practical matter have rather greater prospects to do so. Aid recipients' choices are made among a huge variety of possible careers, of which only a small handful are sectarian. In this case, the fact that aid goes to individuals means that the decision to support religious education is made by the individual, not by the State.

Further, and importantly, nothing in the record indicates that, if petitioner succeeds, any significant portion of the aid expended under the Washington program as a whole will end up flowing to religious education. The function of the Washington program is hardly "to provide desired financial support for nonpublic, sectarian institutions." *Id.,*, 783. The program, providing vocational assistance to the visually handicapped, does not seem well suited to serve as the vehicle for such a subsidy. No evidence has been presented indicating that any other person has ever sought to finance religious education or activity pursuant to the State's program. The combination of these factors, we think, makes the link between the State and the school petitioner wishes to attend a highly attenuated one.

On the facts we have set out, it does not seem appropriate to view any aid ultimately flowing to the Inland Empire School of the Bible as resulting from a *state* action sponsoring or subsidizing religion. Nor does the mere circumstance that petitioner has chosen to use neutrally available state aid to help pay for his religious education confer any message of state endorsement of religion. See *Lynch v. Donnelly,* 465 U.S., 688 (O'CONNOR, J., concurring). Thus, while *amici* supporting respondent are correct in pointing out that aid to a religious institution unrestricted in its potential uses, if properly attributable to the State, is "clearly prohibited under the Establishment Clause," *Grand Rapids,* 473 U.S., 395, because it may subsidize the religious functions of that institution, that observation is not apposite to this case. On the facts present here, we think the Washington program works no state support of religion prohibited by the Establishment Clause. . . .

On remand, the state court is of course free to consider the applicability of the "far stricter" dictates of the Washington State Constitution, see *Witters v. Commission for the Blind,* 102 Wash. 2d, 626. . . . We decline petitioner's invitation to leapfrog consideration of those issues by holding that the Free Exercise Clause *requires* Washington to extend vocational rehabilitation aid to petitioner regardless of what the State Constitution commands or further factual development reveals, and we express no opinion on that matter. . . .

⬚ JUSTICE POWELL, with whom THE CHIEF JUSTICE and JUSTICE REHNQUIST join, concurring.

The Court's omission of *Mueller v. Allen,* 463 U.S. 388, from its analysis may mislead courts and litigants by suggesting that *Mueller* is somehow inapplicable to cases such as this one. I write separately to emphasize that *Mueller* strongly supports the result we reach today.

As the Court states, the central question in this case is whether Washington's provision of aid to handicapped students has the "principal or primary effect" of advancing religion. *Lemon v. Kurtzman,* 403 U.S. 602, 612. *Mueller* makes the answer clear: state programs that are wholly neutral in offering educational assistance to a class defined without reference to religion do not violate the second part of the *Lemon v. Kurtzman* test, because any aid to religion results from the private choices of individual beneficiaries. *Mueller,* 463 U.S., 398-399. . . .

The state program at issue here provides aid to handicapped students when their studies are likely to lead to employment. Aid does not depend on whether the student wishes to attend a public university or a private college, nor does it turn on whether the student seeks training for a religious or a secular career. It follows that under *Mueller* the State's program does not have the "principal or primary effect" of advancing religion.[3]

The Washington Supreme Court reached a different conclusion because it found that the program had the practical effect of aiding religion *in this particular case*. *Witters v. Commission for the Blind,* 102 Wash. 2d 624, 628-629. . . .

Nowhere in *Mueller* did we analyze the effect of Minnesota's tax deduction on the parents who were parties to the case; rather, we looked to the nature and consequences of the program *viewed as a whole*. *Mueller,* 463 U.S., 397-400. This is the appropriate perspective for this case as well. Viewed in the proper light, the Washington program easily satisfies the second prong of the *Lemon* test.

I agree, for the reasons stated by the Court, that the State's program has a secular purpose, and that no entanglement challenge is properly raised on this record. I therefore join the Court's judgment. On the understanding that nothing we do today lessens the authority of our decision in *Mueller,* I join the Court's opinion as well.

▓ JUSTICE O'CONNOR, concurring in part and concurring in the judgment.

I join Parts I and III of the Court's opinion, and concur in the judgment. I also agree with the Court that both the purpose and effect of Washington's program of aid to handicapped students are secular. As Justice POWELL's separate opinion persuasively argues, the Court's opinion in *Mueller v. Allen,* 463 U.S. 388, makes clear that "state programs that are wholly neutral in offering educational assistance to a class defined without reference to religion do not violate the second part of the *Lemon v. Kurtzman* test, because any aid to religion results from the private decisions of beneficiaries." (POWELL, J., concurring) (footnote omitted). The aid to religion at issue here is the result of petitioner's private choice. No reasonable observer is likely to draw from the facts before us an inference that the State itself is endorsing a religious practice or belief. See *Lynch v. Donnelly,* 465 U.S. 668, 690 (1984) (O'CONNOR, J., concurring).

Justice White also filed a short concurring opinion, joining in the majority opinion but also stating his agreement with "most of Justice Powell's concurring opinion with respect to the relevance of *Mueller.*"

---

[3] Contrary to the Court's suggestion, this conclusion does not depend on the fact that petitioner appears to be the only handicapped student who has sought to use his assistance to pursue religious training. Over 90% of the tax benefits in *Mueller* ultimately flowed to religious institutions. Compare *Mueller v. Allen,* 463 U.S., 401, with *id.,* 405, (MARSHALL, J., dissenting). Nevertheless, the aid was thus channeled by individual parents and not by the State, making the tax deduction permissible under the "primary effect" test of *Lemon.*

NOTES AND QUESTIONS

1. On remand, the Washington Supreme Court held that providing aid to the Petitioner would violate the stricter dictates of the Washington Constitution. See *Witters v. State Commission for the Blind*, 771 P.2d 1119 (Wash. 1989). This same provision of the Washington Constitution, Art. I, sec. 11, was also in issue in *Locke v. Davey*, 540 U.S. 712 (2004), discussed on p. 501, below.

2. Among the factors the Court believes is significant in this case is the following: "Any aid provided under Washington's program that ultimately flows to religious institutions does so only as a result of the genuinely independent and private choices of aid recipients." Explain the constitutional significance of this factor. For a full discussion of the constitutional significance of "private choice," see Laura Underkuffler, "Vouchers and Beyond: The Individual as Causative Agent in Establishment Clause Jurisprudence," *Indiana Law Journal* 75 (2000): 167.

3. Another factor that was constitutionally significant for the Court in this case was the fact that the program was "in no way skewed toward religion." What does the Court mean by this? How did the Washington program satisfy this element?

4. The Court also notes that "nothing in the record indicates that . . . any significant portion of the aid expended under the Washington program as a whole will end up flowing to religious education." Why is this important? If all other factors had remained constant, but the record had shown that a significant portion of the aid supported religious education, would this have changed this Court's ruling? Should the aggregate amount of aid that flows indirectly to a religious school under a private choice program be a factor? Suppose the majority of state college scholarships, with an aggregate amount in the millions of dollars, are used to obtain a religious education? Does this affect the theory underlying private choice as not offending the Establishment Clause?

5. Does the Court make a ruling in this case under the Free Exercise Clause? Does such a claim exist under the facts?

6. Why do you think the Court majority failed to mention the *Mueller v. Allen* case in its opinion? After all, most observers considered *Mueller* with its tax deduction as an easier case than the cash outlay involved in *Witters*. How do you explain the fact that the *Mueller* decision was decided in 1983 by a 5-4 vote and the *Witters* case was decided unanimously three years later with no change in Court personnel (with the opinion in *Witters* being written by one of the *Mueller* dissenters)?

7. In a concurring opinion, Justice Powell writes: "[S]tate programs that are wholly neutral in offering educational assistance to a class defined without reference to religion do not violate the second part of the *Lemon v. Kurtzman* test, because any aid to religion results from the private choices of individual beneficiaries." How is this description of the case different from the majority

opinion's description of the case? Is Powell's statement consistent with the Supreme Court's case law up to this point in time?

8. In her opinion concurring in part and concurring in the judgment, Justice O'Connor argues: "No reasonable observer is likely to draw from the facts before us an inference that the State itself is endorsing a religious practice or belief." Why would this be constitutionally significant? Do you agree with Justice O'Connor's conclusion on this matter?

A case with a private choice element next came before the Court in 1993. Petitioner, James Zobrest, deaf from birth, requested that the Respondent school district furnish him with a government-funded sign-language interpreter so that he could enroll as a ninth grader in Salpointe Catholic High School. Authorization for the interpreter was authorized by the federal Individuals with Disabilities Education Act (IDEA) and its Arizona state counterpart. The school district denied the request, based on advice from the state attorney general's office, on the ground the provision of a publicly paid interpreter in a religious school would violate the Establishment Clause. Petitioner then filed suit in federal court, alleging that both the Free Exercise Clause and IDEA required the school district to provide the interpreter in a religious school. The District Court granted summary judgment for the school district, ruling that the provision of the interpreter would likely violate the Establishment Clause, a decision affirmed by a divided Ninth Circuit Court of Appeals.

The Supreme Court agreed to hear the case and determined that it would address the constitutional issue rather than first attempting to resolve the case by construing IDEA requirements.

## ZOBREST v. CATALINA FOOTHILLS SCHOOL DISTRICT
## 509 U.S. 1 (1993)

CHIEF JUSTICE REHNQUIST delivered the opinion of the Court, . . .

We have never said that "religious institutions are disabled by the First Amendment from participating in publicly sponsored social welfare programs." *Bowen v. Kendrick,* 487 U.S. 589, 609. For if the Establishment Clause did bar religious groups from receiving general government benefits, then "a church could not be protected by the police and fire departments, or have its public sidewalk kept in repair." *Widmar v. Vincent,* 454 U.S. 263, 274-275 (internal quotation marks omitted). Given that a contrary rule would lead to such absurd results, we have consistently held that government programs that neutrally provide benefits to a broad class of citizens defined without reference to religion are not readily subject to an Establishment Clause challenge just because sectarian institutions may also receive an attenuated financial benefit. . . .

That same reasoning applies with equal force here. The service at issue in this case is part of a general government program that distributes benefits neutrally to any child qualifying as "disabled" under the IDEA, without regard to the "sectarian-nonsectarian, or public-nonpublic nature" of the school the child attends. By according parents freedom to select a school of their choice, the statute ensures that a government-paid interpreter will be present in a sectarian school only as a result of the private decision of individual parents. In other words, because the IDEA creates no financial incentive for parents to choose a sectarian school, an interpreter's presence there cannot be attributed to state decision-making. When the government offers a neutral service on the premises of a sectarian school as part of a general program that "is in no way skewed towards religion," *Witters,* 488, it follows under our prior decisions that provision of that service does not offend the Establishment Clause. See *Wolman v. Walter,* 433 U.S. 229, 244. Indeed, this is an even easier case than *Mueller* and *Witters* in the sense that, under the IDEA, no funds traceable to the government ever find their way into sectarian schools' coffers. The only indirect economic benefit a sectarian school might receive by dint of the IDEA is the disabled child's tuition; that, without an IDEA interpreter, the child would have gone to school elsewhere; and that the school, then, would have been unable to fill that child's spot.

Respondent contends, however, that this case differs from *Mueller* and *Witters,* in that petitioners seek to have a public employee physically present in a sectarian school to assist in James' religious education. In light of this distinction, respondent argues that this case more closely resembles *Meek v. Pittenger,* 421 U.S. 349, and *School Dist. of Grand Rapids v. Ball,* 473 U.S. 373. In *Meek,* we struck down a statute that, *inter alia,* provided "massive aid" to private schools—more than 75% of which were church related—through a direct loan of teaching material and equipment. . . . According to respondent, if the government could not place a tape recorder in a sectarian school in *Meek,* then it surely cannot place an interpreter in Salpointe. The statute[s] in *Meek* [and *Ball*] also authorized state-paid personnel to furnish "auxiliary services"—which included remedial and accelerated instruction and guidance counseling—on the premises of religious schools. We determined that this part of the statute offended the First Amendment as well. . . .

Respondent's reliance on *Meek* and *Ball* is misplaced for two reasons. First, the programs in *Meek* and *Ball*—through direct grants of government aid—relieved sectarian schools of costs they otherwise would have borne in educating their students. For example, the religious schools in *Meek* received teaching material and equipment from the State, relieving them of an otherwise necessary cost of performing their educational function. 421 U.S., 365-366. "Substantial aid to the educational function of such schools," we explained, "necessarily results in aid to the sectarian school enterprise as a whole," and therefore brings about "the direct and substantial advancement of religious activity." *Id.,* 366. So, too, was the case in *Ball:* The programs challenged there, which provided teachers in addition to instructional equipment and material, "in effect subsidize[d] the religious functions of the parochial schools by taking over a substantial portion of their responsibility for teaching secular subjects." 473 U.S., 397. "This kind of direct aid," we determined, "is indistinguishable from the provision of a direct cash subsidy to the religious school." *Id.,* 395. The extension of aid to petitioners, however, does not amount to "an impermissible 'direct subsidy'" of Salpointe, *Witters,* 474 U.S.,

487, for Salpointe is not relieved of an expense that it otherwise would have assumed in educating its students. And, as we noted above, any attenuated financial benefit that parochial schools do ultimately receive from the IDEA is attributable to "the private choices of individual parents." *Mueller,* 463 U.S., 400. Disabled children, not sectarian schools, are the primary beneficiaries of the IDEA; to the extent sectarian schools benefit at all from the IDEA, they are only incidental beneficiaries. . . .

Second, the task of a sign-language interpreter seems to us quite different from that of a teacher or guidance counselor. . . . [T]he Establishment Clause lays down no absolute bar to the placing of a public employee in a sectarian school. Such a flat rule, smacking of antiquated notions of "taint," would indeed exalt form over substance. Nothing in this record suggests that a sign-language interpreter would do more than accurately interpret whatever material is presented to the class as a whole. In fact, ethical guidelines require interpreters to "transmit everything that is said in exactly the same way it was intended." James' parents have chosen of their own free will to place him in a pervasively sectarian environment. The sign-language interpreter they have requested will neither add to nor subtract from that environment, and hence the provision of such assistance is not barred by the Establishment Clause. . . .

*Reversed.*

🀫 JUSTICE BLACKMUN, with whom JUSTICE SOUTER joins, dissenting. . . .

Let us be clear about exactly what is going on here. The parties have stipulated to the following facts. James Zobrest requested the State to supply him with a sign-language interpreter at Salpointe High School, a private Roman Catholic school operated by the Carmelite Order of the Catholic Church. . . .

At Salpointe, where the secular and the sectarian are "inextricably intertwined," governmental assistance to the educational function of the school necessarily entails governmental participation in the school's inculcation of religion. A state-employed sign-language interpreter would be required to communicate the material covered in religion class, the nominally secular subjects that are taught from a religious perspective, and the daily Masses at which Salpointe encourages attendance for Catholic students. In an environment so pervaded by discussions of the divine, the interpreter's every gesture would be infused with religious significance. . . .

[T]he majority's arguments are unavailing. As to the first two, even a general welfare program may have specific applications that are constitutionally forbidden under the Establishment Clause. For example, a general program granting remedial assistance to disadvantaged schoolchildren attending public and private, secular and sectarian schools alike would clearly offend the Establishment Clause insofar as it authorized the provision of teachers. See *Aguilar v. Felton,* 473 U.S. 402, 410; *School Dist. of Grand Rapids v. Ball,* 473 U.S. 373, 385; *Meek v. Pittenger,* 421 U.S. 349, 371. Such a program would not be saved simply because it supplied teachers to secular as well as sectarian schools. Nor would the fact that teachers were furnished to pupils and their parents, rather than directly to sectarian schools, immunize such a program from Establishment Clause scrutiny. . . .

*Witters,* and *Mueller v. Allen,* 463 U.S. 388, are not to the contrary. Those cases dealt with the payment of cash or a tax deduction, where governmental involvement ended with the disbursement of funds or lessening of tax. This case, on the other hand, involves ongoing, daily, and intimate governmental participation in the teaching and propagation of religious doctrine. When government dispenses public funds to individuals who employ them to finance private choices, it is difficult to argue that government is actually endorsing religion. But the graphic symbol of the concert of church and state that results when a public employee or instrumentality mouths a religious message is likely to "enlis[t]—at least in the eyes of impressionable youngsters—the powers of government to the support of the religious denomination operating the school." *Ball*, 473 U.S., 385. And the union of church and state in pursuit of a common enterprise is likely to place the imprimatur of governmental approval upon the favored religion, conveying a message of exclusion to all those who do not adhere to its tenets. . . .

Justices Stevens and O'Connor also dissented on the ground that the Court should avoid reaching the constitutional issue by first determining whether IDEA required public school districts to provide services in nonpublic schools.

## NOTES AND QUESTIONS

1. What considerations prompted the Court majority to find that this aid did not offend the Establishment Clause? How did the element of private choice work in this case?

2. How does the Court majority attempt to distinguish earlier Supreme Court cases finding that certain state-funded educational and instructional services could not be provided to religious elementary and secondary schools? What arguments does the dissent make in response? Which side do you believe makes the more persuasive arguments on these issues? Why?

3. The Court majority argues that the duties of a sign language interpreter are "quite different from that of a teacher or guidance counselor." Why is this significant? One *amicus* brief argued that because sign language interpreters do not usually sign what is being said verbatim, they will necessarily be reinterpreting the content of what is being communicated to the recipient. The majority rejected this argument. Why would this matter for constitutional purposes?

4. According to the dissent, what constitutional rules have been violated in this case? Is it that the facts are too close to earlier holdings to the contrary (e.g., *Lemon; Ball*), that private choice is an ineffective constitutional shield, or that private choice does not work in this case?

5. The dissent argues that "even a general welfare program may have specific applications that are constitutionally forbidden under the Establishment Clause." It also states that "[w]hen government dispenses public funds to individuals who employ them to finance private choices, it is difficult to argue that government is actually endorsing religion," suggesting that, while it is difficult, it is not impossible to do so. Given your reading of the majority opinion, would the Court majority agree with either or both of these statements?

---

Increasingly through the 1990s, the twin notions of even-handed financial assistance and private choice came to be seen as solutions to the Establishment Clause bar to religious school funding. These notions soon found application outside the specific context of indirect aid programs. In the following two cases—*Agostini v. Felton* and *Mitchell v. Helms*, see if you can identify how the Court majorities apply those concepts with direct aid programs.

In *Agostini v. Felton*, the Court reconsidered its holding from *Aguilar v. Felton*,[2] a companion case to *Grand Rapids School District v. Ball* (see p. 434). As described in *Agostini*, *Aguilar* involved a federally funded program, Title I of the Elementary and Secondary Education Act, that provides government funding for remedial education, counseling and guidance counseling for low income students in both public and private schools.

Under that program, state paid instructors provided the services on the campuses of the public and private schools. The *Aguilar* Court struck down the provisions of the services on religious campuses, citing entanglement concerns. Justice William Brennan, who wrote for a five justice majority, noted that the supervisory system established by the New York City Board of Education to ensure that government funds would not be spent on religious activity resulted in the very type of "pervasive monitoring by public authorities in the sectarian schools" that was the root of the nonentanglement principle.[3] Justice Brennan also identified religious divisiveness concerns as a ground for striking the program: "The numerous judgments that must be made by agents of the city concern matters that may be subtle and controversial, yet may be of deep religious significance to the controlling denominations. As government agents must make these judgments, the dangers of political divisiveness along religious lines increase." As Brennan summarized the basis for the holding, "We have long recognized that underlying the Establishment Clause is 'the objective . . . to prevent, as far as possible, the intrusion of either [church or state] into the precincts of the other.' . . . [T]he detailed monitoring and close administrative contact required to maintain New York's Title I program can only produce 'a kind of continuing day-to-day relationship which the policy of neutrality seeks to minimize.'"

As a result of the *Aguilar* holding, public school authorities were required to provide the services to religious school students on "neutral" sites—in either nearby public school buildings or instructional vans parked adjacent to the religious schools. The administrative burden cause by this requirement, and the additional expenses it produced, eventually brought the New York City Board of Education to request a release from the permanent injunction and a reconsideration of the *Aguilar* holding.

---

## AGOSTINI v. FELTON
### 521 U.S. 203 (1997)

▓ JUSTICE O'CONNOR delivered the opinion of the Court.

In *Aguilar v. Felton*, 473 U.S. 402, this Court held that the Establishment Clause of the First Amendment barred the city of New York from sending public school teachers into parochial schools to provide remedial education to disadvantaged children pursuant to a congressionally mandated program. On remand, the District Court for the Eastern District of New York entered a permanent injunction reflecting our ruling. Twelve years later, petitioners— the parties bound by that injunction—seek relief from its operation. Petitioners maintain that *Aguilar* cannot be squared with our intervening Establishment Clause jurisprudence and ask that we explicitly recognize what our more recent cases already dictate: *Aguilar* is no longer good law. We agree with petitioners that *Aguilar* is not consistent with our subsequent Establishment Clause decisions and further conclude that, on the facts presented here, petitioners are entitled to relief from the operation of the District Court's prospective injunction.

I

In 1965, Congress enacted Title I of the Elementary and Secondary Education Act of 1965, 79 Stat. 27, as modified, 20 U.S.C. § 6301 *et seq.*, to "provid[e] full educational opportunity to every child regardless of economic background." S.Rep. No. 146, 89th Cong., 1st Sess., 5 (1965), (hereinafter Title I). Toward that end, Title I channels federal funds, through the States, to "local educational agencies" (LEAs). 20 U.S.C. §§ 6311, 6312. The LEAs spend these funds to provide remedial education, guidance, and job counseling to eligible students. §§ 6315(c)(1)(A) (LEAs must use funds to "help participating children meet . . . State student performance standards"), 6315(c)(1)(E) (LEAs may use funds to provide "counseling, mentoring, and other pupil services"); see also §§ 6314(b)(1)(B)(i), (iv). An eligible student is one (i) who resides within the attendance boundaries of a public school located in a low-income area, § 6313(a)(2)(B); and (ii) who is failing, or is at risk of failing, the State's student performance standards, § 6315(b)(1)(B). Title I funds must be made available to *all* eligible children, regardless of whether they attend public schools, § 6312(c)(1)(F), and the services provided to children attending private schools must be "equitable in comparison to services and other benefits for public school children," § 6321(a)(3); see § 6321(a)(1); 34 C.F.R. §§ 200.10(a), 200.11(b) (1996).

An LEA providing services to children enrolled in private schools is subject to a number of constraints that are not imposed when it provides aid to public schools. Title I services may be provided only to those private school students eligible for aid, and cannot be used to provide services on a "school-wide" basis. Compare 34 C.F.R. § 200.12(b) (1996) with 20 U.S.C. § 6314 (allowing "school-wide" programs at public schools). In addition, the LEA must retain complete control over Title I funds; retain title to all materials used to provide Title I services; and provide those services through public employees or other persons independent of the private school and any religious institution. §§ 6321(c)(1), (2). The Title I services themselves must be "secular, neutral, and nonideological," § 6321(a)(2), and must "supplement, and in no case supplant, the level of services" already provided by the private school, 34 C.F.R. § 200.12(a) (1996). . . .

The Court described the history of the Title I program of New York City, noting that 10% of the eligible students attended private schools, 90% of which were pervasively sectarian. In order to comply with the *Aguilar* holding, the Board of Education initially offered the services in public school buildings, but experienced poor participation by eligible religious school students. The Board then tried providing services in religious school buildings after instructional hours, which also had mixed results. Finally, the Board began offering services in instructional vans parked adjacent to religious schools. The Court noted that since the *Aguilar* decision the Board had spent approximately $100 million in "providing computer-aided instruction, leasing sites and mobile instructional units, and transporting students to those sites." These "Aguilar costs" came "off-the-top" of the city's allocation, resulting in less money available for remedial education and other services.

Based on the various opinions and holdings in *Board of Education of Kiryas Joel Village School District v. Grumet* and *Zobrest v. Catalina Foothills School District*, the Board in 1995 petitioned the district court for relief from the injunction, claiming that "the decisional law had changed to make legal what the injunction was designed to prevent." The district court denied relief, holding that "*Aguilar's* demise had not yet occurred." The court of appeals affirmed for substantially the same reasons.

III

A

In order to evaluate whether *Aguilar* has been eroded by our subsequent Establishment Clause cases, it is necessary to understand the rationale upon which *Aguilar*, as well as its companion case, *School Dist. of Grand Rapids v. Ball*, 473 U.S. 373, rested.

In *Ball*, the Court evaluated two programs implemented by the School District of Grand Rapids, Michigan. The district's Shared Time program, the one most analogous to Title I, provided remedial and "enrichment" classes, at public expense, to students attending nonpublic schools. The classes were taught during regular school hours by publicly employed teachers, using materials purchased with public funds, on the premises of nonpublic schools. The Shared Time courses were in subjects designed to supplement the "core curriculum" of the nonpublic schools. *Id.*, 375-376. Of the 41 nonpublic schools eligible for the program, 40 were "'pervasively sectarian'" in character—that is, "'the purpos[e] of [those] schools [was] to advance their particular religions.'" *Id.*, 379.

The Court conducted its analysis by applying the three-part test set forth in *Lemon v. Kurtzman*, 403 U.S. 602: . . .

The Court acknowledged that the Shared Time program served a purely secular purpose, . . . Nevertheless, it ultimately concluded that the program had the impermissible effect of advancing religion. *Id.*, 385.

The Court found that the program violated the Establishment Clause's prohibition against "government-financed or government-sponsored indoctrination into the beliefs of a particular religious faith" in at least three ways. *Ibid.* First, drawing upon the analysis in *Meek v. Pittenger*, 421 U.S. 349, the Court observed that "the teachers participating in the programs may become involved in intentionally or inadvertently inculcating particular religious tenets or beliefs." . . . Although the auxiliary services themselves were secular, they were mostly dispensed on the premises of parochial schools, where "an atmosphere dedicated to the advancement of religious belief [was] constantly maintained." *Meek*, 421 U.S., 371. Instruction in that atmosphere was sufficient to create "[t]he potential for impermissible fostering of religion." *Id.*, 372. . . .

The Court concluded that the Grand Rapids' program shared these defects. 473 U.S., 386. As in *Meek*, classes were conducted on the premises of religious schools. Accordingly, a majority found a "'substantial risk'" that teachers—

even those who were not employed by the private schools—might "subtly (or overtly) conform their instruction to the [pervasively sectarian] environment in which they [taught]." 473 U.S., 388. The danger of "state-sponsored indoctrination" was only exacerbated by the school district's failure to monitor the courses for religious content. *Id.*, 387. . . .

The presence of public teachers on parochial school grounds had a second, related impermissible effect: It created a "graphic symbol of the 'concert or union or dependency' of church and state," *id.*, 391 (quoting *Zorach v. Clauson,* 343 U.S. 306, 312), especially when perceived by "children in their formative years," 473 U.S., 390. The Court feared that this perception of a symbolic union between church and state would "conve[y] a message of government endorsement . . . of religion" and thereby violate a "core purpose" of the Establishment Clause. *Id.*, 389.

Third, the Court found that the Shared Time program impermissibly financed religious indoctrination by subsidizing "the primary religious mission of the institutions affected." *Id.*, 385. The Court separated its prior decisions evaluating programs that aided the secular activities of religious institutions into two categories: those in which it concluded that the aid resulted in an effect that was "indirect, remote, or incidental" (and upheld the aid); and those in which it concluded that the aid resulted in "a direct and substantial advancement of the sectarian enterprise" (and invalidated the aid). *Id.*, 393 (internal quotation marks omitted). In light of *Meek* and *Wolman,* Grand Rapids' program fell into the latter category. In those cases, the Court ruled that a state loan of instructional equipment and materials to parochial schools was an impermissible form of "direct aid" because it "advanced the primary, religion-oriented educational function of the sectarian school," 473 U.S., 395 (citations and internal quotation marks omitted), by providing "in kind" aid (e.g., instructional materials) that could be used to teach religion and by freeing up money for religious indoctrination that the school would otherwise have devoted to secular education. . . .

The New York City Title I program challenged in *Aguilar* closely resembled the Shared Time program struck down in *Ball,* but the Court found fault with an aspect of the Title I program not present in *Ball:* The Board had "adopted a system for monitoring the religious content of publicly funded Title I classes in the religious schools." 473 U.S., 409. Even though this monitoring system might prevent the Title I program from being used to inculcate religion, the Court concluded, as it had in *Lemon* and *Meek,* that the level of monitoring necessary to be "certain" that the program had an exclusively secular effect would "inevitably resul[t] in the excessive entanglement of church and state," thereby running afoul of *Lemon* 's third prong. 473 U.S., 409. In the majority's view, New York City's Title I program suffered from the "same critical elements of entanglement" present in *Lemon* and *Meek:* the aid was provided "in a pervasively sectarian environment . . . in the form of teachers," requiring "ongoing inspection . . . to ensure the absence of a religious message." 473 U.S., 412. Such "pervasive monitoring by public authorities in the sectarian schools infringes precisely those Establishment Clause values at the root of the prohibition of excessive entanglement." *Id.*, 413. The Court noted two further forms of entanglement inherent in New York City's Title I program: the "administrative cooperation" required to implement Title I services and the "dangers of political divisiveness" that might grow out of the day-to-day decisions public officials would have to make in order to provide Title I services. *Id.*, 413-414.

Distilled to essentials, the Court's conclusion that the Shared Time program in *Ball* had the impermissible effect of advancing religion rested on three assumptions: (i) any public employee who works on the premises of a religious school is presumed to inculcate religion in her work; (ii) the presence of public employees on private school premises creates a symbolic union between church and state; and (iii) any and all public aid that directly aids the educational function of religious schools impermissibly finances religious indoctrination, even if the aid reaches such schools as a consequence of private decision-making. Additionally, in *Aguilar* there was a fourth assumption: that New York City's Title I program necessitated an excessive government entanglement with religion because public employees who teach on the premises of religious schools must be closely monitored to ensure that they do not inculcate religion.

B

Our more recent cases have undermined the assumptions upon which *Ball* and *Aguilar* relied. To be sure, the general principles we use to evaluate whether government aid violates the Establishment Clause have not changed since *Aguilar* was decided. For example, we continue to ask whether the government acted with the purpose of advancing or inhibiting religion, and the nature of that inquiry has remained largely unchanged. See *Witters,* 474 U.S., 485-486; *Bowen v. Kendrick,* 487 U.S. 589, 602-604 (concluding that Adolescent Family Life Act had a secular purpose); *Board of Ed. of Westside Community Schools v. Mergens,* 496 U.S. 226, 248-249 (concluding that Equal Access Act has a secular purpose); cf. *Edwards v. Aguillard,* 482 U.S. 578 (striking down Louisiana law that required creationism to be discussed with evolution in public schools because the law lacked a legitimate secular purpose). Likewise, we continue to explore whether the aid has the "effect" of advancing or inhibiting religion. What has changed since we decided *Ball* and *Aguilar* is our understanding of the criteria used to assess whether aid to religion has an impermissible effect.

1

As we have repeatedly recognized, government inculcation of religious beliefs has the impermissible effect of advancing religion. Our cases subsequent to *Aguilar* have, however, modified in two significant respects the approach we use to assess indoctrination. First, we have abandoned the presumption erected in *Meek* and *Ball* that the placement of public employees on parochial school grounds inevitably results in the impermissible effect of state-sponsored indoctrination or constitutes a symbolic union between government and religion. . . . [In *Zobrest*, we expressly disavowed] the notion that "the Establishment Clause [laid] down [an] absolute bar to the placing of a public employee in a sectarian school." 509 U.S., 13. "Such a flat rule, smacking of antiquated notions of 'taint,' would indeed exalt form over substance." *Ibid.* We refused to presume that a publicly employed interpreter would be pressured by the pervasively sectarian surroundings to inculcate religion by "add[ing] to [or] subtract[ing] from" the lectures translated. *Ibid.* In the absence of evidence to the contrary, we assumed instead that the interpreter would dutifully discharge her responsibilities as a full-time public employee and comply with the ethical guidelines of her profession by accurately translating what was said. *Id.,* 12. Because the only *government* aid in *Zobrest* was the interpreter, who was herself not inculcating any religious messages, no *government* indoctrination took place and we were able to conclude that "the provision of such assistance [was] not barred by the Establishment Clause." *Id.*, 13. *Zobrest* therefore expressly rejected the notion—relied on in *Ball* and *Aguilar*—that, solely because of her presence on private school property, a public employee will be presumed to inculcate religion in the students. *Zobrest* also implicitly repudiated another assumption on which *Ball* and *Aguilar* turned: that the presence of a public employee on private school property creates an impermissible "symbolic link" between government and religion.

JUSTICE SOUTER contends that *Zobrest* did not undermine the "presumption of inculcation" . . . [but held only] that the Establishment Clause tolerates the presence of public employees in sectarian schools "only. . . in . . . limited circumstances"—i.e., when the employee "simply translates for one student the material presented to the class for the benefit of all students." . . .

The signer in *Zobrest*[, however,] had the same opportunity to inculcate religion in the performance of her duties as do Title I employees, and there is no genuine basis upon which to confine *Zobrest's* underlying rationale—that public employees will not be presumed to inculcate religion—to sign-language interpreters. . . .

Second, we have departed from the rule relied on in *Ball* that all government aid that directly assists the educational function of religious schools is invalid. In *Witters v. Washington Dept. of Servs. for Blind,* 474 U.S. 481, we held that the Establishment Clause did not bar a State from issuing a vocational tuition grant to a blind person who wished to use the grant to attend a Christian college and become a pastor, missionary, or youth director. Even though the grant recipient clearly would use the money to obtain religious education, we observed that the tuition grants were "'made available generally without regard to the sectarian-nonsectarian, or public-nonpublic nature of the institution benefitted.'" *Id.*, 487, (quoting *Committee for Public Ed. & Religious Liberty v. Nyquist,* 413 U.S. 756, 782-783, n. 38). The grants were disbursed directly to students, who then used the money to pay for tuition at the educational institution of their choice. In our view, this transaction was no different from a State's issuing a paycheck to one of its employees, knowing that the employee would donate part or all of the check to a religious institution. In both situations, any money that ultimately went to religious institutions did so "only as a result of the genuinely independent and private choices of" individuals. 474 U.S., 487. The same logic applied in *Zobrest.* . . .

*Zobrest* and *Witters* make clear that, under current law, the Shared Time program in *Ball* and New York City's Title I program in *Aguilar* will not, as a matter of law, be deemed to have the effect of advancing religion through indoctrination. Indeed, each of the premises upon which we relied in *Ball* to reach a contrary conclusion is no longer valid. First, there is no reason to presume that, simply because she enters a parochial school classroom, a full-time public employee such as a Title I teacher will depart from her assigned duties and instructions and embark on religious indoctrination, any more than there was a reason in *Zobrest* to think an interpreter would inculcate religion by altering her translation of classroom lectures. Certainly, no evidence has ever shown that any New York City Title I instructor teaching on parochial school premises attempted to inculcate religion in students. . . .

As discussed above, *Zobrest* also repudiates *Ball's* assumption that the presence of Title I teachers in parochial school classrooms will, without more, create the impression of a "symbolic union" between church and state. . . . JUSTICE SOUTER does not disavow the notion, uniformly adopted by lower courts, that Title I services may be provided to sectarian school students in off campus locations, even though that notion necessarily presupposes that the danger of "symbolic union" evaporates once the services are provided off campus. Taking this view, the only difference between a constitutional program and an unconstitutional one is the location of the classroom, since the degree of cooperation between Title I instructors and parochial school faculty is the same no matter where the services are provided. We do not see any perceptible (let alone dispositive) difference in the degree of symbolic union between a student receiving remedial instruction in a classroom on his sectarian school's campus and one receiving instruction in a van parked just at the school's curbside. To draw this line based solely on the location of the public employee is neither "sensible" nor "sound," and the Court in *Zobrest* rejected it.

Nor under current law can we conclude that a program placing full-time public employees on parochial campuses to provide Title I instruction would impermissibly finance religious indoctrination. In all relevant respects, the provision of instructional services under Title I is indistinguishable from the provision of sign-language interpreters under the IDEA. Both programs make aid available only to eligible recipients. That aid is provided to students at whatever school they choose to attend. Although Title I instruction is provided to several students at once, whereas an interpreter provides translation to a single student, this distinction is not constitutionally significant. Moreover, as in *Zobrest,* Title I services are by law supplemental to the regular curricula. 34 C.F.R. § 200.12(a) (1996). These services do not, therefore, "reliev[e] sectarian schools of costs they otherwise would have borne in educating their students." 509 U.S., 12.

JUSTICE SOUTER finds our conclusion that the IDEA and Title I programs are similar to be "puzzling," and points to three differences he perceives between the programs: (i) Title I services are distributed by LEAs "directly to the religious schools" instead of to individual students pursuant to a formal application process; (ii) Title I services "necessarily reliev[e] a religious school of 'an expense that it otherwise would have assumed'"; and (iii) Title I provides services to more students than did the programs in *Witters* and *Zobrest.* None of these distinctions is meaningful. While it is true that individual students may not directly apply for Title I services, it does not follow from this premise that those services are distributed "directly to the religious schools." In fact, they are not. No Title I funds ever reach the coffers of religious schools, cf. *Committee for Public Ed. and Religious Liberty v. Regan,* 444 U.S. 646, 657-659 (involving a program giving "direct cash reimbursement" to *religious schools* for performing certain state-mandated tasks), and Title I services may not be provided to religious schools on a schoolwide basis, 34 C.F.R. § 200.12(b) (1996). Title I funds are instead distributed to a *public* agency (an LEA) that dispenses services directly to the eligible students within its boundaries, no matter where they choose to attend school. 20 U.S.C. §§ 6311, 6312. Moreover, we fail to see how providing Title I services directly to eligible students results in a greater financing of religious indoctrination simply because those students are not first required to submit a formal application.

We are also not persuaded that Title I services supplant the remedial instruction and guidance counseling already provided in New York City's sectarian schools. Although JUSTICE SOUTER maintains that the sectarian schools provide such services and that those schools reduce those services once their students begin to receive Title I instruction, his claims rest on speculation about the impossibility of drawing any line between supplemental and general education, and not on any evidence in the record that the Board is in fact violating Title I regulations by providing services that supplant those offered in the sectarian schools. See 34 C.F.R. § 200.12(a) (1996). We are unwilling to speculate that all sectarian schools provide remedial instruction and guidance counseling to their students, and are unwilling to presume that the Board would violate Title I regulations by continuing to provide Title I services to students who attend a sectarian school that has curtailed its remedial instruction program in response to Title I. Nor are we willing to conclude that the constitutionality of an aid program depends on the number of sectarian school students who happen to receive the otherwise neutral aid. *Zobrest* did not turn on the fact that James Zobrest had, at the time of litigation, been the only child using a publicly funded sign-language interpreter to attend a parochial school.

What is most fatal to the argument that New York City's Title I program directly subsidizes religion is that it applies with equal force when those services are provided off campus, and *Aguilar* implied that providing the services off campus is entirely consistent with the Establishment Clause. . . . JUSTICE SOUTER does not explain why a sectarian school would not have the same incentive to "make patently significant cut backs" in its curriculum no matter where Title I services are offered, since the school would ostensibly be excused from having to provide the Title I-type services itself. Because the incentive is the same either way, we find no logical basis upon which to conclude that Title I services are an impermissible subsidy of religion when offered on campus, but not when offered off campus. Accordingly, contrary to our conclusion in *Aguilar,* placing full-time employees on parochial school campuses does not as a matter of law have the impermissible effect of advancing religion through indoctrination.

2

Although we examined in *Witters* and *Zobrest* the criteria by which an aid program identifies its beneficiaries, we did so solely to assess whether any use of that aid to indoctrinate religion could be attributed to the State. A number of our Establishment Clause cases have found that the criteria used for identifying beneficiaries are relevant in a second respect, apart from enabling a court to evaluate whether the program subsidizes religion. Specifically, the criteria might themselves have the effect of advancing religion by creating a financial incentive to undertake religious indoctrination. Cf. *Witters,* 474 U.S., 488 (upholding neutrally available program because it did not "creat[e a] financial incentive for students to undertake sectarian education"); *Zobrest,* 10, (upholding neutrally available IDEA aid because it "creates no financial incentive for parents to choose a sectarian school"); accord, (SOUTER, J., dissenting) ("[E]venhandedness is a necessary but not a sufficient condition for an aid program to satisfy constitutional scrutiny"). This incentive is not present, however, where the aid is allocated on the basis of neutral, secular criteria that neither favor nor disfavor religion, and is made available to both religious and secular beneficiaries on a nondiscriminatory basis. Under such circumstances, the aid is less likely to have the effect of advancing religion.

In *Ball* and *Aguilar,* the Court gave this consideration no weight. Before and since those decisions, we have sustained programs that provided aid to *all* eligible children regardless of where they attended school. . . .

Applying this reasoning to New York City's Title I program, it is clear that Title I services are allocated on the basis of criteria that neither favor nor disfavor religion. 34 C.F.R. § 200.10(b) (1996). The services are available to all children who meet the Act's eligibility requirements, no matter what their religious beliefs or where they go to school, 20 U.S.C. § 6312(c)(1)(F). The Board's program does not, therefore, give aid recipients any incentive to modify their religious beliefs or practices in order to obtain those services.

3

We turn now to *Aguilar* 's conclusion that New York City's Title I program resulted in an excessive entanglement between church and state. Whether a government aid program results in such an entanglement has consistently been an aspect of our Establishment Clause analysis. We have considered entanglement both in the course of assessing whether an aid program has an impermissible effect of advancing religion, *Walz v. Tax Comm'n of City of New York,* 397 U.S. 664, 674, and as a factor separate and apart from "effect," *Lemon v. Kurtzman,* 403 U.S., 612-613. Regardless of how we have characterized the issue, however, the factors we use to assess whether an entanglement is "excessive" are similar to the factors we use to examine "effect." That is, to assess entanglement, we have looked to "the character and purposes of the institutions that are benefitted, the nature of the aid that the State provides, and the resulting relationship between the government and religious authority." *Id.,* 615. Similarly, we have assessed a law's "effect" by examining the character of the institutions benefitted (e.g., whether the religious institutions were "predominantly religious"), and the nature of the aid that the State provided (e.g., whether it was neutral and nonideological). Indeed, in *Lemon* itself, the entanglement that the Court found "independently" to necessitate the program's invalidation also was found to have the effect of inhibiting religion. Thus, it is simplest to recognize why entanglement is significant and treat it—as we did in *Walz*—as an aspect of the inquiry into a statute's effect.

Not all entanglements, of course, have the effect of advancing or inhibiting religion. Interaction between church and state is inevitable, see 403 U.S., 614, and we have always tolerated some level of involvement between the two. Entanglement must be "excessive" before it runs afoul of the Establishment Clause. . . .

The pre-*Aguilar* Title I program does not result in an "excessive" entanglement that advances or inhibits religion. As discussed previously, the Court's finding of "excessive" entanglement in *Aguilar* rested on three grounds: (i) the program would require "pervasive monitoring by public authorities" to ensure that Title I employees did not inculcate religion; (ii) the program required "administrative cooperation" between the Board and parochial schools; and (iii) the program might increase the dangers of "political divisiveness." 473 U.S., 413-414. Under our current understanding of the Establishment Clause, the last two considerations are insufficient by themselves to create an "excessive" entanglement. . . . Further, the assumption underlying the first consideration has been undermined. . . . [A]fter *Zobrest* we no longer presume that public employees will inculcate religion simply because they happen to be in a sectarian environment. Since we have abandoned the assumption that properly instructed public employees will fail to discharge their duties faithfully, we must also discard the assumption that *pervasive* monitoring of Title I teachers is required. . . .

To summarize, New York City's Title I program does not run afoul of any of three primary criteria we currently use to evaluate whether government aid has the effect of advancing religion: It does not result in governmental indoctrination; define its recipients by reference to religion; or create an excessive entanglement. We therefore hold that a federally funded program providing supplemental, remedial instruction to disadvantaged children on a neutral basis is not invalid under the Establishment Clause when such instruction is given on the premises of sectarian schools by government employees pursuant to a program containing safeguards such as those present here. The same considerations that justify this holding require us to conclude that this carefully constrained program also cannot reasonably be viewed as an endorsement of religion. . . . Accordingly, we must acknowledge that *Aguilar*, as well as the portion of *Ball* addressing Grand Rapids' Shared Time program, are no longer good law.

[Finally, the Court held that the doctrine of *stare decisis* did not preclude it from "recognizing a change in the law and overruling *Aguilar* and those portions of *Ball* inconsistent with our more recent decisions."]

As discussed above, our Establishment Clause jurisprudence has changed significantly since we decided *Ball* and *Aguilar*, so our decision to overturn those cases rests on far more than "a present doctrinal disposition to come out differently from the Court of [1985]." *Planned Parenthood v. Casey*, 505 U.S. 833, 864. We therefore overrule *Ball* and *Aguilar* to the extent those decisions are inconsistent with our current understanding of the Establishment Clause. . . .

*It is so ordered.*

JUSTICE SOUTER, with whom JUSTICE STEVENS and JUSTICE GINSBURG join, and with whom JUSTICE BREYER joins as to Part II, dissenting. . . .

I believe *Aguilar* was a correct and sensible decision, and my only reservation about its opinion is that the emphasis on the excessive entanglement produced by monitoring religious instructional content obscured those facts that independently called for the application of two central tenets of Establishment Clause jurisprudence. The State is forbidden to subsidize religion directly and is just as surely forbidden to act in any way that could reasonably be viewed as religious endorsement. . . .

[T]he flat ban on subsidization antedates the Bill of Rights and has been an unwavering rule in Establishment Clause cases, qualified only by the conclusion two Terms ago that state exactions from college students are not the sort of public revenues subject to the ban. See *Rosenberger v. Rector and Visitors of Univ. of Va.*, 515 U.S. 819, 868-876, (SOUTER, J., dissenting). The rule expresses the hard lesson learned over and over again in the American past and in the experiences of the countries from which we have come, that religions supported by governments are compromised just as surely as the religious freedom of dissenters is burdened when the government supports religion. . . . The ban against state endorsement of religion addresses the same historical lessons. Governmental approval of religion tends to reinforce the religious message (at least in the short run) and, by the same token, to carry a message of exclusion to those of less favored views. . . . The human tendency, of course, is to forget the hard lessons, and to overlook the history of governmental partnership with religion when a cause is worthy, and bureaucrats have programs. That tendency to forget is the reason for having the Establishment Clause (along with the Constitution's other structural and libertarian guarantees), in the hope of stopping the corrosion before it starts.

These principles were violated by the programs at issue in *Aguilar* and *Ball,* as a consequence of several significant features common to both Title I, as implemented in New York City before *Aguilar,* and the Grand Rapids Shared Time program: each provided classes on the premises of the religious schools, covering a wide range of subjects including some at the core of primary and secondary education, like reading and mathematics; while their services were termed "supplemental," the programs and their instructors necessarily assumed responsibility for teaching subjects that the religious schools would otherwise have been obligated to provide; the public employees carrying out the programs had broad responsibilities involving the exercise of considerable discretion; while the programs offered aid to nonpublic school students generally (and Title I went to public school students as well), participation by religious school students in each program was extensive, and, finally, aid under Title I and Shared Time flowed directly to the schools in the form of classes and programs, as distinct from indirect aid that reaches schools only as a result of independent private choice. . . .

While it would be an obvious sham, say, to channel cash to religious schools to be credited only against the expense of "secular" instruction, the line between "supplemental" and general education is likewise impossible to draw. If a State may constitutionally enter the schools to teach in the manner in question, it must in constitutional principle be free to assume, or assume payment for, the entire cost of instruction provided in any ostensibly secular subject in any religious school. . . .

It may be objected that there is some subsidy in remedial education even when it takes place off the religious premises, some subsidy, that is, even in the way New York City has administered the Title I program after *Aguilar.* . . . [However,] the off-premises teaching is arguably less likely to open the door to relieving religious schools of their responsibilities for secular subjects simply because these schools are less likely (and presumably legally unable) to dispense with those subjects from their curriculums or to make patently significant cutbacks in basic teaching within the schools to offset the outside instruction; if the aid is delivered outside of the schools, it is less likely to supplant some of what would otherwise go on inside them and to subsidize what remains. [Finally,] the difference in the degree of reasonably perceptible endorsement is substantial. . . . When the aid goes overwhelmingly to one religious denomination, minimal contact between state and church is less likely to feed the resentment of other religions that would like access to public money for their own worthy projects.

In sum, if a line is to be drawn short of barring all state aid to religious schools for teaching standard subjects, the *Aguilar-Ball* line was a sensible one capable of principled adherence. It is no less sound, and no less necessary, today. . . .

*Mitchell v. Helms* dealt with a different federal program that provided educational assistance to public and private schools, in this instance, educational materials and equipment, including computers and library books. Several of these forms of aid had been considered in *Meek* and *Wolman*, but *Agostini* now called the authority of those holdings into question. But *Mitchell* also presented a harder case factually for the Court. Unlike the assistance in *Agostini*, which remained under the control of public school employees entering the religious schools, the aid in *Mitchell* was loaned to the religious schools directly. Also, the type of aid involved—computers and library books—lent itself to potential diversion for religious uses, a concern not as present when public employees administered the educational aid as in *Agostini*. And similar to *Agostini*, *Mitchell* raised questions about where the Court should draw the constitutional line with respect to the amount and types of educational assistance. In essence, could the state constitutionally assume financial responsibility for any aspect of a religious school's educational program except for its religious activities? But as much as anything, the justices, lawyers, and observers were aware of the implications of the case for the inevitable voucher case just over the horizon. In reading *Mitchell*, note any differences between the plurality opinion and that of the majority in *Agostini*.

## MITCHELL v. HELMS
### 530 U.S. 793 (2000)

JUSTICE THOMAS announced the judgment of the Court and delivered an opinion, in which THE CHIEF JUSTICE, JUSTICE SCALIA, and JUSTICE KENNEDY join.

As part of a longstanding school-aid program known as Chapter 2, the Federal Government distributes funds to state and local governmental agencies, which in turn lend educational materials and equipment to public and private schools, with the enrollment of each participating school determining the amount of aid that it receives.[1] . . .

Among other things, Chapter 2 provides aid "for the acquisition and use of instructional and educational materials, including library services and materials (including media materials), assessments, reference materials, computer software and hardware for instructional use, and other curricular materials." 20 U.S.C. § 7351(b)(2).

LEAs and SEAs* must offer assistance to both public and private schools (although any private school must be nonprofit). §§ 7312(a), 7372(a)(1). Participating private schools receive Chapter 2 aid based on the number of children enrolled in each school, see § 7372(a)(1), and allocations of Chapter 2 funds for those schools must generally be "equal (consistent with the number of children to be served) to expenditures for programs . . . for children enrolled in the public schools of the [LEA]." § 7372(b).

[T]he "services, materials, and equipment" provided to private schools must be "secular, neutral, and nonideological." § 7372(a)(1). In addition, private schools may not acquire control of Chapter 2 funds or title to Chapter 2 materials, equipment, or property. . . .

[I]n an average year, about 30% of Chapter 2 funds spent in Jefferson Parish, Louisiana are allocated for private schools. For the 1985–1986 fiscal year, 41 private schools participated in Chapter 2. For the following year, 46 participated, and the participation level has remained relatively constant since then. Of these 46, 34 were Roman Catholic; 7 were otherwise religiously affiliated; and 5 were not religiously affiliated. . . .

## II

The Establishment Clause of the First Amendment dictates that "Congress shall make no law respecting an establishment of religion." In the over 50 years since *Everson v. Board of Ed. of Ewing*, 330 U.S. 1, we have consistently struggled to apply these simple words in the context of governmental aid to religious schools . . . .

In *Agostini,* however, . . . we modified *Lemon* for purposes of evaluating aid to schools and examined only the first and second factors. . . . We then set out revised criteria for determining the effect of a statute: "To summarize, New York City's Title I program does not run afoul of any of three primary criteria we currently use to evaluate whether government aid has the effect of advancing religion: It does not result in governmental indoctrination; define its recipients by reference to religion; or create an excessive entanglement." . . .

Considering Chapter 2 in light of our more recent case law, we conclude that it neither results in religious indoctrination by the government nor defines its recipients by reference to religion. In so holding, we acknowledge what both the Ninth and Fifth Circuits saw was inescapable—*Meek* and

---

[1] Chapter 2 is now technically Subchapter VI of Chapter 70 of 20 U.S.C., where it was codified by the Improving America's Schools Act of 1994, Pub. L. 103-382, 108 Stat. 3707. For convenience, we will use the term "Chapter 2," as the lower courts did. Prior to 1994, Chapter 2 was codified at 20 U.S.C. §§ 2911-2976 (1988 ed.).

\* Editors' note: "Local Education Agency"; "State Education Agency."

*Wolman* are anomalies in our case law. We therefore conclude that they are no longer good law.

## A

As we indicated in *Agostini,* and have indicated elsewhere, the question whether governmental aid to religious schools results in governmental indoctrination is ultimately a question whether any religious indoctrination that occurs in those schools could reasonably be attributed to governmental action. . . . We have also indicated that the answer to the question of indoctrination will resolve the question whether a program of educational aid "subsidizes" religion, as our religion cases use that term.

In distinguishing between indoctrination that is attributable to the State and indoctrination that is not, we have consistently turned to the principle of neutrality, upholding aid that is offered to a broad range of groups or persons without regard to their religion. If the religious, irreligious, and areligious are all alike eligible for governmental aid, no one would conclude that any indoctrination that any particular recipient conducts has been done at the behest of the government. For attribution of indoctrination is a relative question. If the government is offering assistance to recipients who provide, so to speak, a broad range of indoctrination, the government itself is not thought responsible for any particular indoctrination. To put the point differently, if the government, seeking to further some legitimate secular purpose, offers aid on the same terms, without regard to religion, to all who adequately further that purpose, see *Allen,* 392 U.S., 245-247 (discussing dual secular and religious purposes of religious schools), then it is fair to say that any aid going to a religious recipient only has the effect of furthering that secular purpose. . . .

As a way of assuring neutrality, we have repeatedly considered whether any governmental aid that goes to a religious institution does so "only as a result of the genuinely independent and private choices of individuals." *Agostini,* 226, (internal quotation marks omitted). We have viewed as significant whether the "private choices of individual parents," as opposed to the "unmediated" will of government, *Ball,* 473 U.S., 395, n. 13, (internal quotation marks omitted), determine what schools ultimately benefit from the governmental aid, and how much. For if numerous private choices, rather than the single choice of a government, determine the distribution of aid pursuant to neutral eligibility criteria, then a government cannot, or at least cannot easily, grant special favors that might lead to a religious establishment. Private choice also helps guarantee neutrality by mitigating the preference for pre-existing recipients that is arguably inherent in any governmental aid program, and that could lead to a program inadvertently favoring one religion or favoring religious private schools in general over nonreligious ones. . . .

*Agostini's* second primary criterion for determining the effect of governmental aid is closely related to the first. The second criterion requires a court to consider whether an aid program "define[s] its recipients by reference to religion." 521 U.S., 234. As we briefly explained in *Agostini, id.,* 230-231, this second criterion looks to the same set of facts as does our focus, under the first criterion, on neutrality, see *id.,* 225-226, but the second criterion uses those facts to answer a somewhat different question—whether the criteria for allocating the aid "creat[e] a financial incentive to undertake religious indoctrination," *id.,* 231 In *Agostini* we set out the following rule for answering this question: "This incentive is not present, however, where the aid is allocated on the basis of neutral, secular criteria that neither favor nor disfavor religion, and is made available to both religious and secular beneficiaries on a nondiscriminatory basis. Under such circumstances, the aid is less likely to have the effect of advancing religion." *Ibid.*

The cases on which *Agostini* relied for this rule, and *Agostini* itself, make clear the close relationship between this rule, incentives, and private choice. For to say that a program does not create an incentive to choose religious schools is to say that the private choice is truly "independent." . . . When such an incentive does exist, there is a greater risk that one could attribute to the government any indoctrination by the religious schools. See *Zobrest*, 10.

We hasten to add, . . . that simply because an aid program offers private schools, and thus religious schools, a benefit that they did not previously receive does not mean that the program, by reducing the cost of securing a religious education, creates, under *Agostini's* second criterion, an "incentive" for parents to choose such an education for their children. For *any* aid will have some such effect.

B

Respondents inexplicably make no effort to address Chapter 2 under the *Agostini* test. Instead, . . . [t]hey argue first, and chiefly, that "direct, nonincidental" aid to the primary educational mission of religious schools is always impermissible. Second, they argue that provision to religious schools of aid that is divertible to religious use is similarly impermissible. . . .

1

Although some of our earlier cases, particularly *Ball*, 473 U.S., 393-394, did emphasize the distinction between direct and indirect aid, the purpose of this distinction was merely to prevent "subsidization" of religion, . . . If aid to schools, even "direct aid," is neutrally available and, before reaching or benefiting any religious school, first passes through the hands (literally or figuratively) of numerous private citizens who are free to direct the aid elsewhere, the government has not provided any "support of religion," *Witters*, 489. Although the presence of private choice is easier to see when aid literally passes through the hands of individuals—which is why we have mentioned directness in the same breath with private choice, see, e.g., *Agostini*, 521 U.S., 226; *Witters*, 487; *Mueller*, 399—there is no reason why the Establishment Clause requires such a form.

Indeed, *Agostini* expressly rejected the absolute line that respondents would have us draw. We there explained that "we have departed from the rule relied on in *Ball* that all government aid that directly assists the educational function of religious schools is invalid." 521 U.S., 225. *Agostini* relied primarily on *Witters* for this conclusion and made clear that private choice and neutrality would resolve the concerns formerly addressed by the rule in *Ball*. It was undeniable in *Witters* that the aid (tuition) would ultimately go to the Inland Empire School of the Bible and would support religious education. We viewed this arrangement, however, as no different from a government issuing a paycheck to one of its employees knowing that the employee would direct the funds to a religious institution. Both arrangements would be valid, for the same reason: "[A]ny money that ultimately went to religious institutions did so 'only as a result of the genuinely independent and private choices of' individuals." . . .

To the extent that respondents intend their direct/indirect distinction to require that any aid be literally placed in the hands of schoolchildren rather than given directly to the school for teaching those same children, the very cases on which respondents most rely, *Meek* and *Wolman,* demonstrate the irrelevance of such formalism. In *Meek,* we justified our rejection of a program that loaned instructional materials and equipment by, among other things, pointing out that the aid was loaned to the schools, and thus was "direct aid." 421 U.S., 362-363. The materials-and-equipment program in *Wolman* was essentially identical, except that the State, in an effort to comply with *Meek,* see *Wolman,* 433 U.S., 233, 250, loaned the aid to the students. . . . Yet we dismissed as "technical" the difference between the two programs: "[I]t would exalt form over substance if this distinction were found to justify a result different from that in *Meek.*" 433 U.S., 250. *Wolman* thus, although purporting to reaffirm *Meek,* actually undermined that decision, as is evident from the similarity between the reasoning of *Wolman* and that of the *Meek* dissent. . . .

Further, respondents' formalistic line breaks down in the application to real-world programs. In *Allen,* for example, although we did recognize that students themselves received and owned the textbooks, we also noted that the books provided were those that the private schools required for courses, that the schools could collect students' requests for books and submit them to the board of education, that the schools could store the textbooks, and that the textbooks were essential to the schools' teaching of secular subjects. Whether one chooses to label this program "direct" or "indirect" is a rather arbitrary choice, one that does not further the constitutional analysis.

Of course, we have seen "special Establishment Clause dangers," *Rosenberger,* 515 U.S., 842, when *money* is given to religious schools or entities directly rather than, as in *Witters* and *Mueller,* indirectly. . . .[8] But direct payments of money are not at issue in this case, and we refuse to allow a "special" case to create a rule for all cases.

Respondents also contend that the Establishment Clause requires that aid to religious schools not be impermissibly religious in nature or be divertible to religious use. We agree with the first part of this argument but not the second. Respondents' "no divertibility" rule is inconsistent with our more recent case law and is unworkable. So long as the governmental aid is not itself "unsuitable for use in the public schools because of religious content," *Allen,* 245, and eligibility for aid is determined in a constitutionally permissible manner, any use of that aid to indoctrinate cannot be attributed to the government and is thus not of constitutional concern. And, of course, the use to which the aid is put does not affect the criteria governing the aid's allocation and thus does not create any impermissible incentive under *Agostini's* second criterion.

Our recent precedents, particularly *Zobrest,* require us to reject respondents' argument. For *Zobrest* gave no consideration to divertibility or even to actual diversion. . . .

Similarly, had we, in *Witters,* been concerned with divertibility or diversion, we would have unhesitatingly, perhaps summarily, struck down the tuition-reimbursement program, because it was certain that Witters sought to

---

[8] The reason for such concern is not that the form *per se* is bad, but that such a form creates special risks that governmental aid will have the effect of advancing religion (or, even more, a purpose of doing so). An indirect form of payment reduces these risks. . . .

participate in it to acquire an education in a religious career from a sectarian institution. Diversion was guaranteed. *Mueller* took the same view as *Zobrest* and *Witters,* for we did not in *Mueller* require the State to show that the tax deductions were only for the costs of education in secular subjects. We declined to impose any such segregation requirement for either the tuition-expense deductions or the deductions for items strikingly similar to those at issue in *Meek* and *Wolman,* and here. . . .

Respondents appear to rely on *Meek* and *Wolman* to establish their rule against "divertible" aid. But those cases offer little, if any, support for respondents. *Meek* mentioned divertibility only briefly in a concluding footnote, see 421 U.S., 366, n. 16, and that mention was, at most, peripheral to the Court's reasoning in striking down the lending of instructional materials and equipment. The aid program in *Wolman* explicitly barred divertible aid, so a concern for divertibility could not have been part of our reason for finding that program invalid.

The issue is not divertibility of aid but rather whether the aid itself has an impermissible content. Where the aid would be suitable for use in a public school, it is also suitable for use in any private school. Similarly, the prohibition against the government providing impermissible content resolves the Establishment Clause concerns that exist if aid is actually diverted to religious uses. . . .

A concern for divertibility, as opposed to improper content, is misplaced not only because it fails to explain why the sort of aid that we have allowed is permissible, but also because it is boundless—enveloping all aid, no matter how trivial—and thus has only the most attenuated (if any) link to any realistic concern for preventing an "establishment of religion." Presumably, for example, government-provided lecterns, chalk, crayons, pens, paper, and paintbrushes would have to be excluded from religious schools under respondents' proposed rule. But we fail to see how indoctrination by means of (i.e., diversion of) such aid could be attributed to the government. . . .

One of the dissent's factors deserves special mention: whether a school that receives aid (or whose students receive aid) is pervasively sectarian. The dissent is correct that there was a period when this factor mattered, particularly if the pervasively sectarian school was a primary or secondary school. But that period is one that the Court should regret, and it is thankfully long past.

There are numerous reasons to formally dispense with this factor. First, its relevance in our precedents is in sharp decline. Although our case law has consistently mentioned it even in recent years, we have not struck down an aid program in reliance on this factor since 1985. . . .

Second, the religious nature of a recipient should not matter to the constitutional analysis, so long as the recipient adequately furthers the government's secular purpose. If a program offers permissible aid to the religious (including the pervasively sectarian), the areligious, and the irreligious, it is a mystery which view of religion the government has established, and thus a mystery what the constitutional violation would be. The pervasively sectarian recipient has not received any special favor, and it is most bizarre that the Court would, as the dissent seemingly does, reserve special hostility for those who take their religion seriously, who think that their religion should affect the whole of their lives, or who make the mistake of being effective in transmitting their views to children.

Third, the inquiry into the recipient's religious views required by a focus on whether a school is pervasively sectarian is not only unnecessary but also offensive. It is well established, in numerous other contexts, that courts should refrain from trolling through a person's or institution's religious beliefs. . . . In addition, and related, the application of the "pervasively sectarian" factor collides with our decisions that have prohibited governments from discriminating in the distribution of public benefits based upon religious status or sincerity. See *Rosenberger v. Rector and Visitors of Univ. of Va.*, 515 U.S. 819; *Lamb's Chapel v. Center Moriches Union Free School Dist.*, 508 U.S. 384; *Widmar v. Vincent*, 454 U.S. 263.

Finally, hostility to aid to pervasively sectarian schools has a shameful pedigree that we do not hesitate to disavow. . . . Opposition to aid to "sectarian" schools acquired prominence in the 1870's with Congress' consideration (and near passage) of the Blaine Amendment, which would have amended the Constitution to bar any aid to sectarian institutions. Consideration of the amendment arose at a time of pervasive hostility to the Catholic Church and to Catholics in general, and it was an open secret that "sectarian" was code for "Catholic." . . .

In short, nothing in the Establishment Clause requires the exclusion of pervasively sectarian schools from otherwise permissible aid programs, and other doctrines of this Court bar it. This doctrine, born of bigotry, should be buried now.

## III

Applying the two relevant *Agostini* criteria, we see no basis for concluding that Jefferson Parish's Chapter 2 program "has the effect of advancing religion.". . .

Taking the second criterion first, it is clear that Chapter 2 aid "is allocated on the basis of neutral, secular criteria that neither favor nor disfavor religion, and is made available to both religious and secular beneficiaries on a nondiscriminatory basis." *Agostini*, 521 U.S., 231. Aid is allocated based on enrollment: "Private schools receive Chapter 2 materials and equipment based on the per capita number of students at each school," *Walker*, 46 F.3d, 1464, and allocations to private schools must "be equal (consistent with the number of children to be served) to expenditures for programs under this subchapter for children enrolled in the public schools of the [LEA]," 20 U.S.C. § 7372(b). . . .

Chapter 2 also satisfies the first *Agostini* criterion. The program makes a broad array of schools eligible for aid without regard to their religious affiliations or lack thereof. . . . Chapter 2 aid also, like the aid in *Agostini, Zobrest,* and *Witters,* reaches participating schools only "as a consequence of private decision-making." *Agostini*, 222. Private decision-making controls because of the per capita allocation scheme, and those decisions are independent because of the program's neutrality. It is the students and their parents—not the government—who, through their choice of school, determine who receives Chapter 2 funds. The aid follows the child.

Because Chapter 2 aid is provided pursuant to private choices, it is not problematic that one could fairly describe Chapter 2 as providing "direct" aid. The materials and equipment provided under Chapter 2 are presumably used from time to time by entire classes rather than by individual students (although individual students are likely the chief consumers of library books and, perhaps, of computers and computer software), and students themselves do not need to apply for Chapter 2 aid in order for their schools to receive it, but, as we explained in *Agostini*, these traits are not constitutionally significant or meaningful. Nor, for reasons we have already explained, is it of constitutional significance that the schools themselves, rather than the students, are the bailees of the Chapter 2 aid. The ultimate beneficiaries of Chapter 2 aid are the students who attend the schools that receive that aid, and this is so regardless of whether individual students lug computers to school each day. . . .

Finally, Chapter 2 satisfies the first *Agostini* criterion because it does not provide to religious schools aid that has an impermissible content. The statute explicitly bars anything of the sort, providing that all Chapter 2 aid for the benefit of children in private schools shall be "secular, neutral, and nonideological," § 7372(a)(1), and the record indicates that the Louisiana SEA and the Jefferson Parish LEA have faithfully enforced this requirement insofar as relevant to this case. . . .

There is evidence that equipment has been, or at least easily could be, diverted for use in religious classes. JUSTICE O'CONNOR, however, finds the safeguards against diversion adequate to prevent and detect actual diversion. . . . [W]e agree with the dissent that there is evidence of actual diversion and that, were the safeguards anything other than anemic, there would almost certainly be more such evidence. In any event, for reasons we discussed in Part II-B-2, the evidence of actual diversion and the weakness of the safeguards against actual diversion are not relevant to the constitutional inquiry, whatever relevance they may have under the statute and regulations.

Respondents do, however, point to some religious books that the LEA improperly allowed to be loaned to several religious schools, and they contend that the monitoring programs of the SEA and the Jefferson Parish LEA are insufficient to prevent such errors. The evidence, however, establishes just the opposite, for the improper lending of library books occurred—and was discovered and remedied—before this litigation began almost 15 years ago. In other words, the monitoring system worked. . . .

We are unwilling to elevate scattered *de minimis* statutory violations, discovered and remedied by the relevant authorities themselves prior to any litigation, to such a level as to convert an otherwise unobjectionable parishwide program into a law that has the effect of advancing religion.

IV

In short, Chapter 2 satisfies both the first and second primary criteria of *Agostini*. It therefore does not have the effect of advancing religion. For the same reason, Chapter 2 also "cannot reasonably be viewed as an endorsement of religion," *Agostini*, 521 U.S., 235. Accordingly, we hold that Chapter 2 is not a law respecting an establishment of religion. Jefferson Parish need not exclude religious schools from its Chapter 2 program. To the extent that *Meek* and *Wolman* conflict with this holding, we overrule them. . . .

The judgment of the Fifth Circuit is reversed.

*It is so ordered.*

⧫ JUSTICE O'CONNOR, with whom JUSTICE BREYER joins, concurring in the judgment. . . .

I

I write separately because, in my view, the plurality announces a rule of unprecedented breadth for the evaluation of Establishment Clause challenges to government school aid programs. Reduced to its essentials, the plurality's rule states that government aid to religious schools does not have the effect of advancing religion so long as the aid is offered on a neutral basis and the aid is secular in content. The plurality also rejects the distinction between direct and indirect aid, and holds that the actual diversion of secular aid by a religious school to the advancement of its religious mission is permissible. Although the expansive scope of the plurality's rule is troubling, two specific aspects of the opinion compel me to write separately. First, the plurality's treatment of neutrality comes close to assigning that factor singular importance in the future adjudication of Establishment Clause challenges to government school aid programs. Second, the plurality's approval of actual diversion of government aid to religious indoctrination is in tension with our precedents and, in any event, unnecessary to decide the instant case. . . .

I agree with JUSTICE SOUTER that the plurality, by taking such a stance, "appears to take evenhandedness neutrality and in practical terms promote it to a single and sufficient test for the establishment constitutionality of school aid."

I do not quarrel with the plurality's recognition that neutrality is an important reason for upholding government-aid programs against Establishment Clause challenges. Our cases have described neutrality in precisely this manner, and we have emphasized a program's neutrality repeatedly in our decisions approving various forms of school aid. Nevertheless, we have never held that a government-aid program passes constitutional muster *solely* because of the neutral criteria it employs as a basis for distributing aid. For example, in *Agostini,* neutrality was only one of several factors we considered in determining that New York City's Title I program did not have the impermissible effect of advancing religion. See 521 U.S., 226-228 (noting lack of evidence of inculcation of religion by Title I instructors, legal requirement that Title I services be supplemental to regular curricula, and that no Title I funds reached religious schools' coffers). Indeed, given that the aid in *Agostini* had secular content and was distributed on the basis of wholly neutral criteria, our consideration of additional factors demonstrates that the plurality's rule does not accurately describe our recent Establishment Clause jurisprudence. . . .

I agree with JUSTICE SOUTER's conclusion that our "most recent use of 'neutrality' to refer to generality or evenhandedness of distribution . . . is relevant in judging whether a benefit scheme so characterized should be seen as aiding a sectarian school's religious mission, but this neutrality is not alone sufficient to qualify the aid as constitutional."

I also disagree with the plurality's conclusion that actual diversion of government aid to religious indoctrination is consistent with the Establishment Clause. Although "[o]ur cases have permitted some government funding of secular functions performed by sectarian organizations," our decisions "provide no precedent for the use of public funds to finance religious activities." *Rosenberger,* 847 (O'CONNOR, J., concurring). . . . In both *Agostini,* our most recent school aid case, and *Board of Ed. v. Allen,* 392 U.S. 236, we rested our approval of the relevant programs in part on the fact that the aid had not been used to advance the religious missions of the recipient schools. . . . Of course, our focus on the lack of such evidence would have been entirely unnecessary if we had believed that the Establishment Clause permits the actual diversion of secular government aid to religious indoctrination. . . .

The plurality bases its holding that actual diversion is permissible on *Witters* and *Zobrest.* Those decisions, however, rested on a significant factual premise missing from this case, as well as from the majority of cases thus far considered by the Court involving Establishment Clause challenges to school aid programs. Specifically, we decided *Witters* and *Zobrest* on the understanding that the aid was provided directly to the individual student who, in turn, made the choice of where to put that aid to use. . . . This characteristic of both programs made them less like a direct subsidy, which would be impermissible under the Establishment Clause, and more akin to the government issuing a paycheck to an employee who, in turn, donates a portion of that check to a religious institution. . . .

Like JUSTICE SOUTER, I do not believe that we should treat a per-capita-aid program the same as the true private-choice programs considered in *Witters* and *Zobrest*. First, when the government provides aid directly to the student beneficiary, that student can attend a religious school and yet retain control over whether the secular government aid will be applied toward the religious education. The fact that aid flows to the religious school and is used for the advancement of religion is therefore *wholly* dependent on the student's private decision. . . .

Second, I believe the distinction between a per capita school aid program and a true private-choice program is significant for purposes of endorsement. In terms of public perception, a government program of direct aid to religious schools based on the number of students attending each school differs meaningfully from the government distributing aid directly to individual students who, in turn, decide to use the aid at the same religious schools. In the former example, if the religious school uses the aid to inculcate religion in its students, it is reasonable to say that the government has communicated a message of endorsement. Because the religious indoctrination is supported by government assistance, the reasonable observer would naturally perceive the aid program as *government* support for the advancement of religion. That the amount of aid received by the school is based on the school's enrollment does not separate the government from the endorsement of the religious message. The aid formula does not—and could not—indicate to a reasonable observer that the inculcation of religion is endorsed only by the individuals attending the religious school, who each affirmatively choose to direct the secular government aid to the school and its religious mission. No such choices have been made. In contrast, when government aid supports a school's religious mission only because of independent decisions made by numerous individuals to guide their secular aid to that school, "[n]o reasonable observer is likely to draw from the facts . . . an inference that the State itself is endorsing a religious practice or belief." *Witters*, 493 (O'CONNOR, J., concurring in part and concurring in judgment). Rather, endorsement of the religious message is reasonably attributed to the individuals who select the path of the aid.

Finally, the distinction between a per-capita-aid program and a true private-choice program is important when considering aid that consists of direct monetary subsidies. . . . If, as the plurality contends, a per-capita-aid program is identical in relevant constitutional respects to a true private-choice program, then there is no reason that, under the plurality's reasoning, the government should be precluded from providing direct money payments to religious organizations (including churches) based on the number of persons belonging to each organization. And, because actual diversion is permissible under the plurality's holding, the participating religious organizations (including churches) could use that aid to support religious indoctrination. To be sure, the plurality does not actually hold that its theory extends to direct money payments.

That omission, however, is of little comfort. In its logic—as well as its specific advisory language—the plurality opinion foreshadows the approval of direct monetary subsidies to religious organizations, even when they use the money to advance their religious objectives. . . .

II

In *Agostini,* after reexamining our jurisprudence since *School Dist. of Grand Rapids v. Ball,* 473 U.S. 373, we explained that the general principles used to determine whether government aid violates the Establishment Clause have remained largely unchanged. Thus, we still ask "whether the government acted with the purpose of advancing or inhibiting religion" and "whether the aid has the 'effect' of advancing or inhibiting religion." 521 U.S., 222-223. We also concluded in *Agostini,* however, that the specific criteria used to determine whether government aid has an impermissible effect had changed. Looking to our recently decided cases, we articulated three primary criteria to guide the determination whether a government-aid program impermissibly advances religion: (1) whether the aid results in governmental indoctrination, (2) whether the aid program defines its recipients by reference to religion, and (3) whether the aid creates an excessive entanglement between government and religion. *Id.,* 234. Finally, we noted that the same criteria could be reviewed to determine whether a government-aid program constitutes an endorsement of religion. . . .

Second, we noted that the Court had "departed from the rule relied on in *Ball* that all government aid that directly assists the educational function of religious schools is invalid." *Agostini,* 225. Relying on *Witters* and *Zobrest,* we noted that our cases had taken a more forgiving view of neutral government programs that make aid available generally without regard to the religious or nonreligious character of the recipient school. . . .

The Chapter 2 program at issue here bears the same hallmarks of the New York City Title I program that we found important in *Agostini.* First, as explained above, Chapter 2 aid is distributed on the basis of neutral, secular criteria. The aid is available to assist students regardless of whether they attend public or private nonprofit religious schools. Second, the statute requires participating SEAs and LEAs to use and allocate Chapter 2 funds only to supplement the funds otherwise available to a religious school. 20 U.S.C. § 7371(b). Chapter 2 funds must in no case be used to supplant funds from non-Federal sources. *Ibid.* Third, no Chapter 2 funds ever reach the coffers of a religious school. Like the Title I program considered in *Agostini,* all Chapter 2 funds are controlled by public agencies—the SEAs and LEAs. § 7372(c)(1). The LEAs purchase instructional and educational materials and then lend those materials to public and private schools. With respect to lending to private schools under Chapter 2, the statute specifically provides that the relevant public agency must retain title to the materials and equipment. § 7372(c)(1). Together with the supplantation restriction, this provision ensures that religious schools reap no financial benefit by virtue of receiving loans of materials and equipment. Finally, the statute provides that all Chapter 2 materials and equipment must be "secular, neutral, and nonideological." § 7372(a)(1). That restriction is reinforced by a further statutory prohibition on "the making of any payment . . . for religious worship or instruction." § 8897. Although respondents claim that Chapter 2 aid has been diverted to religious instruction, that evidence is *de minimis.* . . .

III . . .

Respondents insist that there is a reasoned basis under the Establishment Clause for the distinction between textbooks and instructional materials and equipment. They claim that the presumption that religious schools will use instructional materials and equipment to inculcate religion is sound because such materials and equipment, unlike textbooks, are reasonably divertible to religious uses. . . . Respondents therefore claim that the Establishment Clause prohibits the government from giving or lending aid to religious schools when that aid is reasonably divertible to religious uses. JUSTICE SOUTER also states that the divertibility of secular government aid is an important consideration under the Establishment Clause, although he apparently would not ascribe it the constitutionally determinative status that respondents do.

I would reject respondents' proposed divertibility rule. . . .

For JUSTICE SOUTER, secular school aid presents constitutional problems not only when it is actually diverted to religious ends, but also when it simply has the capacity for, or presents the possibility of, such diversion. . . .

Stated simply, the theory does not provide a logical distinction between the lending of textbooks and the lending of instructional materials and equipment. An educator can use virtually any instructional tool, whether it has ascertainable content or not, to teach a religious message. In this respect, I agree with the plurality that "it is hard to imagine any book that could not, in even moderately skilled hands, serve to illustrate a religious message." In today's case, for example, we are asked to draw a constitutional distinction between lending a textbook and lending a library book. JUSTICE SOUTER's try at justifying that distinction only demonstrates the absurdity on which such a difference must rest. . . .

To the extent JUSTICE SOUTER believes several related Establishment Clause decisions require application of a divertibility rule in the context of this case, I respectfully disagree. JUSTICE SOUTER is correct to note our continued recognition of the special dangers associated with direct money grants to religious institutions. It does not follow, however, that we should treat as constitutionally suspect any form of secular aid that might conceivably be diverted to a religious use. As the cases JUSTICE SOUTER cites demonstrate, our concern with direct monetary aid is based on more than just diversion. In fact, the most important reason for according special treatment to direct money grants is that this form of aid falls precariously close to the original object of the Establishment Clause's prohibition. . . .

IV

Because divertibility fails to explain the distinction our cases have drawn between textbooks and instructional materials and equipment, there remains the question of which of the two irreconcilable strands of our Establishment Clause jurisprudence we should now follow. Between the two, I would adhere to the rule that we have applied in the context of textbook lending programs: To establish a First Amendment violation, plaintiffs must prove that the aid in question actually is, or has been, used for religious purposes. See *Meek*, 421 U.S., 361-362; *Allen*, 392 U.S., 248. Just as we held in *Agostini* that our more recent cases had undermined the assumptions underlying *Ball* and *Aguilar*, I would now hold that *Agostini* and the cases on which it relied have undermined the assumptions underlying *Meek* and *Wolman*. . . . In *Agostini*, we repeatedly emphasized that it would be inappropriate to presume inculcation of religion; rather, plaintiffs raising an Establishment Clause challenge must present evidence that the government aid in question has resulted in religious indoctrination. . . .

## V

Respondents do not rest, however, on their divertibility argument alone. Rather, they also contend that the evidence respecting the actual administration of Chapter 2 in Jefferson Parish demonstrates that the program violated the Establishment Clause. . . . I disagree with both the plurality and JUSTICE SOUTER. The limited evidence amassed by respondents during 4 years of discovery (which began approximately 15 years ago) is at best *de minimis* and therefore insufficient to affect the constitutional inquiry. . . .

To find that actual diversion will flourish, one must presume bad faith on the part of the religious school officials who report to the JPPSS monitors regarding the use of Chapter 2 aid. I believe that it is entirely proper to presume that these school officials will act in good faith. That presumption is especially appropriate in this case, since there is no proof that religious school officials have breached their schools' assurances or failed to tell government officials the truth. . . .

Given the important similarities between the Chapter 2 program here and the Title I program at issue in *Agostini,* respondents' Establishment Clause challenge must fail. As in *Agostini,* the Chapter 2 aid is allocated on the basis of neutral, secular criteria; the aid must be supplementary and cannot supplant non-Federal funds; no Chapter 2 funds ever reach the coffers of religious schools; the aid must be secular; any evidence of actual diversion is *de minimis;* and the program includes adequate safeguards. Regardless of whether these factors are constitutional requirements, they are surely sufficient to find that the program at issue here does not have the impermissible effect of advancing religion. . . .

▦ JUSTICE SOUTER, with whom JUSTICE STEVENS and JUSTICE GINSBURG join, dissenting. . . .

The establishment prohibition of government religious funding serves more than one end. It is meant to guarantee the right of individual conscience against compulsion, to protect the integrity of religion against the corrosion of secular support, and to preserve the unity of political society against the implied exclusion of the less favored and the antagonism of controversy over public support for religious causes. . . .

[A] few fundamental generalizations are nonetheless possible. There may be no aid supporting a sectarian school's religious exercise or the discharge of its religious mission, while aid of a secular character with no discernible benefit to such a sectarian objective is allowable. Because the religious and secular spheres largely overlap in the life of many such schools, the Court has tried to identify some facts likely to reveal the relative religious or secular intent or effect of the government benefits in particular circumstances. We have asked whether the government is acting neutrally in distributing its money, and about the form of the aid itself, its path from government to religious institution, its divertibility to religious nurture, its potential for reducing traditional expenditures of religious institutions, and its relative importance to the recipient, among other things. . . .

After *Everson* and *Allen*, the state of the law applying the Establishment Clause to public expenditures producing some benefit to religious schools was this:

1. Government aid to religion is forbidden, and tax revenue may not be used to support a religious school or religious teaching.

2. Government provision of such paradigms of universally general welfare benefits as police and fire protection does not count as aid to religion.

3. Whether a law's benefit is sufficiently close to universally general welfare paradigms to be classified with them, as distinct from religious aid, is a function of the purpose and effect of the challenged law in all its particularity. The judgment is not reducible to the application of any formula. Evenhandedness of distribution as between religious and secular beneficiaries is a relevant factor, but not a sufficiency test of constitutionality. There is no rule of religious equal protection to the effect that any expenditure for the benefit of religious school students is necessarily constitutional so long as public school pupils are favored on ostensibly identical terms.

4. Government must maintain neutrality as to religion, "neutrality" being a conclusory label for the required position of government as neither aiding religion nor impeding religious exercise by believers. "Neutrality" was not the name of any test to identify permissible action, and in particular, was not synonymous with evenhandedness in conferring benefit on the secular as well as the religious.

Today, the substantive principle of no aid to religious mission remains the governing understanding of the Establishment Clause as applied to public benefits inuring to religious schools. The governing opinions on the subject in the 35 years since *Allen* have never challenged this principle. The cases have, however, recognized that in actual Establishment Clause litigation over school aid legislation, there is no pure aid to religion and no purely secular welfare benefit; the effects of the laws fall somewhere in between, with the judicial task being to make a realistic allocation between the two possibilities. . . .

## II
### A

The most deceptively familiar of those considerations is "neutrality," the presence or absence of which, in some sense, we have addressed from the moment of *Everson* itself. . . .

"[N]eutrality" originally entered this field of jurisprudence as a conclusory term, a label for the required relationship between the government and religion as a state of equipoise between government as ally and government as adversary. Reexamining *Everson's* paradigm cases to derive a prescriptive guideline, we first determined that "neutral" aid was secular, nonideological, or unrelated to religious education. Our subsequent reexamination of *Everson* and *Allen*, beginning in *Nyquist* and culminating in *Mueller* and most recently in *Agostini*, recast neutrality as a concept of "evenhandedness.". . .

In the days when "neutral" was used in *Everson's* sense of equipoise, neutrality was tantamount to constitutionality; the term was conclusory, but when it applied it meant that the government's position was constitutional under the Establishment Clause. This is not so at all, however, under the most recent use of "neutrality" to refer to generality or evenhandedness of distribution. This kind of neutrality is relevant in judging whether a benefit scheme so characterized should be seen as aiding a sectarian school's religious mission, but this neutrality is not alone sufficient to qualify the aid as constitutional. It is to be considered only along with other characteristics of aid, its administration, its recipients, or its potential that have been emphasized over the years as indicators of just how religious the intent and effect of a given aid scheme really is. . . .

## B

The insufficiency of evenhandedness neutrality as a stand-alone criterion of constitutional intent or effect has been clear from the beginning of our interpretative efforts, for an obvious reason. Evenhandedness in distributing a benefit approaches the equivalence of constitutionality in this area only when the term refers to such universality of distribution that it makes no sense to think of the benefit as going to any discrete group. Conversely, when evenhandedness refers to distribution to limited groups within society, like groups of schools or schoolchildren, it does make sense to regard the benefit as aid to the recipients. . . .

At least three main lines of enquiry addressed particularly to school aid have emerged to complement evenhandedness neutrality. First, we have noted that two types of aid recipients heighten Establishment Clause concern: pervasively religious schools and primary and secondary religious schools. Second, we have identified two important characteristics of the method of distributing aid: directness or indirectness of distribution and distribution by genuinely independent choice. Third, we have found relevance in at least five characteristics of the aid itself: its religious content; its cash form; its divertibility or actually diversion to religious support; its supplantation of traditional items of religious school expense; and its substantiality. . . .

## III
## A

The nub of the plurality's new position is this:

> [I]f the government, seeking to further some legitimate secular purpose, offers aid on the same terms, without regard to religion, to all who adequately further that purpose, then it is fair to say that any aid going to a religious recipient only has the effect of furthering that secular purpose. The government, in crafting such an aid program, has had to conclude that a given level of aid is necessary to further that purpose among secular recipients and has provided no more than that same level to religious recipients.

As a break with consistent doctrine the plurality's new criterion is unequaled in the history of Establishment Clause interpretation. Simple on its face, it appears to take evenhandedness neutrality and in practical terms promote it to a single and sufficient test for the establishment constitutionality of school aid. Even on its own terms, its errors are manifold, and attention to at least three of its mistaken assumptions will show the degree to which the plurality's proposal would replace the principle of no aid with a formula for generous religious support.

First, the plurality treats an external observer's attribution of religious support to the government as the sole impermissible effect of a government aid scheme. ("[N]o one would conclude that any indoctrination that any particular recipient conducts has been done at the behest of the government"). While perceived state endorsement of religion is undoubtedly a relevant concern under the Establishment Clause, it is certainly not the only one. *Everson* made this clear from the start: secret aid to religion by the government is also barred. 330 U.S., 16. State aid not attributed to the government would still violate a taxpayer's liberty of conscience, threaten to corrupt religion, and generate disputes over aid. . . .

Second, the plurality apparently assumes as a fact that equal amounts of aid to religious and nonreligious schools will have exclusively secular and equal effects, on both external perception and on incentives to attend different schools. But there is no reason to believe that this will be the case; we have long recognized that unrestricted aid to religious schools will support religious teaching in addition to secular education, a fact that would be true no matter what the supposedly secular purpose of the law might be.

Third, the plurality assumes that per capita distribution rules safeguard the same principles as independent, private choices. But that is clearly not so. . . .

## B

The plurality's conception of evenhandedness does not, however, control the case, whose disposition turns on the misapplication of accepted categories of school aid analysis. The facts most obviously relevant to the Chapter 2 scheme in Jefferson Parish are those showing divertibility and actual diversion in the circumstance of pervasively sectarian religious schools. The type of aid, the structure of the program, and the lack of effective safeguards clearly demonstrate the divertibility of the aid. While little is known about its use, owing to the anemic enforcement system in the parish, even the thin record before us reveals that actual diversion occurred. . . .

## IV

The plurality would break with the law. The majority misapplies it. That misapplication is, however, the only consolation in the case, which reaches an erroneous result but does not stage a doctrinal coup. But there is no mistaking the abandonment of doctrine that would occur if the plurality were to become a majority. It is beyond question that the plurality's notion of evenhandedness neutrality as a practical guarantee of the validity of aid to sectarian schools would be the end of the principle of no aid to the schools' religious mission. And if that were not so obvious it would become so after reflecting on the plurality's thoughts about diversion and about giving attention to the pervasiveness of a school's sectarian teaching.

The plurality is candid in pointing out the extent of actual diversion of Chapter 2 aid to religious use in the case before us, and equally candid in saying it does not matter. To the plurality there is nothing wrong with aiding a school's religious mission; the only question is whether religious teaching obtains its tax support under a formally evenhanded criterion of distribution. The principle of no aid to religious teaching has no independent significance.

And if this were not enough to prove that no aid in religious school aid is dead under the plurality's First Amendment, the point is nailed down in the plurality's attack on the legitimacy of considering a school's pervasively sectarian character when judging whether aid to the school is likely to aid its religious mission. The relevance of this consideration is simply a matter of common sense: where religious indoctrination pervades school activities of children and adolescents, it takes great care to be able to aid the school without supporting the doctrinal effort. This is obvious. The plurality nonetheless condemns any enquiry into the pervasiveness of doctrinal content as a remnant of anti-Catholic bigotry (as if evangelical Protestant schools and Orthodox Jewish yeshivas were never pervasively sectarian), and it equates a refusal to aid religious schools with hostility to religion (as if aid to religious teaching were not opposed in this very case by at least one religious respondent and numerous religious *amici curiae* in a tradition claiming descent from Roger Williams). My concern with these arguments goes not so much to their details as it does to the fact that the plurality's choice to employ imputations of bigotry and irreligion as terms in the Court's debate makes one point clear: that in rejecting the principle of no aid to a school's religious mission the plurality is attacking the most fundamental assumption underlying the Establishment Clause, that government can in fact operate with neutrality in its relation to religion. I believe that it can, and so respectfully dissent.

## NOTES AND QUESTIONS

1. Describe the plurality's holding and what it sees as necessary for a funding program to satisfy the Establishment Clause.

2. Many scholars agree with Justices O'Connor and Souter that the plurality opinion is sweeping in the changes it would implement in Establishment Clause law. Can you identify what those changes would be? Considering the programs in many of the cases at the beginning of this chapter, what would be the practical effect of a jurisprudence that looked only to evenhanded neutrality to determine whether a program is constitutional?

3. Justice O'Connor is highly critical of the plurality's approach to resolving the case. Yet she concurs in the judgment. How do you explain the differences in her opinion and what brings her, in the end, to concur in the result? Conversely, Justice O'Connor appears to be in agreement with much of Justice Souter's dissent. Does she emphasize different constitutional principles or consider different facts from the dissenters, or does she merely place different emphases on those principles and facts?

4. *Mitchell* raised several issues about the substantiality and divertibility of the aid involved. All sides acknowledged that, unlike the amount of funds involved in *Zobrest*, the federal programs in *Mitchell* involved substantial amounts of money. How did the plurality, concurrence, and dissent address those concerns?

5. How do you understand Justice Thomas' comment about the pervasively sectarian doctrine? If he is correct in his criticism, what does that say about the validity of earlier Establishment Clause holdings? Are holdings such as *Everson* and *Lemon* suspect?

In *Zelman v. Simmons-Harris*, the Court considered the constitutionality of publicly funded vouchers for religious school tuition at the elementary and secondary school levels. Private school vouchers had been controversial for some time. The state of Wisconsin instituted the first publicly funded voucher program in Milwaukee in 1989. Initially, that program excluded participation by religious schools, but the state amended the law in 1995 to permit the use of the voucher for religious-based education. The Wisconsin Supreme Court upheld the constitutionality of the Milwaukee program in 1998 as against an Establishment Clause challenge. The United States Supreme Court later denied review. See *Jackson v. Beason*, 578 N.W.2d 602 (Wis. 1998). Over the same period, state courts had considered the constitutionality of several local and state-wide voucher programs in Florida, Maine, Pennsylvania, Puerto Rico, and Vermont, with a majority of the programs being struck down on Establishment Clause and state constitutional grounds. The high court finally entered the fray by reviewing the constitutionality of a voucher program enacted in 1996 for Cleveland, Ohio.

## ZELMAN v. SIMMONS-HARRIS
## 536 U.S. 639 (2002)

CHIEF JUSTICE REHNQUIST delivered the opinion of the Court.

The State of Ohio has established a pilot program designed to provide educational choices to families with children who reside in the Cleveland City School District. The question presented is whether this program offends the Establishment Clause of the United States Constitution. We hold that it does not.

There are more than 75,000 children enrolled in the Cleveland City School District. The majority of these children are from low-income and minority families. Few of these families enjoy the means to send their children to any school other than an inner-city public school. For more than a generation, however, Cleveland's public schools have been among the worst performing public schools in the Nation. . . .

It is against this backdrop that Ohio enacted, among other initiatives, its Pilot Project Scholarship Program. . . .

The program provides two basic kinds of assistance to parents of children in a covered district. First, the program provides tuition aid for students in kindergarten through third grade, expanding each year through eighth grade, to attend a participating public or private school of their parent's choosing. Ohio Rev. Code Ann. §§ 3313.975(B) and (C)(1). Second, the program provides tutorial aid for students who choose to remain enrolled in public school. § 3313.975(A).

The tuition aid portion of the program is designed to provide educational choices to parents who reside in a covered district. Any private school, whether religious or nonreligious, may participate in the program and accept program students so long as the school is located within the boundaries of a covered district and meets statewide educational standards. § 313.976(A)

(3). Participating private schools must agree not to discriminate on the basis of race, religion, or ethnic background, or to "advocate or foster unlawful behavior or teach hatred of any person or group on the basis of race, ethnicity, national origin, or religion." § 3313.976(A)(6). Any public school located in a school district adjacent to the covered district may also participate in the program. § 3313.976(C). Adjacent public schools are eligible to receive a $2,250 tuition grant for each program student accepted in addition to the full amount of per-pupil state funding attributable to each additional student. §§ 3313.976(C), 3317.03(I)(1). All participating schools, whether public or private, are required to accept students in accordance with rules and procedures established by the state superintendent. §§ 3313.977(A)(1)(a)-(c).

Tuition aid is distributed to parents according to financial need. Families with incomes below 200% of the poverty line are given priority and are eligible to receive 90% of private school tuition up to $2,250. . . . For all other families, the program pays 75% of tuition costs, up to $1,875. These families receive tuition aid only if the number of available scholarships exceeds the number of low-income children who choose to participate. Where tuition aid is spent depends solely upon where parents who receive tuition aid choose to enroll their child. If parents choose a private school, checks are made payable to the parents who then endorse the checks over to the chosen school. § 3313.979.

The tutorial aid portion of the program provides tutorial assistance through grants to any student in a covered district who chooses to remain in public school. Parents arrange for registered tutors to provide assistance to their children and then submit bills for those services to the State for payment. §§ 3313.976(D), 3313.979(C). Students from low-income families receive 90% of the amount charged for such assistance up to $360. All other students receive 75% of that amount. § 3313.978(B). The number of tutorial assistance grants offered to students in a covered district must equal the number of tuition aid scholarships provided to students enrolled at participating private or adjacent public schools. § 3313.975(A).

The program has been in operation within the Cleveland City School District since the 1996-1997 school year. In the 1999–2000 school year, 56 private schools participated in the program, 46 (or 82%) of which had a religious affiliation. None of the public schools in districts adjacent to Cleveland have elected to participate. More than 3,700 students participated in the scholarship program, most of whom (96%) enrolled in religiously affiliated schools. Sixty percent of these students were from families at or below the poverty line. In the 1998–1999 school year, approximately 1,400 Cleveland public school students received tutorial aid. This number was expected to double during the 1999–2000 school year.

The program is part of a broader undertaking by the State to enhance the educational options of Cleveland's schoolchildren. That undertaking includes programs governing community and magnet schools. Community schools are funded under state law but are run by their own school boards, not by local school districts. §§ 3314.01(B), 3314.04. These schools enjoy academic independence to hire their own teachers and to determine their own curriculum. They can have no religious affiliation and are required to accept students by lottery. During the 1999–2000 school year, there were 10 startup community schools in the Cleveland City School District with more than 1,900 students enrolled. For each child enrolled in a community school, the school receives state funding of $4,518, twice the funding a participating program school may receive.

Magnet schools are public schools operated by a local school board that emphasize a particular subject area, teaching method, or service to students. For each student enrolled in a magnet school, the school district receives $7,746, including state funding of $4,167, the same amount received per student enrolled at a traditional public school. As of 1999, parents in Cleveland were able to choose from among 23 magnet schools, which together enrolled more than 13,000 students in kindergarten through eighth grade. These schools provide specialized teaching methods, such as Montessori, or a particularized curriculum focus, such as foreign language, computers, or the arts. . . .

In July 1999, respondents filed this action in United States District Court, seeking to enjoin the reenacted program on the ground that it violated the Establishment Clause of the United States Constitution. . . . In December 1999, the District Court granted summary judgment for respondents. 72 F. Supp.2d 834. In December 2000, a divided panel of the Court of Appeals affirmed the judgment of the District Court, finding that the program had the "primary effect" of advancing religion in violation of the Establishment Clause. 234 F.3d 945 (C.A. 6). We granted certiorari, 533 U.S. 976, and now reverse the Court of Appeals.

The Establishment Clause of the First Amendment, applied to the States through the Fourteenth Amendment, prevents a State from enacting laws that have the "purpose" or "effect" of advancing or inhibiting religion. . . .There is no dispute that the program challenged here was enacted for the valid secular purpose of providing educational assistance to poor children in a demonstrably failing public school system. Thus, the question presented is whether the Ohio program nonetheless has the forbidden "effect" of advancing or inhibiting religion.

To answer that question, our decisions have drawn a consistent distinction between government programs that provide aid directly to religious schools, *Mitchell v. Helms,* 530 U.S. 793, 810-814 (plurality opinion); *id.,* 841-844, (O'CONNOR, J., concurring in judgment); *Agostini v. Felton* 521 U.S. 203, 225-227; *Rosenberger v. Univ. of Va.,* 515 U.S. 819, 842 (collecting cases), and programs of true private choice, in which government aid reaches religious schools only as a result of the genuine and independent choices of private individuals, *Mueller v. Allen,* 463 U.S. 388; *Witters v. Washington Dept. of Servs. for Blind,* 474 U.S. 481; *Zobrest v. Catalina Foothills School Dist.,* 509 U.S. 1. While our jurisprudence with respect to the constitutionality of direct aid programs has "changed significantly" over the past two decades, *Agostini,* 236, our jurisprudence with respect to true private choice programs has remained consistent and unbroken. Three times we have confronted Establishment Clause challenges to neutral government programs that provide aid directly to a broad class of individuals, who, in turn, direct the aid to religious schools or institutions of their own choosing. Three times we have rejected such challenges.

In *Mueller,* we rejected an Establishment Clause challenge to a Minnesota program authorizing tax deductions for various educational expenses, including private school tuition costs, even though the great majority of the program's beneficiaries (96%) were parents of children in religious schools. We began by focusing on the class of beneficiaries, finding that because the class included "*all* parents," including parents with "children [who] attend nonsectarian private schools or sectarian private schools," 463 U.S., 397 (emphasis in original), the program was "not readily subject to challenge under the Establishment Clause." Then, viewing the program as a whole, we emphasized the principle of private choice, noting that public funds were made available to religious schools "only as a result of numerous, private choices of individual parents of school-age children." 463 U.S., 399-400. This, we said, ensured that "no 'imprimatur of state approval' can be deemed to have been conferred on any particular religion, or on religion generally." *Id.*, 399 (quoting *Widmar v. Vincent,* 454 U.S. 263, 274). We thus found it irrelevant to the constitutional inquiry that the vast majority of beneficiaries were parents of children in religious schools, saying: "We would be loath to adopt a rule grounding the constitutionality of a facially neutral law on annual reports reciting the extent to which various classes of private citizens claimed benefits under the law." 463 U.S., 401. That the program was one of true private choice, with no evidence that the State deliberately skewed incentives toward religious schools, was sufficient for the program to survive scrutiny under the Establishment Clause.

In *Witters,* we used identical reasoning to reject an Establishment Clause challenge to a vocational scholarship program that provided tuition aid to a student studying at a religious institution to become a pastor. Looking at the program as a whole, we observed that "[a]ny aid . . . that ultimately flows to religious institutions does so only as a result of the genuinely independent and private choices of aid recipients." 474 U.S., 487. We further remarked that, as in *Mueller,* "[the] program is made available generally without regard to the sectarian-nonsectarian, or public-nonpublic nature of the institution benefitted." . . .

Five Members of the Court, in separate opinions, emphasized the general rule from *Mueller* that the amount of government aid channeled to religious institutions by individual aid recipients was not relevant to the constitutional inquiry. 474 U.S., 490-491 (POWELL, J., joined by BURGER, C. J., and REHNQUIST, J., concurring) (citing *Mueller,* 398-399); 474 U.S., 493, (O'CONNOR, J., concurring in part and concurring in judgment); *id.* at 490 (WHITE, J., concurring). Our holding thus rested not on whether few or many recipients chose to expend government aid at a religious school but, rather, on whether recipients generally were empowered to direct the aid to schools or institutions of their own choosing.

Finally, in *Zobrest,* we applied *Mueller* and *Witters* to reject an Establishment Clause challenge to a federal program that permitted sign-language interpreters to assist deaf children enrolled in religious schools. Reviewing our earlier decisions, we stated that "government programs that neutrally provide benefits to a broad class of citizens defined without reference to religion are not readily subject to an Establishment Clause challenge." 509 U.S., 8. Looking once again to the challenged program as a whole, we observed that the program "distributes benefits neutrally to any child qualifying as 'disabled.'" *Id.*, 10. Its "primary beneficiaries," we said, were "disabled children, not sectarian schools." *Id.*, 12.

We further observed that "[b]y according parents freedom to select a school of their choice, the statute ensures that a government-paid interpreter will be present in a sectarian school only as a result of the private decision of individual parents." *Id.*, 10. Our focus again was on neutrality and the principle of private choice, not on the number of program beneficiaries attending religious schools. . . . Because the program ensured that parents were the ones to select a religious school as the best learning environment for their handicapped child, the circuit between government and religion was broken, and the Establishment Clause was not implicated.

Mueller, Witters, and Zobrest thus make clear that where a government aid program is neutral with respect to religion, and provides assistance directly to a broad class of citizens who, in turn, direct government aid to religious schools wholly as a result of their own genuine and independent private choice, the program is not readily subject to challenge under the Establishment Clause. A program that shares these features permits government aid to reach religious institutions only by way of the deliberate choices of numerous individual recipients. The incidental advancement of a religious mission, or the perceived endorsement of a religious message, is reasonably attributable to the individual recipient, not to the government, whose role ends with the disbursement of benefits. . . .

We believe that the program challenged here is a program of true private choice, consistent with Mueller, Witters, and Zobrest, and thus constitutional. As was true in those cases, the Ohio program is neutral in all respects toward religion. It is part of a general and multifaceted undertaking by the State of Ohio to provide educational opportunities to the children of a failed school district. It confers educational assistance directly to a broad class of individuals defined without reference to religion, i.e., any parent of a school-age child who resides in the Cleveland City School District. The program permits the participation of all schools within the district, religious or nonreligious. Adjacent public schools also may participate and have a financial incentive to do so. Program benefits are available to participating families on neutral terms, with no reference to religion. The only preference stated anywhere in the program is a preference for low-income families, who receive greater assistance and are given priority for admission at participating schools.

There are no "financial incentive[s]" that "ske[w]" the program toward religious schools. Witters, 487-488. Such incentives "[are] not present . . . where the aid is allocated on the basis of neutral, secular criteria that neither favor nor disfavor religion, and is made available to both religious and secular beneficiaries on a nondiscriminatory basis." Agostini, 231. The program here in fact creates financial disincentives for religious schools, with private schools receiving only half the government assistance given to community schools and one-third the assistance given to magnet schools. Adjacent public schools, should any choose to accept program students, are also eligible to receive two to three times the state funding of a private religious school. Families too have a financial disincentive to choose a private religious school over other schools. Parents that choose to participate in the scholarship program and then to enroll their children in a private school (religious or nonreligious) must copay a portion of the school's tuition. Families that choose a community school, magnet school, or traditional public school pay nothing. Although such features of the program are not necessary to its constitutionality, they clearly dispel the claim that the program "creates . . . financial incentive[s] for parents to choose a sectarian school." Zobrest, 509 U.S., 10.[3]

---

[3] JUSTICE SOUTER suggests the program is not "neutral" because program students cannot spend scholarship vouchers at traditional public schools. This objection is mistaken: Public schools in Cleveland already receive $7,097 in public funding per pupil—$4,167 of which is attributable to the State. . . .

Respondents suggest that even without a financial incentive for parents to choose a religious school, the program creates a "public perception that the State is endorsing religious practices and beliefs." Brief for Respondents Simmons-Harris et al. 37-38. But we have repeatedly recognized that no reasonable observer would think a neutral program of private choice, where state aid reaches religious schools solely as a result of the numerous independent decisions of private individuals, carries with it the *imprimatur* of government endorsement. The argument is particularly misplaced here since "the reasonable observer in the endorsement inquiry must be deemed aware" of the "history and context" underlying a challenged program. *Good News Club v. Milford School*, 533 U.S. 98, 119. Any objective observer familiar with the full history and context of the Ohio program would reasonably view it as one aspect of a broader undertaking to assist poor children in failed schools, not as an endorsement of religious schooling in general.

There also is no evidence that the program fails to provide genuine opportunities for Cleveland parents to select secular educational options for their school-age children. Cleveland schoolchildren enjoy a range of educational choices: They may remain in public school as before, remain in public school with publicly funded tutoring aid, obtain a scholarship and choose a religious school, obtain a scholarship and choose a nonreligious private school, enroll in a community school, or enroll in a magnet school. That 46 of the 56 private schools now participating in the program are religious schools does not condemn it as a violation of the Establishment Clause. The Establishment Clause question is whether Ohio is coercing parents into sending their children to religious schools, and that question must be answered by evaluating *all* options Ohio provides Cleveland schoolchildren, only one of which is to obtain a program scholarship and then choose a religious school.

JUSTICE SOUTER speculates that because more private religious schools currently participate in the program, the program itself must somehow discourage the participation of private nonreligious schools. But Cleveland's preponderance of religiously affiliated private schools certainly did not arise as a result of the program; it is a phenomenon common to many American cities. . . . It is true that 82% of Cleveland's participating private schools are religious schools, but it is also true that 81% of private schools in Ohio are religious schools. To attribute constitutional significance to this figure, moreover, would lead to the absurd result that a neutral school-choice program might be permissible in some parts of Ohio, such as Columbus, where a lower percentage of private schools are religious schools. . . . Likewise, an identical private choice program might be constitutional in some States, such as Maine or Utah, where less than 45% of private schools are religious schools, but not in other states, such as Nebraska or Kansas, where over 90% of private schools are religious schools.

Respondents and JUSTICE SOUTER claim that even if we do not focus on the number of participating schools that are religious schools, we should attach constitutional significance to the fact that 96% of scholarship recipients have enrolled in religious schools. They claim that this alone proves parents lack genuine choice, even if no parent has ever said so. We need not consider this argument in detail, since it was flatly rejected in *Mueller*, where we found it irrelevant that 96% of parents taking deductions for tuition expenses paid tuition at religious schools. Indeed, we have recently found it irrelevant even to the constitutionality of a direct aid program that a vast majority of program benefits went to religious schools. See *Agostini,* 521 U.S., 229. The constitutionality of a neutral educational aid program simply does not turn on whether and why, in a particular area, at a particular time, most private schools are run by religious organizations, or most recipients choose to use the aid at a religious school. . . .

In sum, the Ohio program is entirely neutral with respect to religion. It provides benefits directly to a wide spectrum of individuals, defined only by financial need and residence in a particular school district. It permits such individuals to exercise genuine choice among options public and private, secular and religious. The program is therefore a program of true private choice. In keeping with an unbroken line of decisions rejecting challenges to similar programs, we hold that the program does not offend the Establishment Clause.

The judgment of the Court of Appeals is reversed.

*It is so ordered.*

⌗ JUSTICE O'CONNOR, concurring.

The Court holds that Ohio's Pilot Project Scholarship Program, Ohio Rev. Code Ann. §§ 3313.974-3313.979 (Anderson 1999 and Supp. 2000) (voucher program), survives respondents' Establishment Clause challenge. While I join the Court's opinion, I write separately for two reasons. First, although the Court takes an important step, I do not believe that today's decision, when considered in light of other longstanding government programs that impact religious organizations and our prior Establishment Clause jurisprudence, marks a dramatic break from the past. Second, given the emphasis the Court places on verifying that parents of voucher students in religious schools have exercised "true private choice," I think it is worth elaborating on the Court's conclusion that this inquiry should consider all reasonable educational alternatives to religious schools that are available to parents. To do otherwise is to ignore how the educational system in Cleveland actually functions.

I

These cases are different from prior indirect aid cases in part because a significant portion of the funds appropriated for the voucher program reach religious schools without restrictions on the use of these funds. The share of public resources that reach religious schools is not, however, as significant as respondents suggest. Data from the 1999–2000 school year indicate that 82 percent of schools participating in the voucher program were religious and that 96 percent of participating students enrolled in religious schools, but these data are incomplete. These statistics do not take into account all of the reasonable educational choices that may be available to students in Cleveland public schools. When one considers the option to attend community schools, the percentage of students enrolled in religious schools falls to 62.1 percent. If magnet schools are included in the mix, this percentage falls to 16.5 percent. . . .

Even these numbers do not paint a complete picture. The Cleveland program provides voucher applicants from low-income families with up to $2,250 in tuition assistance and provides the remaining applicants with up to $1,875 in tuition assistance. . . . Even if one assumes that all voucher students came from low-income families and that each voucher student used up the entire $2,250 voucher, at most $8.2 million of public funds flowed to religious schools under the voucher program in 1999–2000. Although just over one-half as many students attended community schools as religious private schools on the state fisc, the State spent over $1 million more—$9.4 million—on students in community schools than on students in religious private schools because per-pupil aid to community schools is more than double the per-pupil aid to private schools under the voucher program. Moreover, the amount spent on religious private schools is minor compared to the $114.8 million the State spent on students in the Cleveland magnet schools.

Although $8.2 million is no small sum, it pales in comparison to the amount of funds that federal, state, and local governments already provide religious institutions. Religious organizations may qualify for exemptions from the federal corporate income tax, see 26 U.S.C. § 501(c) (3); the corporate income tax in many States, see, e.g., Cal. Rev. & Tax.Code Ann. § 23701d (West 1992); and property taxes in all 50 States, see Turner, Property Tax Exemptions for Nonprofits, 12 Probate & Property 25 (Sept./Oct. 1998); and clergy qualify for a federal tax break on income used for housing expenses, 26 U.S.C. § 1402(a)(8). In addition, the Federal Government provides individuals, corporations, trusts, and estates a tax deduction for charitable contributions to qualified religious groups. See §§ 170, 642(c). Finally, the Federal Government and certain state governments provide tax credits for educational expenses, many of which are spent on education at religious schools. See, e.g., § 25A (Hope tax credit); Minn. Stat. § 290.0674 (Supp. 2001).

Most of these tax policies are well established, see, e.g., *Mueller v. Allen,* 463 U.S. 388, (upholding Minnesota tax deduction for educational expenses); *Walz v. Tax Comm'n of City of New York,* 397 U.S. 664 (1970) (upholding an exemption for religious organizations from New York property tax), yet confer a significant relative benefit on religious institutions. The state property tax exemptions for religious institutions alone amount to very large sums annually. . . . As for the Federal Government, the tax deduction for charitable contributions reduces federal tax revenues by nearly $25 billion annually, and it is reported that over 60 percent of household charitable contributions go to religious charities. Even the relatively minor exemptions lower federal tax receipts by substantial amounts. The parsonage exemption, for example, lowers revenues by around $500 million. . . .

These tax exemptions, which have "much the same effect as [cash grants] . . . of the amount of tax [avoided]," *Regan v. Taxation With Representation,* 461 U.S. 540, 544, are just part of the picture. Federal dollars also reach religiously affiliated organizations through public health programs such as Medicare, 42 U.S.C. §§ 1395-1395ggg and Medicaid, § 1396 *et seq.,* through educational programs such as the Pell Grant program, 20 U.S.C. § 1070a, and the G.I. Bill of Rights, 38 U.S.C. §§ 3451, 3698; and through childcare programs such as the Child Care and Development Block Grant Program (CCDBG), 42 U.S.C. § 9858 (1994 ed., Supp. V). . . . These programs are well-established parts of our social welfare system. . . .

A significant portion of the funds appropriated for these programs reach religiously affiliated institutions, typically without restrictions on its subsequent use. . . . Moreover, taking into account both Medicare and Medicaid, religious hospitals received nearly $45 billion from the federal fisc in 1998. Federal aid to religious schools is also substantial. . . .

Against this background, the support that the Cleveland voucher program provides religious institutions is neither substantial nor atypical of existing government programs. While this observation is not intended to justify the Cleveland voucher program under the Establishment Clause, see SOUTER, J., dissenting, it places in broader perspective alarmist claims about implications of the Cleveland program and the Court's decision in these cases.

## II

Nor does today's decision signal a major departure from this Court's prior Establishment Clause jurisprudence. . . .

The Court's opinion in these cases focuses on a narrow question related to the *Lemon* test: how to apply the primary effects prong in indirect aid cases? Specifically, it clarifies the basic inquiry when trying to determine whether a program that distributes aid to beneficiaries, rather than directly to service providers, has the primary effect of advancing or inhibiting religion, *Lemon v. Kurtzman,* 613-614, or, as I have put it, of "endors[ing] or disapprov[ing] . . . religion, *Lynch v. Donnelly,* 691-692 (concurring opinion). Courts are instructed to consider two factors: first, whether the program administers aid in a neutral fashion, without differentiation based on the religious status of beneficiaries or providers of services; second, and more importantly, whether beneficiaries of indirect aid have a genuine choice among religious and nonreligious organizations when determining the organization to which they will direct that aid. If the answer to either query is "no," the program should be struck down under the Establishment Clause. . . .

## III

There is little question in my mind that the Cleveland voucher program is neutral as between religious schools and nonreligious schools. JUSTICE SOUTER rejects the Court's notion of neutrality, proposing that the neutrality of a program should be gauged not by the opportunities it presents but rather by its effects. In particular, a "neutrality test . . . [should] focus on a category of aid that may be directed to religious as well as secular schools, and ask whether the scheme favors a religious direction." JUSTICE SOUTER doubts that the Cleveland program is neutral under this view. . . .

I do not agree that the nonreligious schools have failed to provide Cleveland parents reasonable alternatives to religious schools in the voucher program. For nonreligious schools to qualify as genuine options for parents, they need not be superior to religious schools in every respect. They need only be adequate substitutes for religious schools in the eyes of parents. The District Court record demonstrates that nonreligious schools were able to compete effectively with Catholic and other religious schools in the Cleveland voucher program. The best evidence of this is that many parents with vouchers selected nonreligious private schools over religious alternatives and an even larger number of parents send their children to community and magnet schools rather than seeking vouchers at all. Moreover, there is no record evidence that any voucher-eligible student was turned away from a nonreligious private school in the voucher program, let alone a community or magnet school. . . .

In my view Cleveland parents who use vouchers to send their children to religious private schools do so as a result of true private choice. The Court rejects, correctly, the notion that the high percentage of voucher recipients who enroll in religious private schools necessarily demonstrates that parents do not actually have the option to send their children to nonreligious schools. Likewise, the mere fact that some parents enrolled their children in religious schools associated with a different faith than their own, says little about whether these parents had reasonable nonreligious options. Indeed, no voucher student has been known to be turned away from a nonreligious private school participating in the voucher program. This is impressive given evidence in the record that the present litigation has discouraged the entry of some nonreligious private schools into the voucher program. Finally, as demonstrated above, the Cleveland program does not establish financial incentives to undertake a religious education.

I find the Court's answer to the question whether parents of students eligible for vouchers have a genuine choice between religious and nonreligious schools persuasive. In looking at the voucher program, all the choices available to potential beneficiaries of the government program should be considered. In these cases, parents who were eligible to apply for a voucher also had the option, at a minimum, to send their children to community schools. Yet the Court of Appeals chose not to look at community schools, let alone magnet schools, when evaluating the Cleveland voucher program. See 234 F.3d, 958. That decision was incorrect. Focusing in these cases only on the program challenged by respondents ignores how the educational system in Cleveland actually functions. The record indicates that, in 1999, two nonreligious private schools that had previously served 15 percent of the students in the voucher program were prompted to convert to community schools because parents were concerned about the litigation surrounding the program, and because a new community schools program provided more per-pupil financial aid. Many of the students that enrolled in the two schools under the voucher program transferred to the community schools program and continued to attend these schools. See Affidavit of David L. Brennan ¶ ¶ 3, 10, App. 145 a, 147 a; Declaration of David P. Zanotti ¶ ¶ 4-10, id., at 225a-227a. This incident provides strong evidence that both parents and nonreligious schools view the voucher program and the community schools program as reasonable alternatives.

Considering all the educational options available to parents whose children are eligible for vouchers, including community and magnet schools, the Court finds that parents in the Cleveland schools have an array of nonreligious options. Not surprisingly, respondents present no evidence that any students who were candidates for a voucher were denied slots in a community school or a magnet school. Indeed, the record suggests the opposite with respect to community schools. See Affidavit of David L. Brennan ¶ 8, App. 147a.

Justice O'Connor responded to Justice Souter's claims that of the ten community schools, four were unavailable to voucher students and another four had poor test scores, making them unappealing to parents.

One year of poor test scores at four community schools targeted at the most challenged students from the inner city says little about the value of those schools, let alone the quality of the 6 other community schools and 24 magnet schools in Cleveland. JUSTICE SOUTER's use of statistics confirms the Court's wisdom in refusing to consider them when assessing the Cleveland program's constitutionality. . . . [T]he goal of the Court's Establishment Clause jurisprudence is to determine whether, after the Cleveland voucher program was enacted, parents were free to direct state educational aid in either a nonreligious or religious direction. That inquiry requires an evaluation of all reasonable educational options Ohio provides the Cleveland school system, regardless of whether they are formally made available in the same section of the Ohio Code as the voucher program. . . .

🔳 JUSTICE THOMAS, concurring. . . .

[I]n the context of the Establishment Clause, it may well be that State action should be evaluated on different terms than similar action by the Federal Government. "States, while bound to observe strict neutrality, should be freer to experiment with involvement [in religion]—on a neutral basis—than the Federal Government." *Walz,* 397 U.S. 664, 699, (HARLAN, J., concurring). Thus, while the Federal Government may "make no law respecting an establishment of religion," the States may pass laws that include or touch on religious matters so long as these laws do not impede free exercise rights or any other individual religious liberty interest. By considering the particular religious liberty right alleged to be invaded by a State, federal courts can strike a proper balance between the demands of the Fourteenth Amendment on the one hand and the federalism prerogatives of States on the other. . . .

[F]ailing urban public schools disproportionately affect minority children most in need of educational opportunity. At the time of Reconstruction, blacks considered public education "a matter of personal liberation and a necessary function of a free society." J. Anderson, Education of Blacks in the South, 1860-1935, p. 18 (1988). Today, the promise of public school education has failed poor inner-city blacks. While in theory providing education to everyone, the quality of public schools varies significantly across districts. . . .

The failure to provide education to poor urban children perpetuates a vicious cycle of poverty, dependence, criminality, and alienation that continues for the remainder of their lives. If society cannot end racial discrimination, at least it can arm minorities with the education to defend themselves from some of discrimination's effects.

Ten states have enacted some form of publicly funded private school choice as one means of raising the quality of education provided to underprivileged urban children. These programs address the root of the problem with failing urban public schools that disproportionately affect minority students. Society's other solution to these educational failures is often to provide racial preferences in higher education. Such preferences, however, run afoul of the Fourteenth Amendment's prohibition against distinctions based on race. See *Plessy v. Ferguson,* 163 U.S., 555 (HARLAN, J., dissenting). By contrast, school choice programs that involve religious schools appear unconstitutional only to those who would twist the Fourteenth Amendment against itself by expansively incorporating the Establishment Clause. Converting the Fourteenth Amendment from a guarantee of opportunity to an obstacle against education reform distorts our constitutional values and disserves those in the greatest need.

🔳 JUSTICE STEVENS, dissenting. . . .

[T]he wide range of choices that have been made available to students *within the public school system* has no bearing on the question whether the State may pay the tuition for students who wish to reject public education entirely and attend private schools that will provide them with a sectarian education. The fact that the vast majority of the voucher recipients who have entirely rejected public education receive religious indoctrination at state expense does, however, support the claim that the law is one "respecting an establishment of religion." The State may choose to divide up its public schools into a dozen different options and label them magnet schools, community schools, or whatever else it decides to call them, but the State is still required to provide a public education and it is the State's decision to fund private school education over and above its traditional obligation that is at issue in these cases. . . .

For the reasons stated by JUSTICE SOUTER and JUSTICE BREYER, I am convinced that the Court's decision is profoundly misguided. Admittedly, in reaching that conclusion I have been influenced by my understanding of the impact of religious strife on the decisions of our forbears to migrate to this continent, and on the decisions of neighbors in the Balkans, Northern Ireland, and the Middle East to mistrust one another. Whenever we remove a brick from the wall that was designed to separate religion and government, we increase the risk of religious strife and weaken the foundation of our democracy.

I respectfully dissent.

JUSTICE SOUTER, with whom JUSTICE STEVENS, JUSTICE GINSBURG, and JUSTICE BREYER join, dissenting. . . .

Today, the majority holds that the Establishment Clause is not offended by Ohio's Pilot Project Scholarship Program, under which students may be eligible to receive as much as $2,250 in the form of tuition vouchers transferable to religious schools. In the city of Cleveland the overwhelming proportion of large appropriations for voucher money must be spent on religious schools if it is to be spent at all, and will be spent in amounts that cover almost all of tuition. The money will thus pay for eligible students' instruction not only in secular subjects but in religion as well, in schools that can fairly be characterized as founded to teach religious doctrine and to imbue teaching in all subjects with a religious dimension. Public tax money will pay at a systemic level for teaching the covenant with Israel and Mosaic law in Jewish schools, the primacy of the Apostle Peter and the Papacy in Catholic schools, the truth of reformed Christianity in Protestant schools, and the revelation to the Prophet in Muslim schools, to speak only of major religious groupings in the Republic. . . .

Viewed with the necessary generality, the [Court's Establishment Clause] cases can be categorized in three groups. In the period from 1947 to 1968, the basic principle of no aid to religion through school benefits was unquestioned. Thereafter for some 15 years, the Court termed its efforts as attempts to draw a line against aid that would be divertible to support the religious, as distinct from the secular, activity of an institutional beneficiary. Then, starting in 1983, concern with divertibility was gradually lost in favor of approving aid in amounts unlikely to afford substantial benefits to religious schools, when offered evenhandedly without regard to a recipient's religious character, and when channeled to a religious institution only by the genuinely free choice of some private individual. Now, the three stages are succeeded by a fourth, in which the substantial character of government aid is held to have no constitutional significance, and the espoused criteria of neutrality in offering aid, and private choice in directing it, are shown to be nothing but examples of verbal formalism. . . .

Justice Souter discussed the Court's early Establishment Clause cases, noting that the Court had consistently struck funding programs to religious schools that provided either substantial aid or aid that could be diverted to religious uses. Also, according to Souter, the Court had "rejected the idea that the path of state aid to religious schools might be dispositive: 'far from providing a *per se* immunity from examination of the substance of the State's program, the fact that aid is disbursed to parents rather than to the schools is only one among many factors to be considered.'" Souter acknowledged that beginning in *Mueller* and continuing with *Witters*, the Court upheld unrestricted benefits that flowed to religious schools, with the Court "emphasizing the [ ] neutral availability for religious and secular educational expenses and the role of private choice in taking them." But, even though those "cases emphasiz[ed] the form of neutrality and private choice over the substance of aid to religious uses, [it was] always in circumstances where any aid to religion was isolated and insubstantial."

> Hence it seems fair to say that it was not until today that substantiality of aid has clearly been rejected as irrelevant by a majority of this Court, just as it has not been until today that a majority, not a plurality, has held purely formal criteria to suffice for scrutinizing aid that ends up in the coffers of religious schools. . . .
>
> Consider first the criterion of neutrality. . . .
>
> In order to apply the neutrality test, it makes sense to focus on a category of aid that may be directed to religious as well as secular schools, and ask whether the scheme favors a religious direction. Here, one would ask whether the voucher provisions, allowing for as much as $2,250 toward private school tuition (or a grant to a public school in an adjacent district), were written in a way that skewed the scheme toward benefiting religious schools.
>
> This, however, is not what the majority asks. The majority looks not to the provisions for tuition vouchers, Ohio Rev.Code Ann. § 3313.976 (West Supp. 2002), but to every provision for educational opportunity. . . . The majority then finds confirmation that "participation of *all* schools" satisfies neutrality by noting that the better part of total state educational expenditure goes to public schools, thus showing there is no favor of religion.
>
> The illogic is patent. If regular, public schools (which can get no voucher payments) "participate" in a voucher scheme with schools that can, and public expenditure is still predominantly on public schools, then the majority's reasoning would find neutrality in a scheme of vouchers available for private tuition in districts with no secular private schools at all. "Neutrality" as the majority employs the term is, literally, verbal and nothing more. . . .
>
> The majority addresses the issue of choice the same way it addresses neutrality, by asking whether recipients or potential recipients of voucher aid have a choice of public schools among secular alternatives to religious schools. Again, however, the majority asks the wrong question and misapplies the criterion. The majority has confused choice in spending scholarships with choice from the entire menu of possible educational placements, most of them open to anyone willing to attend a public school.[8] . . . The majority's view that all educational choices are comparable for purposes of choice thus ignores the

---

[8] In some earlier cases, "private choice" was sensibly understood to go beyond the mere formalism of path, to ensure that aid was neither systemic nor predestined to go to religious uses. Witters, for example, had a virtually unlimited choice among professional training schools, only a few of which were religious; and Zobrest was simply one recipient who chose to use a government-funded interpreter at a religious school over a secular school, either of which was open to him. But recent decisions seem to have stripped away any substantive bite, as "private choice" apparently means only that government aid follows individuals to religious schools. . . .

whole point of the choice test: it is a criterion for deciding whether indirect aid to a religious school is legitimate because it passes through private hands that can spend or use the aid in a secular school. The question is whether the private hand is genuinely free to send the money in either a secular direction or a religious one. The majority now has transformed this question about private choice in channeling aid into a question about selecting from examples of state spending (on education) including direct spending on magnet and community public schools that goes through no private hands and could never reach a religious school under any circumstance. When the choice test is transformed from where to spend the money to where to go to school, it is cut loose from its very purpose.

Defining choice as choice in spending the money or channeling the aid is, moreover, necessary if the choice criterion is to function as a limiting principle at all. If "choice" is present whenever there is any educational alternative to the religious school to which vouchers can be endorsed, then there will always be a choice and the voucher can always be constitutional, even in a system in which there is not a single private secular school as an alternative to the religious school. And because it is unlikely that any participating private religious school will enroll more pupils than the generally available public system, it will be easy to generate numbers suggesting that aid to religion is not the significant intent or effect of the voucher scheme. . . .

If the choice of relevant alternatives is an open one, proponents of voucher aid will always win, because they will always be able to find a "choice" somewhere that will show the bulk of public spending to be secular. The choice enquiry will be diluted to the point that it can screen out nothing, and the result will always be determined by selecting the alternatives to be treated as choices. . . .

If, contrary to the majority, we ask the right question about genuine choice to use the vouchers, the answer shows that something is influencing choices in a way that aims the money in a religious direction: of 56 private schools in the district participating in the voucher program (only 53 of which accepted voucher students in 1999–2000), 46 of them are religious; 96.6% of all voucher recipients go to religious schools, only 3.4% to nonreligious ones. . . .

Second, the $2,500 cap that the program places on tuition for participating low-income pupils has the effect of curtailing the participation of nonreligious schools: "nonreligious schools with higher tuition (about $4,000) stated that they could afford to accommodate just a few voucher students." By comparison, the average tuition at participating Catholic schools in Cleveland in 1999–2000 was $1,592, almost $1,000 below the cap. . . .

There is, in any case, no way to interpret the 96.6% of current voucher money going to religious schools as reflecting a free and genuine choice by the families that apply for vouchers. The 96.6% reflects, instead, the fact that too few nonreligious school desks are available and few but religious schools can afford to accept more than a handful of voucher students. And contrary to the majority's assertion, public schools in adjacent districts hardly have a financial incentive to participate in the Ohio voucher program, and none has. For the overwhelming number of children in the voucher scheme, the only alternative to the public schools is religious. . . .

The scale of the aid to religious schools approved today is unprecedented, both in the number of dollars and in the proportion of systemic school expenditure supported. Each measure has received attention in previous cases.

On one hand, the sheer quantity of aid, when delivered to a class of religious primary and secondary schools, was suspect on the theory that the greater the aid, the greater its proportion to a religious school's existing expenditures, and the greater the likelihood that public money was supporting religious as well as secular instruction. . . .

On the other hand, the Court has found the gross amount unhelpful for Establishment Clause analysis when the aid afforded a benefit solely to one individual, however substantial as to him, but only an incidental benefit to the religious school at which the individual chose to spend the State's money. See *Witters,* 474 U.S., 488; *Zobrest,* 509 U.S., 12. When neither the design nor the implementation of an aid scheme channels a series of individual students' subsidies toward religious recipients, the relevant beneficiaries for establishment purposes, the Establishment Clause is unlikely to be implicated. The majority's reliance on the observations of five Members of the Court in *Witters* as to the irrelevance of substantiality of aid in that case, is therefore beside the point in the matter before us, which involves considerable sums of public funds systematically distributed through thousands of students attending religious elementary and middle schools in the city of Cleveland. . . .

The gross amounts of public money contributed are symptomatic of the scope of what the taxpayers' money buys for a broad class of religious-school students. In paying for practically the full amount of tuition for thousands of qualifying students, cf. *Nyquist,* 781-783 (state aid amounting to 50% of tuition was unconstitutional), the scholarships purchase everything that tuition purchases, be it instruction in math or indoctrination in faith. The consequences of "substantial" aid hypothesized in *Meek* are realized here: the majority makes no pretense that substantial amounts of tax money are not systematically underwriting religious practice and indoctrination. . . .

Justice Breyer wrote a dissenting opinion "to emphasize the risk that publicly financed voucher programs pose in terms of religiously based social conflict."

---

### NOTES AND QUESTIONS

1. According to the Court majority, what kind of genuine secular choices are open to Cleveland parents of school-age children? How does this finding affect the Court's analysis of the voucher plan's constitutionality? In contrast, how would dissenter Justice Stevens define the range of secular choices for purposes of evaluating the constitutional question? Further, what criticisms does Justice Souter make of the majority's approach to this issue?

2. What other factors confirm the voucher plan's constitutionality, according to the majority? Briefly describe Justice Souter's critique of the Court's framework for decision making in this case.

3. In the *Nyquist* case, the Court majority held New York's tuition reimbursement program for religious elementary and secondary schools to be unconstitutional. It stated:

> There can be no question that these grants could not, consistently with the Establishment Clause, be given directly to sectarian schools, since they would suffer from the same deficiency that renders invalid the grants for maintenance and repair. In the absence of an effective means of guaranteeing that

the state aid derived from public funds will be used exclusively for secular, neutral, and nonideological purposes, it is clear from our cases that direct aid in whatever form is invalid. . .

The controlling question here, then, is whether the fact that the grants are delivered to parents rather than schools is of such significance as to compel a contrary result. . . . It is true that [in the *Everson* and *Allen* cases] the Court upheld laws that provided benefits to children attending religious schools and to their parents. . . . But those decisions make clear that, far from providing a *per se* immunity from examination of the substance of the State's program, the fact that aid is disbursed to parents rather than to the schools is only one among many factors to be considered.

In the *Nyquist* case, the Court majority also rebutted an argument by dissenting Chief Justice Burger that tuition reimbursement grants for parents provide comparable benefits to parents of all school children regardless of whether they are enrolled in public or nonpublic schools. The Court wrote:

The grants to parents of private schoolchildren are given in addition to the right they have to send their children to public schools "totally at state expense." And in any event, the argument proves too much, for it would also provide a basis for approving through tuition grants the complete subsidization of all religious schools on the ground that such action is necessary if the State is fully to equalize the position of parents who elect such schools—a result wholly at variance with the Establishment Clause.

Compare the approach of the *Nyquist* Court to these issues with the approach of the *Zelman* Court to similar issues. Are they more dissimilar than similar? More specifically, how does the Court majority distinguish the *Nyquist* case? Do you find the Court's arguments on this issue convincing? Why or why not?

4. The Court majority states: "[O]ver the past two decades, our jurisprudence with respect to true private choices has remained consistent and unbroken." If so, are the dissenters and some critics incorrect that *Zelman* represents a watershed decision? Or is the majority's statement an inaccurate characterization of Supreme Court precedent? In essence, does the holding in *Zelman* flow naturally from the previous holdings in *Mueller*, *Witters*, and *Zobrest*? Additionally, how relevant are the holdings in *Agostini* and *Mitchell* for *Zelman*? Is it fair to say that *Zelman* builds on those holdings but still expands their scope?

5. According to the *Zelman* majority, its holding is consistent with *Witters*. How does Justice Souter distinguish the Court's decision in the *Witters* case? Who has the better argument? Can they both be partially correct?

6. What additional arguments does Justice O'Connor make in favor of the voucher program in her concurring opinion? According to Justice O'Connor, what is required in order for nonreligious schools to be deemed a "reasonable alternative" to religious schools in a voucher program?

7. In his concurring opinion, Justice Thomas argues that "States may pass laws that include or touch on religious matters so long as these laws do not impede

free exercise rights or any other individual religious liberty interest." What does he mean by this? How would this change current constitutional interpretation?

8. What are the four "stages" of the Court's reasoning on these issues, according to Justice Souter? Does this characterization of the Court's precedent seem accurate?

9. In the *Nyquist* case, the Court stated:

> Although Establishment Clause jurisprudence is characterized by few absolutes, the Clause does absolutely prohibit government-financed or government-sponsored indoctrination into the beliefs of a particular religious faith. Such indoctrination, if permitted to occur, would have devastating effects on the right of each individual voluntarily to determine what to believe (and what not to believe) free of any coercive pressures from the State, while at the same time tainting the resulting religious beliefs with a corrosive secularism.

> According to Justice Souter, "the [Court] majority makes no pretense that substantial amounts of tax money are not systematically underwriting religious practice and indoctrination." Is this a fair characterization of the majority's opinion? Are the fears of the *Nyquist* majority relevant in the wake of the *Zelman* decision? Or, is Justice O'Connor right when she insists that the decision does not "signal a major departure from th[e] Court's prior Establishment Clause jurisprudence"?

10. In a portion of his dissenting opinion not reproduced here, Justice Souter writes:

> [The Ohio voucher program] insists that no participating school "advocate or foster unlawful behavior or teach hatred of any person or group on the basis of race, ethnicity, national origin, or religion." And it requires the State to "revoke the registration of any school if, after a hearing, the superintendent determines that the school is in violation" of the program's rules. As one *amicus* argues, "it is difficult to imagine a more divisive activity" than the appointment of state officials as referees to determine whether a particular religious doctrine "teaches hatred or advocates lawlessness."
>
> How are state officials to adjudicate claims that one religion or another is advocating, for example, civil disobedience in response to unjust laws, the use of illegal drugs in a religious ceremony, or resort to force to call attention to what it views as an immoral social practice? What kind of public hearing will there be in response to claims that one religion or another is continuing to teach a view of history that casts members of other religions in the worst possible light? How will the public react to government funding for schools that take controversial religious positions on topics that are of current popular interest—say, the conflict in the Middle East or the war on terrorism? Yet any major funding program for primary religious education will require criteria. And the selection of those criteria, as well as their application, inevitably poses problems that are divisive. Efforts to respond to these problems not only will seriously entangle church and state, but also will promote division

among religious groups, as one group or another fears (often legitimately) that it will receive unfair treatment at the hands of the government.

Does Justice Souter make a fair point? Does the Court majority address this point?

11. Aside from the specific facts and competing doctrines discussed in the various opinions, what religion clause values do the *Zelman* dissenters see as being threatened in a voucher program? How do the majority and concurrence view the elements of neutrality and private choice as addressing those values, or do they place different weight on those constitutional values?

---

*Zelman* upheld the constitutionality of publicly funded vouchers used to finance education at religious schools. That meant that states could fashion educational funding programs that benefited religious schools, provided those programs met the criteria enunciated in *Zelman*. But merely because vouchers were now constitutional under the Establishment Clause, did that mean that states were prohibited from excluding religious uses for its educational scholarships under an otherwise neutral funding program? To put the question in more practical terms, many states contain express constitutional provisions governing public financial aid to religious institutions, some of which have been interpreted more restrictively than the federal Establishment Clause. After *Zelman*, could a state offer a scholarship program but prohibit recipients from using the proceeds to obtain a religious education? Consider the following case and the various intersecting constitutional claims raised by the litigants.

---

## LOCKE v. DAVEY
### 540 U.S. 712 (2004)

CHIEF JUSTICE REHNQUIST delivered the opinion of the Court.

The State of Washington established the Promise Scholarship Program to assist academically gifted students with postsecondary education expenses. . . .

Students may spend their funds on any education-related expense, including room and board. The scholarships are funded through the State's general fund, and their amount varies each year depending on the annual appropriation, which is evenly prorated among the eligible students.

To be eligible for the scholarship, a student must meet academic, income, and enrollment requirements. . . . Finally, the student must enroll "at least half time in an eligible postsecondary institution in the state of Washington," and may not pursue a degree in theology at that institution while receiving the scholarship. Private institutions, including those religiously affiliated, qualify as "eligible postsecondary institution[s]" if they are accredited by a nationally recognized accrediting body. A "degree in theology" is not defined in the statute, but, as both parties concede, the statute simply codifies the State's constitutional prohibition on providing funds to students to pursue degrees that are "devotional in nature or designed to induce religious faith." . . .

Respondent, Joshua Davey, was awarded a Promise Scholarship, and chose to attend Northwest College. Northwest is a private, Christian college affiliated with the Assemblies of God denomination, and is an eligible institution under the Promise Scholarship Program. Davey had "planned for many years to attend a Bible college and to prepare [himself] through that college training for a lifetime of ministry, specifically as a church pastor." . . . There is no dispute that the pastoral ministries degree is devotional and therefore excluded under the Promise Scholarship Program. . . .

[Davey filed suit in federal court arguing that the State's denial of aid violated the Free Exercise, Establishment, and Free Speech Clauses of the First Amendment and the Equal Protection Clause of the Fourteenth Amendment. The District Court rejected Davey's constitutional claims and granted summary judgment in favor of the State.]

A divided panel of the United States Court of Appeals for the Ninth Circuit reversed. 299 F.3d 748 (2002). The court concluded that the State had singled out religion for unfavorable treatment and thus under our decision in *Church of Lukumi Babalu Aye, Inc. v. Hialeah*, 508 U.S. 520, the State's exclusion of theology majors must be narrowly tailored to achieve a compelling state interest. 299 F.3d, 757-758. Finding that the State's own antiestablishment concerns were not compelling, the court declared Washington's Promise Scholarship Program unconstitutional. . . .

The Religion Clauses of the First Amendment . . . are frequently in tension. Yet we have long said that "there is room for play in the joints" between them. *Walz v. Tax Comm'n*, 397 U.S. 664, 669. In other words, there are some state actions permitted by the Establishment Clause but not required by the Free Exercise Clause.

This case involves that "play in the joints" described above. Under our Establishment Clause precedent, the link between government funds and religious training is broken by the independent and private choice of recipients. See *Zelman v. Simmons-Harris*, 536 U.S. 639, 652. As such, there is no doubt that the State could, consistent with the Federal Constitution, permit Promise Scholars to pursue a degree in devotional theology, and the State does not contend otherwise. The question before us, however, is whether Washington, pursuant to its own constitution, which has been authoritatively interpreted as prohibiting even indirectly funding religious instruction that will prepare students for the ministry, can deny them such funding without violating the Free Exercise Clause.

Davey urges us to answer that question in the negative. He contends that under the rule we enunciated in *Church of Lukumi Babalu Aye, Inc. v. Hialeah*, the program is presumptively unconstitutional because it is not facially neutral with respect to religion.[3] We reject his claim of presumptive unconstitution-

---

[3] Davey, relying on *Rosenberger v. Rector and Visitors of Univ. of Va.*, 515 U.S. 819, contends that the Promise Scholarship Program is an unconstitutional viewpoint restriction on speech. But the Promise Scholarship Program is not a forum for speech. The purpose of the Promise Scholarship Program is to assist students from low- and middle-income families with the cost of postsecondary education, not to "'encourage a diversity of views from private speakers.'" *United States v. American Library Assn.*, 539 U.S. 194, 206, (plurality opinion) (quoting *Rosenberger*, 834). Our cases dealing with speech forums are simply inapplicable. . . .

ality, however; to do otherwise would extend the *Lukumi* line of cases well beyond not only their facts but their reasoning. In *Lukumi,* the city of Hialeah made it a crime to engage in certain kinds of animal slaughter. We found that the law sought to suppress ritualistic animal sacrifices of the Santeria religion. 508 U.S., 535. In the present case, the State's disfavor of religion (if it can be called that) is of a far milder kind. It imposes neither criminal nor civil sanctions on any type of religious service or rite. It does not deny to ministers the right to participate in the political affairs of the community. See *McDaniel v. Paty*, 435 U.S. 618. And it does not require students to choose between their religious beliefs and receiving a government benefit. The State has merely chosen not to fund a distinct category of instruction.

JUSTICE SCALIA argues, however, that . . . because the Promise Scholarship Program funds training for all secular professions, the State must also fund training for religious professions. But training for religious professions and training for secular professions are not fungible. Training someone to lead a congregation is an essentially religious endeavor. Indeed, majoring in devotional theology is akin to a religious calling as well as an academic pursuit. . . . And the subject of religion is one in which both the United States and state constitutions embody distinct views—in favor of free exercise, but opposed to establishment—that find no counterpart with respect to other callings or professions. That a State would deal differently with religious education for the ministry than with education for other callings is a product of these views, not evidence of hostility toward religion.

Even though the differently worded Washington Constitution draws a more stringent line than that drawn by the United States Constitution, the interest it seeks to further is scarcely novel. In fact, we can think of few areas in which a State's antiestablishment interests come more into play. Since the founding of our country, there have been popular uprisings against procuring taxpayer funds to support church leaders, which was one of the hallmarks of an "established" religion. . . .

Most States that sought to avoid an establishment of religion around the time of the founding placed in their constitutions formal prohibitions against using tax funds to support the ministry. . . . The plain text of these constitutional provisions prohibited *any* tax dollars from supporting the clergy. We have found nothing to indicate, as JUSTICE SCALIA contends, that these provisions would not have applied so long as the State equally supported other professions or if the amount at stake was *de minimis*. That early state constitutions saw no problem in explicitly excluding *only* the ministry from receiving state dollars reinforces our conclusion that religious instruction is of a different ilk.[7]

Far from evincing the hostility toward religion which was manifest in *Lukumi,* we believe that the entirety of the Promise Scholarship Program goes a long way toward including religion in its benefits. The program permits students to attend pervasively religious schools, so long as they are accredited. . . .

---

[7] The *amici* contend that Washington's Constitution was born of religious bigotry because it contains a so-called "Blaine Amendment," which has been linked with anti-Catholicism. . . . As the State notes and Davey does not dispute, however, the provision in question is not a Blaine Amendment. . . . Neither Davey nor *amici* have established a credible connection between the Blaine Amendment and Article I, § 11, the relevant constitutional provision. Accordingly, the Blaine Amendment's history is simply not before us. . . .

And under the Promise Scholarship Program's current guidelines, students are still eligible to take devotional theology courses. . . .

In short, we find neither in the history or text of Article I, § 11 of the Washington Constitution, nor in the operation of the Promise Scholarship Program, anything that suggests animus towards religion. Given the historic and substantial state interest at issue, we therefore cannot conclude that the denial of funding for vocational religious instruction alone is inherently constitutionally suspect.

Without a presumption of unconstitutionality, Davey's claim must fail. The State's interest in not funding the pursuit of devotional degrees is substantial and the exclusion of such funding places a relatively minor burden on Promise Scholars. If any room exists between the two Religion Clauses, it must be here. . . .

The judgment of the Court of Appeals is therefore

*Reversed.*

JUSTICE SCALIA, with whom JUSTICE THOMAS joins, dissenting. . . .

I

We articulated the principle that governs this case more than 50 years ago in *Everson v. Board of Ed.*, 330 U.S. 1. . . .

When the State makes a public benefit generally available, that benefit becomes part of the baseline against which burdens on religion are measured; and when the State withholds that benefit from some individuals solely on the basis of religion, it violates the Free Exercise Clause no less than if it had imposed a special tax.

That is precisely what the State of Washington has done here. It has created a generally available public benefit, whose receipt is conditioned only on academic performance, income, and attendance at an accredited school. It has then carved out a solitary course of study for exclusion: theology. . . .

The Court does not dispute that the Free Exercise Clause places some constraints on public benefits programs, but finds none here, based on a principle of "'play in the joints.'". . .

Even if "play in the joints" were a valid legal principle, surely it would apply only when it was a close call whether complying with one of the Religion Clauses would violate the other. But that is not the case here. It is not just that "the State could, consistent with the Federal Constitution, permit Promise Scholars to pursue a degree in devotional theology." The establishment question *would not even be close,* as is evident from the fact that this Court's decision in *Witters v. Washington Dept. of Servs. for Blind*, 474 U.S. 481, was unanimous. Perhaps some formally neutral public benefits programs are so gerrymandered and devoid of plausible secular purpose that they might raise specters of state aid to religion, but an evenhanded Promise Scholarship Program is not among them. . . .

[Moreover,] the interest to which the Court defers is not fear of a conceivable Establishment Clause violation, budget constraints, avoidance of endorsement, or substantive neutrality—none of these. It is a pure philosophical preference: the State's opinion that it would violate taxpayers' freedom of conscience *not* to discriminate against candidates for the ministry. This sort of protection of "freedom of conscience" has no logical limit and can justify the singling out of religion for exclusion from public programs in virtually any context. . . .

II

The Court makes no serious attempt to defend the program's neutrality, and instead identifies two features thought to render its discrimination less offensive. The first is the lightness of Davey's burden. The Court offers no authority for approving facial discrimination against religion simply because its material consequences are not severe. . . . The indignity of being singled out for special burdens on the basis of one's religious calling is so profound that the concrete harm produced can never be dismissed as insubstantial. The Court has not required proof of "substantial" concrete harm with other forms of discrimination, see, e.g., *Brown v. Board of Education*, 347 U.S. 483, 493-495; *Craig v. Boren*, 429 U.S. 190, and it should not do so here. . . .

The other reason the Court thinks this particular facial discrimination less offensive is that the scholarship program was not motivated by animus toward religion. The Court does not explain why the legislature's motive matters, and I fail to see why it should. If a State deprives a citizen of trial by jury or passes an *ex post facto* law, we do not pause to investigate whether it was actually trying to accomplish the evil the Constitution prohibits. . . .

It may be that Washington's original purpose in excluding the clergy from public benefits was benign, and the same might be true of its purpose in maintaining the exclusion today. But those singled out for disfavor can be forgiven for suspecting more invidious forces at work. Let there be no doubt: This case is about discrimination against a religious minority. Most citizens of this country identify themselves as professing some religious belief, but the State's policy poses no obstacle to practitioners of only a tepid, civic version of faith. Those the statutory exclusion actually affects—those whose belief in their religion is so strong that they dedicate their study and their lives to its ministry—are a far narrower set. One need not delve too far into modern popular culture to perceive a trendy disdain for deep religious conviction. In an era when the Court is so quick to come to the aid of other disfavored groups, see, e.g., *Romer v. Evans*, 517 U.S. 620, its indifference in this case, which involves a form of discrimination to which the Constitution actually speaks, is exceptional. . . .

---

### NOTES AND QUESTIONS

1. The holdings in *Zelman* and *Locke* seem inconsistent (or are they?). *Zelman* holds that a publicly funded voucher that can be applied in religious schools does not violate the Establishment Clause. *Locke* seems to hold that the public funding of ministerial training, even under a voucher program, contravenes core Establishment Clause principles. How do you reconcile the two holdings coming only two years apart (and both decisions written by Chief Justice Rehnquist) with the same Court membership? Is this simply a difference between what the Constitution allows but does not require?

2. *Locke* is primarily a free exercise and equal protection case (e.g., Davey claimed that Washington's refusal to provide a voucher to obtain a religious education unfairly discriminated against him based on his religious beliefs). Did the state discriminate against Davey based on his *beliefs*, or on the basis of how he intended to *use* his state benefit? Is this distinction significant?

3. How did the Court majority distinguish *Lukumi* and *McDaniel*? Are the Court's distinctions convincing? Why or why not?

4. What does the Court majority mean when it says that the Religion Clauses allow for "play in the joints"?

5. What is the significance of the Washington state constitutional provisions for the case? Are there limits on state constitutional provisions that deviate from interpretations of the Establishment Clause? Could a state constitution (as interpreted by its state supreme court) prohibit property tax exemptions for churches but allow them for nonreligious charities?

6. Justice Scalia claims that the majority's opinion is inconsistent with earlier affirmations of "neutrality" toward religion. Isn't he correct that principles of neutrality toward religion compel the opposite result? What does the majority holding suggest about any limits to the evenhanded neutrality theory vis-a-vis separationism? For various perspectives, see Frank S. Ravitch, "Locke v. Davey and the Lose-Lose Scenario: What Davey Could Have Said, But Didn't," *Tulsa Law Review* 40 (2004): 55; Steven K. Green, "Locke v. Davey and the Limits to Neutrality Theory," *Temple Law Review* 77 (2004): 913.

## CHAPTER 13

# GOVERNMENT AID TO HIGHER EDUCATION

In the previous chapter, dealing with financial support to parochial schools, we observed that the road from *Everson* to *Zelman* was long and tortuous. Some issues have yet to be fully resolved (e.g., issues related to certain forms of direct government aid that flow to what have traditionally been called "pervasively sectarian" schools). In contrast, the high court's consideration of government financial assistance to religious colleges and universities has been brief, involving only three cases and taking place over a five-year period. This is somewhat surprising, considering the variety of religious institutions of higher education (e.g., secular colleges with historical religious ties [e.g., Harvard]; church-related colleges [e.g., Wake Forest]; Bible and other sectarian colleges [e.g., Moody Bible]; seminaries and divinity schools [e.g., Union Theological]), and the plethora of federal and state funding programs available to both college students (e.g., student loans and grants) and the institutions (e.g., construction and research grants; low interest loans and bonding arrangements).

From the beginning, the Court appeared to take a different approach to college funding controversies. (Of note, the Court handed down its decision in *Tilton v. Richardson* on the same day as *Lemon v. Kurtzman*.) See if you can identify the distinctions, whether they involve the character of the institutions, the nature of the financial aid, or a combination of factors.

---

## TILTON v. RICHARDSON
### 403 U.S. 672 (1971)

MR. CHIEF JUSTICE BURGER announced the judgment of the Court and an opinion in which MR. JUSTICE HARLAN, MR. JUSTICE STEWART and MR. JUSTICE BLACKMUN join. . . .

I

The Higher Education Facilities Act was passed in 1963 in response to a strong nationwide demand for the expansion of college and university facilities to meet the sharply rising number of young people demanding higher education. The Act authorizes federal grants and loans to "institutions of higher education" for the construction of a wide variety of "academic facilities." But § 751(a) (2) (1964 ed., Supp. V) expressly excludes "any facility used or to be used for sectarian instruction or as a place for religious worship, or . . . any facility which . . . is used or to be used primarily in connection with any part of the program of a school or department of divinity. . . ."

The United States retains a 20-year interest in any facility constructed with Title I funds. If, during this period, the recipient violates the statutory conditions, the United States is entitled to recover an amount equal to the proportion of its present value that the federal grant bore to the original cost of the facility. During the 20-year period, the statutory restrictions are enforced by the Office of Education primarily by way of on-site inspections.

Appellants brought this suit for injunctive relief against the officials who administer the Act. Four church-related colleges and universities in Connecticut receiving federal construction grants under Title I were also named as defendants. Federal funds were used for five projects at these four institutions: (1) a library building at Sacred Heart University; (2) a music, drama, and arts building at Annhurst College; (3) a science building at Fairfield University; (4) a library building at Fairfield; and (5) a language laboratory at Albertus Magnus College. . . .

The District Court . . . sustained the constitutionality of the Act, finding that it had neither the purpose nor the effect of promoting religion. . . .

III

Numerous cases considered by the Court have noted the internal tension in the First Amendment between the Establishment Clause and the Free Exercise Clause. . . . [T]he three main concerns against which the Establishment Clause sought to protect [are]: "sponsorship, financial support, and active involvement of the sovereign in religious activity." *Walz v. Tax Comm'm*, 397 U.S. 664, 668.

Every analysis must begin with the candid acknowledgment that there is no single constitutional caliper that can be used to measure the precise degree to which these three factors are present or absent. Instead, our analysis in this area must begin with a consideration of the cumulative criteria developed over many years and applying to a wide range of governmental action challenged as violative of the Establishment Clause.

There are always risks in treating criteria discussed by the Court from time to time as "tests" in any limiting sense of that term. Constitutional adjudication does not lend itself to the absolutes of the physical sciences or mathematics. The standards should rather be viewed as guidelines with which to identify instances in which the objectives of the Religion Clauses have been impaired. And, as we have noted in *Lemon v. Kurtzman* and *Early v. DiCenso*, 403 U.S. 602, 612 (1971), candor compels the acknowledgment that we can only dimly perceive the boundaries of permissible government activity in this sensitive area of constitutional adjudication.

Against this background we consider four questions: First, does the Act reflect a secular legislative purpose? Second, is the primary effect of the Act to advance or inhibit religion? Third, does the administration of the Act foster an excessive government entanglement with religion? Fourth, does the implementation of the Act inhibit the free exercise of religion?

(a) . . .

[The Court found a legitimate secular purpose existed in enhancing educational opportunities.]

The simplistic argument that every form of financial aid to church sponsored activity violates the Religion Clauses was rejected long ago in *Bradfield v. Roberts*, 175 U.S. 291 (1899). There a federal construction grant to a hospital operated by a religious order was upheld. Here the Act is challenged on the ground that its primary effect is to aid the religious purposes of church-related colleges and universities. Construction grants surely aid these institutions in the sense that the construction of buildings will assist them to perform their various functions. But bus transportation, textbooks, and tax exemptions all gave aid in the sense that religious bodies would otherwise have been forced to find other sources from which to finance these services. Yet all of these forms of governmental assistance have been upheld. *Everson v. Board of Education*, 330 U.S. 1 (1947); *Board of Education v. Allen*, 392 U.S. 236 (1968); *Walz v. Tax Comm'n*. See also *Bradfield v. Roberts*. The crucial question is not whether some benefit accrues to a religious institution as a consequence of the legislative program, but whether its principal or primary effect advances religion. . . .

The Act itself was carefully drafted to ensure that the federally subsidized facilities would be devoted to the secular and not the religious function of the recipient institutions. It authorizes grants and loans only for academic facilities that will be used for defined secular purposes and expressly prohibits their use for religious instruction, training, or worship. These restrictions have been enforced in the Act's actual administration, and the record shows that some church-related institutions have been required to disgorge benefits for failure to obey them.

Finally, this record fully supports the findings of the District Court that none of the four church-related institutions in this case has violated the statutory restrictions. The institutions presented evidence that there had been no religious services or worship in the federally financed facilities, that there are no religious symbols or plaques in or on them, and that they had been used solely for nonreligious purposes. On this record, therefore, these buildings are indistinguishable from a typical state university facility. . . .

Appellants instead rely on the argument that government may not subsidize any activities of an institution of higher learning that in some of its programs teaches religious doctrines. . . .

Under this concept appellants' position depends on the validity of the proposition that religion so permeates the secular education provided by church-related colleges and universities that their religious and secular educational functions are in fact inseparable. The argument that government grants would thus inevitably advance religion did not escape the notice of Congress. It was carefully and thoughtfully debated, but was found unpersuasive. It was also considered by this Court in *Allen*. There the Court refused to assume that religiosity in parochial elementary and secondary schools necessarily permeates the secular education that they provide.

This record, similarly, provides no basis for any such assumption here. Two of the five federally financed buildings involved in this case are libraries. The District Court found that no classes had been conducted in either of these facilities and that no restrictions were imposed by the institutions on the books that they acquired. There is no evidence to the contrary. The third building was a language laboratory at Albertus Magnus College. The evidence showed that this facility was used solely to assist students with their pronunciation in modern foreign languages—a use which would seem peculiarly unrelated and unadaptable to religious indoctrination. Federal grants were also used to build a science building at Fairfield University and a music, drama, and arts building at Annhurst College.

There is no evidence that religion seeps into the use of any of these facilities. . . . Although appellants introduced several institutional documents that stated certain religious restrictions on what could be taught, other evidence showed that these restrictions were not in fact enforced and that the schools were characterized by an atmosphere of academic freedom rather than religious indoctrination. All four institutions, for example, subscribe to the 1940 Statement of Principles on Academic Freedom and Tenure endorsed by the American Association of University Professors and the Association of American Colleges.

Rather than focus on the four defendant colleges and universities involved in this case, however, appellants seek to shift our attention to a "composite profile" that they have constructed of the "typical sectarian" institution of higher education. We are told that such a "composite" institution imposes religious restrictions on admissions, requires attendance at religious activities, compels obedience to the doctrines and dogmas of the faith, requires instruction in theology and doctrine, and does everything it can to propagate a particular religion. Perhaps some church-related schools fit the pattern that appellants describe. Indeed, some colleges have been declared ineligible for aid by the authorities that administer the Act. But appellants do not contend that these four institutions fall within this category. . . . We cannot, however, strike down an Act of Congress on the basis of a hypothetical "profile."

(b)

Although we reject appellants' broad constitutional arguments we do perceive an aspect in which the statute's enforcement provisions are inadequate to ensure that the impact of the federal aid will not advance religion. . . .

Under § 754(b)(2) a recipient institution's obligation not to use the facility for sectarian instruction or religious worship would appear to expire at the end of 20 years. We note, for example, that under § 718(b)(7)(C) (1964 ed., Supp. V), an institution applying for a federal grant is only required to provide assurances that the facility will not be used for sectarian instruction or religious worship "during at least the period of the Federal interest therein (as defined in section 754 of this title)."

Limiting the prohibition for religious use of the structure to 20 years obviously opens the facility to use for any purpose at the end of that period. It cannot be assumed that a substantial structure has no value after that period and hence the unrestricted use of a valuable property is in effect a contribution of some value to a religious body. Congress did not base the 20-year provision on any contrary conclusion. If, at the end of 20 years, the building is, for example, converted into a chapel or otherwise used to promote religious interests, the original federal grant will in part have the effect of advancing religion.

To this extent the Act therefore trespasses on the Religion Clauses. The restrictive obligations of a recipient institution under § 751(a)(2) cannot, compatibly with the Religion Clauses, expire while the building has substantial value. This circumstance does not require us to invalidate the entire Act, however. . . .

IV

We next turn to the question of whether excessive entanglements characterize the relationship between government and church under the Act. . . .

There are generally significant differences between the religious aspects of church-related institutions of higher learning and parochial elementary and secondary schools. The "affirmative if not dominant policy" of the instruction in pre-college church schools is "to assure future adherents to a particular faith by having control of their total education at an early age." *Walz v. Tax Comm'n*, 671.There is substance to the contention that college students are less impressionable and less susceptible to religious indoctrination. . . . Furthermore, by their very nature, college and postgraduate courses tend to limit the opportunities for sectarian influence by virtue of their own internal disciplines. Many church-related colleges and universities are characterized by a high degree of academic freedom and seek to evoke free and critical responses from their students.

The record here would not support a conclusion that any of these four institutions departed from this general pattern. All four schools are governed by Catholic religious organizations, and the faculties and student bodies at each are predominantly Catholic. Nevertheless, the evidence shows that non-Catholics were admitted as students and given faculty appointments. Not one of these four institutions requires its students to attend religious services. Although all four schools require their students to take theology courses, the parties stipulated that these courses are taught according to the academic requirements of the subject matter and the teacher's concept of professional standards. The parties also stipulated that the courses covered a range of human religious experiences and are not limited to courses about the Roman Catholic religion. The schools introduced evidence that they made no attempt to indoctrinate students or to proselytize. Indeed, some of the required theology courses at Albertus Magnus and Sacred Heart are taught by rabbis. Finally, as we have noted, these four schools subscribe to a well-established set of principles of academic freedom, and nothing in this record shows that these principles are not in fact followed. In short, the evidence shows institutions with admittedly religious functions but whose predominant higher education mission is to provide their students with a secular education.

Since religious indoctrination is not a substantial purpose or activity of these church-related colleges and universities, there is less likelihood than in primary and secondary schools that religion will permeate the area of secular education. This reduces the risk that government aid will in fact serve to support religious activities. Correspondingly, the necessity for intensive government surveillance is diminished and the resulting entanglements between government and religion lessened. Such inspection as may be necessary to ascertain that the facilities are devoted to secular education is minimal and indeed hardly more than the inspections that States impose over all private schools within the reach of compulsory education laws.

The entanglement between church and state is also lessened here by the nonideological character of the aid that the Government provides. Our cases from *Everson* to *Allen* have permitted church-related schools to receive government aid in the form of secular, neutral, or nonideological services, facilities, or materials that are supplied to all students regardless of the affiliation of the school that they attend. In *Lemon* and *DiCenso*, however, the state programs subsidized teachers, either directly or indirectly. Since teachers are not necessarily religiously neutral, greater governmental surveillance would be required to guarantee that state salary aid would not in fact subsidize religious instruction. There we found the resulting entanglement excessive. Here, on the other hand, the Government provides facilities that are themselves religiously neutral. The risks of Government aid to religion and the corresponding need for surveillance are therefore reduced.

Finally, government entanglements with religion are reduced by the circumstance that, unlike the direct and continuing payments under the Pennsylvania program, and all the incidents of regulation and surveillance, the Government aid here is a one-time, single-purpose construction grant. There are no continuing financial relationships or dependencies, no annual audits, and no government analysis of an institution's expenditures on secular as distinguished from religious activities. Inspection as to use is a minimal contact. . . .

We think that cumulatively these three factors also substantially lessen the potential for divisive religious fragmentation in the political arena. . . . Possibly this can be explained by the character and diversity of the recipient colleges and universities and the absence of any intimate continuing relationship or dependency between government and religiously affiliated institutions. The potential for divisiveness inherent in the essentially local problems of primary and secondary schools is significantly less with respect to a college or university whose student constituency is not local but diverse and widely dispersed. . . .

*Vacated and remanded.*

▓ MR. JUSTICE DOUGLAS, with whom MR. JUSTICE BLACK and MR. JUSTICE MARSHALL concur, dissenting in part. . . .

Title I of the Higher Education Facilities Act of 1963 authorizes grants and loans up to 50% of the cost for the construction of undergraduate academic facilities in both public and private colleges and universities. . . .

The public purpose in secular education is, to be sure, furthered by the program. Yet the sectarian purpose is aided by making the parochial school system viable. The purpose is to increase "student enrollment" and the students obviously aimed at are those of the particular faith now financed by taxpayers' money. Parochial schools are not beamed at agnostics, atheists, or those of a competing sect. The more sophisticated institutions may admit minorities; but the dominant religious character is not changed. . . .

The Federal Government is giving religious schools a block grant to build certain facilities. The fact that money is given once at the beginning of a program rather than apportioned annually as in *Lemon* and *DiCenso* is without constitutional significance. . . . The plurality's distinction is in effect that small violations of the First Amendment over a period of years are unconstitutional (see *Lemon* and *DiCenso*) while a huge violation occurring only once is *de minimis*. I cannot agree with such sophistry.

What I have said in *Lemon* and in the *DiCenso* cases decided today is relevant here. The facilities financed by taxpayers' funds are not to be used for "sectarian" purposes. Religious teaching and secular teaching are so enmeshed in parochial schools that only the strictest supervision and surveillance would insure compliance with the condition. Parochial schools may require religious exercises, even in the classroom. A parochial school operates on one budget. Money not spent for one purpose becomes available for other purposes. Thus the fact that there are no religious observances in federally financed facilities is not controlling because required religious observances will take place in other buildings. . . .

I dissent not because of any lack of respect for parochial schools but out of a feeling of despair that the respect which through history has been accorded the First Amendment is this day lost.

It should be remembered that in this case we deal with federal grants and with the command that "Congress shall make no law respecting an establishment of religion, or prohibiting the free exercise thereof." The million-dollar grants sustained today put Madison's miserable "three pence" to shame. But he even thought, as I do, that even a small amount coming out of the pocket of taxpayers and going into the coffers of a church was not in keeping with our constitutional ideal.

I would reverse the judgment below.

---

*Hunt v. McNair* challenged the validity of a South Carolina statutory scheme for aiding colleges by issuing revenue bonds for the construction and financing of projects, such as buildings and facilities, but not to include any facility for sectarian instruction or religious worship. Under the scheme, neither the State nor the South Carolina Educational Facilities Authority was obligated, directly or indirectly, to pay the principal of or interest on the bonds; nor was the State's taxing power pledged or implicated. All expenses of the Authority also were paid solely from the revenues of the projects.

The Authority gave preliminary approval to an application submitted by a Baptist-controlled college, 60% of whose students at the time were Baptists. As subsequently modified, the application requested the issuance of revenue bonds of $1,250,000 to be used for refinancing capital improvements and completing the dining hall. Under the statutory scheme the project would be conveyed to the Authority, which would lease it back to the college, with reconveyance to the college on full payment of the bonds. The lease agreement would contain a clause obligating the institution to observe the Act's restrictions on sectarian use and enabling the Authority to conduct inspections. The provision for reconveyance would restrict the project to nonsectarian use.

The advantage of financing educational institutions through a state-created authority derives from relevant provisions of federal and South Carolina state income tax laws which provide in effect that the interest on such bonds is not subject to income taxation. The income-tax-exempt status of the interest enables the Authority, as an instrumentality of the State, to market the bonds at a significantly lower rate of interest than the educational institution would be forced to pay if it borrowed the money by conventional private financing.

A South Carolina taxpayer challenged the constitutionality of the approval, claiming the issuance of the bonds would violate the Establishment Clause. The trial court denied the taxpayer relief, and the State Supreme Court affirmed.

---

## HUNT v. McNAIR
### 413 U.S. 734 (1973)

▨ MR. JUSTICE POWELL delivered the opinion of the Court. . . .

### II

As we reaffirm today in *Committee for Public Education and Religious Liberty v. Nyquist*, 413 U.S. 756 (1973), the principles which govern our consideration of challenges to statutes as violative of the Establishment Clause are three:

"First, the statute must have a secular legislative purpose; second, its principal or primary effect must be one that neither advances nor inhibits religion . . .; finally, the statute must not foster 'an excessive government entanglement with religion." *Lemon v. Kurtzman*, 403 U.S., 612-613.

The purpose of the statute is manifestly a secular one. The benefits of the Act are available to all institutions of higher education in South Carolina, whether or not having a religious affiliation. . . .

### B

To identify "primary effect," we narrow our focus from the statute as a whole to the only transaction presently before us. Whatever may be its initial appeal, the proposition that the Establishment Clause prohibits any program which in some manner aids an institution with a religious affiliation has consistently been rejected. Stated another way, the Court has not accepted the recurrent argument that all aid is forbidden because aid to one aspect of an institution frees it to spend its other resources on religious ends.

Aid normally may be thought to have a primary effect of advancing religion when it flows to an institution in which religion is so pervasive that a substantial portion of its functions are subsumed in the religious mission or when it funds a specifically religious activity in an otherwise substantially secular setting. . . .

Appellant has introduced no evidence in the present case placing the College in such a category. It is true that the members of the College Board of Trustees are elected by the South Carolina Baptist Convention, that the approval of the Convention is required for certain financial transactions, and that the charter of the College may be amended only by the Convention. But it was likewise true of the institutions involved in *Tilton* that they were "governed by Catholic religious organizations." What little there is in the record concerning the College establishes that there are no religious qualifications for faculty membership or student admission, and that only 60% of the College student body is Baptist, a percentage roughly equivalent to the percentage of Baptists in that area of South Carolina. On the record in this case there is no basis to conclude that the College's operations are oriented significantly towards sectarian rather than secular education.

Nor can we conclude that the proposed transaction will place the Authority in the position of providing aid to the religious as opposed to the secular activities of the College. The scope of the Authority's power to assist institutions of higher education extends only to "projects," and the Act specifically states that a project "shall not include" any buildings or facilities used for religious purposes. . . . In addition, as we have indicated, every lease agreement must contain a clause forbidding religious use and another allowing inspections to enforce the agreement. For these reasons, we are satisfied that implementation of the proposal will not have the primary effect of advancing or inhibiting religion.[7]

## C

The final question posed by this case is whether under the arrangement there would be an unconstitutional degree of entanglement between the State and the College. Appellant argues that the Authority would become involved in the operation of the College both by inspecting the project to insure that it is not being used for religious purposes and by participating in the management decisions of the College. . . .

[First,] the degree of entanglement arising from inspection of facilities as to use varies in large measure with the extent to which religion permeates the institution. . . . As we have indicated above, there is no evidence here to demonstrate that the College is any more an instrument of religious indoctrination than were the colleges and universities involved in *Tilton*.

A closer issue under our precedents is presented by the contention that the Authority could become deeply involved in the day-to-day financial and policy decisions of the College. The Authority is empowered by the Act:

> "(g) (g)enerally, to fix and revise from time to time and charge and collect rates, rents, fees and charges for the use of and for the services furnished or to be furnished by a project; . . .

> "(h) (t)o establish rules and regulations for the use of a project or any portion thereof and to designate a participating institution for higher education as its agent to establish rules and regulations for the use of a project undertaken for such participating institution for higher education. . . ." S.C.Code Ann. § 22-41.4 (Supp.1971).

These powers are sweeping ones, and were there a realistic likelihood that they would be exercised in their full detail, the entanglement problems with the proposed transaction would not be insignificant. . . .

As we read the College's proposal, [however,] the Lease Agreement between the Authority and the College will place on the College the responsibility for making the detailed decisions regarding the government of the campus and the fees to be charged for particular services. . . .

In short, under the proposed Lease Agreement, neither the Authority nor a trustee bank would be justified in taking action unless the College fails to make the prescribed rental payments or otherwise defaults in its obligations. Only if the College refused to meet rental payments or was unable to do so would the Authority or the trustee be obligated to take further action. In that

---

[7] The "state aid" involved in this case is of a very special sort. We have here no expenditure of public funds, either by grant or loan, no reimbursement by a State for expenditures made by a parochial school or college, and no extending or committing of a State's credit. Rather, the only state aid consists, not of financial assistance directly or indirectly which would implicate public funds or credit, but the creation of an instrumentality (the Authority) through which educational institutions may borrow funds on the basis of their own credit and the security of their own property upon more favorable interest terms than otherwise would be available. . . .

event, the Authority or trustee might either foreclose on the mortgage or take a hand in the setting of rules, charges, and fees. It may be argued that only the former would be consistent with the Establishment Clause, but we do not now have that situation before us. . . .

*Affirmed.*

▨ MR. JUSTICE BRENNAN, with whom MR. JUSTICE DOUGLAS and MR. JUSTICE MARSHALL join, dissenting. . . .

The act authorizes a financing arrangement between the Authority and the Baptist College at Charleston, a South Carolina educational corporation operated by the South Carolina Baptist Convention. Under that arrangement, the College would convey a substantial portion of its campus to the Authority, and the Authority would lease back the property to the College at an agreed rental. The Authority would then issue revenue bonds of the State of South Carolina in the amount of $3,500,000, which bonds would be payable, principal and interest, from the rents paid by the College to the Authority under the lease. . . . Upon payment in full of the principal and interest on the bonds, the arrangement requires that the Authority reconvey title to the campus properties to the College free and clear of all liens and encumbrances. The arrangement does not, however, amount merely to a mortgage on the campus property. The Authority is also empowered, *inter alia*, to determine the location and character of any project financed under the act; to construct, maintain, manage, operate, lease as lessor or lessee, and regulate the same; to enter into contracts for the management and operation of such project; to establish rules and regulations for the use of the project or any portion thereof; and to fix and revise from time to time rates, rents, fees, and charges for the use of a project and for the services furnished or to be furnished by a project or any portion thereof. In other words, the College turns over to the State Authority control of substantial parts of the fiscal operation of the school—its very life's blood.

Thus, it is crystal clear, I think, that this scheme involves the State in a degree of policing of the affairs of the College far exceeding that called for by the statutes struck down in *Lemon I*. Indeed, under this scheme the policing by the State can become so extensive that the State may well end up in complete control of the operation of the College, at least for the life of the bonds. The College's freedom to engage in religious activities and to offer religious instruction is necessarily circumscribed by this pervasive state involvement forced upon the College if it is not to lose its benefits under the Act. For it seems inescapable that the content of courses taught in facilities financed under the agreement must be closely monitored by the State Authority in discharge of its duty to ensure that the facilities are not being used for sectarian instruction. The Authority must also involve itself deeply in the fiscal affairs of the College, even to the point of fixing tuition rates, as part of its duty to assure sufficient revenues to meet bond and interest obligations. And should the College find itself unable to meet these obligations, its continued existence as a viable sectarian institution is almost completely in the hands of the State Authority. Thus this agreement, with its consequent state surveillance and ongoing administrative relationships, inescapably entails mutually damaging Church-State involvements. . . .

*Tilton* is clearly not controlling here. The plurality opinion in *Tilton* was expressly based on the premise, erroneous in my view, that the Federal Higher

Education Facilities Act contained no significant intrusions into the everyday affairs of sectarian educational institutions. . . .

But under the South Carolina scheme "continuing financial relationships or dependencies," "annual audits," "government analysis," and "regulation and surveillance" are the core features of the arrangement. In short, the South Carolina statutory scheme as applied to this sectarian institution presents the very sort of "intimate continuing relationship or dependency between government and religiously affiliated institutions" that in the plurality's view was lacking in *Tilton*.

Nor is the South Carolina arrangement between the State and this College any less offensive to the Constitution because it involves, as the Court asserts, no direct financial support to the College by the State. The Establishment Clause forbids far more than payment of public funds directly to support sectarian institutions. It forbids any official involvement with religion, whatever its form, which tends to foster or discourage religious worship or belief. . . .

The State forthrightly aids the College by permitting the College to avail itself of the State's unique ability to borrow money at low interest rates, and the College, in turn, surrenders to the State a comprehensive and continuing surveillance of the educational, religious, and fiscal affairs of the College. The conclusion is compelled that this involves the State in the "essentially religious activities of religious institutions" and "employ(s) the organs of government for essentially religious purposes."

---

The third in the 1970s trilogy of college-aid cases, *Roemer v. Board of Public Works of Maryland*, involved a state program that gives grants to private colleges for a variety of academic activities and programs. In *Roemer*, several church-related colleges applied for and were awarded grants, the only restriction on their use being that the money could not be applied for sectarian activities. Taxpayers filed suit, claiming that the safeguards were inadequate and that several of the colleges were pervasively sectarian and thus ineligible to receive the direct grants. The Court disagreed.

---

## ROEMER v. BOARD OF PUBLIC WORKS OF MARYLAND
### 426 U.S. 736 (1976)

MR. JUSTICE BLACKMUN announced the judgment of the Court and delivered an opinion in which THE CHIEF JUSTICE and MR. JUSTICE POWELL joined.

Maryland has enacted a statute which, as amended, provides for annual noncategorical grants to private colleges, among them religiously affiliated institutions, subject only to the restrictions that the funds not be used for "sectarian purposes." A three-judge District Court, by a divided vote, refused to enjoin the operation of the statute, and a direct appeal has been taken to this Court pursuant to 28 U.S.C. § 1253.

I

The challenged grant program provides funding for "any private institution of higher learning within the State of Maryland," provided the institution is accredited by the State Department of Education, was established in Maryland prior to July 1, 1970, maintains one or more "associate of arts or baccalaureate degree" programs, and refrains from awarding "only seminarian or theological degrees." The aid is in the form of an annual fiscal year subsidy to qualifying colleges and universities. It now provides for a qualifying institution to receive, for each full-time student (excluding students enrolled in seminarian or theological academic programs), an amount equal to 15% of the State's per-full-time-pupil appropriation for a student in the state college system. As first enacted, the grants were completely unrestricted. They remain noncategorical in nature, and a recipient institution may put them to whatever use it prefers, with but one exception. . . . "None of the moneys payable under this subtitle shall be utilized by the institutions for sectarian purposes."

The administration of the grant program is entrusted to the State's Board of Public Works "assisted by the Maryland Council for Higher Education." . . .

The Council performs what the District Court described as a "two-step screening process" to insure compliance with the statutory restrictions on the grants. First, it determines whether an institution applying for aid is eligible at all, or is one "awarding primarily theological or seminary degrees." Several applicants have been disqualified at this stage of the process. Second, the Council requires that those institutions that are eligible for funds not put them to any sectarian use. An application must be accompanied by an affidavit of the institution's chief executive officer stating that the funds will not be used for sectarian purposes, and by a description of the specific nonsectarian uses that are planned. . . . The recipient institution is further required to segregate state funds in a "special revenue account" and to identify aided nonsectarian expenditures separately in its budget. It must retain "sufficient documentation of the State funds expended to permit verification by the Council that funds were not spent for sectarian purposes." . . .

In 1971, $1.7 million was disbursed to 17 private institutions in Maryland. The disbursements were under the statute as originally enacted, and were therefore not subject to § 68A's specific prohibition on sectarian use. Of the 17 institutions, five were church related, and these received $520,000 of the $1.7 million. A total of $1.8 million was to be awarded to 18 institutions in 1972, the second year of the grant program; of this amount, $603,000 was to go to church-related institutions. . . .

Plaintiffs in this suit, appellants here, are four individual Maryland citizens and taxpayers. Their complaint sought a declaration of the statute's invalidity, an order enjoining payments under it to church-affiliated institutions, and a declaration that the State was entitled to recover from such institutions any amounts already disbursed. . . .

II

A system of government that makes itself felt as pervasively as ours could hardly be expected never to cross paths with the church. In fact, our State and Federal Governments impose certain burdens upon, and impart certain benefits to, virtually all our activities, and religious activity is not an exception. The

Court has enforced a scrupulous neutrality by the State, as among religions, and also as between religious and other activities, but a hermetic separation of the two is an impossibility it has never required. It long has been established, for example, that the State may send a cleric, indeed even a clerical order, to perform a wholly secular task. . . .

And religious institutions need not be quarantined from public benefits that are neutrally available to all. . . . The Court has not been blind to the fact that in aiding a religious institution to perform a secular task, the State frees the institution's resources to be put to sectarian ends. If this were impermissible, however, a church could not be protected by the police and fire departments, or have its public sidewalk kept in repair. The Court never has held that religious activities must be discriminated against in this way.

Neutrality is what is required. The State must confine itself to secular objectives, and neither advance nor impede religious activity. Of course, that principle is more easily stated than applied. The Court has taken the view that a secular purpose and a facial neutrality may not be enough, if in fact the State is lending direct support to a religious activity. The State may not, for example, pay for what is actually a religious education, even though it purports to be paying for a secular one, and even though it makes its aid available to secular and religious institutions alike. The Court also has taken the view that the State's efforts to perform a secular task, and at the same time avoid aiding in the performance of a religious one, may not lead it into such an intimate relationship with religious authority that it appears either to be sponsoring or to be excessively interfering with that authority. . . .

### III

The first part of *Lemon I*'s three-part test is not in issue; appellants do not challenge the District Court's finding that the purpose of Maryland's aid program is the secular one of supporting private higher education generally, as an economic alternative to a wholly public system. The focus of the debate is on the second and third parts, those concerning the primary effect of advancing religion, and excessive church state entanglement. We consider them in the same order. . . .

### A

While entanglement is essentially a procedural problem, the primary-effect question is the substantive one of what private educational activities, by whatever procedure, may be supported by state funds. *Hunt* requires (1) that no state aid at all go to institutions that are so "pervasively sectarian" that secular activities cannot be separated from sectarian ones, and (2) that if secular activities can be separated out, they alone may be funded.

(1) The District Court's finding in this case was that the appellee colleges are not "pervasively sectarian." This conclusion it supported with a number of subsidiary findings concerning the role of religion on these campuses:

(a) Despite their formal affiliation with the Roman Catholic Church, the colleges are "characterized by a high degree of institutional autonomy." None of the four receives funds from, or makes reports to, the Catholic Church. The Church is represented on their governing boards, but, as with Mount Saint Mary's, "no instance of entry of Church considerations into college decisions was shown."

(b) The colleges employ Roman Catholic chaplains and hold Roman Catholic religious exercises on campus. Attendance at such is not required; the encouragement of spiritual development is only "one secondary objective" of each college; and "at none of these institutions does this encouragement go beyond providing the opportunities or occasions for religious experience." It was the District Court's general finding that "religious indoctrination is not a substantial purpose or activity of any of these defendants."

(c) Mandatory religion or theology courses are taught at each of the colleges, primarily by Roman Catholic clerics, but these only supplement a curriculum covering "the spectrum of a liberal arts program." Nontheology courses are taught in an "atmosphere of intellectual freedom" and without "religious pressures." Each college subscribes to, and abides by, the 1940 Statement of Principles on Academic Freedom of the American Association of University Professors.

(d) Some classes are begun with prayer. The percentage of classes in which this is done varies with the college, from a "minuscule" percentage at Loyola and Mount Saint Mary's, to a majority at Saint Joseph. There is no "actual college policy" of encouraging the practice. "It is treated as a facet of the instructor's academic freedom." *Ibid.* Classroom prayers were therefore regarded by the District Court as "peripheral to the subject of religious permeation," as were the facts that some instructors wear clerical garb and some classrooms have religious symbols. . . .

(e) The District Court found that, apart from the theology departments, faculty hiring decisions are not made on a religious basis. At two of the colleges, Notre Dame and Mount Saint Mary's, no inquiry at all is made into an applicant's religion. Religious preference is to be noted on Loyola's application form, but the purpose is to allow full appreciation of the applicant's background. Loyola also attempts to employ each year two members of a particular religious order which once staffed a college recently merged into Loyola. Budgetary considerations lead the colleges generally to favor members of religious orders, who often receive less than full salary. Still, the District Court found that "academic quality" was the principal hiring criterion, and that any "hiring bias," or "effort by any defendant to stack its faculty with members of a particular religious group," would have been noticed by other faculty members, who had never been heard to complain.

(f) The great majority of students at each of the colleges are Roman Catholic, but the District Court concluded from a "thorough analysis of the student admission and recruiting criteria" that the student bodies "are chosen without regard to religion."

We cannot say that the foregoing findings as to the role of religion in particular aspects of the colleges are clearly erroneous. Appellants ask us to set those findings aside in certain respects. Not surprisingly, they have gleaned from this record of thousands of pages, compiled during several weeks of trial, occasional evidence of a more sectarian character than the District Court ascribes to the colleges. It is not our place, however, to reappraise the evidence, unless it plainly fails to support the findings of the trier of facts. . . . To answer the question whether an institution is so "pervasively sectarian" that it may receive no direct state aid of any kind, it is necessary to paint a general picture of the institution, composed of many elements. The general picture that the District Court has painted of the appellee institutions is similar in almost all respects to that of the church-affiliated colleges considered in *Tilton* and *Hunt*.[21] We find no constitutionally significant distinction between them, at least for purposes of the "pervasive sectarianism" test.

(2) Having found that the appellee institutions are not "so permeated by religion that the secular side cannot be separated from the sectarian," the District Court proceeded to the next question posed by *Hunt*: whether aid in fact was extended only to "the secular side." This requirement the court regarded as satisfied by the statutory prohibition against sectarian use, and by the administrative enforcement of that prohibition through the Council for Higher Education. We agree. *Hunt* requires only that state funds not be used to support "specifically religious activity." It is clear that fund uses exist that meet this requirement. . . . Funds are put to the use of the college's choice, provided it is not a sectarian use, of which the college must satisfy the Council. If the question is whether the statute sought to be enjoined authorizes state funds for "specifically religious activity," that question fairly answers itself. The statute in terms forbids the use of funds for "sectarian purposes," and this prohibition appears to be at least as broad as *Hunt*'s prohibition of the public funding of "specifically religious activity." We must assume that the colleges, and the Council, will exercise their delegated control over use of the funds in compliance with the statutory, and therefore the constitutional, mandate. It is to be expected that they will give a wide berth to "specifically religious activity," and thus minimize constitutional questions.[22] . . .

---

[21] To be sure, in this case the District Court was unable to find, as was stipulated in *Tilton*, that mandatory theology or religion courses are taught without taint of religious indoctrination. This is not inconsistent, however, with the District Court's finding of a lack of pervasive sectarianism. The latter condition would exist only if, because of the institution's general character, courses other than religion or theology courses could not be funded without fear of religious indoctrination.

The role of the affiliated church appears, if anything, to have been stronger in *Hunt* than in this case. The Baptist College at Charleston, before us in *Hunt*, was controlled by the South Carolina Baptist Convention to the extent that the Convention elected all members of the Board of Trustees, and retained the power to approve certain financial transactions, as well as any amendment of the College's charter.

[22] Maryland [law] prohibits recipient institutions from using State funds for "sectarian purposes." That provision generally proscribes the use of State funds to support religious instruction, religious worship, or other activities of a religious nature. Listed below are several potential uses of State funds which would violate the sectarian use prohibition. The list is not intended to be all-inclusive. . . .

"(1) Student Aid: State Funds may not be used for student aid if the institution imposes religious restrictions or qualifications on eligibility for student aid, nor may they be paid to students then enrolled in a religious, seminarian or theological academic program.

"(2) Salaries: State funds may not be used to pay in whole or in part the salary of any person who is engaged in the teaching of religion or theology, who serves as chaplain or director of the campus ministry, or who administers or supervises any program of religious activities.

"(3) Maintenance and Repair: State funds may not be used to pay any portion of the cost of maintenance or repair of any building or facility used for the teaching of religion or theology or for religious worship or for any religious activity. . .

"(5) Capital Construction and Improvements: If State funds are used to construct a new building or facility or to renovate an existing one, the building or facility may not be used for the teaching of religion or theology or for religious worship or for any religious activity at any time in the future." Regulation 01.03.06A.

B

If the foregoing answer to the "primary effect" question seems easy, it serves to make the "excessive entanglement" problem more difficult. The statute itself clearly denies the use of public funds for "sectarian purposes." It seeks to avert such use, however, through a process of annual interchange proposal and approval, expenditure and review between the colleges and the Council. In answering the question whether this will be an "excessively entangling" relationship, we must consider the several relevant factors identified in prior decisions:

(1) First is the character of the aided institutions. This has been fully described above. As the District Court found, the colleges perform "essentially secular educational functions," that are distinct and separable from religious activity. This finding, which is a prerequisite under the "pervasive sectarianism" test to any state aid at all, is also important for purposes of the entanglement test because it means that secular activities, for the most part, can be taken at face value. There is no danger, or at least only a substantially reduced danger, that an ostensibly secular activity—the study of biology, the learning of a foreign language, an athletic event—will actually be infused with religious content or significance. The need for close surveillance of purportedly secular activities is correspondingly reduced. . . .

(2) As for the form of aid, we have already noted that no particular use of state funds is before us in this case. The process by which aid is disbursed, and a use for it chosen, is before us. We address this as a matter of the "resulting relationship" of secular and religious authority.

(3) As noted, the funding process is an annual one. The subsidies are paid out each year, and they can be put to annually varying uses. The colleges propose particular uses for the Council's approval, and, following expenditure, they report to the Council on the use to which the funds have been put. . . .

We agree with the District Court that "excessive entanglement" does not necessarily result from the fact that the subsidy is an annual one. It is true that the Court favored the "one-time, single-purpose" construction grants in *Tilton* because they entailed "no continuing financial relationships or dependencies, no annual audits, and no government analysis of an institution's expenditures." The present aid program cannot claim these aspects. But if the question is whether this case is more like *Lemon I* or more like *Tilton*—and surely that is the fundamental question before us—the answer must be that it is more like *Tilton*.

*Tilton* is distinguishable only by the form of aid. We cannot discount the distinction entirely, but neither can we regard it as decisive. As the District Court pointed out, ongoing, annual supervision of college facilities was explicitly foreseen in *Tilton*, 403 U.S., 675 and even more so in *Hunt*, 413 U.S., 739-40, 745-49. *Tilton* and *Hunt* would be totally indistinguishable, at least in terms of annual supervision, if funds were used under the present statute to build or maintain physical facilities devoted to secular use. The present statute contemplates annual decisions by the Council as to what is a "sectarian purpose," but, as we have noted, the secular and sectarian activities of the colleges are easily separated. Occasional audits . . . and the other contacts between the Council and the colleges are not likely to be any more entangling than the inspections and audits incident to the normal process of the colleges' accreditations by the State.

While the form-of-aid distinctions of *Tilton* are thus of questionable importance, the character-of-institution distinctions of *Lemon I* are most impressive. . . .

(4) As for political divisiveness, the District Court recognized that the annual nature of the subsidy, along with its promise of an increasing demand for state funds as the colleges' dependency grew, aggravated the danger of "(p)olitical fragmentation . . . on religious lines." Nonetheless, the District Court found that the program "does not create a substantial danger of political entanglement." Several reasons were given. As was stated in *Tilton*, the danger of political divisiveness is "substantially less" when the aided institution is not an elementary or secondary school, but a college, "whose student constituency is not local but diverse and widely dispersed." Furthermore, political divisiveness is diminished by the fact that the aid is extended to private colleges generally, more than two thirds of which have no religious affiliation; this is in sharp contrast to *Nyquist*, for example, where 95% of the aided schools were Roman Catholic parochial schools. Finally, the substantial autonomy of the colleges was thought to mitigate political divisiveness, in that controversies surrounding the aid program are not likely to involve the Catholic Church itself, or even the religious character of the schools, but only their "fiscal responsibility and educational requirements." . . .

There is no exact science in gauging the entanglement of church and state. The wording of the test, which speaks of "excessive entanglement," itself makes that clear. The relevant factors we have identified are to be considered "cumulatively" in judging the degree of entanglement. They may cut different ways, as certainly they do here. In reaching the conclusion that it did, the District Court gave dominant importance to the character of the aided institutions and to its finding that they are capable of separating secular and religious functions. For the reasons stated above, we cannot say that the emphasis was misplaced or the finding erroneous. The judgment of the District Court is

*Affirmed.*

◫ MR. JUSTICE WHITE, with whom MR. JUSTICE REHNQUIST joins, concurring in the judgment.

While I join in the judgment of the Court, I am unable to concur in the plurality opinion. . . .

"It is enough for me that the (State is) financing a separable secular function of overriding importance in order to sustain the legislation here challenged." *Lemon I,* 403 U.S., 664 (opinion of WHITE, J.). As long as there is a secular legislative purpose, and as long as the primary effect of the legislation is neither to advance nor inhibit religion, I see no reason—particularly in light of the "sparse language of the Establishment Clause," *Committee for Public Education v. Nyquist,* 413 U.S., 820—to take the constitutional inquiry further. . . . It is not clear that the "weight and contours of entanglement as a separate constitutional criterion," *Nyquist,* 413 U.S., 822, are any more settled now than when they first surfaced. Today's plurality opinion leaves the impression that the criterion really may not be "separate" at all. . . . It is unclear to me how the first and third parts of the *Lemon I* test are substantially different. The "excessive entanglement" test appears no less "curious and mystifying" than when it was first announced. *Lemon I,* 403 U.S., 666. . . .

▓ MR. JUSTICE BRENNAN, with whom MR. JUSTICE MARSHALL joins, dissenting. . . .

[T]he Act provides for payment of general subsidies to religious institutions from public funds and I have heretofore expressed my view that "(g)eneral subsidies of religious activities would, of course, constitute impermissible state involvement with religion." *Walz v. Tax Comm'n,* 397 U.S. 664, 690 (1970) (concurring opinion). This is because general subsidies "tend to promote that type of interdependence between religion and state which the First Amendment was designed to prevent." *Abington School Dist. v. Schempp,* 374 U.S. 203, 236 (1963) (BRENNAN, J., concurring). "What the Framers meant to foreclose, and what our decisions under the Establishment Clause have forbidden, are those involvements of religious with secular institutions which . . . serve the essentially religious activities of religious institutions." *Id.,* 294-295. . . .

The discrete interests of government and religion are mutually best served when each avoids too close a proximity to the other. "It is not only the nonbeliever who fears the injection of sectarian doctrines and controversies into the civil polity, but in as high degree it is the devout believer who fears the secularization of a creed which becomes too deeply involved with and dependent upon the government." *Abington School Dist.,* 374 U.S., 259 (BRENNAN, J., concurring). The Maryland Act requires "too close a proximity" of government to the subsidized sectarian institutions and in my view creates real dangers of the "secularization of a creed." *Ibid.* . . .

▓ MR. JUSTICE STEVENS, dissenting.

My views are substantially those expressed by Mr. JUSTICE BRENNAN. However, I would add emphasis to the pernicious tendency of a state subsidy to tempt religious schools to compromise their religious mission without wholly abandoning it. The disease of entanglement may infect a law discouraging wholesome religious activity as well as a law encouraging the propagation of a given faith.

---

### NOTES AND QUESTIONS

1. How does the Court distinguish religious parochial schools and church-related colleges for the purpose of receiving government financial aid? Based on your own experience and/or observations, do these distinctions make sense?

2. Are there any differences in the facts of the three college cases (e.g., type of aid; manner of distribution and its application; degree of government supervision) that suggest a progression in the Court's thinking? In essence, after *Roemer,* how would you characterize the Court's rule with respect to aiding church-related colleges? Is it the same rule you would have devised based solely on *Tilton?*

3. Does the Court establish two different presumptions in its parochial school and college aid cases—that all parochial schools will be presumed to be pervasively sectarian in character whereas church-related colleges will have the opposite presumption, absent evidence to the contrary? If so, how many of the

criteria of sectarianism must a college have in order to be disqualified from receiving financial aid? Does the Court indicate whether any of the criteria are more compelling than others?

4. Problem: *Columbia Union College v. Clarke*.

Consider the same program that was in issue in *Roemer*.

To qualify for aid under the Maryland program (ironically, now named the Sellinger Program, after a Maryland Catholic educator), an institution must: (1) be a nonprofit private college or university established in Maryland before July 1, 1970; (2) be approved by the Commission; (3) be accredited; (4) have awarded associate of arts or baccalaureate degrees to at least one graduating class; (5) maintain one or more degreed programs in subjects other than the seminarian or theological programs; and (6) demonstrate that no Sellinger funds will be used for "sectarian purposes" including "religious instruction, religious worship, or other activities of a religious nature."

Columbia Union College is a private four-year college affiliated with the Seventh-day Adventist Church that otherwise meets the first five eligibility criteria. However, at the time of litigation, Columbia Union College: receives 21.5% of its funding from the Seventh-day Adventist Church; requires that 34 of 38 members of the Board of Trustees be members of the Seventh-day Adventist Church; requires once-weekly mandatory prayer services for resident students and three out of six smaller meetings for these same students in their dormitories (although commuter students are not so required); and, 36 of 40 full-time faculty are Seventh-day Adventists and the faculty handbook directs faculty to "bear in mind their peculiar obligation as Christian scholars and members of a Seventh-day Adventist College" and notes that they have "complete freedom so long as their speech and actions are in harmony with the philosophies and principles of the college—a Seventh-day Adventist institution of higher education." Finally, the district court found that while the college offers a wide variety of traditional liberal arts courses (e.g., biology, chemistry, physics, nursing, history, philosophy, psychology), several "nominally secular academic departments are replete with references to secular religion."

Applying the *Hunt-Roemer* factors, is Columbia Union College pervasively sectarian and thus ineligible for undesignated financial aid? How does Columbia Union College compare to the colleges in issue in *Roemer*? See Columbia Union College v. Clarke, 159 F.3d 151 (4th Cir. 1998) (ruling that the above facts could lead a reasonable fact-finder to conclude either way on whether the college was pervasively sectarian, and remanding the case to the trial court). One judge argued in dissent that courts should abandon the pervasively sectarian designation, as it invites judges to scrutinize an institution's religious character and may encourage those institutions "to disown their own religious character in order to gain funding." Id., 175 (Wilkinson, J., dissenting). Are these valid concerns? If so, how should courts approach these issues?

Now consider the above facts in light of the Supreme Court's holdings in *Agostini* and *Mitchell*. Does the Court still adhere to the pervasively sectarian formula after those cases, and even if it does, would Columbia Union be barred from receiving state aid? For the case on appeal after remand, see *Columbia Union College v. Oliver*, 254 F.3d 496 (4th Cir. 2001) (affirming the district court finding that the college was not pervasively sectarian).

## CHAPTER 14

# RELIGIOUS ORGANIZATIONS AND GOVERNMENT-FUNDED SOCIAL SERVICES

For the first forty years of modern Establishment Clause jurisprudence involving government funding of religion, the cases revolved around funding programs that aided religious and parochial schools. This should be expected. As discussed in chapter 13, the controversy over government funding of religious schools reaches back to the early years of the nineteenth century. Also, the funding of children's education represents one of the larger expenditures—and more important functions—of the states (and increasingly, of the federal government). Therefore, it is not surprising that the majority of the Supreme Court's decisions interpreting the Establishment Clause limitations on government funding of religion would arise within the education context.

Issues of government funding of religious activity have arisen in another important context: government grants to religiously affiliated charities to provide human services to the sick and needy. For example, a significant percentage of nongovernmental hospitals in this country are owned by or affiliated with religious denominations. The same could be said for many of the nation's orphanages, nursing homes, and retirement centers. The vast majority of these institutions receive various forms of financial aid from federal, state, and local governments: Medicare; Medicaid; research and construction grants and government-insured bonds. Such funding programs have been common for a long time, and they usually have been relatively noncontroversial.

Notwithstanding this longstanding practice, the government funding of religiously affiliated charities raises Establishment Clause issues. On one level, funding of religiously affiliated social service institutions may present constitutional issues similar to those that occur with the funding of parochial and religious schools: e.g., are the government funds being spent on worship, proselytizing, or other religious activities or are they paying for identifiably secular functions and services; are the institutions able to separate their religious functions from their secular functions; does government regulation and oversight designed to ensure accountability result in excessive government entanglement with the religious operations of the institutions? On a different level, other aspects of these funding programs may implicate fewer Establishment Clause concerns than cases that involve government funding and religious elementary and secondary schools. These aspects include the fact that religiously based charities serve predominately older and less impressionable populations than exist in school settings, that the services are frequently more discrete and less comprehensive than curriculum programs, and that religious instruction or indoctrination has often not been a primary function of services to the poor and infirm.

However, with the passage of "Charitable Choice" legislation in the late 1990s and the advent of the "Faith-Based Initiative" under the second President Bush—both of which advocate the funding of more spiritually integrated human service activities—issues of government funding of religious social service programs became more controversial. (For further discussion of "Charitable Choice" and the "Faith-based Initiative," see the middle part of this chapter.)

A little background may be helpful. Religious groups and agencies have long been active players in the social welfare system—at times and in many locales, they were the only providers of social services. Religious charity work predates many government welfare programs. For over 150 years, denominational entities have run orphanages and homes for the aged and provided adoption services, foodstuffs, clothing, housing, job assistance and counseling, often in the absence of government programs.[1] Although cities and towns also provided "poor relief" throughout the eighteenth and nineteenth centuries, religious organizations were the primary sources of charitable services well into the twentieth century. Even with the increased involvement of the government in social welfare as a result of New Deal programs in the 1930s and Great Society innovations of the 1960s, religious organizations remained active participants in the social service network. For example, in 1995 the Salvation Army served over 27 million people; Catholic Charities served 11 million. This does not count thousands of social service programs run by local agencies and congregations.[2]

Moreover, many religiously affiliated agencies such as Catholic Charities, Lutheran Social Services and the Salvation Army have long received government referrals and even government funding for their programs. As far back as 1803, the Senate approved a treaty with the Kaskaskia Indians that included a grant of one hundred dollars a year for the support of a Catholic mission to the tribe, as well as three hundred dollars for the construction of a Catholic church. Fast forwarding to 1996, the year Charitable Choice was first enacted, Catholic Charities USA received 1.3 billion in public dollars for its programming, accounting for 62 percent of its overall budget.[3] Catholic Charities has long been the largest nongovernmental social service agency in the nation and receives more government funding of any other nongovernmental nonprofit entity. Though accounting for lesser percentages of their budgets, the Salvation Army, Lutheran, and Jewish social services have all received hundreds of millions in government funds for their programs.[4] All of this indicates that religiously affiliated charities have long been active participants in providing social services to the sick and needy and have frequently partnered with the federal, state, and local governments through their offerings. Usually, the constitutional issue has not been whether religiously affiliated charities can distribute or receive government funds for their social service programs, but under what conditions and for what type of activities.

One of the first cases to consider this issue was also one of the earlier Establishment Clause cases decided by the U.S. Supreme Court. In 1897, Congress enacted an appropriation bill for the District of Columbia that authorized the District commissioners to contract with a local hospital to construct a building that would provide medical services for indigent residents of the city. Under the contract, the federal government would also reimburse the hospital for the medical care and treatment of those indigent persons served. The commissioners subsequently entered into a contract with a Catholic-owned hospital, Providence Hospital, which provided funds for the construction of the building and provision of medical services. A local taxpayer objected to the contract with the Catholic hospital and brought an Establishment Clause challenge in federal court. The district court enjoined the contract, but that decision was reversed by the Court of Appeals. The taxpayer then appealed to the Supreme Court, giving that body the opportunity to opine on its understanding of the Establishment Clause limits to government funding of a religiously affiliated institution.

---

## BRADFIELD v. ROBERTS
### 175 U.S. 291 (1899)

The plaintiff-appellant sued the District of Columbia and the Treasurer of the United States (Roberts) to block an agreement under which the federal government would provide funding for the construction of building for Providence Hospital, a Catholic-owned hospital in the District of Columbia. Under the agreement, "two thirds of the entire capacity of said isolating building or ward shall be reserved for the use of such poor patients as shall be sent there by the commissioners of the District from time to time through the proper officers." The District would reimburse the Hospital $250 per annum for each patient referred. The complaint charged that Providence Hospital was owned and operated by a "sisterhood of the Roman Catholic Church, and is conducted under the auspices of said church; that the title to its property is vested in the 'Sisters of Charity of Emmitsburg, Maryland.'"

▨ MR. JUSTICE PECKHAM, after stating the facts, delivered the opinion of the court: . . .

The act shows that the individuals named therein and their successors in office were incorporated under the name of "The Directors of Providence Hospital," with power to receive, hold, and convey personal and real property. . . . Nothing is said about religion or about the religious faith of the incorporators of this institution in the act of incorporation. It is simply the ordinary case of the incorporation of a hospital for the purposes for which such an institution is generally conducted. It is claimed that the allegation in the complainant's bill, that the said "Providence Hospital is a private eleemosynary corporation, and that to the best of complainant's knowledge and belief it is composed of members of a monastic order or sisterhood of the Roman Catholic Church, and is conducted under the auspices of said church; that the title to its property is vested in the Sisters of Charity of Emmitsburg, Maryland," renders the agreement void for the reason therein stated, which is that Congress has no power to make "a law respecting a religious establishment," a phrase which is not synonymous with that used in the Constitution, which prohibits the passage of a law "respecting an establishment of religion." . . .

[W]e are unable to see that the complainant in his bill shows that the corporation is of the kind described, but on the contrary he has clearly shown that it is not.

The above-mentioned allegations in the complainant's bill do not change the legal character of the corporation or render it on that account a religious or sectarian body. Assuming that the hospital is a private eleemosynary corporation, the fact that its members, according to the belief of the complainant, are members of a monastic order or sisterhood of the Roman Catholic Church, and the further fact that the hospital is conducted under the auspices of said church, are wholly immaterial. . . . The facts above stated do not in the least change the legal character of the hospital, or make a religious corporation out of a purely secular one as constituted by the law of its being. Whether the individuals who compose the corporation under its charter happen to be all Roman Catholics, or all Methodists, or Presbyterians, or Unitarians, or members of any other religious organization, or of no organization at all, is of not the slightest consequence with reference to the law of its incorporation, nor can the individual beliefs upon religious matters of the various incorporators be inquired into. Nor is it material that the hospital may be conducted under the auspices of the Roman Catholic Church. To be conducted under the auspices is to be conducted under the influence or patronage of that church. The meaning of the allegation is that the church exercises great and perhaps controlling influence over the management of the hospital. It must, however, be managed pursuant to the law of its being. That the influence of any particular church may be powerful over the members of a nonsectarian and secular corporation, incorporated for a certain defined purpose and with clearly stated powers, is surely not sufficient to convert such a corporation into a religious or sectarian body. . . . There is no allegation that its hospital work is confined to members of that church or that in its management the hospital has been conducted so as to violate its charter in the smallest degree. It is simply the case of a secular corporation being managed by people who hold to the doctrines of the Roman Catholic Church, but who nevertheless are managing the corporation according to the law under which it exists. . . .

The act of Congress . . . shows there is nothing sectarian in the corporation, and 'the specific and limited object of its creation' is the opening and keeping a hospital in the city of Washington for the care of such sick and invalid persons as may place themselves under the treatment and care of the corporation. To make the agreement was within the discretion of the commissioners, and was a fair exercise thereof. . . .

*Affirmed.*

---

The *Bradfield* Court appeared to equate the purpose and operations of the Catholic hospital with that of its secular counterparts, writing that its legal designation did nothing to turn it into a religious entity. By deemphasizing the possible religious characteristics of the hospital and focusing on its secular functions, the Court established precedent authorizing government funding of the secular operations of religious organizations. To a degree, *Bradfield* constitutionalized the dominant practice within the social service community where the government would pay for services that had a secular quality (e.g., food, clothing, shelter, medical care, job training). In order to receive such assistance, religious charities would usually separate government-funded services from any religious or worship activities. All observers agreed that the religious organizations were motivated by their faith and acknowledged that government-funded services were sometimes accompanied by a religious component (e.g., a prayer preceding a meal). But the general understanding of the law was that the government could not fund those programs of religious organizations that integrated religious instruction or worship activities.

That this model worked within the religious social service community is evinced by the near absence of litigation for eighty years. However, this model was put to the test in a lawsuit that arose in the 1980s. With support from a Reagan Administration that was sympathetic to religious groups that were politically conservative, Congress enacted the Adolescent Family Life Act that provided federal grants to nongovernmental agencies, including religious organizations, to provide counseling and related services aimed at reducing teenage sexual activity and pregnancy. The law also prohibited any funding of programs that counseled in favor of or offered abortion-related services. Finally, the law expressly sought out grantees that offered integrated approaches to teenage sexuality and pregnancy that involved families, religious and charitable organizations, and other community and voluntary associations. Several religiously affiliated organizations received grant monies to pay for counseling and education programs that integrated religious values into their services. Opponents of the Act charged that the law violated the Establishment Clause both as written and as administered by the religious groups. Thus the courts had to decide four issues: whether the Act had the dominant purpose or effect of advancing religion; whether religious groups generally could participate as grant recipients; whether religious groups whose services were "pervasively sectarian" in character could receive federal grants; and whether the government funds could be spent on identifiable religious activities. Although the Court appeared to say "yes" to the first two issues and "no" to the second two, see if you can identify any differences in the Court's articulation and application of the legal standard from its school-funding decisions.

---

## BOWEN v. KENDRICK
### 487 U.S. 589 (1988)

CHIEF JUSTICE REHNQUIST delivered the opinion of the Court.

This litigation involves a challenge to a federal grant program that provides funding for services relating to adolescent sexuality and pregnancy. Considering the federal statute both "on its face" and "as applied," the District Court ruled that the statute violated the Establishment Clause of the First Amendment insofar as it provided for the involvement of religious organizations in the federally funded programs. We conclude, however, that the statute is not unconstitutional on its face, and that a determination of whether any of the grants made pursuant to the statute violate the Establishment Clause requires further proceedings in the District Court.

I

The Adolescent Family Life Act (AFLA or Act), 95 Stat. 578, *et seq.*, 42 U.S.C. § 300z (1982 ed. and Supp. IV), was passed by Congress in 1981 in response to the "severe adverse health, social, and economic consequences" that often follow pregnancy and childbirth among unmarried adolescents. . . . AFLA is essentially a scheme for providing grants to public or nonprofit private organizations or agencies "for services and research in the area of premarital adolescent sexual relations and pregnancy." S. Rep. No. 97-161, p. 1

(1981) (hereinafter Senate Report). These grants are intended to serve several purposes, including the promotion of "self discipline and other prudent approaches to the problem of adolescent premarital sexual relations," § 300z(b)(1), the promotion of adoption as an alternative for adolescent parents, the establishment of new approaches to the delivery of care services for pregnant adolescents, and the support of research and demonstration projects "concerning the societal causes and consequences of adolescent premarital sexual relations, contraceptive use, pregnancy, and child rearing," § 300z(b)(1-4). . . .

While the AFLA leaves it up to the Secretary of Health and Human Services (the Secretary) to define exactly what types of services a grantee must provide, see §§ 300z-1(a)(7), (8), 300z-1(b), the statute contains a listing of "necessary services" that may be funded. These services include pregnancy testing and maternity counseling, adoption counseling and referral services, prenatal and postnatal health care, nutritional information, counseling, child care, mental health services, and perhaps most importantly for present purposes, "educational services relating to family life and problems associated with adolescent premarital sexual relations," § 300z-1(a)(4).

> In drawing up the AFLA and determining what services to provide under the Act, . . . Congress expressly recognized that legislative or governmental action alone would be insufficient: "[S]uch problems are best approached through a variety of integrated and essential services provided to adolescents and their families by other family members, religious and charitable organizations, voluntary associations, and other groups in the private sector as well as services provided by publicly sponsored initiatives." § 300z(a)(8)(B). . . .

The AFLA implements this goal by providing in § 300z-2 that demonstration projects funded by the government "shall use such methods as will strengthen the capacity of families to deal with the sexual behavior, pregnancy, or parenthood of adolescents and to make use of support systems such as other family members, friends, religious and charitable organizations, and voluntary associations." . . .

This broad-based involvement of groups outside of the government was intended by Congress to "establish better coordination, integration, and linkages" among existing programs in the community, § 300z(b)(3) (1982 ed., Supp.IV), to aid in the development of "strong family values and close family ties," § 300z(a)(10)(A), and to "help adolescents and their families deal with complex issues of adolescent premarital sexual relations and the consequences of such relations." § 300z(a)(10)(C).

In line with its purposes, the AFLA also imposes limitations on the use of funds by grantees. . . . Second, the AFLA restricts the awarding of grants to "programs or projects which do not provide abortions or abortion counseling or referral," except that the program may provide referral for abortion counseling if the adolescent and her parents request such referral. § 300z-10(a). Finally, the AFLA states that "grants may be made only to projects or programs which do not advocate, promote, or encourage abortion." § 300z-10(a). . . .

Funding has gone to a wide variety of recipients, including state and local health agencies, private hospitals, community health associations, privately operated health care centers, and community and charitable organizations. It is undisputed that a number of grantees or subgrantees were organizations with institutional ties to religious denominations. . . .

The [district] court concluded that the AFLA has a valid secular purpose: the prevention of social and economic injury caused by teenage pregnancy and premarital sexual relations. In the court's view, however, the AFLA does not survive the second prong of the *Lemon* test because it has the "direct and immediate" effect of advancing religion insofar as it expressly requires grant applicants to describe how they will involve religious organizations in the provision of services. § 300z-5(a)(21)(B). The statute also permits religious organizations to be grantees and "envisions a direct role for those organizations in the education and counseling components of AFLA grants." 657 F. Supp., 1562. As written, the AFLA makes it possible for religiously affiliated grantees to teach adolescents on issues that can be considered "fundamental elements of religious doctrine." The AFLA does all this without imposing any restriction whatsoever against the teaching of "religion *qua* religion" or the inculcation of religious beliefs in federally funded programs. As the District Court put it, "[t]o presume that AFLA counselors from religious organizations can put their beliefs aside when counseling an adolescent on matters that are part of religious doctrine is simply unrealistic." *Id.*, 1563 (citing *Grand Rapids School District v. Ball*, 473 U.S. 373 (1985)). . . .

In the District Court's view, the record clearly established that the AFLA, as it has been administered by the Secretary, has in fact directly advanced religion, provided funding for institutions that were "pervasively sectarian," or allowed federal funds to be used for education and counseling that "amounts to the teaching of religion." *Ibid.* As to the entanglement prong of *Lemon,* the court ruled that because AFLA funds are used largely for counseling and teaching, it would require overly intrusive monitoring or oversight to ensure that religion is not advanced by religiously affiliated AFLA grantees. Indeed, the court felt that "it is impossible to comprehend entanglement more extensive and continuous than that necessitated by the AFLA." 657 F. Supp., 1568. . . .

## II

The District Court in this lawsuit held the AFLA unconstitutional both on its face and as applied. Few of our cases in the Establishment Clause area have explicitly distinguished between facial challenges to a statute and attacks on the statute as applied. Several cases have clearly involved challenges to a statute "on its face." For example, in *Edwards v. Aguillard*, 482 U.S. 578 (1987), we considered the validity of the Louisiana "Creationism Act," finding the Act "facially invalid." Indeed, in that case it was clear that only a facial challenge could have been considered, as the Act had not been implemented. . . .

In other cases we have, in the course of determining the constitutionality of a statute, referred not only to the language of the statute but also to the manner in which it had been administered in practice. . . . In several cases we have expressly recognized that an otherwise valid statute authorizing grants might be challenged on the grounds that the award of a grant in a particular case would be impermissible. . . .

There is, then, precedent in this area of constitutional law for distinguishing between the validity of the statute on its face and its validity in particular applications. . . .

This said, we turn to consider whether the District Court was correct in concluding that the AFLA was unconstitutional on its face. As in previous cases involving facial challenges on Establishment Clause grounds, e.g., *Edwards v. Aguillard; Mueller v. Allen*, 463 U.S 388 (1983), we assess the constitutionality of an enactment by reference to the three factors first articulated in *Lemon v. Kurtzman*, 403 U.S. 602 (1971). Under the *Lemon* standard, which guides "[t] he general nature of our inquiry in this area," *Mueller v. Allen*, 463 U.S., 394, a court may invalidate a statute only if it is motivated wholly by an impermissible purpose, if its primary effect is the advancement of religion, or if it requires excessive entanglement between church and state. We consider each of these factors in turn.

As we see it, it is clear from the face of the statute that the AFLA was motivated primarily, if not entirely, by a legitimate secular purpose—the elimination or reduction of social and economic problems caused by teenage sexuality, pregnancy, and parenthood. Appellees cannot, and do not, dispute that, on the whole, religious concerns were not the sole motivation behind the Act. . . . In the court below, however, appellees argued that the *real* purpose of the AFLA could only be understood in reference to the AFLA's predecessor, Title VI. Appellees contended that Congress had an impermissible purpose in adopting the AFLA because it specifically amended Title VI to increase the role of religious organizations in the programs sponsored by the Act. In particular, they pointed to the fact that the AFLA, unlike Title VI, requires grant applicants to describe how they will involve religious organizations in the programs funded by the AFLA. § 300z-5(a)(21)(B).

The District Court rejected this argument, however, reasoning that even if it is assumed that the AFLA was motivated in part by improper concerns, the parts of the statute to which appellees object were also motivated by other, entirely legitimate secular concerns. We agree with this conclusion. As the District Court correctly pointed out, Congress amended Title VI in a number of ways, most importantly for present purposes by attempting to enlist the aid of not only "religious organizations," but also "family members, . . . charitable organizations, voluntary associations, and other groups in the private sector," in addressing the problems associated with adolescent sexuality. § 300z(a)(8)(B); see also §§ 300z-5(a)(21)(A), (B). Cf. Title VI, § 601(a)(5) ("[T]he problems of adolescent [sexuality] . . . are best approached through a variety of integrated and essential services"). Congress' decision to amend the statute in this way reflects the entirely appropriate aim of increasing broad-based community involvement "in helping adolescent boys and girls understand the implications of premarital sexual relations, pregnancy, and parenthood." See Senate Report, at 2, 15-16. In adopting the AFLA, Congress expressly intended to expand the services already authorized by Title VI, to insure the increased participation of parents in education and support services, to increase the flexibility of the programs, and to spark the development of new, innovative services. *Id.,* 7-9. These are all legitimate secular goals that are furthered by the AFLA's additions to Title VI, including the challenged provisions that refer to religious organizations. There simply is no evidence that Congress' "actual purpose" in passing the AFLA was one of "endorsing religion." . . .

As usual in Establishment Clause cases, the more difficult question is whether the primary effect of the challenged statute is impermissible. Before we address this question, however, it is useful to review again just what the AFLA sets out to do. Simply stated, it authorizes grants to institutions that are capable of providing certain care and prevention services to adolescents. Because of the complexity of the problems that Congress sought to remedy, potential grantees are required to describe how they will involve other organizations, including religious organizations, in the programs funded by the federal grants. There is no requirement in the Act that grantees be affiliated with any religious denomination, although the Act clearly does not rule out grants to religious organizations. The services to be provided under the AFLA are not religious in character, nor has there been any suggestion that religious institutions or organizations with religious ties are uniquely well qualified to carry out those services. Certainly it is true that a substantial part of the services listed as "necessary services" under the Act involve some sort of education or counseling, but there is nothing inherently religious about these activities and appellees do not contend that, by themselves, the AFLA's "necessary services" somehow have the primary effect of advancing religion. Finally, it is clear that the AFLA takes a particular approach toward dealing with adolescent sexuality and pregnancy—for example, two of its stated purposes are to "promote self discipline and other prudent approaches to the problem of adolescent premarital sexual relations," § 300z(b)(1), and to "promote adoption as an alternative," 300z(b)(2)—but again, that approach is not inherently religious, although it may coincide with the approach taken by certain religions.

Given this statutory framework, there are two ways in which the statute, considered "on its face," might be said to have the impermissible primary effect of advancing religion. First, it can be argued that the AFLA advances religion by expressly recognizing that "religious organizations have a role to play" in addressing the problems associated with teenage sexuality. In this view, even if no religious institution receives aid or funding pursuant to the AFLA, the statute is invalid under the Establishment Clause because, among other things, it expressly enlists the involvement of religiously affiliated organizations in the federally subsidized programs, it endorses religious solutions to the problems addressed by the Act, or it creates symbolic ties between church and state. Secondly, it can be argued that the AFLA is invalid on its face because it allows religiously affiliated organizations to participate as grantees or subgrantees in AFLA programs. From this standpoint, the Act is invalid because it authorizes direct federal funding of religious organizations which, given the AFLA's educational function and the fact that the AFLA's "viewpoint" may coincide with the grantee's "viewpoint" on sexual matters, will result unavoidably in the impermissible "inculcation" of religious beliefs in the context of a federally funded program.

We consider the former objection first. . . .

Putting aside for the moment the possible role of religious organizations as grantees, these provisions of the statute reflect at most Congress' considered judgment that religious organizations can help solve the problems to which the AFLA is addressed. Nothing in our previous cases prevents Congress from making such a judgment or from recognizing the important part that religion or religious organizations may play in resolving certain secular problems. Particularly when, as Congress found, "prevention of adolescent sexual activity and adolescent pregnancy depends primarily upon developing strong family values and close family ties," § 300z(a)(10)(A), it seems quite sensible for Congress to recognize that religious organizations can influence values and can have some influence on family life, including parents' relations with their adolescent children. To the extent that this congressional recognition has any effect of advancing religion, the effect is at most "incidental and remote." In addition, although the AFLA does require potential grantees to describe how they will involve religious organizations in the provision of services under the Act, it also requires grantees to describe the involvement of "charitable organizations, voluntary associations, and other groups in the private sector," § 300z-5(a)(21)(B). In our view, this reflects the statute's successful mainte-nance of "a course of neutrality among religions, and between religion and non-religion," *Grand Rapids School District v. Ball*, 473 U.S., 382.

This brings us to the second ground for objecting to the AFLA: the fact that it allows religious institutions to participate as recipients of federal funds. The AFLA defines an "eligible grant recipient" as a "public or nonprofit private or-ganization or agency" which demonstrates the capability of providing the req-uisite services. § 300z-1(a)(3). As this provision would indicate, a fairly wide spectrum of organizations is eligible to apply for and receive funding under the Act, and nothing on the face of the Act suggests it is anything but neutral with respect to the grantee's status as a sectarian or purely secular institution. See Senate Report, 16 ("Religious affiliation is not a criterion for selection as a grantee . . ."). In this regard, then, the AFLA is similar to other statutes that this Court has upheld against Establishment Clause challenges in the past. In *Roemer v. Maryland Board of Public Works*, 426 U.S. 736 (1976), for example, we upheld a Maryland statute that provided annual subsidies directly to qualifying colleges and universities in the State, including religiously affiliated institu-tions. As the plurality stated, "religious institutions need not be quarantined from public benefits that are neutrally available to all." . . . In other cases in-volving indirect grants of state aid to religious institutions, we have found it important that the aid is made available regardless of whether it will ultimately flow to a secular or sectarian institution. *Witters v. Washington Dept. of Services for Blind*, 474 U.S. 481, 487 (1986); *Mueller v. Allen*, 463 U.S., 398; *Everson v. Board of Education*, 330 U.S., 17-18; *Walz v. Tax Comm'n*, 397 U.S., 676.

We note in addition that this Court has never held that religious insti-tutions are disabled by the First Amendment from participating in publicly sponsored social welfare programs. To the contrary, in *Bradfield v. Roberts*, 175 U.S. 291 (1899), the Court upheld an agreement between the Commission-ers of the District of Columbia and a religiously affiliated hospital whereby the Federal Government would pay for the construction of a new building on the grounds of the hospital. In effect, the Court refused to hold that the mere fact that the hospital was "conducted under the auspices of the Roman Catholic Church" was sufficient to alter the purely secular legal character of the corporation, *id.*, 298, particularly in the absence of any allegation that the hospital discriminated on the basis of religion or operated in any way inconsis-tent with its secular charter. In the Court's view, the giving of federal aid to the hospital was entirely consistent with the Establishment Clause, and the fact that the hospital was religiously affiliated was "wholly immaterial." *Ibid.* . . .

Of course, even when the challenged statute appears to be neutral on its face, we have always been careful to ensure that direct government aid to re-ligiously affiliated institutions does not have the primary effect of advancing religion. One way in which direct government aid might have that effect is if the aid flows to institutions that are "pervasively sectarian." We stated in *Hunt* that "[a]id normally may be thought to have a primary effect of advancing religion when it flows to an institution in which religion is so pervasive that a substantial portion of its functions are subsumed in the religious mission. . . ." 413 U.S., 743.

The reason for this is that there is a risk that direct government fund-ing, even if it is designated for specific secular purposes, may nonetheless advance the pervasively sectarian institution's "religious mission." See *Grand*

*Rapids School District v. Ball*, 473 U.S., 385 (discussing how aid to religious schools may impermissibly advance religion). Accordingly, a relevant factor in deciding whether a particular statute on its face can be said to have the improper effect of advancing religion is the determination of whether, and to what extent, the statute directs government aid to pervasively sectarian institutions. In *Grand Rapids School District,* for example, the Court began its "effects" inquiry with "a consideration of the nature of the institutions in which the [challenged] programs operate." *Id.*, 384.

In this lawsuit, nothing on the face of the AFLA indicates that a significant proportion of the federal funds will be disbursed to "pervasively sectarian" institutions. Indeed, the contention that there is a substantial risk of such institutions receiving direct aid is undercut by the AFLA's facially neutral grant requirements, the wide spectrum of public and private organizations which are capable of meeting the AFLA's requirements, and the fact that, of the eligible religious institutions, many will not deserve the label of "pervasively sectarian." This is not a case like *Grand Rapids,* where the challenged aid flowed almost entirely to parochial schools. . . . Instead, this litigation more closely resembles *Tilton* and *Roemer,* where it was foreseeable that some proportion of the recipients of government aid would be religiously affiliated, but that only a small portion of these, if any, could be considered "pervasively sectarian." In those cases we upheld the challenged statutes on their face and as applied to the institutions named in the complaints, but left open the consequences which would ensue if they allowed federal aid to go to institutions that were in fact pervasively sectarian. *Tilton,* 403 U.S., 682; *Roemer,* 426 U.S., 760. As in *Tilton* and *Roemer,* we do not think the possibility that AFLA grants may go to religious institutions that can be considered "pervasively sectarian" is sufficient to conclude that no grants whatsoever can be given under the statute to religious organizations. . . .

Nor do we agree with the District Court that the AFLA necessarily has the effect of advancing religion because the religiously affiliated AFLA grantees will be providing educational and counseling services to adolescents. Of course, we have said that the Establishment Clause does "prohibit government-financed or government-sponsored indoctrination into the beliefs of a particular religious faith," *Grand Rapids,* 473 U.S., 385, and we have accordingly struck down programs that entail an unacceptable risk that government funding would be used to "advance the religious mission" of the religious institution receiving aid. See, e.g., *Meek,* 421 U.S., 370. But nothing in our prior cases warrants the presumption adopted by the District Court that religiously affiliated AFLA grantees are not capable of carrying out their functions under the AFLA in a lawful, secular manner. Only in the context of aid to "pervasively sectarian" institutions have we invalidated an aid program on the grounds that there was a "substantial" risk that aid to these religious institutions would, knowingly or unknowingly, result in religious indoctrination. In contrast, when the aid is to flow to religiously affiliated institutions that were not pervasively sectarian, as in *Roemer,* we refused to presume that it would be used in a way that would have the primary effect of advancing religion. . . .

We also disagree with the District Court's conclusion that the AFLA is invalid because it authorizes "teaching" by religious grant recipients on "matters [that] are fundamental elements of religious doctrine," such as the harm of premarital sex and the reasons for choosing adoption over abortion. 657 F. Supp., 1562. On an issue as sensitive and important as teenage sexuality, it is not surprising that the Government's secular concerns would either coincide or conflict with those of religious institutions. But the possibility or even the likelihood that some of the religious institutions who receive AFLA funding will agree with the message that Congress intended to deliver to adolescents through the AFLA is insufficient to warrant a finding that the statute on its face has the primary effect of advancing religion. . . . Nor does the alignment of the statute and the religious views of the grantees run afoul of our proscription against "fund[ing] a specifically religious activity in an otherwise substantially secular setting." *Hunt*, 413 U.S., 743. The facially neutral projects authorized by the AFLA—including pregnancy testing, adoption counseling and referral services, prenatal and postnatal care, educational services, residential care, child care, consumer education, etc.—are not themselves "specifically religious activities," and they are not converted into such activities by the fact that they are carried out by organizations with religious affiliations.

As yet another reason for invalidating parts of the AFLA, the District Court found that the involvement of religious organizations in the Act has the impermissible effect of creating a "crucial symbolic link" between government and religion. If we were to adopt the District Court's reasoning, it could be argued that any time a government aid program provides funding to religious organizations in an area in which the organization also has an interest, an impermissible "symbolic link" could be created, no matter whether the aid was to be used solely for secular purposes. This would jeopardize government aid to religiously affiliated hospitals, for example, on the ground that patients would perceive a "symbolic link" between the hospital—part of whose "religious mission" might be to save lives—and whatever government entity is subsidizing the purely secular medical services provided to the patient. . . .

A final argument that has been advanced for striking down the AFLA on "effects" grounds is the fact that the statute lacks an express provision preventing the use of federal funds for religious purposes. Clearly, if there were such a provision in this statute, it would be easier to conclude that the statute on its face could not be said to have the primary effect of advancing religion, but we have never stated that a *statutory* restriction is constitutionally required. . . . In this litigation, although there is no express statutory limitation on religious use of funds, there is also no intimation in the statute that at some point, or for some grantees, religious uses are permitted. To the contrary, the 1984 Senate Report on the AFLA states that "the use of Adolescent Family Life Act funds to promote religion, or to teach the religious doctrines of a particular sect, is contrary to the intent of this legislation." S.Rep. No. 98-496, p. 10 (1984). We note in addition that the AFLA requires each grantee to undergo evaluations of the services it provides, § 300z-5(b)(1), and also requires grantees to "make such reports concerning its use of Federal funds as the Secretary may require," § 300z-5(c). The application requirements of the Act, as well, require potential grantees to disclose in detail exactly what services they intend to provide and how they will be provided. § 300z-5(a). These provisions, taken together, create a mechanism whereby the Secretary can police the grants that are given out under the Act to ensure that federal funds are not used for impermissible purposes. Unlike some other grant programs, in which aid might be given out in one-time grants without ongoing supervision by the Government, the programs established under the authority of the AFLA can be monitored to determine whether the funds are, in effect, being used by the grantees in such a way as to advance religion. Given this statutory scheme, we do not think that the absence of an express limitation on the use of federal funds for religious purposes means that the statute, on its face, has the primary effect of advancing religion.

This, of course, brings us to the third prong of the *Lemon* Establishment Clause "test"—the question whether the AFLA leads to "'an excessive government entanglement with religion.'" *Lemon*, 403 U.S., 613 (quoting *Walz v. Tax Comm'n*, 397 U.S., 674.) There is no doubt that the monitoring of AFLA grants is necessary if the Secretary is to ensure that public money is to be spent in the way that Congress intended and in a way that comports with the Establishment Clause. Accordingly, this litigation presents us with yet another "Catch-22" argument: the very supervision of the aid to assure that it does not further religion renders the statute invalid. . . . Most of the cases in which the Court has divided over the "entanglement" part of the *Lemon* test have involved aid to parochial schools. . . .

Here, by contrast, there is no reason to assume that the religious organizations which may receive grants are "pervasively sectarian" in the same sense as the Court has held parochial schools to be. There is accordingly no reason to fear that the less intensive monitoring involved here will cause the Government to intrude unduly in the day-to-day operation of the religiously affiliated AFLA grantees. Unquestionably, the Secretary will review the programs set up and run by the AFLA grantees, and undoubtedly this will involve a review of, for example, the educational materials that a grantee proposes to use. The Secretary may also wish to have Government employees visit the clinics or offices where AFLA programs are being carried out to see whether they are in fact being administered in accordance with statutory and constitutional requirements. But in our view, this type of grant monitoring does not amount to "excessive entanglement," at least in the context of a statute authorizing grants to religiously affiliated organizations that are not necessarily "pervasively sectarian." . . .

For the foregoing reasons we conclude that the AFLA does not violate the Establishment Clause "on its face."

III . . .

On the merits of the "as applied" challenge, it seems to us that the District Court did not follow the proper approach in assessing appellees' claim that the Secretary is making grants under the Act that violate the Establishment Clause of the First Amendment. Although the District Court stated several times that AFLA aid had been given to religious organizations that were "pervasively sectarian," it did not identify which grantees it was referring to, nor did it discuss with any particularity the aspects of those organizations which in its view warranted classification as "pervasively sectarian."[16] The District Court did identify certain instances in which it felt AFLA funds were used for constitutionally improper purposes, but in our view the court did not adequately design its remedy to address the specific problems it found in the Secretary's administration

---

[16] The closest the court came was to identify "at least ten AFLA grantees or subgrantees [that] were themselves 'religious organizations,' in the sense that they have explicit corporate ties to a particular religious faith and by-laws or policies that prohibit any deviation from religious doctrine." 657 F. Supp., 1565. While these factors are relevant to the determination of whether an institution is "pervasively sectarian," they are not conclusive, and we do not find the court's conclusion that these institutions are "religious organizations" to be equivalent to a finding that their secular purposes and religious mission are "inextricably intertwined."

of the statute. Accordingly, although there is no dispute that the record contains evidence of specific incidents of impermissible behavior by AFLA grantees, we feel that this lawsuit should be remanded to the District Court for consideration of the evidence presented by appellees insofar as it sheds light on the manner in which the statute is presently being administered. . . .

In particular, it will be open to appellees on remand to show that AFLA aid is flowing to grantees that can be considered "pervasively sectarian" religious institutions, such as we have held parochial schools to be. As our previous discussion has indicated, and as *Tilton, Hunt,* and *Roemer* make clear, it is not enough to show that the recipient of a challenged grant is affiliated with a religious institution or that it is "religiously inspired."

The District Court should also consider on remand whether in particular cases AFLA aid has been used to fund "specifically religious activit[ies] in an otherwise substantially secular setting." . . . Here it would be relevant to determine, for example, whether the Secretary has permitted AFLA grantees to use materials that have an explicitly religious content or are designed to inculcate the views of a particular religious faith. As we have pointed out in our previous discussion, evidence that the views espoused on questions such as premarital sex, abortion, and the like happen to coincide with the religious views of the AFLA grantee would not be sufficient to show that the grant funds are being used in such a way as to have a primary effect of advancing religion. . . .

IV

We conclude, first, that the District Court erred in holding that the AFLA is invalid on its face, and second, that the court should consider on remand whether particular AFLA grants have had the primary effect of advancing religion. Should the court conclude that the Secretary's current practice does allow such grants, it should devise a remedy to insure that grants awarded by the Secretary comply with the Constitution and the statute. The judgment of the District Court is accordingly

*Reversed.*

JUSTICE O'CONNOR, concurring. . . .

The dissent says, and I fully agree, that "[p]ublic funds may not be used to endorse the religious message." As the Court notes, "there is no dispute that the record contains evidence of specific incidents of impermissible behavior by AFLA grantees." . . . In this circumstance, two points deserve to be emphasized. First, *any* use of public funds to promote religious doctrines violates the Establishment Clause. Second, *extensive* violations—if they can be proved in this case—will be highly relevant in shaping an appropriate remedy that ends such abuses. For that reason, appellees may yet prevail on remand, and I do not believe that the Court's approach entails a relaxation of "the unwavering vigilance that the Constitution requires against any law 'respecting an establishment of religion.'"

The need for detailed factual findings by the District Court stems in part from the delicacy of the task given to the Executive Branch by the Adolescent Family Life Act (AFLA). Government has a strong and legitimate secular interest in encouraging sexual restraint among young people. At the same time, as the dissent rightly points out, "[t]here is a very real and important difference between running a soup kitchen or a hospital, and counseling pregnant teenagers on how to make the difficult decisions facing them." Using religious organizations to advance the secular goals of the AFLA, without thereby permitting religious indoctrination, is inevitably more difficult than in other projects, such as ministering to the poor and the sick. I nonetheless agree with the Court that the partnership between governmental and religious institutions contemplated by the AFLA need not result in constitutional violations, despite an undeniably greater risk than is present in cooperative undertakings that involve less sensitive objectives. . . .

▓ JUSTICE KENNEDY, with whom JUSTICE SCALIA joins, concurring.

I join the Court's opinion, and write this separate concurrence to discuss one feature of the proceedings on remand. The Court states that "it will be open to appellees on remand to show that AFLA aid is flowing to grantees that can be considered 'pervasively sectarian' religious institutions, such as we have held parochial schools to be." In my view, such a showing will not alone be enough, in an as-applied challenge, to make out a violation of the Establishment Clause.

Though I am not confident that the term "pervasively sectarian" is a well-founded juridical category, I recognize the thrust of our previous decisions that a statute which provides for exclusive or disproportionate funding to pervasively sectarian institutions may impermissibly advance religion and as such be invalid on its face. We hold today, however, that the neutrality of the grant requirements and the diversity of the organizations described in the statute before us foreclose the argument that it is disproportionately tied to pervasively sectarian groups. Having held that the statute is not facially invalid, the only purpose of further inquiring whether any particular grantee institution is pervasively sectarian is as a preliminary step to demonstrating that the funds are in fact being used to further religion. In sum, where, as in this litigation, a statute provides that the benefits of a program are to be distributed in a neutral fashion to religious and nonreligious applicants alike, and the program withstands a facial challenge, it is not unconstitutional as applied solely by reason of the religious character of a specific recipient. The question in an as-applied challenge is not whether the entity is of a religious character, but how it spends its grant.

▓ JUSTICE BLACKMUN, with whom JUSTICE BRENNAN, JUSTICE MARSHALL, and JUSTICE STEVENS join, dissenting.

In 1981, Congress enacted the Adolescent Family Life Act (AFLA), . . . in a broad-scale effort to alleviate some of the problems associated with teenage pregnancy. It is unclear whether Congress ever envisioned that public funds would pay for a program during a session of which parents and teenagers would be instructed: "You want to know the church teachings on sexuality. . . . You are the church. You people sitting here are the body of Christ. The teachings of you and the things you value are, in fact, the values of the Catholic Church." Or of curricula that taught: "The Church has always taught that the marriage act, or intercourse, seals the union of husband and wife, (and is a representation of their union on all levels.) Christ commits Himself to us when we come to ask for the sacrament of marriage. We ask Him to be active in our life. God is love. We ask Him to share His love in ours, and God procreates with us, He enters into our physical union with Him, and we begin new life." Or the teaching of a method of family planning described on the grant application as "not only a method of birth regulation but also a philosophy of procreation," and promoted as helping "spouses who are striving . . . to transform their married life into testimony[,] . . . to cultivate their matrimonial spirituality[, and] to make themselves better instruments in God's plan," and as "facilitat[ing] the evangelization of homes."

Whatever Congress had in mind, however, it enacted a statute that facilitated and, indeed, encouraged the use of public funds for such instruction, by giving religious groups a central pedagogical and counseling role without imposing any restraints on the sectarian quality of the participation. As the record developed thus far in this litigation makes all too clear, federal tax dollars appropriated for AFLA purposes have been used, with Government approval, to support religious teaching. . . .

## II

Before proceeding to apply *Lemon's* three-part analysis to the AFLA, I pause to note a particular flaw in the majority's method. A central premise of the majority opinion seems to be that the primary means of ascertaining whether a statute that appears to be neutral on its face in fact has the effect of advancing religion is to determine whether aid flows to "pervasively sectarian" institutions. This misplaced focus leads the majority to ignore the substantial body of case law the Court has developed in analyzing programs providing direct aid to parochial schools, and to rely almost exclusively on the few cases in which the Court has upheld the supplying of aid to private colleges, including religiously affiliated institutions.

"Pervasively sectarian," a vaguely defined term of art, has its roots in this Court's recognition that government must not engage in detailed supervision of the inner workings of religious institutions, and the Court's sensible distaste for the "picture of state inspectors prowling the halls of parochial schools and auditing classroom instruction," . . .

The majority first skews the Establishment Clause analysis by adopting a cramped view of what constitutes a pervasively sectarian institution. Perhaps because most of the Court's decisions in this area have come in the context of aid to parochial schools, which traditionally have been characterized as pervasively sectarian, the majority seems to equate the characterization with the institution. . . . In sharp contrast, the District Court here concluded that AFLA grantees and participants included "organizations with institutional ties to religious denominations *and corporate requirements that the organizations abide by and not contradict religious doctrines.* In addition, other recipients of AFLA funds, while not explicitly affiliated with a religious denomination, are religiously inspired *and dedicated to teaching the dogma that inspired them*" (emphasis added). 657 F. Supp., 1564. On a continuum of "sectarianism" running from parochial schools at one end to the colleges funded by the statutes upheld in *Tilton, Hunt,* and *Roemer* at the other, the AFLA grantees described by the District Court clearly are much closer to the former than to the latter. . . .

## III

As is often the case, it is the effect of the statute, rather than its purpose, that creates Establishment Clause problems. Because I have no meaningful disagreement with the majority's discussion of the AFLA's essentially secular purpose, and because I find the statute's effect of advancing religion dispositive, I turn to that issue directly.

A

The majority's holding that the AFLA is not unconstitutional on its face marks a sharp departure from our precedents. While aid programs providing nonmonetary, verifiably secular aid have been upheld notwithstanding the indirect effect they might have on the allocation of an institution's own funds for religious activities, see, e.g., *Board of Education v. Allen*, 392 U.S. 236 (1968) (lending secular textbooks to parochial schools); *Everson v. Board of Education*, 330 U.S. 1 (1947) (providing bus services to parochial schools), direct cash subsidies have always required much closer scrutiny into the expected and potential uses of the funds, and much greater guarantees that the funds would not be used inconsistently with the Establishment Clause. Parts of the AFLA prescribing various forms of outreach, education, and counseling services specifically authorize the expenditure of funds in ways previously held unconstitutional. . . . The teaching materials that may be purchased, developed, or disseminated with AFLA funding are in no way restricted to those already selected and approved for use in secular contexts.[7]

Notwithstanding the fact that Government funds are paying for religious organizations to teach and counsel impressionable adolescents on a highly sensitive subject of considerable religious significance, often on the premises of a church or parochial school and without any effort to remove religious symbols from the sites, the majority concludes that the AFLA is not facially invalid. The majority acknowledges the constitutional proscription on government-sponsored religious indoctrination but, on the basis of little more than an indefensible assumption that AFLA recipients are not pervasively sectarian and consequently are presumed likely to comply with statutory and constitutional mandates, dismisses as insubstantial the risk that indoctrination will enter counseling. Similarly, the majority rejects the District Court's conclusion that the subject matter renders the risk of indoctrination unacceptable, and does so, it says, because "the likelihood that some of the religious institutions who receive AFLA funding will agree with the message that Congress intended to deliver to adolescents through the AFLA" does not amount to the advancement of religion. I do not think the statute can be so easily and conveniently saved.

(1) . . .

The AFLA, unlike any statute this Court has upheld, pays for teachers and counselors, employed by and subject to the direction of religious authorities, to educate impressionable young minds on issues of religious moment. Time and again we have recognized the difficulties inherent in asking even the best-intentioned individuals in such positions to make "a total separation between secular teaching and religious doctrine." *Lemon*, 403 U.S., 619. . . .

---

[7] Thus, for example, until discovery began in this lawsuit, St. Ann's, a home for unmarried pregnant teenagers, operated by the Order of the Daughters of Charity and owned by the Archdiocese of Washington, D.C., purchased books containing Catholic doctrine on chastity, masturbation, homosexuality, and abortion, using AFLA funds, and distributed them to participants. Catholic Family Services of Amarillo, Tex., used a curriculum outline guide for AFLA-funded parent workshops with explicit theological references, as well as religious "reference" materials, including the film "Everyday Miracle," described as "depicting the miracle of the process of human reproduction as a gift from God." Record 155, Plaintiffs' Appendix, Vol. IV, p. 119. . . .

(2)

By observing that the alignment of the statute and the religious views of the grantees do not render the AFLA a statute which funds "specifically religious activity," the majority makes light of the religious significance in the counseling provided by some grantees. Yet this is a dimension that Congress specifically sought to capture by enlisting the aid of religious organizations in battling the problems associated with teenage pregnancy. See S.Rep. No. 97-161, pp. 15-16 (1981); S.Rep. No. 98-496, pp. 9-10 (1984). Whereas there may be secular values promoted by the AFLA, including the encouragement of adoption and premarital chastity and the discouragement of abortion, it can hardly be doubted that when promoted in theological terms by religious figures, those values take on a religious nature. Not surprisingly, the record is replete with observations to that effect. It should be undeniable by now that religious dogma may not be employed by government even to accomplish laudable secular purposes such as "the promotion of moral values, the contradiction to the materialistic trends of our times, the perpetuation of our institutions and the teaching of literature." *Schempp*, 374 U.S., 223. . . .

It is true, of course, that the Court has recognized that the Constitution does not prohibit the government from supporting secular social-welfare services solely because they are provided by a religiously affiliated organization. But such recognition has been closely tied to the nature of the subsidized social service: "the State may send a cleric, indeed even a clerical order, to perform *a wholly secular task*" (emphasis added). *Roemer v. Maryland Public Works Board*, 426 U.S., 746 (plurality opinion). There is a very real and important difference between running a soup kitchen or a hospital, and counseling pregnant teenagers on how to make the difficult decisions facing them. The risk of advancing religion at public expense, and of creating an appearance that the government is endorsing the medium and the message, is much greater when the religious organization is directly engaged in pedagogy, with the express intent of shaping belief and changing behavior, than where it is neutrally dispensing medication, food, or shelter.[11]

There is also, of course, a fundamental difference between government's employing religion *because* of its unique appeal to a higher authority and the transcendental nature of its message, and government's enlisting the aid of religiously committed individuals or organizations without regard to their sectarian motivation. In the latter circumstance, religion plays little or no role; it merely explains why the individual or organization has chosen to get involved in the publicly funded program. In the former, religion is at the core of the subsidized activity, and it affects the manner in which the "service" is dispensed. . . .

---

[11] In arguing that providing "social welfare services" is categorically different from educating schoolchildren for Establishment Clause purposes, appellants relied heavily on *Bradfield v. Roberts*, 175 U.S. 291 (1899), a case in which the Court upheld the appropriation of money for the construction of two buildings to be part of a religiously affiliated hospital. Unlike the AFLA, however, which seeks "to promote self discipline and other prudent approaches to the problem of adolescent premarital sexual relations," § 300z(b)(1), the Act of Congress by which the hospital at issue in *Bradfield* had been incorporated expressed that "'the specific and limited object of its creation' is the opening and keeping a hospital in the city of Washington for the care of such sick and invalid persons as may place themselves under the treatment and care of the corporation." 175 U.S., 299-300.

B

The problems inherent in a statutory scheme specifically designed to involve religious organizations in a government-funded pedagogical program are compounded by the lack of any statutory restrictions on the use of federal tax dollars to promote religion. Conscious of the remarkable omission from the AFLA of any restriction whatsoever on the use of public funds for sectarian purposes, the Court disingenuously argues that we have "never stated that a *statutory* restriction is constitutionally required." . . .

Despite the glaring omission of a restriction on the use of funds for religious purposes, the Court attempts to resurrect the AFLA by noting a legislative intent not to promote religion, and observing that various reporting provisions of the statute "create a mechanism whereby the Secretary can police the grants." However effective this "mechanism" might prove to be in enforcing clear statutory directives, it is of no help where, as here, no restrictions are found on the face of the statute, and the Secretary has not promulgated any by regulation. . . . Furthermore, the "enforcement" of the limitation on sectarian use of AFLA funds, such as it is, lacks any bite. There is no procedure pursuant to which funds used to promote religion must be refunded to the Government, . . .

Indeed, nothing in the AFLA precludes the funding of even "pervasively sectarian" organizations, whose work by definition cannot be segregated into religious and secular categories. . . .

IV

While it is evident that the AFLA does not pass muster under *Lemon's* "effects" prong, the unconstitutionality of the statute becomes even more apparent when we consider the unprecedented degree of entanglement between Church and State required to prevent subsidizing the advancement of religion with AFLA funds. . . .

As to the Court's conclusion that our precedents do not indicate that the Secretary's monitoring will have to be exceedingly intensive or entangling, because the grant recipients are not sufficiently like parochial schools, I must disagree. . . .

To determine whether a statute fosters excessive entanglement, a court must look at three factors: (1) the character and purpose of the institutions benefited; (2) the nature of the aid; and (3) the nature of the relationship between the government and the religious organization. . . .

In *Roemer, Tilton,* and *Hunt,* the Court relied on "the ability of the State to identify and subsidize separate secular functions carried out at the school, *without on-the-site inspections being necessary to prevent diversion of the funds to sectarian purposes," Roemer v. Maryland Public Works Board,* 426 U.S., 765 (emphasis added), and on the fact that one-time grants require "no continuing financial relationships or dependencies, no annual audits, and no government analysis of an institution's expenditures on secular as distinguished from religious activities." *Tilton v. Richardson,* 403 U.S., 688. AFLA grants, of course, are not simply one-time construction grants. As the majority readily acknowledges, the Secretary will have to "review the programs set up and run by the AFLA grantees[, including] a review of, for example, the educational materials that a grantee proposes to use." And, as the majority intimates, monitoring the use of AFLA funds will undoubtedly require more than the "minimal" inspection "necessary to ascertain that the facilities are devoted to secular education."

*Tilton*, 403 U.S., 687. Since teachers and counselors, unlike buildings, "are not necessarily religiously neutral, greater governmental surveillance would be required to guarantee that state salary aid would not in fact subsidize religious instruction." *Id.*, 687-688.

V

The AFLA, without a doubt, endorses religion. Because of its expressed solicitude for the participation of religious organizations in all AFLA programs in one form or another, the statute creates a symbolic and real partnership between the clergy and the fisc in addressing a problem with substantial religious overtones. Given the delicate subject matter and the impressionable audience, the risk that the AFLA will convey a message of Government endorsement of religion is overwhelming. . . .

## NOTES AND QUESTIONS

1. Does the holding in *Bowen* follow from that in *Bradfield,* or are there some differences in the character of services provided by the organizations in these cases? What is the *Bowen* majority's rationale for holding that the funding of religious charities does not violate the Establishment Clause, particularly when the law discourages agencies from separating their religious from non-religious functions? Compare the majority's presumption about the character and operations of the charities in *Bowen* with the presumption that existed in school funding cases up until *Agostini*. How does the majority's rejection of the presumption that the funding of religious institutions will advance religion affect the *Lemon* standard?

2. The majority appeared to hold that pervasively sectarian organizations would be barred as grant recipients and that government funds could not be spent on religious activities. If this is correct, what is the concern of the dissenters?

3. Remember the discussion in *Mitchell v. Helms* from chapter 13 about the legal designation of a pervasively sectarian organization. In *Bowen*, Justices Kennedy and Scalia raise a similar argument, albeit twelve years earlier. What is their argument? What rights or interests do they claim the designation implicates: free exercise; free expression; equal protection under the law? What alternative to the designation do they suggest?

4. Are social service programs run by religious charities sufficiently different from education in religious and parochial schools such that the pervasively sectarian designation is inappropriate? What similarities and differences exist? Are there any shared concerns?

5. Justice O'Connor's concurring opinion—providing the necessary fifth vote to uphold the constitutionality of the Act—acknowledges the "risk" in greater government partnering with religious organizations. What are these risks? What constitutional interests are implicated? Are some types of government-funded programs or services more risk-inclined than others?

## "Charitable Choice" and the "Faith-based Initiative"

In the mid-1990s Congress engaged in a comprehensive overhaul of the nation's welfare system. As then-President Bill Clinton declared, the nation had to "change welfare as we know it." Two of the goals of "welfare reform" were to enlist nongovernmental groups in the delivery of many of the services previously administered by government agencies (frequently matched by a decrease in government funding) and to emphasize programs that encouraged lifestyle changes of beneficiaries rather than simply providing them with financial assistance. With these goals front-and-center, then-Missouri Senator John Ashcroft sponsored provisions in the law to articulate a new approach in this area. Among other things, Ashcroft charged that government officials were suspicious of and biased against religious organizations and that government rules unnecessarily discriminated against "faith-based organizations" in the award of government grants and contracts. Ashcroft said his "Charitable Choice" provision would put an end to such discrimination by allowing religious organizations to compete for government grants and contracts on an equal basis with their nonreligious counterparts. Opponents of Charitable Choice argued that the proposed changes were unnecessary—pointing to participation by groups such as Catholic Charities and the Salvation Army—and that the changes would result in government funding of religious activity.

In 1996, President Clinton signed into law the first Charitable Choice provision: The Personal Responsibility and Work Reconciliation Act, which replaced the Aid to Families with Dependent Children program (AFDC). Charitable Choice provisions were added to three additional federal social service funding programs between 1996 and 2000. In reading the PRWRA below, see if you can identify the constitutional concerns critics claim exist in the language.[5]

## Charitable Choice Provision in Welfare Reform Law

Services provided by charitable, religious, or private organizations, 42 U.S.C. § 604a

(a) In general
    (1) State options
        A State may—
        (A) administer and provide services under the programs described in subparagraphs (A) and (B)(i) of paragraph (2) through contracts with charitable, religious, or private organizations; and
        (B) provide beneficiaries of assistance under the programs described in subparagraphs (A) and (B)(ii) of paragraph (2) with certificates, vouchers, or other forms of disbursement which are redeemable with such organizations.
    (2) Programs described
        The programs described in this paragraph are the following programs:

(A) A State program funded under part A of title IV of the Social Security Act [42 U.S.C.A. § 601 et seq.] (as amended by section 103(a) of this Act).

(B) Any other program established or modified under title I or II of this Act, that—

 (i) permits contracts with organizations; or

 (ii) permits certificates, vouchers, or other forms of disbursement to be provided to beneficiaries, as a means of providing assistance.

(b) Religious organizations

The purpose of this section is to allow States to contract with religious organizations, or to allow religious organizations to accept certificates, vouchers, or other forms of disbursement under any program described in subsection (a)(2) of this section, on the same basis as any other nongovernmental provider without impairing the religious character of such organizations, and without diminishing the religious freedom of beneficiaries of assistance funded under such program.

(c) Nondiscrimination against religious organizations

In the event a State exercises its authority under subsection (a) of this section, religious organizations are eligible, on the same basis as any other private organization, as contractors to provide assistance, or to accept certificates, vouchers, or other forms of disbursement, under any program described in subsection (a)(2) of this section so long as the programs are implemented consistent with the Establishment Clause of the United States Constitution. Except as provided in subsection (k) of this section, neither the Federal Government nor a State receiving funds under such programs shall discriminate against an organization which is or applies to be a contractor to provide assistance, or which accepts certificates, vouchers, or other forms of disbursement, on the basis that the organization has a religious character.

(d) Religious character and freedom

(1) Religious organizations

A religious organization with a contract described in subsection (a)(1)(A) of this section, or which accepts certificates, vouchers, or other forms of disbursement under subsection (a)(1)(B) of this section, shall retain its independence from Federal, State, and local governments, including such organization's control over the definition, development, practice, and expression of its religious beliefs.

(2) Additional safeguards

Neither the Federal Government nor a State shall require a religious organization to—

(A) alter its form of internal governance; or

(B) remove religious art, icons, scripture, or other symbols;

in order to be eligible to contract to provide assistance, or to accept certificates, vouchers, or other forms of disbursement, funded under a program described in subsection (a)(2) of this section.

(e) Rights of beneficiaries of assistance

(1) In general

If an individual described in paragraph (2) has an objection to the religious character of the organization or institution from which the individual receives, or would receive, assistance funded under any program described in subsection (a)(2) of this section, the State in which the individual resides shall provide such individual (if otherwise eligible for such assistance) within a reasonable period of time after the date of such objection with assistance from an alternative provider that is accessible to the individual and the value of which is not less than the value of the assistance which the individual would have received from such organization.

(2) Individual described

An individual described in this paragraph is an individual who receives, applies for, or requests to apply for, assistance under a program described in subsection (a)(2) of this section.

(f) Employment practices

A religious organization's exemption provided under section 2000e-1 of this title regarding employment practices shall not be affected by its participation in, or receipt of funds from, programs described in subsection (a)(2) of this section.

(g) Nondiscrimination against beneficiaries

Except as otherwise provided in law, a religious organization shall not discriminate against an individual in regard to rendering assistance funded under any program described in subsection (a)(2) of this section on the basis of religion, a religious belief, or refusal to actively participate in a religious practice.

(h) Fiscal accountability

(1) In general

Except as provided in paragraph (2), any religious organization contracting to provide assistance funded under any program described in subsection (a)(2) of this section shall be subject to the same regulations as other contractors to account in accord with generally accepted auditing principles for the use of such funds provided under such programs.

(2) Limited audit

If such organization segregates Federal funds provided under such programs into separate accounts, then only the financial assistance provided with such funds shall be subject to audit.

(i) Compliance

Any party which seeks to enforce its rights under this section may assert a civil action for injunctive relief exclusively in an appropriate State court against the entity or agency that allegedly commits such violation.

(j) Limitations on use of funds for certain purposes

No funds provided directly to institutions or organizations to provide services and administer programs under subsection (a)(1)(A) of this section shall be expended for sectarian worship, instruction, or proselytization.

(k) Preemption

Nothing in this section shall be construed to preempt any provision of a State constitution or State statute that prohibits or restricts the expenditure of State funds in or by religious organizations.

---

## The Bush Administration's Faith-based Initiative

Even though President Clinton signed four federal laws that included Charitable Choice provisions, his administration never aggressively pursued full implementation of the law. For example, some of the signing statements Clinton issued to accompany these laws contained cautionary language regarding some of these provisions.

That changed with the election of George W. Bush in 2000. Then-Governor Bush had campaigned on a platform to increase government partnering with and funding of religious and community-based agencies. Immediately upon assuming office, President Bush created the White House Office of Faith-Based and Community Initiatives to encourage and facilitate participation in government-funded programs by religious groups and smaller social service groups. He also created faith-based offices in a number of the federal agencies that administered moneys and social service programs that were susceptible to greater participation by religious and community-based organizations. Finally, President Bush encouraged Congress to enact legislation that would expand Charitable Choice by including similar provisions in all federal social service programs.

Significant opposition to Bush's program arose in Congress. Opponents cited concerns about a range of issues, most prominently the provisions that allow religious organizations to employ co-religionists in government-funded positions. When legislation stalled in Congress over expansion of Charitable Choice in 2002, President Bush issued the following Executive Order that provided for implementation of the faith-based initiative without Congressional approval.

---

### Executive Order 13279
### Equal Protection of the Laws for Faith-Based and Community Organizations

December 12, 2002

By the authority vested in me as President by the Constitution and the laws of the United States of America, including section 121(a) of title 40, United States Code, and section 301 of title 3, United States Code, and in order to guide Federal agencies in formulating and developing policies with implications for faith-based organizations and other community organizations, to ensure equal protection of the laws for faith-based and community organizations, to further the national effort to expand opportunities for, and strengthen the capacity of, faith-based and other community organizations so that they may better meet social needs in America's communities, and to ensure the economical and efficient administration and completion of Government contracts, it is hereby ordered as follows:

Section 1. Definitions. For purposes of this order:

(a) "Federal financial assistance" means assistance that non-Federal entities receive or administer in the form of grants, contracts, loans, loan guarantees, property, cooperative agreements, food commodities, direct appropriations, or other assistance, but does not include a tax credit, deduction, or exemption.

(b) Social service program" means a program that is administered by the Federal Government, or by a State or local government using Federal financial assistance, and that provides services directed at reducing poverty, improving opportunities for low-income children, revitalizing low-income communities, empowering low-income families and low-income individuals to become self-sufficient, or otherwise helping people in need. Such programs include, but are not limited to, the following:

    (i)    child care services, protective services for children and adults, services for children and adults in foster care, adoption services, services related to the management and maintenance of the home, day care services for adults, and services to meet the special needs of children, older individuals, and individuals with disabilities (including physical, mental, or emotional disabilities);

    (ii)    transportation services;

    (iii)    job training and related services, and employment services;

    (iv)    information, referral, and counseling services;

    (v)    the preparation and delivery of meals and services related to soup kitchens or food banks;

    (vi)    health support services;

    (vii)    literacy and mentoring programs;

    (viii)    services for the prevention and treatment of juvenile delinquency and substance abuse, services for the prevention of crime and the provision of assistance to the victims and the families of criminal offenders, and services related to intervention in, and prevention of, domestic violence; and

    (ix)    services related to the provision of assistance for housing under Federal law.

(c) "Policies that have implications for faith-based and community organizations" refers to all policies, programs, and regulations, including official guidance and internal agency procedures, that have significant effects on faith-based organizations participating in or seeking to participate in social service programs supported with Federal financial assistance.

(d) "Agency" means a department or agency in the executive branch.

(e) "Specified agency heads" mean the Attorney General, the Secretaries of Agriculture, Education, Health and Human Services, Housing and Urban Development, and Labor, and the Administrator of the Agency for International Development.

Sec. 2. Fundamental Principles and Policymaking Criteria.

In formulating and implementing policies that have implications for faith-based and community organizations, agencies that administer social service programs supported with Federal financial assistance shall, to the extent permitted by law, be guided by the following fundamental principles:

(a) Federal financial assistance for social service programs should be distributed in the most effective and efficient manner possible;

(b) The Nation's social service capacity will benefit if all eligible organizations, including faith-based and other community organizations, are able to compete on an equal footing for Federal financial assistance used to support social service programs;

(c) No organization should be discriminated against on the basis of religion or religious belief in the administration or distribution of Federal financial assistance under social service programs;

(d) All organizations that receive Federal financial assistance under social services programs should be prohibited from discriminating against beneficiaries or potential beneficiaries of the social services programs on the basis of religion or religious belief. Accordingly, organizations, in providing services supported in whole or in part with Federal financial assistance, and in their outreach activities related to such services, should not be allowed to discriminate against current or prospective program beneficiaries on the basis of religion, a religious belief, a refusal to hold a religious belief, or a refusal to actively participate in a religious practice;

(e) The Federal Government must implement Federal programs in accordance with the Establishment Clause and the Free Exercise Clause of the First Amendment to the Constitution. Therefore, organizations that engage in inherently religious activities, such as worship, religious instruction, and proselytization, must offer those services separately in time or location from any programs or services supported with direct Federal financial assistance, and participation in any such inherently religious activities must be voluntary for the beneficiaries of the social service program supported with such Federal financial assistance; and

(f) Consistent with the Free Exercise Clause and the Free Speech Clause of the Constitution, faith-based organizations should be eligible to compete for Federal financial assistance used to support social service programs and to participate fully in the social service programs supported with Federal financial assistance without impairing their independence, autonomy, expression, or religious character. Accordingly, a faith-based organization that applies for or participates in a social service program supported with Federal financial assistance may retain its independence and may continue to carry out its mission, including the definition, development, practice, and expression of its religious beliefs, provided that it does not use direct Federal financial assistance to support any inherently religious activities, such as worship, religious instruction, or proselytization. Among other things, faith-based organizations that receive Federal financial assistance may use their facilities to provide social services supported with Federal financial assistance, without removing or altering religious art, icons, scriptures, or other symbols from these facilities. In addition, a faith-based organization that applies for or participates in a social service program supported with Federal financial assistance may retain religious terms in its organization's name, select its board members on a religious basis, and include religious references in its organization's mission statements and other chartering or governing documents.

Sec. 3. Agency Implementation.

(a) Specified agency heads shall, in coordination with the White House Office of Faith-Based and Community Initiatives (White House OFBCI), review and evaluate existing policies that have implications for faith-based and community organizations in order to assess the consistency of such policies with the fundamental principles and policymaking criteria articulated in section 2 of this order.

(b) Specified agency heads shall ensure that all policies that have implications for faith-based and community organizations are consistent with the fundamental principles and policymaking criteria articulated in section 2 of this order. Therefore, specified agency heads shall, to the extent permitted by law:

    (i)    amend all such existing policies of their respective agencies to ensure that they are consistent with the fundamental principles and policymaking criteria articulated in section 2 of this order;

    (ii)    where appropriate, implement new policies for their respective agencies that are consistent with and necessary to further the fundamental principles and policymaking criteria set forth in section 2 of this order; and

    (iii)    implement new policies that are necessary to ensure that their respective agencies collect data regarding the participation of faith-based and community organizations in social service programs that receive Federal financial assistance.

(c)  Within 90 days after the date of this order, each specified agency head shall report to the President, through the Director of the White House OFBCI, the actions it proposes to undertake to accomplish the activities set forth in sections 3(a) and (b) of this order.

Sec. 4. Amendment of Executive Order 11246.

Pursuant to section 121(a) of title 40, United States Code, and section 301 of title 3, United States Code, and in order to further the strong Federal interest in ensuring that the cost and progress of Federal procurement contracts are not adversely affected by an artificial restriction of the labor pool caused by the unwarranted exclusion of faith-based organizations from such contracts, section 204 of Executive Order 11246 of September 24, 1965, as amended, is hereby further amended to read as follows:

"SEC. 204 (a) The Secretary of Labor may, when the Secretary deems that special circumstances in the national interest so require, exempt a contracting agency from the requirement of including any or all of the provisions of Section 202 of this Order in any specific contract, subcontract, or purchase order.

(b) The Secretary of Labor may, by rule or regulation, exempt certain classes of contracts, subcontracts, or purchase orders (1) whenever work is to be or has been performed outside the United States and no recruitment of workers within the limits of the United States is involved; (2) for standard commercial supplies or raw materials; (3) involving less than specified amounts of money or specified numbers of workers; or (4) to the extent that they involve subcontracts below a specified tier.

(c) Section 202 of this Order shall not apply to a Government contractor or subcontractor that is a religious corporation, association, educational institution, or society, with respect to the employment of individuals of a particular religion to perform work connected with the carrying on by such corporation, association, educational institution, or society of its activities. Such contractors and subcontractors are not exempted or excused from complying with the other requirements contained in this Order.

(d) The Secretary of Labor may also provide, by rule, regulation, or order, for the exemption of facilities of a contractor that are in all respects separate and distinct from activities of the contractor related to the performance of the contract: provided, that such an exemption will not interfere with or impede the effectuation of the purposes of this Order: and provided further, that in the absence of such an exemption all facilities shall be covered by the provisions of this Order."

Sec. 5. General Provisions.

(a)  This order supplements but does not supersede the requirements contained in Executive Orders 13198 and 13199 of January 29, 2001.

(b) The agencies shall coordinate with the White House OFBCI concerning the implementation of this order.

(c) Nothing in this order shall be construed to require an agency to take any action that would impair the conduct of foreign affairs or the national security.

Sec. 6. Responsibilities of Executive Departments and Agencies. All executive departments and agencies (agencies) shall:

(a) designate an agency employee to serve as the liaison and point of contact with the White House OFBCI; and

(b) cooperate with the White House OFBCI and provide such information, support, and assistance to the White House OFBCI as it may request, to the extent permitted by law.

Sec. 7. Judicial Review.

This order is intended only to improve the internal management of the executive branch, and it is not intended to, and does not, create any right or benefit, substantive or procedural, enforceable at law or in equity by a party against the United States, its agencies, or entities, its officers, employees or agents, or any person.

GEORGE W. BUSH
THE WHITE HOUSE,
December 12, 2002.

Exec. Order No. 13279, 67 FR 77141

---

As this book goes to print, the Supreme Court has yet to rule on the constitutionality of the various provisions from Charitable Choice, this executive order, or accompanying administrative regulations. Several challenges have arisen, with a handful of decisions existing at the trial and appellate levels. But to date, the Supreme Court has ruled only on whether parties have standing to challenge the Executive's expenditure of funds drawn from general Executive branch appropriations that were used by the White House to conduct regional conferences promoting the Faith-Based and Community Initiative (see *Hein v. Freedom from Religion Foundation*, in chapter 5).

Still, Charitable Choice raises several constitutional issues upon which the high court will eventually be required to rule. In announcing an equal right to participate in government grants and programs, the Charitable Choice provisions do not differentiate between organizations that are pervasively religious—those that integrate religious worship and instruction into their social service programs—and those that are religiously affiliated but segregate their religious activities from government-funded programs. [The authors of this book acknowledge that religious social service organizations may do these things to varying degrees.] The provisions do prohibit, however, subsidizing "sectarian worship, instruction, or proselytization" with direct government funds. The Bush executive order contains a similar prohibition, barring the use of direct government funds for what it calls "inherently religious activities." But the Bush executive order also goes further than charitable choice by requiring that any privately funded "inherently religious activities" be offered "separately in time or location from any programs or services supported with direct Federal financial assistance. . . ."[6]

These provisions raise a number of constitutional issues that will be litigated all the way to the Supreme Court. Those issues include the following ones: Should certain overall characteristics of a religious organization make the organization ineligible to receive at least direct government funds? Or should any religious group be permitted to receive direct government funds, so long as it pays for any religious activities with private money and offers those activities separate in time or location from the government program? If the latter is sufficient, how will the government ensure that these requirements are enforced without becoming excessively entangled with the religious body? Does the Constitution prohibit the use of direct funds for religious activities or only for "inherently religious" activities, whatever that term means? Or will the Court instead say that it is not constitutionally problematic for an organization to use any type of government funds for religious activities so long as those funds were offered to a broad range of religious and nonreligious providers on an equal basis? Based on the *Agostini* and *Mitchell* holdings, current law says that direct government grants still may not pay for religious worship or indoctrination. However, *Mitchell* raises doubts about the resiliency of the "pervasively sectarian" doctrine, and the *Mitchell* plurality opinion raises questions about a number of other aspects of traditional Establishment Clause doctrine.

An additional unresolved issue raised by Charitable Choice legislation is whether the provision authorizing religious organizations to prefer co-religionists in their employment practices—an exception from the general prohibition on employment discrimination contained in Title VII (see *Corporation of Presiding Bishop v. Amos* in chapter 20)—is unconstitutional as an establishment of religion when the employment action takes place with regard to government-funded job positions. For more background on this issue and contrasting arguments, see Carl H. Esbeck, et al., *The Freedom of Faith-Based Organizations to Staff on a Religious Basis* (Washington, D.C.: Center for Public Justice, 2004); Steven K. Green, "Religious Discrimination, Public Funding, and Constitutional Values," *Hastings Constitutional Law Quarterly* 30 (2002): 1; and Melissa Rogers "Federal Funding and Religion-based Employment Decisions," in *Sanctioning Religion? Politics, Law, and Faith-based Public Services*, edited by David K. Ryden and Jeffrey Polet (Boulder, Colo.: Lynne Reinner Publishers, 2005).

An example of how lower courts have approached the constitutionality of the funding issues presented by Charitable Choice is presented below. In *Freedom from Religion Foundation v. McCallum*, taxpayer members of Freedom from Religion Foundation (FFRF) challenged a Wisconsin program that used federal Welfare-to-Work funds (a law with a Charitable Choice provision) to contract with private charitable agencies to provide job training and substance abuse counseling to ex-offenders and recipients of Temporary Assistance to Needy Families (TANF). Faith Works, a self-described "Christian faith-based treatment" organization that provides long-term residential treatment for drug and alcohol addicts, entered into contracts with the Wisconsin Department of Workforce Development and Department of Corrections to provide rehabilitation and training services to eligible TANF recipients and ex-offenders, respectively. The former contracts were direct funding grants, while the latter contracts with the Department of Corrections had elements of both a direct and indirect funding program. Excerpted below are decisions of the District Court and the Court of Appeals for the Seventh Circuit.

## FREEDOM FROM RELIGION FOUNDATION v. McCALLUM
## 179 F. Supp. 2d 950 (W.D. Wisc. 2002).

### FACTS . . .

B. *The Faith Works Program*

Faith Works provides long-term residential treatment to male drug and alcohol addicts. It is an independent "faith-based program designed to meet the needs of individuals recovering from addiction to alcohol and other drugs" and to assist them in becoming employed and fully functioning members of society. . . .

The Faith Works program is "committed from day one of [the] clients' enrollment to empower them to live in their community with the best possible chance for societal and economic success." Faith Works strives to incorporate all available community services into the participants' recovery process, on the theory that the participants need to learn how to gain access to those services after completion of the program "for continued support for themselves and the family for whom they have now taken responsibility." A goal of the program is to have each participant have either a spiritual mentor or an Alcoholics Anonymous sponsor (a spiritual person with the AA 12-step program perspective). The Faith Works Milwaukee Annual Report 2000 states that the program has four important aspects: recovery; employment; family services; and spiritual enrichment.

Faith Works counselors work 40 hours a week. The counselors estimate that they spend approximately eight hours a week, or 20 percent of their time, addressing questions of faith or spirituality. They are open to spiritual discussions at any time. The rest of their time is spent on the day-to-day efforts necessary to help recovering alcoholics and drug abusers reorder their lives so that they do not fall back into their addictions.

Commitment to Christian beliefs and values is a hiring consideration for counseling staff, but Faith Works does not impose religious restrictions on staff appointments. Church attendance is expected for Faith Works staff. Faith Works staff counsel participants to develop a personal relationship with God. Counselors discuss issues of faith in order to promote the state objectives of providing alcohol and other drug addiction treatment to non-custodial parents and obtaining unsubsidized employment. . . .

The Department of Workforce Development grant agreement and the Department of Corrections contract require Faith Works not to discriminate by hiring on the basis of religion.

The Faith Works Standards of Practice list the following guidelines for all staff:

> We are a Christian faith-based treatment center. This means all staff is to serve as Jesus served; with compassion, concern and love for all persons, regardless of race, creed, background or whatever sins a person is struggling to overcome through this program.
>
> We are serving the Lord in evangelistic outreach and will respect the Holy Spirit's ability to work in each person's life whether staff or resident. We need to be mature in our faith and work habits in order to be truly able to be witnesses to the Lord and His Grace. . . .

As the name implies, Faith Works is a faith-based organization. As a practical matter, this means that, although the majority of time staff spends at Faith Works involves the everyday aspects of helping the participants recover from addiction, become gainfully employed and re-establish ties with their families and reintegrate with their communities, staff members also offer those who acknowledge some spiritual significance to their lives an opportunity to develop that aspect in their recovery. In its grant proposals, Faith Works promotes spirituality as a basis of the program's success, along with the extended length of the program.

According to Faith Works, recovery is accomplished when participants address their spirituality. Faith Works seeks to help its participants grow and define their spirituality. It describes its residential recovery program facility as a spiritual center because part of the program offerings are spiritually based. It requires its residents to participate in a faith-enhanced 12-step AA program that is mandatory for participants. Faith Works' version of AA involves more explicit references to God than the standard AA. Faith Works makes Bible studies, prayer time and chapel services available on a voluntary basis.

Staff meetings at Faith Works begin with a prayer. The Faith Works Standards of Practice for all staff includes the requirement that staff members "[grow] in [their] own faith life by regular church attendance, prayer, Bible study and seeking Spiritual direction from a Pastor/Shepard in our faith community." The Faith Works counseling staff has an extensive knowledge of scripture.

According to Robert Polito, the former executive director of Faith Works, Milwaukee, the majority of Faith Works clients are not in a practicing faith when they enter the program but most graduates have some sort of relationship with God when they leave. Participants are not required to profess any religious faith; at the same time, discussion about spiritual matters occurs during mandatory meetings. Active participation in the faith component of these meetings is not required but attendance is mandatory. Discussion of faith in these meetings is encouraged. . . .

Faith Works' bylaws state that its program addresses the needs of "[a]ddiction recovery, relying on a faith enhanced model of the 12-step program." The bylaws state that the "program seeks to put a holistic, faith-based approach to bring healing to mind, body, heart and soul. While the program is inherently Christian, services will be offered to all persons who seek it, regardless of their faith background."

Faith Works identified the religious component of its program in grant proposals submitted to the Wisconsin Department of Workforce Development. In one, the author states that Faith Works "is a faith based, long-term residential, holistic program that emphasizes spiritual, physical, emotional and economic wellness." He adds that Faith Works offers a "12-step recovery process in a faith based setting provided by counselors and 12-step volunteer leaders." According to the proposal, one of the goals of Faith Works is to "facilitate stability in employment and recovery, successfully transition to independent living after nine months residency, with assistance in locating housing, as well as support services, church affiliation, 12-step meetings and other support programs that would replace in the new neighborhood what was supplied in the [Faith Works] resident program." . . .

Faith Works [also] has a contract with the Wisconsin Department of Corrections to operate a halfway house providing twenty-four hour supervised residential care and related services. The department reimburses Faith Works for the services it provides on a monthly basis; it funds Faith Works only when supervised offenders enroll in the program. A service provider such as Faith Works must have a state-approved contract as a condition to being paid for providing alcohol and other drug addiction services. . . .

[Editors' note: In fiscal year 1998, Faith Works was awarded $150,000 from the governor's discretionary funds under the Workforce development program. These funds were not disbursed on the basis of the number of individuals referred to Faith Works but rather as a block amount. In fiscal year 1999, Faith Works received a second grant in the amount of $450,000. In 1999, Faith Works received approximately $50,000 from the Department of Corrections for five beds in its halfway house for ex-offenders and parolees.]

OPINION . . .

B. First Amendment: Establishment Clause . . .

[Editors' note: The District Court set out four factors to consider whether a funding program violates the Establishment Clause: (1) it has a secular purpose; (2) it does not result in governmental indoctrination; (3) it does not define its participants by reference to religion; and (4) it does not create excessive entanglement. The plaintiffs conceded that Faith Works was not unconstitutional under the first prong because it has a secular purpose: providing drug treatment and employment training. Plaintiffs also did not assert that Faith Works defines its recipients by reference to religion. The court found that the contracts did not excessively entangle the state with religion. It then turned to the second criterion.]

It is well settled that the establishment clause prohibits "government-financed or government-sponsored indoctrination into the beliefs of a particular religious faith." *Bowen v. Roy*, 487 U.S., 611. Although it is "inappropriate to presume inculcation of religion," *Mitchell v. Helms*, 530 U.S., 858, it is not necessary to make any presumptions to conclude that the Faith Works program inculcates religion. As its name suggests, Faith Works is a faith-based treatment program whose bylaws state that it employs a Christian-enhanced model of the Alcoholics Anonymous 12-step program. Participants are told at an intake interview that the program is faith-based. They are not required to discuss issues of spirituality at the AA meetings or at any other time, but that attendance at the enhanced AA meetings is mandatory. Although AA is not a traditional form of religious worship, the First Amendment applies to "any religious activit[y] or institution[ ], whatever [it] may be called, or whatever form [it] may adopt to teach or practice religion." *Everson v. Bd. of Ed.*, 330 U.S. 1, 16. . . .

In addition to its AA programming, Faith Works sponsors other religious activities, such as Bible study, chapel services and prayer time each day. Faith Works counselors are available to "facilitate a transformation of the mind and soul" and they are prepared to study the Bible, pray with participants and provide guidance on getting connected with a local faith community. Counselors are not required to be of a particular faith, but their Christian-based spirituality is considered a factor in the hiring process. . . . Although faith is only one aspect of the participants' lives that counselors strive to improve,

Faith Works staff encourage participants to integrate spirituality into their recovery program. In the employee handbook distributed to all employees, Faith Works includes a statement of faith that describes in detail the Christian beliefs that provide the framework for the Faith Works program: "The essence of this ministry is to develop a community of believers that would foster rigorous honesty; first with God, second with oneself and third with the Body of Christ." . . .

Although Faith Works may have the secular purposes of providing drug treatment, education and job training, this does not mean that religion does not permeate the programming. A "pervasively sectarian" institution is one in which the organization's "secular activities cannot be separated from sectarian ones." *Roemer v. Bd of Public Works*, 426 U.S. 736, 755 (1976).

Defendants contend that the religious components of Faith Works can be separated from its secular ones. They point to the Department of Workforce Development grant, which funds secular services such as room, board, job readiness training, employment placement services, housing assistance and family reunification, but ostensibly not religious indoctrination. Defendants neglect to point out that they used the integration of religion into Faith Works' recovery model as a strong selling point for obtaining funding. The governor chose to fund Faith Works from his discretionary funds because of its unique holistic recovery model and the extended length of the program. Faith Works won the Department of Corrections grant in part because of its unique long-term, faith-based approach to drug treatment. Faith Works cannot now try to excise religion from its offerings, saying that it contracted with the state to provide the wholly secular services of room and board without any reference to religion. This assertion rings hollow in light of the literature Faith Works provided the state. Taking into consideration Faith Works' daily activities as well as its faith-based approach to drug treatment, I conclude that the Faith Works program indoctrinates its participants in religion, primarily through its counselors. . . .

Simply because a state-funded program engages in indoctrination does not mean that the program's funding is unconstitutional. The establishment clause targets only indoctrination that "could reasonably be attributed to governmental action." *Mitchell*, 530 U.S., 809. To determine whether the religious activities of Faith Works constitute governmental indoctrination, it must be determined whether the activities are supported by unrestricted, direct state funding.

"[S]tates may not make unrestricted cash payments directly to religious institutions." Direct subsidies are viewed as governmental advancement or indoctrination of religion. In contrast, when public funding flows to faith-based organizations solely as a result of the "genuinely independent and private choices of individuals," the funding is considered indirect. *Agostini*, 521 U.S., 226. When a program receives indirect funding, it is the individual participant, and not the state, who chooses to support the religious organization, reducing the likelihood that the public funding has the primary effect of advancing religion in violation of the establishment clause.

[Editors' note: The District Court found that the funding Faith Works received from the governor's discretionary fund through the Department of Workforce Development constituted direct funding and was thus unconstitutional. The court rejected Faith Works' argument that because it operated through a combination of public and private grants, any indoctrination that took place did so with private funds.]

> The Supreme Court has systematically rejected attempts to unbundle religious activities through statistics and accounting. . . . Not only are the public funds paid to Faith Works not targeted for a discrete purpose, but the funding takes the form of money rather than materials. . . . In the present case, the governor's discretionary funds given to Faith Works are not targeted or earmarked for discrete, identified secular activities. Although defendants assert that Faith Works receives sufficient private funds to pay for the counselors' salaries, this accounting procedure does not guarantee that public funds are not put to sectarian use. . . .
>
> Faith Works is one of several drug treatment programs that has entered into a contract with the Department of Corrections to provide treatment to offenders on probation and parole. The payments that Faith Works receives from the state are based upon the number of supervised offenders enrolled in the program, but the state plays a role in the supervised offender's decision to attend Faith Works. The undisputed facts establish that the Department of Corrections funding of Faith Works has some characteristics of direct funding and some characteristics of indirect funding, but they do not allow a determination whether the funding reaches Faith Works only as a result of the genuinely independent, private choice of the offenders.
>
> Because the state has pre-selected Faith Works as one of several treatment programs, the offender's choice is restricted. Defendants assert that it is typical for the government to pre-approve service providers. Nevertheless, the offender does not receive a brochure listing his options; instead, probation and parole agents determine which of the pre-selected programs best suits his assessed needs and "direct" the offender to Faith Works. The undisputed facts do not describe the circumstances surrounding the offender's choice, such as the words that the probation and parole agents use when "directing" the offender to Faith Works or whether the offender's court order specifies *long-term* alcohol and other drug addiction treatment. Offenders do not have to accept treatment at Faith Works, but Faith Works is the only treatment program in the Milwaukee area that provides a nine-month residential program; the other residential treatment programs last only three months. From the undisputed facts, it is not clear whether an offender who has been assessed as needing a nine-month treatment program and who refuses to attend Faith Works has any appropriate treatment alternatives. In addition, the detailed contract between the Department of Corrections and Faith Works indicates that the state is not a disinterested third party that is merely providing offenders with funding to spend at a treatment program of their choosing. . . . I am unable to conclude whether the Department of Corrections contract constitutes direct or indirect funding.

[Editors' note: following a trial on this latter issue, the District Court determined that the Faith Works contract with the Department of Corrections constituted indirect funding and dismissed this claim. Freedom From Religion Foundation appealed this latter decision to the Seventh Circuit Court of Appeals.]

## FREEDOM FROM RELIGION FOUNDATION v. McCALLUM
### 324 F.3d 880 (7th Cir. 2003)

POSNER, CIRCUIT JUDGE.

This is a taxpayer suit to enjoin Wisconsin correctional authorities from funding Faith Works, a halfway house that, like Alcoholics Anonymous, incorporates Christianity into its treatment program. The plaintiffs argue that this funding constitutes an establishment of religion, in violation of the Constitution. The district judge rejected the argument after a bench trial.

If a convicted criminal is out on parole (or probation, but we need not discuss that separately) and living in Milwaukee and he violates the terms of the parole, his parole officer may offer him, as an alternative to being sent back to prison, enrollment in one of several halfway houses with which the state has contracts. The officer can recommend a specific halfway house—the one he thinks best for the particular offender—but the offender is free to choose one of the others. One of the authorized halfway houses, Faith Works, which focuses on employment needs, drug and alcohol addiction, and parental responsibility, has a religious theme: it encourages the offender to establish a personal relationship with God through the mediation of Jesus Christ. Parole officers have recommended Faith Works to some parolees, but have been careful to explain that it is a nonbinding recommendation and that Faith Works is a Christian institution and its program of rehabilitation has a significant Christian element. Parole officers who recommend Faith Works are required to offer the offender a secular halfway house as an alternative. And although Faith Works will enroll an offender even if he is not a Christian, a parole officer will not recommend Faith Works to an offender who has no Christian identity and religious interest and will not advise anyone to convert to Christianity in order to get the most out of Faith Works.

There is no evidence that in recommending Faith Works a parole officer will be influenced by his own religious beliefs. His end is secular, the rehabilitation of a criminal, though the means include religion when the offender chooses Faith Works. Because the Supreme Court will not allow a public agency to force religion on people even if the agency honestly and indeed correctly believes that it is the best way of achieving a secular end that is within government's constitutional authority to promote, the state may not require offenders to enroll in Faith Works even if it is the best halfway house in Milwaukee for any or even all offenders. The choice must be private, to provide insulating material between government and religion. It is private; it is the offender's choice.

The success of Alcoholics Anonymous is evidence that Christianity can be a valuable element in a program for treating addiction. And alone among the approved halfway houses in Milwaukee, Faith Works offers a nine-month residential program; the secular programs are only three months. The longer term makes Faith Works uniquely attractive to the correctional authorities because they believe that many offenders need the longer period of supervised residence in order to succeed in becoming reintegrated into civil society. So the state waived the usual bidding requirements when it contracted with Faith Works, which it had not done with the other halfway houses in Milwaukee. . . .

If an offender enrolls in Faith Works, the state reimburses a part of the cost in accordance with the terms of the contract, just as it does in the case of offenders who enroll in secular halfway houses. . . .

The district judge was right to dismiss the suit. A city does not violate the establishment clause by giving parents vouchers that they can use to purchase private school education for their children, even if most of the private schools in the city are parochial schools—provided, of course, that the parents are not required to use the vouchers to attend a parochial school rather than a secular school. *Zelman v. Simmons-Harris,* 536 U.S. 639 (2002). The practice challenged in the present case is similar. The state in effect gives eligible offenders "vouchers" that they can use to purchase a place in a halfway house, whether the halfway house is "parochial" or secular. We have put "vouchers" in scare quotes because the state has dispensed with the intermediate step by which the recipient of the publicly funded private service hands his voucher to the service provider. But so far as the policy of the establishment clause is concerned, there is no difference between giving the voucher recipient a piece of paper that directs the public agency to pay the service provider and the agency's asking the recipient to indicate his preference and paying the provider whose service he prefers.

Nor does it make a difference that the state, rather than accrediting halfway houses, enters into contracts with them. Obviously it has not refused to enter into contracts with halfway houses that are secular—all but one of its contracts are with secular houses. The only evidence of favoritism, the bid waiver, is unpersuasive; it was granted because Faith Works' program has such attractive features from a purely secular standpoint, such as the length of the program, that the state was eager to have it on its menu of halfway-house choices. That most of the halfway houses with which the state has contracts are secular makes this an easier case than the school voucher case. Most private schools in this country are parochial schools, so that a voucher system, at least in the short run (in the long run the existence of such a system is likely to stimulate the creation of new secular private schools), will give a definite boost to religion. Most halfway houses are secular.

The plaintiffs argue that by recommending Faith Works to some offenders, parole officers steer the offenders to a religious program and by doing so provide governmental support to religion. The implications of the argument are unacceptable. If recommending a religious institution constituted an establishment of religion, a public school guidance counselor could not recommend that a student apply to a Catholic college even if the counselor thought that the particular college would be the best choice for the particular student. And, coming closer to home, a parole officer could not recommend to a parolee who had a serious drinking problem that he enroll in Alcoholics Anonymous, even if the officer believed that this was the only alcoholic-treatment program that would keep the parolee from committing further crimes. To suppose such recommendations unlawful would be to adopt a doctrinaire interpretation of the establishment clause remote from its underlying purpose and historical understanding. Suggestion is not a synonym for coercion. . . .

If religiously oriented halfway houses were *obviously* of little value from a correctional standpoint, the danger of seepage of religious preferences or aversions into the process of rating or recommendation might tip the scale against allowing such halfway houses to receive public funding even as mediated by private choice. But on the contrary—and quite apart from the evidence, confirmed by long experience with the parallel case of Alcoholics Anonymous, that for some substance abusers religion is an effective treatment—there is the fact that Faith Works offers a program that lasts three times as long as that of any of its secular competitors. To exclude Faith Works from this competition on the basis of a speculative fear that parole or probation officers might recommend its program because of their own Christian faith would involve the sacrifice of a real good to avoid a conjectured bad. It would be perverse if the Constitution required this result.

The plaintiffs try to turn the real good of Faith Works' program in their favor by arguing that because it is indeed the best program, offenders who are advised to enroll in it—perhaps all offenders who are eligible for a halfway house—have no real choice. But quality cannot be coercion. That would amount to saying that a city cannot adopt a school voucher system if the parochial schools in the city are better than the public or secular private schools. Faith Works, penalized because its secular competitors were unwilling to invest as much in the rehabilitation of offenders, would have an incentive to reduce the quality of its program, while those competitors would have an incentive to reduce the quality of their own programs in order to make Faith Works' "violation" of the establishment clause more perspicuous and encourage it to curtail its program. There would be a race to the bottom.

It is a misunderstanding of freedom (another paradox, given the name of the principal plaintiff) to suppose that choice is not free when the objects between which the chooser must choose are not equally attractive to him. It would mean that a person was not exercising his free will when in response to the question whether he preferred vanilla or chocolate ice cream he said vanilla, because it was the only honest answer that he could have given and therefore "he had no choice."

*Affirmed.*

## NOTES AND QUESTIONS

1. Lower courts are bound to follow existing Supreme Court precedent. Therefore, once the district court determined that Faith Works' programs were pervasively sectarian they were ineligible to receive direct grants from the state. What factors did the court consider? Should it matter that Faith Works received only a portion of its funding from the state and that some of the religious activities were optional for the program participants?

2. The District Court's holding with respect to the direct funding of Faith Works' programs is consistent with *Bowen*. Is the Court of Appeals holding that the Faith Works contract with the Department of Corrections involves indirect funding akin to a voucher system equally consistent with existing precedent? Looking back on the *Zelman* decision, are there any factors under the Faith Works' contract with the Wisconsin Department of Corrections that distinguish it from the type of voucher program upheld in *Zelman*? Are Judge Posner's distinctions compelling?

CHAPTER 15

# GOVERNMENT FUNDS AND RELIGIOUS INSTITUTIONS: A LOOK TOWARD THE FUTURE

The cases of *Agostini v. Felton,*[1] *Mitchell v. Helms,*[2] *Zelman v. Simmons-Harris,*[3] and *Locke v. Davey*[4] represent a watershed in Supreme Court Establishment Clause jurisprudence. The transition away from the doctrine of "strict separation" or "no-aid" to religious institutions espoused in *Everson v. Board of Education*[5] was long in the making. The cases of *Meek v. Pittenger,*[6] *Aguliar v. Felton,*[7] and *Grand Rapids School District v. Ball*[8] can be seen as the high water marks of the no-aid doctrine. In those cases the Court reaffirmed that "the [Establishment] Clause does absolutely prohibit government-financed or government-sponsored indoctrination into the beliefs of a particular religious faith."[9] This prohibition existed even under benefits programs that were generally available to secular and religious institutions alike. As the Court remarked in 1976, "a facial neutrality [of a program] may not be enough, if in fact the State is lending direct support to a religious activity. The State may not, for example, pay for what is actually a religious education, even though it purports to be paying for a secular one, and even though it makes its aid available to secular and religious institutions alike."[10] Finally, the Court during the 70s and 80s declared that some institutions were simply too religious to participate in general funding or benefits programs because their religious and secular components were "inextricably intertwined" (i.e., the institutions were "pervasively sectarian" in their missions or functions).[11]

Some would argue, however, that *strict* separation with respect to funding of religious institutions was never the rule—that critics used strict separation primarily as a straw man. A close reading of *Everson* reveals competing (or complementary) theories about the appropriate relationship between government and religious institutions, with the Court emphasizing the importance of both the equal treatment of religion and the prohibition on aiding religion.[12] During the same period that the Court struck down teacher-salary supplements for parochial school teachers (*Lemon v. Kurtzman*[13]) and divertable forms of aid to religious schools (*Meek*[14]) the Court upheld supplemental aid in the form of textbooks (*Board of Education v. Allen*[15]) and non-divertable educational equipment and services (*Wolman v. Walter*[16]). And, only two years after *Lemon*, the Court struck down a law that awarded tuition tax credits to parents of children attending religious schools (*Committee for Public Education and Religious Liberty v. Nyquist*[17]). In that same case, however, the Court intimated that some indirect forms of financial aid to religious schools were permissible under programs that were generally available to public and religious school students alike, an approach the Court affirmed ten years later in *Mueller v. Allen*.[18] In essence, the Court's funding jurisprudence during the period from 1947 to 2000 was mixed, with the justices at times placing greater emphasis on the evils of funding religious institutions, while at other times noting the value of equal participation in benefits programs. Still, the dominant theme in funding jurisprudence through the end of the twentieth century was that the government kept tight reins on aid that flowed to religious institutions, particularly direct aid. In *Agostini*, however, by reversing *Aguilar* and part of *Ball*, the Court declared that its "understanding of the criteria used to assess whether [direct] aid to religion has an impermissible effect" had "changed."[19]

Several factors brought about this shift away from "no aid" separationism and toward evenhanded neutrality in funding matters. Understanding the significance of these factors may also provide insight into the future of funding jurisprudence.

The first factor responsible for a change in judicial and popular attitudes toward government funding of religion was the rise of the social welfare state in the latter half of the twentieth century. Prior to the New Deal era of the 1930s, state and federal governments provided little in the way of public services or benefits to private individuals; the federal government provided for our national defense and regulated trade and commerce, while the states' primary obligations were to provide for public education, criminal justice, and public highways. Thus, early on, a rule prohibiting public funding of religious institutions did not appear that inequitable, in that government was not generally in the business of providing financial benefits to its citizens.

The primary exception, of course, was public education, a benefit some cities and states had been providing since the early 1800s. As discussed in chapter 13, government bodies generally refused to fund parochial school education, even though they were funding public schools where nonsectarian religion was often taught. Although Catholic leaders during the nineteenth and early twentieth centuries pointed to this apparent inequality, they were arguing against the trend toward making public education more secular, not more religious. Excluding parochial schools from the benefits of public funding, based on concerns for church-state separation, was not atypical when compared to the overall lack of government benefits programs generally.[20]

This relationship between the government and its citizens began to change with the New Deal and more dramatically with the advent of the Great Society in the 1960s. Beginning with Social Security and then Medicare, Medicaid, Aid to Families with Dependent Children (welfare), college student-loans and other similar programs at the federal and state levels, the government became increasingly responsible for the support, care, and education of individuals. One such crucial federal program was the Elementary and Secondary Education Act of 1965, which provides federal grants to state and local education agencies for supplemental instruction and educational materials to benefit low-income children. Ever since its enactment, ESEA has required state and local education agencies to provide services to all eligible children, including those attending private schools. By the last quarter of the twentieth century, therefore, government grant and benefits programs, including the funds and the regulations that followed the funds, had become ubiquitous in ways that the founders of the nation could hardly have envisioned.

The complement to the rise of the welfare state has been the trend toward privatizing human service programs. As far back as the nineteenth century, local governmental entities occasionally provided government funds to private charitable or educational institutions for research or to perform quasi-government functions. In one of the first such partnerships, in 1803 Congress authorized and President Thomas Jefferson approved federal support for Catholic missions to American Indians, a practice that continued until 1897. Also, one of the earlier Establishment Clause cases involved an 1899 challenge to a federal grant to a Catholic hospital in the District of Columbia, which provided charitable medical services (*Bradfeld v. Roberts*).[21] But such funding and partnering was modest until the latter half of the twentieth century. With the advent of the social welfare state, again, government contracting with nongovernmental entities to provide essential human services became increasingly common, if not the rule in some segments.[22] At the same time that the government took on greater responsibility for human services—sometimes displacing private and religious operations—it in turn began to fund nongovernmental entities to perform these now "government" functions. Government grants flowed to nongovernmental providers, many of them with religious affiliations. For example, a primary recipient of the federal Hill-Burton program providing government grants for hospital construction has been religiously affiliated hospitals. Similarly, much of the government funds to underwrite housing for low-income and disabled persons has gone to religiously affiliated agencies. In fact, in 1996, the same year as Congress enacted "Charitable Choice" to regularize a certain set of rules governing religious participation in welfare grant programs, Catholic Charities U.S.A., was already receiving 1.3 billion dollars per year from various government sources to fund its social programs. It is not surprising, therefore, that when the modern Court first approved the constitutionality of religious participation in a general grant program, it came within the context of a social service program (*Bowen v. Kendrick*[23]).

Thus, the combination of these two factors—ubiquitous benefit programs and the privatization of government services—meant that the earlier rules excluding government funding of religious institutions and activities, primarily religious schools, seemed out of step with the prevailing trend. With many government benefits now being universally available, excluding certain religious institutions from participating in government largesse now was seen by some in a different light.

These institutional and structural changes alone, however, cannot explain the shift in the Court's jurisprudence or provide a road map to where the high court may be headed. Two other factors, already mentioned in the commentary accompanying the cases in chapter 13, fueled the shift in Court jurisprudence and will be instrumental in future funding developments: the rise of neutrality theory and private choice.

Government neutrality toward religion, as a constitutional value, has been part of the Court's jurisprudence since the 1947 decision of *Everson*. As discussed, the Court there identified the twin values of separationism and neutrality toward religion, noting of the latter that the state could not "exclude the members of any . . . faith, *because of their faith, or lack of it*, from receiving the benefits of public welfare legislation."[24] In the forty years following *Everson*, the Court occasionally spoke in terms of neutrality, but usually as a complement to separationist principles, not as representing a competing theorem. Possibly because of its subordinate role, the Court's early use of neutrality was frequently discordant. Following *Everson*, the high court identified neutrality as a goal in rulings as seemingly inconsistent as upholding tax exemptions for churches and prohibiting tax credits for tuition at parochial schools.[25] Maintaining "neutrality" was also the rationale for prohibiting school-sponsored prayer and Bible readings but permitting student religious clubs on secondary school campuses.[26] One explanation for this seeming inconsistency is that the concept of neutrality is difficult to define.[27] Neutrality is "a coat of many colors," the second Justice Harlan once remarked, and the concept is open to many interpretations.[28] Between 1947 and 1995 the Court used the term to represent quite distinct concepts—as a median between encouraging and discouraging religion, as synonym for "secular," and as a form of evenhanded treatment.[29]

The notion of evenhanded treatment of religious and secular entities under generally applicable laws[30] first appeared in cases decided in the 1980s involving access of religious speakers to government forums. In *Widmar v. Vincent* (1981) and *Board of Education v. Mergens* (1990), both involving religious group use of public educational facilities, the Court looked to the general access allowed other speakers under the programs to allay Establishment Clause concerns.[31] The application of evenhanded-neutrality principles to religious speech in public fora is not surprising, given the Court has long reproved subject-matter and viewpoint-based regulations of nongovernmental expression.[32] Indeed, a number of the same justices who took the "strict separationist" position regarding government aid or other support for religious messages, activities, and institutions also voted to uphold policies of equal treatment or equal access for religious speakers to governmental forums. According to these justices, allowing religious speakers to have the same access to government forums as other nongovernmental speakers did not raise the specter of government support for religion. Thus, equal treatment of religion and nonreligion by government was viewed as being appropriate in this context.

But soon this notion of equal treatment or evenhanded neutrality became increasingly significant in the context of government funding questions, and here "strict separationist" justices generally resisted its application. The Court's affinity for the principle of evenhanded neutrality in the funding context became evident in the cases of *Mueller v. Allen* (1983), *Witters v. Washington Department of Services for the Blind* (1986), and *Zobrest v. Catalina Foothills School District* (1993), where it upheld indirect forms of financial assistance to religious schools and colleges.[33] Relying on the access case of *Widmar*, the Court held that programs "that neutrally provide[ ] state assistance to a broad spectrum of citizens [are] not readily subject to challenge under the Establishment Clause."[34] But in none of those cases did neutrality principles dominate. Responding to separationist concerns, the various Court majorities underscored that the financial benefits were "attenuated,"[35] afforded only an "indirect economic benefit,"[36] were insubstantial in the aggregate,[37] and lacked appearances of state approval of religion.[38] In the most recent of the trilogy—*Zobrest*—the Court went out of its way to distinguish the "indirect" and "attenuated financial benefit" of the sign language interpreter[39] from "direct grants of government aid" that "relieve[] sectarian schools of costs they otherwise would [bear] in educating their students."[40] Thus, while program neutrality was crucial, that fact did not predetermine the outcome of the various cases nor obviate other concerns traditionally resolved under a separationist analysis.

Therefore, it was the 2000 decision of *Mitchell v. Helms* where four members of the Court anointed evenhanded-neutrality as the dominant analytical standard for funding cases. Speaking for a plurality, Justice Clarence Thomas declared that, "if the government, seeking to further some legitimate secular purpose, offers aid on the same terms, without regard to religion, to all who adequately further that purpose, then it is fair to say that any aid going to a religious recipient only has the effect of furthering that secular purpose."[41] This is a particularly potent version of neutrality, one that stands independent of private choice or concerns about the actual diversion of public funds for religious purposes.[42] Provided the generally available aid does not have religious content, then it may be used to support religious activity.

The *Mitchell* plurality's sole reliance on evenhanded-neutrality led Justice Sandra O'Connor to call the formula "a rule of unprecedented breadth," one that comes close "to assigning that factor singular importance in the future adjudication of Establishment Clause challenges."[43] She explained:

> I do not quarrel with the plurality's recognition that neutrality is an important reason for upholding government-aid programs against Establishment Clause challenges. Our cases have described neutrality in precisely this manner, and we have emphasized a program's neutrality repeatedly in our decisions approving various forms of school aid. Nevertheless, we have never held that a government-aid program passes constitutional muster *solely* because of the neutral criteria it employs as a basis for distributing aid.[44]

O'Connor strenuously objected to the fact that "the plurality opinion foreshadow[ed] the approval of direct monetary subsidies to religious organizations, even when they use the money to advance their religious objectives."

Yet, despite her criticism of the *Mitchell* plurality's approach,[45] O'Connor agreed that the Court has "emphasized a program's neutrality repeatedly in our decisions approving various forms of school aid," a point she reiterated in her *Zelman* concurrence.[46] These decisions all indicate that evenhanded neutrality is not merely one element in the Court's analytical arsenal but is increasingly the dominant factor.[47]

Complementing neutrality is the element of "private choice," discussed in the notes accompanying *Mueller, Witters, Zobrest,* and *Zelman*. Financial aid that flows to religious institutions "only as a result of the genuinely independent and private choices of aid recipients" does not represent the same type of threats to Establishment Clause values as exist with direct aid programs, the Court indicated in *Witters*.[48] "[I]f numerous private choices, rather than the single choice of a government, determine the distribution of aid, pursuant to neutral eligibility criteria, then a government cannot, or at least cannot easily, grant special favors that might lead to a religious establishment."[49]

Accordingly, the neutrality or general availability of a program and the existence of private choice for transferring funds from the government to a religious institution go hand-in-hand. The *Mitchell* plurality appeared ready to uphold the direct funding of religious activities solely under a neutral program, even in the absence of private choice, but to date a Court majority has been unwilling to deviate so far from earlier Establishment Clause jurisprudence. The addition of two new justices to the Court since *Zelman*—with Justice Samuel Alito replacing Justice Sandra O'Connor—may herald future changes in Establishment Clause jurisprudence. For the present, however, future funding programs will need both elements to survive Establishment Clause scrutiny. The mutually reinforcing nature of the two elements of neutrality and private choice can be seen in the *Zelman* holding, where the Court summed up the rule:

> [W]here a government aid program is neutral with respect to religion, and provides assistance directly to a broad class of citizens who, in turn, direct government aid to religious [institutions] wholly as a result of their own genuine and independent private choice, the program is not readily subject to challenge under the Establishment Clause. A program that shares these features permits government aid to reach

religious institutions only by way of the deliberate choices of numerous individual recipients. The incidental advancement of a religious mission, or the perceived endorsement of a religious message, is reasonably attributable to the individual recipient, not
to the government, whose role ends with the disbursement of benefits.[50]

The rule requiring both neutrality and private choice for funds to flow to religious institutions applies, however, where the funds may be put to religious purposes, such that the
institution's religious mission may be advanced. The 1997 *Agostini* decision indicates that
the government may fund the secular programs of a religious institution, such as Catholic
Charities, without needing to revert to a private choice formula. Provided the government program is neutral toward religion in its goals, does not award grants based on the
religious identity of the recipient, contains sufficient safeguards to ensure the government
is not paying for religious indoctrination, and provides only an attenuated benefit to religion, then religious institutions may participate in direct funding programs.

What was left unanswered by *Agostini* and *Mitchell*, however, is whether anything remains of the pervasively sectarian doctrine (barring government funding of institutions "in
which religion is so pervasive that a substantial portion of [their] functions are subsumed
in the religious mission. . . .").[51] Many scholars believe the pervasively sectarian doctrine
is dead, particularly following the condemnation of the rule by the *Mitchell* plurality as
"not only unnecessary but also offensive."[52] Others believe that the doctrine still controls
situations where churches or other houses of worship are involved or where religious institutions choose to integrate religious teachings into their services, such that it becomes
impossible to ensure that the government is not paying for religious indoctrination. Lower
courts post-*Mitchell* continue to apply the pervasively sectarian doctrine to exclude some
religious institutions from receiving government grants for their social service programs.
Ultimately, the Supreme Court will have to decide whether there is anything left to the
pervasively sectarian doctrine.

The final factor to consider for the future of Supreme Court funding jurisprudence
is the overlay of state and federal discretion on funding matters and the existence of state
constitutional prohibitions. The Court has long been deferential to legislative authority to
make funding determinations. Legislatures, as the popularly elected branches authorized
to make policy judgments, are best equipped to balance perpetual revenue constraints
with competing allocation demands. Accordingly, the Court has held that despite the
existence of a constitutionally protected right (e.g., the right to religious education), there
is no corresponding right to demand government funding in order to enhance the exercise
of that right.[53] Recent decisions touting neutral treatment (e.g., *Rosenberger*) have led some
to suggest that the exclusion of similarly situated religious entities from a government
program may constitute impermissible discrimination. But most scholars and observers
believe that the government is under no obligation to fund a religious alternative to every
secular-based program, provided it has not created an open forum for diverse expressive
views. Therefore, for example, a state may continue to fund public schools without having to fund private religious schools. And courts have held that states may choose to pay
tuition expenses for students to attend private, nonreligious schools without having to
extend the same benefit to students attending religious schools.

A partial answer to this last example was provided in *Locke v. Davey* (2004) and leads
to the second point: that state constitutional provisions must also be considered in any
discussion of the future of government funding and religion. As discussed in chapters 1
and 13, many states have more detailed, and stricter, provisions prohibiting the govern-

ment funding of religious institutions, including religious schools. *Locke* indicated two important points: first, the mere fact that a particular form of aid is permissible under the federal constitution does not mean that states are required to provide such assistance. States may enforce their own visions of religious freedom provided those interpretations do not infringe upon a right protected under the federal constitution; and second, that there is some room for flexibility—"play in the joints" as the Court remarked—between what may be required by the Free Exercise, Free Speech, or Equal Protection Clauses and what is prohibited under the Establishment Clause. On the one hand, this flexibility allows for permissible legislative accommodations of religion not required by free exercise or prohibited by nonestablishment, e.g., an exemption from paying parking meters on Sundays). On the other hand, it allows the state sometimes to exclude certain religious entities from discretionary spending programs. Thus, no state is required to establish a voucher program for religious (and nonreligious) school tuition, even though the Supreme Court has indicated some such programs are permissible under the federal Establishment Clause. And, a state may be justified in excluding religious schools from participating in a voucher program offering private school tuition based on its own constitutional language. This is the general lesson from *Locke*, although some of these specific issues are sure to be litigated because the breadth of *Locke*'s holding is contested.

Given the loosening of constitutional restrictions in this area, it seems clear that more government aid will flow to religious institutions in the future. A handful of states may adopt voucher programs on the model of those in operation in Wisconsin and Ohio. More likely, states will adopt tax relief measures such as tax deductions or credits which are less controversial than vouchers. Also, it is likely that states and the federal government will increase financial arrangements with religious social service agencies as a result of "Charitable Choice" or various "faith-based initiatives." There are, and will continue to be, numerous lawsuits about access to this kind of aid and the types of regulatory conditions that may be placed on such aid. It is in this latter area that the Court will likely next apply its developing funding jurisprudence.

# PART IV

# THE ESTABLISHMENT CLAUSE II

# CHAPTER 16

# RELIGIOUS EXPRESSION AND PUBLIC SCHOOLS
## BACKGROUND, RELEASED-TIME PROGRAMS, AND THE 1960S SCHOOL-PRAYER DECISIONS

A major front in the battle over the constitutional rules governing the relationship between religion and the state has been, and continues to be, our nation's public schools. May public school teachers or students lead a classroom of students in prayer or Bible readings? May public schools release students to religious authorities during the school day for a period of off-site religious instruction? Must public schools allow student religious organizations to use school facilities for after-school meetings when other student organizations are permitted to do so? Does the recitation in public schools of the Pledge of Allegiance with the words "under God" amount to state advancement of religion, and thus constitute an unconstitutional practice?

These are just a few of the controversial questions the United States Supreme Court has addressed in the last sixty years. Before examining the selection of cases and other materials that follow, it is helpful briefly to recall the constitutional significance of the people and institutions involved in these questions—students, parents, schools, and teachers.

Like other citizens, public school students possess First Amendment rights to express themselves religiously and to practice their faith in other ways. Although schools enjoy substantial latitude to impose rules of conduct and determine pedagogical matters, students retain these basic rights within the confines of public schools. Parents' constitutional rights also can be relevant in this arena—parents have the basic right, for example, to raise their children in a particular faith or none without interference from the state.

As governmental institutions, public schools are bound by the constitutional obligations that bind the state. While public schools must protect students' rights to express themselves religiously and practice their religion in other ways, they also must ensure that the school itself takes no part in advancing religion generally or preferring particular religions over others. In general, the school must neither encourage nor discourage religious belief and observance. And school officials are obligated to ensure that the school is not used as a mechanism for imposing religion on students. Finally, while school administrators and teachers enjoy certain First Amendment rights to express their personal faith in their nongovernmental capacities, they also are representatives of the government and therefore have constitutional obligations in their official capacities. Accordingly matters of religious expression in public schools require a delicate balancing of interests and rights.

It also is important to remember that the Court often has drawn important distinctions between public universities and colleges on the one hand, and public elementary and secondary schools on the other. Public elementary and, to a lesser extent, secondary schools, educate impressionable youth who could perceive official support or discouragement of religion even where none would be perceived by a more mature audience. Young children are also more susceptible to peer pressure and more likely to view their teachers as role models to be emulated. A teacher's defense of his or her religious convictions could be understood by the teacher's young students as an official, rather than a personal, endorsement of those beliefs, for example. Writing for the Court, Justice William Brennan noted in 1987:

> The Court has been particularly vigilant in monitoring compliance with the Establishment Clause in elementary and secondary schools. Families entrust public schools with the education of their children, but condition their trust on the understanding that the classroom will not purposely be used to advance religious views that may conflict with the private beliefs of the student and his or her family. Students in such institutions are impressionable and their attendance is involuntary. The State exerts great authority and coercive power through mandatory attendance requirements, and because of the students' emulation of teachers as role models and the children's susceptibility to peer pressure.[1]

This chapter first briefly discusses the history of the common school movement in the United States and then considers cases that have arisen in public elementary and secondary schools, including ones involving a practice known as "released time" as well as prayer in the public schools.

## HISTORICAL BACKGROUND: THE COMMON SCHOOL MOVEMENT

The following essay examines the history of the common school movement in the United States. It provides a glimpse of the history of public elementary and secondary schools and helps to explain the tensions on their mission. Professor Warren Nord has sketched out this history of the issue of religion's relationship to public schools.

> Control over education remained in local hands in the early years of the new republic, and schooling remained religious. Some states retained religious establishments into the nineteenth century and as the idea of a truly nonreligious education was unimaginable, considerable tax support was provided for religious schools. Horace Mann wrote of the Massachusetts schools of the 1830s: "I found books in the schools as strictly and exclusively *doctrinal* as any on the shelves of a theological library. I hear teachers giving oral instructions as strictly and purely *doctrinal* as any ever heard from the pulpit or from the professor's chair."
>
> The movement for tax-supported state systems of "common schools" began in the 1830s. There is a great deal of scholarly controversy regarding the motivation of those who fought for common schools. Some scholars see the movement as a natural extension of democracy and liberalism, making education available to all children, others as a conservative effort to shore up the status quo and defend economic privilege by providing trained workers, socialized to accept the values of order and discipline. It has also been argued that the common schools were designed to preserve religious privilege, that is, Protestant culture and values, in the face of growing religious pluralism.
>
> The common schools were officially nonsectarian. Horace Mann, their most influential spokesman, argued in the spirit of James Madison and Thomas Jefferson

that establishments of religion have always led to persecution and tyranny. In America a different principle had been embraced, "that government should do all that it can to facilitate the acquisition of religious truth, but shall leave the decision of the question, what religious truth is, to the arbitrament, without human appeal, of each man's reasons and conscience." The terms "public school" and "common school," Mann argued, "bear upon their face that they are schools which the children of the entire community may attend. Every man not on the pauper-list is taxed for their support; but he is not taxed to support them as special religious institutions; if he were, it would satisfy at once the largest definition of a religious establishment."

Nonetheless, Mann declared that "religious instruction in our schools, to the extent which the constitution and laws of the State allowed and prescribed, was indispensable to [the students'] highest welfare, and essential to the vitality of moral education." Sectarian no; religious, yes. "Our system," he wrote, "earnestly inculcates all Christian morals; it founds its morals on the basis of religion; it welcomes the religion of the Bible; and in receiving the Bible, it allows it to do what is allowed to do in no other system—to *speak for itself.* But here it stops." That is, Bible reading was to be allowed—the Bible could "speak for itself"—but no doctrinal gloss was to be given; no denominational interpretation of religion was to be permitted. Religious education was not for the purpose of converting students to any denomination but was to underwrite moral values and enable a student "to judge for himself, according to the dictates of his own reason and conscience, what his religious obligations are."

By the middle of the nineteenth century William Ruffner (sometimes called the "Horace Mann of the South") had established in Virginia common schools that taught a "common" or nonsectarian Christianity, largely through the use of the Bible. In 1869 the National Teachers Association passed resolutions declaring that the Bible should be "devotionally read, and its precepts inculcated in all the common schools of the land." But it also held that the teaching of "partisan or sectarian principles in our public schools is a violation of the fundamental principles of our American system of education." In his study of the history of religion in American education Robert Michaelson writes that "by 1870 Protestants generally had arrived at the conclusion that the public school system was best for America, that sectarianism—as they understood it—had no place in that system, but that religion—'nonsectarian,' 'common' religion—was essential to the school."

Of course, the claim that public schools were nonsectarian was disingenuous. Horace Mann and most of his fellow reformers in Massachusetts were Unitarians, committed to a liberal religion of moral duty and enlightenment. The foe was traditional, revealed religion, which they took to be divisive and socially dangerous. Hence, Charles Glenn has argued, the common schools were "profoundly subversive of the beliefs of most Protestants," at least most conservative Protestants. Indeed most of the early opposition to common schools came from conservative Protestants.

Eventually, Protestants united behind common schools because of the growing flood of immigration—particularly, in the case of Massachusetts, from Catholic Ireland. The Protestant hope was that nonsectarian schools would be acceptable to Catholics, who would be socialized into becoming good Americans. To this end, Protestants were willing to dispense with much doctrinal content. The Congregationalist journal *New Englander* editorialized: "It is better that Roman Catholic children should be educated in public schools in which the Bible is not read, than that they should not be educated at all, or educated in schools under the absolute control of their priesthood." Of course, the Bible continued to be read—and this was a major reason Catholics would not attend public schools. But even if there was no denominational catechism, schools used the Protestant rather than the Catholic Bible.

Indeed, to read the Bible without comment itself was not neutral but was a Protestant notion; for Catholics, the Bible required the gloss of the church to be understood. In response, Catholics developed a massive parochial school system.

In some places Catholics pressed for tax support of parochial schools—after all, Protestant common schools were tax supported. Not only was no such aid forthcoming but several states adopted constitutional amendments prohibiting the use of tax funds for "sectarian" schools. In 1875 Congress fell a few votes short of passing a constitutional amendment that would have prohibited the use of public funds (at all levels of government) for the support of sectarian education. Nonetheless, Congress did pass a law requiring that states admitted to the Union after 1876 include provisions for establishing public schools "free from sectarian control," and many states adopted constitutional amendments prohibiting the use of state funds for sectarian schools. By 1900 most states prohibited the use of public funds for sectarian purposes, and many prohibited religious instruction in the public schools. So by the end of the century there were legal impediments to religious education in many states, though unadorned Bible reading was often taken to be nonsectarian and hence permissible. . . .

Even if nineteenth-century common schools were rather less nonsectarian than they claimed to be, the logic of secularization was clearly at work. In a religiously pluralistic culture, peace is achieved by eliminating what is divisive—that is, religion—from public institutions. In the twentieth century Bible reading and prayer became increasingly uncommon as the schools attempted to become truly common schools, acceptable to all religious and secular communities.[2]

Note that Justice Felix Frankfurter's concurring opinion in *McCollum v. Board of Education* and Justice William Brennan's concurring opinion in *Abingdon Township School District v. Schempp* contain additional information about the history of the common school movement. Bear this information in mind as we explore cases that wrestle with the appropriate place of history in the analysis of First Amendment issues.

## "Released-Time" Programs

In 1948, the U.S. Supreme Court decided a case, *McCollum v. Board of Education*, that dealt with a policy of the Champaign, Illinois, Board of Education that allowed teachers employed by private religious groups to offer a weekly period of devotional religious instruction during the school day on public school premises for students whose parents desired such instruction for their children. In his concurring opinion in this case, Justice Frankfurter described the genesis of this practice, commonly known as "released time." Frankfurter wrote:

[In nineteenth century America, religious people were] naturally concerned about the part of the child's education entrusted "to the family altar, the church, and the private school." The promotion of religious education took many forms. Laboring under financial difficulties and exercising only persuasive authority, various denominations felt handicapped in their task of religious education. Abortive attempts were therefore frequently made to obtain public funds for religious schools. But the major efforts of religious inculcation were a recognition of the principle of Separation by the establishment of church schools privately supported. Parochial schools were maintained by various denominations. These, however, were often beset by serious handicaps, financial and otherwise, so that the religious aims which they represented found other directions. There were experiments with vacation schools, with Saturday as well as Sunday schools. They all fell short of their purpose. It was urged that by appearing to make religion a one-day-a-week matter, the Sunday school, which acquired national acceptance, tended to relegate the child's religious education, and thereby his religion, to a minor role not unlike the enforced piano lesson.

Out of these inadequate efforts evolved the week-day church school, held on one or more afternoons a week after the close of the public school. But children continued to be children; they wanted to play when school was out, particularly when other children were free to do so. Church leaders decided that if the week-day church school was to succeed, a way had to be found to give the child his religious education during what the child conceived to be his "business hours."

The initiation of the [released-time] movement may fairly be attributed to Dr. George U. Wenner. The underlying assumption of his proposal, made at the Interfaith Conference on Federation held in New York City in 1905, was that the public school unduly monopolized the child's time and that the churches were entitled to their share of it. This, the schools should "release." Accordingly, the Federation, citing the example of the Third Republic of France, urged that upon the request of their parents children be excused from public school on Wednesday afternoon, so that the churches could provide "Sunday school on Wednesday." This was to be carried out on church premises under church authority. Those not desiring to attend church schools would continue their normal classes. Lest these public school classes unfairly compete with the church education, it was requested that the school authorities refrain from scheduling courses or activities of compelling interest or importance.

The proposal aroused considerable opposition and it took another decade for a "released time" scheme to become part of a public school system. Gary, Indiana, inaugurated the movement [in 1914]. . . . The religious teaching was held on church premises and the public schools had no hand in the conduct of these church schools. They did not supervise the choice of instructors or the subject matter taught. Nor did they assume responsibility for the attendance, conduct or achievement of the child in a church school; and he received no credit for it. The period of attendance in the religious schools would otherwise have been a play period for the child, with the result that the arrangement did not cut into public school instruction or truly affect the activities or feelings of the children who did not attend the church schools. . . .

In the *McCollum* case, the Court ruled the Champaign released-time program unconstitutional under the First and Fourteenth Amendments. As you read the case, see if you can identify the elements or nature of the policy that caused it to run afoul of the Constitution.

---

## McCOLLUM v. BOARD OF EDUCATION
### 333 U.S. 203 (1948)

▨ MR. JUSTICE BLACK delivered the opinion of the court.

This case relates to the power of a state to utilize its tax-supported public school system in aid of religious instruction insofar as that power may be restricted by the First and Fourteenth Amendments to the Federal Constitution.

The appellant, Vashti McCollum, began this action for mandamus against the Champaign Board of Education in the Circuit Court of Champaign County,

Illinois. Her asserted interest was that of a resident and taxpayer of Champaign and of a parent whose child was then enrolled in the Champaign public schools. Illinois has a compulsory education law which, with exceptions, requires parents to send their children, aged seven to sixteen, to its tax-supported public schools where the children are to remain in attendance during the hours when the schools are regularly in session. . . .

Appellant's petition for mandamus alleged that religious teachers, employed by private religious groups, were permitted to come weekly into the school buildings during the regular hours set apart for secular teaching, and then and there for a period of thirty minutes substitute their religious teaching for the secular education provided under the compulsory education law. The petitioner charged that this joint public-school religious-group program violated the First and Fourteenth Amendments to the United States Constitution. The prayer of her petition was that the Board of Education be ordered to "adopt and enforce rules and regulations prohibiting all instruction in and teaching of religious education in all public schools in Champaign School District Number 71, . . . and in all public school houses and buildings in said district when occupied by public schools." . . .

Although there are disputes between the parties as to various inferences that may or may not properly be drawn from the evidence concerning the religious program, the following facts are shown by the record without dispute. In 1940 interested members of the Jewish, Roman Catholic, and a few of the Protestant faiths formed a voluntary association called the Champaign Council on Religious Education. They obtained permission from the Board of Education to offer classes in religious instruction to public school pupils in grades four to nine inclusive. Classes were made up of pupils whose parents signed printed cards requesting that their children be permitted to attend; they were held weekly, thirty minutes for the lower grades, forty-five minutes for the higher. The council employed the religious teachers at no expense to the school authorities, but the instructors were subject to the approval and supervision of the superintendent of schools.[3] The classes were taught in three separate religious groups by Protestant teachers, Catholic priests, and a Jewish rabbi, although for the past several years there have apparently been no classes instructed in the Jewish religion. Classes were conducted in the regular classrooms of the school building. Students who did not choose to take the religious instruction were not released from public school duties; they were required to leave their classrooms and go to some other place in the school building for pursuit of their secular studies. On the other hand, students who were released from secular study for the religious instructions were required to be present at the religious classes. Reports of their presence or absence were to be made to their secular teachers.

---

[3] The trial court found: "Before any faith or other group may obtain permission from the defendant for the similar, free and equal use of rooms in the public school buildings said faith or group must make application to the superintendent of schools of said School District Number 71, who in turn will determine whether or not it is practical for said group to teach in said school system." The president of the local school board testified: ". . . The Protestants would have one group and the Catholics, and would be given a room where they would have the class and we would go along with the plan of the religious people. They were all to be treated alike, with the understanding that the teachers they would bring into the school were approved by the superintendent. . . . The superintendent was the last word so far as the individual was concerned. . . ."

The foregoing facts, without reference to others that appear in the record, show the use of tax-supported property for religious instruction and the close cooperation between the school authorities and the religious council in promoting religious education. The operation of the State's compulsory education system thus assists and is integrated with the program of religious instruction carried on by separate religious sects. Pupils compelled by law to go to school for secular education are released in part from their legal duty upon the condition that they attend the religious classes. This is beyond all question a utilization of the tax-established and tax-supported public school system to aid religious groups to spread their faith. And it falls squarely under the ban of the First Amendment (made applicable to the States by the Fourteenth) as we interpreted it in *Everson v. Board of Education,* 330 U.S. 1.

Recognizing that the Illinois program is barred by the First and Fourteenth Amendments if we adhere to the views expressed both by the majority and the minority in the *Everson* case, counsel for the respondents challenge those views as dicta and urge that we reconsider and repudiate them. They argue that historically the First Amendment was intended to forbid only government preference of one religion over another, not an impartial governmental assistance of all religions. In addition they ask that we distinguish or overrule our holding in the *Everson* case that the Fourteenth Amendment made the "establishment of religion" clause of the First Amendment applicable as a prohibition against the States. After giving full consideration to the arguments presented we are unable to accept either of these contentions.

To hold that a state cannot consistently with the First and Fourteenth Amendments utilize its public school system to aid any or all religious faiths or sects in the dissemination of their doctrines and ideals does not, as counsel urge, manifest a governmental hostility to religion or religious teachings. A manifestation of such hostility would be at war with our national tradition as embodied in the First Amendment's guaranty of the free exercise of religion. For the First Amendment rests upon the premise that both religion and government can best work to achieve their lofty aims if each is left free from the other within its respective sphere. Or, as we said in the *Everson* case, the First Amendment has erected a wall between Church and State which must be kept high and impregnable.

Here not only are the State's tax-supported public school buildings used for the dissemination of religious doctrines. The State also affords sectarian groups an invaluable aid in that it helps to provide pupils for their religious classes through use of the State's compulsory public school machinery. This is not separation of Church and State.

The cause is reversed and remanded to the State Supreme Court for proceedings not inconsistent with this opinion.

*Reversed and remanded.*

⊞ MR. JUSTICE FRANKFURTER delivered the following opinion, in which MR. JUSTICE JACKSON, MR. JUSTICE RUTLEDGE and MR. JUSTICE BURTON join.*

⊞ *MR. JUSTICE RUTLEDGE and MR. JUSTICE BURTON concurred also in the Court's opinion.

We dissented in *Everson v. Board of Education*, 330 U.S. 1, because in our view the Constitutional principle requiring separation of Church and State compelled invalidation of the ordinance sustained by the majority. Illinois has here authorized the commingling of sectarian with secular instruction in the public schools. The Constitution of the United States forbids this.

This case, in the light of the *Everson* decision, demonstrates anew that the mere formulation of a relevant Constitutional principle is the beginning of the solution of a problem, not its answer. This is so because the meaning of a spacious conception like that of the separation of Church from State is unfolded as appeal is made to the principle from case to case. We are all agreed that the First and the Fourteenth Amendments have a secular reach far more penetrating in the conduct of Government than merely to forbid an "established church." But agreement, in the abstract, that the First Amendment was designed to erect a "wall of separation between church and State," does not preclude a clash of views as to what the wall separates. . . .

To understand the particular program now before us as a conscientious attempt to accommodate the allowable functions of Government and the special concerns of the Church within the framework of our Constitution and with due regard to the kind of society for which it was designed, we must put this Champaign program of 1940 in its historic setting. Traditionally, organized education in the Western world was Church education. It could hardly be otherwise when the education of children was primarily study of the Word and the ways of God. Even in the Protestant countries, where there was a less close identification of Church and State, the basis of education was largely the Bible, and its chief purpose inculcation of piety. To the extent that the State intervened, it used its authority to further aims of the Church.

The emigrants who came to these shores brought this view of education with them. Colonial schools certainly started with a religious orientation. When the common problems of the early settlers of the Massachusetts Bay Colony revealed the need for common schools, the object was the defeat of "one chief project of that old deluder, Satan, to keep men from the knowledge of the Scriptures." The Laws and Liberties of Massachusetts, 1648 edition (Cambridge 1929) 47.

The evolution of colonial education, largely in the service of religion, into the public school system of today is the story of changing conceptions regarding the American democratic society, of the functions of State-maintained education in such a society, and of the role therein of the free exercise of religion by the people. The modern public school derived from a philosophy of freedom reflected in the First Amendment. It is appropriate to recall that the Remonstrance of James Madison, an event basic in the history of religious liberty, was called forth by a proposal which involved support to religious education. As the momentum for popular education increased and in turn evoked strong claims for State support of religious education, contests not unlike that which in Virginia had produced Madison's Remonstrance appeared in various forms in other States. New York and Massachusetts provide famous chapters in the history that established dissociation of religious teaching from State-maintained schools. In New York, the rise of the common schools led, despite fierce sectarian opposition, to the barring of tax funds to church schools, and later to any school in which sectarian doctrine was taught. In Massachusetts, largely through the efforts of Horace Mann, all sectarian teachings were barred from the common school to save it from being rent by denominational conflict. The upshot of these controversies, often long and fierce, is fairly summarized by saying that long before the Fourteenth Amendment subjected the States to new limitations, the prohibition of furtherance by the State of religious instruction became the guiding principle, in law and feeling, of the American people. In sustaining Stephen Girard's will, this Court referred to the inevitable conflicts engendered by matters "connected with religious polity" and particularly "in a country composed of such a variety of religious sects as our country." *Vidal v. Girard's Executors*, 2 How. 127, 198. That was more than one hundred years ago.

Separation in the field of education, then, was not imposed upon unwilling States by force of superior law. In this respect the Fourteenth Amendment merely reflected a principle then dominant in our national life. To the extent that the Constitution thus made it binding upon the States, the basis of the restriction is the whole experience of our people. Zealous watchfulness against fusion of secular and religious activities by Government itself, through any of its instruments but especially through its educational agencies, was the democratic response of the American community to the particular needs of a young and growing nation, unique in the composition of its people. A totally different situation elsewhere, as illustrated for instance by the English provisions for religious education in State-maintained schools, only serves to illustrate that free societies are not cast in one mould. Different institutions evolve from different historic circumstances.

It is pertinent to remind that the establishment of this principle of Separation in the field of education was not due to any decline in the religious beliefs of the people. Horace Mann was a devout Christian, and the deep religious feeling of James Madison is stamped upon the Remonstrance. The secular public school did not imply indifference to the basic role of religion in the life of the people, nor rejection of religious education as a means of fostering it. The claims of religion were not minimized by refusing to make the public schools agencies for their assertion. The non-sectarian or secular public school was the means of reconciling freedom in general with religious freedom. The sharp confinement of the public schools to secular education was a recognition of the need of a democratic society to educate its children, insofar as the State undertook to do so, in an atmosphere free from pressures in a realm in which pressures are most resisted and where conflicts are most easily and most bitterly engendered. Designed to serve as perhaps the most powerful agency for promoting cohesion among a heterogeneous democratic people, the public school must keep scrupulously free from entanglement in the strife of sects. The preservation of the community from divisive conflicts, of Government from irreconcilable pressures by religious groups, of religion from censorship and coercion however subtly exercised, requires strict confinement of the State to instruction other than religious, leaving to the individual's church and home, indoctrination in the faith of his choice.

This development of the public school as a symbol of our secular unity was not a sudden achievement nor attained without violent conflict. While in small communities of comparatively homogeneous religious beliefs, the need for absolute separation presented no urgencies, elsewhere the growth of the secular school encountered the resistance of feeling strongly engaged against it. But the inevitability of such attempts is the very reason for Constitutional provisions primarily concerned with the protection of minority groups. And such sects are shifting groups, varying from time to time, and place to place, thus representing in their totality the common interest of the nation.

Enough has been said to indicate that we are dealing not with a full-blown principle, nor one having the definiteness of a surveyor's metes and bounds. But by 1875 the separation of public education from Church entanglements, of the State from the teaching of religion, was firmly established in the consciousness of the nation. In that year President Grant made his famous remarks to the Convention of the Army of the Tennessee:

> Encourage free schools, and resolve that not one dollar appropriated for their support shall be appropriated to the support of any sectarian schools. Resolve that neither the State nor nation, nor both combined, shall support institutions of learning other than those sufficient to afford every child growing up in the land the opportunity of a good common-school education, unmixed with sectarian, pagan, or atheistical dogmas. Leave the matter of religion to the family altar, the church, and the private school, supported entirely by private contributions. Keep the church and the state forever separate. "The President's Speech at Des Moines," 22 Catholic World 433, 434-435 (1876).

So strong was this conviction, that rather than rest on the comprehensive prohibitions of the First and Fourteenth Amendments, President Grant urged that there be written into the United States Constitution particular elaborations, including a specific prohibition against the use of public funds for sectarian education, such as had been written into many State constitutions. By 1894, in urging the adoption of such a provision in the New York Constitution, Elihu Root was able to summarize a century of the nation's history: "It is not a question of religion, or of creed, or of party; it is a question of declaring and maintaining the great American principle of eternal separation between Church and State." Root, Addresses on Government and Citizenship, 137, 140. The extent to which this principle was deemed a presupposition of our Constitutional system is strikingly illustrated by the fact that every State admitted into the Union since 1876 was compelled by Congress to write into its constitution a requirement that it maintain a school system "free from sectarian control."

[After describing the origins of the "released-time movement (see the introduction to the case), Justice Frankfurter returns to the facts of this particular case.] How does "released time" operate in Champaign? Public school teachers distribute to their pupils cards supplied by church groups, so that the parents may indicate whether they desire religious instruction for their children. For those desiring it, religious classes are conducted in the regular classrooms of the public schools by teachers of religion paid by the churches and appointed by them, but, as the State court found, "subject to the approval and supervision of the superintendent." The courses do not profess to give secular instruction in subjects concerning religion. Their candid purpose is sectarian teaching. While a child can go to any of the religious classes offered, a particular sect wishing a teacher for its devotees requires the permission of the school superintendent "who in turn will determine whether or not it is practical for said group to teach in said school system." If no provision is made for religious instruction in the particular faith of a child, or if for other reasons the child is not enrolled in any of the offered classes, he is required to attend a regular school class, or a study period during which he is often left to his own devices. Reports of attendance in the religious classes are submitted by the religious instructor to the school authorities, and the child who fails to attend is presumably deemed a truant.

Religious education so conducted on school time and property is patently woven into the working scheme of the school. The Champaign arrangement thus presents powerful elements of inherent pressure by the school system in the interest of religious sects. The fact that this power has not been used to discriminate is beside the point. Separation is a requirement to abstain from fusing functions of Government and of religious sects, not merely to treat them all equally. That a child is offered an alternative may reduce the constraint; it does not eliminate the operation of influence by the school in matters sacred to conscience and outside the school's domain. The law of imitation operates, and non-conformity is not an outstanding characteristic of children. The result is an obvious pressure upon children to attend.[18] Again, while the Champaign school population represents only a fraction of the more than two hundred and fifty sects of the nation, not even all the practicing sects in Champaign are willing or able to provide religious instruction. The children belonging to these non-participating sects will thus have inculcated in them a feeling of separatism when the school should be the training ground for habits of community, or they will have religious instruction in a faith which is not that of their parents. As a result, the public school system of Champaign actively furthers inculcation in the religious tenets of some faiths, and in the process sharpens the consciousness of religious differences at least among some of the children committed to its care. These are consequences not amenable to statistics. But they are precisely the consequences against which the Constitution was directed when it prohibited the Government common to all from becoming embroiled, however innocently, in the destructive religious conflicts of which the history of even this country records some dark pages. . . .

Nor can the intrusion of religious instruction into the public school system of Champaign be minimized by saying that it absorbs less than an hour a week; in fact, that affords evidence of a design constitutionally objectionable. If it were merely a question of enabling a child to obtain religious instruction with a receptive mind, the thirty or forty-five minutes could readily be found on Saturday or Sunday. If that were all, Champaign might have drawn upon the French system, known in its American manifestation as "dismissed time," whereby one school day is shortened to allow all children to go where they please, leaving those who so desire to go to a religious school. The momentum of the whole school atmosphere and school planning is presumably put behind religious instruction, as given in Champaign, precisely in order to secure for the religious instruction such momentum and planning. To speak of "released time" as being only half or three quarters of an hour is to draw a thread from a fabric.

We do not consider, as indeed we could not, school programs not before us which, though colloquially characterized as "released time," present situations differing in aspects that may well be constitutionally crucial. Different forms which "released time" has taken during more than thirty years of growth

---

[18] It deserves notice that in discussing with the relator her son's inability to get along with his classmates, one of his teachers suggested that "allowing him to take the religious education course might help him to become a member of the group."

include programs which, like that before us, could not withstand the test of the Constitution; others may be found unexceptionable. We do not now attempt to weigh in the Constitutional scale every separate detail or various combination of factors which may establish a valid "released time" program. We find that the basic Constitutional principle of absolute Separation was violated when the State of Illinois, speaking through its Supreme Court, sustained the school authorities of Champaign in sponsoring and effectively furthering religious beliefs by its educational arrangement.

Separation means separation, not something less. Jefferson's metaphor in describing the relation between Church and State speaks of a "wall of separation," not of a fine line easily overstepped. The public school is at once the symbol of our democracy and the most pervasive means for promoting our common destiny. In no activity of the State is it more vital to keep out divisive forces than in its schools, to avoid confusing, not to say fusing, what the Constitution sought to keep strictly apart. "The great American principle of eternal separation"—Elihu Root's phrase bears repetition—is one of the vital reliances of our Constitutional system for assuring unities among our people stronger than our diversities. It is the Court's duty to enforce this principle in its full integrity.

We renew our conviction that "we have staked the very existence of our country on the faith that complete separation between the state and religion is best for the state and best for religion." *Everson v. Board of Education*, 330 U.S., 59. If nowhere else, in the relation between Church and State, "good fences make good neighbors."

MR. JUSTICE JACKSON, concurring

I join the opinion of MR. JUSTICE FRANKFURTER, and concur in the result reached by the Court, but with these reservations: I think it is doubtful whether the facts of this case establish jurisdiction in this Court, but in any event that we should place some bounds on the demands for interference with local schools that we are empowered or willing to entertain. I make these reservations a matter of record in view of the number of litigations likely to be started as a result of this decision. . . .

If, however, jurisdiction is found to exist, it is important that we circumscribe our decision with some care. What is asked is not a defensive use of judicial power to set aside a tax levy or reverse a conviction, or to enjoin threats of prosecution or taxation. The relief demanded in this case is the extraordinary writ of mandamus to tell the local Board of Education what it must do. The prayer for relief is that a writ issue against the Board of Education "ordering it to immediately adopt and enforce rules and regulations prohibiting all instruction in and teaching of religious education in all public schools . . . and in all public school houses and buildings in said district when occupied by public schools." The plaintiff, as she has every right to be, is an avowed atheist. What she has asked of the courts is that they not only end the "released time" plan but also ban every form of teaching which suggests or recognizes that there is a God. She would ban all teaching of the Scriptures. She especially mentions as an example of invasion of her rights "having pupils learn and recite such statements as, 'The Lord is my Shepherd, I shall not want.'" And she objects to teaching that the King James version of the Bible "is called the Christian's Guide Book, the Holy Writ and the Word of God," and many other similar matters. This Court is directing the Illinois courts generally to sustain plaintiff's complaint without exception of any of these grounds of complaint, without discriminating between them and without laying down any standards to define the limits of the effect of our decision.

To me, the sweep and detail of these complaints is a danger signal which warns of the kind of local controversy we will be required to arbitrate if we do not place appropriate limitation on our decision and exact strict compliance with jurisdictional requirements. Authorities list 256 separate and substantial religious bodies to exist in the continental United States. Each of them, through the suit of some discontented but unpenalized and untaxed representative, has as good a right as this plaintiff to demand that the courts compel the schools to sift out of their teaching everything inconsistent with its doctrines. If we are to eliminate everything that is objectionable to any of these warring sects or inconsistent with any of their doctrines, we will leave public education in shreds. Nothing but educational confusion and a discrediting of the public school system can result from subjecting it to constant law suits.

While we may and should end such formal and explicit instruction as the Champaign plan and can at all times prohibit teaching of creed and catechism and ceremonial and can forbid forthright proselyting in the schools, I think it remains to be demonstrated whether it is possible, even if desirable, to comply with such demands as plaintiff's completely to isolate and cast out of secular education all that some people may reasonably regard as religious instruction. Perhaps subjects such as mathematics, physics or chemistry are, or can be, completely secularized. But it would not seem practical to teach either practice or appreciation of the arts if we are to forbid exposure of youth to any religious influences. Music without sacred music, architecture minus the cathedral, or painting without the scriptural themes would be eccentric and incomplete, even from a secular point of view. Yet the inspirational appeal of religion in these guises is often stronger than in forthright sermon. Even such a "science" as biology raises the issue between evolution and creation as an explanation of our presence on this planet. Certainly a course in English literature that omitted the Bible and other powerful uses of our mother tongue for religious ends would be pretty barren. And I should suppose it is a proper, if not an indispensable, part of preparation for a worldly life to know the roles that religion and religions have played in the tragic story of mankind. The fact is that, for good or for ill, nearly everything in our culture worth transmitting, everything which gives meaning to life, is saturated with religious influences, derived from paganism, Judaism, Christianity—both Catholic and Protestant—and other faiths accepted by a large part of the world's peoples. One can hardly respect a system of education that would leave the student wholly ignorant of the currents of religious thought that move the world society for a part in which he is being prepared.

But how one can teach, with satisfaction or even with justice to all faiths, such subjects as the story of the Reformation, the Inquisition, or even the New England effort to found "a Church without a Bishop and a State without a King," is more than I know. It is too much to expect that mortals will teach subjects about which their contemporaries have passionate controversies with the detachment they may summon to teaching about remote subjects such as Confucius or Mohammed. When instruction turns to proselyting and imparting knowledge becomes evangelism is, except in the crudest cases, a subtle inquiry.

The opinions in this case show that public educational authorities have evolved a considerable variety of practices in dealing with the religious problem. Neighborhoods differ in racial, religious and cultural compositions. It must be expected that they will adopt different customs which will give emphasis to different values and will induce different experiments. And it must be expected that, no matter what practice prevails, there will be many discontented and possibly belligerent minorities. We must leave some flexibility to meet local conditions, some chance to progress by trial and error. While I agree that the religious classes involved here go beyond permissible limits, I also think the complaint demands more than plaintiff is entitled to have granted. So far as I can see this Court does not tell the State court where it may stop, nor does it set up any standards by which the State court may determine that question for itself.

The task of separating the secular from the religious in education is one of magnitude, intricacy and delicacy. To lay down a sweeping constitutional doctrine as demanded by complainant and apparently approved by the Court, applicable alike to all school boards of the nation, "to immediately adopt and enforce rules and regulations prohibiting all instruction in and teaching of religious education in all public schools," is to decree a uniform, rigid and, if we are consistent, an unchanging standard for countless school boards representing and serving highly localized groups which not only differ from each other but which themselves from time to time change attitudes. It seems to me that to do so is to allow zeal for our own ideas of what is good in public instruction to induce us to accept the role of a super board of education for every school district in the nation.

It is idle to pretend that this task is one for which we can find in the Constitution one word to help us as judges to decide where the secular ends and the sectarian begins in education. Nor can we find guidance in any other legal source. It is a matter on which we can find no law but our own prepossessions. If with no surer legal guidance we are to take up and decide every variation of this controversy, raised by persons not subject to penalty or tax but who are dissatisfied with the way schools are dealing with the problem, we are likely to have much business of the sort. And, more importantly, we are likely to make the legal "wall of separation between church and state" as winding as the famous serpentine wall designed by Mr. Jefferson for the University he founded.

[※] MR. JUSTICE REED, dissenting.

The decisions reversing the judgment of the Supreme Court of Illinois interpret the prohibition of the First Amendment against the establishment of religion, made effective as to the states by the Fourteenth Amendment, to forbid pupils of the public schools electing, with the approval of their parents, courses in religious education. The courses are given, under the school laws of Illinois as approved by the Supreme Court of that state, by lay or clerical teachers supplied and directed by an interdenominational, local council of religious education. The classes are held in the respective school buildings of the pupils at study or released time periods so as to avoid conflict with recitations. The teachers and supplies are paid for by the interdenominational group. As I am convinced that this interpretation of the First Amendment is erroneous, I feel impelled to express the reasons for my disagreement. By directing attention to the many instances of close association of church and state in American society and by recalling that many of these relations are so much a part of our tradition and culture that they are accepted without more, this dissent may help in an appraisal of the meaning of the clause of the First Amendment concerning the establishment of religion and of the reasons which lead to the approval or disapproval of the judgment below. . . .

I find it difficult to extract from the opinions any conclusion as to what it is in the Champaign plan that is unconstitutional. Is it the use of school buildings for religious instruction; the release of pupils by the schools for religious instruction during school hours; the so-called assistance by teachers in handing out the request cards to pupils, in keeping lists of them for release and records of their attendance; or the action of the principals in arranging an opportunity for the classes and the appearance of the Council's instructors? None of the reversing opinions say whether the purpose of the Champaign plan for religious instruction during school hours is unconstitutional or whether it is some ingredient used in or omitted from the formula that makes the plan unconstitutional.

From the tenor of the opinions I conclude that their teachings are that any use of a pupil's school time, whether that use is on or off the school grounds, with the necessary school regulations to facilitate attendance, falls under the ban. I reach this conclusion notwithstanding one sentence of indefinite meaning in the second opinion: "We do not consider, as indeed we could not, school programs not before us which, though colloquially characterized as 'released time,' present situations differing in aspects that may well be constitutionally crucial." The use of the words "cooperation," "fusion," "complete hands-off," "integrate" and "integrated" to describe the relations between the school and the Council in the plan evidences this. So does the interpretation of the word "aid." The criticized "momentum of the whole school atmosphere," "feeling of separatism" engendered in the non-participating sects, "obvious pressure . . . to attend," and "divisiveness" lead to the stated conclusion. From the holding and the language of the opinions, I can only deduce that religious instruction of public school children during school hours is prohibited. The history of American education is against such an interpretation of the First Amendment. . . .

The phrase "an establishment of religion" may have been intended by Congress to be aimed only at a state church. When the First Amendment was pending in Congress in substantially its present form, "Mr. Madison said, he apprehended the meaning of the words to be, that Congress should not establish a religion, and enforce the legal observation of it by law, nor compel men to worship God in any manner contrary to their conscience." Passing years, however, have brought about acceptance of a broader meaning, although never until today, I believe, has this Court widened its interpretation to any such degree as holding that recognition of the interest of our nation in religion, through the granting, to qualified representatives of the principal faiths, of opportunity to present religion as an optional, extracurricular subject during released school time in public school buildings, was equivalent to an establishment of religion. A reading of the general statements of eminent statesmen of former days, referred to in the opinions in this case and in *Everson v. Board of Education*, will show that circumstances such as those in this case were far from the minds of the authors. The words and spirit of those statements may be wholeheartedly accepted without in the least impugning the judgment of the State of Illinois.

Mr. Jefferson, as one of the founders of the University of Virginia, a school which from its establishment in 1819 has been wholly governed, managed and controlled by the State of Virginia, was faced with the same problem that is before this Court today: the question of the constitutional limitation upon religious education in public schools. In his annual report as Rector, to the President and Directors of the Literary Fund, dated October 7, 1822, approved by the Visitors of the University of whom Mr. Madison was one, Mr. Jefferson set forth his views at some length. These suggestions of Mr. Jefferson were adopted and ch. II, § 1, of the Regulations of the University of October 4, 1824, provided that:

> Should the religious sects of this State, or any of them, according to the invitation held out to them, establish within, or adjacent to, the precincts of the University, schools for instruction in the religion of their sect, the students of the University will be free, and expected to attend religious worship at the establishment of their respective sects, in the morning, and in time to meet their school in the University at its stated hour. ·

Thus, the "wall of separation between church and State" that Mr. Jefferson built at the University which he founded did not exclude religious education from that school. The difference between the generality of his statements on the separation of church and state and the specificity of his conclusions on education are considerable. A rule of law should not be drawn from a figure of speech. . . .

This Court summarized the amendment's accepted reach into the religious field, as I understand its scope, in *Everson v. Board of Education*. The Court's opinion quotes the gist of the Court's reasoning in *Everson*. I agree, as there stated, that none of our governmental entities can "set up a church." I agree that they cannot "aid" all or any religions or prefer one "over another." But "aid" must be understood as a purposeful assistance directly to the church itself or to some religious group or organization doing religious work of such a character that it may fairly be said to be performing ecclesiastical functions. "Prefer" must give an advantage to one "over another." I agree that pupils cannot "be released in part from their legal duty" of school attendance upon condition that they attend religious classes. But as Illinois has held that it is within the discretion of the School Board to permit absence from school for religious instruction no legal duty of school attendance is violated. If the sentence in the Court's opinion, concerning the pupils' release from legal duty, is intended to mean that the Constitution forbids a school to excuse a pupil from secular control during school hours to attend voluntarily a class in religious education, whether in or out of school buildings, I disagree. Of course, no tax can be levied to support organizations intended "to teach or practice religion." I agree too that the state cannot influence one toward religion against his will or punish him for his beliefs. Champaign's religious education course does none of these things.

It seems clear to me that the "aid" referred to by the Court in the *Everson* case could not have been those incidental advantages that religious bodies, with other groups similarly situated, obtain as a by-product of organized society. This explains the well-known fact that all churches receive "aid" from government in the form of freedom from taxation. The *Everson* decision itself justified the transportation of children to church schools by New Jersey for safety reasons. It accords with *Cochran v. Louisiana State Board of Education*, 281

U.S. 370, where this Court upheld a free textbook statute of Louisiana against a charge that it aided private schools on the ground that the books were for the education of the children, not to aid religious schools. Likewise the National School Lunch Act aids all school children attending tax-exempt schools. In *Bradfield v. Roberts*, 175 U.S. 291, this Court held proper the payment of money by the Federal Government to build an addition to a hospital, chartered by individuals who were members of a Roman Catholic sisterhood, and operated under the auspices of the Roman Catholic Church. This was done over the objection that it aided the establishment of religion. While obviously in these instances the respective churches, in a certain sense, were aided, this Court has never held that such "aid" was in violation of the First or Fourteenth Amendment.

Well-recognized and long-established practices support the validity of the Illinois statute here in question. That statute, as construed in this case, is comparable to those in many states. All differ to some extent. New York may be taken as a fair example. In many states the program is under the supervision of a religious council composed of delegates who are themselves communicants of various faiths. As is shown by *Bradfield v. Roberts*, the fact that the members of the council have religious affiliations is not significant. In some, instruction is given outside of the school buildings; in others, within these buildings. Metropolitan centers like New York usually would have available quarters convenient to schools. Unless smaller cities and rural communities use the school building at times that do not interfere with recitations, they may be compelled to give up religious education. I understand that pupils not taking religious education usually are given other work of a secular nature within the schools. Since all these states use the facilities of the schools to aid the religious education to some extent, their desire to permit religious education to school children is thwarted by this Court's judgment. Under it, as I understand its language, children cannot be released or dismissed from school to attend classes in religion while other children must remain to pursue secular education. Teachers cannot keep the records as to which pupils are to be dismissed and which retained. To do so is said to be an "aid" in establishing religion; the use of public money for religion.

Cases running into the scores have been in the state courts of last resort that involved religion and the schools. Except where the exercises with religious significance partook of the ceremonial practice of sects or groups, their constitutionality has been generally upheld. Illinois itself promptly struck down as violative of its own constitution required exercises partaking of a religious ceremony. *People ex rel. Ring v. Board of Education*, 92 N. E. 251. In that case compulsory religious exercises—a reading from the King James Bible, the Lord's Prayer and the singing of hymns—were forbidden as "worship services." In this case, the Supreme Court of Illinois pointed out that in the *Ring* case, the activities in the school were ceremonial and compulsory; in this, voluntary and educational.

The practices of the federal government offer many examples of this kind of "aid" by the state to religion. The Congress of the United States has a chaplain for each House who daily invokes divine blessings and guidance for the proceedings. The armed forces have commissioned chaplains from early days. They conduct the public services in accordance with the liturgical requirements of their respective faiths, ashore and afloat, employing for the purpose property belonging to the United States and dedicated to the services of religion. Under the Servicemen's Readjustment Act of 1944, eligible veterans may receive training at government expense for the ministry in denominational schools. The schools of the District of Columbia have opening exercises which "include a reading from the Bible without note or comment, and the Lord's prayer." . . .

With the general statements in the opinions concerning the constitutional requirement that the nation and the states, by virtue of the First and Fourteenth Amendments may "make no law respecting an establishment of religion," I am in agreement. But, in the light of the meaning given to those words by the precedents, customs, and practices which I have detailed above, I cannot agree with the Court's conclusion that when pupils compelled by law to go to school for secular education are released from school so as to attend the religious classes, churches are unconstitutionally aided. Whatever may be the wisdom of the arrangement as to the use of the school buildings made with the Champaign Council of Religious Education, it is clear to me that past practice shows such cooperation between the schools and a non-ecclesiastical body is not forbidden by the First Amendment. When actual church services have always been permitted on government property, the mere use of the school buildings by a non-sectarian group for religious education ought not to be condemned as an establishment of religion. For a non-sectarian organization to give the type of instruction here offered cannot be said to violate our rule as to the establishment of religion by the state. The prohibition of enactments respecting the establishment of religion do not bar every friendly gesture between church and state. It is not an absolute prohibition against every conceivable situation

---

### RELIGIOUS EDUCATION CARD DISTRIBUTED TO PARENTS BY PUBLIC SCHOOL TEACHERS

Parent's Request Card

Please permit _____ in Grade ___ at _____ School to attend a class in Religious Education one period a week under the Auspices of the Champaign Council of Religious Education.

(Check which)

Date_____

( ) Interdenominational

( ) Protestant

( ) Roman Catholic

( ) Jewish

Signed _____ (Parent Name) _____

Parent's Church _____ Telephone No. _____

Address _____

A fee of 25 cents a semester is charged each pupil to help cover the cost of material used.

If you wish your child to receive religious instruction, please sign this card and return to the school.

Mae Chapin, Director.

[Mae Chapin, the Director, was not a school employee.]

where the two may work together, any more than the other provisions of the First Amendment—free speech, free press—are absolutes. If abuses occur, such as the use of the instruction hour for sectarian purposes, I have no doubt, in view of the *Ring* case, that Illinois will promptly correct them. If they are of a kind that tend to the establishment of a church or interfere with the free exercise of religion, this Court is open for a review of any erroneous decision. This Court cannot be too cautious in upsetting practices embedded in our society by many years of experience. A state is entitled to have great leeway in its legislation when dealing with the important social problems of its population. A definite violation of legislative limits must be established. The Constitution should not be stretched to forbid national customs in the way courts act to reach arrangements to avoid federal taxation. Devotion to the great principle of religious liberty should not lead us into a rigid interpretation of the constitutional guarantee that conflicts with accepted habits of our people. This is an instance where, for me, the history of past practices is determinative of the meaning of a constitutional clause, not a decorous introduction to the study of its text. The judgment should be affirmed.

---

Four years later the Court heard a case involving related facts. That case, *Zorach v. Clauson*, involved a New York City program that permitted public schools to release students during the school day to religious centers for devotional instruction. Thus, the program was largely the same as the one at issue in *McCollum*, except that the religious instruction took place off school premises.

The Court, including three justices who had been in the majority in the *McCollum* case (Justices Douglas and Burton and Chief Justice Vinson), ruled this practice constitutional. The majority opinion in *Zorach*, however, triggered bitter dissents from three other justices who had been in the *McCollum* majority (Justices Black, Frankfurter, and Jackson). As you read this case excerpt, consider whether the difference in facts between the two cases warrants the difference in the judgments.

---

## ZORACH V. CLAUSON
### 343 U.S. 306 (1952)

MR. JUSTICE DOUGLAS delivered the opinion of the Court.

New York City has a program which permits its public schools to release students during the school day so that they may leave the school buildings and school grounds and go to religious centers for religious instruction or devotional exercises. A student is released on written request of his parents. Those not released stay in the classrooms. The churches make weekly reports to the schools, sending a list of children who have been released from public school but who have not reported for religious instruction.

This "released time" program involves neither religious instruction in public school classrooms nor the expenditure of public funds. All costs, including the application blanks, are paid by the religious organizations. The case is therefore unlike *McCollum v. Board of Education*, which involved a "released time" program from Illinois. In that case the classrooms were turned over to religious instructors. We accordingly held that the program violated the First Amendment which (by reason of the Fourteenth Amendment) prohibits the states from establishing religion or prohibiting its free exercise. . . .

It takes obtuse reasoning to inject any issue of the "free exercise" of religion into the present case. No one is forced to go to the religious classroom and no religious exercise or instruction is brought to the classrooms of the public schools. A student need not take religious instruction. He is left to his own desires as to the manner or time of his religious devotions, if any.

There is a suggestion that the system involves the use of coercion to get public school students into religious classrooms. There is no evidence in the record before us that supports that conclusion. The present record indeed tells us that the school authorities are neutral in this regard and do no more than release students whose parents so request. If in fact coercion were used, if it were established that any one or more teachers were using their office to persuade or force students to take the religious instruction, a wholly different case would be presented. Hence we put aside that claim of coercion both as respects the "free exercise" of religion and "an establishment of religion" within the meaning of the First Amendment.

Moreover, apart from that claim of coercion, we do not see how New York by this type of "released time" program has made a law respecting an establishment of religion within the meaning of the First Amendment. There is much talk of the separation of Church and State in the history of the Bill of Rights and in the decisions clustering around the First Amendment. There cannot be the slightest doubt that the First Amendment reflects the philosophy that Church and State should be separated. And so far as interference with the "free exercise" of religion and an "establishment" of religion are concerned, the separation must be complete and unequivocal. The First Amendment within the scope of its coverage permits no exception; the prohibition is absolute. The First Amendment, however, does not say that in every and all respects there shall be a separation of Church and State. Rather, it studiously defines the manner, the specific ways, in which there shall be no concern or union or dependency one on the other. That is the common sense of the matter. Otherwise the state and religion would be aliens to each other—hostile, suspicious, and even unfriendly. Churches could not be required to pay even property taxes. Municipalities would not be permitted to render police or fire protection to religious groups. Policemen who helped parishioners into their places of worship would violate the Constitution. Prayers in our legislative halls; the appeals to the Almighty in the messages of the Chief Executive; the proclamations making Thanksgiving Day a holiday; "so help me God" in our courtroom oaths—these and all other references to the Almighty that run through our laws, our public rituals, our ceremonies would be flouting the First Amendment. A fastidious atheist or agnostic could even object to the supplication with which the Court opens each session: "God save the United States and this Honorable Court."

We would have to press the concept of separation of Church and State to these extremes to condemn the present law on constitutional grounds. The nullification of this law would have wide and profound effects. A Catholic student applies to his teacher for permission to leave the school during hours on a Holy Day of Obligation to attend a mass. A Jewish student asks his teacher for permission to be excused for Yom Kippur. A Protestant wants the afternoon off for a family baptismal ceremony. In each case the teacher requires parental consent in writing. In each case the teacher, in order to make sure the student is not a truant, goes further and requires a report from the priest, the rabbi, or the minister. The teacher in other words cooperates in a religious program to the extent of making it possible for her students to participate in it. Whether she does it occasionally for a few students, regularly for one, or pursuant to a systematized program designed to further the religious needs of all the students does not alter the character of the act.

We are a religious people whose institutions presuppose a Supreme Being. We guarantee the freedom to worship as one chooses. We make room for as wide a variety of beliefs and creeds as the spiritual needs of man deem necessary. We sponsor an attitude on the part of government that shows no partiality to any one group and that lets each flourish according to the zeal of its adherents and the appeal of its dogma. When the state encourages religious instruction or cooperates with religious authorities by adjusting the schedule of public events to sectarian needs, it follows the best of our traditions. For it then respects the religious nature of our people and accommodates the public service to their spiritual needs. To hold that it may not would be to find in the Constitution a requirement that the government show a callous indifference to religious groups. That would be preferring those who believe in no religion over those who do believe. Government may not finance religious groups nor undertake religious instruction nor blend secular and sectarian education nor use secular institutions to force one or some religion on any person. But we find no constitutional requirement which makes it necessary for government to be hostile to religion and to throw its weight against efforts to widen the effective scope of religious influence. The government must be neutral when it comes to competition between sects. It may not thrust any sect on any person. It may not make a religious observance compulsory. It may not coerce anyone to attend church, to observe a religious holiday, or to take religious instruction. But it can close its doors or suspend its operations as to those who want to repair to their religious sanctuary for worship or instruction. No more than that is undertaken here.

This program may be unwise and improvident from an educational or a community viewpoint. That appeal is made to us on a theory, previously advanced, that each case must be decided on the basis of "our own preposessions." See McCollum v. Board of Education, 238. Our individual preferences, however, are not the constitutional standard. The constitutional standard is the separation of Church and State. The problem, like many problems in constitutional law, is one of degree. See McCollum v. Board of Education, 231.

In the McCollum case the classrooms were used for religious instruction and the force of the public school was used to promote that instruction. Here, as we have said, the public schools do no more than accommodate their schedules to a program of outside religious instruction. We follow the McCollum case. But we cannot expand it to cover the present released time program unless separation of Church and State means that public institutions can make no adjustments of their schedules to accommodate the religious needs of the people. We cannot read into the Bill of Rights such a philosophy of hostility to religion.

🔳 MR. JUSTICE BLACK, dissenting. . . .

I see no significant difference between the invalid Illinois system and that of New York here sustained. Except for the use of the school buildings in Illinois, there is no difference between the systems which I consider even worthy of mention. In the New York program, as in that of Illinois, the school authorities release some of the children on the condition that they attend the religious classes, get reports on whether they attend, and hold the other children in the school building until the religious hour is over. As we attempted to make categorically clear, the *McCollum* decision would have been the same if the religious classes had not been held in the school buildings. We said:

> Here *not only* are the State's tax-supported public school buildings used for the dissemination of religious doctrines. The State *also* affords sectarian groups an invaluable aid in that it helps to provide pupils for their religious classes through use of the State's compulsory public school machinery. *This* is not separation of Church and State. (Emphasis supplied.) *McCollum v. Board of Education*, 212.

*McCollum* thus held that Illinois could not constitutionally manipulate the compelled classroom hours of its compulsory school machinery so as to channel children into sectarian classes. Yet that is exactly what the Court holds New York can do. . . .

Difficulty of decision in the hypothetical situations mentioned by the Court, but not now before us, should not confuse the issues in this case. Here the sole question is whether New York can use its compulsory education laws to help religious sects get attendants presumably too unenthusiastic to go unless moved to do so by the pressure of this state machinery. That this is the plan, purpose, design and consequence of the New York program cannot be denied. The state thus makes religious sects beneficiaries of its power to compel children to attend secular schools. Any use of such coercive power by the state to help or hinder some religious sects or to prefer all religious sects over nonbelievers or vice versa is just what I think the First Amendment forbids. In considering whether a state has entered this forbidden field the question is not whether it has entered too far but whether it has entered at all. New York is manipulating its compulsory education laws to help religious sects get pupils. This is not separation but combination of Church and State.

The Court's validation of the New York system rests in part on its statement that Americans are "a religious people whose institutions presuppose a Supreme Being." This was at least as true when the First Amendment was adopted; and it was just as true when eight Justices of this Court invalidated the released time system in *McCollum* on the premise that a state can no more "aid all religions" than it can aid one. It was precisely because Eighteenth Century Americans were a religious people divided into many fighting sects that we were given the constitutional mandate to keep Church and State completely separate. Colonial history had already shown that, here as elsewhere zealous sectarians entrusted with governmental power to further their causes would sometimes torture, maim and kill those they branded "heretics," "atheists" or "agnostics." The First Amendment was therefore to insure that no one powerful sect or combination of sects could use political or governmental power to punish dissenters whom they could not convert to their faith. Now as then, it is only by wholly isolating the state from the religious sphere and compelling it to be completely neutral, that the freedom of each and every denomination and of all nonbelievers can be maintained. It is this neutrality the Court abandons today when it treats New York's coercive system as a program which *merely* "encourages religious instruction or cooperates with religious authorities." The abandonment is all the more dangerous to liberty because of the Court's legal exaltation of the orthodox and its derogation of unbelievers.

Under our system of religious freedom, people have gone to their religious sanctuaries not because they feared the law but because they loved their God. The choice of all has been as free as the choice of those who answered the call to worship moved only by the music of the old Sunday morning church bells. The spiritual mind of man has thus been free to believe, disbelieve, or doubt, without repression, great or small, by the heavy hand of government. Statutes authorizing such repression have been stricken. Before today, our judicial opinions have refrained from drawing invidious distinctions between those who believe in no religion and those who do believe. The First Amendment has lost much if the religious follower and the atheist are no longer to be judicially regarded as entitled to equal justice under law.

State help to religion injects political and party prejudices into a holy field. It too often substitutes force for prayer, hate for love, and persecution for persuasion. Government should not be allowed, under cover of the soft euphemism of "co-operation," to steal into the sacred area of religious choice.

### ✳ MR. JUSTICE FRANKFURTER, dissenting.

By way of emphasizing my agreement with MR. JUSTICE JACKSON'S dissent, I add a few words.

The Court tells us that in the maintenance of its public schools, "[The State government] can close its doors or suspend its operations" so that its citizens may be free for religious devotions or instruction. If that were the issue, it would not rise to the dignity of a constitutional controversy. Of course, a State may provide that the classes in its schools shall be dismissed, for any reason, or no reason, on fixed days, or for special occasions. The essence of this case is that the school system did not "close its doors" and did not "suspend its operations." There is all the difference in the world between letting the children out of school and letting some of them out of school into religious classes. If every one is free to make what use he will of time wholly unconnected from schooling required by law—those who wish sectarian instruction devoting it to that purpose, those who have ethical instruction at home, to that, those who study music, to that—then of course there is no conflict with the Fourteenth Amendment.

The pith of the case is that formalized religious instruction is substituted for other school activity which those who do not participate in the released-time program are compelled to attend. The school system is very much in operation during this kind of released time. If its doors are closed, they are closed upon those students who do not attend the religious instruction, in order to keep them within the school. That is the very thing which raises the constitutional issue. It is not met by disregarding it. Failure to discuss this issue does not take it out of the case.

Again, the Court relies upon the absence from the record of evidence of coercion in the operation of the system. "If in fact coercion were used," according to the Court, "if it were established that any one or more teachers were using their office to persuade or force students to take the religious instruction, a wholly different case would be presented." Thus, "coercion" in the abstract is acknowledged to be fatal. But the Court disregards the fact that as the case comes to us, there could be no proof of coercion, for the appellants were not allowed to make proof of it. Appellants alleged that "The operation of the released time program has resulted and inevitably results in the exercise of pressure and coercion upon parents and children to secure attendance by the children for religious instruction." This allegation—that coercion was in fact present and is inherent in the system, no matter what disavowals might be made in the operating regulations—was denied by appellees. Thus were drawn issues of fact which cannot be determined, on any conceivable view of judicial notice, by judges out of their own knowledge or experience. Appellants sought an opportunity to adduce evidence in support of these allegations at an appropriate trial. And though the courts below cited the concurring opinion in *McCollum v. Board of Education*, 333 U.S. 203, 226, to "emphasize the importance of detailed analysis of the facts to which the Constitutional test of Separation is to be applied," they denied that opportunity on the ground that such proof was irrelevant to the issue of constitutionality.

When constitutional issues turn on facts, it is a strange procedure indeed not to permit the facts to be established. . . .

The result in the *McCollum* case, was based on principles that received unanimous acceptance by this Court, barring only a single vote. I agree with MR. JUSTICE BLACK that those principles are disregarded in reaching the result in this case. Happily they are not disavowed by the Court. From this I draw the hope that in future variations of the problem which are bound to come here, these principles may again be honored in the observance.

The deeply divisive controversy aroused by the attempts to secure public school pupils for sectarian instruction would promptly end if the advocates of such instruction were content to have the school "close its doors or suspend its operations"—that is, dismiss classes in their entirety, without discrimination—instead of seeking to use the public schools as the instrument for securing attendance at denominational classes. The unwillingness of the promoters of this movement to dispense with such use of the public schools betrays a surprising want of confidence in the inherent power of the various faiths to draw children to outside sectarian classes—an attitude that hardly reflects the faith of the greatest religious spirits.

▨ MR. JUSTICE JACKSON, dissenting.

This released time program is founded upon a use of the State's power of coercion, which, for me, determines its unconstitutionality. Stripped to its essentials, the plan has two stages: first, that the State compel each student to yield a large part of his time for public secular education; and, second, that some of it be "released" to him on condition that he devote it to sectarian religious purposes.

No one suggests that the Constitution would permit the State directly to require this "released" time to be spent "under the control of a duly constituted religious body." This program accomplishes that forbidden result by indirection. If public education were taking so much of the pupils' time as to injure the public or the students' welfare by encroaching upon their religious opportunity, simply shortening everyone's school day would facilitate voluntary and optional attendance at Church classes. But that suggestion is rejected upon the ground that if they are made free many students will not go to the Church. Hence, they must be deprived of freedom for this period, with Church attendance put to them as one of the two permissible ways of using it.

The greater effectiveness of this system over voluntary attendance after school hours is due to the truant officer who, if the youngster fails to go to the Church school, dogs him back to the public schoolroom. Here schooling is more or less suspended during the "released time" so the nonreligious attendants will not forge ahead of the churchgoing absentees. But it serves as a temporary jail for a pupil who will not go to Church. It takes more subtlety of mind than I possess to deny that this is governmental constraint in support of religion. It is as unconstitutional, in my view, when exerted by indirection as when exercised forthrightly.

As one whose children, as a matter of free choice, have been sent to privately supported Church schools, I may challenge the Court's suggestion that opposition to this plan can only be antireligious, atheistic, or agnostic. My evangelistic brethren confuse an objection to compulsion with an objection to religion. It is possible to hold a faith with enough confidence to believe that what should be rendered to God does not need to be decided and collected by Caesar.

The day that this country ceases to be free for irreligion it will cease to be free for religion—except for the sect that can win political power. The same epithetical jurisprudence used by the Court today to beat down those who oppose pressuring children into some religion can devise as good epithets tomorrow against those who object to pressuring them into a favored religion. And, after all, if we concede to the State power and wisdom to single out "duly constituted religious" bodies as exclusive alternatives for compulsory secular instruction, it would be logical to also uphold the power and wisdom to choose the true faith among those "duly constituted." We start down a rough road when we begin to mix compulsory public education with compulsory godliness.

A number of Justices just short of a majority of the majority that promulgates today's passionate dialectics joined in answering them in *Illinois ex rel. McCollum v. Board of Education.* The distinction attempted between that case and this is trivial, almost to the point of cynicism, magnifying its nonessential details and disparaging compulsion which was the underlying reason for invalidity. A reading of the Court's opinion in that case along with its opinion in this case will show such difference of overtones and undertones as to make clear that the *McCollum* case has passed like a storm in a teacup. The wall which the Court was professing to erect between Church and State has become even more warped and twisted than I expected. Today's judgment will be more interesting to students of psychology and of the judicial processes than to students of constitutional law.

## Notes and Questions

1. What is the crux of the constitutional problem that the *McCollum* case presents, according to the Court majority? What kinds of arguments were made for upholding the released-time program? How does the Court respond to those arguments?

2. In his concurring opinion in the *McCollum* case, Justice Frankfurter argues that the release-time program is "patently woven into the working scheme of the school." How so, according to Frankfurter? In Justice Frankfurter's view, what negative effects are caused by such a partnership between public schools

and religious authorities? What evidence do you find in both the majority and concurring opinions that the Court is particularly sensitive to church-state constitutional boundaries within the context of public elementary and secondary schools?

3. In the majority opinion in the *McCollum* case, Justice Black says that "the First Amendment rests upon the premise that both religion and government can best work to achieve their lofty aims if each is left free from the other within its respective sphere." How would this standard apply in other cases? Would it prevent, for example, religious organizations from lobbying the government on policy issues? (See chapter 21.) Would it prevent government aid from flowing to religious communities, even if that aid is designated and used for secular activities? (See chapters 11–15.) Would it prevent the government from enforcing anti-discrimination laws to the extent that those laws might apply to people who work within a church body? (See chapter 10.)

4. One of the concerns Justice Jackson expresses in his concurring opinion in the *McCollum* case is that the Court will "allow zeal for our own ideas of what is good in public instruction to induce us to accept the role of a super board of education for every school district in the nation." Does the Court inevitably take on this role if it insists upon uniform enforcement of the First Amendment's religion clauses nationwide, or can it avoid the concern if it limits its role to that particular function and steers clear of attempts to determine what is, or is not, good education policy? What other concerns does Justice Jackson mention in this opinion?

5. In his dissenting opinion in the *McCollum* case, Justice Reed says that he "find[s] it difficult to extract from the [other] opinions any conclusion as to what it is in the Champaign plan that is unconstitutional." Reed also says he concludes that the Court majority is saying "that religious instruction of public school children during school hours is prohibited." Is that a fair reading of the other opinions in this case?

6. In the *McCollum* case, Justice Reed cites some statements by Thomas Jefferson to buttress his argument that the result in cases like *McCollum* and *Everson* "were far from the minds of the authors" of the First Amendment. Can you think of an argument that would undermine Reed's attempt to apply Jefferson's statements to this case? How does Justice Reed define the word "aid"? What examples does Reed offer in support of his understanding of the term "aid"? Must one accept Reed's definition of the word "aid" in order to find these examples to be constitutionally permissible? Finally, Justice Reed argues that "[t]his Court cannot be too cautious in upsetting practices embedded in our society by many years of experience." Is Reed's caution an appropriate or inappropriate one, both in this case and in others involving constitutional rights and restrictions?

7. What are the differences between the programs at issue in *McCollum* and *Zorach*? Do they justify the difference in constitutional judgments?

8. In the *Zorach* case, the Court majority says it "cannot expand [the *McCollum* case] to cover the present released time program unless separation of

Church and State means that public institutions can make no adjustments of their schedules to accommodate the religious needs of the people." Would the Court's hands really be tied in such a way if it had ruled the other way in the *Zorach* case? Conversely, why doesn't the *Zorach* accommodation principle apply in McCollum?

9. In the majority opinion in the *Zorach* case, Justice Douglas states: "We are a religious people whose institutions presuppose a Supreme Being." What point do you think Justice Douglas was attempting to make with this statement? Does this statement strengthen or weaken the opinion? How does Justice Black respond to this argument in his dissenting opinion in this case?

10. In his dissenting opinion, Justice Black argues that "New York is manipulating its compulsory education laws to help religious sects get pupils." What evidence does he depend on to make this argument? Do you think Justice Black is correct about the facts in this case? If Black is correct, should this finding have the effect of making the practice unconstitutional? Or is the *Zorach* majority correct in saying that, "[w]hen the state encourages religious instruction . . . , it follows the best of our traditions"?

11. In his dissenting opinion in the *Zorach* case, what solution does Justice Frankfurter advocate for public schools in situations like these? Why do you think a solution like the one he proposes was not embraced by the school in this case?

12. At the conclusion of his dissenting opinion, Justice Jackson cites "the Court's suggestion that opposition to [the released-time] plan can only be antireligious, atheistic, or agnostic." What response does Jackson make to this point? Why is this charge of governmental hostility to religion made so often by various members of the Court?

## STATE-SPONSORED PRAYER AND BIBLE READING: THE 1960S CASES

In 1962, the Court heard an Establishment Clause challenge by parents of children enrolled in the New York City public schools to the practice of leading public school students in the recitation of a prayer written by the New York State Board of Regents (the state Board of Education). One year later, the Court addressed a related but different question: whether requiring, at the opening of the school day, the reading of verses from the Bible and the recitation of the Lord's Prayer by students violated the Establishment Clause. In both cases, the Court found that the religious practices at issue were sponsored by the school and thus unconstitutional.

These are the landmark school prayer rulings that shook the nation. Until these decisions were handed down by the Supreme Court, it was common in many parts of the country for the public school day to begin with teacher- or student-led prayer and Bible readings (although the number of schools holding religious exercises had been declining for years). One indication of the deep support these religious practices had is the fact that, in each of these cases, attorneys general from twenty-two states filed "friend of the court" briefs with the Supreme Court on behalf of states that sought to defend the constitution-ality of the religious practices. Public reaction to both decisions was generally negative. North Carolina Senator Sam Ervin remarked that "the Supreme Court has made God un-constitutional." Following the second case, proponents of school prayer sought to amend the Constitution to permit religious exercises in the public schools. That effort failed, as did subsequent attempts at a "school prayer amendment," due in large part to opposition by the National Council of Churches, the Baptist Joint Committee on Public Affairs, and other religious and civil rights groups.[3]

As you read these cases, pay close attention to the reasoning the Court articulates, the legal tests it develops, and its use of history.

## ENGEL v. VITALE
### 370 U.S. 421 (1962)

MR. JUSTICE BLACK delivered the opinion of the Court.

The respondent Board of Education of Union Free School District No. 9, New Hyde Park, New York, acting in its official capacity under state law, directed the School District's principal to cause the following prayer to be said aloud by each class in the presence of a teacher at the beginning of each school day: "Almighty God, we acknowledge our dependence upon Thee, and we beg Thy blessings upon us, our parents, our teachers and our Country."

This daily procedure was adopted on the recommendation of the State Board of Regents, a governmental agency created by the State Constitution to which the New York Legislature has granted broad supervisory, executive, and legislative powers over the State's public school system. These state officials composed the prayer which they recommended and published as a part of their "Statement on Moral and Spiritual Training in the Schools," saying: "We believe that this Statement will be subscribed to by all men and women of good will, and we call upon all of them to aid in giving life to our program."

Shortly after the practice of reciting the Regents' prayer was adopted by the School District, the parents of ten pupils brought this action in a New York State Court insisting that use of this official prayer in the public schools was contrary to the beliefs, religions, or religious practices of both themselves and their children. Among other things, these parents challenged the constitu-tionality of both the state law authorizing the School District to direct the use of prayer in public schools and the School District's regulation ordering the recitation of this particular prayer on the ground that these actions of official governmental agencies violate that part of the First Amendment of the Federal Constitution which commands that "Congress shall make no law respecting an establishment of religion"—a command which was "made applicable to the State of New York by the Fourteenth Amendment of the said Constitution."

We think that by using its public school system to encourage recitation of the Regents' prayer, the State of New York has adopted a practice wholly inconsistent with the Establishment Clause. There can, of course, be no doubt that New York's program of daily classroom invocation of God's blessings as prescribed in the Regents' prayer is a religious activity. It is a solemn avowal of divine faith and supplication for the blessings of the Almighty. . . .

The petitioners contend among other things that the state laws requiring or permitting use of the Regents' prayer must be struck down as a violation of the Establishment Clause because that prayer was composed by governmental officials as a part of a governmental program to further religious beliefs. For this reason, petitioners argue, the State's use of the Regents' prayer in its public school system breaches the constitutional wall of separation between Church and State. We agree with that contention since we think that the constitutional prohibition against laws respecting an establishment of religion must at least mean that in this country it is no part of the business of government to compose official prayers for any group of the American people to recite as a part of a religious program carried on by government.

It is a matter of history that this very practice of establishing governmentally composed prayers for religious services was one of the reasons which caused many of our early colonists to leave England and seek religious freedom in America. The Book of Common Prayer, which was created under governmental direction and which was approved by Acts of Parliament in 1548 and 1549, set out in minute detail the accepted form and content of prayer and other religious ceremonies to be used in the established, tax-supported Church of England. The controversies over the Book and what should be its content repeatedly threatened to disrupt the peace of that country as the accepted forms of prayer in the established church changed with the views of the particular ruler that happened to be in control at the time. Powerful groups representing some of the varying religious views of the people struggled among themselves to impress their particular views upon the Government and obtain amendments of the Book more suitable to their respective notions of how religious services should be conducted in order that the official religious establishment would advance their particular religious beliefs. Other groups, lacking the necessary political power to influence the Government on the matter, decided to leave England and its established church and seek freedom in America from England's governmentally ordained and supported religion.

It is an unfortunate fact of history that when some of the very groups which had most strenuously opposed the established Church of England found themselves sufficiently in control of colonial governments in this country to write their own prayers into law, they passed laws making their own religion the official religion of their respective colonies. Indeed, as late as the time of the Revolutionary War, there were established churches in at least eight of the thirteen former colonies and established religions in at least four of the other five. But the successful Revolution against English political domination was shortly followed by intense opposition to the practice of establishing religion by law. This opposition crystallized rapidly into an effective political force in Virginia where the minority religious groups such as Presbyterians, Lutherans, Quakers and Baptists had gained such strength that the adherents to the established Episcopal Church were actually a minority themselves. In 1785-1786, those opposed to the established Church, led by James Madison and Thomas Jefferson, who, though themselves not members of any of these dissenting religious groups, opposed all religious establishments by law on grounds of principle, obtained the enactment of the famous "Virginia Bill for Religious Liberty" by which all religious groups were placed on an equal footing so far as the State was concerned. Similar though less far-reaching legislation was being considered and passed in other States.

By the time of the adoption of the Constitution, our history shows that there was a widespread awareness among many Americans of the dangers of a union of Church and State. These people knew, some of them from bitter personal experience, that one of the greatest dangers to the freedom of the individual to worship in his own way lay in the Government's placing its official stamp of approval upon one particular kind of prayer or one particular form of religious services. They knew the anguish, hardship and bitter strife that could come when zealous religious groups struggled with one another to obtain the Government's stamp of approval from each King, Queen, or Protector that came to temporary power. The Constitution was intended to avert a part of this danger by leaving the government of this country in the hands of the people rather than in the hands of any monarch. But this safeguard was not enough. Our Founders were no more willing to let the content of their prayers and their privilege of praying whenever they pleased be influenced by the ballot box than they were to let these vital matters of personal conscience depend upon the succession of monarchs. The First Amendment was added to the Constitution to stand as a guarantee that neither the power nor the prestige of the Federal Government would be used to control, support or influence the kinds of prayer the American people can say—that the people's religions must not be subjected to the pressures of government for change each time a new political administration is elected to office. Under that Amendment's prohibition against governmental establishment of religion, as reinforced by the provisions of the Fourteenth Amendment, government in this country, be it state or federal, is without power to prescribe by law any particular form of prayer which is to be used as an official prayer in carrying on any program of governmentally sponsored religious activity.

There can be no doubt that New York's state prayer program officially establishes the religious beliefs embodied in the Regents' prayer. The respondents' argument to the contrary, which is largely based upon the contention that the Regents' prayer is "non-denominational" and the fact that the program, as modified and approved by state courts, does not require all pupils to recite the prayer but permits those who wish to do so to remain silent or be excused from the room, ignores the essential nature of the program's constitutional defects. Neither the fact that the prayer may be denominationally neutral nor the fact that its observance on the part of the students is voluntary can serve to free it from the limitations of the Establishment Clause, as it might from the Free Exercise Clause, of the First Amendment, both of which are operative against the States by virtue of the Fourteenth Amendment. Although these two clauses may in certain instances overlap, they forbid two quite different kinds of governmental encroachment upon religious freedom. The Establishment Clause, unlike the Free Exercise Clause, does not depend upon any showing of direct governmental compulsion and is violated by the enactment of laws which establish an official religion whether those laws operate directly to coerce non-observing individuals or not. This is not to say, of course, that laws officially prescribing a particular form of religious worship do not involve coercion of such individuals. When the power, prestige and financial support of government is placed behind a particular religious belief, the indirect coercive pressure upon religious minorities to conform to the prevailing officially approved religion is plain. But the purposes underlying the Establishment Clause go much further than that. Its first and most immediate purpose rested on the belief that a union of government and religion tends to destroy government and to degrade religion. The history of governmentally established religion, both in England and in this country, showed that whenever government had allied itself with one particular form of religion, the inevitable result had been that it had incurred the hatred, disrespect and even contempt of those who held contrary beliefs. That same history showed that many people had lost their respect for any religion that had relied upon the support of government to spread its faith. The Establishment Clause thus stands as an expression of principle on the part of the Founders of our Constitution that religion is too personal, too sacred, too holy, to permit its "unhallowed perversion" by a civil magistrate. Another purpose of the Establishment Clause rested upon an awareness of the historical fact that governmentally established religions and religious persecutions go hand in hand. The Founders knew that only a few years after the Book of Common Prayer became the only accepted form of religious services in the established Church of England, an Act of Uniformity was passed to compel all Englishmen to attend those services and to make it a criminal offense to conduct or attend religious gatherings of any other kind—a law which was consistently flouted by dissenting religious groups in England and which contributed to widespread persecutions of people like John Bunyan who persisted in holding "unlawful [religious] meetings . . . to the great disturbance and distraction of the good subjects of this kingdom . . . ." And they knew that similar persecutions had received the sanction of law in several of the colonies in this country soon after the establishment of official religions in those colonies. It was in large part to get completely away from this sort of systematic religious persecution that the Founders brought into being our Nation, our Constitution, and our Bill of Rights with its prohibition against any governmental establishment of religion. The New York laws officially prescribing the Regents' prayer are inconsistent both with the purposes of the Establishment Clause and with the Establishment Clause itself.

It has been argued that to apply the Constitution in such a way as to prohibit state laws respecting an establishment of religious services in public schools is to indicate a hostility toward religion or toward prayer. Nothing, of course, could be more wrong. The history of man is inseparable from the history of religion. And perhaps it is not too much to say that since the beginning of that history many people have devoutly believed that "More things are wrought by prayer than this world dreams of." It was doubtless largely due to men who believed this that there grew up a sentiment that caused men to leave the cross-currents of officially established state religions and religious persecution in Europe and come to this country filled with the hope that they could find a place in which they could pray when they pleased to the God of their faith in the language they chose. And there were men of this same faith in the power of prayer who led the fight for adoption of our Constitution and also for our Bill of Rights with the very guarantees of religious freedom that forbid the sort of governmental activity which New York has attempted here. These men knew that the First Amendment, which tried to put an end to governmental control of religion and of prayer, was not written to destroy either. They knew rather that it was written to quiet well-justified fears which nearly all of them felt arising out of an awareness that governments of the past had shackled men's tongues to make them speak only the religious thoughts that government wanted them to speak and to pray only to the God that government wanted them to pray to. It is neither sacrilegious nor antireligious to say that each separate government in this country should stay out of the business of writing or sanctioning official prayers and leave that purely religious function to the people themselves and to those the people choose to look to for religious guidance.[21]

It is true that New York's establishment of its Regents' prayer as an officially approved religious doctrine of that State does not amount to a total establishment of one particular religious sect to the exclusion of all others—that, indeed, the governmental endorsement of that prayer seems relatively insignificant when compared to the governmental encroachments upon religion which were commonplace 200 years ago. To those who may subscribe to the view that because the Regents' official prayer is so brief and general there can be no danger to religious freedom in its governmental establishment, however, it may be appropriate to say in the words of James Madison, the author of the First Amendment:

> It is proper to take alarm at the first experiment on our liberties. . . . Who does not see that the same authority which can establish Christianity, in exclusion of all other Religions, may establish with the same ease any particular sect of Christians, in exclusion of all other Sects? That the same authority which can force a citizen to contribute three pence only of his property for the support of any one establishment, may force him to conform to any other establishment in all cases whatsoever?

*Reversed and remanded.*

MR. JUSTICE DOUGLAS, concurring.

It is customary in deciding a constitutional question to treat it in its narrowest form. Yet at times the setting of the question gives it a form and content which no abstract treatment could give. The point for decision is whether the Government can constitutionally finance a religious exercise. Our system at the federal and state levels is presently honeycombed with such financing. Nevertheless, I think it is an unconstitutional undertaking whatever form it takes.

Plainly, our Bill of Rights would not permit a State or the Federal Government to adopt an official prayer and penalize anyone who would not utter it. This, however, is not that case, for there is no element of compulsion or coercion in New York's regulation. . . .

The prayer is said upon the commencement of the school day, immediately following the pledge of allegiance to the flag. The prayer is said aloud in the presence of a teacher, who either leads the recitation or selects a student to do so. No student, however, is compelled to take part. The respondents have adopted a regulation which provides that "Neither teachers nor any school authority shall comment on participation or non-participation . . . nor suggest

---

[21] There is of course nothing in the decision reached here that is inconsistent with the fact that school children and others are officially encouraged to express love for our country by reciting historical documents such as the Declaration of Independence which contain references to the Deity or by singing officially espoused anthems which include the composer's professions of faith in a Supreme Being, or with the fact that there are many manifestations in our public life of belief in God. Such patriotic or ceremonial occasions bear no true resemblance to the unquestioned religious exercise that the State of New York has sponsored in this instance.

or request that any posture or language be used or dress be worn or be not used or not worn." Provision is also made for excusing children, upon written request of a parent or guardian, from the saying of the prayer or from the room in which the prayer is said. A letter implementing and explaining this regulation has been sent to each taxpayer and parent in the school district. As I read this regulation, a child is free to stand or not stand, to recite or not recite, without fear of reprisal or even comment by the teacher or any other school official. . . .

In New York the teacher who leads in prayer is on the public payroll; and the time she takes seems minuscule as compared with the salaries appropriated by state legislatures and Congress for chaplains to conduct prayers in the legislative halls. Only a bare fraction of the teacher's time is given to reciting this short 22-word prayer, about the same amount of time that our Crier spends announcing the opening of our sessions and offering a prayer for this Court. Yet for me the principle is the same, no matter how briefly the prayer is said, for in each of the instances given the person praying is a public official on the public payroll, performing a religious exercise in a governmental institution. . . .

At the same time I cannot say that to authorize this prayer is to establish a religion in the strictly historic meaning of those words. A religion is not established in the usual sense merely by letting those who choose to do so say the prayer that the public school teacher leads. Yet once government finances a religious exercise it inserts a divisive influence into our communities. The New York Court said that the prayer given does not conform to all of the tenets of the Jewish, Unitarian, and Ethical Culture groups. One of the petitioners is an agnostic.

"We are a religious people whose institutions presuppose a Supreme Being." *Zorach v. Clauson*, 343 U.S. 306, 313. Under our Bill of Rights free play is given for making religion an active force in our lives. But "if a religious leaven is to be worked into the affairs of our people, it is to be done by individuals and groups, not by the Government." *McGowan v. Maryland*, 366 U.S. 420, 563 (dissenting opinion). By reason of the First Amendment government is commanded "to have no interest in theology or ritual" (*id.*, 564), for on those matters "government must be neutral." *Ibid.* The First Amendment leaves the Government in a position not of hostility to religion but of neutrality. The philosophy is that the atheist or agnostic—the nonbeliever—is entitled to go his own way. The philosophy is that if government interferes in matters spiritual, it will be a divisive force. The First Amendment teaches that a government neutral in the field of religion better serves all religious interests. . . .

What New York does with this prayer is a break with that tradition. I therefore join the Court in reversing the judgment below.

▓ MR. JUSTICE STEWART, dissenting.

A local school board in New York has provided that those pupils who wish to do so may join in a brief prayer at the beginning of each school day, acknowledging their dependence upon God and asking His blessing upon them and upon their parents, their teachers, and their country. The Court today decides that in permitting this brief nondenominational prayer the school board has violated the Constitution of the United States. I think this decision is wrong.

The Court does not hold, nor could it, that New York has interfered with the free exercise of anybody's religion. For the state courts have made clear that those who object to reciting the prayer must be entirely free of any compulsion to do so, including any "embarrassments and pressures." Cf. *West Virginia State Board of Education v. Barnette*, 319 U.S. 624. But the Court says that in permitting school children to say this simple prayer, the New York authorities have established "an official religion."

With all respect, I think the Court has misapplied a great constitutional principle. I cannot see how an "official religion" is established by letting those who want to say a prayer say it. On the contrary, I think that to deny the wish of these school children to join in reciting this prayer is to deny them the opportunity of sharing in the spiritual heritage of our Nation.

The Court's historical review of the quarrels over the Book of Common Prayer in England throws no light for me on the issue before us in this case. England had then and has now an established church. Equally unenlightening, I think, is the history of the early establishment and later rejection of an official church in our own States. For we deal here not with the establishment of a state church, which would, of course, be constitutionally impermissible, but with whether school children who want to begin their day by joining in prayer must be prohibited from doing so. Moreover, I think that the Court's task, in this as in all areas of constitutional adjudication, is not responsibly aided by the uncritical invocation of metaphors like the "wall of separation," a phrase nowhere to be found in the Constitution. What is relevant to the issue here is not the history of an established church in sixteenth century England or in eighteenth century America, but the history of the religious traditions of our people, reflected in countless practices of the institutions and officials of our government.

At the opening of each day's Session of this Court we stand, while one of our officials invokes the protection of God. Since the days of John Marshall our Crier has said, "God save the United States and this Honorable Court." Both the Senate and the House of Representatives open their daily Sessions with prayer. Each of our Presidents, from George Washington to John F. Kennedy, has upon assuming his Office asked the protection and help of God.

The Court today says that the state and federal governments are without constitutional power to prescribe any particular form of words to be recited by any group of the American people on any subject touching religion.[4] One of the stanzas of "The Star-Spangled Banner," made our National Anthem by Act of Congress in 1931, contains these verses:

Blest with victory and peace, may the heav'n rescued land
Praise the Pow'r that hath made and preserved us a nation!
Then conquer we must, when our cause it is just,
And this be our motto "In God is our Trust."

In 1954 Congress added a phrase to the Pledge of Allegiance to the Flag so that it now contains the words "one Nation *under God*, indivisible, with

---

[4] My brother DOUGLAS says that the only question before us is whether government "can constitutionally finance a religious exercise." The official chaplains of Congress are paid with public money. So are military chaplains. So are state and federal prison chaplains.

liberty and justice for all." In 1952 Congress enacted legislation calling upon the President each year to proclaim a National Day of Prayer. Since 1865 the words "IN GOD WE TRUST" have been impressed on our coins.

Countless similar examples could be listed, but there is no need to belabor the obvious. It was all summed up by this Court just ten years ago in a single sentence: "We are a religious people whose institutions presuppose a Supreme Being." *Zorach v. Clauson*, 343 U.S. 306, 313.

I do not believe that this Court, or the Congress, or the President has by the actions and practices I have mentioned established an "official religion" in violation of the Constitution. And I do not believe the State of New York has done so in this case. What each has done has been to recognize and to follow the deeply entrenched and highly cherished spiritual traditions of our Nation—traditions which come down to us from those who almost two hundred years ago avowed their "firm Reliance on the Protection of divine Providence" when they proclaimed the freedom and independence of this brave new world.

I dissent.

---

## NOTES AND QUESTIONS

1. In the majority opinion, Justice Black noted that the prayers in this case were "nondenominational" and that students who did not wish to join in the prayers could be silent or excused from the room. Nonetheless, the Court still found the program to be constitutionally defective. Why? And what does that say about the nature of the prohibition on governmental establishments of religion?

2. Justice Black writes that "[t]he First Amendment was added to the Constitution to stand as a guarantee that neither the power nor the prestige of the Federal Government would be used to control, support or influence the kinds of prayer the American people can say. . . ." What historical evidence does Black rely on for this statement? Why is it so clearly wrong for the government to do this type of thing, according to Black? Do you find this argument persuasive?

3. Once again, the Court responds to the charge that its decision "indicate[s] a hostility toward religion or toward prayer." What is the Court's defense in this case? Do you find the Court's defense to be convincing?

4. The majority argues that the "first and most immediate purpose [of the Establishment Clause] rested on the belief that a union of government and religion tends to destroy government and to degrade religion." In what ways could such unions have this effect? Is protecting religion from degradation an appropriate purpose of the First Amendment?

5. Why did Justice Douglas write a concurring opinion? In other words, what argument does he make that is different from those made by Court majority? How does he reconcile the language in his majority opinion in *Zorach* with his vote in *Engel*?

6. In his dissent, Justice Stewart argues that the majority's historical arguments are unconvincing. Why? Which side do you think has the better of the argument on this point?

7. Justice Stewart argues that the decision in *Engel v. Vitale* denies school children "the opportunity of sharing in the spiritual heritage of our Nation." Should this argument have been given some weight by the Court majority? Why or why not?

Just one year later, the Supreme Court agreed to hear another case in this controversial area. This time the facts involved daily Bible readings and the recitation of the Lord's Prayer with the context of the public schools in Pennsylvania and Maryland. As you read the opinions, consider the ways in which the Court further develops its rationales and legal tests in this case.

## SCHOOL DISTRICT OF ABINGTON TOWNSHIP v. SCHEMPP
## 374 U.S. 203 (1963)

**Together with Murray v. Curlett**

⊞ MR. JUSTICE CLARK delivered the opinion of the Court.

Once again we are called upon to consider the scope of the provision of the First Amendment to the United States Constitution which declares that "Congress shall make no law respecting an establishment of religion, or prohibiting the free exercise thereof. . . ." These companion cases present the issues in the context of state action requiring that schools begin each day with readings from the Bible. While raising the basic questions under slightly different factual situations, the cases permit of joint treatment. In light of the history of the First Amendment and of our cases interpreting and applying its requirements, we hold that the practices at issue and the laws requiring them are unconstitutional under the Establishment Clause, as applied to the States through the Fourteenth Amendment.

I

*The Facts in Each Case*: (Schempp). The Commonwealth of Pennsylvania by law, 24 Pa. Stat. § 15-1516, as amended, Pub. Law 1928 (Supp. 1960), Dec. 17, 1959, requires that "At least ten verses from the Holy Bible shall be read, without comment, at the opening of each public school on each school day. Any child shall be excused from such Bible reading, or attending such Bible reading, upon the written request of his parent or guardian." The Schempp family, husband and wife and two of their three children, brought suit to enjoin enforcement of the statute, contending that their rights under the Fourteenth Amendment to the Constitution of the United States are, have been, and will continue to be violated unless this statute be declared unconstitutional as violative of these provisions of the First Amendment. They sought to enjoin the appellant school district, wherein the Schempp children attend school, and its officers and the Superintendent of Public Instruction of the Commonwealth from continuing to conduct such readings and recitation of the Lord's Prayer in the public schools of the district pursuant to the statute. A three-judge statutory District Court for the Eastern District of Pennsylvania held that the statute is violative of the Establishment Clause of the First Amendment as applied to the States by the Due Process Clause of the Fourteenth Amendment and directed that appropriate injunctive relief issue

The appellees Edward Lewis Schempp, his wife Sidney, and their children, Roger and Donna, are of the Unitarian faith and are members of the Unitarian Church in Germantown, Philadelphia, Pennsylvania, where they, as well as another son, Ellory, regularly attend religious services. The latter was originally a party but having graduated from the school system *pendente lite* was voluntarily dismissed from the action. The other children attend the Abington Senior High School, which is a public school operated by appellant district.

On each school day at the Abington Senior High School between 8:15 and 8:30 a.m., while the pupils are attending their home rooms or advisory sections, opening exercises are conducted pursuant to the statute. The exercises are broadcast into each room in the school building through an intercommunications system and are conducted under the supervision of a teacher by students attending the school's radio and television workshop. Selected students from this course gather each morning in the school's workshop studio for the exercises, which include readings by one of the students of 10 verses of the Holy Bible, broadcast to each room in the building. This is followed by the recitation of the Lord's Prayer, likewise over the intercommunications system, but also by the students in the various classrooms, who are asked to stand and join in repeating the prayer in unison. The exercises are closed with the flag salute and such pertinent announcements as are of interest to the students. Participation in the opening exercises, as directed by the statute, is voluntary. The student reading the verses from the Bible may select the passages and read from any version he chooses, although the only copies furnished by the school are the King James version, copies of which were circulated to each teacher by the school district. During the period in which the exercises have been conducted the King James, the Douay and the Revised Standard versions of the Bible have been used, as well as the Jewish Holy Scriptures. There are no prefatory statements, no questions asked or solicited, no comments or explanations made and no interpretations given at or during the exercises. The students and parents are advised that the student may absent himself from the classroom or, should he elect to remain, not participate in the exercises.

It appears from the record that in schools not having an intercommunications system the Bible reading and the recitation of the Lord's Prayer were conducted by the home-room teacher,[2] who chose the text of the verses and read them herself or had students read them in rotation or by volunteers. This was

---

[2] The statute as amended imposes no penalty upon a teacher refusing to obey its mandate. However, it remains to be seen whether one refusing could have his contract of employment terminated for "wilful violation of the school laws." 24 Pa. Stat. (Supp. 1960) § 11-1122.

followed by a standing recitation of the Lord's Prayer, together with the Pledge of Allegiance to the Flag by the class in unison and a closing announcement of routine school items of interest.

At the first trial Edward Schempp and the children testified as to specific religious doctrines purveyed by a literal reading of the Bible "which were contrary to the religious beliefs which they held and to their familial teaching." The children testified that all of the doctrines to which they referred were read to them at various times as part of the exercises. Edward Schempp testified at the second trial that he had considered having Roger and Donna excused from attendance at the exercises but decided against it for several reasons, including his belief that the children's relationships with their teachers and classmates would be adversely affected.[3]

Expert testimony was introduced by both appellants and appellees at the first trial, which testimony was summarized by the trial court as follows:

"Dr. Solomon Grayzel testified that there were marked differences between the Jewish Holy Scriptures and the Christian Holy Bible, the most obvious of which was the absence of the New Testament in the Jewish Holy Scriptures. Dr. Grayzel testified that portions of the New Testament were offensive to Jewish tradition and that, from the standpoint of Jewish faith, the concept of Jesus Christ as the Son of God was 'practically blasphemous.' He cited instances in the New Testament which, assertedly, were not only sectarian in nature but tended to bring the Jews into ridicule or scorn. Dr. Grayzel gave as his expert opinion that such material from the New Testament could be explained to Jewish children in such a way as to do no harm to them. But if portions of the New Testament were read without explanation, they could be, and in his specific experience with children Dr. Grayzel observed, had been, psychologically harmful to the child and had caused a divisive force within the social media of the school.

"Dr. Grayzel also testified that there was significant difference in attitude with regard to the respective Books of the Jewish and Christian Religions in that Judaism attaches no special significance to the reading of the Bible *per se* and that the Jewish Holy Scriptures are source materials to be studied. But Dr. Grayzel did state that many portions of the New, as well as of the Old, Testament contained passages of great literary and moral value.

"Dr. Luther A. Weigle, an expert witness for the defense, testified in some detail as to the reasons for and the methods employed in developing the King James and the Revised Standard Versions of the Bible. On direct examina-

---

[3] The trial court summarized his testimony as follows:

"Edward Schempp, the children's father, testified that after careful consideration he had decided that he should not have Roger or Donna excused from attendance at these morning ceremonies. Among his reasons were the following. He said that he thought his children would be 'labeled as "odd balls"' before their teachers and classmates every school day; that children, like Roger's and Donna's classmates, were liable 'to lump all particular religious difference[s] or religious objections [together] as 'atheism' and that today the word 'atheism' is often connected with 'atheistic communism,' and has 'very bad' connotations, such as 'un-American' or 'anti-Red,' with overtones of possible immorality. Mr. Schempp pointed out that due to the events of the morning exercises following in rapid succession, the Bible reading, the Lord's Prayer, the Flag Salute, and the announcements, excusing his children from the Bible reading would mean that probably they would miss hearing the announcements so important to children. He testified also that if Roger and Donna were excused from Bible reading they would have to stand in the hall outside their 'homeroom' and that this carried with it the imputation of punishment for bad conduct." 201 F. Supp., 818.

tion, Dr. Weigle stated that the Bible was non-sectarian. He later stated that the phrase 'non-sectarian' meant to him non-sectarian within the Christian faiths. Dr. Weigle stated that his definition of the Holy Bible would include the Jewish Holy Scriptures, but also stated that the 'Holy Bible' would not be complete without the New Testament. He stated that the New Testament 'conveyed the message of Christians.' In his opinion, reading of the Holy Scriptures to the exclusion of the New Testament would be a sectarian practice. Dr. Weigle stated that the Bible was of great moral, historical and literary value. This is conceded by all the parties and is also the view of the court." 177 F. Supp. 398, 401-402.

The trial court, in striking down the practices and the statute requiring them, made specific findings of fact that the children's attendance at Abington Senior High School is compulsory and that the practice of reading 10 verses from the Bible is also compelled by law. It also found that:

> The reading of the verses, even without comment, possesses a devotional and religious character and constitutes in effect a religious observance. The devotional and religious nature of the morning exercises is made all the more apparent by the fact that the Bible reading is followed immediately by a recital in unison by the pupils of the Lord's Prayer. The fact that some pupils, or theoretically all pupils, might be excused from attendance at the exercises does not mitigate the obligatory nature of the ceremony for . . . Section 1516 . . . unequivocally requires the exercises to be held every school day in every school in the Commonwealth. The exercises are held in the school buildings and perforce are conducted by and under the authority of the local school authorities and during school sessions. Since the statute requires the reading of the "Holy Bible," a Christian document, the practice . . . prefers the Christian religion. The record demonstrates that it was the intention of . . . the Commonwealth . . . to introduce a religious ceremony into the public schools of the Commonwealth. 201 F. Supp., 819.

(Murray) In 1905 the Board of School Commissioners of Baltimore City adopted a rule . . . [providing] for the holding of opening exercises in the schools of the city, consisting primarily of the "reading, without comment, of a chapter in the Holy Bible and/or the use of the Lord's Prayer." The petitioners, Mrs. Madalyn Murray and her son, William J. Murray III, are both professed atheists. Following unsuccessful attempts to have the respondent school board rescind the rule, this suit was filed for mandamus to compel its rescission and cancellation. It was alleged that William was a student in a public school of the city and Mrs. Murray, his mother, was a taxpayer therein; that it was the practice under the rule to have a reading on each school morning from the King James version of the Bible; that at petitioners' insistence the rule was amended[4] to permit children to be excused from the exercise on request of the parent and that William had been excused pursuant thereto; that nevertheless

---

[4] The rule as amended provides as follows:

"Opening Exercises. Each school, either collectively or in classes, shall be opened by the reading, without comment, of a chapter in the Holy Bible and/or the use of the Lord's Prayer. The Douay version may be used by those pupils who prefer it. Appropriate patriotic exercises should be held as a part of the general opening exercise of the school or class. Any child shall be excused from participating in the opening exercises or from attending the opening exercises upon the written request of his parent or guardian."

the rule as amended was in violation of the petitioners' rights "to freedom of religion under the First and Fourteenth Amendments" and in violation of "the principle of separation between church and state, contained therein. . . ." The petition particularized the petitioners' atheistic beliefs and stated that the rule, as practiced, violated their rights "in that it threatens their religious liberty by placing a premium on belief as against non-belief and subjects their freedom of conscience to the rule of the majority; it pronounces belief in God as the source of all moral and spiritual values, equating these values with religious values, and thereby renders sinister, alien and suspect the beliefs and ideals of your Petitioners, promoting doubt and question of their morality, good citizenship and good faith."

The respondents demurred and the trial court, recognizing that the demurrer admitted all facts well pleaded, sustained it without leave to amend. The Maryland Court of Appeals affirmed, the majority of four justices holding the exercise not in violation of the First and Fourteenth Amendments, with three justices dissenting. 179 A. 2d 698. We granted certiorari.

## II

It is true that religion has been closely identified with our history and government. As we said in *Engel v. Vitale*, 370 U.S. 421, 434 (1962), "The history of man is inseparable from the history of religion. And . . . since the beginning of that history many people have devoutly believed that 'More things are wrought by prayer than this world dreams of.'" In *Zorach v. Clauson*, 343 U.S. 306, 313 (1952), we gave specific recognition to the proposition that "[w]e are a religious people whose institutions presuppose a Supreme Being." The fact that the Founding Fathers believed devotedly that there was a God and that the unalienable rights of man were rooted in Him is clearly evidenced in their writings, from the Mayflower Compact to the Constitution itself. This background is evidenced today in our public life through the continuance in our oaths of office from the Presidency to the Alderman of the final supplication, "So help me God." Likewise each House of the Congress provides through its Chaplain an opening prayer, and the sessions of this Court are declared open by the crier in a short ceremony, the final phrase of which invokes the grace of God. Again, there are such manifestations in our military forces, where those of our citizens who are under the restrictions of military service wish to engage in voluntary worship. Indeed, only last year an official survey of the country indicated that 64% of our people have church membership, Bureau of the Census, U.S. Department of Commerce, Statistical Abstract of the United States (83d ed. 1962), 48, while less than 3% profess no religion whatever. *Id.*, 46. It can be truly said, therefore, that today, as in the beginning, our national life reflects a religious people who, in the words of Madison, are "earnestly praying, as . . . in duty bound, that the Supreme Lawgiver of the Universe . . . guide them into every measure which may be worthy of his [blessing . . . .]" Memorial and Remonstrance Against Religious Assessments, quoted in *Everson v. Board of Education*, 330 U.S. 1, 71-72 (1947). . . .

This is not to say, however, that religion has been so identified with our history and government that religious freedom is not likewise as strongly imbedded in our public and private life. Nothing but the most telling of personal experiences in religious persecution suffered by our forebears, could have planted our belief in liberty of religious opinion any more deeply in our heritage. It is true that this liberty frequently was not realized by the colonists, but this is readily accountable by their close ties to the Mother Country.

However, the views of Madison and Jefferson, preceded by Roger Williams, came to be incorporated not only in the Federal Constitution but likewise in those of most of our States. This freedom to worship was indispensable in a country whose people came from the four quarters of the earth and brought with them a diversity of religious opinion. Today authorities list 83 separate religious bodies, each with membership exceeding 50,000, existing among our people, as well as innumerable smaller groups.

## III

Almost a hundred years ago in *Minor v. Board of Education of Cincinnati*, Judge Alphonso Taft, father of the revered Chief Justice, in an unpublished opinion stated the ideal of our people as to religious freedom as one of "absolute equality before the law, of all religious opinions and sects . . . ." "The government is neutral, and, while protecting all, it prefers none, and it *disparages* none."

Before examining this "neutral" position in which the Establishment and Free Exercise Clauses of the First Amendment place our Government it is well that we discuss the reach of the Amendment under the cases of this Court.

First, this Court has decisively settled that the First Amendment's mandate that "Congress shall make no law respecting an establishment of religion, or prohibiting the free exercise thereof" has been made wholly applicable to the States by the Fourteenth Amendment. . . .

Second, this Court has rejected unequivocally the contention that the Establishment Clause forbids only governmental preference of one religion over another. Almost 20 years ago in *Everson*, the Court said that "neither a state nor the Federal Government can set up a church. Neither can pass laws which aid one religion, aid all religions, or prefer one religion over another." . . .

The same conclusion has been firmly maintained ever since that time, see *Illinois ex rel. McCollum*; *McGowan v. Maryland*; *Torcaso v. Watkins*, and we reaffirm it now.

While none of the parties to either of these cases has questioned these basic conclusions of the Court, both of which have been long established, recognized and consistently reaffirmed, others continue to question their history, logic and efficacy. Such contentions, in the light of the consistent interpretation in cases of this Court, seem entirely untenable and of value only as academic exercises. . . .

## V

The wholesome "neutrality" of which this Court's cases speak thus stems from a recognition of the teachings of history that powerful sects or groups might bring about a fusion of governmental and religious functions or a concert or dependency of one upon the other to the end that official support of the State or Federal Government would be placed behind the tenets of one or of all orthodoxies. This the Establishment Clause prohibits. And a further reason for neutrality is found in the Free Exercise Clause, which recognizes the value of religious training, teaching and observance and, more particularly, the right of every person to freely choose his own course with reference thereto, free of any compulsion from the state. This the Free Exercise Clause guarantees. Thus, as we have seen, the two clauses may overlap. As we have indicated, the Establishment Clause has been directly considered by this Court eight times in the past score of years and, with only one Justice dissenting on the point, it has consistently held that the clause withdrew all legislative power respecting religious belief or the expression thereof. The test may be stated as follows: what are the purpose and the primary effect of the enactment? If either is the advancement or inhibition of religion then the enactment exceeds the scope of legislative power as circumscribed by the Constitution. That is to say that to withstand the strictures of the Establishment Clause there must be a secular legislative purpose and a primary effect that neither advances nor inhibits religion. The Free Exercise Clause, likewise considered many times here, withdraws from legislative power, state and federal, the exertion of any restraint on the free exercise of religion. Its purpose is to secure religious liberty in the individual by prohibiting any invasions thereof by civil authority. Hence it is necessary in a free exercise case for one to show the coercive effect of the enactment as it operates against him in the practice of his religion. The distinction between the two clauses is apparent—a violation of the Free Exercise Clause is predicated on coercion while the Establishment Clause violation need not be so attended.

Applying the Establishment Clause principles to the cases at bar we find that the States are requiring the selection and reading at the opening of the school day of verses from the Holy Bible and the recitation of the Lord's Prayer by the students in unison. These exercises are prescribed as part of the curricular activities of students who are required by law to attend school. They are held in the school buildings under the supervision and with the participation of teachers employed in those schools. None of these factors, other than compulsory school attendance, was present in the program upheld in *Zorach v. Clauson*. The trial court in [Schempp] has found that such an opening exercise is a religious ceremony and was intended by the State to be so. We agree with the trial court's finding as to the religious character of the exercises. Given that finding, the exercises and the law requiring them are in violation of the Establishment Clause.

There is no such specific finding as to the religious character of the exercises in [Murray], and the State contends (as does the State in [Schempp]) that the program is an effort to extend its benefits to all public school children without regard to their religious belief. Included within its secular purposes, it says, are the promotion of moral values, the contradiction to the materialistic trends of our times, the perpetuation of our institutions and the teaching of literature. The case came up on demurrer, of course, to a petition which alleged that the uniform practice under the rule had been to read from the King James version of the Bible and that the exercise was sectarian. The short answer, therefore, is that the religious character of the exercise was admitted by the State. But even if its purpose is not strictly religious, it is sought to be accomplished through readings, without comment, from the Bible. Surely the place of the Bible as an instrument of religion cannot be gainsaid, and the State's recognition of the pervading religious character of the ceremony is evident from the rule's specific permission of the alternative use of the Catholic Douay version as well as the recent amendment permitting nonattendance at the exercises. None of these factors is consistent with the contention that the Bible is here used either as an instrument for nonreligious moral inspiration or as a reference for the teaching of secular subjects.

The conclusion follows that in both cases the laws require religious exercises and such exercises are being conducted in direct violation of the rights of the appellees and petitioners. Nor are these required exercises mitigated by the fact that individual students may absent themselves upon parental request, for that fact furnishes no defense to a claim of unconstitutionality under the Establishment Clause. Further, it is no defense to urge that the religious practices here may be relatively minor encroachments on the First Amendment. The breach of neutrality that is today a trickling stream may all too soon become a raging torrent and, in the words of Madison, "it is proper to take alarm at the first experiment on our liberties." Memorial and Remonstrance Against Religious Assessments, quoted in *Everson*, 330 U.S., 65.

It is insisted that unless these religious exercises are permitted a "religion of secularism" is established in the schools. We agree of course that the State may not establish a "religion of secularism" in the sense of affirmatively opposing or showing hostility to religion, thus "preferring those who believe in no religion over those who do believe." *Zorach v. Clauson*, 343 U.S., 314. We do not agree, however, that this decision in any sense has that effect. In addition, it might well be said that one's education is not complete without a study of comparative religion or the history of religion and its relationship to the advancement of civilization. It certainly may be said that the Bible is worthy of study for its literary and historic qualities. Nothing we have said here indicates that such study of the Bible or of religion, when presented objectively as part of a secular program of education, may not be effected consistently with the First Amendment. But the exercises here do not fall into those categories. They are religious exercises, required by the States in violation of the command of the First Amendment that the Government maintain strict neutrality, neither aiding nor opposing religion.

Finally, we cannot accept that the concept of neutrality, which does not permit a State to require a religious exercise even with the consent of the majority of those affected, collides with the majority's right to free exercise of religion.[10] While the Free Exercise Clause clearly prohibits the use of state action to deny the rights of free exercise to *anyone*, it has never meant that a majority could use the machinery of the State to practice its beliefs. Such a contention was effectively answered by Mr. Justice Jackson for the Court in *West Virginia Board of Education v. Barnette*, 319 U.S. 624, 638 (1943):

> The very purpose of a Bill of Rights was to withdraw certain subjects from the vicissitudes of political controversy, to place them beyond the reach of majorities and officials and to establish them as legal principles to be applied by the courts. One's right to . . . freedom of worship . . . and other fundamental rights may not be submitted to vote; they depend on the outcome of no elections.

The place of religion in our society is an exalted one, achieved through a long tradition of reliance on the home, the church and the inviolable citadel of the individual heart and mind. We have come to recognize through bitter experience that it is not within the power of government to invade that citadel, whether its purpose or effect be to aid or oppose, to advance or retard. In the relationship between man and religion, the State is firmly committed to a position of neutrality. Though the application of that rule requires interpretation of

---

[10] We are not of course presented with and therefore do not pass upon a situation such as military service, where the Government regulates the temporal and geographic environment of individuals to a point that, unless it permits voluntary religious services to be conducted with the use of government facilities, military personnel would be unable to engage in the practice of their faiths.

a delicate sort, the rule itself is clearly and concisely stated in the words of the First Amendment. Applying that rule to the facts of these cases, we affirm the judgment in [*Schempp*]. In [*Murray*], the judgment is reversed and the cause remanded to the Maryland Court of Appeals for further proceedings consistent with this opinion.

*It is so ordered.*

### ▥ MR. JUSTICE DOUGLAS, concurring.

I join the opinion of the Court and add a few words in explanation. . . .

These regimes violate the Establishment Clause in two different ways. In each case the State is conducting a religious exercise; and, as the Court holds, that cannot be done without violating the "neutrality" required of the State by the balance of power between individual, church and state that has been struck by the First Amendment. But the Establishment Clause is not limited to precluding the State itself from conducting religious exercises. It also forbids the State to employ its facilities or funds in a way that gives any church, or all churches, greater strength in our society than it would have by relying on its members alone. Thus, the present regimes must fall under that clause for the additional reason that public funds, though small in amount, are being used to promote a religious exercise. Through the mechanism of the State, all of the people are being required to finance a religious exercise that only some of the people want and that violates the sensibilities of others. . . .

### ▥ MR. JUSTICE BRENNAN, concurring.

Almost a century and a half ago, John Marshall, in *M'Culloch v. Maryland*, enjoined: ". . . we must never forget, that it is a *constitution* we are expounding." 4 Wheat. 316, 407. The Court's historic duty to expound the meaning of the Constitution has encountered few issues more intricate or more demanding than that of the relationship between religion and the public schools. Since undoubtedly we are "a religious people whose institutions presuppose a Supreme Being," *Zorach v. Clauson*, 343 U.S. 306, 313, deep feelings are aroused when aspects of that relationship are claimed to violate the injunction of the First Amendment that government may make "no law respecting an establishment of religion, or prohibiting the free exercise thereof; . . ." Americans regard the public schools as a most vital civic institution for the preservation of a democratic system of government. It is therefore understandable that the constitutional prohibitions encounter their severest test when they are sought to be applied in the school classroom. Nevertheless it is this Court's inescapable duty to declare whether exercises in the public schools of the States, such as those of Pennsylvania and Maryland questioned here, are involvements of religion in public institutions of a kind which offends the First and Fourteenth Amendments.

When John Locke ventured in 1689, "I esteem it above all things necessary to distinguish exactly the business of civil government from that of religion and to settle the just bounds that lie between the one and the other," he anticipated the necessity which would be thought by the Framers to require adoption of a First Amendment, but not the difficulty that would be experienced in defining those "just bounds." The fact is that the line which separates the secular from the sectarian in American life is elusive. The difficulty of defining the boundary with precision inheres in a paradox central to our scheme of liberty. While our institutions reflect a firm conviction that we are a religious people, those institutions by solemn constitutional injunction may not officially involve religion in such a way as to prefer, discriminate against, or oppress, a particular sect or religion. Equally the Constitution enjoins those involvements of religious with secular institutions which (a) serve the essentially religious activities of religious institutions; (b) employ the organs of government for essentially religious purposes; or (c) use essentially religious means to serve governmental ends where secular means would suffice. The constitutional mandate expresses a deliberate and considered judgment that such matters are to be left to the conscience of the citizen, and declares as a basic postulate of the relation between the citizen and his government that "the rights of conscience are, in their nature, of peculiar delicacy, and will little bear the gentlest touch of governmental hand. . . ."

I join fully in the opinion and the judgment of the Court. I see no escape from the conclusion that the exercises called in question in these two cases violate the constitutional mandate. The reasons we gave only last Term in *Engel v. Vitale*, 370 U.S. 421, for finding in the New York Regents' prayer an impermissible establishment of religion, compel the same judgment of the practices at bar. The involvement of the secular with the religious is no less intimate here; and it is constitutionally irrelevant that the State has not composed the material for the inspirational exercises presently involved. It should be unnecessary to observe that our holding does not declare that the First Amendment manifests hostility to the practice or teaching of religion, but only applies prohibitions incorporated in the Bill of Rights in recognition of historic needs shared by Church and State alike. While it is my view that not every involvement of religion in public life is unconstitutional, I consider the exercises at bar a form of involvement which clearly violates the Establishment Clause.

The importance of the issue and the deep conviction with which views on both sides are held seem to me to justify detailing at some length my reasons for joining the Court's judgment and opinion.

I

The First Amendment forbids both the abridgment of the free exercise of religion and the enactment of laws "respecting an establishment of religion." The two clauses, although distinct in their objectives and their applicability, emerged together from a common panorama of history. The inclusion of both restraints upon the power of Congress to legislate concerning religious matters shows unmistakably that the Framers of the First Amendment were not content to rest the protection of religious liberty exclusively upon either clause. "In assuring the free exercise of religion," Mr. Justice Frankfurter has said, "the Framers of the First Amendment were sensitive to the then recent history of those persecutions and impositions of civil disability with which sectarian majorities in virtually all of the Colonies had visited deviation in the matter of conscience. This protection of unpopular creeds, however, was not to be the full extent of the Amendment's guarantee of freedom from governmental intrusion in matters of faith. The battle in Virginia, hardly four years won, where James Madison had led the forces of disestablishment in successful opposition to Patrick Henry's proposed Assessment Bill levying a general tax for the support of Christian teachers, was a vital and compelling memory in 1789." *McGowan v. Maryland*, 366 U.S. 420, 464-465.

It is true that the Framers' immediate concern was to prevent the setting up of an official federal church of the kind which England and some of the Colonies had long supported. But nothing in the text of the Establishment Clause supports the view that the prevention of the setting up of an official church was meant to be the full extent of the prohibitions against official involvements in religion. It has rightly been said:

> If the framers of the Amendment meant to prohibit Congress merely from the establishment of a "church," one may properly wonder why they didn't so state. That the words *church* and *religion* were regarded as synonymous seems highly improbable, particularly in view of the fact that the contemporary state constitutional provisions dealing with the subject of establishment used definite phrases such as "religious sect," "sect," or "denomination." . . . With such specific wording in contemporary state constitutions, why was not a similar wording adopted for the First Amendment if its framers intended to prohibit nothing more than what the States were prohibiting? Lardner, How Far Does the Constitution Separate Church and State? 45 Am. Pol. Sci. Rev. 110, 112 (1951).

Plainly, the Establishment Clause, in the contemplation of the Framers, "did not limit the constitutional proscription to any particular, dated form of state-supported theological venture."

> What Virginia had long practiced, and what Madison, Jefferson and others fought to end, was the extension of civil government's support to religion in a manner which made the two in some degree interdependent, and thus threatened the freedom of each. The purpose of the Establishment Clause was to assure that the national legislature would not exert its power in the service of any purely religious end; that it would not, as Virginia and virtually all of the Colonies had done, make of religion, as religion, an object of legislation. . . . The Establishment Clause withdrew from the sphere of legitimate legislative concern and competence a specific, but comprehensive, area of human conduct: man's belief or disbelief in the verity of some transcendental idea and man's expression in action of that belief or disbelief. *McGowan v. Maryland*, 465-466 (opinion of Frankfurter, J.).

In sum, the history which our prior decisions have summoned to aid interpretation of the Establishment Clause permits little doubt that its prohibition was designed comprehensively to prevent those official involvements of religion which would tend to foster or discourage religious worship or belief.

But an awareness of history and an appreciation of the aims of the Founding Fathers do not always resolve concrete problems. The specific question before us has, for example, aroused vigorous dispute whether the architects of the First Amendment—James Madison and Thomas Jefferson particularly— understood the prohibition against any "law respecting an establishment of religion" to reach devotional exercises in the public schools. It may be that Jefferson and Madison would have held such exercises to be permissible— although even in Jefferson's case serious doubt is suggested by his admonition against "putting the Bible and Testament into the hands of the children at an age when their judgments are not sufficiently matured for religious inquiries. . . ." But I doubt that their view, even if perfectly clear one way or the other, would supply a dispositive answer to the question presented by these cases. A more fruitful inquiry, it seems to me, is whether the practices here challenged threaten those consequences which the Framers deeply feared; whether, in short, they tend to promote that type of interdependence between religion and state which the First Amendment was designed to prevent. Our task is to translate "the majestic generalities of the Bill of Rights, conceived as part of the pattern of liberal government in the eighteenth century, into concrete restraints on officials dealing with the problems of the twentieth century. . . ." *West Virginia State Board of Education v. Barnette*, 319 U.S. 624, 639.

A too literal quest for the advice of the Founding Fathers upon the issues of these cases seems to me futile and misdirected for several reasons: First, on our precise problem the historical record is at best ambiguous, and statements can readily be found to support either side of the proposition. The ambiguity of history is understandable if we recall the nature of the problems upper-most in the thinking of the statesmen who fashioned the religious guarantees; they were concerned with far more flagrant intrusions of government into the realm of religion than any that our century has witnessed. While it is clear to me that the Framers meant the Establishment Clause to prohibit more than the creation of an established federal church such as existed in England, I have no doubt that, in their preoccupation with the imminent question of estab-lished churches, they gave no distinct consideration to the particular question whether the clause also forbade devotional exercises in public institutions.

Second, the structure of American education has greatly changed since the First Amendment was adopted. In the context of our modern emphasis upon public education available to all citizens, any views of the eighteenth century as to whether the exercises at bar are an "establishment" offer little aid to deci-sion. Education, as the Framers knew it, was in the main confined to private schools more often than not under strictly sectarian supervision. Only gradu-ally did control of education pass largely to public officials.[7] It would, there-fore, hardly be significant if the fact was that the nearly universal devotional

---

[7] The origins of the modern movement for free state-supported education cannot be fixed with precision. In England, the Levellers unavailingly urged in their platform of 1649 the establishment of free primary education for all, or at least for boys. See Brailsford, The Levellers and the English Revolution (1961), 534. In the North American Colonies, educa-tion was almost without exception under private sponsorship and supervision, frequently under control of the dominant Protestant sects. This condition prevailed after the Revolu-tion and into the first quarter of the nineteenth century. Thus, Virginia's colonial Governor Berkeley exclaimed in 1671: "I thank God there are no free schools nor printing, and I hope we shall not have them these hundred years; for learning has brought disobedience, and heresy, and sects into the world. . . ." (Emphasis deleted.) Bates, Religious Liberty: An Inquiry (1945), 327.

The exclusively private control of American education did not, however, quite survive Berkeley's expectations. Benjamin Franklin's proposals in 1749 for a Philadelphia Academy heralded the dawn of publicly supported secondary education, although the proposal did not bear immediate fruit. Jefferson's elaborate plans for a public school system in Virginia came to naught after the defeat in 1796 of his proposed Elementary School Bill, which found little favor among the wealthier legislators. It was not until the 1820's and 1830's, under the impe-tus of Jacksonian democracy, that a system of public education really took root in the United States. One force behind the development of secular public schools may have been a growing dissatisfaction with the tightly sectarian control over private education, see Harner, Religion's Place in General Education (1949), 29-30. Yet the burgeoning public school systems did not immediately supplant the old sectarian and private institutions; Alexis de Tocqueville, for example, remarked after his tour of the Eastern States in 1831 that "almost all education is

exercises in the schools of the young Republic did not provoke criticism; even today religious ceremonies in church-supported private schools are constitutionally unobjectionable.

Third, our religious composition makes us a vastly more diverse people than were our forefathers. They knew differences chiefly among Protestant sects. Today the Nation is far more heterogeneous religiously, including as it does substantial minorities not only of Catholics and Jews but as well of those who worship according to no version of the Bible and those who worship no God at all. In the face of such profound changes, practices which may have been objectionable to no one in the time of Jefferson and Madison may today be highly offensive to many persons, the deeply devout and the nonbelievers alike.

Whatever Jefferson or Madison would have thought of Bible reading or the recital of the Lord's Prayer in what few public schools existed in their day, our use of the history of their time must limit itself to broad purposes, not specific practices. By such a standard, I am persuaded, as is the Court, that the devotional exercises carried on in the Baltimore and Abington schools offend the First Amendment because they sufficiently threaten in our day those substantive evils the fear of which called forth the Establishment Clause of the First Amendment. It is "a *constitution* we are expounding," and our interpretation of the First Amendment must necessarily be responsive to the much more highly charged nature of religious questions in contemporary society.

---

entrusted to the clergy." 1 Democracy in America (Bradley ed. 1945) 309, n. 4. And compare Lord Bryce's observations, a half century later, on the still largely denominational character of American higher education, 2 The American Commonwealth (1933), 734-735.

Efforts to keep the public schools of the early nineteenth century free from sectarian influence were of two kinds. One took the form of constitutional provisions and statutes adopted by a number of States forbidding appropriations from the public treasury for the support of religious instruction in any manner. The other took the form of measures directed against the use of sectarian reading and teaching materials in the schools. The texts used in the earliest public schools had been largely taken over from the private academies, and retained a strongly religious character and content. In 1827, however, Massachusetts enacted a statute providing that school boards might not thereafter "direct any school books to be purchased or used, in any of the schools . . . which are calculated to favour any particular religious sect or tenet." 2 Stokes, Church and State in the United States (1950), 53. As other States followed the example of Massachusetts, the use of sectarian texts was in time as widely prohibited as the appropriation of public funds for religious instruction.

Concerning the evolution of the American public school systems free of sectarian influence, compare Mr. Justice Frankfurter's account:

"It is pertinent to remind that the establishment of this principle of Separation in the field of education was not due to any decline in the religious beliefs of the people. Horace Mann was a devout Christian, and the deep religious feeling of James Madison is stamped upon the Remonstrance. The secular public school did not imply indifference to the basic role of religion in the life of the people, nor rejection of religious education as a means of fostering it. The claims of religion were not minimized by refusing to make the public schools agencies for their assertion. The non-sectarian or secular public school was the means of reconciling freedom in general with religious freedom. The sharp confinement of the public schools to secular education was a recognition of the need of a democratic society to educate its children, insofar as the State undertook to do so, in an atmosphere free from pressures in a realm in which pressures are most resisted and where conflicts are most easily and most bitterly engendered." *Illinois ex rel. McCollum v. Board of Education*, 333 U.S. 203, 216.

Fourth, the American experiment in free public education available to all children has been guided in large measure by the dramatic evolution of the religious diversity among the population which our public schools serve. The interaction of these two important forces in our national life has placed in bold relief certain positive values in the consistent application to public institutions generally, and public schools particularly, of the constitutional decree against official involvements of religion which might produce the evils the Framers meant the Establishment Clause to forestall. The public schools are supported entirely, in most communities, by public funds—funds exacted not only from parents, nor alone from those who hold particular religious views, nor indeed from those who subscribe to any creed at all. It is implicit in the history and character of American public education that the public schools serve a uniquely *public* function: the training of American citizens in an atmosphere free of parochial, divisive, or separatist influences of any sort—an atmosphere in which children may assimilate a heritage common to all American groups and religions. This is a heritage neither theistic nor atheistic, but simply civic and patriotic.

Attendance at the public schools has never been compulsory; parents remain morally and constitutionally free to choose the academic environment in which they wish their children to be educated. The relationship of the Establishment Clause of the First Amendment to the public school system is preeminently that of reserving such a choice to the individual parent, rather than vesting it in the majority of voters of each State or school district. The choice which is thus preserved is between a public secular education with its uniquely democratic values, and some form of private or sectarian education, which offers values of its own. In my judgment the First Amendment forbids the State to inhibit that freedom of choice by diminishing the attractiveness of either alternative—either by restricting the liberty of the private schools to inculcate whatever values they wish, or by jeopardizing the freedom of the public schools from private or sectarian pressures. The choice between these very different forms of education is one—very much like the choice of whether or not to worship—which our Constitution leaves to the individual parent. It is no proper function of the state or local government to influence or restrict that election. The lesson of history—drawn more from the experiences of other countries than from our own—is that a system of free public education forfeits its unique contribution to the growth of democratic citizenship when that choice ceases to be freely available to each parent. . . .

## IV

I turn now to the cases before us. The religious nature of the exercises here challenged seems plain. Unless *Engel v. Vitale* is to be overruled, or we are to engage in wholly disingenuous distinction, we cannot sustain these practices. Daily recital of the Lord's Prayer and the reading of passages of Scripture are quite as clearly breaches of the command of the Establishment Clause as was the daily use of the rather bland Regents' Prayer in the New York public schools. Indeed, I would suppose that, if anything, the Lord's Prayer and the Holy Bible are more clearly sectarian, and the present violations of the First Amendment consequently more serious. But the religious exercises challenged in these cases have a long history. And almost from the beginning, Bible reading and daily prayer in the schools have been the subject of debate, criticism by educators and other public officials, and proscription by courts and legislative councils. At the outset, then, we must carefully canvass both aspects of this history.

The use of prayers and Bible readings at the opening of the school day long antedates the founding of our Republic. The Rules of the New Haven Hopkins Grammar School required in 1684 "that the Scholars being called together, the Mr. shall every morning begin his work with a short prayer for a blessing on his Laboures and their learning. . . ." More rigorous was the provision in a 1682 contract with a Dutch schoolmaster in Flatbush, New York: "When the school begins, one of the children shall read the morning prayer, as it stands in the catechism, and close with the prayer before dinner; in the afternoon it shall begin with the prayer after dinner, and end with the evening prayer. The evening school shall begin with the Lord's prayer, and close by singing a psalm."

After the Revolution, the new States uniformly continued these long-established practices in the private and the few public grammar schools. The school committee of Boston in 1789, for example, required the city's several schoolmasters "daily to commence the duties of their office by prayer and reading a portion of the Sacred Scriptures. . . ." That requirement was mirrored throughout the original States, and exemplified the universal practice well into the nineteenth century. As the free public schools gradually supplanted the private academies and sectarian schools between 1800 and 1850, morning devotional exercises were retained with few alterations. Indeed, public pressures upon school administrators in many parts of the country would hardly have condoned abandonment of practices to which a century or more of private religious education had accustomed the American people. The controversy centered, in fact, principally about the elimination of plainly sectarian practices and textbooks, and led to the eventual substitution of nonsectarian, though still religious, exercises and materials.

Statutory provision for daily religious exercises is, however, of quite recent origin. At the turn of this century, there was but one State—Massachusetts—which had a law making morning prayer or Bible reading obligatory. Statutes elsewhere either permitted such practices or simply left the question to local option. It was not until after 1910 that 11 more States, within a few years, joined Massachusetts in making one or both exercises compulsory. The Pennsylvania law with which we are concerned in the *Schempp* case, for example, took effect in 1913; and even the Rule of the Baltimore School Board involved in the *Murray* case dates only from 1905. In no State has there ever been a constitutional or statutory prohibition against the recital of prayers or the reading of Scripture, although a number of States have outlawed these practices by judicial decision or administrative order. What is noteworthy about the panoply of state and local regulations from which these cases emerge is the relative recency of the statutory codification of practices which have ancient roots, and the rather small number of States which have ever prescribed compulsory religious exercises in the public schools.

The purposes underlying the adoption and perpetuation of these practices are somewhat complex. It is beyond question that the religious benefits and values realized from daily prayer and Bible reading have usually been considered paramount, and sufficient to justify the continuation of such practices. To Horace Mann, embroiled in an intense controversy over the role of *sectarian* instruction and textbooks in the Boston public schools, there was little question that the regular use of the Bible—which he thought essentially nonsectarian—

would bear fruit in the spiritual enlightenment of his pupils. A contemporary of Mann's, the Commissioner of Education of a neighboring State, expressed a view which many enlightened educators of that day shared:

> As a textbook of morals the Bible is pre-eminent, and should have a prominent place in our schools, either as a reading book or as a source of appeal and instruction. Sectarianism, indeed, should not be countenanced in the schools; but the Bible is not sectarian. . . . The Scriptures should at least be read at the opening of the school, if no more. Prayer may also be offered with the happiest effects.

Wisconsin's Superintendent of Public Instruction, writing a few years later in 1858, reflected the attitude of his eastern colleagues, in that he regarded "with special favor the use of the Bible in public schools, as pre-eminently first in importance among text-books for teaching the noblest principles of virtue, morality, patriotism, and good order—love and reverence for God—charity and good will to man."

Such statements reveal the understanding of educators that the daily religious exercises in the schools served broader goals than compelling formal worship of God or fostering church attendance. The religious aims of the educators who adopted and retained such exercises were comprehensive, and in many cases quite devoid of sectarian bias—but the crucial fact is that they were nonetheless religious. While it has been suggested, that daily prayer and reading of Scripture now serve secular goals as well, there can be no doubt that the origins of these practices were unambiguously religious, even where the educator's aim was not to win adherents to a particular creed or faith.

Almost from the beginning religious exercises in the public schools have been the subject of intense criticism, vigorous debate, and judicial or administrative prohibition. Significantly, educators and school boards early entertained doubts about both the legality and the soundness of opening the school day with compulsory prayer or Bible reading. Particularly in the large Eastern cities, where immigration had exposed the public schools to religious diversities and conflicts unknown to the homogeneous academies of the eighteenth century, local authorities found it necessary even before the Civil War to seek an accommodation. In 1843, the Philadelphia School Board adopted the following resolutions:

"RESOLVED, that no children be required to attend or unite in the reading of the Bible in the Public Schools, whose parents are conscientiously opposed thereto:

"RESOLVED, that those children whose parents conscientiously prefer and desire any particular version of the Bible, without note or comment, be furnished with same."

A decade later, the Superintendent of Schools of New York State issued an even bolder decree that prayers could no longer be required as part of public school activities, and that where the King James Bible was read, Catholic students could not be compelled to attend. This type of accommodation was not restricted to the East Coast; the Cincinnati Board of Education resolved in 1869 that "religious instruction and the reading of religious books, including the Holy Bible, are prohibited in the common schools of Cincinnati, it being the true object and intent of this rule to allow the children of the parents of all sects and opinions, in matters of faith and worship, to enjoy alike the benefit of the common-school fund." The Board repealed at the same time an earlier regulation which had required the singing of hymns and psalms to accompany the Bible reading at the start of the school day. And in 1889, one commentator ventured the view that "there is not enough to be gained from Bible reading to justify the quarrel that has been raised over it."

Thus a great deal of controversy over religion in the public schools had preceded the debate over the Blaine Amendment, precipitated by President Grant's insistence that matters of religion should be left "to the family altar, the church, and the private school, supported entirely by private contributions." There was ample precedent, too, for Theodore Roosevelt's declaration that in the interest of "absolutely nonsectarian public schools" it was "not our business to have the Protestant Bible or the Catholic Vulgate or the Talmud read in those schools." The same principle appeared in the message of an Ohio Governor who vetoed a compulsory Bible-reading bill in 1925:

> It is my belief that religious teaching in our homes, Sunday schools, churches, by the good mothers, fathers, and ministers of Ohio is far preferable to compulsory teaching of religion by the state. The spirit of our federal and state constitutions from the beginning . . . [has] been to leave religious instruction to the discretion of parents.

The same theme has recurred in the opinions of the Attorneys General of several States holding religious exercises or instruction to be in violation of the state or federal constitutional command of separation of church and state. Thus the basic principle upon which our decision last year in *Engel v. Vitale* necessarily rested, and which we reaffirm today, can hardly be thought to be radical or novel.

Particularly relevant for our purposes are the decisions of the state courts on questions of religion in the public schools. Those decisions, while not, of course, authoritative in this Court, serve nevertheless to define the problem before us and to guide our inquiry. . . . The earliest of such decisions declined to review the propriety of actions taken by school authorities, so long as those actions were within the purview of the administrators' powers. . . .

The last quarter of the nineteenth century found the courts beginning to question the constitutionality of public school religious exercises. The legal context was still, of course, that of the state constitutions, since the First Amendment had not yet been held applicable to state action. And the state constitutional prohibitions against church-state cooperation or governmental aid to religion were generally less rigorous than the Establishment Clause of the First Amendment. It is therefore remarkable that the courts of a half dozen States found compulsory religious exercises in the public schools in violation of their respective state constitutions. These courts attributed much significance to the clearly religious origins and content of the challenged practices, and to the impossibility of avoiding sectarian controversy in their conduct. . . .

Even those state courts which have sustained devotional exercises under state law have usually recognized the primarily religious character of prayers and Bible readings. If such practices were not for that reason unconstitutional, it was necessarily because the state constitution forbade only public expenditures for *sectarian* instruction, or for activities which made the schoolhouse a "place of worship," but said nothing about the subtler question of laws "respecting an establishment of religion." Thus the panorama of history permits no other conclusion than that daily prayers and Bible readings in the public schools have always been designed to be, and have been regarded as, essentially religious exercises. Unlike the Sunday closing laws, these exercises appear neither to have been divorced from their religious origins nor deprived of their centrally religious character by the passage of time. . . .

## A

First, it is argued that however clearly religious may have been the origins and early nature of daily prayer and Bible reading, these practices today serve so clearly secular educational purposes that their religious attributes may be overlooked. I do not doubt, for example, that morning devotional exercises may foster better discipline in the classroom, and elevate the spiritual level on which the school day opens. The Pennsylvania Superintendent of Public Instruction, testifying by deposition in the *Schempp* case, offered his view that daily Bible reading "places upon the children or those hearing the reading of this, and the atmosphere which goes on in the reading . . . one of the last vestiges of moral value that we have left in our school system.". . .

It is not the business of this Court to gainsay the judgments of experts on matters of pedagogy. Such decisions must be left to the discretion of those administrators charged with the supervision of the Nation's public schools. The limited province of the courts is to determine whether the means which the educators have chosen to achieve legitimate pedagogical ends infringe the constitutional freedoms of the First Amendment. The secular purposes which devotional exercises are said to serve fall into two categories—those which depend upon an immediately religious experience shared by the participating children; and those which appear sufficiently divorced from the religious content of the devotional material that they can be served equally by nonreligious materials. With respect to the first objective, much has been written about the moral and spiritual values of infusing some religious influence or instruction into the public school classroom. To the extent that only *religious* materials will serve this purpose, it seems to me that the purpose as well as the means is so plainly religious that the exercise is necessarily forbidden by the Establishment Clause. The fact that purely secular benefits may eventually result does not seem to me to justify the exercises, for similar indirect nonreligious benefits could no doubt have been claimed for the released time program invalidated in *McCollum*.

The second justification assumes that religious exercises at the start of the school day may directly serve solely secular ends—for example, by fostering harmony and tolerance among the pupils, enhancing the authority of the teacher, and inspiring better discipline. To the extent that such benefits result not from the content of the readings and recitation, but simply from the holding of such a solemn exercise at the opening assembly or the first class of the day, it would seem that less sensitive materials might equally well serve the same purpose. I have previously suggested that *Torcaso* and the *Sunday Law Cases* forbid the use of religious means to achieve secular ends where nonreligious means will suffice. That principle is readily applied to these cases. It has not been shown that readings from the speeches and messages of great Americans, for example, or from the documents of our heritage of liberty, daily recitation of the Pledge of Allegiance, or even the observance of a moment of reverent silence at the opening of class, may not adequately serve the solely secular purposes of the devotional activities without jeopardizing either the religious liberties of any members of the community or the proper degree of separation between the spheres of religion and government. Such substitutes would, I think, be unsatisfactory or inadequate only to the extent that the present activities do in fact serve religious goals. While I do not question the judgment of experienced educators that the challenged practices may well achieve valuable secular ends, it seems to me that the State acts unconstitutionally if it either sets about to attain even indirectly religious ends by religious means, or if it uses religious means to serve secular ends where secular means would suffice.

B

Second, it is argued that the particular practices involved in the two cases before us are unobjectionable because they prefer no particular sect or sects at the expense of others. Both the Baltimore and Abington procedures permit, for example, the reading of any of several versions of the Bible, and this flexibility is said to ensure neutrality sufficiently to avoid the constitutional prohibition. One answer, which might be dispositive, is that any version of the Bible is inherently sectarian, else there would be no need to offer a system of rotation or alternation of versions in the first place, that is, to allow different sectarian versions to be used on different days. The sectarian character of the Holy Bible has been at the core of the whole controversy over religious practices in the public schools throughout its long and often bitter history. To vary the version as the Abington and Baltimore schools have done may well be less offensive than to read from the King James version every day, as once was the practice. But the result even of this relatively benign procedure is that majority sects are preferred in approximate proportion to their representation in the community and in the student body, while the smaller sects suffer commensurate discrimination. So long as the subject matter of the exercise is sectarian in character, these consequences cannot be avoided.

The argument contains, however, a more basic flaw. There are persons in every community—often deeply devout—to whom any version of the Judaeo-Christian Bible is offensive. There are others whose reverence for the Holy Scriptures demands private study or reflection and to whom public reading or recitation is sacrilegious, as one of the expert witnesses at the trial of the *Schempp* case explained. To such persons it is not the fact of using the Bible in the public schools, nor the content of any particular version, that is offensive, but only the *manner* in which it is used. For such persons, the anathema of public communion is even more pronounced when prayer is involved. Many deeply devout persons have always regarded prayer as a necessarily private experience. One Protestant group recently commented, for example: "When one thinks of prayer as sincere outreach of a human soul to the Creator, 'required prayer' becomes an absurdity." There is a similar problem with respect to comment upon the passages of Scripture which are to be read. Most present statutes forbid comment, and this practice accords with the views of many religious groups as to the manner in which the Bible should be read. However, as a recent survey discloses, scriptural passages read without comment frequently convey no message to the younger children in the school. Thus there has developed a practice in some schools of bridging the gap between faith and understanding by means of "definitions," even where "comment" is forbidden by statute. The present practice therefore poses a difficult dilemma: While Bible reading is almost universally required to be without comment, since only by such a prohibition can sectarian interpretation be excluded from the classroom, the rule breaks down at the point at which rudimentary definitions of Biblical terms are necessary for comprehension if the exercise is to be meaningful at all.

It has been suggested that a tentative solution to these problems may lie in the fashioning of a "common core" of theology tolerable to all creeds but preferential to none. But as one commentator has recently observed, "history is not encouraging to" those who hope to fashion a "common denominator of religion detached from its manifestation in any organized church." Sutherland, Establishment According to Engel, 76 Harv. L. Rev. 25, 51 (1962). Thus, the notion of a "common core" litany or supplication offends many deeply devout worshippers who do not find clearly sectarian practices objectionable. Father Gustave Weigel has recently expressed a widely shared view: "The moral code held by each separate religious community can reductively be unified, but the consistent particular believer wants no such reduction." And, as the American Council on Education warned several years ago, "The notion of a common core suggests a watering down of the several faiths to the point where common essentials appear. This might easily lead to a new sect—a public school sect— which would take its place alongside the existing faiths and compete with them." Engel is surely authority that nonsectarian religious practices, equally with sectarian exercises, violate the Establishment Clause. Moreover, even if the Establishment Clause were oblivious to nonsectarian religious practices, I think it quite likely that the "common core" approach would be sufficiently objectionable to many groups to be foreclosed by the prohibitions of the Free Exercise Clause.

## C

A third element which is said to absolve the practices involved in these cases from the ban of the religious guarantees of the Constitution is the provision to excuse or exempt students who wish not to participate. Insofar as these practices are claimed to violate the Establishment Clause, I find the answer which the District Court gave after our remand of *Schempp* to be altogether dispositive:

> The fact that some pupils, or theoretically all pupils, might be excused from attendance at the exercises does not mitigate the obligatory nature of the ceremony. . . . The exercises are held in the school buildings and perforce are conducted by and under the authority of the local school authorities and during school sessions. Since the statute requires the reading of the "Holy Bible," a Christian document, the practice, as we said in our first opinion, prefers the Christian religion. The record demonstrates that it was the intention of the General Assembly of the Commonwealth of Pennsylvania to introduce a religious ceremony into the public schools of the Commonwealth.

Thus the short, and to me sufficient, answer is that the availability of excusal or exemption simply has no relevance to the establishment question, if it is once found that these practices are essentially religious exercises designed at least in part to achieve religious aims through the use of public school facilities during the school day.

The more difficult question, however, is whether the availability of excusal for the dissenting child serves to refute challenges to these practices under the Free Exercise Clause. While it is enough to decide these cases to dispose of the establishment questions, questions of free exercise are so inextricably interwoven into the history and present status of these practices as to justify disposition of this second aspect of the excusal issue. The answer is that the excusal procedure itself necessarily operates in such a way as to infringe the rights of free exercise of those children who wish to be excused. We have held in *Barnette* and *Torcaso*, respectively, that a State may require neither public school students nor candidates for an office of public trust to profess beliefs offensive to religious principles. By the same token the State could not constitutionally require a student to profess publicly his disbelief as the prerequisite to the exercise of his constitutional right of abstention. And apart from *Torcaso* and *Barnette*, I think *Speiser v. Randall*, 357 U.S. 513, suggests a further answer. We held there that a State may not condition the grant of a tax exemption upon the willingness of those entitled to the exemption to affirm their loyalty to the Government, even though the exemption was itself a matter of grace rather than of constitutional right. We concluded that to impose upon the eligible taxpayers the affirmative burden of proving their loyalty impermissibly jeopardized the freedom to engage in constitutionally protected activities close to the area to which the loyalty oath related. *Speiser v. Randall* seems to me to dispose of two aspects of the excusal or exemption procedure now before us. First, by requiring what is tantamount in the eyes of teachers and schoolmates to a profession of disbelief, or at least of nonconformity, the procedure may well deter those children who do not wish to participate for any reason based upon the dictates of conscience from exercising an indisputably constitutional right to be excused.[68] Thus the excusal provision in its operation subjects them to a cruel dilemma. In consequence, even devout children may well avoid claiming their right and simply continue to participate in exercises distasteful to them because of an understandable reluctance to be stigmatized as atheists or nonconformists simply on the basis of their request.

Such reluctance to seek exemption seems all the more likely in view of the fact that children are disinclined at this age to step out of line or to flout "peer-group norms." Such is the widely held view of experts who have studied the behaviors and attitudes of children. . . .

The history, the purpose and the operation of the daily prayer recital and Bible reading leave no doubt that these practices standing by themselves constitute an impermissible breach of the Establishment Clause. Such devotional exercises may well serve legitimate nonreligious purposes. To the extent, however, that such purposes are really without religious significance, it has never

---

[68] See the testimony of Edward L. Schempp, the father of the children in the Abington schools and plaintiff-appellee in No. 142, concerning his reasons for not asking that his children be excused from the morning exercises after excusal was made available through amendment of the statute:

"We originally objected to our children being exposed to the reading of the King James version of the Bible . . . and under those conditions we would have theoretically liked to have had the children excused. But we felt that the penalty of having our children labelled as 'odd balls' before their teachers and classmates every day in the year was even less satisfactory than the other problem. . . .

"The children, the classmates of Roger and Donna are very liable to label and lump all particular religious difference or religious objections as atheism, particularly, today the word 'atheism' is so often tied to atheistic communism, and atheism has very bad connotations in the minds of children and many adults today."

A recent opinion of the Attorney General of California gave as one reason for finding devotional exercises unconstitutional the likelihood that "children forced by conscience to leave the room during such exercises would be placed in a position inferior to that of students adhering to the State-endorsed religion." 25 *Cal. Op. Atty. Gen.* 316, 319 (1955).

been demonstrated that secular means would not suffice. Indeed, I would suggest that patriotic or other nonreligious materials might provide adequate substitutes—inadequate only to the extent that the purposes now served are indeed directly or indirectly religious. Under such circumstances, the States may not employ religious means to reach a secular goal unless secular means are wholly unavailing. I therefore agree with the Court that the judgment in *Schempp*, must be affirmed, and that in *Murray*, must be reversed.

V

These considerations bring me to a final contention of the school officials in these cases: that the invalidation of the exercises at bar permits this Court no alternative but to declare unconstitutional every vestige, however slight, of cooperation or accommodation between religion and government. I cannot accept that contention. While it is not, of course, appropriate for this Court to decide questions not presently before it, I venture to suggest that religious exercises in the public schools present a unique problem. For not every involvement of religion in public life violates the Establishment Clause. Our decision in these cases does not clearly forecast anything about the constitutionality of other types of interdependence between religious and other public institutions.

Specifically, I believe that the line we must draw between the permissible and the impermissible is one which accords with history and faithfully reflects the understanding of the Founding Fathers. It is a line which the Court has consistently sought to mark in its decisions expounding the religious guarantees of the First Amendment. What the Framers meant to foreclose, and what our decisions under the Establishment Clause have forbidden, are those involvements of religious with secular institutions which (a) serve the essentially religious activities of religious institutions; (b) employ the organs of government for essentially religious purposes; or (c) use essentially religious means to serve governmental ends, where secular means would suffice. When the secular and religious institutions become involved in such a manner, there inhere in the relationship precisely those dangers—as much to church as to state—which the Framers feared would subvert religious liberty and the strength of a system of secular government. On the other hand, there may be myriad forms of involvements of government with religion which do not import such dangers and therefore should not, in my judgment, be deemed to violate the Establishment Clause. Nothing in the Constitution compels the organs of government to be blind to what everyone else perceives—that religious differences among Americans have important and pervasive implications for our society. Likewise nothing in the Establishment Clause forbids the application of legislation having purely secular ends in such a way as to alleviate burdens upon the free exercise of an individual's religious beliefs. Surely the Framers would never have understood that such a construction sanctions that involvement which violates the Establishment Clause. Such a conclusion can be reached, I would suggest, only by using the words of the First Amendment to defeat its very purpose.

The line between permissible and impermissible forms of involvement between government and religion has already been considered by the lower federal and state courts. I think a brief survey of certain of these forms of accommodation will reveal that the First Amendment commands not official hostility toward religion, but only a strict neutrality in matters of religion.

Moreover, it may serve to suggest that the scope of our holding today is to be measured by the special circumstances under which these cases have arisen, and by the particular dangers to church and state which religious exercises in the public schools present. It may be helpful for purposes of analysis to group these other practices and forms of accommodation into several rough categories.

A. *The Conflict Between Establishment and Free Exercise.*—There are certain practices, conceivably violative of the Establishment Clause, the striking down of which might seriously interfere with certain religious liberties also protected by the First Amendment. Provisions for churches and chaplains at military establishments for those in the armed services may afford one such example. The like provision by state and federal governments for chaplains in penal institutions may afford another example. It is argued that such provisions may be assumed to contravene the Establishment Clause, yet be sustained on constitutional grounds as necessary to secure to the members of the Armed Forces and prisoners those rights of worship guaranteed under the Free Exercise Clause. Since government has deprived such persons of the opportunity to practice their faith at places of their choice, the argument runs, government may, in order to avoid infringing the free exercise guarantees, provide substitutes where it requires such persons to be. Such a principle might support, for example, the constitutionality of draft exemptions for ministers and divinity students; of the excusal of children from school on their respective religious holidays; and of the allowance by government of temporary use of public buildings by religious organizations when their own churches have become unavailable because of a disaster or emergency.

Such activities and practices seem distinguishable from the sponsorship of daily Bible reading and prayer recital. For one thing, there is no element of coercion present in the appointment of military or prison chaplains; the soldier or convict who declines the opportunities for worship would not ordinarily subject himself to the suspicion or obloquy of his peers. Of special significance to this distinction is the fact that we are here usually dealing with adults, not with impressionable children as in the public schools. Moreover, the school exercises are not designed to provide the pupils with general opportunities for worship denied them by the legal obligation to attend school. The student's compelled presence in school for five days a week in no way renders the regular religious facilities of the community less accessible to him than they are to others. The situation of the school child is therefore plainly unlike that of the isolated soldier or the prisoner.

The State must be steadfastly neutral in all matters of faith, and neither favor nor inhibit religion. In my view, government cannot sponsor religious exercises in the public schools without jeopardizing that neutrality. On the other hand, hostility, not neutrality, would characterize the refusal to provide chaplains and places of worship for prisoners and soldiers cut off by the State from all civilian opportunities for public communion, the withholding of draft exemptions for ministers and conscientious objectors, or the denial of the temporary use of an empty public building to a congregation whose place of worship has been destroyed by fire or flood. I do not say that government *must* provide chaplains or draft exemptions, or that the courts should intercede if it fails to do so.

B. *Establishment and Exercises in Legislative Bodies.*—The saying of invocational prayers in legislative chambers, state or federal, and the appointment of legislative chaplains, might well represent no involvements of the kind pro-hibited by the Establishment Clause. Legislators, federal and state, are ma-ture adults who may presumably absent themselves from such public and ceremonial exercises without incurring any penalty, direct or indirect. It may also be significant that, at least in the case of the Congress, Art. I, § 5, of the Constitution makes each House the monitor of the "Rules of its Proceedings" so that it is at least arguable whether such matters present "political questions" the resolution of which is exclusively confided to Congress. Finally, there is the difficult question of who may be heard to challenge such practices.

C. *Non-Devotional Use of the Bible in the Public Schools.*—The holding of the Court today plainly does not foreclose teaching *about* the Holy Scriptures or about the differences between religious sects in classes in literature or history. Indeed, whether or not the Bible is involved, it would be impossible to teach meaningfully many subjects in the social sciences or the humanities without some mention of religion. To what extent, and at what points in the curricu-lum, religious materials should be cited are matters which the courts ought to entrust very largely to the experienced officials who superintend our Nation's public schools. They are experts in such matters, and we are not. . . .

Any attempt to impose rigid limits upon the mention of God or references to the Bible in the classroom would be fraught with dangers. If it should some-time hereafter be shown that in fact religion can play no part in the teaching of a given subject without resurrecting the ghost of the practices we strike down today, it will then be time enough to consider questions we must now defer.

D. *Uniform Tax Exemptions Incidentally Available to Religious Institutions.*—Nothing we hold today questions the propriety of certain tax deductions or ex-emptions which incidentally benefit churches and religious institutions, along with many secular charities and nonprofit organizations. If religious institu-tions benefit, it is in spite of rather than because of their religious character. For religious institutions simply share benefits which government makes gen-erally available to educational, charitable, and eleemosynary groups. There is no indication that taxing authorities have used such benefits in any way to subsidize worship or foster belief in God. And as among religious beneficia-ries, the tax exemption or deduction can be truly nondiscriminatory, available on equal terms to small as well as large religious bodies, to popular and un-popular sects, and to those organizations which reject as well as those which accept a belief in God.

E. *Religious Considerations in Public Welfare Programs.*—Since government may not support or directly aid religious *activities* without violating the Es-tablishment Clause, there might be some doubt whether nondiscriminatory programs of governmental aid may constitutionally include *individuals* who become eligible wholly or partially for religious reasons. For example, it might be suggested that where a State provides unemployment compensation gen-erally to those who are unable to find suitable work, it may not extend such benefits to persons who are unemployed by reason of religious beliefs or prac-tices without thereby establishing the religion to which those persons belong. Therefore, the argument runs, the State may avoid an establishment only by singling out and excluding such persons on the ground that religious beliefs or practices have made them potential beneficiaries. Such a construction would, it seems to me, require government to impose religious discriminations and disabilities, thereby jeopardizing the free exercise of religion, in order to avoid what is thought to constitute an establishment.

The inescapable flaw in the argument, I suggest, is its quite unrealistic view of the aims of the Establishment Clause. The Framers were not concerned with the effects of certain incidental aids to individual worshippers which come about as by-products of general and nondiscriminatory welfare programs. If such benefits serve to make easier or less expensive the practice of a particular creed, or of all religions, it can hardly be said that the purpose of the program is in any way religious, or that the consequence of its nondiscriminatory application is to create the forbidden degree of interdependence between secular and sectarian institutions. I cannot therefore accept the suggestion, which seems to me implicit in the argument outlined here, that every judicial or administrative construction which is designed to prevent a public welfare program from abridging the free exercise of religious beliefs, is for that reason *ipso facto* an establishment of religion.

F. *Activities Which, Though Religious in Origin, Have Ceased to Have Religious Meaning.*—As we noted in our *Sunday Law* decisions, nearly every criminal law on the books can be traced to some religious principle or inspiration. But that does not make the present enforcement of the criminal law in any sense an establishment of religion, simply because it accords with widely held religious principles. As we said in *McGowan v. Maryland*, 366 U.S. 420, 442, "the 'Establishment' Clause does not ban federal or state regulation of conduct whose reason or effect merely happens to coincide or harmonize with the tenets of some or all religions." This rationale suggests that the use of the motto "In God We Trust" on currency, on documents and public buildings and the like may not offend the clause. It is not that the use of those four words can be dismissed as "*de minimis*"—for I suspect there would be intense opposition to the abandonment of that motto. The truth is that we have simply interwoven the motto so deeply into the fabric of our civil polity that its present use may well not present that type of involvement which the First Amendment prohibits.

This general principle might also serve to insulate the various patriotic exercises and activities used in the public schools and elsewhere which, whatever may have been their origins, no longer have a religious purpose or meaning. The reference to divinity in the revised pledge of allegiance, for example, may merely recognize the historical fact that our Nation was believed to have been founded "under God." Thus reciting the pledge may be no more of a religious exercise than the reading aloud of Lincoln's Gettysburg Address, which contains an allusion to the same historical fact.

The principles which we reaffirm and apply today can hardly be thought novel or radical. They are, in truth, as old as the Republic itself, and have always been as integral a part of the First Amendment as the very words of that charter of religious liberty. No less applicable today than they were when first pronounced a century ago, one year after the very first court decision involving religious exercises in the public schools, are the words of a distinguished Chief Justice of the Commonwealth of Pennsylvania, Jeremiah S. Black:

> The manifest object of the men who framed the institutions of this country, was to have a *State without religion*, and a *Church without politics*—that is to say, they meant that one should never be used as an engine for any purpose of the other, and that no man's rights in one should be tested by his opinions about the other. As the Church takes no note of men's political differences, so the State looks with equal eye on all the modes of religious faith. . . . Our fathers seem to have been perfectly sincere in their belief that the members of the Church would be more patriotic, and the

citizens of the State more religious, by keeping their respective functions entirely separate. Essay on Religious Liberty, in Black, ed., Essays and Speeches of Jeremiah S. Black (1886), 53.

⊞ MR. JUSTICE GOLDBERG, with whom MR. JUSTICE HARLAN joins, concurring.

As is apparent from the opinions filed today, delineation of the constitutionally permissible relationship between religion and government is a most difficult and sensitive task, calling for the careful exercise of both judicial and public judgment and restraint. . . .

The fullest realization of true religious liberty requires that government neither engage in nor compel religious practices, that it effect no favoritism among sects or between religion and nonreligion, and that it work deterrence of no religious belief. But devotion even to these simply stated objectives presents no easy course, for the unavoidable accommodations necessary to achieve the maximum enjoyment of each and all of them are often difficult of discernment. There is for me no simple and clear measure which by precise application can readily and invariably demark the permissible from the impermissible.

It is said, and I agree, that the attitude of government toward religion must be one of neutrality. But untutored devotion to the concept of neutrality can lead to invocation or approval of results which partake not simply of that noninterference and noninvolvement with the religious which the Constitution commands, but of a brooding and pervasive devotion to the secular and a passive, or even active, hostility to the religious. Such results are not only not compelled by the Constitution, but, it seems to me, are prohibited by it.

Neither government nor this Court can or should ignore the significance of the fact that a vast portion of our people believe in and worship God and that many of our legal, political and personal values derive historically from religious teachings. Government must inevitably take cognizance of the existence of religion and, indeed, under certain circumstances the First Amendment may require that it do so. . . .

The practices here involved do not fall within any sensible or acceptable concept of compelled or permitted accommodation and involve the state so significantly and directly in the realm of the sectarian as to give rise to those very divisive influences and inhibitions of freedom which both religion clauses of the First Amendment preclude. The state has ordained and has utilized its facilities to engage in unmistakably religious exercises—the devotional reading and recitation of the Holy Bible—in a manner having substantial and significant import and impact. That it has selected, rather than written, a particular devotional liturgy seems to me without constitutional import. The pervasive religiosity and direct governmental involvement inhering in the prescription of prayer and Bible reading in the public schools, during and as part of the curricular day, involving young impressionable children whose school attendance is statutorily compelled, and utilizing the prestige, power, and influence of school administration, staff, and authority, cannot realistically be termed simply accommodation, and must fall within the interdiction of the First Amendment. . . .

The First Amendment does not prohibit practices which by any realistic measure create none of the dangers which it is designed to prevent and which do not so directly or substantially involve the state in religious exercises or in the favoring of religion as to have meaningful and practical impact. It is of course true that great consequences can grow from small beginnings, but the measure of constitutional adjudication is the ability and willingness to distinguish between real threat and mere shadow.

▦ MR. JUSTICE STEWART, dissenting.

I think the records in the two cases before us are so fundamentally deficient as to make impossible an informed or responsible determination of the constitutional issues presented. Specifically, I cannot agree that on these records we can say that the Establishment Clause has necessarily been violated. But I think there exist serious questions under both that provision and the Free Exercise Clause—insofar as each is imbedded in the Fourteenth Amendment—which require the remand of these cases for the taking of additional evidence.

I

The First Amendment declares that "Congress shall make no law respecting an establishment of religion, or prohibiting the free exercise thereof; . . ." It is, I think, a fallacious oversimplification to regard these two provisions as establishing a single constitutional standard of "separation of church and state," which can be mechanically applied in every case to delineate the required boundaries between government and religion. We err in the first place if we do not recognize, as a matter of history and as a matter of the imperatives of our free society, that religion and government must necessarily interact in countless ways. Secondly, the fact is that while in many contexts the Establishment Clause and the Free Exercise Clause fully complement each other, there are areas in which a doctrinaire reading of the Establishment Clause leads to irreconcilable conflict with the Free Exercise Clause.

A single obvious example should suffice to make the point. Spending federal funds to employ chaplains for the armed forces might be said to violate the Establishment Clause. Yet a lonely soldier stationed at some faraway outpost could surely complain that a government which did *not* provide him the opportunity for pastoral guidance was affirmatively prohibiting the free exercise of his religion. And such examples could readily be multiplied. The short of the matter is simply that the two relevant clauses of the First Amendment cannot accurately be reflected in a sterile metaphor which by its very nature may distort rather than illumine the problems involved in a particular case.

II

As a matter of history, the First Amendment was adopted solely as a limitation upon the newly created National Government. The events leading to its adoption strongly suggest that the Establishment Clause was primarily an attempt to insure that Congress not only would be powerless to establish a national church, but would also be unable to interfere with existing state establishments. . . . Each State was left free to go its own way and pursue its own policy with respect to religion. Thus Virginia from the beginning pursued a policy of disestablishmentarianism. Massachusetts, by contrast, had an established church until well into the nineteenth century.

So matters stood until the adoption of the Fourteenth Amendment, or more accurately, until this Court's decision in *Cantwell v. Connecticut*, in 1940,

310 U.S. 296. In that case the Court said: "The First Amendment declares that Congress shall make no law respecting an establishment of religion or prohibiting the free exercise thereof. The Fourteenth Amendment has rendered the legislatures of the states as incompetent as Congress to enact such laws."

I accept without question that the liberty guaranteed by the Fourteenth Amendment against impairment by the States embraces in full the right of free exercise of religion protected by the First Amendment, and I yield to no one in my conception of the breadth of that freedom. . . . I accept too the proposition that the Fourteenth Amendment has somehow absorbed the Establishment Clause, although it is not without irony that a constitutional provision evidently designed to leave the States free to go their own way should now have become a restriction upon their autonomy. But I cannot agree with what seems to me the insensitive definition of the Establishment Clause contained in the Court's opinion, nor with the different but, I think, equally mechanistic definitions contained in the separate opinions which have been filed.

### III

Since the *Cantwell* pronouncement in 1940, this Court has only twice held invalid state laws on the ground that they were laws "respecting an establishment of religion" in violation of the Fourteenth Amendment. *McCollum v. Board of Education*, 333 U.S. 203; *Engel v. Vitale*, 370 U.S. 421. On the other hand, the Court has upheld against such a challenge laws establishing Sunday as a compulsory day of rest, *McGowan v. Maryland*, 366 U.S. 420, and a law authorizing reimbursement from public funds for the transportation of parochial school pupils. *Everson v. Board of Education*, 330 U.S. 1.

Unlike other First Amendment guarantees, there is an inherent limitation upon the applicability of the Establishment Clause's ban on state support to religion. That limitation was succinctly put in *Everson v. Board of Education*, 330 U.S. 1, 18: "State power is no more to be used so as to handicap religions than it is to favor them." And in a later case, this Court recognized that the limitation was one which was itself compelled by the free exercise guarantee. "To hold that a state cannot consistently with the First and Fourteenth Amendments utilize its public school system to aid any or all religious faiths or sects in the dissemination of their doctrines and ideals does not . . . manifest a governmental hostility to religion or religious teachings. A manifestation of such hostility would be at war with our national tradition as embodied in the First Amendment's guaranty of the free exercise of religion." *McCollum v. Board of Education*, 333 U.S. 203, 211-212.

That the central value embodied in the First Amendment—and, more particularly, in the guarantee of "liberty" contained in the Fourteenth—is the safeguarding of an individual's right to free exercise of his religion has been consistently recognized. . . .

It is this concept of constitutional protection embodied in our decisions which makes the cases before us such difficult ones for me. For there is involved in these cases a substantial free exercise claim on the part of those who affirmatively desire to have their children's school day open with the reading of passages from the Bible.

It has become accepted that the decision in *Pierce v. Society of Sisters*, 268 U.S. 510, upholding the right of parents to send their children to nonpublic schools, was ultimately based upon the recognition of the validity of the free exercise claim involved in that situation. It might be argued here that parents who wanted their children to be exposed to religious influences in school could, under *Pierce*, send their children to private or parochial schools. But the consideration which renders this contention too facile to be determinative has already been recognized by the Court: "Freedom of speech, freedom of the press, freedom of religion are available to all, not merely to those who can pay their own way." *Murdock v. Pennsylvania*, 319 U.S. 105, 111.

It might also be argued that parents who want their children exposed to religious influences can adequately fulfill that wish off school property and outside school time. With all its surface persuasiveness, however, this argument seriously misconceives the basic constitutional justification for permitting the exercises at issue in these cases. For a compulsory state educational system so structures a child's life that if religious exercises are held to be an impermissible activity in schools, religion is placed at an artificial and state-created disadvantage. Viewed in this light, permission of such exercises for those who want them is necessary if the schools are truly to be neutral in the matter of religion. And a refusal to permit religious exercises thus is seen, not as the realization of state neutrality, but rather as the establishment of a religion of secularism, or at the least, as government support of the beliefs of those who think that religious exercises should be conducted only in private.

What seems to me to be of paramount importance, then, is recognition of the fact that the claim advanced here in favor of Bible reading is sufficiently substantial to make simple reference to the constitutional phrase "establishment of religion" as inadequate an analysis of the cases before us as the ritualistic invocation of the nonconstitutional phrase "separation of church and state." What these cases compel, rather, is an analysis of just what the "neutrality" is which is required by the interplay of the Establishment and Free Exercise Clauses of the First Amendment, as imbedded in the Fourteenth.

## IV

Our decisions make clear that there is no constitutional bar to the use of government property for religious purposes. On the contrary, this Court has consistently held that the discriminatory barring of religious groups from public property is itself a violation of First and Fourteenth Amendment guarantees. *Fowler v. Rhode Island*, 345 U.S. 67; *Niemotko v. Maryland*, 340 U.S. 268. A different standard has been applied to public school property, because of the coercive effect which the use by religious sects of a compulsory school system would necessarily have upon the children involved. *McCollum v. Board of Education*, 333 U.S. 203. But insofar as the *McCollum* decision rests on the Establishment rather than the Free Exercise Clause, it is clear that its effect is limited to religious instruction—to government support of proselytizing activities of religious sects by throwing the weight of secular authority behind the dissemination of religious tenets.

The dangers both to government and to religion inherent in official support of instruction in the tenets of various religious sects are absent in the present cases, which involve only a reading from the Bible unaccompanied by comments which might otherwise constitute instruction. Indeed, since, from all that appears in either record, any teacher who does not wish to do so is free not to participate, it cannot even be contended that some infinitesimal part of the salaries paid by the State are made contingent upon the performance of a religious function.

In the absence of evidence that the legislature or school board intended to prohibit local schools from substituting a different set of readings where parents requested such a change, we should not assume that the provisions before us—as actually administered—may not be construed simply as authorizing religious exercises, nor that the designations may not be treated simply as indications of the promulgating body's view as to the community's preference. We are under a duty to interpret these provisions so as to render them constitutional if reasonably possible. In the *Schempp* case there is evidence which indicates that variations were in fact permitted by the very school there involved, and that further variations were not introduced only because of the absence of requests from parents. And in the *Murray* case the Baltimore rule itself contains a provision permitting another version of the Bible to be substituted for the King James version.

If the provisions are not so construed, I think that their validity under the Establishment Clause would be extremely doubtful, because of the designation of a particular religious book and a denominational prayer. But since, even if the provisions are construed as I believe they must be, I think that the cases before us must be remanded for further evidence on other issues—thus affording the plaintiffs an opportunity to prove that local variations are not in fact permitted—I shall for the balance of this dissenting opinion treat the provisions before us as making the variety and content of the exercises, as well as a choice as to their implementation, matters which ultimately reflect the consensus of each local school community. In the absence of coercion upon those who do not wish to participate—because they hold less strong beliefs, other beliefs, or no beliefs at all—such provisions cannot, in my view, be held to represent the type of support of religion barred by the Establishment Clause. For the only support which such rules provide for religion is the withholding of state hostility—a simple acknowledgment on the part of secular authorities that the Constitution does not require extirpation of all expression of religious belief.

V

I have said that these provisions authorizing religious exercises are properly to be regarded as measures making possible the free exercise of religion. But it is important to stress that, strictly speaking, what is at issue here is a privilege rather than a right. In other words, the question presented is not whether exercises such as those at issue here are constitutionally compelled, but rather whether they are constitutionally invalid. And that issue, in my view, turns on the question of coercion.

It is clear that the dangers of coercion involved in the holding of religious exercises in a schoolroom differ qualitatively from those presented by the use of similar exercises or affirmations in ceremonies attended by adults. Even as to children, however, the duty laid upon government in connection with religious exercises in the public schools is that of refraining from so structuring the school environment as to put any kind of pressure on a child to participate in those exercises; it is not that of providing an atmosphere in which children are kept scrupulously insulated from any awareness that some of their fellows may want to open the school day with prayer, or of the fact that there exist in our pluralistic society differences of religious belief.

These are not, it must be stressed, cases like *Brown v. Board of Education*, 347 U.S. 483, in which this Court held that, in the sphere of public education, the Fourteenth Amendment's guarantee of equal protection of the laws required that race not be treated as a relevant factor. A segregated school system is not invalid because its operation is coercive; it is invalid simply because our Constitution presupposes that men are created equal, and that therefore racial differences cannot provide a valid basis for governmental action. Accommodation of religious differences on the part of the State, however, is not only permitted but required by that same Constitution.

The governmental neutrality which the First and Fourteenth Amendments require in the cases before us, in other words, is the extension of evenhanded treatment to all who believe, doubt, or disbelieve—a refusal on the part of the State to weight the scales of private choice. In these cases, therefore, what is involved is not state action based on impermissible categories, but rather an attempt by the State to accommodate those differences which the existence in our society of a variety of religious beliefs makes inevitable. The Constitution requires that such efforts be struck down only if they are proven to entail the use of the secular authority of government to coerce a preference among such beliefs.

It may well be, as has been argued to us, that even the supposed benefits to be derived from noncoercive religious exercises in public schools are incommensurate with the administrative problems which they would create. The choice involved, however, is one for each local community and its school board, and not for this Court. For, as I have said, religious exercises are not constitutionally invalid if they simply reflect differences which exist in the society from which the school draws its pupils. They become constitutionally invalid only if their administration places the sanction of secular authority behind one or more particular religious or irreligious beliefs.

To be specific, it seems to me clear that certain types of exercises would present situations in which no possibility of coercion on the part of secular officials could be claimed to exist. Thus, if such exercises were held either before or after the official school day, or if the school schedule were such that participation were merely one among a number of desirable alternatives, it could hardly be contended that the exercises did anything more than to provide an opportunity for the voluntary expression of religious belief. On the other hand, a law which provided for religious exercises during the school day and which contained no excusal provision would obviously be unconstitutionally coercive upon those who did not wish to participate. And even under a law containing an excusal provision, if the exercises were held during the school day, and no equally desirable alternative were provided by the school authorities, the likelihood that children might be under at least some psychological compulsion to participate would be great. In a case such as the latter, however, I think we would err if we *assumed* such coercion in the absence of any evidence.

## VI

Viewed in this light, it seems to me clear that the records in both of the cases before us are wholly inadequate to support an informed or responsible decision. Both cases involve provisions which explicitly permit any student who wishes, to be excused from participation in the exercises. There is no evidence in either case as to whether there would exist any coercion of any kind upon a student who did not want to participate. No evidence at all was adduced in the *Murray* case, because it was decided upon a demurrer. All that we have in that case, therefore, is the conclusory language of a pleading.

While such conclusory allegations are acceptable for procedural purposes, I think that the nature of the constitutional problem involved here clearly demands that no decision be made except upon evidence. In the *Schempp* case the record shows no more than a subjective prophecy by a parent of what he thought would happen if a request were made to be excused from participation in the exercises under the amended statute. No such request was ever made, and there is no evidence whatever as to what might or would actually happen, nor of what administrative arrangements the school actually might or could make to free from pressure of any kind those who do not want to participate in the exercises. There were no District Court findings on this issue, since the case under the amended statute was decided exclusively on Establishment Clause grounds.

What our Constitution indispensably protects is the freedom of each of us, be he Jew or Agnostic, Christian or Atheist, Buddhist or Freethinker, to believe or disbelieve, to worship or not worship, to pray or keep silent, according to his own conscience, uncoerced and unrestrained by government. It is conceivable that these school boards, or even all school boards, might eventually find it impossible to administer a system of religious exercises during school hours in such a way as to meet this constitutional standard—in such a way as completely to free from any kind of official coercion those who do not affirmatively want to participate. But I think we must not assume that school boards so lack the qualities of inventiveness and good will as to make impossible the achievement of that goal.

I would remand both cases for further hearings.

## NOTES AND QUESTIONS

1. Why did the Court accept the *Schempp* case having ruled on school-sponsored prayer the year before in *Engel*? What issues did it present that the *Engel* case did not?

2. What "test" is articulated by the *Schempp* court majority to analyze whether there has been a violation of the Establishment Clause? Could it be argued that the prohibition of school-sponsored prayer and Bible reading inhibits religion and thus runs afoul of this test? Or, is this prohibition consistent with this standard because, rather than inhibiting religion, it merely ensures that the state does not become involved in favoring or opposing religion or religious practices, thus leaving those decisions and activities to individuals rather than government? What alternative tests could the Court have used to judge the constitutionality of school-sponsored religious exercises? Both the *Engel* and *Schempp* majorities discuss and reject "coercion" as a possible legal test—why?

3. In the majority opinion in *Schempp*, the Court says: "While the Free Exercise Clause clearly prohibits the use of state action to deny the rights of free exercise to *anyone*, it has never meant that a majority could use the machinery of the State to practice its beliefs." Justice Brennan joined the majority opinion in full and yet, in his concurring opinion, he suggests that the national motto "In God We Trust" and official legislative prayers may be constitutional and

that it could be legitimate for churches to use government property temporarily for their religious services when their own structures "have become unavailable because of a disaster or emergency." Can all of these things be made consistent, constitutionally speaking?

4. In his concurring opinion, Justice Brennan sets out a test for judging the constitutionality of governmental action under the Establishment Clause. What are the three prongs of that test? How does that test differ from the one the majority articulates in this case? For example, does it seem more or less restrictive than the majority's test?

5. In his concurring opinion in the *Schempp* case, Justice Brennan states: "A too literal quest for the advice of the Founding Fathers upon the issues of these cases seems to me futile and misdirected for several reasons." What are the reasons? How does he use the phrase "it is a *constitution* we are expounding" to make his case? Do you agree with Justice Brennan's conclusion on this issue? Is it necessary to accept Justice Brennan's philosophy about the use of history when judging constitutional matters in order to come to the conclusion he did in this case?

6. Why do you think Justice Brennan added a section to his concurring opinion in *Schempp* describing some of the ways in which the government might accommodate religion? Does this part of his opinion seem ill-advised in that it address issues that were not at stake in this case, or is this portion of his opinion useful and appropriate?

7. In their concurring opinion, Justices Goldberg and Harlan warn that "untutored devotion to the concept of neutrality can lead to invocation or approval of results which partake not simply of noninterference and noninvolvement with the religious which the Constitution commands, but of a brooding and pervasive devotion to the secular and a passive, or even active, hostility to the religious. Such results are not only not compelled by the Constitution, but, it seems to me, are prohibited by it." What does this mean? How might the Court cross this line?

8. Why does Justice Stewart dissent in this case? Does he believe that the practices at issue in these cases are clearly constitutional? As a general matter, where would Justice Stewart draw the constitutional line in these kinds of cases?

9. Justice Stewart argues that "there is involved in these cases a substantial free exercise claim on the part of those who affirmatively desire to have their children's school day open with the reading of passages from the Bible." Is his argument persuasive? Why or why not?

10. Is Justice Stewart right when he argues that it is a "fallacious oversimplification" to regard the religion clauses of the Constitution "as establishing a single constitutional standard of 'separation of church and state,' which can be mechanically applied in every case to delinate the required boundaries between government and religion"? Is that how the Court majority uses this metaphor in this and other cases?

In striking school-sponsored prayer and Bible reading, the Supreme Court knew their decisions would be controversial. In part for that reason, the justices sought to write measured and persuasive opinions, ones they hoped would resolve these constitutional controversies and minimize religious dissension.

Any hope that the *Engel* and *Schempp* decisions would provide an amenable solution to an intractable controversy was dashed almost immediately. Many school boards that had policies or practices of prayer and Bible reading defied the Court's holdings or simply ignored them, particularly many schools in the South and Midwest. Politicians chastised the Court's decisions, with Senator Strom Thurman calling the holdings "another major triumph of secularism and atheism which are bent on throwing God completely out of our national life." Alabama Governor George Wallace challenged the Court to stop him from going into a public school and reading the Bible to the students. Congressional proponents of prayer and Bible reading introduced the 1964 Prayer and Bible Reading Amendment to the Constitution, also known as the "Becker Amendment" after its lead sponsor Representative Frank Becker of Illinois. The amendment initially had traction, but it was defeated primarily through the efforts of a coalition of religious groups, led by the National Council of Churches and the Baptist Joint Committee on Public Affairs.[4] Later efforts to amend the Constitution to permit prayer and Bible reading occurred in 1966 and 1982. Both of these efforts failed.

The Supreme Court faced these issues again in 1982 when it summarily affirmed a decision of the Fifth Circuit Court of Appeals striking down a Louisiana statute and accompanying school board regulation authorizing "voluntary" school prayer. See *Karen B. v. Treen*, 653 F.2d 897 (5th Cir. 1981), aff'd, 455 U.S. 913 (1982). The statute and regulation allowed each classroom teacher to ask whether any student wished to offer a prayer, and if no student volunteered, to permit the teacher to pray. Objecting students were not required to participate or be present in the classroom when the prayers were offered. The Fifth Circuit found the authorized practices were controlled by *Engel* and *Schempp*. The statute and regulation had a predominately religious purpose, the court held, and had the effect of encouraging religious devotion in the public schools. The state and school board argued, however, that unlike the situations in *Engel* and *Schempp*, no government official was prescribing or directing any particular prayer, that the practice was religiously neutral. The court rejected this argument:

> That the challenged provisions do not prescribe any particular form of prayer and do not promote some sectarian religious practice is without constitutional significance. The Supreme Court consistently had expressed the view that the First Amendment demands absolute government neutrality with respect to religion, neither advancing not inhibiting any particular religious belief or practice and neither encouraging nor discouraging religious belief or unbelief. *Id.*, 901.

The summary affirmance of *Treen* by the Supreme Court means that the decision is legally binding, though not the rationale expressed by the Fifth Circuit.

These developments kept the issue of religion in public schools at the center of public attention for years, tying together the *Engel* and *Schempp* cases with those cases discussed in the following chapters. For more background on this controversy, see Joan DelFattore, *The Fourth R: Conflicts Over Religion in America's Public Schools* (New Haven: Yale

University Press, 2004); Frank S. Ravitch, *School Prayer and Discrimination: The Civil Rights of Religious Minorities and Dissenters* (Boston: Northeastern University Press, 1999); Robert S. Alley, *School Prayer: The Court, the Congress, and the First Amendment* (Buffalo, N.Y.: Prometheus Press, 1994); and Steven K. Green, "Evangelicals and the Becker Amendment: A Lesson in Church-State Moderation," *Journal of Church and State* 33 (Summer 1991): 541-567.

CHAPTER 17

# RELIGIOUS EXPRESSION IN PUBLIC SCHOOLS
## MOMENTS OF SILENCE AND
## POST-1960S SCHOOL-PRAYER CASES

Once the Supreme Court had firmly established that school-sponsored classroom prayer and Bible readings fell outside constitutional boundaries, other practices moved to the forefront of the debate about religious expression in public schools. This next level involved questions about the constitutionality of moments of silence and school-organized prayers at graduation and sporting events.

The Court first re-engaged the debate in 1985, when it considered whether an Alabama statute mandating a moment of silence in classrooms was constitutional. The law, passed by the Alabama legislature in 1981, stated: "At the commencement of the first class of each day in all grades in all public schools the teacher in charge of the room in which each class is held may announce that a period of silence not to exceed one minute in duration shall be observed for meditation or voluntary prayer, and during any such period no other activities shall be engaged in." As you read the case, consider whether it was the text of this law that caused the Court to strike it down or the context in which it was adopted or some combination of the two.

## WALLACE v. JAFFREE
472 U.S. 38 (1985)

JUSTICE STEVENS delivered the opinion of the Court.

At an early stage of this litigation, the constitutionality of three Alabama statutes was questioned: (1) § 16-1-20, enacted in 1978, which authorized a 1-minute period of silence in all public schools "for meditation"; (2) § 16-1-20.1, enacted in 1981, which authorized a period of silence "for meditation or voluntary prayer"; and (3) § 16-1-20.2, enacted in 1982, which authorized teachers to lead "willing students" in a prescribed prayer to "Almighty God . . . the Creator and Supreme Judge of the world." . . .

645

The Court of Appeals agreed with the District Court's initial interpretation of the purpose of both § 16-1-20.1 and § 16-1-20.2, and held them both unconstitutional. We have already affirmed the Court of Appeals' holding with respect to § 16-1-20.2. Moreover, appellees have not questioned the holding that § 16-1-20 is valid. Thus, the narrow question for decision is whether § 16-1-20.1, which authorizes a period of silence for "meditation or voluntary prayer," is a law respecting the establishment of religion within the meaning of the First Amendment. . . .

Just as the right to speak and the right to refrain from speaking are complementary components of a broader concept of individual freedom of mind, so also the individual's freedom to choose his own creed is the counterpart of his right to refrain from accepting the creed established by the majority. At one time it was thought that this right merely proscribed the preference of one Christian sect over another, but would not require equal respect for the conscience of the infidel, the atheist, or the adherent of a non-Christian faith such as Islam or Judaism.[36] But when the underlying principle has been examined in the crucible of litigation, the Court has unambiguously concluded that the individual freedom of conscience protected by the First Amendment embraces the right to select any religious faith or none at all. This conclusion derives support not only from the interest in respecting the individual's freedom of conscience, but also from the conviction that religious beliefs worthy of respect are the product of free and voluntary choice by the faithful, and from recognition of the fact that the political interest in forestalling intolerance extends beyond intolerance among Christian sects—or even intolerance among "religions"—to encompass intolerance of the disbeliever and the uncertain. As Justice Jackson eloquently stated in *West Virginia Board of Education v. Barnette*, 319 U.S. 624, 642 (1943): "If there is any fixed star in our constitutional constellation, it is that no official, high or petty, can prescribe what shall be orthodox in politics, nationalism, religion, or other matters of opinion or force citizens to confess by word or act their faith therein."

The State of Alabama, no less than the Congress of the United States, must respect that basic truth.

### III

When the Court has been called upon to construe the breadth of the Establishment Clause, it has examined the criteria developed over a period of

---

[36] Thus Joseph Story wrote:

"Probably at the time of the adoption of the constitution, and of the amendment to it, now under consideration [First Amendment], the general, if not the universal sentiment in America was, that [C]hristianity ought to receive encouragement from the state, so far as was not incompatible with the private rights of conscience, and the freedom of religious worship. An attempt to level all religions, and to make it a matter of state policy to hold all in utter indifference, would have created universal disapprobation, if not universal indignation." 2 J. Story, Commentaries on the Constitution of the United States § 1874, p. 593 (1851) (footnote omitted).

In the same volume, Story continued:

"The real object of the amendment was, not to countenance, much less to advance, Mahometanism, or Judaism, or infidelity, by prostrating [C]hristianity; *but to exclude all rivalry among [C]hristian sects, and to prevent any national ecclesiastical establishment, which should give to a hierarchy the exclusive patronage of the national government. It thus cut off the means of religious persecution, (the vice and pest of former ages,) and of the subversion of the rights of conscience in matters of religion,* which had been trampled upon almost from the days of the Apostles to the present age. . . ." *Id.*, § 1877, 594 (emphasis added).

many years. Thus, in *Lemon v. Kurtzman*, 403 U.S. 602, 612-613 (1971), we wrote:

> Every analysis in this area must begin with consideration of the cumula-
> tive criteria developed by the Court over many years. Three such tests
> may be gleaned from our cases. First, the statute must have a secular
> legislative purpose; second, its principal or primary effect must be one
> that neither advances nor inhibits religion, *Board of Education v. Allen*, 392
> U.S. 236, 243 (1968); finally, the statute must not foster "an excessive
> government entanglement with religion." [*Walz v. Tax Comm'n*, 397 U.S.
> 664, 674 (1970)].

It is the first of these three criteria that is most plainly implicated by this
case. As the District Court correctly recognized, no consideration of the second
or third criteria is necessary if a statute does not have a clearly secular purpose.
For even though a statute that is motivated in part by a religious purpose may
satisfy the first criterion, the First Amendment requires that a statute must be
invalidated if it is entirely motivated by a purpose to advance religion.

In applying the purpose test, it is appropriate to ask "whether government's actual purpose is to endorse or disapprove of religion." In this case, the
answer to that question is dispositive. For the record not only provides us with
an unambiguous affirmative answer, but it also reveals that the enactment of
§ 16-1-20.1 was not motivated by any clearly secular purpose—indeed, the
statute had *no* secular purpose.

IV

The sponsor of the bill that became § 16-1-20.1, Senator Donald Holmes,
inserted into the legislative record—apparently without dissent—a statement
indicating that the legislation was an "effort to return voluntary prayer" to the
public schools.[43] Later Senator Holmes confirmed this purpose before the District Court. In response to the question whether he had any purpose for the
legislation other than returning voluntary prayer to public schools, he stated:
"No, I did not have no other purpose in mind."[44] The State did not present
evidence of *any* secular purpose.[45]

---

[43] The statement indicated, in pertinent part:
"Gentlemen, by passage of this bill by the Alabama Legislature our children in this state
will have the opportunity of sharing in the spiritual heritage of this state and this country.
The United States as well as the State of Alabama was founded by people who believe in
God. I believe this effort to return voluntary prayer to our public schools for its return to us
to the original position of the writers of the Constitution, this local philosophies and beliefs
hundreds of Alabamians have urged my continuous support for permitting school prayer.
Since coming to the Alabama Senate I have worked hard on this legislation to accomplish the
return of voluntary prayer in our public schools and return to the basic moral fiber." App.
50 (emphasis added).
[44] *Id.*, 52. The District Court and the Court of Appeals agreed that the purpose of § 16-
1-20.1 was "an effort on the part of the State of Alabama to encourage a religious activity."
*Jaffree v. James*, 544 F. Supp., 732; 705 F.2d, 1535. . . .
[45] Appellant Governor George C. Wallace now argues that § 16-1-20.1 "is best understood as a permissible accommodation of religion" and that viewed even in terms of the
*Lemon* test, the "statute conforms to acceptable constitutional criteria." Brief for Appellant
Wallace 5; see also Brief for Appellants Smith et al. 39 (§ 16-1-20.1 "accommodates the
free exercise of the religious beliefs and free exercise of speech and belief of those affected");
*id.*, 47. These arguments seem to be based on the theory that the free exercise of religion of
some of the State's citizens was burdened before the statute was enacted. The United States,

The unrebutted evidence of legislative intent contained in the legislative record and in the testimony of the sponsor of § 16-1-20.1 is confirmed by a consideration of the relationship between this statute and the two other measures that were considered in this case. The District Court found that the 1981 statute and its 1982 sequel had a common, nonsecular purpose. The wholly religious character of the later enactment is plainly evident from its text. When the differences between § 16-1-20.1 and its 1978 predecessor, § 16-1-20, are examined, it is equally clear that the 1981 statute has the same wholly religious character. . . . [T]he earlier statute refers only to "meditation" whereas § 16-1-20.1 refers to "meditation or voluntary prayer." . . . Thus, the only significant textual difference is the addition of the words "or voluntary prayer."

The legislative intent to return prayer to the public schools is, of course, quite different from merely protecting every student's right to engage in voluntary prayer during an appropriate moment of silence during the schoolday. The 1978 statute already protected that right, containing nothing that prevented any student from engaging in voluntary prayer during a silent minute of meditation. Appellants have not identified any secular purpose that was not fully served by § 16-1-20 before the enactment of § 16-1-20.1. Thus, only two conclusions are consistent with the text of § 16-1-20.1: (1) the statute was enacted to convey a message of state endorsement and promotion of prayer; or (2) the statute was enacted for no purpose. No one suggests that the statute was nothing but a meaningless or irrational act.

We must, therefore, conclude that the Alabama Legislature intended to change existing law and that it was motivated by the same purpose that the Governor's answer to the second amended complaint expressly admitted; that the statement inserted in the legislative history revealed; and that Senator Holmes' testimony frankly described. The legislature enacted § 16-1-20.1, despite the existence of § 16-1-20 for the sole purpose of expressing the State's endorsement of prayer activities for one minute at the beginning of each schoolday. The addition of "or voluntary prayer" indicates that the State intended to characterize prayer as a favored practice. Such an endorsement is not consistent with the established principle that the government must pursue a course of complete neutrality toward religion.

---

appearing as amicus curiae in support of the appellants, candidly acknowledges that "it is unlikely that in most contexts a strong Free Exercise claim could be made that time for personal prayer must be set aside during the school day." Brief for United States as *Amicus Curiae* 10. There is no basis for the suggestion that § 16-1-20.1 "is a means for accommodating the religious and meditative needs of students without in any way diminishing the school's own neutrality or secular atmosphere." *Id.*, 11. In this case, it is undisputed that at the time of the enactment of § 16-1-20.1 there was no governmental practice impeding students from silently praying for one minute at the beginning of each schoolday; thus, there was no need to "accommodate" or to exempt individuals from any general governmental requirement because of the dictates of our cases interpreting the Free Exercise Clause. See, e.g., *Thomas v. Review Board, Indiana Employment Security Div.*, 450 U.S. 707 (1981); *Sherbert v. Verner*, 374 U.S. 398 (1963); see also *Abington School District v. Schempp*, 374 U.S., 226 ("While the Free Exercise Clause clearly prohibits the use of state action to deny the rights of free exercise to anyone, it has never meant that a majority could use the machinery of the State to practice its beliefs"). What was missing in the appellants' eyes at the time of the enactment of § 16-1-20.1—and therefore what is precisely the aspect that makes the statute unconstitutional—was the State's endorsement and promotion of religion and a particular religious practice.

The importance of that principle does not permit us to treat this as an inconsequential case involving nothing more than a few words of symbolic speech on behalf of the political majority. For whenever the State itself speaks on a religious subject, one of the questions that we must ask is "whether the government intends to convey a message of endorsement or disapproval of religion." The well-supported concurrent findings of the District Court and the Court of Appeals—that § 16-1-20.1 was intended to convey a message of state approval of prayer activities in the public schools—make it unnecessary, and indeed inappropriate, to evaluate the practical significance of the addition of the words "or voluntary prayer" to the statute. Keeping in mind, as we must, "both the fundamental place held by the Establishment Clause in our constitutional scheme and the myriad, subtle ways in which Establishment Clause values can be eroded," we conclude that § 16-1-20.1 violates the First Amendment.

The judgment of the Court of Appeals is affirmed.

*It is so ordered.*

### JUSTICE POWELL, concurring.

I concur in the Court's opinion and judgment that Ala. Code § 16-1-20.1 violates the Establishment Clause of the First Amendment. My concurrence is prompted by Alabama's persistence in attempting to institute state-sponsored prayer in the public schools by enacting three successive statutes. I agree fully with JUSTICE O'CONNOR's assertion that some moment-of-silence statutes may be constitutional, a suggestion set forth in the Court's opinion as well.

I write separately to express additional views and to respond to criticism of the three-pronged *Lemon* test. *Lemon v. Kurtzman*, 403 U.S. 602 (1971), identifies standards that have proved useful in analyzing case after case both in our decisions and in those of other courts. It is the only coherent test a majority of the Court has ever adopted. Only once since our decision in *Lemon*, have we addressed an Establishment Clause issue without resort to its three-pronged test. See *Marsh v. Chambers*, 463 U.S. 783 (1983). *Lemon* has not been overruled or its test modified. Yet, continued criticism of it could encourage other courts to feel free to decide Establishment Clause cases on an ad hoc basis.

The first inquiry under *Lemon* is whether the challenged statute has a "secular legislative purpose." *Lemon v. Kurtzman*, 612. As JUSTICE O'CONNOR recognizes, this secular purpose must be "sincere"; a law will not pass constitutional muster if the secular purpose articulated by the legislature is merely a "sham." In *Stone v. Graham*, 449 U.S. 39 (1980) (*per curiam*), for example, we held that a statute requiring the posting of the Ten Commandments in public schools violated the Establishment Clause, even though the Kentucky Legislature asserted that its goal was educational. We have not interpreted the first prong of *Lemon*, however, as requiring that a statute have "exclusively secular" objectives. If such a requirement existed, much conduct and legislation approved by this Court in the past would have been invalidated.

The record before us, however, makes clear that Alabama's purpose was solely religious in character. Senator Donald Holmes, the sponsor of the bill that became Alabama Code § 16-1-20.1, freely acknowledged that the purpose of this statute was "to return voluntary prayer" to the public schools. I agree with JUSTICE O'CONNOR that a single legislator's statement, particularly if made following enactment, is not necessarily sufficient to establish

purpose. But, as noted in the Court's opinion, the religious purpose of §
16-1-20.1 is manifested in other evidence, including the sequence and history
of the three Alabama statutes. . . .

I would vote to uphold the Alabama statute if it also had a clear secular
purpose. See *Mueller v. Allen*, 463 U.S. 388, 394-395 (1983) (the Court is "[re-
luctant] to attribute unconstitutional motives to the States, particularly when
a plausible secular purpose for the State's program may be discerned from the
face of the statute"). Nothing in the record before us, however, identifies a
clear secular purpose, and the State also has failed to identify any nonreligious
reason for the statute's enactment. Under these circumstances, the Court is
required by our precedents to hold that the statute fails the first prong of the
*Lemon* test and therefore violates the Establishment Clause.

Although we do not reach the other two prongs of the *Lemon* test, I note
that the "effect" of a straightforward moment-of-silence statute is unlikely to
"[advance] or [inhibit] religion." See *Board of Education v. Allen*, 392 U.S. 236,
243 (1968). Nor would such a statute "foster 'an excessive government entanglement with religion.'" *Lemon v. Kurtzman*, 403 U.S., 612-613, quoting
*Walz v. Tax Comm'n*, 397 U.S., 674.

I join the opinion and judgment of the Court.

☒ JUSTICE O'CONNOR, concurring in the judgment.

Nothing in the United States Constitution as interpreted by this Court
or in the laws of the State of Alabama prohibits public school students from
voluntarily praying at any time before, during, or after the schoolday. Alabama
has facilitated voluntary silent prayers of students who are so inclined by enacting Ala. Code § 16-1-20, which provides a moment of silence in appellees'
schools each day. The parties to these proceedings concede the validity of this
enactment. At issue in these appeals is the constitutional validity of an additional and subsequent Alabama statute, Ala. Code § 16-1-20.1, which both
the District Court and the Court of Appeals concluded was enacted solely to
officially encourage prayer during the moment of silence. I agree with the
judgment of the Court that, in light of the findings of the courts below and
the history of its enactment, § 16-1-20.1 of the Alabama Code violates the
Establishment Clause of the First Amendment. In my view, there can be little
doubt that the purpose and likely effect of this subsequent enactment is to
endorse and sponsor voluntary prayer in the public schools. I write separately
to identify the peculiar features of the Alabama law that render it invalid,
and to explain why moment of silence laws in other States do not necessarily
manifest the same infirmity. I also write to explain why neither history nor the
Free Exercise Clause of the First Amendment validates the Alabama law struck
down by the Court today.

I . . .

JUSTICE REHNQUIST today suggests that we abandon *Lemon* entirely,
and in the process limit the reach of the Establishment Clause to state discrimination between sects and government designation of a particular church
as a "state" or "national" one.

Perhaps because I am new to the struggle, I am not ready to abandon all
aspects of the *Lemon* test. I do believe, however, that the standards announced
in *Lemon* should be reexamined and refined in order to make them more useful

in achieving the underlying purpose of the First Amendment. We must strive to do more than erect a constitutional "signpost," *Hunt v. McNair,* 413 U.S. 734, 741 (1973), to be followed or ignored in a particular case as our -predilections may dictate. Instead, our goal should be "to frame a principle for constitutional adjudication that is not only grounded in the history and language of the first amendment, but one that is also capable of consistent application to the relevant problems." . . . Last Term, I proposed a refinement of the *Lemon* test with this goal in mind. *Lynch v. Donnelly,* 465 U.S., 687-689 (concurring opinion).

The *Lynch* concurrence suggested that the religious liberty protected by the Establishment Clause is infringed when the government makes adherence to religion relevant to a person's standing in the political community. Direct government action endorsing religion or a particular religious practice is invalid under this approach because it "sends a message to nonadherents that they are outsiders, not full members of the political community, and an accompanying message to adherents that they are insiders, favored members of the political community." *Id.,* 688. Under this view, *Lemon's* inquiry as to the purpose and effect of a statute requires courts to examine whether government's purpose is to endorse religion and whether the statute actually conveys a message of endorsement.

The endorsement test is useful because of the analytic content it gives to the *Lemon*-mandated inquiry into legislative purpose and effect. In this country, church and state must necessarily operate within the same community. Because of this coexistence, it is inevitable that the secular interests of government and the religious interests of various sects and their adherents will frequently intersect, conflict, and combine. A statute that ostensibly promotes a secular interest often has an incidental or even a primary effect of helping or hindering a sectarian belief. Chaos would ensue if every such statute were invalid under the Establishment Clause. For example, the State could not criminalize murder for fear that it would thereby promote the Biblical command against killing. The task for the Court is to sort out those statutes and government practices whose purpose and effect go against the grain of religious liberty protected by the First Amendment.

The endorsement test does not preclude government from acknowledging religion or from taking religion into account in making law and policy. It does preclude government from conveying or attempting to convey a message that religion or a particular religious belief is favored or preferred. Such an endorsement infringes the religious liberty of the nonadherent, for "[when] the power, prestige and financial support of government is placed behind a particular religious belief, the indirect coercive pressure upon religious minorities to conform to the prevailing officially approved religion is plain." *Engel v. Vitale,* 370 U.S. 421, 431. At issue today is whether state moment of silence statutes in general, and Alabama's moment of silence statute in particular, embody an impermissible endorsement of prayer in public schools.

## A . . .

The *Engel* and *Abington* decisions are not dispositive on the constitutionality of moment of silence laws. In those cases, public school teachers and students led their classes in devotional exercises. In *Engel,* a New York statute required teachers to lead their classes in a vocal prayer. The Court concluded that "it is no part of the business of government to compose official prayers for any group of the American people to recite as part of a religious program carried on by the government." 370 U.S., 425. In *Abington*, the Court addressed Pennsylvania and Maryland statutes that authorized morning Bible readings in public schools. The Court reviewed the purpose and effect of the statutes, concluded that they required religious exercises, and therefore found them to violate the Establishment Clause. 374 U.S., 223-224. Under all of these statutes, a student who did not share the religious beliefs expressed in the course of the exercise was left with the choice of participating, thereby compromising the nonadherent's beliefs, or withdrawing, thereby calling attention to his or her nonconformity. The decisions acknowledged the coercion implicit under the statutory schemes, but they expressly turned only on the fact that the government was sponsoring a manifestly religious exercise.

A state-sponsored moment of silence in the public schools is different from state-sponsored vocal prayer or Bible reading. First, a moment of silence is not inherently religious. Silence, unlike prayer or Bible reading, need not be associated with a religious exercise. Second, a pupil who participates in a moment of silence need not compromise his or her beliefs. During a moment of silence, a student who objects to prayer is left to his or her own thoughts, and is not compelled to listen to the prayers or thoughts of others. For these simple reasons, a moment of silence statute does not stand or fall under the Establishment Clause according to how the Court regards vocal prayer or Bible reading. . . .

By mandating a moment of silence, a State does not necessarily endorse any activity that might occur during the period. Even if a statute specifies that a student may choose to pray silently during a quiet moment, the State has not thereby encouraged prayer over other specified alternatives. Nonetheless, it is also possible that a moment of silence statute, either as drafted or as actually implemented, could effectively favor the child who prays over the child who does not. For example, the message of endorsement would seem inescapable if the teacher exhorts children to use the designated time to pray. Similarly, the face of the statute or its legislative history may clearly establish that it seeks to encourage or promote voluntary prayer over other alternatives, rather than merely provide a quiet moment that may be dedicated to prayer by those so inclined. The crucial question is whether the State has conveyed or attempted to convey the message that children should use the moment of silence for prayer. This question cannot be answered in the abstract, but instead requires courts to examine the history, language, and administration of a particular statute to determine whether it operates as an endorsement of religion. *Lynch*, 465 U.S., 694 (concurring opinion) ("Every government practice must be judged in its unique circumstances to determine whether it constitutes an endorsement or disapproval of religion").

Before reviewing Alabama's moment of silence law to determine whether it endorses prayer, some general observations on the proper scope of the inquiry are in order. First, the inquiry into the purpose of the legislature in enacting a moment of silence law should be deferential and limited. In determining whether the government intends a moment of silence statute to convey a message of endorsement or disapproval of religion, a court has no license to psychoanalyze the legislators. If a legislature expresses a plausible secular purpose for a moment of silence statute in either the text or the legislative history, or if the statute disclaims an intent to encourage prayer over alternatives during a moment of silence, then courts should generally defer to that stated intent.

It is particularly troublesome to denigrate an expressed secular purpose due to postenactment testimony by particular legislators or by interested persons who witnessed the drafting of the statute. Even if the text and official history of a statute express no secular purpose, the statute should be held to have an improper purpose only if it is beyond purview that endorsement of religion or a religious belief "was and is the law's reason for existence." *Epperson v. Arkansas*, 393 U.S. 97, 108 (1968). Since there is arguably a secular pedagogical value to a moment of silence in public schools, courts should find an improper purpose behind such a statute only if the statute on its face, in its official legislative history, or in its interpretation by a responsible administrative agency suggests it has the primary purpose of endorsing prayer.

JUSTICE REHNQUIST suggests that this sort of deferential inquiry into legislative purpose "means little," because "it only requires the legislature to express any secular purpose and omit all sectarian references." It is not a trivial matter, however, to require that the legislature manifest a secular purpose and omit all sectarian endorsements from its laws. That requirement is precisely tailored to the Establishment Clause's purpose of assuring that government not intentionally endorse religion or a religious practice. It is of course possible that a legislature will enunciate a sham secular purpose for a statute. I have little doubt that our courts are capable of distinguishing a sham secular purpose from a sincere one, or that the *Lemon* inquiry into the effect of an enactment would help decide those close cases where the validity of an expressed secular purpose is in doubt. While the secular purpose requirement alone may rarely be determinative in striking down a statute, it nevertheless serves an important function. It reminds government that when it acts it should do so without endorsing a particular religious belief or practice that all citizens do not share. In this sense the secular purpose requirement is squarely based in the text of the Establishment Clause it helps to enforce.

Second, the *Lynch* concurrence suggested that the effect of a moment of silence law is not entirely a question of fact:

> [Whether] a government activity communicates endorsement of religion is not a question of simple historical fact. Although evidentiary submissions may help answer it, the question is, like the question whether racial or sex-based classifications communicate an invidious message, in large part a legal question to be answered on the basis of judicial interpretation of social facts. 465 U.S., 693-694.

The relevant issue is whether an objective observer, acquainted with the text, legislative history, and implementation of the statute, would perceive it as a state endorsement of prayer in public schools. A moment of silence law that is clearly drafted and implemented so as to permit prayer, meditation, and reflection within the prescribed period, without endorsing one alternative over the others, should pass this test.

B

The analysis above suggests that moment of silence laws in many States should pass Establishment Clause scrutiny because they do not favor the child who chooses to pray during a moment of silence over the child who chooses to meditate or reflect. Alabama Code § 16-1-20.1 does not stand on the same footing. However deferentially one examines its text and legislative history, however objectively one views the message attempted to be conveyed to the public, the conclusion is unavoidable that the purpose of the statute is to endorse prayer in public schools. I accordingly agree with the Court of Appeals that the Alabama statute has a purpose which is in violation of the Establishment Clause, and cannot be upheld.

In finding that the purpose of § 16-1-20.1 is to endorse voluntary prayer during a moment of silence, the Court relies on testimony elicited from State Senator Donald G. Holmes during a preliminary injunction hearing. Senator Holmes testified that the sole purpose of the statute was to return voluntary prayer to the public schools. For the reasons expressed above, I would give little, if any, weight to this sort of evidence of legislative intent. Nevertheless, the text of the statute in light of its official legislative history leaves little doubt that the purpose of this statute corresponds to the purpose expressed by Senator Holmes at the preliminary injunction hearing.

First, it is notable that Alabama already had a moment of silence statute before it enacted § 16-1-20.1. Appellees do not challenge this statute—indeed, they concede its validity. The only significant addition made by § 16-1-20.1 is to specify expressly that voluntary prayer is one of the authorized activities during a moment of silence. Any doubt as to the legislative purpose of that addition is removed by the official legislative history. The sole purpose reflected in the official history is "to return voluntary prayer to our public schools." Nor does anything in the legislative history contradict an intent to encourage children to choose prayer over other alternatives during the moment of silence. Given this legislative history, it is not surprising that the State of Alabama conceded in the courts below that the purpose of the statute was to make prayer part of daily classroom activity, and that both the District Court and the Court of Appeals concluded that the law's purpose was to encourage religious activity. In light of the legislative history and the findings of the courts below, I agree with the Court that the State intended § 16-1-20.1 to convey a message that prayer was the endorsed activity during the state-prescribed moment of silence.[5] While it is therefore unnecessary also to determine the effect of the statute, it also seems likely that the message actually conveyed to objective observers by § 16-1-20.1 is approval of the child who selects prayer over other alternatives during a moment of silence.

Given this evidence in the record, candor requires us to admit that this Alabama statute was intended to convey a message of state encouragement and endorsement of religion. In *Walz v. Tax Comm'n*, 397 U.S., 669, the Court stated that the Religion Clauses of the First Amendment are flexible enough to "permit religious exercise to exist without sponsorship and without interference." Alabama Code § 16-1-20.1 does more than permit prayer to occur during a moment of silence "without interference." It endorses the decision to

---

[5] THE CHIEF JUSTICE suggests that one consequence of the Court's emphasis on the difference between § 16-1-20.1 and its predecessor statute might be to render the Pledge of Allegiance unconstitutional because Congress amended it in 1954 to add the words "under God." I disagree. In my view, the words "under God" in the Pledge, as codified at 36 U. S. C. § 172, serve as an acknowledgment of religion with "the legitimate secular purposes of solemnizing public occasions, [and] expressing confidence in the future." *Lynch v. Donnelly*, 465 U.S. 668, 693 (1984) (concurring opinion).

I also disagree with THE CHIEF JUSTICE's suggestion that the Court's opinion invalidates any moment of silence statute that includes the word "prayer." As noted, "[even] if a statute specifies that a student may choose to pray silently during a quiet moment, the State has not thereby encouraged prayer over other specified alternatives."

pray during a moment of silence, and accordingly sponsors a religious exercise. For that reason, I concur in the judgment of the Court.

## II

In his dissenting opinion, JUSTICE REHNQUIST reviews the text and history of the First Amendment Religion Clauses. His opinion suggests that a long line of this Court's decisions are inconsistent with the intent of the drafters of the Bill of Rights. He urges the Court to correct the historical inaccuracies in its past decisions by embracing a far more restricted interpretation of the Establishment Clause, an interpretation that presumably would permit vocal group prayer in public schools.

The United States, in an *amicus* brief, suggests a less sweeping modification of Establishment Clause principles. In the Federal Government's view, a state-sponsored moment of silence is merely an "accommodation" of the desire of some public school children to practice their religion by praying silently. Such an accommodation is contemplated by the First Amendment's guarantee that the Government will not prohibit the free exercise of religion. Because the moment of silence implicates free exercise values, the United States suggests that the *Lemon*-mandated inquiry into purpose and effect should be modified. Brief for United States as *Amicus Curiae* 22.

There is an element of truth and much helpful analysis in each of these suggestions. Particularly when we are interpreting the Constitution, "a page of history is worth a volume of logic." *New York Trust Co. v. Eisner*, 256 U.S. 345, 349 (1921). Whatever the provision of the Constitution that is at issue, I continue to believe that "fidelity to the notion of *constitutional*—as opposed to purely judicial—limits on governmental action requires us to impose a heavy burden on those who claim that practices accepted when [the provision] was adopted are now constitutionally impermissible." The Court properly looked to history in upholding legislative prayer, *Marsh v. Chambers*, 463 U.S. 783 (1983), property tax exemptions for houses of worship, *Walz v. Tax Comm'n*, and Sunday closing laws, *McGowan v. Maryland*, 366 U.S. 420 (1961). As Justice Holmes once observed, "[if] a thing has been practised for two hundred years by common consent, it will need a strong case for the Fourteenth Amendment to affect it." *Jackman v. Rosenbaum Co.*, 260 U.S. 22, 31 (1922).

JUSTICE REHNQUIST does not assert, however, that the drafters of the First Amendment expressed a preference for prayer in public schools, or that the practice of prayer in public schools enjoyed uninterrupted government endorsement from the time of enactment of the Bill of Rights to the present era. The simple truth is that free public education was virtually nonexistent in the late 18th century. Since there then existed few government-run schools, it is unlikely that the persons who drafted the First Amendment, or the state legislators who ratified it, anticipated the problems of interaction of church and state in the public schools. Even at the time of adoption of the Fourteenth Amendment, education in Southern States was still primarily in private hands, and the movement toward free public schools supported by general taxation had not taken hold.

This uncertainty as to the intent of the Framers of the Bill of Rights does not mean we should ignore history for guidance on the role of religion in public education. The Court has not done so. When the intent of the Framers is unclear, I believe we must employ both history and reason in our analysis. The primary issue raised by JUSTICE REHNQUIST's dissent is whether the historical fact that our Presidents have long called for public prayers of Thanks should be dispositive on the constitutionality of prayer in public schools. I think not. At the very least, Presidential Proclamations are distinguishable from school prayer in that they are received in a noncoercive setting and are primarily directed at adults, who presumably are not readily susceptible to unwilling religious indoctrination. This Court's decisions have recognized a distinction when government-sponsored religious exercises are directed at impressionable children who are required to attend school, for then government endorsement is much more likely to result in coerced religious beliefs. Although history provides a touchstone for constitutional problems, the Establishment Clause concern for religious liberty is dispositive here.

The element of truth in the United States' arguments, I believe, lies in the suggestion that Establishment Clause analysis must comport with the mandate of the Free Exercise Clause that government make no law prohibiting the free exercise of religion. Our cases have interpreted the Free Exercise Clause to compel the government to exempt persons from some generally applicable government requirements so as to permit those persons to freely exercise their religion. Even where the Free Exercise Clause does not compel the government to grant an exemption, the Court has suggested that the government in some circumstances may voluntarily choose to exempt religious observers without violating the Establishment Clause. The challenge posed by the United States' argument is how to define the proper Establishment Clause limits on voluntary government efforts to facilitate the free exercise of religion. On the one hand, a rigid application of the *Lemon* test would invalidate legislation exempting religious observers from generally applicable government obligations. By definition, such legislation has a religious purpose and effect in promoting the free exercise of religion. On the other hand, judicial deference to all legislation that purports to facilitate the free exercise of religion would completely vitiate the Establishment Clause. Any statute pertaining to religion can be viewed as an "accommodation" of free exercise rights. Indeed, the statute at issue in *Lemon*, which provided salary supplements, textbooks, and instructional materials to Pennsylvania parochial schools, can be viewed as an accommodation of the religious beliefs of parents who choose to send their children to religious schools.

It is obvious that either of the two Religion Clauses, "if expanded to a logical extreme, would tend to clash with the other." *Walz*, 397 U.S., 668-669. The Court has long exacerbated the conflict by calling for government "neutrality" toward religion. It is difficult to square any notion of "complete neutrality" with the mandate of the Free Exercise Clause that government must sometimes exempt a religious observer from an otherwise generally applicable obligation. A government that confers a benefit on an explicitly religious basis is not neutral toward religion.

The solution to the conflict between the Religion Clauses lies not in "neutrality," but rather in identifying workable limits to the government's license to promote the free exercise of religion. The text of the Free Exercise Clause speaks of laws that prohibit the free exercise of religion. On its face, the Clause is directed at government interference with free exercise. Given that concern, one can plausibly assert that government pursues Free Exercise Clause values when it lifts a government-imposed burden on the free exercise of religion. If a statute falls within this category, then the standard Establishment Clause test should be modified accordingly. It is disingenuous to look for a purely secular purpose when the manifest objective of a statute is to facilitate the free exercise of religion by lifting a government-imposed burden. Instead, the Court should simply acknowledge that the religious purpose of such a statute is legitimated by the Free Exercise Clause. I would also go further. In assessing the effect of such a statute—that is, in determining whether the statute conveys the message of endorsement of religion or a particular religious belief—courts should assume that the "objective observer" is acquainted with the Free Exercise Clause and the values it promotes. Thus individual perceptions, or resentment that a religious observer is exempted from a particular government requirement, would be entitled to little weight if the Free Exercise Clause strongly supported the exemption.

While this "accommodation" analysis would help reconcile our Free Exercise and Establishment Clause standards, it would not save Alabama's moment of silence law. If we assume that the religious activity that Alabama seeks to protect is silent prayer, then it is difficult to discern any state-imposed burden on that activity that is lifted by Alabama Code § 16-1-20.1. No law prevents a student who is so inclined from praying silently in public schools. Moreover, state law already provided a moment of silence to these appellees irrespective of § 16-1-20.1. See Ala. Code § 16-1-20. Of course, the State might argue that § 16-1-20.1 protects not silent prayer, but rather group silent prayer under state sponsorship. Phrased in these terms, the burden lifted by the statute is not one imposed by the State of Alabama, but by the Establishment Clause as interpreted in *Engel* and *Abington*. In my view, it is beyond the authority of the State of Alabama to remove burdens imposed by the Constitution itself. I conclude that the Alabama statute at issue today lifts no state-imposed burden on the free exercise of religion, and accordingly cannot properly be viewed as an accommodation statute.

### III

The Court does not hold that the Establishment Clause is so hostile to religion that it precludes the States from affording schoolchildren an opportunity for voluntary silent prayer. To the contrary, the moment of silence statutes of many States should satisfy the Establishment Clause standard we have here applied. The Court holds only that Alabama has intentionally crossed the line between creating a quiet moment during which those so inclined may pray, and affirmatively endorsing the particular religious practice of prayer. This line may be a fine one, but our precedents and the principles of religious liberty require that we draw it. In my view, the judgment of the Court of Appeals must be affirmed.

▨ CHIEF JUSTICE BURGER, dissenting. . . .

The notion that the Alabama statute is a step toward creating an established church borders on, if it does not trespass into, the ridiculous. The statute does not remotely threaten religious liberty; it affirmatively furthers the values of religious freedom and tolerance that the Establishment Clause was designed to protect. Without pressuring those who do not wish to pray, the statute simply creates an opportunity to think, to plan, or to pray if one wishes—as Congress does by providing chaplains and chapels. It accommodates the purely private, voluntary religious choices of the individual pupils who wish to pray while at the same time creating a time for nonreligious reflection for those who do not choose to pray. The statute also provides a meaningful opportunity for schoolchildren to appreciate the absolute constitutional right of each individual to worship and believe as the individual wishes. The statute "endorses" only the view that the religious observances of others should be tolerated and, where possible, accommodated. If the government may not accommodate religious needs when it does so in a wholly neutral and noncoercive manner, the "benevolent neutrality" that we have long considered the correct constitutional standard will quickly translate into the "callous indifference" that the Court has consistently held the Establishment Clause does not require. . . .

▨ JUSTICE REHNQUIST, dissenting.

Thirty-eight years ago this Court, in *Everson v. Board of Education*, 330 U.S. 1, 16 (1947), summarized its exegesis of Establishment Clause doctrine thus: "In the words of Jefferson, the clause against establishment of religion by law was intended to erect 'a wall of separation between church and State.' *Reynolds v. United States* (98 U.S. 145, 164 [1879])."

This language from *Reynolds*, a case involving the Free Exercise Clause of the First Amendment rather than the Establishment Clause, quoted from Thomas Jefferson's letter to the Danbury Baptist Association the phrase "I contemplate with sovereign reverence that act of the whole American people which declared that their legislature should 'make no law respecting an establishment of religion, or prohibiting the free exercise thereof,' thus building a wall of separation between church and State." 8 Writings of Thomas Jefferson 113 (H. Washington ed. 1861).

It is impossible to build sound constitutional doctrine upon a mistaken understanding of constitutional history, but unfortunately the Establishment Clause has been expressly freighted with Jefferson's misleading metaphor for nearly 40 years. Thomas Jefferson was of course in France at the time the constitutional Amendments known as the Bill of Rights were passed by Congress and ratified by the States. His letter to the Danbury Baptist Association was a short note of courtesy, written 14 years after the Amendments were passed by Congress. He would seem to any detached observer as a less than ideal source of contemporary history as to the meaning of the Religion Clauses of the First Amendment.

Jefferson's fellow Virginian, James Madison, with whom he was joined in the battle for the enactment of the Virginia Statute of Religious Liberty of 1786, did play as large a part as anyone in the drafting of the Bill of Rights. He had two advantages over Jefferson in this regard: he was present in the United States, and he was a leading Member of the First Congress. But when we turn to the record of the proceedings in the First Congress leading up to the adoption of the Establishment Clause of the Constitution, including Madison's significant contributions thereto, we see a far different picture of its purpose than the highly simplified "wall of separation between church and State."

During the debates in the Thirteen Colonies over ratification of the Constitution, one of the arguments frequently used by opponents of ratification was that without a Bill of Rights guaranteeing individual liberty the new general Government carried with it a potential for tyranny. The typical response to this argument on the part of those who favored ratification was that the general Government established by the Constitution had only delegated powers, and that these delegated powers were so limited that the Government would have no occasion to violate individual liberties. This response satisfied some, but not others, and of the 11 Colonies which ratified the Constitution by early 1789, 5 proposed one or another amendments guaranteeing individual liberty.

Three—New Hampshire, New York, and Virginia—included in one form or another a declaration of religious freedom. Rhode Island and North Carolina flatly refused to ratify the Constitution in the absence of amendments in the nature of a Bill of Rights. Virginia and North Carolina proposed identical guarantees of religious freedom: "[All] men have an equal, natural and unalienable right to the free exercise of religion, according to the dictates of conscience, and . . . no particular religious sect or society ought to be favored or established, by law, in preference to others."

On June 8, 1789, James Madison rose in the House of Representatives and "reminded the House that this was the day that he had heretofore named for bringing forward amendments to the Constitution." 1 Annals of Cong. 424. Madison's subsequent remarks in urging the House to adopt his drafts of the proposed amendments were less those of a dedicated advocate of the wisdom of such measures than those of a prudent statesman seeking the enactment of measures sought by a number of his fellow citizens which could surely do no harm and might do a great deal of good. He said, *inter alia*:

> It appears to me that this House is bound by every motive of prudence, not to let the first session pass over without proposing to the State Legislatures, some things to be incorporated into the Constitution, that will render it as acceptable to the whole people of the United States, as it has been found acceptable to a majority of them. I wish, among other reasons why something should be done, that those who had been friendly to the adoption of this Constitution may have the opportunity of proving to those who were opposed to it that they were as sincerely devoted to liberty and a Republican Government, as those who charged them with wishing the adoption of this Constitution in order to lay the foundation of an aristocracy or despotism. It will be a desirable thing to extinguish from the bosom of every member of the community, any apprehensions that there are those among his countrymen who wish to deprive them of the liberty for which they valiantly fought and honorably bled. And if there are amendments desired of such a nature as will not injure the Constitution, and they can be ingrafted so as to give satisfaction to the doubting part of our fellow-citizens, the friends of the Federal Government will evince that spirit of deference and concession for which they have hitherto been distinguished. *Id.*, 431-432.

The language Madison proposed for what ultimately became the Religion Clauses of the First Amendment was this: "The civil rights of none shall be abridged on account of religious belief or worship, nor shall any national religion be established, nor shall the full and equal rights of conscience be in any manner, or on any pretext, infringed." *Id.*, 434.

On the same day that Madison proposed them, the amendments which formed the basis for the Bill of Rights were referred by the House to a Committee of the Whole, and after several weeks' delay were then referred to a Select Committee consisting of Madison and 10 others. The Committee revised Madison's proposal regarding the establishment of religion to read: "[No] religion shall be established by law, nor shall the equal rights of conscience be infringed." *Id.*, 729.

The Committee's proposed revisions were debated in the House on August 15, 1789. The entire debate on the Religion Clauses is contained in two full columns of the "Annals," and does not seem particularly illuminating. Representative Peter Sylvester of New York expressed his dislike for the revised version, because it might have a tendency "to abolish religion altogether." Representative John Vining suggested that the two parts of the sentence be transposed; Representative Elbridge Gerry thought the language should be changed to read "that no religious doctrine shall be established by law." *Id.*, 729. Roger Sherman of Connecticut had the traditional reason for opposing provisions of a Bill of Rights—that Congress had no delegated authority to "make religious establishments"—and therefore he opposed the adoption of the amendment. Representative Daniel Carroll of Maryland thought it desirable to adopt the words proposed, saying "[he] would not contend with gentlemen about the phraseology, his object was to secure the substance in such a manner as to satisfy the wishes of the honest part of the community."

Madison then spoke, and said that "he apprehended the meaning of the words to be, that Congress should not establish a religion, and enforce the legal observation of it by law, nor compel men to worship God in any manner contrary to their conscience." *Id.*, 730. He said that some of the state conventions had thought that Congress might rely on the Necessary and Proper Clause to infringe the rights of conscience or to establish a national religion, and "to prevent these effects he presumed the amendment was intended, and he thought it as well expressed as the nature of the language would admit." *Ibid.*

Representative Benjamin Huntington then expressed the view that the Committee's language might "be taken in such latitude as to be extremely hurtful to the cause of religion. He understood the amendment to mean what had been expressed by the gentleman from Virginia; but others might find it convenient to put another construction upon it." Huntington, from Connecticut, was concerned that in the New England States, where state-established religions were the rule rather than the exception, the federal courts might not be able to entertain claims based upon an obligation under the bylaws of a religious organization to contribute to the support of a minister or the building of a place of worship. He hoped that "the amendment would be made in such a way as to secure the rights of conscience, and a free exercise of the rights of religion, but not to patronise those who professed no religion at all." *Id.*, 730-731.

Madison responded that the insertion of the word "national" before the word "religion" in the Committee version should satisfy the minds of those who had criticized the language. "He believed that the people feared one sect might obtain a preeminence, or two combine together, and establish a religion to which they would compel others to conform. He thought that if the word 'national' was introduced, it would point the amendment directly to the object it was intended to prevent." *Id.*, 731. Representative Samuel Livermore expressed himself as dissatisfied with Madison's proposed amendment, and thought it would be better if the Committee language were altered to read that "Congress shall make no laws touching religion, or infringing the rights of conscience." *Ibid.*

Representative Gerry spoke in opposition to the use of the word "national" because of strong feelings expressed during the ratification debates that a federal government, not a national government, was created by the Constitution. Madison thereby withdrew his proposal but insisted that his reference to a "national religion" only referred to a national establishment and did not mean that the Government was a national one. The question was taken on Representative Livermore's motion, which passed by a vote of 31 for and 20 against. *Ibid.*

The following week, without any apparent debate, the House voted to alter the language of the Religion Clauses to read "Congress shall make no law establishing religion, or to prevent the free exercise thereof, or to infringe the rights of conscience." Id., 766. The floor debates in the Senate were secret, and therefore not reported in the Annals. The Senate on September 3, 1789, considered several different forms of the Religion Amendment, and reported this language back to the House: "Congress shall make no law establishing articles of faith or a mode of worship, or prohibiting the free exercise of religion." C. Antieau, A. Downey, & E. Roberts, Freedom From Federal Establishment 130 (1964).

The House refused to accept the Senate's changes in the Bill of Rights and asked for a conference; the version which emerged from the conference was that which ultimately found its way into the Constitution as a part of the First Amendment. "Congress shall make no law respecting an establishment of religion, or prohibiting the free exercise thereof."

The House and the Senate both accepted this language on successive days, and the Amendment was proposed in this form.

On the basis of the record of these proceedings in the House of Representatives, James Madison was undoubtedly the most important architect among the Members of the House of the Amendments which became the Bill of Rights, but it was James Madison speaking as an advocate of sensible legislative compromise, not as an advocate of incorporating the Virginia Statute of Religious Liberty into the United States Constitution. During the ratification debate in the Virginia Convention, Madison had actually opposed the idea of any Bill of Rights. His sponsorship of the Amendments in the House was obviously not that of a zealous believer in the necessity of the Religion Clauses, but of one who felt it might do some good, could do no harm, and would satisfy those who had ratified the Constitution on the condition that Congress propose a Bill of Rights.[3] His original language "nor shall any national religion be established" obviously does not conform to the "wall of separation" between church and State idea which latter-day commentators have ascribed to him. His explanation on the floor of the meaning of his language—"that Congress should not establish a religion, and enforce the legal observation of it by law" is of the same ilk. When he replied to Huntington in the debate over the proposal which came from the Select Committee of the House, he urged that the language "no religion shall be established by law" should be amended by inserting the word "national" in front of the word "religion."

It seems indisputable from these glimpses of Madison's thinking, as reflected by actions on the floor of the House in 1789, that he saw the Amendment as designed to prohibit the establishment of a national religion, and perhaps to prevent discrimination among sects. He did not see it as requiring neutrality on the part of government between religion and irreligion. Thus the Court's opinion in Everson—while correct in bracketing Madison and Jefferson together in their exertions in their home State leading to the enactment of the Virginia Statute of Religious Liberty—is totally incorrect in suggesting that Madison carried these views onto the floor of the United States House

---

[3] In a letter he sent to Jefferson in France, Madison stated that he did not see much importance in a Bill of Rights but he planned to support it because it was "anxiously desired by others . . . [and] it might be of use, and if properly executed could not be of disservice." 5 Writings of James Madison 271 (G. Hunt ed. 1904).

of Representatives when he proposed the language which would ultimately become the Bill of Rights.

The repetition of this error in the Court's opinion in *Illinois ex rel. McCollum v. Board of Education*, 333 U.S. 203 (1948), and, *inter alia, Engel v. Vitale*, 370 U.S. 421 (1962), does not make it any sounder historically. Finally, in *Abington School District v. Schempp*, 374 U.S. 203, 214 (1963), the Court made the truly remarkable statement that "the views of Madison and Jefferson, preceded by Roger Williams, came to be incorporated not only in the Federal Constitution but likewise in those of most of our States" (footnote omitted). On the basis of what evidence we have, this statement is demonstrably incorrect as a matter of history.[4] And its repetition in varying forms in succeeding opinions of the Court can give it no more authority than it possesses as a matter of fact; *stare decisis* may bind courts as to matters of law, but it cannot bind them as to matters of history.

None of the other Members of Congress who spoke during the August 15th debate expressed the slightest indication that they thought the language before them from the Select Committee, or the evil to be aimed at, would require that the Government be absolutely neutral as between religion and irreligion. The evil to be aimed at, so far as those who spoke were concerned, appears to have been the establishment of a national church, and perhaps the preference of one religious sect over another; but it was definitely not concerned about whether the Government might aid all religions evenhandedly. If one were to follow the advice of JUSTICE BRENNAN, concurring in *Abington School District v. Schempp*, 236, and construe the Amendment in the light of what particular "practices . . . challenged threaten those consequences which the Framers deeply feared; whether, in short, they tend to promote that type of interdependence between religion and state which the First Amendment was designed to prevent," one would have to say that the First Amendment Establishment Clause should be read no more broadly than to prevent the establishment of a national religion or the governmental preference of one religious sect over another.

The actions of the First Congress, which reenacted the Northwest Ordinance for the governance of the Northwest Territory in 1789, confirm the view that Congress did not mean that the Government should be neutral between religion and irreligion. The House of Representatives took up the Northwest Ordinance on the same day as Madison introduced his proposed amendments which became the Bill of Rights; while at that time the Federal Government was of course not bound by draft amendments to the Constitution which had not yet been proposed by Congress, say nothing of ratified by the States, it seems highly unlikely that the House of Representatives would simultaneously consider proposed amendments to the Constitution and enact an important piece of territorial legislation which conflicted with the intent of those proposals. The Northwest Ordinance, 1 Stat. 50, reenacted the Northwest Ordinance of 1787 and provided that "[religion], morality, and knowledge, being necessary to good government and the happiness of mankind, schools and the means of education shall forever be encouraged." *Id.*, 52, n. (*a*). Land grants for schools in the Northwest Territory were not limited to public schools. It

---

[4] State establishments were prevalent throughout the late 18th and early 19th centuries. See Mass. Const. of 1780, Part 1, Art. III; N. H. Const. of 1784, Art. VI; Md. Declaration of Rights of 1776, Art. XXXIII; R. I. Charter of 1633 (superseded 1842).

was not until 1845 that Congress limited land grants in the new States and Territories to nonsectarian schools. 5 Stat. 788; C. Antieau, A. Downey, & E. Roberts, Freedom From Federal Establishment 163 (1964).

On the day after the House of Representatives voted to adopt the form of the First Amendment Religion Clauses which was ultimately proposed and ratified, Representative Elias Boudinot proposed a resolution asking President George Washington to issue a Thanksgiving Day proclamation. Boudinot said he "could not think of letting the session pass over without offering an opportunity to all the citizens of the United States of joining with one voice, in returning to Almighty God their sincere thanks for the many blessings he had poured down upon them." 1 Annals of Cong. 914 (1789). Representative Aedanas Burke objected to the resolution because he did not like "this mimicking of European customs"; Representative Thomas Tucker objected that whether or not the people had reason to be satisfied with the Constitution was something that the States knew better than the Congress, and in any event "it is a religious matter, and, as such, is proscribed to us." Id., 915. Representative Sherman supported the resolution "not only as a laudable one in itself, but as warranted by a number of precedents in Holy Writ: for instance, the solemn thanksgivings and rejoicings which took place in the time of Solomon, after the building of the temple, was a case in point. This example, he thought, worthy of Christian imitation on the present occasion . . . ." Ibid.

Boudinot's resolution was carried in the affirmative on September 25, 1789. Boudinot and Sherman, who favored the Thanksgiving Proclamation, voted in favor of the adoption of the proposed amendments to the Constitution, including the Religion Clauses; Tucker, who opposed the Thanksgiving Proclamation, voted against the adoption of the amendments which became the Bill of Rights.

Within two weeks of this action by the House, George Washington responded to the Joint Resolution which by now had been changed to include the language that the President "recommend to the people of the United States a day of public thanksgiving and prayer, to be observed by acknowledging with grateful hearts the many and signal favors of Almighty God, especially by affording them an opportunity peaceably to establish a form of government for their safety and happiness." 1 J. Richardson, Messages and Papers of the Presidents, 1789–1897, p. 64 (1897). The Presidential Proclamation was couched in these words:

> Now, therefore, I do recommend and assign Thursday, the 26th day of November next, to be devoted by the people of these States to the service of that great and glorious Being who is the beneficent author of all the good that was, that is, or that will be; that we may then all unite in rendering unto Him our sincere and humble thanks for His kind care and protection of the people of this country previous to their becoming a nation; for the signal and manifold mercies and the favorable interpositions of His providence in the course and conclusion of the late war; for the great degree of tranquillity, union, and plenty which we have since enjoyed; for the peaceable and rational manner in which we have been enabled to establish constitutions of government for our safety and happiness, and particularly the national one now lately instituted; for the civil and religious liberty with which we are blessed, and the means we have of acquiring and diffusing useful knowledge; and, in general, for all the great and various favors which He has been pleased to confer upon us.

And also that we may then unite in most humbly offering our prayers and supplications to the great Lord and Ruler of Nations, and beseech Him to pardon our national and other transgressions; to enable us all, whether in public or private stations, to perform our several and relative duties properly and punctually; to render our National Government a blessing to all the people by constantly being a Government of wise, just, and constitutional laws, discreetly and faithfully executed and obeyed; to protect and guide all sovereigns and nations (especially such as have shown kindness to us), and to bless them with good governments, peace, and concord; to promote the knowledge and practice of true religion and virtue, and the increase of science among them and us; and, generally, to grant unto all mankind such a degree of temporal prosperity as He alone knows to be best. *Ibid.*

George Washington, John Adams, and James Madison all issued Thanksgiving Proclamations; Thomas Jefferson did not, saying:

"Fasting and prayer are religious exercises; the enjoining them an act of discipline. Every religious society has a right to determine for itself the times for these exercises, and the objects proper for them, according to their own particular tenets; and this right can never be safer than in their own hands, where the Constitution has deposited it." 11 Writings of Thomas Jefferson 429 (A. Lipscomb ed. 1904).

As the United States moved from the 18th into the 19th century, Congress appropriated time and again public moneys in support of sectarian Indian education carried on by religious organizations. Typical of these was Jefferson's treaty with the Kaskaskia Indians, which provided annual cash support for the Tribe's Roman Catholic priest and church. It was not until 1897, when aid to sectarian education for Indians had reached $500,000 annually, that Congress decided thereafter to cease appropriating money for education in sectarian schools. See Act of June 7, 1897, 30 Stat. 62, 79. This history shows the fallacy of the notion found in *Everson* that "no tax in any amount" may be levied for religious activities in any form. 330 U.S., 15-16.

Joseph Story, a Member of this Court from 1811 to 1845, and during much of that time a professor at the Harvard Law School, published by far the most comprehensive treatise on the United States Constitution that had then appeared. Volume 2 of Story's Commentaries on the Constitution of the United States 630-632 (5th ed. 1891) discussed the meaning of the Establishment Clause of the First Amendment this way:

Probably at the time of the adoption of the Constitution, and of the amendment to it now under consideration [First Amendment], the general if not the universal sentiment in America was, that Christianity ought to receive encouragement from the State so far as was not incompatible with the private rights of conscience and the freedom of religious worship. An attempt to level all religions, and to make it a matter of state policy to hold all in utter indifference, would have created universal disapprobation, if not universal indignation. . . .

The real object of the [First] [Amendment] was not to countenance, much less to advance, Mahometanism, or Judaism, or infidelity, by prostrating Christianity; but to exclude all rivalry among Christian sects, and to prevent any national ecclesiastical establishment which should give to a hierarchy the exclusive patronage of the national government. It thus cut off the means of religious persecution (the vice and pest of former ages), and of the subversion of the rights of conscience in matters of religion, which had been trampled upon almost from the days of the Apostles to the present age. . . . (Footnotes omitted.)

Thomas Cooley's eminence as a legal authority rivaled that of Story. Cooley stated in his treatise entitled Constitutional Limitations that aid to a particular religious sect was prohibited by the United States Constitution, but he went on to say:

> But while thus careful to establish, protect, and defend religious freedom and equality, the American constitutions contain no provisions which prohibit the authorities from such solemn recognition of a superintending Providence in public transactions and exercises as the general religious sentiment of mankind inspires, and as seems meet and proper in finite and dependent beings. Whatever may be the shades of religious belief, all must acknowledge the fitness of recognizing in important human affairs the superintending care and control of the Great Governor of the Universe, and of acknowledging with thanksgiving his boundless favors, or bowing in contrition when visited with the penalties of his broken laws. No principle of constitutional law is violated when thanksgiving or fast days are appointed; when chaplains are designated for the army and navy; when legislative sessions are opened with prayer or the reading of the Scriptures, or when religious teaching is encouraged by a general exemption of the houses of religious worship from taxation for the support of State government. Undoubtedly the spirit of the Constitution will require, in all these cases, that care be taken to avoid discrimination in favor of or against any one religious denomination or sect; but the power to do any of these things does not become unconstitutional simply because of its susceptibility to abuse. . . . Id., 470-471.

Cooley added that

> [this] public recognition of religious worship, however, is not based entirely, perhaps not even mainly, upon a sense of what is due to the Supreme Being himself as the author of all good and of all law; but the same reasons of state policy which induce the government to aid institutions of charity and seminaries of instruction will incline it also to foster religious worship and religious institutions, as conservators of the public morals and valuable, if not indispensable, assistants to the preservation of the public order. Id., 470.

It would seem from this evidence that the Establishment Clause of the First Amendment had acquired a well-accepted meaning: it forbade establishment of a national religion, and forbade preference among religious sects or denominations. Indeed, the first American dictionary defined the word "establishment" as "the act of establishing, founding, ratifying or ordaining," such as in "[the] episcopal form of religion, so called, in England." 1 N. Webster, American Dictionary of the English Language (1st ed. 1828). The Establishment Clause did not require government neutrality between religion and irreligion nor did it prohibit the Federal Government from providing nondiscriminatory aid to religion. There is simply no historical foundation for the proposition that the Framers intended to build the "wall of separation" that was constitutionalized in Everson.

Notwithstanding the absence of a historical basis for this theory of rigid separation, the wall idea might well have served as a useful albeit misguided analytical concept, had it led this Court to unified and principled results in Establishment Clause cases. The opposite, unfortunately, has been true; in the 38 years since *Everson* our Establishment Clause cases have been neither principled nor unified. Our recent opinions, many of them hopelessly divided pluralities, have with embarrassing candor conceded that the "wall of separation" is merely a "blurred, indistinct, and variable barrier," which "is not wholly accurate" and can only be "dimly perceived." *Lemon v. Kurtzman*, 403 U.S. 602, 614 (1971); *Tilton v. Richardson*, 403 U.S. 672, 677-678, (1971); *Wolman v. Walter*, 433 U.S. 229, 236 (1977); *Lynch v. Donnelly*, 465 U.S. 668, 673 (1984).

Whether due to its lack of historical support or its practical unworkability, the *Everson* "wall" has proved all but useless as a guide to sound constitutional adjudication. It illustrates only too well the wisdom of Benjamin Cardozo's observation that "[metaphors] in law are to be narrowly watched, for starting as devices to liberate thought, they end often by enslaving it." *Berkey v. Third Avenue R. Co.*, 155 N. E. 58, 61 (1926).

But the greatest injury of the "wall" notion is its mischievous diversion of judges from the actual intentions of the drafters of the Bill of Rights. The "crucible of litigation," is well adapted to adjudicating factual disputes on the basis of testimony presented in court, but no amount of repetition of historical errors in judicial opinions can make the errors true. The "wall of separation between church and State" is a metaphor based on bad history, a metaphor which has proved useless as a guide to judging. It should be frankly and explicitly abandoned.

The Court has more recently attempted to add some mortar to *Everson's* wall through the three-part test of *Lemon v. Kurtzman*, which served at first to offer a more useful test for purposes of the Establishment Clause than did the "wall" metaphor. Generally stated, the *Lemon* test proscribes state action that has a sectarian purpose or effect, or causes an impermissible governmental entanglement with religion.

*Lemon* cited *Board of Education v. Allen*, 392 U.S. 236, 243 (1968), as the source of the "purpose" and "effect" prongs of the three-part test. The *Allen* opinion explains, however, how it inherited the purpose and effect elements from *Schempp* and *Everson*, both of which contain the historical errors described above. Thus the purpose and effect prongs have the same historical deficiencies as the wall concept itself: they are in no way based on either the language or intent of the drafters.

The secular purpose prong has proved mercurial in application because it has never been fully defined, and we have never fully stated how the test is to operate. If the purpose prong is intended to void those aids to sectarian institutions accompanied by a stated legislative purpose to aid religion, the prong will condemn nothing so long as the legislature utters a secular purpose and says nothing about aiding religion. Thus the constitutionality of a statute may depend upon what the legislators put into the legislative history and, more importantly, what they leave out. The purpose prong means little if it only requires the legislature to express any secular purpose and omit all sectarian references, because legislators might do just that. Faced with a valid legislative secular purpose, we could not properly ignore that purpose without a factual basis for doing so.

However, if the purpose prong is aimed to void all statutes enacted with the intent to aid sectarian institutions, whether stated or not, then most statutes providing any aid, such as textbooks or bus rides for sectarian school children, will fail because one of the purposes behind every statute, whether stated or not, is to aid the target of its largesse. In other words, if the purpose prong requires an absence of *any* intent to aid sectarian institutions, whether or not expressed, few state laws in this area could pass the test, and we would be required to void some state aids to religion which we have already upheld.

The entanglement prong of the *Lemon* test came from *Walz v. Tax Comm'n,* 397 U.S. 664, 674 (1970). *Walz* involved a constitutional challenge to New York's time-honored practice of providing state property tax exemptions to church property used in worship. The *Walz* opinion refused to "undermine the ultimate constitutional objective [of the Establishment Clause] as illuminated by history," *id.*, 671, and upheld the tax exemption. The Court examined the historical relationship between the State and church when church property was in issue, and determined that the challenged tax exemption did not so entangle New York with the church as to cause an intrusion or interference with religion. Interferences with religion should arguably be dealt with under the Free Exercise Clause, but the entanglement inquiry in *Walz* was consistent with that case's broad survey of the relationship between state taxation and religious property.

We have not always followed *Walz'* reflective inquiry into entanglement, however. One of the difficulties with the entanglement prong is that, when divorced from the logic of *Walz*, it creates an "insoluable paradox" in school aid cases: we have required aid to parochial schools to be closely watched lest it be put to sectarian use, yet this close supervision itself will create an entanglement. For example, in *Wolman*, the Court in part struck the State's nondiscriminatory provision of buses for parochial school field trips, because the state supervision of sectarian officials in charge of field trips would be too onerous. This type of self-defeating result is certainly not required to ensure that States do not establish religions.

The entanglement test as applied in cases like *Wolman* also ignores the myriad state administrative regulations properly placed upon sectarian institutions such as curriculum, attendance, and certification requirements for sectarian schools, or fire and safety regulations for churches. Avoiding entanglement between church and State may be an important consideration in a case like *Walz*, but if the entanglement prong were applied to all state and church relations in the automatic manner in which it has been applied to school aid cases, the State could hardly require anything of church-related institutions as a condition for receipt of financial assistance.

These difficulties arise because the *Lemon* test has no more grounding in the history of the First Amendment than does the wall theory upon which it rests. The three-part test represents a determined effort to craft a workable rule from a historically faulty doctrine; but the rule can only be as sound as the doctrine it attempts to service. The three-part test has simply not provided adequate standards for deciding Establishment Clause cases, as this Court has slowly come to realize. Even worse, the *Lemon* test has caused this Court to fracture into unworkable plurality opinions, depending upon how each of the three factors applies to a certain state action. The results from our school services cases show the difficulty we have encountered in making the *Lemon* test yield principled results.

For example, a State may lend to parochial school children geography textbooks that contain maps of the United States, but the State may not lend maps of the United States for use in geography class. A State may lend textbooks on American colonial history, but it may not lend a film on George Washington, or a film projector to show it in history class. A State may lend classroom workbooks, but may not lend workbooks in which the parochial school children write, thus rendering them nonreusable. A State may pay for bus transportation to religious schools but may not pay for bus transportation from the parochial school to the public zoo or natural history museum for a field trip. A State may pay for diagnostic services conducted in the parochial school but therapeutic services must be given in a different building; speech and hearing "services" conducted by the State inside the sectarian school are forbidden, *Meek v. Pittenger*, 421 U.S. 349, 367, 371 (1975), but the State may conduct speech and hearing diagnostic testing inside the sectarian school. *Wolman*, 433 U.S., 241. Exceptional parochial school students may receive counseling, but it must take place outside of the parochial school, such as in a trailer parked down the street. A State may give cash to a parochial school to pay for the administration of state-written tests and state-ordered reporting services, but it may not provide funds for teacher-prepared tests on secular subjects. Religious instruction may not be given in public school, but the public school may release students during the day for religion classes elsewhere, and may enforce attendance at those classes with its truancy laws.

These results violate the historically sound principle "that the Establishment Clause does not forbid governments . . . to [provide] general welfare under which benefits are distributed to private individuals, even though many of those individuals may elect to use those benefits in ways that 'aid' religious instruction or worship." *Nyquist*, 413 U.S. 756, 799. It is not surprising in the light of this record that our most recent opinions have expressed doubt on the usefulness of the *Lemon* test.

Although the test initially provided helpful assistance, we soon began describing the test as only a "guideline," and lately we have described it as "no more than [a] useful [signpost]." . . . In *Lynch* we reiterated that the *Lemon* test has never been binding on the Court, and we cited two cases where we had declined to apply it. 465 U.S., 679, citing *Marsh v. Chambers*, 463 U.S. 783 (1983); *Larson v. Valente*, 456 U.S. 228 (1982).

If a constitutional theory has no basis in the history of the amendment it seeks to interpret, is difficult to apply and yields unprincipled results, I see little use in it. The "crucible of litigation," has produced only consistent unpredictability, and today's effort is just a continuation of "the sisyphean task of trying to patch together the 'blurred, indistinct and variable barrier' described in *Lemon v. Kurtzman*." *Regan*, 444 U.S. 646, 671. We have done much straining since 1947, but still we admit that we can only "dimly perceive" the *Everson* wall. Our perception has been clouded not by the Constitution but by the mists of an unnecessary metaphor.

The true meaning of the Establishment Clause can only be seen in its history. As drafters of our Bill of Rights, the Framers inscribed the principles that control today. Any deviation from their intentions frustrates the permanence of that Charter and will only lead to the type of unprincipled decisionmaking that has plagued our Establishment Clause cases since *Everson*.

The Framers intended the Establishment Clause to prohibit the designation of any church as a "national" one. The Clause was also designed to stop the Federal Government from asserting a preference for one religious denomination or sect over others. Given the "incorporation" of the Establishment Clause as against the States via the Fourteenth Amendment in *Everson*, States are prohibited as well from establishing a religion or discriminating between sects. As its history abundantly shows, however, nothing in the Establishment Clause requires government to be strictly neutral between religion and irreligion, nor does that Clause prohibit Congress or the States from pursuing legitimate secular ends through nondiscriminatory sectarian means.

The Court strikes down the Alabama statute because the State wished to "characterize prayer as a favored practice." It would come as much of a shock to those who drafted the Bill of Rights as it will to a large number of thoughtful Americans today to learn that the Constitution, as construed by the majority, prohibits the Alabama Legislature from "endorsing" prayer. George Washington himself, at the request of the very Congress which passed the Bill of Rights, proclaimed a day of "public thanksgiving and prayer, to be observed by acknowledging with grateful hearts the many and signal favors of Almighty God." History must judge whether it was the Father of his Country in 1789, or a majority of the Court today, which has strayed from the meaning of the Establishment Clause.

The State surely has a secular interest in regulating the manner in which public schools are conducted. Nothing in the Establishment Clause of the First Amendment, properly understood, prohibits any such generalized "endorsement" of prayer. I would therefore reverse the judgment of the Court of Appeals.

## NOTES AND QUESTIONS

1. What test does the Court majority use to analyze the issues in this case? Why does the Alabama law fail that test?

2. How significant to the Court's ruling was the fact that a 1978 Alabama moment of silence law already existed? How does that statute impact the Court's ultimate conclusion as to why the subsequent law is unconstitutional? Suppose the earlier statute did not exist; do you believe the Court would still be willing to strike down the later law providing for "meditation or voluntary prayer"?

3. Assume a hypothetical legislature enacts a statute that explicitly states that the moment of silence could be used for mediation or for voluntary silent prayer by students. Assume also that the legislative record indicates that there was a clear secular purpose for such a law (e.g., to provide for a moment of reflection before the start of school activities, the method to be decided by each individual student). Would such a statute be facially constitutional under *Wallace v. Jaffree*? If you believe the statute would be constitutional on its face, suppose that after a five-year period the record reflects that voluntary, student-led silent prayer is taking place in some Alabama classrooms. Would this practice authorized by a facially constitutional statute be otherwise constitutional?

4. Why did Justice Powell write a concurring opinion in this case? In the debate over the adequacy of the *Lemon* test, who do you think has the better of the argument, Justices Powell and O'Connor or Justice Rehnquist?

5. In her opinion concurring in the judgment, Justice O'Connor counsels against "abandon[ing] all aspects of the *Lemon* test." Instead, she urges that it be "refined." In her view, O'Connor writes, "*Lemon's* inquiry as to the purpose and effect of a statute requires courts to examine whether government's purpose is to endorse religion and whether the statute actually conveys a message of endorsement." Does the endorsement "refinement" of the *Lemon* test provide a better mechanism for evaluation of Establishment Clause issues than the traditional *Lemon* test? Can you think of some shortcomings of the endorsement inquiry?

6. According to Justice O'Connor, what are the differences between a state-sponsored moment of silence and state-sponsored prayer? Assume a student is the only atheist in his kindergarten class and everyone else bows their heads when the teacher calls for a moment of silence. Is that child subject to state-sponsored pressure along religious lines? Alternatively, suppose that a Muslim student, observing his classmates bowing their heads in prayer during the moment of silence period, requests to be allowed to use his prayer mat. If the teacher denies the request, does the Muslim student have a legal claim under either the Free Exercise or Establishment Clauses? Or, suppose that another student would like to pray during the moment of silence period, but that student's religious tradition requires that prayers be said aloud. If the teacher denies that request, does the school violate the Free Exercise or Establishment Clause? In the case of these children, would the denials be unconstitutional even if courts have already found the moment of silence statute to have a secular purpose?

7. According to Justice O'Connor, what are some guidelines for courts when applying the purpose prong of the *Lemon* test? Is Justice Rehnquist correct when he argues that, if the purpose prong is understood in this way, it is of little importance?

8. According to Justice O'Connor, what is the problem with the Court's call for governmental neutrality toward religion? In her view, when is it appropriate for the government to accommodate religious practices; in other words, when may the government do so without running afoul of the Establishment Clause? Why does the Alabama law at issue in this case fail to constitute an appropriate accommodation of religious exercise, according to Justice O'Connor? Do you agree?

9. According to Justices O'Connor and Powell, is it possible to enact constitutionally defensible moment-of-silence laws? If so, how would one have to craft and apply such laws?

10. In his dissenting opinion, Chief Justice Burger says "[t]he notion that the Alabama statute is a step toward creating an established church borders on, if it does not trespass into, the ridiculous." Does his statement seem correct? Whether it does or does not, should this be the standard for judging whether the law passes muster under the Establishment Clause?

11. At the conclusion of his dissenting opinion, Chief Justice Burger writes: "If the government may not accommodate religious needs when it does so in a

wholly neutral and noncoercive manner, the 'benevolent neutrality' that we have long considered the correct constitutional standard will quickly translate into the 'callous indifference' that the Court has consistently held the Establishment Clause does not require." Do the standards articulated and applied by the justices who supported the result in this case amount to "callous indifference" to religion? If so, are those standards themselves unconstitutional under the Establishment Clause, the Free Exercise Clause, or both?

12. What does Justice Rehnquist believe that the Establishment Clause forbids? What tools does he say he relies on to arrive at that judgment? How different is his interpretation of the Establishment Clause from the one applied by the Court in this case? If Justice Rehnquist's interpretation of the Establishment Clause had been accepted by Court majorities in the *McCollum*, *Engel*, *Schempp* cases, would that have changed the result in those cases?

13. Should the original intent or the original meaning of the First Amendment matter in these cases? What is the difference between the positions of Justices O'Connor and Rehnquist on this issue?

14. Once again, the "wall of separation" metaphor is criticized by a dissenter on the Court. Is then-Justice Rehnquist correct in saying that "the greatest injury of the 'wall' notion is its mischievous diversion of judges from the actual intentions of the drafters of the Bill of Rights" and that it is "a metaphor based on bad history, a metaphor which has proved useless as a guide to judging" and thus "should be frankly and explicitly abandoned"? Is Rehnquist correct in suggesting that this metaphor has played a large role in the decisions of the Court?

---

In two later cases, the Court considered school prayer outside the classroom. The first case, *Lee v. Weisman*, examined the issue of whether prayers offered by an invited member of the clergy at middle and high school graduations were constitutional. As you read this case, pay close attention to the different legal tests that are articulated and applied by the various justices.

---

### LEE v. WEISMAN
### 505 U.S. 577 (1992)

JUSTICE KENNEDY delivered the opinion of the Court.

School principals in the public school system of the city of Providence, Rhode Island, are permitted to invite members of the clergy to offer invocation and benediction prayers as part of the formal graduation ceremonies for middle schools and for high schools. The question before us is whether including clerical members who offer prayers as part of the official school graduation ceremony is consistent with the Religion Clauses of the First Amendment, provisions the Fourteenth Amendment makes applicable with full force to the States and their school districts.

I
A

Deborah Weisman graduated from Nathan Bishop Middle School, a public school in Providence, at a formal ceremony in June 1989. She was about 14 years old. For many years it has been the policy of the Providence School Committee and the Superintendent of Schools to permit principals to invite members of the clergy to give invocations and benedictions at middle school and high school graduations. Many, but not all, of the principals elected to include prayers as part of the graduation ceremonies. Acting for himself and his daughter, Deborah's father, Daniel Weisman, objected to any prayers at Deborah's middle school graduation, but to no avail. The school principal, petitioner Robert E. Lee, invited a rabbi to deliver prayers at the graduation exercises for Deborah's class. Rabbi Leslie Gutterman, of the Temple Beth El in Providence, accepted.

---

### RABBI GUTTERMAN'S PRAYERS

Rabbi Gutterman's prayers were as follows:

INVOCATION

"God of the Free, Hope of the Brave:

"For the legacy of America where diversity is celebrated and the rights of minorities are protected, we thank You. May these young men and women grow up to enrich it.

"For the liberty of America, we thank You. May these new graduates grow up to guard it.

"For the political process of America in which all its citizens may participate, for its court system where all may seek justice we thank You. May those we honor this morning always turn to it in trust.

"For the destiny of America we thank You. May the graduates of Nathan Bishop Middle School so live that they might help to share it.

"May our aspirations for our country and for these young people, who are our hope for the future, be richly fulfilled.

AMEN"

BENEDICTION

"O God, we are grateful to You for having endowed us with the capacity for learning which we have celebrated on this joyous commencement.

"Happy families give thanks for seeing their children achieve an important milestone. Send Your blessings upon the teachers and administrators who helped prepare them.

"The graduates now need strength and guidance for the future, help them to understand that we are not complete with academic knowledge alone. We must each strive to fulfill what You require of us all: To do justly, to love mercy, to walk humbly.

"We give thanks to You, Lord, for keeping us alive, sustaining us and allowing us to reach this special, happy occasion.

AMEN" 507 U.S., 581-583, 22-23.

It has been the custom of Providence school officials to provide invited clergy with a pamphlet entitled "Guidelines for Civic Occasions," prepared by the National Conference of Christians and Jews. The Guidelines recommend that public prayers at nonsectarian civic ceremonies be composed with "inclusiveness and sensitivity," though they acknowledge that "prayer of any kind may be inappropriate on some civic occasions." The principal gave Rabbi Gutterman the pamphlet before the graduation and advised him the invocation and benediction should be nonsectarian.

The record in this case is sparse in many respects, and we are unfamiliar with any fixed custom or practice at middle school graduations, referred to by the school district as "promotional exercises." We are not so constrained with reference to high schools, however. High school graduations are such an integral part of American cultural life that we can with confidence describe their customary features, confirmed by aspects of the record and by the parties' representations at oral argument. In the Providence school system, most high school graduation ceremonies are conducted away from the school, while most middle school ceremonies are held on school premises. Classical High School, which Deborah now attends, has conducted its graduation ceremonies on school premises. The parties stipulate that attendance at graduation ceremonies is voluntary. The graduating students enter as a group in a processional, subject to the direction of teachers and school officials, and sit together, apart from their families. We assume the clergy's participation in any high school graduation exercise would be about what it was at Deborah's middle school ceremony. There the students stood for the Pledge of Allegiance and remained standing during the rabbi's prayers. Even on the assumption that there was a respectful moment of silence both before and after the prayers, the rabbi's two presentations must not have extended much beyond a minute each, if that. We do not know whether he remained on stage during the whole ceremony, or whether the students received individual diplomas on stage, or if he helped to congratulate them.

The school board (and the United States, which supports it as *amicus curiae*) argued that these short prayers and others like them at graduation exercises are of profound meaning to many students and parents throughout this country who consider that due respect and acknowledgment for divine guidance and for the deepest spiritual aspirations of our people ought to be expressed at an event as important in life as a graduation. We assume this to be so in addressing the difficult case now before us, for the significance of the prayers lies also at the heart of Daniel and Deborah Weisman's case. . . .

II

These dominant facts mark and control the confines of our decision: State officials direct the performance of a formal religious exercise at promotional and graduation ceremonies for secondary schools. Even for those students who object to the religious exercise, their attendance and participation in the state-sponsored religious activity are in a fair and real sense obligatory, though the school district does not require attendance as a condition for receipt of the diploma.

This case does not require us to revisit the difficult questions dividing us in recent cases, questions of the definition and full scope of the principles governing the extent of permitted accommodation by the State for the religious beliefs and practices of many of its citizens. For without reference to those principles in other contexts, the controlling precedents as they relate to prayer and religious exercise in primary and secondary public schools compel the holding here that the policy of the city of Providence is an unconstitutional one. We can decide the case without reconsidering the general constitutional framework by which public schools' efforts to accommodate religion are measured. Thus we do not accept the invitation of petitioners and *amicus* the United States to reconsider our decision in *Lemon v. Kurtzman*. The government involvement with religious activity in this case is pervasive, to the point of creating a state-sponsored and state-directed religious exercise in a public school. Conducting this formal religious observance conflicts with settled rules pertaining to prayer exercises for students, and that suffices to determine the question before us.

The principle that government may accommodate the free exercise of religion does not supersede the fundamental limitations imposed by the Establishment Clause. It is beyond dispute that, at a minimum, the Constitution guarantees that government may not coerce anyone to support or participate in religion or its exercise, or otherwise act in a way which "establishes a [state] religion or religious faith, or tends to do so." The State's involvement in the school prayers challenged today violates these central principles.

That involvement is as troubling as it is undenied. A school official, the principal, decided that an invocation and a benediction should be given; this is a choice attributable to the State, and from a constitutional perspective it is as if a state statute decreed that the prayers must occur. The principal chose the religious participant, here a rabbi, and that choice is also attributable to the State. The reason for the choice of a rabbi is not disclosed by the record, but the potential for divisiveness over the choice of a particular member of the clergy to conduct the ceremony is apparent.

Divisiveness, of course, can attend any state decision respecting religions, and neither its existence nor its potential necessarily invalidates the State's attempts to accommodate religion in all cases. The potential for divisiveness is of particular relevance here though, because it centers around an overt religious exercise in a secondary school environment where, as we discuss below, subtle coercive pressures exist and where the student had no real alternative which would have allowed her to avoid the fact or appearance of participation.

The State's role did not end with the decision to include a prayer and with the choice of a clergyman. Principal Lee provided Rabbi Gutterman with a copy of the "Guidelines for Civic Occasions," and advised him that his prayers should be nonsectarian. Through these means the principal directed and controlled the content of the prayers. Even if the only sanction for ignoring the instructions were that the rabbi would not be invited back, we think no religious representative who valued his or her continued reputation and effectiveness in the community would incur the State's displeasure in this regard. It is a cornerstone principle of our Establishment Clause jurisprudence that "it is no part of the business of government to compose official prayers for any group of the American people to recite as a part of a religious program carried on by government," *Engel v. Vitale*, 370 U.S. 421, 425 (1962), and that is what the school officials attempted to do.

Petitioners argue, and we find nothing in the case to refute it, that the directions for the content of the prayers were a good-faith attempt by the school to ensure that the sectarianism which is so often the flashpoint for religious animosity be removed from the graduation ceremony. The concern is understandable, as a prayer which uses ideas or images identified with a particular religion may foster a different sort of sectarian rivalry than an invocation or benediction in terms more neutral. The school's explanation, however, does not resolve the dilemma caused by its participation. The question is not the good faith of the school in attempting to make the prayer acceptable to most persons, but the legitimacy of its undertaking that enterprise at all when the object is to produce a prayer to be used in a formal religious exercise which students, for all practical purposes, are obliged to attend.

We are asked to recognize the existence of a practice of nonsectarian prayer, prayer within the embrace of what is known as the Judeo-Christian tradition, prayer which is more acceptable than one which, for example, makes explicit references to the God of Israel, or to Jesus Christ, or to a patron saint. There may be some support, as an empirical observation, to the statement of the Court of Appeals for the Sixth Circuit, picked up by Judge Campbell's dissent in the Court of Appeals in this case, that there has emerged in this country a civic religion, one which is tolerated when sectarian exercises are not. . . . If common ground can be defined which permits once conflicting faiths to express the shared conviction that there is an ethic and a morality which transcend human invention, the sense of community and purpose sought by all decent societies might be advanced. But though the First Amendment does not allow the government to stifle prayers which aspire to these ends, neither does it permit the government to undertake that task for itself.

The First Amendment's Religion Clauses mean that religious beliefs and religious expression are too precious to be either proscribed or prescribed by the State. The design of the Constitution is that preservation and transmission of religious beliefs and worship is a responsibility and a choice committed to the private sphere, which itself is promised freedom to pursue that mission. It must not be forgotten then, that while concern must be given to define the protection granted to an objector or a dissenting nonbeliever, these same Clauses exist to protect religion from government interference. James Madison, the principal author of the Bill of Rights, did not rest his opposition to a religious establishment on the sole ground of its effect on the minority. A principal ground for his view was: "Experience witnesseth that ecclesiastical establishments, instead of maintaining the purity and efficacy of Religion, have had a contrary operation." Memorial and Remonstrance Against Religious Assessments (1785).

These concerns have particular application in the case of school officials, whose effort to monitor prayer will be perceived by the students as inducing a participation they might otherwise reject. Though the efforts of the school officials in this case to find common ground appear to have been a good-faith attempt to recognize the common aspects of religions and not the divisive ones, our precedents do not permit school officials to assist in composing prayers as an incident to a formal exercise for their students. Engel v. Vitale, 425. And these same precedents caution us to measure the idea of a civic religion against the central meaning of the Religion Clauses of the First Amendment, which is that all creeds must be tolerated and none favored. The suggestion that government may establish an official or civic religion as a means of avoiding the establishment of a religion with more specific creeds strikes us as a contradiction that cannot be accepted.

The degree of school involvement here made it clear that the graduation prayers bore the imprint of the State and thus put school-age children who objected in an untenable position. We turn our attention now to consider the position of the students, both those who desired the prayer and she who did not.

To endure the speech of false ideas or offensive content and then to counter it is part of learning how to live in a pluralistic society, a society which insists upon open discourse towards the end of a tolerant citizenry. And tolerance presupposes some mutuality of obligation. It is argued that our constitutional vision of a free society requires confidence in our own ability to accept or reject ideas of which we do not approve, and that prayer at a high school graduation does nothing more than offer a choice. By the time they are seniors, high school students no doubt have been required to attend classes and assemblies and to complete assignments exposing them to ideas they find distasteful or immoral or absurd or all of these. Against this background, students may consider it an odd measure of justice to be subjected during the course of their educations to ideas deemed offensive and irreligious, but to be denied a brief, formal prayer ceremony that the school offers in return. This argument cannot prevail, however. It overlooks a fundamental dynamic of the Constitution.

The First Amendment protects speech and religion by quite different mechanisms. Speech is protected by ensuring its full expression even when the government participates, for the very object of some of our most important speech is to persuade the government to adopt an idea as its own. The method for protecting freedom of worship and freedom of conscience in religious matters is quite the reverse. In religious debate or expression the government is not a prime participant, for the Framers deemed religious establishment antithetical to the freedom of all. The Free Exercise Clause embraces a freedom of conscience and worship that has close parallels in the speech provisions of the First Amendment, but the Establishment Clause is a specific prohibition on forms of state intervention in religious affairs with no precise counterpart in the speech provisions. The explanation lies in the lesson of history that was and is the inspiration for the Establishment Clause, the lesson that in the hands of government what might begin as a tolerant expression of religious views may end in a policy to indoctrinate and coerce. A state-created orthodoxy puts at grave risk that freedom of belief and conscience which are the sole assurance that religious faith is real, not imposed.

The lessons of the First Amendment are as urgent in the modern world as in the 18th century when it was written. One timeless lesson is that if citizens are subjected to state-sponsored religious exercises, the State disavows its own duty to guard and respect that sphere of inviolable conscience and belief which is the mark of a free people. To compromise that principle today would be to deny our own tradition and forfeit our standing to urge others to secure the protections of that tradition for themselves.

As we have observed before, there are heightened concerns with protecting freedom of conscience from subtle coercive pressure in the elementary and secondary public schools. Our decisions in *Engel v. Vitale* and *School Dist. of Abington* recognize, among other things, that prayer exercises in public schools carry a particular risk of indirect coercion. The concern may not be limited to the context of schools, but it is most pronounced there. What to most believers may seem nothing more than a reasonable request that the nonbeliever respect their religious practices, in a school context may appear to the nonbeliever or dissenter to be an attempt to employ the machinery of the State to enforce a religious orthodoxy.

We need not look beyond the circumstances of this case to see the phenomenon at work. The undeniable fact is that the school district's supervision and control of a high school graduation ceremony places public pressure, as well as peer pressure, on attending students to stand as a group or, at least, maintain respectful silence during the invocation and benediction. This pressure, though subtle and indirect, can be as real as any overt compulsion. Of course, in our culture standing or remaining silent can signify adherence to a view or simple respect for the views of others. And no doubt some persons who have no desire to join a prayer have little objection to standing as a sign of respect for those who do. But for the dissenter of high school age, who has a reasonable perception that she is being forced by the State to pray in a manner her conscience will not allow, the injury is no less real. There can be no doubt that for many, if not most, of the students at the graduation, the act of standing or remaining silent was an expression of participation in the rabbi's prayer. That was the very point of the religious exercise. It is of little comfort to a dissenter, then, to be told that for her the act of standing or remaining in silence signifies mere respect, rather than participation. What matters is that, given our social conventions, a reasonable dissenter in this milieu could believe that the group exercise signified her own participation or approval of it.

Finding no violation under these circumstances would place objectors in the dilemma of participating, with all that implies, or protesting. We do not address whether that choice is acceptable if the affected citizens are mature adults, but we think the State may not, consistent with the Establishment Clause, place primary and secondary school children in this position. Research in psychology supports the common assumption that adolescents are often susceptible to pressure from their peers towards conformity, and that the influence is strongest in matters of social convention. To recognize that the choice imposed by the State constitutes an unacceptable constraint only acknowledges that the government may no more use social pressure to enforce orthodoxy than it may use more direct means.

The injury caused by the government's action, and the reason why Daniel and Deborah Weisman object to it, is that the State, in a school setting, in effect required participation in a religious exercise. It is, we concede, a brief exercise during which the individual can concentrate on joining its message, meditate on her own religion, or let her mind wander. But the embarrassment and the intrusion of the religious exercise cannot be refuted by arguing that these prayers, and similar ones to be said in the future, are of a *de minimis* character. To do so would be an affront to the rabbi who offered them and to all those for whom the prayers were an essential and profound recognition of divine authority. And for the same reason, we think that the intrusion is greater than the two minutes or so of time consumed for prayers like these. Assuming, as we must, that the prayers were offensive to the student and the parent who now object, the intrusion was both real and, in the context of a secondary school, a violation of the objectors' rights. That the intrusion was in the course of promulgating religion that sought to be civic or nonsectarian rather than pertaining to one sect does not lessen the offense or isolation to the objectors. At best it narrows their number, at worst increases their sense of isolation and affront.

There was a stipulation in the District Court that attendance at graduation and promotional ceremonies is voluntary. Petitioners and the United States, as *amicus*, made this a center point of the case, arguing that the option of not attending the graduation excuses any inducement or coercion in the ceremony itself. The argument lacks all persuasion. Law reaches past formalism. And to say a teenage student has a real choice not to attend her high school graduation is formalistic in the extreme. True, Deborah could elect not to attend commencement without renouncing her diploma; but we shall not allow the case to turn on this point. Everyone knows that in our society and in our culture high school graduation is one of life's most significant occasions. A school rule which excuses attendance is beside the point. Attendance may not be required by official decree, yet it is apparent that a student is not free to absent herself from the graduation exercise in any real sense of the term "voluntary," for absence would require forfeiture of those intangible benefits which have motivated the student through youth and all her high school years. Graduation is a time for family and those closest to the student to celebrate success and express mutual wishes of gratitude and respect, all to the end of impressing upon the young person the role that it is his or her right and duty to assume in the community and all of its diverse parts.

The importance of the event is the point the school district and the United States rely upon to argue that a formal prayer ought to be permitted, but it becomes one of the principal reasons why their argument must fail. Their contention, one of considerable force were it not for the constitutional constraints applied to state action, is that the prayers are an essential part of these ceremonies because for many persons an occasion of this significance lacks meaning if there is no recognition, however brief, that human achievements cannot be understood apart from their spiritual essence. We think the Government's position that this interest suffices to force students to choose between compliance or forfeiture demonstrates fundamental inconsistency in its argumentation. It fails to acknowledge that what for many of Deborah's classmates and their parents was a spiritual imperative was for Daniel and Deborah Weisman religious conformance compelled by the State. While in some societies the wishes of the majority might prevail, the Establishment Clause of the First Amendment is addressed to this contingency and rejects the balance urged upon us. The Constitution forbids the State to exact religious conformity from a student as the price of attending her own high school graduation. This is the calculus the Constitution commands.

The Government's argument gives insufficient recognition to the real conflict of conscience faced by the young student. The essence of the Government's position is that with regard to a civic, social occasion of this importance it is the objector, not the majority, who must take unilateral and private action to avoid compromising religious scruples, hereby electing to miss the graduation exercise. This turns conventional First Amendment analysis on its head. It is a tenet of the First Amendment that the State cannot require one of its citizens to forfeit his or her rights and benefits as the price of resisting conformance to state-sponsored religious practice. To say that a student must remain apart from the ceremony at the opening invocation and closing benediction is to risk compelling conformity in an environment analogous to the classroom setting, where we have said the risk of compulsion is especially high. Just as in *Engel v. Vitale*, 370 U.S., 430, and *School Dist. of Abington v. Schempp*, 374 U.S., 224-225, where we found that provisions within the challenged legislation permitting a student to be voluntarily excused from attendance or participation in the daily prayers did not shield those practices from invalidation, the fact that attendance at the graduation ceremonies is voluntary in a legal sense does not save the religious exercise.

Inherent differences between the public school system and a session of a state legislature distinguish this case from *Marsh v. Chambers*, 463 U.S. 783 (1983). The considerations we have raised in objection to the invocation and benediction are in many respects similar to the arguments we considered in *Marsh*. But there are also obvious differences. The atmosphere at the opening of a session of a state legislature where adults are free to enter and leave with little comment and for any number of reasons cannot compare with the constraining potential of the one school event most important for the student to attend. The influence and force of a formal exercise in a school graduation are far greater than the prayer exercise we condoned in *Marsh*. The *Marsh* majority in fact gave specific recognition to this distinction and placed particular reliance on it in upholding the prayers at issue there. Today's case is different. At a high school graduation, teachers and principals must and do retain a high degree of control over the precise contents of the program, the speeches, the timing, the movements, the dress, and the decorum of the students. In this atmosphere the state-imposed character of an invocation and benediction by clergy selected by the school combine to make the prayer a state-sanctioned religious exercise in which the student was left with no alternative but to submit. This is different from *Marsh* and suffices to make the religious exercise a First Amendment violation. Our Establishment Clause jurisprudence remains a delicate and fact-sensitive one, and we cannot accept the parallel relied upon by petitioners and the United States between the facts of *Marsh* and the case now before us. Our decisions in *Engel v. Vitale* and *School Dist. of Abington v. Schempp* require us to distinguish the public school context.

We do not hold that every state action implicating religion is invalid if one or a few citizens find it offensive. People may take offense at all manner of religious as well as nonreligious messages, but offense alone does not in every case show a violation. We know too that sometimes to endure social isolation or even anger may be the price of conscience or nonconformity. But, by any reading of our cases, the conformity required of the student in this case was too high an exaction to withstand the test of the Establishment Clause. The prayer exercises in this case are especially improper because the State has in every practical sense compelled attendance and participation in an explicit religious exercise at an event of singular importance to every student, one the objecting student had no real alternative to avoid.

Our jurisprudence in this area is of necessity one of line-drawing, of determining at what point a dissenter's rights of religious freedom are infringed by the State.

> The First Amendment does not prohibit practices which by any realistic measure create none of the dangers which it is designed to prevent and which do not so directly or substantially involve the state in religious exercises or in the favoring of religion as to have meaningful and practical impact. It is of course true that great consequences can grow from small beginnings, but the measure of constitutional adjudication is the ability and willingness to distinguish between real threat and mere shadow. *School Dist. of Abington v. Schempp*, 308 (GOLDBERG, J., concurring).

Our society would be less than true to its heritage if it lacked abiding concern for the values of its young people, and we acknowledge the profound belief of adherents to many faiths that there must be a place in the student's life for precepts of a morality higher even than the law we today enforce. We express no hostility to those aspirations, nor would our oath permit us to do so. A relentless and all-pervasive attempt to exclude religion from every aspect of public life could itself become inconsistent with the Constitution. We recognize that, at graduation time and throughout the course of the educational process, there will be instances when religious values, religious practices, and religious persons will have some interaction with the public schools and their students. But these matters, often questions of accommodation of religion, are not before us. The sole question presented is whether a religious exercise may be conducted at a graduation ceremony in circumstances where, as we have found, young graduates who object are induced to conform. No holding by this Court suggests that a school can persuade or compel a student to participate in a religious exercise. That is being done here, and it is forbidden by the Establishment Clause of the First Amendment.

For the reasons we have stated, the judgment of the Court of Appeals is

*Affirmed.*

■ JUSTICE BLACKMUN, with whom JUSTICE STEVENS and JUSTICE O'CONNOR join, concurring.

Nearly half a century of review and refinement of Establishment Clause jurisprudence has distilled one clear understanding: Government may neither promote nor affiliate itself with any religious doctrine or organization, nor may it obtrude itself in the internal affairs of any religious institution. The application of these principles to the present case mandates the decision reached today by the Court. . . .

II

I join the Court's opinion today because I find nothing in it inconsistent with the essential precepts of the Establishment Clause developed in our precedents. The Court holds that the graduation prayer is unconstitutional because the State "in effect required participation in a religious exercise." Although our precedents make clear that proof of government coercion is not necessary to prove an Establishment Clause violation, it is sufficient. Government pressure to participate in a religious activity is an obvious indication that the government is endorsing or promoting religion.

But it is not enough that the government restrain from compelling religious practices: It must not engage in them either. The Court repeatedly has recognized that a violation of the Establishment Clause is not predicated on coercion. The Establishment Clause proscribes public schools from "conveying or attempting to convey a message that religion or a particular religious belief is *favored* or *preferred*," even if the schools do not actually "impose pressure upon a student to participate in a religious activity."[6] . . .

There is no doubt that attempts to aid religion through government coercion jeopardize freedom of conscience. Even subtle pressure diminishes the

---

[6] As a practical matter, of course, anytime the government endorses a religious belief there will almost always be some pressure to conform. "When the power, prestige and financial support of government is placed behind a particular religious belief, the indirect coercive pressure upon religious minorities to conform to the prevailing officially approved religion is plain." *Engel v. Vitale,* 370 U.S. 421, 431 (1962).

right of each individual to choose voluntarily what to believe. Representative Carroll explained during congressional debate over the Establishment Clause: "The rights of conscience are, in their nature, of peculiar delicacy, and will little bear the gentlest touch of governmental hand." 1 Annals of Cong. 757 (1789).

Our decisions have gone beyond prohibiting coercion, however, because the Court has recognized that "the fullest possible scope of religious liberty," entails more than freedom from coercion. The Establishment Clause protects religious liberty on a grand scale; it is a social compact that guarantees for generations a democracy and a strong religious community—both essential to safeguarding religious liberty. "Our fathers seem to have been perfectly sincere in their belief that the members of the Church would be more patriotic, and the citizens of the State more religious, by keeping their respective functions entirely separate." Religious Liberty, in Essays and Speeches of Jeremiah S. Black 53 (C. Black ed. 1885) (Chief Justice of the Commonwealth of Pennsylvania).

The mixing of government and religion can be a threat to free government, even if no one is forced to participate. When the government puts its *imprimatur* on a particular religion, it conveys a message of exclusion to all those who do not adhere to the favored beliefs. A government cannot be premised on the belief that all persons are created equal when it asserts that God prefers some. Only "anguish, hardship and bitter strife" result "when zealous religious groups struggle with one another to obtain the Government's stamp of approval." *Engel*, 370 U.S., 429.

When the government arrogates to itself a role in religious affairs, it abandons its obligation as guarantor of democracy. Democracy requires the nourishment of dialog and dissent, while religious faith puts its trust in an ultimate divine authority above all human deliberation. When the government appropriates religious truth, it "transforms rational debate into theological decree." Those who disagree no longer are questioning the policy judgment of the elected but the rules of a higher authority who is beyond reproach.

Madison warned that government officials who would use religious authority to pursue secular ends "exceed the commission from which they derive their authority and are Tyrants. The People who submit to it are governed by laws made neither by themselves, nor by an authority derived from them, and are slaves." Memorial and Remonstrance against Religious Assessments (1785). Democratic government will not last long when proclamation replaces persuasion as the medium of political exchange.

Likewise, we have recognized that "religion flourishes in greater purity, without than with the aid of Government." To "make room for as wide a variety of beliefs and creeds as the spiritual needs of man deem necessary," the government must not align itself with any one of them. When the government favors a particular religion or sect, the disadvantage to all others is obvious, but even the favored religion may fear being "tainted . . . with a corrosive secularism." The favored religion may be compromised as political figures reshape the religion's beliefs for their own purposes; it may be reformed as government largesse brings government regulation. Keeping religion in the hands of private groups minimizes state intrusion on religious choice and best enables each religion to "flourish according to the zeal of its adherents and the appeal of its dogma."

It is these understandings and fears that underlie our Establishment Clause jurisprudence. We have believed that religious freedom cannot exist in the absence of a free democratic government, and that such a government cannot endure when there is fusion between religion and the political regime. We have believed that religious freedom cannot thrive in the absence of a vibrant religious community and that such a community cannot prosper when it is bound to the secular. And we have believed that these were the animating principles behind the adoption of the Establishment Clause. To that end, our cases have prohibited government endorsement of religion, its sponsorship, and active involvement in religion, whether or not citizens were coerced to conform.

I remain convinced that our jurisprudence is not misguided, and that it requires the decision reached by the Court today. Accordingly, I join the Court in affirming the judgment of the Court of Appeals.

◼ JUSTICE SOUTER, with whom JUSTICE STEVENS and JUSTICE O'CONNOR join, concurring.

I join the whole of the Court's opinion, and fully agree that prayers at public school graduation ceremonies indirectly coerce religious observance. I write separately nonetheless on two issues of Establishment Clause analysis that underlie my independent resolution of this case: whether the Clause applies to governmental practices that do not favor one religion or denomination over others, and whether state coercion of religious conformity, over and above state endorsement of religious exercise or belief, is a necessary element of an Establishment Clause violation.

I . . .
B

Some have challenged [our] precedent by reading the Establishment Clause to permit "nonpreferential" state promotion of religion. The challengers argue that, as originally understood by the Framers, "the Establishment Clause did not require government neutrality between religion and irreligion nor did it prohibit the Federal Government from providing nondiscriminatory aid to religion." *Wallace*, 106 (REHNQUIST, J., dissenting); see also R. Cord, Separation of Church and State: Historical Fact and Current Fiction (1988). While a case has been made for this position, it is not so convincing as to warrant reconsideration of our settled law; indeed, I find in the history of the Clause's textual development a more powerful argument supporting the Court's jurisprudence following *Everson*.

When James Madison arrived at the First Congress with a series of proposals to amend the National Constitution, one of the provisions read that "the civil rights of none shall be abridged on account of religious belief or worship, nor shall any national religion be established, nor shall the full and equal rights of conscience be in any manner, or on any pretext, infringed." 1 Annals of Cong. 434 (1789). Madison's language did not last long. It was sent to a Select Committee of the House, which, without explanation, changed it to read that "no religion shall be established by law, nor shall the equal rights of conscience be infringed." *Id.*, 729. Thence the proposal went to the Committee of the Whole, which was in turn dissatisfied with the Select Committee's language and adopted an alternative proposed by Samuel Livermore of New Hampshire: "Congress shall make no laws touching religion, or infringing the rights of conscience." See *id.*, 731. Livermore's proposal would have forbidden laws having anything to do with religion and was thus not only far broader than Madison's version, but broader even than the scope of the Establishment Clause as we now understand it.

The House rewrote the amendment once more before sending it to the Senate, this time adopting, without recorded debate, language derived from a proposal by Fisher Ames of Massachusetts: "Congress shall make no law establishing Religion, or prohibiting the free exercise thereof, nor shall the rights of conscience be infringed." 1 Annals of Cong. 765 (1789). Perhaps, on further reflection, the Representatives had thought Livermore's proposal too expansive, or perhaps, as one historian has suggested, they had simply worried that his language would not "satisfy the demands of those who wanted something said specifically against establishments of religion." L. Levy, The Establishment Clause 81 (1986) (hereinafter Levy). We do not know; what we do know is that the House rejected the Select Committee's version, which arguably ensured only that "no religion" enjoyed an official preference over others, and deliberately chose instead a prohibition extending to laws establishing "religion" in general.

The sequence of the Senate's treatment of this House proposal, and the House's response to the Senate, confirm that the Framers meant the Establishment Clause's prohibition to encompass nonpreferential aid to religion. In September 1789, the Senate considered a number of provisions that would have permitted such aid, and ultimately it adopted one of them. First, it briefly entertained this language: "Congress shall make no law establishing One Religious Sect or Society in preference to others, nor shall the rights of conscience be infringed." See 1 Documentary History, 151 (Senate Journal); id., 136. After rejecting two minor amendments to that proposal, see id., 151, the Senate dropped it altogether and chose a provision identical to the House's proposal, but without the clause protecting the "rights of conscience," ibid. With no record of the Senate debates, we cannot know what prompted these changes, but the record does tell us that, six days later, the Senate went half circle and adopted its narrowest language yet: "Congress shall make no law establishing articles of faith or a mode of worship, or prohibiting the free exercise of religion." Id., 166. The Senate sent this proposal to the House along with its versions of the other constitutional amendments proposed.

Though it accepted much of the Senate's work on the Bill of Rights, the House rejected the Senate's version of the Establishment Clause and called for a joint conference committee, to which the Senate agreed. The House conferees ultimately won out, persuading the Senate to accept this as the final text of the Religion Clauses: "Congress shall make no law respecting an establishment of religion, or prohibiting the free exercise thereof." What is remarkable is that, unlike the earliest House drafts or the final Senate proposal, the prevailing language is not limited to laws respecting an establishment of "a religion," "a national religion," "one religious sect," or specific "articles of faith."[2] The Framers

---

[2] Some commentators have suggested that by targeting laws respecting "an" establishment of religion, the Framers adopted the very nonpreferentialist position whose much clearer articulation they repeatedly rejected. Yet the indefinite article before the word "establishment" is better seen as evidence that the Clause forbids any kind of establishment, including a non-preferential one. If the Framers had wished, for some reason, to use the indefinite term to achieve a narrow meaning for the Clause, they could far more aptly have placed it before the word "religion." See Laycock, "Nonpreferential" Aid to Religion: A False Claim About Original Intent, 27 Wm. & Mary L. Rev. 875, 884-885 (1986) (hereinafter Laycock, "Non-preferential" Aid).

repeatedly considered and deliberately rejected such narrow language and instead extended their prohibition to state support for "religion" in general.

Implicit in their choice is the distinction between preferential and non-preferential establishments, which the weight of evidence suggests the Framers appreciated. See, e.g., Laycock, "Nonpreferential" Aid, 902-906; Levy, 91-119. But cf. T. Curry, The First Freedoms, 208-222 (1986). Of particular note, the Framers were vividly familiar with efforts in the Colonies and, later, the States to impose general, nondenominational assessments and other incidents of ostensibly ecumenical establishments. The Virginia statute for religious freedom, written by Jefferson and sponsored by Madison, captured the separationist response to such measures. Condemning all establishments, however nonpreferentialist, the statute broadly guaranteed that "no man shall be compelled to frequent or support any religious worship, place, or ministry whatsoever," including his own. Act for Establishing Religious Freedom (1785), in 5 The Founders' Constitution 84, 85 (P. Kurland & R. Lerner eds. 1987). Forcing a citizen to support even his own church would, among other things, deny "the ministry those temporary rewards, which proceeding from an approbation of their personal conduct, are an additional incitement to earnest and unremitting labours for the instruction of mankind." Id., 84. In general, Madison later added, "religion & Govt. will both exist in greater purity, the less they are mixed together." Letter from J. Madison to E. Livingston (July 10, 1822), in 5 The Founders' Constitution, 105, 106.

What we thus know of the Framers' experience underscores the observation of one prominent commentator, that confining the Establishment Clause to a prohibition on preferential aid "requires a premise that the Framers were extraordinarily bad drafters—that they believed one thing but adopted language that said something substantially different, and that they did so after repeatedly attending to the choice of language." Laycock, "Nonpreferential" Aid, 882-883. We must presume, since there is no conclusive evidence to the contrary, that the Framers embraced the significance of their textual judgment.[3] Thus, on balance, history neither contradicts nor warrants reconsideration of the settled principle that the Establishment Clause forbids support for religion in general no less than support for one religion or some.

## C

While these considerations are, for me, sufficient to reject the nonpreferentialist position, one further concern animates my judgment. In many contexts, including this one, non-preferentialism requires some distinction between "sectarian" religious practices and those that would be, by some measure,

---

[3] In his dissent in *Wallace v. Jaffree*, 472 U.S. 38 (1985), THE CHIEF JUSTICE rested his nonpreferentialist interpretation partly on the post-ratification actions of the early National Government. Aside from the willingness of some (but not all) early Presidents to issue ceremonial religious proclamations, which were at worst trivial breaches of the Establishment Clause, he cited such seemingly preferential aid as a treaty provision, signed by Jefferson, authorizing federal subsidization of a Roman Catholic priest and church for the Kaskaskia Indians. But this proves too much, for if the Establishment Clause permits a special appropriation of tax money for the religious activities of a particular sect, it forbids virtually nothing. See Laycock, "Non-preferential" Aid 915. Although evidence of historical practice can indeed furnish valuable aid in the interpretation of contemporary language, acts like the one in question prove only that public officials, no matter when they serve, can turn a blind eye to constitutional principle.

ecumenical enough to pass Establishment Clause muster. Simply by requiring the enquiry, nonpreferentialists invite the courts to engage in comparative theology. I can hardly imagine a subject less amenable to the competence of the federal judiciary, or more deliberately to be avoided where possible.

This case is nicely in point. Since the nonpreferentiality of a prayer must be judged by its text, JUSTICE BLACKMUN pertinently observes, that Rabbi Gutterman drew his exhortation "'to do justly, to love mercy, to walk humbly'" straight from the King James version of Micah, chapter 6, verse 8. At some undefinable point, the similarities between a state-sponsored prayer and the sacred text of a specific religion would so closely identify the former with the latter that even a nonpreferentialist would have to concede a breach of the Establishment Clause. And even if Micah's thought is sufficiently generic for most believers, it still embodies a straightforwardly theistic premise, and so does the rabbi's prayer. Many Americans who consider themselves religious are not theistic; some, like several of the Framers, are deists who would question Rabbi Gutterman's plea for divine advancement of the country's political and moral good. Thus, a nonpreferentialist who would condemn subjecting public school graduates to, say, the Anglican liturgy would still need to explain why the government's preference for theistic over nontheistic religion is constitutional.

Nor does it solve the problem to say that the State should promote a "diversity" of religious views; that position would necessarily compel the government and, inevitably, the courts to make wholly inappropriate judgments about the number of religions the State should sponsor and the relative frequency with which it should sponsor each. In fact, the prospect would be even worse than that. As Madison observed in criticizing religious Presidential proclamations, the practice of sponsoring religious messages tends, over time, "to narrow the recommendation to the standard of the predominant sect." Madison's "Detached Memoranda," 3 Wm. & Mary Q., 534, 561 (E. Fleet ed. 1946) (hereinafter Madison's "Detached Memoranda"). We have not changed much since the days of Madison, and the judiciary should not willingly enter the political arena to battle the centripetal force leading from religious pluralism to official preference for the faith with the most votes.

II

Petitioners rest most of their argument on a theory that, whether or not the Establishment Clause permits extensive nonsectarian support for religion, it does not forbid the state to sponsor affirmations of religious belief that coerce neither support for religion nor participation in religious observance. I appreciate the force of some of the arguments supporting a "coercion" analysis of the Clause. See generally *County of Allegheny*, 655-679 (opinion of KENNEDY, J.); McConnell, Coercion: The Lost Element of Establishment, 27 Wm. & Mary L. Rev.: 933 (1986). But we could not adopt that reading without abandoning our settled law, a course that, in my view, the text of the Clause would not readily permit. Nor does the extratextual evidence of original meaning stand so unequivocally at odds with the textual premise inherent in existing precedent that we should fundamentally reconsider our course. . . .

B

Like the provisions about "due" process and "unreasonable" searches and seizures, the constitutional language forbidding laws "respecting an

establishment of religion" is not pellucid. But virtually everyone acknowledges that the Clause bans more than formal establishments of religion in the
traditional sense, that is, massive state support for religion through, among
other means, comprehensive schemes of taxation. This much follows from the
Framers' explicit rejection of simpler provisions prohibiting either the establishment of a religion or laws "establishing religion" in favor of the broader ban
on laws "respecting an establishment of religion."

While some argue that the Framers added the word "respecting" simply
to foreclose federal interference with state establishments of religion, see, e.g.,
Amar, The Bill of Rights as a Constitution, 100 Yale L. J.: 1131, 1157 (1991),
the language sweeps more broadly than that. In Madison's words, the Clause
in its final form forbids "everything like" a national religious establishment,
see Madison's "Detached Memoranda" 558, and, after incorporation, it forbids
"everything like" a state religious establishment.

While petitioners insist that the prohibition extends only to the "coercive" features and incidents of establishment, they cannot easily square that
claim with the constitutional text. The First Amendment forbids not just laws
"respecting an establishment of religion," but also those "prohibiting the free
exercise thereof." Yet laws that coerce nonadherents to "support or participate
in any religion or its exercise," would virtually by definition violate their right
to religious free exercise. Thus, a literal application of the coercion test would
render the Establishment Clause a virtual nullity, as petitioners' counsel essentially conceded at oral argument.

Our cases presuppose as much; as we said in *School Dist. of Abington*, "the
distinction between the two clauses is apparent—a violation of the Free Exercise Clause is predicated on coercion while the Establishment Clause violation
need not be so attended." . . .

## C

Petitioners argue from the political setting in which the Establishment
Clause was framed, and from the Framers' own political practices following
ratification, that government may constitutionally endorse religion so long
as it does not coerce religious conformity. The setting and the practices warrant canvassing, but while they yield some evidence for petitioners' argument,
they do not reveal the degree of consensus in early constitutional thought that
would raise a threat to *stare decisis* by challenging the presumption that the Establishment Clause adds something to the Free Exercise Clause that follows it.

The Framers adopted the Religion Clauses in response to a long tradition of coercive state support for religion, particularly in the form of tax assessments, but their special antipathy to religious coercion did not exhaust
their hostility to the features and incidents of establishment. Indeed, Jefferson
and Madison opposed any political appropriation of religion, and, even when
challenging the hated assessments, they did not always temper their rhetoric with distinctions between coercive and noncoercive state action. When,
for example, Madison criticized Virginia's general assessment bill, he invoked
principles antithetical to all state efforts to promote religion. An assessment, he
wrote, is improper not simply because it forces people to donate "three pence"
to religion, but, more broadly, because "it is itself a signal of persecution. It
degrades from the equal rank of Citizens all those whose opinions in Religion
do not bend to those of the Legislative authority." J. Madison, Memorial and
Remonstrance Against Religious Assessments (1785). Madison saw that, even

without the tax collector's participation, an official endorsement of religion can impair religious liberty.

Petitioners contend that because the early Presidents included religious messages in their inaugural and Thanksgiving Day addresses, the Framers could not have meant the Establishment Clause to forbid noncoercive state endorsement of religion. The argument ignores the fact, however, that Americans today find such proclamations less controversial than did the founding generation, whose published thoughts on the matter belie petitioners' claim. President Jefferson, for example, steadfastly refused to issue Thanksgiving proclamations of any kind, in part because he thought they violated the Religion Clauses. Letter from Thomas Jefferson to Rev. S. Miller (Jan. 23, 1808), in 5 The Founders' Constitution, 98. In explaining his views to the Reverend Samuel Miller, Jefferson effectively anticipated, and rejected, petitioners' position:

> It is only proposed that I should *recommend*, not prescribe a day of fasting & prayer. That is, that I should *indirectly* assume to the U.S. an authority over religious exercises which the Constitution has directly precluded from them. It must be meant too that this recommendation is to carry some authority, and to be sanctioned by some penalty on those who disregard it; not indeed of fine and imprisonment, but of some degree of proscription perhaps in public opinion. *Id.*, 98-99 (emphasis in original).

By condemning such noncoercive state practices that, in "recommending" the majority faith, demean religious dissenters "in public opinion," Jefferson necessarily condemned what, in modern terms, we call official endorsement of religion. He accordingly construed the Establishment Clause to forbid not simply state coercion, but also state endorsement, of religious belief and observance. And if he opposed impersonal Presidential addresses for inflicting "proscription in public opinion," all the more would he have condemned less diffuse expressions of official endorsement.

During his first three years in office, James Madison also refused to call for days of thanksgiving and prayer, though later, amid the political turmoil of the War of 1812, he did so on four separate occasions. See Madison's "Detached Memoranda," 562 and n. 54. Upon retirement, in an essay condemning as an unconstitutional "establishment" the use of public money to support congressional and military chaplains, *id.*, 558-560,[6] he concluded that "religious proclamations by the Executive recommending thanksgivings & fasts are shoots from the same root with the legislative acts reviewed. Altho' recommendations only, they imply a religious agency, making no part of the trust delegated to political rulers." *Id.*, 560. Explaining that "the members of a Govt . . . can in no sense, be regarded as possessing an advisory trust from their Constituents in their religious capacities," *ibid.*, he further observed that the state necessarily freights all of its religious messages with political ones: "the idea of policy [is]

---

[6] Madison found this practice "a palpable violation of . . . Constitutional principles." Madison's "Detached Memoranda" 558. Although he sat on the committee recommending the congressional chaplainship, see R. Cord, Separation of Church and State: Historical Fact and Current Fiction 23 (1988), he later insisted that "it was not with my approbation, that the deviation from [the immunity of religion from civil jurisdiction] took place in Congs., when they appointed Chaplains, to be paid from the Natl. Treasury." Letter from J. Madison to E. Livingston (July 10, 1822), in 5 The Founders' Constitution, at 105.

associated with religion, whatever be the mode or the occasion, when a function of the latter is assumed by those in power." *Id.*, 562 (footnote omitted).

Madison's failure to keep pace with his principles in the face of congressional pressure cannot erase the principles. He admitted to backsliding, and explained that he had made the content of his wartime proclamations inconsequential enough to mitigate much of their impropriety. See *ibid.*; see also Letter from J. Madison to E. Livingston (July 10, 1822), in 5 The Founders' Constitution, 105. While his writings suggest mild variations in his interpretation of the Establishment Clause, Madison was no different in that respect from the rest of his political generation. That he expressed so much doubt about the constitutionality of religious proclamations, however, suggests a brand of separationism stronger even than that embodied in our traditional jurisprudence. So too does his characterization of public subsidies for legislative and military chaplains as unconstitutional "establishments," for the federal courts, however expansive their general view of the Establishment Clause, have upheld both practices. . . .

To be sure, the leaders of the young Republic engaged in some of the practices that separationists like Jefferson and Madison criticized. The First Congress did hire institutional chaplains, and Presidents Washington and Adams unapologetically marked days of "'public thanksgiving and prayer,'" see R. Cord, Separation of Church and State 53 (1988). Yet in the face of the separationist dissent, those practices prove, at best, that the Framers simply did not share a common understanding of the Establishment Clause, and, at worst, that they, like other politicians, could raise constitutional ideals one day and turn their backs on them the next. "Indeed, by 1787 the provisions of the state bills of rights had become what Madison called mere 'paper parchments'— expressions of the most laudable sentiments, observed as much in the breach as in practice." Kurland, The Origins of the Religion Clauses of the Constitution, 27 Wm. & Mary L. Rev.: 839, 852 (1986) (footnote omitted). Sometimes the National Constitution fared no better. Ten years after proposing the First Amendment, Congress passed the Alien and Sedition Acts, measures patently unconstitutional by modern standards. If the early Congress's political actions were determinative, and not merely relevant, evidence of constitutional meaning, we would have to gut our current First Amendment doctrine to make room for political censorship.

While we may be unable to know for certain what the Framers meant by the Clause, we do know that, around the time of its ratification, a respectable body of opinion supported a considerably broader reading than petitioners urge upon us. This consistency with the textual considerations is enough to preclude fundamentally reexamining our settled law, and I am accordingly left with the task of considering whether the state practice at issue here violates our traditional understanding of the Clause's proscriptions.

### III

While the Establishment Clause's concept of neutrality is not self-revealing, our recent cases have invested it with specific content: the State may not favor or endorse either religion generally over nonreligion or one religion over others. This principle against favoritism and endorsement has become the foundation of Establishment Clause jurisprudence, ensuring that religious belief is irrelevant to every citizen's standing in the political community, and protecting religion from the demeaning effects of any governmental embrace.

Now, as in the early Republic, "religion & Govt. will both exist in greater purity, the less they are mixed together." Letter from J. Madison to E. Livingston (July 10, 1822), in 5 The Founders' Constitution, 106. Our aspiration to religious liberty, embodied in the First Amendment, permits no other standard.

## A

That government must remain neutral in matters of religion does not foreclose it from ever taking religion into account. The State may "accommodate" the free exercise of religion by relieving people from generally applicable rules that interfere with their religious callings. Contrary to the views of some, such accommodation does not necessarily signify an official endorsement of religious observance over disbelief.

In everyday life, we routinely accommodate religious beliefs that we do not share. A Christian inviting an Orthodox Jew to lunch might take pains to choose a kosher restaurant; an atheist in a hurry might yield the right of way to an Amish man steering a horse-drawn carriage. In so acting, we express respect for, but not endorsement of, the fundamental values of others. We act without expressing a position on the theological merit of those values or of religious belief in general, and no one perceives us to have taken such a position.

The government may act likewise. Most religions encourage devotional practices that are at once crucial to the lives of believers and idiosyncratic in the eyes of nonadherents. By definition, secular rules of general application are drawn from the nonadherent's vantage and, consequently, fail to take such practices into account. Yet when enforcement of such rules cuts across religious sensibilities, as it often does, it puts those affected to the choice of taking sides between God and government. In such circumstances, accommodating religion reveals nothing beyond a recognition that general rules can unnecessarily offend the religious conscience when they offend the conscience of secular society not at all. Thus, in freeing the Native American Church from federal laws forbidding peyote use, . . . the government conveys no endorsement of peyote rituals, the Church, or religion as such; it simply respects the centrality of peyote to the lives of certain Americans.

## B

Whatever else may define the scope of accommodation permissible under the Establishment Clause, one requirement is clear: accommodation must lift a discernible burden on the free exercise of religion. Concern for the position of religious individuals in the modern regulatory State cannot justify official solicitude for a religious practice unburdened by general rules; such gratuitous largesse would effectively favor religion over disbelief. By these lights one easily sees that, in sponsoring the graduation prayers at issue here, the State has crossed the line from permissible accommodation to unconstitutional establishment.

Religious students cannot complain that omitting prayers from their graduation ceremony would, in any realistic sense, "burden" their spiritual callings. To be sure, many of them invest this rite of passage with spiritual significance, but they may express their religious feelings about it before and after the ceremony. They may even organize a privately sponsored baccalaureate if they desire the company of like-minded students. Because they accordingly have no need for the machinery of the State to affirm their beliefs, the government's sponsorship of prayer at the graduation ceremony is most reasonably understood as an official endorsement of religion and, in this instance, of theistic religion. One may fairly say, as one commentator has suggested, that the government brought prayer into the ceremony "precisely because some people want a symbolic affirmation that government approves and endorses their religion, and because many of the people who want this affirmation place little or no value on the costs to religious minorities."[8]

Petitioners would deflect this conclusion by arguing that graduation prayers are no different from Presidential religious proclamations and similar official "acknowledgments" of religion in public life. But religious invocations in Thanksgiving Day addresses and the like, rarely noticed, ignored without effort, conveyed over an impersonal medium, and directed at no one in particular, inhabit a pallid zone worlds apart from official prayers delivered to a captive audience of public school students and their families. Madison himself respected the difference between the trivial and the serious in constitutional practice. Realizing that his contemporaries were unlikely to take the Establishment Clause seriously enough to forgo a legislative chaplainship, he suggested that "rather than let this step beyond the landmarks of power have the effect of a legitimate precedent, it will be better to apply to it the legal aphorism *de minimis non curat lex* . . . ." Madison's "Detached Memoranda," 559; see also Letter from J. Madison to E. Livingston (July 10, 1822), in 5 The Founders' Constitution, 105. But that logic permits no winking at the practice in question here. When public school officials, armed with the State's authority, convey an endorsement of religion to their students, they strike near the core of the Establishment Clause. However "ceremonial" their messages may be, they are flatly unconstitutional.

▓ JUSTICE SCALIA, with whom THE CHIEF JUSTICE, JUSTICE WHITE, and JUSTICE THOMAS join, dissenting.

Three Terms ago, I joined an opinion recognizing that the Establishment Clause must be construed in light of the "government policies of accommodation, acknowledgment, and support for religion [that] are an accepted part of our political and cultural heritage." That opinion affirmed that "the meaning of the Clause is to be determined by reference to historical practices and understandings." It said that "[a] test for implementing the protections of the Establishment Clause that, if applied with consistency, would invalidate longstanding traditions cannot be a proper reading of the Clause." *County of Allegheny v. American Civil Liberties Union*, 492 U.S. 573, 657, 670 (1989) (KENNEDY, J., concurring in judgment in part and dissenting in part).

These views of course prevent me from joining today's opinion, which is conspicuously bereft of any reference to history. In holding that the Establishment Clause prohibits invocations and benedictions at public school graduation ceremonies, the Court—with nary a mention that it is doing so—

---

[8] If the State had chosen its graduation day speakers according to wholly secular criteria, and if one of those speakers (not a state actor) had individually chosen to deliver a religious message, it would have been harder to attribute an endorsement of religion to the State. But that is not our case. Nor is this a case where the State has, without singling out religious groups or individuals, extended benefits to them as members of a broad class of beneficiaries defined by clearly secular criteria. . . . Finally, this is not a case like *Marsh v. Chambers*, in which government officials invoke spiritual inspiration entirely for their own benefit without directing any religious message at the citizens they lead.

lays waste a tradition that is as old as public school graduation ceremonies themselves, and that is a component of an even more longstanding American tradition of nonsectarian prayer to God at public celebrations generally. As its instrument of destruction, the bulldozer of its social engineering, the Court invents a boundless, and boundlessly manipulable, test of psychological coercion, which promises to do for the Establishment Clause what the *Durham* rule did for the insanity defense. See *Durham v. United States*, 214 F.2d 862 (1954). Today's opinion shows more forcefully than volumes of argumentation why our Nation's protection, that fortress which is our Constitution, cannot possibly rest upon the changeable philosophical predilections of the Justices of this Court, but must have deep foundations in the historic practices of our people.

I

JUSTICE HOLMES' aphorism that "a page of history is worth a volume of logic," *New York Trust Co. v. Eisner*, 256 U.S. 345, 349 (1921), applies with particular force to our Establishment Clause jurisprudence. As we have recognized, our interpretation of the Establishment Clause should "comport with what history reveals was the contemporaneous understanding of its guarantees." *Lynch v. Donnelly*, 465 U.S. 668, 673 (1984). . . .

The history and tradition of our Nation are replete with public ceremonies featuring prayers of thanksgiving and petition. Illustrations of this point have been amply provided in our prior opinions, but since the Court is so oblivious to our history as to suggest that the Constitution restricts "preservation and transmission of religious beliefs . . . to the private sphere," it appears necessary to provide another brief account.

From our Nation's origin, prayer has been a prominent part of governmental ceremonies and proclamations. The Declaration of Independence, the document marking our birth as a separate people, "appealed to the Supreme Judge of the world for the rectitude of our intentions" and avowed "a firm reliance on the protection of divine Providence." In his first inaugural address, after swearing his oath of office on a Bible, George Washington deliberately made a prayer a part of his first official act as President:

> It would be peculiarly improper to omit in this first official act my fervent supplications to that Almighty Being who rules over the universe, who presides in the councils of nations, and whose providential aids can supply every human defect, that His benediction may consecrate to the liberties and happiness of the people of the United States a Government instituted by themselves for these essential purposes. Inaugural Addresses of the Presidents of the United States, S. Doc. 101-10, p. 2 (1989).

Such supplications have been a characteristic feature of inaugural addresses ever since. Thomas Jefferson, for example, prayed in his first inaugural address: "May that Infinite Power which rules the destinies of the universe lead our councils to what is best, and give them a favorable issue for your peace and prosperity." *Id.*, 17. In his second inaugural address, Jefferson acknowledged his need for divine guidance and invited his audience to join his prayer:

> I shall need, too, the favor of that Being in whose hands we are, who led our fathers, as Israel of old, from their native land and planted them in a country flowing with all the necessaries and comforts of life; who has covered our infancy with His providence and our riper years with His

wisdom and power, and to whose goodness I ask you to join in supplications with me that He will so enlighten the minds of your servants, guide their councils, and prosper their measures that whatsoever they do shall result in your good, and shall secure to you the peace, friendship, and approbation of all nations. *Id.*, 22-23.

Similarly, James Madison, in his first inaugural address, placed his confidence

in the guardianship and guidance of that Almighty Being whose power regulates the destiny of nations, whose blessings have been so conspicuously dispensed to this rising Republic, and to whom we are bound to address our devout gratitude for the past, as well as our fervent supplications and best hopes for the future. *Id.*, 28.

Most recently, President Bush, continuing the tradition established by President Washington, asked those attending his inauguration to bow their heads, and made a prayer his first official act as President. *Id.*, 346.

Our national celebration of Thanksgiving likewise dates back to President Washington. As we recounted in *Lynch*:

The day after the First Amendment was proposed, Congress urged President Washington to proclaim "a day of public thanksgiving and prayer, to be observed by acknowledging with grateful hearts the many and signal favours of Almighty God." President Washington proclaimed November 26, 1789, a day of thanksgiving to "offer our prayers and supplications to the Great Lord and Ruler of Nations, and beseech Him to pardon our national and other transgressions . . . ." 465 U.S. 675, n. 2 (citations omitted).

This tradition of Thanksgiving Proclamations—with their religious theme of prayerful gratitude to God—has been adhered to by almost every President.

The other two branches of the Federal Government also have a long-established practice of prayer at public events. As we detailed in *Marsh*, congressional sessions have opened with a chaplain's prayer ever since the First Congress. And this Court's own sessions have opened with the invocation "God save the United States and this Honorable Court" since the days of Chief Justice Marshall.

In addition to this general tradition of prayer at public ceremonies, there exists a more specific tradition of invocations and benedictions at public school graduation exercises. By one account, the first public high school graduation ceremony took place in Connecticut in July 1868—the very month, as it happens, that the Fourteenth Amendment (the vehicle by which the Establishment Clause has been applied against the States) was ratified—when "15 seniors from the Norwich Free Academy marched in their best Sunday suits and dresses into a church hall and waited through majestic music and long prayers." As the Court obliquely acknowledges in describing the "customary features" of high school graduations, and as respondents do not contest, the invocation and benediction have long been recognized to be "as traditional as any other parts of the [school] graduation program and are widely established."

## II

The Court presumably would separate graduation invocations and benedictions from other instances of public "preservation and transmission of

religious beliefs" on the ground that they involve "psychological coercion."
. . . A few citations of "research in psychology" that have no particular bearing
upon the precise issue here, cannot disguise the fact that the Court has gone
beyond the realm where judges know what they are doing. The Court's argument that state officials have "coerced" students to take part in the invocation
and benediction at graduation ceremonies is, not to put too fine a point on it,
incoherent.

The Court identifies two "dominant facts" that it says dictate its ruling that
invocations and benedictions at public school graduation ceremonies violate
the Establishment Clause. Neither of them is in any relevant sense true.

A

The Court declares that students' "attendance and participation in the [in-
vocation and benediction] are in a fair and real sense obligatory." But what
exactly is this "fair and real sense"? According to the Court, students at graduation who want "to avoid the fact or appearance of participation," in the invocation and benediction are *psychologically* obligated by "public pressure, as
well as peer pressure, . . . to stand as a group or, at least, maintain respectful
silence" during those prayers. This assertion—*the very linchpin of the Court's
opinion*—is almost as intriguing for what it does not say as for what it says. It
does not say, for example, that students are psychologically coerced to bow
their heads, place their hands in a Durer-like prayer position, pay attention to
the prayers, utter "Amen," or in fact pray. (Perhaps further intensive psychological research remains to be done on these matters.) It claims only that students are psychologically coerced "to stand . . . *or*, at least, maintain respectful
silence." Both halves of this disjunctive (*both* of which must amount to the fact
or appearance of participation in prayer if the Court's analysis is to survive on
its own terms) merit particular attention.

To begin with the latter: The Court's notion that a student who simply *sits*
in "respectful silence" during the invocation and benediction (when all others are standing) has somehow joined—or would somehow be perceived as
having joined—in the prayers is nothing short of ludicrous. We indeed live in
a vulgar age. But surely "our social conventions," have not coarsened to the
point that anyone who does not stand on his chair and shout obscenities can
reasonably be deemed to have assented to everything said in his presence.
Since the Court does not dispute that students exposed to prayer at graduation ceremonies retain (despite "subtle coercive pressures,") the free will to
sit, there is absolutely no basis for the Court's decision. It is fanciful enough
to say that "a reasonable dissenter," standing head erect in a class of bowed
heads, "could believe that the group exercise signified her own participation
or approval of it." It is beyond the absurd to say that she could entertain such
a belief while pointedly declining to rise.

But let us assume the very worst, that the nonparticipating graduate is
"subtly coerced" . . . to stand! Even that half of the disjunctive does not remotely establish a "participation" (or an "appearance of participation") in a
religious exercise. The Court acknowledges that "in our culture standing . . .
can signify adherence to a view or simple respect for the views of others."
(Much more often the latter than the former, I think, except perhaps in the
proverbial town meeting, where one votes by standing.) But if it is a permissible inference that one who is standing is doing so simply out of respect for
the prayers of others that are in progress, then how can it possibly be said
that a "reasonable dissenter . . . could believe that the group exercise signified

her own participation or approval"? Quite obviously, it cannot. I may add, moreover, that maintaining respect for the religious observances of others is a fundamental civic virtue that government (including the public schools) can and should cultivate—so that even if it were the case that the displaying of such respect might be mistaken for taking part in the prayer, I would deny that the dissenter's interest in avoiding *even the false appearance of participation* constitutionally trumps the government's interest in fostering respect for religion generally.

The opinion manifests that the Court itself has not given careful consideration to its test of psychological coercion. For if it had, how could it observe, with no hint of concern or disapproval, that students stood for the Pledge of Allegiance, which immediately preceded Rabbi Gutterman's invocation? The government can, of course, no more coerce political orthodoxy than religious orthodoxy. *West Virginia Bd. of Ed. v. Barnette*, 319 U.S. 624, 642 (1943). Moreover, since the Pledge of Allegiance has been revised since *Barnette* to include the phrase "under God," recital of the Pledge would appear to raise the same Establishment Clause issue as the invocation and benediction. If students were psychologically coerced to remain standing during the invocation, they must also have been psychologically coerced, moments before, to stand for (and thereby, in the Court's view, take part in or appear to take part in) the Pledge. Must the Pledge therefore be barred from the public schools (both from graduation ceremonies and from the classroom)? In *Barnette* we held that a public school student could not be compelled to *recite* the Pledge; we did not even hint that she could not be compelled to observe respectful silence—indeed, even to *stand* in respectful silence—when those who wished to recite it did so. Logically, that ought to be the next project for the Court's bulldozer.

I also find it odd that the Court concludes that high school graduates may not be subjected to this supposed psychological coercion, yet refrains from addressing whether "mature adults" may. I had thought that the reason graduation from high school is regarded as so significant an event is that it is generally associated with transition from adolescence to young adulthood. Many graduating seniors, of course, are old enough to vote. Why, then, does the Court treat them as though they were first-graders? Will we soon have a jurisprudence that distinguishes between mature and immature adults?

### B

The other "dominant fact" identified by the Court is that "state officials direct the performance of a formal religious exercise" at school graduation ceremonies. "Directing the performance of a formal religious exercise" has a sound of liturgy to it, summoning up images of the principal directing acolytes where to carry the cross, or showing the rabbi where to unroll the Torah. A Court professing to be engaged in a "delicate and fact-sensitive" line-drawing, would better describe what it means as "prescribing the content of an invocation and benediction." But even that would be false. All the record shows is that principals of the Providence public schools, acting within their delegated authority, have invited clergy to deliver invocations and benedictions at graduations; and that Principal Lee invited Rabbi Gutterman, provided him a two-page pamphlet, prepared by the National Conference of Christians and Jews, giving general advice on inclusive prayer for civic occasions, and advised him that his prayers at graduation should be nonsectarian. How these facts can fairly be transformed into the charges that Principal Lee "directed and controlled the content of [Rabbi Gutterman's] prayer," that school officials "monitor prayer," and attempted to "'compose official prayers,'" and that the "government involvement with religious activity in this case is pervasive," is difficult to fathom. The Court identifies nothing in the record remotely suggesting that school officials have ever drafted, edited, screened, or censored graduation prayers, or that Rabbi Gutterman was a mouthpiece of the school officials.

These distortions of the record are, of course, not harmless error: without them the Court's solemn assertion that the school officials could reasonably be perceived to be "enforcing a religious orthodoxy," would ring as hollow as it ought.

### III

The deeper flaw in the Court's opinion does not lie in its wrong answer to the question whether there was state-induced "peer-pressure" coercion; it lies, rather, in the Court's making violation of the Establishment Clause hinge on such a precious question. The coercion that was a hallmark of historical establishments of religion was coercion of religious orthodoxy and of financial support *by force of law and threat of penalty*. Typically, attendance at the state church was required; only clergy of the official church could lawfully perform sacraments; and dissenters, if tolerated, faced an array of civil disabilities. L. Levy, The Establishment Clause 4 (1986). Thus, for example, in the Colony of Virginia, where the Church of England had been established, ministers were required by law to conform to the doctrine and rites of the Church of England; and all persons were required to attend church and observe the Sabbath, were tithed for the public support of Anglican ministers, and were taxed for the costs of building and repairing churches. *Id.*, 3-4.

The Establishment Clause was adopted to prohibit such an establishment of religion at the federal level (and to protect state establishments of religion from federal interference). I will further acknowledge for the sake of argument that, as some scholars have argued, by 1790 the term "establishment" had acquired an additional meaning—"financial support of religion generally, by public taxation"—that reflected the development of "general or multiple" establishments, not limited to a single church. But that would still be an establishment coerced *by force of law*. And I will further concede that our constitutional tradition, from the Declaration of Independence and the first inaugural address of Washington, quoted earlier, down to the present day, has, with a few aberrations, see *Church of Holy Trinity v. United States*, 143 U.S. 457 (1892), ruled out of order government-sponsored endorsement of religion—even when no legal coercion is present, and indeed even when no ersatz, "peer-pressure" psycho-coercion is present—where the endorsement is sectarian, in the sense of specifying details upon which men and women who believe in a benevolent, omnipotent Creator and Ruler of the world are known to differ (for example, the divinity of Christ). But there is simply no support for the proposition that the officially sponsored nondenominational invocation and benediction read by Rabbi Gutterman—with no one legally coerced to recite them—violated the Constitution of the United States. To the contrary, they are so characteristically American they could have come from the pen of George Washington or Abraham Lincoln himself.

Thus, while I have no quarrel with the Court's general proposition that the Establishment Clause "guarantees that government may not coerce anyone to support or participate in religion or its exercise," I see no warrant for expanding the concept of coercion beyond acts backed by threat of penalty—a brand of coercion that, happily, is readily discernible to those of us who have made a career of reading the disciples of Blackstone rather than of Freud. The Framers were indeed opposed to coercion of religious worship by the National Government; but, as their own sponsorship of nonsectarian prayer in public events demonstrates, they understood that "speech is not coercive; the listener may do as he likes."

This historical discussion places in revealing perspective the Court's extravagant claim that the State has "for all practical purposes,"and "in every practical sense," compelled students to participate in prayers at graduation. Beyond the fact, stipulated to by the parties, that attendance at graduation is voluntary, there is nothing in the record to indicate that failure of attending students to take part in the invocation or benediction was subject to any penalty or discipline. Contrast this with, for example, the facts of *Barnette*: Schoolchildren were required by law to recite the Pledge of Allegiance; failure to do so resulted in expulsion, threatened the expelled child with the prospect of being sent to a reformatory for criminally inclined juveniles, and subjected his parents to prosecution (and incarceration) for causing delinquency. To characterize the "subtle coercive pressures," allegedly present here as the "practical" equivalent of the legal sanctions in *Barnette* is . . . well, let me just say it is not a "delicate and fact-sensitive" analysis.

The Court relies on our "school prayer" cases, [*Engel* and *Schempp*]. But whatever the merit of those cases, they do not support, much less compel, the Court's psycho-journey. In the first place, *Engel* and *Schempp* do not constitute an exception to the rule, distilled from historical practice, that public ceremonies may include prayer; rather, they simply do not fall within the scope of the rule (for the obvious reason that school instruction is not a public ceremony). Second, we have made clear our understanding that school prayer occurs within a framework in which legal coercion to attend school (i.e., coercion under threat of penalty) provides the ultimate backdrop. In *Schempp*, for example, we emphasized that the prayers were "prescribed as part of the curricular activities of students who are *required by law* to attend school." 374 U.S., 223 (emphasis added). *Engel's* suggestion that the school prayer program at issue there—which permitted students "to remain silent or be excused from the room," 370 U.S., 430—involved "indirect coercive pressure," *id.*, 431, should be understood against this backdrop of legal coercion. The question whether the opt-out procedure in *Engel* sufficed to dispel the coercion resulting from the mandatory attendance requirement is quite different from the question whether forbidden coercion exists in an environment *utterly devoid of legal compulsion*. And finally, our school prayer cases turn in part on the fact that the classroom is inherently an instructional setting, and daily prayer there—where parents are not present to counter "the students' emulation of teachers as role models and the children's susceptibility to peer pressure," *Edwards v. Aguillard*, 482 U.S. 578, 584 (1987)—might be thought to raise special concerns regarding state interference with the liberty of parents to direct the religious upbringing of their children: "Families entrust public schools with the education of their children, but condition their trust on the understanding that the classroom will not purposely be used to advance religious views that may conflict with the private beliefs of the student and his or her family." Voluntary prayer at graduation—a one-time ceremony at which parents, friends, and relatives are present—can hardly be thought to raise the same concerns.

IV

Our Religion Clause jurisprudence has become bedeviled (so to speak) by reliance on formulaic abstractions that are not derived from, but positively conflict with, our long-accepted constitutional traditions. Foremost among these has been the so-called *Lemon* test, which has received well-earned criticism from many Members of this Court. The Court today demonstrates the irrelevance of *Lemon* by essentially ignoring it, and the interment of that case may be the one happy byproduct of the Court's otherwise lamentable decision. Unfortunately, however, the Court has replaced *Lemon* with its psycho-coercion test, which suffers the double disability of having no roots whatever in our people's historic practice, and being as infinitely expandable as the reasons for psychotherapy itself.

Another happy aspect of the case is that it is only a jurisprudential disaster and not a practical one. Given the odd basis for the Court's decision, invocations and benedictions will be able to be given at public school graduations next June, as they have for the past century and a half, so long as school authorities make clear that anyone who abstains from screaming in protest does not necessarily participate in the prayers. All that is seemingly needed is an announcement, or perhaps a written insertion at the beginning of the graduation program, to the effect that, while all are asked to rise for the invocation and benediction, none is compelled to join in them, nor will be assumed, by rising, to have done so. That obvious fact recited, the graduates and their parents may proceed to thank God, as Americans have always done, for the blessings He has generously bestowed on them and on their country. . . .

The reader has been told much in this case about the personal interest of Mr. Weisman and his daughter, and very little about the personal interests on the other side. They are not inconsequential. Church and state would not be such a difficult subject if religion were, as the Court apparently thinks it to be, some purely personal avocation that can be indulged entirely in secret, like pornography, in the privacy of one's room. For most believers it is *not* that, and has never been. Religious men and women of almost all denominations have felt it necessary to acknowledge and beseech the blessing of God as a people, and not just as individuals, because they believe in the "protection of divine Providence," as the Declaration of Independence put it, not just for individuals but for societies; because they believe God to be, as Washington's first Thanksgiving Proclamation put it, the "Great Lord and Ruler of Nations." One can believe in the effectiveness of such public worship, or one can deprecate and deride it. But the longstanding American tradition of prayer at official ceremonies displays with unmistakable clarity that the Establishment Clause does not forbid the government to accommodate it.

The narrow context of the present case involves a community's celebration of one of the milestones in its young citizens' lives, and it is a bold step for this Court to seek to banish from that occasion, and from thousands of similar celebrations throughout this land, the expression of gratitude to God that a majority of the community wishes to make. The issue before us today is not the abstract philosophical question whether the alternative of frustrating this desire of a religious majority is to be preferred over the alternative of imposing "psychological coercion," or a feeling of exclusion, upon nonbelievers. Rather, the question is *whether a mandatory choice in favor of the former has been imposed by the United States Constitution*. As the age-old practices of our people show, the answer to that question is not at all in doubt.

I must add one final observation: The Founders of our Republic knew the fearsome potential of sectarian religious belief to generate civil dissension and civil strife. And they also knew that nothing, absolutely nothing, is so inclined to foster among religious believers of various faiths a toleration—no, an affection—for one another than voluntarily joining in prayer together, to the God whom they all worship and seek. Needless to say, no one should be compelled to do that, but it is a shame to deprive our public culture of the opportunity, and indeed the encouragement, for people to do it voluntarily. The Baptist or Catholic who heard and joined in the simple and inspiring prayers of Rabbi Gutterman on this official and patriotic occasion was inoculated from religious bigotry and prejudice in a manner that cannot be replicated. To deprive our society of that important unifying mechanism, in order to spare the nonbeliever what seems to me the minimal inconvenience of standing or even sitting in respectful nonparticipation, is as senseless in policy as it is unsupported in law.

For the foregoing reasons, I dissent.

## Notes and Questions

1. In the view of the Court majority, what are the "dominant facts" that made the practice at issue unconstitutional? How and why does the majority stress the public school's control over the graduation ceremonies? What are some of the purposes of the First Amendment, according to the majority, and how are they threatened by school-sponsored graduation prayer?

2. Why did the majority reject the invitation of the petitioners and the United States (as a friend-of-the-court) to reconsider its decision in *Lemon v. Kurtzman*? Other than a refusal to reconsider *Lemon*, do you find any support for the *Lemon* test in Justice Kennedy's opinion?

3. What is "indirect coercion," as defined by Justice Kennedy? How does Kennedy attempt to tie this case to the precedents set in *Engel v. Vitale* and *School Dist. of Abington v. Schempp*? Is it fair to say that the public school in *Lee v. Weisman* "assist[ed] in composing prayers" that were offered in this case? What facts does the majority rely on to draw this conclusion? How does Justice Scalia respond to these points in his dissenting opinion?

4. Justice Kennedy says the Constitution protects free speech and the right to religious freedom in different ways. Explain his reasoning.

5. How does the majority opinion distinguish the *Marsh v. Chambers* case, the case in which the Court found prayer before legislative sessions to be constitutional?

6. What if class valedictorians were allowed to give speeches at their graduations and the class valedictorian choose to engage in an impromptu prayer and invited the audience to stand for the prayer and bow their heads? Under *Lee v. Weisman*, would this action be constitutional? What would the analysis be under the majority opinion? The concurring opinions? The dissent?

7. What differences are there between the rationale presented by the majority and concurring opinions in this case? Which rationale is the most narrow, i.e., which one would tend to cast constitutional doubt on fewer forms of interaction between government and religion?

8. What are the two issues that Justice Souter addresses in his concurring opinion? Compare then-Justice Rehnquist's dissent in *Wallace v. Jaffree* with Justice Souter's concurring opinion in this case. What differences are there between their respective accounts of historical events surrounding the framing of the First Amendment? How do their analyses of these events differ? By joining the dissenting opinion written by Justice Scalia in *Lee v. Weisman*, does Justice Rehnquist seem to back off of some of the historical claims he made in his dissent in the *Wallace* case?

9. According to Justice Scalia, what should the standard be for the evaluation of claims brought under the Establishment Clause? How does he arrive at this standard? Do Justice Scalia's historical claims necessarily support approval of school-sponsored prayer? In other words, can you think of some arguments that would distinguish his historical examples from the case at hand?

10. In his dissent, Scalia argues that the ruling is, in the final analysis, rather inconsequential because "[a]ll that is seemingly needed [to cure the situation] is an announcement, or perhaps a written insertion at the beginning of the graduation program, to the effect that, while all are asked to rise for the invocation and benediction, none is compelled to join in them, nor will be assumed by rising to have done so." Would that cure the constitutional defect?

11. Justice Scalia says that the founders "knew that nothing, absolutely nothing, is so inclined to foster among religious believers of various faiths a toleration—no, an affection—for one another than voluntarily joining in prayer together, to the God whom they are worship and seek." Scalia then suggests that approval of, and engagement in, school-sponsored graduation prayer is a way to carry forward that tradition today. Does Scalia's statement presume that all religious people worship the same God, both then and now? Is that presumption correct? Do you think Scalia's statement contemplates the existence of people who believe in more than one god, i.e. polytheists? Should any of this matter, constitutionally speaking?

---

The next case the Court agreed to hear in this area was one about prayers offered at high school football games in Texas. Prior to 1995, a high school student who occupied an elected office as chaplain led attendees in prayer over the stadium public-address system prior to the commencement of the game. This practice, among others, was challenged by two sets of current and former students and their respective mothers. The trial court permitted these plaintiffs to litigate anonymously to protect them from harassment. While this lawsuit was pending, the school adopted another policy that "permit[ted], but d[id] not require" prayer initiated and led by a student at all home games. As you read, pay close attention to a key issue in this case—whether the prayers are "*government* speech endorsing religion, which the Establishment Clause forbids," or "*private* speech endorsing religion, which the Free Speech and Free Exercise Clauses protect."

---

## SANTA FE INDEPENDENT SCHOOL DISTRICT v. DOE
## 530 U.S. 290 (2000)

■ JUSTICE STEVENS delivered the opinion of the Court.

Prior to 1995, the Santa Fe High School student who occupied the school's elective office of student council chaplain delivered a prayer over the public address system before each varsity football game for the entire season. This practice, along with others, was challenged in District Court as a violation of the Establishment Clause of the First Amendment. While these proceedings were pending in the District Court, the school district adopted a different policy that permits, but does not require, prayer initiated and led by a student at all home games. The District Court entered an order modifying that policy to permit only nonsectarian, nonproselytizing prayer. The Court of Appeals held that, even as modified by the District Court, the football prayer policy was invalid. We granted the school district's petition for certiorari to review that holding.

I

The Santa Fe Independent School District (District) is a political subdivision of the State of Texas, responsible for the education of more than 4,000 students in a small community in the southern part of the State. The District includes the Santa Fe High School, two primary schools, an intermediate school and the junior high school. Respondents are two sets of current or former students and their respective mothers. One family is Mormon and the other is Catholic. The District Court permitted respondents (Does) to litigate anonymously to protect them from intimidation or harassment.[1]

Respondents commenced this action in April 1995 and moved for a temporary restraining order to prevent the District from violating the Establishment Clause at the imminent graduation exercises. In their complaint the Does alleged that the District had engaged in several proselytizing practices, such as promoting attendance at a Baptist revival meeting, encouraging membership in religious clubs, chastising children who held minority religious beliefs, and distributing Gideon Bibles on school premises. They also alleged that the District allowed students to read Christian invocations and benedictions from the stage at graduation ceremonies, and to deliver overtly Christian prayers over the public address system at home football games.

---

[1] A decision, the Fifth Circuit Court of Appeals noted, that many District officials "apparently neither agreed with nor particularly respected." About a month after the complaint was filed, the District Court entered an order that provided, in part:

"Any further attempt on the part of District or school administration, officials, counsellors, teachers, employees or servants of the School District, parents, students or anyone else, overtly or covertly to ferret out the identities of the Plaintiffs in this cause, by means of bogus petitions, questionnaires, individual interrogation, or downright 'snooping', will cease immediately. ANYONE TAKING ANY ACTION ON SCHOOL PROPERTY, DURING SCHOOL HOURS, OR WITH SCHOOL RESOURCES OR APPROVAL FOR PURPOSES OF ATTEMPTING TO ELICIT THE NAMES OR IDENTITIES OF THE PLAINTIFFS IN THIS CAUSE OF ACTION, BY OR ON BEHALF OF ANY OF THESE INDIVIDUALS, WILL FACE THE HARSHEST POSSIBLE CONTEMPT SANCTIONS FROM THIS COURT, AND MAY ADDITIONALLY FACE CRIMINAL LIABILITY. The Court wants these proceedings addressed on their merits, and not on the basis of intimidation or harassment of the participants on either side."

On May 10, 1995, the District Court entered an interim order addressing a number of different issues. . . .

In response to that portion of the order, the District adopted a series of policies over several months dealing with prayer at school functions. The policies enacted in May and July for graduation ceremonies provided the format for the August and October policies for football games. . . .

The August policy, which was titled "Prayer at Football Games," was similar to the July policy for graduations. It also authorized two student elections, the first to determine whether "invocations" should be delivered, and the second to select the spokesperson to deliver them. Like the July policy, it contained two parts, an initial statement that omitted any requirement that the content of the invocation be "nonsectarian and nonproselytising," and a fall-back provision that automatically added that limitation if the preferred policy should be enjoined. On August 31, 1995, according to the parties' stipulation, "the district's high school students voted to determine whether a student would deliver prayer at varsity football games. . . . The students chose to allow a student to say a prayer at football games." A week later, in a separate election, they selected a student "to deliver the prayer at varsity football games."

The final policy (October policy) is essentially the same as the August policy, though it omits the word "prayer" from its title, and refers to "messages" and "statements" as well as "invocations."[5] It is the validity of that policy that is before us. . . .

---

[5] Despite these changes, the school did not conduct another election, under the October policy, to supersede the results of the August policy election.

---

## Santa Fe School District Policy

"STUDENT ACTIVITIES:
"PRE-GAME CEREMONIES AT FOOTBALL GAMES
"The board has chosen to permit students to deliver a brief invocation and/or message to be delivered during the pre-game ceremonies of home varsity football games to solemnize the event, to promote good sportsmanship and student safety, and to establish the appropriate environment for the competition.

"Upon advice and direction of the high school principal, each spring, the high school student council shall conduct an election, by the high school student body, by secret ballot, to determine whether such a statement or invocation will be a part of the pre-game ceremonies and if so, shall elect a student, from a list of student volunteers, to deliver the statement or invocation. The student volunteer who is selected by his or her classmates may decide what message and/or invocation to deliver, consistent with the goals and purposes of this policy.

"If the District is enjoined by a court order from the enforcement of this policy, then and only then will the following policy automatically become the applicable policy of the school district.

"The board has chosen to permit students to deliver a brief invocation and/or message to be delivered during the pre-game ceremonies of home varsity football games to solemnize the event, to promote good sportsmanship and student safety, and to establish the appropriate environment for the competition.

"Upon advice and direction of the high school principal, each spring, the high school student council shall conduct an election, by the high school student body, by secret ballot, to determine whether such a message or invocation will be a part of the pre-game ceremonies and if so, shall elect a student, from a list of student volunteers, to deliver the statement or invocation. The student volunteer who is selected by his or her classmates may decide what statement or invocation to deliver, consistent with the goals and purposes of this policy. Any message and/or invocation delivered by a student must be nonsectarian and nonproselytizing. *Doe v. Santa Fe Indep. Sch. Dist.*, 530 U.S. 290, footnote 6 (2000).

We granted the District's petition for certiorari, limited to the following question: "Whether petitioner's policy permitting student-led, student-initiated prayer at football games violates the Establishment Clause." We conclude, as did the Court of Appeals, that it does.

## II

The first Clause in the First Amendment to the Federal Constitution provides that "Congress shall make no law respecting an establishment of religion, or prohibiting the free exercise thereof." The Fourteenth Amendment imposes those substantive limitations on the legislative power of the States and their political subdivisions. In *Lee v. Weisman*, we held that a prayer delivered by a rabbi at a middle school graduation ceremony violated that Clause. Although this case involves student prayer at a different type of school function, our analysis is properly guided by the principles that we endorsed in *Lee*.

As we held in that case:

> The principle that government may accommodate the free exercise of religion does not supersede the fundamental limitations imposed by the Establishment Clause. It is beyond dispute that, at a minimum, the Constitution guarantees that government may not coerce anyone to support or participate in religion or its exercise, or otherwise act in a way which "establishes a [state] religion or religious faith, or tends to do so." *Id.*, 587 (citations omitted) (quoting *Lynch v. Donnelly*, 465 U.S. 668, 678 (1984)).

In this case the District first argues that this principle is inapplicable to its October policy because the messages are private student speech, not public speech. It reminds us that "there is a crucial difference between *government* speech endorsing religion, which the Establishment Clause forbids, and *private* speech endorsing religion, which the Free Speech and Free Exercise Clauses protect." *Board of Ed. of Westside Community Schools (Dist. 66) v. Mergens*, 496 U.S. 226, 250 (1990) (opinion of O'CONNOR, J.). We certainly agree with that distinction, but we are not persuaded that the pregame invocations should be regarded as "private speech."

These invocations are authorized by a government policy and take place on government property at government-sponsored school-related events. Of course, not every message delivered under such circumstances is the government's own. We have held, for example, that an individual's contribution to a government-created forum was not government speech. See *Rosenberger v. Rector and Visitors of Univ. of Va.*, 515 U.S. 819 (1995). Although the District relies heavily on *Rosenberger* and similar cases involving such forums, it is clear that the pregame ceremony is not the type of forum discussed in those cases. The Santa Fe school officials simply do not "evince either 'by policy or by practice,' any intent to open the [pregame ceremony] to 'indiscriminate use,' . . . by the student body generally." Rather, the school allows only one student, the same student for the entire season, to give the invocation. The statement or invocation, moreover, is subject to particular regulations that confine the content and topic of the student's message. By comparison, in *Perry* [Ed. Assn. v. Perry Local Educators' Assn., 460 U.S. 37 (1983)] we rejected a claim that the school had created a limited public forum in its school mail system despite the fact that it had allowed far more speakers to address a much broader range of topics than the policy at issue here. As we concluded in *Perry*, "selective access does not transform government property into a public forum."

Granting only one student access to the stage at a time does not, of course, necessarily preclude a finding that a school has created a limited public forum. Here, however, Santa Fe's student election system ensures that only those messages deemed "appropriate" under the District's policy may be delivered. That is, the majoritarian process implemented by the District guarantees, by definition, that minority candidates will never prevail and that their views will be effectively silenced.

Recently, in *Board of Regents of Univ. of Wis. System v. Southworth*, 529 U.S. 217 (2000), we explained why student elections that determine, by majority vote, which expressive activities shall receive or not receive school benefits are constitutionally problematic:

> To the extent the referendum substitutes majority determinations for viewpoint neutrality it would undermine the constitutional protection the program requires. The whole theory of viewpoint neutrality is that minority views are treated with the same respect as are majority views. Access to a public forum, for instance, does not depend upon majoritarian consent. That principle is controlling here.

Like the student referendum for funding in *Southworth*, this student election does nothing to protect minority views but rather places the students who hold such views at the mercy of the majority. Because "fundamental rights may not be submitted to vote; they depend on the outcome of no elections," *West Virginia Bd. of Ed. v. Barnette*, 319 U.S. 624, 638 (1943), the District's elections are insufficient safeguards of diverse student speech.

In *Lee*, the school district made the related argument that its policy of endorsing only "civic or nonsectarian" prayer was acceptable because it minimized the intrusion on the audience as a whole. We rejected that claim by explaining that such a majoritarian policy "does not lessen the offense or isolation to the objectors. At best it narrows their number, at worst increases their sense of isolation and affront." 505 U.S., 594. Similarly, while Santa Fe's majoritarian election might ensure that *most* of the students are represented, it does nothing to protect the minority; indeed, it likely serves to intensify their offense.

Moreover, the District has failed to divorce itself from the religious content in the invocations. It has not succeeded in doing so, either by claiming that its policy is "'one of neutrality rather than endorsement'" or by characterizing the individual student as the "circuit-breaker" in the process. Contrary to the District's repeated assertions that it has adopted a "hands-off" approach to the pregame invocation, the realities of the situation plainly reveal that its policy involves both perceived and actual endorsement of religion. In this case, as we found in *Lee*, the "degree of school involvement" makes it clear that the pregame prayers bear "the imprint of the State and thus put school-age children who objected in an untenable position." 505 U.S., 590.

The District has attempted to disentangle itself from the religious messages by developing the two-step student election process. The text of the October policy, however, exposes the extent of the school's entanglement. The elections take place at all only because the school "board *has chosen to permit* students to deliver a brief invocation and/or message." The elections thus "shall" be conducted "by the high school student council" and "upon advice and direction of the high school principal." The decision whether to deliver a message is first made by majority vote of the entire student body, followed by a choice of the speaker in a separate, similar majority election. Even though the particular words used by the speaker are not determined by those votes, the policy mandates that the "statement or invocation" be "consistent with the goals and purposes of this policy," which are "to solemnize the event, to promote good sportsmanship and student safety, and to establish the appropriate environment for the competition."

In addition to involving the school in the selection of the speaker, the policy, by its terms, invites and encourages religious messages. The policy itself states that the purpose of the message is "to solemnize the event." A religious message is the most obvious method of solemnizing an event. Moreover, the requirements that the message "promote good citizenship" and "establish the appropriate environment for competition" further narrow the types of message deemed appropriate, suggesting that a solemn, yet nonreligious, message, such as commentary on United States foreign policy, would be prohibited. Indeed, the only type of message that is expressly endorsed in the text is an "invocation"—a term that primarily describes an appeal for divine assistance.[19] In fact, as used in the past at Santa Fe High School, an "invocation" has always entailed a focused religious message. Thus, the expressed purposes of the policy encourage the selection of a religious message, and that is precisely how the students understand the policy. The results of the elections described in the parties' stipulation make it clear that the students understood that the central question before them was whether prayer should be a part of the pregame ceremony. We recognize the important role that public worship plays in many communities, as well as the sincere desire to include public prayer as a part of various occasions so as to mark those occasions' significance. But such religious activity in public schools, as elsewhere, must comport with the First Amendment.

The actual or perceived endorsement of the message, moreover, is established by factors beyond just the text of the policy. Once the student speaker is selected and the message composed, the invocation is then delivered to a large audience assembled as part of a regularly scheduled, school-sponsored function conducted on school property. The message is broadcast over the school's public address system, which remains subject to the control of school officials. It is fair to assume that the pregame ceremony is clothed in the traditional indicia of school sporting events, which generally include not just the team, but also cheerleaders and band members dressed in uniforms sporting the school name and mascot. The school's name is likely written in large print across the field and on banners and flags. The crowd will certainly include many who display the school colors and insignia on their school T-shirts, jackets, or hats and who may also be waving signs displaying the school name. It is in a setting such as this that "the board has chosen to permit" the elected student to rise and give the "statement or invocation."

In this context the members of the listening audience must perceive the pregame message as a public expression of the views of the majority of the student body delivered with the approval of the school administration. In cases involving state participation in a religious activity, one of the relevant questions is "whether an objective observer, acquainted with the text, legislative history, and implementation of the statute, would perceive it as a state

---

[19] See, e.g., *Webster's Third New International Dictionary* 1190 (1993) (defining "invocation" as "a prayer of entreaty that is usually a call for the divine presence and is offered at the beginning of a meeting or service of worship").

endorsement of prayer in public schools." Regardless of the listener's support for, or objection to, the message, an objective Santa Fe High School student will unquestionably perceive the inevitable pregame prayer as stamped with her school's seal of approval.

The text and history of this policy, moreover, reinforce our objective student's perception that the prayer is, in actuality, encouraged by the school. When a governmental entity professes a secular purpose for an arguably religious policy, the government's characterization is, of course, entitled to some deference. But it is nonetheless the duty of the courts to "distinguish a sham secular purpose from a sincere one."

According to the District, the secular purposes of the policy are to "foster free expression of private persons . . . as well [as to] solemnize sporting events, promote good sportsmanship and student safety, and establish an appropriate environment for competition." We note, however, that the District's approval of only one specific kind of message, an "invocation," is not necessary to further any of these purposes. Additionally, the fact that only one student is permitted to give a content-limited message suggests that this policy does little to "foster free expression." Furthermore, regardless of whether one considers a sporting event an appropriate occasion for solemnity, the use of an invocation to foster such solemnity is impermissible when, in actuality, it constitutes prayer sponsored by the school. And it is unclear what type of message would be both appropriately "solemnizing" under the District's policy and yet non-religious.

Most striking to us is the evolution of the current policy from the long-sanctioned office of "Student Chaplain" to the candidly titled "Prayer at Football Games" regulation. This history indicates that the District intended to preserve the practice of prayer before football games. The conclusion that the District viewed the October policy simply as a continuation of the previous policies is dramatically illustrated by the fact that the school did not conduct a new election, pursuant to the current policy, to replace the results of the previous election, which occurred under the former policy. Given these observations, and in light of the school's history of regular delivery of a student-led prayer at athletic events, it is reasonable to infer that the specific purpose of the policy was to preserve a popular "state-sponsored religious practice." *Lee*, 505 U.S., 596.

School sponsorship of a religious message is impermissible because it sends the ancillary message to members of the audience who are nonadherents "that they are outsiders, not full members of the political community, and an accompanying message to adherents that they are insiders, favored members of the political community." *Lynch*, 465 U.S., 688 (O'CONNOR, J., concurring). The delivery of such a message—over the school's public address system, by a speaker representing the student body, under the supervision of school faculty, and pursuant to a school policy that explicitly and implicitly encourages public prayer—is not properly characterized as "private" speech.

### III

The District next argues that its football policy is distinguishable from the graduation prayer in *Lee* because it does not coerce students to participate in religious observances. Its argument has two parts: first, that there is no impermissible government coercion because the pregame messages are the product of student choices; and second, that there is really no coercion at all because attendance at an extracurricular event, unlike a graduation ceremony, is voluntary.

The reasons just discussed explaining why the alleged "circuit-breaker" mechanism of the dual elections and student speaker do not turn public speech into private speech also demonstrate why these mechanisms do not insulate the school from the coercive element of the final message. In fact, this aspect of the District's argument exposes anew the concerns that are created by the majoritarian election system. The parties' stipulation clearly states that the issue resolved in the first election was "whether a student would deliver prayer at varsity football games," and the controversy in this case demonstrates that the views of the students are not unanimous on that issue.

One of the purposes served by the Establishment Clause is to remove debate over this kind of issue from governmental supervision or control. We explained in *Lee* that the "preservation and transmission of religious beliefs and worship is a responsibility and a choice committed to the private sphere." 505 U.S., 589. The two student elections authorized by the policy, coupled with the debates that presumably must precede each, impermissibly invade that private sphere. The election mechanism, when considered in light of the history in which the policy in question evolved, reflects a device the District put in place that determines whether religious messages will be delivered at home football games. The mechanism encourages divisiveness along religious lines in a public school setting, a result at odds with the Establishment Clause. Although it is true that the ultimate choice of student speaker is "attributable to the students," the District's decision to hold the constitutionally problematic election is clearly "a choice attributable to the State," *Lee*, 505 U.S., 587.

The District further argues that attendance at the commencement ceremonies at issue in *Lee* "differs dramatically" from attendance at high school football games, which it contends "are of no more than passing interest to many students" and are "decidedly extracurricular," thus dissipating any coercion. Attendance at a high school football game, unlike showing up for class, is certainly not required in order to receive a diploma. Moreover, we may assume that the District is correct in arguing that the informal pressure to attend an athletic event is not as strong as a senior's desire to attend her own graduation ceremony.

There are some students, however, such as cheerleaders, members of the band, and, of course, the team members themselves, for whom seasonal commitments mandate their attendance, sometimes for class credit. The District also minimizes the importance to many students of attending and participating in extracurricular activities as part of a complete educational experience. As we noted in *Lee*, "law reaches past formalism." 505 U.S., 595. To assert that high school students do not feel immense social pressure, or have a truly genuine desire, to be involved in the extracurricular event that is American high school football is "formalistic in the extreme." We stressed in *Lee* the obvious observation that "adolescents are often susceptible to pressure from their peers towards conformity, and that the influence is strongest in matters of social convention." *Id.*, 593. High school home football games are traditional gatherings of a school community; they bring together students and faculty as well as friends and family from years present and past to root for a common cause. Undoubtedly, the games are not important to some students, and they voluntarily choose not to attend. For many others, however, the choice between whether to attend these games or to risk facing a personally offensive religious ritual is in no practical sense an easy one. The Constitution, moreover, demands that the school may not force this difficult choice upon these students for "it is a tenet of the First Amendment that the State cannot require one of its citizens to forfeit his or her rights and benefits as the price of resisting conformance to state-sponsored religious practice." *Id.*, 596.

Even if we regard every high school student's decision to attend a home football game as purely voluntary, we are nevertheless persuaded that the delivery of a pregame prayer has the improper effect of coercing those present to participate in an act of religious worship. For "the government may no more use social pressure to enforce orthodoxy than it may use more direct means." *Id.*, 594. As in *Lee*, "what to most believers may seem nothing more than a reasonable request that the nonbeliever respect their religious practices, in a school context may appear to the nonbeliever or dissenter to be an attempt to employ the machinery of the State to enforce a religious orthodoxy." *Id.*, 592. The constitutional command will not permit the District "to exact religious conformity from a student as the price" of joining her classmates at a varsity football game.

The Religion Clauses of the First Amendment prevent the government from making any law respecting the establishment of religion or prohibiting the free exercise thereof. By no means do these commands impose a prohibition on all religious activity in our public schools. Indeed, the common purpose of the Religion Clauses "is to secure religious liberty." *Engel v. Vitale*, 370 U.S. 421, 430 (1962). Thus, nothing in the Constitution as interpreted by this Court prohibits any public school student from voluntarily praying at any time before, during, or after the schoolday. But the religious liberty protected by the Constitution is abridged when the State affirmatively sponsors the particular religious practice of prayer.

## IV

Finally, the District argues repeatedly that the Does have made a premature facial challenge to the October policy that necessarily must fail. The District emphasizes, quite correctly, that until a student actually delivers a solemnizing message under the latest version of the policy, there can be no certainty that any of the statements or invocations will be religious. Thus, it concludes, the October policy necessarily survives a facial challenge.

This argument, however, assumes that we are concerned only with the serious constitutional injury that occurs when a student is forced to participate in an act of religious worship because she chooses to attend a school event. But the Constitution also requires that we keep in mind "the myriad, subtle ways in which Establishment Clause values can be eroded," *Lynch*, 465 U.S., 694 (O'CONNOR, J., concurring), and that we guard against other different, yet equally important, constitutional injuries. One is the mere passage by the District of a policy that has the purpose and perception of government establishment of religion. Another is the implementation of a governmental electoral process that subjects the issue of prayer to a majoritarian vote.

The District argues that the facial challenge must fail because "Santa Fe's Football Policy cannot be invalidated on the basis of some 'possibility or even likelihood' of an unconstitutional application." Our Establishment Clause cases involving facial challenges, however, have not focused solely on the possible applications of the statute, but rather have considered whether the statute has an unconstitutional purpose. . . . Under the *Lemon* standard, a court must invalidate a statute if it lacks "a secular legislative purpose." *Lemon v. Kurtz-man*, 403 U.S. 602, 612 (1971). It is therefore proper, as part of this facial challenge, for us to examine the purpose of the October policy.

As discussed, the text of the October policy alone reveals that it has an unconstitutional purpose. The plain language of the policy clearly spells out the extent of school involvement in both the election of the speaker and the content of the message. Additionally, the text of the October policy specifies only one, clearly preferred message—that of Santa Fe's traditional religious "invocation." Finally, the extremely selective access of the policy and other content restrictions confirm that it is not a content-neutral regulation that creates a limited public forum for the expression of student speech. Our examination, however, need not stop at an analysis of the text of the policy.

This case comes to us as the latest step in developing litigation brought as a challenge to institutional practices that unquestionably violated the Establishment Clause. One of those practices was the District's long-established tradition of sanctioning student-led prayer at varsity football games. The narrow question before us is whether implementation of the October policy insulates the continuation of such prayers from constitutional scrutiny. It does not. Our inquiry into this question not only can, but must, include an examination of the circumstances surrounding its enactment. Whether a government activity violates the Establishment Clause is "in large part a legal question to be answered on the basis of judicial interpretation of social facts. . . . Every government practice must be judged in its unique circumstances. . . ." *Lynch*, 465 U.S., 693-694 (O'CONNOR, J., concurring). Our discussion in the previous sections demonstrates that in this case the District's direct involvement with school prayer exceeds constitutional limits.

The District, nevertheless, asks us to pretend that we do not recognize what every Santa Fe High School student understands clearly—that this policy is about prayer. The District further asks us to accept what is obviously untrue: that these messages are necessary to "solemnize" a football game and that this single-student, year-long position is essential to the protection of student speech. We refuse to turn a blind eye to the context in which this policy arose, and that context quells any doubt that this policy was implemented with the purpose of endorsing school prayer.

Therefore, the simple enactment of this policy, with the purpose and perception of school endorsement of student prayer, was a constitutional violation. We need not wait for the inevitable to confirm and magnify the constitutional injury. In *Wallace*, for example, we invalidated Alabama's as yet unimplemented and voluntary "moment of silence" statute based on our conclusion that it was enacted "for the sole purpose of expressing the State's endorsement of prayer activities for one minute at the beginning of each school day." Therefore, even if no Santa Fe High School student were ever to offer a religious message, the October policy fails a facial challenge because the attempt by the District to encourage prayer is also at issue. Government efforts to endorse religion cannot evade constitutional reproach based solely on the remote possibility that those attempts may fail.

This policy likewise does not survive a facial challenge because it impermissibly imposes upon the student body a majoritarian election on the issue of prayer. Through its election scheme, the District has established a governmental electoral mechanism that turns the school into a forum for religious debate. It further empowers the student body majority with the authority to subject students of minority views to constitutionally improper messages. The award of that power alone, regardless of the students' ultimate use of it, is not acceptable.[23] Like the referendum in *Southworth*, the election mechanism established by the District undermines the essential protection of minority viewpoints. Such a system encourages divisiveness along religious lines and threatens the imposition of coercion upon those students not desiring to participate in a religious exercise. Simply by establishing this school-related procedure, which entrusts the inherently nongovernmental subject of religion to a majoritarian vote, a constitutional violation has occurred.[24] No further injury is required for the policy to fail a facial challenge.

To properly examine this policy on its face, we "must be deemed aware of the history and context of the community and forum," *Pinette*, 515 U.S., 780 (O'CONNOR, J., concurring in part and concurring in judgment). Our examination of those circumstances above leads to the conclusion that this policy does not provide the District with the constitutional safe harbor it sought. The policy is invalid on its face because it establishes an improper majoritarian election on religion, and unquestionably has the purpose and creates the perception of encouraging the delivery of prayer at a series of important school events.

The judgment of the Court of Appeals is, accordingly, affirmed.

*It is so ordered.*

CHIEF JUSTICE REHNQUIST, with whom JUSTICE SCALIA and JUSTICE THOMAS join, dissenting.

The Court distorts existing precedent to conclude that the school district's student-message program is invalid on its face under the Establishment Clause. But even more disturbing than its holding is the tone of the Court's opinion; it bristles with hostility to all things religious in public life. Neither the holding nor the tone of the opinion is faithful to the meaning of the Establishment Clause, when it is recalled that George Washington himself, at the request of the very Congress which passed the Bill of Rights, proclaimed a day of "public thanksgiving and prayer, to be observed by acknowledging with grateful hearts the many and signal favors of Almighty God."

We do not learn until late in the Court's opinion that respondents in this case challenged the district's student-message program at football games before it had been put into practice. As the Court explained in *United States v.*

---

[23] THE CHIEF JUSTICE accuses us of "essentially invalidating all student elections." This is obvious hyperbole. We have concluded that the resulting religious message under this policy would be attributable to the school, not just the student. For this reason, we now hold only that the District's decision to allow the student majority to control whether students of minority views are subjected to a school-sponsored prayer violates the Establishment Clause.

[24] THE CHIEF JUSTICE contends that we have "misconstrued the nature . . . [of] the policy as being an election on 'prayer' and 'religion.'" We therefore reiterate that the District has stipulated to the facts that the most recent election was held "to determine whether a student would deliver prayer at varsity football games," that the "students chose to allow a student to say a prayer at football games," and that a second election was then held "to determine which student would deliver the prayer." Furthermore, the policy was titled "Prayer at Football Games." Although the District has since eliminated the word "prayer" from the policy, it apparently viewed that change as sufficiently minor as to make holding a new election unnecessary.

*Salerno*, 481 U.S. 739, 745 (1987), the fact that a policy might "operate un-constitutionally under some conceivable set of circumstances is insufficient to render it wholly invalid." While there is an exception to this principle in the First Amendment overbreadth context because of our concern that people may refrain from speech out of fear of prosecution, there is no similar justification for Establishment Clause cases. No speech will be "chilled" by the existence of a government policy that might unconstitutionally endorse religion over nonreligion. Therefore, the question is not whether the district's policy *may be* applied in violation of the Establishment Clause, but whether it inevitably will be.

The Court, venturing into the realm of prophesy, decides that it "need not wait for the inevitable" and invalidates the district's policy on its face. To do so, it applies the most rigid version of the oft-criticized test of *Lemon v. Kurtzman*, 403 U.S. 602 (1971).[1]

*Lemon* has had a checkered career in the decisional law of this Court. . . .

Even if it were appropriate to apply the *Lemon* test here, the district's student-message policy should not be invalidated on its face. The Court applies *Lemon* and holds that the "policy is invalid on its face because it establishes an improper majoritarian election on religion, and unquestionably has the purpose and creates the perception of encouraging the delivery of prayer at a series of important school events." The Court's reliance on each of these conclusions misses the mark.

First, the Court misconstrues the nature of the "majoritarian election" permitted by the policy as being an election on "prayer" and "religion."[2] To the contrary, the election permitted by the policy is a two-fold process whereby students vote first on whether to have a student speaker before football games at all, and second, if the students vote to have such a speaker, on who that speaker will be. It is conceivable that the election could become one in which student candidates campaign on platforms that focus on whether or not they will pray if elected. It is also conceivable that the election could lead to a Christian prayer before 90 percent of the football games. If, upon implementation, the policy operated in this fashion, we would have a record before us to review whether the policy, as applied, violated the Establishment Clause or unduly suppressed minority viewpoints. But it is possible that the students might vote not to have a pregame speaker, in which case there would be no threat of a constitutional violation. It is also possible that the election would not focus on prayer, but on public speaking ability or social popularity. And if student cam-

---

[1] The Court rightly points out that in facial challenges in the Establishment Clause context, we have looked to *Lemon's* three factors to "guide the general nature of our inquiry." (citing *Bowen v. Kendrick*, 487 U.S. 589, 602 [1988]). In *Bowen*, we looked to *Lemon* as such a guide and determined that a federal grant program was not invalid on its face, noting that "it has not been the Court's practice, in considering facial challenges to statutes of this kind, to strike them down in anticipation that particular applications may result in unconstitutional use of funds." 487 U.S., 612. But here the Court, rather than look to *Lemon* as a guide, applies *Lemon's* factors stringently and ignores *Bowen's* admonition that mere anticipation of unconstitutional applications does not warrant striking a policy on its face.

[2] The Court attempts to support its misinterpretation of the nature of the election process by noting that the district stipulated to facts about the most recent election. Of course, the most recent election was conducted under the *previous* policy—a policy that required an elected student speaker to give a pregame invocation. There has not been an election under the policy at issue here, which expressly allows the student speaker to give a message as opposed to an invocation.

paigning did begin to focus on prayer, the school might decide to implement reasonable campaign restrictions.[3]

But the Court ignores these possibilities by holding that merely granting the student body the power to elect a speaker that may choose to pray, "regardless of the students' ultimate use of it, is not acceptable." The Court so holds despite that any speech that may occur as a result of the election process here would be *private*, not *government*, speech. The elected student, not the government, would choose what to say. Support for the Court's holding cannot be found in any of our cases. And it essentially invalidates all student elections. A newly elected student body president, or even a newly elected prom king or queen, could use opportunities for public speaking to say prayers. Under the Court's view, the mere grant of power to the students to vote for such offices, in light of the fear that those elected might publicly pray, violates the Establishment Clause.

Second, with respect to the policy's purpose, the Court holds that "the simple enactment of this policy, with the purpose and perception of school endorsement of student prayer, was a constitutional violation." But the policy itself has plausible secular purposes: "To solemnize the event, to promote good sportsmanship and student safety, and to establish the appropriate environment for the competition." Where a governmental body "expresses a plausible secular purpose" for an enactment, "courts should generally defer to that stated intent." The Court grants no deference to—and appears openly hostile toward—the policy's stated purposes, and wastes no time in concluding that they are a sham.

For example, the Court dismisses the secular purpose of solemnization by claiming that it "invites and encourages religious messages." The Court so concludes based on its rather strange view that a "religious message is the most obvious means of solemnizing an event." But it is easy to think of solemn messages that are not religious in nature, for example urging that a game be fought fairly. And sporting events often begin with a solemn rendition of our national anthem, with its concluding verse "And this be our motto: 'In God is our trust.'" Under the Court's logic, a public school that sponsors the singing of the national anthem before football games violates the Establishment Clause. Although the Court apparently believes that solemnizing football games is an illegitimate purpose, the voters in the school district seem to disagree. Nothing in the Establishment Clause prevents them from making this choice.[4]

The Court bases its conclusion that the true purpose of the policy is to endorse student prayer on its view of the school district's history of

---

[3] The Court's reliance on language regarding the student referendum in *Southworth* to support its conclusion with respect to the election process is misplaced. That case primarily concerned free speech, and, more particularly, mandated financial support of a public forum. But as stated above, if this case were in the "as applied" context and we were presented with the appropriate record, our language in *Southworth* could become more applicable. In fact, *Southworth* itself demonstrates the impropriety of making a decision with respect to the election process without a record of its operation. There we remanded in part for a determination of how the referendum functions.

[4] The Court also determines that the use of the term "invocation" in the policy is an express endorsement of that type of message over all others. A less cynical view of the policy's text is that it permits many types of messages, including invocations. That a policy tolerates religion does not mean that it improperly endorses it. Indeed, as the majority reluctantly admits, the Free Exercise Clause mandates such tolerance. . . .

Establishment Clause violations and the context in which the policy was written, that is, as "the latest step in developing litigation brought as a challenge to institutional practices that unquestionably violated the Establishment Clause." But the context—attempted compliance with a District Court order—actually demonstrates that the school district was acting diligently to come within the governing constitutional law. The District Court ordered the school district to formulate a policy consistent with Fifth Circuit precedent, which permitted a school district to have a prayer-only policy. See *Jones v. Clear Creek Independent School Dist.*, 977 F.2d 963 (CA5 1992). But the school district went further than required by the District Court order and eventually settled on a policy that gave the student speaker a choice to deliver either an invocation or a message. In so doing, the school district exhibited a willingness to comply with, and exceed, Establishment Clause restrictions. Thus, the policy cannot be viewed as having a sectarian purpose.

The Court also relies on our decision in *Lee v. Weisman*, 505 U.S. 577 (1992), to support its conclusion. In *Lee*, we concluded that the content of the speech at issue, a graduation prayer given by a rabbi, was "directed and controlled" by a school official. In other words, at issue in *Lee* was *government* speech. Here, by contrast, the potential speech at issue, if the policy had been allowed to proceed, would be a message or invocation selected or created by a student. That is, if there were speech at issue here, it would be *private* speech. The "crucial difference between *government* speech endorsing religion, which the Establishment Clause forbids, and *private* speech endorsing religion, which the Free Speech and Free Exercise Clauses protect," applies with particular force to the question of endorsement. *Board of Ed. of Westside Community Schools v. Mergens*, 496 U.S. 226, 250 (1990) (plurality opinion) (emphasis in original).

Had the policy been put into practice, the students may have chosen a speaker according to wholly secular criteria—like good public speaking skills or social popularity—and the student speaker may have chosen, on her own accord, to deliver a religious message. Such an application of the policy would likely pass constitutional muster.

Finally, the Court seems to demand that a government policy be completely neutral as to content or be considered one that endorses religion. This is undoubtedly a new requirement, as our Establishment Clause jurisprudence simply does not mandate "content neutrality." That concept is found in our First Amendment *speech* cases and is used as a guide for determining when we apply strict scrutiny. . . . The Court seems to think that the fact that the policy is not content neutral somehow controls the Establishment Clause inquiry.

But even our speech jurisprudence would not require that all public school actions with respect to student speech be content neutral. Schools do not violate the First Amendment every time they restrict student speech to certain categories. But under the Court's view, a school policy under which the student body president is to solemnize the graduation ceremony by giving a favorable introduction to the guest speaker would be facially unconstitutional. Solemnization "invites and encourages" prayer and the policy's content limitations prohibit the student body president from giving a solemn, yet non-religious, message like "commentary on United States foreign policy."

The policy at issue here may be applied in an unconstitutional manner, but it will be time enough to invalidate it if that is found to be the case. I would reverse the judgment of the Court of Appeals.

## NOTES AND QUESTIONS

1. What were the factors that led the Court majority to conclude that the policy permitted state-endorsed religious speech rather than private religious speech? By what route do the dissenters arrive at the opposite conclusion?

2. How large a role did the history surrounding the development of the policy play in the Court's decision? Is the Court's focus on this context appropriate? The dissenters argue that the Court interprets at least some of this history incorrectly. Do they have a point?

3. According to the Court majority, the election component of the policy, which was portrayed by the school as a way to "break the circuit" between the school and the prayers, actually had the effect of exacerbating the constitutional violation. Why?

4. Should the Court have waited for the new policy to be implemented before rejecting it, as the dissent argues? In the final section of the opinion, how does the Court majority characterize the school district's arguments regarding the purpose and effect of the policy? How is the Court's analysis on the issue similar to its analysis in the *Wallace v. Jaffree* case?

5. How does the Court majority in the *Santa Fe* case use the *Lee v. Weisman* precedent? As you know, Justice Kennedy wrote the majority opinion in *Lee v. Weisman*. Kennedy joined the majority opinion in the *Santa Fe* case. Is this evidence that Justice Kennedy's Establishment Clause views have changed or stayed the same? Explain your reasoning.

6. Do you agree with Chief Justice Rehnquist that the tone of the majority opinion "bristles with hostility to all things religious in public life"? If so, what would you point to in the majority opinion that reflects this tone? What evidence would you cite that cuts against Rehnquist's argument on this point? Are the dissenters suggesting that the majority opposes any visible or vocal place for religion in American life? Or, are they arguing that the majority opposes any religious expression on government property or in other government settings? In either case, is the characterization fair?

While these cases resolved important questions of law, they also left open many related issues for litigants to wrestle over in the lower courts. For example, in 1999 a federal court of appeals considered a challenge to the constitutionality of an Alabama statute permitting "non-sectarian, non-proselytizing," student-initiated prayers, invocations, and benedictions during compulsory and non-compulsory school-related events, including sporting events and graduation ceremonies. In this case, *Chandler v. James*,[1] the trial court ruled in favor of the plaintiffs and issued a permanent injunction barring the official organization and sponsorship by the school of religious activities.

On appeal, the state challenged the permanent injunction issued by the trial court insofar as it prohibited the school from "permitting" vocal student prayer or other "devotional speech."[2] The appellate court stated:

While the injunction makes clear that it does not prohibit students from voluntarily praying while at school or at school-related events, either individually or with each other, so long as the prayer is purely *private*, it prohibits all prayer or other devotional speech in situations which are not purely private, such as aloud in the classroom, over the public address system, or as part of the program at school-related assemblies and sporting events, or at a graduation ceremony. Furthermore, the prohibition applies to bar not only school personnel from leading or participating in such public or vocal prayer or other devotional speech or Bible reading, but also *requires school officials to forbid students or other private individuals from doing so while in school or at school-related events.*[3]

The appellate court ruled that the district court improperly enjoined the school "from permitting student initiated religious speech in its schools."[4] The court of appeals stated:

It is true that ordinarily religious speech by private parties cannot establish religion, even if it occurs in a public institution, such as a school. *Mergens*, 496 U.S., 250. On the other hand, it is clear that private parties' religious speech can violate the Establishment Clause if the State uses such parties as surrogates to accomplish what the State may not do. For example, if a school board may not constitutionally write and require students to recite a prayer, as it most assuredly may not, *Engel v. Vitale*, 370 U.S. 421 (1962), the school board may not avoid this prohibition by delegating this function to others. *Lee*, 505 U.S., 577 (invalidating school board policy permitting clergy to give prayers at graduation); *Karen B. v. Treen*, 653 F.2d 897 (5th Cir. 1981) (invalidating school board guidelines which required student or teacher-led prayers in classrooms). Nor may the State establish a policy which "permits" private parties to speak, but then limits their speech to prayer or other devotional speech.

When the State *commands* religious speech, it steps over the Constitution to establish religion. In each of these cases, it is the *State's decision to create an exclusively religious medium* which violates the Establishment Clause; *not* the private parties' religious speech. It is not the "permitting" of religious speech which dooms these policies, but rather the *requirement* that the speech be religious, i.e., invocations, benedictions, or prayers.[5]

The court explained that this reasoning was consistent with the Supreme Court's reasoning in *Engel v. Vitale*, where it held that the government could not prescribe any form of prayer. The court said that, although "[s]ome lower courts have extended *Engel* to require government to prohibit *any* public expression of religious belief in schools," . . . "this is not what the Court said . . ."[6] The appellate court read *Engel* to "merely make clear that the Establishment Clause prohibits the government from commanding prayer and prescribing its form."[7]

The court summarized the issues before it:

Ultimately, the issue in this case is not whether school officials may prescribe prayer or enlist surrogates to that end. They may not. Nor is the issue whether school officials may prohibit religious speech in schools, or censor the content of that speech. They may not. The real issue is what sort of time, place, and manner limits may be imposed upon genuinely student-initiated religious speech in schools? When may students pray? Where may they pray? Under what circumstances may they pray?[8]

The court then articulated some principles to guide these inquiries. It stated "that genuinely student-initiated religious speech must be permitted" but "[o]n the other hand, even genuinely student-intiated religious speech may constitute state action if the State *participates in or supervises* the speech."[9] Thus, "student religious speech must be without oversight, without supervision, subject only to the same reasonable time, place, and manner restrictions as all other student speech in school." The court also noted that "a student's right to express his personal religious beliefs does not extend to using the machinery of the state as a vehicle for converting his audience" and that "[p]roselytizing speech is inherently coercive and, the Constitution prohibits it from the government's pulpit."[10]

The court concluded:

> The Permanent Injunction [ ] forbids [the school district] from "permitting" students to speak religiously. This it cannot constitutionally do. So long as school personnel do not participate in or actively supervise student-initiated speech, DeKalb cannot constitutionally prohibit students from speaking religiously and the Permanent Injunction cannot require it to.[11]

When the Supreme Court handed down its decision in the *Santa Fe* case, it vacated the judgment of the federal appellate court in *Chandler v. James* and remanded the case for further proceedings in light of its decision in the *Santa Fe* case. Upon reconsideration, the appellate court concluded that its earlier decision was "not in conflict with the Supreme Court's decision in *Santa Fe*" and therefore reinstated its original opinion in this case. It explained how its judgment was consistent with the Court's ruling in *Santa Fe*:

> It is not the public context that makes some speech the State's. It is the entanglement with the State. What the Court condemned in *Santa Fe* was not private speech endorsing religion, but the delivery of a school-sponsored prayer. Remove the school sponsorship, and the prayer is private. In *Chandler I*, we held that such prayer must be permitted.
>
> Therefore, if "nothing in the Constitution . . . prohibits any public school student from voluntarily praying at any time before, during, or after the school day," *Santa Fe*, then it does not prohibit prayer aloud or in front of others, as in the case of an audience assembled for some other purpose. *Chandler I*, 180 F.3d, 1261. So long as the prayer is *genuinely student-initiated*, and not the product of any school policy which actively or surreptitiously encourages it, the speech is private and it is protected.[12]

---

### NOTES AND QUESTIONS

1. Consider the last two sentences of the above opinion in *Chandler II*. Is the court saying that students may engage in vocal prayer and other religious expression in front of fellow classmates in a school-run event, provided the expression is "genuinely student-initiated?" Is this consistent with the Supreme Court's holdings in *Lee* or *Santa Fe*?

2. Assume a public high school organized an assembly and invited five students who had been voted the best speakers in their communications classes to give speeches on topics of their choosing, as long as the speeches addressed a matter of public importance and did not cause disruption or include any foul language. No school officials reviewed the speeches in advance. One student argued that his fellow students should support a particular candidate in an upcoming presidential election, another spoke against legal prohibitions on downloading music from the Internet and another spoke in favor of school

uniforms. The other two students included religious themes in their speeches. One student told the story of how he had been inspired by his minister to oppose the Iraq war and another spoke against abortion and suicide, citing Bible verses and concluding by urging her fellow students "to choose life, the abundant life that Christ Jesus called you to live." Would these latter two students' speeches pass constitutional muster under the *Chandler* decision and Supreme Court precedent?

CHAPTER 18

# RELIGION AND THE PUBLIC SCHOOLS
## RELIGION AND THE CURRICULUM AND PRESIDENTIAL
## GUIDELINES ON RELIGION AND PUBLIC SCHOOLS

The U.S. Supreme Court's decisions on released time and school prayer are not the only instances in which the Court has intervened in the sensitive area of religion and public schools. Another issue the Court has addressed concerns some of the ways in which religion has intersected with the curricula that is taught in our nation's public schools.

Should the government be permitted to alter certain secular courses of study due to religious objections? Alternatively, must particular students be excused from aspects of courses of study due to their personal religious objections to certain materials? May schools present academic courses that study religion's place in history, its influence on literature and the arts, and the nature and trajectory of the world's great religions? Is it constitutionally permissible for secondary public schools to teach about the Bible and other sacred texts in a scholarly manner? These are some of the issues courts have grappled with in this challenging area.

The first part of this chapter focuses mostly on aspects of the debate that the Supreme Court has had the occasion to address directly. It begins with a consideration of two attempts to alter public school science curricula due to religious objections. The chapter then considers the issue of what are called "opt outs"—requests made by particular students and their parents to refrain from reading certain books or studying particular aspects of school curricula due to their personal religious objections to such materials. Cases involving these kinds of facts have not yet reached the Supreme Court, so this chapter highlights one prominent lower court case that addresses these issues. Next the chapter focuses on religious displays in the public school classroom by focusing on the 1980 case of *Stone v. Graham*. This case involved a Kentucky statute that required the posting of a copy of the Ten Commandments in every public school classroom in the state. Here the Court considered whether these displays were properly integrated into an academic course of study or whether they were constitutionally impermissible attempts by the public schools to inspire religious devotion. Finally, this part of the chapter briefly considers the drive to teach about religion in an academic way in the public schools, including some of the promise and perils of that movement.

The second part of this chapter steps back from the specific controversies over religion and the public schools. It presents the attempts of two presidents, Bill Clinton and George

717

*Jones*, 13 Wallace [80 U.S.] 679, 728. This has been the interpretation of the great First Amendment which this Court has applied in the many and subtle problems which the ferment of our national life has presented for decision within the Amendment's broad command.

Judicial interposition in the operation of the public school system of the Nation raises problems requiring care and restraint. Our courts, however, have not failed to apply the First Amendment's mandate in our educational system where essential to safeguard the fundamental values of freedom of speech and inquiry and of belief. By and large, public education in our Nation is committed to the control of state and local authorities. Courts do not and cannot intervene in the resolution of conflicts which arise in the daily operation of school systems and which do not directly and sharply implicate basic constitutional values. On the other hand, "the vigilant protection of constitutional freedoms is nowhere more vital than in the community of American schools," *Shelton v. Tucker*, 364 U.S. 479, 487 (1960). As this Court said in *Keyishian v. Board of Regents*, the First Amendment "does not tolerate laws that cast a pall of orthodoxy over the classroom." 385 U.S. 589, 603 (1967). . . .

There is and can be no doubt that the First Amendment does not permit the State to require that teaching and learning must be tailored to the principles or prohibitions of any religious sect or dogma. In *Everson v. Board of Education*, this Court, in upholding a state law to provide free bus service to school children, including those attending parochial schools, said: "Neither [a State nor the Federal Government] can pass laws which aid one religion, aid all religions, or prefer one religion over another." 330 U.S. 1, 15 (1947).

At the following Term of Court, in *McCollum v. Board of Education*, 333 U.S. 203 (1948), the Court held that Illinois could not release pupils from class to attend classes of instruction in the school buildings in the religion of their choice. This, it said, would involve the State in using tax-supported property for religious purposes, thereby breaching the "wall of separation" which, according to Jefferson, the First Amendment was intended to erect between church and state. *Id.*, 211. . . . While study of religions and of the Bible from a literary and historic viewpoint, presented objectively as part of a secular program of education, need not collide with the First Amendment's prohibition, the State may not adopt programs or practices in its public schools or colleges which "aid or oppose" any religion. This prohibition is absolute. It forbids alike the preference of a religious doctrine or the prohibition of theory which is deemed antagonistic to a particular dogma. As Mr. Justice Clark stated in *Joseph Burstyn, Inc. v. Wilson*, "the state has no legitimate interest in protecting any or all religions from views distasteful to them . . . ." 343 U.S. 495, 505 (1952). The test was stated as follows in *Abington School District v. Schempp* 374 U.S. 203, 222: "What are the purpose and the primary effect of the enactment? If either is the advancement or inhibition of religion then the enactment exceeds the scope of legislative power as circumscribed by the Constitution."

These precedents inevitably determine the result in the present case. The State's undoubted right to prescribe the curriculum for its public schools does not carry with it the right to prohibit, on pain of criminal penalty, the teaching of a scientific theory or doctrine where that prohibition is based upon reasons that violate the First Amendment. It is much too late to argue that the State may impose upon the teachers in its schools any conditions that it chooses, however restrictive they may be of constitutional guarantees. *Keyishian*, 385 U.S., 605-606.

In the present case, there can be no doubt that Arkansas has sought to pre-vent its teachers from discussing the theory of evolution because it is contrary to the belief of some that the Book of Genesis must be the exclusive source of doctrine as to the origin of man. No suggestion has been made that Arkansas' law may be justified by considerations of state policy other than the religious views of some of its citizens. It is clear that fundamentalist sectarian conviction was and is the law's reason for existence. Its antecedent, Tennessee's "monkey law," candidly stated its purpose: to make it unlawful "to teach any theory that denies the story of the Divine Creation of man as taught in the Bible, and to teach instead that man has descended from a lower order of animals." Perhaps the sensational publicity attendant upon the *Scopes* trial induced Arkansas to adopt less explicit language. It eliminated Tennessee's reference to "the story of the Divine Creation of man" as taught in the Bible, but there is no doubt that the motivation for the law was the same: to suppress the teaching of a theory which, it was thought, "denied" the divine creation of man.

Arkansas' law cannot be defended as an act of religious neutrality. Arkansas did not seek to excise from the curricula of its schools and universities all discussion of the origin of man. The law's effort was confined to an attempt to blot out a particular theory because of its supposed conflict with the Biblical account, literally read. Plainly, the law is contrary to the mandate of the First, and in violation of the Fourteenth, Amendment to the Constitution.

The judgment of the Supreme Court of Arkansas is

*Reversed.*

▦ MR. JUSTICE BLACK, concurring. . . .

It is plain that a state law prohibiting all teaching of human development or biology is constitutionally quite different from a law that compels a teacher to teach as true only one theory of a given doctrine. It would be difficult to make a First Amendment case out of a state law eliminating the subject of higher mathematics, or astronomy, or biology from its curriculum. And, for all the Supreme Court of Arkansas has said, this particular Act may prohibit that and nothing else. This Court, however, treats the Arkansas Act as though it made it a misdemeanor to teach or to use a book that teaches that evolution is true. But it is not for this Court to arrogate to itself the power to determine the scope of Arkansas statutes. Since the highest court of Arkansas has deliberately refused to give its statute that meaning, we should not presume to do so.

It seems to me that in this situation the statute is too vague for us to strike it down on any ground but that: vagueness. Under this statute as construed by the Arkansas Supreme Court, a teacher cannot know whether he is forbidden to mention Darwin's theory at all or only free to discuss it as long as he refrains from contending that it is true. It is an established rule that a statute which leaves an ordinary man so doubtful about its meaning that he cannot know when he has violated it denies him the first essential of due process. . . .

I find it difficult to agree with the Court's statement that "there can be no doubt that Arkansas has sought to prevent its teachers from discussing the theory of evolution because it is contrary to the belief of some that the Book of Genesis must be the exclusive source of doctrine as to the origin of man." It may be instead that the people's motive was merely that it would be best to remove this controversial subject from its schools; there is no reason I can imagine why a State is without power to withdraw from its curriculum any subject deemed too emotional and controversial for its public schools. And this Court has consistently held that it is not for us to invalidate a statute because of our views that the "motives" behind its passage were improper; it is simply too difficult to determine what those motives were.

A second question that arises for me is whether this Court's decision forbidding a State to exclude the subject of evolution from its schools infringes the religious freedom of those who consider evolution an anti-religious doctrine. If the theory is considered anti-religious, as the Court indicates, how can the State be bound by the Federal Constitution to permit its teachers to advocate such an "anti-religious" doctrine to schoolchildren? The very cases cited by the Court as supporting its conclusion hold that the State must be neutral, not favoring one religious or anti-religious view over another. The Darwinian theory is said to challenge the Bible's story of creation; so too have some of those who believe in the Bible, along with many others, challenged the Darwinian theory. Since there is no indication that the literal Biblical doctrine of the origin of man is included in the curriculum of Arkansas schools, does not the removal of the subject of evolution leave the State in a neutral position toward these supposedly competing religious and anti-religious doctrines? Unless this Court is prepared simply to write off as pure nonsense the views of those who consider evolution an anti-religious doctrine, then this issue presents problems under the Establishment Clause far more troublesome than are discussed in the Court's opinion. . . .

I would either strike down the Arkansas Act as too vague to enforce, or remand to the State Supreme Court for clarification of its holding and opinion.

[The concurring opinions of Justices Harlan and Stewart are omitted.]

---

## NOTES AND QUESTIONS

1. Writing for the Court, Justice Fortas says that "The First Amendment mandates governmental neutrality between religion and religion, and between religion and nonreligion." Can the government truly be neutral between religion and nonreligion when it is forbidden from inculcating religious doctrine but permitted to promote nonreligious ideas? Or, is this statement more directed at emphasizing the need for the government to refrain from promoting or denigrating religion? Can public schools refrain from promoting or denigrating religion when they are required to teach in a secular manner? How do you react to Justice Black's suggestion that teaching evolution may itself be anti-religious?

2. In his concurring opinion, Justice Black quarrels with the Court's statement that there was "no doubt" that the motivation for the prohibition on teaching evolutionary theory was religious in nature. What is the nature of Black's objections to this statement? Are his objections persuasive?

3. Suppose a school board directed school teachers to refrain from discussing homosexual family relationships in a unit about the family because it believes such relationships are heretical. Is that omission constitutional under the First Amendment? What if the school board gave the same direction but did so, it said, solely because the issue of homosexuality was too controversial?

4. In the majority opinion, Justice Abe Fortas begins his opinion by mentioning that the Arkansas law "was a product of the upsurge of 'fundamentalist' religious fervor of the [1920s]." He ends his opinion by stating, "[t]he law's effort was confined to an attempt to blot out a particular theory because of its supposed conflict with the Biblical account, literally read." Why do you think Justice Fortas made these kinds of specific references to a particular faith? Was it necessary and appropriate for him to refer to a particular strain of religious belief in these ways? Do you believe that these references strengthen or weaken the opinion?

5. Would it be constitutional for a school to teach about the fact that some people do not believe in evolutionary theory due to their religious convictions? How and when should such a discussion occur in the public schools?

---

Almost twenty years later, the Court faced a somewhat different issue in this area: whether it was constitutional for the state to forbid the teaching of evolution in public schools unless it was accompanied by instruction in "creation science." Louisiana passed such a law and defended it on the ground that it furthered the legitimate secular interest of academic freedom. The Court however, found that "the Creationism Act is designed either to promote the theory of creation science which embodies a particular religious tenet by requiring that creation science be taught whenever evolution is taught *or* to prohibit the teaching of a scientific theory disfavored by certain religious sects by forbidding the teaching of evolution when creation science is not also taught." Thus, it had an unconstitutional purpose—"restructur[ing] the science curriculum to conform with a particular religious viewpoint." As you read the opinions, consider the differences between the Court majority and the dissenters on both the merits of the case and the rationales used to decide it.

---

## EDWARDS v. AGUILLARD
## 482 U.S. 578 (1987)

JUSTICE BRENNAN delivered the opinion of the Court. (JUSTICE O'CONNOR joins all but Part II of this opinion.)

The question for decision is whether Louisiana's "Balanced Treatment for Creation-Science and Evolution-Science in Public School Instruction" Act (Creationism Act), La. Rev. Stat. Ann. §§ 17:286.1-17:286.7 (West 1982), is facially invalid as violative of the Establishment Clause of the First Amendment.

I

The Creationism Act forbids the teaching of the theory of evolution in public schools unless accompanied by instruction in "creation science." § 17:286.4A. No school is required to teach evolution or creation science.

If either is taught, however, the other must also be taught. The theories of evolution and creation science are statutorily defined as "the scientific evidences for [creation or evolution] and inferences from those scientific evidences." §§ 17.286.3(2) and (3).

Appellees, who include parents of children attending Louisiana public schools, Louisiana teachers, and religious leaders, challenged the constitutionality of the Act in District Court, seeking an injunction and declaratory relief. Appellants, Louisiana officials charged with implementing the Act, defended on the ground that the purpose of the Act is to protect a legitimate secular interest, namely, academic freedom. . . .

## II

The Establishment Clause forbids the enactment of any law "respecting an establishment of religion." The Court has applied a three-pronged test to determine whether legislation comports with the Establishment Clause. First, the legislature must have adopted the law with a secular purpose. Second, the statute's principal or primary effect must be one that neither advances nor inhibits religion. Third, the statute must not result in an excessive entanglement of government with religion. *Lemon v. Kurtzman*, 403 U.S. 602, 612-613 (1971). State action violates the Establishment Clause if it fails to satisfy any of these prongs.

In this case, the Court must determine whether the Establishment Clause was violated in the special context of the public elementary and secondary school system. States and local school boards are generally afforded considerable discretion in operating public schools. "At the same time . . . we have necessarily recognized that the discretion of the States and local school boards in matters of education must be exercised in a manner that comports with the transcendent imperatives of the First Amendment." *Board of Education, Island Trees Union Free School Dist. No. 26 v. Pico*, 457 U.S. 853, 864 (1982).

The Court has been particularly vigilant in monitoring compliance with the Establishment Clause in elementary and secondary schools. Families entrust public schools with the education of their children, but condition their trust on the understanding that the classroom will not purposely be used to advance religious views that may conflict with the private beliefs of the student and his or her family. Students in such institutions are impressionable and their attendance is involuntary. The State exerts great authority and coercive power through mandatory attendance requirements, and because of the students' emulation of teachers as role models and the children's susceptibility to peer pressure. Furthermore, "the public school is at once the symbol of our democracy and the most pervasive means for promoting our common destiny. In no activity of the State is it more vital to keep out divisive forces than in its schools . . . ." *McCollum v. Board of Education*, 333 U.S. 203, 231 (1948) (opinion of FRANKFURTER, J.). . . .

Therefore, in employing the three-pronged *Lemon* test, we must do so mindful of the particular concerns that arise in the context of public elementary and secondary schools. We now turn to the evaluation of the Act under the *Lemon* test.

## III

*Lemon*'s first prong focuses on the purpose that animated adoption of the Act. "The purpose prong of the *Lemon* test asks whether government's actual purpose is to endorse or disapprove of religion." *Lynch v. Donnelly*, 465 U.S. 668, 690 (1984) (O'CONNOR, J., concurring). A governmental intention to promote religion is clear when the State enacts a law to serve a religious purpose. This intention may be evidenced by promotion of religion in general, . . . or by advancement of a particular religious belief. . . . . If the law was enacted for the purpose of endorsing religion, "no consideration of the second or third criteria [of *Lemon*] is necessary." *Wallace v. Jaffree*, 472 U.S. 38, 56. In this case, appellants have identified no clear secular purpose for the Louisiana Act.

True, the Act's stated purpose is to protect academic freedom. This phrase might, in common parlance, be understood as referring to enhancing the freedom of teachers to teach what they will. The Court of Appeals, however, correctly concluded that the Act was not designed to further that goal. We find no merit in the State's argument that the "legislature may not [have] used the terms 'academic freedom' in the correct legal sense. They might have [had] in mind, instead, a basic concept of fairness; teaching all of the evidence." Even if "academic freedom" is read to mean "teaching all of the evidence" with respect to the origin of human beings, the Act does not further this purpose. The goal of providing a more comprehensive science curriculum is not furthered either by outlawing the teaching of evolution or by requiring the teaching of creation science.

## A

While the Court is normally deferential to a State's articulation of a secular purpose, it is required that the statement of such purpose be sincere and not a sham. As JUSTICE O'CONNOR stated in *Wallace*: "It is not a trivial matter, however, to require that the legislature manifest a secular purpose and omit all sectarian endorsements from its laws. That requirement is precisely tailored to the Establishment Clause's purpose of assuring that Government not intentionally endorse religion or a religious practice." 472 U.S., 75 (concurring in judgment).

It is clear from the legislative history that the purpose of the legislative sponsor, Senator Bill Keith, was to narrow the science curriculum. During the legislative hearings, Senator Keith stated: "My preference would be that neither [creationism nor evolution] be taught." Such a ban on teaching does not promote—indeed, it undermines—the provision of a comprehensive scientific education.

It is equally clear that requiring schools to teach creation science with evolution does not advance academic freedom. The Act does not grant teachers a flexibility that they did not already possess to supplant the present science curriculum with the presentation of theories, besides evolution, about the origin of life. Indeed, the Court of Appeals found that no law prohibited Louisiana public school teachers from teaching any scientific theory. As the president of the Louisiana Science Teachers Association testified, "any scientific concept that's based on established fact can be included in our curriculum already, and no legislation allowing this is necessary." The Act provides Louisiana schoolteachers with no new authority. Thus the stated purpose is not furthered by it. . . .

Furthermore, the goal of basic "fairness" is hardly furthered by the Act's discriminatory preference for the teaching of creation science and against the teaching of evolution. While requiring that curriculum guides be developed for creation science, the Act says nothing of comparable guides for evolution. Similarly, resource services are supplied for creation science but not for evolution. Only "creation scientists" can serve on the panel that supplies the resource services. The Act forbids school boards to discriminate against anyone who "chooses to be a creation-scientist" or to teach "creationism," but fails to protect those who choose to teach evolution or any other noncreation science theory, or who refuse to teach creation science.

If the Louisiana Legislature's purpose was solely to maximize the comprehensiveness and effectiveness of science instruction, it would have encouraged the teaching of all scientific theories about the origins of humankind.[8] But under the Act's requirements, teachers who were once free to teach any and all facets of this subject are now unable to do so. Moreover, the Act fails even to ensure that creation science will be taught, but instead requires the teaching of this theory only when the theory of evolution is taught. Thus we agree with the Court of Appeals' conclusion that the Act does not serve to protect academic freedom, but has the distinctly different purpose of discrediting "evolution by counterbalancing its teaching at every turn with the teaching of creationism. . . ."

B . . .

As in *Stone* and *Abington*, we need not be blind in this case to the legislature's preeminent religious purpose in enacting this statute. There is a historic and contemporaneous link between the teachings of certain religious denominations and the teaching of evolution. It was this link that concerned the Court in *Epperson v. Arkansas*, 393 U.S. 97 (1968), which also involved a facial challenge to a statute regulating the teaching of evolution. . . .

These same historic and contemporaneous antagonisms between the teachings of certain religious denominations and the teaching of evolution are present in this case. The preeminent purpose of the Louisiana Legislature was clearly to advance the religious viewpoint that a supernatural being created humankind.[11] The term "creation science" was defined as embracing this particular religious doctrine by those responsible for the passage of the Creationism Act. Senator Keith's leading expert on creation science, Edward Boudreaux, testified at the legislative hearings that the theory of creation science included belief in the existence of a supernatural creator.[12] Senator Keith also

---

[8] The dissent concludes that the Act's purpose was to protect the academic freedom of students, and not that of teachers. Such a view is not at odds with our conclusion that if the Act's purpose was to provide comprehensive scientific education (a concern shared by students and teachers, as well as parents), that purpose was not advanced by the statute's provisions.

Moreover, it is astonishing that the dissent, to prove its assertion, relies on a section of the legislation that was eventually deleted by the legislature. The dissent contends that this deleted section—which was explicitly rejected by the Louisiana Legislature—reveals the legislature's "obviously intended meaning of the statutory terms 'academic freedom.'" Quite to the contrary, Boudreaux, the main expert relied on by the sponsor of the Act, cautioned the legislature that the words "academic freedom" meant "freedom to teach science." His testimony was given at the time the legislature was deciding whether to delete this section of the Act.

[11] While the belief in the instantaneous creation of humankind by a supernatural creator may require the rejection of every aspect of the theory of evolution, an individual instead may choose to accept some or all of this scientific theory as compatible with his or her spiritual outlook.

[12] Boudreaux repeatedly defined creation science in terms of a theory that supports the existence of a supernatural creator. ("Creation . . . requires the direct involvement of a supernatural intelligence.") The lead witness at the hearings introducing the original bill, Luther Sunderland, described creation science as postulating "that everything was created by some intelligence or power external to the universe."

cited testimony from other experts to support the creation-science view that "a creator [was] responsible for the universe and everything in it."[13] The legislative history therefore reveals that the term "creation science," as contemplated by the legislature that adopted this Act, embodies the religious belief that a supernatural creator was responsible for the creation of humankind.

Furthermore, it is not happenstance that the legislature required the teaching of a theory that coincided with this religious view. The legislative history documents that the Act's primary purpose was to change the science curriculum of public schools in order to provide persuasive advantage to a particular religious doctrine that rejects the factual basis of evolution in its entirety. The sponsor of the Creationism Act, Senator Keith, explained during the legislative hearings that his disdain for the theory of evolution resulted from the support that evolution supplied to views contrary to his own religious beliefs. According to Senator Keith, the theory of evolution was consonant with the "cardinal principle[s] of religious humanism, secular humanism, theological liberalism, aetheistism [sic]." The state senator repeatedly stated that scientific evidence supporting his religious views should be included in the public school curriculum to redress the fact that the theory of evolution incidentally coincided with what he characterized as religious beliefs antithetical to his own. The legislation therefore sought to alter the science curriculum to reflect endorsement of a religious view that is antagonistic to the theory of evolution.

In this case, the purpose of the Creationism Act was to restructure the science curriculum to conform with a particular religious viewpoint. Out of many possible science subjects taught in the public schools, the legislature chose to affect the teaching of the one scientific theory that historically has been opposed by certain religious sects. As in *Epperson*, the legislature passed the Act to give preference to those religious groups which have as one of their tenets the creation of humankind by a divine creator. The "overriding fact" that confronted the Court in *Epperson* was "that Arkansas' law selects from the body of knowledge a particular segment which it proscribes for the sole reason that it is deemed to conflict with . . . a particular interpretation of the Book of Genesis by a particular religious group." 393 U.S., 103. Similarly, the Creationism Act is designed *either* to promote the theory of creation science which embodies a particular religious tenet by requiring that creation science be taught whenever evolution is taught *or* to prohibit the teaching of a scientific theory disfavored by certain religious sects by forbidding the teaching of evolution when creation science is not also taught. The Establishment Clause, however, "forbids *alike* the preference of a religious doctrine or the prohibition of theory which is deemed antagonistic to a particular dogma." *Id.*, 106-107 (emphasis added). Because the primary purpose of the Creationism Act is to advance a particular religious belief, the Act endorses religion in violation of the First Amendment.

We do not imply that a legislature could never require that scientific critiques of prevailing scientific theories be taught. Indeed, the Court acknowledged in *Stone* that its decision forbidding the posting of the Ten Commandments did not mean that no use could ever be made of the

---

[13] Senator Keith believed that creation science embodied this view: "One concept is that a creator however you define a creator was responsible for everything that is in this world. The other concept is that it just evolved." Besides Senator Keith, several of the most vocal legislators also revealed their religious motives for supporting the bill in the official legislative history.

Ten Commandments, or that the Ten Commandments played an exclusively religious role in the history of Western Civilization. In a similar way, teaching a variety of scientific theories about the origins of humankind to schoolchildren might be validly done with the clear secular intent of enhancing the effectiveness of science instruction. But because the primary purpose of the Creationism Act is to endorse a particular religious doctrine, the Act furthers religion in violation of the Establishment Clause. . . .

## V

The Louisiana Creationism Act advances a religious doctrine by requiring either the banishment of the theory of evolution from public school classrooms or the presentation of a religious viewpoint that rejects evolution in its entirety. The Act violates the Establishment Clause of the First Amendment because it seeks to employ the symbolic and financial support of government to achieve a religious purpose. The judgment of the Court of Appeals therefore is

*Affirmed.*

JUSTICE POWELL, with whom JUSTICE O'CONNOR joins, concurring.

I write separately to note certain aspects of the legislative history, and to emphasize that nothing in the Court's opinion diminishes the traditionally broad discretion accorded state and local school officials in the selection of the public school curriculum.

## I . . .
## A

"The starting point in every case involving construction of a statute is the language itself." The Balanced Treatment for Creation-Science and Evolution-Science Act (Act or Balanced Treatment Act), La. Rev. Stat. Ann. § 17:286.1 *et seq.* (West 1982), provides in part:

> Public schools within [the] state shall give balanced treatment to creation-science and to evolution-science. Balanced treatment of these two models shall be given in classroom lectures taken as a whole for each course, in textbook materials taken as a whole for each course, in library materials taken as a whole for the sciences and taken as a whole for the humanities, and in other educational programs in public schools, to the extent that such lectures, textbooks, library materials, or educational programs deal in any way with the subject of the origin of man, life, the earth, or the universe. When creation or evolution is taught, each shall be taught as a theory, rather than as proven scientific fact. § 17:286.4(A).

"Balanced treatment" means "providing whatever information and instruction in both creation and evolution models the classroom teacher determines is necessary and appropriate to provide insight into both theories in view of the textbooks and other instructional materials available for use in his classroom." § 17:286.3(1). "Creation-science" is defined as "the scientific evidences for creation and inferences from those scientific evidences." § 17:286.3(2). "Evolution-science" means "the scientific evidences for evolution and inferences from those scientific evidences." § 17:286.3(3).

Although the Act requires the teaching of the scientific evidences of both creation and evolution whenever either is taught, it does not define either term. . . . The "doctrine or theory of creation" is commonly defined as "holding that matter, the various forms of life, and the world were created by a transcendent God out of nothing." Webster's Third New International Dictionary 532 (unabridged 1981). "Evolution" is defined as "the theory that the various types of animals and plants have their origin in other preexisting types, the distinguishable differences being due to modifications in successive generations." *Id.*, 789. Thus, the Balanced Treatment Act mandates that public schools present the scientific evidence to support a theory of divine creation whenever they present the scientific evidence to support the theory of evolution. "Concepts concerning God or a supreme being of some sort are manifestly religious . . . . These concepts do not shed that religiosity merely because they are presented as a philosophy or as a science." *Malnak v. Yogi*, 440 F. Supp. 1284, 1322 (NJ 1977), aff'd *per curiam*, 592 F.2d 197 (CA3 1979). From the face of the statute, a purpose to advance a religious belief is apparent.

A religious purpose alone is not enough to invalidate an act of a state legislature. The religious purpose must predominate. The Act contains a statement of purpose: to "protec[t] academic freedom." § 17:286.2. This statement is puzzling. Of course, the "academic freedom" of teachers to present information in public schools, and students to receive it, is broad. But it necessarily is circumscribed by the Establishment Clause. "Academic freedom" does not encompass the right of a legislature to structure the public school curriculum in order to advance a particular religious belief. *Epperson v. Arkansas*, 393 U.S. 97, 106 (1968). Nevertheless, I read this statement in the Act as rendering the purpose of the statute at least ambiguous. Accordingly, I proceed to review the legislative history of the Act.

B

In June 1980, Senator Bill Keith introduced Senate Bill 956 in the Louisiana Legislature. The stated purpose of the bill was to "assure academic freedom by requiring the teaching of the theory of creation ex nihilo in all public schools where the theory of evolution is taught."[2] The bill defined the "theory of creation ex nihilo" as "the belief that the origin of the elements, the galaxy, the solar system, of life, of all the species of plants and animals, the origin of man, and the origin of all things and their processes and relationships were created ex nihilo and fixed by God." This theory was referred to by Senator Keith as "scientific creationism."

While a Senate committee was studying scientific creationism, Senator Keith introduced a second draft of the bill, requiring balanced treatment of "evolution-science" and "creation-science." Although the Keith bill prohibited "instruction in any religious doctrine or materials," it defined "creation-science" to include

---

[2] Creation "ex nihilo" means creation "from nothing" and has been found to be an "inherently religious concept." *McLean v. Arkansas Board of Education*, 529 F. Supp. 1255, 1266 (ED Ark. 1982). The District Court in McLean found:

"The argument that creation from nothing in [the substantially similar Arkansas Balanced Treatment Act] does not involve a supernatural deity has no evidentiary or rational support. To the contrary, 'creation out of nothing' is a concept unique to Western religions. In traditional Western religious thought, the conception of a creator of the world is a conception of God. Indeed, creation of the world 'out of nothing' is the ultimate religious statement because God is the only actor." *Id.*, 1265.

"the scientific evidences and related inferences that indicate (a) sudden creation of the universe, energy, and life from nothing; (b) the insufficiency of mutation and natural selection in bringing about development of all living kinds from a single organism; (c) changes only within fixed limits or originally created kinds of plants and animals; (d) separate ancestry for man and apes; (e) explanation of the earth's geology by catastrophism, including the occurrence of a worldwide flood; and (f) a relatively recent inception of the earth and living kinds." . . .

The legislature then held hearings on the amended bill that became the Balanced Treatment Act under review. The principal creation scientist to testify in support of the Act was Dr. Edward Boudreaux. He did not elaborate on the nature of creation science except to indicate that the "scientific evidences" of the theory are "the objective information of science [that] point[s] to conditions of a creator." He further testified that the recognized creation scientists in the United States, who "numbe[r] something like a thousand [and] who hold doctorate and masters degrees in all areas of science," are affiliated with either or both the Institute for Creation Research and the Creation Research Society. Information on both of these organizations is part of the legislative history, and a review of their goals and activities sheds light on the nature of creation science as it was presented to, and understood by, the Louisiana Legislature.

The Institute for Creation Research is an affiliate of the Christian Heritage College in San Diego, California. The Institute was established to address the "urgent need for our nation to return to belief in a personal, omnipotent Creator, who has a purpose for His creation and to whom all people must eventually give account." A goal of the Institute is "a revival of belief in special creation as the true explanation of the origin of the world." Therefore, the Institute currently is working on the "development of new methods for teaching scientific creationism in public schools." The Creation Research Society (CRS) is located in Ann Arbor, Michigan. A member must subscribe to the following statement of belief: "The Bible is the written word of God, and because it is inspired throughout, all of its assertions are historically and scientifically true." To study creation science at the CRS, a member must accept "that the account of origins in Genesis is a factual presentation of simple historical truth."

## C

When, as here, "both courts below are unable to discern an arguably valid secular purpose, this Court normally should hesitate to find one." *Wallace v. Jaffree*, 472 U.S., 66 (POWELL, J., concurring). My examination of the language and the legislative history of the Balanced Treatment Act confirms that the intent of the Louisiana Legislature was to promote a particular religious belief. The legislative history of the Arkansas statute prohibiting the teaching of evolution examined in *Epperson v. Arkansas*, 393 U.S. 97 (1968), was strikingly similar to the legislative history of the Balanced Treatment Act. . . .

Here, it is clear that religious belief is the Balanced Treatment Act's "reason for existence." The tenets of creation science parallel the Genesis story of creation, and this is a religious belief. "No legislative recitation of a supposed secular purpose can blind us to that fact." *Stone v. Graham*, 449 U.S. 39, 41 (1980). Although the Act as finally enacted does not contain explicit reference to its religious purpose, there is no indication in the legislative history that the deletion of "creation ex nihilo" and the four primary tenets of the theory was intended to alter the purpose of teaching creation science. Instead, the statements of purpose of the sources of creation science in the United States make clear that their purpose is to promote a religious belief. I find no persuasive evidence in the legislative history that the legislature's purpose was any different. The fact that the Louisiana Legislature purported to add information to the school curriculum rather than detract from it as in *Epperson* does not affect my analysis. Both legislatures acted with the unconstitutional purpose of structuring the public school curriculum to make it compatible with a particular religious belief: the "divine creation of man." . . .

## II

Even though I find Louisiana's Balanced Treatment Act unconstitutional, I adhere to the view "that the States and locally elected school boards should have the responsibility for determining the educational policy of the public schools." *Board of Education, Island Trees Union Free School Dist. No. 26 v. Pico*, 457 U.S. 853, 893 (1982) (POWELL, J., dissenting). A decision respecting the subject matter to be taught in public schools does not violate the Establishment Clause simply because the material to be taught "'happens to coincide or harmonize with the tenets of some or all religions.'" *Harris v. McRae*, 448 U.S. 297, 319 (1980) (quoting *McGowan v. Maryland*, 366 U.S. 420, 442 (1961)). In the context of a challenge under the Establishment Clause, interference with the decisions of these authorities is warranted only when the purpose for their decisions is clearly religious. . . .

## III

In sum, I find that the language and the legislative history of the Balanced Treatment Act unquestionably demonstrate that its purpose is to advance a particular religious belief. Although the discretion of state and local authorities over public school curricula is broad, "the First Amendment does not permit the State to require that teaching and learning must be tailored to the principles or prohibitions of any religious sect or dogma." *Epperson v. Arkansas*, 393 U.S.,106. Accordingly, I concur in the opinion of the Court and its judgment that the Balanced Treatment Act violates the Establishment Clause of the Constitution. . . .

[JUSTICE WHITE's opinion concurring in the judgment has been omitted]

▨ JUSTICE SCALIA, with whom THE CHIEF JUSTICE joins, dissenting.

Even if I agreed with the questionable premise that legislation can be invalidated under the Establishment Clause on the basis of its motivation alone, without regard to its effects, I would still find no justification for today's decision. The Louisiana legislators who passed the "Balanced Treatment for Creation-Science and Evolution-Science Act, each of whom had sworn to support the Constitution, were well aware of the potential Establishment Clause problems and considered that aspect of the legislation with great care. After seven hearings and several months of study, resulting in substantial revision of the original proposal, they approved the Act overwhelmingly and specifically articulated the secular purpose they meant it to serve. Although the record contains abundant evidence of the sincerity of that purpose (the only issue pertinent to this case), the Court today holds, essentially on the basis of "its visceral knowledge regarding what *must* have motivated the legislators," that the members of the Louisiana Legislature knowingly violated their oaths and then lied about it. I dissent. Had requirements of the Balanced Treatment Act that are not apparent on its face been clarified by an interpretation of the Louisiana Supreme Court, or by the manner of its implementation, the Act might well be found unconstitutional; but the question of its constitutionality cannot rightly be disposed of on the gallop, by impugning the motives of its supporters.

I

This case arrives here in the following posture: The Louisiana Supreme Court has never been given an opportunity to interpret the Balanced Treatment Act, State officials have never attempted to implement it, and it has never been the subject of a full evidentiary hearing. We can only guess at its meaning. We know that it forbids instruction in either "creation-science" or "evolution-science" without instruction in the other, but the parties are sharply divided over what creation science consists of. Appellants insist that it is a collection of educationally valuable scientific data that has been censored from classrooms by an embarrassed scientific establishment. Appellees insist it is not science at all but thinly veiled religious doctrine. Both interpretations of the intended meaning of that phrase find considerable support in the legislative history.

At least at this stage in the litigation, it is plain to me that we must accept appellants' view of what the statute means. To begin with, the statute itself *defines* "creation-science" as "the *scientific evidences* for creation and inferences from those *scientific evidences*." If, however, that definition is not thought sufficiently helpful, the means by which the Louisiana Supreme Court will give the term more precise content is quite clear—and again, at this stage in the litigation, favors the appellants' view. "Creation science" is unquestionably a "term of art," and thus, under Louisiana law, is "to be interpreted according to [its] received meaning and acceptance with the learned in the art, trade or profession to which [it] refer[s]." The only evidence in the record of the "received meaning and acceptance" of "creation science" is found in five affidavits filed by appellants. In those affidavits, two scientists, a philosopher, a theologian, and an educator, all of whom claim extensive knowledge of creation science, swear that it is essentially a collection of scientific data supporting the theory that the physical universe and life within it appeared suddenly and have not changed substantially since appearing. These experts insist that creation science is a strictly scientific concept that can be presented without religious reference. At this point, then, we must assume that the Balanced Treatment Act does *not* require the presentation of religious doctrine.

Nothing in today's opinion is plainly to the contrary, but what the statute means and what it requires are of rather little concern to the Court. Like the Court of Appeals, the Court finds it necessary to consider only the motives of the legislators who supported the Balanced Treatment Act. After examining the statute, its legislative history, and its historical and social context, the Court holds that the Louisiana Legislature acted without "a secular legislative purpose" and that the Act therefore fails the "purpose" prong of the three-part test set forth in *Lemon v. Kurtzman.* As I explain below, I doubt whether that "purpose" requirement of Lemon is a proper interpretation of the Constitution; but even if it were, I could not agree with the Court's assessment that the requirement was not satisfied here.

This Court has said little about the first component of the *Lemon* test. Almost invariably, we have effortlessly discovered a secular purpose for measures challenged under the Establishment Clause, typically devoting no more than a sentence or two to the matter. . . . In fact, only once before deciding *Lemon*, and twice since, have we invalidated a law for lack of a secular purpose. See *Wallace v. Jaffree*, 472 U.S. 38 (1985); *Stone v. Graham*, 449 U.S. 39 (1980) (*per curiam*); *Epperson v. Arkansas*, 393 U.S. 97 (1968).

Nevertheless, a few principles have emerged from our cases, principles which should, but to an unfortunately large extent do not, guide the Court's application of *Lemon* today. It is clear, first of all, that regardless of what "legislative purpose" may mean in other contexts, for the purpose of the *Lemon* test it means the "actual" motives of those responsible for the challenged action. The Court recognizes this, as it has in the past. Thus, if those legislators who supported the Balanced Treatment Act *in fact* acted with a "sincere" secular purpose, the Act survives the first component of the *Lemon* test, regardless of whether that purpose is likely to be achieved by the provisions they enacted.

Our cases have also confirmed that when the *Lemon* Court referred to "a secular . . . purpose," it meant "*a* secular purpose." The author of *Lemon*, writing for the Court, has said that invalidation under the purpose prong is appropriate when "there [is] *no question* that the statute or activity was motivated *wholly* by religious considerations." *Lynch v. Donnelly* , 465 U.S. 668, 680 (1984) (BURGER, C. J.) (emphasis added); see also *Wallace v. Jaffree*, 56 ("The First Amendment requires that a statute must be invalidated if it is *entirely* motivated by a purpose to advance religion"). In all three cases in which we struck down laws under the Establishment Clause for lack of a secular purpose, we found that the legislature's sole motive was to promote religion. . . . Thus, the majority's invalidation of the Balanced Treatment Act is defensible only if the record indicates that the Louisiana Legislature had *no* secular purpose.

It is important to stress that the purpose forbidden by *Lemon* is the purpose to "advance religion." . . . Our cases in no way imply that the Establishment Clause forbids legislators merely to act upon their religious convictions. We surely would not strike down a law providing money to feed the hungry or shelter the homeless if it could be demonstrated that, but for the religious beliefs of the legislators, the funds would not have been approved. Also, political activism by the religiously motivated is part of our heritage. Notwithstanding the majority's implication to the contrary, we do not presume that the sole purpose of a law is to advance religion merely because it was supported strongly by organized religions or by adherents of particular faiths. To do so would deprive religious men and women of their right to participate in the political process. Today's religious activism may give us the Balanced Treatment Act, but yesterday's resulted in the abolition of slavery, and tomorrow's may bring relief for famine victims.

Similarly, we will not presume that a law's purpose is to advance religion merely because it "'happens to coincide or harmonize with the tenets of some or all religions,'" *Harris v. McRae*, 319, or because it benefits religion, even substantially. We have, for example, turned back Establishment Clause challenges to restrictions on abortion funding, *Harris v. McRae*, and to Sunday closing laws, *McGowan v. Maryland*, despite the fact that both "agre[e] with the dictates of [some] Judaeo-Christian religions." "In many instances, the Congress or state legislatures conclude that the general welfare of society, wholly apart from any religious considerations, demands such regulation." On many past occasions we have had no difficulty finding a secular purpose for governmental action far more likely to advance religion than the Balanced Treatment Act. . . . Thus, the fact that creation science coincides with the beliefs of certain religions, a fact upon which the majority relies heavily, does not itself justify invalidation of the Act.

Finally, our cases indicate that even certain kinds of governmental actions undertaken with the specific intention of improving the position of religion do not "advance religion" as that term is used in *Lemon*. Rather, we have said that in at least two circumstances government *must* act to advance religion, and that in a third it *may* do so.

First, since we have consistently described the Establishment Clause as forbidding not only state action motivated by the desire to advance religion, but also that intended to "disapprove," "inhibit," or evince "hostility" toward religion, and since we have said that governmental "neutrality" toward religion is the preeminent goal of the First Amendment, a State which discovers that its employees are inhibiting religion must take steps to prevent them from doing so, even though its purpose would clearly be to advance religion. Thus, if the Louisiana Legislature sincerely believed that the State's science teachers were being hostile to religion, our cases indicate that it could act to eliminate that hostility without running afoul of *Lemon's* purpose test.

Second, we have held that intentional governmental advancement of religion is sometimes required by the Free Exercise Clause. For example, in *Hobbie v. Unemployment Appeals Comm'n of Fla.*, 480 U.S. 136 (1987); *Thomas v. Review Bd., Indiana Employment Security Div.*, 450 U.S. 707 (1981); *Wisconsin v. Yoder*, 406 U.S. 205 (1972); and *Sherbert v. Verner*, 374 U.S. 398 (1963), we held that in some circumstances States must accommodate the beliefs of religious citizens by exempting them from generally applicable regulations. We have not yet come close to reconciling *Lemon* and our Free Exercise cases, and typically we do not really try. It is clear, however, that members of the Louisiana Legislature were not impermissibly motivated for purposes of the *Lemon* test if they believed that approval of the Balanced Treatment Act was *required* by the Free Exercise Clause.

We have also held that in some circumstances government may act to accommodate religion, even if that action is not required by the First Amendment. It is well established that "the limits of permissible state accommodation to religion are by no means co-extensive with the noninterference mandated by the Free Exercise Clause." *Walz v. Tax Comm'n of New York City*, 673. We have implied that voluntary governmental accommodation of religion is not only permissible, but desirable. Thus, few would contend that Title VII of the Civil Rights Act of 1964, which both forbids religious discrimination by private-sector employers, and requires them reasonably to accommodate the religious practices of their employees, violates the Establishment Clause, even though its "purpose" is, of course, to advance religion, and even though it is almost certainly not required by the Free Exercise Clause. While we have warned that at some point, accommodation may devolve into "an unlawful fostering of religion," *Hobbie v. Unemployment Appeals Comm'n of Fla.*, 145, we have not suggested precisely (or even roughly) where that point might be. It is possible, then, that even if the sole motive of those voting for the Balanced Treatment Act was to advance religion, and its passage was not actually required, or even believed to be required, by either the Free Exercise or Establishment Clauses, the Act would nonetheless survive scrutiny under *Lemon's* purpose test.

One final observation about the application of that test: Although the Court's opinion gives no hint of it, in the past we have repeatedly affirmed "our reluctance to attribute unconstitutional motives to the States." *Mueller v.*

*Allen*, 394. We "presume that legislatures act in a constitutional manner." *Illinois v. Krull,* 480 U.S. 340, 351 (1987). Whenever we are called upon to judge the constitutionality of an act of a state legislature, "we must have 'due regard to the fact that this Court is not exercising a primary judgment but is sitting in judgment upon those who also have taken the oath to observe the Constitution and who have the responsibility for carrying on government.'" *Rostker v. Goldberg,* 64. This is particularly true, we have said, where the legislature has specifically considered the question of a law's constitutionality.

With the foregoing in mind, I now turn to the purposes underlying adoption of the Balanced Treatment Act.

II

A

We have relatively little information upon which to judge the motives of those who supported the Act. About the only direct evidence is the statute itself and transcripts of the seven committee hearings at which it was considered. Unfortunately, several of those hearings were sparsely attended, and the legislators who were present revealed little about their motives. We have no committee reports, no floor debates, no remarks inserted into the legislative history, no statement from the Governor, and no postenactment statements or testimony from the bill's sponsor or any other legislators. Nevertheless, there is ample evidence that the majority is wrong in holding that the Balanced Treatment Act is without secular purpose.

At the outset, it is important to note that the Balanced Treatment Act did not fly through the Louisiana Legislature on wings of fundamentalist religious fervor—which would be unlikely, in any event, since only a small minority of the State's citizens belong to fundamentalist religious denominations. The Act had its genesis (so to speak) in legislation introduced by Senator Bill Keith in June 1980. After two hearings before the Senate Committee on Education, Senator Keith asked that his bill be referred to a study commission composed of members of both Houses of the Louisiana Legislature. He expressed hope that the joint committee would give the bill careful consideration and determine whether his arguments were "legitimate." The committee met twice during the interim, heard testimony (both for and against the bill) from several witnesses, and received staff reports. Senator Keith introduced his bill again when the legislature reconvened. The Senate Committee on Education held two more hearings and approved the bill after substantially amending it (in part over Senator Keith's objection). After approval by the full Senate, the bill was referred to the House Committee on Education. That committee conducted a lengthy hearing, adopted further amendments, and sent the bill on to the full House, where it received favorable consideration. The Senate concurred in the House amendments and on July 20, 1981, the Governor signed the bill into law.

Senator Keith's statements before the various committees that considered the bill hardly reflect the confidence of a man preaching to the converted. He asked his colleagues to "keep an open mind" and not to be "biased" by misleading characterizations of creation science. He also urged them to "look at this subject on its merits and not on some preconceived idea." Senator Keith's reception was not especially warm. Over his strenuous objection, the Senate Committee on Education voted 5-1 to amend his bill to deprive it of any force; as amended, the bill merely gave teachers *permission* to balance the teaching of creation science or evolution with the other. The House Committee restored the "mandatory" language to the bill by a vote of only 6-5, and both the full

House (by vote of 52-35), and full Senate (23-15), had to repel further efforts to gut the bill.

The legislators understood that Senator Keith's bill involved a "unique" subject, and they were repeatedly made aware of its potential constitutional problems. Although the Establishment Clause, including its secular purpose requirement, was of substantial concern to the legislators, they eventually voted overwhelmingly in favor of the Balanced Treatment Act: The House approved it 71-19 (with 15 members absent), the Senate 26-12 (with all members present). The legislators specifically designated the protection of "academic freedom" as the purpose of the Act. We cannot accurately assess whether this purpose is a "sham," until we first examine the evidence presented to the legislature far more carefully than the Court has done.

Before summarizing the testimony of Senator Keith and his supporters, I wish to make clear that I by no means intend to endorse its accuracy. But my views (and the views of this Court) about creation science and evolution are (or should be) beside the point. Our task is not to judge the debate about teaching the origins of life, but to ascertain what the members of the Louisiana Legislature believed. The vast majority of them voted to approve a bill which explicitly stated a secular purpose; what is crucial is not their *wisdom* in believing that purpose would be achieved by the bill, but their *sincerity* in believing it would be.

Most of the testimony in support of Senator Keith's bill came from the Senator himself and from scientists and educators he presented, many of whom enjoyed academic credentials that may have been regarded as quite impressive by members of the Louisiana Legislature. To a substantial extent, their testimony was devoted to lengthy, and, to the layman, seemingly expert scientific expositions on the origin of life. These scientific lectures touched upon, *inter alia*, biology, paleontology, genetics, astronomy, astrophysics, probability analysis, and biochemistry. The witnesses repeatedly assured committee members that "hundreds and hundreds" of highly respected, internationally renowned scientists believed in creation science and would support their testimony.

Senator Keith and his witnesses testified essentially as set forth in the following numbered paragraphs:

(1) There are two and only two scientific explanations for the beginning of life—evolution and creation science. Both posit a theory of the origin of life and subject that theory to empirical testing. Evolution posits that life arose out of inanimate chemical compounds and has gradually evolved over millions of years. Creation science posits that all life forms now on earth appeared suddenly and relatively recently and have changed little. Since there are only two possible explanations of the origin of life, any evidence that tends to disprove the theory of evolution necessarily tends to prove the theory of creation science, and vice versa. For example, the abrupt appearance in the fossil record of complex life, and the extreme rarity of transitional life forms in that record, are evidence for creation science.

(2) The body of scientific evidence supporting creation science is as strong as that supporting evolution. In fact, it may be *stronger*. The evidence for evolution is far less compelling than we have been led to believe. Evolution is not a scientific "fact," since it cannot actually be observed in a laboratory. Rather, evolution is merely a scientific theory or "guess." It is a very bad guess at that. The scientific problems with evolution are so serious that it could accurately be termed a "myth."

(3) Creation science is educationally valuable. Students exposed to it better understand the current state of scientific evidence about the origin of life. Creation science can and should be presented to children without any religious content.

(4) Although creation science is educationally valuable and strictly scientific, it is now being censored from or misrepresented in the public schools. Evolution, in turn, is misrepresented as an absolute truth. Teachers have been brainwashed by an entrenched scientific establishment composed almost exclusively of scientists to whom evolution is like a "religion." These scientists discriminate against creation scientists so as to prevent evolution's weaknesses from being exposed.

(5) The censorship of creation science has at least two harmful effects. First, it deprives students of knowledge of one of the two scientific explanations for the origin of life and leads them to believe that evolution is proven fact; thus, their education suffers and they are wrongly taught that science has proved their religious beliefs false. Second, it violates the Establishment Clause. The United States Supreme Court has held that secular humanism is a religion. Thus, by censoring creation science and instructing students that evolution is fact, public school teachers are *now* advancing religion in violation of the Establishment Clause.

Senator Keith repeatedly and vehemently denied that his purpose was to advance a particular religious doctrine. At the outset of the first hearing on the legislation, he testified: "We are not going to say today that you should have some kind of religious instructions in our schools. . . . We are not talking about religion today. . . . I am not proposing that we take the Bible in each science class and read the first chapter of Genesis." At a later hearing, Senator Keith stressed: "To . . . teach religion and disguise it as creationism . . . is not my intent. My intent is to see to it that our textbooks are not censored." He made many similar statements throughout the hearings.

We have no way of knowing, of course, how many legislators believed the testimony of Senator Keith and his witnesses. But in the absence of evidence to the contrary,[4] we have to assume that many of them did. Given that assumption, the Court today plainly errs in holding that the Louisiana Legislature passed the Balanced Treatment Act for exclusively religious purposes.

B

Even with nothing more than this legislative history to go on, I think it would be extraordinary to invalidate the Balanced Treatment Act for lack of a valid secular purpose. Striking down a law approved by the democratically elected representatives of the people is no minor matter. "The cardinal principle of statutory construction is to save and not to destroy. We have repeatedly held that as between two possible interpretations of a statute, by one of which it would be unconstitutional and by the other valid, our plain duty is to adopt that which will save the act." *NLRB v. Jones & Laughlin Steel Corp.,* 301 U.S. 1, 30 (1937). So, too, it seems to me, with discerning statutory purpose. Even if

---

[4] Although appellees and *amici* dismiss the testimony of Senator Keith and his witnesses as pure fantasy, they did not bother to submit evidence of that to the District Court, making it difficult for us to agree with them. The State, by contrast, submitted the affidavits of two scientists, a philosopher, a theologian, and an educator, whose academic credentials are rather impressive.

the legislative history were silent or ambiguous about the existence of a secular purpose—and here it is not—the statute should survive *Lemon*'s purpose
test. But even more validation than mere legislative history is present here.
The Louisiana Legislature explicitly set forth its secular purpose ("protecting
academic freedom") in the very text of the Act. We have in the past repeatedly
relied upon or deferred to such expressions,

The Court seeks to evade the force of this expression of purpose by stub-
bornly misinterpreting it, and then finding that the provisions of the Act do
not advance that misinterpreted purpose, thereby showing it to be a sham.
The Court first surmises that "academic freedom" means "enhancing the freedom of teachers to teach what they will"—even though "academic freedom"
in that sense has little scope in the structured elementary and secondary curriculums with which the Act is concerned. Alternatively, the Court suggests
that it might mean "maximiz[ing] the comprehensiveness and effectiveness of
science instruction"—though that is an exceedingly strange interpretation
of the words, and one that is refuted on the very face of the statute. Had the
Court devoted to this central question of the meaning of the legislatively expressed purpose a small fraction of the research into legislative history that
produced its quotations of religiously motivated statements by individual
legislators, it would have discerned quite readily what "academic freedom"
meant: *students'* freedom from *indoctrination*. The legislature wanted to ensure
that students would be free to decide for themselves how life began, based
upon a fair and balanced presentation of the scientific evidence—that is, to
protect "the right of each [student] voluntarily to determine what to believe
(and what not to believe) free of any coercive pressures from the State." *Grand
Rapids School District v. Ball*, 473 U.S., 385. The legislature did not care *whether*
the topic of origins was taught; it simply wished to ensure that *when* the topic
was taught, students would receive "'all of the evidence.'"

As originally introduced, the "purpose" section of the Balanced Treatment
Act read: "This Chapter is enacted for the purposes of protecting academic
freedom . . . *of students* . . . and assisting *students* in their search for truth."
Among the proposed findings of fact contained in the original version of the
bill was the following: "Public school instruction in only evolution-science
. . . *violates the principle of academic freedom because it denies students a choice
between scientific models and instead indoctrinates them in evolution science alone*"
(emphasis added).[5] Senator Keith unquestionably understood "academic freedom" to mean "freedom from indoctrination" (purpose of bill is "to protect
academic freedom by providing student choice") (purpose of bill is to protect
"academic freedom" by giving students a "choice" rather than subjecting them
to "indoctrination on origins").

If one adopts the obviously intended meaning of the statutory term "academic freedom," there is no basis whatever for concluding that the purpose

---

[5] The majority finds it "astonishing" that I would cite a portion of Senator Keith's original bill that was later deleted as evidence of the legislature's understanding of the phrase
"academic freedom." What is astonishing is the majority's implication that the deletion of
that section deprives it of value as a clear indication of what the phrase meant—there and
in the other, retained, sections of the bill. The Senate Committee on Education deleted most
of the lengthy "purpose" section of the bill (with Senator Keith's consent) because it resembled legislative "findings of fact," which, committee members felt, should generally not
be incorporated in legislation. The deletion had absolutely nothing to do with the manner in
which the section described "academic freedom."

they express is a "sham." To the contrary, the Act pursues that purpose plainly and consistently. It requires that, whenever the subject of origins is covered, evolution be "taught as a theory, rather than as proven scientific fact" and that scientific evidence inconsistent with the theory of evolution (viz., "creation science") be taught as well. Living up to its title of "*Balanced Treatment for Creation-Science and Evolution-Science Act*," it treats the teaching of creation the same way. It does *not* mandate instruction in creation science; *forbids* teachers to present creation science "as proven scientific fact;" and *bans* the teaching of creation science unless the theory is (to use the Court's terminology) "discredit[ed] '. . . at every turn'" with the teaching of evolution. It surpasses understanding how the Court can see in this a purpose "to restructure the science curriculum to conform with a particular religious viewpoint," "to provide a persuasive advantage to a particular religious doctrine," "to promote the theory of creation science which embodies a particular religious tenet," and "to endorse a particular religious doctrine."

The Act's reference to "creation" is not convincing evidence of religious purpose. The Act defines creation science as "*scientific evidenc[e]*," and Senator Keith and his witnesses repeatedly stressed that the subject can and should be presented without religious content. We have no basis on the record to conclude that creation science need be anything other than a collection of scientific data supporting the theory that life abruptly appeared on earth. Creation science, its proponents insist, no more must explain whence life came than evolution must explain *whence* came the inanimate materials from which it says life evolved. But even if that were not so, to posit a past creator is not to posit the eternal and personal God who is the object of religious veneration. Indeed, it is not even to posit the "*unmoved* mover" hypothesized by Aristotle and other notably nonfundamentalist philosophers. Senator Keith suggested this when he referred to "a creator *however you define a creator*."

The Court cites three provisions of the Act which, it argues, demonstrate a "discriminatory preference for the teaching of creation science" and no interest in "academic freedom." First, the Act prohibits discrimination only against creation scientists and those who teach creation science. Second, the Act requires local school boards to develop and provide to science teachers "a curriculum guide on presentation of creation-science." Finally, the Act requires the Governor to designate seven creation scientists who shall, upon request, assist local school boards in developing the curriculum guides. But none of these provisions casts doubt upon the sincerity of the legislators' articulated purpose of "academic freedom"—unless, of course, one gives that term the obviously erroneous meanings preferred by the Court. The Louisiana legislators had been told repeatedly that creation scientists were scorned by most educators and scientists, who themselves had an almost religious faith in evolution. It is hardly surprising, then, that in seeking to achieve a balanced, "nonindoctrinating" curriculum, the legislators protected from discrimination only those teachers whom they thought were *suffering* from discrimination. (Also, the legislators were undoubtedly aware of *Epperson v. Arkansas*, 393 U.S. 97 (1968), and thus could quite reasonably have concluded that discrimination against evolutionists was already prohibited.) The two provisions respecting the development of curriculum guides are also consistent with "academic freedom" as the Louisiana Legislature understood the term. Witnesses had informed the legislators that, because of the hostility of most scientists and educators to creation science, the topic had been censored from or badly misrepresented in elementary and secondary school texts. In light of the unavailability of works on creation science suitable for classroom use and the existence of ample materials on evolution, it was entirely reasonable for the legislature to conclude that science teachers attempting to implement the Act would need a curriculum guide on creation science, but not on evolution, and that those charged with developing the guide would need an easily accessible group of creation scientists. Thus, the provisions of the Act of so much concern to the Court *support* the conclusion that the legislature acted to advance "academic freedom."

The legislative history gives ample evidence of the sincerity of the Balanced Treatment Act's articulated purpose. Witness after witness urged the legislators to support the Act so that students would not be "indoctrinated" but would instead be free to decide for themselves, based upon a fair presentation of the scientific evidence, about the origin of life. . . .

Legislators other than Senator Keith made only a few statements providing insight into their motives, but those statements cast no doubt upon the sincerity of the Act's articulated purpose. The legislators were concerned primarily about the manner in which the subject of origins was presented in Louisiana schools—specifically, about whether scientifically valuable information was being censored and students misled about evolution. Representatives Cain, Jenkins, and F. Thompson seemed impressed by the scientific evidence presented in support of creation science. At the first study commission hearing, Senator Picard and Representative M. Thompson questioned Senator Keith about Louisiana teachers' treatment of evolution and creation science. At the close of the hearing, Representative M. Thompson told the audience: "We as members of the committee will also receive from the staff information of what is currently being taught in the Louisiana public schools. We really want to see [it]. I . . . have no idea in what manner [biology] is presented and in what manner the creationist theories [are] excluded in the public school[s]. We want to look at what the status of the situation is."

Legislators made other comments suggesting a concern about censorship and misrepresentation of scientific information.

It is undoubtedly true that what prompted the legislature to direct its attention to the misrepresentation of evolution in the schools (rather than the inaccurate presentation of other topics) was its awareness of the tension between evolution and the religious beliefs of many children. But even appellees concede that a valid secular purpose is not rendered impermissible simply because its pursuit is prompted by concern for religious sensitivities. If a history teacher falsely told her students that the bones of Jesus Christ had been discovered, or a physics teacher that the Shroud of Turin had been conclusively established to be inexplicable on the basis of natural causes, I cannot believe that legislators or school board members would be constitutionally prohibited from taking corrective action, simply because that action was prompted by concern for the religious beliefs of the misinstructed students.

In sum, even if one concedes, for the sake of argument, that a majority of the Louisiana Legislature voted for the Balanced Treatment Act partly in order to foster (rather than merely eliminate discrimination against) Christian fundamentalist beliefs, our cases establish that that alone would not suffice to invalidate the Act, so long as there was a genuine secular purpose as well. We have, moreover, no adequate basis for disbelieving the secular purpose set forth in the Act itself, or for concluding that it is a sham enacted to conceal the legislators' violation of their oaths of office. I am astonished by the Court's unprecedented readiness to reach such a conclusion, which I can only attribute to an intellectual predisposition created by the facts and the legend of *Scopes v. State,* 289 S. W. 363 (1927)—an instinctive reaction that any governmentally imposed requirements bearing upon the teaching of evolution must be a manifestation of Christian fundamentalist repression. In this case, however, it seems to me the Court's position is the repressive one. The people of Louisiana, including those who are Christian fundamentalists, are quite entitled, as a secular matter, to have whatever scientific evidence there may be against evolution presented in their schools, just as Mr. Scopes was entitled to present whatever scientific evidence there was for it. Perhaps what the Louisiana Legislature has done is unconstitutional because there is no such evidence, and the scheme they have established will amount to no more than a presentation of the Book of Genesis. But we cannot say that on the evidence before us in this summary judgment context, which includes ample uncontradicted testimony that "creation science" is a body of scientific knowledge rather than revealed belief. *Infinitely less* can we say (or should we say) that the scientific evidence for evolution is so conclusive that no one could be gullible enough to believe that there is any real scientific evidence to the contrary, so that the legislation's stated purpose must be a lie. Yet that illiberal judgment, that *Scopes*-in-reverse, is ultimately the basis on which the Court's facile rejection of the Louisiana Legislature's purpose must rest. . . .

Because I believe that the Balanced Treatment Act had a secular purpose, which is all the first component of the *Lemon* test requires, I would reverse the judgment of the Court of Appeals and remand for further consideration.

### III

I have to this point assumed the validity of the *Lemon* "purpose" test. In fact, however, I think the pessimistic evaluation that THE CHIEF JUSTICE made of the totality of *Lemon* is particularly applicable to the "purpose" prong: it is "a constitutional theory [that] has no basis in the history of the amendment it seeks to interpret, is difficult to apply and yields unprincipled results . . . ." *Wallace v. Jaffree,* 472 U.S., 112 (REHNQUIST, J., dissenting).

Our cases interpreting and applying the purpose test have made such a maze of the Establishment Clause that even the most conscientious governmental officials can only guess what motives will be held unconstitutional. We have said essentially the following: Government may not act with the purpose of advancing religion, except when forced to do so by the Free Exercise Clause (which is now and then); or when eliminating existing governmental hostility to religion (which exists sometimes); or even when merely accommodating governmentally uninhibited religious practices, except that at some point (it is unclear where) intentional accommodation results in the fostering of religion, which is of course unconstitutional.

But the difficulty of knowing what vitiating purpose one is looking for is as nothing compared with the difficulty of knowing how or where to find it. For while it is possible to discern the objective "purpose" of a statute (i.e., the public good at which its provisions appear to be directed), or even the formal motivation for a statute where that is explicitly set forth (as it was, to no avail, here), discerning the subjective motivation of those enacting the statute is, to be honest, almost always an impossible task. The number of possible motivations, to begin with, is not binary, or indeed even finite. In the present case, for example, a particular legislator need not have voted for the Act either because he wanted to foster religion or because he wanted to improve education. He may have thought the bill would provide jobs for his district, or may have wanted to make amends with a faction of his party he had alienated on another vote, or he may have been a close friend of the bill's sponsor, or he may have been repaying a favor he owed the Majority Leader, or he may have hoped the Governor would appreciate his vote and make a fundraising appearance for him, or he may have been pressured to vote for a bill he disliked by a wealthy contributor or by a flood of constituent mail, or he may have been seeking favorable publicity, or he may have been reluctant to hurt the feelings of a loyal staff member who worked on the bill, or he may have been settling an old score with a legislator who opposed the bill, or he may have been mad at his wife who opposed the bill, or he may have been intoxicated and utterly *unmotivated* when the vote was called, or he may have accidentally voted "yes" instead of "no," or, of course, he may have had (and very likely did have) a combination of some of the above and many other motivations. To look for *the sole purpose* of even a single legislator is probably to look for something that does not exist.

Putting that problem aside, however, where ought we to look for the individual legislator's purpose? We cannot of course assume that every member present (if, as is unlikely, we know who or even how many they were) agreed with the motivation expressed in a particular legislator's preenactment floor or committee statement. Quite obviously, "what motivates one legislator to make a speech about a statute is not necessarily what motivates scores of others to enact it." *United States v. O'Brien*, 391 U.S. 367, 384 (1968). Can we assume, then, that they all agree with the motivation expressed in the staff-prepared committee reports they might have read—even though we are unwilling to assume that they agreed with the motivation expressed in the very statute that they voted for? Should we consider postenactment floor statements? Or postenactment testimony from legislators, obtained expressly for the lawsuit? Should we consider media reports on the realities of the legislative bargaining? All of these sources, of course, are eminently manipulable. Legislative histories can be contrived and sanitized, favorable media coverage orchestrated, and postenactment recollections conveniently distorted. Perhaps most valuable of all would be more objective indications—for example, evidence regarding the individual legislators' religious affiliations. And if that, why not evidence regarding the fervor or tepidity of their beliefs?

Having achieved, through these simple means, an assessment of what individual legislators intended, we must still confront the question (yet to be addressed in any of our cases) how *many* of them must have the invalidating intent. If a state senate approves a bill by vote of 26 to 25, and only one of the 26 intended solely to advance religion, is the law unconstitutional? What if 13 of the 26 had that intent? What if 3 of the 26 had the impermissible intent, but 3 of the 25 voting against the bill were motivated by religious hostility or were simply attempting to "balance" the votes of their impermissibly motivated colleagues? Or is it possible that the intent of the bill's sponsor is alone enough to invalidate it—on a theory, perhaps, that even though everyone else's intent was pure, what they produced was the fruit of a forbidden tree?

Because there are no good answers to these questions, this Court has recognized from CHIEF JUSTICE MARSHALL, to CHIEF JUSTICE WARREN, that determining the subjective intent of legislators is a perilous enterprise. It is perilous, I might note, not just for the judges who will very likely reach the wrong result, but also for the legislators who find that they must assess the validity of proposed legislation—and risk the condemnation of having voted for an unconstitutional measure—not on the basis of what the legislation contains, nor even on the basis of what they themselves intend, but on the basis of what *others* have in mind.

Given the many hazards involved in assessing the subjective intent of governmental decisionmakers, the first prong of *Lemon* is defensible, I think, only if the text of the Establishment Clause demands it. That is surely not the case. The Clause states that "Congress shall make no law respecting an establishment of religion." One could argue, I suppose, that any time Congress acts with the *intent* of advancing religion, it has enacted a "law respecting an establishment of religion"; but far from being an unavoidable reading, it is quite an unnatural one. . . . It is, in short, far from an inevitable reading of the Establishment Clause that it forbids all governmental action intended to advance religion; and if not inevitable, any reading with such untoward consequences must be wrong.

In the past we have attempted to justify our embarrassing Establishment Clause jurisprudence on the ground that it "sacrifices clarity and predictability for flexibility." *Committee for Public Education & Religious Liberty v. Regan*, 444 U.S., 662. One commentator has aptly characterized this as "a euphemism . . . for . . . the absence of any principled rationale." I think it time that we sacrifice some "flexibility" for "clarity and predictability." Abandoning *Lemon's* purpose test—a test which exacerbates the tension between the Free Exercise and Establishment Clauses, has no basis in the language or history of the Amendment, and, as today's decision shows, has wonderfully flexible consequences—would be a good place to start.

## Notes and Questions

1. How does the Court majority interpret the legislature's stated purpose for the Act, academic freedom? What does the Court majority say is the preeminent purpose for the legislation, and what evidence does it point to for this finding? How do the dissenters interpret the stated purpose for the Act? According to the dissenters, what is problematic about the majority's analysis on this point? More generally, what defects plague the "purpose prong" of the *Lemon* test, according to the dissenters?

2. The majority opinion states: "We do not imply that a legislature could never require that scientific critiques of prevailing scientific theories be taught." Today, some have advanced the teaching of the theory of "intelligent design" as a scientific critique of certain aspects of evolutionary theory. Do you think a law stating that evolution could not be taught unless intelligent design theory also was taught would pass constitutional muster today? For further reading on this topic, see *Kitzmiller v. Dover Area School District.*, 400 F. Supp. 2d 707 (M.D. Pa. 2005). In that case, a federal district court judge considered a policy that required public school science teachers to read to ninth grade biology students a statement emphasizing "gaps" in evolutionary theory and referencing "intelligent design" as a different "explanation of the origin of life" for students to consider. The court found that the policy was unconstitutional under the Establishment Clause. It ruled that the policy constituted an impermissible governmental endorsement of religion and that

the "real purpose" and primary effect of the policy was to promote religion in
the public school classroom.

3.  In light of *Edwards*, if a religious purpose is one of several purposes of a
    legislative act, is the act unconstitutional? Is curriculum material necessarily
    unconstitutional if it is consistent with certain religious tenets?

4.  In his dissenting opinion, Justice Scalia writes: "Notwithstanding the major-
    ity's implication to the contrary, we do not presume that the sole purpose
    of a law is to advance religion merely because it was supported strongly by
    organized religions or by adherents of particular faiths." To what comments
    in the majority opinion is Justice Scalia pointing? Is his characterization of
    the majority opinion fair?

5.  In his dissenting opinion, Justice Scalia argues that the purpose of a provision
    of federal law that requires private employers to make reasonable accom-
    modation of employees' religious practices is to advance religion. Yet, Scalia
    argues, no one has suggested that that law is unconstitutional. Could the
    purpose of that provision of federal law be understood to advance religious
    freedom rather than religion? Can the *Edwards* case be differentiated from
    this example?

## "*Opt Outs*"

The cases discussed above dealt with keeping certain materials out of public schools or tailoring them for all students following a particular course of study. In these cases, the Court
made it clear that altering the curricula in public schools for the purpose of advancing a
religious objective violates the Establishment Clause.

Other cases pose a related but different question: Must individual students be excused
from certain aspects of public school curricula due to their religious objections to such
curricula? The Supreme Court has not yet confronted such a case. A representative case
heard by the lower courts is the case of *Mozert v. Hawkins County Board of Education*,
which was decided by the United States Court of Appeals for the Sixth Circuit in 1987.
This case involved a group of students and their families who objected to certain required
reading materials in Tennessee public schools. Among other issues, this case considers
whether a school requirement that a student be exposed to ideas he or she finds objectionable on religious grounds constitutes a burden on that student's free exercise of religion. As
you read the case, consider the differences between the two opinions in this case in terms
of their analyses of the free exercise issues.

## MOZERT v. HAWKINS COUNTY BOARD OF EDUCATION
### 827 F.2d 1058 (6th Circuit, 1987)

LIVELY, CHIEF JUDGE. . . .

I

A

Early in 1983 the Hawkins County, Tennessee Board of Education adopted the Holt, Rinehart and Winston basic reading series (the Holt series) for use in grades 1-8 of the public schools of the county. In grades 1-4, reading is not taught as a separate subject at a designated time in the school day. Instead, the teachers in these grades use the reading texts throughout the day in conjunction with other subjects. In grades 5-8, reading is taught as a separate subject at a designated time in each class. However, the schools maintain an integrated curriculum which requires that ideas appearing in the reading programs reoccur in other courses. By statute public schools in Tennessee are required to include "character education" in their curricula. The purpose of this requirement is "to help each student develop positive values and to improve student conduct as students learn to act in harmony with their positive values and learn to become good citizens in their school, community, and society." . . .

The plaintiff Vicki Frost is the mother of four children, three of whom were students in Hawkins County public schools in 1983. At the beginning of the 1983-84 school year Mrs. Frost read a story in a daughter's sixth grade reader that involved mental telepathy. Mrs. Frost, who describes herself as a "born again Christian," has a religious objection to any teaching about mental telepathy. Reading further, she found additional themes in the reader to which she had religious objections. After discussing her objections with other parents, Mrs. Frost talked with the principal of Church Hill Middle School and obtained an agreement for an alternative reading program for students whose parents objected to the assigned Holt reader. The students who elected the alternative program left their classrooms during the reading sessions and worked on assignments from an older textbook series in available office or library areas. Other students in two elementary schools were excused from reading the Holt books.

B

In November 1983 the Hawkins County School Board voted unanimously to eliminate all alternative reading programs and require every student in the public schools to attend classes using the Holt series. Thereafter the plaintiff students refused to read the Holt series or attend reading classes where the series was being used. The children of several of the plaintiffs were suspended for brief periods for this refusal. Most of the plaintiff students were ultimately taught at home, or attended religious schools, or transferred to public schools outside Hawkins County. One student returned to school because his family was unable to afford alternate schooling. Even after the board's order, two students were allowed some accommodation, in that the teacher either excused them from reading the Holt stories, or specifically noted on worksheets that the student was not required to believe the stories.

On December 2, 1983, the plaintiffs, consisting of seven families—14 parents and 17 children—filed this action pursuant to 42 U.S.C. § 1983. In their complaint the plaintiffs asserted that they have sincere religious beliefs which are contrary to the values taught or inculcated by the reading textbooks and that it is a violation of the religious beliefs and convictions of the plaintiff students to be required to read the books and a violation of the religious beliefs of the plaintiff parents to permit their children to read the books. The plaintiffs sought to hold the defendants liable because "forcing the student-plaintiffs

to read school books which teach or inculcate values in violation of their religious beliefs and convictions is a clear violation of their rights to the free
exercise of religion protected by the First and Fourteenth Amendments to the
United States Constitution." . . .

II

B

Vicki Frost was the first witness for the plaintiffs and she presented the
most complete explanation of the plaintiffs' position. The plaintiffs do not
belong to a single church or denomination, but all consider themselves born
again Christians. Mrs. Frost testified that the word of God as found in the
Christian Bible "is the totality of my beliefs." There was evidence that other
members of their churches, and even their pastors, do not agree with their
position in this case.

Mrs. Frost testified that she had spent more than 200 hours reviewing
the Holt series and had found numerous passages that offended her religious
beliefs. She stated that the offending materials fell into seventeen categories
which she listed. These ranged from such familiar concerns of fundamentalist
Christians as evolution and "secular humanism" to less familiar themes such as
"futuristic supernaturalism," pacifism, magic and false views of death.

In her lengthy testimony Mrs. Frost identified passages from stories and
poems used in the Holt series that fell into each category. Illustrative is her
first category, futuristic supernaturalism, which she defined as teaching "Man
As God." Passages that she found offensive described Leonardo da Vinci as the
human with a creative mind that "came closest to the divine touch." Similarly,
she felt that a passage entitled "Seeing Beneath the Surface" related to an occult theme, by describing the use of imagination as a vehicle for seeing things
not discernible through our physical eyes. She interpreted a poem, "Look at
Anything," as presenting the idea that by using imagination a child can become part of anything and thus understand it better. Mrs. Frost testified that
it is an "occult practice" for children to use imagination beyond the limitation
of scriptural authority. She testified that the story that alerted her to the problem with the reading series fell into the category of futuristic supernaturalism.
Entitled "A Visit to Mars," the story portrays thought transfer and telepathy
in such a way that "it could be considered a scientific concept," according to
this witness. This theme appears in the testimony of several witnesses, i.e., the
materials objected to "could" be interpreted in a manner repugnant to their
religious beliefs.

Mrs. Frost described objectionable passages from other categories in
much the same way. Describing evolution as a teaching that there is no God,
she identified 24 passages that she considered to have evolution as a theme.
She admitted that the textbooks contained a disclaimer that evolution is a
theory, not a proven scientific fact. Nevertheless, she felt that references to
evolution were so pervasive and presented in such a factual manner as to
render the disclaimer meaningless. After describing her objection to passages
that encourage children to make moral judgments about whether it is right or
wrong to kill animals, the witness stated, "I thought they would be learning
to read, to have good English and grammar, and to be able to do other subject
work." Asked by plaintiffs' attorney to define her objection to the text books,
Mrs. Frost replied:

Very basically, I object to the Holt, Rhinehart [sic] Winston series as a whole, what the message is as a whole. There are some contents which are objectionable by themselves, but my most withstanding [sic] objection would be to the series as a whole.

Another witness for the plaintiffs was Bob Mozert, father of a middle school and an elementary school student in the Hawkins County system. His testimony echoed that of Vicki Frost in large part, though his answers to questions tended to be much less expansive. He also found objectionable passages in the readers that dealt with magic, role reversal or role elimination, particularly biographical material about women who have been recognized for achievements outside their homes, and emphasis on one world or a planetary society. Both witnesses testified under cross-examination that the plaintiff parents objected to passages that expose their children to other forms of religion and to the feelings, attitudes and values of other students that contradict the plaintiffs' religious views without a statement that the other views are incorrect and that the plaintiffs' views are the correct ones. . . .

### III
### A

The first question to be decided is whether a governmental requirement that a person be exposed to ideas he or she finds objectionable on religious grounds constitutes a burden on the free exercise of that person's religion as forbidden by the First Amendment. . . .

[T]he plaintiffs' own testimony casts serious doubt on their claim that a more balanced presentation would satisfy their religious views. Mrs. Frost testified that it would be acceptable for the schools to teach her children about other philosophies and religions, but if the practices of other religions were described in detail, or if the philosophy was "profound" in that it expressed a world view that deeply undermined her religious beliefs, then her children "would have to be instructed to [the] error [of the other philosophy]." It is clear that to the plaintiffs there is but one acceptable view—the Biblical view, as they interpret the Bible. Furthermore, the plaintiffs view every human situation and decision, whether related to personal belief and conduct or to public policy and programs, from a theological or religious perspective. Mrs. Frost testified that many political issues have theological roots and that there would be "no way" certain themes could be presented without violating her religious beliefs. She identified such themes as evolution, false supernaturalism, feminism, telepathy and magic as matters that could not be presented in any way without offending her beliefs. The only way to avoid conflict with the plaintiffs' beliefs in these sensitive areas would be to eliminate all references to the subjects so identified. However, the Supreme Court has clearly held that it violates the Establishment Clause to tailor a public school's curriculum to satisfy the principles or prohibitions of any religion. *Epperson v. Arkansas*, 393 U.S. 97, 106 (1968).

The testimony of the plaintiffs' expert witness, Dr. Vitz, illustrates the pitfalls of trying to achieve a balance of materials concerning religion in a reading course. He found "markedly little reference to religion, particularly Christianity, and also remarkably little to Judaism" in the Holt series. His solution would be to "beef up" the references to these two dominant religions in the United States. However, an adherent to a less widely professed religion might then object to the slighting of his or her faith. Balance in the treatment of religion lies in the eye of the beholder. Efforts to achieve the particular "balance" desired by any individual or group by the addition or deletion of religious material would lead to a forbidden entanglement of the public schools in religious matters, if done with the purpose or primary effect of advancing or inhibiting religion.

### B . . .

In *Sherbert, Thomas* and *Hobbie* there was governmental compulsion to engage in conduct that violated the plaintiffs' religious convictions. That element is missing in the present case. The requirement that students read the assigned materials and attend reading classes, in the absence of a showing that this participation entailed affirmation or denial of a religious belief, or performance or non-performance of a religious exercise or practice, does not place an unconstitutional burden on the students' free exercise of religion.

### C . . .

It is abundantly clear that the exposure to materials in the Holt series did not compel the plaintiffs to "declare a belief," "communicate by word and sign [their] acceptance" of the ideas presented, or make an "affirmation of a belief and an attitude of mind." In *Barnette* the unconstitutional burden consisted of compulsion either to do an act that violated the plaintiff's religious convictions or communicate an acceptance of a particular idea or affirm a belief. No similar compulsion exists in the present case.

It is clear that governmental compulsion either to do or refrain from doing an act forbidden or required by one's religion, or to affirm or disavow a belief forbidden or required by one's religion, is the evil prohibited by the Free Exercise Clause. In *Abington School District v. Schempp*, 374 U.S. 203, 223 (1963), the Court described the Free Exercise Clause as follows:

> Its purpose is to secure religious liberty in the individual by prohibiting any invasions thereof by civil authority. Hence it is necessary in a free exercise case for one to show the coercive effect of the enactment as it operates against him in the practice of his religion. The distinction between the two clauses is apparent—a violation of the Free Exercise Clause is predicated on coercion while the Establishment Clause violation need not be so attended. . .

The plaintiffs appear to contend that the element of compulsion was supplied by the requirement of class participation in the reading exercises. As we have pointed out earlier, there is no proof in the record that any plaintiff student was required to engage in role play, make up magic chants, read aloud or engage in the activity of haggling. . . . .

### D

The third Supreme Court decision relied upon by the plaintiffs is the only one that might be read to support the proposition that requiring mere exposure to materials that offend one's religious beliefs creates an unconstitutional burden on the free exercise of religion. *Wisconsin v. Yoder*, 406 U.S. 205 (1972). However, Yoder rested on such a singular set of facts that we do not believe it can be held to announce a general rule that exposure without compulsion to act, believe, affirm or deny creates an unconstitutional burden. . . .

The parents in *Yoder* were required to send their children to some school that prepared them for life in the outside world, or face official sanctions. The parents in the present case want their children to acquire all the skills required to live in modern society. They also want to have them excused from exposure to some ideas they find offensive. Tennessee offers two options to accommodate this latter desire. The plaintiff parents can either send their children to church schools or private schools, as many of them have done, or teach them at home. Tennessee law prohibits any state interference in the education process of church schools. . . . Similarly the statute permitting home schooling by parents or other teachers prescribes nothing with respect to curriculum or the content of class work.

*Yoder* was decided in large part on the impossibility of reconciling the goals of public education with the religious requirement of the Amish that their children be prepared for life in a separated community. As the Court noted, the requirement of school attendance to age 16 posed a "very real threat of undermining the Amish community and religious practice as they exist today. . . ." 406 U.S., 218. No such threat exists in the present case, and Tennessee's school attendance laws offer several options to those parents who want their children to have the benefit of an education which prepares for life in the modern world without being exposed to ideas which offend their religious beliefs. . . .

IV

A

The Supreme Court has recently affirmed that public schools serve the purpose of teaching fundamental values "essential to a democratic society." These values "include tolerance of divergent political and religious views" while taking into account "consideration of the sensibilities of others." *Bethel School District No. 403 v. Fraser*, 478 U.S. 675 (1986). The Court has noted with apparent approval the view of some educators who see public schools as an "assimilative force" that brings together "diverse and conflicting elements" in our society "on a broad but common ground." *Ambach v. Norwick*, 441 U.S. 68 (1979), citing works of J. Dewey, N. Edwards and H. Richey. The critical reading approach furthers these goals. Mrs. Frost stated specifically that she objected to stories that develop "a religious tolerance that all religions are merely different roads to God." Stating that the plaintiffs reject this concept, presented as a recipe for an ideal world citizen, Mrs. Frost said, "We cannot be tolerant in that we accept other religious views on an equal basis with ours." While probably not an uncommon view of true believers in any religion, this statement graphically illustrates what is lacking in the plaintiffs' case.

The "tolerance of divergent . . . religious views" referred to by the Supreme Court is a civil tolerance, not a religious one. It does not require a person to accept any other religion as the equal of the one to which that person adheres. It merely requires a recognition that in a pluralistic society we must "live and let live." If the Hawkins County schools had required the plaintiff students either to believe or say they believe that "all religions are merely different roads to God," this would be a different case. No instrument of government can, consistent with the Free Exercise Clause, require such a belief or affirmation. However, there was absolutely no showing that the defendant school board sought to do this; indeed, the school board agreed at oral argument that it could not constitutionally do so. . . .

The only conduct compelled by the defendants was reading and discussing the material in the Holt series, and hearing other students' interpretations of those materials. This is the exposure to which the plaintiffs objected. What is absent from this case is the critical element of compulsion to affirm or deny a religious belief or to engage or refrain from engaging in a practice forbidden or required in the exercise of a plaintiff's religion.

B . . .

Since we have found none of the prohibited forms of governmental compulsion in this case, we conclude that the plaintiffs failed to establish the existence of an unconstitutional burden. Having determined that no burden was shown, we do not reach the issue of the defendants' compelling interest in requiring a uniform reading series or the question, raised by the defendant, of whether awarding damages violated the Establishment Clause.

※ BOGGS, CIRCUIT JUDGE, concurring. . . .

I concur with my colleagues that Hawkins County is not required by the Constitution to allow plaintiffs the latitude they seek in the educational program of these children. However, I reach that result on a somewhat different view of the facts and governing principles here. . . .

The school board recognizes no limitation on its power to require any curriculum, no matter how offensive or one-sided, and to expel those who will not study it, so long as it does not violate the Establishment Clause. Our opinion today confirms that right, and I would like to make plain my reasons for taking that position.

I

Preliminarily, as my colleagues indicate, we make no judgment on the educational, political or social soundness of the school board's decision to adopt this particular set of books and this general curricular approach. This is not a case about fundamentalist Christians or any particular set of beliefs. It is about the constitutional limits on the powers of school boards to prescribe a curriculum. For myself, I approach this case with a profound sense of sadness. At the classroom level, the pupils and teachers in these schools had in most cases reached a working accommodation. Only by the decisions of higher levels of political authority, and by more conceptualized presentations of the plaintiffs' positions, have we reached the point where we must decide these harsh questions today. . . .

As this case now reaches us, the school board rejects any effort to reach out and take in these children and their concerns. At oral argument, the board specifically argued that it was better for both plaintiffs' children and other children that they not be in the public schools, despite the children's obvious desire to obtain some of the benefits of public schooling. Though the board recognized that their allegedly compelling interests in shaping the education of Tennessee children could not be served at all if they drove the children from the school, the board felt it better not to be associated with any hybrid program.

Plaintiffs' requests were unusual, but a variety of accommodations in fact were made, with no evidence whatsoever of bad effects. Given the masses of speculative testimony as to the hypothetical future evils of accommodating plaintiffs in any way, had there been any evidence of bad effects from what actually occurred, the board would surely have presented it. As we ultimately decide here, on the present state of constitutional law, the school board is indeed entitled to say, "my way or the highway." But in my view the school board's decision here is certainly not required by the Establishment Clause.[3]

## II

Returning to the treatment of plaintiffs' free exercise claim, I believe this is a more difficult case than outlined in the court's opinion. . . . A reasonable reading of plaintiffs' testimony shows they object to the overall effect of the Holt series, not simply to any exposure to any idea opposing theirs. . . .

Ultimately, I think we must address plaintiffs' claims as they actually impact their lives: it is their belief that they should not take a course of study which, on balance, to them, denigrates and opposes their religion, and which the state is compelling them to take on pain of forfeiting all other benefits of public education.

Their view may seem silly or wrong-headed to some, but it is a sincerely held religious belief. By focusing narrowly on references that make plaintiffs appear so extreme that they could never be accommodated, the court simply leaves resolution of the underlying issues here to another case, when we have plaintiffs with a more sophisticated understanding of our own and Supreme Court precedent, and a more careful and articulate presentation of their own beliefs. . . .

I believe we must take plaintiffs' claims as they have stated them—that they desire the accommodation of an opt-out, or alternative reading books, and no more. That is all they have ever asked for in their pleadings, in the arguments at trial and in appellate briefing and argument.

## III

I also disagree with the court's view that there can be no burden here because there is no requirement of conduct contrary to religious belief. That view both slights plaintiffs' honest beliefs that studying the full Holt series would be conduct contrary to their religion, and overlooks other Supreme Court Free Exercise cases which view "conduct" that may offend religious exercise at least as broadly as do plaintiffs. . . .

Here, plaintiffs have drawn their line as to what required school activities, what courses of study, do and do not offend their beliefs to the point of prohibition. I would hold that if they are forced over that line, they are "engaging in conduct" forbidden by their religion. The court's excellent summary of its holding on this point appears to concede that what plaintiffs were doing in school was conduct, but that there "was no evidence that the conduct required of the students was forbidden by their religion." I cannot agree. The plaintiffs provided voluminous testimony of the conflict (in their view) between reading the Holt readers and their religious beliefs, including extensive Scriptural references. The district court found that "plaintiffs' religious beliefs *compel* them to refrain from exposure to the Holt series." 647 F. Supp., 1200 (emphasis supplied). I would think it could hardly be clearer that they believe their religion commands, not merely suggests, their course of action.

If plaintiffs did not use the exact words "reading these books is forbidden by our religion," they certainly seemed to me to make that point clearly. The

---

[3] A different situation would be presented if the purpose or primary effect of any accommodation were to be the advancement of plaintiffs' religion. I see no evidence of such purpose or effect from the accommodation in this case.

court's summary also re-emphasizes my point that the importance of this holding would be greatly diminished in a future case where plaintiffs can articulate
the right set of words. . . .

## V

Thus, I believe the plaintiffs' objection is to the Holt series as a whole, and
that being forced to study the books is "conduct" contrary to their beliefs. In
the absence of a narrower basis that can withstand scrutiny, we must address
the hard issues presented by this case: (1) whether compelling this conduct
forbidden by plaintiffs' beliefs places a burden on their free exercise of their religion, in the sense of earlier Supreme Court holdings; and (2) whether *within
the context of the public schools,* teaching material which offends a person's religious beliefs, but does not violate the Establishment Clause, can be a burden
on free exercise. . . .

For me, the key fact is that the Court has almost never interfered with the
prerogative of school boards to set curricula, based on free exercise claims.
*West Virginia State Board of Education v. Barnette,* 319 U.S. 624 (1943), may be
the only case, and even there a specific affirmation was required, implicating a
non-religious First Amendment basis, as well.

From a common sense view of the word "burden," *Sherbert* and *Thomas*
are very strong cases for plaintiffs. In any sensible meaning of a burden, the
burden in our case is greater than in *Thomas* or *Sherbert.* Both of these cases involved workers who wanted unemployment compensation because they gave
up jobs based on their religious beliefs. Their actual losses that the Court made
good, the actual burden that the Court lifted, was one or two thousand dollars
at most. Although this amount of money was certainly important to them, the
Court did not give them their jobs back. The Court did not guarantee they
would get any future job. It only provided them access to a sum of money
equally with those who quit work for other "good cause" reasons.

Here, the burden is many years of education, being required to study
books that, in plaintiffs' view, systematically undervalue, contradict and ignore
their religion. I trust it is not simply because I am chronologically somewhat
closer than my colleagues to the status of the students involved here that I
interpret the choice forced upon the plaintiffs here as a "burden."

## VI . . .

Running a public school system of today's magnitude is quite a different
proposition. A constitutional challenge to the content of instruction (as opposed to participation in ritual such as magic chants, or prayers) is a challenge
to the notion of a politically-controlled school system. Imposing on school
boards the delicate task of satisfying the "compelling interest" test to justify
failure to accommodate pupils is a significant step. It is a substantial imposition on the schools to *require* them to justify each instance of not dealing with
students' individual, religiously compelled, objections (as opposed to *permitting* a local, rough and ready, adjustment), and I do not see that the Supreme
Court has authorized us to make such a requirement. . . .

Therefore, I reluctantly conclude that under the Supreme Court's decisions as we have them, school boards may set curricula bounded only by the
Establishment Clause, as the state contends. Thus, contrary to the analogy
plaintiffs suggest, pupils may indeed be expelled if they will not read from
the King James Bible, so long as it is only used as literature, and not taught

as religious truth. See *Abington School Dist. v. Schempp*, 374 U.S. 203 (1963); *Donahoe v. Richards*, 38 Me. 379 (1854). Contrary to the position of *amicus* American Jewish Committee, Jewish students may not assert a burden on their religion if their reading materials overwhelmingly provide a negative view of Jews or factual or historical issues important to Jews, so long as such materials do not assert any propositions as religious truth, or do not otherwise violate the Establishment Clause.

The court's opinion well illustrates the distinction between the goals and values that states may try to impose and those they cannot, by distinguishing between teaching civil toleration of other religions, and teaching *religious* toleration of other religions. It is an accepted part of public schools to teach the former, and plaintiffs do not quarrel with that. Thus, the state may teach that all religions have the same civil and political rights, and must be dealt with civilly in civil society. The state itself concedes it may not do the latter. It may not teach as truth that the religions of others are just as correct *as religions* as plaintiffs' own.

It is a more difficult question when, as here, the state presents materials that plaintiffs sincerely believe preach religious toleration of religions by consistent omission of plaintiffs' religion and favorable presentation of opposing views. Our holding requires plaintiffs to put up with what they perceive as an unbalanced public school curriculum, so long as the curriculum does not violate the Establishment Clause. Every other sect or type of religious belief is bound by the same requirement. The rule here is not a rule just for fundamentalist dissenters, for surely the rule cannot be that when the school authorities disagree with non-fundamentalist dissenters, the school loses. . . .

Schools are very important, and some public schools offend some people deeply. That is one major reason private schools of many denominations— fundamentalist, Lutheran, Jewish—are growing. But a response to that phenomenon is a political decision for the schools to make. I believe that such a significant change in school law and expansion in the religious liberties of pupils and parents should come only from [the] Supreme Court itself, and not simply from our interpretation. It may well be that we would have a better society if children and parents were not put to the hard choice posed by this case. But our mandate is limited to carrying out the commands of the Constitution and the Supreme Court.

I therefore concur in the result and reverse the judgment of the District Court.

## NOTES AND QUESTIONS

1. What are the differences between the ways in which Judge Lively and Judge Boggs assess whether exposure to these readers violated the students' free exercise rights? How can judges distinguish, as another court put it, "between those governmental actions that actually interfere with the exercise of religion, and those that merely require or result in exposure to attitudes and outlooks at odds with perspectives prompted by religion"? What difficulties might arise in making this determination? Did the school's reader requirements force the plaintiffs to engage in conduct forbidden by their religion? Should it matter to the constitutional analysis whether the plaintiff understands their religious beliefs to forbid, as opposed merely to frown on, certain conduct?

2. Describe the difference between "religious tolerance" and "civil tolerance," as explained by Judge Lively. Do you think this distinction is a useful one?

3. Judge Boggs notes that "[a]t the classroom level, the pupils and teachers in these schools had in most cases reached a working accommodation." What was that accommodation, and how did it come to an end? Do you agree with Judge Boggs' suggestion that it would have been better to continue such ad-hoc accommodations rather than force the choices presented by this case? In the wake of this case, would it be constitutionally permissible for schools in this jurisdiction to allow certain students to opt out of particular aspects of course due to their religious objections?

4. Do you think the case might have turned out differently if it had involved only one or two students objecting to one book of many assigned in a literature class?

## School-Sponsored Religious Displays

In the 1980 case of *Stone v. Graham*, the Court took the unusual step of summarily reversing a lower court's decision without benefit of oral argument. If the Court agrees to hear a case, usually it orders briefs to be written and sets a date for oral argument of the case. On rare occasions, however, the Court believes that it is able to decide the case based on the briefs asking the court to hear the case (the petition for certiorari and the response to that petition) without further briefing or oral argument. On such occasions, it summarily reverses or affirms a lower court's decision.

*Stone v. Graham*, 449 U.S. 39 (1980), involved a Kentucky law that required the posting of the Ten Commandments in public elementary and secondary schools. See page 756 for text of Kentucky law. A Kentucky trial court held that the purpose of this law was secular rather than religious and the state's highest court affirmed by an equally divided court. The Supreme Court disagreed and summarily reversed the lower court decision. The Court issued a *per curiam* decision in this case, which is an opinion by all of the justices in the majority rather than an opinion written any one justice.

In its *per curiam* opinion, the Court concluded:

The pre-eminent purpose for posting the Ten Commandments on schoolroom walls is plainly religious in nature. The Ten Commandments are undeniably a sacred text in the Jewish and Christian faiths, and no legislative recitation of a supposed secular purpose can blind us to that fact. The Commandments do not confine themselves to arguably secular matters, such as honoring one's parents, killing or murder, adultery, stealing, false witness, and covetousness. See Exodus 20:12-17; Deuteronomy 5:16-21. Rather, the first part of the Commandments concerns the religious duties of believers: worshipping the Lord God alone, avoiding idolatry, not using the Lord's name in vain, and observing the Sabbath Day. See Exodus 20:1-11; Deuteronomy 5:6-15.

This is not a case in which the Ten Commandments are integrated into the school curriculum, where the Bible may constitutionally be used in an appropriate study of history, civilization, ethics, comparative religion, or the like. *Abington School*

*District v. Schempp*, 225. Posting of religious texts on the wall serves no such educational function. If the posted copies of the Ten Commandments are to have any effect at all, it will be to induce the schoolchildren to read, meditate upon, perhaps to venerate and obey, the Commandments. However desirable this might be as a matter of private devotion, it is not a permissible state objective under the Establishment Clause.

It does not matter that the posted copies of the Ten Commandments are financed by voluntary private contributions, for the mere posting of the copies under the auspices of the legislature provides the "official support of the State . . . Government" that the Establishment Clause prohibits. 374 U.S., 222; see *Engel v. Vitale*, 370 U.S. 421, 431 (1962).[4] Nor is it significant that the Bible verses involved in this case are merely posted on the wall, rather than read aloud as in *Schempp* and *Engel*, for "it is no defense to urge that the religious practices here may be relatively minor encroachments on the First Amendment." *Abington School District v. Schempp*, 225. We conclude that Ky. Rev. Stat. § 158.178 (1980) violates the first part of the *Lemon v. Kurtzman* test, and thus the Establishment Clause of the Constitution.

Chief Justice Warren Burger and Justice Harry Blackmun dissented in this case. They would have granted certiorari and given the case full consideration with briefing and oral argument. Justice Potter Stewart noted that he too dissented "from this summary reversal of the courts of Kentucky, which, so far as appears, applied wholly constitutional criteria in reaching their decisions." Then-Justice William Rehnquist dissented as well, issuing a vigorous objection to what he called "a cavalier summary reversal" of Kentucky's highest court. He wrote: "The Court's summary rejection of a secular purpose articulated by the legislature and confirmed by the state court is without precedent in Establishment Clause jurisprudence." Rehnquist argued that "[t]he fact that the asserted secular purpose may overlap with what some may see as a religious objective does not render it unconstitutional." Rehnquist noted that the Court had said that the Ten Commandments is "undeniably a sacred text" and responded:

> It is equally undeniable, however, as the elected representatives of Kentucky determined, that the Ten Commandments have had a significant impact on the development of secular legal codes of the Western World. The trial court concluded that evidence submitted substantiated this determination. See *Anderson v. Salt Lake City Corp.*, 475 F.2d 29, 33 (CA10 1973) (upholding construction on public land of monument inscribed with Ten Commandments because they have "substantial secular attributes"). Certainly the State was permitted to conclude that a document with such secular significance should be placed before its students, with an appropriate statement of the document's secular import.

The Court majority in *Stone* was of the opinion that the state of Kentucky wanted public school students to venerate the religious principles contained in the Ten Commandments. Would it make a difference if the Ten Commandments were posted in a school classroom temporarily while the class studied the way in which they had influenced American law and if other historical codes had been posted temporarily when they were the focus of class study?

---

[4] Moreover, while the actual copies of the Ten Commandments were purchased through private contributions, the State nevertheless expended public money in administering the statute. For example, the statute requires that the state treasurer serve as a collecting agent for the contributions. Ky. Rev. Stat. § 158.178 (3) (1980).

> ### KENTUCKY STATUTE
> The statute provided in its entirety:
> "(1) It shall be the duty of the superintendent of public instruction, provided sufficient funds are available as provided in subsection (3) of this Section, to ensure that a durable, permanent copy of the Ten Commandments shall be displayed on a wall in each public elementary and secondary school classroom in the Commonwealth. The copy shall be sixteen (16) inches wide by twenty (20) inches high.
> "(2) In small print below the last commandment shall appear a notation concerning the purpose of the display, as follows: 'The secular application of the Ten Commandments is clearly seen in its adoption as the fundamental legal code of Western Civilization and the Common Law of the United States.'
> "(3) The copies required by this Act shall be purchased with funds made available through voluntary contributions made to the state treasurer for the purposes of this Act." 1978 Ky. Acts, ch. 436, § 1 (effective June 17, 1978), Ky. Rev. Stat. § 158.178 (1980).

Suppose a different state law requires the permanent posting in public school classrooms of the Ten Commandments along with other documents of historical significance (e.g., the Declaration of Independence, Washington's "Farewell Address," Lincoln's "Gettysburg Address," etc.). The stated purpose in the law, supported by the legislative history, is for students to appreciate the historical, civic, and moral values contained in the various documents. Assume that several of the other historical documents contain devotional references to God or a deity. Is this law distinguishable from the law in *Stone*?

Should a court analyze the issue differently if a Ten Commandments monument is present in a city park instead of a public school classroom? What about the posting of the Ten Commandments in a courtroom? Does it make a difference if other historical documents (e.g., Hammarubi's Code, the Magna Charta) also are posted with the Ten Commandments in these various places? Should it matter whether the Ten Commandments display was posted several decades ago or recently? Some of these issues are discussed in chapter 20.

### TEACHING ABOUT RELIGION IN AN ACADEMIC, RATHER THAN A DEVOTIONAL, MANNER

The *Abington Township v. Schempp* case is best remembered, of course, for its holding—public schools may not engage in devotional teaching of religion. In other words, public schools could not encourage or permit school-sponsored prayers or readings of sacred texts that were intended to inculcate religion or inspire faith commitments. But the *Schempp* Court also noted that academic teaching about religion could be constitutional and even desirable within public school classrooms. In the Court majority opinion in the *Schempp* case, Justice Clark wrote:

> [I]t might well be said that one's education is not complete without a study of comparative religion or the history of religion and its relationship to the advancement of civilization. It certainly may be said that the Bible is worthy of study for its literary and historic qualities. Nothing we have said here indicates that such study of the Bible or of religion, when presented objectively as part of a secular program of education, may not be effected consistently with the First Amendment.

Justice Brennan echoed and expanded on these sentiments in his concurring in this case. Brennan wrote:

> *Non-Devotional Use of the Bible in the Public Schools.*—The holding of the Court today plainly does not foreclose teaching about the Holy Scriptures or about the differences between religious sects in classes in literature or history. Indeed, whether or not the Bible is involved, it would be impossible to teach meaningfully many subjects in the social sciences or the humanities without some mention of religion. To what extent, and at what points in the curriculum, religious materials should be cited are matters which the courts ought to entrust very largely to the experienced officials who superintend our Nation's public schools. They are experts in such matters, and we are not. We should heed Mr. Justice Jackson's caveat that any attempt by this Court to announce curricular standards would be "to decree a uniform, rigid and, if we are consistent, an unchanging standard for countless school boards representing and serving highly localized groups which not only differ from each other but which themselves from time to time change attitudes." *Illinois ex rel. McCollum v. Board of Education,* 237.
>
> We do not, however, in my view usurp the jurisdiction of school administrators by holding as we do today that morning devotional exercises in any form are constitutionally invalid. But there is no occasion now to go further and anticipate problems we cannot judge with the material now before us. Any attempt to impose rigid limits upon the mention of God or references to the Bible in the classroom would be fraught with dangers. If it should sometime hereafter be shown that in fact religion can play no part in the teaching of a given subject without resurrecting the ghost of the practices we strike down today, it will then be time enough to consider questions we must now defer.

With these statements, the Court made it clear that the door was open for the academic study of religion in our nation's public schools. But these comments did not receive much attention when they were made or in the years immediately following this decision. They were eclipsed by the fierce backlash against the 1960s school-prayer decisions.

In subsequent years, however, the notion of academic teaching about religion began to gain more attention and traction. In 1987, the Court reaffirmed the statements it made in the *Schempp* case in the case of *Edwards v. Aguillard.* Writing for the *Edwards* majority, Justice Brennan noted that the academic study of religion in public schools does not present the same constitutional concerns as the devotional use of religion.

> As a matter of history, schoolchildren can and should properly be informed of all aspects of this Nation's religious heritage. I would see no constitutional problem if schoolchildren were taught the nature of the Founding Father's religious beliefs and how these beliefs affected the attitudes of the times and the structure of our government. Courses in comparative religion of course are customary and constitutionally appropriate. In fact, since religion permeates our history, a familiarity with the nature of religious beliefs is necessary to understand many historical as well as contemporary events. In addition, it is worth noting that the Establishment Clause does not prohibit *per se* the educational use of religious documents in public school education. Although this Court has recognized that the Bible is "an instrument of religion," *Abington School District v. Schempp,* 224, it also has made clear that the Bible "may constitutionally be used in an appropriate study of history, civilization, ethics, comparative religion, or the like." *Stone v. Graham,* 449 U.S., 42 (citing *Abington School District v. Schempp,* 225). The book is, in fact, "the world's all-time best seller" with

undoubted literary and historic value apart from its religious content. The Establishment Clause is properly understood to prohibit the use of the Bible and other religious documents in public school education only when the purpose of the use is to advance a particular religious belief.

These comments played a role in spurring a movement to teach about religion, in an academic and neutral way, in our nation's elementary and secondary schools. In 1988, for example, eighteen diverse religious and educational groups released "Religion and the Public School Curriculum," the first consensus guidelines on study about religion in the public schools. The guidelines state in part:

> Because religion plays a significant role in history and society, study about religion is essential to understanding both our nation and the world. Omission of facts about religion can give students the false impression that the religious life of humankind is insignificant or unimportant. . . . Study about religion is also important if students are to value religious liberty, the first freedom guaranteed in the Bill of Rights. Moreover, knowledge of the roles of religion in the past and present promotes cross-cultural understanding essential to democracy and world peace.[1]

The guidelines helped trigger further discussion of religion in history textbooks, state standards, and classrooms in many parts of the nation. Especially in the wake of the 9/11 attacks on the United States, the argument for increased teaching about religion in public schools has gathered steam. Progress in this area, however, has not been clear-cut or universally embraced. Critics of the current curriculum, including Warren Nord and Charles Haynes, authors of *Taking Religion Seriously Across the Curriculum*,[2] argue that these modest changes do not add up to serious treatment of religion or religious diversity across the curriculum. At the same time, scholars have highlighted the challenges that must be addressed if religion is to be more comprehensively taught in our nation's public schools in ways that comport with constitutional principles, sound pedagogy, and basic fairness. See Kent Greenawalt, "Teaching About Religion in the Public Schools," *Journal of Law and Politics* 18 (Spring 2002): 329.

More recently, conflict has flared around efforts to study the Bible in public schools and appropriate curricula for doing so. For example, in 2006 the state of Georgia enacted a law requiring the State Board of Education to create two optional courses on the history and literature of the Old and New Testament. Most agree that such courses may be constitutionally taught, but there is litigation over whether some courses resemble Sunday school lessons more than they do academic courses. In another example, in 2007 the American Civil Liberties Union brought a lawsuit against public schools in Odessa, Texas, charging that a Bible course taught in these schools impermissibly promotes religion. It also should be noted that there is disagreement from an educational and fairness standpoint about whether Bible courses should be taught if they are the only religion-related course offerings in particular schools. For more on current debates surrounding efforts to teach about religion in public schools, visit the Web site of the First Amendment Center of the Freedom Forum.[3]

## Presidential Guidelines on Religious Expression in Public Elementary and Secondary Schools

There often has been confusion among school officials about exactly what rules they must observe regarding religious expression in public elementary and secondary schools. Amidst emotional claims that "God had been kicked out of our public schools," dispassionate guidance on these issues is needed but often not widely available. For these and other reasons, Presidents William J. Clinton and George W. Bush issued guidelines for schools to try to help them understand the constitutional rules governing religious expression in the public schools.

President Clinton issued guidelines in 1998 based on a document drafted by a diverse group of religious and civil liberties lawyers, including two of this book's authors. In an accompanying letter to public school officials, Clinton's Secretary of Education, Richard Riley, noted that "[t]he purpose of promulgating these presidential guidelines was to end much of the confusion regarding religious expression in our nation's public schools that had developed over more than thirty years since the U.S. Supreme Court decision in 1962 regarding state sponsored school prayer." These guidelines may be found at http://www.ed.gov/Speeches/08-1995/religion.html.

In 2003, President George W. Bush offered guidelines of his own on "constitutionally protected prayer in public elementary and secondary schools." These guidelines were required by the provisions of the No Child Left Behind Act of 2001. The most obvious difference between the Clinton and Bush guidelines is that the No Child Left Behind Act stated that local education authorities would not receive federal funding unless they certified in writing that they had no policies that prevented or otherwise denied participation in "constitutionally protected prayer as set forth in [the Bush] guidelines." Bush administration officials explained that they believed that the Clinton guidelines had not been adequately observed because they had no "teeth" in them; in other words, school officials were under no legal obligation to honor them. Hence, the threat of losing federal funding was designed to force schools into compliance with the Bush guidelines. The following is an excerpt from the Bush guidelines.[4]

GUIDANCE ON CONSTITUTIONALLY PROTECTED PRAYER IN PUBLIC
ELEMENTARY AND SECONDARY SCHOOLS
February 7, 2003

## OVERVIEW OF GOVERNING CONSTITUTIONAL PRINCIPLES

The relationship between religion and government in the United States is governed by the First Amendment to the Constitution, which both prevents the government from establishing religion and protects privately initiated religious expression and activities from government interference and discrimination. The First Amendment thus establishes certain limits on the conduct of public school officials as it relates to religious activity, including prayer.

The legal rules that govern the issue of constitutionally protected prayer in the public schools are similar to those that govern religious expression generally. Thus, in discussing the operation of Section 9524 of the ESEA, this guidance sometimes speaks in terms of "religious expression." There are a variety of issues relating to religion in the public schools, however, that this guidance is not intended to address.

The Supreme Court has repeatedly held that the First Amendment requires public school officials to be neutral in their treatment of religion, showing neither favoritism toward nor hostility against religious expression such as prayer. Accordingly, the First Amendment forbids religious activity that is sponsored by the government but protects religious activity that is initiated by private individuals, and the line between government-sponsored and privately initiated religious expression is vital to a proper understanding of the First Amendment's scope. As the Court has explained in several cases, "there is a crucial difference between *government* speech endorsing religion, which the Establishment Clause forbids, and *private* speech endorsing religion, which the Free Speech and Free Exercise Clauses protect."

The Supreme Court's decisions over the past forty years set forth principles that distinguish impermissible governmental religious speech from the constitutionally protected private religious speech of students. For example, teachers and other public school officials may not lead their classes in prayer, devotional readings from the Bible, or other religious activities. Nor may school officials attempt to persuade or compel students to participate in prayer or other religious activities. Such conduct is "attributable to the State" and thus violates the Establishment Clause.

Similarly, public school officials may not themselves decide that prayer should be included in school-sponsored events. In *Lee v. Weisman*, for example, the Supreme Court held that public school officials violated the Constitution in inviting a member of the clergy to deliver a prayer at a graduation ceremony. Nor may school officials grant religious speakers preferential access to public audiences, or otherwise select public speakers on a basis that favors religious speech. In *Santa Fe Independent School District v. Doe*, for example, the Court invalidated a school's football game speaker policy on the ground that it was designed by school officials to result in pregame prayer, thus favoring religious expression over secular expression.

Although the Constitution forbids public school officials from directing or favoring prayer, students do not "shed their constitutional rights to freedom of speech or expression at the schoolhouse gate," and the Supreme Court has made clear that "private religious speech, far from being a First Amendment orphan, is as fully protected under the Free Speech Clause as secular private expression." Moreover, not all religious speech that takes place in the public schools or at school-sponsored events is governmental speech. For example, "nothing in the Constitution . . . prohibits any public school student from voluntarily praying at any time before, during, or after the school day," and students may pray with fellow students during the school day on the same terms and conditions that they may engage in other conversation or speech. Likewise, local school authorities possess substantial discretion to impose rules of order and pedagogical restrictions on student activities, but they may not structure or administer such rules to discriminate against student prayer or religious speech. For instance, where schools permit student expression on the basis of genuinely neutral criteria and students retain primary control over the content of their expression, the speech of students who choose to express themselves through religious means such as prayer is not attributable to the state and therefore may not be restricted because of its religious content. Student remarks are not attributable to the state simply because they are delivered in a public setting or to a public audience. As the Supreme Court has explained: "The proposition that schools do not endorse everything they fail to censor is not complicated," and the Constitution mandates neutrality rather than hostility toward privately initiated religious expression.

## APPLYING THE GOVERNING PRINCIPLES IN PARTICULAR CONTEXTS

### Prayer During Noninstructional Time

Students may pray when not engaged in school activities or instruction, subject to the same rules designed to prevent material disruption of the educational program that are applied to other privately initiated expressive activities. Among other things, students may read their Bibles or other scriptures, say grace before meals, and pray or study religious materials with fellow students during recess, the lunch hour, or other noninstructional time to the same extent that they may engage in nonreligious activities. While school authorities may impose rules of order and pedagogical restrictions on student activities, they may not discriminate against student prayer or religious speech in applying such rules and restrictions.

### Organized Prayer Groups and Activities

Students may organize prayer groups, religious clubs, and "see you at the pole" gatherings before school to the same extent that students are permitted to organize other non-curricular student activities groups. Such groups must be given the same access to school facilities for assembling as is given to other non-curricular groups, without discrimination because of the religious content of their expression. School authorities possess substantial discretion concerning whether to permit the use of school media for student advertising or announcements regarding non-curricular activities. However, where student groups that meet for nonreligious activities are permitted to advertise or announce their meetings—for example, by advertising in a student newspaper, making announcements on a student activities bulletin board or public address system, or handing out leaflets—school authorities may not discriminate against groups who meet to pray. School authorities may disclaim sponsorship of non-curricular groups and events, provided they administer such disclaimers in a manner that neither favors nor disfavors groups that meet to engage in prayer or religious speech.

### Teachers, Administrators, and Other School Employees

When acting in their official capacities as representatives of the state, teachers, school administrators, and other school employees are prohibited by the Establishment Clause from encouraging or discouraging prayer, and from actively participating in such activity with students. Teachers may, however, take part in religious activities where the overall context makes clear that they are not participating in their official capacities. Before school or during lunch, for example, teachers may meet with other teachers for prayer or Bible study to the same extent that they may engage in other conversation or nonreligious activities. Similarly, teachers may participate in their personal capacities in privately sponsored baccalaureate ceremonies.

### Moments of Silence

If a school has a "minute of silence" or other quiet periods during the school day, students are free to pray silently, or not to pray, during these periods of time. Teachers and other school employees may neither encourage nor discourage students from praying during such time periods.

Accommodation of Prayer During Instructional Time

It has long been established that schools have the discretion to dismiss students to off-premises religious instruction, provided that schools do not encourage or discourage participation in such instruction or penalize students for attending or not attending. Similarly, schools may excuse students from class to remove a significant burden on their religious exercise, where doing so would not impose material burdens on other students. For example, it would be lawful for schools to excuse Muslim students briefly from class to enable them to fulfill their religious obligations to pray during Ramadan.

Where school officials have a practice of excusing students from class on the basis of parents' requests for accommodation of nonreligious needs, religiously motivated requests for excusal may not be accorded less favorable treatment. In addition, in some circumstances, based on federal or state constitutional law or pursuant to state statutes, schools may be required to make accommodations that relieve substantial burdens on students' religious exercise. Schools officials are therefore encouraged to consult with their attorneys regarding such obligations.

Religious Expression and Prayer in Class Assignments

Students may express their beliefs about religion in homework, artwork, and other written and oral assignments free from discrimination based on the religious content of their submissions. Such home and classroom work should be judged by ordinary academic standards of substance and relevance and against other legitimate pedagogical concerns identified by the school. Thus, if a teacher's assignment involves writing a poem, the work of a student who submits a poem in the form of a prayer (for example, a psalm) should be judged on the basis of academic standards (such as literary quality) and neither penalized nor rewarded on account of its religious content.

Student Assemblies and Extracurricular Events

Student speakers at student assemblies and extracurricular activities such as sporting events may not be selected on a basis that either favors or disfavors religious speech. Where student speakers are selected on the basis of genuinely neutral, evenhanded criteria and retain primary control over the content of their expression, that expression is not attributable to the school and therefore may not be restricted because of its religious (or anti-religious) content. By contrast, where school officials determine or substantially control the content of what is expressed, such speech is attributable to the school and may not include prayer or other specifically religious (or anti-religious) content. To avoid any mistaken perception that a school endorses student speech that is not in fact attributable to the school, school officials may make appropriate, neutral disclaimers to clarify that such speech (whether religious or nonreligious) is the speaker's and not the school's.

Prayer at Graduation

School officials may not mandate or organize prayer at graduation or select speakers for such events in a manner that favors religious speech such as prayer. Where students or other private graduation speakers are selected on the basis of genuinely neutral, evenhanded criteria and retain primary control over the content of their expression, however, that expression is not attributable to the school and therefore may not be restricted because of its religious (or anti-religious) content. To avoid any mistaken perception that a school endorses student or other private speech that is not in fact attributable to the school, school officials may make appropriate, neutral disclaimers to clarify that such speech (whether religious or nonreligious) is the speaker's and not the school's.

Baccalaureate Ceremonies

School officials may not mandate or organize religious ceremonies. However, if a school makes its facilities and related services available to other private groups, it must make its facilities and services available on the same terms to organizers of privately sponsored religious baccalaureate ceremonies. In addition, a school may disclaim official endorsement of events sponsored by private groups, provided it does so in a manner that neither favors nor disfavors groups that meet to engage in prayer or religious speech.

---

## Notes and Questions

1. The Bush guidance states: "Teachers may . . . take part in religious activities where the overall context makes clear that they are not participating in their official capacities." In light of this statement, is a teacher permitted to participate in a student-organized prayer meeting before school? Should he or she be permitted to offer religious counsel and encouragement to a student who goes to the same church as they walk down the halls between classes?

2. The Bush guidance states: "Student may express their beliefs about religion in homework, artwork, and other written and oral assignments free from discrimination based on the religious content of their submissions." Assume a teacher asks the students to write a dramatic speech and share it with the class. One student writes a speech about the horrible fate that will befall non-Muslims when they die. In light of the guidelines and constitutional precepts, should the student be permitted to focus on the topic and share the speech with the class? Would it matter if it was a high school class instead of a middle or elementary school class?

3. Some disagreed with the notion that the Bush guidelines were a fair and accurate statement of the law. The following excerpt from a document by Americans United for Separation of Church and State, for example, provides a critical analysis of part of the Bush guidelines:

   [T]he Guidance overstates the case when it asserts that the law mandates that prayers must be permitted at school events under certain circumstances. Within the Eleventh Circuit—which consists of Georgia, Alabama, and Florida—prayers may be permitted at graduation ceremonies in certain circumstances, but this holding does not extend beyond the graduation context. Elsewhere in the country, whether prayers may be permitted at graduation ceremonies and/or other school-sponsored events is an unresolved question, and the pronouncements of the Supreme Court and two federal circuits suggest that they may not be.

4. As stated above, the law that triggered these guidelines provided that a school would lose its funding if it fails to comply with the guidelines. Can you think of some drawbacks of such a policy? In your opinion, is this funding cut-off mostly helpful or mostly harmful?

# CHAPTER 19

# EQUAL ACCESS

Earlier chapters have explored some of the applicable constitutional principles when government speech includes religious references or elements. For example, in the previous chapter, we noted that public schools may teach about religion, but they may not preach religion. This chapter considers a different issue: what are the constitutional rules that apply to nongovernmental religious speech on government property?

An important rule to bear in mind in these settings is the following one articulated by the Supreme Court: "[T]here is a crucial difference between government[al] speech endorsing religion, which the Establishment Clause forbids, and [nongovernmental] speech endorsing religion, which the Free Speech and Free Exercise Clauses protect."[1] In other words, if it is clear that the speech endorsing religion is nongovernmental, then it is protected rather than prohibited by the Constitution, even if such speech takes place on governmental property. (As you will see in this chapter and the next two, this does not mean that every parcel of government property must be equally open to nongovernmental speech, including nongovernmental religious speech, but it is an important basic guideline to bear in mind.)

In this vein, this chapter focuses on what is often called the "equal access" principle. It basically means that if the government opens its property for a wide variety of nongovernmental speech, it generally must welcome nongovernmental religious speech to be part of that mix. This chapter discusses a number of cases that deal with the equal access principle as it applies to the use of public school property by students and to the use of such property after school hours by nongovernmental community groups. Note that in these cases the Court regularly analyzes the issues as implicating the Free Speech Clause, rather than the Free Exercise Clause. This approach is consistent with that taken in several of the early Jehovah's Witness cases, discussed in chapter 8. The chief reason for relying on the Free Speech Clause is that it has a strong "equality" element (i.e., regulations affecting speech are to be content and viewpoint neutral), whereas it may be difficult to show that exclusion of religious speech from government property rises to the level of a substantial burden on religious belief or practice.

The Court addressed the equal access issue for the first time in 1981 in the higher education context, considering "whether a state university, which makes its facilities generally available for the activities of registered student groups, may close its facilities to a registered student group desiring to use the facilities for religious worship and religious discussion." As you read the case, pay particular attention to the debate about whether this kind of equal access for nongovernmental religious speech is merely something the university may choose to do, or whether it is a constitutional obligation.

———————————

## WIDMAR v. VINCENT
### 454 U.S. 263 (1981)

▩ JUSTICE POWELL delivered the opinion of the court.

This case presents the question whether a state university, which makes its facilities generally available for the activities of registered student groups, may close its facilities to a registered student group desiring to use the facilities for religious worship and religious discussion.

I

It is the stated policy of the University of Missouri at Kansas City to encourage the activities of student organizations. The University officially recognizes over 100 student groups. It routinely provides University facilities for the meetings of registered organizations. Students pay an activity fee of $41 per semester (1978-1979) to help defray the costs to the University.

From 1973 until 1977 a registered religious group named Cornerstone regularly sought and received permission to conduct its meetings in University facilities.[2] In 1977, however, the University informed the group that it could no longer meet in University buildings. The exclusion was based on a regulation, adopted by the Board of Curators in 1972, that prohibits the use of University buildings or grounds "for purposes of religious worship or religious teaching."

There is no chapel on the campus of UMKC. The nearest University chapel is at the Columbia campus, approximately 125 miles east of UMKC.

Although the University had routinely approved Cornerstone meetings before 1977, the District Court found that University officials had never "authorized a student organization to utilize a University facility for a meeting where they had full knowledge that the purposes of the meeting [included] religious worship or religious teaching."

Eleven University students, all members of Cornerstone, brought suit to challenge the regulation in the Federal District Court for the Western District of Missouri. They alleged that the University's discrimination against religious activity and discussion violated their rights to free exercise of religion, equal

---

[2] Cornerstone is an organization of evangelical Christian students from various denominational backgrounds. According to an affidavit filed in 1977, "perhaps twenty students . . . participate actively in Cornerstone and form the backbone of the campus organization." Cornerstone held its on-campus meetings in classrooms and in the student center. These meetings were open to the public and attracted up to 125 students. A typical Cornerstone meeting included prayer, hymns, Bible commentary, and discussion of religious views and experiences.

---

### POLICY OF UNIVERSITY OF MISSOURI AT KANSAS CITY

The pertinent regulations provided as follows:

"4.0314.0107 No University buildings or grounds (except chapels as herein provided) may be used for purposes of religious worship or religious teaching by either student or non-student groups. . . . The general prohibition against use of University buildings and grounds for religious worship or religious teaching is a policy required, in the opinion of The Board of Curators, by the Constitution and laws of the State and is not open to any other construction. No regulations shall be interpreted to forbid the offering of prayer or other appropriate recognition of religion at public functions held in University facilities. . . .

"4.0314.0108 Regular chapels established on University grounds may be used for religious services but not for regular recurring services of any groups. Special rules and procedures shall be established for each such chapel by the Chancellor. It is specifically directed that no advantage shall be given to any religious group." [These regulations appear as note 3 in the text of the case.]

---

protection, and freedom of speech under the First and Fourteenth Amendments to the Constitution of the United States. . . .

## II

Through its policy of accommodating their meetings, the University has created a forum generally open for use by student groups. Having done so, the University has assumed an obligation to justify its discriminations and exclusions under applicable constitutional norms.[5] The Constitution forbids a State to enforce certain exclusions from a forum generally open to the public, even if it was not required to create the forum in the first place. See, e.g., *Southeastern Promotions, Ltd. v. Conrad,* 420 U.S. 546, 555-559 (1975) (because municipal theater was a public forum, city could not exclude a production without satisfying constitutional safeguards applicable to prior restraints).

The University's institutional mission, which it describes as providing a "*secular* education" to its students, does not exempt its actions from constitutional scrutiny. With respect to persons entitled to be there, our cases leave no doubt that the First Amendment rights of speech and association extend to the campuses of state universities.

---

[5] This Court has recognized that the campus of a public university, at least for its students, possesses many of the characteristics of a public forum. "The college classroom with its surrounding environs is peculiarly 'the marketplace of ideas.'" *Healy v. James,* 408 U.S. 169, 180 (1972). Moreover, the capacity of a group or individual "to participate in the intellectual give and take of campus debate . . . [would be] limited by denial of access to the customary media for communicating with the administration, faculty members, and other students." *Id.,* 181-182. We therefore have held that students enjoy First Amendment rights of speech and association on the campus, and that the "denial [to particular groups] of use of campus facilities for meetings and other appropriate purposes" must be subjected to the level of scrutiny appropriate to any form of prior restraint. *Id.,* 181, 184.

At the same time, however, our cases have recognized that First Amendment rights must be analyzed "in light of the special characteristics of the school environment." *Tinker v. Des Moines Independent School District,* 393 U.S. 503, 506 (1969). We continue to adhere to that view. A university differs in significant respects from public forums such as streets or parks or even municipal theaters. A university's mission is education, and decisions of this Court have never denied a university's authority to impose reasonable regulations compatible with that mission upon the use of its campus and facilities. We have not held, for example, that a campus must make all of its facilities equally available to students and nonstudents alike, or that a university must grant free access to all of its grounds or buildings.

Here UMKC has discriminated against student groups and speakers based on their desire to use a generally open forum to engage in religious worship and discussion. These are forms of speech and association protected by the First Amendment.[6] In order to justify discriminatory exclusion from a public forum based on the religious content of a group's intended speech, the University must therefore satisfy the standard of review appropriate to content-based exclusions. It must show that its regulation is necessary to serve a compelling state interest and that it is narrowly drawn to achieve that end.

III

In this case the University claims a compelling interest in maintaining strict separation of church and State. It derives this interest from the "Establishment Clauses" of both the Federal and Missouri Constitutions.

A

The University first argues that it cannot offer its facilities to religious groups and speakers on the terms available to other groups without violating the Establishment Clause of the Constitution of the United States. We agree that the interest of the University in complying with its constitutional obligations may be characterized as compelling. It does not follow, however, that an "equal access" policy would be incompatible with this Court's Establishment Clause cases. Those cases hold that a policy will not offend the Establishment Clause if it can pass a three-pronged test: "First, the [governmental policy] must have a secular legislative purpose; second, its principal

---

[6] The dissent argues that "religious worship" is not speech generally protected by the "free speech" guarantee of the First Amendment and the "equal protection" guarantee of the Fourteenth Amendment. If "religious worship" were protected "speech," the dissent reasons, "the Religion Clauses would be emptied of any independent meaning in circumstances in which religious practice took the form of speech." This is a novel argument. The dissent does not deny that speech *about* religion is speech entitled to the general protections of the First Amendment. It does not argue that descriptions of religious experiences fail to qualify as "speech." Nor does it repudiate last Term's decision in *Heffron v. International Society for Krishna Consciousness, Inc.*, which assumed that religious appeals to nonbelievers constituted protected "speech." Rather, the dissent seems to attempt a distinction between the kinds of religious speech explicitly protected by our cases and a new class of religious "speech [acts]," constituting "worship." There are at least three difficulties with this distinction.

First, the dissent fails to establish that the distinction has intelligible content. There is no indication when "singing hymns, reading scripture, and teaching biblical principles," cease to be "singing, teaching, and reading"—all apparently forms of "speech," despite their religious subject matter—and become unprotected "worship."

Second, even if the distinction drew an arguably principled line, it is highly doubtful that it would lie within the judicial competence to administer. Merely to draw the distinction would require the university—and ultimately the courts—to inquire into the significance of words and practices to different religious faiths, and in varying circumstances by the same faith. Such inquiries would tend inevitably to entangle the State with religion in a manner forbidden by our cases.

Finally, the dissent fails to establish the *relevance* of the distinction on which it seeks to rely. The dissent apparently wishes to preserve the vitality of the Establishment Clause. But it gives no reason why the Establishment Clause, or any other provision of the Constitution, would require different treatment for religious speech designed to win religious converts, than for religious worship by persons already converted. It is far from clear that the State gives greater support in the latter case than in the former.

or primary effect must be one that neither advances nor inhibits religion . . . ; finally, the [policy] must not foster 'an excessive government entanglement with religion.'" *Lemon v. Kurtzman*, 403 U.S. 602, 612-613 (1971).

In this case two prongs of the test are clearly met. Both the District Court and the Court of Appeals held that an open-forum policy, including nondiscrimination against religious speech,[9] would have a secular purpose[10] and would avoid entanglement with religion.[11] But the District Court concluded, and the University argues here, that allowing religious groups to share the limited public forum would have the "primary effect" of advancing religion.

The University's argument misconceives the nature of this case. The question is not whether the creation of a religious forum would violate the Establishment Clause. The University has opened its facilities for use by student groups, and the question is whether it can now exclude groups because of the content of their speech. In this context we are unpersuaded that the primary effect of the public forum, open to all forms of discourse, would be to advance religion.

We are not oblivious to the range of an open forum's likely effects. It is possible—perhaps even foreseeable—that religious groups will benefit from access to University facilities. But this Court has explained that a religious organization's enjoyment of merely "incidental" benefits does not violate the prohibition against the "primary advancement" of religion.

We are satisfied that any religious benefits of an open forum at UMKC would be "incidental" within the meaning of our cases. Two factors are especially relevant.

First, an open forum in a public university does not confer any imprimatur of state approval on religious sects or practices. As the Court of Appeals quite aptly stated, such a policy "would no more commit the University . . . to religious goals" than it is "now committed to the goals of the Students for a

---

[9] As the dissent emphasizes, the Establishment Clause requires the State to distinguish between "religious" speech—speech, undertaken or approved by the State, the primary effect of which is to support an establishment of religion—and "nonreligious" speech—speech, undertaken or approved by the State, the primary effect of which is not to support an establishment of religion. This distinction is required by the plain text of the Constitution. It is followed in our cases. The dissent attempts to equate this distinction with its view of an alleged constitutional difference between religious "speech" and religious "worship." We think that the distinction advanced by the dissent lacks a foundation in either the Constitution or in our cases, and that it is judicially unmanageable.

[10] It is the avowed purpose of UMKC to provide a forum in which students can exchange ideas. The University argues that use of the forum for religious speech would undermine this secular aim. But by creating a forum the University does not thereby endorse or promote any of the particular ideas aired there. Undoubtedly many views are advocated in the forum with which the University desires no association.

Because this case involves a forum already made generally available to student groups, it differs from those cases in which this Court has invalidated statutes permitting school facilities to be used for instruction by religious groups, but not by others. In those cases the school may appear to sponsor the views of the speaker.

[11] We agree with the Court of Appeals that the University would risk greater "entanglement" by attempting to enforce its exclusion of "religious worship" and "religious speech." Initially, the University would need to determine which words and activities fall within "religious worship and religious teaching." This alone could prove "an impossible task in an age where many and various beliefs meet the constitutional definition of religion." There would also be a continuing need to monitor group meetings to ensure compliance with the rule.

Democratic Society, the Young Socialist Alliance," or any other group eligible to use its facilities.

Second, the forum is available to a broad class of nonreligious as well as religious speakers; there are over 100 recognized student groups at UMKC. The provision of benefits to so broad a spectrum of groups is an important index of secular effect. If the Establishment Clause barred the extension of general benefits to religious groups, "a church could not be protected by the police and fire departments, or have its public sidewalk kept in repair." *Roemer v. Maryland Public Works Bd.*, 426 U.S. 736, 747 (plurality opinion). At least in the absence of empirical evidence that religious groups will dominate UMKC's open forum, we agree with the Court of Appeals that the advancement of religion would not be the forum's "primary effect." . . .

IV

Our holding in this case in no way undermines the capacity of the University to establish reasonable time, place, and manner regulations. Nor do we question the right of the University to make academic judgments as to how best to allocate scarce resources or "to determine for itself on academic grounds who may teach, what may be taught, how it shall be taught, and who may be admitted to study." *Sweezy v. New Hampshire*, 354 U.S. 234, 263 (1957) (FRANKFURTER, J., concurring in result). Finally, we affirm the continuing validity of cases that recognize a university's right to exclude even First Amendment activities that violate reasonable campus rules or substantially interfere with the opportunity of other students to obtain an education.

The basis for our decision is narrow. Having created a forum generally open to student groups, the University seeks to enforce a content-based exclusion of religious speech. Its exclusionary policy violates the fundamental principle that a state regulation of speech should be content-neutral, and the University is unable to justify this violation under applicable constitutional standards.

For this reason, the decision of the Court of Appeals is

*Affirmed.*

JUSTICE STEVENS, concurring in the judgment.

As the Court recognizes, every university must "make academic judgments as to how best to allocate scarce resources." The Court appears to hold, however, that those judgments must "serve a compelling state interest" whenever they are based, even in part, on the content of speech. This conclusion apparently flows from the Court's suggestion that a student activities program—from which the public may be excluded—must be managed as though it were a "public forum." In my opinion, the use of the terms "compelling state interest" and "public forum" to analyze the question presented in this case may needlessly undermine the academic freedom of public universities. . . .

Because every university's resources are limited, an educational institution must routinely make decisions concerning the use of the time and space that is available for extracurricular activities. In my judgment, it is both necessary and appropriate for those decisions to evaluate the content of a proposed student activity. I should think it obvious, for example, that if two groups of

25 students requested the use of a room at a particular time—one to view Mickey Mouse cartoons and the other to rehearse an amateur performance of Hamlet—the First Amendment would not require that the room be reserved for the group that submitted its application first. Nor do I see why a university should have to establish a "compelling state interest" to defend its decision to permit one group to use the facility and not the other. In my opinion, a university should be allowed to decide for itself whether a program that illuminates the genius of Walt Disney should be given precedence over one that may duplicate material adequately covered in the classroom. Judgments of this kind should be made by academicians, not by federal judges, and their standards for decision should not be encumbered with ambiguous phrases like "compelling state interest." . . .

▓ JUSTICE WHITE, dissenting.

In affirming the decision of the Court of Appeals, the majority rejects petitioners' argument that the Establishment Clause of the Constitution prohibits the use of university buildings for religious purposes. A state university may permit its property to be used for purely religious services without violating the First and Fourteenth Amendments. With this I agree. The Establishment Clause, however, sets limits only on what the State may do with respect to religious organizations; it does not establish what the State is *required* to do. I have long argued that Establishment Clause limits on state action which incidentally aids religion are not as strict as the Court has held. The step from the permissible to the necessary, however, is a long one. In my view, just as there is room under the Religion Clauses for state policies that may have some beneficial effect on religion, there is also room for state policies that may incidentally burden religion. In other words, I believe the States to be a good deal freer to formulate policies that affect religion in divergent ways than does the majority. The majority's position will inevitably lead to those contradictions and tensions between the Establishment and Free Exercise Clauses warned against by JUSTICE STEWART in *Sherbert v. Verner*, 374 U.S. 398, 416.

The University regulation at issue here provides in pertinent part:

> No University buildings or grounds (except chapels as herein provided) may be used for purposes of religious worship or religious teaching by either student or nonstudent groups. Student congregations of local churches or of recognized denominations or sects, although not technically recognized campus groups, may use the facilities . . . under the same regulations that apply to recognized campus organizations, provided that no University facilities may be used for purposes of religious worship or religious teaching.

Although there may be instances in which it would be difficult to determine whether a religious group used university facilities for "worship" or "religious teaching," rather than for secular ends, this is not such a case. The regulation was applied to respondents' religious group, Cornerstone, only after the group explicitly informed the University that it sought access to the facilities for the purpose of offering prayer, singing hymns, reading scripture, and teaching biblical principles. Cornerstone described their meetings as follows: "Although these meetings would not appear to a casual observer to correspond precisely to a traditional worship service, there is no doubt that worship is an important part of the general atmosphere."[1] The issue here is only whether the University regulation as applied and interpreted in this case is impermissible under the Federal Constitution. If it is impermissible, it is because it runs afoul of either the Free Speech or the Free Exercise Clause of the First Amendment.

A large part of respondents' argument, accepted by the court below and accepted by the majority, is founded on the proposition that because religious worship uses speech, it is protected by the Free Speech Clause of the First Amendment.[2] Not only is it protected, they argue, but religious worship *qua* speech is not different from any other variety of protected speech as a matter of constitutional principle. I believe that this proposition is plainly wrong. Were it right, the Religion Clauses would be emptied of any independent meaning in circumstances in which religious practice took the form of speech.

Although the majority describes this argument as "novel," I believe it to be clearly supported by our previous cases. Just last Term, the Court found it sufficiently obvious that the Establishment Clause prohibited a State from posting a copy of the Ten Commandments on the classroom wall that a statute requiring such a posting was summarily struck down. *Stone v. Graham*, 449 U.S. 39 (1980). That case necessarily presumed that the State could not ignore the religious content of the written message, nor was it permitted to treat that content as it would, or must, treat other—secular—messages under the First Amendment's protection of speech. Similarly, the Court's decisions prohibiting prayer in the public schools rest on a content-based distinction between varieties of speech: as a speech act, apart from its content, a prayer is

---

[1] Cornerstone was denied access to University facilities because it intended to use those facilities for regular religious services in which "worship is an important part of the general atmosphere." There is no issue here as to the application of the regulation to "religious teaching." Reaching this issue is particularly inappropriate in this case because nothing in the record indicates how the University has interpreted the phrase "religious teaching" or even whether it has ever been applied to activity that was not clearly "religious worship." The District Court noted that plaintiffs did not contend that they were "limited, in any way, from holding on-campus meetings that do not include religious worship services." At oral argument, counsel for the University indicated that the regulation would not bar discussion of biblical texts under circumstances that did not constitute "religious worship." The sole question in this case involves application of the regulation to prohibit regular religious worship services in University buildings.

[2] Given that the majority's entire argument turns on this description of religious services as speech, it is surprising that the majority assumes this proposition to require no argument. The majority assumes the conclusion by describing the University's action as discriminating against "speakers based on their desire to . . . engage in religious worship and discussion." As noted above, it is not at all clear that the University has discriminated or intends to discriminate against "religious discussion"—as a preliminary matter; it is not even clear what the majority means by "religious discussion" or how it entered the case. That religious worship is a form of speech, the majority takes to have been established by three cases. *Heffron v. International Society for Krishna Consciousness, Inc.*, 452 U.S. 640 (1981); *Niemotko v. Maryland*, 340 U.S. 268 (1951); *Saia v. New York*, 334 U.S. 558 (1948). None of these cases stand for this proposition. *Heffron* and *Saia* involved the communication of religious views to a nonreligious, public audience. Talk about religion and about religious beliefs, however, is not the same as religious services of worship. *Niemotko* was an equal protection challenge to a discriminatory denial of one religious group's access to a public park. The Court specifically stated that it was not addressing the question of whether the State could uniformly deny all religious groups access to public parks. 340 U.S., 272.

indistinguishable from a biology lesson. See *Abington School District v. Schempp,* 374 U.S. 203 (1963); *Engel v. Vitale,* 370 U.S. 421 (1962). Operation of the Free Exercise Clause is equally dependent, in certain circumstances, on recognition of a content-based distinction between religious and secular speech. Thus, in *Torcaso v. Watkins,* 367 U.S. 488 (1961), the Court struck down, as violative of the Free Exercise Clause, a state requirement that made a declaration of belief in God a condition of state employment. A declaration is again a speech act, but it was the content of the speech that brought the case within the scope of the Free Exercise Clause.

If the majority were right that no distinction may be drawn between verbal acts of worship and other verbal acts, all of these cases would have to be reconsidered. Although I agree that the line may be difficult to draw in many cases, surely the majority cannot seriously suggest that no line may ever be drawn.[3] If that were the case, the majority would have to uphold the University's right to offer a class entitled "Sunday Mass." Under the majority's view, such a class would be—as a matter of constitutional principle—indistinguishable from a class entitled "The History of the Catholic Church."

There may be instances in which a State's attempt to disentangle itself from religious worship would intrude upon secular speech about religion. In such a case, the State's action would be subject to challenge under the Free Speech Clause of the First Amendment. This is not such a case. This case involves religious worship only; the fact that that worship is accomplished through speech does not add anything to respondents' argument. That argument must rely upon the claim that the State's action impermissibly interferes with the free exercise of respondents' religious practices. Although this is a close question, I conclude that it does not.

Plausible analogies on either side suggest themselves. Respondents argue, and the majority agrees, that by permitting any student group to use its facilities for communicative purposes other than religious worship, the University has created a "public forum." With ample support, they argue that the State may not make content-based distinctions as to what groups may use, or what messages may be conveyed in, such a forum. The right of the religious to nondiscriminatory access to the public forum is well established.

Moreover, it is clear that there are bounds beyond which the University could not go in enforcing its regulation: I do not suppose it could prevent students from saying grace before meals in the school cafeteria, or prevent distribution of religious literature on campus.[5]

Petitioners, on the other hand, argue that allowing use of their facilities for religious worship is constitutionally indistinguishable from directly subsidizing such religious services: It would "[fund] a specifically religious activity in

---

[3] Indeed, while footnote 6 of the majority opinion suggests that no intelligible distinction may be drawn between worship and other forms of speech, footnote 9 recognizes that the Establishment Clause "requires" that such a line be drawn. The majority does not adequately explain why the State is "required" to observe a line in one context, but prohibited from voluntarily recognizing it in another context.

[5] There are obvious limits on the scope of this analogy. I know of no precedent holding that simply because a public forum is open to all kinds of speech—including speech about religion—it must be open to regular religious worship services as well. I doubt that the State need stand by and allow its public forum to become a church for any religious sect that chooses to stand on its right of access to that forum.

an otherwise substantially secular setting." *Hunt v. McNair,* 413 U.S. 734, 743 (1973). They argue that the fact that secular student groups are entitled to the in-kind subsidy at issue here does not establish that a religious group is entitled to the same subsidy. They could convincingly argue, for example, that a state university that pays for basketballs for the basketball team is not thereby required to pay for Bibles for a group like Cornerstone.[6]

A third analogy suggests itself, one that falls between these two extremes. There are a variety of state policies which incidentally benefit religion that this Court has upheld without implying that they were constitutionally required of the State. See *Board of Education v. Allen,* 392 U.S. 236 (1968) (state loan of textbooks to parochial school students); *Zorach v. Clauson,* 343 U.S. 306 (1952) (release of students from public schools, during school hours, to perform religious activities away from the school grounds); *Everson v. Board of Education,* 330 U.S. 1 (1947) (state provision of transportation to parochial school students). Provision of university facilities on a uniform basis to all student groups is not very different from provision of textbooks or transportation. From this perspective the issue is not whether the State must, or must not, open its facilities to religious worship; rather, it is whether the State may choose not to do so.

Each of these analogies is persuasive. Because they lead to different results, however, they are of limited help in reaching a decision here. They also demonstrate the difficulty in reconciling the various interests expressed in the Religion Clauses. In my view, therefore, resolution of this case is best achieved by returning to first principles. This requires an assessment of the burden on respondents' ability freely to exercise their religious beliefs and practices and of the State's interest in enforcing its regulation.

Respondents complain that compliance with the regulation would require them to meet "about a block and a half" from campus under conditions less comfortable than those previously available on campus.[7] I view this burden on free exercise as minimal. Because the burden is minimal, the State need do no more than demonstrate that the regulation furthers some permissible state end. The State's interest in avoiding claims that it is financing or otherwise supporting religious worship—in maintaining a definitive separation between church and State—is such an end. That the State truly does mean to act toward this end is amply supported by the treatment of religion in the State Constitution.[8] Thus, I believe the interest of the State is sufficiently strong to justify the imposition of the minimal burden on respondents' ability freely to exercise their religious beliefs.

---

[6] There are, of course, limits to this subsidy argument. *Sherbert v. Verner,* 374 U.S. 398 (1963), and *Thomas v. Indiana Employment Security Division,* 450 U.S. 707 (1981), demonstrate that in certain circumstances the State may be required to "subsidize," at least indirectly, religious practices, under circumstances in which it does not and need not subsidize similar behavior founded on secular motives.

[7] Respondents also complain that the University action has made their religious message less attractive by suggesting that it is not appropriate fare for the college campus. I give no weight to this because it is indistinguishable from an argument that respondents are entitled to the appearance of an endorsement of their beliefs and practices from the University.

[8] Since 1820, the Missouri Constitution has contained provisions requiring a separation of church and State. The Missouri Supreme Court has held that the state constitutional provisions are "not only more explicit but more restrictive than the Establishment Clause of the United States Constitution." *Paster v. Tussey,* 512 S. W. 2d 97, 102 (1974).

On these facts, therefore, I cannot find that the application of the regulation to prevent Cornerstone from holding religious worship services in University facilities violates the First and Fourteenth Amendments. I would not hold as the majority does that if a university permits students and others to use its property for secular purposes, it must also furnish facilities to religious groups for the purposes of worship and the practice of their religion. Accordingly, I would reverse the judgment of the Court of Appeals.

## NOTES AND QUESTIONS

1. The trial court in *Widmar v. Vincent* found that allowing equal access to University facilities for groups like Cornerstone would be unconstitutional because it would have the primary effect of advancing religion. The court referenced the Supreme Court's ruling in *Tilton v. Richardson*, in which the Court found that a college building constructed through a grant of federal financial assistance must be prohibited from "sectarian use" in perpetuity rather than simply for twenty years, as the statute had provided. How do you think the lower court could have applied this decision to arrive at its ruling? Can you think of a way to distinguish the *Tilton* case from the case at hand?

2. The Court majority argues that the open forum at the university "does not confer any imprimatur of state approval on religious sects or practices." How does it explain this conclusion? Would the Court have ruled differently if it had been faced with a case involving a state college in the Bible Belt that recognized 50 student clubs, 35 of which were Christian groups? What if the case had instead involved a state college in the North that recognized 50 student clubs, 10 of which were Christian, 10 of which were Jewish, 5 Muslim, 3 Buddhist, 2 Hindu, 3 ecumenical, and 2 atheistic?

3. The dissent states: "The sole question in this case involves application of the regulation to prohibit regular worship services in University buildings." Justice White proceeds to argue that "[t]alk about religion and religious beliefs . . . is not the same as religious services of worship." White cites the *Stone v. Graham* case and the school prayer cases and concludes: "If the majority were right that no distinction may be drawn between verbal acts of worship and other verbal acts, all of these cases would have to be reconsidered." Justice White also states that, if the majority is right on this issue,

   If that were the case, the majority would have to uphold the University's right to offer a class entitled "Sunday Mass." Under the majority's view, such a class would be—as a matter of constitutional principle—indistinguishable from a class entitled "The History of the Catholic Church."

   Is Justice White correct? How does the majority analyze this issue of religious worship on government property?

4. In the first paragraph of his dissenting opinion, Justice White summarizes his view of the case. If he agrees that a state university may permit its property to be used for purely religious services without violating the Establishment Clause, why did White file a dissenting opinion in this case?

5. Justice White's chief philosophical complaint with the reasoning of the majority is that in equating religious worship with religious (and secular) speech, it empties the Free Exercise Clause of any independent meaning. Has Justice White identified an important matter of concern? Can you think of any down side to equating religious speech with secular speech and relying primarily on the Free Speech Clause to protect religious expression? Keep this question in mind as you read the remaining cases in this chapter.

6. In a footnote in his dissenting opinion, Justice White cites the following statements made during oral argument of the case:

> Counsel for respondents was somewhat more forthright in recognizing the extraordinary breadth of his argument, than is the majority. Counsel explicitly stated that once the distinction between speech and worship is collapsed a university that generally provides student groups access to its facilities would be constitutionally required to allow its facilities to be used as a church for the purpose of holding "regular church services." Similarly, although the majority opinion limits its discussion to student groups, counsel for respondents recognized that the First Amendment argument relied upon would apply equally to nonstudent groups. He recognized that respondents' submission would require the University to make available its buildings to the Catholic Church and other denominations for the purpose of holding religious services, if University facilities were made available to nonstudent groups. In other words, the University could not avoid the conversion of one of its buildings into a church, as long as the religious group meets the same neutral requirements of entry—e.g., rent—as are imposed on other groups.

Is the result suggested by respondents' counsel commanded by the majority's decision?

7. Do you agree with Justice White's argument that requiring Cornerstone to meet about a block and a half from campus in less comfortable facilities would constitute only a minimal burden on free exercise? Is the Free Exercise Clause relevant in this case?

---

Partially in response to the *Widmar v. Vincent* case, the U.S. Congress passed legislation in 1984 extending the Court's "equal access" principle to public secondary schools. The Equal Access Act essentially prohibits public secondary schools from denying equal access to religious clubs if they allow other "non-curriculum related" clubs to meet during non-instructional time on school property.

In 1990, the Supreme Court heard a case that involved the application and constitutionality of the Equal Access Act. The case began when certain students and their parents sued an Omaha, Nebraska, public secondary school for denying their request to form a Christian club at the school that would have the same privileges and meet on the same terms and conditions as the other approximately 30 student groups recognized by the

**The Federal Equal Access Act (20 U.S.C. § 4071 *et seq.*) provides in part:**

§ 4071. Denial of equal access prohibited

(a) Restriction of limited open forum on basis of religious, political, philosophical, or other speech context prohibited. It shall be unlawful for any public secondary school which receives Federal financial assistance and which has a limited open forum to deny equal access or a fair opportunity to, or discriminate against, any students who wish to conduct a meeting within that limited open forum on the basis of the religious, political, philosophical, or other content of the speech at such meetings.

(b) "Limited open forum" defined. A public secondary school has a limited open forum whenever such school grants an offering to or opportunity for one or more noncurriculum related student groups to meet on school premises during noninstructional time.

(c) Fair opportunity criteria. Schools shall be deemed to offer a fair opportunity to students who wish to conduct a meeting within its limited open forum if such school uniformly provides that—
  (1) the meeting is voluntary and student-initiated;
  (2) there is no sponsorship of the meeting by the school, the government, or its agents or employees;
  (3) employees or agents of the school or government are present at religious meetings only in a nonparticipatory capacity;
  (4) the meeting does not materially and substantially interfere with the orderly conduct of educational activities within the school; and
  (5) nonschool persons may not direct, conduct, control, or regularly attend activities of student groups.

(d) Construction of title [20 USCS §§ 4071 et seq.] with respect to certain rights. Nothing in this title [20 USCS §§ 4071 et seq.] shall be construed to authorize the United States or any State or political subdivision thereof—
  (1) to influence the form or content of any prayer or other religious activity;
  (2) to require any person to participate in prayer or other religious activity;
  (3) to expend public funds beyond the incidental cost of providing the space for student-initiated meetings;
  (4) to compel any school agent or employee to attend a school meeting if the content of the speech at the meeting is contrary to the beliefs of the agent or employee;
  (5) to sanction meetings that are otherwise unlawful;
  (6) to limit the rights of groups of students which are not of a specified numerical size; or
  (7) to abridge the constitutional rights of any person.

(e) Federal financial assistance to schools unaffected. Notwithstanding the availability of any other remedy under the Constitution or the laws of the United States, nothing in this title [20 USCS §§ 4071 et seq.] shall be construed to authorize the United States to deny or withhold Federal financial assistance to any school.

(f) Authority of schools with respect to order, discipline, well-being, and attendance concerns. Nothing in this title [20 USCS §§ 4071 et seq.] shall be construed to limit the authority of the school, its agents or employees, to maintain order and discipline on school premises, to protect the well-being of students and faculty, and to assure that attendance of students at meetings is voluntary.

school. The school's policy was to recognize clubs as a "vital part of the total education program as a means of developing citizenship, wholesome attitudes, good human relations, knowledge and skills." It also provided that each club should have a faculty sponsor and that organizations "shall not be sponsored by any political or religious organization. . . ." School officials denied the request to form a student religious club because the school policy required that all clubs have a faculty sponsor and "the proposed religious club would not or could not have [such a sponsor], and that a religious club at the school would violate the Establishment Clause" of the First Amendment.

The Supreme Court agreed to hear the case, *Board of Education v. Mergens*, to determine the meaning of certain statutory provisions of the Equal Access Act and to determine the law's constitutionality under the Establishment Clause. Note that the Court's discussion about the equal access principle in *Mergens* concerns a statutory "right" conferred by Congress, rather than a constitutionally based right arising under the Free Speech Clause. As you will see, much turned on how broadly one defined the term "noncurriculm related student groups" from the Equal Access law.

---

## BOARD OF EDUCATION v. MERGENS
## 496 U.S. 226 (1990)

☒ JUSTICE O'CONNOR announced the judgment of the Court and delivered the opinion of the Court with respect to Parts I, II-A, II-B, and II-C, in which CHIEF JUSTICE REHNQUIST and JUSTICES WHITE, BLACKMUN, SCALIA, and KENNEDY joined, and an opinion with respect to Part III, in which CHIEF JUSTICE REHNQUIST and JUSTICES WHITE and BLACKMUN joined.

This case requires us to decide whether the Equal Access Act, 98 Stat. 1302, 20 U.S.C. §§ 4071-4074, prohibits Westside High School from denying a student religious group permission to meet on school premises during noninstructional time, and if so, whether the Act, so construed, violates the Establishment Clause of the First Amendment. . . .

II

A

In *Widmar v. Vincent*, 454 U.S. 263 (1981), we invalidated, on free speech grounds, a state university regulation that prohibited student use of school facilities "'for purposes of religious worship or religious teaching.'" *Id.*, 265. In doing so, we held that an "equal access" policy would not violate the Establishment Clause under our decision in *Lemon v. Kurtzman*, 403 U.S. 602, 612-613 (1971). In particular, we held that such a policy would have a secular purpose, would not have the primary effect of advancing religion, and would not result in excessive entanglement between government and religion. *Widmar*, 454 U.S., 271-274. We noted, however, that "university students are, of course, young adults. They are less impressionable than younger students and should be able to appreciate that the University's policy is one of neutrality toward religion." *Id.*, 274, n. 14.

In 1984, Congress extended the reasoning of *Widmar* to public secondary schools. Under the Equal Access Act, a public secondary school with a "limited open forum" is prohibited from discriminating against students who wish to conduct a meeting within that forum on the basis of the "religious, political, philosophical, or other content of the speech at such meetings." 20 U.S.C. §§ 4071(a) and (b). Specifically, the Act provides:

> It shall be unlawful for any public secondary school which receives Federal financial assistance and which has a limited open forum to deny equal access or a fair opportunity to, or discriminate against, any students who wish to conduct a meeting within that limited open forum on the basis of the religious, political, philosophical, or other content of the speech at such meetings. 20 U.S.C. § 4071(a).

A "limited open forum" exists whenever a public secondary school "grants an offering to or opportunity for one or more noncurriculum related student groups to meet on school premises during noninstructional time." § 4071(b). "Meeting" is defined to include "those activities of student groups which are permitted under a school's limited open forum and are not *directly related* to the school curriculum." § 4072(3). "Noninstructional time" is defined to mean "time set aside by the school before actual classroom instruction begins or after actual classroom instruction ends." § 4072(4). Thus, even if a public secondary school allows only one "noncurriculum related student group" to meet, the Act's obligations are triggered and the school may not deny other clubs, on the basis of the content of their speech, equal access to meet on school premises during noninstructional time.

The Act further specifies that "schools shall be deemed to offer a fair opportunity to students who wish to conduct a meeting within its limited open forum" if the school uniformly provides that the meetings are voluntary and student-initiated; are not sponsored by the school, the government, or its agents or employees; do not materially and substantially interfere with the orderly conduct of education activities within the school; and are not directed, controlled, conducted, or regularly attended by "nonschool persons." §§ 4071(c)(1), (2), (4), and (5). "Sponsorship" is defined to mean "the acting of promoting, leading, or participating in a meeting. The assignment of a teacher, administrator, or other school employee to a meeting for custodial purposes does not constitute sponsorship of the meeting." § 4072(2). If the meetings are religious, employees or agents of the school or government may attend only in a "nonparticipatory capacity." § 4071(c)(3). Moreover, a State may not influence the form of any religious activity, require any person to participate in such activity, or compel any school agent or employee to attend a meeting if the content of the speech at the meeting is contrary to that person's beliefs. §§ 4071(d)(1), (2), and (3).

Finally, the Act does not "authorize the United States to deny or withhold Federal financial assistance to any school," § 4071(e), or "limit the authority of the school, its agents or employees, to maintain order and discipline on school premises, to protect the well-being of students and faculty, and to assure that attendance of students at the meetings is voluntary," § 4071(f).

## B

The parties agree that Westside High School receives federal financial assistance and is a public secondary school within the meaning of the Act. The Act's obligation to grant equal access to student groups is therefore triggered if Westside maintains a "limited open forum"—i.e., if it permits one or more "noncurriculum related student groups" to meet on campus before or after classes.

Unfortunately, the Act does not define the crucial phrase "noncurriculum related student group." Our immediate task is therefore one of statutory interpretation. We begin, of course, with the language of the statute. The common meaning of the term "curriculum" is "the whole body of courses offered by an educational institution or one of its branches." Webster's Third New International Dictionary 557 (1976); see also Black's Law Dictionary 345 (5th ed. 1979) ("The set of studies or courses for a particular period, designated by a school or branch of a school"). Any sensible interpretation of "noncurriculum related student group" must therefore be anchored in the notion that such student groups are those that are not related to the body of courses offered by the school. The difficult question is the degree of "unrelatedness to the curriculum" required for a group to be considered "noncurriculum related."

The Act's definition of the sort of "meetings" that must be accommodated under the statute, § 4071(a), sheds some light on this question. "The term 'meeting' includes those activities of student groups which are . . . not *directly related* to the school curriculum." § 4072(3) (emphasis added). Congress' use of the phrase "directly related" implies that student groups directly related to the subject matter of courses offered by the school do not fall within the "noncurriculum related" category and would therefore be considered "curriculum related."

The logic of the Act also supports this view, namely, that a curriculum-related student group is one that has more than just a tangential or attenuated relationship to courses offered by the school. Because the purpose of granting equal access is to prohibit discrimination between religious or political clubs on the one hand and other noncurriculum-related student groups on the other, the Act is premised on the notion that a religious or political club is itself likely to be a noncurriculum-related student group. It follows, then, that a student group that is "curriculum related" must at least have a more direct relationship to the curriculum than a religious or political club would have.

Although the phrase "noncurriculum related student group" nevertheless remains sufficiently ambiguous that we might normally resort to legislative history, we find the legislative history on this issue less than helpful. Because the bill that led to the Act was extensively rewritten in a series of multilateral negotiations after it was passed by the House and reported out of committee by the Senate, the committee reports shed no light on the language actually adopted. During congressional debate on the subject, legislators referred to a number of different definitions, and thus both petitioners and respondents can cite to legislative history favoring their interpretation of the phrase. Compare 130 Cong. Rec. 19223 (1984) (statement of Sen. Hatfield) (curriculum-related clubs are those that are "really a kind of extension of the classroom"), with *ibid*. (statement of Sen. Hatfield) (in response to question whether school districts would have full authority to decide what was curriculum-related, "we in no way seek to limit that discretion"). See Laycock, Equal Access and Moments of Silence: The Equal Status of Religious Speech by Private Speakers, 81 Nw. U. L. Rev. 1, 37-39 (1986).

We think it significant, however, that the Act, which was passed by wide, bipartisan majorities in both the House and the Senate, reflects at least some consensus on a broad legislative purpose. The committee reports indicate that the Act was intended to address perceived widespread discrimination against religious speech in public schools, and, as the language of the Act indicates, its sponsors contemplated that the Act would do more than merely validate the status quo. The committee reports also show that the Act was enacted in part in response to two federal appellate court decisions holding that student religious groups could not, consistent with the Establishment Clause, meet on school premises during noninstructional time. A broad reading of the Act would be consistent with the views of those who sought to end discrimination by allowing students to meet and discuss religion before and after classes.

In light of this legislative purpose, we think that the term "noncurriculum related student group" is best interpreted broadly to mean any student group that does not directly relate to the body of courses offered by the school. In our view, a student group directly relates to a school's curriculum if the subject matter of the group is actually taught, or will soon be taught, in a regularly offered course; if the subject matter of the group concerns the body of courses as a whole; if participation in the group is required for a particular course; or if participation in the group results in academic credit. We think this limited definition of groups that directly relate to the curriculum is a commonsense interpretation of the Act that is consistent with Congress' intent to provide a low threshold for triggering the Act's requirements.

For example, a French club would directly relate to the curriculum if a school taught French in a regularly offered course or planned to teach the subject in the near future. A school's student government would generally relate directly to the curriculum to the extent that it addresses concerns, solicits opinions, and formulates proposals pertaining to the body of courses offered by the school. If participation in a school's band or orchestra were required for the band or orchestra classes, or resulted in academic credit, then those groups would also directly relate to the curriculum. The existence of such groups at a school would not trigger the Act's obligations.

On the other hand, unless a school could show that groups such as a chess club, a stamp collecting club, or a community service club fell within our description of groups that directly relate to the curriculum, such groups would be "noncurriculum related student groups" for purposes of the Act. The existence of such groups would create a "limited open forum" under the Act and would prohibit the school from denying equal access to any other student group on the basis of the content of that group's speech. Whether a specific student group is a "noncurriculum related student group" will therefore depend on a particular school's curriculum, but such determinations would be subject to factual findings well within the competence of trial courts to make.

Petitioners contend that our reading of the Act unduly hinders local control over schools and school activities, but we think that schools and school districts nevertheless retain a significant measure of authority over the type of officially recognized activities in which their students participate. First, schools and school districts maintain their traditional latitude to determine appropriate subjects of instruction. To the extent that a school chooses to structure its course offerings and existing student groups to avoid the Act's obligations, that result is not prohibited by the Act. On matters of statutory interpretation, "our task is to apply the text, not to improve on it." Second, the Act expressly does not limit a school's authority to prohibit meetings that would "materially and substantially interfere with the orderly conduct of educational activities within the school." § 4071(c)(4); cf. *Tinker v. Des Moines Independent Community School Dist.*, 393 U.S. 503, 509 (1969). The Act also preserves "the

authority of the school, its agents or employees, to maintain order and discipline on school premises, to protect the well-being of students and faculty,
and to assure that attendance of students at meetings is voluntary." § 4071(f).
Finally, because the Act applies only to public secondary schools that receive
federal financial assistance, § 4071(a), a school district seeking to escape the
statute's obligations could simply forgo federal funding. Although we do not
doubt that in some cases this may be an unrealistic option, Congress clearly sought to prohibit schools from discriminating on the basis of the content of a student group's speech, and that obligation is the price a federally
funded school must pay if it opens its facilities to noncurriculum-related
student groups.

The dissent suggests that "an extracurricular student organization is 'noncurriculum related' if it has as its purpose (or as part of its purpose) the advocacy of partisan theological, political, or ethical views." This interpretation
of the Act, we are told, is mandated by Congress' intention to "track our own
Free Speech Clause jurisprudence," by incorporating *Widmar*'s notion of a
"limited public forum" into the language of the Act.

This suggestion is flawed for at least two reasons. First, the Act itself neither uses the phrase "limited public forum" nor so much as hints that that
doctrine is somehow "incorporated" into the words of the statute. The operative language of the statute, 20 U.S.C. § 4071(a), of course, refers to a "limited open forum," a term that is specifically defined in the next subsection, §
4071(b). Congress was presumably aware that "limited public forum," as used
by the Court, is a term of art, see, e.g., *Perry Ed. Assn. v. Perry Local Educators'
Assn.*, 460 U.S. 37, 45-49 (1983), and had it intended to import that concept
into the Act, one would suppose that it would have done so explicitly. Indeed,
Congress' deliberate choice to use a different term—and to define that term—
can only mean that it intended to establish a standard different from the one
established by our free speech cases. See Laycock, 81 Nw. U. L. Rev., 36 ("The
statutory 'limited open forum' is an artificial construct, and comparisons with
the constitutional ['limited public forum'] cases can be misleading"). To paraphrase the dissent, "if Congress really intended to [incorporate] *Widmar* for
reasons of administrative clarity, Congress kept its intent well hidden, both in
the statute and in the debates preceding its passage."

Second, and more significant, the dissent's reliance on the legislative history to support its interpretation of the Act shows just how treacherous that
task can be. The dissent appears to agree with our view that the legislative
history of the Act, even if relevant, is highly unreliable, yet the interpretation
it suggests rests solely on a few passing, general references by legislators to our
decision in *Widmar*. We think that reliance on legislative history is hazardous
at best, but where "'not even the sponsors of the bill knew what it meant,'"
such reliance cannot form a reasonable basis on which to interpret the text of
a statute. . . .The only thing that can be said with any confidence is that some
Senators may have thought that the obligations of the Act would be triggered
only when a school permits advocacy groups to meet on school premises during noninstructional time. That conclusion, of course, cannot bear the weight
the dissent places on it.

## C

The parties in this case focus their dispute on 10 of Westside's approximately 30 voluntary student clubs: Interact (a service club related to Rotary

International); Chess; Subsurfers (a club for students interested in scuba diving); National Honor Society; Photography; Welcome to Westside (a club to introduce new students to the school); Future Business Leaders of America; Zonta (the female counterpart to Interact); Student Advisory Board (student government); and Student Forum (student government). Petitioners contend that all of these student activities are curriculum-related because they further the goals of particular aspects of the school's curriculum. Welcome to Westside, for example, helps "further the School's overall goal of developing effective citizens by requiring student members to contribute to their fellow students." The student government clubs "advance the goals of the School's political science classes by providing an understanding and appreciation of government processes." Subsurfers furthers "one of the essential goals of the Physical Education Department—enabling students to develop life-long recreational interests." Chess "supplements math and science courses because it enhances students' ability to engage in critical thought processes." Participation in Interact and Zonta "promotes effective citizenship, a critical goal of the WHS curriculum, specifically the Social Studies Department."

To the extent that petitioners contend that "curriculum related" means anything remotely related to abstract educational goals, however, we reject that argument. To define "curriculum related" in a way that results in almost no schools having limited open fora, or in a way that permits schools to evade the Act by strategically describing existing student groups, would render the Act merely hortatory. See 130 Cong. Rec. 19222 (1984) (statement of Sen. Leahy) ("[A] limited open forum should be triggered by what a school does, not by what it says"). As the court below explained:

> Allowing such a broad interpretation of "curriculum-related" would make the [Act] meaningless. A school's administration could simply declare that it maintains a closed forum and choose which student clubs it wanted to allow by tying the purposes of those clubs to some broadly defined educational goal. At the same time the administration could arbitrarily deny access to school facilities to any unfavored student club on the basis of its speech content. This is exactly the result that Congress sought to prohibit by enacting the [Act]. A public secondary school cannot simply declare that it maintains a closed forum and then discriminate against a particular student group on the basis of the content of the speech of that group. 867 F.2d 1076, 1078 (1989).

Rather, we think it clear that Westside's existing student groups include one or more "noncurriculum related student groups." Although Westside's physical education classes apparently include swimming, counsel stated at oral argument that scuba diving is not taught in any regularly offered course at the school. Based on Westside's own description of the group, Subsurfers does not directly relate to the curriculum as a whole in the same way that a student government or similar group might. Moreover, participation in Subsurfers is not required by any course at the school and does not result in extra academic credit. Thus, Subsurfers is a "noncurriculum related student group" for purposes of the Act. Similarly, although math teachers at Westside have encouraged their students to play chess, chess is not taught in any regularly offered course at the school, and participation in the chess club is not required for any class and does not result in extra credit for any class. The chess club is therefore another "noncurriculum related student group" at Westside.

Moreover, Westside's principal acknowledged at trial that the Peer Advocates program—a service group that works with special education classes—does not directly relate to any courses offered by the school and is not required by any courses offered by the school. Peer Advocates would therefore also fit within our description of a "noncurriculum related student group." The record therefore supports a finding that Westside has maintained a limited open forum under the Act.

Although our definition of "noncurriculum related student activities" looks to a school's actual practice rather than its stated policy, we note that our conclusion is also supported by the school's own description of its student activities. . . . [T]he school states that Band "is included in our regular curriculum"; Choir "is a course offered as part of the curriculum"; Distributive Education "is an extension of the Distributive Education class"; International Club is "developed through our foreign language classes"; Latin Club is "designed for those students who are taking Latin as a foreign language"; Student Publications "includes classes offered in preparation of the yearbook (Shield) and the student newspaper (Lance)"; Dramatics "is an extension of a regular academic class"; and Orchestra "is an extension of our regular curriculum." These descriptions constitute persuasive evidence that these student clubs directly relate to the curriculum. By inference, however, the fact that the descriptions of student activities such as Subsurfers and chess do not include such references strongly suggests that those clubs do not, by the school's own admission, directly relate to the curriculum. We therefore conclude that Westside permits "one or more noncurriculum related student groups to meet on school premises during noninstructional time," § 4071(b). Because Westside maintains a "limited open forum" under the Act, it is prohibited from discriminating, based on the content of the students' speech, against students who wish to meet on school premises during noninstructional time.

The remaining statutory question is whether petitioners' denial of respondents' request to form a religious group constitutes a denial of "equal access" to the school's limited open forum. Although the school apparently permits respondents to meet informally after school, respondents seek equal access in the form of official recognition by the school. Official recognition allows student clubs to be part of the student activities program and carries with it access to the school newspaper, bulletin boards, the public address system, and the annual Club Fair. Given that the Act explicitly prohibits denial of "equal access . . . to . . . any students who wish to conduct a meeting within [the school's] limited open forum" on the basis of the religious content of the speech at such meetings, § 4071(a), we hold that Westside's denial of respondents' request to form a Christian club denies them "equal access" under the Act.

Because we rest our conclusion on statutory grounds, we need not decide—and therefore express no opinion on—whether the First Amendment requires the same result.

III

Petitioners contend that even if Westside has created a limited open forum within the meaning of the Act, its denial of official recognition to the proposed Christian club must nevertheless stand because the Act violates the Establishment Clause of the First Amendment, as applied to the States through the Fourteenth Amendment. Specifically, petitioners maintain that because the school's recognized student activities are an integral part of its educational mission, official recognition of respondents' proposed club would effectively incorporate religious activities into the school's official program, endorse participation in the religious club, and provide the club with an official platform to proselytize other students.

We disagree. In *Widmar*, we applied the three-part *Lemon* test to hold that an "equal access" policy, at the university level, does not violate the Establishment Clause. We concluded that "an open-forum policy including nondiscrimination against religious speech, would have a secular purpose," and would in fact avoid entanglement with religion. . . . We also found that although incidental benefits accrued to religious groups who used university facilities, this result did not amount to an establishment of religion. First, we stated that a university's forum does not "confer any imprimatur of state approval on religious sects or practices." Indeed, the message is one of neutrality rather than endorsement; if a State refused to let religious groups use facilities open to others, then it would demonstrate not neutrality but hostility toward religion. "The Establishment Clause does not license government to treat religion and those who teach or practice it, simply by virtue of their status as such, as subversive of American ideals and therefore subject to unique disabilities." *McDaniel v. Paty*, 435 U.S. 618, 641 (1978) (BRENNAN, J., concurring in judgment). Second, we noted that "the [University's] provision of benefits to [a] broad . . . spectrum of groups"—both nonreligious and religious speakers—was "an important index of secular effect."

We think the logic of *Widmar* applies with equal force to the Equal Access Act. As an initial matter, the Act's prohibition of discrimination on the basis of "political, philosophical, or other" speech as well as religious speech is a sufficient basis for meeting the secular purpose prong of the *Lemon* test. See *Edwards v. Aguillard*, 482 U.S. 578, 586 (1987) (Court "is normally deferential to a [legislative] articulation of a secular purpose"). Congress' avowed purpose—to prevent discrimination against religious and other types of speech—is undeniably secular. Even if some legislators were motivated by a conviction that religious speech in particular was valuable and worthy of protection, that alone would not invalidate the Act, because what is relevant is the legislative purpose of the statute, not the possibly religious motives of the legislators who enacted the law. Because the Act on its face grants equal access to both secular and religious speech, we think it clear that the Act's purpose was not to "'endorse or disapprove of religion.'"

Petitioners' principal contention is that the Act has the primary effect of advancing religion. Specifically, petitioners urge that, because the student religious meetings are held under school aegis, and because the state's compulsory attendance laws bring the students together (and thereby provide a ready-made audience for student evangelists), an objective observer in the position of a secondary school student will perceive official school support for such religious meetings.

We disagree. First, although we have invalidated the use of public funds to pay for teaching state-required subjects at parochial schools, in part because of the risk of creating "a crucial symbolic link between government and religion, thereby enlisting—at least in the eyes of impressionable youngsters—the powers of government to the support of the religious denomination operating the school," *Grand Rapids School Dist. v. Ball*, 473 U.S. 373, 385 (1985), there is a crucial difference between *government* speech endorsing religion, which the Establishment Clause forbids, and *private* speech endorsing religion, which the Free Speech and Free Exercise Clauses protect. We think that secondary school students are mature enough and are likely to understand that a school does not endorse or support student speech that it merely permits on a non-discriminatory basis. The proposition that schools do not endorse everything they fail to censor is not complicated. "Particularly in this age of massive media information . . . the few years difference in age between high school and college students [does not] justify departing from *Widmar*." *Bender v. Williamsport Area School Dist.*, 475 U.S. 534, 556 (1986) (POWELL, J. dissenting).

Indeed, we note that Congress specifically rejected the argument that high school students are likely to confuse an equal access policy with state sponsorship of religion. See S. Rep. No. 98-357, p. 35 ("Students below the college level are capable of distinguishing between State-initiated, school sponsored, or teacher-led religious speech on the one hand and student-initiated, student-led religious speech on the other"). Given the deference due "the duly enacted and carefully considered decision of a coequal and representative branch of our Government," we do not lightly second-guess such legislative judgments, particularly where the judgments are based in part on empirical determinations.

Second, we note the Act expressly limits participation by school officials at meetings of student religious groups, §§ 4071(c)(2) and (3), and that any such meetings must be held during "noninstructional time," § 4071(b). The Act therefore avoids the problems of "the students' emulation of teachers as role models" and "mandatory attendance requirements." To be sure, the possibility of *student* peer pressure remains, but there is little if any risk of official state endorsement or coercion where no formal classroom activities are involved and no school officials actively participate. Moreover, petitioners' fear of a mistaken inference of endorsement is largely self-imposed, because the school itself has control over any impressions it gives its students. To the extent a school makes clear that its recognition of respondents' proposed club is not an endorsement of the views of the club's participants, students will reasonably understand that the school's official recognition of the club evinces neutrality toward, rather than endorsement of, religious speech.

Third, the broad spectrum of officially recognized student clubs at Westside, and the fact that Westside students are free to initiate and organize additional student clubs counteract any possible message of official endorsement of or preference for religion or a particular religious belief. See *Widmar*, 454 U.S., 274 ("The provision of benefits to so broad a spectrum of groups is an important index of secular effect"). Although a school may not itself lead or direct a religious club, a school that permits a student-initiated and student-led religious club to meet after school, just as it permits any other student group to do, does not convey a message of state approval or endorsement of the particular religion. Under the Act, a school with a limited open forum may not lawfully deny access to a Jewish students' club, a Young Democrats club, or a philosophy club devoted to the study of Neitzsche. To the extent that a religious club is merely one of many different student-initiated voluntary clubs, students should perceive no message of government endorsement of religion. Thus, we conclude that the Act does not, at least on its face and as applied to Westside, have the primary effect of advancing religion.

Petitioners' final argument is that by complying with the Act's requirement, the school risks excessive entanglement between government and religion. The proposed club, petitioners urge, would be required to have a faculty sponsor who would be charged with actively directing the activities of the group, guiding its leaders, and ensuring balance in the presentation of controversial ideas. Petitioners claim that this influence over the club's religious program would entangle the government in day-to-day surveillance of religion of the type forbidden by the Establishment Clause.

Under the Act, however, faculty monitors may not participate in any religious meetings, and nonschool persons may not direct, control, or regularly attend activities of student groups. §§ 4071(c)(3) and (5). Moreover, the Act prohibits school "sponsorship" of any religious meetings, § 4071(c)(2), which means that school officials may not promote, lead, or participate in any such meeting, § 4072(2). Although the Act permits "the assignment of a teacher, administrator, or other school employee to the meeting for custodial purposes," *ibid.*, such custodial oversight of the student-initiated religious group, merely to ensure order and good behavior, does not impermissibly entangle government in the day-to-day surveillance or administration of religious activities. Indeed, as the Court noted in *Widmar*, a denial of equal access to religious speech might well create greater entanglement problems in the form of invasive monitoring to prevent religious speech at meetings at which such speech might occur.

Accordingly, we hold that the Equal Access Act does not on its face contravene the Establishment Clause. Because we hold that petitioners have violated the Act, we do not decide respondents' claims under the Free Speech and Free Exercise Clauses. For the foregoing reasons, the judgment of the Court of Appeals is affirmed.

*It is so ordered. . . .*

▓ JUSTICE KENNEDY, with whom JUSTICE SCALIA joins, concurring in part and concurring in the judgment.

The Court's interpretation of the statutory term "non-curriculum related groups" is proper and correct, in my view, and I join Parts I and II of the Court's opinion. I further agree that the Act does not violate the Establishment Clause, and so I concur in the judgment; but my view of the analytic premise that controls the establishment question differs from that employed by the plurality. I write to explain why I cannot join all that is said in Part III of JUSTICE O'CONNOR'S opinion. . . .

II

I agree with the plurality that a school complying with the statute by satisfying the criteria in § 4071(c) does not violate the Establishment Clause. The accommodation of religion mandated by the Act is a neutral one, and in the context of this case it suffices to inquire whether the Act violates either one of two principles. The first is that the government cannot "give direct benefits to religion in such a degree that it in fact 'establishes a [state] religion or religious faith, or tends to do so.'" *Allegheny v. ACLU*, 492 U.S. 573, 655. Any incidental benefits that accompany official recognition of a religious club under the criteria set forth in the § 4071(c) do not lead to the establishment of religion under this standard. The second principle controlling the case now before us, in my view, is that the government cannot coerce any student to participate in a religious activity. The Act is consistent with this standard as well. Nothing on the face of the Act or in the facts of the case as here presented demonstrate that enforcement of the statute will result in the coercion of any student to participate in a religious activity. The Act does not authorize school authorities to require, or even to encourage, students to become members of a religious club or to attend a club's meetings, see §§ 4071(c), (d), 4072(2); the meetings take place while school is not in session, see §§ 4071(b) 4072(4); and the Act does not compel any school employee to participate in, or to attend, a club's meetings or activities, see §§ 4071(c), (d)(4).

The plurality uses a different test, one which asks whether school officials, by complying with the Act, have endorsed religion. It is true that when government gives impermissible assistance to a religion it can be said to have "endorsed" religion; but endorsement cannot be the test. The word endorsement has insufficient content to be dispositive. And for reasons I have explained elsewhere, see *Allegheny County*, its literal application may result in neutrality in name but hostility in fact when the question is the government's proper relation to those who express some religious preference.

I should think it inevitable that a public high school "endorses" a religious club, in a common-sense use of the term, if the club happens to be one of many activities that the school permits students to choose in order to further the development of their intellect and character in an extracurricular setting. But no constitutional violation occurs if the school's action is based upon a recognition of the fact that membership in a religious club is one of many permissible ways for a student to further his or her own personal enrichment. The inquiry with respect to coercion must be whether the government imposes pressure upon a student to participate in a religious activity. This inquiry, of course, must be undertaken with sensitivity to the special circumstances that exist in a secondary school where the line between voluntary and coerced participation may be difficult to draw. No such coercion, however, has been shown to exist as a necessary result of this statute, either on its face or as respondents seek to invoke it on the facts of this case.

For these reasons, I join Parts I and II of the Court's opinion, and concur in the judgment.

JUSTICE MARSHALL, with whom JUSTICE BRENNAN joins, concurring in the judgment.

I agree with the majority that "noncurriculum" must be construed broadly to "prohibit schools from discriminating on the basis of the content of a student group's speech." As the majority demonstrates, such a construction "is consistent with Congress' intent to provide a low threshold for triggering the Act's requirements." In addition, to the extent that Congress intended the Act to track this Court's free speech jurisprudence, as the dissent argues, the majority's construction is faithful to our commitment to nondiscriminatory access to open fora in public schools. When a school allows student-initiated clubs not directly tied to the school's curriculum to use school facilities, it has "created a forum generally open to student groups" and is therefore constitutionally prohibited from enforcing a "content-based exclusion" of other student speech. In this respect, the Act as construed by the majority simply codifies in statute what is already constitutionally mandated: schools may not discriminate among student-initiated groups that seek access to school facilities for expressive purposes not directly related to the school's curriculum.

The Act's low threshold for triggering equal access, however, raises serious Establishment Clause concerns where secondary schools with fora that differ substantially from the forum in *Widmar* are required to grant access to student religious groups. Indeed, as applied in the present case, the Act mandates a religious group's access to a forum that is dedicated to promoting fundamental values and citizenship as defined by the school. The Establishment Clause does not forbid the operation of the Act in such circumstances, but it does require schools to change their relationship to their fora so as to disassociate themselves effectively from religious clubs' speech. Thus, although I agree with the plurality that the Act as applied to Westside could withstand Establishment Clause scrutiny, I write separately to emphasize the steps Westside must take to avoid appearing to endorse the Christian Club's goals. The plurality's Establishment Clause analysis pays inadequate attention to the differences between this case and *Widmar* and dismisses too lightly the distinctive pressures created by Westside's highly structured environment.

I . . .
B . . .

[T]he plurality fails to recognize that the wide-open and independent character of the student forum in *Widmar* differs substantially from the forum at Westside.

Westside currently does not recognize any student club that advocates a controversial viewpoint. Indeed, the clubs at Westside that trigger the Act involve scuba diving, chess, and counseling for special education students. As a matter of school policy, Westside encourages student participation in clubs based on a broad conception of its educational mission. That mission comports with the Court's acknowledgment "that public schools are vitally important 'in the preparation of individuals for participation as citizens,' and as vehicles for 'inculcating fundamental values necessary to the maintenance of a democratic political system.'" *Board of Education, Island Trees Union Free School Dist. No. 26 v. Pico*, 457 U.S. 853, 864 (1982) (plurality). Given the nature and function of student clubs at Westside, the school makes no effort to disassociate itself from the activities and goals of its student clubs.

The entry of religious clubs into such a realm poses a real danger that those clubs will be viewed as part of the school's effort to inculcate fundamental values. The school's message with respect to its existing clubs is not one of toleration but one of endorsement. As the majority concedes, the program is part of the "district's commitment to teaching academic, physical, civic, and personal skills and values." But although a school may permissibly encourage its students to become well-rounded as student-athletes, student-musicians, and student-tutors, the Constitution forbids schools to encourage students to become well-rounded as student-worshippers. Neutrality toward religion, as required by the Constitution, is not advanced by requiring a school that endorses the goals of some noncontroversial secular organizations to endorse the goals of religious organizations as well.

The fact that the Act, when triggered, provides access to political as well as religious speech does not ameliorate the potential threat of endorsement. The breadth of beneficiaries under the Act does suggest that the Act may satisfy the "secular purpose" requirement of the Establishment Clause inquiry we identified in Lemon, 403 U.S., 612-613. But the crucial question is how the Act affects each school. If a school already houses numerous ideological organizations, then the addition of a religion club will most likely not violate the Establishment Clause because the risk that students will erroneously attribute the views of the religion club to the school is minimal. To the extent a school tolerates speech by a wide range of ideological clubs, students cannot reasonably understand the school to endorse all of the groups' divergent and contradictory views. But if the religion club is the sole advocacy-oriented group in the forum, or one of a very limited number, and the school continues to promote its student-club program as instrumental to citizenship, then the school's failure to disassociate itself from the religious activity will reasonably be understood as an endorsement of that activity. That political and other advocacy-oriented groups are permitted to participate in a forum that, through school support and encouragement, is devoted to fostering a student's civic identity does not ameliorate the appearance of school endorsement unless the invitation is accepted and the forum is transformed into a forum like that in *Widmar*.

For this reason, the plurality's reliance on *Widmar* is misplaced. The University of Missouri took concrete steps to ensure "that the University's name will not 'be identified in any way with the aims, policies, programs, products, or opinions of any organization or its members.'" Westside, in contrast, explicitly promotes its student clubs "as a vital part of the total education program [and] as a means of developing citizenship." And while the University of Missouri recognized such clubs as the Young Socialist alliance and the Young Democrats, Westside has recognized no such political clubs.

The different approaches to student clubs embodied in these policies reflect a significant difference, for Establishment Clause purposes, between the respective roles that Westside High School and the University of Missouri attempt to play in their students' lives. To the extent that a school emphasizes the autonomy of its students, as does the University of Missouri, there is a corresponding decrease in the likelihood that student speech will be regarded as school speech. Conversely, where a school such as Westside regards its student clubs as a mechanism for defining and transmitting fundamental values, the inclusion of a religious club in the school's program will almost certainly signal school endorsement of the religious practice.

Thus, the underlying difference between this case and *Widmar* is not that college and high school students have varying capacities to perceive the subtle differences between toleration and endorsement, but rather that the University of Missouri and Westside actually choose to define their respective missions in different ways. That high schools tend to emphasize student autonomy less than universities may suggest that high school administrators tend to perceive a difference in the maturity of secondary and university students. But the school's behavior, not the purported immaturity of high school students, is dispositive. If Westside stood apart from its club program and expressed the view, endorsed by Congress through its passage of the Act, that high school students are capable of engaging in wide-ranging discussion of sensitive and controversial speech, the inclusion of religious groups in Westside's forum would confirm the school's commitment to nondiscrimination. Here, though, the Act requires the school to permit religious speech in a forum explicitly designed to advance the school's interest in shaping the character of its students.

The comprehensiveness of the access afforded by the Act further highlights the Establishment Clause dangers posed by the Act's application to fora such as Westside's. The Court holds that "official recognition allows student clubs to be part of the student activities program and carries with it access to the school newspaper, bulletin boards, the public address system, and the annual Club Fair." Students would be alerted to the meetings of the religion club over the public address system; they would see religion club material posted on the official school bulletin board and club notices in the school newspaper, they would be recruited to join the religion club at the school-sponsored Club Fair. If a school has a variety of ideological clubs, as in *Widmar*, I agree with the plurality that a student is likely to understand that "a school does not endorse or support student speech that it merely permits on a nondiscriminatory basis." When a school has a religion club but no other political or ideological organizations, however, that relatively fine distinction may be lost.

Moreover, in the absence of a truly robust forum that includes the participation of more than one advocacy-oriented group, the presence of a religious club could provide a fertile ground for peer pressure, especially if the club commanded support from a substantial portion of the student body. Indeed, it is precisely in a school without such a forum that intolerance for different religious and other views would be most dangerous and that a student who does not share the religious beliefs of his classmates would perceive "that religion or a particular religious belief is favored or preferred." *Wallace v. Jaffree*, 472 U.S. 38, 70 (1985) (O'CONNOR, J., concurring in judgment).

The plurality concedes that there is a "possibility of student peer pressure," but maintains that this does not amount to "official state endorsement." This dismissal is too facile. We must remain sensitive, especially in the public schools, to "the numerous more subtle ways that government can show favoritism to particular beliefs or convey a message of disapproval to others." *Allegheny v. ACLU*, 492 U.S. 573, 627. When the government, through mandatory attendance laws, brings students together in a highly controlled environment every day for the better part of their waking hours and regulates virtually every aspect of their existence during that time, we should not be so quick to dismiss the problem of peer pressure as if the school environment had nothing to do with creating and fostering it. The State has structured an environment in which students holding mainstream views may be able to coerce adherents of minority religions to attend club meetings or to adhere to club beliefs. Thus, the State cannot disclaim its responsibility for those resulting pressures.

## II

Given these substantial risks posed by the inclusion of the proposed Christian Club within Westside's present forum, Westside must redefine its relationship to its club program. The plurality recognizes that such redefinition is necessary to avoid the risk of endorsement and construes the Act accordingly. The plurality holds that the Act "limits participation by school officials at meetings of student religious groups," and requires religious club meetings to be held during noninstructional time. It also holds that schools may not sponsor any religious meetings. Finally, and perhaps most importantly, the plurality states that schools bear the responsibility for taking whatever further steps are necessary to make clear that their recognition of a religious club does not reflect their endorsement of the views of the club's participants.

Westside thus must do more than merely prohibit faculty members from actively participating in the Christian Club's meetings. It must fully disassociate itself from the Club's religious speech and avoid appearing to sponsor or endorse the Club's goals. It could, for example, entirely discontinue encouraging student participation in clubs and clarify that the clubs are not instrumentally related to the school's overall mission. Or, if the school sought to continue its general endorsement of those student clubs that did not engage in controversial speech, it could do so if it also affirmatively disclaimed any endorsement of the Christian Club.

III

The inclusion of the Christian Club in the type of forum presently established at Westside, without more, will not assure government neutrality toward religion. Rather, because the school endorses the extracurricular program as part of its educational mission, the inclusion of the Christian Club in that program will convey to students the school-sanctioned message that involvement in religion develops "citizenship, wholesome attitudes, good human relations, knowledge and skills." We need not question the value of that message to affirm that it is not the place of schools to issue it. Accordingly, schools such as Westside must be responsive not only to the broad terms of the Act's coverage, but also to this Court's mandate that they effectively disassociate themselves from the religious speech that now may become commonplace in their facilities.

▓ JUSTICE STEVENS, dissenting.

The dictionary is a necessary, and sometimes sufficient, aid to the judge confronted with the task of construing an opaque act of Congress. In a case like this, however, I believe we must probe more deeply to avoid a patently bizarre result. Can Congress really have intended to issue an order to every public high school in the nation stating, in substance, that if you sponsor a chess club, a scuba diving club, or a French club—without having formal classes in those subjects—you must also open your doors to every religious, political, or social organization, no matter how controversial or distasteful its views may be? I think not. A fair review of the legislative history of the Equal Access Act (Act), 20 U.S.C. §§ 4071-4074, discloses that Congress intended to recognize a much narrower forum than the Court has legislated into existence today.

I . . .

Our decision in *Widmar* encompassed two constitutional holdings. First, we interpreted the Free Speech Clause of the First Amendment to determine whether the University of Missouri at Kansas City had, by its own policies, abdicated discretion that it would otherwise have to make content-based discriminations among student groups seeking to meet on its campus. We agreed that it had. Next, we interpreted the Establishment Clause of the First Amendment to determine whether the University was prohibited from permitting student-initiated religious groups to participate in that forum. We agreed that it was not.

To extend *Widmar* to high schools, then, would require us to pose two questions. We would first ask whether a high school had established a forum comparable under our Free Speech Clause jurisprudence to that which existed in *Widmar*. Only if this question were answered affirmatively would we then need to test the constitutionality of the Act by asking whether the Establishment Clause has different consequences when applied to a high school's open forum than when applied to a college's. . . .

The forum at Westside is considerably different from that which existed at the University of Missouri. In *Widmar*, we held that the University had created "a generally open forum." Over 100 officially recognized student groups routinely participated in that forum. They included groups whose activities not only were unrelated to any specific courses, but also were of a kind that a state university could not properly sponsor or endorse. Thus, for example, they included such political organizations as the Young Socialist Alliance, the Women's Union, and the Young Democrats. The University permitted use of its facilities for speakers advocating transcendental meditation and humanism. Since the University had allowed such organizations and speakers the use of campus facilities, we concluded that the University could not discriminate against a religious group on the basis of the content of its speech. The forum established by the state university accommodated participating groups that were "noncurriculum related" not only because they did not mirror the school's classroom instruction, but also because they advocated controversial positions that a state university's obligation of neutrality prevented it from endorsing. . . .

   Nor would it be wise to ignore this difference. High school students may be adult enough to distinguish between those organizations that are sponsored by the school and those which lack school sponsorship even though they participate in a forum that the school does sponsor. But high school students are also young enough that open fora may be less suitable for them than for college students. The need to decide whether to risk treating students as adults too soon, or alternatively to risk treating them as children too long, is an enduring problem for all educators. The youth of these students, whether described in terms of "impressionability" or "maturity," may be irrelevant to our application of the constitutional restrictions that limit educational discretion in the public schools, but it surely is not irrelevant to our interpretation of the educational policies that have been adopted. . . .

   For these reasons, I believe that the distinctions between Westside's program and the University of Missouri's program suggest what is the best understanding of the Act: an extracurricular student organization is "noncurriculum related" if it has as its purpose (or as part of its purpose) the advocacy of partisan theological, political, or ethical views. A school that admits at least one such club has apparently made the judgment that students are better off if the student community is permitted to, and perhaps even encouraged to, compete along ideological lines. This pedagogical strategy may be defensible or even desirable. But it is wrong to presume that Congress endorsed that strategy—and dictated its nationwide adoption—simply because it approved the application of *Widmar* to high schools. And it seems absurd to presume that Westside has invoked the same strategy by recognizing clubs like Swim Timing Team and Subsurfers which, though they may not correspond directly to anything in Westside's course offerings, are no more controversial than a grilled cheese sandwich.

   Accordingly, as I would construe the Act, a high school could properly sponsor a French club, a chess club, or a scuba diving club simply because their activities are fully consistent with the school's curricular mission. It would not matter whether formal courses in any of those subjects—or in directly related subjects—were being offered as long as faculty encouragement of student participation in such groups would be consistent with both the school's obligation of neutrality and its legitimate pedagogical concerns. Nothing in *Widmar* implies that the existence of a French club, for example, would create constitutional obligation to allow student members of the Ku Klux Klan or the

Communist Party to have access to school facilities. More importantly, nothing in that case suggests that the constitutional issue should turn on whether French is being taught in a formal course while the club is functioning.

Conversely, if a high school decides to allow political groups to use its facilities, it plainly cannot discriminate among controversial groups because it agrees with the positions of some and disagrees with the ideas advocated by others. Again, the fact that the history of the Republican party might be taught in a political science course could not justify a decision to allow the young Republicans to form a club while denying Communists, white supremacists, or Christian Scientists the same privilege. In my judgment, the political activities of the young Republicans are "noncurriculum related" for reasons that have nothing to do with the content of the political science course. The statutory definition of what is "noncurriculum related" should depend on the constitutional concern that motivated our decision in *Widmar*.

In this case, the district judge reviewed each of the clubs in the high school program and found that they are all "tied to the educational function of the institution." He correctly concluded that this club system "differs dramatically from those found to create an open forum policy in *Widmar* and *Bender*." I agree with his conclusion that, under a proper interpretation of the Act, this dramatic difference requires a different result. . . .

For all of these reasons, the argument for construing "noncurriculum related" by recourse to the facts of *Widmar*, and so by reference to the existence of advocacy groups, seems to me overwhelming. It provides a test that is both more simple and more easily administered than what the majority has crafted. Indeed, the only plausible answer to this construction of the statute is that it could easily be achieved without reference to the exotic concept of "noncurriculum related" organizations. This point was made at length on the Senate floor by Senator Gorton. Senator Hatfield answered that the term had been recommended to him by lawyers, apparently in an effort to capture the distinctions important to the judiciary's construction of the Free Speech Clause. . . .

II

My construction of the Act makes it unnecessary to reach the Establishment Clause question that the Court decides. It is nevertheless appropriate to point out that the question is much more difficult than the Court assumes. The Court focuses upon whether the Act might run afoul of the Establishment Clause because of the danger that some students will mistakenly believe that the student-initiated religious clubs are sponsored by the school. I believe that the plurality's construction of the statute obliges it to answer a further question: whether the Act violates the Establishment Clause by authorizing religious organizations to meet on high school grounds even when the high school's teachers and administrators deem it unwise to admit controversial or partisan organizations of any kind.

Under the Court's interpretation of the Act, Congress has imposed a difficult choice on public high schools receiving federal financial assistance. If such a school continues to allow students to participate in such familiar and innocuous activities as a school chess or scuba diving club, it must also allow religious groups to make use of school facilities. Indeed, it is hard to see how a cheerleading squad or a pep club, among the most common student groups in American high schools, could avoid being "noncurriculum related" under the majority's test. The Act, as construed by the majority, comes perilously close to an outright command to allow organized prayer, and perhaps the kind of religious ceremonies involved in *Widmar*, on school premises.

We have always treated with special sensitivity the Establishment Clause problems that result when religious observances are moved into the public schools. As the majority recognizes, student-initiated religious groups may exert a considerable degree of pressure even without official school sponsorship. Testimony in this case indicated that one purpose of the proposed Bible Club was to convert students to Christianity. The influence that could result is the product not only of the Equal Access Act and student-initiated speech, but also of the compulsory attendance laws, which we have long recognized to be of special constitutional importance in this context. . . .

I tend to agree with the Court that the Constitution does not forbid a local school district, or Congress, from bringing organized religion into the schools so long as all groups, religious or not, are welcome equally if "they do not break either the laws or the furniture." That Congress has such authority, however, does not mean that the concerns underlying the Establishment Clause are irrelevant when, and if, that authority is exercised. Certainly we should not rush to embrace the conclusion that Congress swept aside these concerns by the hurried passage of clumsily drafted legislation. . . .

The Court's construction of this Act, however, leads to a sweeping intrusion by the federal government into the operation of our public schools, and does so despite the absence of any indication that Congress intended to divest local school districts of their power to shape the educational environment. If a high school administration continues to believe that it is sound policy to exclude controversial groups, such as political clubs, the Ku Klux Klan, and perhaps gay rights advocacy groups, from its facilities, it now must also close its doors to traditional extracurricular activities that are non-controversial but not directly related to any course being offered at the school. Congress made frequent reference to the primacy of local control in public education, and the legislative history of the Act is thus inconsistent with the Court's rigid definition of "noncurriculum related groups." Indeed, the very fact that Congress omitted any definition in the statute itself is persuasive evidence of an intent to allow local officials broad discretion in deciding whether or not to create limited public fora. I see no reason—and no evidence of congressional intent—to constrain that discretion any more narrowly than our holding in *Widmar* requires. . . .

I respectfully dissent.

## NOTES AND QUESTIONS

1. By its terms, when does the Equal Access Act apply to public secondary schools? Why do you think it applies only to public secondary schools rather than public elementary and secondary schools? If religious groups meet on school property pursuant to the Equal Access Act, what are the limits on the school's participation in those meetings and any nonschool participants involvement in those meetings? What would you guess would be the rationales for those limits?

2. Contrast the ways in which Justice O'Connor and Justice Stevens defined the statutory term "noncurriculum related." How do the justices arrive at these

different definitions? What impact would each have on the operation of the Equal Access Act? Which definition seems more correct to you, in terms of the interpretation of legislative history, effectuating the purposes of the statute, or in terms of a common-sense reading of the words?

3. According to Justice O'Connor's opinion, if the Equal Access Act did not exist, would the First Amendment have required the same result in this case?

4. Justice O'Connor's opinion includes the following statement: "Even if some legislators were motivated [to vote for the Equal Access Act] by a conviction that religious speech in particular was valuable and worthy of protection, that alone would not invalidate the Act, because what is relevant is the legislative purpose of the statute, not the possibly religious motives of the legislators who enacted the law." Does this seem like a workable distinction when applying the first prong of the *Lemon* test?

5. In her opinion, Justice O'Connor makes a point about the "broad spectrum of officially recognized student clubs at Westside. . . ." How does the breadth of clubs that exist in this case compare to the breadth of clubs that existed in the *Widmar* case? Does such a comparison tell us anything, constitutionally speaking?

6. Describe the different tests used by Justice O'Connor and Justice Kennedy to evaluate the Establishment Clause issues in this case. What are Justice Kennedy's criticisms of the ways in which Justice O'Connor analyzes these issues? Are those criticisms persuasive?

7. Do Justices Marshall and Brennan make a convincing case that high school students are much more likely than college students to assume that the school supports the message of student organizations recognized by the school? What other distinctions do Justices Marshall, Brennan, and Stevens (in his dissenting opinion) draw between this case and the *Widmar* case? According to Justices Marshall and Brennan, what must Westside school do in order "redefine its relationship to its club program" and thereby "avoid appearing to sponsor or endorse [the religious club's] goals"? What responses does Justice O'Connor offer to these arguments in the opinion she wrote in this case?

8. Describe the similarities and differences between Justice Stevens' dissenting opinion and the opinion concurring in the judgment by Justices Marshall and Brennan. What explains their different votes?

9. Justice Stevens argues that "[t]he [Equal Access] Act, as construed by the majority, comes perilously close to an outright command to allow organized prayer, and perhaps the kind of religious ceremonies involved in *Widmar*, on school premises." Is Justice Stevens correct to indicate that these prospects are troubling from a constitutional standpoint?

10. The Equal Access Act defines "noninstructional time" in the following way: "time set aside by the school before actual classroom instruction begins or after actual classroom instruction ends." 20 U.S.C. 4072(4). Could lunch time be fairly characterized as "noninstructional time," and thus time in which

noncurriculum related clubs, including religious clubs could meet? See *Ceniceros v. Board of Trustees*, 106 F.3d 878 (9th Cir. 1997).

11. Assume that a school has a policy of requiring all student organizations to refrain from discriminating on the basis of race, gender, disability, ethnicity or religion. Assume also that a student Christian club has a policy of allowing only Christians to hold offices within the club and that the school threatens to prohibit the club's meetings on campus unless the club revokes its religious test for club officers. What is the proper result in such a case? See *Hsu v. Roslyn Union Free School District*, 85 F.3d 839 (2d Cir. 1996).

---

Do religious groups that are sponsored by adults, rather than by students, have some right of equal access to public school property after school hours? For example, should a religious organization be able to hold meetings on school property after school hours if other civic organizations are permitted to do so? Should a church whose sanctuary is being remodeled be able to use school facilities temporarily for worship services if other community groups are permitted similar access to school facilities?

In *Lamb's Chapel v. Center Moriches Union Free School District*, the Court confronted a case in which a religious group wished to use public school property in the evenings in order to show an evangelical Christian film series containing lectures by religious commentator James Dobson. The Center Moriches School District denied the application of an evangelical church, Lamb's Chapel, to show the film series based on New York Education Law § 414, that authorized school districts to open their facilities after hours to the public for "social, civic and recreational meetings and entertainments, and other uses pertaining to the welfare of the community." The law provided, however, that the list of permitted uses "does not include meetings for religious purposes." The school district had adopted its own rules that conformed to the state law ("Rule 7").

The church filed suit, alleging that the denial of access violated its rights under the Free Speech, Free Exercise, Establishment, and Equal Protection Clauses of the Constitution. The church's attorneys raised two closely related arguments alleging religious discrimination: that the school district had already granted public access for religious uses by other groups in contravention of its own rules; and, even if not, the film series discussed topics already permitted under the law, but from a religious rather than a secular perspective. Both the trial and appellate courts held for the school district on the ground that its building was not a traditional public forum but either a limited or nonpublic forum that permitted the district to distinguish access on the basis of subject matter and group identity. [For an explanation of the Court's public forum doctrine, see chapter 6.] The lower courts found that the district had not opened its facilities to organizations similar to Lamb's Chapel for religious purposes, such that the denial was viewpoint neutral and not a violation of the Free Speech Clause.

The Supreme Court reversed, but reached only the second claim raised by the church, the one of viewpoint discrimination. The Court also had to consider whether granting a religious group access to public school property would contravene the Establishment Clause. It held that it would not.

## LAMB'S CHAPEL v. CENTER MORICHES UNION FREE SCHOOL DISTRICT
508 U.S. 384 (1993)

▦ JUSTICE WHITE delivered the opinion of the Court. . . .

### II

There is no question that the District, like the private owner of property, may legally preserve the property under its control for the use to which it is dedicated. . . . It is also common ground that the District need not have permitted after-hours use of its property for any of the uses permitted by New York Educ. Law § 414. The District, however, did open its property for 2 of the 10 uses permitted by § 414. . . .

With respect to public property that is not a designated public forum open for indiscriminate public use for communicative purposes, we have said that "[c]ontrol over access to a nonpublic forum can be based on subject matter and speaker identity so long as the distinctions drawn are reasonable in light of the purpose served by the forum and are viewpoint neutral." *Cornelius v. NAACP Legal Defense and Ed. Fund,* 473 U.S. 788, 806. . . . The Court of Appeals thought that the application of Rule 7 in this case was viewpoint neutral because it had been, and would be, applied in the same way to all uses of school property for religious purposes. That all religions and all uses for religious purposes are treated alike under Rule 7, however, does not answer the critical question whether it discriminates on the basis of viewpoint to permit school property to be used for the presentation of all views about family issues and child rearing except those dealing with the subject matter from a religious standpoint.

There is no suggestion from the courts below or from the District or the State that a lecture or film about child rearing and family values would not be a use for social or civic purposes otherwise permitted by Rule 10. That subject matter is not one that the District has placed off limits to any and all speakers. Nor is there any indication in the record before us that the application to exhibit the particular film series involved here was, or would have been, denied for any reason other than the fact that the presentation would have been from a religious perspective. . . .

The film series involved here no doubt dealt with a subject otherwise permissible under Rule 10, and its exhibition was denied solely because the series dealt with the subject from a religious standpoint. The principle that has emerged from our cases "is that the First Amendment forbids the government to regulate speech in ways that favor some viewpoints or ideas at the expense of others." *City Council of Los Angeles v. Taxpayers for Vincent,* 466 U.S. 789, 804 (1984). . . .

The District, as a respondent, would save its judgment below on the ground that to permit its property to be used for religious purposes would be an establishment of religion forbidden by the First Amendment. This Court suggested in *Widmar v. Vincent,* 454 U.S. 263, 271 (1981), that the interest of the State in avoiding an Establishment Clause violation "may be [a] compelling" one justifying an abridgment of free speech otherwise protected by the First Amendment; but the Court went on to hold that permitting use of university property for religious purposes under the open access policy involved there would not be incompatible with the Court's Establishment Clause cases.

We have no more trouble than did the *Widmar* Court in disposing of the claimed defense on the ground that the posited fears of an Establishment Clause violation are unfounded. The showing of this film series would not have been during school hours, would not have been sponsored by the school, and would have been open to the public, not just to church members. The District property had repeatedly been used by a wide variety of private organizations. Under these circumstances, as in *Widmar*, there would have been no realistic danger that the community would think that the District was endorsing religion or any particular creed, and any benefit to religion or to the Church would have been no more than incidental. As in *Widmar*, permitting District property to be used to exhibit the film series involved in this case would not have been an establishment of religion under the three-part test articulated in *Lemon v. Kurtzman* (1971): The challenged governmental action has a secular purpose, does not have the principal or primary effect of advancing or inhibiting religion, and does not foster an excessive entanglement with religion.[7] . . .

For the reasons stated in this opinion, the judgment of the Court of Appeals is

*Reversed.* . . .

■ JUSTICE SCALIA, with whom JUSTICE THOMAS joins, concurring in the judgment.

I join the Court's conclusion that the District's refusal to allow use of school facilities for petitioners' film viewing, while generally opening the schools for community activities, violates petitioners' First Amendment free-speech rights. . . . I also agree with the Court that allowing Lamb's Chapel to use school facilities poses "no realistic danger" of a violation of the Establishment Clause, but I cannot accept most of its reasoning in this regard. . . .

As to the Court's invocation of the *Lemon* test: Like some ghoul in a late-night horror movie that repeatedly sits up in its grave and shuffles abroad, after being repeatedly killed and buried, *Lemon* stalks our Establishment Clause jurisprudence once again, frightening the little children and school attorneys of Center Moriches Union Free School District. Its most recent burial, only last Term, was, to be sure, not fully six feet under: Our decision in *Lee v. Weisman*, 505 U.S. 577 conspicuously avoided using the supposed "test" but also declined the invitation to repudiate it. Over the years, however, no fewer than five of the currently sitting Justices have, in their own opinions, personally driven pencils through the creature's heart (the author of today's opinion repeatedly), and a sixth has joined an opinion doing so.

---

[7] While we are somewhat diverted by JUSTICE SCALIA's evening at the cinema, we return to the reality that there is a proper way to inter an established decision and *Lemon*, however frightening it might be to some, has not been overruled. This case, like *Corporation of Presiding Bishop v. Amos*, 483 U.S. 327 (1987), presents no occasion to do so. JUSTICE SCALIA apparently was less haunted by the ghosts of the living when he joined the opinion of the Court in that case.

The secret of the *Lemon* test's survival, I think, is that it is so easy to kill. It is there to scare us (and our audience) when we wish it to do so, but we can command it to return to the tomb at will. When we wish to strike down a practice it forbids, we invoke it; when we wish to uphold a practice it forbids, we ignore it entirely, see *Marsh v. Chambers* 463 U.S. 783 (upholding state legislative chaplains). Sometimes, we take a middle course, calling its three prongs "no more than helpful signposts," *Hunt v. McNair,* 413 U.S. 734, 741 (1973). Such a docile and useful monster is worth keeping around, at least in a somnolent state; one never knows when one might need him. . . .

I cannot join for yet another reason: the Court's statement that the proposed use of the school's facilities is constitutional because (among other things) it would not signal endorsement of religion in general. What a strange notion, that a Constitution which *itself* gives "religion in general" preferential treatment (I refer to the Free Exercise Clause) forbids endorsement of religion in general. . . . That was *not* the view of those who adopted our Constitution, who believed that the public virtues inculcated by religion are a public good. . . . [I]ndifference to "religion in general" is *not* what our cases, both old and recent, demand.

## NOTES AND QUESTIONS

1. Is *Lamb's Chapel* primarily a free speech case or an Establishment Clause case? Is the holding that the free speech interests—here, not being subjected to viewpoint discrimination in a limited or non-public forum—outweigh the no-establishment values or that those values were not threatened by granting the church access to the school building after hours?

   Both the American Civil Liberties Union and Americans United for Separation of Church and State filed an *amicus* brief on behalf of *Lamb's Chapel* arguing that establishment concerns were not implicated by a religious use of a school that did not involve access to public school students. Assuming that this was a correct legal position to take, was it a strategic error for the separationist organizations? *Lamb's Chapel,* with its expansion of viewpoint discrimination doctrine, served as authority for *Rosenberger v. Rectors and Visitors of University of Virginia* (1995), requiring not equal access to a facility by a religious group but equal funding of its religious activity (see p. 821), and for *Good News Club v. Milford Central School* (2001), requiring a school to allow facility access to a religious group to hold religious instruction with elementary school students immediately following the school day (see p. 802). ACLU and Americans United opposed the holdings in these latter two cases. Viewed together, the three cases provide a nice illustration of how later cases build on precedent to develop legal doctrine, at times authorizing practices that the initial supporters of the precedent would have opposed.

2. Are there some Establishment Clause limits to the *Lamb's Chapel* holding? Suppose *Lamb's Chapel* had not applied to use the school to show a six-night film series but had asked to use the school building to conduct Sunday worship services on an indefinite basis (in fact, *Lamb's Chapel* made such a request, which was denied, but it declined to challenge that denial). Assume the school district requires only a minimal cleaning fee for such uses by charitable

organizations. The church uses the school facility for many years which allows it to avoid the financial costs of building its own sanctuary. Does such an arrangement—common in many cities—violate the Establishment Clause by subsidizing the church and thus advancing religion? How is this benefit to religion different from the city giving the church money to build its sanctuary?

Finally, what about Justice O'Connor's argument from her concurring opinion in *Capitol Square Review and Advisory Board v. Pinette* (1995) (see chapter 20) that "[a]t some point, . . . a private religious group may so dominate a public forum that a formal policy of equal access is transformed into a demonstration of approval," thus violating the no-endorsement rule? Returning to the hypothetical, what if the church is only one of twenty other nongovernmental groups that uses school property on a weekly basis?

3. Is "religion" a viewpoint or a subject matter? Stated differently, is religion a unique and distinct way of organizing thought, such that it has no secular counterpart, or is there a religious perspective to most nonreligious epistemologies, such that it should be treated no different from its secular counterparts? In *Rosenberger v. University of Virginia* (see p. 821), Justice Kennedy makes the following statement:

> It is, in a sense, something of an understatement to speak of religious thought and discussion as just a viewpoint, as distinct from a comprehensive body of thought. The nature of our origins and destiny and their dependence upon the existence of a divine being have been subjects of philosophic inquiry throughout human history. . . . Religion may be a vast area of inquiry, but it also provides, as it did here, a specific premise, a perspective, a standpoint from which a variety of subjects may be discussed and considered.

If religion can be both a perspective and a distinct body of thought, how far does the holding in *Lamb's Chapel* extend? Must the state provide an opportunity for a religious perspective on every secular subject it opens up for public discussion? Suppose a public elementary school holds assemblies on various scientific subjects to inspire students to pursue science. The school invites a paleontologist to speak about dinosaurs and the age of the earth, and she comments that the earth is over four billion years old. Must the school now allow a "young-earth" creationist to address the students about how the earth is between 6,000 to 8,000 years old? Or, does the holding in *Lamb's Chapel* clearly not address situations in which there are captive audiences of schoolchildren?

4. Could it be argued that requiring equal access in these kinds of situations plays a crucial role in ensuring that religion is not fenced out of public debate or denied some important recognition or visibility in the public square? A bit of background is helpful in addressing this question. The Establishment Clause has been read to prohibit the government from promoting religion, and thus the state is usually forbidden from speaking religiously. The equal access principle, however, ensures that in many cases speech endorsing religion may take place on government property so long as it is clear that that speech is attributable to nongovernmental rather than governmental speakers.

Given the large amount of government property in the modern era, can it be argued that the equal-access concept plays an important role in ensuring that religious people and messages may be recognized and participate in public discussion, even as it also ensures that the government itself doesn't promote religion? Or, would it be sufficient to find that religious messages may indeed be expressed in the public square, as long as the forum or property is nongovernmental in nature?

5.  Justice Scalia's melodrama aside, how accurate is his assessment about the Court's use of the *Lemon* test? If he is correct, is this a weakness of the *Lemon* test or a strength? Scalia's argument could be summed up as thus: that the Court's sporadic and uneven use of *Lemon* leads to legal uncertainty; that public officials and lower court judges do not know what standard to apply in Establishment Clause matters (or how to apply it); and that the inconsistent use of *Lemon* undermines the integrity of the Court and the legitimacy of its decisions. Are these concerns compelling? What arguments support the Court's selective use of *Lemon* and its sensitivity to the different facts in each case?

Should a religious organization for children be permitted to use school facilities after school hours for biblical instruction and related activities if other nongovernmental groups may do likewise? Remember in *McCollum v. Board of Education* (1948), the Court struck down a program that allowed a community organization to provide religious instruction to willing students during the school day. Do the constitutional concerns expressed in *McCollum* lessen when the religious instruction takes place immediately following the school bell?

The Court agreed to address some of these issues in 2001. In 1996, Stephen and Darleen Fournier, residents of the Milford School District, in New York, submitted a proposal to conduct weekly meetings of the Good News Club, a private Christian organization for children ages 6-12, after school in the school cafeteria. The Fourniers described their proposed use of the facilities as to have "a fun time of singing songs, hearing a Bible lesson and memorizing scripture." The school denied the Fourniers' request, referring to a community use policy that prohibits use of school facilities "by an individual or organization for religious purposes." When the Supreme Court heard the case, however, it ruled in favor of the Good News Club. Citing its earlier rulings in cases such as *Widmar* and *Lamb's Chapel*, the Court found that the school had engaged in impermissible viewpoint discrimination and that the club's use of school facilities presented no Establishment Clause violation.

## GOOD NEWS CLUB v. MILFORD CENTRAL SCHOOL
### 533 U.S. 98 (2001)

JUSTICE THOMAS delivered the opinion of the Court.

This case presents two questions. The first question is whether Milford Central School violated the free speech rights of the Good News Club when it excluded the Club from meeting after hours at the school. The second question is whether any such violation is justified by Milford's concern that permitting the Club's activities would violate the Establishment Clause. We conclude that Milford's restriction violates the Club's free speech rights and that no Establishment Clause concern justifies that violation.

I

The State of New York authorizes local school boards to adopt regulations governing the use of their school facilities. In particular, N.Y. Educ. Law § 414 (McKinney 2000) enumerates several purposes for which local boards may open their schools to public use. In 1992, respondent Milford Central School (Milford) enacted a community use policy adopting seven of § 414's purposes for which its building could be used after school. Two of the stated purposes are relevant here. First, district residents may use the school for "instruction in any branch of education, learning or the arts." Second, the school is available for "social, civic and recreational meetings and entertainment events, and other uses pertaining to the welfare of the community, provided that such uses shall be nonexclusive and shall be opened to the general public."

Stephen and Darleen Fournier reside within Milford's district and therefore are eligible to use the school's facilities as long as their proposed use is approved by the school. Together they are sponsors of the local Good News Club, a private Christian organization for children ages 6 to 12. Pursuant to Milford's policy, in September 1996 the Fourniers submitted a request to Dr. Robert McGruder, interim superintendent of the district, in which they sought permission to hold the Club's weekly afterschool meetings in the school cafeteria. The next month, McGruder formally denied the Fourniers' request on the ground that the proposed use—to have "a fun time of singing songs, hearing a Bible lesson and memorizing scripture"—was "the equivalent of religious worship." According to McGruder, the community use policy, which prohibits use "by any individual or organization for religious purposes," foreclosed the Club's activities.

In response to a letter submitted by the Club's counsel, Milford's attorney requested information to clarify the nature of the Club's activities. The Club sent a set of materials used or distributed at the meetings and the following description of its meeting:

> The Club opens its session with Ms. Fournier taking attendance. As she calls a child's name, if the child recites a Bible verse the child receives a treat. After attendance, the Club sings songs. Next Club members engage in games that involve, *inter alia,* learning Bible verses. Ms. Fournier then relates a Bible story and explains how it applies to Club members' lives. The Club closes with prayer. Finally, Ms. Fournier distributes treats and the Bible verses for memorization.

McGruder and Milford's attorney reviewed the materials and concluded that "the kinds of activities proposed to be engaged in by the Good News Club were not a discussion of secular subjects such as child rearing, development of character and development of morals from a religious perspective, but were in fact the equivalent of religious instruction itself." In February 1997, the Milford Board of Education adopted a resolution rejecting the Club's request to use Milford's facilities "for the purpose of conducting religious instruction and Bible study."

In March 1997, petitioners, the Good News Club, Ms. Fournier, and her daughter Andrea Fournier (collectively, the Club), filed an action . . . alleg[ing] that Milford's denial of its application violated its free speech rights under the First and Fourteenth Amendments, its right to equal protection under the Fourteenth Amendment, and its right to religious freedom under the Religious Freedom Restoration Act of 1993, 42 U.S.C. § 2000bb et seq. . . .

There is a conflict among the Courts of Appeals on the question whether speech can be excluded from a limited public forum on the basis of the religious nature of the speech. . . . We granted certiorari to resolve this conflict.

## II

The standards that we apply to determine whether a State has unconstitutionally excluded a private speaker from use of a public forum depend on the nature of the forum. See *Perry Ed. Assn. v. Perry Local Educators' Assn.*, 460 U.S. 37, 44 (1983). If the forum is a traditional or open public forum, the State's restrictions on speech are subject to stricter scrutiny than are restrictions in a limited public forum. We have previously declined to decide whether a school district's opening of its facilities pursuant to N.Y. Educ. Law § 414 creates a limited or a traditional public forum. See *Lamb's Chapel v. Center Moriches School District,* 508 U.S. 384 (1993). Because the parties have agreed that Milford created a limited public forum when it opened its facilities in 1992, we need not resolve the issue here. Instead, we simply will assume that Milford operates a limited public forum.

When the State establishes a limited public forum, the State is not required to and does not allow persons to engage in every type of speech. The State may be justified "in reserving [its forum] for certain groups or for the discussion of certain topics." *Rosenberger v. Rector and Visitors of Univ. of Va.*, 515 U.S. 819, 829 (1995); see also *Lamb's Chapel,* 392–393. The State's power to restrict speech, however, is not without limits. The restriction must not discriminate against speech on the basis of viewpoint, *Rosenberger,* 829, and the restriction must be "reasonable in light of the purpose served by the forum," *Cornelius v. NAACP Legal Defense & Ed. Fund, Inc.,* 473 U.S. 788, 806 (1985).

## III

Applying this test, we first address whether the exclusion constituted viewpoint discrimination. We are guided in our analysis by two of our prior opinions, *Lamb's Chapel* and *Rosenberger*. In *Lamb's Chapel*, we held that a school district violated the Free Speech Clause of the First Amendment when it excluded a private group from presenting films at the school based solely on the films' discussions of family values from a religious perspective. Likewise, in *Rosenberger*, we held that a university's refusal to fund a student publication because the publication addressed issues from a religious perspective violated the Free Speech Clause. Concluding that Milford's exclusion of the Good News Club based on its religious nature is indistinguishable from the exclusions in these cases, we hold that the exclusion constitutes viewpoint discrimination. Because the restriction is viewpoint discriminatory, we need not decide whether it is unreasonable in light of the purposes served by the forum.[2]

Milford has opened its limited public forum to activities that serve a variety of purposes, including events "pertaining to the welfare of the community." Milford interprets its policy to permit discussions of subjects such as child rearing, and of "the development of character and morals from a religious perspective." For example, this policy would allow someone to use Aesop's Fables to teach children moral values. Additionally, a group could sponsor a debate on whether there should be a constitutional amendment to permit prayer in public schools, and the Boy Scouts could meet "to influence a boy's character, development and spiritual growth." In short, any group that "promotes the moral and character development of children" is eligible to use the school building.

Just as there is no question that teaching morals and character development to children is a permissible purpose under Milford's policy, it is clear that the Club teaches morals and character development to children. For example, no one disputes that the Club instructs children to overcome feelings of jealousy, to treat others well regardless of how they treat the children, and to be obedient, even if it does so in a nonsecular way. Nonetheless, because Milford found the Club's activities to be religious in nature—"the equivalent of religious instruction itself," it excluded the Club from use of its facilities.

Applying *Lamb's Chapel*, we find it quite clear that Milford engaged in viewpoint discrimination when it excluded the Club from the afterschool forum. In *Lamb's Chapel*, the local New York school district similarly had adopted § 414's "social, civic or recreational use" category as a permitted use in its limited public forum. The district also prohibited use "by any group for religious purposes." Citing this prohibition, the school district excluded a church that wanted to present films teaching family values from a Christian perspective. We held that, because the films "no doubt dealt with a subject otherwise permissible" under the rule, the teaching of family values, the district's exclusion of the church was unconstitutional viewpoint discrimination.

Like the church in *Lamb's Chapel*, the Club seeks to address a subject otherwise permitted under the rule, the teaching of morals and character, from a religious standpoint. Certainly, one could have characterized the film presentations in *Lamb's Chapel* as a religious use. And one easily could conclude that the films' purpose to instruct that "'society's slide toward humanism . . . can only be counterbalanced by a loving home where Christian values are instilled from an early age,'" was "quintessentially religious." The only apparent difference between the activity of *Lamb's Chapel* and the activities of the Good News Club is that the Club

---

[2] Although Milford argued below that, under § 414, it could not permit its property to be used for the purpose of religious activity, here it merely asserts in one sentence that it has, "in accordance with state law, closed [its] limited open forum to purely religious instruction and services." Because Milford does not elaborate, it is difficult to discern whether it is arguing that it is required by state law to exclude the Club's activities.

Before the Court of Appeals, Milford cited *Trietley v. Board of Ed. of Buffalo*, 65 A.D.2d 1, 409 N.Y.S.2d 912 (1978), in which a New York court held that a local school district could not permit a student Bible club to meet on school property because "religious purposes are not included in the enumerated purposes for which a school may be used under section 414 of the Education Law." Although the court conceded that the Bible clubs might provide incidental secular benefits, it nonetheless concluded that the school would have violated the Establishment Clause had it permitted the club's activities on campus. Because we hold that the exclusion of the Club on the basis of its religious perspective constitutes unconstitutional viewpoint discrimination, it is no defense for Milford that purely religious purposes can be excluded under state law.

chooses to teach moral lessons from a Christian perspective through live storytell-ing and prayer, whereas *Lamb's Chapel* taught lessons through films. This distinc-tion is inconsequential. Both modes of speech use a religious viewpoint. Thus, the exclusion of the Good News Club's activities, like the exclusion of *Lamb's Chapel's* films, constitutes unconstitutional viewpoint discrimination.

Our opinion in *Rosenberger* also is dispositive. . . . Given the obvious reli-gious content of Wide Awake [magazine], we cannot say that the Club's activi-ties are any more "religious" or deserve any less First Amendment protection than did the publication of Wide Awake in *Rosenberger*.

Despite our holdings in *Lamb's Chapel* and *Rosenberger*, the Court of Ap-peals, like Milford, believed that its characterization of the Club's activities as religious in nature warranted treating the Club's activities as different in kind from the other activities permitted by the school. The "Christian viewpoint" is unique, according to the court, because it contains an "additional layer" that other kinds of viewpoints do not. That is, the Club "is focused on teaching children how to cultivate their relationship with God through Jesus Christ," which it characterized as "quintessentially religious." With these observations, the court concluded that, because the Club's activities "fall outside the bounds of pure 'moral and character development,'" the exclusion did not constitute viewpoint discrimination.

We disagree that something that is "quintessentially religious" or "decid-edly religious in nature" cannot also be characterized properly as the teaching of morals and character development from a particular viewpoint. See 202 F.3d, 512 (JACOBS, J., dissenting) ("When the subject matter is morals and character, it is quixotic to attempt a distinction between religious viewpoints and religious subject matters"). What matters for purposes of the Free Speech Clause is that we can see no logical difference in kind between the invoca-tion of Christianity by the Club and the invocation of teamwork, loyalty, or patriotism by other associations to provide a foundation for their lessons. It is apparent that the unstated principle of the Court of Appeals' reasoning is its conclusion that any time religious instruction and prayer are used to dis-cuss morals and character, the discussion is simply not a "pure" discussion of those issues. According to the Court of Appeals, reliance on Christian prin-ciples taints moral and character instruction in a way that other foundations for thought or viewpoints do not. We, however, have never reached such a conclusion. Instead, we reaffirm our holdings in *Lamb's Chapel* and *Rosenberg-er* that speech discussing otherwise permissible subjects cannot be excluded from a limited public forum on the ground that the subject is discussed from a religious viewpoint. Thus, we conclude that Milford's exclusion of the Club from use of the school, pursuant to its community use policy, constitutes im-permissible viewpoint discrimination.[4]

## IV

Milford argues that, even if its restriction constitutes viewpoint discrimi-nation, its interest in not violating the Establishment Clause outweighs the Club's interest in gaining equal access to the school's facilities. In other words,

---

[4] Despite Milford's insistence that the Club's activities constitute "religious worship," the Court of Appeals made no such determination. It did compare the Club's activities to

according to Milford, its restriction was required to avoid violating the Establishment Clause. We disagree.

We have said that a state interest in avoiding an Establishment Clause violation "may be characterized as compelling," and therefore may justify content-based discrimination. *Widmar v. Vincent*, 454 U.S. 263, 271 (1981). However, it is not clear whether a State's interest in avoiding an Establishment Clause violation would justify viewpoint discrimination. We need not, however, confront the issue in this case, because we conclude that the school has no valid Establishment Clause interest.

We rejected Establishment Clause defenses similar to Milford's in two previous free speech cases, *Lamb's Chapel* and *Widmar*. In particular, in *Lamb's Chapel*, we explained that "the showing of the film series would not have been during school hours, would not have been sponsored by the school, and would have been open to the public, not just to church members." 508 U.S., 395. Accordingly, we found that "there would have been no realistic danger that the community would think that the District was endorsing religion or any particular creed." *Ibid.* Likewise, in *Widmar*, where the university's forum was already available to other groups, this Court concluded that there was no Establishment Clause problem. 454 U.S., 272-273, and n. 13.

The Establishment Clause defense fares no better in this case. As in *Lamb's Chapel*, the Club's meetings were held after school hours, not sponsored by the school, and open to any student who obtained parental consent, not just to Club members. As in *Widmar*, Milford made its forum available to other organizations. The Club's activities are materially indistiguishable from those in *Lamb's Chapel* and *Widmar*. Thus, Milford's reliance on the Establishment Clause is unavailing.

Milford attempts to distinguish *Lamb's Chapel* and *Widmar* by emphasizing that Milford's policy involves elementary school children. According to Milford, children will perceive that the school is endorsing the Club and will feel coercive pressure to participate, because the Club's activities take place on school grounds, even though they occur during nonschool hours.[5] This argument is unpersuasive.

First, we have held that "a significant factor in upholding governmental programs in the face of Establishment Clause attack is their *neutrality* towards

---

"religious worship," but ultimately it concluded merely that the Club's activities "fall outside the bounds of pure 'moral and character development.'" In any event, we conclude that the Club's activities do not constitute mere religious worship, divorced from any teaching of moral values.

JUSTICE SOUTER's recitation of the Club's activities is accurate. But in our view, religion is used by the Club in the same fashion that it was used by Lamb's Chapel and by the students in Rosenberger: religion is the viewpoint from which ideas are conveyed. We did not find the Rosenberger students' attempt to cultivate a personal relationship with Christ to bar their claim that religion was a viewpoint. And we see no reason to treat the Club's use of religion as something other than a viewpoint merely because of any evangelical message it conveys. According to JUSTICE SOUTER, the Club's activities constitute "an evangelical service of worship." Regardless of the label JUSTICE SOUTER wishes to use, what matters is the substance of the Club's activities, which we conclude are materially indistinguishable from the activities in Lamb's Chapel and Rosenberger.

[5] It is worth noting that, although Milford repeatedly has argued that the Club's meeting time directly after the schoolday is relevant to its Establishment Clause concerns, the record

religion." *Rosenberger*, 515 U.S., 839 (emphasis added). . . . Milford's implication that granting access to the Club would do damage to the neutrality principle defies logic. For the "guarantee of neutrality is respected, not offended, when the government, following neutral criteria and evenhanded policies, extends benefits to recipients whose ideologies and viewpoints, including religious ones, are broad and diverse." *Rosenberger*, 839. The Good News Club seeks nothing more than to be treated neutrally and given access to speak about the same topics as are other groups. Because allowing the Club to speak on school grounds would ensure neutrality, not threaten it, Milford faces an uphill battle in arguing that the Establishment Clause compels it to exclude the Good News Club.

Second, to the extent we consider whether the community would feel coercive pressure to engage in the Club's activities, the relevant community would be the parents, not the elementary school children. It is the parents who choose whether their children will attend the Good News Club meetings. Because the children cannot attend without their parents' permission, they cannot be coerced into engaging in the Good News Club's religious activities. Milford does not suggest that the parents of elementary school children would be confused about whether the school was endorsing religion. Nor do we believe that such an argument could be reasonably advanced.

Third, whatever significance we may have assigned in the Establishment Clause context to the suggestion that elementary school children are more impressionable than adults, we have never extended our Establishment Clause jurisprudence to foreclose private religious conduct during nonschool hours merely because it takes place on school premises where elementary school children may be present.

None of the cases discussed by Milford persuades us that our Establishment Clause jurisprudence has gone this far. For example, Milford cites *Lee v. Weisman* for the proposition that "there are heightened concerns with protecting freedom of conscience from subtle coercive pressure in the elementary and secondary public schools," 505 U.S., 592. In *Lee*, however, we concluded that attendance at the graduation exercise was obligatory. *Id.*, 586. We did not place independent significance on the fact that the graduation exercise might take place on school premises, *Lee*, 583. Here, where the school facilities are being used for a nonschool function and there is no government sponsorship of the Club's activities, *Lee* is inapposite.

Equally unsupportive is *Edwards v. Aguillard*, 482 U.S. 578 (1987), in which we held that a Louisiana law that proscribed the teaching of evolution as part of the public school curriculum, unless accompanied by a lesson on creationism, violated the Establishment Clause. In *Edwards*, we mentioned that students are susceptible to pressure in the classroom, particularly given their possible reliance on teachers as role models. But we did not discuss this

---

does not reflect any offer by the school district to permit the Club to use the facilities at a different time of day. The superintendent's stated reason for denying the applications was simply that the Club's activities were "religious instruction." In any event, consistent with Lamb's Chapel and Widmar, the school could not deny equal access to the Club for any time that is generally available for public use.

concern in our application of the law to the facts. Moreover, we did note that mandatory attendance requirements meant that State advancement of religion in a school would be particularly harshly felt by impressionable students.[6] But we did not suggest that, when the school was not actually advancing religion, the impressionability of students would be relevant to the Establishment Clause issue. Even if *Edwards* had articulated the principle Milford believes it did, the facts in *Edwards* are simply too remote from those here to give the principle any weight. *Edwards* involved the content of the curriculum taught by state teachers *during the schoolday* to children required to attend. Obviously, when individuals who are not schoolteachers are giving lessons after school to children permitted to attend only with parental consent, the concerns expressed in *Edwards* are not present.[7]

Fourth, even if we were to consider the possible misperceptions by schoolchildren in deciding whether Milford's permitting the Club's activities would violate the Establishment Clause, the facts of this case simply do not support Milford's conclusion. There is no evidence that young children are permitted to loiter outside classrooms after the schoolday has ended. Surely even young children are aware of events for which their parents must sign permission forms. The meetings were held in a combined high school resource room and middle school special education room, not in an elementary school classroom. The instructors are not schoolteachers. And the children in the group are not all the same age as in the normal classroom setting; their ages range from 6 to 12.[8] In sum, these circumstances simply do not support the theory that small children would perceive endorsement here.

---

[6] Milford also cites *Illinois ex rel. McCollum v. Board of Ed.*, 333 U.S. 203 (1948), for its position that the Club's religious element would be advanced by the State through compulsory attendance laws. In McCollum, the school district excused students from their normal classroom study during the regular schoolday to attend classes taught by sectarian religious teachers, who were subject to approval by the school superintendent. Under these circumstances, this Court found it relevant that "the operation of the State's compulsory education system . . . assisted and was integrated with the program of religious instruction carried on by separate religious sects." *Id.*, 209. In the present case, there is simply no integration and cooperation between the school district and the Club. The Club's activities take place after the time when the children are compelled by state law to be at the school.

[7] Milford also refers to *Board of Ed. of Westside Community Schools v. Mergens*, 496 U.S. 226 (1990), to support its view that "assumptions about the ability of students to make . . . subtle distinctions [between schoolteachers during the schoolday and Reverend Fournier after school] are less valid for elementary age children who tend to be less informed, more impressionable, and more subject to peer pressure than average adults." Four Justices in *Mergens* believed that high school students likely are capable of distinguishing between government and private endorsement of religion. The opinion, however, made no statement about how capable of discerning endorsement elementary school children would have been in the context of *Mergens*, where the activity at issue was after school. In any event, even to the extent elementary school children are more prone to peer pressure than are older children, it simply is not clear what, in this case, they could be pressured to do.

In further support of the argument that the impressionability of elementary school children even after school is significant, Milford points to several cases in which we have found Establishment Clause violations in public schools. For example, Milford relies heavily on *School Dist. of Abington Township v. Schempp*, 374 U.S. 203 (1963), in which we found unconstitutional Pennsylvania's practice of permitting public schools to read Bible verses at the opening of each schoolday. *Schempp*, however, is inapposite because this case does not involve activity by the school during the schoolday.

[8] Milford also relies on the Equal Access Act, as evidence that Congress has recognized the vulnerability of elementary school children to misperceiving endorsement of religion.

Finally, even if we were to inquire into the minds of schoolchildren in this case, we cannot say the danger that children would misperceive the endorsement of religion is any greater than the danger that they would perceive a hostility toward the religious viewpoint if the Club were excluded from the public forum. This concern is particularly acute given the reality that Milford's building is not used only for elementary school children. Students, from kindergarten through the 12th grade, all attend school in the same building. There may be as many, if not more, upperclassmen than elementary school children who occupy the school after hours. For that matter, members of the public writ large are permitted in the school after hours pursuant to the community use policy. Any bystander could conceivably be aware of the school's use policy and its exclusion of the Good News Club, and could suffer as much from viewpoint discrimination as elementary school children could suffer from perceived endorsement.

We cannot operate, as Milford would have us do, under the assumption that any risk that small children would perceive endorsement should counsel in favor of excluding the Club's religious activity. We decline to employ Establishment Clause jurisprudence using a modified heckler's veto, in which a group's religious activity can be proscribed on the basis of what the youngest members of the audience might misperceive. There are countervailing constitutional concerns related to rights of other individuals in the community. In this case, those countervailing concerns are the free speech rights of the Club and its members. And, we have already found that those rights have been violated, not merely perceived to have been violated, by the school's actions toward the Club.

We are not convinced that there is any significance in this case to the possibility that elementary school children may witness the Good News Club's activities on school premises, and therefore we can find no reason to depart from our holdings in *Lamb's Chapel* and *Widmar*. Accordingly, we conclude that permitting the Club to meet on the school's premises would not have violated the Establishment Clause.[9]

V

When Milford denied the Good News Club access to the school's limited public forum on the ground that the Club was religious in nature, it discrimi-

---

The Act, however, makes no express recognition of the impressionability of elementary school children. It applies only to public secondary schools and makes no mention of elementary schools. We can derive no meaning from the choice by Congress not to address elementary schools.

[9] Both parties have briefed the Establishment Clause issue extensively, and neither suggests that a remand would be of assistance on this issue. Although JUSTICE SOUTER would prefer that a record be developed on several facts, and JUSTICE BREYER believes that development of those facts could yet be dispositive in this case, none of these facts is relevant to the Establishment Clause inquiry. For example, JUSTICE SOUTER suggests that we cannot determine whether there would be an Establishment Clause violation unless we know when, and to what extent, other groups use the facilities. When a limited public forum is available for use by groups presenting any viewpoint, however, we would not find an Establishment Clause violation simply because only groups presenting a religious viewpoint have opted to take advantage of the forum at a particular time.

nated against the Club because of its religious viewpoint in violation of the Free Speech Clause of the First Amendment. Because Milford has not raised a valid Establishment Clause claim, we do not address the question whether such a claim could excuse Milford's viewpoint discrimination.

The judgment of the Court of Appeals is reversed, and the case is remanded for further proceedings consistent with this opinion.

*It is so ordered.*

JUSTICE SCALIA, concurring.

I join the Court's opinion but write separately to explain further my views on two issues.

I

First, I join Part IV of the Court's opinion, regarding the Establishment Clause issue, with the understanding that its consideration of coercive pressure and perceptions of endorsement "to the extent" that the law makes such factors relevant, is consistent with the belief (which I hold) that in this case that extent is zero. As to coercive pressure: Physical coercion is not at issue here; and so-called "peer pressure," if it can even been considered coercion, is, when it arises from private activities, one of the attendant consequences of a freedom of association that is constitutionally protected. What is at play here is not coercion, but the compulsion of ideas—and the private right to exert and receive that compulsion (or to have one's children receive it) is *protected* by the Free Speech and Free Exercise Clauses, not banned by the Establishment Clause. A priest has as much liberty to proselytize as a patriot.

As to endorsement, I have previously written that "religious expression cannot violate the Establishment Clause where it (1) is purely private and (2) occurs in a traditional or designated public forum, publicly announced and open to all on equal terms." *Capitol Square Review and Advisory Bd. v. Pinette,* 515 U.S. 753, 770 (1995). The same is true of private speech that occurs in a limited public forum, publicly announced, whose boundaries are not drawn to favor religious groups but instead permit a cross-section of uses. In that context, which is this case, "erroneous conclusions [about endorsement] do not count." *Id.*, 765.

II

Second, since we have rejected the only reason that respondent gave for excluding the Club's speech from a forum that clearly included it (the forum was opened to any "use pertaining to the welfare of the community"), I do not suppose it matters whether the exclusion is characterized as viewpoint or subject-matter discrimination. Lacking *any* legitimate reason for excluding the Club's speech from its forum—"because it's religious" will not do—respondent would seem to fail First Amendment scrutiny regardless of how its action is characterized. Even subject-matter limits must at least be "reasonable in light of the purpose served by the forum," *Cornelius v. NAACP Legal Defense & Ed. Fund, Inc.,* 473 U.S. 788, 806 (1985). But I agree, in any event, that respondent did discriminate on the basis of viewpoint.

As I understand it, the point of disagreement between the Court and the dissenters (and the Court of Appeals) with regard to petitioner's Free Speech Clause claim is not whether the Good News Club must be permitted to present religious viewpoints on morals and character in respondent's forum, which has been opened to secular discussions of that subject. The answer to that is established by our decision in *Lamb's Chapel*. The point of disagreement is not even whether *some* of the Club's religious speech fell within the protection of *Lamb's Chapel*. It certainly did.

The disagreement, rather, regards the portions of the Club's meetings that are not "purely" "discussions" of morality and character from a religious viewpoint. The Club, for example, urges children "who already believe in the Lord Jesus as their Savior" to "stop and ask God for the strength and the 'want' . . . to obey Him," and it invites children who "don't know Jesus as Savior" to "trust the Lord Jesus to be [their] Savior from sin." The dissenters and the Second Circuit say that the presence of such additional speech, because it is purely religious, transforms the Club's meetings into something different in kind from other, nonreligious activities that teach moral and character development. Therefore, the argument goes, excluding the Club is not viewpoint discrimination. I disagree.

Respondent has opened its facilities to any "use pertaining to the welfare of the community, provided that such use shall be nonexclusive and shall be opened to the general public." Shaping the moral and character development of children certainly "pertains to the welfare of the community." Thus, respondent has agreed that groups engaged in the endeavor of developing character may use its forum. The Boy Scouts, for example, may seek "to influence a boy's character, development and spiritual growth," and a group may use Aesop's Fables to teach moral values. When the Club attempted to teach Biblical-based moral values, however, it was excluded because its activities "did not involve merely a religious perspective on the secular subject of morality" and because "it [was] clear from the conduct of the meetings that the Good News Club goes far beyond merely stating its viewpoint." 202 F.3d, 510.

From no other group does respondent require the sterility of speech that it demands of petitioners. The Boy Scouts could undoubtedly buttress their exhortations to keep "morally straight" and live "clean" lives by giving *reasons* why that is a good idea—because parents want and expect it, because it will make the scouts "better" and "more successful" people, because it will emulate such admired past Scouts as former President Gerald Ford. The Club, however, may only discuss morals and character, and cannot give *its* reasons why they should be fostered—because God wants and expects it, because it will make the Club members "saintly" people, and because it emulates Jesus Christ. The Club may not, in other words, independently discuss the religious premise on which its views are based—that God exists and His assistance is necessary to morality. It may not defend the premise, and it absolutely must not seek to persuade the children that the premise is true. The children must, so to say, take it on faith. This is blatant viewpoint discrimination. Just as calls to character based on patriotism will go unanswered if the listeners do not believe their country is good and just, calls to moral behavior based on God's will are useless if the listeners do not believe that God exists. Effectiveness in presenting a viewpoint rests on the persuasiveness with which the speaker defends his premise—and in respondent's facilities every premise but a religious one may be defended.

In *Rosenberger* we struck down a similar viewpoint restriction. There, a private student newspaper sought funding from a student-activity fund on the same basis as its secular counterparts. And though the paper printed such directly religious material as exhortations to belief, we held that refusing to provide the funds discriminated on the basis of viewpoint, because the religious speech had been used to "provide . . . a specific premise . . . from which a variety of subjects may be discussed and considered." The right to present a viewpoint based on a religion premise carried with it the right to defend the premise.

The dissenters emphasize that the religious speech used by the Club as the foundation for its views on morals and character is not just any type of religious speech—although they cannot agree exactly what type of religious speech it is. In JUSTICE STEVENS' view, it is speech "aimed principally at proselytizing or inculcating belief in a particular religious faith." This does not, to begin with, distinguish *Rosenberger*, which also involved proselytizing speech, as the above quotations show. But in addition, it does not distinguish the Club's activities from those of the other groups using respondent's forum—which have not, as JUSTICE STEVENS suggests, been restricted to roundtable "discussions" of moral issues. Those groups may seek to inculcate children with their beliefs, and they may furthermore "recruit others to join their respective groups." The Club must therefore have liberty to do the same, even if, as JUSTICE STEVENS fears without support in the record, its actions may prove (shudder!) divisive.

JUSTICE SOUTER, while agreeing that the Club's religious speech "may be characterized as proselytizing," thinks that it is even more clearly excludable from respondent's forum because it is essentially "an evangelical service of worship." But we have previously rejected the attempt to distinguish worship from other religious speech, saying that "the distinction has [no] intelligible content," and further, no *"relevance"* to the constitutional issue. *Widmar v. Vincent*, 454 U.S. 263, 269, n. 6 (1981); see also *Murdock v. Pennsylvania*, 319 U.S., 109 (refusing to distinguish evangelism from worship).[3] Those holdings are surely proved correct today by the dissenters' inability to agree, even between themselves, into which subcategory of religious speech the Club's activities fell. If the distinction did have content, it would be beyond the courts' competence to administer. And if courts (and other government officials) were competent, applying the distinction would require state monitoring of private, religious speech with a degree of pervasiveness that we have previously found unacceptable. I will not endorse an approach that suffers such a wondrous diversity of flaws.

With these words of explanation, I join the opinion of the Court.

▓ JUSTICE BREYER, concurring in part.

I agree with the Court's conclusion and join its opinion to the extent that they are consistent with the following three observations. First, the government's "neutrality" in respect to religion is one, but only one, of the considerations relevant to deciding whether a public school's policy violates the Establishment Clause. As this Court previously has indicated, a child's perception that the school has endorsed a particular religion or religion in general may also

---

[3] We have drawn a different distinction—between religious speech generally and speech about religion—but only with regard to restrictions the State must place on its own speech, where pervasive state monitoring is unproblematic. See *School Dist. of Abington Township v. Schempp*, 374 U.S. 203, 225 (1963) (State schools in their official capacity may not teach religion but may teach about religion). Whatever the rule there, licensing and monitoring private religious speech is an entirely different matter, even in a limited public forum where the state has some authority to draw subject-matter distinctions.

prove critically important. . . . Today's opinion does not purport to change that legal principle.

Second, the critical Establishment Clause question here may well prove to be whether a child, participating in the Good News Club's activities, could reasonably perceive the school's permission for the club to use its facilities as an endorsement of religion. . . . The time of day, the age of the children, the nature of the meetings, and other specific circumstances are relevant in helping to determine whether, in fact, the Club "so dominates" the "forum" that, in the children's minds, "a formal policy of equal access is transformed into a demonstration of approval."

Third, the Court cannot fully answer the Establishment Clause question this case raises, given its procedural posture. The specific legal action that brought this case to the Court of Appeals was the District Court's decision to grant Milford Central School's motion for summary judgment. The Court of Appeals affirmed the grant of summary judgment. We now hold that the school was not entitled to summary judgment, either in respect to the Free Speech or the Establishment Clause issue. Our holding must mean that, *viewing the disputed facts* (including facts about the children's perceptions) *favorably to the Club* (the nonmoving party), the school has not shown an Establishment Clause violation.

To deny one party's motion for summary judgment, however, is not to grant summary judgment for the other side. There may be disputed "genuine issues" of "material fact," particularly about how a reasonable child participant would understand the school's role. Indeed, the Court itself points to facts not in evidence ("There is no evidence that young children are permitted to loiter outside classrooms after the schoolday has ended") ("There may be as many, if not more, upperclassmen than elementary school children who occupy the school after hours"), identifies facts in evidence which may, depending on other facts not in evidence, be of legal significance (discussing the type of room in which the meetings were held and noting that the Club's participants "are not all the same age as in the normal classroom setting"), and makes assumptions about other facts. ("Surely even young children are aware of events for which their parents must sign permission forms") ("Any bystander could conceivably be aware of the school's use policy and its exclusion of the Good News Club, and could suffer as much from viewpoint discrimination as elementary school children could suffer from perceived endorsement"). The Court's invocation of what is missing from the record and its assumptions about what is present in the record only confirm that both parties, if they so desire, should have a fair opportunity to fill the evidentiary gap in light of today's opinion.

⊞ JUSTICE STEVENS, dissenting.

The Milford Central School has invited the public to use its facilities for educational and recreational purposes, but not for "religious purposes." Speech for "religious purposes" may reasonably be understood to encompass three different categories. First, there is religious speech that is simply speech about a particular topic from a religious point of view. The film in *Lamb's Chapel* illustrates this category. Second, there is religious speech that amounts to worship, or its equivalent. Our decision in *Widmar* concerned such speech. Third, there is an intermediate category that is aimed principally at proselytizing or inculcating belief in a particular religious faith.

A public entity may not generally exclude even religious worship from an open public forum. Similarly, a public entity that creates a limited public forum for the discussion of certain specified topics may not exclude a speaker simply because she approaches those topics from a religious point of view. Thus, in *Lamb's Chapel* we held that a public school that permitted its facilities to be used for the discussion of family issues and child rearing could not deny access to speakers presenting a religious point of view on those issues.

But, while a public entity may not censor speech about an authorized topic based on the point of view expressed by the speaker, it has broad discretion to "preserve the property under its control for the use to which it is lawfully dedicated." *Greer v. Spock*, 424 U.S. 828, 836 (1976). Accordingly, "control over access to a nonpublic forum can be based on subject matter and speaker identity so long as the distinctions drawn are reasonable in light of the purpose served by the forum and are viewpoint neutral." *Cornelius v. NAACP Legal Defense & Ed. Fund, Inc.*, 473 U.S. 788, 806 (1985). The novel question that this case presents concerns the constitutionality of a public school's attempt to limit the scope of a public forum it has created. More specifically, the question is whether a school can, consistently with the First Amendment, create a limited public forum that admits the first type of religious speech without allowing the other two.

Distinguishing speech from a religious viewpoint, on the one hand, from religious proselytizing, on the other, is comparable to distinguishing meetings to discuss political issues from meetings whose principal purpose is to recruit new members to join a political organization. If a school decides to authorize after school discussions of current events in its classrooms, it may not exclude people from expressing their views simply because it dislikes their particular political opinions. But must it therefore allow organized political groups—for example, the Democratic Party, the Libertarian Party, or the Ku Klux Klan—to hold meetings, the principal purpose of which is not to discuss the current-events topic from their own unique point of view but rather to recruit others to join their respective groups? I think not. Such recruiting meetings may introduce divisiveness and tend to separate young children into cliques that undermine the school's educational mission.

School officials may reasonably believe that evangelical meetings designed to convert children to a particular religious faith pose the same risk. And, just as a school may allow meetings to discuss current events from a political perspective without also allowing organized political recruitment, so too can a school allow discussion of topics such as moral development from a religious (or nonreligious) perspective without thereby opening its forum to religious proselytizing or worship. Moreover, any doubt on a question such as this should be resolved in a way that minimizes "intrusion by the Federal Government into the operation of our public schools." . . .

The particular limitation of the forum at issue in this case is one that prohibits the use of the school's facilities for "religious purposes." It is clear that, by "religious purposes," the school district did not intend to exclude all speech from a religious point of view. Instead, it sought only to exclude religious speech whose principal goal is to "promote the gospel." In other words, the school sought to allow the first type of religious speech while excluding the second and third types. As long as this is done in an even handed manner, I see no constitutional violation in such an effort.[1] The line between the various categories of religious speech may be difficult to draw, but I think that the distinctions are valid, and that a school, particularly an elementary school, must be permitted to draw them.

This case is undoubtedly close. Nonetheless, regardless of whether the Good News Club's activities amount to "worship," it does seem clear, based on the facts in the record, that the school district correctly classified those activities as falling within the third category of religious speech and therefore beyond the scope of the school's limited public forum. In short, I am persuaded that the school district could (and did) permissibly exclude from its limited public forum proselytizing religious speech that does not rise to the level of actual worship. I would therefore affirm the judgment of the Court of Appeals.

Even if I agreed with Part II of the majority opinion, however, I would not reach out, as it does in Part IV, to decide a constitutional question that was not addressed by either the District Court or the Court of Appeals. Accordingly, I respectfully dissent.

JUSTICE SOUTER, with whom JUSTICE GINSBURG joins, dissenting.

The majority rules on two issues. First, it decides that the Court of Appeals failed to apply the rule in *Lamb's Chapel*, which held that the government may not discriminate on the basis of viewpoint in operating a limited public forum. The majority applies that rule and concludes that Milford violated *Lamb's Chapel* in denying Good News the use of the school. The majority then goes on to determine that it would not violate the Establishment Clause of the First Amendment for the Milford School District to allow the Good News Club to hold its intended gatherings of public school children in Milford's elementary school. The majority is mistaken on both points. The Court of Appeals unmistakably distinguished this case from *Lamb's Chapel*, though not by name, and accordingly affirmed the application of a policy, unchallenged in the District Court, that Milford's public schools may not be used for religious purposes. As for the applicability of the Establishment Clause to the Good News Club's intended use of Milford's school, the majority commits error even in reaching the issue, which was addressed neither by the Court of Appeals nor by the District Court. I respectfully dissent.

I . . .

The appeals court agreed with the District Court that the undisputed facts in this case differ from those in *Lamb's Chapel*, as night from day. A sampling of those facts shows why both courts were correct.

Good News's classes open and close with prayer. In a sample lesson considered by the District Court, children are instructed that "the Bible tells us how we can have our sins forgiven by receiving the Lord Jesus Christ. It tells us how to live to please Him. . . . If you have received the Lord Jesus as your Saviour from sin, you belong to God's special group—His family." The lesson plan instructs the teacher to "lead a child to Christ," and, when reading a Bible verse,

---

[1] The school district, for example, could not, consistently with its present policy, allow school facilities to be used by a group that affirmatively attempted to inculcate nonbelief in God or in the view that morality is wholly unrelated to belief in God. Nothing in the record, however, indicates that any such group was allowed to use school facilities.

to "emphasize that this verse is from the Bible, God's Word" and is "important—and true—because God said it." The lesson further exhorts the teacher to "be sure to give an opportunity for the 'unsaved' children in your class to respond to the Gospel" and cautions against "neglecting this responsibility."

While Good News's program utilizes songs and games, the heart of the meeting is the "challenge" and "invitation," which are repeated at various times throughout the lesson. During the challenge, "saved" children who "already believe in the Lord Jesus as their Savior" are challenged to "'stop and ask God for the strength and the "want" . . . to obey Him.'" They are instructed that "if you know Jesus as your Savior, you need to place God first in your life. And if you don't know Jesus as Savior and if you would like to, then we will—we will pray with you separately, individually. . . . And the challenge would be, those of you who know Jesus as Savior, you can rely on God's strength to obey Him."

During the invitation, the teacher "invites" the "unsaved" children "'to trust the Lord Jesus to be your Savior from sin,'" and "'receive [him] as your Savior from sin.'" The children are then instructed that

> if you believe what God's Word says about your sin and how Jesus died and rose again for you, you can have His forever life today. Please bow your heads and close your eyes. If you have never believed on the Lord Jesus as your Savior and would like to do that, please show me by raising your hand. If you raised your hand to show me you want to believe on the Lord Jesus, please meet me so I can show you from God's Word how you can receive His everlasting life.

It is beyond question that Good News intends to use the public school premises not for the mere discussion of a subject from a particular, Christian point of view, but for an evangelical service of worship calling children to commit themselves in an act of Christian conversion.[3] The majority avoids this reality only by resorting to the bland and general characterization of Good News's activity as "teaching of morals and character, from a religious standpoint." If the majority's statement ignores reality, as it surely does, then today's holding may be understood only in equally generic terms. Otherwise, indeed, this case would stand for the remarkable proposition that any public school opened for civic meetings must be opened for use as a church, synagogue, or mosque.

## II

I also respectfully dissent from the majority's refusal to remand on all other issues, insisting instead on acting as a court of first instance in reviewing Milford's claim that it would violate the Establishment Clause to grant Good

---

[3] The majority rejects Milford's contention that Good News's activities fall outside the purview of the limited forum because they constitute "religious worship" on the ground that the Court of Appeals made no such determination regarding the character of the club's program. This distinction is merely semantic, in light of the Court of Appeals's conclusion that "it is difficult to see how the Club's activities differ materially from the 'religious worship' described" in other case law 202 F.3d 510, and the record below.

JUSTICE STEVENS distinguishes between proselytizing and worship and distinguishes each from discussion reflecting a religious point of view. I agree with JUSTICE STEVENS that Good News's activities may be characterized as proselytizing and therefore as outside the purpose of Milford's limited forum. Like the Court of Appeals, I also believe Good News's meetings have elements of worship that put the club's activities further afield of Milford's limited forum policy, the legitimacy of which was unchallenged in the summary judgment proceeding.

News's application. Milford raised this claim to demonstrate a compelling interest for saying no to Good News, even on the erroneous assumption that *Lamb's Chapel's* public forum analysis would otherwise require Milford to say yes. Whereas the District Court and Court of Appeals resolved this case entirely on the ground that Milford's actions did not offend the First Amendment's Speech Clause, the majority now sees fit to rule on the application of the Establishment Clause, in derogation of this Court's proper role as a court of review. . . .

Of course, I am in no better position than the majority to perform an Establishment Clause analysis in the first instance. Like the majority, I lack the benefit that development in the District Court and Court of Appeals might provide, and like the majority I cannot say for sure how complete the record may be. I can, however, speak to the doubtful underpinnings of the majority's conclusion. . . .

What we know about this case looks very little like *Widmar* or *Lamb's Chapel*. The cohort addressed by Good News is not university students with relative maturity, or even high school pupils, but elementary school children as young as six.[4] The Establishment Clause cases have consistently recognized the particular impressionability of schoolchildren, see *Edwards v. Aguillard*, 482 U.S. 578, 583-584, and the special protection required for those in the elementary grades in the school forum. We have held the difference between college students and grade school pupils to be a "distinction [that] warrants a difference in constitutional results," *Edwards*, 584, n. 5.

Nor is Milford's limited forum anything like the sites for wide-ranging intellectual exchange that were home to the challenged activities in *Widmar* and *Lamb's Chapel*. In *Widmar*, the nature of the university campus and the sheer number of activities offered precluded the reasonable college observer from seeing government endorsement in any one of them, and so did the time and variety of community use in the *Lamb's Chapel* case. . . .

The timing and format of Good News's gatherings, on the other hand, may well affirmatively suggest the *imprimatur* of officialdom in the minds of the young children. The club is open solely to elementary students (not the entire community, as in *Lamb's Chapel*), only four outside groups have been identified as meeting in the school, and Good News is, seemingly, the only one whose instruction follows immediately on the conclusion of the official school day. Although school is out at 2:56 p.m., Good News apparently requested use of the school beginning at 2:30 on Tuesdays "during the school year," so that instruction could begin promptly at 3:00, at which time children who are

---

[4] It is certainly correct that parents are required to give permission for their children to attend Good News's classes (as parents are often required to do for a host of official school extracurricular activities), and correct that those parents would likely not be confused as to the sponsorship of Good News's classes. But the proper focus of concern in assessing effects includes the elementary school pupils who are invited to meetings, who see peers heading into classrooms for religious instruction as other classes end, and who are addressed by the "challenge" and "invitation."

The fact that there may be no evidence in the record that individual students were confused during the time the Good News Club met on school premises pursuant to the District Court's preliminary injunction is immaterial. As JUSTICE O'CONNOR explained in *Capitol Square Review Bd. v. Pinette*, the endorsement test does not focus "on the actual perception of individual observers, who naturally have differing degrees of knowledge," but on "the perspective of a hypothetical observer."

compelled by law to attend school surely remain in the building. Good News's religious meeting follows regular school activities so closely that the Good News instructor must wait to begin until "the room is clear," and "people are out of the room" before starting proceedings in the classroom located next to the regular third- and fourth-grade rooms. In fact, the temporal and physical continuity of Good News's meetings with the regular school routine seems to be the whole point of using the school. When meetings were held in a community church, 8 or 10 children attended; after the school became the site, the number went up three-fold.

Even on the summary judgment record, then, a record lacking whatever supplementation the trial process might have led to, and devoid of such insight as the trial and appellate judges might have contributed in addressing the Establishment Clause, we can say this: there is a good case that Good News's exercises blur the line between public classroom instruction and private religious indoctrination, leaving a reasonable elementary school pupil unable to appreciate that the former instruction is the business of the school while the latter evangelism is not. Thus, the facts we know (or think we know) point away from the majority's conclusion, and while the consolation may be that nothing really gets resolved when the judicial process is so truncated, that is not much to recommend today's result.

---

### NOTES AND QUESTIONS

1. Did the school district exclude all speech from a religious point of view from its limited public forum? If not, where did it draw the line?

2. According to the Court majority, what kind of forum is the school property in this case and what are the rules that apply regarding the government's restrictions on the use of such a forum? How does the Court define "viewpoint discrimination"? Would a state's interest in avoiding an Establishment Clause violation justify viewpoint discrimination?

3. The Court has long expressed its concern with protecting impressionable school children from coercive religious practices in the public schools. Is the impressionability of school children a relevant consideration here? Does your answer turn on whether *Good News Club* is characterized primarily as a Free Speech case or an Establishment Clause case? What is the emphasis of the majority opinion? Does this emphasis help explain why the expressive rights of outsiders to the school prevailed over the potential conscience rights of school children? Or, would it be fairer to say that the Court simply did not view the case as presenting any legitimate concerns regarding the students' rights of conscience?

4. Note that the majority addresses *McCollum v. Board of Education* in a footnote. The majority adopts a formal line between religious instruction during the school day and religious instruction that may take place immediately *following* the school day. Is this distinction convincing? Why or why not?

5. The majority argues that "we cannot say the danger that children would misperceive [governmental] endorsement of religion is any greater than the danger that they would perceive [governmental] hostility toward the religious viewpoint if the [Good News] Club were excluded from the public forum."

Does Justice Thomas mean that the absence of religious expression from a public forum, such as the absence of a Good News Club from a public school facility in the afternoons, would be perceived as hostility toward religion if Boy and Girl Scouts meet at the school? Or is Justice Thomas merely concerned that school children will be aware that a religious group had asked to use the space but was excluded by the school?

6. In his concurring opinion, Justice Scalia argues that the Court has already "rejected the attempt to distinguish worship from other religious speech. . . ." To what case is he referring? How does Justice Stevens approach this issue in his dissenting opinion? Who has the better of the argument on this point?

7. Why do Justices Souter and Breyer believe that the case should have been remanded in part? Are their arguments persuasive?

8. According to Justice Souter's dissent, requiring a public school that opened for civic meetings to also open for use "as a church, synagogue or mosque" is a "remarkable" proposition not intended by the majority opinion. Would such a requirement be a remarkably bad idea, constitutionally speaking, and is Souter correct that such a result is not suggested by the Court's ruling? How does Justice Souter distinguish the *Widmar* decision from this case? For further reading on this topic, compare *Bronx Household of Faith v. Board of Education*, 400 F. Supp. 2d 581 (2005) (striking down a school district policy that opened school property to a range of community uses but prohibited rental of the property for the purpose of religious worship) with *Faith Center Church Evangelical Ministries v. Glover*, 462 F.3d 1194 (9th Cir. 2006) (upholding county's policy that allowed community groups to have wide access to a public library meeting room but prohibited the use of the room for worship services).

## OTHER RELIGIOUS EXPRESSION/ACCESS ISSUES

Do the same constitutional values that inform the equal access principle apply when the government access sought is not merely spatial but is also financial? If so, are greater establishment concerns present when a claimant asks not simply for public space to "preach the Word," but also for government financial support for his religious expression? In essence, does or should the existence of a "financial" public forum change the Court's approach to the application of equal access/treatment issues?

In 1995, the Court confronted a case that arose at the school Thomas Jefferson founded, the University of Virginia, and involved religious expression and notions of access to a speech forum. The twist on this case is that it also involved funds held by this state university and asked whether a religious student group was entitled to a share of those funds, along with other student groups.

The University had established a system whereby it used student activity funds to pay an outside contractor to print a variety of student publications. When a religious student group sought to have the University of Virginia pay for its evangelical magazine, the University balked, citing school regulations that prohibited the use of such funds for religious activities. The student group sued, claiming, among other things, unlawful governmental discrimination based on its viewpoint.

The students prevailed in the Supreme Court. As the Court's majority opinion indicates, its decision hinged in large part on its desire not to suppress "free speech and creative inquiry in one of the vital centers for the Nation's intellectual life, its college and university campuses." As you read the opinions, see if you can identify some of the cross-cutting constitutional principles presented in this case.

## ROSENBERGER v. RECTOR AND VISITORS OF THE UNIVER-SITY OF VIRGINIA
## 515 U.S. 819 (1995)

JUSTICE KENNEDY delivered the opinion of the Court.

The University of Virginia, an instrumentality of the Commonwealth for which it is named and thus bound by the First and Fourteenth Amendments, authorizes the payment of outside contractors for the printing costs of a variety of student publications. It withheld any authorization for payments on behalf of petitioners for the sole reason that their student paper "primarily promotes or manifests a particular belief in or about a deity or an ultimate reality." That the paper did promote or manifest views within the defined exclusion seems plain enough. The challenge is to the University's regulation and its denial of authorization, the case raising issues under the Speech and Establishment Clauses of the First Amendment.

I

Founded by Thomas Jefferson in 1819, and ranked by him, together with the authorship of the Declaration of Independence and of the Virginia Act for Religious Freedom as one of his proudest achievements, the University [of Virginia] is among the Nation's oldest and most respected seats of higher learning. It has more than 11,000 undergraduate students, and 6,000 graduate and professional students. An understanding of the case requires a somewhat detailed description of the program the University created to support extracurricular student activities on its campus.

Before a student group is eligible to submit bills from its outside contractors for payment by the fund described below, it must become a "Contracted Independent Organization" (CIO). CIO status is available to any group the majority of whose members are students, whose managing officers are full-time students, and that complies with certain procedural requirements. A CIO must file its constitution with the University; must pledge not to discriminate in its membership; and must include in dealings with third parties and in all written materials a disclaimer, stating that the CIO is independent of the University and that the University is not responsible for the CIO. CIOs enjoy access to University facilities, including meeting rooms and computer terminals. A standard agreement signed between each CIO and the University provides that the benefits and opportunities afforded to CIOs "should not be misinterpreted as meaning that those organizations are part of or controlled by the University, that the University is responsible for the organizations' contracts or other acts or omissions, or that the University approves of the organizations' goals or activities."

All CIOs may exist and operate at the University, but some are also entitled to apply for funds from the Student Activities Fund (SAF). Established and governed by University Guidelines, the purpose of the SAF is to support a broad range of extracurricular student activities that "are related to the educational purpose of the University." The SAF is based on the University's "recognition that the availability of a wide range of opportunities" for its students "tends to enhance the University environment." The Guidelines require that it be administered "in a manner consistent with the educational purpose of the University as well as with state and federal law." The SAF receives its money from a mandatory fee of $14 per semester assessed to each full-time student. The Student Council, elected by the students, has the initial authority to disburse the funds, but its actions are subject to review by a faculty body chaired by a designee of the Vice President for Student Affairs.

Some, but not all, CIOs may submit disbursement requests to the SAF. The Guidelines recognize 11 categories of student groups that may seek payment to third-party contractors because they "are related to the educational purpose of the University of Virginia." One of these is "student news, information, opinion, entertainment, or academic communications media groups." The Guidelines also specify, however, that the costs of certain activities of CIOs that are otherwise eligible for funding will not be reimbursed by the SAF. The student activities that are excluded from SAF support are religious activities, philanthropic contributions and activities, political activities, activities that would jeopardize the University's tax-exempt status, those which involve payment of honoraria or similar fees, or social entertainment or related expenses. The prohibition on "political activities" is defined so that it is limited to electioneering and lobbying. The Guidelines provide that "these restrictions on funding political activities are not intended to preclude funding of any otherwise eligible student organization which . . . espouses particular positions or ideological viewpoints, including those that may be unpopular or are not generally accepted." A "religious activity," by contrast, is defined as any activity that "primarily promotes or manifests a particular belief in or about a deity or an ultimate reality."

The Guidelines prescribe these criteria for determining the amounts of third-party disbursements that will be allowed on behalf of each eligible student organization: the size of the group, its financial self-sufficiency, and the University-wide benefit of its activities. If an organization seeks SAF support, it must submit its bills to the Student Council, which pays the organization's creditors upon determining that the expenses are appropriate. No direct payments are made to the student groups. During the 1990–1991 academic year, 343 student groups qualified as CIOs. One hundred thirty-five of them applied for support from the SAF, and 118 received funding. Fifteen of the groups were funded as "student news, information, opinion, entertainment, or academic communications media groups."

Petitioners' organization, Wide Awake Productions (WAP), qualified as a CIO. Formed by petitioner Ronald Rosenberger and other undergraduates in 1990, WAP was established "to publish a magazine of philosophical and religious expression," "to facilitate discussion which fosters an atmosphere of sensitivity to and tolerance of Christian viewpoints," and "to provide a unifying focus for Christians of multicultural backgrounds." WAP publishes Wide Awake: A Christian Perspective at the University of Virginia. The paper's Christian viewpoint was evident from the first issue, in which its editors wrote that the journal "offers a Christian perspective on both personal and community issues, especially those relevant to college students at the University of Virginia." The editors committed the paper to a two-fold mission: "to challenge Christians to live, in word and deed, according to the faith they proclaim and to encourage students to consider what a personal relationship with Jesus Christ means." The first issue had articles about racism, crisis pregnancy, stress, prayer, C. S. Lewis' ideas about evil and free will, and reviews of religious music. In the next two issues, Wide Awake featured stories about homosexuality, Christian missionary work, and eating disorders, as well as music reviews and interviews with University professors. Each page of Wide Awake, and the end of each article or review, is marked by a cross. The advertisements carried in Wide Awake also reveal the Christian perspective of the journal. For the most part, the advertisers are churches, centers for Christian study, or Christian bookstores. By June 1992, WAP had distributed about 5,000 copies of Wide Awake to University students, free of charge. . . .

A few months after being given CIO status, WAP requested the SAF to pay its printer $5,862 for the costs of printing its newspaper. The Appropriations Committee of the Student Council denied WAP's request on the ground that Wide Awake was a "religious activity" within the meaning of the Guidelines, i.e., that the newspaper "promoted or manifested a particular belief in or about a deity or an ultimate reality." . . .

WAP, Wide Awake, and three of its editors and members [subsequently] filed suit in the United States District Court for the Western District of Virginia. . . . They alleged that refusal to authorize payment of the printing costs of the publication, solely on the basis of its religious editorial viewpoint, violated their rights to freedom of speech and press, to the free exercise of religion, and to equal protection of the law. . . .

## II

It is axiomatic that the government may not regulate speech based on its substantive content or the message it conveys. Other principles follow from this precept. In the realm of private speech or expression, government regulation may not favor one speaker over another. When the government targets not subject matter, but particular views taken by speakers on a subject, the violation of the First Amendment is all the more blatant. Viewpoint discrimination is thus an egregious form of content discrimination. The government must abstain from regulating speech when the specific motivating ideology or the opinion or perspective of the speaker is the rationale for the restriction.

These principles provide the framework forbidding the State from exercising viewpoint discrimination, even when the limited public forum is one of its own creation. . . . [I]n determining whether the State is acting to preserve the limits of the forum it has created so that the exclusion of a class of speech is legitimate, we have observed a distinction between, on the one hand, content discrimination, which may be permissible if it preserves the purposes of that limited forum, and, on the other hand, viewpoint discrimination, which is presumed impermissible when directed against speech otherwise within the forum's limitations.

The SAF is a forum more in a metaphysical than in a spatial or geographic sense, but the same principles are applicable. . . .

The University does acknowledge (as it must in light of our precedents) that "ideologically driven attempts to suppress a particular point of view are presumptively unconstitutional in funding, as in other contexts," but insists that this case does not present that issue because the Guidelines draw lines based on content, not viewpoint. As we have noted, discrimination against one set of views or ideas is but a subset or particular instance of the more general phenomenon of content discrimination. And, it must be acknowledged, the distinction is not a precise one. It is, in a sense, something of an understatement to speak of religious thought and discussion as just a viewpoint, as distinct from a comprehensive body of thought. The nature of our origins and destiny and their dependence upon the existence of a divine being have been subjects of philosophic inquiry throughout human history. We conclude, nonetheless, that here, as in *Lamb's Chapel*, viewpoint discrimination is the proper way to interpret the University's objections to Wide Awake. By the very terms of the SAF prohibition, the University does not exclude religion as a subject matter but selects for disfavored treatment those student journalistic efforts with religious editorial viewpoints. Religion may be a vast area of inquiry, but it also provides, as it did here, a specific premise, a perspective, a standpoint from which a variety of subjects may be discussed and considered. The prohibited perspective, not the general subject matter, resulted in the refusal to make third-party payments, for the subjects discussed were otherwise within the approved category of publications.

The dissent's assertion that no viewpoint discrimination occurs because the Guidelines discriminate against an entire class of viewpoints reflects an insupportable assumption that all debate is bipolar and that antireligious speech is the only response to religious speech. Our understanding of the complex and multifaceted nature of public discourse has not embraced such a contrived description of the marketplace of ideas. If the topic of debate is, for example, racism, then exclusion of several views on that problem is just as offensive to the First Amendment as exclusion of only one. It is as objectionable to exclude both a theistic and an atheistic perspective on the debate as it is to exclude one, the other, or yet another political, economic, or social viewpoint. The dissent's declaration that debate is not skewed so long as multiple voices are silenced is simply wrong; the debate is skewed in multiple ways.

The University's denial of WAP's request for third-party payments in the present case is based upon viewpoint discrimination not unlike the discrimination the school district relied upon in *Lamb's Chapel* and that we found invalid. The church group in *Lamb's Chapel* would have been qualified as a social or civic organization, save for its religious purposes. Furthermore, just as the school district in *Lamb's Chapel* pointed to nothing but the religious views of the group as the rationale for excluding its message, so in this case the University justifies its denial of SAF participation to WAP on the ground that the contents of Wide Awake reveal an avowed religious perspective. . . .

The University tries to escape the consequences of our holding in *Lamb's Chapel* by urging that this case involves the provision of funds rather than access to facilities. The University begins with the unremarkable proposition that the State must have substantial discretion in determining how to allocate scarce resources to accomplish its educational mission. Citing our decisions in *Rust v. Sullivan*, 500 U.S. 173 (1991), *Regan v. Taxation with Representation of Wash.*, 461 U.S. 540 (1983), and *Widmar v. Vincent*, 454 U.S. 263 (1981), the University argues that content-based funding decisions are both inevitable and lawful. Were the reasoning of *Lamb's Chapel* to apply to funding decisions as well as to those involving access to facilities, it is urged, its holding "would become a judicial juggernaut, constitutionalizing the ubiquitous content-based decisions that schools, colleges, and other government entities routinely make in the allocation of public funds."

To this end the University relies on our assurance in *Widmar v. Vincent*. There, in the course of striking down a public university's exclusion of religious groups from use of school facilities made available to all other student groups, we stated: "Nor do we question the right of the University to make academic judgments as to how best to allocate scarce resources." 454 U.S., 276. The quoted language in *Widmar* was but a proper recognition of the principle that when the State is the speaker, it may make content-based choices. When the University determines the content of the education it provides, it is the University speaking, and we have permitted the government to regulate the content of what is or is not expressed when it is the speaker or when it enlists private entities to convey its own message. In the same vein, in *Rust v. Sullivan*, we upheld the government's prohibition on abortion-related advice applicable to recipients of federal funds for family planning counseling. There, the government did not create a program to encourage private speech but instead used private speakers to transmit specific information pertaining to its own program. We recognized that when the government appropriates public funds to promote a particular policy of its own it is entitled to say what it wishes. When the government disburses public funds to private entities to convey a governmental message, it may take legitimate and appropriate steps to ensure that its message is neither garbled nor distorted by the grantee.

It does not follow, however, and we did not suggest in *Widmar*, that viewpoint-based restrictions are proper when the University does not itself speak or subsidize transmittal of a message it favors but instead expends funds to encourage a diversity of views from private speakers. A holding that the University may not discriminate based on the viewpoint of private persons whose speech it facilitates does not restrict the University's own speech, which is controlled by different principles. . . .

The distinction between the University's own favored message and the private speech of students is evident in the case before us. The University itself has taken steps to ensure the distinction in the agreement each CIO must sign. The University declares that the student groups eligible for SAF support are not the University's agents, are not subject to its control, and are not its responsibility. Having offered to pay the third-party contractors on behalf of private speakers who convey their own messages, the University may not silence the expression of selected viewpoints.

The University urges that, from a constitutional standpoint, funding of speech differs from provision of access to facilities because money is scarce and physical facilities are not. Beyond the fact that in any given case this proposition might not be true as an empirical matter, the underlying premise that the University could discriminate based on viewpoint if demand for space exceeded its availability is wrong as well. The government cannot justify viewpoint discrimination among private speakers on the economic fact of scarcity. Had the meeting rooms in *Lamb's Chapel* been scarce, had the demand been greater than the supply, our decision would have been no different. It would have been incumbent on the State, of course, to ration or allocate the scarce resources on some acceptable neutral principle; but nothing in our decision indicated that scarcity would give the State the right to exercise viewpoint discrimination that is otherwise impermissible.

Vital First Amendment speech principles are at stake here. The first danger to liberty lies in granting the State the power to examine publications to determine whether or not they are based on some ultimate idea and, if so, for the State to classify them. The second, and corollary, danger is to speech from the chilling of individual thought and expression. That danger is especially real in the University setting, where the State acts against a background and tradition of thought and experiment that is at the center of our intellectual and philosophic tradition. . . . For the University, by regulation, to cast disapproval on particular viewpoints of its students risks the suppression of free speech and creative inquiry in one of the vital centers for the Nation's intellectual life, its college and university campuses.

The Guideline invoked by the University to deny third-party contractor payments on behalf of WAP effects a sweeping restriction on student thought and student inquiry in the context of University sponsored publications. The prohibition on funding on behalf of publications that "primarily promote or manifest a particular belief in or about a deity or an ultimate reality," in its ordinary and common-sense meaning, has a vast potential reach. . . . Were the prohibition applied with much vigor at all, it would bar funding of essays by hypothetical student contributors named Plato, Spinoza, and Descartes. And if the regulation covers, as the University says it does, those student journalistic efforts that primarily manifest or promote a belief that there is no deity and no ultimate reality, then undergraduates named Karl Marx, Bertrand Russell, and Jean-Paul Sartre would likewise have some of their major essays excluded from student publications. If any manifestation of beliefs in first principles disqualifies the writing, as seems to be the case, it is indeed difficult to name renowned thinkers whose writings would be accepted, save perhaps for articles disclaiming all connection to their ultimate philosophy. Plato could contrive perhaps to submit an acceptable essay on making pasta or peanut butter cookies, provided he did not point out their (necessary) imperfections.

Based on the principles we have discussed, we hold that the regulation invoked to deny SAF support, both in its terms and in its application to these petitioners, is a denial of their right of free speech guaranteed by the First Amendment. It remains to be considered whether the violation following from the University's action is excused by the necessity of complying with the Constitution's prohibition against state establishment of religion. We turn to that question.

### III

Before its brief on the merits in this Court, the University had argued at all stages of the litigation that inclusion of WAP's contractors in SAF funding authorization would violate the Establishment Clause. Indeed, that is the ground on which the University prevailed in the Court of Appeals. We granted certiorari on this question: "Whether the Establishment Clause compels a state university to exclude an otherwise eligible student publication from participation in the student activities fund, solely on the basis of its religious viewpoint, where such exclusion would violate the Speech and Press Clauses if the viewpoint of the publication were nonreligious." Pet. for Cert. i. The University now seems to have abandoned this position, contending that "the fundamental objection to petitioners' argument is not that it implicates the Establishment Clause but that it would defeat the ability of public education at all levels to control the use of public funds." That the University itself no longer presses the Establishment Clause claim is some indication that it lacks force; but as the Court of Appeals rested its judgment on the point and our dissenting colleagues would find it determinative, it must be addressed.

The Court of Appeals ruled that withholding SAF support from Wide Awake contravened the Speech Clause of the First Amendment, but proceeded to hold that the University's action was justified by the necessity of avoiding a violation of the Establishment Clause, an interest it found compelling. Recognizing that this Court has regularly "sanctioned awards of direct non-monetary benefits to religious groups where government has created open fora to which all similarly situated organizations are invited," the Fourth Circuit asserted that direct monetary subsidization of religious organizations and projects is "a beast of an entirely different color." The court declared that the Establishment Clause would not permit the use of public funds to support "'a specifically religious activity in an otherwise substantially secular setting.'" 18 F.3d, 285 (quoting *Hunt v. McNair,* 413 U.S. 734, 743 [1973] [emphasis deleted]). It reasoned that because Wide Awake is "a journal pervasively devoted to the discussion and advancement of an avowedly Christian theological and personal philosophy," the University's provision of SAF funds for its publication would "send an unmistakably clear signal that the University of Virginia supports Christian values and wishes to promote the wide promulgation of such values."

If there is to be assurance that the Establishment Clause retains its force in guarding against those governmental actions it was intended to prohibit, we must in each case inquire first into the purpose and object of the governmental action in question and then into the practical details of the program's operation. Before turning to these matters, however, we can set forth certain general principles that must bear upon our determination.

A central lesson of our decisions is that a significant factor in upholding governmental programs in the face of Establishment Clause attack is their neutrality towards religion. We have decided a series of cases addressing the receipt of government benefits where religion or religious views are implicated in some degree. The first case in our modern Establishment Clause jurisprudence was *Everson v. Board of Ed. of Ewing,* 330 U.S. 1 (1947). There we cautioned that in enforcing the prohibition against laws respecting establishment of religion, we must "be sure that we do not inadvertently prohibit [the government] from extending its general state law benefits to all its citizens without regard to their religious belief." *Id.,* 16. We have held that the guarantee of neutrality is respected, not offended, when the government, following neutral criteria and evenhanded policies, extends benefits to recipients whose ideologies and viewpoints, including religious ones, are broad and diverse. More than once have we rejected the position that the Establishment Clause even justifies, much less requires, a refusal to extend free speech rights to religious speakers who participate in broad-reaching government programs neutral in design.

The governmental program here is neutral toward religion. There is no suggestion that the University created it to advance religion or adopted some ingenious device with the purpose of aiding a religious cause. The object of the SAF is to open a forum for speech and to support various student enterprises, including the publication of newspapers, in recognition of the diversity and creativity of student life. The University's SAF Guidelines have a separate classification for, and do not make third-party payments on behalf of, "religious organizations," which are those "whose purpose is to practice a devotion to an acknowledged ultimate reality or deity." The category of support here is for "student news, information, opinion, entertainment, or academic communications media groups," of which Wide Awake was 1 of 15 in the 1990 school year. WAP did not seek a subsidy because of its Christian editorial viewpoint; it sought funding as a student journal, which it was.

The neutrality of the program distinguishes the student fees from a tax levied for the direct support of a church or group of churches. A tax of that sort, of course, would run contrary to Establishment Clause concerns dating from the earliest days of the Republic. The apprehensions of our predecessors involved the levying of taxes upon the public for the sole and exclusive purpose of establishing and supporting specific sects. The exaction here, by contrast, is a student activity fee designed to reflect the reality that student life in its many dimensions includes the necessity of wide-ranging speech and inquiry and that student expression is an integral part of the University's educational mission. The fee is mandatory, and we do not have before us the question whether an objecting student has the First Amendment right to demand a pro rata return to the extent the fee is expended for speech to which he or she does not subscribe. We must treat it, then, as an exaction upon the students. But the $14 paid each semester by the students is not a general tax designed to raise revenue for the University. The SAF cannot be used for unlimited purposes, much less the illegitimate purpose of supporting one religion. Much like the arrangement in *Widmar*, the money goes to a special fund from which any group of students with CIO status can draw for purposes consistent with the University's educational mission; and to the extent the student is interested in speech, withdrawal is permitted to cover the whole spectrum of speech, whether it manifests a religious view, an antireligious view, or neither. Our decision, then, cannot be read as addressing an expenditure from a general tax fund. Here, the disbursements from the fund go to private contractors for the cost of printing that which is protected under the Speech Clause of the First Amendment. This is a far cry from a general public assessment designed and effected to provide financial support for a church.

Government neutrality is apparent in the State's overall scheme in a further meaningful respect. The program respects the critical difference "between *government* speech endorsing religion, which the Establishment Clause forbids, and *private* speech endorsing religion, which the Free Speech and Free Exercise Clauses protect." In this case, "the government has not fostered or encouraged" any mistaken impression that the student newspapers speak for the University. The University has taken pains to disassociate itself from the private speech involved in this case. The Court of Appeals' apparent concern that Wide Awake's religious orientation would be attributed to the University is not a plausible fear, and there is no real likelihood that the speech in question is being either endorsed or coerced by the State.

The Court of Appeals (and the dissent) are correct to extract from our decisions the principle that we have recognized special Establishment Clause dangers where the government makes direct money payments to sectarian institutions. The error is not in identifying the principle, but in believing that it controls this case. Even assuming that WAP is no different from a church and that its speech is the same as the religious exercises conducted in *Widmar* (two points much in doubt), the Court of Appeals decided a case that was, in essence, not before it, and the dissent would have us do the same. We do not confront a case where, even under a neutral program that includes nonsectarian recipients, the government is making direct money payments to an institution or group that is engaged in religious activity. Neither the Court of Appeals nor the dissent, we believe, takes sufficient cognizance of the undisputed fact that no public funds flow directly to WAP's coffers.

It does not violate the Establishment Clause for a public university to grant access to its facilities on a religion-neutral basis to a wide spectrum of student groups, including groups that use meeting rooms for sectarian activities, accompanied by some devotional exercises. This is so even where the upkeep, maintenance, and repair of the facilities attributed to those uses is paid from a student activities fund to which students are required to contribute. The government usually acts by spending money. Even the provision of a meeting room, as in *Mergens* and *Widmar*, involved governmental expenditure, if only in the form of electricity and heating or cooling costs. The error made by the Court of Appeals, as well as by the dissent, lies in focusing on the money that is undoubtedly expended by the government, rather than on the nature of the benefit received by the recipient. If the expenditure of governmental funds is prohibited whenever those funds pay for a service that is, pursuant to a religion-neutral program, used by a group for sectarian purposes, then *Widmar*, *Mergens*, and *Lamb's Chapel* would have to be overruled. Given our holdings in these cases, it follows that a public university may maintain its own computer facility and give student groups access to that facility, including the use of the printers, on a religion neutral, say first-come-first-served, basis. If a religious student organization obtained access on that religion-neutral basis and used a computer to compose or a printer or copy machine to print speech with a religious content or viewpoint, the State's action in providing the group with access would no more violate the Establishment Clause than would giving those groups access to an assembly hall. There is no difference in logic or principle, and no difference of constitutional significance, between a school using its funds to operate a facility to which students have access, and a school paying a third-party contractor to operate the facility on its behalf. The latter occurs here. The University provides printing services to a broad spectrum of student newspapers qualified as CIOs by reason of their officers and membership. Any benefit to religion is incidental to the government's provision of secular services for secular purposes on a religion-neutral basis. Printing is a routine, secular, and recurring attribute of student life.

By paying outside printers, the University in fact attains a further degree of separation from the student publication, for it avoids the duties of supervision, escapes the costs of upkeep, repair, and replacement attributable to student use, and has a clear record of costs. As a result, and as in *Widmar*, the University can charge the SAF, and not the taxpayers as a whole, for the discrete activity in question. It would be formalistic for us to say that the University must forfeit these advantages and provide the services itself in order to comply with the Establishment Clause. It is, of course, true that if the State pays a church's bills it is subsidizing it, and we must guard against this abuse. That is not a danger here, based on the considerations we have advanced and for the additional reason that the student publication is not a religious institution, at least in the usual sense of that term as used in our case law, and it is not a religious organization as used in the University's own regulations. It is instead a publication involved in a pure forum for the expression of ideas, ideas that would be both incomplete and chilled were the Constitution to be interpreted to require that state officials and courts scan the publication to ferret out views that principally manifest a belief in a divine being.

Were the dissent's view to become law, it would require the University, in order to avoid a constitutional violation, to scrutinize the content of student speech, lest the expression in question—speech otherwise protected by the Constitution—contain too great a religious content. The dissent, in fact, anticipates such censorship as "crucial" in distinguishing between "works characterized by the evangelism of Wide Awake and writing that merely happens to express views that a given religion might approve." That eventuality raises the specter of governmental censorship, to ensure that all student writings and publications meet some baseline standard of secular orthodoxy. To impose that standard on student speech at a university is to imperil the very sources of free speech and expression. As we recognized in *Widmar*, official censorship would be far more inconsistent with the Establishment Clause's dictates than would governmental provision of secular printing services on a religion-blind basis. . . .

To obey the Establishment Clause, it was not necessary for the University to deny eligibility to student publications because of their viewpoint. The neutrality commanded of the State by the separate Clauses of the First Amendment was compromised by the University's course of action. The viewpoint discrimination inherent in the University's regulation required public officials to scan and interpret student publications to discern their underlying philosophic assumptions respecting religious theory and belief. That course of action was a denial of the right of free speech and would risk fostering a pervasive bias or hostility to religion, which could undermine the very neutrality the Establishment Clause requires. There is no Establishment Clause violation in the University's honoring its duties under the Free Speech Clause.

The judgment of the Court of Appeals must be, and is, reversed.

*It is so ordered.*

JUSTICE O'CONNOR, concurring.

"We have time and again held that the government generally may not treat people differently based on the God or gods they worship, or do not worship." *Board of Ed. of Kiryas Joel Village School Dist. v. Grumet*, 512 U.S. 687, 714 (1994) (O'CONNOR, J., concurring in part and concurring in judgment). This insistence on government neutrality toward religion explains why we have held that schools may not discriminate against religious groups by denying them equal access to facilities that the schools make available to all. Withholding access would leave an impermissible perception that religious activities are disfavored: "The message is one of neutrality rather than endorsement; if a State refused to let religious groups use facilities open to others, then it would demonstrate not neutrality but hostility toward religion." *Board of Ed. of Westside Community Schools v. Mergens*, 496 U.S. 226, 248 (1990) (plurality opinion). "The Religion Clauses prohibit the government from favoring religion, but they provide no warrant for discriminating *against* religion." *Kiryas Joel*, 717 (O'CONNOR, J.). Neutrality, in both form and effect, is one hallmark of the Establishment Clause.

As JUSTICE SOUTER demonstrates, however (dissenting opinion), there exists another axiom in the history and precedent of the Establishment Clause. "Public funds may not be used to endorse the religious message." *Bowen v. Kendrick*, 487 U.S. 589, 642 (1988) (BLACKMUN, J., dissenting). Our cases have permitted some government funding of secular functions performed by sectarian organizations. See, e.g., *id.*, 617 (funding for sex education); *Roemer*

v. *Board of Public Works of Md.*, 426 U.S. 736, 741 (1976) (cash grant to colleges not to be used for "sectarian purposes"); *Bradfield v. Roberts*, 175 U.S. 291, 299-300 (1899) (funding of health care for indigent patients). These decisions, however, provide no precedent for the use of public funds to finance religious activities.

This case lies at the intersection of the principle of government neutrality and the prohibition on state funding of religious activities. It is clear that the University has established a generally applicable program to encourage the free exchange of ideas by its students, an expressive marketplace that includes some 15 student publications with predictably divergent viewpoints. It is equally clear that petitioners' viewpoint is religious and that publication of Wide Awake is a religious activity, under both the University's regulation and a fair reading of our precedents. Not to finance Wide Awake, according to petitioners, violates the principle of neutrality by sending a message of hostility toward religion. To finance Wide Awake, argues the University, violates the prohibition on direct state funding of religious activities.

When two bedrock principles so conflict, understandably neither can provide the definitive answer. Reliance on categorical platitudes is unavailing. Resolution instead depends on the hard task of judging—sifting through the details and determining whether the challenged program offends the Establishment Clause. Such judgment requires courts to draw lines, sometimes quite fine, based on the particular facts of each case. . . .

In *Witters v. Washington Dept. of Servs. for Blind,* 474 U.S. 481 (1986), for example, we unanimously held that the State may, through a generally applicable financial aid program, pay a blind student's tuition at a sectarian theological institution. The Court so held, however, only after emphasizing that "vocational assistance provided under the Washington program is paid directly to the student, who transmits it to the educational institution of his or her choice." *Id.*, 487. The benefit to religion under the program, therefore, is akin to a public servant contributing her government paycheck to the church. We thus resolved the conflict between the neutrality principle and the funding prohibition, not by permitting one to trump the other, but by relying on the elements of choice peculiar to the facts of that case: "The aid to religion at issue here is the result of petitioner's private choice. No reasonable observer is likely to draw from the facts before us an inference that the State itself is endorsing a religious practice or belief." *Id.*, 493 (O'CONNOR, J., concurring in part and concurring in judgment). . . .

The nature of [this] dispute does not admit of categorical answers, nor should any be inferred from the Court's decision today. Instead, certain considerations specific to the program at issue lead me to conclude that by providing the same assistance to Wide Awake that it does to other publications, the University would not be endorsing the magazine's religious perspective.

First, the student organizations, at the University's insistence, remain strictly independent of the University. . . . [T]he agreement requires that student organizations include in every letter, contract, publication, or other written materials the following disclaimer: "Although this organization has members who are University of Virginia students (faculty) (employees), the organization is independent of the corporation which is the University and which is not responsible for the organization's contracts, acts or omissions." Any reader of Wide Awake would be on notice of the publication's independence from the University.

Second, financial assistance is distributed in a manner that ensures its use only for permissible purposes. A student organization seeking assistance must submit disbursement requests; if approved, the funds are paid directly to the third-party vendor and do not pass through the organization's coffers. This safeguard accompanying the University's financial assistance, when provided to a publication with a religious viewpoint such as Wide Awake, ensures that the funds are used only to further the University's purpose in maintaining a free and robust marketplace of ideas, from whatever perspective. This feature also makes this case analogous to a school providing equal access to a generally available printing press (or other physical facilities), and unlike a block grant to religious organizations.

Third, assistance is provided to the religious publication in a context that makes improbable any perception of government endorsement of the religious message. Wide Awake does not exist in a vacuum. It competes with 15 other magazines and newspapers for advertising and readership. The widely divergent viewpoints of these many purveyors of opinion, all supported on an equal basis by the University, significantly diminishes the danger that the message of any one publication is perceived as endorsed by the University. Besides the general news publications, for example, the University has provided support to The Yellow Journal, a humor magazine that has targeted Christianity as a subject of satire, and Al-Salam, a publication to "promote a better understanding of Islam to the University Community." Given this wide array of nonreligious, anti-religious and competing religious viewpoints in the forum supported by the University, any perception that the University endorses one particular viewpoint would be illogical. This is not the harder case where religious speech threatens to dominate the forum.

Finally, although the question is not presented here, I note the possibility that the student fee is susceptible to a Free Speech Clause challenge by an objecting student that she should not be compelled to pay for speech with which she disagrees. There currently exists a split in the lower courts as to whether such a challenge would be successful. While the Court does not resolve the question here, the existence of such an opt-out possibility not available to citizens generally, provides a potential basis for distinguishing proceeds of the student fees in this case from proceeds of the general assessments in support of religion that lie at the core of the prohibition against religious funding, and from government funds generally. Unlike moneys dispensed from state or federal treasuries, the Student Activities Fund is collected from students who themselves administer the fund and select qualifying recipients only from among those who originally paid the fee. The government neither pays into nor draws from this common pool, and a fee of this sort appears conducive to granting individual students proportional refunds. The Student Activities Fund, then, represents not government resources, whether derived from tax revenue, sales of assets, or otherwise, but a fund that simply belongs to the students.

The Court's decision today therefore neither trumpets the supremacy of the neutrality principle nor signals the demise of the funding prohibition in Establishment Clause jurisprudence. As I observed last Term, "experience proves that the Establishment Clause, like the Free Speech Clause, cannot easily be reduced to a single test." *Kiryas Joel,* 512 U.S., 720. When bedrock principles collide, they test the limits of categorical obstinacy and expose the flaws and dangers of a Grand Unified Theory that may turn out to be neither grand nor unified. The Court today does only what courts must do in many Establishment Clause cases—focus on specific features of a particular government action to ensure that it does not violate the Constitution. By withholding from Wide Awake assistance that the University provides generally to all other student publications, the University has discriminated on the basis of the magazine's religious viewpoint in violation of the Free Speech Clause. And particular features of the University's program—such as the explicit disclaimer, the disbursement of funds directly to third-party vendors, the vigorous nature of the forum at issue, and the possibility for objecting students to opt out—convince me that providing such assistance in this case would not carry the danger of impermissible use of public funds to endorse Wide Awake's religious message.

Subject to these comments, I join the opinion of the Court.

### JUSTICE THOMAS, concurring.

I agree with the Court's opinion and join it in full, but I write separately to express my disagreement with the historical analysis put forward by the dissent. Although the dissent starts down the right path in consulting the original meaning of the Establishment Clause, its misleading application of history yields a principle that is inconsistent with our Nation's long tradition of allowing religious adherents to participate on equal terms in neutral government programs.

Even assuming that the Virginia debate on the so-called "Assessment Controversy" was indicative of the principles embodied in the Establishment Clause, this incident hardly compels the dissent's conclusion that government must actively discriminate against religion. The dissent's historical discussion glosses over the fundamental characteristic of the Virginia assessment bill that sparked the controversy: The assessment was to be imposed for the support of clergy in the performance of their function of teaching religion. Thus, the "Bill Establishing a Provision for Teachers of the Christian Religion" provided for the collection of a specific tax, the proceeds of which were to be appropriated "by the Vestries, Elders, or Directors of each religious society . . . to a provision for a Minister or Teacher of the Gospel of their denomination, or the providing places of divine worship, and to none other use whatsoever."[1]

---

[1] The dissent suggests that the assessment bill would have created a "generally available subsidy program" comparable to respondent's Student Activities Fund (SAF). The dissent's characterization of the bill, however, is squarely at odds with the bill's clear purpose and effect to provide "for the support of Christian teachers." *Everson*, 330 U.S., at 72. Moreover, the section of the bill cited by the dissent, simply indicated that funds would be "disposed of under the direction of the General Assembly, for the encouragement of seminaries of learning within the Counties whence such sums shall arise," *Everson*, 74. This provision disposing of undesignated funds hardly transformed the "Bill Establishing a Provision for Teachers of the Christian Religion" into a truly neutral program that would benefit religious adherents as part of a large class of beneficiaries defined without reference to religion. Indeed, the only appropriation of money made by the bill would have been to promote "the general diffusion of Christian knowledge," 330 U.S., 72; any possible appropriation for "seminaries of learning" depended entirely on future legislative action.

Even assuming that future legislators would adhere to the bill's directive in appropriating the undesignated tax revenues, nothing in the bill would prevent use of those funds solely for sectarian educational institutions. To the contrary, most schools at the time of the founding were affiliated with some religious organization, see C. Antieau, A. Downey,

James Madison's Memorial and Remonstrance must be understood in this context. Contrary to the dissent's suggestion, Madison's objection to the assessment bill did not rest on the premise that religious entities may never participate on equal terms in neutral government programs. Nor did Madison embrace the argument that forms the linchpin of the dissent: that monetary subsidies are constitutionally different from other neutral benefits programs. Instead, Madison's comments are more consistent with the neutrality principle that the dissent inexplicably discards. According to Madison, the Virginia assessment was flawed because it "violated that equality which ought to be the basis of every law." The assessment violated the "equality" principle not because it allowed religious groups to participate in a generally available government program, but because the bill singled out religious entities for special benefits. See *ibid.* (arguing that the assessment violated the equality principle "by subjecting some to peculiar burdens" and "by granting to others peculiar exemptions").

Legal commentators have disagreed about the historical lesson to take from the Assessment Controversy. For some, the experience in Virginia is consistent with the view that the Framers saw the Establishment Clause simply as a prohibition on governmental preferences for some religious faiths over others. . . . Other commentators have rejected this view, concluding that the Establishment Clause forbids not only government preferences for some religious sects over others, but also government preferences for religion over irreligion. . . .

I find much to commend the former view. Madison's focus on the preferential nature of the assessment was not restricted to the fourth paragraph of the Remonstrance discussed above. The funding provided by the Virginia assessment was to be extended only to Christian sects, and the Remonstrance seized on this defect: "Who does not see that the same authority which can establish Christianity, in exclusion of all other Religions, may establish with the same ease any particular sect of Christians, in exclusion of all other Sects."

In addition to the third and fourth paragraphs of the Remonstrance, "Madison's seventh, ninth, eleventh, and twelfth arguments all speak, in some way, to the same intolerance, bigotry, unenlightenment, and persecution that had generally resulted from previous exclusive religious establishments." The conclusion that Madison saw the principle of nonestablishment as barring

---

& E. Roberts, Freedom From Federal Establishment, Formation and Early History of the First Amendment Religion Clauses 163 (1964), and in fact there was no system of public education in Virginia until several decades after the assessment bill was proposed, see A. Morrison, The Beginnings of Public Education in Virginia, 1776–1860, p. 9 (1917); see also A. Johnson, The Legal Status of Church-State Relationships in the United States 4 (1982) ("In Virginia the parish institutions transported from England were the earliest educational agencies. Although much of the teaching took place in the home and with the aid of tutors, every minister had a school, and it was the duty of the vestry to see that all the poor children were taught to read and write") (footnote omitted). Further, the clearly religious tenor of the Virginia assessment would seem to point toward appropriation of residual funds to sectarian "seminaries of learning." Finally, although modern historians have focused on the opt-out provision, the dissent provides no indication that Madison viewed the Virginia assessment as an evenhanded program; in fact, several of the objections expressed in Madison's Memorial and Remonstrance Against Religious Assessments, reprinted in *Everson,* 63, focus clearly on the bill's violation of the principle of "equality," or evenhandedness.

governmental preferences for *particular* religious faiths seems especially clear in light of statements he made in the more-relevant context of the House debates on the First Amendment. . . . Moreover, even if more extreme notions of the separation of church and state can be attributed to Madison, many of them clearly stem from "arguments reflecting the concepts of natural law, natural rights, and the social contract between government and a civil society," rather than the principle of nonestablishment in the Constitution. In any event, the views of one man do not establish the original understanding of the First Amendment.

But resolution of this debate is not necessary to decide this case. Under any understanding of the Assessment Controversy, the history cited by the dissent cannot support the conclusion that the Establishment Clause "categorically condemn[s] state programs directly aiding religious activity" when that aid is part of a neutral program available to a wide array of beneficiaries. Even if Madison believed that the principle of nonestablishment of religion precluded government financial support for religion *per se* (in the sense of government benefits specifically targeting religion), there is no indication that at the time of the framing he took the dissent's extreme view that the government must discriminate against religious adherents by excluding them from more generally available financial subsidies.[2]

In fact, Madison's own early legislative proposals cut against the dissent's suggestion. In 1776, when Virginia's Revolutionary Convention was drafting its Declaration of Rights, Madison prepared an amendment that would have disestablished the Anglican Church. This amendment (which went too far for the Convention and was not adopted) is not nearly as sweeping as the dissent's version of disestablishment; Madison merely wanted the Convention to declare that "no man or class of men ought, on account of religion[,] to be invested with *peculiar* emoluments or privileges . . . ." Likewise, Madison's Remonstrance stressed that "just government" is "best supported by protecting every citizen in the enjoyment of his Religion with the same equal hand which protects his person and his property; by neither invading the equal rights of any Sect, nor suffering any Sect to invade those of another." . . .

Stripped of its flawed historical premise, the dissent's argument is reduced to the claim that our Establishment Clause jurisprudence permits neutrality in the context of access to government *facilities* but requires discrimination in access to government *funds*. The dissent purports to locate the prohibition against "direct public funding" at the "heart" of the Establishment Clause, but this conclusion fails to confront historical examples of funding that date back to the time of the founding. To take but one famous example, both Houses of the First Congress elected chaplains, and that Congress enacted legislation providing for an annual salary of $500 to be paid out of the Treasury. Madison

---

[2] To the contrary, Madison's Remonstrance decried the fact that the assessment bill would require civil society to take "cognizance" of religion. Madison's Remonstrance P 1, reprinted in *Everson v. Board of Ed. of Ewing*, 330 U.S. 1, 64. Respondents' exclusion of religious activities from SAF funding creates this very problem. It requires University officials to classify publications as "religious activities," and to discriminate against the publications that fall into that category. Such a policy also contravenes the principles expressed in Madison's Remonstrance by encouraging religious adherents to cleanse their speech of religious overtones, thus "degrading from the equal rank of Citizens all those whose opinions in Religion do not bend to those of the Legislative authority." Madison's Remonstrance, P 9.

himself was a member of the committee that recommended the chaplain system in the House. This same system of "direct public funding" of congressional chaplains has "continued without interruption ever since that early session of Congress." *Marsh v. Chambers*, 463 U.S. 783, 788 (1983).

The historical evidence of government support for religious entities through property tax exemptions is also overwhelming. As the dissent concedes, property tax exemptions for religious bodies "have been in place for over 200 years without disruption to the interests represented by the Establishment Clause." In my view, the dissent's acceptance of this tradition puts to rest the notion that the Establishment Clause bars monetary aid to religious groups even when the aid is equally available to other groups. . . .

Though our Establishment Clause jurisprudence is in hopeless disarray, this case provides an opportunity to reaffirm one basic principle that has enjoyed an uncharacteristic degree of consensus: The Clause does not compel the exclusion of religious groups from government benefits programs that are generally available to a broad class of participants. Under the dissent's view, however, the University of Virginia may provide neutral access to the University's own printing press, but it may not provide the same service when the press is owned by a third party. Not surprisingly, the dissent offers no logical justification for this conclusion, and none is evident in the text or original meaning of the First Amendment.

If the Establishment Clause is offended when religious adherents benefit from neutral programs such as the University of Virginia's Student Activities Fund, it must also be offended when they receive the same benefits in the form of in-kind subsidies. The constitutional demands of the Establishment Clause may be judged against either a baseline of "neutrality" or a baseline of "no aid to religion," but the appropriate baseline surely cannot depend on the fortuitous circumstances surrounding the *form* of aid. The contrary rule would lead to absurd results that would jettison centuries of practice respecting the right of religious adherents to participate on neutral terms in a wide variety of government-funded programs.

Our Nation's tradition of allowing religious adherents to participate in evenhanded government programs is hardly limited to the class of "essential public benefits" identified by the dissent. A broader tradition can be traced at least as far back as the First Congress, which ratified the Northwest Ordinance of 1787. Article III of that famous enactment of the Confederation Congress had provided: "Religion, morality, and knowledge . . . being necessary to good government and the happiness of mankind, schools and the means of education shall forever be encouraged." Congress subsequently set aside federal lands in the Northwest Territory and other territories for the use of schools. Many of the schools that enjoyed the benefits of these land grants undoubtedly were church-affiliated sectarian institutions as there was no requirement that the schools be "public." Nevertheless, early Congresses found no problem with the provision of such neutral benefits. . . .

Thus, history provides an answer for the constitutional question posed by this case, but it is not the one given by the dissent. The dissent identifies no evidence that the Framers intended to disable religious entities from participating on neutral terms in evenhanded government programs. The evidence that does exist points in the opposite direction and provides ample support for today's decision.

JUSTICE SOUTER, with whom JUSTICE STEVENS, JUSTICE GINSBURG, and JUSTICE BREYER join, dissenting.

The Court today, for the first time, approves direct funding of core religious activities by an arm of the State. It does so, however, only after erroneous treatment of some familiar principles of law implementing the First Amendment's Establishment and Speech Clauses, and by viewing the very funds in question as beyond the reach of the Establishment Clause's funding restrictions as such. Because there is no warrant for distinguishing among public funding sources for purposes of applying the First Amendment's prohibition of religious establishment, I would hold that the University's refusal to support petitioners' religious activities is compelled by the Establishment Clause. I would therefore affirm.

I

The central question in this case is whether a grant from the Student Activities Fund to pay Wide Awake's printing expenses would violate the Establishment Clause. Although the Court does not dwell on the details of Wide Awake's message, it recognizes something sufficiently religious in the publication to demand Establishment Clause scrutiny. Although the Court places great stress on the eligibility of secular as well as religious activities for grants from the Student Activities Fund, it recognizes that such evenhanded availability is not by itself enough to satisfy constitutional requirements for any aid scheme that results in a benefit to religion. Something more is necessary to justify any religious aid. Some Members of the Court, at least, may think the funding permissible on a view that it is indirect, since the money goes to Wide Awake's printer, not through Wide Awake's own checking account. The Court's principal reliance, however, is on an argument that providing religion with economically valuable services is permissible on the theory that services are economically indistinguishable from religious access to governmental speech forums, which sometimes is permissible. But this reasoning would commit the Court to approving direct religious aid beyond anything justifiable for the sake of access to speaking forums. The Court implicitly recognizes this in its further attempt to circumvent the clear bar to direct governmental aid to religion. Different Members of the Court seek to avoid this bar in different ways. The opinion of the Court makes the novel assumption that only direct aid financed with tax revenue is barred, and draws the erroneous conclusion that the involuntary Student Activities Fee is not a tax. I do not read JUSTICE O'CONNOR's opinion as sharing that assumption; she places this Student Activities Fund in a category of student funding enterprises from which religious activities in public universities may benefit, so long as there is no consequent endorsement of religion. The resulting decision is in unmistakable tension with the accepted law that the Court continues to avow.

A

The Court's difficulties will be all the more clear after a closer look at Wide Awake than the majority opinion affords. The character of the magazine is candidly disclosed on the opening page of the first issue, where the editor-in-chief announces Wide Awake's mission in a letter to the readership signed, "Love in Christ": it is "to challenge Christians to live, in word and deed, according to the faith they proclaim and to encourage students to consider what a personal relationship with Jesus Christ means." The masthead of every issue bears St. Paul's exhortation, that "the hour has come for you to awake from your slumber, because our salvation is nearer now than when we first believed. Romans 13:11."

Each issue of Wide Awake contained in the record makes good on the editor's promise and echoes the Apostle's call to accept salvation:

> The only way to salvation through Him is by confessing and repenting of sin. It is the Christian's duty to make sinners aware of their need for salvation. Thus, Christians must confront and condemn sin, or else they fail in their duty of love. Mourad & Prince, A Love/Hate Relationship, Nov./Dec. 1990, p. 3.

> When you get to the final gate, the Lord will be handing out boarding passes, and He will examine your ticket. If, in your lifetime, you did not request a seat on His Friendly Skies Flyer by trusting Him and asking Him to be your pilot, then you will not be on His list of reserved seats (and the Lord will know you not). You will not be able to buy a ticket then; no amount of money or desire will do the trick. You will be met by your chosen pilot and flown straight to Hell on an express jet (without air conditioning or toilets, of course). Ace, The Plane Truth, *ibid.*

> "Go into all the world and preach the good news to all creation." (Mark 16:15) The Great Commission is the prime-directive for our lives as Christians . . . . Liu, Christianity and the Five-legged Stool, Sept./Oct. 1991, p. 3.

> The Spirit provides access to an intimate relationship with the Lord of the Universe, awakens our minds to comprehend spiritual truth and empowers us to serve as effective ambassadors for the Lord Jesus in our earthly lives. Buterbaugh, A Spiritual Advantage, Mar./Apr. 1991, p. 21.

There is no need to quote further from articles of like tenor, but one could examine such other examples as religious poetry, see Macpherson, I Have Started Searching for Angels, Nov./Dec. 1990, p. 18; religious textual analysis and commentary, see Buterbaugh, Colossians 1:1-14: Abundant Life, *id.*, 20; Buterbaugh, John 14-16: A Spiritual Advantage, Mar./Apr. 1991, pp. 20-21; and instruction on religious practice, see Early, Thanksgiving and Prayer, Nov./ Dec. 1990, p. 21 (providing readers with suggested prayers and posing contemplative questions about biblical texts); Early, Hope and Spirit, Mar./Apr. 1991, p. 21 (similar).

Even featured essays on facially secular topics become platforms from which to call readers to fulfill the tenets of Christianity in their lives. Although a piece on racism has some general discussion on the subject, it proceeds beyond even the analysis and interpretation of biblical texts to conclude with the counsel to take action because that is the Christian thing to do:

> God calls us to take the risks of voluntarily stepping out of our comfort zones and to take joy in the whole richness of our inheritance in the body of Christ. We must take the love we receive from God and share it with all peoples of the world.
>
> Racism is a disease of the heart, soul, and mind, and only when it is extirpated from the individual consciousness and replaced with the love

and peace of God will true personal and communal healing begin. Liu, Rosenberger, Mourad, and Prince, "Eracing" Mistakes, Nov./Dec. 1990, p. 14.

The same progression occurs in an article on eating disorders, which begins with descriptions of anorexia and bulimia and ends with this religious message:

> As thinking people who profess a belief in God, we must grasp firmly the truth, the reality of who we are because of Christ. Christ is the Bread of Life (John 6:35). Through Him, we are full. He alone can provide the ultimate source of spiritual fulfillment which permeates the emotional, psychological, and physical dimensions of our lives. Ferguson & Lassiter, From Calorie to Calvary, Sept./Oct. 1991, p. 14.

This writing is no merely descriptive examination of religious doctrine or even of ideal Christian practice in confronting life's social and personal problems. Nor is it merely the expression of editorial opinion that incidentally coincides with Christian ethics and reflects a Christian view of human obligation. It is straightforward exhortation to enter into a relationship with God as revealed in Jesus Christ, and to satisfy a series of moral obligations derived from the teachings of Jesus Christ. These are not the words of "student news, information, opinion, entertainment, or academic communication . . ." (in the language of the University's funding criterion, but the words of "challenge [to] Christians to live, in word and deed, according to the faith they proclaim and . . . to consider what a personal relationship with Jesus Christ means" (in the language of Wide Awake's founder). The subject is not the discourse of the scholar's study or the seminar room, but of the evangelist's mission station and the pulpit. It is nothing other than the preaching of the word, which (along with the sacraments) is what most branches of Christianity offer those called to the religious life.

Using public funds for the direct subsidization of preaching the word is categorically forbidden under the Establishment Clause, and if the Clause was meant to accomplish nothing else, it was meant to bar this use of public money. Evidence on the subject antedates even the Bill of Rights itself, as may be seen in the writings of Madison, whose authority on questions about the meaning of the Establishment Clause is well settled. Four years before the First Congress proposed the First Amendment, Madison gave his opinion on the legitimacy of using public funds for religious purposes, in the Memorial and Remonstrance Against Religious Assessments, which played the central role in ensuring the defeat of the Virginia tax assessment bill in 1786 and framed the debate upon which the Religion Clauses stand:

> Who does not see that . . . the same authority which can force a citizen to contribute three pence only of his property for the support of any one establishment, may force him to conform to any other establishment in all cases whatsoever? James Madison, Memorial and Remonstrance Against Religious Assessments ¶ 3.

Madison wrote against a background in which nearly every Colony had exacted a tax for church support, the practice having become "so commonplace as to shock the freedom-loving colonials into a feeling of abhorrence." Madison's Remonstrance captured the colonists' "conviction that individual religious liberty could be achieved best under a government which was stripped of all power to tax, to support, or otherwise to assist any or all religions, or to interfere with the beliefs of any religious individual or group."[1] Their sentiment, as expressed by Madison in Virginia, led not only to the defeat of Virginia's tax assessment bill, but also directly to passage of the Virginia Bill for Establishing Religious Freedom, written by Thomas Jefferson. That bill's preamble declared that "to compel a man to furnish contributions of money for the propagation of opinions which he disbelieves, is sinful and tyrannical," and its text provided "that no man shall be compelled to frequent or support any religious worship, place, or ministry whatsoever . . . ." We have "previously recognized that the provisions of the First Amendment, in the drafting and adoption of which Madison and Jefferson played such leading roles, had the same objective and were intended to provide the same protection against governmental intrusion on religious liberty as the Virginia statute."[2]

---

[1] JUSTICE THOMAS suggests that Madison would have approved of the assessment bill if only it had satisfied the principle of evenhandedness. Nowhere in the Remonstrance, however, did Madison advance the view that Virginia should be able to provide financial support for religion as part of a generally available subsidy program. Indeed, while JUSTICE THOMAS claims that the "funding provided by the Virginia assessment was to be extended only to Christian sects," it is clear that the bill was more general in scope than this. While the bill . . ., which is reprinted in *Everson v. Board of Ed. of Ewing*, 330 U.S. 1, 72-74 (1947), provided that each taxpayer could designate a religious society to which he wanted his levy paid, *id.*, 73, it would also have allowed a taxpayer to refuse to appropriate his levy to any religious society, in which case the legislature was to use these unappropriated sums to fund "seminaries of learning." *Id.*, 74 (contrary to JUSTICE THOMAS's unsupported assertion, this portion of the bill was no less obligatory than any other). While some of these seminaries undoubtedly would have been religious in character, others would not have been, as a seminary was generally understood at the time to be "any school, academy, college or university, in which young persons are instructed in the several branches of learning which may qualify them for their future employments." N. Webster, An American Dictionary of the English Language (1st ed. 1828); see also 14 The Oxford English Dictionary 956 (2d ed. 1989). Not surprisingly, then, scholars have generally agreed that the bill would have provided funding for nonreligious schools. See, e.g., Laycock, "Nonpreferential" Aid to Religion: A False Claim About Original Intent, 27 Wm. & Mary L. Rev. 875, 897, and n. 108 (1986) ("Any taxpayer could refuse to designate a church, with undesignated church taxes going to a fund for schools. . . . The bill used the phrase 'seminaries of learning,' which almost certainly meant schools generally and not just schools for the training of ministers"); T. Buckley, Church and State in Revolutionary Virginia, 1776–1787, p. 133 (1977) ("The assessment had been carefully drafted to permit those who preferred to support education rather than religion to do so"); T. Curry, The First Freedoms 141 (1986) ("Those taxes not designated for any specific denomination [were] allocated to education"). It is beside the point that "there was no system of public education in Virginia until several decades after the assessment bill was proposed," because the bill was never passed, the funds that it would have made available for secular, public schools never materialized. The fact that the bill, if passed, would have funded secular as well as religious instruction did nothing to soften Madison's opposition to it.

Nor is it fair to argue that Madison opposed the bill only because it treated religious groups unequally. In various paragraphs of the Remonstrance, Madison did complain about the bill's peculiar burdens and exemptions, *Everson*, 66, but to identify this factor as the sole point of Madison's opposition to the bill is unfaithful to the Remonstrance's text. Madison strongly inveighed against the proposed aid for religion for a host of reasons (the Remonstrance numbers 15 paragraphs, each containing at least one point in opposition), and crucial here is the fact that many of those reasons would have applied whether or not the state aid was being distributed equally among sects, and whether or not the aid was going to those sects in the context of an evenhanded government program. See, e.g., Madison's

The principle against direct funding with public money is patently violated by the contested use of today's student activity fee. Like today's taxes generally, the fee is Madison's threepence. The University exercises the power of the State to compel a student to pay it, and the use of any part of it for the direct support of religious activity thus strikes at what we have repeatedly held to be the heart of the prohibition on establishment. *Everson,* 15-16 ("The 'establishment of religion' clause . . . means at least this . . . . No tax in any amount, large or small, can be levied to support any religious activities or institutions, whatever they may be called, or whatever form they may adopt to teach or practice religion"); see *School Dist. of Grand Rapids v. Ball,* 473 U.S. 373, 385

---

Remonstrance, reprinted in *Everson,* 330 U.S. at 64, P 1 ("In matters of Religion, no man's right is abridged by the institution of Civil Society, and . . . Religion is wholly exempt from its cognizance"); *id.,* 67, P 6 (arguing that State support of religion "is a contradiction to the Christian Religion itself; for every page of it disavows a dependence on the powers of this world"); *ibid.,* P 7 ("Experience witnesseth that ecclesiastical establishments, instead of maintaining the purity and efficacy of Religion, have had a contrary operation"). Madison's objections were supplemented by numerous other petitions in opposition to the bill that likewise do not suggest that the lack of evenhandedness was its dispositive flaw. L. Levy, The Establishment Clause: Religion and the First Amendment 63-67 (2d ed. 1994). For example, the petition that received the largest number of signatories was motivated by the view that religion should only be supported voluntarily. *Id.,* 63-64. Indeed, Madison's Remonstrance did not argue for a bill distributing aid to all sects and religions on an equal basis, and the outgrowth of the Remonstrance and the defeat of the Virginia assessment was not such a bill; rather, it was the Virginia Bill for Establishing Religious Freedom, which, as discussed in the text, proscribed the use of tax dollars for religious purposes.

In attempting to recast Madison's opposition as having principally been targeted against "governmental preferences for *particular* religious faiths," (emphasis in original), JUSTICE THOMAS wishes to wage a battle that was lost long ago, for "this Court has rejected unequivocally the contention that the Establishment Clause forbids only governmental preference of one religion over another," *School Dist. of Abington Township v. Schempp,* 374 U.S. 203, 216 (1963); see also *Texas Monthly, Inc. v. Bullock,* 489 U.S. 1, 17 (1989) (plurality opinion); *id.,* 28 (BLACKMUN, J., concurring in judgment); *Wallace v. Jaffree,* 472 U.S. 38, 52-53 (1985); *Torcaso v. Watkins,* 367 U.S. 488 (1961); *Engel v. Vitale,* 370 U.S. 421, 430 (1962); *Everson,,* 15; see generally *Lee v. Weisman,* 505 U.S. 577, 609-616 (1992) (SOUTER, J., concurring).

[2] JUSTICE THOMAS attempts to cast doubt on this accepted version of Establishment Clause history by reference to historical facts that are largely inapposite. As I have said elsewhere, individual Acts of Congress, especially when they are few and far between, scarcely serve as an authoritative guide to the meaning of the religion clauses, for "like other politicians, [members of the early Congresses] could raise constitutional ideals one day and turn their backs on them the next. [For example,] . . . [t]en years after proposing the First Amendment, Congress passed the Alien and Sedition Acts, measures patently unconstitutional by modern standards. If the early Congress's political actions were determinative, and not merely relevant, evidence of constitutional meaning, we would have to gut our current First Amendment doctrine to make room for political censorship." *Lee v. Weisman,* 505 U.S. 577, 626 (1992) (concurring opinion). The legislation cited by JUSTICE THOMAS, including the Northwest Ordinance, is no more dispositive than the Alien and Sedition Acts in interpreting the First Amendment. Even less persuasive, then, are citations to constitutionally untested Acts dating from the mid-19th century, for without some rather innovative argument, they cannot be offered as providing an authoritative gloss on the Framers' intent.

JUSTICE THOMAS's references to Madison's actions as a legislator also provide little support for his cause. JUSTICE THOMAS seeks to draw a significant lesson out of the fact that, in seeking to disestablish the Anglican Church in Virginia in 1776, Madison did not inveigh against state funding of religious activities. That was not the task at hand, however. Madison was acting with the specific goal of eliminating the special privileges enjoyed by

(1985) ("Although Establishment Clause jurisprudence is characterized by few absolutes, the Clause does absolutely prohibit government-financed or government-sponsored indoctrination into the beliefs of a particular religious faith"); *Committee for Public Ed. v. Nyquist*, 413 U.S. 780 ("In the absence of an effective means of guaranteeing that the state aid derived from public funds will be used exclusively for secular, neutral, and nonideological purposes, it is clear from our cases that direct aid in whatever form is invalid"); *id.*, 772 ("Primary among those evils" against which the Establishment Clause guards "have been sponsorship, financial support, and active involvement of the sovereign in religious activity") (citations and internal quotation marks omitted); see also *Lee v. Weisman*, 505 U.S. 577, 640 (1992) (SCALIA, J., dissenting) ("The coercion that was a hallmark of historical establishments of religion was coercion of religious orthodoxy and of financial support by force of law and threat of penalty") (emphasis deleted).

The Court, accordingly, has never before upheld direct state funding of the sort of proselytizing published in Wide Awake and, in fact, has categorically condemned state programs directly aiding religious activity.

Even when the Court has upheld aid to an institution performing both secular and sectarian functions, it has always made a searching enquiry to ensure that the institution kept the secular activities separate from its sectarian ones, with any direct aid flowing only to the former and never the latter.

Reasonable minds may differ over whether the Court reached the correct result in each of these cases, but their common principle has never been questioned or repudiated. "Although Establishment Clause jurisprudence is characterized by few absolutes, the Clause does absolutely prohibit government-financed . . . indoctrination into the beliefs of a particular religious faith." *School Dist. v. Ball*, 473 U.S., 385.

B

Why does the Court not apply this clear law to these clear facts and conclude, as I do, that the funding scheme here is a clear constitutional violation? The answer must be in part that the Court fails to confront the evidence set out in the preceding section. Throughout its opinion, the Court refers unin-

---

Virginia Anglicans, and he made no effort to lay out the broader views of church and state that came to bear in his drafting of the First Amendment some 13 years later. That Madison did not speak in more expansive terms than necessary in 1776 was hardly surprising for, as it was, his proposal was defeated by the Virginia Convention as having gone too far. *Ibid.*

Similarly, the invocation of Madison's tenure on the congressional committee that approved funding for legislative chaplains provides no support for more general principles that run counter to settled Establishment Clause jurisprudence. As I have previously pointed out, Madison, upon retirement, "insisted that 'it was not with my approbation, that the deviation from [the immunity of religion from civil jurisdiction] took place in Congs., when they appointed Chaplains, to be paid from the Natl. Treasury.'" *Lee*, 625, n. 6, quoting Letter from J. Madison to E. Livingston (July 10, 1822), in 5 The Founders' Constitution, 105. And when we turned our attention to deciding whether funding of legislative chaplains posed an establishment problem, we did not address the practice as one instance of a larger class of permissible government funding of religious activities. Instead, *Marsh v. Chambers*, 463 U.S. 783, 791 (1983), explicitly relied on the singular, 200-year pedigree of legislative chaplains, noting that "[t]his unique history" justified carving out an exception for the specific practice in question. Given that the decision upholding this practice was expressly limited to its facts, then, it would stand the Establishment Clause on its head to extract from it a broad rule permitting the funding of religious activities.

formatively to Wide Awake's "Christian viewpoint," or its "religious perspective," and in distinguishing funding of Wide Awake from the funding of a church, the Court maintains that "[Wide Awake] is not a religious institution, at least in the usual sense."[4] The Court does not quote the magazine's adoption of Saint Paul's exhortation to awaken to the nearness of salvation, or any of its articles enjoining readers to accept Jesus Christ, or the religious verses, or the religious textual analyses, or the suggested prayers. And so it is easy for the Court to lose sight of what the University students and the Court of Appeals found so obvious, and to blanch the patently and frankly evangelistic character of the magazine by unrevealing allusions to religious points of view.

Nevertheless, even without the encumbrance of detail from Wide Awake's actual pages, the Court finds something sufficiently religious about the magazine to require examination under the Establishment Clause, and one may therefore ask why the unequivocal prohibition on direct funding does not lead the Court to conclude that funding would be unconstitutional. The answer is that the Court focuses on a subsidiary body of law, which it correctly states but ultimately misapplies. That subsidiary body of law accounts for the Court's substantial attention to the fact that the University's funding scheme is "neutral," in the formal sense that it makes funds available on an evenhanded basis to secular and sectarian applicants alike. While this is indeed true and relevant under our cases, it does not alone satisfy the requirements of the Establishment Clause, as the Court recognizes when it says that evenhandedness is only a "significant factor" in certain Establishment Clause analysis, not a dispositive one. . . . This recognition reflects the Court's appreciation of two general rules: that whenever affirmative government aid ultimately benefits religion, the Establishment Clause requires some justification beyond evenhandedness on the government's part; and that direct public funding of core sectarian activities, even if accomplished pursuant to an evenhanded program, would be entirely inconsistent with the Establishment Clause and would strike at the very heart of the Clause's protection. . . .

In order to understand how the Court thus begins with sound rules but ends with an unsound result, it is necessary to explore those rules in greater detail than the Court does. As the foregoing quotations from the Court's opinion indicate, the relationship between the prohibition on direct aid and the requirement of evenhandedness when affirmative government aid does result in some benefit to religion reflects the relationship between basic rule and marginal criterion. At the heart of the Establishment Clause stands the prohibition against direct public funding, but that prohibition does not answer the questions that occur at the margins of the Clause's application. Is any government activity that provides any incidental benefit to religion likewise unconstitutional? Would it be wrong to put out fires in burning churches, wrong to pay the bus fares of students on the way to parochial schools, wrong to allow a grantee of special education funds to spend them at a religious college? These are the questions that call for drawing lines, and it is in drawing them that evenhandedness becomes important. However the Court may in the past have phrased its line-drawing test, the question whether such benefits are provided on an evenhanded basis has been relevant, for the question addresses

---

[4] To the extent the Court perceives some distinction between the printing and dissemination of evangelism and proselytization, and core religious activity "in [its] usual sense," this distinction goes entirely unexplained in the Court's opinion.

one aspect of the issue whether a law is truly neutral with respect to religion (that is, whether the law either "advances [or] inhibits religion.") . . . In *Widmar v. Vincent*, 454 U.S. 263, 274 (1981), for example, we noted that "the provision of benefits to [a] broad . . . spectrum of [religious and nonreligious] groups is an important index of secular effect." In the doubtful cases (those not involving direct public funding), where there is initially room for argument about a law's effect, evenhandedness serves to weed out those laws that impermissibly advance religion by channelling aid to it exclusively. Evenhandedness is therefore a prerequisite to further enquiry into the constitutionality of a doubtful law, but evenhandedness goes no further. It does not guarantee success under Establishment Clause scrutiny.

Three cases permitting indirect aid to religion, *Mueller v. Allen*, 463 U.S. 388 (1983), *Witters v. Washington Dept. of Servs. for Blind,* 474 U.S. 481 (1986), and *Zobrest v. Catalina Foothills School Dist.*, 509 U.S. 1 (1993), are among the latest of those to illustrate this relevance of evenhandedness when advancement is not so obvious as to be patently unconstitutional. Each case involved a program in which benefits given to individuals on a religion-neutral basis ultimately were used by the individuals, in one way or another, to support religious institutions. In each, the fact that aid was distributed generally and on a neutral basis was a necessary condition for upholding the program at issue. But the significance of evenhandedness stopped there. We did not, in any of these cases, hold that satisfying the condition was sufficient, or dispositive. Even more importantly, we never held that evenhandedness might be sufficient to render direct aid to religion constitutional. Quite the contrary. Critical to our decisions in these cases was the fact that the aid was indirect; it reached religious institutions "only as a result of the genuinely independent and private choices of aid recipients," *Witters*, 487. In noting and relying on this particular feature of each of the programs at issue, we in fact reaffirmed the core prohibition on direct funding of religious activities. Thus, our holdings in these cases were little more than extensions of the unremarkable proposition that "a State may issue a paycheck to one of its employees, who may then donate all or part of that paycheck to a religious institution, all without constitutional barrier . . . ." *Witters*, 486-487. Such "attenuated financial benefits, ultimately controlled by the private choices of individuals," we have found, are simply not within the contemplation of the Establishment Clause's broad prohibition. . . .

Evenhandedness as one element of a permissibly attenuated benefit is, of course, a far cry from evenhandedness as a sufficient condition of constitutionality for direct financial support of religious proselytization, and our cases have unsurprisingly repudiated any such attempt to cut the Establishment Clause down to a mere prohibition against unequal direct aid. And nowhere has the Court's adherence to the preeminence of the no-direct-funding principle over the principle of evenhandedness been as clear as in *Bowen v. Kendrick,* 487 U.S. 589 (1988).

*Bowen* involved consideration of the Adolescent Family Life Act (AFLA), a federal grant program providing funds to institutions for counseling and educational services related to adolescent sexuality and pregnancy. At the time of the litigation, 141 grants had been awarded under the AFLA to a broad array of both secular and religiously affiliated institutions. . . .

With respect to the claim that the program was unconstitutional as applied, we remanded the case to the District Court "for consideration of the evidence presented by appellees insofar as it sheds light on the manner in which the statute is presently being administered." . . . At no point in our opinion did we suggest that the breadth of potential recipients, or distribution on an evenhanded basis, could have justified the use of federal funds for religious activities, a position that would have made no sense after we had pegged the Act's facial constitutionality to our conclusion that advancement of religion was not inevitable. . . .

Bowen was no sport; its pedigree was the line of *Everson v. Board of Ed.*, 330 U.S., 16-18, *Board of Ed. v. Allen*, 392 U.S., 243-249, *Tilton v. Richardson*, 678-682, *Hunt v. McNair*, 742-745, and *Roemer v. Board of Public Works of Md.*, 426 U.S., 759-761. Each of these cases involved a general aid program that provided benefits to a broad array of secular and sectarian institutions on an evenhanded basis, but in none of them was that fact dispositive. The plurality opinion in *Roemer* made this point exactly:

> The Court has taken the view that a secular purpose and a facial neutral-ity may not be enough, if in fact the State is lending direct support to a religious activity. The State may not, for example, pay for what is actually a religious education, even though it purports to be paying for a secular one, and even though it makes its aid available to secular and religious institutions alike. 426 U.S., 747.

Instead, the central enquiry in each of these general aid cases, as in *Bowen*, was whether secular activities could be separated from the sectarian ones suf-ficiently to ensure that aid would flow to the secular alone.

*Witters, Mueller*, and *Zobrest* expressly preserve the standard thus exhibit-ed so often. Each of these cases explicitly distinguished the indirect aid in issue from contrasting examples in the line of cases striking down direct aid, and each thereby expressly preserved the core constitutional principle that direct aid to religion is impermissible. . . . It appears that the University perfectly un-derstood the primacy of the no-direct-funding rule over the evenhandedness principle when it drew the line short of funding "any activity which primarily promotes or manifests a particular belief(s) in or about a deity or an ultimate reality."

## C

Since conformity with the marginal or limiting principle of evenhanded-ness is insufficient of itself to demonstrate the constitutionality of providing a government benefit that reaches religion, the Court must identify some fur-ther element in the funding scheme that does demonstrate its permissibility. For one reason or another, the Court's chosen element appears to be the fact that under the University's Guidelines, funds are sent to the printer chosen by Wide Awake, rather than to Wide Awake itself.

### 1

If the Court's suggestion is that this feature of the funding program brings this case into line with *Witters, Mueller*, and *Zobrest*, the Court has misread those cases, which turned on the fact that the choice to benefit religion was made by a nonreligious third party standing between the government and a religious institution. Here there is no third party standing between the government and the ultimate religious beneficiary to break the circuit by its independent discre-tion to put state money to religious use. The printer, of course, has no option to take the money and use it to print a secular journal instead of Wide Awake.

It only gets the money because of its contract to print a message of religious evangelism at the direction of Wide Awake, and it will receive payment only for doing precisely that. The formalism of distinguishing between payment to Wide Awake so it can pay an approved bill and payment of the approved bill itself cannot be the basis of a decision of constitutional law. If this indeed were a critical distinction, the Constitution would permit a State to pay all the bills of any religious institution;[10] in fact, despite the Court's purported adherence to the no-direct-funding principle, the State could simply hand out credit cards to religious institutions and honor the monthly statements (so long as someone could devise an evenhanded umbrella to cover the whole scheme). *Witters* and the other cases cannot be distinguished out of existence this way.

2

It is more probable, however, that the Court's reference to the printer goes to a different attempt to justify the payment. On this purported justification, the payment to the printer is significant only as the last step in an argument resting on the assumption that a public university may give a religious group the use of any of its equipment or facilities so long as secular groups are likewise eligible. The Court starts with the cases of *Widmar v. Vincent, Board of Ed. of Westside Community Schools v. Mergens,* and *Lamb's Chapel v. Center Moriches Union Free School Dist.,* in which religious groups were held to be entitled to access for speaking in government buildings open generally for that purpose. The Court reasons that the availability of a forum has economic value (the government built and maintained the building, while the speakers saved the rent for a hall); and that economically there is no difference between the University's provision of the value of the room and the value, say, of the University's printing equipment; and that therefore the University must be able to provide the use of the latter. Since it may do that, the argument goes, it would be unduly formalistic to draw the line at paying for an outside printer, who simply does what the magazine's publishers could have done with the University's own printing equipment.

The argument is as unsound as it is simple, and the first of its troubles emerges from an examination of the cases relied upon to support it. The common factual thread running through *Widmar, Mergens,* and *Lamb's Chapel* is that a governmental institution created a limited forum for the use of students in a school or college, or for the public at large, but sought to exclude speakers with religious messages. In each case the restriction was struck down either as an impermissible attempt to regulate the content of speech in an open forum (as in *Widmar* and *Mergens*) or to suppress a particular religious viewpoint (as in *Lamb's Chapel*). In each case, to be sure, the religious speaker's use of the room passed muster as an incident of a plan to facilitate speech generally for a secular purpose, entailing neither secular entanglement with religion nor risk that the religious speech would be taken to be the speech of the govern-

---

[10] The Court acknowledges that "if the State pays a church's bills it is subsidizing it," and concedes that "we must guard against this abuse." These concerns are not present here, the Court contends, because Wide Awake "is not a religious institution, at least in the usual sense of that term as used in our case law." The Court's concession suggests that its distinction between paying a religious institution and paying a religious institution's bills is not really significant. But if the Court is relying on its characterization of Wide Awake as not a religious institution, "at least in the usual sense," the Court could presumably stop right there.

ment or that the government's endorsement of a religious message would be inferred. But each case drew ultimately on unexceptionable Speech Clause doctrine treating the evangelist, the Salvation Army, the millennialist, or the Hare Krishna like any other speaker in a public forum. It was the preservation of free speech on the model of the street corner that supplied the justification going beyond the requirement of evenhandedness.

The Court's claim of support from these forum-access cases is ruled out by the very scope of their holdings. While they do indeed allow a limited benefit to religious speakers, they rest on the recognition that all speakers are entitled to use the street corner (even though the State paves the roads and provides police protection to everyone on the street) and on the analogy between the public street corner and open classroom space. Thus, the Court found it significant that the classroom speakers would engage in traditional speech activities in these forums, too, even though the rooms (like street corners) require some incidental state spending to maintain them. The analogy breaks down entirely, however, if the cases are read more broadly than the Court wrote them, to cover more than forums for literal speaking. There is no traditional street corner printing provided by the government on equal terms to all comers, and the forum cases cannot be lifted to a higher plane of generalization without admitting that new economic benefits are being extended directly to religion in clear violation of the principle barring direct aid. The argument from economic equivalence thus breaks down on recognizing that the direct state aid it would support is not mitigated by the street corner analogy in the service of free speech. Absent that, the rule against direct aid stands as a bar to printing services as well as printers.

3

It must, indeed, be a recognition of just this point that leads the Court to take a third tack, not in coming up with yet a third attempt at justification within the rules of existing case law, but in recasting the scope of the Establishment Clause in ways that make further affirmative justification unnecessary. JUSTICE O'CONNOR makes a comprehensive analysis of the manner in which the activity fee is assessed and distributed. She concludes that the funding differs so sharply from religious funding out of governmental treasuries generally that it falls outside Establishment Clause's purview in the absence of a message of religious endorsement (which she finds not to be present). The opinion of the Court concludes more expansively that the activity fee is not a tax, and then proceeds to find the aid permissible on the legal assumption that the bar against direct aid applies only to aid derived from tax revenue. I have already indicated why it is fanciful to treat the fee as anything but a tax (noting mandatory nature of the fee), and will not repeat the point again. The novelty of the assumption that the direct aid bar only extends to aid derived from taxation, however, requires some response.

Although it was a taxation scheme that moved Madison to write in the first instance, the Court has never held that government resources obtained without taxation could be used for direct religious support, and our cases on direct government aid have frequently spoken in terms in no way limited to tax revenues. . . .

Allowing nontax funds to be spent on religion would, in fact, fly in the face of clear principle. Leaving entirely aside the question whether public nontax revenues could ever be used to finance religion without violating the endorsement test, any such use of them would ignore one of the dual objectives of the Establishment Clause, which was meant not only to protect individuals and their republics from the destructive consequences of mixing government and religion, but to protect religion from a corrupting dependence on support from the Government. . . . Since the corrupting effect of government support does not turn on whether the Government's own money comes from taxation or gift or the sale of public lands, the Establishment Clause could hardly relax its vigilance simply because tax revenue was not implicated. Accordingly, in the absence of a forthright disavowal, one can only assume that the Court does not mean to eliminate one half of the Establishment Clause's justification.

### D

Nothing in the Court's opinion would lead me to end this enquiry into the application of the Establishment Clause any differently from the way I began it. The Court is ordering an instrumentality of the State to support religious evangelism with direct funding. This is a flat violation of the Establishment Clause.

### II

Given the dispositive effect of the Establishment Clause's bar to funding the magazine, there should be no need to decide whether in the absence of this bar the University would violate the Free Speech Clause by limiting funding as it has done. But the Court's speech analysis may have independent application, and its flaws should not pass unremarked.

The Court acknowledges the necessity for a university to make judgments based on the content of what may be said or taught when it decides, in the absence of unlimited amounts of money or other resources, how to honor its educational responsibilities. Nor does the Court generally question that in allocating public funds a state university enjoys spacious discretion. . . .[11] Accordingly, the Court recognizes that the relevant enquiry in this case is not merely whether the University bases its funding decisions on the subject matter of student speech; if there is an infirmity in the basis for the University's funding decision, it must be that the University is impermissibly distinguishing among competing viewpoints. . . .

The issue whether a distinction is based on viewpoint does not turn simply on whether a government regulation happens to be applied to a speaker who seeks to advance a particular viewpoint; the issue, of course, turns on whether the burden on speech is explained by reference to viewpoint. As when deciding whether a speech restriction is content based or content neu-

---

[11] The Court draws a distinction between a State's use of public funds to advance its own speech and the State's funding of private speech, suggesting that authority to make content-related choices is at its most powerful when the State undertakes the former. I would not argue otherwise, see *Hazelwood School Dist. v. Kuhlmeier*, 484 U.S. 260, 270-273 (1988), but I do suggest that this case reveals the difficulties that can be encountered in drawing this distinction. There is a communicative element inherent in the very act of funding itself, cf. *Buckley v. Valeo*, 424 U.S. 1, 15-19 (1976) (*per curiam*), and although it is the student speakers who choose which particular messages to advance in the forum created by the University, the initial act of defining the boundaries of the forum is a decision attributable to the University, not the students. In any event, even assuming that private and state speech always may be separated by clean lines and that this case involves only the former, I believe the distinction is irrelevant here because this case does not involve viewpoint discrimination.

tral, "the government's purpose is the controlling consideration." *Ward v. Rock Against Racism,* 491 U.S. 781, 791 (1989). . . . So, for example, a city that enforces its excessive noise ordinance by pulling the plug on a rock band using a forbidden amplification system is not guilty of viewpoint discrimination simply because the band wishes to use that equipment to espouse antiracist views. Nor does a municipality's decision to prohibit political advertising on bus placards amount to viewpoint discrimination when in the course of applying this policy it denies space to a person who wishes to speak in favor of a particular political candidate.

Accordingly, the prohibition on viewpoint discrimination serves that important purpose of the Free Speech Clause, which is to bar the government from skewing public debate. Other things being equal, viewpoint discrimination occurs when government allows one message while prohibiting the messages of those who can reasonably be expected to respond. . . . It is precisely this element of taking sides in a public debate that identifies viewpoint discrimination and makes it the most pernicious of all distinctions based on content. Thus, if government assists those espousing one point of view, neutrality requires it to assist those espousing opposing points of view, as well. . . .

If the Guidelines were written or applied so as to limit only such Christian advocacy and no other evangelical efforts that might compete with it, the discrimination would be based on viewpoint. But that is not what the regulation authorizes; it applies to Muslim and Jewish and Buddhist advocacy as well as to Christian. And since it limits funding to activities promoting or manifesting a particular belief not only "in" but "about" a deity or ultimate reality, it applies to agnostics and atheists as well as it does to deists and theists (as the University maintained at oral argument, and as the Court recognizes). The Guidelines, and their application to Wide Awake, thus do not skew debate by funding one position but not its competitors. As understood by their application to Wide Awake, they simply deny funding for hortatory speech that "primarily promotes or manifests" any view on the merits of religion; they deny funding for the entire subject matter of religious apologetics.

The Court, of course, reads the Guidelines differently, but while I believe the Court is wrong in construing their breadth, the important point is that even on the Court's own construction the Guidelines impose no viewpoint discrimination. In attempting to demonstrate the potentially chilling effect such funding restrictions might have on learning in our Nation's universities, the Court describes the Guidelines as "a sweeping restriction on student thought and student inquiry," disentitling a vast array of topics to funding. As the Court reads the Guidelines to exclude "any writing that is explicable as resting upon a premise which presupposes the existence of a deity or ultimate reality," as well as "those student journalistic efforts which primarily manifest or promote a belief that there is no deity and no ultimate reality," the Court concludes that the major works of writers from Descartes to Sartre would be barred from the funding forum. The Court goes so far as to suggest that the Guidelines, properly interpreted, tolerate nothing much more than essays on "making pasta or peanut butter cookies."

Now, the regulation is not so categorically broad as the Court protests. The Court reads the word "primarily" ("primarily promotes or manifests a particular belief(s) in or about a deity or an ultimate reality") right out of the Guidelines, whereas it is obviously crucial in distinguishing between works characterized by the evangelism of Wide Awake and writing that merely happens to express views that a given religion might approve, or simply descriptive writing informing a reader about the position of a given religion. But, as I said, that is not the important point. Even if the Court were indeed correct about the funding restriction's categorical breadth, the stringency of the restriction would most certainly not work any impermissible viewpoint discrimination under any prior understanding of that species of content discrimination. If a university wished to fund no speech beyond the subjects of pasta and cookie preparation, it surely would not be discriminating on the basis of someone's viewpoint, at least absent some controversial claim that pasta and cookies did not exist. The upshot would be an instructional universe without higher education, but not a universe where one viewpoint was enriched above its competitors. . . .

To put the point another way, the Court's decision equating a categorical exclusion of both sides of the religious debate with viewpoint discrimination suggests the Court has concluded that primarily religious and antireligious speech, grouped together, always provides an opposing (and not merely a related) viewpoint to any speech about any secular topic. Thus, the Court's reasoning requires a university that funds private publications about any primarily nonreligious topic also to fund publications primarily espousing adherence to or rejection of religion. But a university's decision to fund a magazine about racism, and not to fund publications aimed at urging repentance before God does not skew the debate either about racism or the desirability of religious conversion. The Court's contrary holding amounts to a significant reformulation of our viewpoint discrimination precedents and will significantly expand access to limited-access forums.

### III

Since I cannot see the future I cannot tell whether today's decision portends much more than making a shambles out of student activity fees in public colleges. Still, my apprehension is whetted by CHIEF JUSTICE BURGER's warning in *Lemon v. Kurtzman*, 403 U.S. 602, 624 (1971): "in constitutional adjudication some steps, which when taken were thought to approach 'the verge,' have become the platform for yet further steps. A certain momentum develops in constitutional theory and it can be a 'downhill thrust' easily set in motion but difficult to retard or stop."

I respectfully dissent.

---

### Notes and Questions

1. Access to funds versus facilities: How convincing is the majority's argument for extending the equal access principle to a "financial" public forum? The majority opinion rejects the University's argument and the dissent's argument that the fact that the case involves the provision of funds rather than the access to facilities is significant. What are the reasons for the Court's rejection of these arguments? Are there other arguments that might have been advanced on this issue by the University or the dissent?

2. According to Justice Kennedy, why is the danger of chilling individual thought and expression particularly worrisome in this case? Is this case more like the equal access cases discussed earlier in this chapter or more like the funding cases discussed in part 3?

3. What is the difference between the way in which the Court majority defines "viewpoint discrimination" and the way in which the dissenters define the term in this case? Which definition do you find more persuasive?

4. What is the difference between the majority opinion and the dissent on the appropriate place of what Justice Souter calls "evenhandedness" in the analysis of claims under the Establishment Clause? Which side do you believe has a better claim on Court precedent?

5. What specific factors do Justices Kennedy and O'Connor enumerate to illustrate the fact that, in their opinion, requiring the University to pay for the publications of groups such as Wide Awake Productions does not trigger an Establishment Clause violation? What is the dissent's critique of these factors, individually and corporately? Is Justice O'Connor's concurring opinion broader or narrower than the majority opinion?

6. What bedrock Establishment Clause rule does the dissent allege the majority breaks? What historical evidence does it rely on to make its case? Why does Justice Thomas fault the dissent for drawing analogies between the Virginia General Assessment and the University program at issue here? Does the Establishment Clause prohibit governmental preferences for religion over irreligion as well as governmental preferences for some religions over others, or does it only prohibit the latter, according to Justice Thomas? How does the dissent respond to this kind of claim?

7. In his concurring opinion, Justice Thomas cites a series of examples in which some government funds have been used to pay for religious activities or activities that benefit religious entities. Are there ways to distinguish these examples from this case?

8. According to Justice Thomas' concurring opinion, should the form of the government aid be a significant factor in the Establishment Clause analysis? What are some Establishment Clause limits that Justice Thomas would apply in this area?

9. Does this decision open the door wide to government funding of religious activities, or is it simply a narrow decision that is basically limited to its facts? Would it be possible, for example, for this decision to be used to validate a government grant for the reconstruction of church facilities that have been damaged by fire and flood or a government grant for a drug-rehabilitation ministry that relies on acceptance of the gospel to get people off drugs?

CHAPTER 20

# RELIGIOUS SYMBOLS ON GOVERNMENT PROPERTY

In a country where an overwhelming majority of people say they practice some religion, it is not surprising that religion often is a prominent feature in public life. It is a common and noncontroversial practice, for example, for churches to place nativity scenes in their front lawns during the Christmas season. But what if a church wants to place its nativity scene in a city park? Or, what if the government places a nativity scene in the lobby of a government courthouse?

When the government interacts with religion in these and other ways, it must strike a careful balance. As we saw in the previous chapter, the U.S. Supreme Court has said: "[T]here is a crucial difference between government speech endorsing religion, which the Establishment Clause [of the First Amendment] forbids, and private speech endorsing religion, which the Free Speech and Free Exercise Clauses [of the First Amendment] protect."[1] Similarly, the Court has held that government action must have a predominantly nonreligious purpose and primary effect. Thus, under the First Amendment, the government must not promote or endorse religion itself, but it must protect the rights of citizens and religious groups to do so.

For several reasons, however, these matters can be more complex than these principles would suggest. First, the Court has held that, not only does the Establishment Clause restrict the government's own expression, it also prohibits the government from supporting or sponsoring religious expression by nongovernmental actors. *The County of Allegheny v. ACLU* case provides an illustration of the application of this rule. Second, under certain circumstances, the Court has upheld even particular governmental expressions and actions that are religious or that have religious elements. The case of *Lynch v. Donnelly* is one example of this kind of reasoning and result. Third, as the cases clearly demonstrate, the Court is deeply divided over which legal tests and principles should govern inquiries into these matters.

This chapter focuses on cases involving displays of the Ten Commandments, nativity scenes, menorahs and other religious symbols. All except one of the displays (the display in the *Lynch v. Donnelly* case) were erected on government property. The cases involve some displays that were erected by the government and some that were erected by nongovernmental groups. As you read, note how the justices struggle to develop legal tests that are sensitive to the facts of each case and yet also broad and clear enough to enable government officials to predict in most cases which displays are constitutionally permissible and which ones are not.

## LYNCH v. DONNELLY
465 U.S. 668 (1984)

⊞ CHIEF JUSTICE BURGER delivered the opinion of the Court.

We granted certiorari to decide whether the Establishment Clause of the First Amendment prohibits a municipality from including a crèche, or Nativity scene, in its annual Christmas display.

### I

Each year, in cooperation with the downtown retail merchants' association, the city of Pawtucket, R. I., erects a Christmas display as part of its observance of the Christmas holiday season. The display is situated in a park owned by a nonprofit organization and located in the heart of the shopping district. The display is essentially like those to be found in hundreds of towns or cities across the Nation—often on public grounds—during the Christmas season. The Pawtucket display comprises many of the figures and decorations traditionally associated with Christmas, including, among other things, a Santa Claus house, reindeer pulling Santa's sleigh, candy-striped poles, a Christmas tree, carolers, cutout figures representing such characters as a clown, an elephant, and a teddy bear, hundreds of colored lights, a large banner that reads "SEASONS GREETINGS," and the crèche at issue here. All components of this display are owned by the city.

The crèche, which has been included in the display for 40 or more years, consists of the traditional figures, including the Infant Jesus, Mary and Joseph, angels, shepherds, kings, and animals, all ranging in height from 5" to 5'. In 1973, when the present crèche was acquired, it cost the city $1,365; it now is valued at $200. The erection and dismantling of the crèche costs the city about $20 per year; nominal expenses are incurred in lighting the crèche. No money has been expended on its maintenance for the past 10 years.

Respondents, Pawtucket residents and individual members of the Rhode Island affiliate of the American Civil Liberties Union, and the affiliate itself, brought this action in the United States District Court for Rhode Island, challenging the city's inclusion of the crèche in the annual display. . . .

### II
#### A . . .
#### C

There is an unbroken history of official acknowledgment by all three branches of government of the role of religion in American life from at least 1789. Seldom in our opinions was this more affirmatively expressed than in JUSTICE DOUGLAS' opinion for the Court validating a program allowing release of public school students from classes to attend off-campus religious exercises. Rejecting a claim that the program violated the Establishment Clause, the Court asserted pointedly: "We are a religious people whose institutions presuppose a Supreme Being." *Zorach v. Clauson*, 343 U.S. 306, 313.

Our history is replete with official references to the value and invocation of Divine guidance in deliberations and pronouncements of the Founding Fathers and contemporary leaders. Beginning in the early colonial period long before Independence, a day of Thanksgiving was celebrated as a religious holiday to give thanks for the bounties of Nature as gifts from God. President Washington and his successors proclaimed Thanksgiving, with all its religious overtones, a day of national celebration and Congress made it a National Holiday more than a century ago. That holiday has not lost its theme of expressing thanks for Divine aid any more than has Christmas lost its religious significance.

Executive Orders and other official announcements of Presidents and of the Congress have proclaimed both Christmas and Thanksgiving National Holidays in religious terms. And, by Acts of Congress, it has long been the practice that federal employees are released from duties on these National Holidays, while being paid from the same public revenues that provide the compensation of the Chaplains of the Senate and the House and the military services. Thus, it is clear that Government has long recognized—indeed it has subsidized—holidays with religious significance.

Other examples of reference to our religious heritage are found in the statutorily prescribed national motto "In God We Trust," which Congress and the President mandated for our currency, and in the language "One nation under God," as part of the Pledge of Allegiance to the American flag. That pledge is recited by many thousands of public school children—and adults—every year.

Art galleries supported by public revenues display religious paintings of the 15th and 16th centuries, predominantly inspired by one religious faith. The National Gallery in Washington, maintained with Government support, for example, has long exhibited masterpieces with religious messages, notably the Last Supper, and paintings depicting the Birth of Christ, the Crucifixion, and the Resurrection, among many others with explicit Christian themes and messages. The very chamber in which oral arguments on this case were heard is decorated with a notable and permanent—not seasonal—symbol of religion: Moses with the Ten Commandments. Congress has long provided chapels in the Capitol for religious worship and meditation.

There are countless other illustrations of the Government's acknowledgment of our religious heritage and governmental sponsorship of graphic manifestations of that heritage. Congress has directed the President to proclaim a National Day of Prayer each year "on which [day] the people of the United States may turn to God in prayer and meditation at churches, in groups, and as individuals." Our Presidents have repeatedly issued such Proclamations. Presidential Proclamations and messages have also [been] issued to commemorate Jewish Heritage Week. One cannot look at even this brief resume without finding that our history is pervaded by expressions of religious beliefs such as are found in *Zorach*. Equally pervasive is the evidence of accommodation of all faiths and all forms of religious expression, and hostility toward none. Through this accommodation, as Justice Douglas observed, governmental action has "[followed] the best of our traditions" and "[respected] the religious nature of our people." 343 U.S., 314.

### III

This history may help explain why the Court consistently has declined to take a rigid, absolutist view of the Establishment Clause. We have refused "to construe the Religion Clauses with a literalness that would undermine the ultimate constitutional objective *as illuminated by history*." In our modern, complex society, whose traditions and constitutional underpinnings rest on and encourage diversity and pluralism in all areas, an absolutist approach in applying the Establishment Clause is simplistic and has been uniformly rejected by the Court.

Rather than mechanically invalidating all governmental conduct or statutes that confer benefits or give special recognition to religion in general or to one faith—as an absolutist approach would dictate—the Court has scrutinized challenged legislation or official conduct to determine whether, in reality, it establishes a religion or religious faith, or tends to do so. Joseph Story wrote a century and a half ago: "The real object of the [First] Amendment was . . . to prevent any national ecclesiastical establishment, which should give to an hierarchy the exclusive patronage of the national government."

In each case, the inquiry calls for line-drawing; no fixed, *per se* rule can be framed. . . .

In the line-drawing process we have often found it useful to inquire whether the challenged law or conduct has a secular purpose, whether its principal or primary effect is to advance or inhibit religion, and whether it creates an excessive entanglement of government with religion. *Lemon.* But, we have repeatedly emphasized our unwillingness to be confined to any single test or criterion in this sensitive area. . . .

In this case, the focus of our inquiry must be on the crèche in the context of the Christmas season. . . . Focus exclusively on the religious component of any activity would inevitably lead to its invalidation under the Establishment Clause.

The Court has invalidated legislation or governmental action on the ground that a secular purpose was lacking, but only when it has concluded there was no question that the statute or activity was motivated wholly by religious considerations. . . .

When viewed in the proper context of the Christmas Holiday season, it is apparent that, on this record, there is insufficient evidence to establish that the inclusion of the crèche is a purposeful or surreptitious effort to express some kind of subtle governmental advocacy of a particular religious message. In a pluralistic society a variety of motives and purposes are implicated. The city, like the Congresses and Presidents, however, has principally taken note of a significant historical religious event long celebrated in the Western World. The crèche in the display depicts the historical origins of this traditional event long recognized as a National Holiday

The narrow question is whether there is a secular purpose for Pawtucket's display of the crèche. The display is sponsored by the city to celebrate the Holiday and to depict the origins of that Holiday. These are legitimate secular purposes.[6] . . .

---

[6] The city contends that the purposes of the display are "exclusively secular." We hold only that Pawtucket has a secular purpose for its display, which is all that *Lemon v. Kurtzman*, 403 U.S. 602 (1971), requires. Were the test that the government must have "exclusively secular" objectives, much of the conduct and legislation this Court has approved in the past would have been invalidated.

We are unable to discern a greater aid to religion deriving from inclusion of the crèche than from these benefits and endorsements previously held not violative of the Establishment Clause. What was said about the legislative prayers in *Marsh* and implied about the Sunday Closing Laws in *McGowan* is true of the city's inclusion of the crèche: its "reason or effect merely happens to coincide or harmonize with the tenets of some . . . religions." *McGowan v. Maryland*, 366 U.S. 420, 442. . . .

The dissent asserts some observers may perceive that the city has aligned itself with the Christian faith by including a Christian symbol in its display and that this serves to advance religion. We can assume, *arguendo*, that the display advances religion in a sense; but our precedents plainly contemplate that on occasion some advancement of religion will result from governmental action. The Court has made it abundantly clear, however, that "not every law that confers an 'indirect,' 'remote,' or 'incidental' benefit upon [religion] is, for that reason alone, constitutionally invalid." *Committee for Public Education & Religious Liberty v. Nyquist*, 413 U.S. 756, 771. Here, whatever benefit there is to one faith or religion or to all religions, is indirect, remote, and incidental; display of the crèche is no more an advancement or endorsement of religion than the Congressional and Executive recognition of the origins of the Holiday itself as "Christ's Mass," or the exhibition of literally hundreds of religious paintings in governmentally supported museums. . . .

In this case, there is no reason to disturb the District Court's finding on the absence of administrative entanglement. There is no evidence of contact with church authorities concerning the content or design of the exhibit prior to or since Pawtucket's purchase of the crèche. No expenditures for maintenance of the crèche have been necessary; and since the city owns the crèche, now valued at $200, the tangible material it contributes is *de minimis*. In many respects the display requires far less ongoing, day-to-day interaction between church and state than religious paintings in public galleries. There is nothing here, of course, like the "comprehensive, discriminating, and continuing state surveillance" or the "enduring entanglement" present in *Lemon*.

The Court of Appeals correctly observed that this Court has not held that political divisiveness alone can serve to invalidate otherwise permissible conduct. And we decline to so hold today. . . . In any event, apart from this litigation there is no evidence of political friction or divisiveness over the crèche in the 40-year history of Pawtucket's Christmas celebration. . . .

We are satisfied that the city has a secular purpose for including the crèche, that the city has not impermissibly advanced religion, and that including the crèche does not create excessive entanglement between religion and government.

## IV . . .

Of course the crèche is identified with one religious faith but no more so than the examples we have set out from prior cases in which we found no conflict with the Establishment Clause. It would be ironic, however, if the inclusion of a single symbol of a particular historic religious event, as part of a celebration acknowledged in the Western World for 20 centuries, and in this country by the people, by the Executive Branch, by the Congress, and the courts for 2 centuries, would so "taint" the city's exhibit as to render it violative of the Establishment Clause. To forbid the use of this one passive symbol—the crèche—at the very time people are taking note of the season with Christmas hymns and carols in public schools and other public places, and while the

Congress and legislatures open sessions with prayers by paid chaplains, would be a stilted overreaction contrary to our history and to our holdings. If the presence of the crèche in this display violates the Establishment Clause, a host of other forms of taking official note of Christmas, and of our religious heritage, are equally offensive to the Constitution.

The Court has acknowledged that the "fears and political problems" that gave rise to the Religion Clauses in the 18th century are of far less concern today. We are unable to perceive the Archbishop of Canterbury, the Bishop of Rome, or other powerful religious leaders behind every public acknowledgment of the religious heritage long officially recognized by the three constitutional branches of government. Any notion that these symbols pose a real danger of establishment of a state church is farfetched indeed.

## V

That this Court has been alert to the constitutionally expressed opposition to the establishment of religion is shown in numerous holdings striking down statutes or programs as violative of the Establishment Clause. . . . Taken together these cases abundantly demonstrate the Court's concern to protect the genuine objectives of the Establishment Clause. It is far too late in the day to impose a crabbed reading of the Clause on the country.

## VI

We hold that, notwithstanding the religious significance of the crèche, the city of Pawtucket has not violated the Establishment Clause of the First Amendment. Accordingly, the judgment of the Court of Appeals is reversed.

*It is so ordered.*

JUSTICE O'CONNOR, concurring.

I concur in the opinion of the Court. I write separately to suggest a clarification of our Establishment Clause doctrine. The suggested approach leads to the same result in this case as that taken by the Court, and the Court's opinion, as I read it, is consistent with my analysis.

## I

The Establishment Clause prohibits government from making adherence to a religion relevant in any way to a person's standing in the political community. Government can run afoul of that prohibition in two principal ways. One is excessive entanglement with religious institutions, which may interfere with the independence of the institutions, give the institutions access to government or governmental powers not fully shared by nonadherents of the religion, and foster the creation of political constituencies defined along religious lines. The second and more direct infringement is government endorsement or disapproval of religion. Endorsement sends a message to nonadherents that they are outsiders, not full members of the political community, and an accompanying message to adherents that they are insiders, favored members of the political community. Disapproval sends the opposite message

Our prior cases have used the three-part test articulated in *Lemon v. Kurtzman* as a guide to detecting these two forms of unconstitutional government action. It has never been entirely clear, however, how the three parts of the test relate to the principles enshrined in the Establishment Clause. Focusing on institutional entanglement and on endorsement or disapproval of religion clarifies the *Lemon* test as an analytical device.

## II . . .

In my view, political divisiveness along religious lines should not be an independent test of constitutionality.

Although several of our cases have discussed political divisiveness under the entanglement prong of *Lemon*, we have never relied on divisiveness as an independent ground for holding a government practice unconstitutional. Guessing the potential for political divisiveness inherent in a government practice is simply too speculative an enterprise, in part because the existence of the litigation, as this case illustrates, itself may affect the political response to the government practice. Political divisiveness is admittedly an evil addressed by the Establishment Clause. Its existence may be evidence that institutional entanglement is excessive or that a government practice is perceived as an endorsement of religion. But the constitutional inquiry should focus ultimately on the character of the government activity that might cause such divisiveness, not on the divisiveness itself. The entanglement prong of the *Lemon* test is properly limited to institutional entanglement.

## III

The central issue in this case is whether Pawtucket has endorsed Christianity by its display of the crèche. To answer that question, we must examine both what Pawtucket intended to communicate in displaying the crèche and what message the city's display actually conveyed. The purpose and effect prongs of the *Lemon* test represent these two aspects of the meaning of the city's action. . . .

The purpose prong of the *Lemon* test asks whether government's actual purpose is to endorse or disapprove of religion. The effect prong asks whether, irrespective of government's actual purpose, the practice under review in fact conveys a message of endorsement or disapproval. An affirmative answer to either question should render the challenged practice invalid.

## A

The purpose prong of the *Lemon* test requires that a government activity have a secular purpose. That requirement is not satisfied, however, by the mere existence of some secular purpose, however dominated by religious purposes. In *Stone v. Graham*, for example, the Court held that posting copies of the Ten Commandments in schools violated the purpose prong of the *Lemon* test, yet the State plainly had some secular objectives, such as instilling most of the values of the Ten Commandments and illustrating their connection to our legal system. The proper inquiry under the purpose prong of *Lemon*, I submit, is whether the government intends to convey a message of endorsement or disapproval of religion.

Applying that formulation to this case, I would find that Pawtucket did not intend to convey any message of endorsement of Christianity or disapproval of non-Christian religions. The evident purpose of including the crèche in the larger display was not promotion of the religious content of the crèche but celebration of the public holiday through its traditional symbols. Celebration of public holidays, which have cultural significance even if they also have religious aspects, is a legitimate secular purpose. . . .

B

Focusing on the evil of government endorsement or disapproval of religion makes clear that the effect prong of the *Lemon* test is properly interpreted not to require invalidation of a government practice merely because it in fact causes, even as a primary effect, advancement or inhibition of religion. The laws upheld in *Walz v. Tax Comm'n*, (tax exemption for religious, educational, and charitable organizations), in *McGowan v. Maryland*, (mandatory Sunday closing law), and in *Zorach v. Clauson*, (released time from school for off-campus religious instruction), had such effects, but they did not violate the Establishment Clause. What is crucial is that a government practice not have the effect of communicating a message of government endorsement or disapproval of religion. It is only practices having that effect, whether intentionally or unintentionally, that make religion relevant, in reality or public perception, to status in the political community.

Pawtucket's display of its crèche, I believe, does not communicate a message that the government intends to endorse the Christian beliefs represented by the crèche. Although the religious and indeed sectarian significance of the crèche, as the District Court found, is not neutralized by the setting, the overall holiday setting changes what viewers may fairly understand to be the purpose of the display—as a typical museum setting, though not neutralizing the religious content of a religious painting, negates any message of endorsement of that content. The display celebrates a public holiday, and no one contends that declaration of that holiday is understood to be an endorsement of religion. The holiday itself has very strong secular components and traditions. Government celebration of the holiday, which is extremely common, generally is not understood to endorse the religious content of the holiday, just as government celebration of Thanksgiving is not so understood. The crèche is a traditional symbol of the holiday that is very commonly displayed along with purely secular symbols, as it was in Pawtucket.

These features combine to make the government's display of the crèche in this particular physical setting no more an endorsement of religion than such governmental "acknowledgments" of religion as legislative prayers of the type approved in *Marsh v. Chambers*, government declaration of Thanksgiving as a public holiday, printing of "In God We Trust" on coins, and opening court sessions with "God save the United States and this honorable court." Those government acknowledgments of religion serve, in the only ways reasonably possible in our culture, the legitimate secular purposes of solemnizing public occasions, expressing confidence in the future, and encouraging the recognition of what is worthy of appreciation in society. For that reason, and because of their history and ubiquity, those practices are not understood as conveying government approval of particular religious beliefs. The display of the crèche likewise serves a secular celebration of a public holiday with traditional symbols. It cannot fairly be understood to convey a message of government endorsement of religion. It is significant in this regard that the crèche display apparently caused no political divisiveness prior to the filing of this lawsuit, although Pawtucket had incorporated the crèche in its annual Christmas display for some years. For these reasons, I conclude that Pawtucket's display of the crèche does not have the effect of communicating endorsement of Christianity. . . .

IV

Every government practice must be judged in its unique circumstances to determine whether it constitutes an endorsement or disapproval of religion. In making that determination, courts must keep in mind both the fundamental place held by the Establishment Clause in our constitutional scheme and the myriad, subtle ways in which Establishment Clause values can be eroded. Government practices that purport to celebrate or acknowledge events with religious significance must be subjected to careful judicial scrutiny.

The city of Pawtucket is alleged to have violated the Establishment Clause by endorsing the Christian beliefs represented by the crèche included in its Christmas display. Giving the challenged practice the careful scrutiny it deserves, I cannot say that the particular crèche display at issue in this case was intended to endorse or had the effect of endorsing Christianity. I agree with the Court that the judgment below must be reversed.

JUSTICE BRENNAN, with whom JUSTICE MARSHALL, JUSTICE BLACK-MUN, and JUSTICE STEVENS join, dissenting. . . .

Despite the narrow contours of the Court's opinion, our precedents in my view compel the holding that Pawtucket's inclusion of a life-sized display depicting the biblical description of the birth of Christ as part of its annual Christmas celebration is unconstitutional. Nothing in the history of such practices or the setting in which the city's crèche is presented obscures or diminishes the plain fact that Pawtucket's action amounts to an impermissible governmental endorsement of a particular faith.

I . . .
A . . .

Applying the three-part [Lemon] test to Pawtucket's crèche, I am persuaded that the city's inclusion of the crèche in its Christmas display simply does not reflect a "clearly secular . . . purpose." Nyquist, 773. Unlike the typical case in which the record reveals some contemporaneous expression of a clear purpose to advance religion, see, e.g., Epperson v. Arkansas, 107-109; Engel v. Vitale, 423, or, conversely, a clear secular purpose, see, e.g., Lemon v. Kurtzman, 613; Wolman v. Walter, 433 U.S. 229, 236, here we have no explicit statement of purpose by Pawtucket's municipal government accompanying its decision to purchase, display, and maintain the crèche. Governmental purpose may nevertheless be inferred. . . .

[T]wo compelling aspects of this case indicate that our generally prudent "reluctance to attribute unconstitutional motives" to a governmental body, Mueller v. Allen, 394, should be overcome. First, as was true in Larkin v. Grendel's Den, Inc., 123-124, all of Pawtucket's "valid secular objectives can be readily accomplished by other means." Plainly, the city's interest in celebrating the holiday and in promoting both retail sales and goodwill are fully served by the elaborate display of Santa Claus, reindeer, and wishing wells that are already a part of Pawtucket's annual Christmas display. More importantly, the nativity scene, unlike every other element of the Hodgson Park display, reflects a sectarian exclusivity that the avowed purposes of celebrating the holiday season and promoting retail commerce simply do not encompass. To be found constitutional, Pawtucket's seasonal celebration must at least be nondenominational and not serve to promote religion. The inclusion of a distinctively religious element like the crèche, however, demonstrates that a narrower sectarian purpose lay behind the decision to include a nativity scene. That the crèche retained this religious character for the people and municipal government of Pawtucket is suggested by the Mayor's testimony at trial in which he stated that for him, as well as others in the city, the effort to eliminate the nativity scene from Pawtucket's Christmas celebration "is a step towards establishing another religion, non-religion that it may be." Plainly, the city and its leaders understood that the inclusion of the crèche in its display would serve the wholly religious purpose of "[keeping] 'Christ in Christmas.'" From this record, therefore, it is impossible to say with the kind of confidence that was possible in *McGowan v. Maryland*, that a wholly secular goal predominates.

The "primary effect" of including a nativity scene in the city's display is, as the District Court found, to place the government's imprimatur of approval on the particular religious beliefs exemplified by the crèche. Those who believe in the message of the nativity receive the unique and exclusive benefit of public recognition and approval of their views. For many, the city's decision to include the crèche as part of its extensive and costly efforts to celebrate Christmas can only mean that the prestige of the government has been conferred on the beliefs associated with the crèche, thereby providing "a significant symbolic benefit to religion . . . ." *Larkin v. Grendel's Den, Inc.*, 125-126. The effect on minority religious groups, as well as on those who may reject all religion, is to convey the message that their views are not similarly worthy of public recognition nor entitled to public support. It was precisely this sort of religious chauvinism that the Establishment Clause was intended forever to prohibit. . . .

Finally, it is evident that Pawtucket's inclusion of a crèche as part of its annual Christmas display does pose a significant threat of fostering "excessive entanglement." As the Court notes, the District Court found no administrative entanglement in this case, primarily because the city had been able to administer the annual display without extensive consultation with religious officials. Of course, there is no reason to disturb that finding, but it is worth noting that after today's decision, administrative entanglements may well develop. Jews and other non-Christian groups, prompted perhaps by the Mayor's remark that he will include a Menorah in future displays, can be expected to press government for inclusion of their symbols, and faced with such requests, government will have to become involved in accommodating the various demands. More importantly, although no political divisiveness was apparent in Pawtucket prior to the filing of respondents' lawsuit, that act, as the District Court found, unleashed powerful emotional reactions which divided the city along religious lines. 525 F. Supp., 1180. . . . In many communities, non-Christian groups can be expected to combat practices similar to Pawtucket's; this will be so especially in areas where there are substantial non-Christian minorities.

In sum, considering the District Court's careful findings of fact under the three-part analysis called for by our prior cases, I have no difficulty concluding that Pawtucket's display of the crèche is unconstitutional.

B

The Court advances two principal arguments to support its conclusion that the Pawtucket crèche satisfies the *Lemon* test. Neither is persuasive. . . .

[I]t blinks reality to claim, as the Court does, that by including such a distinctively religious object as the crèche in its Christmas display, Pawtucket has done no more than make use of a "traditional" symbol of the holiday, and has thereby purged the crèche of its religious content and conferred only an "incidental and indirect" benefit on religion.

The Court's struggle to ignore the clear religious effect of the crèche seems to me misguided for several reasons. In the first place, the city has positioned the crèche in a central and highly visible location within the Hodgson Park display. . . .

Moreover, the city has done nothing to disclaim government approval of the religious significance of the crèche, to suggest that the crèche represents only one religious symbol among many others that might be included in a seasonal display truly aimed at providing a wide catalog of ethnic and religious celebrations, or to disassociate itself from the religious content of the crèche. . . .

Third, we have consistently acknowledged that an otherwise secular setting alone does not suffice to justify a governmental practice that has the effect of aiding religion. In *Hunt v. McNair*, for instance, we observed that "[aid] normally may be thought to have a primary effect of advancing religion . . . when it [supports] a specifically religious activity in an otherwise substantially secular setting." The demonstrably secular context of public education, therefore, did not save the challenged practice of school prayer in *Engel* or in *Schempp*. Similarly, in *Tilton v. Richardson*, despite the generally secular thrust of the financing legislation under review, the Court unanimously struck down that aspect of the program which permitted church-related institutions eventually to assume total control over the use of buildings constructed with federal aid.[12]

Finally, and most importantly, even in the context of Pawtucket's seasonal celebration, the crèche retains a specifically Christian religious meaning. I refuse to accept the notion implicit in today's decision that non-Christians would find that the religious content of the crèche is eliminated by the fact that it appears as part of the city's otherwise secular celebration of the Christmas holiday. The nativity scene is clearly distinct in its purpose and effect from the rest of the Hodgson Park display for the simple reason that it is the only one rooted in a biblical account of Christ's birth. It is the chief symbol of the characteristically Christian belief that a divine Savior was brought into the world and that the purpose of this miraculous birth was to illuminate a path toward salvation and redemption. For Christians, that path is exclusive, precious, and holy. But for those who do not share these beliefs, the symbolic reenactment of the birth of a divine being who has been miraculously incarnated as a man stands as a dramatic reminder of their differences with Christian faith. . . . To be so excluded on religious grounds by one's elected government is an insult and an injury that, until today, could not be countenanced by the Establishment Clause. . . .

The Court apparently believes that once it finds that the designation of Christmas as a public holiday is constitutionally acceptable, it is then free to conclude that virtually every form of governmental association with the celebration of the holiday is also constitutional. The vice of this dangerously

---

[12] Indeed, in the aid-to-sectarian-schools cases, the state financing schemes under review almost always require us to focus on a specific element that may violate the Establishment Clause, even though it is a part of a complex and otherwise secular statutory framework. See, e.g., *Meek v. Pittenger*, 421 U.S. 349 (1975); *Wolman v. Walter*, 433 U.S. 229 (1977). See also *Committee for Public Education & Religious Liberty v. Regan*, 444 U.S. 646, 662 (1980) (BLACKMUN, J., dissenting).

superficial argument is that it overlooks the fact that the Christmas holiday in our national culture contains both secular and sectarian elements. To say that government may recognize the holiday's traditional, secular elements of gift-giving, public festivities, and community spirit, does not mean that government may indiscriminately embrace the distinctively sectarian aspects of the holiday. Indeed, in its eagerness to approve the crèche, the Court has advanced a rationale so simplistic that it would appear to allow the Mayor of Pawtucket to participate in the celebration of a Christmas Mass, since this would be just another unobjectionable way for the city to "celebrate the holiday." As is demonstrated below, the Court's logic is fundamentally flawed both because it obscures the reason why public designation of Christmas Day as a holiday is constitutionally acceptable, and blurs the distinction between the secular aspects of Christmas and its distinctively religious character, as exemplified by the crèche.

When government decides to recognize Christmas Day as a public holiday, it does no more than accommodate the calendar of public activities to the plain fact that many Americans will expect on that day to spend time visiting with their families, attending religious services, and perhaps enjoying some respite from preholiday activities. The Free Exercise Clause, of course, does not necessarily compel the government to provide this accommodation, but neither is the Establishment Clause offended by such a step. Because it is clear that the celebration of Christmas has both secular and sectarian elements, it may well be that by taking note of the holiday, the government is simply seeking to serve the same kinds of wholly secular goals—for instance, promoting goodwill and a common day of rest—that were found to justify Sunday Closing Laws in *McGowan v. Maryland*. If public officials go further and participate in the *secular* celebration of Christmas—by, for example, decorating public places with such secular images as wreaths, garlands, or Santa Claus figures—they move closer to the limits of their constitutional power but nevertheless remain within the boundaries set by the Establishment Clause. But when those officials participate in or appear to endorse the distinctively religious elements of this otherwise secular event, they encroach upon First Amendment freedoms. For it is at that point that the government brings to the forefront the theological content of the holiday, and places the prestige, power, and financial support of a civil authority in the service of a particular faith.

The inclusion of a crèche in Pawtucket's otherwise secular celebration of Christmas clearly violates these principles. Unlike such secular figures as Santa Claus, reindeer, and carolers, a nativity scene represents far more than a mere "traditional" symbol of Christmas. The essence of the crèche's symbolic purpose and effect is to prompt the observer to experience a sense of simple awe and wonder appropriate to the contemplation of one of the central elements of Christian dogma—that God sent His Son into the world to be a Messiah. Contrary to the Court's suggestion, the crèche is far from a mere representation of a "particular historic religious event." It is, instead, best understood as a mystical re-creation of an event that lies at the heart of Christian faith. . . .

It would be another matter if the crèche were displayed in a museum setting, in the company of other religiously inspired artifacts, as an example, among many, of the symbolic representation of religious myths. In that setting, we would have objective guarantees that the crèche could not suggest that a particular faith had been singled out for public favor and recognition. The effect of Pawtucket's crèche, however, is not confined by any of these limiting attributes. In the absence of any other religious symbols or of any neutral disclaimer, the inescapable effect of the crèche will be to remind the average observer of the religious roots of the celebration he is witnessing and to call to mind the scriptural message that the nativity symbolizes. The fact that Pawtucket has gone to the trouble of making such an elaborate public celebration and of including a crèche in that otherwise secular setting inevitably serves to reinforce the sense that the city means to express solidarity with the Christian message of the crèche and to dismiss other faiths as unworthy of similar attention and support.

## II

Although the Court's relaxed application of the *Lemon* test to Pawtucket's crèche is regrettable, it is at least understandable and properly limited to the particular facts of this case. The Court's opinion, however, also sounds a broader and more troubling theme. . . .

Intuition tells us that some official "acknowledgment" is inevitable in a religious society if government is not to adopt a stilted indifference to the religious life of the people. It is equally true, however, that if government is to remain scrupulously neutral in matters of religious conscience, as our Constitution requires, then it must avoid those overly broad acknowledgments of religious practices that may imply governmental favoritism toward one set of religious beliefs. This does not mean, of course, that public officials may not take account, when necessary, of the separate existence and significance of the religious institutions and practices in the society they govern. Should government choose to incorporate some arguably religious element into its public ceremonies, that acknowledgment must be impartial; it must not tend to promote one faith or handicap another; and it should not sponsor religion generally over nonreligion. . . .

[W]e have noted that government cannot be completely prohibited from recognizing in its public actions the religious beliefs and practices of the American people as an aspect of our national history and culture. See *Engel v. Vitale*, 435, n. 21; *Schempp*, 300-304 (BRENNAN, J., concurring). While I remain uncertain about these questions, I would suggest that such practices as the designation of "In God We Trust" as our national motto, or the references to God contained in the Pledge of Allegiance to the flag can best be understood, in Dean Rostow's apt phrase, as a form of "ceremonial deism," protected from Establishment Clause scrutiny chiefly because they have lost through rote repetition any significant religious content. See *Marsh v. Chambers*, 463 U.S., 818 (BRENNAN, J., dissenting). Moreover, these references are uniquely suited to serve such wholly secular purposes as solemnizing public occasions, or inspiring commitment to meet some national challenge in a manner that simply could not be fully served in our culture if government were limited to purely nonreligious phrases. The practices by which the government has long acknowledged religion are therefore probably necessary to serve certain secular functions, and that necessity, coupled with their long history, gives those practices an essentially secular meaning. . . .

[T]he crèche, because of its unique association with Christianity, is clearly more sectarian than those references to God that we accept in ceremonial phrases or in other contexts that assure neutrality. The religious works on display at the National Gallery, Presidential references to God during an Inaugural Address, or the national motto present no risk of establishing religion. To be sure, our understanding of these expressions may begin in contemplation of some religious element, but it does not end there. Their message is dominantly secular. In contrast, the message of the crèche begins and ends with reverence for a particular image of the divine.

By insisting that such a distinctively sectarian message is merely an unobjectionable part of our "religious heritage," the Court takes a long step backwards to the days when JUSTICE BREWER could arrogantly declare for the Court that "this is a Christian nation." *Church of Holy Trinity v. United States*, 143 U.S. 457, 471 (1892). Those days, I had thought, were forever put behind us by the Court's decision in *Engel v. Vitale*, in which we rejected a similar argument advanced by the State of New York that its Regent's Prayer was simply an acceptable part of our "spiritual heritage." 370 U.S., 425.

## III . . .

The intent of the Framers with respect to the public display of nativity scenes is virtually impossible to discern primarily because the widespread celebration of Christmas did not emerge in its present form until well into the 19th century. Carrying a well-defined Puritan hostility to the celebration of Christ's birth with them to the New World, the founders of the Massachusetts Bay Colony pursued a vigilant policy of opposition to any public celebration of the holiday. . . .

The historical evidence with respect to public financing and support for governmental displays of nativity scenes is even more difficult to gauge. What is known suggests that German immigrants who settled in Pennsylvania early in the 18th century, presumably drawing upon European traditions, were probably the first to introduce nativity scenes to the American celebration of Christmas. It also appears likely that this practice expanded as more Roman Catholic immigrants settled during the 19th century. From these modest beginnings, the familiar crèche scene developed and gained wider recognition by the late 19th century. It is simply impossible to tell, however, whether the practice ever gained widespread acceptance, much less official endorsement, until the 20th century.

In sum, there is no evidence whatsoever that the Framers would have expressly approved a federal celebration of the Christmas holiday including public displays of a nativity scene; accordingly, the Court's repeated invocation of the decision in *Marsh*, is not only baffling, it is utterly irrelevant. Nor is there any suggestion that publicly financed and supported displays of Christmas crèches are supported by a record of widespread, undeviating acceptance that extends throughout our history. Therefore, our prior decisions which relied upon concrete, specific historical evidence to support a particular practice simply have no bearing on the question presented in this case. Contrary to today's careless decision, those prior cases have all recognized that the "illumination" provided by history must always be focused on the particular practice at issue in a given case. Without that guiding principle and the intellectual discipline it imposes, the Court is at sea, free to select random elements of America's varied history solely to suit the views of five Members of this Court.

## IV

Under our constitutional scheme, the role of safeguarding our "religious heritage" and of promoting religious beliefs is reserved as the exclusive prerogative of our Nation's churches, religious institutions, and spiritual leaders. Because the Framers of the Establishment Clause understood that "religion is too personal, too sacred, too holy to permit its 'unhallowed perversion' by civil [authorities]," *Engel v. Vitale*, 370 U.S., 432, the Clause demands that government play no role in this effort. The Court today brushes aside these concerns by insisting that Pawtucket has done nothing more than include a "traditional" symbol of Christmas in its celebration of this national holiday, thereby muting the religious content of the crèche. But the city's action should be recognized for what it is: a coercive, though perhaps small, step toward establishing the sectarian preferences of the majority at the expense of the minority, accomplished by placing public facilities and funds in support of the religious symbolism and theological tidings that the crèche conveys. As JUSTICE FRANKFURTER, writing in *McGowan v. Maryland*, observed, the Establishment Clause "[withdraws] from the sphere of legitimate legislative concern and competence a specific, but comprehensive, area of human conduct: man's belief or disbelief in the verity of some transcendental idea and man's expression in action of that belief or disbelief." 366 U.S., 465-466 (separate opinion). That the Constitution sets this realm of thought and feeling apart from the pressures and antagonisms of government is one of its supreme achievements. Regrettably, the Court today tarnishes that achievement.

I dissent. . . .

---

### NOTES AND QUESTIONS

1. Who owns the display at issue in this case? Who owns the land on which the display sits? What role do these factors play in the constitutional analysis?

2. In addition to the legislative chaplaincy involved in the *Marsh* case, what other parallels does Chief Justice Burger find for the Pawtucket display in American culture, history, and traditions? Is Burger correct that these practices help to validate the display, or can these practices be distinguished from the case at hand? Should the fact that a practice has a long tradition immunize it from constitutional scrutiny? Alternatively, should culture, history, and tradition at least factor into the constitutional analysis in some way?

3. Chief Justice Burger writes in *Lynch*:

   Rather than mechanically invalidating all governmental conduct or statutes that confer benefits or give special recognition to religion in general or to one faith—as an absolutist approach would dictate—the Court has scrutinized challenged legislation or official conduct to determine whether, in reality, it establishes a religion or religious faith, or tends to do so. . . . Joseph Story wrote a century and a half ago: "The real object of the [First] Amendment was . . . to prevent any national ecclesiastical establishment, which should give to an hierarchy the exclusive patronage of the national government." (citations omitted)

   Later in the opinion, Burger states: "Any notion that these symbols pose a real danger of establishment of a state church is farfetched indeed." Are these statements consistent or inconsistent with other Supreme Court doctrine interpreting the original aim of the Establishment Clause?

4. According to the majority opinion in *Lynch*, what is the right and wrong focus of inquiry in evaluating the constitutionality of the "holiday display"? What is Justice Brennan's response to this argument?

5. According to Chief Justice Burger, what are the legitimate secular purposes for the Pawtucket display? Under what circumstances should a Court conclude that a governmental action fails the *Lemon* purpose test, according to Burger? How does Justice O'Connor approach this issue? How does Justice Brennan's analysis on this point differ from both that of Chief Justice Burger and Justice O'Connor? Who articulates the most appropriate constitutional standard on this matter, in your view?

6. Would it be appropriate for a court to strike down a government display that includes religious elements simply because it has caused division in the community where it sits? What does Justice Burger have to say about this issue? Justice O'Connor?

7. Chief Justice Burger writes: "[D]isplay of the crèche [in this case] is no more an advancement or endorsement of religion than the Congressional and Executive recognition of the origins of the Holiday itself as 'Christ's Mass,' or the exhibition of literally hundreds of religious paintings in governmentally supported museums." He also argues: "If the presence of the crèche in this display violates the Establishment Clause, a host of other forms of taking official note of Christmas, and of our religious heritage, are equally offensive to the Constitution." Do you agree? If so, where would you draw the line on government acknowledgments of religion? What analytical standard would you apply so as to be consistent with the next case that comes along?

8. Describe Justice O'Connor's endorsement test. How does that test modify the *Lemon* test, according to O'Connor? How does Justice O'Connor suggest that a court should go about determining what a governmental body "intended" to do with its actions? Would it be possible for the government to have unconstitutional intentions and still produce a constitutional action? For example, what if the government did intend to advance Christianity with the Pawtucket display, but it justified the display without explicit reference to those intentions? In such a case, would there be a constitutional problem?

9. At the conclusion of her concurring opinion, Justice O'Connor writes: "[C]ourts must keep in mind both the fundamental place held by the Establishment Clause in our constitutional scheme and the myriad, subtle ways in which Establishment Clause values can be eroded." If you were a lower court judge attempting to decide a case involving a governmental display with religious elements, would this sentence be a help or a hindrance to your decisionmaking?

10. According to Justice Brennan's dissenting opinion, what changes must be made to Pawtucket's display to bring it into compliance with the Constitution? How do these steps reduce Establishment Clause concerns?

11. In his dissenting opinion, Justice Brennan states that religious references such as the national motto ("In God We Trust") and the references to God in the Pledge of Allegiance "are uniquely suited to serve such wholly secular purposes as solemnizing public occasions, or inspiring commitment to meet some national challenge in a manner that simply could not be fully served in

our culture if government were limited to purely nonreligious phrases." Do you agree? Where does Justice Brennan draw the line between government acknowledgments of religion and governmental advancements of religion?

12. According to Justice Brennan, did the framers of the Constitution express an opinion about issues such as the one that is contested in this case? Brennan describes the Court's decision as "careless." Why?

---

In 1989, the Court confronted another religious display case. This one involved two different displays, which the Court considered in turn. The first was a crèche that was placed by itself on the steps of the "Grand Staircase" in a courthouse in Allegheny, Pennsylvania. That display was sponsored by the Holy Name Society, a Catholic group. The second was a display outside a government building that included a menorah, a Christmas tree, and a sign, from the office of the Mayor, saluting liberty. As you will see, the Court split badly in this case, exposing some bitter divisions and emotions in the process. See if you can identify the various analytical approaches used by the majority, concurring justices, and dissenters and which approach provides the most workable standard for resolving such issues.

---

## COUNTY OF ALLEGHENY v. AMERICAN CIVIL LIBERTIES UNION
### 492 U.S. 573 (1989)

JUSTICE BLACKMUN announced the judgment of the Court and delivered the opinion of the Court with respect to Parts III-A, IV, and V, an opinion with respect to Parts I and II, in which JUSTICE STEVENS and JUSTICE O'CONNOR join, an opinion with respect to Part III-B, in which JUSTICE STEVENS joins, an opinion with respect to Part VII, in which JUSTICE O'CONNOR joins, and an opinion with respect to Part VI.

This litigation concerns the constitutionality of two recurring holiday displays located on public property in downtown Pittsburgh. The first is a crèche placed on the Grand Staircase of the Allegheny County Courthouse. The second is a Chanukah menorah placed just outside the City-County Building, next to a Christmas tree and a sign saluting liberty. The Court of Appeals for the Third Circuit ruled that each display violates the Establishment Clause of the First Amendment because each has the impermissible effect of endorsing religion. We agree that the crèche display has that unconstitutional effect but reverse the Court of Appeals' judgment regarding the menorah display.

I

A

The county courthouse is owned by Allegheny County and is its seat of government. It houses the offices of the county commissioners, controller, treasurer, sheriff, and clerk of court. . . . The "main," "most beautiful," and "most public" part of the courthouse is its Grand Staircase, set into one arch and surrounded by others, with arched windows serving as a backdrop.

Since 1981, the county has permitted the Holy Name Society, a Roman Catholic group, to display a crèche in the county courthouse during the Christmas holiday season. . . . As observed in this Nation, Christmas has a secular, as well as a religious, dimension. . . .

The crèche includes figures of the infant Jesus, Mary, Joseph, farm animals, shepherds, and wise men, all placed in or before a wooden representation of a manger, which has at its crest an angel bearing a banner that proclaims "Gloria in Excelsis Deo!"

During the 1986–1987 holiday season, the crèche was on display on the Grand Staircase from November 26 to January 9. It had a wooden fence on three sides and bore a plaque stating: "This Display Donated by the Holy Name Society." Sometime during the week of December 2, the county placed red and white poinsettia plants around the fence. The county also placed a small evergreen tree, decorated with a red bow, behind each of the two end-posts of the fence. These trees stood alongside the manger backdrop and were slightly shorter than it was. The angel thus was at the apex of the crèche display. Altogether, the crèche, the fence, the poinsettias, and the trees occupied a substantial amount of space on the Grand Staircase. No figures of Santa Claus or other decorations appeared on the Grand Staircase.

The county uses the crèche as the setting for its annual Christmas-carol program. During the 1986 season, the county invited high school choirs and other musical groups to perform during weekday lunch hours from December 3 through December 23. The county dedicated this program to world peace and to the families of prisoners-of-war and of persons missing in action in Southeast Asia.

Near the Grand Staircase is an area of the county courthouse known as the "gallery forum" used for art and other cultural exhibits. The crèche, with its fence-and-floral frame, however, was distinct and not connected with any exhibit in the gallery forum. In addition, various departments and offices within the county courthouse had their own Christmas decorations, but these also are not visible from the Grand Staircase.

### B

The City-County Building is separate and a block removed from the county courthouse and, as the name implies, is jointly owned by the city of Pittsburgh and Allegheny County. . . .

For a number of years, the city has had a large Christmas tree under the middle arch outside the Grant Street entrance. Following this practice, city employees on November 17, 1986, erected a 45-foot tree under the middle arch and decorated it with lights and ornaments. A few days later, the city placed at the foot of the tree a sign bearing the mayor's name and entitled "Salute to Liberty." Beneath the title, the sign stated: "During this holiday season, the city of Pittsburgh salutes liberty. Let these festive lights remind us that we are the keepers of the flame of liberty and our legacy of freedom."

At least since 1982, the city has expanded its Grant Street holiday display to include a symbolic representation of Chanukah, an 8-day Jewish holiday that begins on the 25th day of the Jewish lunar month of Kislev. . .

According to Jewish tradition, on the 25th of Kislev in 164 B.C.E. (before the common era [165 B.C.]), the Maccabees rededicated the Temple of Jerusalem after recapturing it from the Greeks, or, more accurately, from the Greek-influenced Seleucid Empire, in the course of a political rebellion. Chanukah is the holiday which celebrates that event. The early history of the celebration of Chanukah is unclear; it appears that the holiday's central ritual—the lighting of lamps—was well established long before a single explanation of that ritual took hold. . . .

Lighting the menorah is the primary tradition associated with Chanukah, but the holiday is marked by other traditions as well. One custom among some Jews is to give children Chanukah gelt, or money. Another is for the children to gamble their gelt using a dreidel, a top with four sides. Each of the four sides contains a Hebrew letter; together the four letters abbreviate a phrase that refers to the Chanukah miracle. . . .

[S]ome have suggested that the proximity of Christmas accounts for the social prominence of Chanukah in this country. Whatever the reason, Chanukah is observed by American Jews to an extent greater than its religious importance would indicate: in the hierarchy of Jewish holidays, Chanukah ranks fairly low in religious significance. This socially heightened status of Chanukah reflects its cultural or secular dimension.[34]

On December 22 of the 1986 holiday season, the city placed at the Grant Street entrance to the City-County Building an 18-foot Chanukah menorah of an abstract tree-and-branch design. The menorah was placed next to the city's 45-foot Christmas tree, against one of the columns that supports the arch into which the tree was set. The menorah is owned by Chabad, a Jewish group, but is stored, erected, and removed each year by the city. The tree, the sign, and the menorah were all removed on January 13. . . .

II

This litigation began on December 10, 1986, when respondents, the Greater Pittsburgh Chapter of the American Civil Liberties Union and seven local residents, filed suit against the county and the city, seeking permanently to enjoin the county from displaying the crèche in the county courthouse and the city from displaying the menorah in front of the City-County Building. Respondents claim that the displays of the crèche and the menorah each violate the Establishment Clause of the First Amendment, made applicable to state governments by the Fourteenth Amendment.[37] . . .

III
A . . .

In the course of adjudicating specific cases, this Court has come to understand the Establishment Clause to mean that government may not promote or affiliate itself with any religious doctrine or organization, may not discriminate among persons on the basis of their religious beliefs and practices, may not delegate a governmental power to a religious institution, and may not involve itself too deeply in such an institution's affairs. . . .

In *Lemon v. Kurtzman*, the Court sought to refine these principles by focusing on three "tests" for determining whether a government practice

---

[34] Additionally, menorahs—like Chanukah itself—have a secular as well as a religious dimension. The record in this litigation contains a passing reference to the fact that menorahs "are used extensively by secular Jewish organizations to represent the Jewish people."

[37] Respondents, however, do not claim that the city's Christmas tree violates the Establishment Clause and do not seek to enjoin its display. Respondents also do not claim that the county's Christmas-carol program is unconstitutional.

violates the Establishment Clause. Under the *Lemon* analysis, a statute or practice which touches upon religion, if it is to be permissible under the Establishment Clause, must have a secular purpose; it must neither advance nor inhibit religion in its principal or primary effect; and it must not foster an excessive entanglement with religion. 403 U.S., 612-613. This trilogy of tests has been applied regularly in the Court's later Establishment Clause cases.

Our subsequent decisions further have refined the definition of governmental action that unconstitutionally advances religion. In recent years, we have paid particularly close attention to whether the challenged governmental practice either has the purpose or effect of "endorsing" religion, a concern that has long had a place in our Establishment Clause jurisprudence. See *Engel v. Vitale*, 370 U.S. 421, 436 (1962). . . .

Of course, the word "endorsement" is not self-defining. Rather, it derives its meaning from other words that this Court has found useful over the years in interpreting the Establishment Clause. Thus, it has been noted that the prohibition against governmental endorsement of religion "preclude[s] government from conveying or attempting to convey a message that religion or a particular religious belief is favored or preferred.". . .

Whether the key word is "endorsement," "favoritism," or "promotion," the essential principle remains the same. The Establishment Clause, at the very least, prohibits government from appearing to take a position on questions of religious belief or from "making adherence to a religion relevant in any way to a person's standing in the political community." *Lynch v. Donnelly*, 465 U.S., 687 (O'CONNOR, J., concurring). . . .

Since *Lynch*, the Court has made clear that, when evaluating the effect of government conduct under the Establishment Clause, we must ascertain whether "the challenged governmental action is sufficiently likely to be perceived by adherents of the controlling denominations as an endorsement, and by the nonadherents as a disapproval, of their individual religious choices." *Grand Rapids*, 473 U.S., 390. Accordingly, our present task is to determine whether the display of the crèche and the menorah, in their respective "particular physical settings," has the effect of endorsing or disapproving religious beliefs.

## IV

We turn first to the county's crèche display. There is no doubt, of course, that the crèche itself is capable of communicating a religious message. Indeed, the crèche in this lawsuit uses words, as well as the picture of the Nativity scene, to make its religious meaning unmistakably clear. "Glory to God in the Highest!" says the angel in the crèche—Glory to God because of the birth of Jesus. This praise to God in Christian terms is indisputably religious—indeed sectarian—just as it is when said in the Gospel or in a church service.

Under the Court's holding in *Lynch*, the effect of a crèche display turns on its setting. Here, unlike in *Lynch*, nothing in the context of the display detracts from the crèche's religious message. The *Lynch* display comprised a series of figures and objects, each group of which had its own focal point. Santa's house and his reindeer were objects of attention separate from the crèche, and had their specific visual story to tell. Similarly, whatever a "talking" wishing well may be, it obviously was a center of attention separate from the crèche. Here, in contrast, the crèche stands alone: it is the single element of the display on the Grand Staircase.

The floral decoration surrounding the crèche cannot be viewed as somehow equivalent to the secular symbols in the overall *Lynch* display. The floral frame, like all good frames, serves only to draw one's attention to the message inside the frame. The floral decoration surrounding the crèche contributes to, rather than detracts from, the endorsement of religion conveyed by the crèche. . . .

Nor does the fact that the crèche was the setting for the county's annual Christmas-carol program diminish its religious meaning. First, the carol program in 1986 lasted only from December 3 to December 23 and occupied at most one hour a day. The effect of the crèche on those who viewed it when the choirs were not singing—the vast majority of the time—cannot be negated by the presence of the choir program. Second, because some of the carols performed at the site of the crèche were religious in nature, those carols were more likely to augment the religious quality of the scene than to secularize it.

Furthermore, the crèche sits on the Grand Staircase, the "main" and "most beautiful part" of the building that is the seat of county government. No viewer could reasonably think that it occupies this location without the support and approval of the government.[50] Thus, by permitting the "display of the crèche in this particular physical setting," *Lynch*, 465 U.S., 692 (O'Connor, J., concurring), the county sends an unmistakable message that it supports and promotes the Christian praise to God that is the crèche's religious message.

The fact that the crèche bears a sign disclosing its ownership by a Roman Catholic organization does not alter this conclusion. On the contrary, the sign simply demonstrates that the government is endorsing the religious message of that organization, rather than communicating a message of its own. But the Establishment Clause does not limit only the religious content of the government's own communications. It also prohibits the government's support and promotion of religious communications by religious organizations. See, e.g., *Texas Monthly, Inc. v. Bullock*, 489 U.S. 1 (1989) (government support of the distribution of religious messages by religious organizations violates the Establishment Clause). Indeed, the very concept of "endorsement" conveys the sense of promoting someone else's message. Thus, by prohibiting government endorsement of religion, the Establishment Clause prohibits precisely what occurred here: the government's lending its support to the communication of a religious organization's religious message.

Finally, the county argues that it is sufficient to validate the display of the crèche on the Grand Staircase that the display celebrates Christmas, and Christmas is a national holiday. This argument obviously proves too much. It would allow the celebration of the Eucharist inside a courthouse on Christmas

---

[50] The Grand Staircase does not appear to be the kind of location in which all were free to place their displays for weeks at a time, so that the presence of the crèche in that location for over six weeks would then not serve to associate the government with the crèche. Even if the Grand Staircase occasionally was used for displays other than the crèche (for example, a display of flags commemorating the 25th anniversary of Israel's independence), it remains true that any display located there fairly may be understood to express views that receive the support and endorsement of the government. In any event, the county's own press releases made clear to the public that the county associated itself with the crèche. Moreover, the county created a visual link between itself and the crèche: it placed next to official county signs two small evergreens identical to those in the crèche display. In this respect, the crèche here does not raise the kind of "public forum" issue, presented by the crèche in *McCreary v. Stone*, 739 F. 2d 716 (CA2 1984), aff'd by an equally divided Court sub nom. *Board of Trustees of Scarsdale v. McCreary*, 471 U.S. 83 (1985) (private crèche in public park).

Eve. While the county may have doubts about the constitutional status of celebrating the Eucharist inside the courthouse under the government's auspices, this Court does not. The government may acknowledge Christmas as a cultural phenomenon, but under the First Amendment it may not observe it as a Christian holy day by suggesting that people praise God for the birth of Jesus.

In sum, *Lynch* teaches that government may celebrate Christmas in some manner and form, but not in a way that endorses Christian doctrine. Here, Allegheny County has transgressed this line. It has chosen to celebrate Christmas in a way that has the effect of endorsing a patently Christian message: Glory to God for the birth of Jesus Christ. Under *Lynch*, and the rest of our cases, nothing more is required to demonstrate a violation of the Establishment Clause. The display of the crèche in this context, therefore, must be permanently enjoined.

## V . . .

### A

In *Marsh*, the Court relied specifically on the fact that Congress authorized legislative prayer at the same time that it produced the Bill of Rights. JUSTICE KENNEDY, however, argues that *Marsh* legitimates all "practices with no greater potential for an establishment of religion" than those "accepted traditions dating back to the Founding." Otherwise, the Justice asserts, such practices as our national motto ("In God We Trust") and our Pledge of Allegiance (with the phrase "under God," added in 1954, Pub. L. 396, 68 Stat. 249) are in danger of invalidity.

Our previous opinions have considered in dicta the motto and the pledge, characterizing them as consistent with the proposition that government may not communicate an endorsement of religious belief. *Lynch*, 465 U.S., 693 (O'CONNOR, J., concurring); *id.*, 716-717 (BRENNAN, J., dissenting). We need not return to the subject of "ceremonial deism," because there is an obvious distinction between crèche displays and references to God in the motto and the pledge. However history may affect the constitutionality of nonsectarian references to religion by the government, history cannot legitimate practices that demonstrate the government's allegiance to a particular sect or creed.

Indeed, in *Marsh* itself, the Court recognized that not even the "unique history" of legislative prayer, 463 U.S., 791, can justify contemporary legislative prayers that have the effect of affiliating the government with any one specific faith or belief. *Id.*, 794-795. The legislative prayers involved in *Marsh* did not violate this principle because the particular chaplain had "removed all references to Christ." *Id.*, 793, n. 14. Thus, *Marsh* plainly does not stand for the sweeping proposition JUSTICE KENNEDY apparently would ascribe to it, namely, that all accepted practices 200 years old and their equivalents are constitutional today. Nor can *Marsh*, given its facts and its reasoning, compel the conclusion that the display of the crèche involved in this lawsuit is constitutional. Although JUSTICE KENNEDY says that he "cannot comprehend" how the crèche display could be invalid after *Marsh*, surely he is able to distinguish between a specifically Christian symbol, like a crèche, and more general religious references, like the legislative prayers in *Marsh*.

JUSTICE KENNEDY's reading of *Marsh* would gut the core of the Establishment Clause, as this Court understands it. The history of this Nation, it is perhaps sad to say, contains numerous examples of official acts that endorsed

Christianity specifically. Some of these examples date back to the Founding of the Republic, but this heritage of official discrimination against non-Christians has no place in the jurisprudence of the Establishment Clause. Whatever else the Establishment Clause may mean (and we have held it to mean no official preference even for religion over nonreligion), it certainly means at the very least that government may not demonstrate a preference for one particular sect or creed (including a preference for Christianity over other religions). "The clearest command of the Establishment Clause is that one religious denomination cannot be officially preferred over another." *Larson v. Valente*, 456 U.S. 228, 244 (1982). There have been breaches of this command throughout this Nation's history, but they cannot diminish in any way the force of the command.

B

Although JUSTICE KENNEDY's misreading of *Marsh* is predicated on a failure to recognize the bedrock Establishment Clause principle that, regardless of history, government may not demonstrate a preference for a particular faith, even he is forced to acknowledge that some instances of such favoritism are constitutionally intolerable. He concedes also that the term "endorsement" long has been another way of defining a forbidden "preference" for a particular sect, but he would repudiate the Court's endorsement inquiry as a "jurisprudence of minutiae," because it examines the particular contexts in which the government employs religious symbols.

This label, of course, could be tagged on many areas of constitutional adjudication . . . . It is perhaps unfortunate, but nonetheless inevitable, that the broad language of many clauses within the Bill of Rights must be translated into adjudicatory principles that realize their full meaning only after their application to a series of concrete cases.

Indeed, not even under JUSTICE KENNEDY's preferred approach can the Establishment Clause be transformed into an exception to this rule. The Justice would substitute the term "proselytization" for "endorsement," but his "proselytization" test suffers from the same "defect," if one must call it that, of requiring close factual analysis. JUSTICE KENNEDY has no doubt, "for example, that the [Establishment] Clause forbids a city to permit the permanent erection of a large Latin cross on the roof of city hall . . . because such an obtrusive year-round religious display would place the government's weight behind an obvious effort to proselytize on behalf of a particular religion." He also suggests that a city would demonstrate an unconstitutional preference for Christianity if it displayed a Christian symbol during every major Christian holiday but did not display the religious symbols of other faiths during other religious holidays. But, for JUSTICE KENNEDY, would it be enough of a preference for Christianity if that city each year displayed a crèche for 40 days during the Christmas season and a cross for 40 days during Lent (and never the symbols of other religions)? If so, then what if there were no cross but the 40-day crèche display contained a sign exhorting the city's citizens "to offer up their devotions to God their Creator, and his Son Jesus Christ, the Redeemer of the world"?

The point of these rhetorical questions is obvious. In order to define precisely what government could and could not do under JUSTICE KENNEDY's "proselytization" test, the Court would have to decide a series of cases with particular fact patterns that fall along the spectrum of government references to religion (from the permanent display of a cross atop city hall to a passing reference to divine Providence in an official address). If one wished to be "un-charitable" to JUSTICE KENNEDY, one could say that his methodology re-quires counting the number of days during which the government displays Christian symbols and subtracting from this the number of days during which non-Christian symbols are displayed, divided by the number of different non-Christian religions represented in these displays, and then somehow factoring into this equation the prominence of the display's location and the degree to which each symbol possesses an inherently proselytizing quality. JUSTICE KENNEDY, of course, could defend his position by pointing to the inevitably fact-specific nature of the question whether a particular governmental prac-tice signals the government's unconstitutional preference for a specific reli-gious faith. But because JUSTICE KENNEDY's formulation of this essential Establishment Clause inquiry is no less fact intensive than the "endorsement" formulation adopted by the Court, JUSTICE KENNEDY should be wary of ac-cusing the Court's formulation as "using little more than intuition and a tape measure," lest he find his own formulation convicted on an identical charge.

Indeed, perhaps the only real distinction between JUSTICE KENNEDY's "proselytization" test and the Court's "endorsement" inquiry is a burden of "unmistakable" clarity that JUSTICE KENNEDY apparently would require of government favoritism for specific sects in order to hold the favoritism in vio-lation of the Establishment Clause. The question whether a particular practice "would place the government's weight behind an obvious effort to proselytize for a particular religion," is much the same as whether the practice demon-strates the government's support, promotion, or "endorsement" of the particu-lar creed of a particular sect—except to the extent that it requires an "obvious" allegiance between the government and the sect.

Our cases, however, impose no such burden on demonstrating that the government has favored a particular sect or creed. On the contrary, we have expressly required "strict scrutiny" of practices suggesting "a denominational preference," *Larson v. Valente*, 456 U.S., 246, in keeping with "'the unwavering vigilance that the Constitution requires'" against any violation of the Establish-ment Clause. *Bowen v. Kendrick*, 487 U.S. 589, 623 (1988) (O'CONNOR, J., concurring), quoting *id.*, 648 (dissenting opinion); see also *Lynch*, 465 U.S., 694 (O'CONNOR, J., concurring) ("[T]he myriad, subtle ways in which Estab-lishment Clause values can be eroded" necessitates "careful judicial scrutiny" of "[g]overnment practices that purport to celebrate or acknowledge events with religious significance"). Thus, when all is said and done, JUSTICE KENNEDY's effort to abandon the "endorsement" inquiry in favor of his "proselytization" test seems nothing more than an attempt to lower considerably the level of scrutiny in Establishment Clause cases. We choose, however, to adhere to the vigilance the Court has managed to maintain thus far, and to the endorsement inquiry that reflects our vigilance.

C

Although JUSTICE KENNEDY repeatedly accuses the Court of harboring a "latent hostility" or "callous indifference" toward religion, nothing could be further from the truth, and the accusations could be said to be as offensive as they are absurd. JUSTICE KENNEDY apparently has misperceived a respect for religious pluralism, a respect commanded by the Constitution, as hostility or indifference to religion. No misperception could be more antithetical to the values embodied in the Establishment Clause.

JUSTICE KENNEDY's accusations are shot from a weapon triggered by the following proposition: if government may celebrate the secular aspects of Christmas, then it must be allowed to celebrate the religious aspects as well because, otherwise, the government would be discriminating against citizens who celebrate Christmas as a religious, and not just a secular, holiday. This proposition, however, is flawed at its foundation. The government does not discriminate against any citizen on the basis of the citizen's religious faith if the government is secular in its functions and operations. On the contrary, the Constitution mandates that the government remain secular, rather than affiliate itself with religious beliefs or institutions, precisely in order to avoid discriminating among citizens on the basis of their religious faiths.

A secular state, it must be remembered, is not the same as an atheistic or antireligious state. A secular state establishes neither atheism nor religion as its official creed. JUSTICE KENNEDY thus has it exactly backwards when he says that enforcing the Constitution's requirement that government remain secular is a prescription of orthodoxy. It follows directly from the Constitution's proscription against government affiliation with religious beliefs or institutions that there is no orthodoxy on religious matters in the secular state. Although JUSTICE KENNEDY accuses the Court of "an Orwellian rewriting of history," perhaps it is JUSTICE KENNEDY himself who has slipped into a form of Orwellian newspeak when he equates the constitutional command of secular government with a prescribed orthodoxy.

To be sure, in a pluralistic society there may be some would-be theocrats, who wish that their religion were an established creed, and some of them perhaps may be even audacious enough to claim that the lack of established religion discriminates against their preferences. But this claim gets no relief, for it contradicts the fundamental premise of the Establishment Clause itself. The antidiscrimination principle inherent in the Establishment Clause necessarily means that would-be discriminators on the basis of religion cannot prevail.

For this reason, the claim that prohibiting government from celebrating Christmas as a religious holiday discriminates against Christians in favor of nonadherents must fail. Celebrating Christmas as a religious, as opposed to a secular, holiday, necessarily entails professing, proclaiming, or believing that Jesus of Nazareth, born in a manger in Bethlehem, is the Christ, the Messiah. If the government celebrates Christmas as a religious holiday (for example, by issuing an official proclamation saying: "We rejoice in the glory of Christ's birth!"), it means that the government really is declaring Jesus to be the Messiah, a specifically Christian belief. In contrast, confining the government's own celebration of Christmas to the holiday's secular aspects does *not* favor the religious beliefs of non-Christians over those of Christians. Rather, it simply permits the government to acknowledge the holiday without expressing an allegiance to Christian beliefs, an allegiance that would truly favor Christians over non-Christians. To be sure, some Christians may wish to see the government proclaim its allegiance to Christianity in a religious celebration of Christmas, but the Constitution does not permit the gratification of that desire, which would contradict the "'the logic of secular liberty'" it is the purpose of the Establishment Clause to protect. See *Larson v. Valente*, 456 U.S., 244, quoting B. Bailyn, The Ideological Origins of the American Revolution 265 (1967).

Of course, not all religious celebrations of Christmas located on government property violate the Establishment Clause. It obviously is not unconstitutional, for example, for a group of parishioners from a local church to go caroling through a city park on any Sunday in Advent or for a Christian club at a public university to sing carols during their Christmas meeting. Cf. *Widmar v. Vincent,* 454 U.S. 263 (1981). The reason is that activities of this nature do not demonstrate the government's allegiance to, or endorsement of, the Christian faith.

Equally obvious, however, is the proposition that not all proclamations of Christian faith located on government property are permitted by the Establishment Clause just because they occur during the Christmas holiday season, as the example of a Mass in the courthouse surely illustrates. And once the judgment has been made that a particular proclamation of Christian belief, when disseminated from a particular location on government property, has the effect of demonstrating the government's endorsement of Christian faith, then it necessarily follows that the practice must be enjoined to protect the constitutional rights of those citizens who follow some creed other than Christianity. It is thus incontrovertible that the Court's decision today, premised on the determination that the crèche display on the Grand Staircase demonstrates the county's endorsement of Christianity, does not represent a hostility or indifference to religion but, instead, the respect for religious diversity that the Constitution requires.

## VI

The display of the Chanukah menorah in front of the City-County Building may well present a closer constitutional question. The menorah, one must recognize, is a religious symbol: it serves to commemorate the miracle of the oil as described in the Talmud. But the menorah's message is not exclusively religious. The menorah is the primary visual symbol for a holiday that, like Christmas, has both religious and secular dimensions.[60]

Moreover, the menorah here stands next to a Christmas tree and a sign saluting liberty. While no challenge has been made here to the display of the tree and the sign, their presence is obviously relevant in determining the effect of the menorah's display. The necessary result of placing a menorah next to a Christmas tree is to create an "overall holiday setting" that represents both Christmas and Chanukah—two holidays, not one. See *Lynch,* 465 U.S., 692 (O'CONNOR, J., concurring).

---

[60] JUSTICE KENNEDY is clever but mistaken in asserting that the description of the menorah, purports to turn the Court into a "national theology board." Any inquiry concerning the government's use of a religious object to determine whether that use results in an unconstitutional religious preference requires a review of the factual record concerning the religious object—even if the inquiry is conducted pursuant to JUSTICE KENNEDY's "proselytization" test. Surely, JUSTICE KENNEDY cannot mean that this Court must keep itself in ignorance of the symbol's conventional use and decide the constitutional question knowing only what it knew before the case was filed. This prescription of ignorance obviously would bias this Court according to the religious and cultural backgrounds of its Members, a condition much more intolerable than any which results from the Court's efforts to become familiar with the relevant facts.

Moreover, the relevant facts concerning Chanukah and the menorah are largely to be found in the record, as indicated by the extensive citation to the Appendix. In any event, Members of this Court have not hesitated in referring to secondary sources in aid of their Establishment Clause analysis, see, e.g., *Lynch,* 465 U.S., 709-712, 721-724 (BRENNAN, J., dissenting), because the question "whether a government activity communicates an endorsement of religion" is "in large part a legal question to be answered on the basis of judicial interpretation of social facts," *id.,* 693-694 (O'CONNOR, J., concurring).

The mere fact that Pittsburgh displays symbols of both Christmas and Chanukah does not end the constitutional inquiry. If the city celebrates both Christmas and Chanukah as religious holidays, then it violates the Establishment Clause. The simultaneous endorsement of Judaism and Christianity is no less constitutionally infirm than the endorsement of Christianity alone.[61]

Conversely, if the city celebrates both Christmas and Chanukah as secular holidays, then its conduct is beyond the reach of the Establishment Clause. Because government may celebrate Christmas as a secular holiday, it follows that government may also acknowledge Chanukah as a secular holiday. Simply put, it would be a form of discrimination against Jews to allow Pittsburgh to celebrate Christmas as a cultural tradition while simultaneously disallowing the city's acknowledgment of Chanukah as a contemporaneous cultural tradition.

Accordingly, the relevant question for Establishment Clause purposes is whether the combined display of the tree, the sign, and the menorah has the effect of endorsing both Christian and Jewish faiths, or rather simply recognizes that both Christmas and Chanukah are part of the same winter-holiday season, which has attained a secular status in our society. Of the two interpretations of this particular display, the latter seems far more plausible and is also in line with *Lynch*.

The Christmas tree, unlike the menorah, is not itself a religious symbol. Although Christmas trees once carried religious connotations, today they typify the secular celebration of Christmas. Numerous Americans place Christmas trees in their homes without subscribing to Christian religious beliefs, and when the city's tree stands alone in front of the City-County Building, it is not considered an endorsement of Christian faith. Indeed, a 40-foot Christmas tree was one of the objects that validated the crèche in *Lynch*. The widely accepted view of the Christmas tree as the preeminent secular symbol of the Christmas holiday season serves to emphasize the secular component of the message communicated by other elements of an accompanying holiday display, including the Chanukah menorah.

The tree, moreover, is clearly the predominant element in the city's display. The 45-foot tree occupies the central position beneath the middle archway in front of the Grant Street entrance to the City-County Building; the 18-foot menorah is positioned to one side. Given this configuration, it is much more sensible to interpret the meaning of the menorah in light of the tree, rather than vice versa. In the shadow of the tree, the menorah is readily understood as simply a recognition that Christmas is not the only traditional way of observing the winter-holiday season. In these circumstances, then, the combination of the tree and the menorah communicates, not a simultaneous endorsement of both the Christian and Jewish faiths, but instead, a secular celebration of Christmas coupled with an acknowledgment of Chanukah as a contemporaneous alternative tradition.

Although the city has used a symbol with religious meaning as its representation of Chanukah, this is not a case in which the city has reasonable

---

[61] The display of a menorah next to a crèche on government property might prove to be invalid. Cf. *Greater Houston Chapter of American Civil Liberties Union v. Eckels*, 589 F. Supp. 222 (SD Tex. 1984), appeal dism'd, 755 F. 2d 426 (CA5), cert. denied, 474 U.S. 980 (1985) (war memorial containing crosses and a Star of David unconstitutionally favored Christianity and Judaism, discriminating against the beliefs of patriotic soldiers who were neither Christian nor Jewish).

alternatives that are less religious in nature. It is difficult to imagine a predominantly secular symbol of Chanukah that the city could place next to its Christmas tree. An 18-foot dreidel would look out of place and might be interpreted
by some as mocking the celebration of Chanukah. The absence of a more
secular alternative symbol is itself part of the context in which the city's actions must be judged in determining the likely effect of its use of the menorah.
Where the government's secular message can be conveyed by two symbols,
only one of which carries religious meaning, an observer reasonably might
infer from the fact that the government has chosen to use the religious symbol
that the government means to promote religious faith. . . . But where, as here,
no such choice has been made, this inference of endorsement is not present.

The mayor's sign further diminishes the possibility that the tree and the
menorah will be interpreted as a dual endorsement of Christianity and Judaism. The sign states that during the holiday season the city salutes liberty.
Moreover, the sign draws upon the theme of light, common to both Chanukah
and Christmas as winter festivals, and links that theme with this Nation's legacy of freedom, which allows an American to celebrate the holiday season in
whatever way he wishes, religiously or otherwise. While no sign can disclaim
an overwhelming message of endorsement, see *Stone v. Graham*, 449 U.S., 41,
an "explanatory plaque" may confirm that in particular contexts the government's association with a religious symbol does not represent the government's
sponsorship of religious beliefs. See *Lynch*, 465 U.S., 707 (BRENNAN, J., dissenting). Here, the mayor's sign serves to confirm what the context already
reveals: that the display of the menorah is not an endorsement of religious
faith but simply a recognition of cultural diversity.

Given all these considerations, it is not "sufficiently likely" that residents
of Pittsburgh will perceive the combined display of the tree, the sign, and the
menorah as an "endorsement" or "disapproval . . . of their individual religious
choices." *Grand Rapids*, 473 U.S., 390. While an adjudication of the display's
effect must take into account the perspective of one who is neither Christian
nor Jewish, as well as of those who adhere to either of these religions, the
constitutionality of its effect must also be judged according to the standard of
a "reasonable observer," see *Witters v. Washington Dept. of Services for Blind*, 474
U.S. 481, 493 (1986) (O'CONNOR, J., concurring in part and concurring in
judgment); see also *Tribe 1296* (challenged government practices should be
judged "from the perspective of a 'reasonable non-adherent'"). When measured against this standard, the menorah need not be excluded from this particular display. The Christmas tree alone in the Pittsburgh location does not
endorse Christian belief; and, on the facts before us, the addition of the menorah "cannot fairly be understood to" result in the simultaneous endorsement
of Christian and Jewish faiths. *Lynch*, 465 U.S., 693 (O'CONNOR, J.). On the
contrary, for purposes of the Establishment Clause, the city's overall display
must be understood as conveying the city's secular recognition of different
traditions for celebrating the winter-holiday season.[69]

The conclusion here that, in this particular context, the menorah's display
does not have an effect of endorsing religious faith does not foreclose the pos-

---

[69] This is not to say that the combined display of a Christmas tree and a menorah is constitutional wherever it may be located on government property. For example, when located
in a public school, such a display might raise additional constitutional considerations. Cf.
*Edwards v. Aguillard*, 482 U.S., 583-584 (Establishment Clause must be applied with special
sensitivity in the public-school context).

sibility that the display of the menorah might violate either the "purpose" or "entanglement" prong of the *Lemon* analysis. These issues were not addressed by the Court of Appeals and may be considered by that court on remand.

### VII

*Lynch v. Donnelly* confirms, and in no way repudiates, the longstanding constitutional principle that government may not engage in a practice that has the effect of promoting or endorsing religious beliefs. The display of the crèche in the county courthouse has this unconstitutional effect. The display of the menorah in front of the City-County Building, however, does not have this effect, given its "particular physical setting."

The judgment of the Court of Appeals is affirmed in part and reversed in part, and the cases are remanded for further proceedings.

*It is so ordered.*

⬛ JUSTICE O'CONNOR, with whom JUSTICE BRENNAN and JUSTICE STE-VENS join as to Part II, concurring in part and concurring in the judgment.

### I

Judicial review of government action under the Establishment Clause is a delicate task. The Court has avoided drawing lines which entirely sweep away all government recognition and acknowledgment of the role of religion in the lives of our citizens for to do so would exhibit not neutrality but hostility to religion. Instead the courts have made case-specific examinations of the challenged government action and have attempted to do so with the aid of the standards described by JUSTICE BLACKMUN in Part III-A of the Court's opinion. Unfortunately, even the development of articulable standards and guidelines has not always resulted in agreement among the Members of this Court on the results in individual cases. And so it is again today.

The constitutionality of the two displays at issue in these cases turns on how we interpret and apply the holding in *Lynch v. Donnelly*, in which we rejected an Establishment Clause challenge to the city of Pawtucket's inclusion of a crèche in its annual Christmas holiday display. . . .

In my concurrence in *Lynch*, I suggested a clarification of our Establishment Clause doctrine to reinforce the concept that the Establishment Clause "prohibits government from making adherence to a religion relevant in any way to a person's standing in the political community." The government violates this prohibition if it endorses or disapproves of religion. "Endorsement sends a message to nonadherents that they are outsiders, not full members of the political community, and an accompanying message to adherents that they are insiders, favored members of the political community." Disapproval of religion conveys the opposite message. . . .

For the reasons stated in Part IV of the Court's opinion in these cases, I agree that the crèche displayed on the Grand Staircase of the Allegheny County Courthouse, the seat of county government, conveys a message to nonadherents of Christianity that they are not full members of the political community, and a corresponding message to Christians that they are favored members of the political community. In contrast to the crèche in *Lynch*, which was displayed in a private park in the city's commercial district as part of a broader display of traditional secular symbols of the holiday season, this crèche stands alone in the county courthouse. The display of religious symbols in public areas of core government buildings runs a special risk of "mak[ing] religion relevant, in reality or public perception, to status in the political community." . . . The Court correctly concludes that placement of the central religious symbol of the Christmas holiday season at the Allegheny County Courthouse has the unconstitutional effect of conveying a government endorsement of Christianity.

## II

In his separate opinion, JUSTICE KENNEDY asserts that the endorsement test "is flawed in its fundamentals and unworkable in practice." In my view, neither criticism is persuasive. As a theoretical matter, the endorsement test captures the essential command of the Establishment Clause, namely, that government must not make a person's religious beliefs relevant to his or her standing in the political community by conveying a message "that religion or a particular religious belief is *favored* or *preferred*." . . .

An Establishment Clause standard that prohibits only "coercive" practices or overt efforts at government proselytization, but fails to take account of the numerous more subtle ways that government can show favoritism to particular beliefs or convey a message of disapproval to others, would not, in my view, adequately protect the religious liberty or respect the religious diversity of the members of our pluralistic political community. Thus, this Court has never relied on coercion alone as the touchstone of Establishment Clause analysis. To require a showing of coercion, even indirect coercion, as an essential element of an Establishment Clause violation would make the Free Exercise Clause a redundancy. . . . Moreover, as even JUSTICE KENNEDY recognizes, any Establishment Clause test limited to "*direct* coercion" clearly would fail to account for forms of "[s]ymbolic recognition or accommodation of religious faith" that may violate the Establishment Clause.

I continue to believe that the endorsement test asks the right question about governmental practices challenged on Establishment Clause grounds, including challenged practices involving the display of religious symbols. . . . I also remain convinced that the endorsement test is capable of consistent application. Indeed, it is notable that the three Courts of Appeals that have considered challenges to the display of a crèche standing alone at city hall have each concluded, relying in part on endorsement analysis, that such a practice sends a message to nonadherents of Christianity that they are outsiders in the political community. . . . To be sure, the endorsement test depends on a sensitivity to the unique circumstances and context of a particular challenged practice and, like any test that is sensitive to context, it may not always yield results with unanimous agreement at the margins. But that is true of many standards in constitutional law, and even the modified coercion test offered by JUSTICE KENNEDY involves judgment and hard choices at the margin. He admits as much by acknowledging that the permanent display of a Latin cross at city hall would violate the Establishment Clause, as would the display of symbols of Christian holidays alone. Would the display of a Latin cross for six months have such an unconstitutional effect, or the display of the symbols of most Christian holidays and one Jewish holiday? Would the Christmastime display of a crèche inside a courtroom be "coercive" if subpoenaed witnesses had no opportunity to "turn their backs" and walk away? Would displaying a crèche in front of a public school violate the Establishment Clause under JUSTICE KENNEDY's test? We cannot avoid the obligation to draw lines, often close and difficult lines, in deciding Establishment Clause cases, and that is not a problem unique to the endorsement test.

JUSTICE KENNEDY submits that the endorsement test is inconsistent with our precedents and traditions because, in his words, if it were "applied without artificial exceptions for historical practice," it would invalidate many traditional practices recognizing the role of religion in our society. This criticism shortchanges both the endorsement test itself and my explanation of the reason why certain longstanding government acknowledgments of religion do not, under that test, convey a message of endorsement. Practices such as legislative prayers or opening Court sessions with "God save the United States and this honorable Court" serve the secular purposes of "solemnizing public occasions" and "expressing confidence in the future." These examples of ceremonial deism do not survive Establishment Clause scrutiny simply by virtue of their historical longevity alone. Historical acceptance of a practice does not in itself validate that practice under the Establishment Clause if the practice violates the values protected by that Clause, just as historical acceptance of racial or gender based discrimination does not immunize such practices from scrutiny under the Fourteenth Amendment. As we recognized in *Walz v. Tax Comm'n of New York City*: "[N]o one acquires a vested or protected right in violation of the Constitution by long use, even when that span of time covers our entire national existence and indeed predates it."

Under the endorsement test, the "history and ubiquity" of a practice is relevant not because it creates an "artificial exception" from that test. On the contrary, the "history and ubiquity" of a practice is relevant because it provides part of the context in which a reasonable observer evaluates whether a challenged governmental practice conveys a message of endorsement of religion. It is the combination of the longstanding existence of practices such as opening legislative sessions with legislative prayers or opening Court sessions with "God save the United States and this honorable Court," as well as their nonsectarian nature, that leads me to the conclusion that those particular practices, despite their religious roots, do not convey a message of endorsement of particular religious beliefs. Similarly, the celebration of Thanksgiving as a public holiday, despite its religious origins, is now generally understood as a celebration of patriotic values rather than particular religious beliefs. The question under endorsement analysis, in short, is whether a reasonable observer would view such longstanding practices as a disapproval of his or her particular religious choices, in light of the fact that they serve a secular purpose rather than a sectarian one and have largely lost their religious significance over time. Although the endorsement test requires careful and often difficult linedrawing and is highly context specific, no alternative test has been suggested that captures the essential mandate of the Establishment Clause as well as the endorsement test does, and it warrants continued application and refinement.

Contrary to JUSTICE KENNEDY's assertions, neither the endorsement test nor its application in these cases reflects "an unjustified hostility toward religion." Instead, the endorsement standard recognizes that the religious liberty so precious to the citizens who make up our diverse country is protected, not impeded, when government avoids endorsing religion or favoring particular beliefs over others. Clearly, the government can *acknowledge* the role of religion in our society in numerous ways that do not amount to an endorsement. Moreover, the government can *accommodate* religion by lifting government-imposed burdens on religion. Indeed, the Free Exercise Clause may mandate that it do so in particular cases. . . . The cases before the Court today, however, do not involve lifting a governmental burden on the free exercise of religion. By repeatedly using the terms "acknowledgment" of religion and "accommodation" of religion interchangeably, however, JUSTICE KENNEDY obscures the fact that the displays at issue in these cases were not placed at city hall in order to remove a government-imposed burden on the free exercise of religion. Christians remain free to display their crèches at their homes and churches. Allegheny County has neither placed nor removed a governmental burden on the free exercise of religion but rather, for the reasons stated in Part IV of the Court's opinion, has conveyed a message of governmental endorsement of Christian beliefs. This the Establishment Clause does not permit.

### III

For reasons which differ somewhat from those set forth in Part VI of JUSTICE BLACKMUN's opinion, I also conclude that the city of Pittsburgh's combined holiday display of a Chanukah menorah, a Christmas tree, and a sign saluting liberty does not have the effect of conveying an endorsement of religion. . . . Although JUSTICE BLACKMUN's opinion acknowledges that a Christmas tree alone conveys no endorsement of Christian beliefs, it formulates the question posed by Pittsburgh's combined display of the tree and the menorah as whether the display "has the effect of endorsing *both* Christian and Jewish faiths, or rather simply recognizes that both Christmas and Chanukah are part of the same winter-holiday season, which has attained a secular status in our society."

That formulation of the question disregards the fact that the Christmas tree is a predominantly secular symbol and, more significantly, obscures the religious nature of the menorah and the holiday of Chanukah. The opinion is correct to recognize that the religious holiday of Chanukah has historical and cultural as well as religious dimensions, and that there may be certain "secular aspects" to the holiday. But that is not to conclude, however, as JUSTICE BLACKMUN seems to do, that Chanukah has become a "secular holiday" in our society. The Easter holiday celebrated by Christians may be accompanied by certain "secular aspects" such as Easter bunnies and Easter egg hunts; but it is nevertheless a religious holiday. Similarly, Chanukah is a religious holiday with strong historical components particularly important to the Jewish people. Moreover, the menorah is the central religious symbol and ritual object of that religious holiday. Under JUSTICE BLACKMUN's view, however, the menorah "has been relegated to the role of a neutral harbinger of the holiday season," almost devoid of any religious significance. In my view, the relevant question for Establishment Clause purposes is whether the city of Pittsburgh's display of the menorah, the religious symbol of a religious holiday, next to a Christmas tree and a sign saluting liberty sends a message of government endorsement of Judaism or whether it sends a message of pluralism and freedom to choose one's own beliefs. . . .

[T]he question here is whether Pittsburgh's holiday display conveys a message of endorsement of Judaism, when the menorah is the only religious symbol in the combined display and when the opinion acknowledges that the tree cannot reasonably be understood to convey an endorsement of Christianity. One need not characterize Chanukah as a "secular" holiday or strain to argue that the menorah has a "secular" dimension, in order to conclude that the city of Pittsburgh's combined display does not convey a message of endorsement of Judaism or of religion in general.

In setting up its holiday display, which included the lighted tree and the menorah, the city of Pittsburgh stressed the theme of liberty and pluralism by accompanying the exhibit with a sign bearing the following message: "'During this holiday season, the city of Pittsburgh salutes liberty. Let these festive lights remind us that we are the keepers of the flame of liberty and our legacy of freedom.'" This sign indicates that the city intended to convey its own distinctive message of pluralism and freedom. By accompanying its display of a Christmas tree—a secular symbol of the Christmas holiday season—with a salute to liberty, and by adding a religious symbol from a Jewish holiday also celebrated at roughly the same time of year, I conclude that the city did not endorse Judaism or religion in general, but rather conveyed a message of pluralism and freedom of belief during the holiday season. . . .

The message of pluralism conveyed by the city's combined holiday display is not a message that endorses religion over nonreligion. Just as government may not favor particular religious beliefs over others, "government may not favor religious belief over disbelief." Here, by displaying a secular symbol of the Christmas holiday season rather than a religious one, the city acknowledged a public holiday celebrated by both religious and nonreligious citizens alike, and it did so without endorsing Christian beliefs. A reasonable observer would, in my view, appreciate that the combined display is an effort to acknowledge the cultural diversity of our country and to convey tolerance of different choices in matters of religious belief or nonbelief by recognizing that the winter holiday season is celebrated in diverse ways by our citizens. In short, in the holiday context, this combined display in its particular physical setting conveys neither an endorsement of Judaism or Christianity nor disapproval of alternative beliefs, and thus does not have the impermissible effect of "mak[ing] religion relevant, in reality or public perception, to status in the political community." . . .

In my view, JUSTICE BLACKMUN's new rule, that an inference of endorsement arises every time government uses a symbol with religious meaning if a "more secular alternative" is available is too blunt an instrument for Establishment Clause analysis, which depends on sensitivity to the context and circumstances presented by each case. Indeed, the opinion appears to recognize the importance of this contextual sensitivity by creating an exception to its new rule in the very case announcing it: the opinion acknowledges that "a purely secular symbol" of Chanukah is available, namely, a dreidel or four-sided top, but rejects the use of such a symbol because it "might be interpreted by some as mocking the celebration of Chanukah." This recognition that the more *religious* alternative may, depending on the circumstances, convey a message that is least likely to implicate Establishment Clause concerns is an excellent example of the need to focus on the specific practice in question in its particular physical setting and context in determining whether government has conveyed or attempted to convey a message that religion or a particular religious belief is favored or preferred.

In sum, I conclude that the city of Pittsburgh's combined holiday display had neither the purpose nor the effect of endorsing religion, but that Allegheny County's crèche display had such an effect. Accordingly, I join Parts I, II, III-A, IV, V, and VII of the Court's opinion and concur in the judgment.

▨ JUSTICE BRENNAN, with whom JUSTICE MARSHALL and JUSTICE STEVENS join, concurring in part and dissenting in part.

I have previously explained at some length my views on the relationship between the Establishment Clause and government-sponsored celebrations of the Christmas holiday. I continue to believe that the display of an object that "retains a specifically Christian [or other] religious meaning," is incompatible with the separation of church and state demanded by our Constitution. I therefore agree with the Court that Allegheny County's display of a crèche at the county courthouse signals an endorsement of the Christian faith in violation of the Establishment Clause, and join Parts III-A, IV, and V of the Court's opinion. I cannot agree, however, that the city's display of a 45-foot Christmas tree and an 18-foot Chanukah menorah at the entrance to the building housing the mayor's office shows no favoritism towards Christianity, Judaism, or both. Indeed, I should have thought that the answer as to the first display supplied the answer to the second. . . .

[T]he decision as to the menorah rests on three premises: the Christmas tree is a secular symbol; Chanukah is a holiday with secular dimensions, symbolized by the menorah; and the government may promote pluralism by sponsoring or condoning displays having strong religious associations on its property. None of these is sound.

I

The first step toward JUSTICE BLACKMUN's conclusion is the claim that, despite its religious origins, the Christmas tree is a secular symbol. . . . JUSTICE O'CONNOR accepts this view of the Christmas tree because, "whatever its origins, [it] is not regarded today as a religious symbol.". . .

Thus, while acknowledging the religious origins of the Christmas tree, JuSTICES BLACKMUN and O'CONNOR dismiss their significance. In my view, this attempt to take the "Christmas" out of the Christmas tree is unconvincing. . . .

Positioned as it was, the Christmas tree's religious significance was bound to come to the fore. Situated next to the menorah—which, JUSTICE BLACKMUN acknowledges, is "a symbol with religious meaning," and indeed, is "the central religious symbol and ritual object of" Chanukah—the Christmas tree's religious dimension could not be overlooked by observers of the display. Even though the tree alone may be deemed predominantly secular, it can hardly be so characterized when placed next to such a forthrightly religious symbol. Consider a poster featuring a star of David, a statue of Buddha, a Christmas tree, a mosque, and a drawing of Krishna. There can be no doubt that, when found in such company, the tree serves as an unabashedly religious symbol. . . .

As a factual matter, it seems to me that the sight of an 18-foot menorah would be far more eye catching than that of a rather conventionally sized Christmas tree. It also seems to me likely that the symbol with the more singular message will predominate over one lacking such a clear meaning. Given the homogenized message that JUSTICE BLACKMUN associates with the Christmas tree, I would expect that the menorah, with its concededly religious character, would tend to dominate the tree. And, though JUSTICE BLACKMUN shunts the point to a footnote at the end of his opinion, it is highly relevant that the menorah was lit during a religious ceremony complete with traditional religious blessings. I do not comprehend how the failure to challenge separately this portion of the city's festivities precludes us from considering it in assessing the message sent by the display as a whole. With such an openly religious introduction, it is most likely that the religious aspects of the menorah would be front and center in this display.

I would not, however, presume to say that my interpretation of the tree's significance is the "correct" one, or the one shared by most visitors to the City-County Building. I do not know how we can decide whether it was the tree that stripped the religious connotations from the menorah, or the menorah that laid bare the religious origins of the tree. Both are reasonable interpretations of the scene the city presented, and thus both, I think, should satisfy JUSTICE BLACKMUN's requirement that the display "be judged according to the standard of a 'reasonable observer.'" I shudder to think that the only "reasonable observer" is one who shares the particular views on perspective, spacing, and accent expressed in JUSTICE BLACKMUN's opinion, thus making analysis under the Establishment Clause look more like an exam in Art 101 than an inquiry into constitutional law.

## II

The second premise on which today's decision rests is the notion that Chanukah is a partly secular holiday, for which the menorah can serve as a secular symbol. It is no surprise and no anomaly that Chanukah has historical and societal roots that range beyond the purely religious. I would venture that most, if not all, major religious holidays have beginnings and enjoy histories studded with figures, events, and practices that are not strictly religious. It does not seem to me that the mere fact that Chanukah shares this kind of background makes it a secular holiday in any meaningful sense. The menorah is indisputably a religious symbol, used ritually in a celebration that has deep religious significance. That, in my view, is all that need be said. Whatever secular practices the holiday of Chanukah has taken on in its contemporary observance are beside the point. . . .

As JUSTICE O'CONNOR rightly observes, JUSTICE BLACKMUN "obscures the religious nature of the menorah and the holiday of Chanukah."

I cannot, in short, accept the effort to transform an emblem of religious faith into the innocuous "symbol for a holiday that . . . has both religious and secular dimensions."

## III

JUSTICE BLACKMUN, in his acceptance of the city's message of "diversity," and, even more so, JUSTICE O'CONNOR, in her approval of the "message of pluralism and freedom to choose one's own beliefs," appear to believe that, where seasonal displays are concerned, more is better. Whereas a display might be constitutionally problematic if it showcased the holiday of just one religion, those problems vaporize as soon as more than one religion is included. I know of no principle under the Establishment Clause, however, that permits us to conclude that governmental promotion of religion is acceptable so long as one religion is not favored. We have, on the contrary, interpreted that Clause to require neutrality, not just among religions, but between religion and nonreligion.

Nor do I discern the theory under which the government is permitted to appropriate particular holidays and religious objects to its own use in celebrating "pluralism." The message of the sign announcing a "Salute to Liberty" is not religious, but patriotic; the government's use of religion to promote its own cause is undoubtedly offensive to those whose religious beliefs are not bound up with their attitude toward the Nation.

The uncritical acceptance of a message of religious pluralism also ignores the extent to which even that message may offend. Many religious faiths are hostile to each other, and indeed, refuse even to participate in ecumenical services designed to demonstrate the very pluralism JUSTICES BLACKMUN and O'CONNOR extol. To lump the ritual objects and holidays of religions together without regard to their attitudes toward such inclusiveness, or to decide which religions should be excluded because of the possibility of offense, is not a benign or beneficent celebration of pluralism: it is instead an interference in religious matters precluded by the Establishment Clause.

The government-sponsored display of the menorah alongside a Christmas tree also works a distortion of the Jewish religious calendar. As JUSTICE BLACKMUN acknowledges, "the proximity of Christmas [may] accoun[t] for the social prominence of Chanukah in this country." It is the proximity of Christmas that undoubtedly accounts for the city's decision to participate in the celebration of Chanukah, rather than the far more significant Jewish holidays of Rosh Hashanah and Yom Kippur. Contrary to the impression the city and JUSTICES BLACKMUN and O'CONNOR seem to create, with their emphasis on "the winter-holiday season," December is not the holiday season for Judaism. Thus, the city's erection alongside the Christmas tree of the symbol of a relatively minor Jewish religious holiday, far from conveying "the city's secular recognition of different traditions for celebrating the winter-holiday season," or "a message of pluralism and freedom of belief," has the effect of promoting a Christianized version of Judaism. The holiday calendar they appear willing to accept revolves exclusively around a Christian holiday. And those religions that have no holiday at all during the period between Thanksgiving and New Year's Day will not benefit, even in a second-class manner, from the city's once-a-year tribute to "liberty" and "freedom of belief." This is not "pluralism" as I understand it.

▓ JUSTICE STEVENS, with whom JUSTICE BRENNAN and JUSTICE MARSHALL join, concurring in part and dissenting in part. . . .

In my opinion the Establishment Clause should be construed to create a strong presumption against the display of religious symbols on public property. There is always a risk that such symbols will offend nonmembers of the faith being advertised as well as adherents who consider the particular advertisement disrespectful. Some devout Christians believe that the crèche should be placed only in reverential settings, such as a church or perhaps a private home; they do not countenance its use as an aid to commercialization of Christ's birthday. In this very suit, members of the Jewish faith firmly opposed the use to which the menorah was put by the particular sect that sponsored the display at Pittsburgh's City-County Building. Even though "[p]assersby who disagree with the message conveyed by these displays are free to ignore them, or even to turn their backs," displays of this kind inevitably have a greater tendency to emphasize sincere and deeply felt differences among individuals than to achieve an ecumenical goal. The Establishment Clause does not allow public bodies to foment such disagreement.

Application of a strong presumption against the public use of religious symbols scarcely will "require a relentless extirpation of all contact between government and religion," for it will prohibit a display only when its message, evaluated in the context in which it is presented, is nonsecular. . . .

I cannot agree with the Court's conclusion that the display at Pittsburgh's City-County Building was constitutional. Standing alone in front of a governmental headquarters, a lighted, 45-foot evergreen tree might convey holiday greetings linked too tenuously to Christianity to have constitutional moment. Juxtaposition of this tree with an 18-foot menorah does not make the latter secular, as Justice Blackmun contends. Rather, the presence of the Chanukah menorah, unquestionably a religious symbol, gives religious significance to the Christmas tree. The overall display thus manifests governmental approval of the Jewish and Christian religions. Although it conceivably might be interpreted as sending "a message of pluralism and freedom to choose one's own beliefs," the message is not sufficiently clear to overcome the strong presumption that the display, respecting two religions to the exclusion of all others, is the very kind of double establishment that the First Amendment was designed to outlaw. . . .

▒ JUSTICE KENNEDY, with whom THE CHIEF JUSTICE, JUSTICE WHITE, and JUSTICE SCALIA join, concurring in the judgment in part and dissenting in part.

The majority holds that the County of Allegheny violated the Establishment Clause by displaying a crèche in the county courthouse, because the "principal or primary effect" of the display is to advance religion within the meaning of *Lemon v. Kurtzman*. This view of the Establishment Clause reflects an unjustified hostility toward religion, a hostility inconsistent with our history and our precedents, and I dissent from this holding. The crèche display is constitutional, and, for the same reasons, the display of a menorah by the city of Pittsburgh is permissible as well. On this latter point, I concur in the result, but not the reasoning, of Part VI of JUSTICE BLACKMUN's opinion.

I

In keeping with the usual fashion of recent years, the majority applies the *Lemon* test to judge the constitutionality of the holiday displays here in question. I am content for present purposes to remain within the *Lemon* framework, but do not wish to be seen as advocating, let alone adopting, that test as our primary guide in this difficult area. Persuasive criticism of *Lemon* has emerged. . . . Substantial revision of our Establishment Clause doctrine may be in order; but it is unnecessary to undertake that task today, for even the *Lemon* test, when applied with proper sensitivity to our traditions and our case law, supports the conclusion that both the crèche and the menorah are permissible displays in the context of the holiday season.

The only *Lemon* factor implicated in these cases directs us to inquire whether the "principal or primary effect" of the challenged government practice is "one that neither advances nor inhibits religion." The requirement of neutrality inherent in that formulation has sometimes been stated in categorical terms. For example, in *Everson v. Board of Education of Ewing*, the first case in our modern Establishment Clause jurisprudence, JUSTICE BLACK wrote that the Clause forbids laws "which aid one religion, aid all religions, or prefer one religion over another." We have stated that government "must be neutral in matters of religious theory, doctrine, and practice" and "may not aid, foster, or promote one religion or religious theory against another or even against the militant opposite." *Epperson v. Arkansas*, 393 U.S. 97, 103-104. And we have spoken of a prohibition against conferring an "'imprimatur of state approval'" on religion, or "favor[ing] the adherents of any sect or religious organization." *Gillette v. United States*, 401 U.S. 437, 450.

These statements must not give the impression of a formalism that does not exist. Taken to its logical extreme, some of the language quoted above would require a relentless extirpation of all contact between government and religion. But that is not the history or the purpose of the Establishment Clause. Government policies of accommodation, acknowledgment, and support for religion are an accepted part of our political and cultural heritage. . . .

Rather than requiring government to avoid any action that acknowledges or aids religion, the Establishment Clause permits government some latitude in recognizing and accommodating the central role religion plays in our society. Any approach less sensitive to our heritage would border on latent hostility toward religion, as it would require government in all its multifaceted roles to acknowledge only the secular, to the exclusion and so to the detriment of the religious. A categorical approach would install federal courts as jealous guardians of an absolute "wall of separation," sending a clear message of disapproval. In this century, as the modern administrative state expands to touch the lives of its citizens in such diverse ways and redirects their financial choices through programs of its own, it is difficult to maintain the fiction that requiring government to avoid all assistance to religion can in fairness be viewed as serving the goal of neutrality. . . .

Nothing in the First Amendment compelled New York City to establish the release-time policy in *Zorach*, but the fact that the policy served to aid religion, and in particular those sects that offer religious education to the young, did not invalidate the accommodation. Likewise, we have upheld government programs supplying textbooks to students in parochial schools, providing grants to church-sponsored universities and colleges, and exempting churches from the obligation to pay taxes. These programs all have the effect of providing substantial benefits to particular religions, but they are nonetheless permissible. . . .

The ability of the organized community to recognize and accommodate religion in a society with a pervasive public sector requires diligent observance of the border between accommodation and establishment. Our cases disclose two limiting principles: government may not coerce anyone to support or participate in any religion or its exercise; and it may not, in the guise of avoiding hostility or callous indifference, give direct benefits to religion in such a degree that it in fact "establishes a [state] religion or religious faith, or tends to do so." These two principles, while distinct, are not unrelated, for it would be difficult indeed to establish a religion without some measure of more or less subtle coercion, be it in the form of taxation to supply the substantial benefits that would sustain a state-established faith, direct compulsion to observance, or governmental exhortation to religiosity that amounts in fact to proselytizing.

It is no surprise that without exception we have invalidated actions that further the interests of religion through the coercive power of government. Forbidden involvements include compelling or coercing participation or attendance at a religious activity, requiring religious oaths to obtain government office or benefits, delegating government power to religious groups. The freedom to worship as one pleases without government interference or oppression is the great object of both the Establishment and the Free Exercise Clauses. Barring all attempts to aid religion through government coercion goes far toward attainment of this object. . . .

As JUSTICE BLACKMUN observes, some of our recent cases reject the view that coercion is the sole touchstone of an Establishment Clause violation. That may be true if by "coercion" is meant *direct* coercion in the classic sense of an establishment of religion that the Framers knew. But coercion need not be a direct tax in aid of religion or a test oath. Symbolic recognition or accommodation of religious faith may violate the Clause in an extreme case. I doubt not, for example, that the Clause forbids a city to permit the permanent erection of a large Latin cross on the roof of city hall. This is not because government speech about religion is *per se* suspect, as the majority would have it, but because such an obtrusive year-round religious display would place the government's weight behind an obvious effort to proselytize on behalf of a particular religion. Speech may coerce in some circumstances, but this does not justify a ban on all government recognition of religion. As CHIEF JUSTICE BURGER wrote for the Court in *Walz*: "The general principle deducible from the First Amendment and all that has been said by the Court is this: that we will not tolerate either governmentally established religion or governmental interference with religion. Short of those expressly proscribed governmental acts there is room for play in the joints productive of a benevolent neutrality which will permit religious exercise to exist without sponsorship and without interference."

This is most evident where the government's act of recognition or accommodation is passive and symbolic, for in that instance any intangible benefit to religion is unlikely to present a realistic risk of establishment. Absent coercion, the risk of infringement of religious liberty by passive or symbolic accommodation is minimal. Our cases reflect this reality by requiring a showing that the symbolic recognition or accommodation advances religion to such a degree that it actually "establishes a religion or religious faith, or tends to do so."

In determining whether there exists an establishment, or a tendency toward one, we refer to the other types of church-state contacts that have existed unchallenged throughout our history, or that have been found permissible in our case law. In *Lynch*, for example, we upheld the city of Pawtucket's holiday display of a crèche, despite the fact that "the display advance[d] religion in a sense." We held that the crèche conferred no greater benefit on religion than did governmental support for religious education, legislative chaplains, "recognition of the origins of the [Christmas] Holiday itself as 'Christ's Mass,'" or many other forms of symbolic or tangible governmental assistance to religious faiths that are ensconced in the safety of national tradition. And in *Marsh v. Chambers*, we found that Nebraska's practice of employing a legislative chaplain did not violate the Establishment Clause, because "legislative prayer presents no more potential for establishment than the provision of school transportation, beneficial grants for higher education, or tax exemptions for religious organizations." Noncoercive government action within the realm of flexible accommodation or passive acknowledgment of existing symbols does not violate the Establishment Clause unless it benefits religion in a way more direct and more substantial than practices that are accepted in our national heritage.

## II

These principles are not difficult to apply to the facts of the cases before us. In permitting the displays on government property of the menorah and the crèche, the city and county sought to do no more than "celebrate the season," and to acknowledge, along with many of their citizens, the historical background and the religious, as well as secular, nature of the Chanukah and Christmas holidays. This interest falls well within the tradition of government accommodation and acknowledgment of religion that has marked our history from the beginning.[2] It cannot be disputed that government, if it chooses,

---

[2] The majority rejects the suggestion that the display of the crèche can "be justified as an 'accommodation' of religion," because it "does not remove any burden on the free exercise of Christianity." Contrary to the assumption implicit in this analysis, however, we have never held that government's power to accommodate and recognize religion extends no further than the requirements of the Free Exercise Clause. To the contrary, "[t]he limits of permissible state accommodation to religion are by no means coextensive with the non-interference mandated by the Free Exercise Clause." *Walz v. Tax Comm'n*, 397 U.S. 664, 673

may participate in sharing with its citizens the joy of the holiday season, by declaring public holidays, installing or permitting festive displays, sponsoring celebrations and parades, and providing holiday vacations for its employees. All levels of our government do precisely that. As we said in *Lynch*, "Government has long recognized—indeed it has subsidized—holidays with religious significance." 465 U.S., 676.

If government is to participate in its citizens' celebration of a holiday that contains both a secular and a religious component, enforced recognition of only the secular aspect would signify the callous indifference toward religious faith that our cases and traditions do not require; for by commemorating the holiday only as it is celebrated by nonadherents, the government would be refusing to acknowledge the plain fact, and the historical reality, that many of its citizens celebrate its religious aspects as well. Judicial invalidation of government's attempts to recognize the religious underpinnings of the holiday would signal not neutrality but a pervasive intent to insulate government from all things religious. The Religion Clauses do not require government to acknowledge these holidays or their religious component; but our strong tradition of government accommodation and acknowledgment permits government to do so.

There is no suggestion here that the government's power to coerce has been used to further the interests of Christianity or Judaism in any way. No one was compelled to observe or participate in any religious ceremony or activity. Neither the city nor the county contributed significant amounts of tax money to serve the cause of one religious faith. The crèche and the menorah are purely passive symbols of religious holidays. Passersby who disagree with the message conveyed by these displays are free to ignore them, or even to turn their backs, just as they are free to do when they disagree with any other form of government speech.

There is no realistic risk that the crèche and the menorah represent an effort to proselytize or are otherwise the first step down the road to an establishment of religion. *Lynch* is dispositive of this claim with respect to the crèche, and I find no reason for reaching a different result with respect to the menorah. Both are the traditional symbols of religious holidays that over time have acquired a secular component. Without ambiguity, *Lynch* instructs that "the focus of our inquiry must be on the [religious symbol] in the context of the [holiday] season." In that context, religious displays that serve "to celebrate the Holiday and to depict the origins of that Holiday" give rise to no Establishment Clause concern. If Congress and the state legislatures do not run afoul of the Establishment Clause when they begin each day with a state-sponsored prayer for divine guidance offered by a chaplain whose salary is paid at government expense, I cannot comprehend how a menorah or a crèche, displayed in the limited context of the holiday season, can be invalid.[4]

---

[4] The majority suggests that our approval of legislative prayer in *Marsh v. Chambers* is to be distinguished from these cases on the ground that legislative prayer is nonsectarian, while crèches and menorahs are not. In the first place, of course, this purported distinction is utterly inconsistent with the majority's belief that the Establishment Clause "mean[s] no official preference even for religion over nonreligion." If year-round legislative prayer does not express "official preference for religion over nonreligion," a crèche or menorah display in the context of the holiday season certainly does not "demonstrate a preference for one particular sect or creed." Moreover, the majority chooses to ignore the Court's opinion in *Lynch v.*

Respondents say that the religious displays involved here are distinguishable from the crèche in *Lynch* because they are located on government property and are not surrounded by the candy canes, reindeer, and other holiday paraphernalia that were a part of the display in *Lynch*. Nothing in CHIEF JUSTICE BURGER's opinion for the Court in *Lynch* provides support for these purported distinctions. After describing the facts, the *Lynch* opinion makes no mention of either of these factors. It concentrates instead on the significance of the crèche as part of the entire holiday season. Indeed, it is clear that the Court did not view the secular aspects of the display as somehow subduing the religious message conveyed by the crèche, for the majority expressly rejected the dissenters' suggestion that it sought "'to explain away the clear religious import of the crèche'" or had "equated the crèche with a Santa's house or reindeer." Crucial to the Court's conclusion was not the number, prominence, or type of secular items contained in the holiday display but the simple fact that, when displayed by government during the Christmas season, a crèche presents no realistic danger of moving government down the forbidden road toward an establishment of religion. Whether the crèche be surrounded by poinsettias, talking wishing wells, or carolers, the conclusion remains the same, for the relevant context is not the items in the display itself but the season as a whole.

The fact that the crèche and menorah are both located on government property, even at the very seat of government, is likewise inconsequential. In the first place, the *Lynch* Court did not rely on the fact that the setting for Pawtucket's display was a privately owned park, and it is difficult to suggest that anyone could have failed to receive a message of government sponsorship after observing Santa Claus ride the city fire engine to the park to join with the mayor of Pawtucket in inaugurating the holiday season by turning on the lights of the city-owned display. Indeed, the District Court in *Lynch* found that "people might reasonably mistake the Park for public property," and rejected as "frivolous" the suggestion that the display was not directly associated with the city.

Our cases do not suggest, moreover, that the use of public property necessarily converts otherwise permissible government conduct into an Establishment Clause violation. To the contrary, in some circumstances the First Amendment may *require* that government property be available for use by religious groups, and even where not required, such use has long been permitted. The prayer approved in *Marsh v. Chambers*, for example, was conducted in the legislative chamber of the State of Nebraska, surely the single place most likely to be thought the center of state authority.

Nor can I comprehend why it should be that placement of a government-owned crèche on private land is lawful while placement of a privately owned crèche on public land is not.[5] If anything, I should have thought government ownership of a religious symbol presented the more difficult question under the Establishment Clause, but as *Lynch* resolved that question to sustain the government action, the sponsorship here ought to be all the easier to sustain.

---

*Donnelly,* which applied *precisely the same analysis* as that I apply today: "[T]o conclude that the primary effect of including the crèche is to advance religion in violation of the Establishment Clause would require that we view it as more beneficial to and more an endorsement of religion . . . than . . . the legislative prayers upheld in *Marsh v. Chambers* . . . ."

[5] The crèche in *Lynch* was owned by Pawtucket. Neither the crèche nor the menorah at issue in this case is owned by a governmental entity.

In short, nothing about the religious displays here distinguishes them in any meaningful way from the crèche we permitted in *Lynch*.

If *Lynch* is still good law—and until today it was—the judgment below cannot stand. I accept and indeed approve both the holding and the reasoning of CHIEF JUSTICE BURGER's opinion in *Lynch*, and so I must dissent from the judgment that the crèche display is unconstitutional. On the same reasoning, I agree that the menorah display is constitutional.

## III

The majority invalidates display of the crèche, not because it disagrees with the interpretation of *Lynch* applied above, but because it chooses to discard the reasoning of the *Lynch* majority opinion in favor of JUSTICE O'CONNOR's concurring opinion in that case. It has never been my understanding that a concurring opinion "suggest[ing] a clarification of our . . . doctrine," *Lynch*, 465 U.S., 687 (O'CONNOR, J., concurring), could take precedence over an opinion joined in its entirety by five Members of the Court. As a general rule, the principle of *stare decisis* directs us to adhere not only to the holdings of our prior cases, but also to their explications of the governing rules of law. Since the majority does not state its intent to overrule *Lynch*, I find its refusal to apply the reasoning of that decision quite confusing.

Even if *Lynch* did not control, I would not commit this Court to the test applied by the majority today. The notion that cases arising under the Establishment Clause should be decided by an inquiry into whether a "'reasonable observer'" may "'fairly understand'" government action to "'sen[d] a message to nonadherents that they are outsiders, not full members of the political community,'" is a recent, and in my view most unwelcome, addition to our tangled Establishment Clause jurisprudence. Although a scattering of our cases have used "endorsement" as another word for "preference" or "*imprimatur*," the endorsement test applied by the majority had its genesis in JUSTICE O'CONNOR's concurring opinion in *Lynch*. . . . Only one opinion for the Court has purported to apply it in full, see *School Dist. of Grand Rapids v. Ball*, but the majority's opinion in these cases suggests that this novel theory is fast becoming a permanent accretion to the law. For the reasons expressed below, I submit that the endorsement test is flawed in its fundamentals and unworkable in practice. The uncritical adoption of this standard is every bit as troubling as the bizarre result it produces in the cases before us.

## A

I take it as settled law that, whatever standard the Court applies to Establishment Clause claims, it must at least suggest results consistent with our precedents and the historical practices that, by tradition, have informed our First Amendment jurisprudence. It is true that, for reasons quite unrelated to the First Amendment, displays commemorating religious holidays were not commonplace in 1791. But the relevance of history is not confined to the inquiry into whether the challenged practice itself is a part of our accepted traditions dating back to the Founding.

Our decision in *Marsh v. Chambers* illustrates this proposition. The dissent in that case sought to characterize the decision as "carving out an exception to the Establishment Clause rather than reshaping Establishment Clause doctrine to accommodate legislative prayer," but the majority rejected the suggestion that "historical patterns ca[n] justify contemporary violations of constitutional guarantees." *Marsh* stands for the proposition, not that specific practices common in 1791 are an exception to the otherwise broad sweep of the Establishment Clause, but rather that the meaning of the Clause is to be determined by reference to historical practices and understandings. Whatever test we choose to apply must permit not only legitimate practices two centuries old but also any other practices with no greater potential for an establishment of religion. The First Amendment is a rule, not a digest or compendium. A test for implementing the protections of the Establishment Clause that, if applied with consistency, would invalidate longstanding traditions cannot be a proper reading of the Clause.

If the endorsement test, applied without artificial exceptions for historical practice, reached results consistent with history, my objections to it would have less force. But, as I understand that test, the touchstone of an Establishment Clause violation is whether nonadherents would be made to feel like "outsiders" by government recognition or accommodation of religion. Few of our traditional practices recognizing the part religion plays in our society can withstand scrutiny under a faithful application of this formula.

Some examples suffice to make plain my concerns. Since the Founding of our Republic, American Presidents have issued Thanksgiving Proclamations establishing a national day of celebration and prayer. The first such proclamation was issued by President Washington at the request of the First Congress, and "recommend[ed] and assign[ed]" a day "to be devoted by the people of these States to the service of that great and glorious Being who is the beneficent author of all the good that was, that is, or that will be," so that "we may then unite in most humbly offering our prayers and supplications to the great Lord and Ruler of Nations, and beseech Him to . . . promote the knowledge and practice of true religion and virtue . . . ." Most of President Washington's successors have followed suit,[8] and the forthrightly religious nature of these proclamations has not waned with the years. President Franklin D. Roosevelt went so far as to "suggest a nationwide reading of the Holy Scriptures during the period from Thanksgiving Day to Christmas" so that "we may bear more earnest witness to our gratitude to Almighty God." It requires little imagination to conclude that these proclamations would cause nonadherents to feel excluded, yet they have been a part of our national heritage from the beginning.

The Executive has not been the only Branch of our Government to recognize the central role of religion in our society. The fact that this Court opens its sessions with the request that "God save the United States and this honorable Court" has been noted elsewhere. The Legislature has gone much further, not only employing legislative chaplains, see 2 U.S.C. § 61d, but also setting aside a special prayer room in the Capitol for use by Members of the House and Senate. The room is decorated with a large stained glass panel that depicts President Washington kneeling in prayer; around him is etched the first verse of the 16th Psalm: "Preserve me, O God, for in Thee do I put my trust." Beneath the panel is a rostrum on which a Bible is placed; next to the rostrum is an American Flag. Some endorsement is inherent in these reasonable accommodations, yet the Establishment Clause does not forbid them.

The United States Code itself contains religious references that would be suspect under the endorsement test. Congress has directed the President to

---

[8] In keeping with his strict views of the degree of separation mandated by the Establishment Clause, Thomas Jefferson declined to follow this tradition.

"set aside and proclaim a suitable day each year . . . as a National Day of Prayer, on which the people of the United States may turn to God in prayer and meditation at churches, in groups, and as individuals." This statute does not require anyone to pray, of course, but it is a straightforward endorsement of the concept of "turn[ing] to God in prayer." Also by statute, the Pledge of Allegiance to the Flag describes the United States as "one Nation under God." To be sure, no one is obligated to recite this phrase, but it borders on sophistry to suggest that the "'reasonable'" atheist would not feel less than a "'full membe[r] of the political community'" every time his fellow Americans recited, as part of their expression of patriotism and love for country, a phrase he believed to be false. Likewise, our national motto, "In God we trust," which is prominently engraved in the wall above the Speaker's dias in the Chamber of the House of Representatives and is reproduced on every coin minted and every dollar printed by the Federal Government, must have the same effect.

If the intent of the Establishment Clause is to protect individuals from mere feelings of exclusion, then legislative prayer cannot escape invalidation. It has been argued that "[these] government acknowledgments of religion serve, in the only ways reasonably possible in our culture, the legitimate secular purposes of solemnizing public occasions, expressing confidence in the future, and encouraging the recognition of what is worthy of appreciation in society." I fail to see why prayer is the only way to convey these messages; appeals to patriotism, moments of silence, and any number of other approaches would be as effective, were the only purposes at issue the ones described by the *Lynch* concurrence. Nor is it clear to me why "encouraging the recognition of what is worthy of appreciation in society" can be characterized as a purely secular purpose, if it can be achieved only through religious prayer. No doubt prayer is "worthy of appreciation," but that is most assuredly not because it is secular. Even accepting the secular-solemnization explanation at face value, moreover, it seems incredible to suggest that the average observer of legislative prayer who either believes in no religion or whose faith rejects the concept of God would not receive the clear message that his faith is out of step with the political norm. Either the endorsement test must invalidate scores of traditional practices recognizing the place religion holds in our culture, or it must be twisted and stretched to avoid inconsistency with practices we know to have been permitted in the past, while condemning similar practices with no greater endorsement effect simply by reason of their lack of historical antecedent.[10] Neither result is acceptable.

B

In addition to disregarding precedent and historical fact, the majority's approach to government use of religious symbolism threatens to trivialize consti-

---

[10] If the majority's test were to be applied logically, it would lead to the elimination of all nonsecular Christmas caroling in public buildings or, presumably, anywhere on public property. It is difficult to argue that lyrics like "Good Christian men, rejoice," "Joy to the world! the Savior reigns," "This, this is Christ the King," "Christ, by highest heav'n adored," and "Come and behold Him, Born the King of angels" have acquired such a secular nature that nonadherents would not feel "left out" by a government-sponsored or approved program that included these carols. We do not think for a moment that the Court will ban such carol programs, however. Like Thanksgiving Proclamations, the reference to God in the Pledge of Allegiance, and invocations to God in sessions of Congress and of this Court, they constitute practices that the Court will not proscribe, but that the Court's reasoning today does not explain.

tutional adjudication. By mischaracterizing the Court's opinion in *Lynch* as an endorsement-in-context test, JUSTICE BLACKMUN embraces a jurisprudence of minutiae. A reviewing court must consider whether the city has included Santas, talking wishing wells, reindeer, or other secular symbols as "a center of attention separate from the crèche." After determining whether these centers of attention are sufficiently "separate" that each "had their specific visual story to tell," the court must then measure their proximity to the crèche. A community that wishes to construct a constitutional display must also take care to avoid floral frames or other devices that might insulate the crèche from the sanitizing effect of the secular portions of the display. The majority also notes the presence of evergreens near the crèche that are identical to two small evergreens placed near official county signs. After today's decision, municipal greenery must be used with care.

Another important factor will be the prominence of the setting in which the display is placed. In this case, the Grand Staircase of the county courthouse proved too resplendent. Indeed, the Court finds that this location itself conveyed an "unmistakable message that [the county] supports and promotes the Christian praise to God that is the crèche's religious message."

My description of the majority's test, though perhaps uncharitable, is intended to illustrate the inevitable difficulties with its application.[11] This test could provide workable guidance to the lower courts, if ever, only after this Court has decided a long series of holiday display cases, using little more than intuition and a tape measure. Deciding cases on the basis of such an unguided examination of marginalia is irreconcilable with the imperative of applying neutral principles in constitutional adjudication. . . .

JUSTICE BLACKMUN employs in many respects a similar analysis with respect to the menorah, principally discussing its proximity to the Christmas tree and whether "it is . . . more sensible to interpret the menorah in light of the tree, rather than vice versa." JUSTICE BLACKMUN goes further, however, and in upholding the menorah as an acknowledgment of a holiday with secular aspects emphasizes the city's lack of "reasonable alternatives that are less religious in nature." This least-religious-means test presents several difficulties.[12] First, it creates an internal inconsistency in JUSTICE BLACKMUN's opinion. JUSTICE BLACKMUN earlier suggests that the display of a crèche is sometimes constitutional. But it is obvious that there are innumerable secular symbols of Christmas, and that there will always be a more secular alternative

---

[11] JUSTICE BLACKMUN and JUSTICE O'CONNOR defend the majority's test by suggesting that the approach followed in *Lynch* would require equally difficult line drawing. It is true that the *Lynch* test may involve courts in difficult line-drawing in the unusual case where a municipality insists on such extreme use of religious speech that an establishment of religion is threatened. Only adoption of the absolutist views that either *all* government involvement with religion is permissible, or that *none* is, can provide a bright line in all cases. That price for clarity is neither exacted nor permitted by the Constitution. But for the most part, JUSTICE BLACKMUN's and JUSTICE O'CONNOR's objections are not well taken. As a practical matter, the only cases of symbolic recognition likely to arise with much frequency are those involving simple holiday displays, and in that context *Lynch* provides unambiguous guidance. I would follow it. The majority's test, on the other hand, demands the Court to draw exquisite distinctions from fine detail in a wide range of cases. The anomalous result the test has produced here speaks for itself.

[12] Of course, a majority of the Court today rejects JUSTICE BLACKMUN's approach in this regard.

available in place of a crèche. Second, the test as applied by JUSTICE BLACK-MUN is unworkable, for it requires not only that the Court engage in the unfamiliar task of deciding whether a particular alternative symbol is more or less religious, but also whether the alternative would "look out of place." Third, although JUSTICE BLACKMUN purports not to be overruling *Lynch*, the more-secular-alternative test contradicts that decision, as it comes not from the Court's opinion, nor even from the concurrence, but from the dissent. The Court in *Lynch* noted that the dissent "argues that the city's objectives could have been achieved without including the crèche in the display." "True or false," we said, "that is irrelevant."

The result the Court reaches in these cases is perhaps the clearest illustration of the unwisdom of the endorsement test. Although JUSTICE O'CONNOR disavows JUSTICE BLACKMUN's suggestion that the minority or majority status of a religion is relevant to the question whether government recognition constitutes a forbidden endorsement, the very nature of the endorsement test, with its emphasis on the feelings of the objective observer, easily lends itself to this type of inquiry. If there be such a person as the "reasonable observer," I am quite certain that he or she will take away a salient message from our holding in these cases: the Supreme Court of the United States has concluded that the First Amendment creates classes of religions based on the relative numbers of their adherents. Those religions enjoying the largest following must be consigned to the status of least favored faiths so as to avoid any possible risk of offending members of minority religions. I would be the first to admit that many questions arising under the Establishment Clause do not admit of easy answers, but whatever the Clause requires, it is not the result reached by the Court today.

IV

The approach adopted by the majority contradicts important values embodied in the Clause. Obsessive, implacable resistance to all but the most carefully scripted and secularized forms of accommodation requires this Court to act as a censor, issuing national decrees as to what is orthodox and what is not. What is orthodox, in this context, means what is secular; the only Christmas the State can acknowledge is one in which references to religion have been held to a minimum. The Court thus lends its assistance to an Orwellian rewriting of history as many understand it. I can conceive of no judicial function more antithetical to the First Amendment.

A further contradiction arises from the majority's approach, for the Court also assumes the difficult and inappropriate task of saying what every religious symbol means. Before studying these cases, I had not known the full history of the menorah, and I suspect the same was true of my colleagues. More important, this history was, and is, likely unknown to the vast majority of people of all faiths who saw the symbol displayed in Pittsburgh. Even if the majority is quite right about the history of the menorah, it hardly follows that this same history informed the observers' view of the symbol and the reason for its presence. This Court is ill equipped to sit as a national theology board, and I question both the wisdom and the constitutionality of its doing so. Indeed, were I required to choose between the approach taken by the majority and a strict separationist view, I would have to respect the consistency of the latter.

The suit before us is admittedly a troubling one. It must be conceded that, however neutral the purpose of the city and county, the eager proselytizer may seek to use these symbols for his own ends. The urge to use them to teach or to taunt is always present. It is also true that some devout adherents of Judaism or Christianity may be as offended by the holiday display as are nonbelievers, if not more so. To place these religious symbols in a common hallway or sidewalk, where they may be ignored or even insulted, must be distasteful to many who cherish their meaning.

For these reasons, I might have voted against installation of these particular displays were I a local legislative official. But we have no jurisdiction over matters of taste within the realm of constitutionally permissible discretion. Our role is enforcement of a written Constitution. In my view, the principles of the Establishment Clause and our Nation's historic traditions of diversity and pluralism allow communities to make reasonable judgments respecting the accommodation or acknowledgment of holidays with both cultural and religious aspects. No constitutional violation occurs when they do so by displaying a symbol of the holiday's religious origins.

---

## NOTES AND QUESTIONS

1. Who owns the crèche that is involved in this case? Who owns the menorah, Christmas tree, and "salute to liberty" sign? On what kind of property does each display sit? What role do these factors play in the case?

2. What proposition does the *Lynch* case stand for, according to Justice Blackmun? How does Blackmun use *Lynch* in this case, or does he? How would you explain the different outcomes in the two displays, based on Justices Blackmun's and O'Connor's opinions?

3. According to Justice Blackmun's opinion, was the "Grand Staircase" of the county courthouse regularly made available to community groups' displays? How significant is this point to the Court's decision?

4. How does Justice O'Connor's analysis of the display at the city-county building differ from Justice Blackmun's? Of the two, who has the more persuasive argument on this issue? Is the Court's ruling on the display at the city-county building correct in your opinion? Explain.

5. In the *Allegheny* case, Justice Blackmun says it is wrong to assume that, if the government may celebrate the secular aspects of Christmas, then it may or must celebrate the religious aspects of the holiday as well. Blackmun explains:

    The government does not discriminate against any citizen on the basis of the citizen's religious faith if the government is secular in its functions and operations. On the contrary, the Constitution mandates that the government remain secular, rather than affiliate itself with religious beliefs or institutions, precisely in order to avoid discriminating among citizens on the basis of their religious faiths.

    In his dissenting opinion in this case, however, Justice Kennedy states:

    If government is to participate in its citizens' celebration of a holiday that contains both a secular and a religious component, enforced recognition of only the secular aspect would signify the callous indifference toward religious faith that our cases and traditions do not require; for by commemorating the holiday only as it is celebrated by nonadherents, the government would be refusing to acknowledge the plain fact, and the historical reality, that many of its citizens celebrate its religious aspects as well. Judicial invalidation of government's attempts to recognize the religious underpinnings of the holiday would signal not neutrality but a pervasive intent to insulate government from all things religious. The Religion Clauses do not require government to acknowledge these holidays or their religious component; but our strong tradition of government accommodation and acknowledgment permits government to do so.

What are the presumptions about the role of the religion clauses (and of religion in public life) that underlie each of these statements? Which justice's arguments are more consistent with prior case law? Who has the better argument? Further, do you agree with Justice Blackmun when he says that a secular state "is not the same as an atheistic or antireligious state"?

6. According to Justice O'Connor, what is the "essential command" of the Establishment Clause? Do the opinions of Justices Blackmun and Brennan agree or disagree with this statement?

7. What are Justice Kennedy's criticisms of the endorsement test and its application to the facts of this case? What test would he use as a substitute for that test? What defenses do Justices O'Connor and Blackmun offer for the endorsement test? What criticisms do Justice O'Connor and Justice Blackmun have for the test Justices Kennedy proposes? Which test provides the most certainty in terms of predicting whether various forms of religious expression will pass constitutional muster? Which test best protects Establishment Clause values?

8. In her concurring opinion Justice O'Connor states: "To require a showing of coercion, even indirect coercion, as an essential element of an Establishment Clause violation would make the Free Exercise Clause a redundancy." What does she mean?

9. In the *Allegheny* case, O'Connor argues that application of the endorsement test would not result in striking down various instances of "ceremonial deism." Is her argument convincing? What limiting principles does she envision for the endorsement test?

10. In the *Lynch* and *Allegheny* cases, Justice Stevens advocates a presumption the Court majority does not adopt. What is that presumption? Would the presumption apply when a religious group temporarily erects a cross in a public park for use during its Easter sunrise service (assume that other nongovernmental groups also use the park and temporarily display their symbols there)? In his opinion concurring in part and dissenting in part, Justice Brennan says that he "continue[s] to believe that the display of an object that 'retains a specifically Christian [or other] religious meaning,' is incompatible with the separation of church and state demanded by our Constitution." How would you guess that Justice Brennan would react to the hypothetical described above?

11. In his opinion concurring in part in the judgment and dissenting in part, Justice Kennedy states: "The ability of the organized community to recognize and accommodate religion in a society with a pervasive public sector requires diligent observance of the border between accommodation and establishment." According to Kennedy, what are the ways in which accommodation should be limited so that it does not result in establishment? In what ways do Justices O'Connor and Kennedy disagree regarding governmental accommodation of religion?

12. Justice Kennedy further criticizes Justice Blackmun's opinion for "embracing a jurisprudence of minutiae," while Justice Brennan says, "I shudder to think that the only 'reasonable observer' is one who shares the particular views on perspective, spacing, and accent expressed in Justice Blackmun's opinion, thus making analysis under the Establishment Clause look more like an exam in Art 101 than an inquiry into constitutional law." Yet Justices Kennedy and Brennan disagree about the proper result in the *Allegheny* case. Explain.

13. Justice Kennedy writes:

> Respondents say that the religious displays involved here are distinguishable from the crèche in *Lynch* because they are located on government property and are not surrounded by the candy canes, reindeer, and other holiday paraphernalia that were a part of the display in *Lynch*. Nothing in Chief Justice Burger's opinion for the Court in *Lynch* provides support for these purported distinctions. . . . The majority invalidates display of the crèche, not because it disagrees with the interpretation of *Lynch* . . . but because it chooses to discard the reasoning of the *Lynch* majority opinion in favor of Justice O'Connor's concurring opinion in that case.

According to Justice Kennedy, what is the essential holding of the *Lynch* case? Is Justice Kennedy's reading of the *Lynch* case a plausible one? In any case, is Kennedy correct to take issue with the fact that Justice Blackmun applies the endorsement test in the *Allegheny* case?

14. Toward the conclusion of his opinion, Justice Kennedy writes:

> If there be such a person as the "reasonable observer," I am quite certain that he or she will take away a salient message from our holding in these cases: the Supreme Court of the United States has concluded that the First Amendment creates classes of religions based on the relative numbers of their adherents. Those religions enjoying the largest following must be consigned to the status of least favored faiths so as to avoid any possible risk of offending members of minority religions.

What constitutional danger is Justice Kennedy referencing? What political danger?

15. Justice Kennedy notes that he "might have voted against installation of these particular displays were [he] a local legislative official." Nonetheless, he rules that they should be upheld as a constitutional matter. In what ways are the roles of a judge and a legislator different, according to Justice Kennedy?

16. Suppose a public high school displays a menorah and a Christmas tree along with a "holiday countdown" sign (a sign counting down the days until the winter break) in the school atrium during the month of December. Would this display be constitutional under these cases and the cases described in previous chapters? Suppose a Christian student complained that her religious holiday was essentially excluded by the display. Alternatively, suppose a Hindu student made a similar complaint. What action(s) should the school take in response to the complaint(s)?

The Supreme Court also has dealt with cases involving religious displays outside the context of religious holidays. For example, in 1995, the Court confronted a case in which the Ku Klux Klan wanted to post an unattended Latin cross on a temporary basis on Capitol Square in Columbus, Ohio. The Square, which surrounds the statehouse in Columbus, had been open to a number of uses over the years, including use by nongovernmental groups that had erected their own temporary displays. Simply stated, the question in this case was whether this display constituted nongovernmental speech endorsing religion that the First Amendment protects, or whether it constituted governmental speech endorsing religion, which the First Amendment forbids. Here again, the Court splintered. Seven of the justices agreed that this speech was constitutionally protected, but they could not fully agree on a rationale to support that result.

## CAPITOL SQUARE REVIEW BOARD v. PINETTE
## 515 U.S. 753 (1995)

JUSTICE SCALIA announced the judgment of the Court and delivered the opinion of the Court with respect to Parts I, II, and III, and an opinion with respect to Part IV, in which THE CHIEF JUSTICE, JUSTICE KENNEDY, and JUSTICE THOMAS join. . . .

The question in this case is whether a State violates the Establishment Clause when, pursuant to a religiously neutral state policy, it permits a private party to display an unattended religious symbol in a traditional public forum located next to its seat of government.

I

Capitol Square is a 10-acre, state-owned plaza surrounding the statehouse in Columbus, Ohio. For over a century the square has been used for public speeches, gatherings, and festivals advocating and celebrating a variety of causes, both secular and religious. [Ohio law] makes the square available "for use by the public . . . for free discussion of public questions, or for activities of a broad public purpose," gives the Capitol Square Review and Advisory Board (Board) responsibility for regulating public access. To use the square, a group must simply fill out an official application form and meet several criteria, which concern primarily safety, sanitation, and noninterference with other uses of the square, and which are neutral as to the speech content of the proposed event.

It has been the Board's policy "to allow a broad range of speakers and other gatherings of people to conduct events on the Capitol Square." Such diverse groups as homosexual rights organizations, the Ku Klux Klan, and the United Way have held rallies. The Board has also permitted a variety of unattended displays on Capitol Square: a state-sponsored lighted tree during the Christmas season, a privately sponsored menorah during Chanukah, a display showing the progress of a United Way fundraising campaign, and booths and exhibits during an arts festival. Although there was some dispute in this litigation regarding the frequency of unattended displays, the District Court found, with ample justification, that there was no policy against them.

In November 1993, after reversing an initial decision to ban unattended holiday displays from the square during December 1993, the Board authorized the State to put up its annual Christmas tree. On November 29, 1993, the Board granted a rabbi's application to erect a menorah. That same day, the Board received an application from respondent Donnie Carr, an officer of the Ohio Ku Klux Klan, to place a cross on the square from December 8, 1993, to December 24, 1993. The Board denied that application on December 3, informing the Klan by letter that the decision to deny "was made upon the advice of counsel, in a good faith attempt to comply with the Ohio and United States Constitutions, as they have been interpreted in relevant decisions by the Federal and State Courts."

Two weeks later, having been unsuccessful in its effort to obtain administrative relief from the Board's decision, the Ohio Klan, through its leader Vincent Pinette, filed the present suit in the United States District Court for the Southern District of Ohio, seeking an injunction requiring the Board to issue the requested permit. . . .

## II . . .

Respondents' religious display in Capitol Square was private expression. Our precedent establishes that private religious speech, far from being a First Amendment orphan, is as fully protected under the Free Speech Clause as secular private expression. . . . Indeed, in Anglo-American history, at least, government suppression of speech has so commonly been directed *precisely* at religious speech that a free-speech clause without religion would be Hamlet without the prince. Accordingly, we have not excluded from free-speech protections religious proselytizing, or even acts of worship. Petitioners do not dispute that respondents, in displaying their cross, were engaging in constitutionally protected expression. They do contend that the constitutional protection does not extend to the length of permitting that expression to be made on Capitol Square.

It is undeniable, of course, that speech which is constitutionally protected against state suppression is not thereby accorded a guaranteed forum on all property owned by the State. The right to use government property for one's private expression depends upon whether the property has by law or tradition been given the status of a public forum, or rather has been reserved for specific official uses. If the former, a State's right to limit protected expressive activity is sharply circumscribed: It may impose reasonable, content-neutral time, place, and manner restrictions (a ban on all unattended displays, which did not exist here, might be one such), but it may regulate expressive *content* only if such a restriction is necessary, and narrowly drawn, to serve a compelling state interest. These strict standards apply here, since the District Court and the Court of Appeals found that Capitol Square was a traditional public forum.

Petitioners do not claim that their denial of respondents' application was based upon a content-neutral time, place, or manner restriction. To the contrary, they concede—indeed it is the essence of their case—that the Board rejected the display precisely because its content was religious. Petitioners advance a single justification for closing Capitol Square to respondents' cross: the State's interest in avoiding official endorsement of Christianity, as required by the Establishment Clause.

## III

There is no doubt that compliance with the Establishment Clause is a state interest sufficiently compelling to justify content-based restrictions on speech. Whether that interest is implicated here, however, is a different question. And we do not write on a blank slate in answering it. We have twice previously addressed the combination of private religious expression, a forum available for public use, content-based regulation, and a State's interest in complying with the Establishment Clause. [*Lamb's Chapel v. Center Moriches Union Free School District; Widmar v. Vincent*] Both times, we have struck down the restriction on religious content. . . .

Quite obviously, the factors that we considered determinative in *Lamb's Chapel* and *Widmar* exist here as well. The State did not sponsor respondents' expression, the expression was made on government property that had been opened to the public for speech, and permission was requested through the same application process and on the same terms required of other private groups.

## IV

Petitioners argue that one feature of the present case distinguishes it from *Lamb's Chapel* and *Widmar*: the forum's proximity to the seat of government, which, they contend, may produce the perception that the cross bears the State's approval. They urge us to apply the so-called "endorsement test," and to find that, because an observer might mistake private expression for officially endorsed religious expression, the State's content-based restriction is constitutional.

We must note, to begin with, that it is not really an "endorsement test" of any sort, much less the "endorsement test" which appears in our more recent Establishment Clause jurisprudence, that petitioners urge upon us. "Endorsement" connotes an expression or demonstration of approval or support. Our cases have accordingly equated "endorsement" with "promotion" or "favoritism." We find it peculiar to say that government "promotes" or "favors" a religious display by giving it the same access to a public forum that all other displays enjoy. And as a matter of Establishment Clause jurisprudence, we have consistently held that it is no violation for government to enact neutral policies that happen to benefit religion. . . . Where we have tested for endorsement of religion, the subject of the test was either expression *by the government itself*, or else government action alleged to *discriminate in favor* of private religious expression or activity. The test petitioners propose, which would attribute to a neutrally behaving government *private* religious expression, has no antecedent in our jurisprudence, and would better be called a "transferred endorsement" test.

Petitioners rely heavily on *Allegheny* and *Lynch*, but each is easily distinguished. In *Allegheny* we held that the display of a privately sponsored crèche on the "Grand Staircase" of the Allegheny County Courthouse violated the Establishment Clause. That staircase was not, however, open to all on an equal basis, so the County was *favoring* sectarian religious expression. 492 U.S., 599-600, and n. 50 ("The Grand Staircase does not appear to be the kind of location in which all were free to place their displays"). We expressly distinguished that site from the kind of public forum at issue here, and made clear that if the staircase were available to all on the same terms, "the presence of the crèche in that location for over six weeks would then *not* serve to associate the government with the crèche." In *Lynch* we held that a city's display of a crèche did not violate the Establishment Clause because, in context, the display did not endorse religion. The opinion does assume, as petitioners contend, that the *government's* use of religious symbols is unconstitutional if it effectively endorses sectarian religious belief. But the case neither holds nor even remotely assumes that the government's neutral treatment of *private* religious expression can be unconstitutional.

Petitioners argue that absence of perceived endorsement was material in *Lamb's Chapel* and *Widmar*. We did state in *Lamb's Chapel* that there was "no realistic danger that the community would think that the District was endorsing religion or any particular creed," But that conclusion was not the result of empirical investigation; it followed directly, we thought, from the fact that the forum was open and the religious activity privately sponsored. It is significant that we referred only to what would be thought by "the community"—not by outsiders or individual members of the community uninformed about the school's practice. Surely some of the latter, hearing of religious ceremonies on school premises, and not knowing of the premises' availability and use for all sorts of other private activities, *might* leap to the erroneous conclusion of state endorsement. But, we in effect said, given an open forum and private sponsorship, erroneous conclusions do not count. So also in *Widmar*. Once we determined that the benefit to religious groups from the public forum was incidental and shared by other groups, we categorically rejected the State's Establishment Clause defense.

What distinguishes *Allegheny* and the dictum in *Lynch* from *Widmar* and *Lamb's Chapel* is the difference between government speech and private speech. "There is a crucial difference between *government* speech endorsing religion, which the Establishment Clause forbids, and *private* speech endorsing religion, which the Free Speech and Free Exercise Clauses protect."[2] Petitioners assert, in effect, that that distinction disappears when the private speech is conducted too close to the symbols of government. But that, of course, must be merely a subpart of a more general principle: that the distinction disappears whenever private speech can be mistaken for government speech. That proposition cannot be accepted, at least where, as here, the government has not fostered or encouraged the mistake.

---

[2] This statement in JUSTICE O'CONNOR's *Mergens* opinion is followed by the observation: "We think that secondary school students are mature enough and are likely to understand that a school does not endorse or support student speech that it merely permits on a nondiscriminatory basis." 496 U.S., 250. JUSTICE O'CONNOR today says this observation means that, even when we recognize private speech to be at issue, we must apply the endorsement test. But that would cause the second sentence to contradict the first, saying in effect that the "difference between government speech . . . and private speech" is not "crucial."

Of course, giving sectarian religious speech preferential access to a forum close to the seat of government (or anywhere else for that matter) would violate the Establishment Clause (as well as the Free Speech Clause, since it would involve content discrimination). And one can conceive of a case in which a governmental entity manipulates its administration of a public forum close to the seat of government (or within a government building) in such a manner that only certain religious groups take advantage of it, creating an impression of endorsement *that is in fact accurate*. But those situations, which involve governmental *favoritism*, do not exist here. Capitol Square is a genuinely public forum, is known to be a public forum, and has been widely used as a public forum for many, many years. Private religious speech cannot be subject to veto by those who see favoritism where there is none.

The contrary view, most strongly espoused by JUSTICE STEVENS, but endorsed by JUSTICE SOUTER and JUSTICE O'CONNOR as well, exiles private religious speech to a realm of less-protected expression heretofore inhabited only by sexually explicit displays and commercial speech. It will be a sad day when this Court casts piety in with pornography, and finds the First Amendment more hospitable to private expletives, than to private prayers. This would be merely bizarre were religious speech simply *as* protected by the Constitution as other forms of private speech; but it is outright perverse when one considers that private religious expression receives *preferential* treatment under the Free Exercise Clause. It is no answer to say that the Establishment Clause tempers religious speech. By its terms that Clause applies only to the words and acts of *government*. It was never meant, and has never been read by this Court, to serve as an impediment to purely *private* religious speech connected to the State only through its occurrence in a public forum.

Since petitioners' "transferred endorsement" principle cannot possibly be restricted to squares in front of state capitols, the Establishment Clause regime that it would usher in is most unappealing. To require (and permit) access by a religious group in *Lamb's Chapel*, it was sufficient that the group's activity was not in fact government sponsored, that the event was open to the public, and that the benefit of the facilities was shared by various organizations. Petitioners' rule would require school districts adopting similar policies in the future to guess whether some undetermined critical mass of the community might nonetheless perceive the district to be advocating a religious viewpoint. Similarly, state universities would be forced to reassess our statement that "an open forum in a public university does not confer any *imprimatur* of state approval on religious sects or practices." *Widmar*, 454 U.S., 274. Whether it does would henceforth depend upon immediate appearances. Policymakers would find themselves in a vise between the Establishment Clause on one side and the Free Speech and Free Exercise Clauses on the other. Every proposed act of private, religious expression in a public forum would force officials to weigh a host of imponderables. How close to government is too close? What kind of building, and in what context, symbolizes state authority? If the State guessed wrong in one direction, it would be guilty of an Establishment Clause violation; if in the other, it would be liable for suppressing free exercise or free speech (a risk not run when the State restrains only its *own* expression).

The "transferred endorsement" test would also disrupt the settled principle that policies providing incidental benefits to religion do not contravene the Establishment Clause. That principle is the basis for the constitutionality of a broad range of laws, not merely those that implicate free-speech issues. It has radical implications for our public policy to suggest that neutral laws are invalid whenever hypothetical observers may—*even reasonably*—confuse an incidental benefit to religion with state endorsement.[3]

If Ohio is concerned about misperceptions, nothing prevents it from requiring all private displays in the square to be identified as such. That would be a content-neutral "manner" restriction that is assuredly constitutional. But the State may not, on the claim of misperception of official endorsement, ban all private religious speech from the public square, or discriminate against it by requiring religious speech alone to disclaim public sponsorship.[4]

Religious expression cannot violate the Establishment Clause where it (1) is purely private and (2) occurs in a traditional or designated public forum, publicly announced and open to all on equal terms. Those conditions are satisfied here, and therefore the State may not bar respondents' cross from Capitol Square.

The judgment of the Court of Appeals is

*Affirmed.*

▧ JUSTICE THOMAS, concurring.

I join the Court's conclusion that petitioner's exclusion of the Ku Klux Klan's cross cannot be justified on Establishment Clause grounds. But the fact

---

[3] If it is true, as JUSTICE O'CONNOR suggests, that she would not "be likely to come to a different result from the plurality where truly private speech is allowed on equal terms in a vigorous public forum that the government has administered properly," then she is extending the "endorsement test" to private speech to cover an eventuality that is "not likely" to occur. Before doing that, it would seem desirable to explore the precise degree of the unlikelihood (is it perhaps 100%?)—for as we point out in text, the extension to private speech has considerable costs. Contrary to what JUSTICE O'CONNOR, JUSTICE SOUTER, and JUSTICE STEVENS argue, the endorsement test does not supply an appropriate standard for the inquiry before us. It supplies no standard whatsoever. The lower federal courts that JUSTICE O'CONNOR's concurrence identifies as having "applied the endorsement test in precisely the context before us today," have reached precisely *differing* results—which is what led the Court to take this case. And if further proof of the invited chaos is required, one need only follow the debate between the concurrence and JUSTICE STEVENS' dissent as to whether the hypothetical beholder who will be the determinant of "endorsement" should be any beholder (no matter how unknowledgeable), or the *average* beholder, or (what JUSTICE STEVENS accuses the concurrence of favoring) the "ultrareasonable" beholder. And, of course, even when one achieves agreement upon that question, it will be unrealistic to expect different judges (or should it be juries?) to reach consistent answers as to what any beholder, the average beholder, or the ultrareasonable beholder (as the case may be) would think. It is irresponsible to make the Nation's legislators walk this minefield.

[4] For this reason, among others, we do not inquire into the adequacy of the identification that was attached to the cross ultimately erected in this case. The difficulties posed by such an inquiry, however, are yet another reason to reject the principle of "transferred endorsement." The only principled line for adequacy of identification would be identification that is legible at whatever distance the cross is visible. Otherwise, the uninformed viewer who does not have time or inclination to come closer to read the sign might be misled, just as (under current law) the uninformed viewer who does not have time or inclination to inquire whether speech in Capitol Square is publicly endorsed speech might be misled. Needless to say, such a rule would place considerable constraint upon religious speech, not to mention that it would be ridiculous. But if one rejects that criterion, courts would have to decide (on what basis we cannot imagine) how large an identifying sign is large enough. Our Religion Clause jurisprudence is complex enough without the addition of this highly litigable feature.

that the legal issue before us involves the Establishment Clause should not lead anyone to think that a cross erected by the Ku Klux Klan is a purely religious symbol. The erection of such a cross is a political act, not a Christian one. . . .

Although the Klan might have sought to convey a message with some religious component, I think that the Klan had a primarily nonreligious purpose in erecting the cross. The Klan simply has appropriated one of the most sacred of religious symbols as a symbol of hate. In my mind, this suggests that this case may not have truly involved the Establishment Clause, although I agree with the Court's disposition because of the manner in which the case has come before us. In the end, there may be much less here than meets the eye.

▒ JUSTICE O'CONNOR, with whom JUSTICE SOUTER and JUSTICE BREYER join, concurring in part and concurring in the judgment.

I join Parts I, II, and III of the Court's opinion and concur in the judgment. Despite the messages of bigotry and racism that may be conveyed along with religious connotations by the display of a Ku Klux Klan cross, at bottom this case must be understood as it has been presented to us—as a case about private religious expression and whether the State's relationship to it violates the Establishment Clause. In my view, "the endorsement test asks the right question about governmental practices challenged on Establishment Clause grounds, including challenged practices involving the display of religious symbols," *Allegheny v. ACLU*, 492 U.S. 573, 628, even where a neutral state policy toward private religious speech in a public forum is at issue. Accordingly, I see no necessity to carve out, as the plurality opinion would today, an exception to the endorsement test for the public forum context.

For the reasons given by JUSTICE SOUTER, whose opinion I also join, I conclude on the facts of this case that there is "no realistic danger that the community would think that the [State] was endorsing religion or any particular creed," by granting respondents a permit to erect their temporary cross on Capitol Square. I write separately, however, to emphasize that, because it seeks to identify those situations in which government makes "'adherence to a religion relevant . . . to a person's standing in the political community,'" *Allegheny*, 492 U.S., 594, the endorsement test necessarily focuses upon the perception of a reasonable, informed observer.

I

"In recent years, we have paid particularly close attention [in Establishment Clause cases] to whether the challenged governmental practice either has the purpose or effect of 'endorsing' religion, a concern that has long had a place in our Establishment Clause jurisprudence." *Allegheny*, 592. A government statement "'that religion or a particular religious belief is favored or preferred,'" violates the prohibition against establishment of religion because such "endorsement sends a message to nonadherents that they are outsiders, not full members of the political community, and an accompanying message to adherents that they are insiders, favored members of the political community." Although "experience proves that the Establishment Clause . . . cannot easily be reduced to a single test," the endorsement inquiry captures the fundamental requirement of the Establishment Clause when courts are called upon to evaluate the constitutionality of religious symbols on public property.

While the plurality would limit application of the endorsement test to "expression *by the government itself*, . . . or else government action alleged to *discriminate in favor* of private religious expression or activity," I believe that an impermissible message of endorsement can be sent in a variety of contexts, not all of which involve direct government speech or outright favoritism. It is true that neither *Allegheny* nor *Lynch,* our two prior religious display cases, involved the same combination of private religious speech and a public forum that we have before us today. Nonetheless, as JUSTICE SOUTER aptly demonstrates, we have on several occasions employed an endorsement perspective in Establishment Clause cases where private religious conduct has intersected with a neutral governmental policy providing some benefit in a manner that parallels the instant case. Thus, while I join the discussion of *Lamb's Chapel* and *Widmar v. Vincent,* in Part III of the Court's opinion, I do so with full recognition that the factors the Court properly identifies ultimately led in each case to the conclusion that there was no endorsement of religion by the State.

There is, as the plurality notes, "a crucial difference between *government* speech endorsing religion, which the Establishment Clause forbids, and *private* speech endorsing religion, which the Free Speech and Free Exercise Clauses protect." But the quoted statement was made while applying the endorsement test itself; indeed, the sentence upon which the plurality relies was followed immediately by the conclusion that "secondary school students are mature enough and are likely to understand that a school does not endorse or support student speech that it merely permits on a nondiscriminatory basis." Thus, as I read the decisions JUSTICE SOUTER carefully surveys, our prior cases do not imply that the endorsement test has no place where private religious speech in a public forum is at issue. Moreover, numerous lower courts (including the Court of Appeals in this case) have applied the endorsement test in precisely the context before us today. Given this background, I see no necessity to draw new lines where "religious expression . . . (1) is purely private and (2) occurs in a traditional or designated public forum."

None of this is to suggest that I would be likely to come to a different result from the plurality where truly private speech is allowed on equal terms in a vigorous public forum that the government has administered properly. That the religious display at issue here was erected by a private group in a public square available "for use by the public . . . for free discussion of public questions, or for activities of a broad public purpose," certainly informs the Establishment Clause inquiry under the endorsement test. Indeed, many of the factors the plurality identifies are some of those I would consider important in deciding cases like this one where religious speakers seek access to public spaces: "The State did not sponsor respondents' expression, the expression was made on government property that had been opened to the public for speech, and permission was requested through the same application process and on the same terms required of other private groups." And, as I read the plurality opinion, a case is not governed by its proposed *per se* rule where such circumstances are otherwise—that is, where preferential placement of a religious symbol in a public space or government manipulation of the forum is involved.

To the plurality's consideration of the open nature of the forum and the private ownership of the display, however, I would add the presence of a sign disclaiming government sponsorship or endorsement on the Klan cross, which would make the State's role clear to the community. This factor is important because, as JUSTICE SOUTER makes clear, certain aspects of the cross display in this case arguably intimate government approval of respondents' private religious message—particularly that the cross is an especially potent sectarian symbol which stood unattended in close proximity to official government buildings. In context, a disclaimer helps remove doubt about state approval of respondents' religious message. On these facts, then, "the message [of inclusion] is one of neutrality rather than endorsement."

Our agreement as to the outcome of this case, however, cannot mask the fact that I part company with the plurality on a fundamental point: I disagree that "it has radical implications for our public policy to suggest that neutral laws are invalid whenever hypothetical observers may—*even reasonably*—confuse an incidental benefit to religion with state endorsement." On the contrary, when the reasonable observer would view a government practice as endorsing religion, I believe that it is our *duty* to hold the practice invalid. The plurality today takes an exceedingly narrow view of the Establishment Clause that is out of step both with the Court's prior cases and with well-established notions of what the Constitution requires. The Clause is more than a negative prohibition against certain narrowly defined forms of government favoritism; it also imposes affirmative obligations that may require a State, in some situations, to take steps to avoid being perceived as supporting or endorsing a private religious message. That is, the Establishment Clause forbids a State from hiding behind the application of formally neutral criteria and remaining studiously oblivious to the effects of its actions. Governmental intent cannot control, and not all state policies are permissible under the Religion Clauses simply because they are neutral in form.

Where the government's operation of a public forum has the effect of endorsing religion, even if the governmental actor neither intends nor actively encourages that result, the Establishment Clause is violated. This is so not because of "'transferred endorsement,'" or mistaken attribution of private speech to the State, but because the State's own actions (operating the forum in a particular manner and permitting the religious expression to take place therein), and their relationship to the private speech at issue, *actually convey* a message of endorsement. At some point, for example, a private religious group may so dominate a public forum that a formal policy of equal access is transformed into a demonstration of approval. Other circumstances may produce the same effect—whether because of the fortuity of geography, the nature of the particular public space, or the character of the religious speech at issue, among others. Our Establishment Clause jurisprudence should remain flexible enough to handle such situations when they arise.

In the end, I would recognize that the Establishment Clause inquiry cannot be distilled into a fixed, *per se* rule. Thus, "every government practice must be judged in its unique circumstances to determine whether it constitutes an endorsement or disapproval of religion." And this question cannot be answered in the abstract, but instead requires courts to examine the history and administration of a particular practice to determine whether it operates as such an endorsement. I continue to believe that government practices relating to speech on religious topics "must be subjected to careful judicial scrutiny," and that the endorsement test supplies an appropriate standard for that inquiry.

## II

Conducting the review of government action required by the Establishment Clause is always a sensitive matter. Unfortunately, as I noted in *Allegheny*, "even the development of articulable standards and guidelines has not always resulted in agreement among the Members of this Court on the results in individual cases." 492 U.S., 623. Today, JUSTICE STEVENS reaches a different conclusion regarding whether the Board's decision to allow respondents' display on Capitol Square constituted an impermissible endorsement of the cross' religious message. Yet I believe it is important to note that we have not simply arrived at divergent results after conducting the same analysis. Our fundamental point of departure, it appears, concerns the knowledge that is properly attributed to the test's "reasonable observer [who] evaluates whether a challenged governmental practice conveys a message of endorsement of religion." In my view, proper application of the endorsement test requires that the reasonable observer be deemed more informed than the casual passerby postulated by JUSTICE STEVENS.

Because an Establishment Clause violation must be moored in government action of some sort, and because our concern is with the political community writ large, the endorsement inquiry is not about the perceptions of particular individuals or saving isolated nonadherents from the discomfort of viewing symbols of a faith to which they do not subscribe. Indeed, to avoid "entirely sweeping away all government recognition and acknowledgment of the role of religion in the lives of our citizens," our Establishment Clause jurisprudence must seek to identify the point at which the government becomes responsible, whether due to favoritism toward or disregard for the evident effect of religious speech, for the injection of religion into the political life of the citizenry.

I therefore disagree that the endorsement test should focus on the actual perception of individual observers, who naturally have differing degrees of knowledge. Under such an approach, a religious display is necessarily precluded so long as some passersby would perceive a governmental endorsement thereof. In my view, however, the endorsement test creates a more collective standard to gauge "the 'objective' meaning of the [government's] statement in the community." In this respect, the applicable observer is similar to the "reasonable person" in tort law, who "is not to be identified with any ordinary individual, who might occasionally do unreasonable things," but is "rather a personification of a community ideal of reasonable behavior, determined by the [collective] social judgment." Thus, "we do not ask whether there is *any* person who could find an endorsement of religion, whether *some* people may be offended by the display, or whether *some* reasonable person *might* think [the State] endorses religion." Saying that the endorsement inquiry should be conducted from the perspective of a hypothetical observer who is presumed to possess a certain level of information that all citizens might not share neither chooses the perceptions of the majority over those of a "reasonable nonadherent," nor invites disregard for the values the Establishment Clause was intended to protect. It simply recognizes the fundamental difficulty inherent in focusing on actual people: There is always *someone* who, with a particular quantum of knowledge, reasonably might perceive a particular action as an endorsement of religion. A State has not made religion relevant to standing in the political community simply because a particular viewer of a display might feel uncomfortable.

It is for this reason that the reasonable observer in the endorsement inquiry must be deemed aware of the history and context of the community and forum in which the religious display appears. As I explained in *Allegheny*, "the 'history and ubiquity' of a practice is relevant because it provides part of the context in which a reasonable observer evaluates whether a challenged governmental practice conveys a message of endorsement of religion." Nor can the knowledge attributed to the reasonable observer be limited to the information gleaned simply from viewing the challenged display. Today's proponents of the endorsement test all agree that we should attribute to the observer knowledge that the cross is a religious symbol, that Capitol Square is owned by the State, and that the large building nearby is the seat of state government. In my view, our hypothetical observer also should know the general history of the place in which the cross is displayed. Indeed, the fact that Capitol Square is a public park that has been used over time by private speakers of various types is as much a part of the display's context as its proximity to the Ohio Statehouse. This approach does not require us to assume an "'ultrareasonable observer' who understands the vagaries of this Court's First Amendment jurisprudence." An informed member of the community will know how the public space in question has been used in the past—and it is that fact, not that the space may meet the legal definition of a public forum, which is relevant to the endorsement inquiry.

JUSTICE STEVENS' property-based argument fails to give sufficient weight to the fact that the cross at issue here was displayed in a forum traditionally open to the public. "The very fact that a sign is installed on public property," his dissent suggests, "implies official recognition and reinforcement of its message." While this may be the case where a government building and its immediate curtilage are involved, it is not necessarily so with respect to those "places which by long tradition or by government fiat have been devoted to assembly and debate, . . . [particularly] streets and parks which 'have immemorially been held in trust for the use of the public and, time out of mind, have been used for purposes of assembly, communicating thoughts between citizens, and discussing public questions.'" *Perry Ed. Assn. v. Perry Local Educators' Assn.,* 460 U.S. 37, 45. To the extent there is a presumption that "structures on government property—and, in particular, in front of buildings plainly identified with the State—imply state approval of their message," that presumption can be rebutted where the property at issue is a forum historically available for private expression. The reasonable observer would recognize the distinction between speech the government supports and speech that it merely allows in a place that traditionally has been open to a range of private speakers accompanied, if necessary, by an appropriate disclaimer.

In this case, I believe, the reasonable observer would view the Klan's cross display fully aware that Capitol Square is a public space in which a multiplicity of groups, both secular and religious, engage in expressive conduct. It is precisely this type of knowledge that we presumed in *Lamb's Chapel,* and in *Mergens.* Moreover, this observer would certainly be able to read and understand an adequate disclaimer, which the Klan had informed the State it would include in the display at the time it applied for the permit, and the content of which the Board could have defined as it deemed necessary as a condition of granting the Klan's application. On the facts of this case, therefore, I conclude that the reasonable observer would not interpret the State's tolerance of the Klan's private religious display in Capitol Square as an endorsement of religion.

## III

"To be sure, the endorsement test depends on a sensitivity to the unique circumstances and context of a particular challenged practice and, like any test that is sensitive to context, it may not always yield results with unanimous agreement at the margins." *Allegheny*, 492 U.S., 629. In my view, however, this flexibility is a virtue and not a vice; "courts must keep in mind both the fundamental place held by the Establishment Clause in our constitutional scheme and the myriad, subtle ways in which Establishment Clause values can be eroded." *Lynch*, 465 U.S., 694.

I agree that "compliance with the Establishment Clause is a state interest sufficiently compelling to justify content-based restrictions on speech." The Establishment Clause "prohibits government from appearing to take a position on questions of religious belief or from 'making adherence to a religion relevant in any way to a person's standing in the political community.'" Because I believe that, under the circumstances at issue here, allowing the Klan cross, along with an adequate disclaimer, to be displayed on Capitol Square presents no danger of doing so, I conclude that the State has not presented a compelling justification for denying respondents their permit.

◪ JUSTICE SOUTER, with whom JUSTICE O'CONNOR and JUSTICE BREYER join, concurring in part and concurring in the judgment.

I concur in Parts I, II, and III of the Court's opinion. I also want to note specifically my agreement with the Court's suggestion that the State of Ohio could ban all unattended private displays in Capitol Square if it so desired. The fact that the capitol lawn has been the site of public protests and gatherings, and is the location of any number of the government's own unattended displays, such as statues, does not disable the State from closing the square to all privately owned, unattended structures. . . .

Otherwise, however, I limit my concurrence to the judgment. Although I agree in the end that, in the circumstances of this case, petitioners erred in denying the Klan's application for a permit to erect a cross on Capitol Square, my analysis of the Establishment Clause issue differs from JUSTICE SCALIA's, and I vote to affirm in large part because of the possibility of affixing a sign to the cross adequately disclaiming any government sponsorship or endorsement of it.

The plurality's opinion declines to apply the endorsement test to the Board's action, in favor of a *per se* rule: religious expression cannot violate the Establishment Clause where it (1) is private and (2) occurs in a public forum, even if a reasonable observer would see the expression as indicating state endorsement. This *per se* rule would be an exception to the endorsement test, not previously recognized and out of square with our precedents.

I

My disagreement with the plurality on the law may receive some focus from attention to a matter of straight fact that we see alike: in some circumstances an intelligent observer may mistake private, unattended religious displays in a public forum for government speech endorsing religion. . . . The Klan concedes this possibility as well, saying that, in its view, "on a different set of facts, the government might be found guilty of violating the endorsement test by permitting a private religious display in a public forum." Brief for Respondents 43.

An observer need not be "obtuse," to presume that an unattended display on government land in a place of prominence in front of a government building either belongs to the government, represents government speech, or enjoys its location because of government endorsement of its message. Capitol Square, for example, is the site of a number of unattended displays owned or sponsored by the government, some permanent (statues), some temporary (such as the Christmas tree and a "Seasons Greetings" banner), and some in between (flags, which are, presumably, taken down and put up from time to time). Given the domination of the square by the government's own displays, one would not be a dimwit as a matter of law to think that an unattended religious display there was endorsed by the government, even though the square has also been the site of three privately sponsored, unattended displays over the years (a menorah, a United Way "thermometer," and some artisans' booths left overnight during an arts festival) . . . . When an individual speaks in a public forum, it is reasonable for an observer to attribute the speech, first and foremost, to the speaker, while an unattended display (and any message it conveys) can naturally be viewed as belonging to the owner of the land on which it stands.

In sum, I do not understand that I am at odds with the plurality when I assume that in some circumstances an intelligent observer would reasonably perceive private religious expression in a public forum to imply the government's endorsement of religion. My disagreement with the plurality is simply that I would attribute these perceptions of the intelligent observer to the reasonable observer of Establishment Clause analysis under our precedents, where I believe that such reasonable perceptions matter.

## II . . .

*Allegheny*'s endorsement test cannot be dismissed, as JUSTICE SCALIA suggests, as applying only to situations in which there is an allegation that the Establishment Clause has been violated through "expression by the government itself" or "government action . . . discriminating in favor of private religious expression." Such a distinction would, in all but a handful of cases, make meaningless the "effect-of-endorsing" part of *Allegheny*'s test. Effects matter to the Establishment Clause, and one, principal way that we assess them is by asking whether the practice in question creates the appearance of endorsement to the reasonable observer. If a reasonable observer would perceive a religious display in a government forum as government speech endorsing religion, then the display has made "religion relevant, in . . . public perception, to status in the political community." Unless we are to retreat entirely to government intent and abandon consideration of effects, it makes no sense to recognize a public perception of endorsement as a harm only in that subclass of cases in which the government owns the display. Indeed, the Court stated in *Allegheny* that "once the judgment has been made that a particular proclamation of Christian belief, when disseminated from a particular location on government property, has the effect of demonstrating the government's endorsement of Christian faith, then it necessarily follows that the practice must be enjoined." Notably, we did not say that it was only a "particular government proclamation" that could have such an unconstitutional effect, nor does the passage imply anything of the kind.

The significance of the fact that the Court in *Allegheny* did not intend to lay down a *per se* rule in the way suggested by the plurality today has been confirmed by subsequent cases. . . .

[E]ven though *Mergens* involved private religious speech in a nondiscriminatory "'limited open forum,'" a majority of the Court reached the conclusion in the case not by applying an irrebuttable presumption, as the plurality does today, but by making a contextual judgment taking account of the circumstances of the specific case. The *Mergens* plurality considered the nature of the likely audience, ("Secondary school students are mature enough . . . to understand that a school does not endorse or support student speech that it merely permits on a nondiscriminatory basis"); the details of the particular forum, (noting "the broad spectrum of officially recognized student clubs" at the school, and the students' freedom "to initiate and organize additional student clubs"); the presumptively secular nature of most student organizations. ("'In the absence of empirical evidence that religious groups will dominate [the] . . . . open forum, . . . the advancement of religion would not be the forum's "primary effect,"'"); and the school's specific action or inaction that would disassociate itself from any religious message ("No school officials actively participate" in the religious group's activities) . . . .

Similarly, in *Lamb's Chapel v. Center Moriches Union Free School Dist.,* we held that an evangelical church, wanting to use public school property to show a series of films about child rearing with a religious perspective, could not be refused access to the premises under a policy that would open the school to other groups showing similar films from a nonreligious perspective. In reaching this conclusion, we expressly concluded that the policy would "not have the principal or primary effect of advancing or inhibiting religion." Again we looked to the specific circumstances of the private religious speech and the public forum: the film would not be shown during school hours or be sponsored by the school, it would be open to the public, and the forum had been used "repeatedly" by "a wide variety" of other private speakers. . . .

*Widmar v. Vincent* is not to the contrary. Although *Widmar* was decided before our adoption of the endorsement test in *Allegheny*, its reasoning fits with such a test and not with the *per se* rule announced today. There, in determining whether it would violate the Establishment Clause to allow private religious speech in a "generally open forum" at a university, the Court looked to the *Lemon* test, and focused on the "effects" prong, in reaching a contextual judgment. It was relevant that university students "should be able to appreciate that the University's policy is one of neutrality toward religion," that students were unlikely, as a matter of fact, to "draw any reasonable inference of University support from the mere fact of a campus meeting place," and that the University's student handbook carried a disclaimer that the University should not "'be identified in any way with the . . . opinions of any [student] organization.'" "In this context," and in the "absence of empirical evidence that religious groups [would] dominate [the] open forum," the Court found that the forum at issue did not "confer any imprimatur of state approval on religious sects or practices."

Even if precedent and practice were otherwise, however, and there were an open question about applying the endorsement test to private speech in public forums, I would apply it in preference to the plurality's view, which creates a serious loophole in the protection provided by the endorsement test. In JUSTICE SCALIA's view, as I understand it, the Establishment Clause is violated in a public forum only when the government itself intentionally endorses religion or willfully "foster[s]" a misperception of endorsement in the forum, or when it "manipulates" the public forum "in such a manner that only certain religious groups take advantage of it." If the list of forbidden acts is truly this short, then governmental bodies and officials are left with generous scope to

encourage a multiplicity of religious speakers to erect displays in public forums. As long as the governmental entity does not "manipulate" the forum in
such a way as to exclude all other speech, the plurality's opinion would seem
to invite such government encouragement, even when the result will be the
domination of the forum by religious displays and religious speakers. By allowing government to encourage what it cannot do on its own, the proposed
*per se* rule would tempt a public body to contract out its establishment of
religion, by encouraging the private enterprise of the religious to exhibit what
the government could not display itself. . . .

## III

As for the specifics of this case, one must admit that a number of facts
known to the Board, or reasonably anticipated, weighed in favor of upholding
its denial of the permit. For example, the Latin cross the Klan sought to erect
is the principal symbol of Christianity around the world, and display of the
cross alone could not reasonably be taken to have any secular point. It was
displayed immediately in front of the Ohio Statehouse, with the government's
flags flying nearby, and the government's statues close at hand. For much of
the time the cross was supposed to stand on the square, it would have been the
only private display on the public plot (the menorah's permit expired several
days before the cross actually went up). There was nothing else on the statehouse lawn that would have suggested a forum open to any and all private,
unattended religious displays.

Based on these and other factors, the Board was understandably concerned
about a possible Establishment Clause violation if it had granted the permit.
But a flat denial of the Klan's application was not the Board's only option to
protect against an appearance of endorsement, and the Board was required
to find its most "narrowly drawn" alternative. Either of two possibilities would
have been better suited to this situation. In support of the Klan's application,
its representative stated in a letter to the Board that the cross would be accompanied by a disclaimer, legible "from a distance," explaining that the cross
was erected by private individuals "'without government support.'" The letter
said that "the contents of the sign" were "open to negotiation." The Board,
then, could have granted the application subject to the condition that the
Klan attach a disclaimer sufficiently large and clear to preclude any reasonable
inference that the cross was there to "demonstrate the government's allegiance
to, or endorsement of, the Christian faith."[2] In the alternative, the Board could
have instituted a policy of restricting all private, unattended displays to one
area of the square, with a permanent sign marking the area as a forum for private speech carrying no endorsement from the State.

With such alternatives available, the Board cannot claim that its flat denial
was a narrowly tailored response to the Klan's permit application and thus
cannot rely on that denial as necessary to ensure that the State did not "appear

---

[2] Of course, the presence of a disclaimer does not always remove the possibility that
a private religious display "convey[s] or attempt[s] to convey a message that religion or a
particular religious belief is favored or preferred," when other indicia of endorsement (e.g.,
objective indications that the government in fact invited the display or otherwise intended
to further a religious purpose) outweigh the mitigating effect of the disclaimer, or when the
disclaimer itself does not sufficiently disclaim government support. In this case, however,
there is no reason to presume that an adequate disclaimer could not have been drafted.

to take a position on questions of religious belief." For these reasons, I concur in the judgment.

▓ JUSTICE STEVENS, dissenting.

The Establishment Clause should be construed to create a strong presumption against the installation of unattended religious symbols on public property. Although the State of Ohio has allowed Capitol Square, the area around the seat of its government, to be used as a public forum, and although it has occasionally allowed private groups to erect other sectarian displays there, neither fact provides a sufficient basis for rebutting that presumption. On the contrary, the sequence of sectarian displays disclosed by the record in this case illustrates the importance of rebuilding the "wall of separation between church and State" that Jefferson envisioned. . . .

II . . .

The Establishment Clause, "at the very least, prohibits government from appearing to take a position on questions of religious belief or from 'making adherence to a religion relevant in any way to a person's standing in the political community.'" *Allegheny v. ACLU*, 492 U.S. 573, 593-594. At least when religious symbols are involved, the question of whether the State is "appearing to take a position" is best judged from the standpoint of a "reasonable observer." It is especially important to take account of the perspective of a reasonable observer who may not share the particular religious belief it expresses. A paramount purpose of the Establishment Clause is to protect such a person from being made to feel like an outsider in matters of faith, and a stranger in the political community. If a reasonable person could perceive a government endorsement of religion from a private display, then the State may not allow its property to be used as a forum for that display. No less stringent rule can adequately protect nonadherents from a well-grounded perception that their sovereign supports a faith to which they do not subscribe.[5]

In determining whether the State's maintenance of the Klan's cross in front of the statehouse conveyed a forbidden message of endorsement, we should be mindful of the power of a symbol standing alone and unexplained. Even on private property, signs and symbols are generally understood to express the owner's views. The location of the sign is a significant component of the message it conveys. . . .

Like other speakers, a person who places a sign on her own property has the autonomy to choose the content of her own message. Thus, the location of a stationary, unattended sign generally is both a component of its message and an implicit endorsement of that message by the party with the power to decide whether it may be conveyed from that location. . . .

---

[5] The ideal human JUSTICE O'CONNOR describes knows and understands much more than meets the eye. Her "reasonable person" comes off as a well-schooled jurist, a being finer than the tort-law model. With respect, I think this enhanced tort-law standard is singularly out of place in the Establishment Clause context. It strips of constitutional protection every reasonable person whose knowledge happens to fall below some "'ideal'" standard. Instead of protecting only the "'ideal'" observer, then, I would extend protection to the universe of reasonable persons and ask whether some viewers of the religious display would be likely to perceive a government endorsement. . . .

The very fact that a sign is installed on public property implies official recognition and reinforcement of its message. That implication is especially strong when the sign stands in front of the seat of the government itself. The "reasonable observer" of any symbol placed unattended in front of any capitol in the world will normally assume that the sovereign—which is not only the owner of that parcel of real estate but also the lawgiver for the surrounding territory—has sponsored and facilitated its message.

That the State may have granted a variety of groups permission to engage in uncensored expressive activities in front of the capitol building does not, in my opinion, qualify or contradict the normal inference of endorsement that the reasonable observer would draw from the unattended, freestanding sign or symbol. Indeed, parades and demonstrations at or near the seat of government are often exercises of the right of the people to petition their government for a redress of grievances—exercises in which the government is the recipient of the message rather than the messenger. Even when a demonstration or parade is not directed against government policy, but merely has made use of a particularly visible forum in order to reach as wide an audience as possible, there usually can be no mistake about the identity of the messengers as persons other than the State. But when a statue or some other free-standing, silent, unattended, immoveable structure—regardless of its particular message—appears on the lawn of the capitol building, the reasonable observer must identify the State either as the messenger, or, at the very least, as one who has endorsed the message. Contrast, in this light, the image of the cross standing alone and unattended, and the image the observer would take away were a hooded Klansman holding, or standing next to, the very same cross.

This Court has never held that a private party has a right to place an unattended object in a public forum.[7] . . .

Because structures on government property—and, in particular, in front of buildings plainly identified with the State—imply state approval of their message, the government must have considerable leeway, outside of the religious arena, to choose what kinds of displays it will allow and what kinds it will not. Although the First Amendment requires the government to allow leafletting or demonstrating outside its buildings, the State has greater power to exclude unattended symbols when they convey a type of message with which the State does not wish to be identified. I think it obvious, for example, that Ohio could prohibit certain categories of signs or symbols in Capitol Square—erotic exhibits, commercial advertising, and perhaps campaign posters as well—without violating the Free Speech Clause.[11] Moreover, our "public forum" cases do not foreclose public entities from enforcing prohibitions against all unattended

---

[7] Despite the absence of any holding on this point, JUSTICE O'CONNOR assumes that a reasonable observer would not impute the content of an unattended display to the government because that observer would know that the State is required to allow all such displays on Capitol Square. JUSTICE O'CONNOR thus presumes a reasonable observer so prescient as to understand legal doctrines that this Court has not yet adopted.

[11] The plurality incorrectly assumes that a decision to exclude a category of speech from an inappropriate forum must rest on a judgment about the value of that speech. Yet, we have upheld the exclusion of all political signs from public vehicles, though political expression is at the heart of the protection afforded by the First Amendment. A view that "private prayers," are most appropriate in private settings is neither novel nor disrespectful to religious speech.

displays in public parks, or possibly even limiting the use of such displays to the communication of noncontroversial messages. Such a limitation would not inhibit any of the traditional forms of expression that have been given full constitutional protection in public fora.

The State's general power to restrict the types of unattended displays does not alone suffice to decide this case, because Ohio did not profess to be exercising any such authority. Instead, the Capitol Square Review Board denied a permit for the cross because it believed the Establishment Clause required as much, and we cannot know whether the Board would have denied the permit on other grounds. Accordingly, we must evaluate the State's rationale on its own terms. But in this case, the endorsement inquiry under the Establishment Clause follows from the State's power to exclude unattended private displays from public property. Just as the Constitution recognizes the State's interest in preventing its property from being used as a conduit for ideas it does not wish to give the appearance of ratifying, the Establishment Clause prohibits government from allowing, and thus endorsing, unattended displays that take a position on a religious issue. If the State allows such stationary displays in front of its seat of government, viewers will reasonably assume that it approves of them. As the picture appended to this opinion demonstrates, a reasonable observer would likely infer endorsement from the location of the cross erected by the Klan in this case. Even if the disclaimer at the foot of the cross (which stated that the cross was placed there by a private organization) were legible, that inference would remain, because a property owner's decision to allow a third party to place a sign on her property conveys the same message of endorsement as if she had erected it herself.[13]

When the message is religious in character, it is a message the State can neither send nor reinforce without violating the Establishment Clause. Accordingly, I would hold that the Constitution generally forbids the placement of a symbol of a religious character in, on, or before a seat of government.

## III

The Court correctly acknowledges that the State's duty to avoid a violation of the Establishment Clause can justify a content-based restriction on speech or expression, even when that restriction would otherwise be prohibited by the Free Speech Clause. The plurality asserts, however, that government cannot be perceived to be endorsing a religious display when it merely accords that display "the same access to a public forum that all other displays enjoy." I find this argument unpersuasive.

The existence of a "public forum" in itself cannot dispel the message of endorsement. A contrary argument would assume an "ultrareasonable observer" who understands the vagaries of this Court's First Amendment jurisprudence. I think it presumptuous to consider such knowledge a precondition of Establishment Clause protection. Many (probably most) reasonable people do not

---

[13] Indeed, I do not think *any* disclaimer could dispel the message of endorsement in this case. Capitol Square's location in downtown Columbus, Ohio makes it inevitable that countless motorists and pedestrians would immediately perceive the proximity of the cross to the Capitol without necessarily noticing any disclaimer of public sponsorship. The plurality thus correctly abjures inquiry into the possible adequacy or significance of a legend identifying the owner of the cross. . . .

know the difference between a "public forum," a "limited public forum," and a "nonpublic forum." They *do* know the difference between a state capitol and a church. Reasonable people have differing degrees of knowledge; that does not make them "'obtuse,'" nor does it make them unworthy of constitutional protection. It merely makes them human. For a religious display to violate the Establishment Clause, I think it is enough that *some* reasonable observers would attribute a religious message to the State.

The plurality appears to rely on the history of this particular public forum—specifically, it emphasizes that Ohio has in the past allowed three other private unattended displays. Even if the State could not reasonably have been understood to endorse the prior displays, I would not find this argument convincing, because it assumes that all reasonable viewers know all about the history of Capitol Square—a highly unlikely supposition. But the plurality's argument fails on its own terms, because each of the three previous displays conveyed the same message of approval and endorsement that this one does.

Most significant, of course, is the menorah that stood in Capitol Square during Chanukah. The display of that religious symbol should be governed by the same rule as the display of the cross. In my opinion, both displays are equally objectionable. Moreover, the fact that the State has placed its stamp of approval on two different religions instead of one only compounds the constitutional violation. The Establishment Clause does not merely prohibit the State from favoring one religious sect over others. It also proscribes state action supporting the establishment of a number of religions, as well as the official endorsement of religion in preference to nonreligion. The State's prior approval of the pro-religious message conveyed by the menorah is fully consistent with its endorsement of one of the messages conveyed by the cross: "The State of Ohio favors religion over irreligion." This message is incompatible with the principles embodied by our Establishment Clause.

The record identifies two other examples of free-standing displays that the State previously permitted in Capitol Square: a "United Way Campaign 'thermometer,'" and "craftsmen's booths and displays erected during an Arts Festival." Both of those examples confirm the proposition that a reasonable observer should infer official approval of the message conveyed by a structure erected in front of the statehouse. Surely the thermometer suggested that the State was encouraging passersby to contribute to the United Way. It seems equally clear that the State was endorsing the creativity of artisans and craftsmen by permitting their booths to occupy a part of the square. Nothing about either of those freestanding displays contradicts the normal inference that the State has endorsed whatever message might be conveyed by permitting an unattended symbol to adorn the capitol grounds. Accordingly, the fact that the menorah, and later the cross, stood in an area available "'for free discussion of public questions, or for activities of a broad public purpose,'" is fully consistent with the conclusion that the State sponsored those religious symbols. They, like the thermometer and the booths, were displayed in a context that connotes state approval.

This case is therefore readily distinguishable from *Widmar v. Vincent,* and *Lamb's Chapel v. Center Moriches Union Free School Dist.* In both of those cases, as we made perfectly clear, there was no danger of incorrect identification of the speakers and no basis for inferring that their messages had been endorsed by any public entity. . . .

In contrast, the installation of the religious symbols in Capitol Square quite obviously did "have the principal or primary effect of advancing or inhibiting religion"; indeed, no other effect is even suggested by the record. The primary difference is that in this case we are dealing with a *visual display*—a symbol readily associated with a religion, in a venue readily associated with the State. This clear image of endorsement was lacking in *Widmar* and *Lamb's Chapel*, in which the issue was access to government facilities. Moreover, there was no question in those cases of an unattended display; private speakers, who could be distinguished from the State, were present. Endorsement might still be present in an access case if, for example, the religious group sought the use of the roof of a public building for an obviously religious ceremony, where many onlookers might witness that ceremony and connect it to the State. But no such facts were alleged in *Widmar* or *Lamb's Chapel*. The religious practices in those cases were simply less obtrusive, and less likely to send a message of endorsement, than the eye-catching symbolism at issue in this case.

The battle over the Klan cross underscores the power of such symbolism. The menorah prompted the Klan to seek permission to erect an antisemitic symbol, which in turn not only prompted vandalism but also motivated other sects to seek permission to place their own symbols in the square. These facts illustrate the potential for insidious entanglement that flows from state-endorsed proselytizing. There is no reason to believe that a menorah placed in front of a synagogue would have motivated any reaction from the Klan, or that a Klan cross placed on a Klansman's front lawn would have produced the same reaction as one that enjoyed the apparent imprimatur of the State of Ohio. Nor is there any reason to believe the placement of the displays in Capitol Square had any purpose other than to connect the State—though perhaps against its will—to the religious or anti-religious beliefs of those who placed them there. The cause of the conflict is the State's apparent approval of a religious or antireligious message. Our Constitution wisely seeks to minimize such strife by forbidding state-endorsed religious activity.

IV . . .

The Court's decision today is unprecedented. It entangles two sovereigns in the propagation of religion, and it disserves the principle of tolerance that underlies the prohibition against state action "respecting an establishment of religion."

*I respectfully dissent.*

JUSTICE GINSBURG, dissenting. . . .

If the aim of the Establishment Clause is genuinely to uncouple government from church, a State may not permit, and a court may not order, a display of this character. . . .

Whether a court order allowing display of a cross, but demanding a sturdier disclaimer, could withstand Establishment Clause analysis is a question more difficult than the one this case poses. I would reserve that question for another day and case. But I would not let the prospect of what might have been permissible control today's decision on the constitutionality of the display the District Court's order in fact authorized.

## Notes and Questions

1. According to Justice Scalia, what rule should be applied in cases like this one? What objections do Justices O'Connor and Souter have to the opinion that Justice Scalia wrote for the plurality? Which test—the one articulated by Justice Scalia or the one articulated by Justices O'Connor and Souter— provides greater certainty in terms of predicting whether various forms of religious expression will pass constitutional muster? Which one is more faithful to Establishment Clause values? How can Justices O'Connor, Souter, and Breyer concur in the result if they disagree so strongly with Justice Scalia's approach?

2. Is the holding in *Pinette* that the free speech claim—here in the form of a content-based distinction prohibiting the display of the cross—out-weighed the no-establishment concerns, or that those latter values were not seriously threatened by this display? Does your answer depend on which value—free expression or non-establishment—you believe is at greater risk by either allowing or disallowing the cross display? Interestingly, the Klan was represented by the American Civil Liberties Union, which frequently challenges government-sponsored displays of religious symbols on public property. Americans United for Separation of Church and State filed an amicus brief supporting the State's action denying the cross display, a brief that was joined by two ACLU affiliates.

3. In the plurality opinion in *Pinette*, Justice Scalia writes:

   Where we have tested for endorsement of religion, the subject of the test was either expression *by the government itself*, or else government action alleged to *discriminate in favor* of private religious expression or activity. The test petitioners propose, which would attribute to a neutrally behaving government *private* religious expression, has no antecedent in our jurisprudence, and would better be called a "transferred endorsement" test. (citations omitted).

   Is this an accurate description of the Court's doctrine in this area?

4. How do you explain the fact that the Court upheld the temporary display of an unattended cross in the *Pinette* case and struck down the temporary display of an unattended nativity scene in the *Allegheny* case? Does the difference in the outcomes turn on the particular facts, the articulation/application of the standard, or some other factor(s)?

5. What level of knowledge should a court attribute to the "reasonable observer," according to Justice O'Connor? In his dissenting opinion, what criticisms does Justice Stevens make of O'Connor's concept of the "reasonable observer"? According to Justice Stevens, what kind of showing is necessary to establish that a religious display violates the endorsement test? What criticisms does Justice O'Connor have of the approach that Justice Stevens advocates?

6. According to Justice Souter's opinion concurring in part and concurring in the judgment, refusing the KKK's request was not the only option open to the government. What were the other options? Contrast Justice Souter's approach to this question with that of Justice Ginsburg.

7. Justice Stevens says that "[t]he Establishment Clause should be construed to create a strong presumption against the installation of unattended religious symbols on public property." What particular concerns does Stevens raise about the nature of unattended religious symbols on government property? How does Justice Stevens distinguish the *Widmar* and *Lamb's Chapel* cases from this case? What constitutional counterweights are there to Stevens' concerns about unattended religious symbols on government property? How should these different concerns be balanced?

8. Suppose a public elementary school classroom allows children to distribute goodies to their classmates on the last day of school before winter break, as long as the treats are wrapped and given to every child in the classroom. Assume a child would like to pass out candy canes with a tag that says, "Jesus loves you" as part of this activity. Should the student be permitted to pass out the candy canes, according to the ruling in the *Pinette* case?

9. If you were the attorney for a particular county, what policy would you advise the city to adopt regarding unattended displays sponsored by nongovernmental community groups or individuals in public parks? Would you recommend a different policy for parks near county courthouses and the statehouse?

In 2005, the Court agreed to hear two cases that involved Ten Commandments displays on state property. The first case, *McCreary County v. ACLU*, involved a recently posted display of the Ten Commandments along with other documents in two Kentucky courthouses. These particular displays were preceded by two other displays that had been rejected at various stages of litigation. The second case, *Van Orden v. Perry*, focused on a Ten Commandments monument that had been given to the state of Texas by the Fraternal Order of Eagles decades ago. It sat with a number of other monuments on the grounds of the State Capitol. The Court handed down its decisions in these cases on the same day, striking down the Kentucky display as unconstitutional, while upholding the Texas monument. Both were 5-4 decisions, and, as you will see, the divisions were even more numerous than that tally would indicate. Interestingly, you will also find that only Justice Stephen Breyer believed both cases were correctly decided.

## McCREARY COUNTY v. AMERICAN CIVIL LIBERTIES UNION
## 545 U.S. 844 (2005)

JUSTICE SOUTER delivered the opinion of the Court.

Executives of two counties posted a version of the Ten Commandments on the walls of their courthouses. . . .

The issues are whether a determination of the counties' purpose is a sound basis for ruling on the Establishment Clause complaints, and whether evaluation of the counties' claim of secular purpose for the ultimate displays may take their evolution into account. We hold that the counties' manifest objective may be dispositive of the constitutional enquiry, and that the development of the presentation should be considered when determining its purpose.

I

In the summer of 1999, petitioners McCreary County and Pulaski County, Kentucky (hereinafter Counties), put up in their respective courthouses large, gold-framed copies of an abridged text of the King James version of the Ten Commandments, including a citation to the Book of Exodus. In McCreary County, the placement of the Commandments responded to an order of the county legislative body requiring "the display [to] be posted in 'a very high traffic area' of the courthouse." In Pulaski County, amidst reported controversy over the propriety of the display, the Commandments were hung in a ceremony presided over by the county Judge-Executive, who called them "good rules to live by" and who recounted the story of an astronaut who became convinced "there must be a divine God" after viewing the Earth from the moon. The Judge-Executive was accompanied by the pastor of his church, who called the Commandments "a creed of ethics" and told the press after the ceremony that displaying the Commandments was "one of the greatest things the judge could have done to close out the millennium." In both counties, this was the version of the Commandments posted:

> Thou shalt have no other gods before me.
> Thou shalt not make unto thee any graven images.
> Thou shalt not take the name of the Lord thy God in vain.
> Remember the sabbath day, to keep it holy.
> Honor thy father and thy mother.
> Thou shalt not kill.
> Thou shalt not commit adultery.
> Thou shalt not steal.
> Thou shalt not bear false witness.
> Thou shalt not covet.
>
> Exodus 20:3-17

In each county, the hallway display was "readily visible to . . . county citizens who use the courthouse to conduct their civic business, to obtain or renew driver's licenses and permits, to register cars, to pay local taxes, and to register to vote."

In November 1999, respondents American Civil Liberties Union of Kentucky et al. sued the Counties in Federal District Court . . . and sought a preliminary injunction against maintaining the displays, which the ACLU charged were violations of the prohibition of religious establishment included in the First Amendment of the Constitution. Within a month, and before the District Court had responded to the request for injunction, the legislative body of each County authorized a second, expanded display, by nearly identical resolutions reciting that the Ten Commandments are "the precedent legal code upon which the civil and criminal codes of . . . Kentucky are founded," and stating several grounds for taking that position: that "the Ten Commandments are codified in Kentucky's civil and criminal laws"; that the Kentucky House of Representatives had in 1993 "voted unanimously . . . to adjourn . . . 'in remembrance and honor of Jesus Christ, the Prince of Ethics'"; that the "County Judge and . . . magistrates agree with the arguments set out by Judge [Roy] Moore" in defense of his "display [of] the Ten Commandments in his courtroom"; and that the "Founding Father[s] [had an] explicit understanding of the duty of elected officials to publicly acknowledge God as the source of America's strength and direction."

As directed by the resolutions, the Counties expanded the displays of the Ten Commandments in their locations, presumably along with copies of the resolution, which instructed that it, too, be posted. In addition to the first display's large framed copy of the edited King James version of the Commandments, the second included eight other documents in smaller frames, each either having a religious theme or excerpted to highlight a religious element. The documents were the "endowed by their Creator" passage from the Declaration of Independence; the Preamble to the Constitution of Kentucky; the national motto, "In God We Trust"; a page from the Congressional Record of February 2, 1983, proclaiming the Year of the Bible and including a statement of the Ten Commandments; a proclamation by President Abraham Lincoln designating April 30, 1863, a National Day of Prayer and Humiliation; an excerpt from President Lincoln's "Reply to Loyal Colored People of Baltimore upon Presentation of a Bible," reading that "[t]he Bible is the best gift God has ever given to man"; a proclamation by President Reagan marking 1983 the Year of the Bible; and the Mayflower Compact.

After argument, the District Court entered a preliminary injunction on May 5, 2000, ordering that the "display . . . be removed from [each] County Courthouse IMMEDIATELY" and that no county official "erect or cause to be erected similar displays."

The Counties . . . then installed another display in each courthouse, the third within a year. No new resolution authorized this one, nor did the Counties repeal the resolutions that preceded the second. The posting consists of nine framed documents of equal size, one of them setting out the Ten Commandments explicitly identified as the "King James Version" at Exodus 20:3-17, and quoted at greater length than before:

> Thou shalt have no other gods before me.
> Thou shalt not make unto thee any graven image, or any likeness of any thing that is in heaven above, or that is in the earth beneath, or that is in the water underneath the earth: Thou shalt not bow down thyself to them, nor serve them: for I the LORD thy God am a jealous God, visiting the iniquity of the fathers upon the children unto the third and fourth generation of them that hate me.
> Thou shalt not take the name of the LORD thy God in vain: for the LORD will not hold him guiltless that taketh his name in vain.
> Remember the sabbath day, to keep it holy.
> Honour thy father and thy mother: that thy days may be long upon the land which the LORD thy God giveth thee.
> Thou shalt not kill.
> Thou shalt not commit adultery.
> Thou shalt not steal.
> Thou shalt not bear false witness against thy neighbour.
> Thou shalt not covet thy neighbour's house, thou shalt not covet th[y] neighbor's wife, nor his manservant, nor his maidservant, nor his ox, nor his ass, nor anything that is th[y] neighbour's.

Assembled with the Commandments are framed copies of the Magna Carta, the Declaration of Independence, the Bill of Rights, the lyrics of the Star Spangled Banner, the Mayflower Compact, the National Motto, the Preamble to the Kentucky Constitution, and a picture of Lady Justice. The collection is entitled "The Foundations of American Law and Government Display" and each document comes with a statement about its historical and legal significance. The comment on the Ten Commandments reads:

> The Ten Commandments have profoundly influenced the formation of Western legal thought and the formation of our country. That influence is clearly seen in the Declaration of Independence, which declared that "We hold these truths to be self-evident, that all men are created equal, that they are endowed by their Creator with certain unalienable Rights, that among these are Life, Liberty, and the pursuit of Happiness." The Ten Commandments provide the moral background of the Declaration of Independence and the foundation of our legal tradition.

The ACLU moved to supplement the preliminary injunction to enjoin the Counties' third display, and the Counties responded with several explanations for the new version, including desires "to demonstrate that the Ten Commandments were part of the foundation of American Law and Government" and "to educate the citizens of the county regarding some of the documents that played a significant role in the foundation of our system of law and government." In light of the Counties' decision to post the Commandments by themselves in the first instance, contrary to *Stone,* and later to "accentuat[e]" the religious objective by surrounding the Commandments with "specific references to Christianity," the District Court understood the Counties' "clear" purpose as being to post the Commandments, not to educate.

[A] divided panel of the Court of Appeals for the Sixth Circuit affirmed. . . . We granted certiorari, and now affirm.

## II

Twenty-five years ago in a case prompted by posting the Ten Commandments in Kentucky's public schools, this Court recognized that the Commandments "are undeniably a sacred text in the Jewish and Christian faiths" and held that their display in public classrooms violated the First Amendment's bar against establishment of religion. *Stone* found a predominantly religious purpose in the government's posting of the Commandments, given their prominence as "'an instrument of religion.'" The Counties ask for a different approach here by arguing that official purpose is unknowable and the search for it inherently vain. . . .

### A

Ever since *Lemon v. Kurtzman* summarized the three familiar considerations for evaluating Establishment Clause claims, looking to whether government action has "a secular legislative purpose" has been a common, albeit seldom dispositive, element of our cases. Though we have found government action motivated by an illegitimate purpose only four times since *Lemon*, and "the secular purpose requirement alone may rarely be determinative, . . . it nevertheless serves an important function."

The touchstone for our analysis is the principle that the "First Amendment mandates governmental neutrality between religion and religion, and between religion and nonreligion." *Epperson v. Arkansas*, 393 U.S. 97, 104 (1968). When the government acts with the ostensible and predominant purpose of advancing religion, it violates that central Establishment Clause value of official religious neutrality, there being no neutrality when the government's ostensible object is to take sides. Manifesting a purpose to favor one faith over another, or adherence to religion generally, clashes with the "understanding, reached . . . after decades of religious war, that liberty and social stability demand a religious tolerance that respects the religious views of all citizens. . . ." *Zelman v. Simmons-Harris*, 536 U.S. 639, 718. By showing a purpose to favor religion, the government "sends the . . . message to . . . nonadherents 'that they are outsiders, not full members of the political community, and an accompanying message to adherents that they are insiders, favored members. . . .'" *Santa Fe School Dist. v. Doe*, 536 U.S. 290, 309-310.

Indeed, the purpose apparent from government action can have an impact more significant than the result expressly decreed: when the government maintains Sunday closing laws, it advances religion only minimally because many working people would take the day as one of rest regardless, but if the government justified its decision with a stated desire for all Americans to honor Christ, the divisive thrust of the official action would be inescapable.

B

Despite the intuitive importance of official purpose to the realization of Establishment Clause values, the Counties ask us to abandon *Lemon's* purpose test, or at least to truncate any enquiry into purpose here. Their first argument is that the very consideration of purpose is deceptive: according to them, true "purpose" is unknowable, and its search merely an excuse for courts to act selectively and unpredictably in picking out evidence of subjective intent. The assertions are as seismic as they are unconvincing.

Examination of purpose is a staple of statutory interpretation that makes up the daily fare of every appellate court in the country. . . . Scrutinizing purpose does make practical sense, as in Establishment Clause analysis, where an understanding of official objective emerges from readily discoverable fact, without any judicial psychoanalysis of a drafter's heart of hearts. The eyes that look to purpose belong to an "'objective observer,'" one who takes account of the traditional external signs that show up in the "'text, legislative history, and implementation of the statute,'" or comparable official act. . . . There is, then, nothing hinting at an unpredictable or disingenuous exercise when a court enquires into purpose after a claim is raised under the Establishment Clause.

The cases with findings of a predominantly religious purpose point to the straightforward nature of the test. In *Wallace*, for example, we inferred purpose from a change of wording from an earlier statute to a later one, each dealing with prayer in schools. And in *Edwards*, we relied on a statute's text and the detailed public comments of its sponsor, when we sought the purpose of a state law requiring creationism to be taught alongside evolution. In other cases, the government action itself bespoke the purpose, as in *Abington*, where the object of required Bible study in public schools was patently religious, in *Stone*, the Court held that the "[p]osting of religious texts on the wall serve[d] no . . . educational function," and found that if "the posted copies of the Ten Commandments [were] to have any effect at all, it [would] be to induce the schoolchildren to read, meditate upon, perhaps to venerate and obey, the Commandments." In each case, the government's action was held unconstitutional only because openly available data supported a commonsense conclusion that a religious objective permeated the government's action.

Nor is there any indication that the enquiry is rigged in practice to finding a religious purpose dominant every time a case is filed. In the past, the test has not been fatal very often, presumably because government does not generally act unconstitutionally, with the predominant purpose of advancing religion. That said, one consequence of the corollary that Establishment Clause analysis does not look to the veiled psyche of government officers could be that in some of the cases in which establishment complaints failed, savvy officials had disguised their religious intent so cleverly that the objective observer just missed it. But that is no reason for great constitutional concern. If someone in the government hides religious motive so well that the "'objective observer, acquainted with the text, legislative history, and implementation of the statute,'" cannot see it, then without something more the government does not make a divisive announcement that in itself amounts to taking religious sides. A secret motive stirs up no strife and does nothing to make outsiders of nonadherents, and it suffices to wait and see whether such government action turns out to have (as it may even be likely to have) the illegitimate effect of advancing religion.

## C

After declining the invitation to abandon concern with purpose wholesale, we also have to avoid the Counties' alternative tack of trivializing the enquiry into it. The Counties would read the cases as if the purpose enquiry were so naive that any transparent claim to secularity would satisfy it, and they would cut context out of the enquiry, to the point of ignoring history, no matter what bearing it actually had on the significance of current circumstances. There is no precedent for the Counties' arguments, or reason supporting them.

## 1

*Lemon* said that government action must have "a secular . . . purpose," and after a host of cases it is fair to add that although a legislature's stated reasons will generally get deference, the secular purpose required has to be genuine, not a sham, and not merely secondary to a religious objective.

True, *Wallace* said government action is tainted by its object "if it is entirely motivated by a purpose to advance religion," a remark that suggests, in isolation, a fairly complaisant attitude. But in that very case the Court declined to credit Alabama's stated secular rationale of "accommodation" for legislation authorizing a period of silence in school for meditation or voluntary prayer, given the implausibility of that explanation in light of another statute already accommodating children wishing to pray. And it would be just as much a mistake to infer that a timid standard underlies the statement in *Lynch v. Donnelly* that the purpose enquiry looks to whether government "activity was motivated wholly by religious considerations," for two cases cited for that proposition had examined and rejected claims of secular purposes that turned out to be implausible or inadequate: *Stone, Abington*. As we said, the Court often does accept governmental statements of purpose, in keeping with the respect owed in the first instance to such official claims. But in those unusual cases where the claim was an apparent sham, or the secular purpose secondary, the unsurprising results have been findings of no adequate secular object, as against a predominantly religious one.[13]

---

[13] The dissent nonetheless maintains that the purpose test is satisfied so long as any secular purpose for the government action is apparent. Leaving aside the fact that this position is inconsistent with the language of the cases just discussed, it would leave the purpose test with no real bite, given the ease of finding some secular purpose for almost any government action. While heightened deference to legislatures is appropriate for the review of economic legislation, an approach that credits any valid purpose, no matter how trivial, has not been the way the Court has approached government action that implicates establishment.

2

The Counties' second proffered limitation can be dispatched quickly. They argue that purpose in a case like this one should be inferred, if at all, only from the latest news about the last in a series of governmental actions, however close they may all be in time and subject. But the world is not made brand new every morning, and the Counties are simply asking us to ignore perfectly probative evidence; they want an absentminded objective observer, not one presumed to be familiar with the history of the government's actions and competent to learn what history has to show. The Counties' position just bucks common sense: reasonable observers have reasonable memories, and our precedents sensibly forbid an observer "to turn a blind eye to the context in which [the] policy arose."[14]

### III . . .

We take *Stone* as the initial legal benchmark, our only case dealing with the constitutionality of displaying the Commandments. *Stone* recognized that the Commandments are an "instrument of religion" and that, at least on the facts before it, the display of their text could presumptively be understood as meant to advance religion: although state law specifically required their posting in public school classrooms, their isolated exhibition did not leave room even for an argument that secular education explained their being there. But *Stone* did not purport to decide the constitutionality of every possible way the Commandments might be set out by the government, and under the Establishment Clause detail is key. Hence, we look to the record of evidence showing the progression leading up to the third display of the Commandments.

### A

The display rejected in *Stone* had two obvious similarities to the first one in the sequence here: both set out a text of the Commandments as distinct from any traditionally symbolic representation, and each stood alone, not part of an arguably secular display. *Stone* stressed the significance of integrating the Commandments into a secular scheme to forestall the broadcast of an otherwise clearly religious message, and for good reason, the Commandments being a central point of reference in the religious and moral history of Jews and Christians. They proclaim the existence of a monotheistic god (no other

---

[14] One consequence of taking account of the purpose underlying past actions is that the same government action may be constitutional if taken in the first instance and unconstitutional if it has a sectarian heritage. This presents no incongruity, however, because purpose matters. Just as Holmes's dog could tell the difference between being kicked and being stumbled over, it will matter to objective observers whether posting the Commandments follows on the heels of displays motivated by sectarianism, or whether it lacks a history demonstrating that purpose. The dissent, apparently not giving the reasonable observer as much credit as Holmes's dog, contends that in practice it will be "absur[d]" to rely upon differences in purpose in assessing government action. As an initial matter, it will be the rare case in which one of two identical displays violates the purpose prong. In general, like displays tend to show like objectives and will be treated accordingly. But where one display has a history manifesting sectarian purpose that the other lacks, it is appropriate that they be treated differently, for the one display will be properly understood as demonstrating a preference for one group of religious believers as against another. While posting the Commandments may not have the effect of causing greater adherence to them, an ostensible indication of a purpose to promote a particular faith certainly will have the effect of causing viewers to understand the government is taking sides.

gods). They regulate details of religious obligation (no graven images, no sabbath breaking, no vain oath swearing). And they unmistakably rest even the universally accepted prohibitions (as against murder, theft, and the like) on the sanction of the divinity proclaimed at the beginning of the text. Displaying that text is thus different from a symbolic depiction, like tablets with 10 roman numerals, which could be seen as alluding to a general notion of law, not a sectarian conception of faith. Where the text is set out, the insistence of the religious message is hard to avoid in the absence of a context plausibly suggesting a message going beyond an excuse to promote the religious point of view. The display in *Stone* had no context that might have indicated an object beyond the religious character of the text, and the Counties' solo exhibit here did nothing more to counter the sectarian implication than the postings at issue in *Stone*.[16] Actually, the posting by the Counties lacked even the *Stone* display's implausible disclaimer that the Commandments were set out to show their effect on the civil law. What is more, at the ceremony for posting the framed Commandments in Pulaski County, the county executive was accompanied by his pastor, who testified to the certainty of the existence of God. The reasonable observer could only think that the Counties meant to emphasize and celebrate the Commandments' religious message.

This is not to deny that the Commandments have had influence on civil or secular law; a major text of a majority religion is bound to be felt. The point is simply that the original text viewed in its entirety is an unmistakably religious statement dealing with religious obligations and with morality subject to religious sanction. When the government initiates an effort to place this statement alone in public view, a religious object is unmistakable.

### B

Once the Counties were sued, they modified the exhibits and invited additional insight into their purpose in a display that hung for about six months. This new one was the product of forthright and nearly identical Pulaski and McCreary County resolutions listing a series of American historical documents with theistic and Christian references, which were to be posted in order to furnish a setting for displaying the Ten Commandments and any "other Kentucky and American historical documen[t]" without raising concern about "any Christian or religious references" in them. As mentioned, the resolutions expressed support for an Alabama judge who posted the Commandments in his courtroom, and cited the fact the Kentucky Legislature once adjourned a session in honor of "Jesus Christ, Prince of Ethics."

In this second display, unlike the first, the Commandments were not hung in isolation, merely leaving the Counties' purpose to emerge from the pervasively religious text of the Commandments themselves. Instead, the second version was required to include the statement of the government's purpose expressly set out in the county resolutions, and underscored it by juxtaposing the Commandments to other documents with highlighted references to God as their sole common element. The display's unstinting focus was on religious passages, showing that the Counties were posting the Commandments precisely because of their sectarian content. That demonstration of the

---

[16] Although the Counties point out that the courthouses contained other displays besides the Ten Commandments, there is no suggestion that the Commandments display was integrated to form a secular display.

government's objective was enhanced by serial religious references and the accompanying resolution's claim about the embodiment of ethics in Christ. Together, the display and resolution presented an indisputable, and undisputed, showing of an impermissible purpose.

Today, the Counties make no attempt to defend their undeniable objective, but instead hopefully describe version two as "dead and buried." Their refusal to defend the second display is understandable, but the reasonable observer could not forget it.

C

1

After the Counties changed lawyers, they mounted a third display, without a new resolution or repeal of the old one. The result was the "Foundations of American Law and Government" exhibit, which placed the Commandments in the company of other documents the Counties thought especially significant in the historical foundation of American government. In trying to persuade the District Court to lift the preliminary injunction, the Counties cited several new purposes for the third version, including a desire "to educate the citizens of the county regarding some of the documents that played a significant role in the foundation of our system of law and government." The Counties' claims did not, however, persuade the court, intimately familiar with the details of this litigation, or the Court of Appeals, neither of which found a legitimizing secular purpose in this third version of the display. "'When both courts [that have already passed on the case] are unable to discern an arguably valid secular purpose, this Court normally should hesitate to find one.'" *Edwards*, 482 U.S., 594, n. 15. The conclusions of the two courts preceding us in this case are well warranted.

These new statements of purpose were presented only as a litigating position, there being no further authorizing action by the Counties' governing boards. And although repeal of the earlier county authorizations would not have erased them from the record of evidence bearing on current purpose, the extraordinary resolutions for the second display passed just months earlier were not repealed or otherwise repudiated. Indeed, the sectarian spirit of the common resolution found enhanced expression in the third display, which quoted more of the purely religious language of the Commandments than the first two displays had done; for additions, see App. to Pet. for Cert. 189a ("I the LORD thy God am a jealous God") (text of Second Commandment in third display); ("the LORD will not hold him guiltless that taketh his name in vain") (from text of Third Commandment); and ("that thy days may be long upon the land which the LORD thy God giveth thee") (text of Fifth Commandment). No reasonable observer could swallow the claim that the Counties had cast off the objective so unmistakable in the earlier displays.

Nor did the selection of posted material suggest a clear theme that might prevail over evidence of the continuing religious object. In a collection of documents said to be "foundational" to American government, it is at least odd to include a patriotic anthem, but to omit the Fourteenth Amendment, the most significant structural provision adopted since the original Framing. And it is no less baffling to leave out the original Constitution of 1787 while quoting the 1215 Magna Carta even to the point of its declaration that "fish-weirs shall be removed from the Thames." If an observer found these choices and omissions perplexing in isolation, he would be puzzled for a different reason when he read the Declaration of Independence seeking confirmation for the Counties' posted explanation that the "Ten Commandments' . . . influence is clearly seen in the Declaration;" in fact the observer would find that the Commandments are sanctioned as divine imperatives, while the Declaration of Independence holds that the authority of government to enforce the law derives "from the consent of the governed." If the observer had not thrown up his hands, he would probably suspect that the Counties were simply reaching for any way to keep a religious document on the walls of courthouses constitutionally required to embody religious neutrality.[22]

### 2

In holding the preliminary injunction adequately supported by evidence that the Counties' purpose had not changed at the third stage, we do not decide that the Counties' past actions forever taint any effort on their part to deal with the subject matter. We hold only that purpose needs to be taken seriously under the Establishment Clause and needs to be understood in light of context; an implausible claim that governmental purpose has changed should not carry the day in a court of law any more than in a head with common sense. . . .

Nor do we have occasion here to hold that a sacred text can never be integrated constitutionally into a governmental display on the subject of law, or American history. We do not forget, and in this litigation have frequently been reminded, that our own courtroom frieze was deliberately designed in the exercise of governmental authority so as to include the figure of Moses holding tablets exhibiting a portion of the Hebrew text of the later, secularly phrased Commandments; in the company of 17 other lawgivers, most of them secular figures, there is no risk that Moses would strike an observer as evidence that the National Government was violating neutrality in religion.[23]

### IV

The importance of neutrality as an interpretive guide is no less true now than it was when the Court broached the principle in *Everson v. Board of Ed. of Ewing* and a word needs to be said about the different view taken in today's dissent. We all agree, of course, on the need for some interpretative help. The First Amendment contains no textual definition of "establishment," and the term is certainly not self-defining. No one contends that the prohibition of establishment stops at a designation of a national (or with Fourteenth Amendment incorporation, *Cantwell v. Connecticut*, a state) church, but nothing in the text says just how much more it covers. There is no simple answer, for more than one reason.

The prohibition on establishment covers a variety of issues from prayer in widely varying settings, to financial aid for religious individuals and institutions, to comment on religious questions. In these varied settings, issues of interpreting inexact Establishment Clause language, like difficult interpretative issues generally, arise from the tension of competing values, each constitutionally respectable, but none open to realization to the logical limit.

---

[22] The Counties grasp at *McGowan v. Maryland*, 366 U.S. 420 (1961), but it bears little resemblance to this case. As noted, *McGowan* held that religious purposes behind centuries-old predecessors of Maryland's Sunday laws were not dispositive of the purposes of modern Sunday laws, where the legislature had removed much of the religious reference in the laws and stated secular and pragmatic justifications for them. . . .

[23] The dissent notes that another depiction of Moses and the Commandments adorns this Court's east pediment. But as with the courtroom frieze, Moses is found in the company of other figures, not only great but secular.

The First Amendment has not one but two clauses tied to "religion," the second forbidding any prohibition on the "the free exercise thereof," and sometimes, the two clauses compete: spending government money on the clergy looks like establishing religion, but if the government cannot pay for military chaplains a good many soldiers and sailors would be kept from the opportunity to exercise their chosen religions. At other times, limits on governmental action that might make sense as a way to avoid establishment could arguably limit freedom of speech when the speaking is done under government auspices.

Given the variety of interpretative problems, the principle of neutrality has provided a good sense of direction: the government may not favor one religion over another, or religion over irreligion, religious choice being the prerogative of individuals under the Free Exercise Clause. The principle has been helpful simply because it responds to one of the major concerns that prompted adoption of the Religion Clauses. The Framers and the citizens of their time intended not only to protect the integrity of individual conscience in religious matters, but to guard against the civic divisiveness that follows when the Government weighs in on one side of religious debate. A sense of the past thus points to governmental neutrality as an objective of the Establishment Clause, and a sensible standard for applying it. To be sure, given its generality as a principle, an appeal to neutrality alone cannot possibly lay every issue to rest, or tell us what issues on the margins are substantial enough for constitutional significance, a point that has been clear from the Founding era to modern times. But invoking neutrality is a prudent way of keeping sight of something the Framers of the First Amendment thought important.

The dissent, however, puts forward a limitation on the application of the neutrality principle, with citations to historical evidence said to show that the Framers understood the ban on establishment of religion as sufficiently narrow to allow the government to espouse submission to the divine will. The dissent identifies God as the God of monotheism, all of whose three principal strains (Jewish, Christian, and Muslim) acknowledge the religious importance of the Ten Commandments. On the dissent's view, it apparently follows that even rigorous espousal of a common element of this common monotheism, is consistent with the establishment ban.

But the dissent's argument for the original understanding is flawed from the outset by its failure to consider the full range of evidence showing what the Framers believed. The dissent is certainly correct in putting forward evidence that some of the Framers thought some endorsement of religion was compatible with the establishment ban; the dissent quotes the first President as stating that "national morality [cannot] prevail in exclusion of religious principle," for example, and it cites his first Thanksgiving proclamation giving thanks to God. Surely if expressions like these from Washington and his contemporaries were all we had to go on, there would be a good case that the neutrality principle has the effect of broadening the ban on establishment beyond the Framers' understanding of it (although there would, of course, still be the question of whether the historical case could overcome some 60 years of precedent taking neutrality as its guiding principle).

But the fact is that we do have more to go on, for there is also evidence supporting the proposition that the Framers intended the Establishment Clause to require governmental neutrality in matters of religion, including neutrality in statements acknowledging religion. The very language of the Establishment

Clause represented a significant departure from early drafts that merely prohibited a single national religion, and, the final language instead "extended [the] prohibition to state support for 'religion' in general."

The historical record, moreover, is complicated beyond the dissent's account by the writings and practices of figures no less influential than Thomas Jefferson and James Madison. Jefferson, for example, refused to issue Thanksgiving Proclamations because he believed that they violated the Constitution. And Madison, whom the dissent claims as supporting its thesis, criticized Virginia's general assessment tax not just because it required people to donate "three pence" to religion, but because "it is itself a signal of persecution. It degrades from the equal rank of Citizens all those whose opinions in Religion do not bend to those of the Legislative authority." *Weisman*, 505 U.S., 622. . . .

The fair inference is that there was no common understanding about the limits of the establishment prohibition, and the dissent's conclusion that its narrower view was the original understanding, stretches the evidence beyond tensile capacity. What the evidence does show is a group of statesmen, like others before and after them, who proposed a guarantee with contours not wholly worked out, leaving the Establishment Clause with edges still to be determined. And none the worse for that. Indeterminate edges are the kind to have in a constitution meant to endure, and to meet "exigencies which, if foreseen at all, must have been seen dimly, and which can be best provided for as they occur." *McCulloch v. Maryland*, 17 U.S. 316.

While the dissent fails to show a consistent original understanding from which to argue that the neutrality principle should be rejected, it does manage to deliver a surprise. As mentioned, the dissent says that the deity the Framers had in mind was the God of monotheism, with the consequence that government may espouse a tenet of traditional monotheism. This is truly a remarkable view. Other members of the Court have dissented on the ground that the Establishment Clause bars nothing more than governmental preference for one religion over another, but at least religion has previously been treated inclusively. Today's dissent, however, apparently means that government should be free to approve the core beliefs of a favored religion over the tenets of others, a view that should trouble anyone who prizes religious liberty. Certainly history cannot justify it; on the contrary, history shows that the religion of concern to the Framers was not that of the monotheistic faiths generally, but Christianity in particular, a fact that no member of this Court takes as a premise for construing the Religion Clauses.

Historical evidence thus supports no solid argument for changing course (whatever force the argument might have when directed at the existing precedent), whereas public discourse at the present time certainly raises no doubt about the value of the interpretative approach invoked for 60 years now. We are centuries away from the St. Bartholomew's Day massacre and the treatment of heretics in early Massachusetts, but the divisiveness of religion in current public life is inescapable. This is no time to deny the prudence of understanding the Establishment Clause to require the Government to stay neutral on religious belief, which is reserved for the conscience of the individual.

■ JUSTICE O'CONNOR, concurring.

I join in the Court's opinion. The First Amendment expresses our Nation's fundamental commitment to religious liberty by means of two provisions—

one protecting the free exercise of religion, the other barring establishment of religion. They were written by the descendents of people who had come to this land precisely so that they could practice their religion freely. Together with the other First Amendment guarantees—of free speech, a free press, and the rights to assemble and petition—the Religion Clauses were designed to safeguard the freedom of conscience and belief that those immigrants had sought. They embody an idea that was once considered radical: Free people are entitled to free and diverse thoughts, which government ought neither to constrain nor to direct.

Reasonable minds can disagree about how to apply the Religion Clauses in a given case. But the goal of the Clauses is clear: to carry out the Founders' plan of preserving religious liberty to the fullest extent possible in a pluralistic society. By enforcing the Clauses, we have kept religion a matter for the individual conscience, not for the prosecutor or bureaucrat. At a time when we see around the world the violent consequences of the assumption of religious authority by government, Americans may count themselves fortunate: Our regard for constitutional boundaries has protected us from similar travails, while allowing private religious exercise to flourish. . . . Those who would renegotiate the boundaries between church and state must therefore answer a difficult question: Why would we trade a system that has served us so well for one that has served others so poorly?

Our guiding principle has been James Madison's—that "[t]he Religion . . . of every man must be left to the conviction and conscience of every man." . . . Government may not coerce a person into worshiping against her will, nor prohibit her from worshiping according to it. It may not prefer one religion over another or promote religion over nonbelief. It may not entangle itself with religion. And government may not, by "endorsing religion or a religious practice," "mak[e] adherence to religion relevant to a person's standing in the political community."

When we enforce these restrictions, we do so for the same reason that guided the Framers—respect for religion's special role in society. Our Founders conceived of a Republic receptive to voluntary religious expression, and provided for the possibility of judicial intervention when government action threatens or impedes such expression. Voluntary religious belief and expression may be as threatened when government takes the mantle of religion upon itself as when government directly interferes with private religious practices. When the government associates one set of religious beliefs with the state and identifies nonadherents as outsiders, it encroaches upon the individual's decision about whether and how to worship. In the marketplace of ideas, the government has vast resources and special status. Government religious expression therefore risks crowding out private observance and distorting the natural interplay between competing beliefs. Allowing government to be a potential mouthpiece for competing religious ideas risks the sort of division that might easily spill over into suppression of rival beliefs. Tying secular and religious authority together poses risks to both.

Given the history of this particular display of the Ten Commandments, the Court correctly finds an Establishment Clause violation. The purpose behind the counties' display is relevant because it conveys an unmistakable message of endorsement to the reasonable observer.

It is true that many Americans find the Commandments in accord with their personal beliefs. But we do not count heads before enforcing the First

Amendment. Nor can we accept the theory that Americans who do not accept the Commandments' validity are outside the First Amendment's protections. There is no list of approved and disapproved beliefs appended to the First Amendment—and the Amendment's broad terms ("free exercise," "establishment," "religion") do not admit of such a cramped reading. It is true that the Framers lived at a time when our national religious diversity was neither as robust nor as well recognized as it is now. They may not have foreseen the variety of religions for which this Nation would eventually provide a home. They surely could not have predicted new religions, some of them born in this country. But they did know that line-drawing between religions is an enterprise that, once begun, has no logical stopping point. They worried that "the same authority which can establish Christianity, in exclusion of all other Religions, may establish with the same ease any particular sect of Christians, in exclusion of all other Sects." The Religion Clauses, as a result, protect adherents of all religions, as well as those who believe in no religion at all.

We owe our First Amendment to a generation with a profound commitment to religion and a profound commitment to religious liberty—visionaries who held their faith "with enough confidence to believe that what should be rendered to God does not need to be decided and collected by Caesar." In my opinion, the display at issue was an establishment of religion in violation of our Constitution. For the reasons given above, I join in the Court's opinion.

▓ JUSTICE SCALIA, with whom THE CHIEF JUSTICE and JUSTICE THOMAS join, and with whom JUSTICE KENNEDY joins as to Parts II and III, dissenting.

I would uphold *McCreary County* and Pulaski County, Kentucky's (hereinafter Counties) displays of the Ten Commandments. I shall discuss first, why the Court's oft repeated assertion that the government cannot favor religious practice is false; second, why today's opinion extends the scope of that falsehood even beyond prior cases; and third, why even on the basis of the Court's false assumptions the judgment here is wrong.

I

A . . .

[JUSTICE SCALIA's opinion begins with several examples of early public figures making religious acknowledgments in their official capacities.]

These actions of our First President and Congress and the Marshall Court were not idiosyncratic; they reflected the beliefs of the period. Those who wrote the Constitution believed that morality was essential to the well-being of society and that encouragement of religion was the best way to foster morality. The "fact that the Founding Fathers believed devotedly that there was a God and that the unalienable rights of man were rooted in Him is clearly evidenced in their writings, from the Mayflower Compact to the Constitution itself." *Abington Township v. Schempp*, 374 U.S. 203. President Washington opened his Presidency with a prayer, and reminded his fellow citizens at the conclusion of it that "reason and experience both forbid us to expect that National morality can prevail in exclusion of religious principle." President John Adams wrote to the Massachusetts Militia, "we have no government armed with power capable of contending with human passions unbridled by morality and religion. . . . Our Constitution was made only for a moral and religious people. It is wholly inadequate to the government of any other." Thomas Jefferson concluded his second inaugural address by inviting his audience to pray[.] . . .

James Madison, in his first inaugural address, likewise placed his confidence "in the guardianship and guidance of that Almighty Being whose power regulates the destiny of nations, whose blessings have been so conspicuously dispensed to this rising Republic, and to whom we are bound to address our devout gratitude for the past, as well as our fervent supplications and best hopes for the future."

Nor have the views of our people on this matter significantly changed. Presidents continue to conclude the Presidential oath with the words "so help me God." Our legislatures, state and national, continue to open their sessions with prayer led by official chaplains. The sessions of this Court continue to open with the prayer "God save the United States and this Honorable Court." Invocation of the Almighty by our public figures, at all levels of government, remains commonplace. Our coinage bears the motto "IN GOD WE TRUST." And our Pledge of Allegiance contains the acknowledgment that we are a Nation "under God." As one of our Supreme Court opinions rightly observed, "We are a religious people whose institutions presuppose a Supreme Being." *Zorach v. Clauson*, 343 U.S. 306, 313.

With all of this reality (and much more) staring it in the face, how can the Court *possibly* assert that "'the First Amendment mandates governmental neutrality between . . . religion and nonreligion,'" and that "[m]anifesting a purpose to favor . . . adherence to religion generally," is unconstitutional? Who says so? Surely not the words of the Constitution. Surely not the history and traditions that reflect our society's constant understanding of those words. Surely not even the current sense of our society, recently reflected in an Act of Congress adopted *unanimously* by the Senate and with only 5 nays in the House of Representatives, criticizing a Court of Appeals opinion that had held "under God" in the Pledge of Allegiance unconstitutional. Nothing stands behind the Court's assertion that governmental affirmation of the society's belief in God is unconstitutional except the Court's own say-so, citing as support only the unsubstantiated say-so of earlier Courts going back no farther than the mid-20th century.[2] . . . And it is, moreover, a thoroughly discredited say-so. It is discredited, to begin with, because a majority of the Justices on the current Court (including at least one Member of today's majority) have, in separate opinions, repudiated the brain-spun "*Lemon* test" that embodies the supposed principle of neutrality between religion and irreligion. . . . And it is discredited because the Court has not had the courage (or the foolhardiness) to apply the neutrality principle consistently.

What distinguishes the rule of law from the dictatorship of a shifting Supreme Court majority is the absolutely indispensable requirement that judicial opinions be grounded in consistently applied principle. That is what prevents judges from ruling now this way, now that—thumbs up or thumbs down—as their personal preferences dictate. Today's opinion forthrightly (or actually,

---

[2] The fountainhead of this jurisprudence, *Everson v. Board of Ed. of Ewing*, based its dictum that "[n]either a state nor the Federal Government . . . can pass laws which . . . aid all religions," on a review of historical evidence that focused on the debate leading up to the passage of the Virginia Bill for Religious Liberty. A prominent commentator of the time remarked (after a thorough review of the evidence himself) that it appeared the Court had been "sold . . . a bill of goods."

somewhat less than forthrightly) admits that it does not rest upon consistently applied principle. . . .

I have cataloged elsewhere the variety of circumstances in which this Court—even *after* its embrace of *Lemon's* stated prohibition of such behavior—has approved government action "undertaken with the specific intention of improving the position of religion," *Edwards v. Aguillard*, 482 U.S. 578, 616, (SCALIA, J., dissenting). Suffice it to say here that when the government relieves churches from the obligation to pay property taxes, when it allows students to absent themselves from public school to take religious classes, and when it exempts religious organizations from generally applicable prohibitions of religious discrimination, it surely means to bestow a benefit on religious practice—but we have approved it. Indeed, we have even approved (post-*Lemon*) government-led prayer to God. In *Marsh v. Chambers*, the Court upheld the Nebraska State Legislature's practice of paying a chaplain to lead it in prayer at the opening of legislative sessions. The Court explained that "[t]o invoke Divine guidance on a public body entrusted with making the laws is not . . . an 'establishment' of religion or a step toward establishment; it is simply a tolerable acknowledgment of beliefs widely held among the people of this country." (Why, one wonders, is not respect for the Ten Commandments a tolerable acknowledgment of beliefs widely held among the people of this country?)

The only "good reason" for ignoring the neutrality principle set forth in any of these cases was the antiquity of the practice at issue. That would be a good reason for finding the neutrality principle a mistaken interpretation of the Constitution, but it is hardly a good reason for letting an unconstitutional practice continue. . . .

Besides appealing to the demonstrably false principle that the government cannot favor religion over irreligion, today's opinion suggests that the posting of the Ten Commandments violates the principle that the government cannot favor one religion over another. That is indeed a valid principle where public aid or assistance to religion is concerned or where the free exercise of religion is at issue, but it necessarily applies in a more limited sense to public acknowledgment of the Creator. If religion in the public forum had to be entirely nondenominational, there could be no religion in the public forum at all. One cannot say the word "God," or "the Almighty," one cannot offer public supplication or thanksgiving, without contradicting the beliefs of some people that there are many gods, or that God or the gods pay no attention to human affairs. With respect to public acknowledgment of religious belief, it is entirely clear from our Nation's historical practices that the Establishment Clause permits this disregard of polytheists and believers in unconcerned deities, just as it permits the disregard of devout atheists. The Thanksgiving Proclamation issued by George Washington at the instance of the First Congress was scrupulously nondenominational—but it was monotheistic. In *Marsh v. Chambers*, we said that the fact the particular prayers offered in the Nebraska Legislature were "in the Judeo-Christian tradition," posed no additional problem, because "there is no indication that the prayer opportunity has been exploited to proselytize or advance any one, or to disparage any other, faith or belief."

Historical practices thus demonstrate that there is a distance between the acknowledgment of a single Creator and the establishment of a religion. The former is, as *Marsh v. Chambers* put it, "a tolerable acknowledgment of beliefs widely held among the people of this country." *Id.*, 792. The three most popular religions in the United States, Christianity, Judaism, and Islam—which combined account for 97.7% of all believers—are monotheistic. All of them, moreover (Islam included), believe that the Ten Commandments were given by God to Moses, and are divine prescriptions for a virtuous life. Publicly honoring the Ten Commandments is thus indistinguishable, insofar as discriminating against other religions is concerned, from publicly honoring God. Both practices are recognized across such a broad and diverse range of the population—from Christians to Muslims—that they cannot be reasonably understood as a government endorsement of a particular religious viewpoint.[4]

## B . . .

A few remarks are necessary in response to the criticism of this dissent by the Court, as well as JUSTICE STEVENS' criticism in the related case of *Van Orden v. Perry*. . . . I have relied primarily upon official acts and official proclamations of the United States or of the component branches of its Government, including the First Congress's beginning of the tradition of legislative prayer to God, its appointment of congressional chaplains, its legislative proposal of a Thanksgiving Proclamation, and its reenactment of the Northwest Territory Ordinance; our first President's issuance of a Thanksgiving Proclamation; and invocation of God at the opening of sessions of the Supreme Court. . . . The Court and JUSTICE STEVENS, by contrast, appeal to no official or even quasi-official action in support of their view of the Establishment Clause—only James Madison's Memorial and Remonstrance Against Religious Assessments, written before the federal Constitution had even been proposed, two letters written by Madison long after he was President, and the quasi-official *inaction* of Thomas Jefferson in refusing to issue a Thanksgiving Proclamation. The Madison Memorial and Remonstrance, dealing as it does with enforced contribution to religion rather than public acknowledgment of God, is irrelevant; one of the letters is utterly ambiguous as to the point at issue here, and should not be read to contradict Madison's statements in his first inaugural address, quoted earlier; even the other letter does not disapprove public acknowledgment of God . . . . And as to Jefferson: the notoriously self-contradicting Jefferson did not choose to have his nonauthorship of a Thanksgiving Proclamation inscribed on his tombstone. What he did have inscribed was his authorship of the Virginia Statute for Religious Freedom, a governmental act which begins "Whereas Almighty God hath created the mind free. . . ."

It is no answer for JUSTICE STEVENS to say that the understanding that these official and quasi-official actions reflect was not "enshrined in the Constitution's text." The Establishment Clause, upon which JUSTICE STEVENS would rely, *was* enshrined in the Constitution's text, and these official actions show *what it meant*. There were doubtless some who thought it should have a broader meaning, but those views were plainly rejected. . . .

JUSTICE STEVENS argues [in his *Van Orden* dissent] that original meaning should not be the touchstone anyway, but that we should rather "expoun[d] the meaning of constitutional provisions with one eye towards our Nation's

---

[4] This is not to say that a display of the Ten Commandments could never constitute an impermissible endorsement of a particular religious view. The Establishment Clause would prohibit, for example, governmental endorsement of a particular version of the Decalogue as authoritative. Here the display of the Ten Commandments alongside eight secular documents, and the plaque's explanation for their inclusion, make clear that they were not posted to take sides in a theological dispute.

history and the other fixed on its democratic aspirations." This is not the place to debate the merits of the "living Constitution." Even assuming, however, that the meaning of the Constitution ought to change according to "democratic aspirations," why are those aspirations to be found in Justices' notions of what the Establishment Clause ought to mean, rather than in the democratically adopted dispositions of our current society? As I have observed above, numerous provisions of our laws and numerous continuing practices of our people demonstrate that the government's invocation of God (and hence the government's invocation of the Ten Commandments) is unobjectionable—including a statute enacted by Congress almost unanimously less than three years ago, stating that "under God" in the Pledge of Allegiance is constitutional. To ignore all this is not to give effect to "democratic aspirations" but to frustrate them.

Finally, I must respond to JUSTICE STEVENS' assertion that I would "marginaliz[e] the belief systems of more than 7 million Americans" who adhere to religions that are not monotheistic. Surely that is a gross exaggeration. The beliefs of those citizens are entirely protected by the Free Exercise Clause, and by those aspects of the Establishment Clause that do not relate to government acknowledgment of the Creator. Invocation of God despite their beliefs is permitted not because nonmonotheistic religions cease to be religions recognized by the religion clauses of the First Amendment, but because governmental invocation of God is not an establishment. JUSTICE STEVENS fails to recognize that in the context of public acknowledgments of God there are legitimate *competing* interests: On the one hand, the interest of that minority in not feeling "excluded"; but on the other, the interest of the overwhelming majority of religious believers in being able to give God thanks and supplication *as a people*, and with respect to our national endeavors. Our national tradition has resolved that conflict in favor of the majority. . . .

## II

As bad as the *Lemon* test is, it is worse for the fact that, since its inception, its seemingly simple mandates have been manipulated to fit whatever result the Court aimed to achieve. Today's opinion is no different. In two respects it modifies *Lemon* to ratchet up the Court's hostility to religion. First, the Court justifies inquiry into legislative purpose, not as an end itself, but as a means to ascertain the appearance of the government action to an "'objective observer.'" Because in the Court's view the true danger to be guarded against is that the objective observer would feel like an "outside[r]" or "not [a] full membe[r] of the political community," its inquiry focuses not on the *actual purpose* of government action, but the "purpose apparent from government action." Under this approach, even if a government could show that its actual purpose was not to advance religion, it would presumably violate the Constitution as long as the Court's objective observer would think otherwise. . . .

I have remarked before that it is an odd jurisprudence that bases the unconstitutionality of a government practice that does not *actually* advance religion on the hopes of the government that it *would* do so. See *Edwards*, 482 U.S., 639. But that oddity pales in comparison to the one invited by today's analysis: the legitimacy of a government action with a wholly secular effect would turn on the *misperception* of an imaginary observer that the government officials behind the action had the intent to advance religion.

Second, the Court replaces *Lemon*'s requirement that the government have "*a* secular . . . purpose," with the heightened requirement that the secular purpose "predominate" over any purpose to advance religion. . . . The new demand that secular purpose predominate contradicts *Lemon's* more limited requirement, and finds no support in our cases. In all but one of the five cases in which this Court has invalidated a government practice on the basis of its purpose to benefit religion, it has first declared that the statute was motivated entirely by the desire to advance religion. . . . In *Edwards*, the Court did say that the state action was invalid because its "primary" or "preeminent" purpose was to advance a particular religious belief, but that statement was unnecessary to the result, since the Court rejected the State's only proffered secular purpose as a sham.

I have urged that *Lemon's* purpose prong be abandoned, because (as I have discussed in Part I) even an *exclusive* purpose to foster or assist religious practice is not necessarily invalidating. But today's extension makes things even worse. By shifting the focus of *Lemon's* purpose prong from the search for a genuine, secular motivation to the hunt for a predominantly religious purpose, the Court converts what has in the past been a fairly limited inquiry into a rigorous review of the full record. . . .

### III

Even accepting the Court's *Lemon*-based premises, the displays at issue here were constitutional.

### A

To any person who happened to walk down the hallway of the McCreary or Pulaski County Courthouse during the roughly nine months when the Foundations Displays were exhibited, the displays must have seemed unremarkable—if indeed they were noticed at all. The walls of both courthouses were already lined with historical documents and other assorted portraits; each Foundations Display was exhibited in the same format as these other displays and nothing in the record suggests that either County took steps to give it greater prominence. . . .

### B

On its face, the Foundations Displays manifested the purely secular purpose that the Counties asserted before the District Court: "to display documents that played a significant role in the foundation of our system of law and government." That the Displays included the Ten Commandments did not transform their apparent secular purpose into one of impermissible advocacy for Judeo-Christian beliefs. Even an isolated display of the Decalogue conveys, at worst, "an equivocal message, perhaps of respect for Judaism, for religion in general, or for law." But when the Ten Commandments appear alongside other documents of secular significance in a display devoted to the foundations of American law and government, the context communicates that the Ten Commandments are included, not to teach their binding nature as a religious text, but to show their unique contribution to the development of the legal system. . . .

Acknowledgment of the contribution that religion has made to our Nation's legal and governmental heritage partakes of a centuries-old tradition. Members of this Court have themselves often detailed the degree to which religious belief pervaded the National Government during the founding era. . . . Display of the Ten Commandments is well within the mainstream of this practice of acknowledgment. Federal, State, and local governments across the

Nation have engaged in such display. The Supreme Court Building itself includes depictions of Moses with the Ten Commandments in the Courtroom and on the east pediment of the building, and symbols of the Ten Commandments "adorn the metal gates lining the north and south sides of the Courtroom as well as the doors leading into the Courtroom." Similar depictions of the Decalogue appear on public buildings and monuments throughout our Nation's capital. The frequency of these displays testifies to the popular understanding that the Ten Commandments are a foundation of the rule of law, and a symbol of the role that religion played, and continues to play, in our system of government.

Perhaps in recognition of the centrality of the Ten Commandments as a widely recognized symbol of religion in public life, the Court is at pains to dispel the impression that its decision will require governments across the country to sandblast the Ten Commandments from the public square. The constitutional problem, the Court says, is with the Counties' *purpose* in erecting the Foundations Displays, not the displays themselves. The Court adds in a footnote: "One consequence of taking account of the purpose underlying past actions is that the same government action may be constitutional if taken in the first instance and unconstitutional if it has a sectarian heritage."

This inconsistency may be explicable in theory, but I suspect that the "objective observer" with whom the Court is so concerned will recognize its absurdity in practice. . . . Displays erected in silence (and under the direction of good legal advice) are permissible, while those hung after discussion and debate are deemed unconstitutional. Reduction of the Establishment Clause to such minutiae trivializes the Clause's protection against religious establishment; indeed, it may inflame religious passions by making the passing comments of every government official the subject of endless litigation.

### C

In any event, the Court's conclusion that the Counties exhibited the Foundations Displays with the purpose of promoting religion is doubtful. . . . If, as discussed above, the Commandments have a proper place in our civic history, even placing them by themselves can be civically motivated—especially when they are placed, not in a school (as they were in the *Stone* case upon which the Court places such reliance), but in a courthouse. . . .

The Court has in the past prohibited government actions that "proselytize or advance any one, or . . . disparage any other, faith or belief," or that apply some level of coercion (though I and others have disagreed about the form that coercion must take). The passive display of the Ten Commandments, even standing alone, does not begin to do either. . . .

Nor is it the case that a solo display of the Ten Commandments advances any one faith. They are assuredly a religious symbol, but they are not so closely associated with a single religious belief that their display can reasonably be understood as preferring one religious sect over another. The Ten Commandments are recognized by Judaism, Christianity, and Islam alike as divinely given.

The Court also points to the Counties' second displays, which featured a number of statements in historical documents reflecting a religious influence, and the resolutions that accompanied their erection, as evidence of an impermissible religious purpose. In the Court's view, "[t]he [second] display's unstinting focus . . . on religious passages, show[s] that the Counties were posting the Commandments precisely because of their sectarian content." No, all it necessarily shows is that the exhibit was meant to focus upon the historic role of religious belief in our national life—which is entirely permissible. And the same can be said of the resolution. To forbid any government focus upon this aspect of our history is to display what Justice Goldberg called "untutored devotion to the concept of neutrality," *Abington Township*, 374 U.S., 306 (concurring opinion), that would commit the Court (and the Nation) to a revisionist agenda of secularization.

Turning at last to the displays actually at issue in this case, the Court faults the Counties for not *repealing* the resolution expressing what the Court believes to be an impermissible intent. . . . [But] it is unlikely that a reasonable observer *would even have been aware* of the resolutions, so there would be nothing to "cast off." . . .

In sum: The first displays did not necessarily evidence an intent to further religious practice; nor did the second displays, or the resolutions authorizing them; and there is in any event no basis for attributing whatever intent motivated the first and second displays to the third. Given the presumption of regularity that always accompanies our review of official action, the Court has identified no evidence of a purpose to advance religion in a way that is inconsistent with our cases. The Court may well be correct in identifying the third displays as the fruit of a desire to display the Ten Commandments, but neither our cases nor our history support its assertion that such a desire renders the fruit poisonous.

For the foregoing reasons, I would reverse the judgment of the Court of Appeals.

---

## VAN ORDEN v. PERRY
545 U.S. 677 (2005)

CHIEF JUSTICE REHNQUIST announced the judgment of the Court and delivered an opinion, in which JUSTICE SCALIA, JUSTICE KENNEDY and JUSTICE THOMAS join.

The question here is whether the Establishment Clause of the First Amendment allows the display of a monument inscribed with the Ten Commandments on the Texas State Capitol grounds. We hold that it does.

The 22 acres surrounding the Texas State Capitol contain 17 monuments and 21 historical markers commemorating the "people, ideals, and events that compose Texan identity."[1] The monolith challenged here stands 6-feet high and 3 1/2-feet wide. It is located to the north of the Capitol building, between the Capitol and the Supreme Court building. Its primary content is the text of the Ten Commandments. An eagle grasping the American flag, an eye inside of a pyramid, and two small tablets with what appears to be an

---

[1] The monuments are: Heroes of the Alamo, Hood's Brigade, Confederate Soldiers, Volunteer Fireman, Terry's Texas Rangers, Texas Cowboy, Spanish-American War, Texas National Guard, Ten Commandments, Tribute to Texas School Children, Texas Pioneer Woman, The Boy Scouts' Statue of Liberty Replica, Pearl Harbor Veterans, Korean War Veterans, Soldiers of World War I, Disabled Veterans, and Texas Peace Officers.

ancient script are carved above the text of the Ten Commandments. Below the text are two Stars of David and the superimposed Greek letters Chi and Rho, which represent Christ. The bottom of the monument bears the inscription "PRESENTED TO THE PEOPLE AND YOUTH OF TEXAS BY THE FRATERNAL ORDER OF EAGLES OF TEXAS 1961."

The legislative record surrounding the State's acceptance of the monument from the Eagles—a national social, civic, and patriotic organization—is limited to legislative journal entries. After the monument was accepted, the State selected a site for the monument based on the recommendation of the state organization responsible for maintaining the Capitol grounds. The Eagles paid the cost of erecting the monument, the dedication of which was presided over by two state legislators. . . .

Forty years after the monument's erection and six years after [Petitioner Thomas] Van Orden began to encounter the monument [during visits to the law library in the Supreme Court building], he sued . . . seeking both a declaration that the monument's placement violates the Establishment Clause and an injunction requiring its removal. . . .

Our cases, Januslike, point in two directions in applying the Establishment Clause. One face looks toward the strong role played by religion and religious traditions throughout our Nation's history. . . . The other face looks toward the principle that governmental intervention in religious matters can itself endanger religious freedom.

This case, like all Establishment Clause challenges, presents us with the difficulty of respecting both faces. Our institutions presuppose a Supreme Being, yet these institutions must not press religious observances upon their citizens. One face looks to the past in acknowledgment of our Nation's heritage, while the other looks to the present in demanding a separation between church and state. Reconciling these two faces requires that we neither abdicate our responsibility to maintain a division between church and state nor evince a hostility to religion by disabling the government from in some ways recognizing our religious heritage: . . .

These two faces are evident in representative cases both upholding and invalidating laws under the Establishment Clause. Over the last 25 years, we have sometimes pointed to *Lemon v. Kurtzman*, as providing the governing test in Establishment Clause challenges. . . . Others have applied it only after concluding that the challenged practice was invalid under a different Establishment Clause test.

Whatever may be the fate of the *Lemon* test in the larger scheme of Establishment Clause jurisprudence, we think it not useful in dealing with the sort of passive monument that Texas has erected on its Capitol grounds. Instead, our analysis is driven both by the nature of the monument and by our Nation's history.

As we explained in *Lynch v. Donnelly*, "There is an unbroken history of official acknowledgment by all three branches of government of the role of religion in American life from at least 1789." For example, both Houses passed resolutions in 1789 asking President George Washington to issue a Thanksgiving Day Proclamation to "recommend to the people of the United States a day of public thanksgiving and prayer, to be observed by acknowledging, with grateful hearts, the many and signal favors of Almighty God." President Washington's proclamation directly attributed to the Supreme Being the foundations and successes of our young Nation:

Now, therefore, I do recommend and assign Thursday, the 26th day of November next, to be devoted by the people of these States to the service of that great and glorious Being who is the beneficent author of all the good that was, that is, or that will be; that we may then all unite in rendering unto Him our sincere and humble thanks for His kind care and protection of the people of this country previous to their becoming a nation; for the signal and manifold mercies and the favorable interpositions of His providence in the course and conclusion of the late war; for the great degree of tranquillity, union, and plenty which we have since enjoyed; for the peaceable and rational manner in which we have been enabled to establish constitutions of government for our safety and happiness, and particularly the national one now lately instituted; for the civil and religious liberty with which we are blessed, and the means we have of acquiring and diffusing useful knowledge; and, in general, for all the great and various favors which He has been pleased to confer upon us. 1 J. Richardson, Messages and Papers of the Presidents, 1789–1897, p. 64 (1899).

Recognition of the role of God in our Nation's heritage has also been reflected in our decisions. We have acknowledged, for example, that "religion has been closely identified with our history and government," and that "[t]he history of man is inseparable from the history of religion," This recognition has led us to hold that the Establishment Clause permits a state legislature to open its daily sessions with a prayer by a chaplain paid by the State. Such a practice, we thought, was "deeply embedded in the history and tradition of this country." As we observed there, "it would be incongruous to interpret [the Establishment Clause] as imposing more stringent First Amendment limits on the states than the draftsmen imposed on the Federal Government." With similar reasoning, we have upheld laws, which originated from one of the Ten Commandments, that prohibited the sale of merchandise on Sunday.

In this case we are faced with a display of the Ten Commandments on government property outside the Texas State Capitol. Such acknowledgments of the role played by the Ten Commandments in our Nation's heritage are common throughout America. We need only look within our own Courtroom. Since 1935, Moses has stood, holding two tablets that reveal portions of the Ten Commandments written in Hebrew, among other lawgivers in the south frieze. Representations of the Ten Commandments adorn the metal gates lining the north and south sides of the Courtroom as well as the doors leading into the Courtroom. Moses also sits on the exterior east facade of the building holding the Ten Commandments tablets.

Similar acknowledgments can be seen throughout a visitor's tour of our Nation's Capital. For example, a large statue of Moses holding the Ten Commandments, alongside a statue of the Apostle Paul, has overlooked the rotunda of the Library of Congress' Jefferson Building since 1897. And the Jefferson Building's Great Reading Room contains a sculpture of a woman beside the Ten Commandments with a quote above her from the Old Testament (Micah 6:8). A medallion with two tablets depicting the Ten Commandments decorates the floor of the National Archives. . . . Moses is also prominently featured in the Chamber of the United States House of Representatives.

Our opinions, like our building, have recognized the role the Decalogue plays in America's heritage. The Executive and Legislative Branches have also acknowledged the historical role of the Ten Commandments. These displays and recognitions of the Ten Commandments bespeak the rich American tradition of religious acknowledgments.

Of course, the Ten Commandments are religious—they were so viewed at their inception and so remain. The monument, therefore, has religious significance. According to Judeo-Christian belief, the Ten Commandments were given to Moses by God on Mount Sinai. But Moses was a lawgiver as well as a religious leader. And the Ten Commandments have an undeniable historical meaning, as the foregoing examples demonstrate. Simply having religious content or promoting a message consistent with a religious doctrine does not run afoul of the Establishment Clause.

There are, of course, limits to the display of religious messages or symbols. For example, we held unconstitutional a Kentucky statute requiring the posting of the Ten Commandments in every public schoolroom. In the classroom context, we found that the Kentucky statute had an improper and plainly religious purpose. As evidenced by *Stone*'s almost exclusive reliance upon two of our school prayer cases, it stands as an example of the fact that we have "been particularly vigilant in monitoring compliance with the Establishment Clause in elementary and secondary schools." Neither *Stone* itself nor subsequent opinions have indicated that *Stone*'s holding would extend to a legislative chamber or to capitol grounds.

The placement of the Ten Commandments monument on the Texas State Capitol grounds is a far more passive use of those texts than was the case in *Stone*, where the text confronted elementary school students every day. Indeed, Van Orden, the petitioner here, apparently walked by the monument for a number of years before bringing this lawsuit. The monument is therefore also quite different from the prayers involved in *Schempp* and *Lee v. Weisman*. Texas has treated her Capitol grounds monuments as representing the several strands in the State's political and legal history. The inclusion of the Ten Commandments monument in this group has a dual significance, partaking of both religion and government. We cannot say that Texas' display of this monument violates the Establishment Clause of the First Amendment.

The judgment of the Court of Appeals is affirmed.

*It is so ordered.*

▦ JUSTICE SCALIA, concurring.

I join the opinion of THE CHIEF JUSTICE because I think it accurately reflects our current Establishment Clause jurisprudence—or at least the Establishment Clause jurisprudence we currently apply some of the time. I would prefer to reach the same result by adopting an Establishment Clause jurisprudence that is in accord with our Nation's past and present practices, and that can be consistently applied—the central relevant feature of which is that there is nothing unconstitutional in a State's favoring religion generally, honoring God through public prayer and acknowledgment, or, in a nonproselytizing manner, venerating the Ten Commandments.

▦ JUSTICE THOMAS, concurring. . . .

This case would be easy if the Court were willing to abandon the inconsistent guideposts it has adopted for addressing Establishment Clause challenges, and return to the original meaning of the Clause. I have previously suggested that the Clause's text and history "resis[t] incorporation" against the States. If the Establishment Clause does not restrain the States, then it has no application here, where only state action is at issue.

Even if the Clause is incorporated, or if the Free Exercise Clause limits the power of States to establish religions, our task would be far simpler if we returned to the original meaning of the word "establishment" than it is under the various approaches this Court now uses. The Framers understood an establishment "necessarily [to] involve actual legal coercion." *Newdow*, 542 U.S. 52 (THOMAS, J., concurring in judgment); *Lee v. Weisman*, 505 U.S. 577, 640 (1992) (SCALIA, J., dissenting) ("The coercion that was a hallmark of historical establishments of religion was coercion of religious orthodoxy and of financial support *by force of law and threat of penalty*"). "In other words, establishment at the founding involved, for example, mandatory observance or mandatory payment of taxes supporting ministers." *Cutter*, 544 U.S. 709, 729 (THOMAS, J., concurring). And "government practices that have nothing to do with creating or maintaining . . . coercive state establishments" simply do not "implicate the possible liberty interest of being free from coercive state establishments." *Newdow*, 542 U.S., 53 (THOMAS, J., concurring in judgment).

There is no question that, based on the original meaning of the Establishment Clause, the Ten Commandments display at issue here is constitutional. In no sense does Texas compel petitioner Van Orden to do anything. The only injury to him is that he takes offense at seeing the monument as he passes it on his way to the Texas Supreme Court Library. He need not stop to read it or even to look at it, let alone to express support for it or adopt the Commandments as guides for his life. The mere presence of the monument along his path involves no coercion and thus does not violate the Establishment Clause.

Returning to the original meaning would do more than simplify our task. It also would avoid the pitfalls present in the Court's current approach to such challenges. . . .

First, this Court's precedent permits even the slightest public recognition of religion to constitute an establishment of religion. For example, individuals frequenting a county courthouse have successfully challenged as an Establishment Clause violation a sign at the courthouse alerting the public that the building was closed for Good Friday and containing a 4-inch high crucifix. Similarly, a park ranger has claimed that a cross erected to honor World War I veterans on a rock in the Mojave Desert Preserve violated the Establishment Clause, and won. If a cross in the middle of a desert establishes a religion, then no religious observance is safe from challenge. . . .

Second, in a seeming attempt to balance out its willingness to consider almost any acknowledgment of religion an establishment, in other cases Members of this Court have concluded that the term or symbol at issue has no religious meaning by virtue of its ubiquity or rote ceremonial invocation. But words such as "God" have religious significance. For example, just last Term this Court had before it a challenge to the recitation of the Pledge of Allegiance, which includes the phrase "one Nation under God." The declaration that our country is "'one Nation under God'" necessarily "entail[s] an affirmation that God exists." This phrase is thus anathema to those who reject God's existence and a validation of His existence to those who accept it. Telling either nonbelievers or believers that the words "under God" have no meaning contradicts what they know to be true. Moreover, repetition does not deprive religious words or symbols of their traditional meaning. Words like "God" are not vulgarities for which the shock value diminishes with each successive utterance.

Even when this Court's precedents recognize the religious meaning of symbols or words, that recognition fails to respect fully religious belief or disbelief. This Court looks for the meaning to an observer of indeterminate religious affiliation who knows all the facts and circumstances surrounding a challenged display. . . .

This analysis is not fully satisfying to either nonadherents or adherents. For the nonadherent, who may well be more sensitive than the hypothetical "reasonable observer," or who may not know all the facts, this test fails to capture completely the honest and deeply felt offense he takes from the government conduct. For the adherent, this analysis takes no account of the message sent by removal of the sign or display, which may well appear to him to be an act hostile to his religious faith. The Court's foray into religious meaning either gives insufficient weight to the views of nonadherents and adherents alike, or it provides no principled way to choose between those views. In sum, this Court's effort to assess religious meaning is fraught with futility.

Finally, the very "flexibility" of this Court's Establishment Clause precedent leaves it incapable of consistent application. The inconsistency between the decisions the Court reaches today in this case and in *McCreary County v. American Civil Liberties Union of Ky.*, only compounds the confusion.

The unintelligibility of this Court's precedent raises the further concern that, either in appearance or in fact, adjudication of Establishment Clause challenges turns on judicial predilections. . . .

Much, if not all, of this would be avoided if the Court would return to the views of the Framers and adopt coercion as the touchstone for our Establishment Clause inquiry. Every acknowledgment of religion would not give rise to an Establishment Clause claim. Courts would not act as theological commissions, judging the meaning of religious matters. Most important, our precedent would be capable of consistent and coherent application. While the Court correctly rejects the challenge to the Ten Commandments monument on the Texas Capitol grounds, a more fundamental rethinking of our Establishment Clause jurisprudence remains in order.

▨ JUSTICE BREYER, concurring in the judgment.

In *School Dist. of Abington Township v. Schempp*, JUSTICE GOLDBERG, joined by JUSTICE HARLAN, wrote, in respect to the First Amendment's Religion Clauses, that there is "no simple and clear measure which by precise application can readily and invariably demark the permissible from the impermissible." One must refer instead to the basic purposes of those Clauses. They seek to "assure the fullest possible scope of religious liberty and tolerance for all." They seek to avoid that divisiveness based upon religion that promotes social conflict, sapping the strength of government and religion alike. They seek to maintain that "separation of church and state" that has long been critical to the "peaceful dominion that religion exercises in [this] country," where the "spirit of religion" and the "spirit of freedom" are productively "united," "reign[ing] together" but in separate spheres "on the same soil."

The Court has made clear, as JUSTICES GOLDBERG and HARLAN noted, that the realization of these goals means that government must "neither engage in nor compel religious practices," that it must "effect no favoritism among sects or between religion and nonreligion," and that it must "work deterrence of no religious belief." The government must avoid excessive interference with, or promotion of, religion. But the Establishment Clause does not compel the government to purge from the public sphere all that in any way partakes of the religious. Such absolutism is not only inconsistent with our national traditions, but would also tend to promote the kind of social conflict the Establishment Clause seeks to avoid.

Thus, as JUSTICES GOLDBERG and HARLAN pointed out, the Court has found no single mechanical formula that can accurately draw the constitutional line in every case. . . .

Neither can this Court's other tests readily explain the Establishment Clause's tolerance, for example, of the prayers that open legislative meetings; certain references to, and invocations of, the Deity in the public words of public officials; the public references to God on coins, decrees, and buildings; or the attention paid to the religious objectives of certain holidays, including Thanksgiving. . . .

If the relation between government and religion is one of separation, but not of mutual hostility and suspicion, one will inevitably find difficult borderline cases. And in such cases, I see no test-related substitute for the exercise of legal judgment. That judgment is not a personal judgment. Rather, as in all constitutional cases, it must reflect and remain faithful to the underlying purposes of the Clauses, and it must take account of context and consequences measured in light of those purposes. While the Court's prior tests provide useful guideposts—and might well lead to the same result the Court reaches today—no exact formula can dictate a resolution to such fact-intensive cases.

The case before us is a borderline case. It concerns a large granite monument bearing the text of the Ten Commandments located on the grounds of the Texas State Capitol. On the one hand, the Commandments' text undeniably has a religious message, invoking, indeed emphasizing, the Diety. On the other hand, focusing on the text of the Commandments alone cannot conclusively resolve this case. Rather, to determine the message that the text here conveys, we must examine how the text is *used*. And that inquiry requires us to consider the context of the display.

In certain contexts, a display of the tablets of the Ten Commandments can convey not simply a religious message but also a secular moral message (about proper standards of social conduct). And in certain contexts, a display of the tablets can also convey a historical message (about a historic relation between those standards and the law). . . .

Here the tablets have been used as part of a display that communicates not simply a religious message, but a secular message as well. The circumstances surrounding the display's placement on the capitol grounds and its physical setting suggest that the State itself intended the latter, nonreligious aspects of the tablets' message to predominate. And the monument's 40-year history on the Texas state grounds indicates that that has been its effect.

The group that donated the monument, the Fraternal Order of Eagles, a private civic (and primarily secular) organization, while interested in the religious aspect of the Ten Commandments, sought to highlight the Commandments' role in shaping civic morality as part of that organization's efforts to combat juvenile delinquency. The Eagles' consultation with a committee composed of members of several faiths in order to find a nonsectarian text underscores the group's ethics-based motives. The tablets, as displayed on the monument, prominently acknowledge that the Eagles donated the display, a factor which, though not sufficient, thereby further distances the State itself from the religious aspect of the Commandments' message.

The physical setting of the monument suggests little or nothing of the sacred. The monument sits in a large park containing 17 monuments and 21 historical markers, all designed to illustrate the "ideals" of those who settled in Texas and of those who have lived there since that time. The setting does not readily lend itself to meditation or any other religious activity. But it does provide a context of history and moral ideals. It (together with the display's inscription about its origin) communicates to visitors that the State sought to reflect moral principles, illustrating a relation between ethics and law that the State's citizens, historically speaking, have endorsed. That is to say, the context suggests that the State intended the display's moral message—an illustrative message reflecting the historical "ideals" of Texans—to predominate.

If these factors provide a strong, but not conclusive, indication that the Commandments' text on this monument conveys a predominantly secular message, a further factor is determinative here. As far as I can tell, 40 years passed in which the presence of this monument, legally speaking, went un-challenged (until the single legal objection raised by petitioner). And I am not aware of any evidence suggesting that this was due to a climate of intimida-tion. Hence, those 40 years suggest more strongly than can any set of formula-ic tests that few individuals, whatever their system of beliefs, are likely to have understood the monument as amounting, in any significantly detrimental way, to a government effort to favor a particular religious sect, primarily to promote religion over nonreligion, to "engage in" any "religious practic[e]," to "compel" any "religious practic[e]," or to "work deterrence" of any "religious belief." Those 40 years suggest that the public visiting the capitol grounds has con-sidered the religious aspect of the tablets' message as part of what is a broader moral and historical message reflective of a cultural heritage. . . .

This case differs from *McCreary County*, where the short (and stormy) history of the courthouse Commandments' displays demonstrates the sub-stantially religious objectives of those who mounted them, and the effect of this readily apparent objective upon those who view them. That history there indicates a governmental effort substantially to promote religion, not simply an effort primarily to reflect, historically, the secular impact of a religiously in-spired document. And, in today's world, in a Nation of so many different reli-gious and comparable nonreligious fundamental beliefs, a more contemporary state effort to focus attention upon a religious text is certainly likely to prove divisive in a way that this longstanding, pre-existing monument has not.

For these reasons, I believe that the Texas display—serving a mixed but primarily nonreligious purpose, not primarily "advanc[ing]" or "inhibit[ing]" religion," and not creating an "excessive government entanglement with religion"—might satisfy this Court's more formal Establishment Clause tests. But, as I have said, in reaching the conclusion that the Texas display falls on the permissible side of the constitutional line, I rely less upon a literal applica-tion of any particular test than upon consideration of the basic purposes of the First Amendment's Religion Clauses themselves. This display has stood apparently uncontested for nearly two generations. That experience helps us understand that as a practical matter of *degree* this display is unlikely to prove divisive. And this matter of degree is, I believe, critical in a borderline case such as this one.

At the same time, to reach a contrary conclusion here, based primarily upon the religious nature of the tablets' text would, I fear, lead the law to exhibit a hostility toward religion that has no place in our Establishment Clause traditions. Such a holding might well encourage disputes concerning the removal of longstanding depictions of the Ten Commandments from public buildings across the Nation. And it could thereby create the very kind of religiously based divisiveness that the Establishment Clause seeks to avoid. . . .

I concur in the judgment of the Court.

JUSTICE STEVENS, with whom JUSTICE GINSBURG joins, dissenting.

The sole function of the monument on the grounds of Texas' State Capitol is to display the full text of one version of the Ten Commandments. The monument is not a work of art and does not refer to any event in the history of the State. . . .

Viewed on its face, Texas' display has no purported connection to God's role in the formation of Texas or the founding of our Nation; nor does it provide the reasonable observer with any basis to guess that it was erected to honor any individual or organization. The message transmitted by Texas' chosen display is quite plain: This State endorses the divine code of the "Judeo-Christian" God. . . .

I

In my judgment, at the very least, the Establishment Clause has created a strong presumption against the display of religious symbols on public property. . . .

Government's obligation to avoid divisiveness and exclusion in the religious sphere is compelled by the Establishment and Free Exercise Clauses, which together erect a wall of separation between church and state.[4] This metaphorical wall protects principles long recognized and often recited in this Court's cases. The first and most fundamental of these principles, one that a majority of this Court today affirms, is that the Establishment Clause demands religious neutrality—government may not exercise a preference for one religious faith over another. This essential command, however, is not merely a prohibition against the government's differentiation among religious sects. We have repeatedly reaffirmed that neither a State nor the Federal Government "can constitutionally pass laws or impose requirements which aid all religions as against non-believers, and neither can aid those religions based on a belief in the existence of God as against those religions founded on different beliefs." This principle is based on the straightforward notion that governmental

---

[4] The accuracy and utility of this metaphor have been called into question. Whatever one may think of the merits of the historical debate surrounding Jefferson and the "wall" metaphor, this Court at a minimum has never questioned the concept of the "separation of church and state" in our First Amendment jurisprudence. THE CHIEF JUSTICE's opinion affirms that principle, (demanding a "separation between church and state"). Indeed, even the Court that famously opined that "[w]e are a religious people whose institutions presuppose a Supreme Being," acknowledged that "[t]here cannot be the slightest doubt that the First Amendment reflects the philosophy that Church and State should be separated." The question we face is how to give meaning to that concept of separation.

promotion of orthodoxy is not saved by the aggregation of several orthodoxies under the State's banner. . . .

In restating this principle, I do not discount the importance of avoiding an overly strict interpretation of the metaphor so often used to define the reach of the Establishment Clause. The plurality is correct to note that "religion and religious traditions" have played a "strong role . . . throughout our nation's history." . . . Given this history, it is unsurprising that a religious symbol may at times become an important feature of a familiar landscape or a reminder of an important event in the history of a community. The wall that separates the church from the State does not prohibit the government from acknowledging the religious beliefs and practices of the American people, nor does it require governments to hide works of art or historic memorabilia from public view just because they also have religious significance.

This case, however, is not about historic preservation or the mere recognition of religion. The issue is obfuscated rather than clarified by simplistic commentary on the various ways in which religion has played a role in American life, and by the recitation of the many extant governmental "acknowledgments" of the role the Ten Commandments played in our Nation's heritage.[9]

The monolith displayed on Texas Capitol grounds cannot be discounted as a passive acknowledgment of religion, nor can the State's refusal to remove it upon objection be explained as a simple desire to preserve a historic relic. This Nation's resolute commitment to neutrality with respect to religion is flatly inconsistent with the plurality's wholehearted validation of an official state endorsement of the message that there is one, and only one, God.

## II

When the Ten Commandments monument was donated to the State of Texas in 1961, it was not for the purpose of commemorating a noteworthy event in Texas history, signifying the Commandments' influence on the development of secular law, or even denoting the religious beliefs of Texans at that time. To the contrary, the donation was only one of over a hundred largely identical monoliths, and of over a thousand paper replicas, distributed to state and local governments throughout the Nation over the course of several decades. . . .

The donors were motivated by a desire to "inspire the youth" and curb juvenile delinquency by providing children with a "code of conduct or standards by which to govern their actions." It is the Eagles' belief that disseminating the message conveyed by the Ten Commandments will help to persuade young men and women to observe civilized standards of behavior, and will lead to more productive lives. . . .

The desire to combat juvenile delinquency by providing guidance to youths is both admirable and unquestionably secular. But achieving that goal

---

[9] Though this Court has subscribed to the view that the Ten Commandments influenced the development of Western legal thought, it has not officially endorsed the far more specific claim that the Ten Commandments played a significant role in the development of our Nation's foundational documents (and the subsidiary implication that it has special relevance to Texas). Although it is perhaps an overstatement to characterize this latter proposition as "idiotic," as one Member of the *plurality* has done, at the very least the question is a matter of intense scholarly debate. Compare Brief for Legal Historians and Law Scholars as Amicus Curiae in *McCreary County v. American Civil Liberties Union of Ky.*, with Brief for American Center for Law and Justice as *Amici Curiae*. . . .

through biblical teachings injects a religious purpose into an otherwise secular endeavor. . . .

Though the State of Texas may genuinely wish to combat juvenile delinquency, and may rightly want to honor the Eagles for their efforts, it cannot effectuate these admirable purposes through an explicitly religious medium. The State may admonish its citizens not to lie, cheat or steal, to honor their parents and to respect their neighbors' property; and it may do so by printed words, in television commercials, or on granite monuments in front of its public buildings. . . . The message at issue in this case, however, is fundamentally different from either a bland admonition to observe generally accepted rules of behavior or a general history lesson.

The reason this message stands apart is that the Decalogue is a venerable religious text. As we held 25 years ago, it is beyond dispute that "[t]he Ten Commandments are undeniably a sacred text in the Jewish and Christian faiths." For many followers, the Commandments represent the literal word of God as spoken to Moses and repeated to his followers after descending from Mount Sinai. The message conveyed by the Ten Commandments thus cannot be analogized to an appendage to a common article of commerce ("In God we Trust") or an incidental part of a familiar recital ("God save the United States and this honorable Court"). Thankfully, the plurality does not attempt to minimize the religious significance of the Ten Commandments. . . .

The profoundly sacred message embodied by the text inscribed on the Texas monument is emphasized by the especially large letters that identify its author: "I AM the LORD thy God." It commands present worship of Him and no other deity. It directs us to be guided by His teaching in the current and future conduct of all of our affairs. It instructs us to follow a code of divine law, some of which has informed and been integrated into our secular legal code ("Thou shalt not kill"), but much of which has not ("Thou shalt not make to thyself any graven images. . . . Thou shalt not covet").

Moreover, despite the Eagles' best efforts to choose a benign nondenominational text, the Ten Commandments display projects not just a religious, but an inherently sectarian message. There are many distinctive versions of the Decalogue, ascribed to by different religions and even different denominations within a particular faith; to a pious and learned observer, these differences may be of enormous religious significance. In choosing to display this version of the Commandments, Texas tells the observer that the State supports this side of the doctrinal religious debate. The reasonable observer, after all, has no way of knowing that this text was the product of a compromise, or that there is a rationale of any kind for the text's selection.

The Establishment Clause, if nothing else, forbids government from "specifying details upon which men and women who believe in a benevolent, omnipotent Creator and Ruler of the world are known to differ." Given that the chosen text inscribed on the Ten Commandments monument invariably places the State at the center of a serious sectarian dispute, the display is unquestionably unconstitutional under our case law.

Even if, however, the message of the monument, despite the inscribed text, fairly could be said to represent the belief system of all Judeo-Christians, it would still run afoul of the Establishment Clause by prescribing a compelled code of conduct from one God, namely a Judeo-Christian God, that is rejected by prominent polytheistic sects, such as Hinduism, as well as nontheistic religions, such as Buddhism. And, at the very least, the text of the

Ten Commandments impermissibly commands a preference for religion over irreligion. . . .

Recognizing the diversity of religious and secular beliefs held by Texans and by all Americans, it seems beyond peradventure that allowing the seat of government to serve as a stage for the propagation of an unmistakably Judeo-Christian message of piety would have the tendency to make nonmonotheists and nonbelievers "feel like [outsiders] in matters of faith, and [strangers] in the political community." . . .

Even more than the display of a religious symbol on government property, displaying this sectarian text at the state capitol should invoke a powerful presumption of invalidity. As JUSTICE SOUTER's opinion persuasively demonstrates, the physical setting in which the Texas monument is displayed—far from rebutting that presumption—actually enhances the religious content of its message. The monument's permanent fixture at the seat of Texas government is of immense significance. . . .

## III

The plurality relies heavily on the fact that our Republic was founded, and has been governed since its nascence, by leaders who spoke then (and speak still) in plainly religious rhetoric. THE CHIEF JUSTICE cites, for instance, George Washington's 1789 Thanksgiving Proclamation in support of the proposition that the Establishment Clause does not proscribe official recognition of God's role in our Nation's heritage.[20] Further, the plurality emphatically endorses the seemingly timeless recognition that our "institutions presuppose a Supreme Being." Many of the submissions made to this Court by the parties and *amici*, in accord with the plurality's opinion, have relied on the ubiquity of references to God throughout our history.

The speeches and rhetoric characteristic of the founding era, however, do not answer the question before us. I have already explained why Texas' display of the full text of the Ten Commandments, given the content of the actual display and the context in which it is situated, sets this case apart from the countless examples of benign government recognitions of religion. But there is another crucial difference. Our leaders, when delivering public addresses, often express their blessings simultaneously in the service of God and their constituents. Thus, when public officials deliver public speeches, we recognize that their words are not exclusively a transmission from *the* government because those oratories have embedded within them the inherently personal views of the speaker as an individual member of the polity.[21] The permanent placement of a textual religious display on state property is different in kind; it amalgamates otherwise discordant individual views into a collective statement of government approval. Moreover, the message never ceases to transmit itself to objecting viewers whose only choices are to accept the message or to ignore the offense by averting their gaze. In this sense, although Thanksgiving Day proclamations and inaugural speeches undoubtedly seem official, in most

---

[20] This is, of course, a rhetorical approach not unique to the plurality's opinion today. Appeals to such religious speeches have frequently been used in support of governmental transmission of religious messages. . . .

[21] It goes without saying that the analysis differs when a listener is coerced into listening to a prayer.

circumstances they will not constitute the sort of governmental endorsement of religion at which the separation of church and state is aimed.[22]

The plurality's reliance on early religious statements and proclamations made by the Founders is also problematic because those views were not espoused at the Constitutional Convention in 1787 nor enshrined in the Constitution's text. Thus, the presentation of these religious statements as a unified historical narrative is bound to paint a misleading picture. It does so here. In according deference to the statements of George Washington and John Adams, THE CHIEF JUSTICE and JUSTICE SCALIA, fail to account for the acts and publicly espoused views of other influential leaders of that time. Notably absent from their historical snapshot is the fact that Thomas Jefferson refused to issue the Thanksgiving proclamations that Washington had so readily embraced based on the argument that to do so would violate the Establishment Clause. THE CHIEF JUSTICE and JUSTICE SCALIA disregard the substantial debates that took place regarding the constitutionality of the early proclamations and acts they cite, see, e.g., Letter from James Madison to Edward Livingston (July 10, 1822), (arguing that Congress' appointment of Chaplains to be paid from the National Treasury was "not with my approbation" and was a "deviation" from the principle of "immunity of Religion from civil jurisdiction"), and paper over the fact that Madison more than once repudiated the views attributed to him by many, stating unequivocally that with respect to government's involvement with religion, the "'tendency to a usurpation on one side, or the other, or to a corrupting coalition or alliance between them, will be best guarded against by an entire abstinence of the Government from interference, in any way whatever, beyond the necessity of preserving public order, & protecting each sect against trespasses on its legal rights by others.'"

These seemingly nonconforming sentiments should come as no surprise. Not insignificant numbers of colonists came to this country with memories of religious persecution by monarchs on the other side of the Atlantic. Others experienced religious intolerance at the hands of colonial Puritans, who regrettably failed to practice the tolerance that some of their contemporaries preached. THE CHIEF JUSTICE and JUSTICE SCALIA ignore the separationist impulses—in accord with the principle of "neutrality"—that these individuals brought to the debates surrounding the adoption of the Establishment Clause.[27]

---

[22] With respect to the "legislative prayers" cited approvingly by THE CHIEF JUSTICE, I reiterate my view that "the designation of a member of one religious faith to serve as the sole official chaplain of a state legislature for a period of 16 years constitutes the preference of one faith over another in violation of the Establishment Clause." Thus, JUSTICE SCALIA and I are in agreement with respect to at least one point—this Court's decision in Marsh "ignor[ed] the neutrality principle" at the heart of the Establishment Clause.

[27] The contrary evidence cited by THE CHIEF JUSTICE and JUSTICE SCALIA only underscores the obvious fact that leaders who have drafted and voted for a text are eminently capable of violating their own rules. The first Congress was—just as the present Congress is—capable of passing unconstitutional legislation. Thus, it is no answer to say that the Founders' separationist impulses were "plainly rejected" simply because the first Congress enacted laws that acknowledged God. To adopt such an interpretive approach would misguidedly give authoritative weight to the fact that the Congress that passed the Fourteenth Amendment also enacted laws that tolerated segregation, and the fact that the Congress that passed the First Amendment also enacted laws, such as the Alien and Sedition Act, that indisputably violated our present understanding of the First Amendment.

Ardent separationists aside, there is another critical nuance lost in the plurality's portrayal of history. Simply put, many of the Founders who are often cited as authoritative expositors of the Constitution's original meaning understood the Establishment Clause to stand for a *narrower* proposition than the plurality, for whatever reason, is willing to accept. Namely, many of the Framers understood the word "religion" in the Establishment Clause to encompass only the various sects of Christianity.

The evidence is compelling. Prior to the Philadelphia Convention, the States had begun to protect "religious freedom" in their various constitutions. Many of those provisions, however, restricted "equal protection" and "free exercise" to Christians, and invocations of the divine were commonly understood to refer to Christ. That historical background likely informed the Framers' understanding of the First Amendment. Accordingly, one influential thinker wrote of the First Amendment that "'[t]he meaning of the term "establishment" in this amendment unquestionably is, the preference and establishment given by law to one sect of Christians over every other.'" Jasper Adams, The Relation of Christianity to Civil Government in the United States (Feb. 13, 1833). That definition tracked the understanding of the text Justice Story adopted in his famous Commentaries, in which he wrote that the "real object" of the Clause was:

> not to countenance, much less to advance Mahometanism, or Judaism, or infidelity, by prostrating Christianity; but to exclude all rivalry among Christian sects, and to prevent any national ecclesiastical establishment, which should give to an hierarchy the exclusive patronage of the national government. It thus sought to cut off the means of religious persecution, (the vice and pest of former ages,) and the power of subverting the rights of conscience in matters of religion, which had been trampled upon almost from the days of the Apostles to the present age.[29] . . .

Along these lines, for nearly a century after the Founding, many accepted the idea that America was not just a *religious* nation, but "a Christian nation."

The original understanding of the type of "religion" that qualified for constitutional protection under the Establishment Clause likely did not include those followers of Judaism and Islam who are among the preferred "monotheistic" religions JUSTICE SCALIA has embraced in his *McCreary County* opinion. The inclusion of Jews and Muslims inside the category of constitutionally favored religions surely would have shocked CHIEF JUSTICE MARSHALL and JUSTICE STORY. Indeed, JUSTICE SCALIA is unable to point to any persuasive historical evidence or entrenched traditions in support of his decision to give specially preferred constitutional status to all monotheistic religions. Perhaps this is because the history of the Establishment Clause's original meaning just as strongly supports a preference for Christianity as it does a preference for monotheism. Generic references to "God" hardly constitute evidence that

---

[29] Justice Story wrote elsewhere that "Christianity is indispensable to the true interests & solid foundations of all free governments. I distinguish . . . between the establishment of a particular sect, as the Religion of the State, & the Establishment of Christianity itself, without any preference of any particular form of it. I know not, indeed, how any deep sense of moral obligation or accountableness can be expected to prevail in the community without a firm persuasion of the great Christian Truths." . . .

those who spoke the word meant to be inclusive of all monotheistic believers; nor do such references demonstrate that those who heard the word spoken understood it broadly to include all monotheistic faiths. JUSTICE SCALIA's inclusion of Judaism and Islam is a laudable act of religious tolerance, but it is one that is unmoored from the Constitution's history and text, and moreover one that is patently arbitrary in its inclusion of some, but exclusion of other (e.g., Buddhism), widely practiced non-Christian religions. Given the original understanding of the men who championed our "Christian nation"—men who had no cause to view anti-Semitism or contempt for atheists as problems worthy of civic concern—one must ask whether JUSTICE SCALIA "has not had the courage (or the foolhardiness) to apply [his originalism] principle consistently."

Indeed, to constrict narrowly the reach of the Establishment Clause to the views of the Founders would lead to more than this unpalatable result; it would also leave us with an unincorporated constitutional provision—in other words, one that limits only the *federal* establishment of "a national religion." Under this view, not only could a State constitutionally adorn all of its public spaces with crucifixes or passages from the New Testament, it would also have full authority to prescribe the teachings of Martin Luther or Joseph Smith as *the* official state religion. Only the Federal Government would be prohibited from taking sides, (and only then as between Christian sects).

A reading of the First Amendment dependent on either of the purported original meanings expressed above would eviscerate the heart of the Establishment Clause. It would replace Jefferson's "wall of separation" with a perverse wall of exclusion—Christians inside, non-Christians out. It would permit States to construct walls of their own choosing—Baptists inside, Mormons out; Jewish Orthodox inside, Jewish Reform out. A Clause so understood might be faithful to the expectations of some of our Founders, but it is plainly not worthy of a society whose enviable hallmark over the course of two centuries has been the continuing expansion of religious pluralism and tolerance.

Unless one is willing to renounce over 65 years of Establishment Clause jurisprudence and cross back over the incorporation bridge, appeals to the religiosity of the Framers ring hollow.[32] But even if there were a coherent way to embrace incorporation with one hand while steadfastly abiding by the Founders' purported religious views on the other, the problem of the

---

[32] JUSTICE SCALIA's answer—that incorporation does not empty "the incorporated provisions of their original meaning"—ignores the fact that the Establishment Clause has its own unique history. There is no evidence, for example, that incorporation of the Confrontation Clause ran contrary to the core of the Clause's original understanding. There is, however, some persuasive evidence to this effect regarding the Establishment Clause. See *Elk Grove Unified School Dist. v. Newdow*, 542 U.S. 1, 49 (2004) (THOMAS, J., concurring in judgment) (arguing that the Clause was originally understood to be a "federalism provision" intended to prevent "Congress from interfering with state establishments"). It is this unique history, not incorporation writ large, that renders incoherent the post-incorporation reliance on the Establishment Clause's original understanding.

JUSTICE THOMAS, at least, has faced this problem head-on. But even if the decision to incorporate the Establishment Clause was misguided, it is at this point unwise to reverse course given the weight of precedent that would have to be cast aside to reach the intended result. . . .

selective use of history remains. As the widely divergent views espoused by the leaders of our founding era plainly reveal, the historical record of the preincorporation Establishment Clause is too indeterminate to serve as an interpretive North Star.[33]

It is our duty, therefore, to interpret the First Amendment's command that "Congress shall make no law respecting an establishment of religion" not by merely asking what those words meant to observers at the time of the founding, but instead by deriving from the Clause's text and history the broad principles that remain valid today. As we have said in the context of statutory interpretation, legislation "often [goes] beyond the principal evil [at which the statute was aimed] to cover reasonably comparable evils, and it is ultimately the provisions of our laws rather than the principal concerns of our legislators by which we are governed." In similar fashion, we have construed the Equal Protection Clause of the Fourteenth Amendment to prohibit segregated schools, even though those who drafted that Amendment evidently thought that separate was not unequal. We have held that the same Amendment prohibits discrimination against individuals on account of their gender, despite the fact that the contemporaries of the Amendment "doubt[ed] very much whether any action of a State not directed by way of discrimination against the negroes as a class, or on account of their race, will ever be held to come within the purview of this provision. And we have construed "evolving standards of decency" to make impermissible practices that were not considered "cruel and unusual" at the founding.

To reason from the broad principles contained in the Constitution does not, as JUSTICE SCALIA suggests, require us to abandon our heritage in favor of unprincipled expressions of personal preference. The task of applying the broad principles that the Framers wrote into the text of the First Amendment is, in any event, no more a matter of personal preference than is one's selection between two (or more) sides in a heated historical debate. We serve our constitutional mandate by expounding the meaning of constitutional provisions with one eye towards our Nation's history and the other fixed on its democratic aspirations. . . .

The principle that guides my analysis is neutrality.[35] The basis for that principle is firmly rooted in our Nation's history and our Constitution's text. I

---

[33] See Lee, 505 U.S., 626 (SOUTER, J., concurring) ("[A]t best, . . . the Framers simply did not share a common understanding of the Establishment Clause," and at worst, their overtly religious proclamations show "that they . . . could raise constitutional ideals one day and turn their backs on them the next"); *Lynch v. Donnelly*, 465 U.S. 668, 716 (1984) (BRENNAN, J., dissenting) (same); cf. Feldman, "Intellectual Origins of the Establishment Clause," 77 N.Y.U.L.Rev. 346, 404-405 (2002) (noting that, for the Framers, "the term 'establishment' was a contested one" and that the word "was used in both narrow and expansive ways in the debates of the time").

[35] JUSTICE THOMAS contends that the Establishment Clause cannot include such a neutrality principle because the Clause reaches only the governmental coercion of individual belief or disbelief. In my view, although actual religious coercion is undoubtedly forbidden by the Establishment Clause, that cannot be the full extent of the provision's reach. Jefferson's "wall" metaphor and his refusal to issue Thanksgiving proclamations, would have been nonsensical if the Clause reached only direct coercion. Further, under the "coercion" view, the Establishment Clause would amount to little more than a replica of our compelled speech

recognize that the requirement that government must remain neutral between religion and irreligion would have seemed foreign to some of the Framers; so too would a requirement of neutrality between Jews and Christians. Fortunately, we are not bound by the Framers' expectations—we are bound by the legal principles they enshrined in our Constitution. Story's vision that States should not discriminate between Christian sects has as its foundation the principle that government must remain neutral between valid systems of belief. As religious pluralism has expanded, so has our acceptance of what constitutes valid belief systems. The evil of discriminating today against atheists, "polytheists[,] and believers in unconcerned deities," is in my view a direct descendent of the evil of discriminating among Christian sects. The Establishment Clause thus forbids it and, in turn, forbids Texas from displaying the Ten Commandments monument the plurality so casually affirms.

## IV

The Eagles may donate as many monuments as they choose to be displayed in front of Protestant churches, benevolent organizations' meeting places, or on the front lawns of private citizens. The expurgated text of the King James version of the Ten Commandments that they have crafted is unlikely to be accepted by Catholic parishes, Jewish synagogues, or even some Protestant denominations, but the message they seek to convey is surely more compatible with church property than with property that is located on the government side of the metaphorical wall.

The judgment of the Court in this case stands for the proposition that the Constitution permits governmental displays of sacred religious texts. This makes a mockery of the constitutional ideal that government must remain neutral between religion and irreligion. If a State may endorse a particular deity's command to "have no other gods before me," it is difficult to conceive of any textual display that would run afoul of the Establishment Clause.

The disconnect between this Court's approval of Texas's monument and the constitutional prohibition against preferring religion to irreligion cannot be reduced to the exercise of plotting two adjacent locations on a slippery

---

doctrine, with a religious flavor. A Clause so interpreted would not prohibit explicit state endorsements of religious orthodoxies of particular sects, actions that lie at the heart of what the Clause was meant to regulate. The government could, for example, take out television advertisements lauding Catholicism as the only pure religion. Under the reasoning endorsed by JUSTICE THOMAS, those programs would not be coercive because the viewer could simply turn off the television or ignore the ad. . . .

Further, the notion that the application of a "coercion" principle would somehow lead to a more consistent jurisprudence is dubious. Enshrining coercion as the Establishment Clause touchstone fails to eliminate the difficult judgment calls regarding "the form that coercion must take." Coercion may seem obvious to some, while appearing nonexistent to others. Compare *Santa Fe Independent School Dist.*, 530 U.S., 312, with *Lee*, 505 U.S., 642 (SCALIA, J., dissenting). It may be a legal requirement or an effect that is indirectly inferred from a variety of factors. See, e.g., *Engel v. Vitale*, 370 U.S. 421, 431 (1962) ("When the power, prestige and financial support of government is placed behind a particular religious belief, the indirect coercive pressure upon religious minorities to conform to the prevailing officially approved religion is plain"). In short, "reasonable people could, and no doubt would, argue about whether coercion existed in a particular situation." Feldman, "The Intellectual Origins of the Establishment Clause," 77 N.Y.U. L.Rev. 346, 415 (2002).

slope. Rather, it is the difference between the shelter of a fortress and exposure to "the winds that would blow" if the wall were allowed to crumble. That wall, however imperfect, remains worth preserving.

*I respectfully dissent.*

▦ JUSTICE O'CONNOR, dissenting.

For essentially the reasons given by JUSTICE SOUTER, as well as the reasons given in my concurrence in *McCreary County v. American Civil Liberties Union of Ky.*, I respectfully dissent.

▦ JUSTICE SOUTER, with whom JUSTICE STEVENS and JUSTICE GINS-BURG join, dissenting.

Although the First Amendment's Religion Clauses have not been read to mandate absolute governmental neutrality toward religion, the Establishment Clause requires neutrality as a general rule, and thus expresses Madison's condemnation of "employ[ing] Religion as an engine of Civil policy." A governmental display of an obviously religious text cannot be squared with neutrality, except in a setting that plausibly indicates that the statement is not placed in view with a predominant purpose on the part of government either to adopt the religious message or to urge its acceptance by others. . . .

[A] pedestrian happening upon the monument at issue here needs no training in religious doctrine to realize that the statement of the Commandments, quoting God himself, proclaims that the will of the divine being is the source of obligation to obey the rules, including the facially secular ones. . . .

To drive the religious point home, and identify the message as religious to any viewer who failed to read the text, the engraved quotation is framed by religious symbols: two tablets with what appears to be ancient script on them, two Stars of David, and the superimposed Greek letters Chi and Rho as the familiar monogram of Christ. Nothing on the monument, in fact, detracts from its religious nature,[2] nothing in the context of the display detracts from the crèche's religious message"), and the plurality does not suggest otherwise. It would therefore be difficult to miss the point that the government of Texas[3] is telling everyone who sees the monument to live up to a moral code because God requires it, with both code and conception of God being rightly understood as the inheritances specifically of Jews and Christians. And it is likewise

---

[2] That the monument also surrounds the text of the Commandments with various American symbols (notably the U.S. flag and a bald eagle) only underscores the impermissibility of Texas's actions: by juxtaposing these patriotic symbols with the Commandments and other religious signs, the monument sends the message that being American means being religious (and not just being religious but also subscribing to the Commandments, i.e., practicing a monotheistic religion).

[3] There is no question that the State in its own right is broadcasting the religious message. When Texas accepted the monument from the Eagles, the state legislature, aware that the Eagles "for the past several years have placed across the country . . . parchment plaques and granite monoliths of the Ten Commandments . . . [in order] to promote youth morality and help stop the alarming increase in delinquency," resolved "that the Fraternal Order of the Eagles of the State of Texas be commended and congratulated for its efforts and contributions in combating juvenile delinquency throughout our nation." The State, then, expressly approved of the Eagles' proselytizing, which it made on its own.

unsurprising that the District Court expressly rejected Texas's argument that the State's purpose in placing the monument on the capitol grounds was related to the Commandments' role as "part of the foundation of modern secular law in Texas and elsewhere."

The monument's presentation of the Commandments with religious text emphasized and enhanced stands in contrast to any number of perfectly constitutional depictions of them, the frieze of our own Courtroom providing a good example, where the figure of Moses stands among history's great lawgivers. While Moses holds the tablets of the Commandments showing some Hebrew text, no one looking at the lines of figures in marble relief is likely to see a religious purpose behind the assemblage or take away a religious message from it. Only one other depiction represents a religious leader, and the historical personages are mixed with symbols of moral and intellectual abstractions like Equity and Authority. Since Moses enjoys no especial prominence on the frieze, viewers can readily take him to be there as a lawgiver in the company of other lawgivers; and the viewers may just as naturally see the tablets of the Commandments (showing the later ones, forbidding things like killing and theft, but without the divine preface) as background from which the concept of law emerged, ultimately having a secular influence in the history of the Nation. Government may, of course, constitutionally call attention to this influence, and may post displays or erect monuments recounting this aspect of our history no less than any other, so long as there is a context and that context is historical. Hence, a display of the Commandments accompanied by an exposition of how they have influenced modern law would most likely be constitutionally unobjectionable.[4] And the Decalogue could, as *Stone* suggested, be integrated constitutionally into a course of study in public schools.

Texas seeks to take advantage of the recognition that visual symbol and written text can manifest a secular purpose in secular company, when it argues that its monument (like Moses in the frieze) is not alone and ought to be viewed as only 1 among 17 placed on the 22 acres surrounding the state capitol. Texas, indeed, says that the Capitol grounds are like a museum for a collection of exhibits, the kind of setting that several Members of the Court have said can render the exhibition of religious artifacts permissible, even though in

---

[4] For similar reasons, the other displays of the Commandments that the plurality mentions, do not run afoul of the Establishment Clause. The statues of Moses and St. Paul in the Main Reading Room of the Library of Congress are 2 of 16 set in close proximity, statues that "represent men illustrious in the various forms of thought and activity. . . ." Moses and St. Paul represent religion, while the other 14 (a group that includes Beethoven, Shakespeare, Michelangelo, Columbus, and Plato) represent the nonreligious categories of philosophy, art, history, commerce, science, law, and poetry. Similarly, the sculpture of the woman beside the Decalogue in the Main Reading Room is one of 8 such figures "represent[ing] eight characteristic features of civilized life and thought," the same 8 features (7 of them nonreligious) that Moses, St. Paul, and the rest of the 16 statues represent.

The inlay on the floor of the National Archives Building is one of four such discs, the collective theme of which is not religious. Rather, the discs "symbolize the various types of Government records that were to come into the National Archive." . . .

As for Moses's "prominen[t] featur[ing]" in the Chamber of the United States House of Representatives," Moses is actually 1 of 23 portraits encircling the House Chamber, each approximately the same size, having no religious theme. The portraits depict "men noted in history for the part they played in the evolution of what has become American law." More importantly for purposes of this case, each portrait consists only of the subject's face; the Ten Commandments appear nowhere in Moses's portrait.

other circumstances their display would be seen as meant to convey a religious message forbidden to the State. So, for example, the Government of the United States does not violate the Establishment Clause by hanging Giotto's Madonna on the wall of the National Gallery.

But 17 monuments with no common appearance, history, or esthetic role scattered over 22 acres is not a museum, and anyone strolling around the lawn would surely take each memorial on its own terms without any dawning sense that some purpose held the miscellany together more coherently than fortuity and the edge of the grass. One monument expresses admiration for pioneer women. One pays respect to the fighters of World War II. And one quotes the God of Abraham whose command is the sanction for moral law. The themes are individual grit, patriotic courage, and God as the source of Jewish and Christian morality; there is no common denominator. In like circumstances, we rejected an argument similar to the State's, noting in *County of Allegheny* that "[t]he presence of Santas or other Christmas decorations elsewhere in the . . . [c]ourthouse, and of the nearby gallery forum, fail to negate the [crèche's] endorsement effect. . . . The record demonstrates . . . that the crèche, with its floral frame, was its own display distinct from any other decorations or exhibitions in the building."[6]

If the State's museum argument does nothing to blunt the religious message and manifestly religious purpose behind it, neither does the plurality's reliance on generalities culled from cases factually different from this one. . . . In fact, it is not until the end of its opinion that the plurality turns to the relevant precedent of *Stone*, a case actually dealing with a display of the Decalogue.

When the plurality finally does confront *Stone*, it tries to avoid the case's obvious applicability by limiting its holding to the classroom setting. The plurality claims to find authority for limiting *Stone's* reach this way in the opinion's citations of two school-prayer cases, *School Dist. of Abington Township v. Schempp* and *Engel v. Vitale*. But *Stone* relied on those cases for widely applicable notions, not for any concept specific to schools. The opinion quoted *Schempp's* statements that "it is no defense to urge that the religious practices here may be relatively minor encroachments on the First Amendment," and that "the place of the Bible as an instrument of religion cannot be gainsaid." And *Engel* was cited to support the proposition that the State was responsible for displaying the Commandments, even though their framed, printed texts were bought with private subscriptions. *Stone*, 42 ("[T]he mere posting of the [Commandments] under the auspices of the legislature provides the official support of the State Government that the Establishment Clause prohibits" (omission and internal quotation marks omitted)). Thus, the schoolroom was beside the point of the citations, and that is presumably why the *Stone* Court failed to discuss

---

[6] It is true that the Commandments monument is unlike the display of the Commandments considered in the other Ten Commandments case we decide today, *McCreary County*. There the Commandments were posted at the behest of the county in the first instance, whereas the State of Texas received the monument as a gift from the Eagles, which apparently conceived of the donation at the suggestion of a movie producer bent on promoting his commercial film on the Ten Commandments. But this distinction fails to neutralize the apparent expression of governmental intent to promote a religious message: although the nativity scene in *Allegheny County* was donated by the Holy Name Society, we concluded that "[n]o viewer could reasonably think that [the scene] occupies [its] location [at the seat of county government] without the support and approval of the government."

the educational setting, as other opinions had done when school was significant. *Stone* did not, for example, speak of children's impressionability or their
captivity as an audience in a school class. In fact, *Stone's* reasoning reached the
classroom only in noting the lack of support for the claim that the State had
brought the Commandments into schools in order to "integrat[e] [them] into
the school curriculum." Accordingly, our numerous prior discussions of *Stone*
have never treated its holding as restricted to the classroom.

Nor can the plurality deflect *Stone* by calling the Texas monument "a far
more passive use of [the Decalogue] than was the case in *Stone*, where the text
confronted elementary school students every day." Placing a monument on the
ground is not more "passive" than hanging a sheet of paper on a wall when
both contain the same text to be read by anyone who looks at it. The problem
in *Stone* was simply that the State was putting the Commandments there to be
seen, just as the monument's inscription is there for those who walk by it.

To be sure, Kentucky's compulsory-education law meant that the schoolchildren were forced to see the display every day, whereas many see the monument by choice, and those who customarily walk the Capitol grounds can
presumably avoid it if they choose. But in my judgment (and under our often
inexact Establishment Clause jurisprudence, such matters often boil down to
judgment), this distinction should make no difference. The monument in this
case sits on the grounds of the Texas State Capitol. There is something significant in the common term "statehouse" to refer to a state capitol building:
it is the civic home of every one of the State's citizens. If neutrality in religion
means something, any citizen should be able to visit that civic home without
having to confront religious expressions clearly meant to convey an official
religious position that may be at odds with his own religion, or with rejection
of religion. . . .

Finally, though this too is a point on which judgment will vary, I do not
see a persuasive argument for constitutionality in the plurality's observation
that Van Orden's lawsuit comes "[f]orty years after the monument's erection
. . . ," an observation that echoes the State's contention that one fact cutting in
its favor is that "the monument stood . . . in Austin . . . for some forty years
without generating any controversy or litigation." It is not that I think the
passage of time is necessarily irrelevant in Establishment Clause analysis. We
have approved framing-era practices because they must originally have been
understood as constitutionally permissible, and we have recognized that Sunday laws have grown recognizably secular over time. There is also an analogous argument, not yet evaluated, that ritualistic religious expression can
become so numbing over time that its initial Establishment Clause violation
becomes at some point too diminished for notice. But I do not understand
any of these to be the State's argument, which rather seems to be that 40 years
without a challenge shows that as a factual matter the religious expression is
too tepid to provoke a serious reaction and constitute a violation. Perhaps,
but the writer of Exodus chapter 20 was not lukewarm, and other explanations may do better in accounting for the late resort to the courts. Suing a
State over religion puts nothing in a plaintiff's pocket and can take a great deal
out, and even with volunteer litigators to supply time and energy, the risk of
social ostracism can be powerfully deterrent. I doubt that a slow walk to the
courthouse, even one that took 40 years, is much evidentiary help in applying
the Establishment Clause.

I would reverse the judgment of the Court of Appeals.

## NOTES AND QUESTIONS

1. How do you explain the different outcomes in the two cases, *McCreary* and *Van Orden*? Is it the facts, the analytical standard applied by each majority, differing views of the relevance of history, or simply the views of one justice, Justice Breyer? How does Justice Breyer reconcile the two competing outcomes?

2. Think back to the questions raised in other parts of the book about the relevance and uses of the history surrounding the adoption of the First Amendment in deciding such controversies. In what ways do the various opinions use that history to reach their conclusions? According to the *McCreary* Court, what are some of the major concerns that promoted the adoption of the First Amendment's religion clauses? How do the *Van Orden* majority and the *McCreary* dissent differ from the *McCreary* majority in terms of its convictions about what the Establishment Clause means? Whose arguments do you find more persuasive? For historical analysis of the legal significance of the Ten Commandments, see Paul Finkelman, "The Ten Commandments on the Courthouse Lawn and Elsewhere," *Fordham Law Review* 73 (2005): 1477-1520, and Steven K. Green, "The Font of Everything Just and Right? The Ten Commandments as a Source of American Law," *Journal of Law and Religion* 14 (1999–2000): 525-558.

3. In his dissenting opinion in the *Van Orden* case, Justice Stevens argues that, when interpreting the Establishment Clause, it is necessary to ask "not merely . . . what [the text of the Clause] meant to observers at the time of the founding, but instead by deriving from the Clause's text and history the broad principles that remain valid today." What is Justice Scalia's response to this argument?

4. How does the majority in *McCreary* articulate and defend the "purpose" part of the *Lemon* test? What are some of the dissent's criticisms of the majority's opinion on these points?

5. In her concurring opinion in the *McCreary* decision, Justice O'Connor says: "Voluntary religious belief and expression may be as threatened when government takes the mantle of religion upon itself as when the government directly interferes with private religious practices." What does she mean? Can you think of arguments other than the ones O'Connor makes to support this statement? What does Justice O'Connor mean when she says "we do not count heads before enforcing the First Amendment"?

6. In his dissent in the *McCreary* case, how does Justice Scalia attempt to attack the notion that the government may not prefer religion over nonreligion? According to Justice Scalia, may the government also prefer one religion over another? What is the *McCreary* majority's response to these arguments? How does Justice Stevens respond to these arguments in his dissenting opinion in the *Van Orden* case?

7. What legal test does the Court plurality apply in *Van Orden*? How would Justice Scalia prefer to approach the case? What test would Justice Thomas

apply? What are the differences between the way Justice Scalia would approach these matters and the way Justice Thomas would do so? Justice Thomas argues that applying his coercion test would clear up much of the confusion in Establishment Clause jurisprudence. Do you agree? Would applying Justice Scalia's preferred test have a similar effect?

8. What legal test does Justice Breyer apply in his opinion concurring in the judgment in the *Van Orden* case? What factual point is most significant to Breyer's legal judgment in this case? How does Justice Stevens criticize Justice Breyer's arguments in the *Van Orden* case? Between the two, whose arguments do you find more persuasive? To what extent should the absence of prior complaints about a religious display affect its constitutionality?

9. How does the plurality in the *Van Orden* case distinguish the case of *Stone v. Graham*? What arguments does Justice Souter make on this matter in his dissenting opinion in this case? Whose argument is more persuasive on this point?

10. Justice Thomas argues that the Establishment Clause should not apply to the states. How does he justify his stand on this issue? Do any of the other justices agree with Justice Thomas on this matter?

11. A number of the justices discuss the notion of divisiveness based on religious difference and how this notion factors into their Establishment Clause analyses in these cases. Discuss some of the different perspectives on this issue. Do they put the right amount of emphasis on this factor or too much?

12. According to Justice Breyer's opinion concurring in the judgment in the *Van Orden* case, why do contemporary government-sponsored displays of religious texts raise more concerns than similar older displays? Do you agree with his analysis? Whether or not you agree, what kind of religions would this sort of approach tend to benefit?

13. In his dissenting opinion in the *McCreary* case, Justice Scalia argues that Justice Stevens

> fails to recognize that in the context of public acknowledgements of God there are legitimate *competing* interests; On the one hand, the interest of that minority in not feeling "excluded"; but on the other, the interest of the overwhelming majority of religious believers in being able to give God thanks and supplication *as a people*, and with respect to our national endeavors. Our national tradition has resolved that conflict in favor of the majority. . . .

Is the competing interest Justice Scalia articulates a legitimate one? If so, why does it not suffice for people to be able to worship God, give thanks, and pray for the nation as part of their services in various houses of worship? Further, does Justice Scalia assume too much about the commonality of even monotheistic faiths?

14. What does the *Van Orden* plurality mean when it calls the Texas Ten Commandments display a "passive display"? How does Justice Souter respond to that argument in his dissenting opinion in that case?

15. Toward the end of his dissenting opinion in the *Van Orden* case, Justice Stevens writes:

    > The Eagles may donate as many monuments as they choose to be displayed in front of Protestant churches, benevolent organizations' meeting places, or on the front lawns of private citizens.

    What point is Stevens trying to make here? If the Court had adopted Stevens' approach, would it have meant that the public square would have been shorn of religious displays? Or, would only displays on government property have been constitutionally forbidden? In other words, is it possible that property can have "public" aspects to it and yet not be government property (at least if we use the word "public" in the colloquial sense rather than the technical legal sense)? In any case, is Justice Stevens' approach correct or is it too rigid?

16. In the *McCreary* case, the Court observed that "[o]ne consequence of taking account of the purpose underlying past actions is that the same government action may be constitutional if taken in the first instance and unconstitutional if it has a sectarian heritage." Note that a display identical to the one struck down in *McCreary* was upheld in a subsequent lower court case. See *ACLU v. Mercer County*, 432 F.3d 624 (6th Cir. 2005). Does it make constitutional sense for one court to strike and another court to uphold otherwise identical displays of the Ten Commandments on the basis of how well the respective county commissions articulated a secular rationale for their displays?

17. In his confirmation hearings, a Senator asked then-Supreme Court nominee John Roberts about these Ten Commandments rulings. While Roberts said he was "not commenting on the correctness" of the decisions, he nonetheless noted that "there's exactly one justice [Justice Breyer] that thinks [that both the Kentucky and Texas Ten Commandments decisions are] right." In short, he chided the Court for its failure to be more cohesive and send a clearer signal in this context. Does Roberts have a point?

18. Dr. Martin Marty, a scholar of American religion, has said that the "bottom line" of "the Nativity-Menorah-Crescent battles [is that they] are not about religion. They are about politics, about preemption of space in the official polis. Wielders of these and other symbols (e.g., Ten Commandments) placed there are saying, 'We belong, and you don't.' 'We own the tradition. You don't.'"[2] Do you agree or disagree with Dr. Marty's assessment?

## CHAPTER 21

# GOVERNMENT ACKNOWLEDGMENTS OF RELIGION, GOVERNMENT CHAPLAINS, RELIGION AND POLITICS, AND RELIGION IN THE GOVERNMENTAL WORKPLACE

A chaplain chosen and paid by the government invites state legislators to bow their heads in prayer before commencing legislative business. A minister seeks to serve as a delegate to his state constitutional convention, but he is thwarted by a state law that prohibits ministers from holding public office. A United States Postal Service clerk places a prominent crucifix in her work area, an area frequented by customers each day.

Does the First Amendment permit or prohibit these kinds of expressions and actions? In this chapter, we explore these and related issues.

As discussed in the previous chapter, the First Amendment protects the rights of nongovernmental groups and individuals to promote their faith, but it prohibits the government from endorsing or advancing religion. Nevertheless, the Court has held that the government may employ legislative chaplains, and at times it has distinguished between permissible governmental acknowledgment of religion and impermissible governmental endorsement or establishment of it. This chapter begins by examining some of those rulings. It then considers the complex relationship of religion and politics and some of the ways in which religion may be expressed and practiced in the federal workplace.

## GOVERNMENTAL ACKNOWLEDGMENTS OF RELIGION AND GOVERNMENT CHAPLAINS

The 1892 case of *Church of Holy Trinity v. United States*[1] involved a church that contracted with a resident of England to come to New York City and serve as rector and pastor of a congregation there. The government alleged that the arrangement was barred by a federal law that prohibited contracting with foreigners in ways that encouraged them to migrate to perform labor or service in this country. The Act's terms were quite broad, such that a literal reading of the law would have made it applicable to this case, but the Court refused to read it that way. It found that the title of the act, the circumstances surrounding its adoption, and its legislative history indicated that Congress had a narrower intent when it drafted the statute—"to stay the influx of [ ] cheap unskilled labor." Writing for the Court, Justice David Brewer continued: "But beyond all these matters no purpose of action against religion can be imputed to any legislation, state or national, because this is a religious people. This is historically true. From the discovery of this continent to the present hour, there is a single voice making this affirmation."[2]

The Court then reviewed the many religious references in original colony charters, the Declaration of Independence and state constitutions. The Court asserted, for example:

> If we examine the constitutions of the various States we find in them a constant recognition of religious obligations. Every constitution of every one of the forty-four States contains language which either directly or by clear implication recognizes a profound reverence for religion and an assumption that its influence in all human affairs is essential to the well being of the community This recognition may be in the preamble, such as is found in the constitution of Illinois, 1870: "We, the people of the State of Illinois, grateful to Almighty God for the civil, political and religious liberty which He hath so long permitted us to enjoy, and looking to Him for a blessing upon our endeavors to secure and transmit the same unimpaired to succeeding generations," etc.[3]

The Court further emphasized the federal Constitution's treatment of religion:

> Even the Constitution of the United States, which is supposed to have little touch upon the private life of the individual, contains in the First Amendment a declaration common to the constitutions of all the States, as follows: "Congress shall make no law respecting an establishment of religion, or prohibiting the free exercise thereof," etc. And also provides in Article 1, section 7, (a provision common to many constitutions,) that the Executive shall have ten days (Sundays excepted) within which to determine whether he will approve or veto a bill.
>
> There is no dissonance in these declarations. There is a universal language pervading them all, having one meaning; they affirm and reaffirm that this is a religious nation.[4]

Finally, the Court looked beyond government documents and actions to the way in which religion pervades American culture:

> If we pass beyond these matters to a view of American life as expressed by its laws, its business, its customs and its society, we find everywhere a clear recognition of the same truth. Among other matters note the following: The form of oath universally prevailing, concluding with an appeal to the Almighty; the custom of opening sessions of all deliberative bodies and most conventions with prayer; the prefatory words of all wills, "In the name of God, amen;" the laws respecting the observance of the Sabbath, with the general cessation of all secular business, and the closing of courts, legislatures, and other similar public assemblies on that day; the churches and church organizations which abound in every city, town and hamlet; the multitude of charitable organizations existing every where under Christian auspices; the gigantic missionary associations, with general support, and aiming to establish Christian missions in every quarter of the globe. These, and many other matters which might be noticed, add a volume of unofficial declarations to the mass of organic utterances that this is a Christian nation. In the face of all these, shall it be believed that a Congress of the United States intended to make it a misdemeanor for a church of this country to contract for the services of a Christian minister residing in another nation?[5] . . .

NOTES AND QUESTIONS

1. Justice Brewer's "Christian nation" declarations in the *Holy Trinity* case elicited some minor criticism at the time, but generally his statements received little attention. Possibly this was because it was more common for public officials in the eighteenth and nineteenth centuries to make statements of a religious nature.

   One question raised by the *Holy Trinity* case has to do with the use of history and tradition in judicial opinions. In this area of church-state law judges tend to rely heavily on prior historical practices and customs. To what extent should contemporaneous historical practices that were not part of the legislative history specific to the statute or constitutional provision in question (e.g., the House debates on the drafting of the First Amendment contained in the Annals of Congress) inform modern deliberations into the appropriateness of government religious expression? If history is important, what weight should it be given, and how does one know whether he or she has gotten the history "right"? Keep these questions in mind as you read the cases and materials in this chapter.

2. Justice Brewer says that "this is a Christian nation." In your opinion, does this statement have more cultural or legal significance? If it is the former, does it then have any constitutional significance? If it is the latter, does the statement mean that governments may enact legislation and enforce policies that favor Christianity over other faiths or that public officials may take into account the fact that the majority of Americans profess allegiance to Christianity when they are developing and implementing policy? Even if the statement only represents the second alternative, does it still violate notions of government neutrality toward religion? Or are Justices Rehnquist and Scalia correct that the nation's Christian heritage means that government is not required to be neutral as between religion and nonreligion?

3. *Holy Trinity* in context: The *Holy Trinity* decision came at a time of a backlash by conservative Protestants to increased immigration, growing religious pluralism, and a perceived secularization of American culture and the public schools. A small but visible religious group, the National Reform Association (N.R.A.), advocated an amendment to the U.S. Constitution, known as the "Christian Amendment," to insert an acknowledgment of God and Jesus Christ in the Preamble. During this period, the phrase "Christian nation" was understood to stand for a Protestant hegemony. The N.R.A. and other religious groups also pushed legislation in Congress, such as a restrictive national Sunday law and a law limiting the availability of divorce. Justice Brewer, a devout Congregationalist, was a popular speaker on the religious and moral issues of the day and sympathized with some of these efforts, though any connection he maintained with the N.R.A. is uncertain. Several years following the issuance of the *Holy Trinity* decision, Brewer wrote a book entitled *The United States a Christian Nation*, in which he advocated for several religious causes including greater Sabbath observance and government acknowledgments of religion. Does this context affect the way in which people should analyze Justice Brewer's statements in *Holy Trinity*? For background on the

opinion and Justice Brewer, see Steven K. Green, "Justice David Josiah Brewer and the "Christian Nation" Maxim," *Albany Law Review* 63 (1999): 427. See also Gaines M. Foster, *Moral Reconstruction: Christian Lobbyists and the Federal Legislation of Morality, 1865-1920* (Chapel Hill: The University of North Carolina Press, 2002).

4. Justice Brewer's "Christian nation" declaration has been criticized in subsequent Supreme Court opinions. Almost a century later, Justice Brennan called this statement "arrogant." See *Lynch v. Donnelly*, 465 U.S. 668, 718 (1984) (Brennan, dissenting). Even Justice Scalia has termed the Christian nation declaration an "aberration." See *Lee v. Weisman*, 505 U.S. 577, 641 (1992) (Scalia, dissenting). Does this criticism reflect a disagreement with the substance of Justice Brewer's statements or a shift in attitude toward the permissibility of judges and other government officials making religious declarations?

5. In 2004, some members of Congress proposed legislation that included the following provision:

> Notwithstanding any other provision of this chapter, the Supreme Court shall not have jurisdiction to review . . . any matter to the extent that relief is sought against an element of Federal, State, or local government, or against an officer of Federal, State, or local government (whether or not acting in official personal capacity), by reason of that element's or officer's acknowledgement of God as the sovereign source of law, liberty, or government.

If this measure were to be enacted, do you believe it would be found constitutional? If so, how might it be interpreted? If this law were enacted, for example, would it permit a judge to invite local clergy to offer prayers before judicial proceedings? Would it permit the judge to limit those invitations to Christian and Jewish clergy if the judge believed the nation was founded on Biblical principles? Would it permit a government official to lead prayers over the public address system each morning in a public building as an "acknowledgement of God as the sovereign source of law, liberty and government"? Would it permit a public school teacher to do the same?

---

More than a century later, the Court continues to consider the ways in which history should shape First Amendment doctrine. One of the most prominent Supreme Court cases in this regard is *Marsh v. Chambers*, which involved a chaplain chosen and paid by the government who offered prayers before the commencement of business in the Nebraska legislature. In 1983, the Court was asked to decide whether this practice violated the First Amendment's Establishment Clause. In its opinion upholding the practice, the Court majority did not apply the *Lemon* test or any other test previously used to determine a practice's constitutionality under the Establishment Clause but instead primarily relied on the "unique" and "unbroken" historical tradition of legislative chaplains. As you read the opinions in *Marsh v. Chambers*, consider whether you believe that the reasoning and result in this case are well-founded and what kind of precedent you believe the ruling sets.

## MARSH v. CHAMBERS
### 463 U.S. 783 (1983)

▨ CHIEF JUSTICE BURGER delivered the opinion of the Court.

The question presented is whether the Nebraska Legislature's practice of opening each legislative day with a prayer by a chaplain paid by the State violates the Establishment Clause of the First Amendment.

I

The Nebraska Legislature begins each of its sessions with a prayer offered by a chaplain who is chosen biennially by the Executive Board of the Legislative Council and paid out of public funds. Robert E. Palmer, a Presbyterian minister, has served as chaplain since 1965 at a salary of $319.75 per month for each month the legislature is in session.

Ernest Chambers is a member of the Nebraska Legislature and a taxpayer of Nebraska. Claiming that the Nebraska Legislature's chaplaincy practice violates the Establishment Clause of the First Amendment, he brought this action, seeking to enjoin enforcement of the practice. . . . Applying the three-part test of *Lemon v. Kurtzman*, the [Court of Appeals] held that the chaplaincy practice violated all three elements of the test: the purpose and primary effect of selecting the same minister for 16 years and publishing his prayers was to promote a particular religious expression; use of state money for compensation and publication led to entanglement. . . .We granted certiorari limited to the challenge to the practice of opening sessions with prayers by a state-employed clergyman and we reverse.

II

The opening of sessions of legislative and other deliberative public bodies with prayer is deeply embedded in the history and tradition of this country. From colonial times through the founding of the Republic and ever since, the practice of legislative prayer has coexisted with the principles of disestablishment and religious freedom. In the very courtrooms in which the United States District Judge and later three Circuit Judges heard and decided this case, the proceedings opened with an announcement that concluded, "God save the United States and this Honorable Court." The same invocation occurs at all sessions of this Court.

The tradition in many of the Colonies was, of course, linked to an established church, but the Continental Congress, beginning in 1774, adopted the traditional procedure of opening its sessions with a prayer offered by a paid chaplain. Although prayers were not offered during the Constitutional Convention,[6] the First Congress, as one of its early items of business, adopted

---

[6] History suggests that this may simply have been an oversight. At one point, Benjamin Franklin suggested that "henceforth prayers imploring the assistance of Heaven, and its blessings on our deliberations, be held in this Assembly every morning before we proceed to business." His proposal was rejected not because the Convention was opposed to prayer, but because it was thought that a midstream adoption of the policy would highlight prior omissions and because "[the] Convention had no funds."

the policy of selecting a chaplain to open each session with prayer. Thus, on April 7, 1789, the Senate appointed a committee "to take under consideration the manner of electing Chaplains On April 9, 1789, a similar committee was appointed by the House of Representatives. On April 25, 1789, the Senate elected its first chaplain; the House followed suit on May 1, 1789. A statute providing for the payment of these chaplains was enacted into law on September 22, 1789.[8]

On September 25, 1789, three days after Congress authorized the appointment of paid chaplains, final agreement was reached on the language of the Bill of Rights. Clearly the men who wrote the First Amendment Religion Clauses did not view paid legislative chaplains and opening prayers as a violation of that Amendment, for the practice of opening sessions with prayer has continued without interruption ever since that early session of Congress. It has also been followed consistently in most of the states, including Nebraska, where the institution of opening legislative sessions with prayer was adopted even before the State attained statehood. Neb. Jour. of Council, General Assembly.

Standing alone, historical patterns cannot justify contemporary violations of constitutional guarantees, but there is far more here than simply historical patterns. In this context, historical evidence sheds light not only on what the draftsmen intended the Establishment Clause to mean, but also on how they thought that Clause applied to the practice authorized by the First Congress—their actions reveal their intent. An Act "passed by the first Congress assembled under the Constitution, many of whose members had taken part in framing that instrument, . . . is contemporaneous and weighty evidence of its true meaning." *Wisconsin v. Pelican Ins. Co.*, 127 U.S 265, 297 (1888).

In *Walz v. Tax Comm'n*, we considered the weight to be accorded to history: "It is obviously correct that no one acquires a vested or protected right in violation of the Constitution by long use, even when that span of time covers our entire national existence and indeed predates it. Yet an unbroken practice . . . is not something to be lightly cast aside."

No more is Nebraska's practice of over a century, consistent with two centuries of national practice, to be cast aside. It can hardly be thought that in the same week Members of the First Congress voted to appoint and to pay a chaplain for each House and also voted to approve the draft of the First Amendment for submission to the states, they intended the Establishment Clause of the Amendment to forbid what they had just declared acceptable. In applying the First Amendment to the states through the Fourteenth Amendment, it would be incongruous to interpret that Clause as imposing more stringent First Amendment limits on the states than the draftsmen imposed on the Federal Government.

This unique history leads us to accept the interpretation of the First Amendment draftsmen who saw no real threat to the Establishment Clause arising from a practice of prayer similar to that now challenged. We conclude that legislative prayer presents no more potential for establishment than the provision of school transportation, beneficial grants for higher education, or tax exemptions for religious organizations.

---

[8] It bears note that James Madison, one of the principal advocates of religious freedom in the Colonies and a drafter of the Establishment Clause, was one of those appointed to undertake this task by the House of Representatives, and voted for the bill authorizing payment of the chaplains.

Respondent cites JUSTICE BRENNAN's concurring opinion in *Abington School Dist. v. Schempp*, and argues that we should not rely too heavily on "the advice of the Founding Fathers" because the messages of history often tend to be ambiguous and not relevant to a society far more heterogeneous than that of the Framers. Respondent also points out that John Jay and John Rutledge opposed the motion to begin the first session of the Continental Congress with prayer.[12]

We do not agree that evidence of opposition to a measure weakens the force of the historical argument; indeed it infuses it with power by demonstrating that the subject was considered carefully and the action not taken thoughtlessly, by force of long tradition and without regard to the problems posed by a pluralistic society. Jay and Rutledge specifically grounded their objection on the fact that the delegates to the Congress "were so divided in religious sentiments . . . that [they] could not join in the same act of worship." Their objection was met by Samuel Adams, who stated that "he was no bigot, and could hear a prayer from a gentleman of piety and virtue, who was at the same time a friend to his country." A. P. Stokes, Church and State in the United States, vol. 1, 449.

This interchange emphasizes that the delegates did not consider opening prayers as a proselytizing activity or as symbolically placing the government's "official seal of approval on one religious view." Rather, the Founding Fathers looked at invocations as "conduct whose . . . effect . . . [harmonized] with the tenets of some or all religions." *McGowan v. Maryland*, 366 U.S. 420, 442. The Establishment Clause does not always bar a state from regulating conduct simply because it "harmonizes with religious canons." Here, the individual claiming injury by the practice is an adult, presumably not readily susceptible to "religious indoctrination."

In light of the unambiguous and unbroken history of more than 200 years, there can be no doubt that the practice of opening legislative sessions with prayer has become part of the fabric of our society. To invoke Divine guidance on a public body entrusted with making the laws is not, in these circumstances, an "establishment" of religion or a step toward establishment; it is simply a tolerable acknowledgment of beliefs widely held among the people of this country. As JUSTICE DOUGLAS observed, "[we] are a religious people whose institutions presuppose a Supreme Being."

### III

We turn then to the question of whether any features of the Nebraska practice violate the Establishment Clause. Beyond the bare fact that a prayer is offered, three points have been made: first, that a clergyman of only one denomination—Presbyterian—has been selected for 16 years; second, that the chaplain is paid at public expense; and third, that the prayers are in the Judeo-Christian tradition.[14] Weighed against the historical background, these factors do not serve to invalidate Nebraska's practice.

---

[12] It also could be noted that objections to prayer were raised, apparently successfully, in Pennsylvania while ratification of the Constitution was debated, and that in the 1820's, Madison expressed doubts concerning the chaplaincy practice.

[14] Palmer characterizes his prayers as "nonsectarian," "Judeo Christian," and with "elements of the American civil religion." Although some of his earlier prayers were often explicitly Christian, Palmer removed all references to Christ after a 1980 complaint from a Jewish legislator.

The Court of Appeals was concerned that Palmer's long tenure has the effect of giving preference to his religious views. We cannot, any more than Members of the Congresses of this century, perceive any suggestion that choosing a clergyman of one denomination advances the beliefs of a particular church. To the contrary, the evidence indicates that Palmer was reappointed because his performance and personal qualities were acceptable to the body appointing him. Palmer was not the only clergyman heard by the legislature; guest chaplains have officiated at the request of various legislators and as substitutes during Palmer's absences. Absent proof that the chaplain's reappointment stemmed from an impermissible motive, we conclude that his long tenure does not in itself conflict with the Establishment Clause.

Nor is the compensation of the chaplain from public funds a reason to invalidate the Nebraska Legislature's chaplaincy; remuneration is grounded in historic practice initiated, as we noted earlier, by the same Congress that drafted the Establishment Clause of the First Amendment. The Continental Congress paid its chaplain, as did some of the states. Currently, many state legislatures and the United States Congress provide compensation for their chaplains. Nebraska has paid its chaplain for well over a century. The content of the prayer is not of concern to judges where, as here, there is no indication that the prayer opportunity has been exploited to proselytize or advance any one, or to disparage any other, faith or belief. That being so, it is not for us to embark on a sensitive evaluation or to parse the content of a particular prayer.

We do not doubt the sincerity of those, who like respondent, believe that to have prayer in this context risks the beginning of the establishment the Founding Fathers feared. But this concern is not well founded, for as JUSTICE GOLDBERG aptly observed in his concurring opinion in *Abington*: "It is of course true that great consequences can grow from small beginnings, but the measure of constitutional adjudication is the ability and willingness to distinguish between real threat and mere shadow."

The unbroken practice for two centuries in the National Congress and for more than a century in Nebraska and in many other states gives abundant assurance that there is no real threat "while this Court sits," *Panhandle Oil Co. v. Mississippi ex rel. Knox*, 277 U.S. 218, 223 (1928) (HOLMES, J., dissenting).

The judgment of the Court of Appeals is

*Reversed.*

JUSTICE BRENNAN, with whom JUSTICE MARSHALL joins, dissenting.

The Court today has written a narrow and, on the whole, careful opinion. In effect, the Court holds that officially sponsored legislative prayer, primarily on account of its "unique history," is generally exempted from the First Amendment's prohibition against "an establishment of religion." The Court's opinion is consistent with dictum in at least one of our prior decisions, and its limited rationale should pose little threat to the overall fate of the Establishment Clause. Moreover, disagreement with the Court requires that I confront the fact that some 20 years ago, in a concurring opinion in one of the cases striking down official prayer and ceremonial Bible reading in the public schools, I came very close to endorsing essentially the result reached by the Court today. Nevertheless, after much reflection, I have come to the conclusion that I was wrong then and that the Court is wrong today. I now believe that the practice of official invocational prayer, as it exists in Nebraska and most other state legislatures, is unconstitutional. It is contrary to the doctrine as well the underlying purposes of the Establishment Clause, and it is not saved either by its history or by any of the other considerations suggested in the Court's opinion.

I

The Court makes no pretense of subjecting Nebraska's practice of legislative prayer to any of the formal "tests" that have traditionally structured our inquiry under the Establishment Clause. That it fails to do so is, in a sense, a good thing, for it simply confirms that the Court is carving out an exception to the Establishment Clause rather than reshaping Establishment Clause doctrine to accommodate legislative prayer. For my purposes, however, I must begin by demonstrating what should be obvious: that, if the Court were to judge legislative prayer through the unsentimental eye of our settled doctrine, it would have to strike it down as a clear violation of the Establishment Clause.

The most commonly cited formulation of prevailing Establishment Clause doctrine is found in *Lemon v. Kurtzman*:

> Every analysis in this area must begin with consideration of the cumulative criteria developed by the Court over many years. Three such tests may be gleaned from our cases. First, the statute [at issue] must have a secular legislative purpose; second, its principal or primary effect must be one that neither advances nor inhibits religion; finally, the statute must not foster 'an excessive government entanglement with religion.' 403 U.S. 602, 612-613.

That the "purpose" of legislative prayer is pre-eminently religious rather than secular seems to me to be self-evident. "To invoke Divine guidance on a public body entrusted with making the laws," is nothing but a religious act. Moreover, whatever secular functions legislative prayer might play—formally opening the legislative session, getting the members of the body to quiet down, and imbuing them with a sense of seriousness and high purpose—could so plainly be performed in a purely nonreligious fashion that to claim a secular purpose for the prayer is an insult to the perfectly honorable individuals who instituted and continue the practice.

The "primary effect" of legislative prayer is also clearly religious. As we said in the context of officially sponsored prayers in the public schools, "prescribing a particular form of religious worship," even if the individuals involved have the choice not to participate, places "indirect coercive pressure upon religious minorities to conform to the prevailing officially approved religion. . . ." *Engel v. Vitale*, 370 U.S. 421, 431. More importantly, invocations in Nebraska's legislative halls explicitly link religious belief and observance to the power and prestige of the State. "[The] mere appearance of a joint exercise of legislative authority by Church and State provides a significant symbolic benefit to religion in the minds of some by reason of the power conferred." *Larkin v. Gendel's Den*, 459 U.S. 116, 125-126.

The Court argues that legislators are adults, "presumably not readily susceptible to . . . peer pressure." I made a similar observation in my concurring opinion in *Schempp*. Quite apart from the debatable constitutional significance of this argument, I am now most uncertain as to whether it is even factually correct: Legislators, by virtue of their instinct for political survival, are often loath to assert in public religious views that their constituents might perceive as hostile or nonconforming.

Finally, there can be no doubt that the practice of legislative prayer leads to excessive "entanglement" between the State and religion. *Lemon* pointed out that "entanglement" can take two forms: First, a state statute or program might involve the state impermissibly in monitoring and overseeing religious affairs. In the case of legislative prayer, the process of choosing a "suitable" chaplain, whether on a permanent or rotating basis, and insuring that the chaplain limits himself or herself to "suitable" prayers, involves precisely the sort of supervision that agencies of government should if at all possible avoid.[8]

Second, excessive "entanglement" might arise out of "the divisive political potential" of a state statute or program. . . .

In this case, this second aspect of entanglement is also clear. The controversy between Senator Chambers and his colleagues, which had reached the stage of difficulty and rancor long before this lawsuit was brought, has split the Nebraska Legislature precisely on issues of religion and religious conformity. The record in this case also reports a series of instances, involving legislators other than Senator Chambers, in which invocations by Reverend Palmer and others led to controversy along religious lines. And in general, the history of legislative prayer has been far more eventful—and divisive—than a hasty reading of the Court's opinion might indicate.[10]

In sum, I have no doubt that, if any group of law students were asked to apply the principles of *Lemon* to the question of legislative prayer, they would nearly unanimously find the practice to be unconstitutional.[11] . . .

---

[8] In *Lemon*, we struck down certain state statutes providing aid to sectarian schools, in part because "the program requires the government to examine the school's records in order to determine how much of the total expenditures is attributable to secular education and how much to religious activity." In this case, by the admission of the very government officials involved, supervising the practice of legislative prayer requires those officials to determine if particular members of the clergy and particular prayers are "too explicitly Christian," (testimony of Rev. Palmer) or consistent with "the various religious preferences that the Senators may or may not have," (same), or likely to "inject some kind of a religious dogma" into the proceedings, (testimony of Frank Lewis, Chairman of the Nebraska Legislature Executive Board).

[10] [P]articular prayers and particular chaplains in the state legislatures have periodically led to serious political divisiveness along religious lines. See, e.g., The Oregonian, Apr. 1, 1983, p. C8 ("Despite protests from at least one representative, a follower of an Indian guru was allowed to give the prayer at the start of Thursday's [Oregon] House [of Representatives] session. Shortly before Ma Anand Sheela began the invocation, about a half-dozen representatives walked off the House floor in apparent protest of the prayer"); Cal. Senate Jour., 37th Sess., 171-173, 307-308 (1907) (discussing request by a State Senator that State Senate Chaplain not use the name of Christ in legislative prayer, and response by one local clergyman claiming that the legislator who made the request had committed a "crowning infamy" and that his "words were those of an irreverent and godless man").

[11] The *Lemon* tests do not, of course, exhaust the set of formal doctrines that can be brought to bear on the issues before us today. Last Term, for example, we made clear that a state program that discriminated among religious faiths, and not merely in favor of all religious faiths, "must be invalidated unless it is justified by a compelling governmental interest." . . . In this case, the appointment of a single chaplain for 16 years, and the evident impossibility of a Buddhist monk or Sioux Indian religious worker being appointed for a similar period, might well justify application of the Larson test. Moreover, given the pains that petitioners have gone through to emphasize the "ceremonial" function of legislative prayer, and given the ease with which a similar "ceremonial" function could be performed without the necessity for prayer, I have little doubt that the Nebraska practice, at least, would fail the Larson test.

## II

The path of formal doctrine, however, can only imperfectly capture the nature and importance of the issues at stake in this case. A more adequate analysis must therefore take into account the underlying function of the Establishment Clause, and the forces that have shaped its doctrine.

### A . . .

The principles of "separation" and "neutrality" implicit in the Establishment Clause serve many purposes. Four of these are particularly relevant here.

The first, which is most closely related to the more general conceptions of liberty found in the remainder of the First Amendment, is to guarantee the individual right to conscience. The right to conscience, in the religious sphere, is not only implicated when the government engages in direct or indirect coercion. It is also implicated when the government requires individuals to support the practices of a faith with which they do not agree. . . .

The second purpose of separation and neutrality is to keep the state from interfering in the essential autonomy of religious life, either by taking upon itself the decision of religious issues, or by unduly involving itself in the supervision of religious institutions or officials. . . .

The third purpose of separation and neutrality is to prevent the trivialization and degradation of religion by too close an attachment to the organs of government. The Establishment Clause "stands as an expression of principle on the part of the Founders of our Constitution that religion is too personal, too sacred, too holy, to permit its 'unhallowed perversion' by a civil magistrate." *Engel*, 370 U.S., 432. . . .[16]

Finally, the principles of separation and neutrality help assure that essentially religious issues, precisely because of their importance and sensitivity, not become the occasion for battle in the political arena. With regard to most issues, the government may be influenced by partisan argument and may act as a partisan itself. In each case, there will be winners and losers in the political battle, and the losers' most common recourse is the right to dissent and the right to fight the battle again another day. With regard to matters that are essentially religious, however, the Establishment Clause seeks that there should be no political battles, and that no American should at any point feel alienated from his government because that government has declared or acted upon some "official" or "authorized" point of view on a matter of religion.

### B

The imperatives of separation and neutrality are not limited to the relationship of government to religious institutions or denominations, but extend

---

[16] Consider, in addition to the formal authorities cited in text, the following words by a leading Methodist clergyman:

"[Some propose] to reassert religious values by posting the Ten Commandments on every school-house wall, by erecting cardboard nativity shrines on every corner, by writing God's name on our money, and by using His Holy Name in political oratory. Is this not the ultimate in profanity? . . .

"What is the result of all this display of holy things in public places? Does it make the market-place more holy? Does it improve people? Does it change their character or motives? On the contrary, the sacred symbols are thereby cheapened and degraded. The effect is often that of a television commercial on a captive audience—boredom and resentment." Dean Kelley, "Beyond Separation of Church and State," *Journal of Church and State* 5 (1963): 181, 190-191.

as well to the relationship of government to religious beliefs and practices. In *Torcaso v. Watkins*, for example, we struck down a state provision requiring a religious oath as a qualification to hold office, not only because it violated principles of free exercise of religion, but also because it violated the principles of nonestablishment of religion. And, of course, in the pair of cases that hang over this one like a reproachful set of parents, we held that official prayer and prescribed Bible reading in the public schools represent a serious encroachment on the Establishment Clause. As we said in *Engel*, "[it] is neither sacrilegious nor antireligious to say that each separate government in this country should stay out of the business of writing or sanctioning official prayers and leave that purely religious function to the people themselves and to those the people choose to look to for religious guidance." 370 U.S., 435.

Nor should it be thought that this view of the Establishment Clause is a recent concoction of an overreaching judiciary. Even before the First Amendment was written, the Framers of the Constitution broke with the practice of the Articles of Confederation and many state constitutions, and did not invoke the name of God in the document. This "omission of a reference to the Deity was not inadvertent; nor did it remain unnoticed." Leo Pfeffer, "The Deity in American Constitutional History," 23 J. Church & State (1981): 215, 217. Moreover, Thomas Jefferson and Andrew Jackson, during their respective terms as President, both refused on Establishment Clause grounds to declare national days of thanksgiving or fasting. And James Madison, writing subsequent to his own Presidency on essentially the very issue we face today, stated:

> Is the appointment of Chaplains to the two Houses of Congress consistent with the Constitution, and with the pure principle of religious freedom?
>
> In strictness, the answer on both points must be in the negative. The Constitution of the U.S. forbids everything like an establishment of a national religion. The law appointing Chaplains establishes a religious worship for the national representatives, to be performed by Ministers of religion, elected by a majority of them; and these are to be paid out of the national taxes. Does not this involve the principle of a national establishment, applicable to a provision for a religious worship for the Constituent as well as of the representative Body, approved by the majority, and conducted by Ministers of religion paid by the entire nation?

## C

Legislative prayer clearly violates the principles of neutrality and separation that are embedded within the Establishment Clause. It is contrary to the fundamental message of *Engel* and *Schempp*. It intrudes on the right to conscience by forcing some legislators either to participate in a "prayer opportunity," with which they are in basic disagreement, or to make their disagreement a matter of public comment by declining to participate. It forces all residents of the State to support a religious exercise that may be contrary to their own beliefs. It requires the State to commit itself on fundamental theological issues. It has the potential for degrading religion by allowing a religious call to worship to be intermeshed with a secular call to order. And it injects religion into the political sphere by creating the potential that each and every selection of a chaplain, or consideration of a particular prayer, or even reconsideration of the practice itself, will provoke a political battle along religious lines and ultimately alienate some religiously identified group of citizens.

D

One response to the foregoing account, of course, is that "neutrality" and "separation" do not exhaust the full meaning of the Establishment Clause as it has developed in our cases. It is indeed true that there are certain tensions inherent in the First Amendment itself, or inherent in the role of religion and religious belief in any free society, that have shaped the doctrine of the Establishment Clause, and required us to deviate from an absolute adherence to separation and neutrality. Nevertheless, these considerations, although very important, are also quite specific, and where none of them is present, the Establishment Clause gives us no warrant simply to look the other way and treat an unconstitutional practice as if it were constitutional. . . .

We have also recognized that government cannot, without adopting a decidedly *anti*-religious point of view, be forbidden to recognize the religious beliefs and practices of the American people as an aspect of our history and culture. Certainly, bona fide classes in comparative religion can be offered in the public schools. And certainly, the text of Abraham Lincoln's Second Inaugural Address which is inscribed on a wall of the Lincoln Memorial need not be purged of its profound theological content. The practice of offering invocations at legislative sessions cannot, however, simply be dismissed as "a tolerable *acknowledgment of beliefs* widely held among the people of this country" (emphasis added). "Prayer is religion *in act*." "Praying means to take hold of a word, the end, so to speak, of a line that leads to God." Reverend Palmer and other members of the clergy who offer invocations at legislative sessions are not museum pieces put on display once a day for the edification of the legislature. Rather, they are engaged by the legislature to lead it—as a body—in an act of religious worship. If upholding the practice requires denial of this fact, I suspect that many supporters of legislative prayer would feel that they had been handed a pyrrhic victory. . . .

[O]ur cases recognize that, in one important respect, the Constitution is *not* neutral on the subject of religion: Under the Free Exercise Clause, religiously motivated claims of conscience may give rise to constitutional rights that other strongly held beliefs do not. Moreover, even when the government is not compelled to do so by the Free Exercise Clause, it may to some extent act to facilitate the opportunities of individuals to practice their religion. This is not, however, a case in which a State is accommodating individual religious interests. We are not faced here with the right of the legislature to allow its members to offer prayers during the course of general legislative debate. We are certainly not faced with the right of legislators to form voluntary groups for prayer or worship. We are not even faced with the right of the State to employ members of the clergy to minister to the private religious needs of individual legislators. Rather, we are faced here with the regularized practice of conducting official prayers, on behalf of the entire legislature, as part of the order of business constituting the formal opening of every single session of the legislative term. If this is free exercise, the Establishment Clause has no meaning whatsoever. . . .

III . . .

I sympathize with the Court's reluctance to strike down a practice so prevalent and so ingrained as legislative prayer. I am, however, unconvinced by the Court's arguments, and cannot shake my conviction that legislative prayer violates both the letter and the spirit of the Establishment Clause.

## A

The Court's main argument for carving out an exception sustaining legislative prayer is historical. . . . This is a case, however, in which—absent the Court's invocation of history—there would be no question that the practice at issue was unconstitutional. And despite the surface appeal of the Court's argument, there are at least three reasons why specific historical practice should not in this case override that clear constitutional imperative.[30]

First, it is significant that the Court's historical argument does not rely on the legislative history of the Establishment Clause itself. Indeed, that formal history is profoundly unilluminating on this and most other subjects. Rather, the Court assumes that the Framers of the Establishment Clause would not have themselves authorized a practice that they thought violated the guarantees contained in the Clause. This assumption, however, is questionable. Legislators, influenced by the passions and exigencies of the moment, the pressure of constituents and colleagues, and the press of business, do not always pass sober constitutional judgment on every piece of legislation they enact, and this must be assumed to be as true of the Members of the First Congress as any other. Indeed, the fact that James Madison, who voted for the bill authorizing the payment of the first congressional chaplains, later expressed the view that the practice was unconstitutional, is instructive on precisely this point. Madison's later views may not have represented so much a change of *mind* as a change of *role*, from a Member of Congress engaged in the hurly-burly of legislative activity to a detached observer engaged in unpressured reflection. Since the latter role is precisely the one with which this Court is charged, I am not at all sure that Madison's later writings should be any less influential in our deliberations than his earlier vote.

Second, the Court's analysis treats the First Amendment simply as an Act of Congress, as to whose meaning the intent of Congress is the single touchstone. Both the Constitution and its Amendments, however, became supreme law only by virtue of their ratification by the States, and the understanding of the States should be as relevant to our analysis as the understanding of Congress. This observation is especially compelling in considering the meaning of the Bill of Rights. The first 10 Amendments were not enacted because the Members of the First Congress came up with a bright idea one morning; rather, their enactment was forced upon Congress by a number of the States as a condition for their ratification of the original Constitution. To treat any practice authorized by the First Congress as presumptively consistent with the Bill of Rights is therefore somewhat akin to treating any action of a party to a contract as presumptively consistent with the terms of the contract. The latter proposition, if it were accepted, would of course resolve many of the heretofore perplexing issues in contract law.

Finally, and most importantly, the argument tendered by the Court is misguided because the Constitution is not a static document whose meaning on

---

[30] Indeed, the sort of historical argument made by the Court should be advanced with some hesitation in light of certain other skeletons in the congressional closet. See, e.g., An Act for the Punishment of certain Crimes against the United States, (enacted by the First Congress and requiring that persons convicted of certain theft offenses "be publicly whipped, not exceeding thirty-nine stripes"); Act of July 23, 1866, (reaffirming the racial segregation of the public schools in the District of Columbia; enacted exactly one week after Congress proposed the Fourteenth Amendment to the States).

every detail is fixed for all time by the life experience of the Framers. We have recognized in a wide variety of constitutional contexts that the practices that were in place at the time any particular guarantee was enacted into the Constitution do not necessarily fix forever the meaning of that guarantee. To be truly faithful to the Framers, "our use of the history of their time must limit itself to broad purposes, not specific practices." *Schempp*, 374 U.S., 241. Our primary task must be to translate "the majestic generalities of the Bill of Rights, conceived as part of the pattern of liberal government in the eighteenth century, into concrete restraints on officials dealing with the problems of the twentieth century . . . ." *West Va. Bd. of Ed. v. Barnette*, 319 U.S. 624, 639.

The inherent adaptability of the Constitution and its amendments is particularly important with respect to the Establishment Clause. "[Our] religious composition makes us a vastly more diverse people than were our forefathers. . . . In the face of such profound changes, practices which may have been objectionable to no one in the time of Jefferson and Madison may today be highly offensive to many persons, the deeply devout and the nonbelievers alike." *Schempp*, 374 U.S., 240-241. President John Adams issued during his Presidency a number of official proclamations calling on all Americans to engage in Christian prayer. Justice Story, in his treatise on the Constitution, contended that the "real object" of the First Amendment "was, not to countenance, much less to advance Mahometanism, or Judaism, or infidelity, by prostrating Christianity; but to exclude all rivalry among Christian sects. . . ." Whatever deference Adams' actions and Story's views might once have deserved in this Court, the Establishment Clause must now be read in a very different light. Similarly, the Members of the First Congress should be treated, not as sacred figures whose every action must be emulated, but as the authors of a document meant to last for the ages. Indeed, a proper respect for the Framers themselves forbids us to give so static and lifeless a meaning to their work. To my mind, the Court's focus here on a narrow piece of history is, in a fundamental sense, a betrayal of the lessons of history.

B

Of course, the Court does not rely entirely on the practice of the First Congress in order to validate legislative prayer. There is another theme which, although implicit, also pervades the Court's opinion. It is exemplified by the Court's comparison of legislative prayer with the formulaic recitation of "God save the United States and this Honorable Court." It is also exemplified by the Court's apparent conclusion that legislative prayer is, at worst, a "'mere shadow'" on the Establishment Clause rather than a "'real threat'" to it. Simply put, the Court seems to regard legislative prayer as at most a *de minimis* violation, somehow unworthy of our attention. I frankly do not know what should be the proper disposition of features of our public life such as "God save the United States and this Honorable Court," "In God We Trust," "One Nation Under God," and the like. I might well adhere to the view expressed in *Schempp* that such mottos are consistent with the Establishment Clause, not because their import is *de minimis*, but because they have lost any true religious significance. Legislative invocations, however, are very different.

First of all, as JUSTICE STEVENS' dissent so effectively highlights, legislative prayer, unlike mottos with fixed wordings, can easily turn narrowly and obviously sectarian. I agree with the Court that the federal judiciary should not sit as a board of censors on individual prayers, but to my mind the better way of avoiding that task is by striking down all official legislative invocations.

More fundamentally, however, *any* practice of legislative prayer, even if it might look "nonsectarian" to nine Justices of the Supreme Court, will inevitably and continuously involve the State in one or another religious debate. Prayer is serious business—serious theological business—and it is not a mere "acknowledgment of beliefs widely held among the people of this country" for the State to immerse itself in that business. Some religious individuals or groups find it theologically problematic to engage in joint religious exercises predominantly influenced by faiths not their own. Some might object even to the attempt to fashion a "nonsectarian" prayer. Some would find it impossible to participate in any "prayer opportunity," marked by Trinitarian references. Some would find a prayer *not* invoking the name of Christ to represent a flawed view of the relationship between human beings and God.[44] Some might find any petitionary prayer to be improper. Some might find any prayer that lacked a petitionary element to be deficient. Some might be troubled by what they consider shallow public prayer, or nonspontaneous prayer, or prayer without adequate spiritual preparation or concentration. Some might, of course, have *theological* objections to any prayer sponsored by an organ of government. Some might object on theological grounds to the level of political neutrality generally expected of government-sponsored invocational prayer. And some might object on theological grounds to the Court's requirement that prayer, even though religious, not be proselytizing. If these problems arose in the context of a religious objection to some otherwise decidedly secular activity, then whatever remedy there is would have to be found in the Free Exercise Clause. But, in this case, we are faced with potential religious objections to an activity at the very center of religious life, and it is simply beyond the competence of government, and inconsistent with our conceptions of liberty, for the State to take upon itself the role of ecclesiastical arbiter.

## IV

The argument is made occasionally that a strict separation of religion and state robs the Nation of its spiritual identity. I believe quite the contrary. It may be true that individuals cannot be "neutral" on the question of religion. But the judgment of the Establishment Clause is that neutrality by the organs of *government* on questions of religion is both possible and imperative. . . .

I respectfully dissent.

▦ JUSTICE STEVENS, dissenting.

In a democratically elected legislature, the religious beliefs of the chaplain tend to reflect the faith of the majority of the lawmakers' constituents. Prayers may be said by a Catholic priest in the Massachusetts Legislature and by a Presbyterian minister in the Nebraska Legislature, but I would not expect to find a Jehovah's Witness or a disciple of Mary Baker Eddy or the Reverend Moon serving as the official chaplain in any state legislature. Regardless of the

---

[44] . . . As the Court points out, Reverend Palmer eliminated the Christological references in his prayers after receiving complaints from some of the State Senators. Suppose, however, that Reverend Palmer had said that he could not in good conscience omit some references. Should he have been dismissed? And, if so, what would have been the implications of *that* action under both the Establishment and the Free Exercise Clauses?

motivation of the majority that exercises the power to appoint the chaplain, it seems plain to me that the designation of a member of one religious faith to serve as the sole official chaplain of a state legislature for a period of 16 years constitutes the preference of one faith over another in violation of the Establishment Clause of the First Amendment. . . .

I would affirm the judgment of the Court of Appeals.

---

## NOTES AND QUESTIONS

1. After *Marsh*, if it can be demonstrated that a particular practice that has been challenged under the Establishment Clause has a history dating back to the founding era, is that enough to guarantee its constitutionality? Or is there something unique about the issue in *Marsh* that lends itself to this analytical approach, an approach that may be less suited to other issues (e.g., the Continental Congress approving the purchase of Bibles)?

2. What are the virtues and vices of relying on historical practice in the way the majority does in this case? Do problems arise when courts rely on history to justify their holdings? Consider Justice Brennan's critique in his dissent. Is the historical record ever clear? On the other hand, are there dangers in placing too little emphasis on the historical record? What critiques could be made of Justice Brennan's approach in this area? For a comprehensive and evenhanded review of the historical origins of the chaplaincy practice, as well as other early religious issues, see Derek H. Davis, *Religion and the Continental Congress 1774–1789* (New York: Oxford University Press, 2000). Does historical evidence become skewed in the adversarial nature of judicial proceedings, and do judges have the training and perspective to appreciate the legal significance of "historical facts"? For one perspective on this issue, see Steven K. Green, "'Bad History': The Lure of History in Establishment Clause Adjudication," *Notre Dame Law Review* 81 (2006): 1717.

3. Assume that you agree with the outcome in *Marsh*. Are there other analytical models or approaches that would arrive at the same conclusion? Some have argued, based in part on *Marsh*, for a *de minimis* approach to such government acknowledgments of religion (i.e., that the harm to Establishment Clause values is minimal and thus the practice should not be deemed a constitutional violation). Is the practice described here "*de minimis*" in nature? What are the pros and cons to such an analytical approach?

4. Suppose members of a town council open their meetings with prayer, usually invoking the name of Jesus Christ. In light of the Court's ruling in *Marsh*, would this practice run afoul of the Constitution? What critiques might the *Marsh* dissenters make of such a practice? Compare *Wynne v. Town of Great Falls*, 376 F.3d 292 (4th Cir. 2004); *Hinrichs v. Bosma*, 400 F. Supp. 2d 1103 (S.D. Ind. 2005); *Rubin v. City of Burbank*, 101 Cal. App. 4th 1194 (2002) with *Pelphrey v. Cobb County*, 448 F. Supp. 2d 1357 (N.D. Ga. 2006).

5. According to the dissent, what are the purposes of "separation" and "neutrality"? In light of your study of case law thus far, do you believe this is an

accurate and helpful characterization of the purposes of the First Amendment's religion clauses?

6. According to Justice Brennan, this case is not about the free exercise of religion. Why?

---

If it is constitutional for a legislature to employ a chaplain, is it constitutional for the military to do so in order to tend to the spiritual needs of service members? What about government-paid prison chaplains? What do these situations have in common with each other and with the case of legislative chaplains? How are they different? The Supreme Court has not directly addressed the constitutionality of the military or prison chaplaincy, but lower courts have. The following are excerpts from two lower court cases dealing with these issues.

---

## KATCOFF v. MARSH
### 755 F.2d 223 (2d Cir. 1985)

⌗ MANSFIELD, Circuit Judge:

This appeal raises the question of whether Congress and the United States Army ("Army"), in furnishing chaplains as part of our armed forces to enable soldiers to practice the religions of their choice, violate the Constitution. We hold that, except in a few respects that require further consideration, they do not. . . .

Congress, in the exercise of its powers under Art. I, § 8, of the Constitution to provide for the conduct of our national defense, has established an Army for the purpose of "preserving the peace and security, and providing for the defense, of the United States," and has directed that the "organized peace establishment of the Army" consist of all organizations and persons "necessary to form the basis for a complete and immediate mobilization for the national defense in the event of a national emergency." It has specifically authorized that as part of this establishment there be "Chaplains in the Army," who shall include the Chief of Chaplains, and commissioned and other officers of the Army appointed as chaplains. 10 U.S.C. § 3073. Under 10 U.S.C. § 3547 each chaplain is required, when practicable, to hold religious services for the command to which he is assigned and to perform burial services for soldiers who die while in that command. The statute also obligates the commanding officer to furnish facilities, including transportation, to assist a chaplain in performing his duties. *Id.*

In providing our armed forces with a military chaplaincy Congress has perpetuated a facility that began during Revolutionary days before the adoption of our Constitution, and that has continued ever since then, with the size of the chaplaincy growing larger in proportion to the increase in the size of our Army. When the Continental Army was formed those chaplains attached to the militia of the 13 colonies became part of our country's first national army. On

July 29, 1775, the Continental Congress authorized that a Continental Army chaplain be paid, and within a year General George Washington directed that regimental Continental Army chaplains be procured.

Upon the adoption of the Constitution and before the December 1791 ratification of the First Amendment Congress authorized the appointment of a commissioned Army chaplain. Since then, as the Army has increased in size the military chaplaincy has been extended and Congress has increased the number of Army chaplains.

In 1981 the Army had approximately 1,427 active-duty commissioned chaplains, 10 auxiliary chaplains, 1,383 chaplain's assistants, and 48 Directors of Religious Education. These chaplains are appointed as commissioned officers with rank and uniform but without command. Before an applicant may be appointed to the position of chaplain he must receive endorsement from an ecclesiastical endorsing agency recognized by the Armed Forces Chaplains Board, of which there are 47 in the United States, representing 120 denominations. In addition to meeting the theological standards of the endorsing agency the applicant must also meet minimum educational requirements established by the Department of Defense, which are more stringent than those of some religious denominations having endorsing agencies and are designed to insure the applicant's ability to communicate with soldiers of all ranks and to administer religious programs. In deciding upon the denominations of chaplains to be appointed the Office of the Chief of Chaplains establishes quotas based on the denominational distribution of the population of the United States as a whole. The entire civilian church population rather than the current military religious population is used in order to assure that in the event of war or total mobilization the denominational breakdown will accurately reflect that of the larger-sized Army.

Upon his appointment the chaplain, except for a number of civilian clerics provided voluntarily or by contract, is subject to the same discipline and training as that given to other officers and soldiers. He is trained in such subjects as Army organization, command relationships, supply, planning, teaching, map-reading, types of warfare, security, battlefield survival, and military administration. When ordered with troops into any area, including a combat zone under fire, he must obey. He must be prepared to meet problems inherent in Army life, including how to handle trauma, death or serious injury of soldiers on the field of battle, marital and family stresses of military personnel, tending the wounded or dying, and psychological treatment of soldiers' drug or alcohol abuse, as well as the alleviation of tensions between soldiers and their commanders. On the other hand, the chaplain is not required to bear arms or receive training in weapons. Under Articles 33 and 35 of the Geneva Conventions Relative to Treatment of Prisoners of War "chaplains" are accorded a noncombatant status, which means that they are not to be considered prisoners of war and they may exercise their ministry among prisoners of war. Promotion of a chaplain within the military ranks is based solely on his military performance and not on his effectiveness as a cleric.

The primary function of the military chaplain is to engage in activities designed to meet the religious needs of a pluralistic military community, including military personnel and their dependents. In view of the Army's huge size (some 788,000 soldiers and 1,300,000 dependents in 1981) and its far-flung distribution (291,000 soldiers stationed abroad and many in remote areas of the United States) the task is an important and formidable one. The Army consists of a wide spectrum of persons of different ethnic, racial and religious backgrounds who go into military service from varied social, economic and educational environments. The great majority of the soldiers in the Army express religious preferences. About 80% are under 30 years of age and a large number are married. As a result it has become necessary to provide religious facilities for soldiers of some 86 different denominations. . . .

Aside from the problems arising out of the sheer size and pluralistic nature of the Army, its members experience increased needs for religion as the result of being uprooted from their home environments, transported often thousands of miles to territories entirely strange to them, and confronted there with new stresses that would not otherwise have been encountered if they had remained at home. In 1981 approximately 37% of the Army's active duty soldiers, amounting to 293,000 persons, were stationed overseas in locations such as Turkey, Sinai, Greece, or Korea. In most of these areas the Judeo-Christian faiths of most American soldiers are hardly represented at all by local clergy and the average soldier is separated from the local populace by a linguistic and cultural wall. Within the United States the same problem exists in a somewhat different way in that, although the linguistic or cultural barrier may be absent, local civilian clergy in the rural areas where most military camps are centered are inadequate to satisfy the soldiers' religious needs because they are too few in number for the task and are usually of different religious denominations from those of most of the nearby troops.

The problem of meeting the religious needs of Army personnel is compounded by the mobile, deployable nature of our armed forces, who must be ready on extremely short notice to be transported from bases (whether or not in the United States) to distant parts of the world for combat duty in fulfillment of our nation's international defense commitments. Unless there were chaplains ready to move simultaneously with the troops and to tend to their spiritual needs as they face possible death, the soldiers would be left in the lurch, religiously speaking. In the opinion of top generals of the Army and those presently in the chaplaincy, unless chaplains were made available in such circumstances the motivation, morale and willingness of soldiers to face combat would suffer immeasurable harm and our national defense would be weakened accordingly.

Many soldiers in the Army also suffer serious stresses from other causes attributable largely to their military service, which can be alleviated by counseling and spiritual assistance from a leader of their respective faiths. Among these are tensions created by separation from their homes, loneliness when on duty in strange surroundings involving people whose language or customs they do not share, fear of facing combat or new assignments, financial hardships, personality conflicts, and drug, alcohol or family problems. The soldier faced with any of these problems at home would usually be able to consult his spiritual adviser. The Army seeks to furnish the same services through military chaplains. In doing so the Army has proceeded on the premise that having uprooted the soldiers from their natural habitats it owes them a duty to satisfy their Free Exercise rights, especially since the failure to do so would diminish morale, thereby weakening our national defense.

To meet the religious needs of our armed forces Army chaplains and their assistants engage in a wide variety of services to military personnel and their families who wish to use them. No chaplain is authorized to proselytize soldiers or their families. The chaplain's principal duties are to conduct religious services (including periodic worship, baptisms, marriages, funerals and the like), to furnish religious education to soldiers and their families, and to counsel soldiers with respect to a wide variety of personal problems. In addition the chaplain, because of his close relationship with the soldiers in his unit, often serves as a liaison between the soldiers and their commanders, advising the latter of racial unrest, drug or alcohol abuse, and other problems affecting the morale and efficiency of the unit, and helps to find solutions. In some areas the Army also makes available religious retreats, in which soldiers voluntarily withdraw for a short period from the routine activities of daily living to another location for spiritual reflection and renewal. . . .

The great majority of the chaplaincy's services, facilities, and supplies are procured by the Army through funds appropriated by Congress, which amounted to over $85 million for the fiscal year 1981, of which more than $62 million was used to pay the salaries and other compensation of chaplains, chaplain's assistants and auxiliary chaplains. Much smaller amounts were paid for the services of contract chaplains ($332,000), directors of religious education ($221,000), and organists and choir directors ($412,000). Some $7.7 million of non-appropriated funds, representing voluntary contributions or designated offerings from soldiers and their dependents, were also used in the fiscal year 1981 to provide for the needs of the Army's chaplaincy program. Generally speaking, non-appropriated funds are used for denominational activities such as the purchase of sacred items and literature and the salaries of organists and choir directors.

Appellants' complaint, filed on November 23, 1979, seeks a declaratory judgment that the foregoing program violates the Establishment Clause and injunctive relief. The complaint alleges that the "constitutional rights of Army personnel and their dependents to freely exercise their religion can better be served by an alternative Chaplaincy program which is privately funded and controlled." In the district court and here appellants have not questioned the need to satisfy the Free Exercise rights of military personnel but have claimed that government funding of the chaplaincy program is unnecessary. . . .

## DISCUSSION

The threshold question, whether plaintiffs have standing to litigate the constitutionality of the Army's military chaplaincy, need not detain us long. . . [W]e agree that as federal taxpayers the plaintiffs satisfy the two-pronged test of *Flast v. Cohen*, 392 U.S. 83 (1968). . . .

Turning to the merits, the Establishment Clause of the First Amendment, which provides that "Congress shall make no law respecting an establishment of religion," was designed by our Founding Fathers to insure religious liberty for our country's citizens by precluding a government from imposing, sponsoring, or supporting religion or forcing a person to remain away from the practice of religion. . . .

The Army chaplaincy does not seek to "establish" a religion according to this simple formula. It observes the basic prohibition expressed by the Court in *Zorach v. Clauson*, 343 U.S. 306 (1952):

> The government must be neutral when it comes to competition between sects. It may not thrust any sect on any person. It may not make a religious observance compulsory. It may not coerce anyone to attend church, to observe a religious holiday, or to take religious instruction.

Since the program meets the requirement of voluntariness by leaving the practice of religion solely to the individual soldier, who is free to worship or not as he chooses without fear of any discipline or stigma, it might be viewed as not proscribed by the Establishment Clause. Indeed, if the Army prevented soldiers from worshipping in their own communities by removing them to areas where religious leaders of their persuasion and facilities were not available it could be accused of violating the Establishment Clause *unless* it provided them with a chaplaincy since its conduct would amount to inhibiting religion. *Everson v. Board of Education* (the government can neither "force nor influence a person . . . to remain away from church against his will. . . ." *Id.*, 15. "State power is no more to be used so as to handicap religions than it is to favor them." *Id.*, 18).

Congress' authorization of a military chaplaincy before and contemporaneous with the adoption of the Establishment Clause is also "weighty evidence" that it did not intend that Clause to apply to such a chaplaincy. Moreover, its "unambiguous and unbroken history of more than 200 years," *Marsh v. Chambers*, 463 U.S. 783 (1983), in continuing that course indicates that, as with the practice of opening legislative sessions with a prayer, "the First Amendment draftsmen . . . saw no real threat to the Establishment Clause," *id.*, 463 U.S., 791, arising from a military chaplaincy. In interpreting the Bill of Rights such "an unbroken practice . . . is not something to be lightly cast aside." *Walz v. Tax Commission*, 397 U.S. 664, 678, (1970); see *McGowan v. Maryland*, 366 U.S. 420, 429-449 (1961). . . .

If the current Army chaplaincy were viewed in isolation, there could be little doubt that it would fail to meet the *Lemon v. Kurtzman* conditions. Although the ultimate objective of the chaplaincy may be secular in the sense that it seeks to maintain the efficiency of the Army by improving the morale of our military personnel, its immediate purpose is to promote religion by making it available, albeit on a voluntary basis, to our armed forces. The effect of the program, moreover, is to advance the practice of religion. Administration of the program, involving arrangements with many church organizations of different denominations, entangles the government with religious accrediting bodies.

However, neither the Establishment Clause nor statutes creating and maintaining the Army chaplaincy may be interpreted as if they existed in a sterile vacuum. They must be viewed in the light of the historical background of their enactment to the extent that it sheds light on the purpose of the Framers of the Constitution. They must also be considered in context, since a test which may be reasonable in one context may be wholly inappropriate in another. The Supreme Court, while noting that it found *Lemon* useful in some contexts, only recently reaffirmed its "unwillingness to be confined to any single test or criterion in this sensitive area," disclaiming a *per se* or "absolutist" approach and pointing out that even in *Lemon* it had stated that the Clause erects a "blurred, indistinct, and variable barrier depending on all the circumstances of a particular relationship," *Lynch v. Donnelly*, 465 U.S. 668 (1984). The need for some flexibility in this respect had earlier been recognized in *Walz v. Tax Commission*, where the Court stated that

> The course of constitutional neutrality in this area cannot be an absolutely straight line; rigidity could well defeat the basic purpose of these provisions, which is to insure that no religion be sponsored or favored, none commanded, and none inhibited. . . . Short of those expressly pro-

scribed governmental acts there is room for play in the joints productive of a benevolent neutrality which will permit religious exercise to exist without sponsorship and without interference. 397 U.S., 669.

Aside from the fact that no single test will meet all contexts, the Establishment Clause must in any event be interpreted to accommodate other equally valid provisions of the Constitution, including the Free Exercise Clause, when they are implicated.

The present case involves two other provisions of our Constitution, which must not only be respected but, to the extent possible, interpreted compatibly with the Establishment Clause. The first of these is the War Power Clause of Art. I, § 8, which provides in pertinent part that Congress shall have the power to "provide for the common Defence," "to raise and support Armies," and to "make Rules for the Government and Regulation of the land and naval Forces." Although military conduct is not immune from judicial review when challenged as violative of the Bill of Rights, the Supreme Court has recognized that:

> Judges are not given the task of running the Army. . . . The military con-
> stitutes a specialized community governed by a separate discipline from
> that of the civilian. Orderly government requires that the judiciary be
> as scrupulous not to interfere with legitimate Army matters as the Army
> must be scrupulous not to intervene in judicial matters. . . . *Orloff v. Wil-
> loughby*, 345 U.S. 83, 93-94 (1953).

In a perilous world our survival as a nation and our enjoyment of the blessings of liberty depend heavily upon our Army and other military institutions, rigid and disciplined as they must be. Those who want the individual liberty embodied in our Bill of Rights must be willing to make sacrifices for it. One of these is the duty of a soldier to obey military orders and forego many of the freedoms that he would otherwise enjoy as a civilian, including the right to travel whenever and wherever he pleases. As the Court noted in *Schlesinger v. Ballard*, 419 U.S. 498, 510 (1975), "responsibility for determining how best our Armed Forces shall attend to [the] business [of fighting or being ready to fight wars should the occasion arise] rests with Congress . . . and with the President." As a result, "while the members of the military are not excluded from the protection granted by the First Amendment, the different character of the military community and of the military mission requires a different application of those protections." *Parker v. Levy*, 417 U.S. 733, 758 (1974); *Brown v. Glines*, 444 U.S. 348 (1980) (First Amendment rights of Army officer limited); *Middendorf v. Henry*, 425 U.S. 25 (1976) (servicemen do not have Sixth Amendment right to counsel in summary court-martial proceedings).

The line where military control requires that enjoyment of civilian rights be regulated or restricted may sometimes be difficult to define. But caution dictates that when a matter provided for by Congress in the exercise of its war power and implemented by the Army appears reasonably relevant and necessary to furtherance of our national defense it should be treated as presumptively valid and any doubt as to its constitutionality should be resolved as a matter of judicial comity in favor of deference to the military's exercise of its discretion.

The second provision of the Constitution which plays a vital role in our interpretation of the Establishment Clause is the Free Exercise Clause of the same Amendment. It is readily apparent that this Clause, like the

Establishment Clause, obligates Congress, upon creating an Army, to make religion available to soldiers who have been moved by the Army to areas of the world where religion of their own denominations is not available to them. Otherwise the effect of compulsory military service could be to violate their rights under both Religion Clauses of the First Amendment. Unless the Army provided a chaplaincy it would deprive the soldier of his right under the Establishment Clause not to have religion inhibited and of his right under the Free Exercise Clause to practice his freely chosen religion. . . .

Members of the Supreme Court have pointed to Congress' provision of churches and chaplains at military establishments as an example of an appropriate accommodation between the two Clauses. *See Abington School Dist. v. Schempp*, 374 U.S. 203, 296-298 (BRENNAN, J., concurring), 308-309 (STEWART, J., dissenting). Congress recognized as early as 1850 that its failure to provide a chaplaincy would deprive soldiers of their Free Exercise rights. H.R. Rep. No. 171, 31st Cong., 1st Sess. (1850). The problem was also noted by the Court in *Abington School Dist. v. Schempp*, 374 U.S., 226 n. 10:

> We are not of course presented with and therefore do not pass upon a situation such as military service, where the Government regulates the temporal and geographic environment of individuals to a point that, unless it permits voluntary religious services to be conducted with the use of government facilities, military personnel would be unable to engage in the practice of their faiths.

The standard to be applied, therefore, in deciding whether the Army's military chaplaincy can survive attack as violative of the Establishment Clause must take into account the deference required to be given to Congress' exercise of its War Power and the necessity of recognizing the Free Exercise rights of military personnel. In our view these additional factors, which were not present in *Lemon v. Kurtzman* or its progeny, relied on by plaintiffs, render its test inappropriate here. On the other hand, we do not agree with the district court that the doctrine of deference to Congress' judgment in military affairs leaves us powerless to review the constitutional permissibility of the military chaplaincy. In our view the test of permissibility in this context is whether, after considering practical alternatives, the chaplaincy program is relevant to and reasonably necessary for the Army's conduct of our national defense.

Applying these principles to the present case, we start with plaintiffs' concession that some chaplaincy is essential. Except for peripheral claims that a few practices of the government's military chaplaincy amount to "religious proselytism," their lawsuit hinges entirely on their contention that a privately funded chaplaincy, patterned on the present military program, would fully meet the government's needs under the War Power Clause and the free-exercise needs of military personnel. They state, "A civilian program could be comprised of the same individuals performing the same functions, with the Army exercising the same military control and providing the same logistical support, coordination and training in military affairs. Only the source of funding for substantive religious practice would differ."

For the most part, we disagree. To begin with, defendants have described in detail the various functions performed by the Army's chaplains and the inability of local civilian clergy or special organizations of civilian clergy to meet the religious needs of the many different denominations in the armed forces. They note that among the inadequacies of a civilian clergy would be the questionable ability of many denominations, particularly the smaller ones, to fund a civilian chaplaincy and the lack of training in the military subjects needed to enable the civilian chaplain to function effectively in the field.

In response to the detailed affidavits submitted by the defendants pursuant to Fed. R. Civ. P. 56(e) plaintiffs have not come forward with any evidence or offer through discovery or depositions to establish that the many religious denominations involved, including the principal Catholic, Protestant and Jewish organizations in the United States, would support and be willing to pay their respective shares of the $85 million required to operate a civilian chaplaincy and to provide such additional sums as may be required in case of war or national emergency. Nor have plaintiffs come forward with assurances from the numerous religious organizations involved that they would seek to agree upon each denomination's proportionate share of the overall financial obligation and that they would be able and willing to honor their respective obligations in the years ahead. It is obvious from the evidence offered by the defendants that without enforceable commitments on the part of these various denominations the Army would be unable to maintain a functioning civilian chaplaincy. Assuming hypothetically that such a program could be launched, it would constantly be teetering on the brink of disaster. An impractical alternative is no alternative at all. . . .

In short, plaintiffs' proposal is so inherently impractical as to border on the frivolous. Absent some substantial evidence that it might be within the realm of the feasible, we do not believe that taxpayers, merely by instituting a lawsuit, are entitled to engage in a costly and time-consuming broad-scale investigation into an entirely speculative suggestion, made without an evidentiary basis for believing that the claim is well-grounded in fact. . . .

Aside from the obvious financial infeasibility of appellants' alternative proposal, plaintiffs offer no evidence that civilian chaplains would accept military discipline which is essential to the efficient operation of our armed forces. This discipline demands willingness to undergo thorough military training except in the use of firearms, to remain with an Army unit for a specified period of time, to obey orders to move overnight with that unit to other locations, which might be thousands of miles away, and to advance as ordered on the battlefield and risk their lives in order to minister to the wounded and dying. Thus, since plaintiffs' suggested alternative of a civilian chaplaincy amounts to nothing more than speculation, unsupported by some showing of practical feasibility, it fails to survive the evidentiary showing advanced by the defendants. . . .

Lastly, even if plaintiffs' proposal were feasible it would, assuming the *Lemon* standard advanced by the plaintiffs were held applicable, violate the Establishment Clause. The Army, financed by Congress, would to at least some extent still be commanding the civilian chaplains and supporting them with taxpayer-provided "logistical support, coordination and training in military affairs," including transport, food and facilities.

We find that the more appropriate standard of relevancy to our national defense and reasonable necessity is met by the great majority of the Army's existing chaplaincy activities. The purpose and effect of the program is to make religion, religious education, counseling and religious facilities available to military personnel and their families under circumstances where the practice of religion would otherwise be denied as a practical matter to all or a substantial number. As a result, the morale of our soldiers, their willingness to serve, and the efficiency of the Army as an instrument for our national defense rests in substantial part on the military chaplaincy, which is vital to our Army's functioning.

In a few areas, however, the reasonable necessity for certain activities of the military chaplaincy is not readily apparent. For instance, it appears that in some large urban centers, such as at the Pentagon in Washington, D.C., in New York City and San Francisco, government funds may be used to provide military chaplains, facilities and retreats to "armchair" military personnel who, like other government civil servants, commute daily to their homes and spend their free hours (including weekends) in locations where civilian clergy and facilities are just as available to them as to other non-military citizens. Plaintiffs also assert that government-financed Army chaplaincy and facilities are provided to retired military personnel and their families. If the ability of such personnel to worship in their own communities is not inhibited by their military service and funds for these chaplains and facilities would not otherwise be expended, the justification for a governmental program of religious support for them is questionable and, notwithstanding our deference to Congress in military matters, requires a showing that they are relevant to and reasonably necessary for the conduct of our national defense by the Army. A remand therefore becomes necessary to determine whether, according to the standard we have outlined, government financing of a military chaplaincy in these limited areas for the purposes indicated is constitutionally permissible.

Accordingly, the order of the district court is affirmed except to the extent so remanded. Costs to the appellees.

---

## DELORES RUDD v. The HONORABLE ROBERT D. RAY
248 N.W. 2d 125 (Iowa 1976)

JUDGE HARRIS:

This is a taxpayer's derivative suit challenging the constitutionality of legislation which provides for salaried chaplains and religious facilities at the state penitentiary. The challenge is grounded on both federal and state constitutions. The trial court held the legislation does not offend the federal constitution but does offend the state constitution. Accordingly the trial court enjoined the use of public funds for such purposes. We believe the legislation violates neither constitution. We reverse the trial court and remand for dissolution of the injunction.

The facts can be simply stated. Plaintiffs are taxpaying citizens of the State of Iowa. Under authority given by statute the Iowa State Penitentiary: (1) employs two full-time chaplains (one Protestant, one Catholic) at annual salaries totaling $25,000, (2) employs a part-time chaplain at a salary of $216 monthly, (3) expends other funds in relation to chapel activities at the penitentiary. Separate chapel areas are reserved in a previously vacant industrial building for Catholic and Protestant congregate worship. Another group, calling themselves the Church of the New Song, utilizes the prison auditorium and also has office and meeting space elsewhere in the penitentiary.

The chaplains at the penitentiary are ordained clergymen who have received advanced training concerning institutional settings and counselling.

They provide sectarian services. The Protestant services are general in nature. The Protestant chaplains provide service for inmates of all religious persuasion, including "minority religions." Attendance by the prisoners at all services is purely voluntary. The chaplains provide substantial counselling service. Counselling is done on both a group and individual basis, at set times or on a crisis basis.

I. The trial court held providing for state supported chaplains and religious facilities does not violate the establishment clause of the First Amendment to the United States Constitution. Plaintiffs appeal from this portion of the trial court's ruling. . . .

Plaintiffs argue the challenged legislation violates all three parts of the *Nyquist* test and thus runs afoul of the establishment clause. The argument has force but ignores the companion free exercise clause with which the establishment clause must be balanced. The free exercise clause prohibits the making of a law which in any way interferes with the free exercise of religion. The prohibition extends to unorthodox as well as orthodox religious beliefs and practices. It extends to religious organizations and individuals. It denies the government any power to proscribe, regulate, favor directly or indirectly any particular religious beliefs or doctrines (though not necessarily the acts which citizens may feel called upon to perform in compliance with their religious views).

The crucial and controlling fact in this case is that it deals with the exercise of religion by prison inmates. Prison inmates are restrained and consequently deprived of their liberty. By reason of their status they are displaced from their homes and communities. They are thereby denied the opportunity to exercise their individual rights to worship in the same manner as could an ordinary citizen.

It is clear prisoners retain some rights to religious freedom.

"While the law in this area is still (1967) in a state of development, it is now established that prisoners do have certain rights and privileges in the religious area which the courts will protect and that the prison authorities may not punish or discriminate against religious beliefs as such. . . . . ." See *Cruz v. Beto*, 405 U.S. 319 (1972). A prisoner's retained rights of religious freedom include some reasonable opportunity to exercise their religion. In *Cruz*, 405 U.S., 322, it is stated:

> We do not suggest, of course, that every religious sect or group within a prison—however few in number—must have identical facilities or personnel. A special chapel or place of worship need not be provided for every faith regardless of size; nor must a chaplain, priest, or minister be provided without regard to the extent of the demand. But reasonable opportunities must be afforded to all prisoners to exercise the religious freedom guaranteed by the First and Fourteenth Amendments without fear of penalty. See . . . *O'Malley v. Brierley*, 477 F.2d 785, 796 (3 Cir. 1973).

The question becomes whether the enhancement of the free exercise clause by state-provided chaplains and religious facilities nevertheless violates the establishment clause. The few cases which have addressed the question seem to agree with our conclusion it does not. *Remmers v. Brewer*, D.C., 361 F. Supp. 537, 543 (1973); *Horn v. People of California*, D. C., 321 F. Supp. 961, 964 (1968). Our view was capsulized by Mr. Justice Brennan in a concurring opinion in *School District of Abington Township*, 374 U.S., 296-299:

There are certain practices, conceivably violative of the Establishment Clause, the striking down of which might seriously interfere with certain religious liberties also protected by the First Amendment. Provisions for churches and chaplains at military establishments for those in the armed services may afford one such example. The like provision by state and federal governments for chaplains in penal institutions may afford another example. It is argued that such provisions may be assumed to contravene the Establishment Clause, yet be sustained on constitutional grounds as necessary to secure to the members of the Armed Forces and prisoners those rights of worship guaranteed under the Free Exercise Clause. Since government has deprived such persons of the opportunity to practice their faith at places of their choice, the argument runs, government may, in order to avoid infringing the free exercise guarantees, provide substitutes where it requires such persons to be. . . .

The State must be steadfastly neutral in all matters of faith, and neither favor nor inhibit religion. . . . On the other hand, hostility, not neutrality, would characterize the refusal to provide chaplains and places of worship for prisoners and soldiers cut off by the State from all civilian opportunities for public communion. . . .

Our holding is consistent with the rule the government must be neutral and not hostile to religion.

The prohibition of the establishment clause is not absolute. This is illustrated by the following examples of governmental actions which benefit religion without violation of the establishment clause: (1) the use by religious organizations of civil courts. *Maryland & Virginia Eldership of Churches of God, Inc. v. Church of God, Inc.*, 396 U.S. 367 (1970); . . . (2) the exemption of property used for religious purposes from taxation. *Walz v. Tax Com. of New York*, 397 U.S. 664 (1970), (3) the Sunday closing or "blue" laws, *McGowan v. Maryland*, 336 U.S. 420 (1961); *Galagher v. Crown Kosher Super Market*, 336 U.S. 617 (1961); *Two Guys from Harrison-Allentown, Inc. v. McGinley*, 336 U.S. 582 (1961).

From the foregoing we conclude there is no violation of the First Amendment to the United States Constitution by the action of the state in providing chaplains and religious facilities to prisoners. Any claim of offense against the establishment clause is balanced by its justification under the free exercise clause. The trial court was correct in so ruling.

## NOTES AND QUESTIONS

1. What reasons did the *Katcoff* court cite for upholding the government-funded military chaplaincy? Did the court find that the chaplaincy was constitutional in all aspects, or did it reserve certain issues? According to this court, to what extent might such a program be constitutionally compelled, as opposed to merely being constitutionally permissible?

   Why did the *Katcoff* court refrain from using the *Lemon* test to evaluate the constitutionality of the military chaplaincy? Could it be argued that the military chaplaincy would pass constitutional muster even under the *Lemon* test?

2. The *Katcoff* court says that "[p]romotion of a chaplain within the military ranks is based solely on his military performance and not on his effectiveness as a cleric." Does this standard seem appropriate? Can you envision any problems it might present?

   In the *Katcoff* decision, the court says that "[n]o chaplain in authorized to proselytize soldiers or their families." Legislation has been introduced in the U.S. Congress that states that "military chaplains shall have the prerogative to pray according to the dictates of their conscience" at military functions, including some functions that service members are required to attend. Supporters of this legislation claim that such legislation is needed at least partially because some chaplains have been prohibited from using language that is exclusive to one faith tradition at such functions. (Of course, when chaplains conduct worship services for service members who choose to attend such services, the chaplain may preach and pray "according to the manner and forms of the church of which he is a member."[6])

   If a chaplain offers prayers to "Jesus Christ" at mandatory military functions, is the chaplain proselytizing? More generally, are prayers at these functions constitutionally permissible? To what extent do chaplains have personal free exercise rights as military chaplains, and to what extent are they simply serving as instruments through which the military accommodates the free exercise interests of soldiers? *See* Ira C. Lupu and Robert W. Tuttle, "Instruments of Accommodation: The Military Chaplaincy and the Establishment Clause," 110 W. Va. L. Rev. 89 (2007).

3. According to the *Rudd* court, what are the reasons for upholding the prison chaplaincy as constitutional? What precedent does the court cite for its holding? Does the court apply the *Lemon* test to the facts of this case?

   Would a system that utilized only nongovernmental chaplains be more likely to work in the prison or the legislative setting than in the military setting? If so, is that constitutionally significant?

---

## Religion and Politics

Does the First Amendment require not only a separation between the institutions of church and state but also a separation between religion and politics? We examine a few aspects of that question in this part of the chapter.

A good place to start in this discussion is to consider the "no religious test" clause of Article VI of the U.S. Constitution. Article VI requires certain government officials to take an oath or affirm that they will support the Constitution, but it also specifies that "no religious Test shall ever be required as a Qualification to any Office or public Trust under the United States." This prevents the federal government from requiring a person to promise allegiance to or against a god, any particular faith or purely religious precept in order to serve in government. The Supreme Court has specifically held that neither the state nor federal government may require someone to say that he or she believes in God in order to hold government office. The case, *Torcaso v. Watkins*, 367 U.S. 488 (1961) (see chapter 22), focused on a requirement under the Maryland Constitution that public officials affirm the existence of God. The Court struck the requirement, holding that a governmental body's "religious test for public office unconstitutionally invades [a person's] freedom of belief and religion and therefore cannot be enforced against him."

In a 1978 case about a similar concept, entitled *McDaniel v. Paty*, the Court found that a state law disqualifying ministers from holding public office violated the Constitution. You will notice that all of the justices agreed on the result in this case, but they differed somewhat on the proper rationale for that result. As you read the case, pay particular attention to the differences among those rationales.

## McDANIEL v. PATY
### 435 U.S. 618 (1978)

🔲 MR. CHIEF JUSTICE BURGER announced the judgment of the Court and delivered an opinion in which MR. JUSTICE POWELL, MR. JUSTICE REHNQUIST, and MR. JUSTICE STEVENS joined.

The question presented by this appeal is whether a Tennessee statute barring "[Ministers] of the Gospel, or [priests] of any denomination whatever" from serving as delegates to the State's limited constitutional convention deprived appellant McDaniel, an ordained minister, of the right to the free exercise of religion guaranteed by the First Amendment and made applicable to the States by the Fourteenth Amendment. The First Amendment forbids all laws "prohibiting the free exercise" of religion.

In its first Constitution, in 1796, Tennessee disqualified ministers from serving as legislators.[1] That disqualifying provision has continued unchanged since its adoption[.][In 1976,] [t]he state legislature applied this provision to candidates for delegate to the State's 1977 limited constitutional convention. . . .

McDaniel, an ordained minister of a Baptist Church in Chattanooga, Tenn., filed as a candidate for delegate to the constitutional convention. An opposing candidate, appellee Selma Cash Paty, sued in the Chancery Court for a declaratory judgment that McDaniel was disqualified from serving as a delegate and for a judgment striking his name from the ballot. . . .

II
A

The disqualification of ministers from legislative office was a practice carried from England by seven of the original States; later six new States similarly excluded clergymen from some political offices. In England the practice of excluding clergy from the House of Commons was justified on a variety of grounds: to prevent dual officeholding, that is, membership by a minister in

---

[1] "Whereas Ministers of the Gospel are by their profession, dedicated to God and the care of Souls, and ought not to be diverted from the great duties of their functions; therefore, no Minister of the Gospel, or priest of any denomination whatever, shall be eligible to a seat in either House of the Legislature." Tenn. Const., Art. VIII, § 1 (1796).

both Parliament and Convocation; to insure that the priest or deacon devoted himself to his "sacred calling" rather than to "such mundane activities as were appropriate to a member of the House of Commons"; and to prevent ministers, who after 1533 were subject to the Crown's powers over the benefices of the clergy, from using membership in Commons to diminish its independence by increasing the influence of the King and the nobility.

The purpose of the several States in providing for disqualification was primarily to assure the success of a new political experiment, the separation of church and state. Prior to 1776, most of the 13 Colonies had some form of an established, or government-sponsored, church. Even after ratification of the First Amendment, which prohibited the Federal Government from following such a course, some States continued pro-establishment provisions. Massachusetts, the last State to accept disestablishment, did so in 1833.

In light of this history and a widespread awareness during that period of undue and often dominant clerical influence in public and political affairs here, in England, and on the Continent, it is not surprising that strong views were held by some that one way to assure disestablishment was to keep clergymen out of public office. Indeed, some of the foremost political philosophers and statesmen of that period held such views regarding the clergy. Earlier, John Locke argued for confining the authority of the English clergy "within the bounds of the church, nor can it in any manner be extended to civil affairs; because the church itself is a thing absolutely separate and distinct from the commonwealth." Thomas Jefferson initially advocated such a position in his 1783 draft of a constitution for Virginia.[4] James Madison, however, disagreed and vigorously urged the position which in our view accurately reflects the spirit and purpose of the Religion Clauses of the First Amendment. Madison's response to Jefferson's position was:

> Does not the exclusion of Ministers of the Gospel as such violate a fundamental principle of liberty by punishing a religious profession with the privation of a civil right? does it [not] violate another article of the plan itself which exempts religion from the cognizance of Civil power? does it not violate justice by at once taking away a right and prohibiting a compensation for it? does it not in fine violate impartiality by shutting the door [against] the Ministers of one Religion and leaving it open for those of every other. 5 Writings of James Madison 288 (G. Hunt ed. 1904).

Madison was not the only articulate opponent of clergy disqualification. When proposals were made earlier to prevent clergymen from holding public office, John Witherspoon, a Presbyterian minister, president of Princeton University, and the only clergyman to sign the Declaration of Independence, made a cogent protest and, with tongue in cheek, offered an amendment to a provision much like that challenged here:

> "No clergyman, of any denomination, shall be capable of being elected a member of the Senate or House of Representatives, because (here insert the grounds of offensive disqualification, which I have not been able to discover) Provided always, and it is the true intent and meaning of this part of the constitution, that if at any time he shall be completely

---

[4] Jefferson later concluded that experience demonstrated there was no need to exclude clergy from elected office. . . .

deprived of the clerical character by those by whom he was invested with it, as by deposition for cursing and swearing, drunkenness or uncleanness, he shall then be fully restored to all the privileges of a free citizen; his offense [of being a clergyman] shall no more be remembered against him; but he may be chosen either to the Senate or House of Representatives, and shall be treated with all the respect due to his brethren, the other members of Assembly." A. P. Stokes, Church and State in the United States, vol. 1, 625.

As the value of the disestablishment experiment was perceived, 11 of the 13 States disqualifying the clergy from some types of public office gradually abandoned that limitation. New York, for example, took that step in 1846 after delegates to the State's constitutional convention argued that the exclusion of clergymen from the legislature was an "odious distinction." Only Maryland and Tennessee continued their clergy-disqualification provisions into this century and, in 1974, a District Court held Maryland's provision violative of the First and Fourteenth Amendments' guarantees of the free exercise of religion. Today Tennessee remains the only State excluding ministers from certain public offices.

The essence of this aspect of our national history is that in all but a few States the selection or rejection of clergymen for public office soon came to be viewed as something safely left to the good sense and desires of the people.

B

This brief review of the history of clergy-disqualification provisions also amply demonstrates, however, that, at least during the early segment of our national life, those provisions enjoyed the support of responsible American statesmen and were accepted as having a rational basis. Against this background we do not lightly invalidate a statute enacted pursuant to a provision of a state constitution which has been sustained by its highest court. The challenged provision came to the Tennessee Supreme Court clothed with the presumption of validity to which that court was bound to give deference.

However, the right to the free exercise of religion unquestionably encompasses the right to preach, proselyte, and perform other similar religious functions, or, in other words, to be a minister of the type McDaniel was found to be. Tennessee also acknowledges the right of its adult citizens generally to seek and hold office as legislators or delegates to the state constitutional convention. Yet under the clergy-disqualification provision, McDaniel cannot exercise both rights simultaneously because the State has conditioned the exercise of one on the surrender of the other. Or, in James Madison's words, the State is "punishing a religious profession with the privation of a civil right." In so doing, Tennessee has encroached upon McDaniel's right to the free exercise of religion. "[To] condition the availability of benefits [including access to the ballot] upon this appellant's willingness to violate a cardinal principle of [his] religious faith [by surrendering his religiously impelled ministry] effectively penalizes the free exercise of [his] constitutional liberties." Sherbert v. Verner, 374 U.S. 398, 406 (1963).

If the Tennessee disqualification provision were viewed as depriving the clergy of a civil right solely because of their religious beliefs, our inquiry would be at an end. The Free Exercise Clause categorically prohibits government from regulating, prohibiting, or rewarding religious beliefs as such. In Torcaso v. Watkins, the Court reviewed the Maryland constitutional requirement that all holders of "any office of profit or trust in this State" declare their belief in the existence of God. In striking down the Maryland requirement, the Court did not evaluate the interests assertedly justifying it but rather held that it violated freedom of religious belief.

In our view, however, *Torcaso* does not govern. By its terms, the Tennessee disqualification operates against McDaniel because of his status as a "minister" or "priest." The meaning of those words is, of course, a question of state law. And although the question has not been examined extensively in state-law sources, such authority as is available indicates that ministerial status is defined in terms of conduct and activity rather than in terms of belief. Because the Tennessee disqualification is directed primarily at status, acts, and conduct it is unlike the requirement in *Torcaso*, which focused on belief. Hence, the Free Exercise Clause's absolute prohibition of infringements on the "freedom to believe" is inapposite here.

This does not mean, of course, that the disqualification escapes judicial scrutiny or that McDaniel's activity does not enjoy significant First Amendment protection. The Court recently declared in *Wisconsin v. Yoder*: "The essence of all that has been said and written on the subject is that only those interests of the highest order and those not otherwise served can overbalance legitimate claims to the free exercise of religion."

Tennessee asserts that its interest in preventing the establishment of a state religion is consistent with the Establishment Clause and thus of the highest order. The constitutional history of the several States reveals that generally the interest in preventing establishment prompted the adoption of clergy disqualification provisions; Tennessee does not appear to be an exception to this pattern. There is no occasion to inquire whether promoting such an interest is a permissible legislative goal, however, for Tennessee has failed to demonstrate that its views of the dangers of clergy participation in the political process have not lost whatever validity they may once have enjoyed. The essence of the rationale underlying the Tennessee restriction on ministers is that if elected to public office they will necessarily exercise their powers and influence to promote the interests of one sect or thwart the interests of another, thus pitting one against the others, contrary to the anti-establishment principle with its command of neutrality. However widely that view may have been held in the 18th century by many, including enlightened statesmen of that day, the American experience provides no persuasive support for the fear that clergymen in public office will be less careful of anti-establishment interests or less faithful to their oaths of civil office than their unordained counterparts.

We hold that § 4 of ch. 848 violates McDaniel's First Amendment right to the free exercise of his religion made applicable to the States by the Fourteenth Amendment. Accordingly, the judgment of the Tennessee Supreme Court is reversed, and the case is remanded to that court for further proceedings not inconsistent with this opinion.

*Reversed and remanded.*

▩ MR. JUSTICE BLACKMUN took no part in the consideration or decision of this case.

▩ MR. JUSTICE BRENNAN, with whom MR. JUSTICE MARSHALL joins, concurring in the judgment.

I would hold that § 4 of the legislative call to the Tennessee constitutional convention, to the extent that it incorporates Art. 9, § 1, of the Tennessee Constitution, violates both the Free Exercise and Establishment Clauses of the First Amendment as applied to the States through the Fourteenth Amendment. I therefore concur in the reversal of the judgment of the Tennessee Supreme Court.

I

The Tennessee Supreme Court sustained Tennessee's exclusion on the ground that it "does not infringe upon religious belief or religious action within the protection of the free exercise clause [, and] that such indirect burden as may be imposed upon ministers and priests by excluding them from the lawmaking process of government is justified by the compelling state interest in maintaining the wall of separation between church and state." In reaching this conclusion, the state court relied on two interrelated propositions which are inconsistent with decisions of this Court. The first is that a distinction may be made between "religious belief or religious action" on the one hand, and the "career or calling" of the ministry on the other. The court stated that "[it] is not religious belief, but the career or calling, by which one is identified as dedicated to the full time promotion of the religious objectives of a particular religious sect, that disqualifies." The second is that the disqualification provision does not interfere with the free exercise of religion because the practice of the ministry is left unimpaired; only candidacy for legislative office is proscribed.

The characterization of the exclusion as one burdening appellant's "career or calling" and not religious belief cannot withstand analysis. Clearly freedom of belief protected by the Free Exercise Clause embraces freedom to profess or practice that belief, even including doing so to earn a livelihood. One's religious belief surely does not cease to enjoy the protection of the First Amendment when held with such depth of sincerity as to impel one to join the ministry.

Whether or not the provision discriminates among religions (and I accept for purposes of discussion the State Supreme Court's construction that it does not[4]), it establishes a religious classification—involvement in protected religious activity—governing the eligibility for office, which I believe is absolutely prohibited. The provision imposes a unique disability upon those who exhibit a defined level of intensity of involvement in protected religious activity. Such a classification as much imposes a test for office based on religious conviction as one based on denominational preference. A law which limits political participation to those who eschew prayer, public worship, or the ministry as much establishes a religious test as one which disqualifies Catholics, or Jews, or Protestants. Because the challenged provision establishes as a condition of office the willingness to eschew certain protected religious practices, compels the conclusion that it violates the Free Exercise Clause. *Torcaso* struck down Maryland's requirement that an appointee to the office of notary public declare his belief in the existence of God, expressly disavowing "the historically and

---

[4] It is arguable that the provision not only discriminates between religion and nonreligion, but may, as well, discriminate among religions by depriving ministers of faiths with established, clearly recognizable ministries from holding elective office, while permitting the members of nonorthodox humanistic faiths having no "counterpart" to ministers, similarly engaged to do so. . . .

constitutionally discredited policy of probing religious beliefs by test oaths or limiting public offices to persons who have, or perhaps more properly profess to have, a belief in some particular kind of religious concept." That principle equally condemns the religious qualification for elective office imposed by Tennessee.

The second proposition—that the law does not interfere with free exercise because it does not directly prohibit religious activity, but merely conditions eligibility for office on its abandonment—is also squarely rejected by precedent. In *Sherbert v. Verner*, a state statute disqualifying from unemployment compensation benefits persons unwilling to work on Saturdays was held to violate the Free Exercise Clause as applied to a Sabbatarian whose religious faith forbade Saturday work. That decision turned upon the fact that "[the] ruling forces her to choose between following the precepts of her religion and forfeiting benefits, on the one hand, and abandoning one of the precepts of her religion in order to accept work, on the other hand. Governmental imposition of such a choice puts the same kind of burden upon the free exercise of religion as would a fine imposed against appellant for her Saturday worship." Similarly, in "prohibiting legislative service because of a person's leadership role in a religious faith," Tennessee's disqualification provision imposed an unconstitutional penalty upon appellant's exercise of his religious faith.

Nor can Tennessee's political exclusion be distinguished from *Sherbert's* welfare disqualification as the Tennessee court thought, by suggesting that the unemployment compensation involved in *Sherbert* was necessary to sustain life while participation in the constitutional convention is a voluntary activity not itself compelled by religious belief. *Torcaso* answers that contention. There we held that "[the] fact . . . that a person is not compelled to hold public office cannot possibly be an excuse for barring him from office by state-imposed criteria forbidden by the Constitution."

The opinion of the Tennessee Supreme Court makes clear that the statute requires appellant's disqualification solely because he is a minister of a religious faith. If appellant were to renounce his ministry, presumably he could regain eligibility for elective office, but if he does not, he must forgo an opportunity for political participation he otherwise would enjoy. *Sherbert* and *Torcaso* compel the conclusion that because the challenged provision requires appellant to purchase his right to engage in the ministry by sacrificing his candidacy it impairs the free exercise of his religion.

The plurality recognizes that *Torcaso* held "categorically [prohibited]," a provision disqualifying from political office on the basis of religious belief, but draws what I respectfully suggest is a sophistic distinction between that holding and Tennessee's disqualification provision. The purpose of the Tennessee provision is not to regulate activities associated with a ministry, such as dangerous snake handling or human sacrifice, which the State validly could prohibit, but to bar from political office persons regarded as deeply committed to religious participation because of that participation—participation itself not regarded as harmful by the State and which therefore must be conceded to be protected. As the plurality recognizes, appellant was disqualified because he "[filled] a 'leadership role in religion,' and . . . 'dedicated [himself] to the full time promotion of the religious objectives of a particular religious sect.' According to the plurality, McDaniel could not be and was not in fact barred for his belief in religion, but was barred because of his commitment to persuade or lead others to accept that belief. I simply cannot fathom why the Free

Exercise Clause "categorically prohibits" hinging qualification for office on the act of declaring a belief in religion, but not on the act of discussing that belief with others.

## II

The State Supreme Court's justification of the prohibition, echoed here by the State, as intended to prevent those most intensely involved in religion from injecting sectarian goals and policies into the lawmaking process, and thus to avoid fomenting religious strife or the fusing of church with state affairs, itself raises the question whether the exclusion violates the Establishment Clause. As construed, the exclusion manifests patent hostility toward, not neutrality respecting, religion; forces or influences a minister or priest to abandon his ministry as the price of public office; and, in sum, has a primary effect which inhibits religion.

The fact that responsible statesmen of the day, including some of the United States Constitution's Framers, were attracted by the concept of clergy disqualification, does not provide historical support for concluding that those provisions are harmonious with the Establishment Clause. Notwithstanding the presence of such provisions in seven state constitutions when the Constitution was being written, the Framers refused to follow suit. That the disqualification provisions contained in state constitutions contemporaneous with the United States Constitution and the Bill of Rights cannot furnish a guide concerning the understanding of the harmony of such provisions with the Establishment Clause is evident from the presence in state constitutions, side by side with disqualification clauses, of provisions which would have clearly contravened the First Amendment had it applied to the States, such as those creating an official church, and limiting political office to Protestants or theistic believers generally. In short, the regime of religious liberty embodied in state constitutions was very different from that established by the Constitution of the United States. When, with the adoption of the Fourteenth Amendment, the strictures of the First Amendment became wholly applicable to the States, earlier conceptions of permissible state action with respect to religion—including those regarding clergy disqualification—were superseded. . . .

[Our] understanding of the interrelationship of the Religion Clauses has permitted government to take religion into account when necessary to further secular purposes unrelated to the advancement of religion, and to exempt, when possible, from generally applicable governmental regulation individuals whose religious beliefs and practices would otherwise thereby be infringed, or to create without state involvement an atmosphere in which voluntary religious exercise may flourish.

Beyond these limited situations in which government may take cognizance of religion for purposes of accommodating our traditions of religious liberty, government may not use religion as a basis of classification for the imposition of duties, penalties, privileges or benefits. "State power is no more to be used so as to handicap religions than it is to favor them." *Everson v. Board of Education*, 330 U.S., 18.

Tennessee nevertheless invokes the Establishment Clause to excuse the imposition of a civil disability upon those deemed to be deeply involved in religion. In my view, that Clause will not permit, much less excuse or condone, the deprivation of religious liberty here involved.

Fundamental to the conception of religious liberty protected by the Religion Clause is the idea that religious beliefs are a matter of voluntary choice by individuals and their associations, and that each sect is entitled to "flourish according to the zeal of its adherents and the appeal of its dogma." Accordingly, religious ideas, no less than any other, may be the subject of debate which is "uninhibited, robust, and wide-open . . . ." Government may not interfere with efforts to proselyte or worship in public places. It may not tax the dissemination of religious ideas. It may not seek to shield its citizens from those who would solicit them with their religious beliefs.

That public debate of religious ideas, like any other, may arouse emotion, may incite, may foment religious divisiveness and strife does not rob it of constitutional protection. The mere fact that a purpose of the Establishment Clause is to reduce or eliminate religious divisiveness or strife, does not place religious discussion, association, or political participation in a status less preferred than rights of discussion, association, and political participation generally. "Adherents of particular faiths and individual churches frequently take strong positions on public issues including . . . vigorous advocacy of legal or constitutional positions. Of course, churches as much as secular bodies and private citizens have that right."

The State's goal of preventing sectarian bickering and strife may not be accomplished by regulating religious speech and political association. The Establishment Clause does not license government to treat religion and those who teach or practice it, simply by virtue of their status as such, as subversive of American ideals and therefore subject to unique disabilities. Government may not inquire into the religious beliefs and motivations of officeholders— it may not remove them from office merely for making public statements regarding religion, or question whether their legislative actions stem from religious conviction.

In short, government may not as a goal promote "safe thinking" with respect to religion and fence out from political participation those, such as ministers, whom it regards as overinvolved in religion. Religionists no less than members of any other group enjoy the full measure of protection afforded speech, association, and political activity generally. The Establishment Clause, properly understood, is a shield against any attempt by government to inhibit religion as it has done here. It may not be used as a sword to justify repression of religion or its adherents from any aspect of public life.

Our decisions under the Establishment Clause prevent government from supporting or involving itself in religion or from becoming drawn into ecclesiastical disputes. These prohibitions naturally tend, as they were designed to, to avoid channeling political activity along religious lines and to reduce any tendency toward religious divisiveness in society. Beyond enforcing these prohibitions, however, government may not go. The antidote which the Constitution provides against zealots who would inject sectarianism into the political process is to subject their ideas to refutation in the marketplace of ideas and their platforms to rejection at the polls. With these safeguards, it is unlikely that they will succeed in inducing government to act along religiously divisive lines, and, with judicial enforcement of the Establishment Clause, any measure of success they achieve must be short-lived, at best. . . .

◈ MR. JUSTICE WHITE, concurring in the judgment.

While I share the view of my Brothers that Tennessee's disqualification of ministers from serving as delegates to the State's constitutional convention is constitutionally impermissible, I disagree as to the basis for this invalidity. Rather than relying on the Free Exercise Clause, as do the other Members of the Court, I would hold ch. 848, § 4, of 1976 Tenn. Pub. Acts unconstitutional under the Equal Protection Clause of the Fourteenth Amendment.

The plurality states that § 4 "has encroached upon McDaniel's right to the free exercise of religion," but fails to explain in what way McDaniel has been deterred in the observance of his religious beliefs. Certainly he has not felt compelled to abandon the ministry as a result of the challenged statute, nor has he been required to disavow any of his religious beliefs. Because I am not persuaded that the Tennessee statute in any way interferes with McDaniel's ability to exercise his religion as he desires, I would not rest the decision on the Free Exercise Clause, but instead would turn to McDaniel's argument that the statute denies him equal protection of the laws.

Our cases have recognized the importance of the right of an individual to seek elective office and accordingly have afforded careful scrutiny to state regulations burdening that right. . . .

The restriction in this case, unlike the ones challenged in the previous cases, is absolute on its face: There is no way in which a Tennessee minister can qualify as a candidate for the State's constitutional convention. The State's asserted interest in this absolute disqualification is its desire to maintain the required separation between church and state. While the State recognizes that not all ministers would necessarily allow their religious commitments to interfere with their duties to the State and to their constituents, it asserts that the potential for such conflict is sufficiently great to justify § 4's candidacy disqualification.

Although the State's interest is a legitimate one, close scrutiny reveals that the challenged law is not "reasonably necessary to the accomplishment of . . ." that objective. All 50 States are required by the First and Fourteenth Amendments to maintain a separation between church and state, and yet all of the States other than Tennessee are able to achieve this objective without burdening ministers' rights to candidacy. This suggests that the underlying assumption on which the Tennessee statute is based—that a minister's duty to the superiors of his church will interfere with his governmental service—is unfounded. Moreover, the rationale of the Tennessee statute is undermined by the fact that it is both underinclusive and overinclusive. While the State asserts an interest in keeping religious and governmental interests separate, the disqualification of ministers applies only to legislative positions, and not to executive and judicial offices. On the other hand, the statute's sweep is also overly broad, for it applies with equal force to those ministers whose religious beliefs would not prevent them from properly discharging their duties as constitutional convention delegates.

The facts of this case show that the voters of McDaniel's district desired to have him represent them at the limited constitutional convention. Because I conclude that the State's justification for frustrating the desires of these voters and for depriving McDaniel and all other ministers of the right to seek this position is insufficient, I would hold § 4 unconstitutional as a violation of the Equal Protection Clause.

## Notes and Questions

1. Prior to the Revolution, ministers of the local established churches (i.e., "settled" ministers) wielded considerable political power and frequently enjoyed unique privileges, such as immunity from many legal obligations and exemptions from paying many taxes (although, even in Puritan Massachusetts, clergy could not hold political office). Colonists scorned the even greater political power clergy wielded in Great Britain and Europe and feared that this pattern could be replicated in the colonies. In fact, widespread opposition to the creation of an Anglican bishopric in America was one of the galvanizing events leading up to the Revolution.

   Even after the Revolution, many people expressed concern about the political influence of the conservative New England "Standing Order" who resisted the dissolution of the remaining state establishments and other democratic reforms. In his *Autobiography*, Rev. Lyman Beecher candidly acknowledged the political power of the Connecticut Standing Order prior to disestablishment:

   > The ministers had always managed [political matters] themselves, for in those days the ministers were all politicians. They had always been used to it from the beginning. On election day they had a festival. All the clergy used to go, walk in procession, smoke pipes, and drink. And, fact is when they got together, they would talk over who should be governor, and who lieutenant-governor and who in the upper house, and their counsels would prevail.[7]

   With this background, can you articulate any establishment concerns that may have motivated early state legislatures to adopt provisions similar to the one struck down in *McDaniel*?

   It should also be noted that some founding-era commentators who supported disestablishment in the states drew a sharp line between special treatment of clergy in the political system and equal treatment of them. For example, in 1790, Baptist minister John Leland (1754–1841) wrote:

   > To have one branch of the legislature composed of clergyman, as is the case in some European powers, is not seemly—to have them entitled to seats of legislation, on account of their Eccesiastical dignity, like the bishops of England, is absurd. But to declare them ineligible, when their neighbors prefer them to any others, is depriving them of the liberty of free citizens, and those who prefer them, the freedom of choice.[8]

2. The plurality, Justice Brennan, and Justice White all agree that the Tennessee exclusion cannot stand, but they each offer different rationales. What are the three rationales for striking the provision, and how are they related or distinguishable? Which rationale is more compelling?

3. How do you understand Justice Brennan's free exercise argument? In what way is Rev. McDaniel's ability to believe and practice his religion burdened by the Tennessee exclusion? What does Brennan argue about the scope of the free exercise right? What aspect of his understanding is likely uncomfortable for the members of the plurality?

4. In *McDaniel*, Justice Brennan writes: "The Establishment Clause, properly understood, is a shield against any attempt by government to inhibit religion as it has done here; *Abington School Dist. v. Schempp*, 374 U.S. 203, 222 (1963). It may not be used as a sword to justify repression of religion or its adherents from any aspect of public life." What does he mean? Brennan also says: "The mere fact that a purpose of the Establishment Clause is to reduce or eliminate religious divisiveness or strife, does not place religious discussion, association or political participation in a status less preferred than rights of discussion, association, and political participation generally." Where is Brennan trying to draw the constitutional line?

5. According to Justice Brennan, when may the government "take religion into account"? How, in his opinion, should the government do so in these situations?

As some of the opinions in *McDaniel v. Paty* suggest, private citizens clearly have a constitutional right to comment on issues of public concern in religious terms. This right also extends to nongovernmental organizations. As the Court said in 1970: "Adherents of particular faiths and individual churches frequently take strong positions on public issues. . . . Of course, churches as much as secular bodies and private citizens have that right." *Walz v. Tax Comm'n*, 397 U.S. 664, 670 (1970).

But what about religious statements by high-ranking legislative or executive branch government officials, such as the president of the United States, a governor or a member of Congress? In other words, when such public officials make statements endorsing religion in the course of their duties, is the government speaking, or do the statements merely reflect the personal sentiments of the speakers?

Some insist that such government officials should be free to publicly discuss their policy-related religious motivations and reasons. For example, Professor Michael Perry has argued:

Does a legislator or other public official, or even an ordinary citizen, violate the non-establishment norm by presenting a religious argument in public political debate? For example, does a legislator violate the nonestablishment norm by presenting, in public debate about whether the law should recognize homosexual marriage, a religious argument that homosexual sexual conduct is immoral? An affirmative answer is wildly implausible. Every citizen, without regard to whether she is a legislator or other public official, is constitutionally free to present in public political debate whatever arguments about morality, including whatever religious arguments, she wants to present. Indeed, the freedom of speech protected by the constitutional law of the United States is so generous that it extends even to arguments, including secular arguments, that may not, as a constitutional matter, serve as a basis of political choice—for example, the argument that persons of nonwhite ancestry are not truly or fully human (which is an unconstitutional basis of political choice under the antidiscrimination part of the Fourteenth Amendment). . . .

Moreover, to disfavor religious arguments relative to secular ones would violate the core meaning—the antidiscrimination meaning—of the free exercise norm. After all, included among the religious practices protected by the free exercise norm are bearing public witness to one's religious beliefs and trying to influence political decisionmaking on the basis of those beliefs . . . .

Although the non-establishment norm . . . forbids any branch or agency of government to do certain things, to engage in certain sorts of actions, it does not forbid any person—including any person who happens to be a legislator or other public official—to say whatever she wants to say, religious or not, in public political debate. The serious question, then, is not whether legislators or public officials, much less citizens, violate the nonestablishment norm by presenting religious arguments in public political debate. The serious question, rather, is whether government would violate the nonestablishment norm by basing a political choice—for example, a law banning abortion—on a religious argument.[9]

In sharp contrast, Professor Steven Gey argues:

A policy-making official's statement about his or her religious views on a matter falling within that official's area of authority is obviously relevant to that official's duties (even when the statement is made off-duty or in a private forum), and the public will assume that the official's religious views have an impact on whatever policy the official ultimately supports. Consider, for example, a congressman who gives an impassioned testimonial at a religious service on Sunday in which he cites the Bible in support of the proposition that abortion is sinful, and then on Monday the same congressman introduces legislation severely restricting abortion. Most members of the public will justifiably assume that the official's legislative actions are motivated by his religious beliefs. Unlike most government administrators—whose public roles are strictly circumscribed by the narrow parameters of their jobs and by their accountability to supervisors and courts—there is no clear line between a policymaker's private life (in which the public expression of strong religious views should be constitutionally protected) and the policymaker's public function (in which the Constitution demands that the official refrain from acting to advance a religious agenda). Certainly even policymakers retain a broad area of purely private belief and behavior in which they may express their religious views. (No one would suggest that the Establishment Clause should permit examination of a politician's statements in the confessional, for example.) But at the very least, the Establishment Clause should support limitations on policymakers' prominent public expression of religious motivations for their official actions.[10]

The Supreme Court has not addressed this issue, but in his dissenting opinion in *Van Orden v. Perry* (see chapter 20), Supreme Court Justice John Paul Stevens suggested that, at least with respect to speeches by high-ranking governmental officials, we should view them as containing both personal and official sentiments. This "dual character" of their statements, commonly recognized as such by the public, is the reason that these references are generally not constitutionally objectionable. Justice Stevens wrote: "Our leaders, when delivering public addresses, often express their blessings simultaneously in the service of God and their constituents. Thus, when [government] officials deliver public speeches, we recognize that their words are not exclusively a transmission from *the* government because those oratories have embedded within them the inherently personal views of the speaker as an individual member of the polity."

Even if constitutional principles are not violated when high-ranking legislative and executive government officials discuss their faith while carrying out their public duties, is it a good idea for them to do so? This question has long been hotly debated by scholars and practitioners alike. Professor Kent Greenawalt says that as a matter of self restraint rather than legal restraint, "public officials acting in their official capacity should rarely state religious reasons as their bases for political decisions." In a section of a speech by Professor Greenawalt addressing the legislative arena, Greenawalt explains:

> At least at a national level, I believe we have reached a general understanding that legislators should not make such religious arguments. They represent all their constituents, members of diverse religions. They should not present as crucial arguments grounds that are applicable only to members of certain religions. . . .
>
> I think this practice respects the religious diversity of our population. Since religious tensions remain significant in the United States, this practice also reduces political and religious conflict in a desirable way. This restraint involves only a minor impairment of the religious liberty of legislators. They have chosen a public role and they often say less than everything that they think about particular issues. Moreover, the number of legislators in the country is small in comparison with the number of citizens. If legislators forego public religious arguments about political issues, that entails only a slight diminution of people's freedom to act upon religious understandings.
>
> How legislators should make up their minds is troubling. Unlike judges, they may often find that public reasons are indecisive. Legislators should focus primarily on public reasons, but we should not expect them systematically to disregard personal reasons and religious grounds. . . . .
>
> [I]t is much simpler to tell whether others are restraining their discourse than whether they are restraining their judgment. The primary restraint on legislators should be conceived as a restraint on public discourse, not on judgment.
>
> Does this proposal endorse dishonesty and concealment? No one expects legislators to reveal all their grounds for decision. If this is not expected, their failure to develop religious arguments that carry considerable weight with them is not really dishonest. The issue of concealment is more difficult. Some people believe that citizens should know as completely as possible the bases on which legislators decide. Such knowledge can help the citizens decide what to do at the next election. This is a telling point, but not telling enough to justify wide political speech cast in religious terms. I do believe legislators appropriately mention that religious grounds matter to them, and certainly they should not lie about that. What they should not do is to make full religious arguments in the public political forum.[11]

Do you agree or disagree with Professor Greenawalt's assessment of these matters? For a number of other responses to this issue, see "Religiously Based Morality: Its Proper Place in American Law and Public Policy?" *Wake Forest Law Review* 36 (2001): 217-570.

As noted earlier, the Supreme Court has not spoken directly to all of these issues, but it has said that governmental action must not have the predominant purpose or primary effect of advancing religion. Determining if an act of government has the requisite non-religious purpose and primary effect can be a complex and difficult inquiry, to be sure. But some basic guidelines can be gleaned from the Court's decisions in this area.

The Court is "normally deferential to a State's articulation of a secular purpose," *Edwards v. Aguillard*, 482 U.S. 482, 586 (1987). But the Court also has "required that the statement of [legislative] purpose be sincere and not a sham." *Edwards*, 482 U.S., 586-587. See also *Bowen v. Kendrick*, 487 U.S. 589, 604 (1988) (quoting *Edwards* on this point).

The Court has said "scrutinizing purpose does make practical sense, as in Establishment Clause analysis, where an understanding of official objective emerges from readily discoverable fact, without any judicial psychoanalysis of a drafter's heart of hearts." *McCreary County v. ACLU*, 545 U.S. 844, 862 (2005). In cases where the Supreme Court has found an impermissible purpose for government action, it says it has done so because "openly available data supported a commonsense conclusion that a religious objective permeated the government's action." *Id.* at 863.

In *Harris v. McRae*, 448 U.S. 297 (1980), the Court considered whether a law that denies government funding for certain medically necessary abortions, a position that coincides with the doctrines of the Roman Catholic Church (among some other religious groups), violated the Establishment Clause. The Court responded:

> It is well settled that "a legislative enactment does not contravene the Establishment Clause if it has a secular legislative purpose, if its principal or primary effect neither advances nor inhibits religion, and if it does not foster an excessive governmental entanglement with religion." *Committee for Public Education v. Regan*, 444 U.S. 646, 653. Applying this standard, the District Court properly concluded that [this law, commonly called] the Hyde Amendment, does not run afoul of the Establishment Clause. Although neither a State nor the Federal Government can constitutionally "pass laws which aid one religion, aid all religions, or prefer one religion over another," *Everson v. Board of Education*, 330 U.S. 1, 15, it does not follow that a statute violates the Establishment Clause because it "happens to coincide or harmonize with the tenets of some or all religions." *McGowan v. Maryland*, 366 U.S. 420, 442. That the Judaeo-Christian religions oppose stealing does not mean that a State or the Federal Government may not, consistent with the Establishment Clause, enact laws prohibiting larceny. Ibid. The Hyde Amendment, as the District Court noted, is as much a reflection of "traditionalist" values towards abortion, as it is an embodiment of the views of any particular religion. 491 F. Supp., 741. See also *Roe v. Wade*, 410 U.S., 138-141. In sum, we are convinced that the fact that the funding restrictions in the Hyde Amendment may coincide with the religious tenets of the Roman Catholic Church does not, without more, contravene the Establishment Clause. *McRae*, 448 U.S., 319-320.

## NOTES AND QUESTIONS

1. As noted above, some argue that certain religious references by high-ranking legislative or executive government officials should be understood as personal rather than governmental. But doesn't the government commonly "speak" through its officials, through speeches, proclamations and/or official reports? Is there any difference between speeches made by such leaders and laws or official reports?

2. Assume that a governor of a state launched a state-wide speaking tour to encourage people to deepen their faith commitments. Would it be appropriate to argue that this speaking tour, or the speeches made during it, are purely personal (nongovernmental)?

3. What about commentary by judges that touches on religious matters? The *Holy Trinity* decision, the case in which the Court claimed that the United States was a "Christian nation," was by a unanimous Supreme Court. Does that make its declarations more "official" than a speech by the president or

a Senator? Could the Court's declarations in *Holy Trinity* be described more as an observation about the culture of the country at that time, or does it constitute an official endorsement of Christianity by the federal judiciary?

4.  Should the personal religious views of judges play any role in their decision-making? Why or why not? In what way is the role of judges different from that of policymakers? Professor Kent Greenawalt addressed some of these issues in a 1996 piece:

> Among public officials, judges are the most constrained in their bases for decision. Since appellate judges justify their results in formal opinions, we know precisely what grounds they use to defend their decisions. Generally, they provide reasons based on legally authoritative sources, like statutes and prior cases. Sometimes however, they must give meaning to basic concepts like fairness and equality. Then they may engage in reasoning that is broader in scope. What one does not find, however, is argument that depends on any source of insight that the judges do not think is available and forceful for lawyers or members of society in general. One does not find religious grounds. Judges rarely say behavior is wrong because it violates one particular authoritative religious point of view. . . .
>
> Judges may employ references to religious morality to indicate traditions in this country, say about abortion or homosexual acts; but judges do not claim that the morality of Christianity, or any other religion, is correct because the religion is correct. Opinions claim to rely on bases for decision that would be authoritative for any judge; no directly religious ground has this status. Present practices preclude judges from advancing directly religious grounds for decision. . . .
>
> On very rare occasions, judges may find all the legal and other arguments of general force to be indecisive. They may find they need to rely on some more personal source of insight to tip the balance. Is this ever appropriate? If it is appropriate, may a judge rely on a religious position as the more personal source of insight? The first point is arguable. Perhaps judges should always strain to be guided by public reasons, reasons that they recognize have force for all judges and that they would feel comfortable putting into an opinion. I think they should strive hard to be guided by public reasons, but that when they find these reasons to be evenly balanced, they may give some weight to more personal reasons they would not put in an opinion. An example would be, "I can't explain why, but I feel deeply that a seventh month old fetus counts just as much as a new born baby." In those rare instances when judges rely on personal reasons they would not put in opinions, I believe they may treat their own religious beliefs as they would other personal sources of judgment. Kent Greenawalt, "Religious Liberty and Democratic Politics," *Northern Kentucky Law Review* 23 (1996): 637-638.

Does Professor Greenawalt's assessment of these matters seem correct? For further discussion of these issues and the articulation of other points of view, see Stephen L. Carter, "The Religiously Devout Judge," *Notre Dame Law Review* 64 (1989): 932; Wendell L. Griffen, "The Case for Religious Values in Judicial Decisionmaking," *Marquette Law Review* 81 (1998): 513; Joan B. Gottschall, "Response to Judge Wendell Griffen," *Marquette Law Review* 81 (1998): 533; Scott C. Idleman, "The Limits of Religious Values in Judicial Decisionmaking," *Marquette Law Review* 81 (1998): 537; Daniel O. Conkle, "Religiously Devout Judges: Issue of Personal Integrity and Public Benefit," *Marquette Law Review* 81 (1998): 523.

5. What about the religious speech of government employees who are not high-ranking officials? Here, there is general agreement that the constitutional analysis would be different.[12] For example, when the supervisor of the local post office makes a speech or releases remarks, we normally don't expect those kinds of remarks to include personal opinions, religious or otherwise. And it is worth noting that the Supreme Court has cut back on the free expression interests that government employees possess when they are engaged in their professional capacities.[13] The rules that apply in these circumstances are discussed in more detail below at pages 1017-1028.

In addition to the U.S. Constitution, other legal restrictions are relevant to the engagement of religion, policy and politics. The most prominent of these legal restrictions are federal statutory limits on the lobbying and political activities of organizations, including religious organizations, that wish to qualify for and maintain tax-exempt status under Section 501(c)(3) of the Internal Revenue Code. The following case discusses some of these restrictions.

## BRANCH MINISTRIES v. ROSSOTTI
## 211 F.3d 137 (D.C. Cir. 2000)

Opinion for the court filed by Senior Judge BUCKLEY.

Four days before the 1992 presidential election, Branch Ministries, a tax-exempt church, placed full-page advertisements in two newspapers in which it urged Christians not to vote for then-presidential candidate Bill Clinton because of his positions on certain moral issues. The Internal Revenue Service concluded that the placement of the advertisements violated the statutory restrictions on organizations exempt from taxation and, for the first time in its history, [but see the very similar case *Christian Echoes National Ministry v. United States*, 470 F.2d 849 (1972), cert. denied 414 U.S. 864 (1973)] it revoked a bona fide church's tax-exempt status because of its involvement in politics. Branch Ministries and its pastor, Dan Little, challenge the revocation on the grounds that (1) the Service acted beyond its statutory authority, (2) the revocation violated its right to the free exercise of religion guaranteed by the First Amendment and the Religious Freedom Restoration Act, and (3) it was the victim of selective prosecution in violation of the Fifth Amendment.

Because these objections are without merit, we affirm the district court's grant of summary judgment to the Service.

I. BACKGROUND

  A. Taxation of Churches

      The Internal Revenue Code ("Code") exempts certain organizations from taxation, including those organized and operated for religious purposes, provided that they do not engage in certain activities, including involvement in "any political campaign on behalf of (or in opposition to) any candidate for public office." Contributions to such organizations are also deductible from the donating taxpayer's taxable income. Although most organizations seeking tax-exempt status are required to apply to the Internal Revenue Service ("IRS" or "Service") for an advance determination that they meet the requirements of section 501(c)(3), *id.* § 508(a), a church may simply hold itself out as tax exempt and receive the benefits of that status without applying for advance recognition from the IRS. . . .

      The unique treatment churches receive in the Internal Revenue Code is further reflected in special restrictions on the IRS's ability to investigate the tax status of a church. The Church Audit Procedures Act ("CAPA") sets out the circumstances under which the IRS may initiate an investigation of a church and the procedures it is required to follow in such an investigation. Upon a "reasonable belief" by a high-level Treasury official that a church may not be exempt from taxation under section 501, the IRS may begin a "church tax inquiry." . . . If the IRS is not able to resolve its concerns through a church tax inquiry, it may proceed to the second level of investigation: a "church tax examination." In such an examination, the IRS may obtain and review the church's records or examine its activities "to determine whether [the] organization claiming to be a church is a church for any period."

  B. Factual and Procedural History

      Branch Ministries, Inc. operates the Church at Pierce Creek ("Church"), a Christian church located in Binghamton, New York. In 1983, the Church requested and received a letter from the IRS recognizing its tax-exempt status. On October 30, 1992, four days before the presidential election, the Church placed full-page advertisements in *USA Today* and the *Washington Times*. Each bore the headline "Christians Beware" and asserted that then-Governor Clinton's positions concerning abortion, homosexuality, and the distribution of condoms to teenagers in schools violated Biblical precepts. The following appeared at the bottom of each advertisement: "This advertisement was co-sponsored by the Church at Pierce Creek, Daniel J. Little, Senior Pastor, and by churches and concerned Christians nationwide. Tax-deductible donations for this advertisement gladly accepted. Make donations to: The Church at Pierce Creek. [mailing address]."

      The advertisements did not go unnoticed. They produced hundreds of contributions to the Church from across the country and were mentioned in a *New York Times* article and an Anthony Lewis column which stated that the sponsors of the advertisement had almost certainly violated the Internal Revenue Code.

      The advertisements also came to the attention of the Regional Commissioner of the IRS, who notified the Church on November 20, 1992 that he had authorized a church tax inquiry based on "a reasonable belief . . . that you may not be tax-exempt or that you may be liable for tax" due to political activities and expenditures. The Church denied that it had engaged in any prohibited political activity and declined to provide the IRS with certain information the Service had requested. On February 11, 1993, the IRS informed the Church that it was beginning a church tax examination. Following two unproductive meetings between the parties, the IRS revoked the Church's section 501(c)(3) tax-exempt status on January 19, 1995, citing the newspaper advertisements as prohibited intervention in a political campaign.

The Church and Pastor Little (collectively, "Church") commenced this lawsuit soon thereafter. This had the effect of suspending the revocation of the Church's tax exemption until the district court entered its judgment in this case. The Church challenged the revocation of its tax-exempt status, alleging that the IRS had no authority to revoke its tax exemption, that the revocation violated its right to free speech and to freely exercise its religion under the First Amendment and the Religious Freedom Restoration Act of 1993, and that the IRS engaged in selective prosecution in violation of the Equal Protection Clause of the Fifth Amendment. After allowing discovery on the Church's selective prosecution claim, the district court granted summary judgment in favor of the IRS.

The Church filed a timely appeal, and we have jurisdiction[.] . . .

II. ANALYSIS

The Church advances a number of arguments in support of its challenges to the revocation. We examine only those that warrant analysis. . . .

B. First Amendment Claims and the RFRA

The Church claims that the revocation of its exemption violated its right to freely exercise its religion under both the First Amendment and the RFRA. To sustain its claim under either the Constitution or the statute, the Church must first establish that its free exercise right has been substantially burdened. . . . We conclude that the Church has failed to meet this test.

The Church asserts, first, that a revocation would threaten its existence. The Church maintains that a loss of its tax-exempt status will not only make its members reluctant to contribute the funds essential to its survival, but may obligate the Church itself to pay taxes.

The Church appears to assume that the withdrawal of a conditional privilege for failure to meet the condition is in itself an unconstitutional burden on its free exercise right. This is true, however, only if the receipt of the privilege (in this case the tax exemption) is conditioned "upon conduct proscribed by a religious faith, or . . . denied . . . because of conduct mandated by religious belief, thereby putting substantial pressure on an adherent to modify his behavior and to violate his beliefs." *Jimmy Swaggart Ministries*, 493 U.S., 391-392 (internal quotation marks and citation omitted). Although its advertisements reflected its religious convictions on certain questions of morality, the Church does not maintain that a withdrawal from electoral politics would violate its beliefs. The sole effect of the loss of the tax exemption will be to decrease the amount of money available to the Church for its religious practices. The Supreme Court has declared, however, that such a burden "is not constitutionally significant." *Id.*, 391.

In actual fact, even this burden is overstated. Because of the unique treatment churches receive under the Internal Revenue Code, the impact of the revocation is likely to be more symbolic than substantial. As the IRS confirmed at oral argument, if the Church does not intervene in future political campaigns, it may hold itself out as a 501(c)(3) organization and receive all the benefits of that status. All that will have been lost, in that event, is the advance assurance of deductibility in the event a donor should be audited. Contributions will remain tax deductible as long as donors are able to establish that the Church meets the requirements of section 501(c)(3).

Nor does the revocation necessarily make the Church liable for the payment of taxes. As the IRS explicitly represented in its brief and reiterated at oral argument, the revocation of the exemption does not convert bona fide donations into income taxable to the Church. Furthermore, we know of no authority, and counsel provided none, to prevent the Church from reapplying for a prospective determination of its tax-exempt status and regaining the advance assurance of deductibility—provided, of course, that it renounces future involvement in political campaigns.

We also reject the Church's argument that it is substantially burdened because it has no alternate means by which to communicate its sentiments about candidates for public office. In *Regan v. Taxation With Representation*, (BLACKMUN, J., concurring), three members of the Supreme Court stated that the availability of such an alternate means of communication is essential to the constitutionality of section 501(c)(3)'s restrictions on lobbying. The Court subsequently confirmed that this was an accurate description of its holding. In *Regan*, the concurring justices noted that "TWR may use its present § 501(c)(3) organization for its nonlobbying activities and may create a § 501(c)(4) affiliate to pursue its charitable goals through lobbying."

The Church has such an avenue available to it. As was the case with TWR, the Church may form a related organization under section 501(c)(4) of the Code. See 26 U.S.C. § 501(c)(4) (tax exemption for "civic leagues or organizations not organized for profit but operated exclusively for the promotion of social welfare"). Such organizations are exempt from taxation; but unlike their section 501(c)(3) counterparts, contributions to them are not deductible. Although a section 501(c)(4) organization is also subject to the ban on intervening in political campaigns, it may form a political action committee (PAC) that would be free to participate in political campaigns. . . .

At oral argument, counsel for the Church doggedly maintained that there can be no "Church at Pierce Creek PAC." True, it may not itself create a PAC; but as we have pointed out, the Church can initiate a series of steps that will provide an alternate means of political communication that will satisfy the standards set by the concurring justices in *Regan*. Should the Church proceed to do so, however, it must understand that the related 501(c)(4) organization must be separately incorporated; and it must maintain records that will demonstrate that tax-deductible contributions to the Church have not been used to support the political activities conducted by the 501(c)(4) organization's political action arm.

That the Church cannot use its tax-free dollars to fund such a PAC unquestionably passes constitutional muster. The Supreme Court has consistently held that, absent invidious discrimination, "Congress has not violated [an organization's] First Amendment rights by declining to subsidize its First Amendment activities." *Regan*, 461 U.S., 548; see also *Cammarano v. United States*, 358 U.S. 498, 513 (1959) ("Petitioners are not being denied a tax deduction because they engage in constitutionally protected activities, but are simply being required to pay for those activities entirely out of their own pockets, as everyone else engaging in similar activities is required to do under the provisions of the Internal Revenue Code.").

Because the Church has failed to demonstrate that its free exercise rights have been substantially burdened, we do not reach its arguments that section 501(c)(3) does not serve a compelling government interest or, if it is indeed compelling, that revocation of its tax exemption was not the least restrictive means of furthering that interest.

Nor does the Church succeed in its claim that the IRS has violated its First Amendment free speech rights by engaging in viewpoint discrimination. The restrictions imposed by section 501(c)(3) are viewpoint neutral; they prohibit intervention in favor of all candidates for public office by all tax-exempt organizations, regardless of candidate, party, or viewpoint.

C. Selective Prosecution (Fifth Amendment)

The Church alleges that the IRS violated the Equal Protection Clause of the Fifth Amendment by engaging in selective prosecution. In support of its claim, the Church has submitted several hundred pages of newspaper excerpts reporting political campaign activities in, or by the pastors of, other churches that have retained their tax-exempt status. These include reports of explicit endorsements of Democratic candidates by clergymen as well as many instances in which favored candidates have been invited to address congregations from the pulpit. The Church complains that despite this widespread and widely reported involvement by other churches in political campaigns, it is the only one to have ever had its tax-exempt status revoked for engaging in political activity. It attributes this alleged discrimination to the Service's political bias.

To establish selective prosecution, the Church must "prove that (1) [it] was singled out for prosecution from among others similarly situated and (2) that [the] prosecution was improperly motivated, i.e., based on race, religion or another arbitrary classification." This burden is a demanding one because "in the absence of clear evidence to the contrary, courts presume that [government prosecutors] have properly discharged their official duties." *United States v. Armstrong*, 517 U.S. 456, 464 (1996). At oral argument, counsel for the IRS conceded that if some of the church-sponsored political activities cited by the Church were accurately reported, they were in violation of section 501(c)(3) and could have resulted in the revocation of those churches' tax-exempt status. But even if the Service could have revoked their tax exemptions, the Church has failed to establish selective prosecution because it has failed to demonstrate that it was similarly situated to any of those other churches. None of the reported activities involved the placement of advertisements in newspapers with nationwide circulations opposing a candidate and soliciting tax deductible contributions to defray their cost. . . .

Because the Church has failed to establish that it was singled out for prosecution from among others who were similarly situated, we need not examine whether the IRS was improperly motivated in undertaking this prosecution.

III. CONCLUSION

For the foregoing reasons, we find that the revocation of the Church's tax-exempt status neither violated the Constitution nor exceeded the IRS's statutory authority. The judgment of the district court is therefore

*Affirmed.*

## Notes and Questions

1. Are the legal restraints on the church in this case statutory or constitutional in nature? Would there be any way for the church to be free of the restrictions placed on tax-exempt 501(c)(3) organizations?

2. The Court has referred to the restriction at issue in the *McDaniel* case as an "unconstitutional condition." What does this mean? The concept is elusive, but it may help to distinguish those situations when the government imposes certain conditions on the application or uses of a government benefit (e.g., a government grant can be spent only on pregnancy related services that do not include abortion services) from situations where the government imposes restrictions on the expressive activity of beneficiaries as a condition of receiving an unrelated benefit (e.g., requiring a loyalty oath as a condition for a veteran to receive his benefits). Which situation is more applicable in *McDaniel*? In *Branch Ministries*?

3. Assume a state legislature passes a constitutional amendment prohibiting gays and lesbians from marrying. The amendment's popular title is the "Sanctity of Marriage" amendment and its primary co-sponsors are prominent members of churches that believe homosexual activity and marriage is a sin. The legislative history of the amendment is replete with references to various legislators' beliefs that homosexuality is, for example, "outside God's plan" for human sexual behavior and family life. Would this amendment be found to have the requisite secular purpose? What additional information in the legislative history would be helpful in answering the question?

   Now assume that the articulated purpose for the law is strictly nonreligious in nature. The legislators instead discuss what is good for families and the role of the family in American society Would courts be likely to find that this law had the requisite secular purpose? Do you believe that there could be a predominantly secular purpose for such a law?

4. In the *Branch Ministries* case, why did the court find that there was no substantial burden on the church's free exercise rights? How is this burden different from the one presented in *McDaniel*, or are they similar? In this case, the court says that the church did not "maintain that a withdrawal from electoral politics would violate its [religious] beliefs." If the church had made such a claim, might the court's conclusion have been different on this matter? If so, what would the next step be in the free-exercise analysis?

5. In the *Branch Ministries* case, the court references a number of instances in which churches made candidate endorsements, but the IRS did not commence a church tax inquiry. Can you venture some guesses as to why the IRS did not act in these cases?

6. The Court approvingly cites a statement from another case that says that "Congress has not violated [an organization's] First Amendment rights by declining to subsidize its First Amendment activities." How, then, can one explain the outcome in the *Sherbert v. Verner* case (see chapter 7)?

7. In 2003, some members of Congress introduced legislation that included the following provision:

An organization described in section 508(c)(1)(A) (relating to churches) shall not fail to be treated as organized and operated exclusively for a religious purpose, or to have participated in, or intervened in any political campaign on behalf of (or in opposition to) any candidate for public office, for purposes of subsection (c)(3), or section 170(c)(2) (relating to charitable contributions), because of the content, preparation, or presentation of any homily, sermon, teaching, dialectic, or other presentation made during religious services or gatherings.

The sponsors of the legislation claimed that the bill was needed partially because it would be unconstitutional for the IRS to revoke a church's tax-exempt status based on a candidate endorsement that occurs as a part of religious services. Do you agree? If enacted, would this law itself pass constitutional muster? (See, e.g., *Texas Monthly*, 489 U.S. 1 (1989)). For further reading on this topic, see Richard W. Garnett, "A Quiet Faith? Taxes, Politics, and the Privatization of Religion," *Boston College Law Review* 42 (2001): 771 and Donald B. Tobin, "Political Campaigning by Churches and Charities: Hazardous for 501(c)(3)s, Dangerous for Democracy," *Georgetown Law Journal* 95 (2007): 1313.

## RELIGION IN THE FEDERAL WORKPLACE

As discussed above, government employees have limited free speech rights to engage in personal expressive activity in the workplace, particularly when that expression concerns their job duties. At the same time, workplaces are not "religion-free" zones, even governmental workplaces. Employers generally must ensure that religious discrimination and religious harassment do not occur in the workplace. Furthermore, while it must guard against any appearance that the government itself is promoting religion, the government must ensure that employees' free speech and free exercise interests are respected. In 1997, the Clinton White House released the following guidelines on religious expression and exercise in the federal workplace to help both federal employers and employees to better understand their rights and responsibilities.

### GUIDELINES ON RELIGIOUS EXERCISE AND RELIGIOUS EXPRESSION IN THE FEDERAL WORKPLACE

The following Guidelines, addressing religious exercise and religious expression, shall apply to all civilian executive branch agencies, officials, and employees in the Federal workplace.

These Guidelines principally address employees' religious exercise and religious expression when the employees are acting in their personal capacity within the Federal workplace and the public does not have regular exposure to the workplace. The Guidelines do not comprehensively address whether and when the government and its employees may engage in religious speech directed at the public. They also do not address religious exercise and religious expression by uniformed military personnel, or the conduct of business by chaplains employed by the Federal Government. Nor do the Guidelines define the rights and responsibilities of non-governmental employers—including religious employers—and their employees. Although these Guidelines, including the examples cited in them, should answer the most frequently encountered questions in the Federal workplace, actual cases sometimes will be complicated by additional facts and circumstances that may require a different result from the one the Guidelines indicate.

Section 1. Guidelines for Religious Exercise and Religious Expression in the Federal Workplace. Executive departments and agencies ("agencies") shall permit personal religious expression by Federal employees to the greatest extent possible, consistent with requirements of law and interests in workplace efficiency as described in this set of Guidelines. Agencies shall not discriminate against employees on the basis of religion, require religious participation or non-participation as a condition of employment, or permit religious harassment. And agencies shall accommodate employees' exercise of their religion in the circumstances specified in these Guidelines. These requirements are but applications of the general principle that agencies shall treat all employees with the same respect and consideration, regardless of their religion (or lack thereof).

A.  Religious Expression. As a matter of law, agencies shall not restrict personal religious expression by employees in the Federal workplace except where the employee's interest in the expression is outweighed by the government's interest in the efficient provision of public services or where the expression intrudes upon the legitimate rights of other employees or creates the appearance, to a reasonable observer, of an official endorsement of religion. The examples cited in these Guidelines as permissible forms of religious expression will rarely, if ever, fall within these exceptions.

As a general rule, agencies may not regulate employees' personal religious expression on the basis of its content or viewpoint. In other words, agencies generally may not suppress employees' private religious speech in the workplace while leaving unregulated other private employee speech that has a comparable effect on the efficiency of the workplace—including ideological speech on politics and other topics—because to do so would be to engage in presumptively unlawful content or viewpoint discrimination. Agencies, however, may, in their discretion, reasonably regulate the time, place and manner of all employee speech, provided such regulations do not discriminate on the basis of content or viewpoint.

The Federal Government generally has the authority to regulate an employee's private speech, including religious speech, where the employee's interest in that speech is outweighed by the government's interest in promoting the efficiency of the public services it performs. Agencies should exercise this authority evenhandedly and with restraint, and with regard for the fact that Americans are used to expressions of disagreement on controversial subjects, including religious ones. Agencies are not required, however, to permit employees to use work time to pursue religious or ideological agendas. Federal employees are paid to perform official work, not to engage in personal religious or ideological campaigns during work hours.

(1) Expression in Private Work Areas. Employees should be permitted to engage in private religious expression in personal work areas not regularly

open to the public to the same extent that they may engage in nonreligious private expression, subject to reasonable content—and viewpoint-neutral standards and restrictions: such religious expression must be permitted so long as it does not interfere with the agency's carrying out of its official responsibilities.

Examples:

(a) An employee may keep a Bible or Koran on her private desk and read it during breaks.

(b) An agency may restrict all posters, or posters of a certain size, in private work areas, or require that such posters be displayed facing the employee, and not on common walls; but the employer typically cannot single out religious or anti-religious posters for harsher or preferential treatment.

(2) Expression Among Fellow Employees. Employees should be permitted to engage in religious expression with fellow employees, to the same extent that they may engage in comparable nonreligious private expression, subject to reasonable and content-neutral standards and restrictions: such expression should not be restricted so long as it does not interfere with workplace efficiency. Though agencies are entitled to regulate such employee speech based on reasonable predictions of disruption, they should not restrict speech based on merely hypothetical concerns, having little basis in fact, that the speech will have a deleterious effect on workplace efficiency.

Examples:

(a) In informal settings, such as cafeterias and hallways, employees are entitled to discuss their religious views with one another, subject only to the same rules of order as apply to other employee expression. If an agency permits unrestricted nonreligious expression of a controversial nature, it must likewise permit equally controversial religious expression.

(b) Employees are entitled to display religious messages on items of clothing to the same extent that they are permitted to display other comparable messages. So long as they do not convey any governmental endorsement of religion, religious messages may not typically be singled out for suppression.

(c) Employees generally may wear religious medallions over their clothes or so that they are otherwise visible. Typically, this alone will not affect workplace efficiency, and therefore is protected.

(3) Expression Directed at Fellow Employees. Employees are permitted to engage in religious expression directed at fellow employees, and may even attempt to persuade fellow employees of the correctness of their religious views, to the same extent as those employees may engage in comparable speech not involving religion. Some religions encourage adherents to spread the faith at every opportunity, a duty that can encompass the adherent's workplace. As a general matter, proselytizing is as entitled to constitutional protection as any other form of speech—as long as a reasonable observer would not interpret the expression as government endorsement of religion. Employees may urge a colleague to participate or not to participate in religious activities to the same extent that, consistent with concerns of workplace efficiency, they may urge their colleagues to engage in or refrain from other personal endeavors. But employees must refrain from such expression when a fellow employee asks that it stop or otherwise demonstrates that it is unwelcome. (Such expression by supervisors

is subject to special consideration as discussed in Section B(2) of these guidelines.)

Examples:

    (a) During a coffee break, one employee engages another in a polite discussion of why his faith should be embraced. The other employee disagrees with the first employee's religious exhortations, but does not ask that the conversation stop. Under these circumstances, agencies should not restrict or interfere with such speech.

    (b) One employee invites another employee to attend worship services at her church, though she knows that the invitee is a devout adherent of another faith. The invitee is shocked, and asks that the invitation not be repeated. The original invitation is protected, but the employee should honor the request that no further invitations be issued.

    (c) In a parking lot, a non-supervisory employee hands another employee a religious tract urging that she convert to another religion lest she be condemned to eternal damnation. The proselytizing employee says nothing further and does not inquire of his colleague whether she followed the pamphlet's urging. This speech typically should not be restricted.

Though personal religious expression such as that described in these examples, standing alone, is protected in the same way, and to the same extent, as other constitutionally valued speech in the Federal workplace, such expression should not be permitted if it is part of a larger pattern of verbal attacks on fellow employees (or a specific employee) not sharing the faith of the speaker. Such speech, by virtue of its excessive or harassing nature, may constitute religious harassment or create a hostile work environment, as described in Part B(3) of these Guidelines, and an agency should not tolerate it.

(4) Expression in Areas Accessible to the Public. Where the public has access to the Federal workplace, all Federal employers must be sensitive to the Establishment Clause's requirement that expression not create the reasonable impression that the government is sponsoring, endorsing, or inhibiting religion generally, or favoring or disfavoring a particular religion. This is particularly important in agencies with adjudicatory functions.

However, even in workplaces open to the public, not all private employee religious expression is forbidden. For example, Federal employees may wear personal religious jewelry absent special circumstances (such as safety concerns) that might require a ban on all similar nonreligious jewelry. Employees may also display religious art and literature in their personal work areas to the same extent that they may display other art and literature, so long as the viewing public would reasonably understand the religious expression to be that of the employee acting in her personal capacity, and not that of the government itself. Similarly, in their private time employees may discuss religion with willing coworkers in public spaces to the same extent as they may discuss other subjects, so long as the public would reasonably understand the religious expression to be that of the employees acting in their personal capacities.

B.   Religious Discrimination. Federal agencies may not discriminate against employees on the basis of their religion, religious beliefs, or views concerning religion.

(1) Discrimination in Terms and Conditions. No agency within the executive branch may promote, refuse to promote, hire, refuse to hire, or otherwise favor or disfavor, an employee or potential employee because of his or her religion, religious beliefs, or views concerning religion.
Examples:

    (a) A Federal agency may not refuse to hire Buddhists, or impose more onerous requirements on applicants for employment who are Buddhists.

    (b) An agency may not impose, explicitly or implicitly, stricter promotion requirements for Christians, or impose stricter discipline on Jews than on other employees, based on their religion. Nor may Federal agencies give advantages to Christians in promotions, or impose lesser discipline on Jews than on other employees, based on their religion.

    (c) A supervisor may not impose more onerous work requirements on an employee who is an atheist because that employee does not share the supervisor's religious beliefs.

(2) Coercion of Employee's Participation or Nonparticipation in Religious Activities. A person holding supervisory authority over an employee may not, explicitly or implicitly, insist that the employee participate in religious activities as a condition of continued employment, promotion, salary increases, preferred job assignments, or any other incidents of employment. Nor may a supervisor insist that an employee refrain from participating in religious activities outside the workplace except pursuant to otherwise legal, neutral restrictions that apply to employees' off-duty conduct and expression in general (e.g., restrictions on political activities prohibited by the Hatch Act).

    This prohibition leaves supervisors free to engage in some kinds of speech about religion. Where a supervisor's religious expression is not coercive and is understood as his or her personal view, that expression is protected in the Federal workplace in the same way and to the same extent as other constitutionally valued speech. For example, if surrounding circumstances indicate that the expression is merely the personal view of the supervisor and that employees are free to reject or ignore the supervisor's point of view or invitation without any harm to their careers or professional lives, such expression is so protected.

    Because supervisors have the power to hire, fire, or promote, employees may reasonably perceive their supervisors' religious expression as coercive, even if it was not intended as such. Therefore, supervisors should be careful to ensure that their statements and actions are such that employees do not perceive any coercion of religious or non-religious behavior (or respond as if such coercion is occurring), and should, where necessary, take appropriate steps to dispel such misperceptions.
Examples:

    (a) A supervisor may invite co-workers to a son's confirmation in a church, a daughter's bat mitzvah in a synagogue, or to his own wedding at a temple. but—A supervisor should not say to an employee: "I didn't see you in church this week. I expect to see you there this Sunday."

    (b) On a bulletin board on which personal notices unrelated to work regularly are permitted, a supervisor may post a flyer announcing an Easter musical service at her church, with a handwritten notice inviting co-workers to attend. but—A supervisor should not circulate a memo announcing that he will be leading a lunch-hour Talmud class that employees should attend in order to participate in a discussion of career advancement that will convene at the conclusion of the class.

(c) During a wide-ranging discussion in the cafeteria about various non-work related matters, a supervisor states to an employee her belief that religion is important in one's life. Without more, this is not coercive, and the statement is protected in the Federal workplace in the same way, and to the same extent, as other constitutionally valued speech.

(d) A supervisor who is an atheist has made it known that he thinks that anyone who attends church regularly should not be trusted with the public weal. Over a period of years, the supervisor regularly awards merit increases to employees who do not attend church routinely, but not to employees of equal merit who do attend church. This course of conduct would reasonably be perceived as coercive and should be prohibited.

(e) At a lunch-table discussion about abortion, during which a wide range of views are vigorously expressed, a supervisor shares with those he supervises his belief that God demands full respect for unborn life, and that he believes it is appropriate for all persons to pray for the unborn. Another supervisor expresses the view that abortion should be kept legal because God teaches that women must have control over their own bodies. Without more, neither of these comments coerces employees' religious conformity or conduct. Therefore, unless the supervisors take further steps to coerce agreement with their view or act in ways that could reasonably be perceived as coercive, their expressions are protected in the Federal workplace in the same way and to the same extent as other constitutionally valued speech.

(3) Hostile Work Environment and Harassment. The law against workplace discrimination protects Federal employees from being subjected to a hostile environment, or religious harassment, in the form of religiously discriminatory intimidation, or pervasive or severe religious ridicule or insult, whether by supervisors or fellow workers. Whether particular conduct gives rise to a hostile environment, or constitutes impermissible religious harassment, will usually depend upon its frequency or repetitiveness, as well as its severity. The use of derogatory language in an assaultive manner can constitute statutory religious harassment if it is severe or invoked repeatedly. A single incident, if sufficiently abusive, might also constitute statutory harassment. However, although employees should always be guided by general principles of civility and workplace efficiency, a hostile environment is not created by the bare expression of speech with which some employees might disagree. In a country where freedom of speech and religion are guaranteed, citizens should expect to be exposed to ideas with which they disagree.

The examples below are intended to provide guidance on when conduct or words constitute religious harassment that should not be tolerated in the Federal workplace. In a particular case, the question of employer liability would require consideration of additional factors, including the extent to which the agency was aware of the harassment and the actions the agency took to address it.

Examples:

    (a) An employee repeatedly makes derogatory remarks to other employees with whom she is assigned to work about their faith or lack of faith. This typically will constitute religious harassment. An agency should not tolerate such conduct.

    (b) A group of employees subjects a fellow employee to a barrage of comments about his sex life, knowing that the targeted employee would be discomforted and offended by such comments because of his religious beliefs. This typically will constitute harassment, and an agency should not tolerate it.

    (c) A group of employees that share a common faith decides that they want to work exclusively with people who share their views. They engage in a pattern of verbal attacks on other employees who do not share their views, calling them heathens, sinners, and the like. This conduct should not be tolerated.

    (d) Two employees have an angry exchange of words. In the heat of the moment, one makes a derogatory comment about the other's religion. When tempers cool, no more is said. Unless the words are sufficiently severe or pervasive to alter the conditions of the insulted employee's employment or create an abusive working environment, this is not statutory religious harassment.

    (e) Employees wear religious jewelry and medallions over their clothes or so that they are otherwise visible. Others wear buttons with a generalized religious or anti-religious message. Typically, these expressions are personal and do not alone constitute religious harassment.

    (f) In her private work area, a Federal worker keeps a Bible or Koran on her private desk and reads it during breaks. Another employee displays a picture of Jesus and the text of the Lord's Prayer in her private work area. This conduct, without more, is not religious harassment, and does not create an impermissible hostile environment with respect to employees who do not share those religious views, even if they are upset or offended by the conduct.

    (g) During lunch, certain employees gather on their own time for prayer and Bible study in an empty conference room that employees are generally free to use on a first-come, first-served basis. Such a gathering does not constitute religious harassment even if other employees with different views on how to pray might feel excluded or ask that the group be disbanded.

C. Accommodation of Religious Exercise. Federal law requires an agency to accommodate employees' exercise of their religion unless such accommodation would impose an undue hardship on the conduct of the agency's operations. Though an agency need not make an accommodation that will result in more than a *de minimis* cost to the agency, that cost or hardship nevertheless must be real rather than speculative or hypothetical: the accommodation should be made unless it would cause an actual cost to the agency or to other employees or an actual disruption of work, or unless it is otherwise barred by law.

In addition, religious accommodation cannot be disfavored vis-à-vis other, nonreligious accommodations. Therefore, a religious accommodation cannot be denied if the agency regularly permits similar accommodations for nonreligious purposes.

Examples:

    (a) An agency must adjust work schedules to accommodate an employee's religious observance—for example, Sabbath or religious holiday observance—if an adequate substitute is available, or if the employee's absence would not otherwise impose an undue burden on the agency.

    (b) An employee must be permitted to wear religious garb, such as a crucifix, a yarmulke, or a head scarf or hijab, if wearing such attire during the work day is part of the employee's religious practice or expression, so long as the wearing of such garb does not unduly interfere with the functioning of the workplace.

    (c) An employee should be excused from a particular assignment if performance of that assignment would contravene the employee's religious beliefs and the agency would not suffer undue hardship in reassigning the employee to another detail.

    (d) During lunch, certain employees gather on their own time for prayer and Bible study in an empty conference room that employees are generally free to use on a first-come, first-served basis. Such a gathering may not be subject to discriminatory restrictions because of its religious content. In those cases where an agency's work rule imposes a substantial burden on a particular employee's exercise of religion, the agency must go further: an agency should grant the employee an exemption from that rule, unless the agency has a compelling interest in denying the exemption and there is no less restrictive means of furthering that interest.

Examples:

    (a) A corrections officer whose religion compels him or her to wear long hair should be granted an exemption from an otherwise generally applicable hair-length policy unless denial of an exemption is the least restrictive means of preserving safety, security, discipline or other compelling interests.

    (b) An applicant for employment in a governmental agency who is a Jehovah's Witness should not be compelled, contrary to her religious beliefs, to take a loyalty oath whose form is religiously objectionable.

D. Establishment of Religion. Supervisors and employees must not engage in activities or expression that a reasonable observer would interpret as Government endorsement or denigration of religion or a particular religion. Activities of employees need not be officially sanctioned in order to violate this principle; if, in all the circumstances, the activities would leave a reasonable observer with the impression that Government was endorsing, sponsoring, or inhibiting religion generally or favoring or disfavoring a particular religion, they are not permissible. Diverse factors, such as the context of the expression or whether official channels of communication are used, are relevant to what a reasonable observer would conclude.

Examples:

    (a) At the conclusion of each weekly staff meeting and before anyone leaves the room, an employee leads a prayer in which nearly all employees participate. All employees are required to attend the weekly meeting. The supervisor neither explicitly recognizes the prayer as an official function nor explicitly states that no one

need participate in the prayer. This course of conduct is not permitted unless under all the circumstances a reasonable observer
would conclude that the prayer was not officially endorsed.
(b) At Christmas time, a supervisor places a wreath over the entrance
to the office's main reception area. This course of conduct is permitted.

Section 2. Guiding Legal Principles. In applying the guidance set forth in section 1 of this order, executive branch departments and agencies should consider the following legal principles.

A. Religious Expression. It is well-established that the Free Speech Clause of
the First Amendment protects Government employees in the workplace.
This right encompasses a right to speak about religious subjects. The Free
Speech Clause also prohibits the Government from singling out religious
expression for disfavored treatment: "[P]rivate religious speech, far from
being a First Amendment orphan, is as fully protected under the Free
Speech Clause as secular private expression," *Capitol Square Review Board
v. Pinette*, 515 U.S. 753 (1995). Accordingly, in the Government workplace, employee religious expression cannot be regulated because of its
religious character, and such religious speech typically cannot be singled
out for harsher treatment than other comparable expression.

Many religions strongly encourage their adherents to spread the faith
by persuasion and example at every opportunity, a duty that can extend
to the adherents' workplace. As a general matter, proselytizing is entitled to the same constitutional protection as any other form of speech.
Therefore, in the governmental workplace, proselytizing should not be
singled out because of its content for harsher treatment than nonreligious
expression.

However, it is also well-established that the Government in its role
as employer has broader discretion to regulate its employees' speech in
the workplace than it does to regulate speech among the public at large.
Employees' expression on matters of public concern can be regulated if
the employees' interest in the speech is outweighed by the interest of the
Government, as an employer, in promoting the efficiency of the public
services it performs through its employees. Governmental employers also
possess substantial discretion to impose content-neutral and viewpoint-
neutral time, place, and manner rules regulating private employee expression in the workplace (though they may not structure or administer
such rules to discriminate against particular viewpoints). Furthermore,
employee speech can be regulated or discouraged if it impairs discipline
by superiors, has a detrimental impact on close working relationships for
which personal loyalty and confidence are necessary, impedes the performance of the speaker's duties or interferes with the regular operation of
the enterprise, or demonstrates that the employee holds views that could
lead his employer or the public reasonably to question whether he can
perform his duties adequately.

Consistent with its fully protected character, employee religious speech
should be treated, within the Federal workplace, like other expression
on issues of public concern: in a particular case, an employer can discipline an employee for engaging in speech if the value of the speech
is outweighed by the employer's interest in promoting the efficiency of
the public services it performs through its employee. Typically, however,

the religious speech cited as permissible in the various examples included in these Guidelines will not unduly impede these interests and should not be regulated. And rules regulating employee speech, like other rules regulating speech, must be carefully drawn to avoid any unnecessary limiting or chilling of protected speech.

B. Discrimination in Terms and Conditions. Title VII of the Civil Rights Act of 1964 makes it unlawful for employers, both private and public, to "fail or refuse to hire or to discharge any individual, or otherwise to discriminate against any individual with respect to compensation, terms, conditions, or privileges of employment, because of such individual's . . . religion." 42 U.S.C. 2000e-2(a)(1). The Federal Government also is bound by the equal protection component of the Due Process Clause of the Fifth Amendment, which bars intentional discrimination on the basis of religion. Moreover, the prohibition on religious discrimination in employment applies with particular force to the Federal Government, for Article VI, clause 3 of the Constitution bars the Government from enforcing any religious test as a requirement for qualification to any Office. In addition, if a Government law, regulation or practice facially discriminates against employees' private exercise of religion or is intended to infringe upon or restrict private religious exercise, then that law, regulation, or practice implicates the Free Exercise Clause of the First Amendment. Last, under the Religious Freedom Restoration Act, 42 U.S.C. 2000bb-1, Federal governmental action that substantially burdens a private party's exercise of religion can be enforced only if it is justified by a compelling interest and is narrowly tailored to advance that interest.

C. Coercion of Employees' Participation or Nonparticipation in Religious Activities. The ban on religious discrimination is broader than simply guaranteeing nondiscriminatory treatment in formal employment decisions such as hiring and promotion. It applies to all terms and conditions of employment. It follows that the Federal Government may not require or coerce its employees to engage in religious activities or to refrain from engaging in religious activity. For example, a supervisor may not demand attendance at (or a refusal to attend) religious services as a condition of continued employment or promotion, or as a criterion affecting assignment of job duties. *Quid pro quo* discrimination of this sort is illegal. Indeed, wholly apart from the legal prohibitions against coercion, supervisors may not insist upon employees' conformity to religious behavior in their private lives any more than they can insist on conformity to any other private conduct unrelated to employees' ability to carry out their duties.

D. Hostile Work Environment and Harassment. Employers violate Title VII's ban on discrimination by creating or tolerating a "hostile environment" in which an employee is subject to discriminatory intimidation, ridicule, or insult sufficiently severe or pervasive to alter the conditions of the victim's employment. This statutory standard can be triggered (at the very least) when an employee, because of her or his religion or lack thereof, is exposed to intimidation, ridicule, and insult. The hostile conduct—which may take the form of speech—need not come from supervisors or from the employer. Fellow employees can create a hostile environment through their own words and actions.

    The existence of some offensive workplace conduct does not necessarily constitute harassment under Title VII. Occasional and isolated utterances of an epithet that engenders offensive feelings in an employee typically would not affect conditions of employment, and therefore would not in and of itself constitute harassment. A hostile environment, for Title VII purposes, is not created by the bare expression of speech with which one disagrees. For religious harassment to be illegal under Title VII, it must be sufficiently severe or pervasive to alter the conditions of employment and create an abusive working environment. Whether conduct can be the predicate for a finding of religious harassment under Title VII depends on the totality of the circumstances, such as the nature of the verbal or physical conduct at issue and the context in which the alleged incidents occurred. As the Supreme Court has said in an analogous context:

"[W]hether an environment is "hostile" or "abusive" can be determined only by looking at all the circumstances. These may include the frequency of the discriminatory conduct; its severity; whether it is physically threatening or humiliating, or a mere offensive utterance; and whether it unreasonably interferes with an employee's work performance. The effect on the employee's psychological well-being is, of course, relevant to determining whether the plaintiff actually found the environment abusive." *Harris v. Forklift Systems, Inc.*, 510 U.S. 17, 23 (1993).

The use of derogatory language directed at an employee can rise to the level of religious harassment if it is severe or invoked repeatedly. In particular, repeated religious slurs and negative religious stereotypes, or continued disparagement of an employee's religion or ritual practices, or lack thereof, can constitute harassment. It is not necessary that the harassment be explicitly religious in character or that the slurs reference religion: it is sufficient that the harassment is directed at an employee because of the employee's religion or lack thereof. That is to say, Title VII can be violated by employer tolerance of repeated slurs, insults and/or abuse not explicitly religious in nature if that conduct would not have occurred but for the targeted employee's religious belief or lack of religious belief. Finally, although proselytization directed at fellow employees is generally permissible (subject to the special considerations relating to supervisor expression discussed elsewhere in these Guidelines), such activity must stop if the listener asks that it stops or otherwise demonstrates that it is unwelcome.

E. Accommodation of Religious Exercise. Title VII requires employers "to reasonably accommodate . . . an employee's or prospective employee's religious observance or practice" unless such accommodation would impose an "undue hardship on the conduct of the employer's business." 42 U.S.C. 2000e(j). For example, by statute, if an employee's religious beliefs require her to be absent from work, the Federal Government must grant that employee compensation time for overtime work, to be applied against the time lost, unless to do so would harm the ability of the agency to carry out its mission efficiently. 5 U.S.C. 5550a.

Though an employer need not incur more than *de minimis* costs in providing an accommodation, the employer hardship nevertheless must be real rather than speculative or hypothetical. Religious accommodation cannot be disfavored relative to other, nonreligious, accommodations. If an employer regularly permits accommodation for nonreligious purposes, it cannot deny comparable religious accommodation: "Such an arrangement would display a discrimination against religious practices that is the antithesis of reasonableness." *Ansonia Board of Education v. Philbrook*, 479 U.S. 60, 71 (1986).

In the Federal Government workplace, if neutral workplace rules—that is, rules that do not single out religious or religiously motivated conduct for disparate treatment—impose a substantial burden on a particular employee's exercise of religion, the Religious Freedom Restoration Act requires the employer to grant the employee an exemption from that neutral rule, unless the employer has a compelling interest in denying an exemption and there is no less restrictive means of furthering that interest. 42 U.S.C. 2000bb-1.

F. Establishment of Religion. The Establishment Clause of the First Amendment prohibits the Government—including its employees—from acting in a manner that would lead a reasonable observer to conclude that the Government is sponsoring, endorsing or inhibiting religion generally or favoring or disfavoring a particular religion. For example, where the public has access to the Federal workplace, employee religious expression should be prohibited where the public reasonably would perceive that the employee is acting in an official, rather than a private, capacity, or under circumstances that would lead a reasonable observer to conclude that the Government is endorsing or disparaging religion. The Establishment Clause also forbids Federal employees from using Government funds or resources (other than those facilities generally available to government employees) for private religious uses. . . .

## Notes and Questions

1. After this document was released, the Supreme Court handed down a decision that is relevant to these matters. In its decision in *Garcetti v. Ceballos*, 547 U.S. 410 (2006), the Court basically held that government employees do not enjoy free speech rights regarding expression that is part of their job duties. Thus, the government may restrict personal speech, including religious or anti-religious speech, that is understood to be part of an employee's work responsibilities. In this same case, however, the Court noted that it has "made clear that [governmental] employees do not surrender all their First Amendment rights by reason of their employment." If a person speaks as a citizen, rather than pursuant to official governmental duties, and the speech addresses a matter of "public concern," then such expression may be constitutionally protected.

   Assume that an elementary school teacher was fired for offering her personal opinion in the classroom on whether teachers should be able to lead prayer in public schools. Is the school's decision justified under the *Garcetti* case? See *Mayer v. Monroe County Community School*, 474 F.3d 477 (7th Cir. 2007).

   Assume that, during a city council meeting, a city employee criticized the council for allowing prayers before the council's meeting. The city employee's job is to oversee financial matters for the municipality, and she reported on those matters during an earlier portion of the meeting. If the employee was fired for her criticism of the council on the prayer issue, was the dismissal proper? See *Lindsey v. City of Orrick*, 2007 U.S. App. LEXIS 15149 (8th Cir. 2007).

2. Assume a supervisor in the Department of Agriculture begins staff meetings with prayer. The supervisor also posts notes about special events at her

church on the communal bulletin board at work and frequently invites her subordinates to attend church with her. Evaluate the constitutionality of each of these actions.

3. As part of her religious practice, a United States Postal Service clerk places a prominent crucifix in her work area, an area frequented by customers each day. Other clerks post pictures of their children, team logos or inspirational sayings in their work areas. Should a supervisor require the worker to remove the crucifix from her work area?

4. Assume the Attorney General of the United States, the top official at the U.S. Department of Justice, holds Bible studies in his office once a week prior to the commencement of the work day. It is made clear that all Department staff are welcome, but it also is emphasized that a person's choice not to attend will in no way affect his or her employment at the agency. Is this practice constitutional? Is it consistent with the guidelines?

5. An employee of the Department of Motor Vehicles tells his customers to "have a blessed day" when he concludes a transaction with them. One of his customers complains that the employee's conduct violates the Establishment Clause. Does it?

6. Some Muslim employees at the federal Department of Transportation have asked for the use of one of the conference rooms for their daily prayers. The conference room has glass walls such that it is visible to both Department employees and to citizen tours of the Department. Should the Department accommodate this request?

7. Assume a state employer installs foot-wash basins in its bathrooms. It does so because it has a number of Muslim employees who need to wash their feet before praying during their break, and they are creating safety hazards (pools of water on the floor) in the bathroom when they attempt to wash their feet in the sinks. Should the state employer's action be seen as an appropriate accommodation of religious practice or an inappropriate governmental endorsement or advancement of such practices?

   Assume that a court finds that the state's action in this case was appropriate. What should the state's response be if a group of Jewish employees now seek to have the work cafeteria offer kosher food? What should the state's response be if a group of Christian employees now asks it to provide rugs for Christians who wish to kneel while praying during their breaks?

## CHAPTER 22

# RELIGIOUS PREFERENCES/DELEGATIONS

In its actions affecting religious faith and institutions, may the government prefer some religions over others? The short answer is "No." The commitment to nonpreferential treatment of religion, or "sect equality," extends back to the founding era. While people during the founding period may have disagreed over the precise understandings of disestablishment and liberty of conscience, there was universal agreement that all religious groups should receive the same treatment from, and stand in the same relationship to, the government (albeit some during the founding period limited that principle of nonpreferential treatment to Protestants or Christians).

Under the no establishment principle, the idea of neutrality includes the notion that government may not prefer one or some religions over others. The no establishment principle commands that government may neither advance nor hinder religion, or, in Justice Sandra Day O'Connor's words, government is neither to communicate a message of endorsement nor disapproval of religion.[1] If government gives preferential treatment to some religions or religious organizations, it advances or endorses the preferred and hinders or disapproves the unpreferred. This is problematic, Justice O'Connor wrote, because:

> The Establishment Clause prohibits government from making adherence to a religion relevant in any way to a person's standing in the political community. . . . Endorsement [of religion] sends a message to nonadherents that they are outsiders, not full members of the political community, and an accompanying message to adherents that they are insiders, favored members of the community. Disapproval sends the opposite message.[2]

Accordingly, the Supreme Court has ruled that "the prohibition against government endorsement of religion 'preclude[s] government from conveying or attempting to convey a message that religion or *a particular religious belief* is favored or preferred.'"[3]

Also, government may not assign its powers to religious organizations. This prohibition implicates two concerns. In delegating authority to a religious body, the government will inevitably assign power to a particular religious group, thereby advancing its religious mission while conveying the impression that the recipient of its authority is favored or preferred. At one point, the Court spoke about the dangers to representative democracy presented by the "graphic symbol of the 'concert or union or dependency' of church and state."[4] The second concern raised by delegations involves the prohibition on excessive government entanglements with religion. Delegations of authority will likely involve more than the mere transfer of power but will necessitate an ongoing relationship through a "fusion of governmental and religious functions."[5] These precepts have been illustrated by many cases in this book in sections that covered other issues. But there are some cases that focus specifically on the issues of preferential treatment and giving governmental authority to religious groups. Those are the subject of this chapter.

## GOVERNMENT PREFERENCES OF RELIGION

Government preferences of religion can take two forms: preferential legal treatment of one denomination or religion over others; and, government preferences of religion over non-religion. The latter form of preferentialism, paradoxically called "nonprefrentialism," has been highly controversial among legal scholars and judges for some time. The debate over whether the Establishment Clause exists only to ensure that aid to religion be given on an equal, nonpreferential basis is addressed in the introductory "Themes and Trends" chapter, and the issue of nonpreferentialism has appeared in several cases discussed in earlier chapters. Compare *Texas Monthly v. Bullock* (1989) (striking a nonpreferential tax benefit for religious publications only); with *Corporation of Presiding Bishop v. Amos* (1987) (holding that when the "government acts with the proper purpose of lifting a regulation that burdens the exercise of religion, we see no reason to require that the exemption comes packaged with benefits to secular entities"). See also Justice Rehnquist's dissent in *Wallace v. Jaffree* (1985) where he endorsed the concept of nonpreferential treatment of religion.

This section is concerned with the former form of preferential treatment of religion: of legal preferences for some expressions of faith over others. Such laws are rarely enacted, at least purposefully, but some cases have made their way through the courts. For example, in *Church of the Lukumi Babalu Aye v. City of Hialeah* (1993) [see chapter 8], the Court held that a city ordinance prohibiting "animal sacrifice" was enacted to impose a burden on a particular religious group, the Santerias. [In Lukumi, the Court chose to resolve the case as involving discrimination under the Free Exercise Clause, rather than as an instance of government disapproval of a particular religion under the Establishment Clause.] As mentioned, the abolition of religious preferences was one aspect of disestablishment upon which all (or almost all) members of the founding generation agreed. Still, religious preferences existed within the operation of the remaining state establishments in New England, despite constitutional guarantees of "equal protection" and that "no subordination of any one sect or denomination to another shall ever be established by law." See Article III of the Massachusetts Constitution of 1780. And many state constitutions and statutes maintained regimes of religious preferentialism by limiting public office holding and voting to Christians or Protestants and imposing religious prerequisites for the taking of oaths.

It was within this last area, that of religious tests or qualifications for public office holding, that the new national constitution broke with tradition and common practice in all the states at that time. Article VI, clause 3 of the Constitution provides that " . . . no religious Test shall ever be required as a Qualification to any office or public Trust under the United States." When proposed and adopted by the Constitutional Convention in 1787, the provision was relatively uncontroversial; because the Constitution applied only to the federal government and not to the states, most delegates supported the ban on religious tests because it would not affect the practices at the state level while it would prevent the President and Congress from aligning the federal government with any religious divisions that existed in parts of the country. During the ratification of the Constitution, however, the ban on religious tests became a contentious issue, with one Anti-federalist charging that "according to this [provision] we may have a Papist, a Mohomatan, a Deist, yea an Atheist at the helm of Government."[6] The question of whether the national constitution should retain at least *this* religious preference was hotly debated in several state ratifying conventions. Opponents of religious preferentialism viewed the test ban as a crucial component in securing religious freedom and equality in the new nation. James Iredell, a future justice on the U. S. Supreme Court, defended Article VI, clause 3 in the North Carolina Convention, stating that "I consider the clause under consideration as one of the strongest proofs that could be adduced, that it was the intention of those who formed this system, to establish a general religious liberty in America."[7] The states ratified the Constitution with the religious test ban in tact, and the clause would serve as an example to the states as they gradually abolished similar legal disabilities and preferences.

A handful of states retained their religious requirements for public office holding well into the twentieth century. One such state was Maryland, whose constitution required that office holders believe in the existence of God. Roy Torcaso was appointed a Notary Public by the Governor of Maryland but was not allowed to assume office because he could not profess a belief in God. Torcaso sued, asserting the state maintained a religious preference. He won at the Supreme Court but not on Article VI grounds. Rather, the Court held that the "Maryland religious test for public office unconstitutionally invades the appellant's freedom of belief and religion." Thus, rather than single out one of the religion clauses, the Court indicated that this requirement violated the First Amendment's religious liberty guarantees generally.

---

## TORCASO v. WATKINS
### 367 U.S. 488 (1961)

MR. JUSTICE BLACK delivered the opinion of the court.

Article 37 of the Declaration of Rights of the Maryland Constitution provides: "[N]o religious test ought ever to be required as a qualification for any office of profit or trust in this State, other than a declaration of belief in the existence of God . . . ."

There is, and can be, no dispute about the purpose or effect of the Maryland Declaration of Rights requirement before us—it sets up a religious test which was designed to and, if valid, does bar every person who refuses to declare a belief in God from holding a public "office of profit or trust" in Maryland. The power and authority of the State of Maryland thus is put on the side of one particular sort of believers—those who are willing to say they believe in "the existence of God." . . .

We repeat and again reaffirm that neither a State nor the Federal Government can constitutionally force a person "to profess a belief or disbelief in any religion." [*Everson v. Board of Education,* 330 U.S. 1, 15.] Neither can constitutionally pass laws or impose requirements which aid all religions as against non-believers, and neither can aid those religions based on a belief in the existence of God as against those religions founded on different beliefs. . . .

This Maryland religious test for public office unconstitutionally invades the appellant's freedom of belief and religion and therefore cannot be enforced against him.

---

As the situation in *Torcaso* indicates, preferential treatment of religion is commonly accompanied with unfavorable treatment of those individuals and religions not in the favored class. They are the ones who will challenge the legal preference, not those in the favored class.

Occasionally, though, a law will not affect a legal preference but work to impose a burden on a particular religious group or practice. Rarely are such laws overt (e.g., a law to banish Baptists from Texas); more commonly, they are in the form of subtle regulations that impose burdens that are particular to a religious group. In the 1960s and 1970s there was considerable apprehension across the country about "cults," frequently called "destructive cults," an indication of the nature of the concern.[8] "Cult," was commonly used (pejoratively) to describe newer, nontraditional religious movements that usually separated themselves from the greater society, at least spiritually, if not physically, in communes. Cults were perceived to be organized and operated by unscrupulous leaders who wanted power and money. Critics charged they used religion to deceive both their members and the general public to get their wealth. Cults were frequently accused of "brainwashing" their recruits and even of holding them in mental, if not physical, captivity. The "brainwashing" often involved indoctrinating new members into thinking that the theology of the cult was the only true theology, in contrast to the faith of the members' traditional religions. This had the effect of inducing the members to reject their parents and extended family. In short, many charged that cults were a threat to the individuals who were recruited into the cults, to, families, and to the society as a whole, in that the cults promoted secrecy and a perversion of religious freedom because they recruited by deception and brainwashing. The worst fears of cult watchers were realized when, on 18 November 1978, 909 members of the People's Temple (including 294 children) died from ingesting poison at the insistence of the group's leader, Jim Jones. The nation was aghast not only at the loss of life, but at the apparent willingness of these cult members to follow the will of their leader even to death. This was but one of many, although the worst, of incidents that convinced people that such groups not only had unusual beliefs, but that they also were potentially dangerous and destructive.

It was in this environment (but before the People's Temple tragedy) that Minnesota amended a law ostensibly to protect Minnesotans from fraud, but probably to target and impair cult groups, although those two goals were not mutually exclusive. In 1961 the legislature passed a law requiring all charitable organizations to register with the Minnesota Department of Commerce and annually file reports detailing the amount and source of their revenue and how much was spent on management, fundraising, and public education and how much revenue went to support the charitable work for which the organization raised funds. Organizations that did not meet state criteria for honest behavior, including excessive administrative expenses, or were guilty of fraudulent solicitation of funds could have their registration revoked.

From 1961 until 1978 all religious organizations were exempt from the reporting requirement. But in March 1978, the legislature amended the law to require religious organizations that received 50 percent or more of their revenue from nonmembers to make the revenue reports to the state. It was common knowledge that groups such as the Unification Church (commonly known as "Moonies" after their founder and leader, Rev. Sun Myung Moon), the Hare Krishnas, the Children of God, Jews for Jesus, and other such groups regularly solicited money from strangers in shopping malls, airports, city parks, and on the streets. However, religious organizations that received 50 percent or more of their revenue from their own members remained exempt from filing the reports.

At that point several members of the Unification Church, including Valente, and the church itself, sued, claiming the law violated their First Amendment rights of free exercise of religion and free expression and their Fourteenth Amendment right to equal protection of the law. They also argued that because the law discriminated among religious organizations, it violated the Establishment Clause. The Court, in an opinion written by Justice William Brennan that focused on the Establishment Clause dimension of the case, found in favor of the Unification Church. The Court stated that the Establishment Clause does not allow government to prefer one religious denomination over another. Yet that was precisely what Minnesota had done with its fifty percent rule, Brennan wrote. In reading the decision, see if you can identify how the fifty percent rule preferred some religions but not others and in what ways this preferential treatment contravened the Establishment Clause. Also look for how the Court addressed the various justifications the state offered for the rule.

---

### LARSON v. VALENTE
456 U.S. 228 (1982)

JUSTICE BRENNAN delivered the opinion of the Court.

The principal question presented by this appeal is whether a Minnesota statute, imposing certain registration and reporting requirements upon only those religious organizations that solicit more than fifty percent of their funds from nonmembers, discriminates against such organizations in violation of the Establishment Clause of the First Amendment. . . .

### III
### A

The clearest command of the Establishment Clause is that one religious denomination cannot be officially preferred over another. . . .

This constitutional prohibition of denominational preferences is inextricably connected with the continuing vitality of the Free Exercise Clause. Madison once noted: "Security for civil rights must be the same as that for religious rights. It consists in the one case in the multiplicity of interests and in the other in the multiplicity of sects." Madison's vision—freedom for all religion being guaranteed by free competition between religions—naturally assumed that every denomination would be equally at liberty to exercise and propagate its beliefs. But such equality would be impossible in an atmosphere of official denominational preference. Free exercise thus can be guaranteed only when legislators—and voters—are required to accord to their own religions the very same treatment given to small, new, or unpopular denominations. . . .

[Also,] since *Everson v. Board of Education*, 330 U.S. 1 (1947), this Court has adhered to the principle, clearly manifested in the history and logic of the Establishment Clause, that no State can "pass laws which aid one religion" or that "prefer one religion over another." *Id.*, 15. This principle of denominational neutrality has been restated on many occasions. In *Zorach v. Clauson*, 343 U.S. 306 (1952), we said that "[t]he government must be neutral when it comes to competition between sects." *Id.*, 314. In short, when we are presented with a state law granting a denominational preference, our precedents demand that we treat the law as suspect and that we apply strict scrutiny in adjudging its constitutionality.

B

The fifty percent rule of § 309.515, subd. 1(b), clearly grants denominational preferences of the sort consistently and firmly deprecated in our precedents. Consequently, that rule must be invalidated unless it is justified by a compelling governmental interest, and unless it is closely fitted to further that interest. With that standard of review in mind, we turn to an examination of the governmental interest asserted by appellants.

Appellants assert, and we acknowledge, that the State of Minnesota has a significant interest in protecting its citizens from abusive practices in the solicitation of funds for charity, and that this interest retains importance when the solicitation is conducted by a religious organization. We thus agree with the Court of Appeals that the Act, "viewed as a whole, has a valid secular purpose," and we will therefore assume, *arguendo*, that the Act generally is addressed to a sufficiently "compelling" governmental interest. But our inquiry must focus more narrowly, upon the distinctions drawn by § 309.515, subd. 1(b), itself: Appellants must demonstrate that the challenged fifty percent rule is closely fitted to further the interest that it assertedly serves.

Appellants argue that § 309.515, subd. 1(b)'s distinction between contributions solicited from members and from nonmembers is eminently sensible. They urge that members are reasonably assumed to have significant control over the solicitation of contributions from themselves to their organization, and over the expenditure of the funds that they contribute, as well. Further, appellants note that as a matter of Minnesota law, members of organizations have greater access than nonmembers to the financial records of the organization. Appellants conclude:

> Where the safeguards of membership funding do not exist, the need for public disclosure is obvious. . . .
>     . . . As public contributions increase as a percentage of total contributions, the need for public disclosure increases. . . . The particular point at which public disclosure should be required . . . is a determination for the legislature. In this case, the Act's 'majority' distinction is a compelling point, since it is at this point that the organization becomes predominantly public-funded.

We reject the argument, for it wholly fails to justify the only aspect of § 309.515, subd. 1(b), under attack—the selective fifty percent rule. Appellants' argument is based on three distinct premises: that members of a religious organization can and will exercise supervision and control over the organization's solicitation activities when membership contributions exceed fifty percent; that membership control, assuming its existence, is an adequate safeguard against abusive solicitations of the public by the organization; and that the need for public disclosure rises in proportion with the *percentage* of nonmember contributions. Acceptance of all three of these premises is necessary to appellants' conclusion, but we find no substantial support for any of them in the record.

Regarding the first premise, there is simply nothing suggested that would justify the assumption that a religious organization will be supervised and controlled by its members simply because they contribute more than half of the organization's solicited income. Even were we able to accept appellants' doubtful assumption that members will *supervise* their religious organization under such circumstances, the record before us is wholly barren of support for appellants' further assumption that members will effectively *control* the organization if they contribute more than half of its solicited income. Appellants have offered no evidence whatever that members of religious organizations exempted by § 309.515, subd. 1(b)'s fifty percent rule in fact control their organizations. Indeed, the legislative history of § 309.515, subd. 1(b), indicates precisely to the contrary. In short, the first premise of appellants' argument has no merit.

Nor do appellants offer any stronger justification for their second premise—that membership control is an adequate safeguard against abusive solicitations of the public by the organization. This premise runs directly contrary to the central thesis of the entire Minnesota charitable solicitations Act—namely, that charitable organizations soliciting contributions from the public cannot be relied upon to regulate themselves, and that state regulation is accordingly necessary. Appellants offer nothing to suggest why religious organizations should be treated any differently in this respect. And even if we were to assume that the members of religious organizations have some incentive, absent in nonreligious organizations, to protect the interests of nonmembers solicited by the organization, appellants' premise would still fail to justify the fifty percent rule: Appellants offer no reason why the members of religious organizations exempted under § 309.515, subd. 1(b)'s fifty percent rule should have any *greater* incentive to protect nonmembers than the members of non-exempted religious organizations have. Thus we also reject appellants' second premise as without merit.

Finally, we find appellants' third premise—that the need for public disclosure rises in proportion with the percentage of nonmember contributions—also without merit. The flaw in appellants' reasoning here may be illustrated by the following example. Church A raises $10 million, 20 percent from nonmembers. Church B raises $50,000, 60 percent from nonmembers. Appellants would argue that although the public contributed $2 million to Church A and only $30,000 to Church B, there is less need for public disclosure with respect to Church A than with respect to Church B. We disagree; the need for public disclosure more plausibly rises in proportion with the *absolute amount*, rather than with the *percentage*, of nonmember contributions. The State of Minnesota has itself adopted this view elsewhere in § 309.515: With qualifications not relevant here, charitable organizations that receive annual nonmember contributions of less than $10,000 are exempted from the registration and reporting requirements of the Act.

We accordingly conclude that appellants have failed to demonstrate that the fifty percent rule in § 309.515, subd. 1(b), is "closely fitted" to further a "compelling governmental interest."

## C

As our citations of *Board of Education v. Allen* and *Walz v. Tax Comm'n*, indicated, the *Lemon v. Kurtzman* "tests" are intended to apply to laws affording a uniform benefit to all religions, and not to provisions, like § 309.515, subd. 1(b)'s fifty percent rule, that discriminate among religions. Although application of the *Lemon* tests is not necessary to the disposition of the case before us, those tests do reflect the same concerns that warranted the application of strict scrutiny to § 309.515, subd. 1(b)'s fifty percent rule. The Court of Appeals found that rule to be invalid under the first two *Lemon* tests. We view the third of those tests as most directly implicated in the present case. . . . Justice Harlan well described the problems of entanglement in his separate opinion in *Walz*, where he observed that governmental involvement in programs concerning religion

> may be so direct or in such degree as to engender a risk of politiciz-
> ing religion. . . . [R]eligious groups inevitably represent certain points of
> view and not infrequently assert them in the political arena, as evidenced
> by the continuing debate respecting birth control and abortion laws. Yet
> history cautions that political fragmentation on sectarian lines must be
> guarded against. . . . 397 U.S., 695

The Minnesota statute challenged here is illustrative of this danger. By their "very nature," the distinctions drawn by § 309.515, subd. 1(b), and its fifty percent rule "engender a risk of politicizing religion"—a risk, indeed, that has already been substantially realized.

It is plain that the principal effect of the fifty percent rule in § 309.515, subd. 1(b), is to impose the registration and reporting requirements of the Act on some religious organizations but not on others. It is also plain that, as the Court of Appeals noted, "[t]he benefit conferred [by exemption] constitutes a substantial advantage; the burden of compliance with the Act is certainly not *de minimis*." We do not suggest that the burdens of compliance with the Act would be intrinsically impermissible if they were imposed evenhandedly. But this statute does not operate evenhandedly, nor was it designed to do so: The fifty percent rule of § 309.515, subd. 1(b), effects the selective legislative imposition of burdens and advantages upon particular denominations. The "risk of politicizing religion" that inheres in such legislation is obvious, and indeed is confirmed by the provision's legislative history. For the history of § 309.515, subd. 1(b)'s fifty percent rule demonstrates that the provision was drafted with the explicit intention of including particular religious denominations and excluding others. . . .

In short, the fifty percent rule's capacity—indeed, its express design—to burden or favor selected religious denominations led the Minnesota Legislature to discuss the characteristics of various sects with a view towards "religious gerrymandering," *Gillette v. United States*, 401 U.S. 437, 452 (1971). As the CHIEF JUSTICE stated in *Lemon*, 403 U.S., 620: "This kind of state inspection and evaluation of the religious content of a religious organization is fraught with the sort of entanglement that the Constitution forbids. It is a relationship pregnant with dangers of excessive government direction . . . of churches."

IV

In sum, we conclude that the fifty percent rule of § 309.515, subd. 1(b), is not closely fitted to the furtherance of any compelling governmental interest asserted by appellants, and that the provision therefore violates the Establishment Clause. Indeed, we think that § 309.515, subd. 1(b)'s fifty percent rule sets up precisely the sort of official denominational preference that the Framers of the First Amendment forbade. Accordingly, we hold that appellees cannot be compelled to register and report under the Act on the strength of that provision.

The judgment of the Court of Appeals is

*Affirmed.* . . .

JUSTICE WHITE, with whom JUSTICE REHNQUIST joins, dissenting. . . .

II

I have several difficulties with this disposition of the case. First, the Court employs a legal standard wholly different from that applied in the courts below. The premise for the Court's standard is that the challenged provision is a deliberate and explicit legislative preference for some religious denominations over others. But there was no such finding in the District Court. . . .

[Second, the Court declares that this] "is not simply a facially neutral statute" but one that makes "explicit and deliberate distinctions between different religious organizations." The rule itself, however, names no churches or denominations that are entitled to or denied the exemption. It neither qualifies nor disqualifies a church based on the kind or variety of its religious belief. Some religions will qualify and some will not, but this depends on the source of their contributions, not on their brand of religion.

To say that the rule on its face represents an explicit and deliberate preference for some religious beliefs over others is not credible. The Court offers no support for this assertion other than to agree with the Court of Appeals that the limitation might burden the less well organized denominations. This conclusion, itself, is a product of assumption and speculation. . . .

Third, I cannot join the Court's easy rejection of the State's submission that a valid secular purpose justifies basing the exemption on the percentage of external funding. This Court, preferring its own judgment of the realities of fundraising by religious organizations to that of the state legislature, rejects the State's submission that organizations depending on their members for more than half of their funds do not pose the same degree of danger as other religious organizations. In the course of doing so, the Court expressly disagrees with the notion that members in general can be relied upon to control their organizations.

I do not share the Court's view of our omniscience. The State has the same interest in requiring registration by organizations soliciting most of their funds from the public as it would have in requiring any charitable organization to register, including a religious organization, if it wants to solicit funds. And if the State determines that its interest in preventing fraud does not extend to those who do not raise a majority of their funds from the public, its interest in imposing the requirement on others is not thereby reduced in the least. . . .

I would reverse the judgment of the Court of Appeals. . . .

## Notes and Questions

1. In *Larson* the Court ruled that government cannot give preferential treatment to some religions. Is this the same as the idea that the government should be able to provide aid to religious groups on a nonpreferential basis? If so, what do you make of the fact that, with regard to nonpreferential aid, the interpretive principle generally is designed to approve of government support for religion whereas in *Larson* the government was commanded to leave religion alone?

2. Can you think of other circumstances, historical or contemporary, in which the *Larson* decision would apply? One example is *Cruz v. Beto*, 405 U.S. 319 (1972), discussed briefly in chapter 7. There, the Texas prison system refused to allow Cruz, a Buddhist, to use the prison chapel to hold religious services, even though it afforded that benefit to Protestant, Catholic and Jewish prisoners. The Court held: "If Cruz was a Buddhist and if he was denied a reasonable opportunity of pursuing his faith comparable to the opportunity afforded fellow prisoners who adhere to conventional religious precepts, then there was palpable discrimination by the State against the Buddhist religion [in violation of the First Amendment]." Ibid., 322.

3. The majority's discussion of how the Minnesota statute "grants denominational preferences" is quite brief; most of the opinion is reserved to scrutinizing the state's justifications for the statute. Does the mere fact that a law imposes reporting requirements on some denominations but not others, but not based on their religious beliefs, turn that law into a forbidden religious preference? As Justice White argues in his dissent: "Some religions will qualify and some will not, but this depends on the source of their contributions, not on their brand of religion." Suppose a state law requires churches and other charitable organizations that receive more than $100,000 in contributions per year to register with the Secretary of State's office and file a yearly report that itemizes receipts and expenditures. How is this law that affects some churches but not others different from the Minnesota statute in *Larson*?

4. The dissenters are correct that the Minnesota statute did not identify a religious group by name or according to any religious practice. Since that is the case, what does *Larson* say about the breadth of the nonpreference rule? Is a legislature prohibited from addressing a perceived social problem simply because it is unique to the practices of one religion? What was the problem in the *Lukumi Babalu Aye* case—that the city council outlawed animal killing, animal sacrifice, or sacrificial practices unique to one religion? Suppose a state requires all parents or guardians to seek medical treatment for children with serious or life-threatening diseases. Is such a law unconstitutional because it places a unique religious burden on Christian Science parents?

5. Does requiring religious groups to register with the government, whether or not they gain more than fifty percent of their revenue from nonmembers, raise other separation of church and state concerns?

## GOVERNMENT DELEGATIONS OF AUTHORITY TO RELIGION

A different kind of Establishment Clause case faced the Court in *Larkin v. Grendel's Den*.[9] The issue was whether it was permissible for a governmental entity to delegate regulatory authority to religious institutions. Land use and zoning laws across the country commonly prohibit adult theaters/bookstores, bars serving alcohol, and related entertainment establishments from locating in close proximity to schools, playgrounds, and places of worship. The required distance between these institutions and places of presumed antithetical character varies according to the jurisdiction, sometimes 500, 750, or even 1,000 feet.

Massachusetts had such a law. It required a 500 foot distance between schools and churches and businesses that served alcohol. What made this law different from the multitude of similar laws around the nation, and what brought it to the Court, was that it vested the veto power denying the liquor license in the school or religious institution. The case originated when a restaurant, Grendel's Den, in Harvard Square in Cambridge, Massachusetts, applied for a liquor license. The problem was that its back wall was ten feet from the back wall of the Holy Cross Armenian Catholic Church. When the church learned that Grendel's Den had applied for the liquor license, it notified the Cambridge License Commission of its objection and the Commission denied the license. After seeking administrative remedy, Grendel's Den sued the Commission, claiming among other things, that the law violated the Establishment Clause.

When the case got to the Supreme Court, Chief Justice Warren Burger wrote an opinion in favor of Grendel's Den, holding that the law did, indeed, violate the Establishment Clause. Burger applied the second and third parts of the *Lemon* test. The law had the principal and primary effect of advancing religion and resulted in excessive governmental entanglement with religion. In reading the opinion, consider how the law advances the religious mission of the church. Also consider whether such delegations of authority implicate any other establishment concerns.

---

## LARKIN v. GRENDEL'S DEN
### 459 U.S. 116 (1982)

CHIEF JUSTICE BURGER delivered the opinion of the Court.

The question presented by this appeal is whether a Massachusetts statute, which vests in the governing bodies of churches and schools the power effectively to veto applications for liquor licenses within a 500-foot radius of the church or school, violates the Establishment Clause of the First Amendment or the Due Process Clause of the Fourteenth Amendment.

I

A

Appellee operates a restaurant located in the Harvard Square area of Cambridge, Mass. The Holy Cross Armenian Catholic Parish is located adjacent to the restaurant; the back walls of the two buildings are 10 feet apart. In 1977, appellee applied to the Cambridge License Commission for approval of an alcoholic beverages license for the restaurant.

Section 16C of Chapter 138 of the Massachusetts General Laws provides: "Premises . . . located within a radius of five hundred feet of a church or school shall not be licensed for the sale of alcoholic beverages if the governing body of such church or school files written objection thereto."

Holy Cross Church objected to appellee's application, expressing concern over "having *so many* licenses so near" (emphasis in original). The License Commission voted to deny the application, citing only the objection of Holy Cross Church and noting that the church "is within 10 feet of the proposed location." . . .

Appellee then sued the License Commission and the Beverages Control Commission in United States District Court. . . .

## II

### A

Appellants contend that the State may, without impinging on the Establishment Clause of the First Amendment, enforce what it describes as a "zoning" law in order to shield schools and places of divine worship from the presence nearby of liquor-dispensing establishments. It is also contended that a zone of protection around churches and schools is essential to protect diverse centers of spiritual, educational, and cultural enrichment. It is to that end that the State has vested in the governing bodies of all schools, public or private, and all churches, the power to prevent the issuance of liquor licenses for any premises within 500 feet of their institutions.

Plainly schools and churches have a valid interest in being insulated from certain kinds of commercial establishments, including those dispensing liquor. Zoning laws have long been employed to this end, and there can be little doubt about the power of a state to regulate the environment in the vicinity of schools, churches, hospitals, and the like by exercise of reasonable zoning laws. . . .

The zoning function is traditionally a governmental task requiring the "balancing [of] numerous competing considerations," and courts should properly "refrain from reviewing the merits of [such] decisions, absent a showing of arbitrariness or irrationality." . . .

However, § 16C is not simply a legislative exercise of zoning power. As the Massachusetts Supreme Judicial Court concluded, § 16C delegates to private, nongovernmental entities power to veto certain liquor license applications. We need not decide whether, or upon what conditions, such power may ever be delegated to nongovernmental entities; here, of two classes of institutions to which the legislature has delegated this important decisionmaking power, one is secular, but one is religious. Under these circumstances, the deference normally due a legislative zoning judgment is not merited.

### B

The purposes of the First Amendment guarantees relating to religion were twofold: to foreclose state interference with the practice of religious faiths, and to foreclose the establishment of a state religion familiar in other 18th-century systems. Religion and government, each insulated from the other, could then coexist. Jefferson's idea of a "wall" was a useful figurative illustration to emphasize the concept of separateness. Some limited and incidental entanglement between church and state authority is inevitable in a complex modern society, but the concept of a "wall" of separation is a useful signpost. Here that "wall"

is substantially breached by vesting discretionary governmental powers in religious bodies. . . .

The purpose of § 16C, as described by the District Court, is to "protec[t]
spiritual, cultural, and educational centers from the 'hurly-burly' associated
with liquor outlets." There can be little doubt that this embraces valid secular
legislative purposes. However, these valid secular objectives can be readily
accomplished by other means—either through an absolute legislative ban on
liquor outlets within reasonable prescribed distances from churches, schools,
hospitals, and like institutions, or by ensuring a hearing for the views of affected institutions at licensing proceedings where, without question, such views
would be entitled to substantial weight.

Appellants argue that § 16C has only a remote and incidental effect on the
advancement of religion. The highest court in Massachusetts, however, has
construed the statute as conferring upon churches a veto power over governmental licensing authority. Section 16C gives churches the right to determine
whether a particular applicant will be granted a liquor license, or even which
one of several competing applicants will receive a license.

The churches' power under the statute is standardless, calling for no reasons, findings, or reasoned conclusions. That power may therefore be used
by churches to promote goals beyond insulating the church from undesirable
neighbors; it could be employed for explicitly religious goals, for example,
favoring liquor licenses for members of that congregation or adherents of that
faith. We can assume that churches would act in good faith in their exercise
of the statutory power, yet § 16C does not by its terms require that churches'
power be used in a religiously neutral way. "[T]he potential for conflict inheres
in the situation," *Levitt v. Committee for Public Education*, 413 U.S. 472, 480
(1973); and appellants have not suggested any "effective means of guaranteeing" that the delegated power "will be used exclusively for secular, neutral, and
nonideological purposes." *Committee for Public Education & Religious Liberty
v. Nyquist*, 413 U.S., 780 (1973). In addition, the mere appearance of a joint
exercise of legislative authority by Church and State provides a significant
symbolic benefit to religion in the minds of some by reason of the power conferred. It does not strain our prior holdings to say that the statute can be seen
as having a "primary" and "principal" effect of advancing religion.

Turning to the third phase of the inquiry called for by *Lemon v. Kurtzman*,
we see that we have not previously had occasion to consider the entanglement
implications of a statute vesting significant governmental authority in churches. This statute enmeshes churches in the exercise of substantial governmental
powers contrary to our consistent interpretation of the Establishment Clause;
"[t]he objective is to prevent, as far as possible, the intrusion of either [Church
or State] into the precincts of the other." *Lemon v. Kurtzman*, 614. . . .

[T]he core rationale underlying the Establishment Clause is preventing
"a fusion of governmental and religious functions," *Abington School District
v. Schempp*, (1963). The Framers did not set up a system of government in
which important, discretionary governmental powers would be delegated to
or shared with religious institutions.

Section 16C substitutes the unilateral and absolute power of a church for
the reasoned decisionmaking of a public legislative body acting on evidence
and guided by standards, on issues with significant economic and political
implications. The challenged statute thus enmeshes churches in the processes of government and creates the danger of "[p]olitical fragmentation and

divisiveness on religious lines," *Lemon v. Kurtzman*, 623. Ordinary human experience and a long line of cases teach that few entanglements could be more offensive to the spirit of the Constitution.

The judgment of the Court of Appeals is

*Affirmed. . . .*

---

### NOTES AND QUESTIONS

1. In *Larkin v. Grendel's Den*, the Court held that by putting into the hands of the religious institution the power to reject an application for a liquor license, a power normally resting with a government agency, the law advanced the religious mission of the church. The Establishment Clause prohibits the awarding of significant government authority to religious entities. Furthermore, the arrangement also violated the excessive entanglement prong of the *Lemon* test. One could hardly imagine a greater degree of entanglement than allowing religious entities to exercise governmental power as well.

2. In *Larkin*, the law allowed the church to object to its neighbor's application for a liquor license. Then the government agency denied the license. What was the constitutional problem presented by this procedure—that the church could object and have the city take cognizance of its concerns? That the church had an absolute veto over the license application? Or that there was a commingling of religious and governmental authority? Do you think this was *really* a religious institution operating as a government agency? That is, was the case correctly decided? Why or why not?

3. In *Larkin* the Court said the law was invalid because it had the primary and principal effect of advancing religion. Do you think this second part of the *Lemon* test was appropriate in this case? How did the ability to block the award of a liquor license advance religion? Suppose the alcohol commission merely took the church's objection into account in denying the license application? Wouldn't this provide the same beneficial effect to the church's religious mission?

4. In *Larkin* and other cases, the Court has occasionally written about the "symbolism" of a "fusion of governmental and religious functions" and the "mere appearance of a joint exercise of legislative authority by Church and State." What are the constitutional and historical bases for this concern? How compelling is this principle as a constitutional doctrine?

5. Suppose as a result of Charitable Choice a state contracts with a religious organization to provide an important government benefit, such as job training. Suppose also that the contract authorizes the religious organization to determine whether a beneficiary has successfully complied with the program requirements in order to continue receiving assistance. Is this an unlawful delegation of government authority to religion under *Larkin*? Does this "joint enterprise" confer an important symbolic benefit to religion?

*Larkin v. Grendel's Den* served as precedent in a case involving the operation of a school for learning disabled children in *Board of Education of Kiryas Joel Village School District v. Grumet.*[10] The principals in this case were Hasidic Jews and the State of New York.

The Hasidic dimension of Judaism arose in Poland in the early eighteenth century (before the Reform, Conservative, or the branch giving itself the label Orthodox). Beginning in 1648 there was a peasant's revolt against the aristocracy and their employees, many of whom were Jews. Approximately 100,000 Jews were killed and Jewish communities in Poland were devastated. Survivors immersed themselves in worship and Talmud study. They also began to believe that God would surely send the Messiah to rescue them from their suffering. Yet not all Jews had the knowledge or the time to be scholars (some had to work in the fields and shops), so a division developed in the Jewish community between scholars and nonscholars. Time passed, but the Messiah did not come.

Fairly early in the eighteenth century, a new leader emerged among the Polish Jews, the Baal Shem Tov, translated as "Master of the Good Name." The message of the Baal Shem Tov, oversimplified, was that Judaism was not just for scholars, but was a matter of the heart, the emotions, feelings, as well as the head. Even if the Messiah did not come, Jews could have an intimate relationship with God. Judaism was a religion of the love of God and of God's law. Jews should be as faithful as possible to God's commandments for life, the Torah. That is, they should be as strict as possible in obedience to God's laws.

This message revitalized Judaism in Poland and, in time, the movement spread throughout eastern Europe. The Hasidim (the "pious ones") began to separate themselves from "the world," that is, not only from Gentiles, but from other, less observant, Jews. Even their clothing and the men's uncut hair and full beards served to separate them from the evil society and to symbolically say to all who paid attention, "We are the true Jews." Certainly by the twentieth century they could be characterized as "ultra orthodox," more orthodox than Orthodox Jews.

There were few Hasidim in the United States prior to 1950. Because Hasidim lived in close-knit enclaves in eastern Europe and because of their distinctive dress and absolute insistence on obeying the Jewish law, they were easy targets for the Nazis and their collaborators in World War II. Approximately one-half of all the 6,000,000 Jews killed during the Holocaust were Hasidim. Survivors, along with non-Hasidic Jews, began to flee Europe, to go anywhere to escape the horror and its aftermath. Many came to America. Unlike other Jews, however, the Hasidim identified themselves with the villages where their particular branch of Hasidism began. Indeed, the various groups are designated by their ancestral place names, Lubavitch, Satmar, Bobovich, and the like.

This case involves the Satmar Hasidim, who are among the most rigorous of all Hasidic Jews in their devotion to Torah and separation from the world. When they first came to America, they lived in Brooklyn, New York. But in the early 1970s they purchased some land outside New York City and began to develop their own town, Kiryas Joel, next to the larger town of Monroe. The problem developed over the education of Hasidic children. Students went to private Hasidic schools, segregated by gender. But those schools had no provision for children with learning disabilities. For a while disabled children went to special education programs in public schools in neighboring towns. But this was most unsatisfactory, given the cultural difference between Hasidic children and other, Jewish and non-Jewish, children. The Hasidim took their children out of the public schools.

At that point the New York Legislature passed a law that allowed the village of Kiryas Joel to have its own public school district, the board of which would all be Hasidic Jews. That way, there could be a publicly-supported school governed by Hasidic Jews and for Hasidic children with learning disabilities. But the New York State School Boards Association filed suit against the State Education Department and various government officials, claiming the Hasidic public school district was an unconstitutional establishment of religion. The Supreme Court, in an opinion written by Justice David Souter, agreed, using *Larkin v. Grendel's Den* as precedent. Authority over public schools belongs to the state: it cannot cede that authority to a religious group without violating the Establishment Clause. To allow a religious group to govern a public school district combines religion and government in a way that cannot avoid invalidation under the principle that government may not give preferential treatment to one religious group over another.

---

## KIRYAS JOEL VILLAGE SCHOOL DISTRICT v. GRUMET
### 512 U.S. 687 (1994)

▓ JUSTICE SOUTER delivered the opinion of the Court (except as to Part II (introduction) and Part IIA)

The Village of Kiryas Joel in Orange County, New York, is a religious enclave of Satmar Hasidim, practitioners of a strict form of Judaism. The village fell within the Monroe-Woodbury Central School District until a special state statute passed in 1989 carved out a separate district, following village lines, to serve this distinctive population. 1989 N.Y.Laws, ch. 748. The question is whether the Act creating the separate school district violates the Establishment Clause of the First Amendment, binding on the States through the Fourteenth Amendment. Because this unusual act is tantamount to an allocation of political power on a religious criterion and neither presupposes nor requires governmental impartiality toward religion, we hold that it violates the prohibition against establishment.

I

The Satmar Hasidic sect takes its name from the town near the Hungarian and Romanian border where, in the early years of this century, Grand Rebbe Joel Teitelbaum molded the group into a distinct community. After World War II and the destruction of much of European Jewry, the Grand Rebbe and most of his surviving followers moved to the Williamsburg section of Brooklyn, New York. Then, 20 years ago, the Satmars purchased an approved but undeveloped subdivision in the town of Monroe and began assembling the community that has since become the Village of Kiryas Joel. When a zoning dispute arose in the course of settlement, the Satmars presented the Town Board of Monroe with a petition to form a new village within the town, a right that New York's Village Law gives almost any group of residents who satisfy certain procedural niceties. Neighbors who did not wish to secede with the Satmars objected strenuously, and, after arduous negotiations, the proposed boundaries of the Village of Kiryas Joel were drawn to include just the 320 acres owned and inhabited entirely by Satmars. The village, incorporated in 1977, has a population of about 8,500 today. Rabbi Aaron Teitelbaum, eldest son of the current Grand Rebbe, serves as the village rov (chief rabbi) and rosh yeshivah (chief authority in the parochial schools).

The residents of Kiryas Joel are vigorously religious people who make few concessions to the modern world and go to great lengths to avoid assimilation into it. They interpret the Torah strictly; segregate the sexes outside the home; speak Yiddish as their primary language; eschew television, radio, and English language publications; and dress in distinctive ways that include headcoverings and special garments for boys and modest dresses for girls. Children are educated in private religious schools, most boys at the United Talmudic Academy, where they receive a thorough grounding in the Torah and limited exposure to secular subjects, and most girls at Bais Rochel, an affiliated school with a curriculum designed to prepare girls for their roles as wives and mothers.

These schools do not, however, offer any distinctive services to handicapped children, who are entitled under state and federal law to special education services even when enrolled in private schools. Starting in 1984 the Monroe-Woodbury Central School District provided such services for the children of Kiryas Joel at an annex to Bais Rochel, but a year later ended that arrangement in response to our decisions in *Aguilar v. Felton* and *School Dist. of Grand Rapids v. Ball*. Children from Kiryas Joel who needed special education (including the deaf, the mentally retarded, and others suffering from a range of physical, mental, or emotional disorders) were then forced to attend public schools outside the village, which their families found highly unsatisfactory. Parents of most of these children withdrew them from the Monroe-Woodbury secular schools, citing "the panic, fear and trauma [the children] suffered in leaving their own community and being with people whose ways were so different," and some sought administrative review of the public school placements.

Monroe-Woodbury, for its part, sought a declaratory judgment in state court that New York law barred the district from providing special education services outside the district's regular public schools. The New York Court of Appeals disagreed, holding that state law left Monroe-Woodbury free to stablish a separate school in the village because it gives educational authorities broad discretion in fashioning an appropriate program. The court added, however, that the Satmars' constitutional right to exercise their religion freely did not require a separate school, since the parents had alleged emotional trauma, not inconsistency with religious practice or doctrine, as the reason for seeking separate treatment.

By 1989, only one child from Kiryas Joel was attending Monroe-Woodbury's public schools; the village's other handicapped children received privately funded special services or went without. It was then that the New York Legislature passed the statute at issue in this litigation, which provided that the Village of Kiryas Joel "is constituted a separate school district, . . . and shall have and enjoy all the powers and duties of a union free school district. . . ." The statute thus empowered a locally elected board of education to take such action as opening schools and closing them, hiring teachers, prescribing textbooks, establishing disciplinary rules, and raising property taxes to fund operations. In signing the bill into law, Governor Cuomo recognized that the residents of the new school district were "all members of the same religious sect," but said that the bill was "a good faith effort to solve th[e] unique problem" associated with providing special education services to handicapped children in the village.

Although it enjoys plenary legal authority over the elementary and secondary education of all school-aged children in the village, the Kiryas Joel Village School District currently runs only a special education program for handicapped children. The other village children have stayed in their parochial schools, relying on the new school district only for transportation, remedial education, and health and welfare services. If any child without handicap in Kiryas Joel were to seek a public school education, the district would pay tuition to send the child into Monroe-Woodbury or another school district nearby. Under like arrangements, several of the neighboring districts send their handicapped Hasidic children into Kiryas Joel, so that two thirds of the full-time students in the village's public school come from outside. In all, the new district serves just over 40 full-time students, and two or three times that many parochial school students on a part-time basis.

Several months before the new district began operations, the New York State School Boards Association brought this action against the State Education Department and various state officials, challenging Chapter 748 under the national and state constitutions as an unconstitutional establishment of religion. On cross-motions for summary judgment, the trial court ruled for the plaintiffs (respondents here), finding that the statute failed all three prongs of the test in *Lemon v. Kurtzman* and was thus unconstitutional under both the National and State Constitutions.

A divided Appellate Division affirmed on the ground that Chapter 748 had the primary effect of advancing religion, in violation of both constitutions, and the state Court of Appeals affirmed on the federal question, while expressly reserving the state constitutional issue. . . .

We stayed the mandate of the Court of Appeals, and granted certiorari.

II

"A proper respect for both the Free Exercise and the Establishment Clauses compels the State to pursue a course of 'neutrality' toward religion," *Committee for Public Ed. & Religious Liberty v. Nyquist* 413 U.S. 756, 792-793 (1973), favoring neither one religion over others nor religious adherents collectively over nonadherents. Chapter 748, the statute creating the Kiryas Joel Village School District, departs from this constitutional command by delegating the State's discretionary authority over public schools to a group defined by its character as a religious community, in a legal and historical context that gives no assurance that governmental power has been or will be exercised neutrally.

*Larkin v. Grendel's Den, Inc.* provides an instructive comparison with the litigation before us. There, the Court was requested to strike down a Massachusetts statute granting religious bodies veto power over applications for liquor licenses. Under the statute, the governing body of any church, synagogue, or school located within 500 feet of an applicant's premises could, simply by submitting written objection, prevent the Alcohol Beverage Control Commission from issuing a license. In spite of the State's valid interest in protecting churches, schools, and like institutions from "'the hurly-burly' associated with liquor outlets," 459 U.S. 116, 123, the Court found that in two respects the statute violated "the wholesome 'neutrality' of which this Court's cases speak," *School Dist. of Abington v. Schempp* 374 U.S. 203, 222 (1963). The Act brought about a "'fusion of governmental and religious functions'" by delegating "important, discretionary governmental powers" to religious bodies, thus impermissibly entangling government and religion. 459 U.S., 126,

127. And it lacked "any 'effective means of guaranteeing' that the delegated power '[would] be used exclusively for secular, neutral, and nonideological purposes;'" 459 U.S., 125; this, along with the "significant symbolic benefit to religion" associated with "the mere appearance of a joint exercise of legislative authority by Church and State," led the Court to conclude that the statute had a "'primary' and 'principal' effect of advancing religion," 459 U.S., 125-126. Comparable constitutional problems inhere in the statute before us.

## A

*Larkin* presented an example of united civic and religious authority, an establishment rarely found in such straightforward form in modern America, and a violation of "the core rationale underlying the Establishment Clause." 459 U.S., 126. . . .

The Establishment Clause problem presented by Chapter 748 is more subtle, but it resembles the issue raised in *Larkin* to the extent that the earlier case teaches that a State may not delegate its civic authority to a group chosen according to a religious criterion. Authority over public schools belongs to the State, and cannot be delegated to a local school district defined by the State in order to grant political control to a religious group. What makes this litigation different from *Larkin* is the delegation here of civic power to the "qualified voters of the village of Kiryas Joel," as distinct from a religious leader such as the village rov, or an institution of religious government like the formally constituted parish council in *Larkin*. In light of the circumstances of this case, however, this distinction turns out to lack constitutional significance.

It is, first, not dispositive that the recipients of state power in this case are a group of religious individuals united by common doctrine, not the group's leaders or officers. Although some school district franchise is common to all voters, the State's manipulation of the franchise for this district limited it to Satmars, giving the sect exclusive control of the political subdivision. In the circumstances of this case, the difference between thus vesting state power in the members of a religious group as such instead of the officers of its sectarian organization is one of form, not substance. It is true that religious people (or groups of religious people) cannot be denied the opportunity to exercise the rights of citizens simply because of their religious affiliations or commitments, for such a disability would violate the right to religious free exercise, see *McDaniel v. Paty* 435 U.S. 618 (1978), which the First Amendment guarantees as certainly as it bars any establishment. But *McDaniel*, which held that a religious individual could not, because of his religious activities, be denied the right to hold political office, is not in point here. That individuals who happen to be religious may hold public office does not mean that a state may deliberately delegate discretionary power to an individual, institution, or community on the ground of religious identity. If New York were to delegate civic authority to "the Grand Rebbe," *Larkin* would obviously require invalidation (even though under *McDaniel* the Grand Rebbe may run for, and serve on his local school board), and the same is true if New York delegates political authority by reference to religious belief. Where "fusion" is an issue, the difference lies in the distinction between a government's purposeful delegation on the basis of religion and a delegation on principles neutral to religion, to individuals whose religious identities are incidental to their receipt of civic authority.

Of course, Chapter 748 delegates power not by express reference to the religious belief of the Satmar community, but to residents of the "territory of the village of Kiryas Joel." Thus the second (and arguably more important) distinction between this case and *Larkin* is the identification here of the group to exercise civil authority in terms not expressly religious. But our analysis does not end with the text of the statute at issue, and the context here persuades us that Chapter 748 effectively identifies these recipients of governmental authority by reference to doctrinal adherence, even though it does not do so expressly. We find this to be the better view of the facts because of the way the boundary lines of the school district divide residents according to religious affiliation, under the terms of an unusual and special legislative act.

It is undisputed that those who negotiated the village boundaries when applying the general village incorporation statute drew them so as to exclude all but Satmars, and that the New York Legislature was well aware that the village remained exclusively Satmar in 1989 when it adopted Chapter 748. The significance of this fact to the state legislature is indicated by the further fact that carving out the village school district ran counter to customary districting practices in the State. Indeed, the trend in New York is not toward dividing school districts but toward consolidating them. The thousands of small common school districts laid out in the early 19th century have been combined and recombined, first into union free school districts and then into larger central school districts, until only a tenth as many remain today. . . . Most of these cover several towns, many of them cross county boundaries, and only one remains precisely coterminous with an incorporated village. The object of the State's practice of consolidation is the creation of districts large enough to provide a comprehensive education at affordable cost, which is thought to require at least 500 pupils for a combined junior-senior high school. The Kiryas Joel Village School District, in contrast, has only 13 local, full-time students in all (even including out-of-area and part-time students leaves the number under 200), and in offering only special education and remedial programs it makes no pretense to be a full-service district.

The origin of the district in a special act of the legislature, rather than the State's general laws governing school district reorganization, is likewise anomalous. Although the legislature has established some 20 existing school districts by special act, all but one of these are districts in name only, having been designed to be run by private organizations serving institutionalized children. They have neither tax bases nor student populations of their own but serve children placed by other school districts or public agencies. The one school district petitioners point to that was formed by special act of the legislature to serve a whole community, as this one was, is a district formed for a new town, much larger and more heterogeneous than this village, being built on land that straddled two existing districts. Thus the Kiryas Joel Village School District is exceptional to the point of singularity, as the only district coming to our notice that the legislature carved from a single existing district to serve local residents. . . .

Because the district's creation ran uniquely counter to state practice, following the lines of a religious community where the customary and neutral principles would not have dictated the same result, we have good reasons to treat this district as the reflection of a religious criterion for identifying the recipients of civil authority. Not even the special needs of the children in this community can explain the legislature's unusual Act, for the State could have responded to the concerns of the Satmar parents without implicating the Establishment Clause, as we explain in some detail further on. We therefore find the legislature's Act to be substantially equivalent to defining a political subdivision and hence the qualification for its franchise by a religious test, resulting in a purposeful and forbidden "fusion of governmental and religious functions." *Larkin v. Grendel's Den*, 459 U.S., 126.[11]

B

The fact that this school district was created by a special and unusual Act of the legislature also gives reason for concern whether the benefit received by the Satmar community is one that the legislature will provide equally to other religious (and nonreligious) groups. This is the second malady the *Larkin* Court identified in the law before it, the absence of an "effective means of guaranteeing" that governmental power will be and has been neutrally employed. But whereas, in *Larkin*, it was religious groups the Court thought might exercise civic power to advance the interests of religion (or religious adherents), here the threat to neutrality occurs at an antecedent stage.

The fundamental source of constitutional concern here is that the legislature itself may fail to exercise governmental authority in a religiously neutral way. The anomalously case-specific nature of the legislature's exercise of state authority in creating this district for a religious community leaves the Court without any direct way to review such state action for the purpose of safeguarding a principle at the heart of the Establishment Clause, that government should not prefer one religion to another, or religion to irreligion. Because the religious community of Kiryas Joel did not receive its new governmental authority simply as one of many communities eligible for equal treatment under a general law, we have no assurance that the next similarly situated group seeking a school district of its own will receive one; unlike an administrative agency's denial of an exemption from a generally applicable law, which "would be entitled to a judicial audience," a legislature's failure to enact a special law is itself unreviewable. Nor can the historical context in this case furnish us with any reason to suppose that the Satmars are merely one in a series of communities receiving the benefit of special school district laws. . . .

The general principle that civil power must be exercised in a manner neutral to religion is one the *Larkin* Court recognized, although it did not discuss the specific possibility of legislative favoritism along religious lines because the statute before it delegated state authority to any religious group assembled near the premises of an applicant for a liquor license, as well as to a further category of institutions not identified by religion. But the principle is well grounded in our case law, as we have frequently relied explicitly on the general availability of any benefit provided religious groups or individuals in turning aside Establishment Clause challenges. In *Walz v. Tax Comm'n* of New York City (1970), for example, the Court sustained a property tax exemption for religious properties in part because the State had "not singled out one particular church or religious group or even churches as such," but had exempted "a broad class of property owned by nonprofit, quasi-public corporations." And *Bowen v.*

---

[11] Because it is the unusual circumstances of this district's creation that persuade us the State has employed a religious criterion for delegating political power, this conclusion does not imply that any political subdivision that is coterminous with the boundaries of a religiously homogeneous community suffers the same constitutional infirmity. The district in this case is distinguishable from one whose boundaries are derived according to neutral historical and geographic criteria, but whose population happens to comprise coreligionists.

*Kendrick* (1988), upheld a statute enlisting a "wide spectrum of organizations" in addressing adolescent sexuality because the law was "neutral with respect to the grantee's status as a sectarian or purely secular institution.". . . Here the benefit flows only to a single sect, but aiding this single, small religious group causes no less a constitutional problem than would follow from aiding a sect with more members or religion as a whole, and we are forced to conclude that the State of New York has violated the Establishment Clause.

C

In finding that Chapter 748 violates the requirement of governmental neutrality by extending the benefit of a special franchise, we do not deny that the Constitution allows the state to accommodate religious needs by alleviating special burdens. Our cases leave no doubt that in commanding neutrality the Religion Clauses do not require the government to be oblivious to impositions that legitimate exercises of state power may place on religious belief and practice. Rather, there is "ample room under the Establishment Clause" for "benevolent neutrality which will permit religious exercise to exist without sponsorship and without interference." The fact that Chapter 748 facilitates the practice of religion is not what renders it an unconstitutional establishment. . . .

But accommodation is not a principle without limits, and what petitioners seek is an adjustment to the Satmars' religiously grounded preferences that our cases do not countenance. Prior decisions have allowed religious communities and institutions to pursue their own interests free from governmental interference, . . . but we have never hinted that an otherwise unconstitutional delegation of political power to a religious group could be saved as a religious accommodation. Petitioners' proposed accommodation singles out a particular religious sect for special treatment, and whatever the limits of permissible legislative accommodations may be, . . . it is clear that neutrality as among religions must be honored.

This conclusion does not, however, bring the Satmar parents, the Monroe-Woodbury school district, or the State of New York to the end of the road in seeking ways to respond to the parents' concerns. Just as the Court in *Larkin* observed that the State's interest in protecting religious meeting places could be "readily accomplished by other means," there are several alternatives here for providing bilingual and bicultural special education to Satmar children. Such services can perfectly well be offered to village children through the Monroe-Woodbury Central School District. Since the Satmars do not claim that separatism is religiously mandated, their children may receive bilingual and bicultural instruction at a public school already run by the Monroe-Woodbury district. Or if the educationally appropriate offering by Monroe-Woodbury should turn out to be a separate program of bilingual and bicultural education at a neutral site near one of the village's parochial schools, this Court has already made it clear that no Establishment Clause difficulty would inhere in such a scheme, administered in accordance with neutral principles that would not necessarily confine special treatment to Satmars.

To be sure, the parties disagree on whether the services Monroe-Woodbury actually provided in the late 1980's were appropriately tailored to the needs of Satmar children, but this dispute is of only limited relevance to the question whether such services could have been provided, had adjustments been made. . . .

III

Justice Cardozo once cast the dissenter as "the gladiator making a last stand against the lions." B. Cardozo, *Law and Literature* 34 (1931). JUSTICE SCALIA's dissent is certainly the work of a gladiator, but he thrusts at lions of his own imagining. We do not disable a religiously homogeneous group from exercising political power conferred on it without regard to religion. Unlike the states of Utah and New Mexico (which were laid out according to traditional political methodologies taking account of lines of latitude and longitude and topographical features), the reference line chosen for the Kiryas Joel Village School District was one purposely drawn to separate Satmars from non-Satmars. Nor do we impugn the motives of the New York Legislature, which no doubt intended to accommodate the Satmar community without violating the Establishment Clause; we simply refuse to ignore that the method it chose is one that aids a particular religious community, as such, rather than all groups similarly interested in separate schooling. The dissent protests it is novel to insist "up front" that a statute not tailor its benefits to apply only to one religious group, but, if this were so, *Texas Monthly, Inc.* would have turned out differently, and language in *Walz v. Tax Comm'n* and *Bowen v. Kendrick* purporting to rely on the breadth of the statutory schemes would have been mere surplusage. Indeed, under the dissent's theory, if New York were to pass a law providing school buses only for children attending Christian day schools, we would be constrained to uphold the statute against Establishment Clause attack until faced by a request from a non-Christian family for equal treatment under the patently unequal law. And to end on the point with which JUSTICE SCALIA begins, the license he takes in suggesting that the Court holds the Satmar sect to be New York's established church is only one symptom of his inability to accept the fact that this Court has long held that the First Amendment reaches more than classic, 18th century establishments. . . .

In this case, we are clearly constrained to conclude that the statute before us fails the test of neutrality. It delegates a power this Court has said "ranks at the very apex of the function of a State," *Wisconsin v. Yoder* 406 U.S. 205, 213 (1972), to an electorate defined by common religious belief and practice, in a manner that fails to foreclose religious favoritism. It therefore crosses the line from permissible accommodation to impermissible establishment. The judgment of the Court of Appeals of the State of New York is accordingly

*Affirmed.* . . .

JUSTICE STEVENS, with whom JUSTICE BLACKMUN and JUSTICE GINSBURG join, concurring.

New York created a special school district for the members of the Satmar religious sect in response to parental concern that children suffered "panic, fear and trauma" when "leaving their own community and being with people whose ways were so different." To meet those concerns, the State could have taken steps to alleviate the children's fear by teaching their schoolmates to be tolerant and respectful of Satmar customs. Action of that kind would raise no constitutional concerns and would further the strong public interest in promoting diversity and understanding in the public schools.

Instead, the State responded with a solution that affirmatively supports a religious sect's interest in segregating itself and preventing its children from associating with their neighbors. The isolation of these children, while it may protect them from "panic, fear and trauma," also unquestionably increased the likelihood that they would remain within the fold, faithful adherents of their parents' religious faith. By creating a school district that is specifically intended to shield children from contact with others who have "different ways," the State provided official support to cement the attachment of young adherents to a particular faith. It is telling, in this regard, that two thirds of the school's full-time students are Hasidic handicapped children from outside the village; the Kiryas Joel school thus serves a population far wider than the village—one defined less by geography than by religion.

Affirmative state action in aid of segregation of this character is unlike the evenhanded distribution of a public benefit or service, a "release time" program for public school students involving no public premises or funds, or a decision to grant an exemption from a burdensome general rule. It is, I believe, fairly characterized as establishing, rather than merely accommodating, religion. For this reason, as well as the reasons set out in JUSTICE SOUTER's opinion, I am persuaded that the New York law at issue in these cases violates the Establishment Clause of the First Amendment.

JUSTICE O'CONNOR, concurring in part and concurring in the judgment.

I

The question at the heart of this case is: what may the government do, consistently with the Establishment Clause, to accommodate people's religious beliefs? . . .

II . . .

We have time and again held that the government generally may not treat people differently based on the God or gods they worship, or don't worship. "The clearest command of the Establishment Clause is that one religious denomination cannot be officially preferred over another." *Larson v. Valente*, 456 U.S. 228, 244 (1982). . . .

This emphasis on equal treatment is, I think, an eminently sound approach. In my view, the Religion Clauses—the Free Exercise Clause, the Establishment Clause, the Religious Test Clause, Art. VI, cl. 3, and the Equal Protection Clause as applied to religion—all speak with one voice on this point: absent the most unusual circumstances, one's religion ought not affect one's legal rights or duties or benefits. As I have previously noted, "the Establishment Clause is infringed when the government makes adherence to religion relevant to a person's standing in the political community." *Wallace v. Jaffree*, 472 U.S. 38, 69 (1985).

That the government is acting to accommodate religion should generally not change this analysis. What makes accommodation permissible, even praiseworthy, is not that the government is making life easier for some particular religious group as such. Rather, it is that the government is accommodating a deeply held belief. Accommodations may thus justify treating those who share this belief differently from those who do not; but they do not justify discriminations based on sect. A state law prohibiting the consumption of alcohol may exempt sacramental wines, but it may not exempt sacramental wine use by Catholics, but not by Jews. . . . The Constitution permits "*nondiscriminatory* religious practice exemption[s]," not sectarian ones.

## III

I join Parts I, II-B, II-C, and III of the Court's opinion because I think this law, rather than being a general accommodation, singles out a particular religious group for favorable treatment. The Court's analysis of the history of this law and of the surrounding statutory scheme persuades me of this.

On its face, this statute benefits one group—the residents of Kiryas Joel. Because this benefit was given to this group based on its religion, it seems proper to treat it as a legislatively drawn religious classification. I realize this is a close question, because the Satmars may be the only group who currently need this particular accommodation. The legislature may well be acting without any favoritism, so that if another group came to ask for a similar district, the group might get it on the same terms as the Satmars. But the nature of the legislative process makes it impossible to be sure of this. A legislature, unlike the judiciary or many administrative decisionmakers, has no obligation to respond to any group's requests. A group petitioning for a law may never get a definite response, or may get a "no" based not on the merits, but on the press of other business or the lack of an influential sponsor. Such a legislative refusal to act would not normally be reviewable by a court. Under these circumstances, it seems dangerous to validate what appears to me a clear religious preference.

Our invalidation of this statute in no way means that the Satmars' needs cannot be accommodated. There is nothing improper about a legislative intention to accommodate a religious group, so long as it is implemented through generally applicable legislation. New York may, for instance, allow all villages to operate their own school districts. If it does not want to act so broadly, it may set forth neutral criteria that a village must meet to have a school district of its own; these criteria can then be applied by a state agency, and the decision would then be reviewable by the judiciary. A district created under a generally applicable scheme would be acceptable even though it coincides with a village which was consciously created by its voters as an enclave for their religious group. I do not think the Court's opinion holds the contrary.

I also think there is one other accommodation that would be entirely permissible: the 1984 scheme, which was discontinued because of our decision in *Aguilar*. The Religion Clauses prohibit the government from favoring religion, but they provide no warrant for discriminating against religion. All handicapped children are entitled by law to government-funded special education. If the government provides this education on-site at public schools and at nonsectarian private schools, it is only fair that it provide it on-site at sectarian schools as well.

I thought this to be true in *Aguilar*, and I still believe it today. The Establishment Clause does not demand hostility to religion, religious ideas, religious people, or religious schools. It is the Court's insistence on disfavoring religion in *Aguilar* that led New York to favor it here. The Court should, in a proper case, be prepared to reconsider *Aguilar*, in order to bring our Establishment Clause jurisprudence back to what I think is the proper track—government impartiality, not animosity, towards religion.

## IV

One aspect of the Court's opinion in this case is worth noting: Like the opinions in two recent cases, *Lee v. Weisman*; *Zobrest v. Catalina Foothills School Dist.*, and the case I think is most relevant to this one, *Larson v. Valente*, the

Court's opinion does not focus on the Establishment Clause test we set forth in *Lemon v. Kurtzman*.

It is always appealing to look for a single test, a Grand Unified Theory that would resolve all the cases that may arise under a particular clause. There is, after all, only one Establishment Clause, one Free Speech Clause, one Fourth Amendment, one Equal Protection Clause.

But the same constitutional principle may operate very differently in different contexts. We have, for instance, no one Free Speech Clause test. We have different tests for content-based speech restrictions, for content-neutral speech restrictions, for restrictions imposed by the government acting as employer, for restrictions in nonpublic fora, and so on. This simply reflects the necessary recognition that the interests relevant to the Free Speech Clause inquiry—personal liberty, an informed citizenry, government efficiency, public order, and so on—are present in different degrees in each context.

And setting forth a unitary test for a broad set of cases may sometimes do more harm than good. Any test that must deal with widely disparate situations risks being so vague as to be useless. . . .

Experience proves that the Establishment Clause, like the Free Speech Clause, cannot easily be reduced to a single test. There are different categories of Establishment Clause cases, which may call for different approaches. Some cases, like this one, involve government actions targeted at particular individuals or groups, imposing special duties or giving special benefits. Cases involving government speech on religious topics, see, e.g., *Lee v. Weisman*; *Allegheny County v. American Civil Liberties Union Greater Pittsburgh Chapter*; *Lynch v. Donnelly*; *Stone v. Graham*, seem to me to fall into a different category, and to require an analysis focusing on whether the speech endorses or disapproves of religion, rather than on whether the government action is neutral with regard to religion.

Another category encompasses cases in which the government must make decisions about matters of religious doctrine and religious law. See *Serbian Eastern Orthodox Diocese v. Milivojevich* (which also did not apply *Lemon*). These cases, which often arise in the application of otherwise neutral property or contract principles to religious institutions, involve complicated questions not present in other situations. . . . Government delegations of power to religious bodies may make up yet another category. As *Larkin* itself suggested, government impartiality towards religion may not be enough in such situations: A law that bars all alcohol sales within some distance of a church, school, or hospital may be valid, but an equally evenhanded law that gives each institution discretionary power over the sales may not be. Of course, there may well be additional categories, or more opportune places to draw the lines between the categories.

As the Court's opinion today shows, the slide away from *Lemon's* unitary approach is well under way. A return to *Lemon*, even if possible, would likely be futile, regardless of where one stands on the substantive Establishment Clause questions. I think a less unitary approach provides a better structure for analysis. If each test covers a narrower and more homogeneous area, the tests may be more precise and therefore easier to apply. There may be more opportunity to pay attention to the specific nuances of each area. There might also be, I hope, more consensus on each of the narrow tests than there has been on a broad test. And abandoning the *Lemon* framework need not mean abandoning some of the insights that the test reflected, nor the insights of the cases that applied it.

Perhaps eventually under this structure we may indeed distill a unified, or at least a more unified, Establishment Clause test from the cases. . . . But it seems to me that the case law will better be able to evolve towards this if it is freed from the *Lemon* test's rigid influence. The hard questions would, of course, still have to be asked; but they will be asked within a more carefully tailored and less distorted framework. . . .

For the reasons stated, I would affirm the judgment of the Court of Appeals of the State of New York.

▨ JUSTICE KENNEDY, concurring in the judgment.

The Court's ruling that the Kiryas Joel Village School District violates the Establishment Clause is in my view correct, but my reservations about what the Court's reasoning implies for religious accommodations in general are sufficient to require a separate writing. As the Court recognizes, a legislative accommodation that discriminates among religions may become an establishment of religion. But the Court's opinion can be interpreted to say that an accommodation for a particular religious group is invalid because of the risk that the legislature will not grant the same accommodation to another religious group suffering some similar burden. This rationale seems to me without grounding in our precedents and a needless restriction upon the legislature's ability to respond to the unique problems of a particular religious group. The real vice of the school district, in my estimation, is that New York created it by drawing political boundaries on the basis of religion. I would decide the issue we confront upon this narrower theory, though in accord with many of the Court's general observations about the State's actions in this case.

I

This is not a case in which the government has granted a benefit to a general class of recipients of which religious groups are just one part. It is, rather, a case in which the government seeks to alleviate a specific burden on the religious practices of a particular religious group. I agree that a religious accommodation demands careful scrutiny to ensure that it does not so burden nonadherents or discriminate against other religions as to become an establishment. I disagree, however, with the suggestion that the Kiryas Joel Village School District contravenes these basic constitutional commands. But for the forbidden manner in which the New York Legislature sought to go about it, the State's attempt to accommodate the special needs of the handicapped Satmar children would have been valid. . . .

New York's object in creating the Kiryas Joel Village School District—to accommodate the religious practices of the handicapped Satmar children—is validated by the principles that emerge from these precedents. First, by creating the district, New York sought to alleviate a specific and identifiable burden on the Satmars' religious practice. The Satmars' way of life, which springs out of their strict religious beliefs, conflicts in many respects with mainstream American culture. They do not watch television or listen to radio; they speak Yiddish in their homes and do not read English language publications; and they have a distinctive hairstyle and dress. Attending the Monroe-Woodbury public schools, where they were exposed to much different ways of life, caused the handicapped Satmar children understandable anxiety and distress. New York was entitled to relieve these significant burdens, even though mainstream public schooling does not conflict with any specific tenet of the Satmars' religious faith. . . .

Second, by creating the district, New York did not impose or increase any burden on non-Satmars, compared to the burden it lifted from the Satmars, that might disqualify the District as a genuine accommodation. . . . There is a point, to be sure, at which an accommodation may impose a burden on non-adherents so great that it becomes an establishment. . . . This case has not been argued, however, on the theory that non-Satmars suffer any special burdens from the existence of the Kiryas Joel Village School District.

Third, the creation of the school district to alleviate the special burdens born by the handicapped Satmar children cannot be said, for that reason alone, to favor the Satmar religion to the exclusion of any other. . . . The Court insists that religious favoritism is a danger here, because the "anomalously case-specific nature of the legislature's exercise of state authority in creating this district for a religious community leaves the Court without any direct way to review such state action" to ensure interdenominational neutrality. "Because the religious community of Kiryas Joel did not receive its new governmental authority simply as one of many communities eligible for equal treatment under a general law," the Court maintains, "we have no assurance that the next similarly situated group seeking a school district of its own will receive one; . . . a legislature's failure to enact a special law is itself unreviewable."

This reasoning reverses the usual presumption that a statute is constitutional and, in essence, adjudges the New York Legislature guilty until it proves itself innocent. No party has adduced any evidence that the legislature has denied another religious community like the Satmars its own school district under analogous circumstances. The legislature, like the judiciary, is sworn to uphold the Constitution, and we have no reason to presume that the New York Legislature would not grant the same accommodation in a similar future case. The fact that New York singled out the Satmars for this special treatment indicates nothing other than the uniqueness of the handicapped Satmar children's plight. It is normal for legislatures to respond to problems as they arise—no less so when the issue is religious accommodation. Most accommodations cover particular religious practices. . . .

## II

The Kiryas Joel Village School District thus does not suffer any of the typical infirmities that might invalidate an attempted legislative accommodation. In the ordinary case, the fact that New York has chosen to accommodate the burdens unique to one religious group would raise no constitutional problems. Without further evidence that New York has denied the same accommodation to religious groups bearing similar burdens, we could not presume from the particularity of the accommodation that the New York Legislature acted with discriminatory intent.

This particularity takes on a different cast, however, when the accommodation requires the government to draw political or electoral boundaries. "The principle that government may accommodate the free exercise of religion does not supersede the fundamental limitations imposed by the Establishment Clause," *Lee v. Weisman* 505 U.S. 577, 587 (1992), and, in my view, one such fundamental limitation is that government may not use religion as a criterion to draw political or electoral lines. Whether or not the purpose is accommodation and whether or not the government provides similar gerrymanders to people of all religious faiths, the Establishment Clause forbids the government to use religion as a line-drawing criterion. In this respect, the Establishment Clause mirrors the Equal Protection Clause. Just as the government may not segregate people on account of their race, so too it may not segregate on the basis of religion. The danger of stigma and stirred animosities is no less acute for religious line-drawing than for racial.

. . . I agree with the Court insofar as it invalidates the school district for being drawn along religious lines. As the plurality observes, the New York Legislature knew that everyone within the village was Satmar when it drew the school district along the village lines, and it determined who was to be included in the district by imposing, in effect, a religious test. There is no serious question that the legislature configured the school district, with purpose and precision, along a religious line. This explicit religious gerrymandering violates the First Amendment Establishment Clause.

It is important to recognize the limits of this principle. We do not confront the constitutionality of the Kiryas Joel Village itself, and the formation of the village appears to differ from the formation of the school district in one critical respect. As the Court notes, the village was formed pursuant to a religion-neutral self-incorporation scheme. Under New York law, a territory with at least 500 residents and not more than five square miles may be incorporated upon petition by at least 20 percent of the voting residents of that territory or by the owners of more than 50 percent of the territory's real property. . . .

As the plurality indicates, the Establishment Clause does not invalidate a town or a state "whose boundaries are derived according to neutral historical and geographic criteria, but whose population happens to comprise coreligionists." People who share a common religious belief or lifestyle may live together without sacrificing the basic rights of self-governance that all American citizens enjoy, so long as they do not use those rights to establish their religious faith. Religion flourishes in community, and the Establishment Clause must not be construed as some sort of homogenizing solvent that forces unconventional religious groups to choose between assimilating to mainstream American culture or losing their political rights. There is more than a fine line, however, between the voluntary association that leads to a political community comprised of people who share a common religious faith, and the forced separation that occurs when the government draws explicit political boundaries on the basis of peoples' faith. In creating the Kiryas Joel Village School District, New York crossed that line, and so we must hold the district invalid.

III . . .

Before 1985, the handicapped Satmar children of Kiryas Joel attended the private religious schools within the village that the other Satmar children attended. Because their handicaps were in some cases acute (ranging from mental retardation and deafness to spina bifida and cerebral palsy), the State of New York provided public funds for special education of these children at annexes to the religious schools. Then came the companion cases of *School Dist. of Grand Rapids v. Ball* and *Aguilar v. Felton* (1985). . . . After these cases, the Monroe-Woodbury School District suspended its special education program at the Kiryas Joel religious schools, and the Kiryas Joel parents were forced to enroll their handicapped children at the Monroe-Woodbury public schools in order for the children to receive special education. The ensuing difficulties, as the Court recounts, led to the creation of the Kiryas Joel Village School District.

The decisions in *Grand Rapids* and *Aguilar* may have been erroneous. In light of the case before us, and in the interest of sound elaboration of constitutional doctrine, it may be necessary for us to reconsider them at a later date. A neutral aid scheme, available to religious and nonreligious alike, is the preferable way to address problems such as the Satmar handicapped children have suffered. But for *Grand Rapids* and *Aguilar*, the Satmars would have had no need to seek special accommodations or their own school district. Our decisions led them to choose that unfortunate course, with the deficiencies I have described.

One misjudgment is no excuse, however, for compounding it with another. We must confront this case as it comes before us, without bending rules to free the Satmars from a predicament into which we put them. The Establishment Clause forbids the government to draw political boundaries on the basis of religious faith. For this reason, I concur in the judgment of the Court.

⊞ JUSTICE SCALIA, with whom THE CHIEF JUSTICE and JUSTICE THOMAS join, dissenting.

The Court today finds that the Powers That Be, up in Albany, have conspired to effect an establishment of the Satmar Hasidim. I do not know who would be more surprised at this discovery: the Founders of our Nation or Grand Rebbe Joel Teitelbaum, founder of the Satmar. The Grand Rebbe would be astounded to learn that, after escaping brutal persecution and coming to America with the modest hope of religious toleration for their ascetic form of Judaism, the Satmar had become so powerful, so closely allied with Mammon, as to have become an "establishment" of the Empire State. And the Founding Fathers would be astonished to find that the Establishment Clause—which they designed "to insure that no one powerful sect or combination of sects could use political or governmental power to punish dissenters," *Zorach v. Clauson* 343 U.S. 306, 319 (1952) (BLACK, J., dissenting)—has been employed to prohibit characteristically and admirably American accommodation of the religious practices (or more precisely, cultural peculiarities) of a tiny minority sect. I, however, am not surprised. Once this Court has abandoned text and history as guides, nothing prevents it from calling religious toleration the establishment of religion.

I

Unlike most of our Establishment Clause cases involving education, these cases involve no public funding, however slight or indirect, to private religious schools. They do not involve private schools at all. The school under scrutiny is a public school specifically designed to provide a public secular education to handicapped students. The superintendent of the school, who is not Hasidic, is a 20-year veteran of the New York City public school system, with expertise in the area of bilingual, bicultural, special education. The teachers and therapists at the school all live outside the village of Kiryas Joel. While the village's private schools are profoundly religious and strictly segregated by sex, classes at the public school are co-ed and the curriculum secular. The school building has the bland appearance of a public school, unadorned by religious symbols or markings; and the school complies with the laws and regulations governing all other New York State public schools. There is no suggestion, moreover, that this public school has gone too far in making special adjustments to the religious needs of its students. In sum, these cases involve only public aid to a school that is public as can be. The only thing distinctive about the school is that all the students share the same religion.

None of our cases has ever suggested that there is anything wrong with that. In fact, the Court has specifically approved the education of students of a single religion on a neutral site adjacent to a private religious school. See *Wolman v. Walter* 433 U.S. 229, 247-248 (1977). In that case, the Court rejected the argument that "any program that isolates the sectarian pupils is impermissible," *id.*, 246, and held that, "[t]he fact that a unit on a neutral site on occasion may serve only sectarian pupils does not provoke [constitutional] concerns," *id.*, 247. And just last Term, the Court held that the State could permit public employees to assist students in a Catholic school. See *Zobrest v. Catalina Foothills School Dist.*, 509 U.S. 1, 13-14 (1993) (sign language translator for deaf student). If a State can furnish services to a group of sectarian students on a neutral site adjacent to a private religious school, or even within such a school, how can there be any defect in educating those same students in a public school? As the Court noted in *Wolman*, the constitutional dangers of establishment arise "from the nature of the institution, not from the nature of the pupils." *Wolman*, 248. There is no danger in educating religious students in a public school.

For these very good reasons, JUSTICE SOUTER's opinion does not focus upon the school, but rather upon the school district and the New York Legislature that created it. His arguments, though sometimes intermingled, are two: that reposing governmental power in the Kiryas Joel School District is the same as reposing governmental power in a religious group, and that, in enacting the statute creating the district, the New York State Legislature was discriminating on the basis of religion, i.e., favoring the Satmar Hasidim over others. I shall discuss these arguments in turn.

## II

For his thesis that New York has unconstitutionally conferred governmental authority upon the Satmar sect, JUSTICE SOUTER relies extensively, and virtually exclusively, upon *Larkin v. Grendel's Den, Inc.* JUSTICE SOUTER believes that the present case "resembles" *Grendel's Den* because that case "teaches that a state may not delegate its civic authority *to a group chosen according to a religious criterion*" (emphasis added). That misdescribes both what that case taught (which is that a state may not delegate its civil authority to a *church*), and what this case involves (which is a group chosen according to cultural characteristics). The statute at issue there gave churches veto power over the State's authority to grant a liquor license to establishments in the vicinity of the church. The Court had little difficulty finding the statute unconstitutional. . . .

JUSTICE SOUTER's steamrolling of the difference between civil authority held by a church, and civil authority held by members of a church, is breathtaking. To accept it, one must believe that large portions of the civil authority exercised during most of our history were unconstitutional, and that much more of it than merely the Kiryas Joel School District is unconstitutional today. The history of the populating of North America is in no small measure the story of groups of people sharing a common religious and cultural heritage striking out to form their own communities. It is preposterous to suggest that the civil institutions of these communities, separate from their churches, were constitutionally suspect. . . .

JUSTICE SOUTER's position boils down to the quite novel proposition that any group of citizens (say, the residents of Kiryas Joel) can be invested with political power, but not if they all belong to the same religion. Of course such *disfavoring* of religion is positively antagonistic to the purposes of the Religion Clauses, and we have rejected it before. . . .

Perhaps appreciating the startling implications for our constitutional jurisprudence of collapsing the distinction between religious institutions and their members, JUSTICE SOUTER tries to limit his "unconstitutional conferral of civil authority" holding by pointing out several features supposedly unique to the present case: that the "boundary lines of the school district divide residents *according to* religious affiliation" (emphasis added); that the school district was created by "a special act of the legislature"; and that the formation of the school district ran counter to the legislature's trend of consolidating districts in recent years. Assuming all these points to be true (and they are not), they would certainly bear upon whether the legislature had an impermissible religious motivation in creating the district. . . . But they have nothing to do with whether conferral of power upon a group of citizens can be the conferral of power upon a religious institution. . . .

## III

I turn, next, to JUSTICE SOUTER's second justification for finding an establishment of religion: his facile conclusion that the New York Legislature's creation of the Kiryas Joel School District was religiously motivated. . . .

There is, of course, no possible doubt of a secular basis here. The New York Legislature faced a unique problem in Kiryas Joel: a community in which all the nonhandicapped children attend private schools, and the physically and mentally disabled children who attend public school suffer the additional handicap of cultural distinctiveness. It would be troublesome enough if these peculiarly dressed, handicapped students were sent to the next town, accompanied by their similarly clad but unimpaired classmates. But all the unimpaired children of Kiryas Joel attend private school. The handicapped children suffered sufficient emotional trauma from their predicament that their parents kept them home from school. Surely the legislature could target this problem, and provide a public education for these students, in the same way it addressed, by a similar law, the unique needs of children institutionalized in a hospital. . . .

But even if the New York Legislature had never before created a school district by special statute (which is not true), and even if it had done nothing but consolidate school districts for over a century (which is not true), how could the departure from those past practices possibly demonstrate that the legislature had religious favoritism in mind? It could not. To be sure, when there is no special treatment, there is no possibility of religious favoritism; but it is not logical to suggest that when there is special treatment, there is proof of religious favoritism.

JUSTICE SOUTER's case against the statute comes down to nothing more, therefore, than the fact that all the residents of the Kiryas Joel Village School District are Satmars. But all its residents also wear unusual dress, have unusual civic customs, and have not much to do with people who are culturally different from them. . . . On what basis does JUSTICE SOUTER conclude that it is the theological distinctiveness, rather than the cultural distinctiveness, that was the basis for New York State's decision? The normal assumption would be that it was the latter, since it was not theology, but dress, language, and cultural alienation that posed the educational problem for the children. . . .

I have little doubt that JUSTICE SOUTER would laud this humanitarian legislation if all of the distinctiveness of the students of Kiryas Joel were attributable to the fact that their parents were nonreligious commune dwellers, or American Indians, or gypsies. The creation of a special, one-culture school district for the benefit of those children would pose no problem. The neutrality demanded by the Religion Clauses requires the same indulgence towards cultural characteristics that are accompanied by religious belief. . . .

At various times, JUSTICE SOUTER intimates, though he does not precisely say, that the boundaries of the school district were intentionally drawn on the basis of religion. He refers, for example, to "[t]he State's manipulation of the franchise for this district . . . , giving the sect exclusive control of the political subdivision"—implying that the "giving" of political power to the religious sect was the object of the "manipulation." There is no evidence of that. The special district was created to meet the special educational needs of distinctive handicapped children, and the geographical boundaries selected for that district were (quite logically) those that already existed for the village. . . . It was a classic drawing of lines on the basis of communality of secular governmental desires, not communality of religion. What happened in the creation of the village is, in fact, precisely what happened in the creation of the school district, so that the former cannot possibly infect the latter, as JUSTICE SOUTER tries to suggest. Entirely secular reasons (zoning for the village, cultural alienation of students for the school district) produced a political unit whose members happened to share the same religion. There is no evidence (indeed, no plausible suspicion) of the legislature's desire to favor the Satmar religion, as opposed to meeting distinctive secular needs or desires of citizens who happened to be Satmars. If there were, JUSTICE SOUTER would say so; instead, he must merely insinuate.

IV

But even if Chapter 748 were intended to create a special arrangement for the Satmars because of their religion, it would be a permissible accommodation. "This Court has long recognized that the government may (and sometimes must) accommodate religious practices and that it may do so without violating the Establishment Clause." . . . Accommodation is permissible, moreover, even when the statute deals specifically with religion, see, e.g., Zorach v. Clauson, and even when accommodation is not commanded by the Free Exercise Clause.

When a legislature acts to accommodate religion, particularly a minority sect, "it follows the best of our traditions." . . .

In today's opinion, however, the Court seems uncomfortable with this aspect of our constitutional tradition. Although it acknowledges the concept of accommodation, it quickly points out that it is "not a principle without limits," and then gives reasons why the present case exceeds those limits, reasons which simply do not hold water. "[W]e have never hinted," the Court says, "that an otherwise unconstitutional delegation of political power to a religious group could be saved as a religious accommodation." Putting aside the circularity inherent in referring to a delegation as "otherwise unconstitutional" when its constitutionality turns on whether there is an accommodation, if this statement is true, it is only because we have never hinted that delegation of political power to citizens who share a particular religion could be unconstitutional. . . .

The second and last reason the Court finds accommodation impermissible is, astoundingly, the mere risk that the State will not offer accommodation to a similar group in the future, and that neutrality will therefore not be preserved. . . .

At bottom, the Court's "no guarantee of neutrality" argument is an assertion of this Court's inability to control the New York Legislature's future denial of comparable accommodation. We have "no assurance," the Court says, "that the next similarly situated group seeking a school district of its own will receive one," since "a legislature's failure to enact a special law is . . . unreviewable." That is true only in the technical (and irrelevant) sense that the later group denied an accommodation may need to challenge the grant of the first accommodation in light of the later denial, rather than challenging the denial directly. . . .

The Court's demand for "up front" assurances of a neutral system is at war with both traditional accommodation doctrine and the judicial role. As we have described, Congress's earliest accommodations exempted duties paid by specific churches on particular items. Moreover, most efforts at accommodation seek to solve a problem that applies to members of only one or a few religions. Not every religion uses wine in its sacraments, but that does not make an exemption from Prohibition for sacramental wine-use impermissible. The record is clear that the necessary guarantee can and will be provided, after the fact, *by the courts*. . . .

V

A few words in response to the separate concurrences: JUSTICE STEVENS adopts, for these cases, a rationale that is almost without limit. The separate Kiryas Joel School District is problematic in his view because "[t]he isolation of these children, while it may protect them from 'panic, fear and trauma,' also unquestionably increased the likelihood that they would remain within the fold, faithful adherents of their parents' religious faith." So much for family values. If the Constitution forbids any state action that incidentally helps parents to raise their children in their own religious faith, it would invalidate a release program permitting public school children to attend the religious instruction program of their parents' choice, of the sort we approved in *Zorach*; indeed, it would invalidate state laws according parents physical control over their children at least insofar as that is used to take the little fellows to church or synagogue. JUSTICE STEVENS' statement is less a legal analysis than a manifesto of secularism. It surpasses mere rejection of accommodation, and announces a positive hostility to religion—which, unlike all other noncriminal values, the state must not assist parents in transmitting to their offspring.

JUSTICE KENNEDY's "political line-drawing" approach founders on its own terms. He concedes that the Constitution does not prevent people who share a faith from forming their own villages and towns, and suggests that the formation of the village of Kiryas Joel was free from defect. He also notes that States are free to draw political lines on the basis of history and geography. I do not see, then, how a school district drawn to mirror the boundaries of an existing village (an existing geographic line), which itself is not infirm, can violate the Constitution. . . . He says the village is constitutional because it was formed (albeit by members of a single religious sect) under a general New

York law; but he finds the school district unconstitutional because it was the product of a specific enactment. In the end, his analysis is no different from the Court's. . . .

Finally, JUSTICE O'CONNOR observes that the Court's opinion does not focus on the so-called *Lemon* test, see *Lemon v. Kurtzman* and she urges that that test be abandoned at least as a "unitary approach" to all Establishment Clause claims. I have previously documented the Court's convenient relationship with *Lemon*, which it cites only when useful, and I no longer take any comfort in the Court's failure to rely on it in any particular case. . . .

Unlike JUSTICE O'CONNOR, however, I would not replace *Lemon* with nothing, and let the case law "evolve" into a series of situation-specific rules (government speech on religious topics, government benefits to particular groups, etc.) unconstrained by any "rigid influence." The problem with (and the allure of) *Lemon* has not been that it is "rigid," but rather that, in many applications, it has been utterly meaningless, validating whatever result the Court would desire. . . . The foremost principle I would apply is fidelity to the longstanding traditions of our people, which surely provide the diversity of treatment that JUSTICE O'CONNOR seeks, but do not leave us to our own devices.

The Court's decision today is astounding. Chapter 748 involves no public aid to private schools, and does not mention religion. In order to invalidate it, the Court casts aside, on the flimsiest of evidence, the strong presumption of validity that attaches to facially neutral laws, and invalidates the present accommodation because it does not trust New York to be as accommodating toward other religions (presumably those less powerful than the Satmar Hasidim) in the future. This is unprecedented—except that it continues, and takes to new extremes, a recent tendency in the opinions of this Court to turn the Establishment Clause into a repealer of our Nation's tradition of religious toleration. I dissent.

. . .

## NOTES AND QUESTIONS

1. The majority/plurality opinion in *Kiryas Joel* offers two rationales for why the special school district is unconstitutional. How are these rationales distinct or related? Justice Kennedy offers a third rationale: religious gerrymandering. Which of these rationales is most compelling?

2. Why is the state's action not seen as a religious accommodation, or at least an attempt to assist a particular religious group in obtaining an appropriate education to their learning disabled children? Is *Kiryas Joel* hypersensitive about the no establishment principle? Why or why not? For a case raising a similar set of facts but with a different result, see *Stark v. Independent School District*, 123 F.3d 1068 (8th Cir. 1997) (rejecting an Establishment Clause challenge to a school district's decision to establish a separate "back-to-basics" elementary school to accommodate the complaints that parents belonging to a conservative religious group had to the "use of technology, including televisions, radios, videos, films, and computers" in the curriculum).

3. In his opinion concurring in the judgment, Justice Kennedy disagrees with the majority that the state's action otherwise fails as a permissible accommodation

of religion. If so, how do you explain his agreement with the majority that the state's action is unconstitutional?

4. Was *Larkin v. Grendel's Den* an appropriate precedent to apply in *Kiryas Joel*? How is the delegation of authority in *Kiryas Joel* different or similar to the award of authority in *Larkin*?

5. Justice Scalia, in his criticism of the *Lemon* test, says that the principal criterion to be used in deciding Establishment Clause cases "is fidelity to the longstanding traditions of our people." Consider whether this an adequate and sufficient test for deciding such cases. Some would argue that many of the cases addressed in this book indicate that there has been a long tradition of the American people violating the no establishment principle by enacting formal and informal preferences of religion (e.g., the common practice of Protestant religious exercises in nineteenth century public schools). If so, would that give precedent to continue to do it?

6. In his dissent, Justice Scalia points to the following statement made by Justice Stevens in this case: "By creating a school district that is specifically intended to shield children from contact with others who have 'different ways,' the State provided official support to cement the attachment of young adherents to a particular faith." Justice Scalia responds by saying: "If the Constitution forbids any state action that incidentally helps parents to raise their children in their own religious faith, it would invalidate a release program permitting public school children to attend the religious instruction program of their parents' choice, of the sort we approved in *Zorach*; indeed, it would invalidate state laws according parents physical control over their children at least insofar as that is used to take the little fellows to church or synagogue." Does Justice Scalia make a fair point here?

## Chapter 23

# Legislative Accommodation of Religious Exercise

As noted in earlier chapters, the government sometimes attempts to accommodate religious practices by passing laws aimed at enhancing religious freedom or at alleviating state interference with such practices. This chapter considers a few of those legislative efforts to accommodate religious exercise. Some of the obstacles these efforts must navigate around are the Establishment Clause's prohibition on government endorsement of or excessive entanglement with religion and its ban on governmental preference for one faith over another.

The Court first embraced accommodation of religious exercise as a positive constitutional value in *Zorach v. Clauson*,[1] where it upheld a program that allowed public schools to release students during the school day so they could attend religious instruction off school campuses. In addition to finding no Establishment Clause bar to the program, the Court majority addressed the ability of legislative bodies to affirmatively accommodate religious practice:

> We are a religious people whose institutions presuppose a Supreme Being. We guarantee the freedom to worship as one chooses. We make room for as wide a variety of beliefs and creeds as the spiritual needs of man deem necessary. We sponsor an attitude on the part of the government that shows no partiality to any one group and that lets each flourish according to the zeal of its adherents and the appeal of its dogma. When the state encourages religious instruction or cooperates with religious authorities by adjusting the schedule of public events to sectarian needs, it follows the best of our traditions. For it then respects the religious nature of our people and accommodates the public service to their spiritual needs. To hold that it may not would be to find in the Constitution a requirement that the government show a callous indifference to religious groups. . . .
>
> In the *McCollum [v. Board of Education]* case the classrooms were used for religious instruction and the force of the public school was used to promote that instruction. Here, as we have said, the public schools do no more than accommodate their schedules to a program of outside religious instruction.[2]

Even though the *Zorach* majority was able to distinguish the religious accommodation there from the forbidden advancement of religion present in *McCollum*, the lines between the two concepts are not always pellucid, as is evinced by the existence of three dissenting opinions in *Zorach*. Many legislative accommodations present close cases. For example, in the case of *McGowan v. Maryland*[3] employees of a Maryland department store were indicted for selling goods on Sunday in violation of the state's "Sunday Closing Law" or "Sunday Blue Law." These laws prohibited Sunday sale of all merchandise except from a list of selected items and prohibited a variety of commercial and other activities on Sunday. The employees challenged these laws as violations of the federal constitution's Establishment Clause, among other grounds, and the Supreme Court agreed to hear their case. The Court found that the laws did not violate the Establishment Clause.

According to the Court, "[t]he essence of appellants' 'establishment' argument is that Sunday is the Sabbath day of the predominant Christian sects; that the purpose of the enforced stoppage of labor on that day is to facilitate and encourage church attendance; that the purpose of setting Sunday as a day of universal rest is to induce people with no religion or people with marginal religious beliefs to join the predominant Christian sects; that the purpose of the atmosphere of tranquility created by Sunday closing is to aid the conduct of church services and religious observance of the sacred day. . . ." The Court responded: "There is no dispute that the original laws which dealt with Sunday labor were motivated by religious forces. But what we must decide is whether present Sunday legislation, having undergone extensive changes from the earliest forms, still retains its religious character."[4]

The Court determined that "the statutes' present purpose and effect is not to aid religion but to set aside a day of rest and recreation." It explained:

> Throughout this century and longer, both the federal and state governments have oriented their activities very largely toward improvement of the health, safety, recreation and general well-being of our citizens. Numerous laws affecting public health, safety factors in industry, laws affecting hours and conditions of labor of women and children, week-end diversion at parks and beaches, and cultural activities of various kinds, now point the way toward the good life for all. Sunday Closing Laws, like those before us, have become part and parcel of this great governmental concern wholly apart from their original purposes or connotations. The present purpose and effect of most of them is to provide a uniform day of rest for all citizens; the fact that this day is Sunday, a day of particular significance for the dominant Christian sects, does not bar the State from achieving its secular goals. To say that the States cannot prescribe Sunday as a day of rest for these purposes solely because centuries ago such laws had their genesis in religion would give a constitutional interpretation of hostility to the public welfare rather than one of mere separation of church and State. . . .[5]

The Court also rejected the argument that it should require Maryland to develop a policy that would allow citizens to select one day each week to be off work. The Court reasoned:

> [T]he State's purpose is not merely to provide a one-day-in-seven work stoppage. In addition to this, the State seeks to set one day apart from all others as a day of rest, repose, recreation and tranquility—a day which all members of the family and community have the opportunity to spend and enjoy together, a day on which there exists relative quiet and disassociation from the everyday intensity of commercial activities, a day on which people may visit friends and relatives who are not available during working days.
>
> Obviously, a State is empowered to determine that a rest-one-day-in-seven statute would not accomplish this purpose; that it would not provide for a general

cessation of activity, a special atmosphere of tranquility, a day which all members of the family or friends and relatives might spend together. Furthermore, it seems plain that the problems involved in enforcing such a provision would be exceedingly more difficult than those in enforcing a common-day-of-rest provision.[6]

The Court also distinguished its ruling in the *McCollum* case.

> The distinctions between the statutes in the case before us and the state action in *McCollum v. Board of Education*, the only case in this Court finding a violation of the "Establishment Clause," lend further substantiation to our conclusion. In *McCollum*, state action permitted religious instruction in public school buildings during school hours and required students not attending the religious instruction to remain in their classrooms during that time. The Court found that this system had the effect of coercing the children to attend religious classes; no such coercion to attend church services is present in the situation at bar. In *McCollum*, the only alternative available to the nonattending students was to remain in their classrooms; the alternatives open to nonlaboring persons in the instant case are far more diverse. In *McCollum*, there was direct cooperation between state officials and religious ministers; no such direct participation exists under the Maryland laws. In *McCollum*, tax-supported buildings were used to aid religion; in the instant case, no tax monies are being used in aid of religion.[7]

Finally, the Court emphasized "that this case deals only with the constitutionality of § 521 of the Maryland statute before us. We do not hold that Sunday legislation may not be a violation of the 'Establishment' Clause if it can be demonstrated that its purpose—evidenced either on the face of the legislation, in conjunction with its legislative history, or in its operative effect—is to use the State's coercive power to aid religion."[8]

In sum, the Court concluded: "In light of the evolution of our Sunday Closing Laws through the centuries, and of their more or less recent emphasis upon secular considerations, it is not difficult to discern that as presently written and administered, most of them, at least, are of a secular rather than of a religious character, and that presently they bear no relationship to establishment of religion as those words are used in the Constitution of the United States."[9]

---

### NOTES AND QUESTIONS

1. The situations in *Zorach* and *McGowan* represent forms of government accommodation of religious practice. But the underlying rationales for the respective accommodations are vastly different. The justification for the released time program in *Zorach* was religious: to support the spiritual needs of school children. In contrast, the stated justification for the Sunday law was secular—a uniform day of rest—though the Court acknowledged that the law also accommodated religious practice. This raises a threshold issue regarding religious accommodations: can or should the government seek to accommodate religious practice for the purpose of enhancing that practice, or should accommodations serve a primarily secular purpose? What about cases in which the government places a burden on religious practices? Does the government then have the responsibility—or at least the latitude—to remove or lessen that burden in order to protect the free exercise of faith? To take one example, do the exemptions from military service for religious conscientious

objectors exist out of respect for religious conscience (or out of a concern about the government coercing matters of faith) or for pragmatic reasons arising out of the need for a reliable and obedient fighting force, or both? Does it matter for constitutional purposes how the government justifies a religious accommodation? Should it? If the government provides an accommodation that is limited to religious entities or activities, what prerequisites should exist—that the accommodation relieves some burden on religious practice? If so, then how great must the burden be on the practitioner and who must impose that burden, the government or a nongovernmental actor? Does it matter if the accommodation of the religious practice imposes burdens on other people? Keep these issues in mind as you read the following questions and cases.

2. According to the *Zorach* Court, what grounds justify accommodations of religious practice? Are they persuasive? Did the Court require a showing that the children's ability to practice their religion was otherwise burdened in order to justify the release-time program? Would the religious practices of the school children in *Zorach* have been burdened in the absence of the release-time program?

3. The *McGowan* decision implies that modern state legislatures employ Sunday laws to achieve secular goals. Could the Court have used a rationale similar to that in *Zorach*, that the Sunday law was justified on the ground that Maryland was accommodating the religious practice of the majority of its citizens who happen to be Sunday observing Christians? Would the lack of a Sunday law impose a burden on the ability to practice one's religion? Or should a religious justification for a Sunday law be sufficient in the absence of any burden on religious practice?

4. The Court has said that "[t]he clearest command of the Establishment Clause is that one religious denomination cannot be officially preferred over another." (*Larson v. Valente*). Even though the Court said that the Sunday law basically had lost its religious significance, is there some denominational preference inherent in prohibiting the sale of goods on Sunday? Relatedly, is the accommodation provided by the Sunday law valid if it imposes a burden on non-Sunday observers? See the companion case to *McGowan*, *Braunfeld v. Brown*, in chapter 7, where Jewish shop owners claimed that the Sunday law burdened their religious practice. The *Braunfeld* Court held that the alleged burden there did not rise to the level of a free exercise violation, but should the burden on the Jewish shop owners have been sufficient to undermine the accommodation provided by the Sunday law?

5. If the legislative history that supported a particular Sunday law reflected a number of legislators' beliefs that commercial activities should be prohibited on Sunday in order to honor the Christian faith, would that law run afoul of the Establishment Clause?

Since the earliest days of our nation, churches and other houses of worship have received exemptions from paying taxes on their property holdings and other assets and income. In chapter 9, we saw that the Court has held that the Free Exercise Clause does not require the state to exempt religious materials from a generally applicable sales and use tax. In that case, the Court found that the burden imposed on religious practice by that tax liability is not substantial. See *Jimmy Swaggart Ministries v. Board of Equalization* (1990). But that holding does not answer the question of whether the state may exempt the property of houses of worship and other nonprofit organizations from taxation. Or, is such an exemption actually unconstitutional because it violates the Establishment Clause? The Supreme Court considered these and other questions when it entertained a challenge to a state law that exempted the property of religious organizations, among other organizations, from taxation.

## WALZ v. TAX COMMISSION OF THE CITY OF NEW YORK
### 397 U.S. 664 (1970)

▨ MR. CHIEF JUSTICE BURGER delivered the opinion of the Court.

Appellant, owner of real estate in Richmond County, New York, sought an injunction in the New York courts to prevent the New York City Tax Commission from granting property tax exemptions to religious organizations for religious properties used solely for religious worship. The exemption from state taxes is authorized by Art. 16, § 1, of the New York Constitution, which provides in relevant part:

> Exemptions from taxation may be granted only by general laws. Exemptions may be altered or repealed except those exempting real or personal property used exclusively for religious, educational or charitable purposes as defined by law and owned by any corporation or association organized or conducted exclusively for one or more of such purposes and not operating for profit.[1]

The essence of appellant's contention was that the New York City Tax Commission's grant of an exemption to church property indirectly requires the appellant to make a contribution to religious bodies and thereby violates provisions prohibiting establishment of religion under the First Amendment which under the Fourteenth Amendment is binding on the States. . . .

---

[1] Art. 16, § 1, of the New York State Constitution is implemented by § 420, subd. 1, of the New York Real Property Tax Law which states in pertinent part:

"Real property owned by a corporation or association organized exclusively for the moral or mental improvement of men and women, or for religious, bible, tract, charitable, benevolent, missionary, hospital, infirmary, educational, public playground, scientific, literary, bar association, medical society, library, patriotic, historical or cemetery purposes . . . and used exclusively for carrying out thereupon one or more of such purposes . . . shall be exempt from taxation as provided in this section."

I

Prior opinions of this Court have discussed the development and historical background of the First Amendment in detail. See *Everson v. Board of Education*, 330 U.S. 1 (1947); *Engel v. Vitale*, 370 U.S. 421 (1962). It would therefore serve no useful purpose to review in detail the background of the Establishment and Free Exercise Clauses of the First Amendment or to restate what the Court's opinions have reflected over the years.

It is sufficient to note that for the men who wrote the Religion Clauses of the First Amendment the "establishment" of a religion connoted sponsorship, financial support, and active involvement of the sovereign in religious activity. . . .

The Establishment and Free Exercise Clauses of the First Amendment are not the most precisely drawn portions of the Constitution. The sweep of the absolute prohibitions in the Religion Clauses may have been calculated; but the purpose was to state an objective, not to write a statute. In attempting to articulate the scope of the two Religion Clauses, the Court's opinions reflect the limitations inherent in formulating general principles on a case-by-case basis. The considerable internal inconsistency in the opinions of the Court derives from what, in retrospect, may have been too sweeping utterances on aspects of these clauses that seemed clear in relation to the particular cases but have limited meaning as general principles.

The Court has struggled to find a neutral course between the two Religion Clauses, both of which are cast in absolute terms, and either of which, if expanded to a logical extreme, would tend to clash with the other. . . .

The course of constitutional neutrality in this area cannot be an absolutely straight line; rigidity could well defeat the basic purpose of these provisions, which is to insure that no religion be sponsored or favored, none commanded, and none inhibited. The general principle deducible from the First Amendment and all that has been said by the Court is this: that we will not tolerate either governmentally established religion or governmental interference with religion. Short of those expressly proscribed governmental acts there is room for play in the joints productive of a benevolent neutrality which will permit religious exercise to exist without sponsorship and without interference.

Each value judgment under the Religion Clauses must therefore turn on whether particular acts in question are intended to establish or interfere with religious beliefs and practices or have the effect of doing so. Adherence to the policy of neutrality that derives from an accommodation of the Establishment and Free Exercise Clauses has prevented the kind of involvement that would tip the balance toward government control of churches or governmental restraint on religious practice.

Adherents of particular faiths and individual churches frequently take strong positions on public issues including, as this case reveals in the several briefs *amici*, vigorous advocacy of legal or constitutional positions. Of course, churches as much as secular bodies and private citizens have that right. No perfect or absolute separation is really possible; the very existence of the Religion Clauses is an involvement of sorts—one that seeks to mark boundaries to avoid excessive entanglement. . . .

In *Everson* the Court declined to construe the Religion Clauses with a literalness that would undermine the ultimate constitutional objective as illuminated by history. Surely, bus transportation and police protection to pupils who receive religious instruction "aid" that particular religion to maintain schools that plainly tend to assure future adherents to a particular faith by having control of their total education at an early age. No religious body that maintains schools would deny this as an affirmative if not dominant policy of church schools. But if as in *Everson* buses can be provided to carry and policemen to protect church school pupils, we fail to see how a broader range of police and fire protection given equally to all churches, along with nonprofit hospitals, art galleries, and libraries receiving the same tax exemption, is different for purposes of the Religion Clauses.

Similarly, making textbooks available to pupils in parochial schools in common with public schools was surely an "aid" to the sponsoring churches because it relieved those churches of an enormous aggregate cost for those books. Supplying of costly teaching materials was not seen either as manifesting a legislative purpose to aid or as having a primary effect of aid contravening the First Amendment. *Board of Education v. Allen*, 392 U.S. 236 (1968). In so holding the Court was heeding both its own prior decisions and our religious tradition. MR. JUSTICE DOUGLAS, in *Zorach v. Clauson*, after recalling that we "are a religious people whose institutions presuppose a Supreme Being," went on to say:

> We make room for as wide a variety of beliefs and creeds as the spiritual needs of man deem necessary. . . . *When the state encourages religious instruction . . . it follows the best of our traditions.* For it then respects the religious nature of our people and accommodates the public service to their spiritual needs. 343 U.S., 313-314 (emphasis added.)

With all the risks inherent in programs that bring about administrative relationships between public education bodies and church-sponsored schools, we have been able to chart a course that preserved the autonomy and freedom of religious bodies while avoiding any semblance of established religion. This is a "tight rope" and one we have successfully traversed.

## II

The legislative purpose of the property tax exemption is neither the advancement nor the inhibition of religion; it is neither sponsorship nor hostility. New York, in common with the other States, has determined that certain entities that exist in a harmonious relationship to the community at large, and that foster its "moral or mental improvement," should not be inhibited in their activities by property taxation or the hazard of loss of those properties for nonpayment of taxes. It has not singled out one particular church or religious group or even churches as such; rather, it has granted exemption to all houses of religious worship within a broad class of property owned by nonprofit, quasi-public corporations which include hospitals, libraries, playgrounds, scientific, professional, historical, and patriotic groups. The State has an affirmative policy that considers these groups as beneficial and stabilizing influences in community life and finds this classification useful, desirable, and in the public interest. Qualification for tax exemption is not perpetual or immutable; some tax-exempt groups lose that status when their activities take them outside the classification and new entities can come into being and qualify for exemption.

Governments have not always been tolerant of religious activity, and hostility toward religion has taken many shapes and forms—economic, political, and sometimes harshly oppressive. Grants of exemption historically reflect the concern of authors of constitutions and statutes as to the latent dangers inherent in the imposition of property taxes; exemption constitutes a reasonable and balanced attempt to guard against those dangers. The limits of permissible state accommodation to religion are by no means co-extensive with the noninterference mandated by the Free Exercise Clause. To equate the two would be to deny a national heritage with roots in the Revolution itself. . . . We cannot read New York's statute as attempting to establish religion; it is simply sparing the exercise of religion from the burden of property taxation levied on private profit institutions.

We find it unnecessary to justify the tax exemption on the social welfare services or "good works" that some churches perform for parishioners and others—family counselling, aid to the elderly and the infirm, and to children. Churches vary substantially in the scope of such services; programs expand or contract according to resources and need. . . . To give emphasis to so variable an aspect of the work of religious bodies would introduce an element of governmental evaluation and standards as to the worth of particular social welfare programs, thus producing a kind of continuing day-to-day relationship which the policy of neutrality seeks to minimize. Hence, the use of a social welfare yardstick as a significant element to qualify for tax exemption could conceivably give rise to confrontations that could escalate to constitutional dimensions.

Determining that the legislative purpose of tax exemption is not aimed at establishing, sponsoring, or supporting religion does not end the inquiry, however. We must also be sure that the end result—the effect—is not an excessive government entanglement with religion. The test is inescapably one of degree. Either course, taxation of churches or exemption, occasions some degree of involvement with religion. Elimination of exemption would tend to expand the involvement of government by giving rise to tax valuation of church property, tax liens, tax foreclosures, and the direct confrontations and conflicts that follow in the train of those legal processes.

Granting tax exemptions to churches necessarily operates to afford an indirect economic benefit and also gives rise to some, but yet a lesser, involvement than taxing them. In analyzing either alternative the questions are whether the involvement is excessive, and whether it is a continuing one calling for official and continuing surveillance leading to an impermissible degree of entanglement. Obviously a direct money subsidy would be a relationship pregnant with involvement and, as with most governmental grant programs, could encompass sustained and detailed administrative relationships for enforcement of statutory or administrative standards, but that is not this case. The hazards of churches supporting government are hardly less in their potential than the hazards of government supporting churches; each relationship carries some involvement rather than the desired insulation and separation. We cannot ignore the instances in history when church support of government led to the kind of involvement we seek to avoid.

The grant of a tax exemption is not sponsorship since the government does not transfer part of its revenue to churches but simply abstains from demanding that the church support the state. No one has ever suggested that tax exemption has converted libraries, art galleries, or hospitals into arms of the state or put employees "on the public payroll." There is no genuine nexus between tax exemption and establishment of religion. As Mr. Justice Holmes commented in a related context "a page of history is worth a volume of logic."

The exemption creates only a minimal and remote involvement between church and state and far less than taxation of churches. It restricts the fiscal relationship between church and state, and tends to complement and reinforce the desired separation insulating each from the other.

Separation in this context cannot mean absence of all contact; the complexities of modern life inevitably produce some contact and the fire and police protection received by houses of religious worship are no more than incidental benefits accorded all persons or institutions within a State's boundaries, along with many other exempt organizations. The appellant has not established even an arguable quantitative correlation between the payment of an ad valorem property tax and the receipt of these municipal benefits.

All of the 50 States provide for tax exemption of places of worship, most of them doing so by constitutional guarantees. For so long as federal income taxes have had any potential impact on churches—over 75 years—religious organizations have been expressly exempt from the tax. Such treatment is an "aid" to churches no more and no less in principle than the real estate tax exemption granted by States. Few concepts are more deeply embedded in the fabric of our national life, beginning with pre-Revolutionary colonial times, than for the government to exercise at the very least this kind of benevolent neutrality toward churches and religious exercise generally so long as none was favored over others and none suffered interference.

It is significant that Congress, from its earliest days, has viewed the Religion Clauses of the Constitution as authorizing statutory real estate tax exemption to religious bodies. In 1802 the 7th Congress enacted a taxing statute for the County of Alexandria, adopting the 1800 Virginia statutory pattern which provided tax exemptions for churches. 2 Stat. 194. As early as 1813 the 12th Congress refunded import duties paid by religious societies on the importation of religious articles. During this period the City Council of Washington, D. C., acting under congressional authority, enacted a series of real and personal property assessments that uniformly exempted church property. In 1870 the Congress specifically exempted all churches in the District of Columbia and appurtenant grounds and property "from any and all taxes or assessments, national, municipal, or county."

It is obviously correct that no one acquires a vested or protected right in violation of the Constitution by long use, even when that span of time covers our entire national existence and indeed predates it. Yet an unbroken practice of according the exemption to churches, openly and by affirmative state action, not covertly or by state inaction, is not something to be lightly cast aside. . . .

Nothing in this national attitude toward religious tolerance and two centuries of uninterrupted freedom from taxation has given the remotest sign of leading to an established church or religion and on the contrary it has operated affirmatively to help guarantee the free exercise of all forms of religious belief. Thus, it is hardly useful to suggest that tax exemption is but the "foot in the door" or the "nose of the camel in the tent" leading to an established church. If tax exemption can be seen as this first step toward "establishment" of religion, as MR. JUSTICE DOUGLAS fears, the second step has been long in coming. Any move that realistically "establishes" a church or tends to do so can be dealt with "while this Court sits." . . .

The argument that making "fine distinctions" between what is and what is not absolute under the Constitution is to render us a government of men, not laws, gives too little weight to the fact that it is an essential part of adjudication to draw distinctions, including fine ones, in the process of interpreting the Constitution. We must frequently decide, for example, what are "reasonable" searches and seizures under the Fourth Amendment. Determining what acts of government tend to establish or interfere with religion falls well within what courts have long been called upon to do in sensitive areas.

It is interesting to note that while the precise question we now decide has not been directly before the Court previously, the broad question was discussed by the Court in relation to real estate taxes assessed nearly a century ago on land owned by and adjacent to a church in Washington, D. C. At that time Congress granted real estate tax exemptions to buildings devoted to art, to institutions of public charity, libraries, cemeteries, and "church buildings, and grounds actually occupied by such buildings." In denying tax exemption as to land owned by but not used for the church, but rather to produce income, the Court concluded:

"In the exercise of this [taxing] power, Congress, like any State legislature unrestricted by constitutional provisions, may at its discretion wholly exempt certain classes of property from taxation, or may tax them at a lower rate than other property." *Gibbons v. District of Columbia*, 116 U.S. 404, 408 (1886).

It appears that at least up to 1885 this Court, reflecting more than a century of our history and uninterrupted practice, accepted without discussion the proposition that federal or state grants of tax exemption to churches were not a violation of the Religion Clauses of the First Amendment. As to the New York statute, we now confirm that view.

*Affirmed.*

▦ MR. JUSTICE BRENNAN, concurring.

I concur for reasons expressed in my opinion in *Abington School Dist. v. Schempp.* I adhere to the view there stated that to give concrete meaning to the Establishment Clause,

> the line we must draw between the permissible and the impermissible is one which accords with history and faithfully reflects the understanding of the Founding Fathers. It is a line which the Court has consistently sought to mark in its decisions expounding the religious guarantees of the First Amendment. What the Framers meant to foreclose, and what our decisions under the Establishment Clause have forbidden, are those involvements of religious with secular institutions which (a) serve the essentially religious activities of religious institutions; (b) employ the organs of government for essentially religious purposes; or (c) use essentially religious means to serve governmental ends, where secular means would suffice. When the secular and religious institutions become involved in such a manner, there inhere in the relationship precisely those dangers—as much to church as to state—which the Framers feared would subvert religious liberty and the strength of a system of secular government. On the other hand, there may be myriad forms of involvements of government with religion which do not import such dangers and therefore should not, in my judgment, be deemed to violate the Establishment Clause.

Thus, in my view, the history, purpose, and operation of real property tax exemptions for religious organizations must be examined to determine whether the Establishment Clause is breached by such exemptions.

I

The existence from the beginning of the Nation's life of a practice, such as tax exemptions for religious organizations, is not conclusive of its constitutionality. But such practice is a fact of considerable import in the interpretation of abstract constitutional language. On its face, the Establishment Clause is reasonably susceptible of different interpretations regarding the exemptions. This Court's interpretation of the clause, accordingly, is appropriately influenced by the reading it has received in the practices of the Nation. . . . The more longstanding and widely accepted a practice, the greater its impact upon constitutional interpretation. History is particularly compelling in the present case because of the undeviating acceptance given religious tax exemptions from our earliest days as a Nation. Rarely if ever has this Court considered the constitutionality of a practice for which the historical support is so overwhelming.

The Establishment Clause, along with the other provisions of the Bill of Rights, was ratified by the States in 1791. Religious tax exemptions were not an issue in the petitions calling for the Bill of Rights, in the pertinent congressional debates, or in the debates preceding ratification by the States. The absence of concern about the exemptions could not have resulted from failure to foresee the possibility of their existence, for they were widespread during colonial days. Rather, it seems clear that the exemptions were not among the evils that the Framers and Ratifiers of the Establishment Clause sought to avoid. Significantly, within a decade after ratification, at least four States passed statutes exempting the property of religious organizations from taxation.

Although the First Amendment may not have applied to the States during this period, practice in Virginia at the time is nonetheless instructive. The Commonwealth's efforts to separate church and state provided the direct antecedents of the First Amendment, and Virginia remained unusually sensitive to the proper relation between church and state during the years immediately following ratification of the Establishment Clause. Virginia's protracted movement to disestablish the Episcopal Church culminated in the passage on January 24, 1799, of "An ACT to repeal certain acts, and to declare the construction of the [Virginia] bill of rights and constitution, concerning religion." The 1799 Act stated that the Virginia Bill of Rights had "excepted from the powers given to the [civil] government, the power of reviving any species of ecclesiastical or church government . . . by referring the subject of religion to conscience" and that the repealed measures had "bestowed property upon [the Anglican] church," had "asserted a legislative right to establish any religious sect," and had "incorporated religious sects, all of which is inconsistent with the principles of the constitution, and of religious freedom, and manifestly tends to the reestablishment of a national church." Yet just one year after the passage of this Act, Virginia re-enacted a measure exempting from taxation property belonging to "any . . . college, houses for divine worship, or seminary of learning." This exemption dated at least from 1777 and had been reaffirmed immediately before and after ratification of the First Amendment. It may reasonably be inferred that the Virginians did not view the exemption for "houses of divine worship" as an establishment of religion.

Similarly, in 1784 the New York Legislature repealed colonial acts establishing the Episcopal Church in several counties of the State. Yet in 1799, the legislature provided that "no house or land belonging to . . . any church or place of public worship, . . . nor any college or incorporated academy, nor any school house, . . . alms house or property belonging to any incorporated library, shall be taxed by virtue of this act." And early practice in the District of Columbia—governed from the outset by the First Amendment—mirrored that in the States. In 1802 the Corporation of the City of Washington, under authority delegated by Congress, exempted "houses for public worship" from real property taxes.

Thomas Jefferson was President when tax exemption was first given Washington churches, and James Madison sat in sessions of the Virginia General Assembly that voted exemptions for churches in that Commonwealth. I have found no record of their personal views on the respective Acts.[5] The absence of such a record is itself significant. It is unlikely that two men so concerned with the separation of church and state would have remained silent had they thought the exemptions established religion. And if they had not either approved the exemptions, or been mild in their opposition, it is probable that their views would be known to us today. Both Jefferson and Madison wrote prolifically about issues they felt important, and their opinions were well known to contemporary chroniclers. . . . Much the same can be said of the other Framers and Ratifiers of the Bill of Rights who remained active in public affairs during the late 18th and early 19th centuries. The adoption of the early exemptions without controversy, in other words, strongly suggests that they were not thought incompatible with constitutional prohibitions against involvements of church and state.

The exemptions have continued uninterrupted to the present day. They are in force in all 50 States. No judicial decision, state or federal, has ever held that they violate the Establishment Clause. . . .

For almost 200 years the view expressed in the actions of legislatures and courts has been that tax exemptions for churches do not threaten "those consequences which the Framers deeply feared" or "tend to promote that type of interdependence between religion and state which the First Amendment was designed to prevent." *Schempp*, 374 U.S., 236. An examination both of the governmental purposes for granting the exemptions and of the type of church-state relationship that has resulted from their existence makes clear that no "strong case" exists for holding unconstitutional this historic practice.[7]

---

[5] In an essay written after he had left the presidency, Madison did argue against tax exemptions for churches, the incorporation of ecclesiastical bodies with the power of acquiring and holding property in perpetuity, the right of the Houses of Congress to choose chaplains who are paid out of public funds, the provision of chaplains in the Army and Navy, and presidential proclamations of days of thanksgiving or prayer—though he admitted proclaiming several such days at congressional request. These arguments were advanced long after the passage of the Virginia exemption discussed in the text, and even longer after the adoption of the Establishment Clause. They represent at most an extreme view of church-state relations, which Madison himself may have reached only late in life. He certainly expressed no such understanding of Establishment during the debates on the First Amendment. And even if he privately held these views at that time, there is no evidence that they were shared by others among the Framers and Ratifiers of the Bill of Rights.

[7] Compare the very different situation regarding prayers in public schools. The practice was not widespread at the time of the adoption of the First Amendment. Legislative authorization for the prayers came much later and then only in a relatively small number of States. Moreover, courts began to question the constitutionality of the practice by the late 19th century. The prayers were found unconstitutional by courts in six States and by state attorneys general in several others.

## II

Government has two basic secular purposes for granting real property tax exemptions to religious organizations. First, these organizations are exempted because they, among a range of other private, nonprofit organizations contribute to the well-being of the community in a variety of nonreligious ways, and thereby bear burdens that would otherwise either have to be met by general taxation, or be left undone, to the detriment of the community. . . .

Appellant seeks to avoid the force of this secular purpose of the exemptions by limiting his challenge to "exemptions from real property taxation to religious organizations on real property used exclusively for religious purposes." Appellant assumes, apparently, that church-owned property is used for exclusively religious purposes if it does not house a hospital, orphanage, weekday school, or the like. Any assumption that a church building itself is used for exclusively religious activities, however, rests on a simplistic view of ordinary church operations. As the appellee's brief cogently observes, "the public welfare activities and the sectarian activities of religious institutions are . . . intertwined. . . . Often a particular church will use the same personnel, facilities and source of funds to carry out both its secular and religious activities." Thus, the same people who gather in church facilities for religious worship and study may return to these facilities to participate in Boy Scout activities, to promote antipoverty causes, to discuss public issues, or to listen to chamber music. Accordingly, the funds used to maintain the facilities as a place for religious worship and study also maintain them as a place for secular activities beneficial to the community as a whole. Even during formal worship services, churches frequently collect the funds used to finance their secular operations and make decisions regarding their nature.

Second, government grants exemptions to religious organizations because they uniquely contribute to the pluralism of American society by their religious activities. Government may properly include religious institutions among the variety of private, nonprofit groups that receive tax exemptions, for each group contributes to the diversity of association, viewpoint, and enterprise essential to a vigorous, pluralistic society. To this end, New York extends its exemptions not only to religious and social service organizations but also to scientific, literary, bar, library, patriotic, and historical groups, and generally to institutions "organized exclusively for the moral or mental improvement of men and women." The very breadth of this scheme of exemptions negates any suggestion that the State intends to single out religious organizations for special preference. The scheme is not designed to inject any religious activity into a nonreligious context, as was the case with school prayers. No particular activity of a religious organization—for example, the propagation of its beliefs—is specially promoted by the exemptions. They merely facilitate the existence of a broad range of private, nonprofit organizations, among them religious groups, by leaving each free to come into existence, then to flourish or wither, without being burdened by real property taxes.

## III

Although governmental purposes for granting religious exemptions may be wholly secular, exemptions can nonetheless violate the Establishment Clause if they result in extensive state involvement with religion. Accordingly, those who urge the exemptions' unconstitutionality argue that exemptions are the equivalent of governmental subsidy of churches. General subsidies of

religious activities would, of course, constitute impermissible state involvement with religion.

Tax exemptions and general subsidies, however, are qualitatively different. Though both provide economic assistance, they do so in fundamentally
different ways. A subsidy involves the direct transfer of public monies to the
subsidized enterprise and uses resources exacted from taxpayers as a whole. An
exemption, on the other hand, involves no such transfer. It assists the exempted
enterprise only passively, by relieving a privately funded venture of the burden
of paying taxes. In other words, "in the case of direct subsidy, the state forcibly
diverts the income of both believers and nonbelievers to churches," while "in
the case of an exemption, the state merely refrains from diverting to its own uses
income independently generated by the churches through voluntary contributions." Thus, "the symbolism of tax exemption is significant as a manifestation
that organized religion is not expected to support the state; by the same token
the state is not expected to support the church." Tax exemptions, accordingly,
constitute mere passive state involvement with religion and not the affirmative
involvement characteristic of outright governmental subsidy.

Even though exemptions produce only passive state involvement with
religion, nonetheless some argue that their termination would be desirable
as a means of reducing the level of church-state contact. But it cannot realistically be said that termination of religious tax exemptions would quantitatively
lessen the extent of state involvement with religion. Appellee contends that "as
a practical matter, the public welfare activities and the sectarian activities of
religious institutions are so intertwined that they cannot be separated for the
purpose of determining eligibility for tax exemptions." If not impossible, the
separation would certainly involve extensive state investigation into church
operations and finances. Moreover, the termination of exemptions would give
rise, as the Court says, to the necessity for "tax valuation of church property,
tax liens, tax foreclosures, and the direct confrontations and conflicts that follow in the train of those legal processes." Taxation, further, would bear unequally on different churches, having its most disruptive effect on those with
the least ability to meet the annual levies assessed against them. And taxation
would surely influence the allocation of church resources. By diverting funds
otherwise available for religious or public service purposes to the support of
the Government, taxation would necessarily affect the extent of church support for the enterprises that they now promote. In many instances, the public
service activities would bear the brunt of the reallocation, as churches looked
first to maintain their places and programs of worship. In short, the cessation of exemptions would have a significant impact on religious organizations.
Whether Government grants or withholds the exemptions, it is going to be
involved with religion.[12]

## IV

Against the background of this survey of the history, purpose, and operation of religious tax exemptions, I must conclude that the exemptions do

---

[12] The state involvement with religion that would be occasioned by any cessation of
exemptions might conflict with the demands of the Free Exercise Clause. It is unnecessary
to reach any questions of free exercise in the present case, however. And while I believe that
"hostility, not neutrality, would characterize the refusal to provide [the exemptions]. . . , I do
not say that government must provide [them], or that the courts should intercede if it fails to
do so." *Schempp*, 374 U.S., 299.

not "serve the essentially religious activities of religious institutions." Their principal effect is to carry out secular purposes—the encouragement of public service activities and of a pluralistic society. During their ordinary operations, most churches engage in activities of a secular nature that benefit the community; and all churches by their existence contribute to the diversity of association, viewpoint, and enterprise so highly valued by all of us.

Nor do I find that the exemptions "employ the organs of government for essentially religious purposes." To the extent that the exemptions further secular ends, they do not advance "essentially religious purposes." To the extent that purely religious activities are benefited by the exemptions, the benefit is passive. Government does not affirmatively foster these activities by exempting religious organizations from taxes, as it would were it to subsidize them. The exemption simply leaves untouched that which adherents of the organization bring into being and maintain.

Finally, I do not think that the exemptions "use essentially religious means to serve governmental ends, where secular means would suffice." The means churches use to carry on their public service activities are not "essentially religious" in nature. They are the same means used by any purely secular organization—money, human time and skills, physical facilities. It is true that each church contributes to the pluralism of our society through its purely religious activities, but the state encourages these activities not because it champions religion *per se* but because it values religion among a variety of private, nonprofit enterprises that contribute to the diversity of the Nation. Viewed in this light, there is no nonreligious substitute for religion as an element in our societal mosaic, just as there is no nonliterary substitute for literary groups.

As I said in *Schempp*, the First Amendment does not invalidate "the propriety of certain tax . . . exemptions which incidentally benefit churches and religious institutions, along with many secular charities and nonprofit organizations. . . . Religious institutions simply share benefits which government makes generally available to educational, charitable, and eleemosynary groups. There is no indication that taxing authorities have used such benefits in any way to subsidize worship or foster belief in God." 374 U.S., 301. . . .

MR. JUSTICE DOUGLAS, dissenting.

Petitioner is the owner of real property in New York and is a Christian. But he is not a member of any of the religious organizations, "rejecting them as hostile." The New York statute exempts from taxation real property "owned by a corporation or association organized exclusively for . . . religious . . . purposes" and used "exclusively for carrying out" such purposes. Yet nonbelievers who own realty are taxed at the usual rate. The question in the case therefore is whether believers—organized in church groups—can be made exempt from real estate taxes, merely because they are believers, while nonbelievers, whether organized or not, must pay the real estate taxes.

My Brother HARLAN says he "would suppose" that the tax exemption extends to "groups whose avowed tenets may be antitheological, atheistic, or agnostic." If it does, then the line between believers and nonbelievers has not been drawn. But, with all respect, there is not even a suggestion in the present record that the statute covers property used exclusively by organizations for "antitheological purposes," "atheistic purposes," or "agnostic purposes."

In *Torcaso v. Watkins*, we held that a State could not bar an atheist from public office in light of the freedom of belief and religion guaranteed by the

First and Fourteenth Amendments. Neither the State nor the Federal Government, we said, "can constitutionally pass laws or impose requirements which aid all religions as against non-believers, and neither can aid those religions based on a belief in the existence of God as against those religions founded on different beliefs."

That principle should govern this case.

There is a line between what a State may do in encouraging "religious" activities, *Zorach v. Clauson*, and what a State may not do by using its resources to promote "religious" activities, *McCollum v. Board of Education*, or bestowing benefits because of them. Yet that line may not always be clear. Closing public schools on Sunday is in the former category; subsidizing churches, in my view, is in the latter. Indeed I would suppose that in common understanding one of the best ways to "establish" one or more religions is to subsidize them, which a tax exemption does. The State may not do that any more than it may prefer "those who believe in no religion over those who do believe."

In affirming this judgment the Court largely overlooks the revolution initiated by the adoption of the Fourteenth Amendment. That revolution involved the imposition of new and far-reaching constitutional restraints on the States. Nationalization of many civil liberties has been the consequence of the Fourteenth Amendment, reversing the historic position that the foundations of those liberties rested largely in state law.

The process of the "selective incorporation" of various provisions of the Bill of Rights into the Fourteenth Amendment, although often provoking lively disagreement at large as well as among the members of this Court, has been a steady one. . . . As regards the religious guarantees of the First Amendment, the Free Exercise Clause was expressly deemed incorporated into the Fourteenth Amendment in 1940 in *Cantwell v. Connecticut*. . . . The Establishment Clause was not incorporated in the Fourteenth Amendment until *Everson v. Board of Education*, was decided in 1947.

Those developments in the last 30 years have had unsettling effects. It was, for example, not until 1962 that state-sponsored, sectarian prayers were held to violate the Establishment Clause. That decision brought many protests, for the habit of putting one sect's prayer in public schools had long been practiced. Yet if the Catholics, controlling one school board, could put their prayer into one group of public schools, the Mormons, Baptists, Moslems, Presbyterians, and others could do the same, once they got control. And so the seeds of Establishment would grow and a secular institution would be used to serve a sectarian end. . . .

[T]he revolution occasioned by the Fourteenth Amendment has progressed as Article after Article in the Bill of Rights has been incorporated in it and made applicable to the States.

Hence the question in the present case makes irrelevant the "two centuries of uninterrupted freedom from taxation," referred to by the Court. If history be our guide, then tax exemption of church property in this country is indeed highly suspect, as it arose in the early days when the church was an agency of the state. The question here, though, concerns the meaning of the Establishment Clause and the Free Exercise Clause made applicable to the States for only a few decades at best.

With all due respect the governing principle is not controlled by *Everson v. Board of Education*. *Everson* involved the use of public funds to bus children to parochial as well as to public schools. Parochial schools teach religion; yet they are also educational institutions offering courses competitive with public schools. They prepare students for the professions and for activities in all walks of life. Education in the secular sense was combined with religious indoctrination at the parochial schools involved in *Everson*. Even so, the *Everson* decision was five to four and, though one of the five, I have since had grave doubts about it, because I have become convinced that grants to institutions teaching a sectarian creed violate the Establishment Clause.

This case, however, is quite different. Education is not involved. The financial support rendered here is to the church, the place of worship. A tax exemption is a subsidy. Is my Brother BRENNAN correct in saying that we would hold that state or federal grants to churches, say, to construct the edifice itself would be unconstitutional? What is the difference between that kind of subsidy and the present subsidy?

The problem takes us back where Madison was in 1784 and 1785 when he battled the Assessment Bill in Virginia. That bill levied a tax for the support of Christian churches, leaving to each taxpayer the choice as to "what society of Christians" he wanted the tax paid; and absent such designation, the tax was to go for education. Even so, Madison was unrelenting in his opposition. . . .

[James Madison's Memorial and] Remonstrance covers some aspects of the present subsidy, including [his] protest in paragraph 3 to a requirement that any person be compelled to contribute even "three pence" to support a church. . . .

The Court seeks to avoid this historic argument as to the meaning of "establishment" and "free exercise" by relying on the long practice of the States in granting the subsidies challenged here.

Certainly government may not lay a tax on either worshiping or preaching. . . .

Churches, like newspapers also enjoying First Amendment rights, have no constitutional immunity from all taxes. . . .

State aid to places of worship, whether in the form of direct grants or tax exemption, takes us back to the Assessment Bill and the Remonstrance. The church *qua* church would not be entitled to that support from believers and from nonbelievers alike. Yet the church *qua* nonprofit, charitable institution is one of many that receive a form of subsidy through tax exemption. To be sure, the New York statute does not single out the church for grant or favor. . . . While the beneficiaries cover a wide range, "atheistic," "agnostic," or "antitheological" groups do not seem to be included.

Churches perform some functions that a State would constitutionally be empowered to perform. I refer to nonsectarian social welfare operations such as the care of orphaned children and the destitute and people who are sick. A tax exemption to agencies performing those functions would therefore be as constitutionally proper as the grant of direct subsidies to them. Under the First Amendment a State may not, however, provide worship if private groups fail to do so. . . .

That is a major difference between churches on the one hand and the rest of the nonprofit organizations on the other. Government could provide or finance operas, hospitals, historical societies, and all the rest because they represent social welfare programs within the reach of the police power. In contrast, government may not provide or finance worship because of the Establishment Clause any more than it may single out "atheistic" or "agnostic" centers or groups and create or finance them.

The Brookings Institution, writing in 1933, before the application of the Establishment Clause of the First Amendment to the States, said about tax exemptions of religious groups:

> Tax exemption, no matter what its form, is essentially a government grant or subsidy. Such grants would seem to be justified only if the purpose for which they are made is one for which the legislative body *would be equally willing to make* a direct appropriation from public funds equal to the amount of the exemption. This test would not be met except in the case where the exemption is granted to encourage certain activities of private interests, which, if not thus performed, would have to be assumed by the government at an expenditure at least as great as the value of the exemption. (Emphasis added.)

Since 1947, when the Establishment Clause was made applicable to the States, that report would have to state that the exemption would be justified only where "the legislative body *could make*" an appropriation for the cause.

On the record of this case, the church *qua* nonprofit, charitable organization is intertwined with the church *qua* church. A church may use the same facilities, resources, and personnel in carrying out both its secular and its sectarian activities. The two are unitary and on the present record have not been separated one from the other. The state has a public policy of encouraging private public welfare organizations, which it desires to encourage through tax exemption. Why may it not do so and include churches *qua* welfare organizations on a nondiscriminatory basis? That avoids, it is argued, a discrimination against churches and in a real sense maintains neutrality toward religion which the First Amendment was designed to foster. Welfare services, whether performed by churches or by nonreligious groups, may well serve the public welfare.

Whether a particular church seeking an exemption for its welfare work could constitutionally pass muster would depend on the special facts. The assumption is that the church is a purely private institution, promoting a sectarian cause. The creed, teaching, and beliefs of one may be undesirable or even repulsive to others. Its sectarian faith sets it apart from all others and makes it difficult to equate its constituency with the general public. The extent that its facilities are open to all may only indicate the nature of its proselytism. Yet though a church covers up its religious symbols in welfare work, its welfare activities may merely be a phase of sectarian activity. I have said enough to indicate the nature of this tax exemption problem.

Direct financial aid to churches or tax exemptions to the church *qua* church is not, in my view, even arguably permitted. Sectarian causes are certainly not antipublic and many would rate their own church or perhaps all churches as the highest form of welfare. The difficulty is that sectarian causes must remain in the private domain not subject to public control or subsidy. That seems to me to be the requirement of the Establishment Clause. . . .

The exemptions provided here insofar as welfare projects are concerned may have the ring of neutrality. But subsidies either through direct grant or tax exemption for sectarian causes, whether carried on by church *qua* church or by church *qua* welfare agency, must be treated differently, lest we in time allow the church *qua* church to be on the public payroll, which, I fear, is imminent. . . .

What Madison would have thought of the present state subsidy to churches—a tax exemption as distinguished from an outright grant—no one can say with certainty. The fact that Virginia early granted church tax exemptions cannot be credited to Madison. Certainly he seems to have been opposed. In his paper Monopolies, Perpetuities, Corporations, Ecclesiastical Endowments he wrote: "Strongly guarded as is the separation between Religion & Govt in the Constitution of the United States the danger of encroachment by Ecclesiastical Bodies, may be illustrated by precedents already furnished in their short history." And he referred, *inter alia*, to the "attempt in Kentucky for example, where it was proposed to exempt Houses of Worship from taxes." From these three statements, Madison, it seems, opposed all state subsidies to churches.

We should adhere to what we said in *Torcaso v. Watkins* that neither a State nor the Federal Government "can constitutionally pass laws or impose requirements *which aid all religions as against nonbelievers*, and neither can aid those religions based on a belief in the existence of God as against those religions founded on different beliefs." (Emphasis added.)

Unless we adhere to that principle, we do not give full support either to the Free Exercise Clause or to the Establishment Clause.

If a church can be exempted from paying real estate taxes, why may not it be made exempt from paying special assessments? The benefits in the two cases differ only in degree; and the burden on nonbelievers is likewise no different in kind.

The religiously used real estate of the churches today constitutes a vast domain. Their assets total over $141 billion and their annual income at least $22 billion.

And the extent to which they are feeding from the public trough in a variety of forms is alarming. We are advised that since 1968 at least five States have undertaken to give subsidies to parochial and other private schools—Pennsylvania, Ohio, New York, Connecticut, and Rhode Island. And it is reported that under two federal Acts, . . . *billions of dollars* have been granted to parochial and other private schools.

The federal grants to elementary and secondary schools were made to the States which in turn made advances to elementary and secondary schools. Those figures are not available.

But the federal grants to private institutions of higher education are revealed in Department of Health, Education, and Welfare (HEW), Digest of Educational Statistics 16 (1969). These show in billions of dollars the following:

| 1965-1966 | $ 1.4 |
|-----------|-------|
| 1966-1967 | $ 1.6 |
| 1967-1968 | $ 1.7 |
| 1968-1969 | $ 1.9 |
| 1969-1970 | $ 2.1 |

It is an old, old problem. Madison adverted to it:

Are there not already examples in the U.S. of ecclesiastical wealth equally beyond its object and the foresight of those who laid the foundation of it? In the U.S. there is a double motive for fixing limits in this case, because wealth may increase not only from additional gifts, but from exorbitant advances in the value of the primitive one. In grants of vacant lands, and of lands in the vicinity of growing towns & Cities the increase of value is often such as if foreseen, would essentially controul the liberality confirming them. The people of the U.S. owe their Independence & their liberty, to the wisdom of descrying in the minute tax of 3 pence on tea, the magnitude of the evil comprized in the precedent. Let them exert the same wisdom, in watching agst every evil lurking under plausible disguises, and growing up from small beginnings." Fleet, Madison's "Detached Memoranda," Wm & Mary Q. (3d ser.), 557-558.

If believers are entitled to public financial support, so are nonbelievers. A believer and nonbeliever under the present law are treated differently because of the articles of their faith. Believers are doubtless comforted that the cause of religion is being fostered by this legislation. Yet one of the mandates of the First Amendment is to promote a viable, pluralistic society and to keep government neutral, not only between sects, but also between believers and nonbelievers. The present involvement of government in religion may seem *de minimis*. But it is, I fear, a long step down the Establishment path. Perhaps I have been misinformed. But as I have read the Constitution and its philosophy, I gathered that independence was the price of liberty.

I conclude that this tax exemption is unconstitutional.

## NOTES AND QUESTIONS

1. In its majority opinion, the Court states: "The limits of permissible state accommodation to religion are by no means co-extensive with the noninterference mandated by the Free Exercise Clause." What does this mean?

2. The Court and the concurring opinion stress the point that the tax-exemption at issue in this case was broad, in that it extended to "all houses of religious worship within a broad class of property owned by nonprofit, quasi-public corporations which include hospitals, libraries, playgrounds, scientific, professional, historical, and patriotic groups." What is the constitutional significance of this fact? Does this mean that legislatures cannot justify an accommodation on how it affects religion? Does this mean that all religious accommodations must also benefit non-religious entities? If so, is this ruling inconsistent with the notion of a religious accommodation?

3. The majority declined to make a "social welfare yardstick" a significant factor in its decision. Does this statement contradict the above statement that appears to place religious organizations within a broader class of charities? What would be the reasons for the Court taking this position?

4. According to Justice Brennan, there are two secular purposes for providing real property tax exemptions to religious organizations. What are they? Can you think of any other valid secular purposes that support this law? As the Court notes, it is safe to assume that many of the exempt churches engage solely in worship activities that benefit their parishioners only. If so, what is the secular purpose of exempting these churches from taxes?

5. According to the majority and Justice Brennan's concurring opinion, what is the constitutional difference between a tax exemption and a direct money subsidy? Many economists would argue that from a financial standpoint, it is a difference without any distinction. If that is true, are there other constitutional values that support this distinction, or is the dissent correct?

6. What is the majority's working definition of "excessive entanglement" between church and state? What does the Court mean when it says that the tax exemption "creates only a minimal and remote involvement between church and state and far less than taxation of churches"? According to the majority opinion and Justice Brennan's concurring opinion, would invalidation of this tax exemption as it applies to religious organizations itself be unconstitutional? In other words, is this kind of exemption not only constitutionally permitted but also constitutionally required?

7. Both the Court majority and Justice Brennan note the longstanding "unbroken practice" of tax exemptions. How do they see that historical fact as impacting constitutional scrutiny? At the same time, Justice Brennan concedes that James Madison argued against tax exemptions for churches after he had left the presidency. How does Justice Brennan view the constitutional significance of this fact?

8. How does Justice Douglas frame the question in this case in his dissenting opinion? How does this characterization differ from that of the majority and concurrence? Is one characterization more accurate than the others? Later, Justice Douglas says: "A believer and nonbeliever under the present law are treated differently because of the articles of their faith." How does the majority deal with this charge?

9. As you will recall, Justice Douglas was in the Court majority in the *Everson* and *Zorach* cases. How does Justice Douglas distinguish those cases from this one? Are these distinctions persuasive? What does Justice Douglas say in retrospect about the *Everson* decision?

10. Justice Douglas argues: "State aid to places of worship, whether in the form of direct grants or tax exemption, takes us back to the Assessment Bill and the Remonstrance." As he continues:

   Direct financial aid to churches or tax exemptions to the church *qua* church is not, in my view, even arguably permitted. Sectarian causes are certainly not antipublic and many would rate their own church or perhaps all churches as the highest form of welfare. The difficulty is that sectarian causes must remain in the private domain not subject to public control or subsidy. That seems to me to be the requirement of the Establishment Clause. . . . But subsidies either through direct grant or tax exemption for sectarian causes, whether carried on by church *qua* church or by church *qua* welfare agency, must be treated differently, lest we in time allow the church *qua* church to be on the public payroll, which, I fear, is imminent.

   What is the Court majority's response to this argument? Under President Bush's faith-based initiative, churches are permitted to receive government grants to provide social services. In light of that fact, do you believe that Justice Douglas' fears have been realized? Do you believe that this policy is a consequence of the *Walz* decision upholding the constitutionality of tax exemptions for religious and other organizations? If the Court had struck down the tax exemption in *Walz*, what do you think the legal and policy consequences might have been?

11. Douglas cites statistics about the "vast domain" of church assets and adds that "the extent to which [religious organizations] are feeding from the public trough in a variety of forms is alarming." To what extent should the assets and outside income of religious organizations be a factor in providing a religious accommodation through a tax exemption? Compare Justice Douglas' dissenting opinion in this case with Justice O'Connor's concurring opinion in the *Zelman* case—what are the similarities and differences?

---

Sometimes legislatures pass measures that require nongovernmental as well as governmental employers to accommodate their employees' religious practices. A series of cases reveal that this is often an area of bitter controversy as such measures sometimes disrupt the functioning of the workplace and cause friction between management and labor. In the case below, the Court considered how far a private company must go to accommodate an employee's religious practices when the law says that such a company must make "reasonable accommodation" of the religious needs of its employees provided the accommodation does not create an "undue hardship" for the employer.

---

## TRANS WORLD AIRLINES v. HARDISON
### 432 U.S. 63 (1977)

▓ MR. JUSTICE WHITE delivered the opinion of the Court.

Section 703(a)(1) of the Civil Rights Act of 1964, Title VII, makes it an unlawful employment practice for an employer to discriminate against an employee or a prospective employee on the basis of his or her religion. At the time of the events involved here, a guideline of the Equal Employment Opportunity Commission (EEOC), required, as the Act itself now does, that an employer, short of "undue hardship," make "reasonable accommodations" to the religious needs of its employees. The issue in this case is the extent of the employer's obligation under Title VII to accommodate an employee whose religious beliefs prohibit him from working on Saturdays.

I

We summarize briefly the facts found by the District Court.

Petitioner Trans World Airlines (TWA) operates a large maintenance and overhaul base in Kansas City, Mo. On June 5, 1967, respondent Larry G. Hardison was hired by TWA to work as a clerk in the Stores Department at its Kansas City base. Because of its essential role in the Kansas City operation, the Stores Department must operate 24 hours per day, 365 days per year, and whenever an employee's job in that department is not filled, an employee must be shifted from another department, or a supervisor must cover the job, even if the work in other areas may suffer.

Hardison, like other employees at the Kansas City base, was subject to a seniority system contained in a collective-bargaining agreement that TWA maintains with petitioner International Association of Machinists and Aerospace Workers (IAM). The seniority system is implemented by the union steward through a system of bidding by employees for particular shift assignments as they become available. The most senior employees have first choice for job and shift assignments, and the most junior employees are required to work when the union steward is unable to find enough people willing to work at a particular time or in a particular job to fill TWA's needs.

In the spring of 1968 Hardison began to study the religion known as the Worldwide Church of God. One of the tenets of that religion is that one must observe the Sabbath by refraining from performing any work from sunset on Friday until sunset on Saturday. The religion also proscribes work on certain specified religious holidays.

When Hardison informed Everett Kussman, the manager of the Stores Department, of his religious conviction regarding observance of the Sabbath, Kussman agreed that the union steward should seek a job swap for Hardison or a change of days off; that Hardison would have his religious holidays off whenever possible if Hardison agreed to work the traditional holidays when asked; and that Kussman would try to find Hardison another job that would be more compatible with his religious beliefs. The problem was temporarily solved when Hardison transferred to the 11 p.m.–7 a.m. shift. Working this shift permitted Hardison to observe his Sabbath.

The problem soon reappeared when Hardison bid for and received a transfer from Building 1, where he had been employed, to Building 2, where he would work the day shift. The two buildings had entirely separate seniority lists; and while in Building 1 Hardison had sufficient seniority to observe the Sabbath regularly, he was second from the bottom on the Building 2 seniority list.

In Building 2 Hardison was asked to work Saturdays when a fellow employee went on vacation. TWA agreed to permit the union to seek a change of work assignments for Hardison, but the union was not willing to violate the seniority provisions set out in the collective-bargaining contract, and Hardison had insufficient seniority to bid for a shift having Saturdays off.

A proposal that Hardison work only four days a week was rejected by the company. Hardison's job was essential, and on weekends he was the only available person on his shift to perform it. To leave the position empty would have impaired supply shop functions, which were critical to airline operations; to fill Hardison's position with a supervisor or an employee from another area would simply have undermanned another operation; and to employ someone not regularly assigned to work Saturdays would have required TWA to pay premium wages.

When an accommodation was not reached, Hardison refused to report for work on Saturdays. A transfer to the twilight shift proved unavailing since that schedule still required Hardison to work past sundown on Fridays. After a hearing, Hardison was discharged on grounds of insubordination for refusing to work during his designated shift. . . .

II

The Court of Appeals found that TWA had committed an unlawful employment practice under § 703(a)(1) of the Act, 42 U.S.C. § 2000e-2(a)(1), which provides:

(a) It shall be an unlawful employment practice for an employer—
(1) to fail or refuse to hire or to discharge any individual, or otherwise to discriminate against any individual with respect to his compensation, terms, conditions, or privileges of employment, because of such individual's race, color, religion, sex, or national origin.

The emphasis of both the language and the legislative history of the statute is on eliminating discrimination in employment; similarly situated employees are not to be treated differently solely because they differ with respect to race, color, religion, sex, or national origin. This is true regardless of whether the discrimination is directed against majorities or minorities. *McDonald v. Santa Fe Trail Transportation Co.*, 427 U.S. 273, 280 (1976). See *Griggs v. Duke Power Co.*, 401 U.S. 424, 431 (1971).

[T]he extent of the required accommodation—remained unsettled when this Court, in *Dewey v. Reynolds Metals Co.*, affirmed by an equally divided Court the Sixth Circuit's decision. The discharge of an employee who for religious reasons had refused to work on Sundays was there held by the Court of Appeals not to be an unlawful employment practice because the manner in which the employer allocated Sunday work assignments was discriminatory in neither its purpose nor effect; and consistent with the 1967 EEOC guidelines, the employer had made a reasonable accommodation of the employee's beliefs by giving him the opportunity to secure a replacement for his Sunday work.

In part "to resolve by legislation" some of the issues raised in *Dewey*, Congress included the following definition of religion in its 1972 amendments to Title VII:

The term "religion" includes all aspects of religious observance and practice, as well as belief, unless an employer demonstrates that he is unable to reasonably accommodate to an employee's or prospective employee's religious observance or practice without undue hardship on the conduct of the employer's business.

The intent and effect of this definition was to make it an unlawful employment practice under § 703(a)(1) for an employer not to make reasonable accommodations, short of undue hardship, for the religious practices of his employees and prospective employees. But like the EEOC guidelines, the statute provides no guidance for determining the degree of accommodation that is required of an employer. The brief legislative history of § 701(j) is likewise of little assistance in this regard. The proponent of the measure, Senator Jennings Randolph, expressed his general desire "to assure that freedom from religious discrimination in the employment of workers is for all time guaranteed by law," but he made no attempt to define the precise circumstances under which the "reasonable accommodation" requirement would be applied.

In brief, the employer's statutory obligation to make reasonable accommodation for the religious observances of its employees, short of incurring an undue hardship, is clear, but the reach of that obligation has never been spelled out by Congress or by EEOC guidelines. With this in mind, we turn to a consideration of whether TWA has met its obligation under Title VII to accommodate the religious observances of its employees.

### III . . .

### A

It might be inferred from the Court of Appeals' opinion and from the brief of the EEOC in this Court that TWA's efforts to accommodate were no more than negligible. The findings of the District Court, supported by the record, are to the contrary. In summarizing its more detailed findings, the District Court observed:

> TWA established as a matter of fact that it did take appropriate action to accommodate as required by Title VII. It held several meetings with plaintiff at which it attempted to find a solution to plaintiff's problems. It did accommodate plaintiff's observance of his special religious holidays. It authorized the union steward to search for someone who would swap shifts, which apparently was normal procedure.

It is also true that TWA itself attempted without success to find Hardison another job. The District Court's view was that TWA had done all that could reasonably be expected within the bounds of the seniority system.

The Court of Appeals observed, however, that the possibility of a variance from the seniority system was never really posed to the union. This is contrary to the District Court's findings and to the record. The District Court found that when TWA first learned of Hardison's religious observances in April 1968, it agreed to permit the union's steward to seek a swap of shifts or days off but that "the steward reported that he was unable to work out scheduling changes and that he understood that no one was willing to swap days with plaintiff." Later, in March 1969, at a meeting held just two days before Hardison first failed to report for his Saturday shift, TWA again "offered to accommodate plaintiff's religious observance by agreeing to any trade of shifts or change of sections that plaintiff and the union could work out. . . . Any shift or change was impossible within the seniority framework and the union was not willing to violate the seniority provisions set out in the contract to make a shift or change." As the record shows, Hardison himself testified that Kussman was willing, but the union was not, to work out a shift or job trade with another employee.

We shall say more about the seniority system, but at this juncture it appears to us that the system itself represented a significant accommodation to the needs, both religious and secular, of all of TWA's employees. As will become apparent, the seniority system represents a neutral way of minimizing the number of occasions when an employee must work on a day that he would prefer to have off. Additionally, recognizing that weekend work schedules are the least popular, the company made further accommodation by reducing its work force to a bare minimum on those days.

### B

We are also convinced, contrary to the Court of Appeals, that TWA itself cannot be faulted for having failed to work out a shift or job swap for Hardison. Both the union and TWA had agreed to the seniority system; the union was unwilling to entertain a variance over the objections of men senior to Hardison; and for TWA to have arranged unilaterally for a swap would have amounted to a breach of the collective-bargaining agreement.

## (1)

Hardison and the EEOC insist that the statutory obligation to accommodate religious needs takes precedence over both the collective-bargaining contract and the seniority rights of TWA's other employees. We agree that neither a collective-bargaining contract nor a seniority system may be employed to violate the statute, but we do not believe that the duty to accommodate requires TWA to take steps inconsistent with the otherwise valid agreement. Collective bargaining, aimed at effecting workable and enforceable agreements between management and labor, lies at the core of our national labor policy, and seniority provisions are universally included in these contracts. Without a clear and express indication from Congress, we cannot agree with Hardison and the EEOC that an agreed-upon seniority system must give way when necessary to accommodate religious observances. The issue is important and warrants some discussion.

Any employer who, like TWA, conducts an around-the-clock operation is presented with the choice of allocating work schedules either in accordance with the preferences of its employees or by involuntary assignment. Insofar as the varying shift preferences of its employees complement each other, TWA could meet its manpower needs through voluntary work scheduling. In the present case, for example, Hardison's supervisor foresaw little difficulty in giving Hardison his religious holidays off since they fell on days that most other employees preferred to work, while Hardison was willing to work on the traditional holidays that most other employees preferred to have off.

Whenever there are not enough employees who choose to work a particular shift, however, some employees must be assigned to that shift even though it is not their first choice. Such was evidently the case with regard to Saturday work; even though TWA cut back its weekend work force to a skeleton crew, not enough employees chose those days off to staff the Stores Department through voluntary scheduling. In these circumstances, TWA and IAM agreed to give first preference to employees who had worked in a particular department the longest.

Had TWA nevertheless circumvented the seniority system by relieving Hardison of Saturday work and ordering a senior employee to replace him, it would have denied the latter his shift preference so that Hardison could be given his. The senior employee would also have been deprived of his contractual rights under the collective-bargaining agreement.

It was essential to TWA's business to require Saturday and Sunday work from at least a few employees even though most employees preferred those days off. Allocating the burdens of weekend work was a matter for collective bargaining. In considering criteria to govern this allocation, TWA and the union had two alternatives: adopt a neutral system, such as seniority, a lottery, or rotating shifts; or allocate days off in accordance with the religious needs of its employees. TWA would have had to adopt the latter in order to assure Hardison and others like him of getting the days off necessary for strict observance of their religion, but it could have done so only at the expense of others who had strong, but perhaps nonreligious, reasons for not working on weekends. There were no volunteers to relieve Hardison on Saturdays, and to give Hardison Saturdays off, TWA would have had to deprive another employee of his shift preference at least in part because he did not adhere to a religion that observed the Saturday Sabbath.

Title VII does not contemplate such unequal treatment. The repeated, unequivocal emphasis of both the language and the legislative history of Title VII is on eliminating discrimination in employment, and such discrimination is proscribed when it is directed against majorities as well as minorities. Indeed, the foundation of Hardison's claim is that TWA and IAM engaged in religious discrimination in violation of 703(a)(1) when they failed to arrange for him to have Saturdays off. It would be anomalous to conclude that by "reasonable accommodation" Congress meant that an employer must deny the shift and job preference of some employees, as well as deprive them of their contractual rights, in order to accommodate or prefer the religious needs of others, and we conclude that Title VII does not require an employer to go that far.

(2)

Our conclusion is supported by the fact that seniority systems are afforded special treatment under Title VII itself. Section 703(h) provides in pertinent part:

> Notwithstanding any other provision of this subchapter, it shall not be an unlawful employment practice for an employer to apply different standards of compensation, or different terms, conditions, or privileges of employment pursuant to a bona fide seniority or merit system . . . provided that such differences are not the result of an intention to discriminate because of race, color, religion, sex, or national origin. . . .

Thus, absent a discriminatory purpose, the operation of a seniority system cannot be an unlawful employment practice even if the system has some discriminatory consequences.

There has been no suggestion of discriminatory intent in this case. . . . The Court of Appeals' conclusion that TWA was not limited by the terms of its seniority system was in substance nothing more than a ruling that operation of the seniority system was itself an unlawful employment practice even though no discriminatory purpose had been shown. That ruling is plainly inconsistent with the dictates of § 703(h), both on its face and as interpreted in the recent decisions of this Court.

As we have said, TWA was not required by Title VII to carve out a special exception to its seniority system in order to help Hardison to meet his religious obligations.[14]

---

[14] Despite its hyperbole and rhetoric, the dissent appears to agree with—at least it stops short of challenging—the fundamental proposition that Title VII does not require an employer and a union who have agreed on a seniority system to deprive senior employees of their seniority rights in order to accommodate a junior employee's religious practices. This is the principal issue on which TWA and the union came to this Court. The dissent is thus reduced to (1) asserting that the statute requires TWA to accommodate Hardison even though substantial expenditures are required to do so; and (2) advancing its own view of the record to show that TWA could have done more than it did to accommodate Hardison without violating the seniority system or incurring substantial additional costs. We reject the former assertion as an erroneous construction of the statute. As for the latter, we prefer the findings of the District Judge who heard the evidence. . . . We accept the District Court's findings that TWA had done all that it could do to accommodate Hardison's religious beliefs without either incurring substantial costs or violating the seniority rights of other employees.

## C

The Court of Appeals also suggested that TWA could have permitted Hardison to work a four-day week if necessary in order to avoid working on his Sabbath. Recognizing that this might have left TWA short-handed on the one shift each week that Hardison did not work, the court still concluded that TWA would suffer no undue hardship if it were required to replace Hardison either with supervisory personnel or with qualified personnel from other departments. Alternatively, the Court of Appeals suggested that TWA could have replaced Hardison on his Saturday shift with other available employees through the payment of premium wages. Both of these alternatives would involve costs to TWA, either in the form of lost efficiency in other jobs or higher wages.

To require TWA to bear more than a *de minimis* cost in order to give Hardison Saturdays off is an undue hardship. Like abandonment of the seniority system, to require TWA to bear additional costs when no such costs are incurred to give other employees the days off that they want would involve unequal treatment of employees on the basis of their religion. By suggesting that TWA should incur certain costs in order to give Hardison Saturdays off the Court of Appeals would in effect require TWA to finance an additional Saturday off and then to choose the employee who will enjoy it on the basis of his religious beliefs. While incurring extra costs to secure a replacement for Hardison might remove the necessity of compelling another employee to work involuntarily in Hardison's place, it would not change the fact that the privilege of having Saturdays off would be allocated according to religious beliefs.

As we have seen, the paramount concern of Congress in enacting Title VII was the elimination of discrimination in employment. In the absence of clear statutory language or legislative history to the contrary, we will not readily construe the statute to require an employer to discriminate against some employees in order to enable others to observe their Sabbath.

*Reversed.*

■ MR. JUSTICE MARSHALL, with whom MR. JUSTICE BRENNAN joins, dissenting. . . .

Today's decision deals a fatal blow to all efforts under Title VII to accommodate work requirements to religious practices. The Court holds, in essence, that although the EEOC regulations and the Act state that an employer must make reasonable adjustments in his work demands to take account of religious observances, the regulation and Act do not really mean what they say. An employer, the Court concludes, need not grant even the most minor special privilege to religious observers to enable them to follow their faith. As a question of social policy, this result is deeply troubling, for a society that truly values religious pluralism cannot compel adherents of minority religions to make the cruel choice of surrendering their religion or their job. And as a matter of law today's result is intolerable, for the Court adopts the very position that Congress expressly rejected in 1972, as if we were free to disregard congressional choices that a majority of this Court thinks unwise. I therefore dissent.

## I

With respect to each of the proposed accommodations to respondent Hardison's religious observances that the Court discusses, it ultimately notes that the accommodation would have required "unequal treatment," in favor of the religious observer. That is quite true. But if an accommodation can be rejected simply because it involves preferential treatment, then the regulation and the statute, while brimming with "sound and fury," ultimately "signif[y] nothing."

The accommodation issue by definition arises only when a neutral rule of general applicability conflicts with the religious practices of a particular employee. In some of the reported cases, the rule in question has governed work attire; in other cases it has required attendance at some religious function; in still other instances, it has compelled membership in a union; and in the largest class of cases, it has concerned work schedules. What all these cases have in common is an employee who could comply with the rule only by violating what the employee views as a religious commandment. In each instance, the question is whether the employee is to be exempt from the rule's demands. To do so will always result in a privilege being "allocated according to religious beliefs," unless the employer gratuitously decides to repeal the rule in toto. What the statute says, in plain words, is that such allocations are required unless "undue hardship" would result. . . .

In reaching this result, the Court seems almost oblivious of the legislative history of the 1972 amendments to Title VII which is briefly recounted in the Court's opinion. That history is far more instructive than the Court allows. After the EEOC promulgated its second set of guidelines requiring reasonable accommodations unless undue hardship would result, at least two courts issued decisions questioning whether the guidelines were consistent with Title VII. These courts reasoned, in language strikingly similar to today's decision, that to excuse religious observers from neutral work rules would "discriminate against . . . other employees" and "constitute unequal administration of the collective-bargaining agreement." They therefore refused to equate "religious discrimination with failure to accommodate." When Congress was reviewing Title VII in 1972, Senator Jennings Randolph informed the Congress of these decisions which, he said, had "clouded" the meaning of religious discrimination. He introduced an amendment, tracking the language of the EEOC regulation, to make clear that Title VII requires religious accommodation, even though unequal treatment would result. The primary purpose of the amendment, he explained, was to protect Saturday Sabbatarians like himself from employers who refuse "to hire or to continue in employment employees whose religious practices rigidly require them to abstain from work in the nature of hire on particular days." His amendment was unanimously approved by the Senate on a roll-call vote, and was accepted by the Conference Committee whose report was approved by both Houses. Yet the Court today, in rejecting any accommodation that involves preferential treatment, follows the *Dewey* decision in direct contravention of congressional intent.

The Court's interpretation of the statute, by effectively nullifying it, has the singular advantage of making consideration of petitioner's constitutional challenge unnecessary. . . . Moreover, while important constitutional questions would be posed by interpreting the law to compel employers (or fellow employees) to incur substantial costs to aid the religious observer,[3] not

---

[3] Because of the view I take of the facts, I find it unnecessary to decide how much cost an employer must bear before he incurs "undue hardship." I also leave for another day the merits of any constitutional objections that could be raised if the law were construed to require employers (or employees) to assume significant costs in accommodating.

all accommodations are costly, and the constitutionality of the statute is not placed in serious doubt simply because it sometimes requires an exemption from a work rule. Indeed, this Court has repeatedly found no Establishment Clause problems in exempting religious observers from state-imposed duties even when the exemption was in no way compelled by the Free Exercise Clause.[4] If the State does not establish religion over nonreligion by excusing religious practitioners from obligations owed the State, I do not see how the State can be said to establish religion by requiring employers to do the same with respect to obligations owed the employer. Thus, I think it beyond dispute that the Act does—and, consistently with the First Amendment, can— require employers to grant privileges to religious observers as part of the accommodation process.

## II

Once it is determined that the duty to accommodate sometimes requires that an employee be exempted from an otherwise valid work requirement, the only remaining question is whether this is such a case: Did TWA prove that it exhausted all reasonable accommodations, and that the only remaining alternatives would have caused undue hardship on TWA's business? To pose the question is to answer it, for all that the District Court found TWA had done to accommodate respondent's Sabbath observance was that it "held several meetings with [respondent] . . . [and] authorized the union steward to search for someone who would swap shifts." To conclude that TWA, one of the largest air carriers in the Nation, would have suffered undue hardship had it done anything more defies both reason and common sense.

The Court implicitly assumes that the only means of accommodation open to TWA were to compel an unwilling employee to replace Hardison; to pay premium wages to a voluntary substitute; or to employ one less person during respondent's Sabbath shift. Based on this assumption, the Court seemingly finds that each alternative would have involved undue hardship not only because Hardison would have been given a special privilege, but also because either another employee would have been deprived of rights under the collective-bargaining agreement, or because "more than a *de minimis* cost," would have been imposed on TWA. But the Court's myopic view of the available options is not supported by either the District Court's findings or the evidence adduced at trial. Thus, the Court's conclusion cannot withstand analysis, even assuming that its rejection of the alternatives it does discuss is justifiable.

To begin with, the record simply does not support the Court's assertion, made without accompanying citations, that "[t]here were no volunteers to relieve Hardison on Saturdays." Everett Kussman, the manager of the department in which respondent worked, testified that he had made no effort to find

---

[4] The exemption here, like those we have upheld, can be claimed by any religious practitioner, a term that the EEOC has sensibly defined to include atheists, and persons not belonging to any organized sect but who hold "'[a] sincere and meaningful belief which occupies in the life of its possessor a place parallel to that filled by the God of those admittedly qualifying for the exemption.'" The purpose and primary effect of requiring such exemptions is the wholly secular one of securing equal economic opportunity to members of minority religions. And the mere fact that the law sometimes requires special treatment of religious practitioners does not present the dangers of "sponsorship, financial support, and active involvement of the sovereign in religious activity," against which the Establishment Clause is principally aimed.

volunteers, and the union stipulated that its steward had not done so either,
Thus, contrary to the Court's assumption, there may have been one or more
employees who, for reasons of either sympathy or personal convenience, willingly would have substituted for respondent on Saturdays until respondent
could either regain the non-Saturday shift he had held for the three preceding
months or transfer back to his old department where he had sufficient seniority to avoid Saturday work. Alternatively, there may have been an employee
who preferred respondent's Thursday-Monday daytime shift to his own; in
fact, respondent testified that he had informed Kussman and the union steward that the clerk on the Sunday-Thursday night shift (the "graveyard" shift)
was dissatisfied with his hours. Thus, respondent's religious observance might
have been accommodated by a simple trade of days or shifts without necessarily depriving any employee of his or her contractual rights and without imposing significant costs on TWA. Of course, it is also possible that no trade—or
none consistent with the seniority system—could have been arranged. But the
burden under the EEOC regulation is on TWA to establish that a reasonable
accommodation was not possible. Because it failed either to explore the possibility of a voluntary trade or to assure that its delegate, the union steward,
did so, TWA was unable to meet its burden.

   Nor was a voluntary trade the only option open to TWA that the Court
ignores; to the contrary, at least two other options are apparent from the record. First, TWA could have paid overtime to a voluntary replacement for
respondent—assuming that someone would have been willing to work Saturdays for premium pay—and passed on the cost to respondent. In fact, one
accommodation Hardison suggested would have done just that by requiring
Hardison to work overtime when needed at regular pay. Under this plan, the
total overtime cost to the employer—and the total number of overtime hours
available for other employees—would not have reflected Hardison's Sabbath
absences. Alternatively, TWA could have transferred respondent back to his
previous department where he had accumulated substantial seniority, as respondent also suggested. Admittedly, both options would have violated the
collective-bargaining agreement; the former because the agreement required
that employees working over 40 hours per week receive premium pay, and the
latter because the agreement prohibited employees from transferring departments more than once every six months. But neither accommodation would
have deprived any other employee of rights under the contract or violated
the seniority system in any way. Plainly an employer cannot avoid his duty to
accommodate by signing a contract that precludes all reasonable accommodations; even the Court appears to concede as much. Thus I do not believe it can
be even seriously argued that TWA would have suffered "undue hardship" to
its business had it required respondent to pay the extra costs of his replacement, or had it transferred respondent to his former department.[13]

---

[13] Of course, the accommodations discussed in the text would have imposed some
administrative inconvenience on TWA. Petitioners do not seriously argue, however, that this
consequence of accommodation makes the statute violative of the Establishment Clause.
Were such an argument to be made, our prior decision upholding exemptions from state-
created duties, would provide a complete answer, since the exemptions we have sustained
have placed not inconsiderable burdens on private parties. For example, the effect of excusing conscientious objectors from military conscription is to require a nonobjector to serve
instead, yet we have repeatedly upheld this exemption.

What makes today's decision most tragic, however, is not that respondent Hardison has been needlessly deprived of his livelihood simply because he chose to follow the dictates of his conscience. Nor is the tragedy exhausted by the impact it will have on thousands of Americans like Hardison who could be forced to live on welfare as the price they must pay for worshiping their God.[14] The ultimate tragedy is that despite Congress' best efforts, one of this Nation's pillars of strength—our hospitality to religious diversity—has been seriously eroded. All Americans will be a little poorer until today's decision is erased.

I respectfully dissent.

---

In 1986, the Court heard another case involving a religious person's claim that his employer, a public school, had unlawfully discriminated against him by failing to reasonably accommodate his religious beliefs. The collective-bargaining agreement involved in the case permitted the employee to take three days annual leave for religious observance, but denied employees the right to use an additional three days of personal leave for religious purposes as well as other purposes.

The employee took issue with the fact that he had to take unauthorized leave for days beyond the three he was granted under the collective bargaining agreement for religious activities, causing him to lose pay for those days. Accordingly, the employee "asked the school board to adopt one of two alternatives. His preferred alternative would allow use of personal business leave for religious observance, effectively giving him three additional days of paid leave for that purpose. Short of this arrangement, respondent suggested that he pay the cost of a substitute and receive full pay for additional days off for religious observances." The employer rejected both proposals.

In this case, *Ansonia v. Philbrook*,[10] the Court stated:

We find no basis in either the statute or its legislative history for requiring an employer to choose any particular reasonable accommodation. By its very terms the statute directs that any reasonable accommodation by the employer is sufficient to meet its accommodation obligation. The employer violates the statute unless it "demonstrates that [it] is unable to reasonably accommodate . . . an employee's . . . religious observance or practice without undue hardship on the conduct of the employer's business." 42 U. S. C. § 2000e(j). Thus, where the employer has already reasonably accommodated the employee's religious needs, the statutory inquiry is at an end. The employer need not further show that each of the employee's alternative accommodations would result in undue hardship. As *Hardison* illustrates, the extent of undue hardship on the employer's business is at issue only where the employer claims that it is unable to offer any reasonable accommodation without such hardship. Once the Court of Appeals assumed that the school board had offered to Philbrook a reasonable alternative, it erred by requiring the Board to nonetheless demonstrate the hardship of Philbrook's alternatives.[11]

---

[14] Ironically, the fiscal costs to society of today's decision may exceed the costs that would accrue if employers were required to make all accommodations without regard to hardship, since it is clear that persons on welfare cannot be denied benefits because they refuse to take jobs that would prevent them from observing religious holy days, see *Sherbert v. Verner*, 374 U.S. 398 (1963).

The Court also found that "the school board policy in this case, requiring respondent to take unpaid leave for holy day observance that exceeded the amount allowed by the collective-bargaining agreement, would generally be a reasonable one." It said "[t]he provision of unpaid leave eliminates the conflict between employment requirements and religious practices by allowing the individual to observe fully religious holy days and requires him only to give up compensation for a day that he did not in fact work. Generally speaking, '[the] direct effect of [unpaid leave] is merely a loss of income for the period the employee is not at work; such an exclusion has no direct effect upon either employment opportunities or job status.'" *Nashville Gas Co. v. Satty*, 434 U.S. 136, 145 (1977).[12]

Finally, the Court noted that "unpaid leave is not a reasonable accommodation when paid leave is provided for all purposes *except* religious ones." It remanded the case for "factual inquiry into past and present administration of the personal business leave provisions of the collective-bargaining agreement"[13] to determine whether the policy ran afoul of this principle.

Justice Thurgood Marshall wrote an opinion concurring in part and dissenting in part. He stated:

> The Court suggests that requiring an employer to consider an employee's proposals would enable the employee to hold his employer hostage in exchange for a particular accommodation. If the employer has offered a reasonable accommodation that *fully* resolves the conflict between the employee's work and religious requirements, I agree that no further consideration of the employee's proposals would normally be warranted. But if the accommodation offered by the employer does not completely resolve the employee's conflict, I would hold that the employer remains under an obligation to consider whatever *reasonable* proposals the employee may submit.[14]

Marshall concluded:

> The Court's analysis in *Trans World Airlines, Inc. v. Hardison*, 432 U.S. 63 (1977), is difficult to reconcile with its holding today. In *Hardison*, the Court held that the employer's chosen work schedule was a reasonable accommodation but nonetheless went on to consider and reject each of the alternative suggested accommodations. The course followed in *Hardison* should have been adopted here as well. "Once it is determined that the duty to accommodate sometimes requires that an employee be exempted from an otherwise valid work requirement, the only remaining question is . . . : Did [the employer] prove that *it exhausted all reasonable accommodations*, and that the *only remaining alternatives would have caused undue hardship* on [the employer's] business?" Ibid., 91 (MARSHALL, J., dissenting) (emphasis added).
>
> Accordingly, I would remand this case for factual findings on both the intended scope of the school board's leave provision *and* the reasonableness and expected hardship of Philbrook's proposals.[15]

As discussed above, the Supreme Court has read the term "undue hardship" in Title VII of the Civil Rights Act in a narrow way. In the wake of these cases, legislation has been introduced in Congress that would provide more protection for worker's rights in this area. The legislation would do so mostly by adding or expanding definitions to various terms found in Title VII. The following is an excerpt from that legislation, which is known as the "Workplace Religious Freedom Act":

> (a)(2)(A) [T]he term "employee" includes an employee (as defined in subsection (f)), or a prospective employee, who, with or without reasonable accommodation, is qualified to perform the essential functions of the employment position that such individual holds or desires.
>
> (B) [T]he term "perform the essential functions" includes carrying out the core requirements of an employment position and does not include carrying out practices relating to clothing, practices relating to taking time off, or other practices that may have a temporary or tangential impact on the ability to perform job functions, if any of the practices described in this subparagraph restrict the ability to wear religious clothing, to take time off for a holy day, or to participate in a religious observance or practice.
>
> (3) [T]he term "undue hardship" means an accommodation requiring significant difficulty or expense. For purposes of determining whether an accommodation requires significant difficulty or expense, factors to be considered in making the determination shall include—
>
> "(A) the identifiable cost of the accommodation, including the costs of loss of productivity and of retraining or hiring employees or transferring employees from 1 facility to another;
>
> "(B) the overall financial resources and size of the employer involved, relative to the number of its employees; and
>
> "(C) for an employer with multiple facilities, the geographic separateness or administrative or fiscal relationship of the facilities." . . .
>
> (b)(2) For purposes of determining whether an employer has committed an unlawful employment practice under this title by failing to provide a reasonable accommodation to the religious observance or practice of an employee, for an accommodation to be considered to be reasonable, the accommodation shall remove the conflict between employment requirements and the religious observance or practice of the employee.
>
> (3) An employer shall be considered to commit such a practice by failing to provide such a reasonable accommodation for an employee if the employer refuses to permit the employee to utilize leave of general usage to remove such a conflict solely because the leave will be used to accommodate the religious observance or practice of the employee.

---

### NOTES AND QUESTIONS

1. How does the Court majority in *Hardison* define the statutory term "undue hardship"? What is the dissent's critique of this definition? Does the dissent offer a competing definition of this term?

2. According to the *Hardison* Court, does Title VII require an employer and a union that have agreed on a seniority system to deviate from that system in order to accommodate the religious practices of employees? Does the dissent agree or disagree with the Court majority on this point?

3. According to the *Hardison* dissent, what other options could the employer have pursued in order to reasonably accommodate the employee in this case? On what ground does the Court majority reject these alternatives?

4. The *Hardison* dissenters state: "[T]he mere fact that the law sometimes requires special treatment of religious practitioners does not present the dangers of 'sponsorship, financial support, and active involvement of the sovereign in religious activity,' against which the Establishment Clause is principally aimed, *Walz v. Tax Comm'n*, 397 U.S. 664, 668 (1970)." Does the majority agree or disagree with this characterization?

5. Why did the Court majority in the *Philbrook* case decline to require employers to accept employees' preferred accommodations?

6. If the *Hardison* and *Philbrook* cases were to be litigated under the standard set forth in the Workplace Religious Freedom Act (WRFA), would their outcomes be different?

7. Assume a police officer refuses for religious reasons to guard a medical facility that offers abortions when there is a protest at the facility. The officer says he is willing to take any other duty, but he will not perform that particular duty. Assume the officer is fired for this reason. Does he have a claim under WRFA? Does it matter if other police officers were available to perform this duty in his stead?

When does the government go too far in trying to accommodate religious exercise? What requirements in a law are necessary to ensure that an accommodation does not turn into an impermissible advancement of religion? Can the government purposefully accommodate religious practice without providing comparable benefits to similarly situated nonreligious entities? To what extent should legislatures and courts consider the impact of the legislative accommodation on third persons? The following three cases explore these issues.

In 1985, the Supreme Court confronted a case that questioned the constitutional latitude of a state to accommodate employees' religious exercise. *Estate of Thornton v. Caldor* involved a state statute that provided employees with an absolute right not to work on their chosen day of Sabbath. The question in this case was: Does that kind of legislative accommodation of religious practice actually constitute a forbidden establishment of faith?

## ESTATE OF THORNTON v. CALDOR
### 472 U.S. 703 (1985)

CHIEF JUSTICE BURGER delivered the opinion of the Court.

We granted certiorari to decide whether a state statute that provides employees with the absolute right not to work on their chosen Sabbath violates the Establishment Clause of the First Amendment.

I

In early 1975, petitioner's decedent Donald E. Thornton began working for respondent Caldor, Inc., a chain of New England retail stores; he managed the men's and boys' clothing department in respondent's Waterbury, Connecticut, store. At that time, respondent's Connecticut stores were closed on Sundays pursuant to state law.

In 1977, following the state legislature's revision of the Sunday-closing laws, respondent opened its Connecticut stores for Sunday business. In order to handle the expanded store hours, respondent required its managerial employees to work every third or fourth Sunday. Thornton, a Presbyterian who observed Sunday as his Sabbath, initially complied with respondent's demand and worked a total of 31 Sundays in 1977 and 1978. In October 1978, Thornton was transferred to a management position in respondent's Torrington store; he continued to work on Sundays during the first part of 1979. In November 1979, however, Thornton informed respondent that he would no longer work on Sundays because he observed that day as his Sabbath; he invoked the protection of Conn. Gen. Stat. § 53-303e(b) (1985), which provides: "No person who states that a particular day of the week is observed as his Sabbath may be required by his employer to work on such day. An employee's refusal to work on his Sabbath shall not constitute grounds for his dismissal."

Thornton rejected respondent's offer either to transfer him to a management job in a Massachusetts store that was closed on Sundays, or to transfer him to a nonsupervisory position in the Torrington store at a lower salary. In March 1980, respondent transferred Thornton to a clerical position in the Torrington store; Thornton resigned two days later and filed a grievance with the State Board of Mediation and Arbitration alleging that he was discharged from his manager's position in violation of Conn. Gen. Stat. § 53-303e(b) (1985). . . .

II

Under the Religion Clauses, government must guard against activity that impinges on religious freedom, and must take pains not to compel people to act in the name of any religion. In setting the appropriate boundaries in Establishment Clause cases, the Court has frequently relied on our holding in *Lemon* for guidance, and we do so here. To pass constitutional muster under *Lemon* a statute must not only have a secular purpose and not foster excessive entanglement of government with religion, its primary effect must not advance or inhibit religion.

The Connecticut statute challenged here guarantees every employee, who "states that a particular day of the week is observed as his Sabbath," the right not to work on his chosen day. The State has thus decreed that those who observe a Sabbath any day of the week as a matter of religious conviction must be relieved of the duty to work on that day, no matter what burden or inconvenience this imposes on the employer or fellow workers. The statute arms Sabbath observers with an absolute and unqualified right not to work on whatever day they designate as their Sabbath.

In essence, the Connecticut statute imposes on employers and employees an absolute duty to conform their business practices to the particular religious practices of the employee by enforcing observance of the Sabbath the employee unilaterally designates. The State thus commands that Sabbath religious concerns automatically control over all secular interests at the workplace; the statute takes no account of the convenience or interests of the employer or those of other employees who do not observe a Sabbath. The employer and others must adjust their affairs to the command of the State whenever the statute is invoked by an employee.

There is no exception under the statute for special circumstances, such as the Friday Sabbath observer employed in an occupation with a Monday through Friday schedule—a school teacher, for example; the statute provides for no special consideration if a high percentage of an employer's work force asserts rights to the same Sabbath. Moreover, there is no exception when honoring the dictates of Sabbath observers would cause the employer substantial economic burdens or when the employer's compliance would require the imposition of significant burdens on other employees required to work in place of the Sabbath observers.[9] Finally, the statute allows for no consideration as to whether the employer has made reasonable accommodation proposals.

This unyielding weighting in favor of Sabbath observers over all other interests contravenes a fundamental principle of the Religion Clauses, so well articulated by Judge Learned Hand: "The First Amendment . . . gives no one the right to insist that in pursuit of their own interests others must conform their conduct to his own religious necessities." *Otten v. Baltimore & Ohio R. Co.*, 205 F.2d 58, 61 (CA2 1953).

As such, the statute goes beyond having an incidental or remote effect of advancing religion. The statute has a primary effect that impermissibly advances a particular religious practice.

### III

We hold that the Connecticut statute, which provides Sabbath observers with an absolute and unqualified right not to work on their Sabbath, violates the Establishment Clause of the First Amendment. Accordingly, the judgment of the Supreme Court of Connecticut is

*Affirmed.*

JUSTICE REHNQUIST dissents.

JUSTICE O'CONNOR, with whom JUSTICE MARSHALL joins, concurring.

The Court applies the test enunciated in *Lemon v. Kurtzman* and concludes that Conn. Gen. Stat. § 53-303e(b) (1985) has a primary effect that impermissibly advances religion. I agree, and I join the Court's opinion and judgment. In my view, the Connecticut Sabbath law has an impermissible effect because it conveys a message of endorsement of the Sabbath observance.

All employees, regardless of their religious orientation, would value the benefit which the statute bestows on Sabbath observers—the right to select

---

[9] Section 53-303e(b) gives Sabbath observers the valuable right to designate a particular weekly day off—typically a weekend day, widely prized as a day off. Other employees who have strong and legitimate, but nonreligious, reasons for wanting a weekend day off have no rights under the statute. For example, those employees who have earned the privilege through seniority to have weekend days off may be forced to surrender this privilege to the Sabbath observer; years of service and payment of "dues" at the workplace simply cannot compete with the Sabbath observer's absolute right under the statute. Similarly, those employees who would like a weekend day off, because that is the only day their spouses are also not working, must take a back seat to the Sabbath observer.

the day of the week in which to refrain from labor. Yet Connecticut requires private employers to confer this valued and desirable benefit only on those employees who adhere to a particular religious belief. The statute singles out Sabbath observers for special and, as the Court concludes, absolute protection without according similar accommodation to ethical and religious beliefs and practices of other private employees. There can be little doubt that an objective observer or the public at large would perceive this statutory scheme precisely as the Court does today. The message conveyed is one of endorsement of a particular religious belief, to the detriment of those who do not share it. As such, the Connecticut statute has the effect of advancing religion, and cannot withstand Establishment Clause scrutiny.

I do not read the Court's opinion as suggesting that the religious accommodation provisions of Title VII of the Civil Rights Act of 1964 are similarly invalid. These provisions preclude employment discrimination based on a person's religion and require private employers to reasonably accommodate the religious practices of employees unless to do so would cause undue hardship to the employer's business. Like the Connecticut Sabbath law, Title VII attempts to lift a burden on religious *practice* that is imposed by private employers, and hence it is not the sort of accommodation statute specifically contemplated by the Free Exercise Clause. The provisions of Title VII must therefore manifest a valid secular purpose and effect to be valid under the Establishment Clause. In my view, a statute outlawing employment discrimination based on race, color, religion, sex, or national origin has the valid secular purpose of assuring employment opportunity to all groups in our pluralistic society. Since Title VII calls for reasonable rather than absolute accommodation and extends that requirement to all religious beliefs and practices rather than protecting only the Sabbath observance, I believe an objective observer would perceive it as an anti-discrimination law rather than an endorsement of religion or a particular religious practice.

---

An earlier chapter discussed several issues that arise when religious organizations act as employers and the extent to which religious employers should be subject to anti-discrimination laws regulating employment relations. The flip side to those cases occurs when legislatures affirmatively accommodate religious organizations by allowing them to engage in employment practices that prefer members of their own faith. It certainly would not surprise anyone to hear that Baptist churches hire Baptist preachers and Jewish temples hire rabbis. But what if a Baptist church insists on hiring only Baptists to fill all of the employee positions at the church, including the secretary and janitor? In 1972, Congress decided that religious organizations should have the freedom to hire and fire on the basis of religion for all employment positions, regardless of whether it could be established in court that each position engaged in religious activities. In the case of *Corporation of Presiding Bishop of the Church of Jesus Christ of Latter-day Saints v. Amos*, the Court considered whether such a provision was constitutionally permissible.

---

## CORPORATION OF THE PRESIDING BISHOP OF THE CHURCH OF JESUS CHRIST OF LATTER-DAY SAINTS v. AMOS
### 483 U.S. 327 (1987)

▓ JUSTICE WHITE delivered the opinion of the Court.

Section 702 of the Civil Rights Act of 1964, exempts religious organizations from Title VII's prohibition against discrimination in employment on the basis of religion.[1] The question presented is whether applying the § 702 exemption to the secular nonprofit activities of religious organizations violates the Establishment Clause of the First Amendment. The District Court held that it does, and these cases are here on direct appeal. We reverse.

### I

The Deseret Gymnasium (Gymnasium) in Salt Lake City, Utah, is a nonprofit facility, open to the public, run by the Corporation of the Presiding Bishop of The Church of Jesus Christ of Latter-day Saints (CPB), and the Corporation of the President of The Church of Jesus Christ of Latter-day Saints (COP). The CPB and the COP are religious entities associated with The Church of Jesus Christ of Latter-day Saints (Church), an unincorporated religious association sometimes called the Mormon or LDS Church.

Appellee Mayson worked at the Gymnasium for some 16 years as an assistant building engineer and then as building engineer. He was discharged in 1981 because he failed to qualify for a temple recommend, that is, a certificate that he is a member of the Church and eligible to attend its temples.[4]

Mayson and others purporting to represent a class of plaintiffs brought an action against the CPB and the COP alleging, among other things, discrimination on the basis of religion in violation of § 703 of the Civil Rights Act of 1964. The defendants moved to dismiss this claim on the ground that § 702 shields them from liability. The plaintiffs contended that if construed to allow religious employers to discriminate on religious grounds in hiring for nonreligious jobs, § 702 violates the Establishment Clause. . . .

### II

"This Court has long recognized that the government may (and sometimes must) accommodate religious practices and that it may do so without violating the Establishment Clause." *Hobbie v. Unemployment Appeals Comm'n,*

---

[1] Section 702 provides in relevant part: "This subchapter [i.e., Title VII of the Civil Rights Act of 1964, 42 U. S. C. § 2000e et seq.] shall not apply . . . to a religious corporation, association, educational institution, or society with respect to the employment of individuals of a particular religion to perform work connected with the carrying on by such corporation, association, educational institution, or society of its activities."

[4] Temple recommends are issued only to individuals who observe the Church's standards in such matters as regular church attendance, tithing, and abstinence from coffee, tea, alcohol, and tobacco.

480 U.S. 136, 144-145. It is well established, too, that "the limits of permissible state accommodation to religion are by no means co-extensive with the noninterference mandated by the Free Exercise Clause." *Walz v. Tax Comm'n*, 397 U.S. 664, 673. There is ample room under the Establishment Clause for "benevolent neutrality which will permit religious exercise to exist without sponsorship and without interference." At some point, accommodation may devolve into "an unlawful fostering of religion," but these are not such cases, in our view. . . .

*Lemon* requires first that the law at issue serve a "secular legislative purpose." This does not mean that the law's purpose must be unrelated to religion—that would amount to a requirement "that the government show a callous indifference to religious groups," and the Establishment Clause has never been so interpreted. Rather, *Lemon*'s "purpose" requirement aims at preventing the relevant governmental decisionmaker—in this case, Congress—from abandoning neutrality and acting with the intent of promoting a particular point of view in religious matters.

Under the *Lemon* analysis, it is a permissible legislative purpose to alleviate significant governmental interference with the ability of religious organizations to define and carry out their religious missions. Appellees argue that there is no such purpose here because § 702 provided adequate protection for religious employers prior to the 1972 amendment, when it exempted only the religious activities of such employers from the statutory ban on religious discrimination. We may assume for the sake of argument that the pre-1972 exemption was adequate in the sense that the Free Exercise Clause required no more. Nonetheless, it is a significant burden on a religious organization to require it, on pain of substantial liability, to predict which of its activities a secular court will consider religious. The line is hardly a bright one, and an organization might understandably be concerned that a judge would not understand its religious tenets and sense of mission. Fear of potential liability might affect the way an organization carried out what it understood to be its religious mission.

After a detailed examination of the legislative history of the 1972 amendment, the District Court concluded that Congress' purpose was to minimize governmental "interfer[ence] with the decision-making process in religions." We agree with the District Court that this purpose does not violate the Establishment Clause.

The second requirement under *Lemon* is that the law in question have "a principal or primary effect . . . that neither advances nor inhibits religion." Undoubtedly, religious organizations are better able now to advance their purposes than they were prior to the 1972 amendment to § 702. But religious groups have been better able to advance their purposes on account of many laws that have passed constitutional muster: for example, the property tax exemption at issue in *Walz v. Tax Comm'n*, or the loans of schoolbooks to schoolchildren, including parochial school students, upheld in *Board of Education v. Allen*. A law is not unconstitutional simply because it allows churches to advance religion, which is their very purpose. For a law to have forbidden "effects" under *Lemon*, it must be fair to say that the *government itself* has advanced religion through its own activities and influence. As the Court observed in *Walz*, "for the men who wrote the Religion Clauses of the First Amendment the 'establishment' of a religion connoted sponsorship, financial support, and active involvement of the sovereign in religious activity." 397 U.S., 668.

The District Court appeared to fear that sustaining the exemption would permit churches with financial resources impermissibly to extend their influence and propagate their faith by entering the commercial, profit-making world. The cases before us, however, involve a nonprofit activity instituted over 75 years ago in the hope that "all who assemble here, and who come for the benefit of their health, and for physical blessings, [may] feel that they are in a house dedicated to the Lord." These cases therefore do not implicate the apparent concerns of the District Court. Moreover, we find no persuasive evidence in the record before us that the Church's ability to propagate its religious doctrine through the Gymnasium is any greater now than it was prior to the passage of the Civil Rights Act in 1964. In such circumstances, we do not see how any advancement of religion achieved by the Gymnasium can be fairly attributed to the Government, as opposed to the Church.[15]

We find unpersuasive the District Court's reliance on the fact that § 702 singles out religious entities for a benefit. Although the Court has given weight to this consideration in its past decisions, it has never indicated that statutes that give special consideration to religious groups are *per se* invalid. That would run contrary to the teaching of our cases that there is ample room for accommodation of religion under the Establishment Clause. Where, as here, government acts with the proper purpose of lifting a regulation that burdens the exercise of religion, we see no reason to require that the exemption come packaged with benefits to secular entities.

We are also unpersuaded by the District Court's reliance on the argument that § 702 is unsupported by long historical tradition. There was simply no need to consider the scope of the § 702 exemption until the 1964 Civil Rights Act was passed, and the fact that Congress concluded after eight years that the original exemption was unnecessarily narrow is a decision entitled to deference, not suspicion.

Appellees argue that § 702 offends equal protection principles by giving less protection to the employees of religious employers than to the employees of secular employers. Appellees rely on *Larson v. Valente*, for the proposition that a law drawing distinctions on religious grounds must be strictly scrutinized. But *Larson* indicates that laws discriminating *among* religions are subject to strict scrutiny, and that laws "affording a uniform benefit to *all* religions" should be analyzed under *Lemon*. In cases such as these, where a statute is neutral on its face and motivated by a permissible purpose of limiting governmental interference with the exercise of religion, we see no justification for applying strict scrutiny to a statute that passes the *Lemon* test. The proper inquiry

---

[15] Undoubtedly, Mayson's freedom of choice in religious matters was impinged upon, but it was the Church (through the COP and the CPB), and not the Government, who put him to the choice of changing his religious practices or losing his job. This is a very different case than *Estate of Thornton v. Caldor, Inc.* In *Caldor*, the Court struck down a Connecticut statute prohibiting an employer from requiring an employee to work on a day designated by the employee as his Sabbath. In effect, Connecticut had given the force of law to the employee's designation of a Sabbath day and required accommodation by the employer regardless of the burden which that constituted for the employer or other employees. In the present cases, appellee Mayson was not legally obligated to take the steps necessary to qualify for a temple recommend, and his discharge was not required by statute. We find no merit in appellees' contention that § 702 "impermissibly delegates governmental power to religious employees and conveys a message of governmental endorsement of religious discrimination."

is whether Congress has chosen a rational classification to further a legitimate end. We have already indicated that Congress acted with a legitimate purpose in expanding the § 702 exemption to cover all activities of religious employers. To dispose of appellees' equal protection argument, it suffices to hold—as we now do—that as applied to the nonprofit activities of religious employers, § 702 is rationally related to the legitimate purpose of alleviating significant governmental interference with the ability of religious organizations to define and carry out their religious missions.

It cannot be seriously contended that § 702 impermissibly entangles church and state; the statute effectuates a more complete separation of the two and avoids the kind of intrusive inquiry into religious belief that the District Court engaged in in this case. The statute easily passes muster under the third part of the *Lemon* test.[17]

The judgment of the District Court is reversed, and the cases are remanded for further proceedings consistent with this opinion.

*It is so ordered.*

JUSTICE BRENNAN, with whom JUSTICE MARSHALL joins, concurring in the judgment.

I write separately to emphasize that my concurrence in the judgment rests on the fact that these cases involve a challenge to the application of § 702's categorical exemption to the activities of a *nonprofit* organization. I believe that the particular character of nonprofit activity makes inappropriate a case-by-case determination whether its nature is religious or secular.

These cases present a confrontation between the rights of religious organizations and those of individuals. Any exemption from Title VII's proscription on religious discrimination necessarily has the effect of burdening the religious liberty of prospective and current employees. An exemption says that a person may be put to the choice of either conforming to certain religious tenets or losing a job opportunity, a promotion, or, as in these cases, employment itself.[1] The potential for coercion created by such a provision is in serious tension with our commitment to individual freedom of conscience in matters of religious belief.

At the same time, religious organizations have an interest in autonomy in ordering their internal affairs, so that they may be free to:

> select their own leaders, define their own doctrines, resolve their own disputes, and run their own institutions. Religion includes important communal

---

[17] We have no occasion to pass on the argument of the COP and the CPB that the exemption to which they are entitled under § 702 is required by the Free Exercise Clause.

Appellees argue that § 702 creates danger of political divisiveness along political lines. As the Court stated in *Lynch v. Donnelly*:

This Court has not held that political divisiveness alone can serve to invalidate otherwise permissible conduct. And we decline to so hold today. This case does not involve a direct subsidy to church-sponsored schools or colleges, or other religious institutions, and hence no inquiry into political divisiveness is even called for, *Mueller v. Allen*, 463 U.S. 388, 403-404, n. 11 (1983).

[1] The fact that a religious organization is permitted, rather than required, to impose this burden is irrelevant; what is significant is that the burden is the effect of the exemption. See *Lemon v. Kurtzman*, 403 U.S. 602, 612 (1971). An exemption by its nature merely permits certain behavior, but that has never stopped this Court from examining the *effect* of exemptions that would free religion from regulations placed on others.

elements for most believers. They exercise their religion through religious organizations, and these organizations must be protected by the [Free Exercise] Clause. Laycock, "Toward a General Theory of the Religion Clauses: . . ." 81 Colm. L. Rev. 1373, 1389 (1981). . . .

For many individuals, religious activity derives meaning in large measure from participation in a larger religious community. Such a community represents an ongoing tradition of shared beliefs, an organic entity not reducible to a mere aggregation of individuals. Determining that certain activities are in furtherance of an organization's religious mission, and that only those committed to that mission should conduct them, is thus a means by which a religious community defines itself. Solicitude for a church's ability to do so reflects the idea that furtherance of the autonomy of religious organizations often furthers individual religious freedom as well.

The authority to engage in this process of self-definition inevitably involves what we normally regard as infringement on free exercise rights, since a religious organization is able to condition employment in certain activities on subscription to particular religious tenets. We are willing to countenance the imposition of such a condition because we deem it vital that, if certain activities constitute part of a religious community's practice, then a religious organization should be able to require that only members of its community perform those activities.

This rationale suggests that, ideally, religious organizations should be able to discriminate on the basis of religion *only* with respect to religious activities, so that a determination should be made in each case whether an activity is religious or secular. This is because the infringement on religious liberty that results from conditioning performance of *secular* activity upon religious belief cannot be defended as necessary for the community's self-definition. Furthermore, the authorization of discrimination in such circumstances is not an accommodation that simply enables a church to gain members by the normal means of prescribing the terms of membership for those who seek to participate in furthering the mission of the community. Rather, it puts at the disposal of religion the added advantages of economic leverage in the secular realm. As a result, the authorization of religious discrimination with respect to nonreligious activities goes beyond reasonable accommodation, and has the effect of furthering religion in violation of the Establishment Clause.

What makes the application of a religious-secular distinction difficult is that the character of an activity is not self-evident. As a result, determining whether an activity is religious or secular requires a searching case-by-case analysis. This results in considerable ongoing government entanglement in religious affairs. Furthermore, this prospect of government intrusion raises concern that a religious organization may be chilled in its free exercise activity. While a church may regard the conduct of certain functions as integral to its mission, a court may disagree. A religious organization therefore would have an incentive to characterize as religious only those activities about which there likely would be no dispute, even if it genuinely believed that religious commitment was important in performing other tasks as well. As a result, the community's process of self-definition would be shaped in part by the prospects of litigation. A case-by-case analysis for all activities therefore would both produce excessive government entanglement with religion and create the danger of chilling religious activity.

The risk of chilling religious organizations is most likely to arise with respect to *nonprofit* activities. The fact that an operation is not organized as a profit-making commercial enterprise makes colorable a claim that it is not purely secular in orientation. In contrast to a for-profit corporation, a non-profit organization must utilize its earnings to finance the continued provision of the goods or services it furnishes, and may not distribute any surplus to the owners. This makes plausible a church's contention that an entity is not operated simply in order to generate revenues for the church, but that the activities themselves are infused with a religious purpose. Furthermore, unlike for-profit corporations, nonprofits historically have been organized specifically to provide certain community services, not simply to engage in commerce. Churches often regard the provision of such services as a means of fulfilling religious duty and of providing an example of the way of life a church seeks to foster.

Nonprofit activities therefore are most likely to present cases in which characterization of the activity as religious or secular will be a close question. If there is a danger that a religious organization will be deterred from classifying as religious those activities it actually regards as religious, it is likely to be in this domain. This substantial potential for chilling religious activity makes inappropriate a case-by-case determination of the character of a nonprofit organization, and justifies a categorical exemption for nonprofit activities. Such an exemption demarcates a sphere of deference with respect to those activities most likely to be religious. It permits infringement on employee free exercise rights in those instances in which discrimination is most likely to reflect a religious community's self-definition. While not every nonprofit activity may be operated for religious purposes, the likelihood that many are makes a categorical rule a suitable means to avoid chilling the exercise of religion.[6]

Sensitivity to individual religious freedom dictates that religious discrimination be permitted only with respect to employment in religious activities. Concern for the autonomy of religious organizations demands that we avoid the entanglement and the chill on religious expression that a case-by-case determination would produce. We cannot escape the fact that these aims are in tension. Because of the nature of nonprofit activities, I believe that a categorical exemption for such enterprises appropriately balances these competing concerns. As a result, I concur in the Court's judgment that the nonprofit Deseret Gymnasium may avail itself of an automatic exemption from Title VII's proscription on religious discrimination. . . .

⬚ JUSTICE O'CONNOR, concurring in the judgment.

Although I agree with the judgment of the Court, I write separately to note that this action once again illustrates certain difficulties inherent in the Court's use of the test articulated in *Lemon v. Kurtzman*. As a result of this problematic analysis, while the holding of the opinion for the Court extends only to nonprofit organizations, its reasoning fails to acknowledge that the

---

[6] It is also conceivable that some for-profit activities could have a religious character, so that religious discrimination with respect to these activities would be justified in some cases. The cases before us, however, involve a nonprofit organization; I believe that a *categorical* exemption authorizing discrimination is particularly appropriate for such entities, because claims that they possess a religious dimension will be especially colorable.

amended § 702, raises different questions as it is applied to profit and non-profit organizations. . . .

While acknowledging that "undoubtedly, religious organizations are better able now to advance their purposes than they were prior to the 1972 amendment to § 702," the Court seems to suggest that the "effects" prong of the *Lemon* test is not at all implicated as long as the government action can be characterized as "allowing" religious organizations to advance religion, in contrast to government action directly advancing religion. This distinction seems to me to obscure far more than to enlighten. Almost any government benefit to religion could be recharacterized as simply "allowing" a religion to better advance itself, unless perhaps it involved actual proselytization by government agents. In nearly every case of a government benefit to religion, the religious mission would not be advanced if the religion did not take advantage of the benefit; even a direct financial subsidy to a religious organization would not advance religion if for some reason the organization failed to make any use of the funds. It is for this same reason that there is little significance to the Court's observation that it was the Church rather than the Government that penalized Mayson's refusal to adhere to Church doctrine. The Church had the power to put Mayson to a choice of qualifying for a temple recommend or losing his job because *the Government* had lifted from religious organizations the general regulatory burden imposed by § 702.

The necessary first step in evaluating an Establishment Clause challenge to a government action lifting from religious organizations a generally applicable regulatory burden is to recognize that such government action *does* have the effect of advancing religion. The necessary second step is to separate those benefits to religion that constitutionally accommodate the free exercise of religion from those that provide unjustifiable awards of assistance to religious organizations. As I have suggested in earlier opinions, the inquiry framed by the *Lemon* test should be "whether government's purpose is to endorse religion and whether the statute actually conveys a message of endorsement." To ascertain whether the statute conveys a message of endorsement, the relevant issue is how it would be perceived by an objective observer, acquainted with the text, legislative history, and implementation of the statute. Of course, in order to perceive the government action as a permissible accommodation of religion, there must in fact be an identifiable burden *on the exercise of religion* that can be said to be lifted by the government action. The determination whether the objective observer will perceive an endorsement of religion "is not a question of simple historical fact. Although evidentiary submissions may help answer it, the question is, like the question whether racial or sex-based classifications communicate an invidious message, in large part a legal question to be answered on the basis of judicial interpretation of social facts." *Lynch v. Donnelly*, 465 U.S. 668, 693-694.

The above framework, I believe, helps clarify why the amended § 702 raises different questions as it is applied to nonprofit and for-profit organizations. . . . These cases involve a Government decision to lift from a nonprofit activity of a religious organization the burden of demonstrating that the particular nonprofit activity is religious as well as the burden of refraining from discriminating on the basis of religion. Because there is a probability that a nonprofit activity of a religious organization will itself be involved in the organization's religious mission, in my view the objective observer should perceive the Government action as an accommodation of the exercise of religion rather than as a Government endorsement of religion.

It is not clear, however, that activities conducted by religious organizations solely as profit-making enterprises will be as likely to be directly involved in the religious mission of the organization. While I express no opinion on the issue, I emphasize that under the holding of the Court, and under my view of the appropriate Establishment Clause analysis, the question of the constitutionality of the § 702 exemption as applied to for-profit activities of religious organizations remains open.

---

*Texas Monthly v. Bullock* presented another instance of a legislative accommodation of religious entities, albeit not in an employment context. The state of Texas exempted from its sales tax religious magazines and books but not any other magazines and books. In this case, the Court found that this provision violated the Establishment Clause. Note, however, that there was no Court majority in terms of the reasoning that supported this result.

---

## TEXAS MONTHLY v. BULLOCK
### 489 U.S. 1 (1989)

JUSTICE BRENNAN announced the judgment of the Court and delivered an opinion, in which JUSTICE MARSHALL and JUSTICE STEVENS join.

Texas exempts from its sales tax "[p]eriodicals that are published or distributed by a religious faith and that consist wholly of writings promulgating the teaching of the faith and books that consist wholly of writings sacred to a religious faith." The question presented is whether this exemption violates the Establishment Clause or the Free Press Clause of the First Amendment when the State denies a like exemption for other publications. We hold that, when confined exclusively to publications advancing the tenets of a religious faith, the exemption runs afoul of the Establishment Clause; accordingly, we need not reach the question whether it contravenes the Free Press Clause as well.

I

Prior to October 2, 1984, Texas exempted from its sales and use tax magazine subscriptions running half a year or longer and entered as second class mail. This exemption was repealed as of October 2, 1984, before being reinstated effective October 1, 1987. Throughout this 3-year period, Texas continued to exempt from its sales and use tax periodicals published or distributed by a religious faith consisting entirely of writings promulgating the teaching of the faith, along with books consisting solely of writings sacred to a religious faith.

Appellant Texas Monthly, Inc., publishes a general interest magazine of the same name. Appellant is not a religious faith, and its magazine does not contain only articles promulgating the teaching of a religious faith. Thus, it was required during this 3-year period to collect and remit to the State the applicable sales tax on the price of qualifying subscription sales. In 1985, appellant paid sales taxes of $149,107.74 under protest and sued to recover those payments in state court. . . .

III

In proscribing all laws "respecting an establishment of religion," the Constitution prohibits, at the very least, legislation that constitutes an endorsement of one or another set of religious beliefs or of religion generally. It is part of our settled jurisprudence that "the Establishment Clause prohibits government from abandoning secular purposes in order to put an imprimatur on one religion, or on religion as such, or to favor the adherents of any sect or religious organization. The core notion animating the requirement that a statute possess "a secular legislative purpose" and that "its principal or primary effect . . . be one that neither advances nor inhibits religion," is not only that government may not be overtly hostile to religion but also that it may not place its prestige, coercive authority, or resources behind a single religious faith or behind religious belief in general, compelling nonadherents to support the practices or proselytizing of favored religious organizations and conveying the message that those who do not contribute gladly are less than full members of the community.

It does not follow, of course, that government policies with secular objectives may not incidentally benefit religion. The nonsectarian aims of government and the interests of religious groups often overlap, and this Court has never required that public authorities refrain from implementing reasonable measures to advance legitimate secular goals merely because they would thereby relieve religious groups of costs they would otherwise incur. Nor have we required that legislative categories make no explicit reference to religion. . . .

In all of these cases, however, we emphasized that the benefits derived by religious organizations flowed to a large number of nonreligious groups as well. Indeed, were those benefits confined to religious organizations, they could not have appeared other than as state sponsorship of religion; if that were so, we would not have hesitated to strike them down for lacking a secular purpose and effect. . . .

Finally, we emphasized in *Walz [v. Tax Comm'n,]* that in granting a property tax deduction, the State "has not singled out one particular church or religious group or even churches as such; rather, it has granted exemption to all houses of religious worship within a broad class of property owned by nonprofit, quasipublic corporations which include hospitals, libraries, playgrounds, scientific, professional, historical, and patriotic groups." 397 U.S., 673. The breadth of New York's property tax exemption was essential to our holding that it was "not aimed at establishing, sponsoring, or supporting religion," *id.*, 674, but rather possessed the legitimate secular purpose and effect of contributing to the community's moral and intellectual diversity and encouraging private groups to undertake projects that advanced the community's well-being and that would otherwise have to be funded by tax revenues or left undone.[2] . . .

---

[2] Although we found it "unnecessary to justify the tax exemption on the social welfare services or 'good works' that some churches perform for parishioners and others," *Walz v. Tax Comm'n*, 397 U.S., 674, we in no way intimated that the exemption would have been valid had it applied only to the property of religious groups or had it lacked a permissible secular objective. Rather, we concluded that the State might reasonably have determined that religious groups generally contribute to the cultural and moral improvement of the community, perform useful social services, and enhance a desirable pluralism of viewpoint and

Texas' sales tax exemption for periodicals published or distributed by a religious faith and consisting wholly of writings promulgating the teaching of the faith lacks sufficient breadth to pass scrutiny under the Establishment Clause. Every tax exemption constitutes a subsidy that affects nonqualifying taxpayers, forcing them to become "indirect and vicarious 'donors.'" Insofar as that subsidy is conferred upon a wide array of nonsectarian groups as well as religious organizations in pursuit of some legitimate secular end,[4] the fact that religious groups benefit incidentally does not deprive the subsidy of the secular purpose and primary effect mandated by the Establishment Clause. However, when government directs a subsidy exclusively to religious organizations that is not required by the Free Exercise Clause and that either burdens nonbeneficiaries markedly or cannot reasonably be seen as removing a significant state-imposed deterrent to the free exercise of religion, as Texas has done, it "provide[s] unjustifiable awards of assistance to religious organizations" and cannot but "conve[y] a message of endorsement" to slighted members of the community. This is particularly true where, as here, the subsidy is targeted at writings that *promulgate* the teachings of religious faiths. It is difficult to view Texas' narrow exemption as anything but state sponsorship of religious belief, regardless of whether one adopts the perspective of beneficiaries or of uncompensated contributors.

How expansive the class of exempt organizations or activities must be to withstand constitutional assault depends upon the State's secular aim in granting a tax exemption. If the State chose to subsidize, by means of a tax exemption, all groups that contributed to the community's cultural, intellectual, and moral betterment, then the exemption for religious publications could be retained, provided that the exemption swept as widely as the property tax exemption we upheld in *Walz*. By contrast, if Texas sought to promote reflection and discussion about questions of ultimate value and the contours of a good or meaningful life, then a tax exemption would have to be available to an extended range of associations whose publications were substantially devoted to such matters; the exemption could not be reserved for publications dealing solely with religious issues, let alone restricted to publications advocating rather than criticizing religious belief or activity, without signaling an endorsement of religion that is offensive to the principles informing the Establishment Clause. . . .

It is not our responsibility to specify which permissible secular objectives, if any, the State should pursue to justify a tax exemption for religious periodicals. That charge rests with the Texas Legislature. Our task, and that of the

---

enterprise, just as do the host of other nonprofit organizations that qualified for the exemption. It is because the set of organizations defined by these secular objectives was so large that we saw no need to inquire into the secular benefits provided by religious groups that sought to avail themselves of the exemption. . . . Had the State defined the class of subsidized activities more narrowly—to encompass only "charitable" works, for example—more searching scrutiny would have been necessary, notwithstanding the greater intermingling of government and religion that would likely result.

[4] The fact that Texas grants other sales tax exemptions (e.g., for sales of food, agricultural items, and property used in the manufacture of articles for ultimate sale) for *different* purposes does not rescue the exemption for religious periodicals from invalidation. What is crucial is that any subsidy afforded religious organizations be warranted by some overarching secular purpose that justifies like benefits for nonreligious groups. . . .

Texas courts, is rather to ensure that any scheme of exemptions adopted by the legislature does not have the purpose or effect of sponsoring certain religious tenets or religious belief in general. . . .

IV

A

In defense of its sales tax exemption for religious publications, Texas claims that it has a compelling interest in avoiding violations of the Free Exercise and Establishment Clauses, and that the exemption serves that end. Without such an exemption, Texas contends, its sales tax might trammel free exercise rights, as did the flat license tax this Court struck down as applied to proselytizing by Jehovah's Witnesses in *Murdock v. Pennsylvania*. In addition, Texas argues that an exemption for religious publications neither advances nor inhibits religion, as required by the Establishment Clause, and that its elimination would entangle church and state to a greater degree than the exemption itself.

We reject both parts of this argument. Although Texas may widen its exemption consonant with some legitimate secular purpose, nothing in our decisions under the Free Exercise Clause prevents the State from eliminating altogether its exemption for religious publications. . . . In this case, the State has adduced no evidence that the payment of a sales tax by subscribers to religious periodicals or purchasers of religious books would offend their religious beliefs or inhibit religious activity. The State therefore cannot claim persuasively that its tax exemption is compelled by the Free Exercise Clause in even a single instance, let alone in every case. No concrete need to accommodate religious activity has been shown.[8]

Moreover, even if members of some religious group succeeded in demonstrating that payment of a sales tax—or, less plausibly, of a sales tax when applied to printed matter—would violate their religious tenets, it is by no means obvious that the State would be required by the Free Exercise Clause to make individualized exceptions for them. In *United States v. Lee*, we ruled unanimously that the Federal Government need not exempt an Amish

---

[8] Contrary to the dissent's claims, we in no way suggest that all benefits conferred exclusively upon religious groups or upon individuals on account of their religious beliefs are forbidden by the Establishment Clause unless they are mandated by the Free Exercise Clause. Our decisions in *Zorach v. Clauson*, and *Corporation of Presiding Bishop of Church of Jesus Christ of Latter-day Saints v. Amos*, offer two examples. Similarly, if the Air Force provided a sufficiently broad exemption from its dress requirements for servicemen whose religious faiths commanded them to wear certain headgear or other attire, see *Goldman v. Weinberger*, 475 U.S. 503 (1986), that exemption presumably would not be invalid under the Establishment Clause even though this Court has not found it to be required by the Free Exercise Clause.

All of these cases, however, involve legislative exemptions that did not, or would not, impose substantial burdens on nonbeneficiaries while allowing others to act according to their religious beliefs, or that were designed to alleviate government intrusions that might significantly deter adherents of a particular faith from conduct protected by the Free Exercise Clause. New York City's decision to release students from public schools so that they might obtain religious instruction elsewhere, which we upheld in *Zorach*, was found not to coerce students who wished to remain behind to alter their religious beliefs, nor did it impose monetary costs on their parents or other taxpayers who opposed, or were indifferent to, the religious instruction given to students who were released. The hypothetical Air Force uniform exemption also would not place a monetary burden on those required to conform to the dress code or subject them to any appreciable privation. And the application of Title VII's

employer from the payment of Social Security taxes, notwithstanding our recognition that compliance would offend his religious beliefs. We noted that "[n]ot all burdens on religion are unconstitutional," and held that "[t]he state may justify a limitation on religious liberty by showing that it is essential to accomplish an overriding governmental interest." Although the balancing test we set forth in *Lee* must be performed on a case-by-case basis, a State's interest in the uniform collection of a sales tax appears comparable to the Federal Government's interest in the uniform collection of Social Security taxes, and mandatory exemptions under the Free Exercise Clause are arguably as difficult to prove. No one has suggested that members of any of the major religious denominations in the United States—the principal beneficiaries of Texas' tax exemption—could demonstrate an infringement of their free exercise rights sufficiently serious to overcome the State's countervailing interest in collecting its sales tax.

### B

Texas' further claim that the Establishment Clause mandates, or at least favors, its sales tax exemption for religious periodicals is equally unconvincing. Not only does the exemption seem a blatant endorsement of religion, but it appears, on its face, to produce greater state entanglement with religion than the denial of an exemption. . . . The prospect of inconsistent treatment and government embroilment in controversies over religious doctrine seems especially baleful where, as in the case of Texas' sales tax exemption, a statute requires that public officials determine whether some message or activity is consistent with "the teaching of the faith."

While Texas is correct in pointing out that compliance with government regulations by religious organizations and the monitoring of their compliance by government agencies would itself enmesh the operations of church and state to some degree, we have found that such compliance would generally not impede the evangelical activities of religious groups and that the "routine and factual inquiries" commonly associated with the enforcement of tax laws "bear no resemblance to the kind of government surveillance the Court has previously held to pose an intolerable risk of government entanglement with religion." *Tony and Susan Alamo Foundation v. Secretary of Labor*, 471 U.S., 305.

On the record before us, neither the Free Exercise Clause nor the Establishment Clause prevents Texas from withdrawing its current exemption for religious publications if it chooses not to expand it to promote some legitimate secular aim.

---

exemption for religious organizations that we approved in Corporation of Presiding Bishop, though it had some adverse effect on those holding or seeking employment with those organizations (if not on taxpayers generally), prevented potentially serious encroachments on protected religious freedoms.

Texas tax exemption, by contrast, does not remove a demonstrated and possibly grave imposition on religious activity sheltered by the Free Exercise Clause. Moreover, it burdens nonbeneficiaries by increasing their tax bills by whatever amount is needed to offset the benefit bestowed on subscribers to religious publications. The fact that such exemptions are of long standing cannot shield them from the strictures of the Establishment Clause. As we said in *Walz v. Tax Comm'n*, "no one acquires a vested or protected right in violation of the Constitution by long use, even when that span of time covers our entire national existence and indeed predates it."

C

Our conclusion today is admittedly in tension with some unnecessarily sweeping statements in *Murdock v. Pennsylvania* and *Follett v. McCormick*. To the extent that language in those opinions is inconsistent with our decision here, based on the evolution in our thinking about the Religion Clauses over the last 45 years, we disavow it. . . .

If one accepts the majority's characterization of the critical issues in *Murdock* and *Follett*, those decisions are easily compatible with our holding here. In striking down application of the town ordinance to Jehovah's Witnesses in *Follett*—an ordinance the Court found to be "in all material respects the same," as the one whose application it restricted in *Murdock*—the Court declared that only a single "narrow" question was presented: "It is whether a flat license tax as applied to one who earns his livelihood as an evangelist or preacher in his home town is constitutional." Regarding *Follett* in this light, we must agree that "we have quite a different case from that of a merchant who sells books at a stand or on the road." There is no doubt that the First Amendment prevents both the States and the Federal Government from imposing a special occupation tax exclusively on those who devote their days to spreading religious messages. Moreover, it is questionable whether, consistent with the Free Exercise Clause, government may exact a facially neutral license fee designed for commercial salesmen from religious missionaries whose principal work is preaching and who only occasionally sell religious tracts for small sums, so long as "the fee is not a nominal one, imposed as a regulatory measure and calculated to defray the expense of protecting those on the streets and at home against the abuses of solicitors." In such a case, equal treatment of commercial and religious solicitation might result in an unconstitutional imposition on religious activity warranting judicial relief, particularly where that activity is deemed central to a given faith, as the Court found this form of proselytizing to be in *Murdock* and *Follett*, and where the tax burden is far from negligible.

Insofar as the Court's holdings in *Murdock* and *Follett* are limited to these points, they are plainly consistent with our decision today. The sales tax that Texas imposes is not an occupation tax levied on religious missionaries. Nor is it a flat tax that "restrains in advance," the free exercise of religion. On the contrary, because the tax is equal to a small fraction of the value of each sale and payable by the buyer, it poses little danger of stamping out missionary work involving the sale of religious publications, and in view of its generality it can hardly be viewed as a covert attempt to curtail religious activity. We therefore see no inconsistency between our former decisions and our present holding.

To the extent that our opinions in *Murdock* and *Follett* might be read, however, to suggest that the States and the Federal Government may never tax the sale of religious or other publications, we reject those dicta. Our intervening decisions make clear that even if the denial of tax benefits "will inevitably have a substantial impact" on religious groups, the refusal to grant such benefits does not offend the Free Exercise Clause when it does not prevent those groups "from observing their religious tenets." In *Murdock* and *Follett*, the application of a flat license or occupation tax to Jehovah's Witnesses arguably did prevent adherents of that sect from acting in accordance with some of their central religious beliefs, in the absence of any overriding government interest in denying them an exemption. In the much more common circumstances exemplified by this case, however, taxes or regulations would not subject religious organizations to undue burdens and the government's interest in their uniform application is far weightier. Hence, there is no bar to Texas' imposing a general sales tax on religious publications.

V

We conclude that Texas' sales tax exemption for religious publications violates the First Amendment, as made applicable to the States by the Fourteenth Amendment. Accordingly, the judgment of the Texas Court of Appeals is reversed, and the case is remanded for further proceedings.

*It is so ordered.* . . .

※ JUSTICE BLACKMUN, with whom JUSTICE O'CONNOR joins, concurring in the judgment. . . .

The Free Exercise Clause value suggests that a State may not impose a tax on spreading the gospel. The Establishment Clause value suggests that a State may not give a tax break to those who spread the gospel that it does not also give to others who actively might advocate disbelief in religion.

It perhaps is fairly easy to reconcile the Free Exercise and Press Clause values. If the Free Exercise Clause suggests that a State may not tax the sale of religious literature by a religious organization, this fact alone would give a State a compelling reason to exclude this category of sales from an otherwise general sales tax. . . .

I find it more difficult to reconcile in this case the Free Exercise and Establishment Clause values. The Free Exercise Clause suggests that a special exemption for religious books is required. The Establishment Clause suggests that a special exemption for religious books is forbidden. This tension between mandated and prohibited religious exemptions is well recognized.

JUSTICE BRENNAN's opinion, in its Part IV, would resolve the tension between the Free Exercise and Establishment Clause values simply by subordinating the Free Exercise value, even, it seems to me, at the expense of longstanding precedents. . . .

Perhaps it is a vain desire, but I would like to decide the present case without necessarily sacrificing either the Free Exercise Clause value or the Establishment Clause value. It is possible for a State to write a tax-exemption statute consistent with both values: for example, a state statute might exempt the sale not only of religious literature distributed by a religious organization but also of philosophical literature distributed by nonreligious organizations devoted to such matters of conscience as life and death, good and evil, being and nonbeing, right and wrong. . . .

I believe we can avoid most of these difficulties with a narrow resolution of the case before us. We need not decide today the extent to which the Free Exercise Clause requires a tax exemption for the sale of religious literature by a religious organization; in other words, defining the ultimate scope of *Follett* and *Murdock* may be left for another day. We need decide here only whether a tax exemption *limited to* the sale of religious literature by religious organizations violates the Establishment Clause. I conclude that it does.

In this case, by confining the tax exemption exclusively to the sale of religious publications, Texas engaged in preferential support for the communication of religious messages. Although some forms of accommodating religion are constitutionally permissible, this one surely is not. A statutory preference for the dissemination of religious ideas offends our most basic understanding of what the Establishment Clause is all about and hence is constitutionally intolerable. Accordingly, whether or not *Follett* and *Murdock* prohibit taxing the sale of religious literature, the Establishment Clause prohibits a tax exemption limited to the sale of religious literature. Cf. *Estate of Thornton v. Caldor, Inc.*, 472 U.S. 703 (1985) (the Establishment Clause prohibits a statute that grants employees an unqualified right not to work on their Sabbath), and *Hobbie v. Unemployment Appeals Comm'n of Fla.*, 480 U.S. 136, 145-146, and n. 11 (1987) (consistent with *Caldor*, the Free Exercise Clause prohibits denying unemployment compensation to employees who refuse to work on their Sabbath).

At oral argument, appellees suggested that the statute at issue here exempted from taxation the sale of atheistic literature distributed by an atheistic organization. If true, this statute might survive Establishment Clause scrutiny, as well as Free Exercise and Press Clause scrutiny. But, as appellees were quick to concede at argument, the record contains nothing to support this facially implausible interpretation of the statute. Thus, constrained to construe this Texas statute as exempting religious literature alone, I concur in the holding that it contravenes the Establishment Clause, and in remanding the case for further proceedings not inconsistent with this holding.

JUSTICE SCALIA, with whom THE CHIEF JUSTICE and JUSTICE KENNEDY join, dissenting.

As a judicial demolition project, today's decision is impressive. The machinery employed by the opinions of JUSTICE BRENNAN and JUSTICE BLACKMUN is no more substantial than the antinomy that accommodation of religion may be required but not permitted, and the bold but unsupportable assertion (given such realities as the text of the Declaration of Independence, the national Thanksgiving Day proclaimed by every President since Lincoln, the inscriptions on our coins, the words of our Pledge of Allegiance, the invocation with which sessions of our Court are opened and, come to think of it, the discriminatory protection of freedom of religion in the Constitution) that government may not "convey a message of endorsement of religion." With this frail equipment, the Court topples an exemption for religious publications of a sort that expressly appears in the laws of at least 15 of the 45 States that have sales and use taxes—States from Maine to Texas, from Idaho to New Jersey. In practice, a similar exemption may well exist in even more States than that, since until today our case law has suggested that it is not only permissible but perhaps required. I expect, for example, that even in States without express exemptions many churches, and many tax assessors, have thought sales taxes inapplicable to the religious literature typically offered for sale in church foyers.

When one expands the inquiry to sales taxes on items other than publications and to other types of taxes such as property, income, amusement, and motor vehicle taxes—all of which are likewise affected by today's holding—the Court's accomplishment is even more impressive. At least 45 States provide exemptions for religious groups without analogous exemptions for other types of nonprofit institutions. For over half a century the federal Internal Revenue Code has allowed "minister[s] of the gospel" (a term interpreted broadly enough to include cantors and rabbis) to exclude from gross income the rental value of their parsonages. In short, religious tax exemptions of the type the

Court invalidates today permeate the state and federal codes, and have done so for many years.

I dissent because I find no basis in the text of the Constitution, the decisions of this Court, or the traditions of our people for disapproving this long-standing and widespread practice.

I . . .

It should be apparent that *Walz*, which we have reaffirmed on numerous occasions in the last two decades, is utterly dispositive of the Establishment Clause claim before us here. The Court invalidates § 151.312 of the Texas Tax Code only by distorting the holding of that case and radically altering the well-settled Establishment Clause jurisprudence which that case represents.

JUSTICE BRENNAN explains away *Walz* by asserting that "[t]he breadth of New York's property tax exemption was essential to our holding that it was 'not aimed at establishing, sponsoring, or supporting religion.'" This is not a plausible reading of the opinion. At the outset of its discussion concerning the permissibility of the legislative purpose, the *Walz* Court did discuss the fact that the New York tax exemption applied not just to religions but to certain other "nonprofit" groups, including "hospitals, libraries, playgrounds, scientific, professional, historical, and patriotic groups." The finding of valid legislative purpose was not rested upon that, however, but upon the more direct proposition that "exemption constitutes a reasonable and balanced attempt to guard against" the "latent dangers" of governmental hostility towards religion "inherent in the imposition of property taxes." . . .

Today's opinions go beyond misdescribing *Walz*, however. In repudiating what *Walz* in fact approved, they achieve a revolution in our Establishment Clause jurisprudence, effectively overruling other cases that were based, as *Walz* was, on the "accommodation of religion" rationale. According to Justice Brennan's opinion, no law is constitutional whose "benefits [are] confined to religious organizations"—except, of course, those laws that are unconstitutional *unless* they contain benefits confined to religious organizations. Our jurisprudence affords no support for this unlikely proposition. *Walz* is just one of a long line of cases in which we have recognized that "the government may (and sometimes must) accommodate religious practices and that it may do so without violating the Establishment Clause." *Hobbie v. Unemployment Appeals Comm'n of Fla.*, 480 U.S. 136, 144-145. In such cases as *Sherbert v. Verner, Wisconsin v. Yoder, Thomas v. Review Bd. of Ind. Employment Security Div.*, and *Hobbie v. Unemployment Appeals Comm'n of Fla.*, we held that the Free Exercise Clause of the First Amendment *required* religious beliefs to be accommodated by granting religion-specific exemptions from otherwise applicable laws. We have often made clear, however, that "[t]he limits of permissible state accommodation to religion are by no means coextensive with the noninterference mandated by the Free Exercise Clause." *Walz.*, 397 U.S., 673. . . .

The novelty of today's holding is obscured by JUSTICE BRENNAN's citation and description of many cases in which "breadth of coverage" *was* relevant to the First Amendment determination. Breadth of coverage is essential to constitutionality whenever a law's benefiting of religious activity is sought to be defended not specifically (or not exclusively) as an intentional and reasonable accommodation of religion, but as merely the incidental consequence of seeking to benefit *all* activity that achieves a particular secular goal. But that is a different rationale—more commonly invoked than accommodation of religion but, as our cases show, not preclusive of it. Where accommodation of religion is the justification, by definition religion is being singled out. . . .

It is not always easy to determine when accommodation slides over into promotion, and neutrality into favoritism, but the withholding of a tax upon the dissemination of religious materials is not even a close case. The subjects of the exemption before us consist exclusively of "writings promulgating the teaching of the faith" and "writings sacred to a religious faith." If there is any close question, it is not whether the exemption is permitted, but whether it is constitutionally compelled in order to avoid "interference with the dissemination of religious ideas." *Gillette.*, 401 U.S., 462. . . .

I am willing to acknowledge, however, that *Murdock* and *Follett* are narrowly distinguishable. But what follows from that is not the facile conclusion that therefore the State has no "compelling interest in avoiding violations of the Free Exercise and Establishment Clauses," and thus the exemption is invalid. . . . The proper lesson to be drawn from the narrow distinguishing of *Murdock* and *Follett* is quite different: If the exemption comes so close to being a constitutionally required accommodation, there is no doubt that it is at least a permissible one.

Although JUSTICE BRENNAN's opinion places almost its entire reliance upon the "purpose" prong of *Lemon*, it alludes briefly to the second prong as well, finding that § 151.312 has the impermissible "effect of sponsoring certain religious tenets or religious belief in general." Once again, *Walz* stands in stark opposition to this assertion, but it may be useful to explain why. Quite obviously, a sales tax exemption aids religion, since it makes it less costly for religions to disseminate their beliefs. But that has never been enough to strike down an enactment under the Establishment Clause. "A law is not unconstitutional simply because it *allows* churches to advance religion, which is their very purpose." . . .

Finally, and least persuasively of all, Justice Brennan suggests that § 151.312 violates the "excessive government entanglement" aspect of *Lemon*. It is plain that the exemption does not foster the sort of "comprehensive, discriminating, and continuing state surveillance" necessary to run afoul of that test. A State does not excessively involve itself in religious affairs merely by examining material to determine whether it is religious or secular in nature. In *Mueller*, for instance, we held that state officials' examination of textbooks to determine whether they were "books and materials used in the teaching of religious tenets, doctrines or worship" did not constitute excessive entanglement. I see no material distinction between that inquiry and the one Texas officials must make in this case. Moreover, here as in *Walz*, it is all but certain that elimination of the exemption will have the effect of *increasing* government's involvement with religion. The Court's invalidation of § 151.312 ensures that Texas churches selling publications that promulgate their religion will now be subject to numerous statutory and regulatory impositions, including audits, requirements for the filing of security, reporting requirements, writs of attachment without bond, and the seizure and sale of property to satisfy tax delinquencies.

II . . .

Today's decision introduces a new strain of irrationality in our Religion Clause jurisprudence. I have no idea how to reconcile it with *Zorach* (which seems a much harder case of accommodation), with *Walz* (which seems precisely in point), and with *Corporation of Presiding Bishop* (on which the ink is hardly dry). It is not right—it is not constitutionally healthy—that this Court should feel authorized to refashion anew our civil society's relationship with religion, adopting a theory of church and state that is contradicted by current practice, tradition, and even our own case law. I dissent.

---

## NOTES AND QUESTIONS

1. The cases of *Thorton*, *Amos*, and *Texas Monthly* came in quick succession, with each holding being separated by only two years. The three cases share similar facts. Each legislative accommodation benefited only religious entities. Each legislative accommodation imposed various burdens on individuals or entities not in the benefited class. Yet the accommodations in *Thorton* and *Texas Monthly* were held unconstitutional. What explains the difference(s)?

2. What was the constitutional problem in *Thornton* – that the intended accommodation under the law was unsupportable; that the law benefited religious persons only; that the accommodation was absolute; or that the accommodation burdened third persons? Assume the accommodation was not "absolute and unqualified" but created a presumption that authorized employers to treat Sabbath observers preferentially. But assume also that this hypothetical accommodation would create the same inconveniences on fellow workers. Would that kind of statute be constitutional?

3. According to the Court in *Amos*, what is the permissible legislative purpose for the § 702 exemption? According to the majority, when is it permissible for the government to single out religion for accommodation, as it did in the § 702 exemption? How was the Title VII 702 exemption broadened in 1972? Was this broadening required by the Free Exercise Clause? How does this fact enter into the majority's holding?

   Contrast this holding with that of the plurality in *Texas Monthly*. According to Justice Brennan, when is it impermissible to single out religion for special accommodation that isn't required by the Free Exercise Clause? More specifically, how does he distinguish the Court's decision in *Amos* from its decision in this case? What is the dissent's critique of these rationales?

4. Is there any constitutional significance to the fact that the religious group involved in *Amos* was a nonprofit organization? How important is this factor for the majority and concurrences?

5. Burdens, part 1. What threshold degree of a burden is necessary to justify an affirmative accommodation of religion? The *Amos* Court said that an infringement on religious practice did not need to rise to the level of an actual free exercise violation in order to justify an accommodation. But how close must it come? How did the *Amos* and *Walz* Courts describe and evaluate the burdens on religious entities that would result if the exemptions at issue in those cases did not shield their activities? Does the necessary degree of a religious burden justifying an accommodation vary depending on whether religion is singled out for the benefit or whether religion enjoys the accommodation along with similarly situated secular entities? Recall the passage from *Amos*: "Where, as

here, government acts with the proper purpose of lifting a regulation, we see no reason to require that the exemption comes packaged with benefits to secular entities." How should this passage be understood?

6. Burdens, part 2. If a religious accommodation is not mandated by the Free Exercise Clause, how serious must the burden be on third parties to override that accommodation? Is it any burden? *Thorton* spoke of an "inconvenience" imposed on third parties, whereas *Texas Monthly* noted the exemption increased the tax bills of nonbeneficiaries. Suppose a church claims under RLU-IPA that a zoning ordinance restricting the size of buildings places a burden on its religious practice by keeping it from building a larger sanctuary. This significantly hampers the church's ability to minister to a growing membership. Nearby neighbors respond that a larger sanctuary will encroach on property lines, affect their property values, obstruct light and create a visual blight, all affecting their quality of life. Who wins?

7. Burdens, part 3. Who must impose the burden on religious practice or third persons in order to justify (or nix) the accommodation, the government or private parties? The *Amos* majority writes that "it was the Church (through the COP and the CPB), and not the Government, who put [Mayson] to the choice of changing his religious practices or losing his job." Justice O'Connor retorts that the Church could only have imposed that choice with the "blessing" of the § 702 exemption. How does the burden on third parties in *Amos* differ from those discussed in *Thorton* and *Texas Monthly*? If this was a matter of concern to Justices Brennan and O'Connor in those two cases, why did they concur in *Amos*?

8. How does Justice O'Connor's rationale differ from the plurality's in *Texas Monthly*? How does O'Connor distinguish this case from the *Amos* case?

9. According to the dissent in *Texas Monthly*, the *Walz* case is "utterly dispositive of the Establishment Clause claim" in that case. How does the plurality distinguish *Walz*? Does the plurality or the dissent have the better of the argument on this point?

10. Describe the contrasting views of the plurality and the dissent in *Texas Monthly* on the issue of whether the invalidation of the tax exemption would cause more or less church-state entanglement. Are these opposing sides working from a common definition of excessive church-state entanglement or different definitions?

*Texas Monthly* was not the final word on legislative accommodations of religion. Issues concerning the permissibility of accommodations have arisen in several later cases discussed in earlier chapters. Two of those cases are excerpted below. Consider whether the Court's position on legislative accommodations has changed since the fractured opinions in *Texas Monthly*.

---

## KIRYAS JOEL VILLAGE SCHOOL DISTRICT v. GRUMET
## 512 U.S. 687 (1994)

[The facts and lower court holdings in *Kiryas Joel* are discussed in chapter 22. In the first two sections of the opinion, Justice Souter, writing first for a plurality and then for a majority, held that in creating the special school district for the village, the state delegated government authority to a religious group and gave preferential treatment to the Satmar Hasidic community. He then turned to the issue of whether the state's action could be upheld as a religious accommodation.]

▓ JUSTICE SOUTER delivered the opinion of the Court.

In finding that Chapter 748 violates the requirement of governmental neutrality by extending the benefit of a special franchise, we do not deny that the Constitution allows the state to accommodate religious needs by alleviating special burdens. Our cases leave no doubt that in commanding neutrality the Religion Clauses do not require the government to be oblivious to impositions that legitimate exercises of state power may place on religious belief and practice. Rather, there is "ample room under the Establishment Clause" for "benevolent neutrality which will permit religious exercise to exist without sponsorship and without interference." The fact that Chapter 748 facilitates the practice of religion is not what renders it an unconstitutional establishment. . . .

But accommodation is not a principle without limits, and what petitioners seek is an adjustment to the Satmars' religiously grounded preferences that our cases do not countenance. Prior decisions have allowed religious communities and institutions to pursue their own interests free from governmental interference, . . . but we have never hinted that an otherwise unconstitutional delegation of political power to a religious group could be saved as a religious accommodation. Petitioners' proposed accommodation singles out a particular religious sect for special treatment, and whatever the limits of permissible legislative accommodations may be, . . . it is clear that neutrality as among religions must be honored.

This conclusion does not, however, bring the Satmar parents, the Monroe-Woodbury school district, or the State of New York to the end of the road in seeking ways to respond to the parents' concerns. Just as the Court in *Larkin* observed that the State's interest in protecting religious meeting places could be "readily accomplished by other means," there are several alternatives here for providing bilingual and bicultural special education to Satmar children. Such services can perfectly well be offered to village children through the Monroe-Woodbury Central School District. Since the Satmars do not claim that separatism is religiously mandated, their children may receive bilingual and bicultural instruction at a public school already run by the Monroe-Woodbury district. Or if the educationally appropriate offering by Monroe-Woodbury should turn out to be a separate program of bilingual and bicultural education at a neutral site near one of the village's parochial schools, this Court has already made it clear that no Establishment Clause difficulty would inhere in such a scheme, administered in accordance with neutral principles that would not necessarily confine special treatment to Satmars.

To be sure, the parties disagree on whether the services Monroe-Woodbury actually provided in the late 1980's were appropriately tailored to the needs of Satmar children, but this dispute is of only limited relevance to the question whether such services could have been provided, had adjustments been made. . . .

■ JUSTICE KENNEDY, concurring in the judgment.

The Court's ruling that the Kiryas Joel Village School District violates the Establishment Clause is in my view correct, but my reservations about what the Court's reasoning implies for religious accommodations in general are sufficient to require a separate writing. As the Court recognizes, a legislative accommodation that discriminates among religions may become an establishment of religion. But the Court's opinion can be interpreted to say that an accommodation for a particular religious group is invalid because of the risk that the legislature will not grant the same accommodation to another religious group suffering some similar burden. This rationale seems to me without grounding in our precedents and a needless restriction upon the legislature's ability to respond to the unique problems of a particular religious group.

■ JUSTICE SCALIA, dissenting.

In today's opinion . . . the Court seems uncomfortable with . . . our constitutional tradition. Although it acknowledges the concept of accommodation, it quickly points out that it is "not a principle without limits," and then gives reasons why the present case exceeds those limits, reasons which simply do not hold water. "[W]e have never hinted," the Court says, "that an otherwise unconstitutional delegation of political power to a religious group could be saved as a religious accommodation." Putting aside the circularity inherent in referring to a delegation as "otherwise unconstitutional" when its constitutionality turns on whether there is an accommodation, if this statement is true, it is only because we have never hinted that delegation of political power to citizens who share a particular religion could be unconstitutional. . . .

The second and last reason the Court finds accommodation impermissible is, astoundingly, the mere risk that the State will not offer accommodation to a similar group in the future, and that neutrality will therefore not be preserved. . . .

At bottom, the Court's "no guarantee of neutrality" argument is an assertion of this Court's inability to control the New York Legislature's future denial of comparable accommodation. We have "no assurance," the Court says, "that the next similarly situated group seeking a school district of its own will receive one" . . . .

The Court's demand for "up front" assurances of a neutral system is at war with both traditional accommodation doctrine and the judicial role. As we have described, Congress's earliest accommodations exempted duties paid by specific churches on particular items. Moreover, most efforts at accommodation seek to solve a problem that applies to members of only one or a few religions. Not every religion uses wine in its sacraments, but that does not make an exemption from Prohibition for sacramental wine-use impermissible. The record is clear that the necessary guarantee can and will be provided, after the fact, *by the courts*. . . .

Eleven years after *Kiryas Joel*, the Supreme Court was called to rule on the constitutionality of a major piece of legislation that accommodates religious practice, the Religious Land Use and Institutionalized Persons Act of 2000 ("RLUIPA"). As discussed in chapter 8, Congress enacted RLUIPA in the wake of the Court's striking down portions of the Religious Freedom Restoration Act of 1993 in *City of Boerne v. Flores*. Congress conducted hearings and made substantial findings, indicating its unmistakable purpose to legislatively accommodate the religious needs of houses of worship and institutionalized persons. The primary issue for the Court in *Cutter v. Wilkinson* was whether RLUIPA violates the Establishment Clause by advancing religion. A unanimous Court found that it did not. In so holding, the Court entered into an extended discussion about legislative accommodations of religion, excerpted below.

## CUTTER v. WILKINSON
### 544 U.S. 709 (2005)

[A more lengthy excerpt from this case appears in chapter 8.]

▦ JUSTICE GINSBURG delivered the opinion of the Court. . . .

Our decisions recognize that "there is room for play in the joints" between the Clauses, some space for legislative action neither compelled by the Free Exercise Clause nor prohibited by the Establishment Clause. . . .[W]e hold that § 3 of RLUIPA fits within the corridor between the Religion Clauses: On its face, the Act qualifies as a permissible legislative accommodation of religion that is not barred by the Establishment Clause.

Foremost, we find RLUIPA's institutionalized-persons provision compatible with the Establishment Clause because it alleviates exceptional government-created burdens on private religious exercise. . . . Furthermore, the Act on its face does not founder on shoals our prior decisions have identified: Properly applying RLUIPA, courts must take adequate account of the burdens a requested accommodation may impose on nonbeneficiaries, and they must be satisfied that the Act's prescriptions are and will be administered neutrally among different faiths.[8]

"The 'exercise of religion' often involves not only belief and profession but the performance of . . . physical acts [such as] assembling with others for a worship service [or] participating in sacramental use of bread and wine . . . ." *Smith*, 494 U.S., 877. Section 3 covers state-run institutions—mental hospitals, prisons, and the like—in which the government exerts a degree of control unparalleled in civilian society and severely disabling to private religious exercise. RLUIPA thus protects institutionalized persons who are unable freely to attend to their religious needs and are therefore dependent on the government's permission and accommodation for exercise of their religion.

---

[8] Directed at obstructions institutional arrangements place on religious observances, RLUIPA does not require a State to pay for an inmate's devotional accessories. . . .

We note in this regard the Federal Government's accommodation of religious practice by members of the military. In *Goldman v. Weinberger*, 475 U.S. 503 (1986), we held that the Free Exercise Clause did not require the Air Force to exempt an Orthodox Jewish officer from uniform dress regulations so that he could wear a yarmulke indoors. In a military community, the Court observed, "there is simply not the same [individual] autonomy as there is in the larger civilian community." Congress responded to *Goldman* by prescribing that "a member of the armed forces may wear an item of religious apparel while wearing the uniform," unless "the wearing of the item would interfere with the performance [of] military duties [or] the item of apparel is not neat and conservative." 10 U.S.C. § 774(a)-(b).

We do not read RLUIPA to elevate accommodation of religious observances over an institution's need to maintain order and safety. Our decisions indicate that an accommodation must be measured so that it does not override other significant interests. In *Caldor*, the Court struck down a Connecticut law that "armed Sabbath observers with an absolute and unqualified right not to work on whatever day they designated as their Sabbath." 472 U.S., 709. We held the law invalid under the Establishment Clause because it "unyieldingly weighted" the interests of Sabbatarians "over all other interests."

We have no cause to believe that RLUIPA would not be applied in an appropriately balanced way, with particular sensitivity to security concerns. . . .

Finally, RLUIPA does not differentiate among bona fide faiths. In *Kiryas Joel*, we invalidated a state law that carved out a separate school district to serve exclusively a community of highly religious Jews, the Satmar Hasidim. We held that the law violated the Establishment Clause, in part because it "singled out a particular religious sect for special treatment." RLUIPA presents no such defect. It confers no privileged status on any particular religious sect, and singles out no bona fide faith for disadvantageous treatment.

Should inmate requests for religious accommodations become excessive, impose unjustified burdens on other institutionalized persons, or jeopardize the effective functioning of an institution, the facility would be free to resist the imposition. In that event, adjudication in as-applied challenges would be in order. . . .

. . .

## NOTES AND QUESTIONS

1. How do you understand the passage from the majority opinion in *Kiryas Joel*? Are governments forbidden from accommodating religious practice if the benefit flows solely to one religious group? Justices Kennedy and Scalia criticize this view as being inconsistent with the notion of a legislative effort to lift a potentially burdening regulation on a group's ability to practice its religion. Is their critique of Souter's opinion correct, or did the accommodation fail for other reasons?

2. Considering the several questions raised at the beginning of this chapter, how do you understand the status of legislative accommodations of religion after *Cutter*? The opinion seeks to reconcile the various issues presented in *Thornton*, *Amos*, *Texas Monthly*, and *Kiryas Joel*. Is the Court successful? Aside from

the Establishment Clause issue, did *Cutter* present an easy case for accommodation? As RLUIPA was applied in that case, it relieved an "exceptional government-created burden" on religious practice, it took account of "the burdens a requested accommodation may impose on nonbeneficiaries," and it was "administered neutrally among different faiths." As such, RLUIPA did not suffer from any of the infirmities present in the earlier cases. If this is an accurate characterization, does *Cutter* clarify the rules governing accommodation or settle the tension that exists between *Amos,* on one side, and *Thorton* and *Texas Monthly* on the other side?

# A Bill Establishing a Provision for Teachers of the Christian Religion*

Whereas the general diffusion of Christian knowledge hath a natural tendency to correct the morals of men, restrain their vices, and preserve the peace of society; which cannot be effected without a competent provision for learned teachers, who may be thereby enabled to devote their time and attention to the duty of instructing such citizens, as from their circumstances and want of education, cannot otherwise attain such knowledge; and it is judged that such provision may be made by the Legislature, without counteracting the liberal principle heretofore adopted and intended to be preserved by abolishing all distinctions of pre-eminence amongst the different societies or communities of Christians;

*Be it therefore enacted by the General Assembly,* That for the support of Christian teachers, per centum on the amount, or in the pound on the sum payable for tax on the property within this Commonwealth, is hereby assessed, and shall be paid by every person chargeable with the said tax at the time the same shall become due; and the Sheriffs of the several Counties shall have power to levy and collect the same in the same manner and under the like restrictions and limitations, as are or may be prescribed by the laws for raising the Revenues of this State.

*And be it enacted,* That for every sum so paid, the Sheriff or Collector shall give a receipt, expressing therein to what society of Christians the person from whom he may receive the same shall direct the money to be paid, keeping a distinct account thereof in his books. The Sheriff of every County, shall, on or before the day of in every year, return to the Court, upon oath, two alphabetical lists of the payments to him made, distinguishing in columns opposite to the names of the persons who shall have paid the same, the society to which the money so paid was by them appropriated; and one column for the names where no appropriation shall be made. One of which lists, after being recorded in a book to be kept for that purpose, shall be filed by the Clerk in his office; the other shall by the Sheriff be fixed up in the Court-house, there to remain for the inspection of all concerned. And the Sheriff, after deducting five per centum for the collection, shall forthwith pay to such person or persons as shall be appointed to receive the same by the Vestry, Elders, or Directors, however denominated of each such society, the sum so stated to be due to that society; or in default thereof, upon the motion of such person or persons to the next or any succeeding Court, execution shall be awarded for the same against the Sheriff and his security, his and their executors or administrators; provided that ten days previous notice be given of such motion. And upon every such execution, the Officer serving the same shall proceed to immediate sale of the estate taken, and shall not accept of security for payment at the end of three months, nor to have the goods forthcoming at the day of sale; for his better direction wherein, the Clerk shall endorse upon every such execution that no security of any kind shall be taken.

*And be it further enacted,* That the money to be raised by virtue of this Act, shall be by the Vestries, Elders, or Directors of each religious society, appropriated to a provision for a Minister or Teacher of the Gospel of their denomination, or the providing places of divine worship, and to none other use whatsoever; except in the denominations of Quakers and Menonists, who may receive what is collected from their members, and place it in their general fund, to be disposed of in a manner which they shall think best calculated to promote their particular mode of worship.

*And be it enacted,* That all sums which at the time of payment to the Sheriff or Collector may not be appropriated by the person paying the same, shall be accounted for with the Court in manner as by this Act is directed; and after deducting for his collection, the Sheriff shall pay the amount thereof (upon account certified by the Court to the Auditors of Public Accounts, and by them to the Treasurer) into the public Treasury, to be disposed of under the direction of the General Assembly, for the encouragement of seminaries of learning within the Counties whence such sums shall arise, and to no other use or purpose whatsoever.

THIS Act shall commence, and be in force, from and after the day of ___ in the year ___.

*A Copy from the Engrossed Bill.*

JOHN BECKLEY, C. H. D.
*Washington Mss. (Papers of George Washington, Vol. 231); Library of Congress.*[1]

# A Bill for Establishing Religious Freedom

SECTION I. Well aware that the opinions and belief of men depend not on their own will, but follow involuntarily the evidence proposed to their minds; that Almighty God hath created the mind free, and manifested his supreme will that free it shall remain by making it altogether insusceptible of restraint; that all attempts to influence it by temporal punishments, or burdens, or by civil incapacitations, tend only to beget habits of hypocrisy and meanness, and are a departure from the plan of the holy author of our religion, who being lord both of body and mind, yet chose not to propagate it by coercions on either, as was in his Almighty power to do, but to extend it by its influence on reason alone; that the impious presumption of legislators and rulers, civil as well as ecclesiastical, who, being themselves but fallible and uninspired men, have assumed dominion over the faith of others, setting up their own opinions and modes of thinking as the only true and infallible, and as such endeavoring to impose them on others, hath established and maintained false religions over the greatest part of the world and through all time: That to compel a man to furnish contributions of money for the propagation of opinions which he disbelieves and abhors, is sinful and tyrannical; that even the forcing him to support this or that teacher of his own religious persuasion, is depriving him of the comfortable liberty of giving his contributions to the particular pastor whose morals he would make his pattern, and whose powers he feels most persuasive to righteousness; and is withdrawing from the ministry those temporary rewards, which proceeding from an approbation of their personal conduct, are an additional incitement to earnest and unremitting labours for the instruction of mankind; that our civil rights have no dependance on our religious opinions, any more than our opinions in physics or geometry; that therefore the proscribing any citizen as unworthy the public confidence by laying upon him an incapacity of being called to offices of trust and emolument, unless he profess or renounce this or that religious opinion, is depriving him injuriously of those privileges and advantages to which, in common with his fellow citizens, he has a natural right; that it tends also to corrupt the principles of that very religion it is meant to encourage, by bribing, with a monopoly of worldly honours and emoluments, those who will externally profess and conform to it; that though indeed these are criminal who do not withstand such temptation, yet neither are those innocent who lay the bait in their way; that the opinions of men are not the object of civil government, nor under its jurisdiction; that to suffer the civil magistrate to intrude his powers into the field of opinion and to restrain the profession or propagation of principles on supposition of their ill tendency is a dangerous fallacy, which at once destroys all religious liberty, because he being of course judge of that tendency will make his opinions the rule of judgment, and approve or condemn the sentiments of others only as they shall square with or differ from his own; that it is time enough for the rightful purposes of civil government for its officers to interfere when principles break out into overt acts against peace and good order; and finally, that truth is great and will prevail if left to herself; that she is the proper and sufficient antagonist to error, and has nothing to fear from the conflict unless by human interposition disarmed of her natural weapons, free argument and debate; errors ceasing to be dangerous when it is permitted freely to contradict them.

SECTION II. WE the General Assembly of Virginia do enact that no man shall be compelled to frequent or support any religious worship, place, or ministry whatsoever, nor shall be enforced, restrained, molested, or burthened in his body or goods, nor shall otherwise suffer, on account of his religious opinions or belief; but that all men shall be free to profess, and by argument to maintain, their opinions in matters of religion, and that the same shall in no wise diminish, enlarge, or affect their civil rights.

SECTION III. AND though we well know that this Assembly, elected by the people for the ordinary purposes of legislation only, have no power to restrain the acts of succeeding Assemblies, constituted with powers equal to our own, and that therefore to declare this act irrevocable would be of no effect in law; yet we are free to declare, and do declare, that the rights hereby asserted are of the natural rights of mankind, and that if any act shall be hereafter passed to repeal the present or to narrow its operation, such act will be an infringement of natural right.

# APPENDIX 3

# MEMORIAL AND REMONSTRANCE AGAINST RELIGIOUS ASSESSMENTS

## TO THE HONORABLE THE GENERAL ASSEMBLY
## OF
## THE COMMONWEALTH OF VIRGINIA.
## A MEMORIAL AND REMONSTRANCE*

We, the subscribers, citizens of the said Commonwealth, having taken into serious consideration, a Bill printed by order of the last Session of General Assembly, entitled "A Bill establishing a provision for Teachers of the Christian Religion," and conceiving that the same, if finally armed with the sanctions of a law, will be a dangerous abuse of power, are bound as faithful members of a free State, to remonstrate against it, and to declare the reasons by which we are determined. We remonstrate against the said Bill,

1. Because we hold it for a fundamental and undeniable truth, "that Religion or the duty which we owe to our Creator and the Manner of discharging it, can be directed only by reason and conviction, not by force or violence."[1] The Religion then of every man must be left to the conviction and conscience of every man; and it is the right of every man to exercise it as these may dictate. This right is in its nature an unalienable right. It is unalienable; because the opinions of men, depending only on the evidence contemplated by their own minds, cannot follow the dictates of other men: It is unalienable also; because what is here a right towards men, is a duty towards the Creator. It is the duty of every man to render to the Creator such homage, and such only, as he believes to be acceptable to him. This duty is precedent both in order of time and degree of obligation, to the claims of Civil Society. Before any man can be considered as a member of Civil Society, he must be considered as a subject of the Governor of the Universe: And if a member of Civil Society, who enters into any subordinate Association, must always do it with a reservation of his duty to the general authority; much more must every man who becomes a member of any particular Civil Society, do it with a saving of his allegiance to the Universal Sovereign. We

---

[1] Decl. Rights, Art: 16. [Note in the original.]

maintain therefore that in matters of Religion, no man's right is abridged by the institution of Civil Society, and that Religion is wholly exempt from its cognizance. True it is, that no other rule exists, by which any question which may divide a Society, can be ultimately determined, but the will of the majority; but it is also true, that the majority may trespass on the rights of the minority.

2. Because if religion be exempt from the authority of the Society at large, still less can it be subject to that of the Legislative Body. The latter are but the creatures and vicegerents of the former. Their jurisdiction is both derivative and limited: it is limited with regard to the coordinate departments, more necessarily is it limited with regard to the constituents. The preservation of a free government requires not merely, that the metes and bounds which separate each department of power may be invariably maintained; but more especially, that neither of them be suffered to overleap the great Barrier which defends the rights of the people. The Rulers who are guilty of such an encroachment, exceed the commission from which they derive their authority, and are Tyrants. The People who submit to it are governed by laws made neither by themselves, nor by an authority derived from them, and are slaves.

3. Because, it is proper to take alarm at the first experiment on our liberties. We hold this prudent jealousy to be the first duty of citizens, and one of [the] noblest characteristics of the late Revolution. The freemen of America did not wait till usurped power had strengthened itself by exercise, and entangled the question in precedents. They saw all the consequences in the principle, and they avoided the consequences by denying the principle. We revere this lesson too much, soon to forget it. Who does not see that the same authority which can establish Christianity, in exclusion of all other Religions, may establish with the same ease any particular sect of Christians, in exclusion of all other Sects? That the same authority which can force a citizen to contribute three pence only of his property for the support of any one establishment, may force him to conform to any other establishment in all cases whatsoever?

4. Because, the bill violates that equality which ought to be the basis of every law, and which is more indispensible, in proportion as the validity or expediency of any law is more liable to be impeached. If "all men are by nature equally free and independent,"[2] all men are to be considered as entering into Society on equal conditions; as relinquishing no more, and therefore retaining no less, one than another, of their natural rights. Above all are they to be considered as retaining an "*equal* title to the free exercise of Religion according to the dictates of conscience."[3] Whilst we assert for ourselves a freedom to embrace, to profess and to observe the Religion which we believe to be of divine origin, we cannot deny an equal freedom to those whose minds have not yet yielded to the evidence which has convinced us. If this freedom be abused, it is an offence against God, not against man: To God, therefore, not to men, must an account of it be rendered. As the Bill violates equality by subjecting some to peculiar burdens; so it violates the same principle, by granting to others peculiar exemptions. Are the Quakers and Menonists the only sects who think a compulsive support of their religions unnecessary and unwarantable? Can their piety alone be intrusted with the care of public worship? Ought their Religions to be endowed above all others, with extraordinary privileges, by which proselytes may be enticed from

---

[2] Decl. Rights, Art. 1. [Note in the original.]

[3] Art: 16. [Note in the original.]

all others? We think too favorably of the justice and good sense of these denominations, to believe that they either covet preeminencies over their fellow citizens, or that they will be seduced by them, from the common opposition to the measure.

5. Because the bill implies either that the Civil Magistrate is a competent Judge of Religious truth; or that he may employ Religion as an engine of Civil policy. The first is an arrogant pretension falsified by the contradictory opinions of Rulers in all ages, and throughout the world: The second an unhallowed perversion of the means of salvation.

6. Because the establishment proposed by the Bill is not requisite for the support of the Christian Religion. To say that it is, is a contradiction to the Christian Religion itself; for every page of it disavows a dependence on the powers of this world: it is a contradiction to fact; for it is known that this Religion both existed and flourished, not only without the support of human laws, but in spite of every opposition from them; and not only during the period of miraculous aid, but long after it had been left to its own evidence, and the ordinary care of Providence: Nay, it is a contradiction in terms; for a Religion not invented by human policy, must have pre-existed and been supported, before it was established by human policy. It is moreover to weaken in those who profess this Religion a pious confidence in its innate excellence, and the patronage of its Author; and to foster in those who still reject it, a suspicion that its friends are too conscious of its fallacies, to trust it to its own merits.

7. Because experience witnesseth that ecclesiastical establishments, instead of maintaining the purity and efficacy of Religion, have had a contrary operation. During almost fifteen centuries, has the legal establishment of Christianity been on trial. What have been its fruits? More or less in all places, pride and indolence in the Clergy; ignorance and servility in the laity; in both, superstition, bigotry and persecution. Enquire of the Teachers of Christianity for the ages in which it appeared in its greatest lustre; those of every sect, point to the ages prior to its incorporation with Civil policy. Propose a restoration of this primitive state in which its Teachers depended on the voluntary rewards of their flocks; many of them predict its downfall. On which side ought their testimony to have greatest weight, when for or when against their interest?

8. Because the establishment in question is not necessary for the support of Civil Government. If it be urged as necessary for the support of Civil Government only as it is a means of supporting Religion, and it be not necessary for the latter purpose, it cannot be necessary for the former. If Religion be not within [the] cognizance of Civil Government, how can its legal establishment be said to be necessary to civil Government? What influence in fact have ecclesiastical establishments had on Civil Society? In some instances they have been seen to erect a spiritual tyranny on the ruins of Civil authority; in many instances they have been seen upholding the thrones of political tyranny; in no instance have they been seen the guardians of the liberties of the people. Rulers who wished to subvert the public liberty, may have found an established clergy convenient auxiliaries. A just government, instituted to secure & perpetuate it, needs them not. Such a government will be best supported by protecting every citizen in the enjoyment of his Religion with the same equal hand which protects his person and his property; by neither invading the equal rights of any Sect, nor suffering any Sect to invade those of another.

9. Because the proposed establishment is a departure from that generous policy, which, offering an asylum to the persecuted and oppressed of every Nation and Religion,

promised a lustre to our country, and an accession to the number of its citizens. What a melancholy mark is the Bill of sudden degeneracy? Instead of holding forth an asylum to the persecuted, it is itself a signal of persecution. It degrades from the equal rank of Citizens all those whose opinions in Religion do not bend to those of the Legislative authority. Distant as it may be, in its present form, from the Inquisition it differs from it only in degree. The one is the first step, the other the last in the career of intolerance. The magnanimous sufferer under this cruel scourge in foreign Regions, must view the Bill as a Beacon on our Coast, warning him to seek some other haven, where liberty and philanthrophy in their due extent may offer a more certain repose from his troubles.

10. Because, it will have a like tendency to banish our Citizens. The allurements presented by other situations are every day thinning their number. To superadd a fresh motive to emigration, by revoking the liberty which they now enjoy, would be the same species of folly which has dishonoured and depopulated flourishing kingdoms.

11. Because, it will destroy that moderation and harmony which the forbearance of our laws to intermeddle with Religion, has produced amongst its several sects. Torrents of blood have been spilt in the old world, by vain attempts of the secular arm to extinguish Religious discord, by proscribing all difference in Religious opinions. Time has at length revealed the true remedy. Every relaxation of narrow and rigorous policy, wherever it has been tried, has been found to assuage the disease. The American Theatre has exhibited proofs, that equal and complete liberty, if it does not wholly eradicate it, sufficiently destroys its malignant influence on the health and prosperity of the State. If with the salutary effects of this system under our own eyes, we begin to contract the bonds of Religious freedom, we know no name that will too severely reproach our folly. At least let warning be taken at the first fruits of the threatened innovation. The very appearance of the Bill has transformed that "Christian forbearance, love and charity,"[4] which of late mutually prevailed, into animosities and jealousies, which may not soon be appeased. What mischiefs may not be dreaded should this enemy to the public quiet be armed with the force of a law?

12. Because, the policy of the bill is adverse to the diffusion of the light of Christianity. The first wish of those who enjoy this precious gift, ought to be that it may be imparted to the whole race of mankind. Compare the number of those who have as yet received it with the number still remaining under the dominion of false Religions; and how small is the former! Does the policy of the Bill tend to lessen the disproportion? No; it at once discourages those who are strangers to the light of [revelation] from coming into the Region of it; and countenances, by example the nations who continue in darkness, in shutting out those who might convey it to them. Instead of levelling as far as possible, every obstacle to the victorious progress of truth, the Bill with an ignoble and unchristian timidity would circumscribe it, with a wall of defence, against the encroachments of error.

13. Because attempts to enforce by legal sanctions, acts obnoxious to so great a proportion of Citizens, tend to enervate the laws in general, and to slacken the bands of Society. If it be difficult to execute any law which is not generally deemed necessary or salutary, what must be the case where it is deemed invalid and dangerous? and what may be the effect of so striking an example of impotency in the Government, on its general authority.

---

[4] Art. 16. [Note in the original.]

14. Because a measure of such singular magnitude and delicacy ought not to be imposed, without the clearest evidence that it is called for by a majority of citizens: and no satisfactory method is yet proposed by which the voice of the majority in this case may be determined, or its influence secured. "The people of the respective counties are indeed requested to signify their opinion respecting the adoption of the Bill to the next Session of Assembly." But the representation must be made equal, before the voice either of the Representatives or of the Counties, will be that of the people. Our hope is that neither of the former will, after due consideration, espouse the dangerous principle of the Bill. Should the event disappoint us, it will still leave us in full confidence, that a fair appeal to the latter will reverse the sentence against our liberties.

15. Because, finally, "the equal right of every citizen to the free exercise of his Religion according to the dictates of conscience" is held by the same tenure with all our other rights. If we recur to its origin, it is equally the gift of nature; if we weigh its importance, it cannot be less dear to us; if we consult the Declaration of those rights which pertain to the good people of Virginia, as the "basis and foundation of Government,"[5] it is enumerated with equal solemnity, or rather studied emphasis. Either then, we must say, that the will of the Legislature is the only measure of their authority; and that in the plenitude of this authority, they may sweep away all our fundamental rights; or, that they are bound to leave this particular right untouched and sacred: Either we must say, that they may control the freedom of the press, may abolish the trial by jury, may swallow up the Executive and Judiciary Powers of the State; nay that they may despoil us of our very right of suffrage, and erect themselves into an independent and hereditary assembly: or we must say, that they have no authority to enact into law the Bill under consideration. We the subscribers say, that the General Assembly of this Commonwealth have no such authority: And that no effort may be omitted on our part against so dangerous an usurpation, we oppose to it, this remonstrance; earnestly praying, as we are in duty bound, that the Supreme Lawgiver of the Universe, by illuminating those to whom it is addressed, may on the one hand, turn their councils from every act which would affront his holy prerogative, or violate the trust committed to them: and on the other, guide them into every measure which may be worthy of his [blessing, may re]dound to their own praise, and may establish more firmly the liberties, the prosperity, and the Happiness of the Commonwealth.

---

[5] Decl. Rights-title. [Note in the original.]

# Supreme Court Opinions by Justice

## Alito, Samuel A. (2006– )
Standing to Sue
*Hein v. FFRF*

## Black, Hugo L. (1937–1971)
Aid to Religious Schools
*Everson v. Board of Education*
Conscientious Objection
*Welsh v. United States*
Devotional Exercises in Public Schools
*Engel v. Vitale*
Flag Salute
*West Virginia Board of Education v.*
*Barnett* (concurring)
Released Time
*McCollum v. Board of Education*
*Zorach v. Clauson* (dissenting)
Religious Tests
*Torcaso v. Watkins*
Teaching Evolution in Public Schools
*Epperson v. Arkansas*
Textbook Loan
*Board of Education v. Allen* (dissenting)

## Blackmun, Harry (1970–1993)
Aid to Religious Schools
*Committee for Public Education and*
*Religious Liberty v. Regan* (dissenting)

*Roemer v. Board of Public Works of*
*Maryland*
*Wolman v. Walter*
*Zobrest v. Catalina Hills School District*
(dissenting)
Church Exercising a Government
Function
*Kiryas Joel v. Grumet* (concurring)
Church Property
*Jones v. Wolf*
Devotional Exercises in Public Schools
*Lee v. Weisman* (concurring)
Free Exercise/Public Benefits
*Bowen v. Roy* (concurring in part)
Labor Relations (including sabbatarian
concerns)
*Church of Jesus Christ of Latter-day*
*Saints v. Amos* (concurring in judgment)
*Employment Division of Oregon v. Smith*
(dissenting)
Public Funding for Social Services
*Bowen v. Kendrick* (dissenting)
Religion in the Military
*Goldman v. Weinberger* (dissenting)
Religious Discrimination
*Church of Lukumi Babalu Aye v. Hialeah*
(concurring in judgment)
Religious Symbols on Public Property
*Allegheny v. ACLU*

## BURGER, WARREN E. (CHIEF JUSTICE, 1969–1986)

Aid to Religious Schools
*Aguilar v. Felton* (dissenting)
*Committee for Public Education and Religious Liberty v. Nyquist* (concurring and dissenting)
*Grand Rapids School District v. Ball* (concurring and dissenting)
*Lemon v. Kurtzman*
*Meek v. Pittenger* (concurring and dissenting)
*Tilton v. Richardson*
Church Exercising a Government Function
*Larkin v. Grendel's Den*
Church Taxation
*Walz v. Tax Commission*
Devotional Exercises in Public Schools
*Wallace v. Jaffree* (dissenting)
Free Exercise/Compulsory Education
*Wisconsin v. Yoder*
Free Exercise/Public Benefits
*Bowen v. Roy*
Labor Relations (including sabbatarian concerns)
*Thomas v. Review Board of the Indiana Employment Security Commission*
*Thornton v. Caldor*
Public Office-Holding by Ministers
*McDaniel v. Paty*
Religious Symbols on Public Property
*Lynch v. Donnelly*
Standing to Sue
*Bender v. Williamsport* (dissenting)
State-Supported Chaplains
*Marsh v. Chambers*
Tax Exemption
*Bob Jones University v. United States*
*United States v. Lee*

## BUTLER, PIERCE (1922–1939)

Conscientious Objection
*Hamilton v. Regents of the University of California*
*United States v. Schwimmer*

## CAMPBELL, JOHN A. (1853–1861)

Church Property
*Baker v. Nachtrieb*

## CARDOZO, BENJAMIN (1932–1938)

Conscientious Objection
*Hamilton v. Regents of the University of California* (concurring)

## CATRON, JOHN (1837–1865)

Free Exercise Application to the States
*Permoli v. First Municipality of New Orleans*

## CLARK, TOM C. (1949–1967)

Conscientious Objection
*United States v. Seeger*
Devotional Exercises in Public Schools
*Abington School District v. Schempp*

## CLIFFORD, NATHAN (1858–1881)

Church Property
*Watson v. Jones* (dissenting)

## DOUGLAS, WILLIAM O. (1939–1975)

Aid to Religious Schools
*Lemon v. Kurtzman* (concurring)
*Tilton v. Richardson* (dissenting in part)
Church Taxation
*Walz v. Tax Commission* (dissenting)
Compulsory Education
*Wisconsin v. Yoder* (dissenting in part)
Conscientious Objection
*Gillette v. United States* (dissenting)
*Girouard v. United States*
*United States v. Seeger* (concurring)
Devotional Exercises in Public Schools
*Abington School District v. Schempp* (concurring)
*Engel v. Vitale* (concurring)

Labor Relations (including sabbatarian concerns)
  *Sherbert v. Verner* (concurring)
Released Time
  *Zorach v. Clauson*
Religious Access/Use of Public Property
  *Murdock v. Pennsylvania*
Standing to Sue
  *Flast v. Cohen* (concurring)
Sunday Closing Laws
  *McGowan v. Maryland* (dissenting)
Test of Faith
  *United States v. Ballard*
Textbook Loan
  *Board of Education v. Allen* (dissenting)

## FIELD, STEPHEN J. (1863–1897)

Mormon Polygamy
  *Davis v. Beason*

## FORTAS, ABE (1965–1969)

Devotional Exercises in Public Schools
  *Stone v. Graham* (per curium)
Standing to Sue
  *Flast v. Cohen* (concurring)
Teaching Evolution in Public Schools
  *Epperson v. Arkansas*
Textbook Loan
  *Board of Education v. Allen* (dissenting)

## FRANKFURTER, FELIX (1939–1962)

Church Property
  *Kedroff v. St. Nicholas Cathedral* (concurring)
Flag Salute
  *Minersville School District v. Gobitis*
  *West Virginia Board of Education v. Barnette* (dissenting)
Released Time
  *McCollum v. Board of Education* (separate opinion)
  *Zorach v. Clauson* (dissenting)
Religious Access/Use of Public Property
  *Murdock v. Pennsylvania* (dissenting)

Sunday Closing Laws
  *McGowan v. Maryland* (separate opinion)

## FULLER, MELVIN W. (CHIEF JUSTICE, 1888–1910)

Aid to Religious Institutions
  *Quick Bear v. Leupp*
Mormon Question
  *The Late Corporation of the Church of Jesus Christ of Latter Day Saints v. United States* (dissenting)

## GINSBURG, RUTH BADER (1993– )

Aid to Religious Schools
  *Agostini v. Felton* (dissenting)
Free Exercise/RLUIPA; Prisoner Rights
  *Cutter v. Wilkinson*
Religious Symbols on Public Property
  *Capitol Square v. Pinette* (dissenting)

## GOLDBERG, ARTHUR J. (1962–1965)

Devotional Exercises in Public Schools
  *Abington School District v. Schempp* (concurring)

## GRAY, HORACE (1882–1902)

Church Property
  *Speidel v. Henrici*

## HARLAN, JOHN M. (1955–1971)

Church Taxation
  *Walz v. Tax Commission* (concurring)
Conscientious Objection
  *Welsh v. United States* (concurring)
Labor Relations (including sabbatarian concerns)
  *Sherbert v. Verner* (dissenting)
Standing to Sue
  *Flast v. Cohen* (dissenting)
Teaching Evolution in Public Schools
  *Epperson v. Arkansas* (concurring)
Textbook Loan
  *Board of Education v. Allen* (concurring)

## HOLMES, OLIVER WENDELL (1902–1932)

Conscientious Objection
*United States v. Schwimmer* (dissenting)

## HUGHES, CHARLES EVANS (ASSOC. JUSTICE, 1910–1916; CHIEF JUSTICE, 1930–1941)

Conscientious Objection
*United States v. Macintosh* (dissenting)
Religious Access/Use of Public Property
*Cox v. New Hampshire*
Textbook Loan
*Cochran v. Board of Education*

## JACKSON, ROBERT H. (1941–1954)

Aid to Religious Schools
*Everson v. Board of Education* (dissenting)
Church Property
*Kedroff v. St. Nicholas Cathedral* (dissenting)
Flag Salute
*West Virginia Board of Education v. Barnette*
Released Time
*McCollum v. Board of Education* (concurring)
*Zorach v. Clauson* (dissenting)
Religious Access/Use of Public Property
*Prince v. Massachusetts* (separate opinion)
Test of Faith
*United States v. Ballard* (dissenting)

## KENNEDY, ANTHONY (1988– )

Religious Access/Use of Public Property
*Lamb's Chapel v. Center Moriches School District* (concurring in part)
Church Exercising a Government Function
*Kiryas Joel v. Grumet* (concurring in judgment)
Devotional Exercises in Public Schools
*Board of Education v. Mergens* (concurring in part)
*Lee v. Weisman*

Public Funding for Social Services
*Bowen v. Kendrick* (concurring)
Religious Discrimination
*Church of Lukumi Babalu Aye v. Hialeah*
Religious Publications in Public Institutions
*Rosenberger v. University of Virginia*
Religious Symbols on Public Property
*Allegheny v. ACLU* (concurring and dissenting)
Free Exercise Standard of Review/RFRA
*City of Boerne v. Flores*
Standing to Sue
*Hein v. FFRF* (concurring)

## McREYNOLDS, JAMES C. (1914–1941)

Right of Religious Schools to Exist
*Pierce v. Society of Sisters*

## MARSHALL, THURGOOD (1967–1991)

Aid to Religious Schools
*Mueller v. Allen* (dissenting)
*Wolman v. Walter* (concurring and dissenting)
Aid for Religious Vocations
*Witters v. Washington Department of Services for the Blind*
Conscientious Objection
*Gillette v. United States*
Devotional Exercises in Public Schools
*Board of Education v. Mergens* (concurring in judgment)
Labor Relations (including sabbatarian concerns)
*Trans World Airlines, Inc. v. Hardison* (dissenting)
Tax Exemption
*Hernandez v. Commissioner of Internal Revenue*

## MATHEWS, STANLEY (1881–1889)

Mormon Polygamy
*Murphy v. Ramsey*

## MILLER, SAMUEL F. (1862–1890)

Church Property
*Watson v. Jones*

## MURPHY, FRANK (1940–1949)

Religious Access/Use of Public Property
*Jones v. Opelika* (dissenting)
*Prince v. Massachusetts* (dissenting)

## O'CONNOR, SANDRA DAY (1981– 2006)

Aid to Religious Schools
*Agostini v. Felton*
*Aguilar v. Felton* (dissenting)
*Grand Rapids School District v. Ball* (concurring and dissenting)
*Mitchell v. Helms* (concurring in judgment)
*Zobrest v. Catalina Foothills School District* (dissenting)
Aid for Religious Vocations
*Witters v. Washington Department of Services for the Blind* (concurring)
Church Exercising a Government Function
*Kiryas Joel v. Grumet* (concurring in part and in judgment)
Devotional Exercises in Public Schools
*Board of Education v. Mergens*
*Wallace v. Jaffree* (concurring)
Free Exercise Standard of Review
*City of Boerne v. Flores* (dissenting)
*Employment Division of Oregon v. Smith* (concurring in judgment)
Free Exercise/Public Benefits
*Bowen v. Roy* (concurring and dissenting)
Free Exercise/Native Rights
*Lyng v. Indian Cemetery Assn.*
Labor Relations (including sabbatarian concerns)
*Church of Jesus Christ of Latter-day Saints v. Amos* (concurring in judgment)
*Thornton v. Caldor* (concurring)
Pledge of Allegiance; Standing
*Elk Grove Unified School District v. Newdow* (concurring in judgment)

Public Funding for Social Services
*Bowen v. Kendrick* (concurring)
Religious Publications in Public Institutions
*Rosenberger v. University of Virginia* (concurring)
Religion in the Military
*Goldman v. Weinberger* (dissenting)
Religious Symbols on Public Property
*Allegheny v. ACLU* (concurring in judgment)
*Capitol Square v. Pinette* (concurring in part and in judgment)
*Lynch v. Donnelly* (concurring)
*McCreary County v. ACLU of Kentucky* (concurring)
*Van Orden v. Perry* (dissenting)
Tax Exemption
*Davis v. United States*
*Hernandez v. Commissioner of Internal Revenue* (dissenting)
*Jimmy Swaggart Ministries v. California*
Religious School Subsidy; Voucher
*Zelman v. Simmons-Harris* (concurring)

## PECKHAM, RUFUS (1896–1909)

Aid for Religious Social Services
*Bradfield v. Roberts*

## POWELL, LEWIS F. (1971–1987)

Aid to Religious Schools
*Aguilar v. Felton* (concurring)
*Committee for Public Education and Religious Liberty v. Nyquist*
*Wolman v .Walter* (concurring and dissenting)
Aid for Religious Vocations
*Witters v. Washington Department of Services for the Blind* (concurring)
Church Property
*Jones v. Wolf* (dissenting)
Devotional Exercises in Public Schools
*Wallace v. Jaffree* (concurring)
Labor Relations (including sabbatarian concerns)

*Hobbie v. Unemployment Comm'n of Florida* (concurring in judgment)

Tax Exemption
*Bob Jones University v. United States* (concurring)

Teaching Evolution in Public Schools
*Edwards v. Aguillard* (concurring)

## REED, STANLEY
## (1938–1957)

Church Property
*Kedroff v. St. Nicholas Cathedral*

Released Time
*McCollum v. Board of Education* (dissenting)

Religious Access/Use of Public Property
*Jones v. Opelika*
*Murdock v. Pennsylvania* (dissenting)

## REHNQUIST, WILLIAM H.
## (ASSOC. JUSTICE, 1971–1986;
## CHIEF JUSTICE, 1986–2006)

Aid for Religious Vocations
*Locke v. Davey*

Aid to Religious Schools
*Aguilar v. Felton* (dissenting)
*Grand Rapids School District v. Ball* (dissenting)
*Meek v. Pittenger* (concurring and dissenting)
*Mueller v. Allen*
*Zobrest v. Catalina Foothills School District*

Church Exercising a Government Function
*Larkin v. Grendel's Den* (dissenting)

Church Property
*Serbian Eastern Orthodox Diocese v. Milivojevich* (dissenting)

Devotional Exercises in Public Schools
*Santa Fe Indep. School Dist. v. Doe* (dissenting)
*Stone v. Graham* (dissenting)
*Wallace v. Jaffree* (dissenting)

Labor Relations (including sabbatarian concerns)

*Hobbie v. Unemployment Comm'n of Florida* (dissenting)
*Thomas v. Review Board of the Indiana Employment Security Division* (dissenting)
*Thornton v. Caldor* (dissenting without opinion)

Licensing
*Watchtower Bible and Tract Society v. Village of Stratton* (dissenting)

Public Funding for Social Services
*Bowen v. Kendrick*

Religion in the Military or Prisons
*Goldman v. Weinberger*
*O'Lone v. Estate of Shabazz*

Religious School Subsidy; Voucher
*Zelman v. Simmons-Harris*

Religious Symbols on Public Property
*Van Orden v. Perry*

Standing to Sue
*Elk Grove Unified School District v. Newdow* (concurring in judgment)
*Valley Forge Christian College v. Americans United*

State Regulation of Church Solicitation
*Larson v. Valente* (dissenting)

Tax Exemption
*Bob Jones University v. United States* (dissenting)

## ROBERTS, JOHN G. (CHIEF
## JUSTICE, 2005– )

Religious Exercise/RFRA
*Gonzales v. O Centro Espirita Beneficente Uniao Do Vegetal*

## ROBERTS, OWEN J.
## (1930–1945)

Religious Access/Use of Public Property
*Cantwell v. Connecticut*

## RUTLEDGE, WILEY
## (1943–1949)

Aid to Religious Schools
*Everson v. Board of Education* (dissenting)

Religious Access/Use of Public Property
*Prince v. Massachusetts*

## SCALIA, ANTONIN (1986– )

Aid for Religious Vocations
  *Locke v. Davey* (dissenting)
Church Exercising a Government
Function
  *Kiryas Joel v. Grumet* (dissenting)
Devotional Exercises in Public Schools
  *Lee v. Weisman* (dissenting)
Free Exercise Standard of Review
  *City of Boerne v. Flores* (concurring in
  part)
  *Employment Division of Oregon v. Smith*
Licensing
  *Watchtower Bible and Tract Society
  v. Village of Stratton* (concurring in
  judgment)
Religious Access/Use of Public Property
  *Good News Club v. Milford Central School*
  (concurring)
  *Lamb's Chapel v. Center Moriches School
  District* (concurring in judgment)
Religious Discrimination
  *Church of Lukumi Babalu Aye v. Hialeah*
  (concurring in part)
Religious Symbols on Public Property
  *Capitol Square v. Pinette*
  *McCreary County v. ACLU of Kentucky*
  (dissenting)
  *Van Orden v. Perry* (concurring)
Standing to Sue
  *Hein v. FFRF* (concurring in judgment)
Teaching Evolution in Public Schools
  *Edwards v. Aguillard* (dissenting)
Tax Exemption
  *Texas Monthly v. Bullock* (dissenting)

## SOUTER, DAVID H. (1990– )

Aid to Religious Schools
  *Agostini v. Felton* (dissenting)
  *Mitchell v. Helms* (dissenting)
Church Exercising a Government
Function
  *Kiryas Joel v. Grumet*
Devotional Exercises in Public Schools
  *Lee v. Weisman* (concurring)
Free Exercise Standard of Review
  *City of Boerne v. Flores* (dissenting)

Religious Access/Use of Public Property
  *Good News Club v. Milford Central School*
  (dissenting)
Religious Discrimination
  *Church of Lukumi Babalu Aye v. Hialeah*
  (concurring in part)
Religious Publications in Public
Institutions
  *Rosenberger v. University of Virginia*
  (dissenting)
Religious School Subsidy; Voucher
  *Zelman v. Simmons-Harris* (dissenting)
Religious Symbols on Public Property
  *Capitol Square v. Pinette* (concurring in
  part and in judgment)
  *McCreary County v. ACLU of Kentucky*
  *Van Orden v. Perry* (dissenting)
Standing to Sue
  *Hein v. FFRF* (dissenting)

## STEVENS, JOHN PAUL (1975– )

Aid to Religious Schools
  *Committee for Public Education and
  Religious Liberty v. Regan* (dissenting)
  *Roemer v. Board of Public Works of
  Maryland* (dissenting)
  *Wolman v. Walter* (concurring and
  dissenting)
Church Exercising a Government
Function
  *Kiryas Joel v. Grumet* (concurring)
Devotional Exercises in Public Schools
  *Board of Education v. Mergens*
  (dissenting)
  *Santa Fe Indep. School Dist. v. Doe*
  *Wallace v. Jaffree*
Free Exercise/Public Benefits
  *Bowen v. Roy* (concurring)
Free Exercise Standard of Review
  *City of Boerne v. Flores* (concurring)
Licensing
  *Watchtower Bible and Tract Society v.
  Village of Stratton*
Mootness
  *Church of Scientology of California v.
  United States*

## WAITE, MORRISON R. (CHIEF JUSTICE, 1874–1888)

Mormon Polygamy
*Reynolds v. United States*

## WARREN, EARL (CHIEF JUSTICE, 1953–1969)

Standing to Sue
*Flast v. Cohen*
Sunday Closing Laws
*Braunfeld v. Brown*
*McGowan v. Maryland*

## WHITE, BYRON R. (1962-1993)

Aid for Religious Vocations
*Witters v. Washington Department of Services for the Blind* (concurring)
Aid to Religious Schools
*Aguilar v. Felton* (dissenting)
*Committee for Public Education and Religious Liberty v. Nyquist* (dissenting)
*Committee for Public Education and Religious Liberty v. Regan*
*Grand Rapids School District v. Ball* (dissenting)
*Lemon v. Kurtzman* (concurring and dissenting)
*Roemer v. Board of Public Works of Maryland* (concurring)
Church Property
*Serbian Eastern Orthodox Diocese v. Milivojevich* (concurring)

Conscientious Objection
*Welsh v. United States* (dissenting)
Devotional Exercises in Public Schools
*Wallace v. Jaffree* (dissenting)
Free Exercise/Public Benefits
*Bowen v. Roy* (dissenting)
Labor Relations (including sabbatarian concerns)
*Church of Jesus Christ of Latter-day Saints v. Amos*
*Frazee v. Illinois Dept. of Employment Security*
*Trans World Airlines, Inc. v. Hardison*
Public Office-Holding by Ministers
*McDaniel v. Paty* (concurring)
Religious Access/Use of Public Property
*Lamb's Chapel v. Center Moriches School District*
*Widmar v. Vincent* (dissenting)
State Regulation of Church Solicitation
*Heffron v. ISKCON*
*Larson v. Valente* (dissenting)
Tax Exemption
*Texas Monthly v. Bullock* (concurring in judgment)
Teaching Evolution in Public Schools
*Edwards v. Aguillard* (concurring in judgment)
Textbook Loan
*Board of Education v. Allen*

# SUPREME COURT CHURCH-STATE CASES

| Justices | Church-State Cases | Other Significant Cases |
|---|---|---|
| **1815–1816**<br>John Marshall, C.J.<br>Bushrod Washington<br>William Johnson<br>Henry B. Livingston<br>Thomas Todd<br>Gabriel Duvall<br>Joseph Story | **Terrett v. Taylor**<br>Story (7-0) | **Martin v. Hunter's Lessee** |
| **1843–1844**<br>Roger Brooke Taney, C.J.<br>Joseph Story<br>John McLean<br>Henry Baldwin<br>James M. Wayne<br>John Catron<br>John McKinley<br>Peter V. Daniel | **Vidal v. Girard's Executors**<br>Story (7-0)<br><br>**Permoli v. First Municipality of New Orleans**<br>Catron (8-0) | |
| **1871–1872**<br>Salmon P. Chase, C.J.<br>Samuel Nelson<br>Nathan Clifford<br>Noah H. Swayne<br>Samuel F. Miller<br>David Davis<br>Stephen J. Field<br>William Strong<br>Joseph P. Bradley | **Watson v. Jones**<br>Miller (6-2)<br>Clifford, dissenting, joined by Davis<br>Chase – sat out | **Slaughterhouse cases**<br>(1873) one different justice |

| Justices | Church-State Cases | Other Significant Cases |
|---|---|---|
| **1878–1879**<br>Morrison R. Waite, C.J.<br>Noah H. Swayne<br>Nathan Clifford<br>Samuel F. Miller<br>Stephen J. Field<br>William Strong<br>Joseph P. Bradley<br>Ward Hunt<br>John Marshall Harlan | **Reynolds v. United States**<br>Waite, C.J. (9-0) | |
| **1885–1886**<br>Morrison R. Waite, C.J.<br>Samuel F. Miller<br>Stephen J. Field<br>Joseph P. Bradley<br>John Marshall Harlan<br>Thomas S. Matthews<br>Horace Gray<br>Samuel Blatchford<br>L.Q.C. Lamar II | **Murphy v. Ramsey**<br>Matthews, J. (9-0) | **Yick Wo v. Hopkins** |
| **1889–1890**<br>Melville W. Fuller, C.J.<br>Samuel F. Miller<br>Stephen J. Field<br>Joseph P. Bradley<br>John Marshall Harlan<br>Horace Gray<br>Samuel Blatchford<br>Lucius Q.C. Lamar<br>David J. Brewer | **Davis v. Beason**<br>Field (9-0)<br><br>**The Late Corporation of the Church of Jesus Christ of Latter Day Saints v. United States**<br>Bradley (6-3)<br>Fuller, C.J., dissenting, joined by Field, Lamar | **Hans v. Louisiana** |
| **1892–1893**<br>Melville W. Fuller, C.J.<br>Stephen J. Field<br>John Marshall Harlan<br>Horace Gray<br>Samuel Blatchford<br>L.Q.C. Lamar II<br>David J. Brewer<br>Henry Billings Brown<br>George Shiras, Jr. | **Church of the Holy Trinity v. United States**<br>Brewer (9-0) | **Plessy v. Ferguson**<br>(1895–1896 term) |
| **1899–1900**<br>Melville W. Fuller, C.J.<br>John Marshall Harlan<br>Horace Gray<br>David J. Brewer<br>Henry Billings Brown<br>George Shiras, Jr.<br>Edward Douglass White<br>Rufus W. Peckham<br>Joseph Mckenna | **Bradfield v. Roberts**<br>Peckham (9-0) | |

| Justices | Church-State Cases | Other Significant Cases |
|---|---|---|
| **1907–1908**<br>Melville W. Fuller, C.J.<br>John Marshal Harlan<br>David J. Brewer<br>Edward Douglas White<br>Rufus Wheeler Peckham<br>Joseph McKenna<br>Oliver Wendell Holmes<br>William R. Day<br>William H. Moody | **Quick Bear v. Leupp**<br>Fuller, C.J. (9-0) | **Adair v. U.S.**<br><br>**Muller v. Oregon** |
| **1923–1924**<br>William Howard Taft, C.J.<br>Joseph McKenna<br>Oliver Wendell Holmes<br>Willis Van De Vanter<br>James C. McReynolds<br>Louis D. Brandeis<br>George Sutherland<br>Pierce Butler<br>Edward T. Sanford | **Meyer v. Nebraska**<br>McReynolds (7-2)<br>Holmes, dissenting, joined by Sutherland<br><br>Dissent attached to **Bartels v. Iowa** | **Frothingham v. Mellon**<br>(1922–1923 term) |
| **1924–1925**<br>William Howard Taft, C.J.<br>Oliver Wendell Holmes<br>Willis Van De Vanter<br>James C. McReynolds<br>Louis D. Brandeis<br>George Sutherland<br>Pierce Butler<br>Edward T. Sanford<br>Harlan F. Stone | **Pierce v. Society of Sisters**<br>McReynolds (9-0) | **Gitlow v. New York** |
| **1928–1929**<br>William Howard Taft, C.J.<br>Oliver Wendell Holmes<br>Willis Van De Vanter<br>James C. McReynolds<br>Louis D. Brandeis<br>George Sutherland<br>Pierce Butler<br>Edward T. Sanford<br>Harlan F. Stone | **United States v. Schwimmer**<br>Butler (6-3)<br>Holmes, dissenting, joined by Brandeis<br>Sanford, dissenting | |
| **1929–1930**<br>Charles Evans Hughes, C.J.<br>Oliver Wendell Holmes<br>Willis Van De Vanter<br>James C. McReynolds<br>Louis D. Brandeis<br>George Sutherland<br>Pierce Butler<br>Harlan F. Stone<br>Owen J. Roberts | **Cochran v. Board of Education**<br>Hughes, C.J. (9-0) | |

| Justices | Church-State Cases | Other Significant Cases |
|---|---|---|
| **1930–1931**<br>Charles Evans Hughes, C.J.<br>Oliver Wendell Holmes<br>Willis Van De Vanter<br>James C. McReynolds<br>Louis D. Brandeis<br>George Sutherland<br>Pierce Butler<br>Harlan F. Stone<br>Owen J. Roberts | **U.S. v. Macintosh**<br>Sutherland (5-4)<br>Hughes, C.J., dissenting, joined by Holmes, Brandeis, Stone | **Near v. Minnesota** |
| **1934–1935**<br>Charles Evans Hughes, C.J.<br>Willis Van De Vanter<br>James C. McReynolds<br>Louis D. Brandeis<br>George Sutherland<br>Pierce Butler<br>Harlan F. Stone<br>Owen J. Roberts<br>Benjamin N. Cardozo | **Hamilton v. Regents of the University of California**<br>Butler (9-0)<br>Cardozo, concurring | |
| **1938–1939**<br>Charles Evans Hughes, C.J.<br>Louis D. Brandeis<br>Pierce Butler<br>Harlan F. Stone<br>Owen J. Roberts<br>Benamin N. Cardozo<br>Hugo Black<br>Stanley F. Reed | **Lovell v. City of Griffin**<br>Hughes, C.J. (8-0) | |
| **1939–1940**<br>Charles Evans Hughes, C.J.<br>James C. McReynolds<br>Pierce Butler<br>Harlan F. Stone<br>Owen J. Roberts<br>Hugo L. Black<br>Stanley F. Reed<br>Felix Frankfurter<br>William O. Douglas | **Schneider v. State of New Jersey (Town of Irvington)**<br>Roberts (7-1)<br>McReynolds voted no (no written dissent)<br><br>**Cantwell v. Connecticut**<br>Roberts (9-0)<br><br>**Minersville School District v. Gobitis**<br>Frankfurter (7/1-1)<br>Stone, dissenting | **Hague v. CIO**<br><br>**Coleman v. Miller** |
| **1940–1941**<br>Charles Evans Hughes, C.J.<br>James C. McReynolds<br>Harlan F. Stone<br>Owen J. Roberts<br>Hugo L. Black<br>Stanley F. Reed<br>Felix Frankfurter<br>William O. Douglas<br>Frank Murphy | **Cox v. New Hampshire**<br>Hughes, C.J. (9-0) | |

| Justices | Church-State Cases | Other Significant Cases |
|---|---|---|
| 1941–1942<br>Harlan F. Stone, C.J.<br>Owen J. Roberts<br>Hugo L. Black<br>Stanley F. Reed<br>Felix Frankfurter<br>William O. Douglas<br>Frank Murphy<br>James F. Byrnes<br>Robert H. Jackson | **Chaplinsky v. New Hampshire**<br>Murphy (9-0)<br><br>**Jones v. Opelika (I)**<br>Reed (5-4)<br>Stone, C.J., dissenting, joined by Black, Douglas, Murphy<br>Murphy, dissenting, joined by Stone, Black, Douglas<br>Black, dissenting, joined by Douglas, Murphy | Edwards v. California<br><br>Skinner v. Oklahoma |
| 1942–1943<br>Harlan F. Stone, C.J.<br>Owen J. Roberts<br>Hugo L. Black<br>Stanley F. Reed<br>Felix Frankfurter<br>William O. Douglas<br>Frank Murphy<br>Robert H. Jackson<br>Wiley B. Rutledge | **Jones v. Opelika (II)**<br>Per curiam (5-4)<br>Relying on Douglas' opinion in Murdock and Stone's dissent in Opelika (I)<br>Reed, dissenting, joined by Roberts, Frankfurter, Jackson<br>Frankfurter, dissenting, joined by Jackson<br><br>**Murdock v. Pennsylvania (City of Jeannette)**<br>Douglas 5-4<br>Reed, dissenting, joined by Roberts, Frankfurter, Jackson<br>Frankfurter, dissenting, joined by Jackson<br><br>**Martin v. Struthers**<br>Black (5-4)<br>Murphy, concurring, joined by Douglas, Rutledge<br>Frankfurter, concurring in the judgment<br>Reed, dissenting, joined by Roberts, Jackson<br>Jackson, dissenting<br><br>**West Virginia State Board of Education v. Barnette**<br>Jackson (6-3)<br>Black, concurring, joined by Douglas<br>Murphy, concurring<br>Frankfurter, dissenting, joined by Roberts, Reed | |
| 1943–1944<br>Harlan F. Stone, C.J.<br>Owen J. Roberts<br>Hugo L. Black<br>Stanley F. Reed<br>Felix Frankfurter<br>William O. Douglas<br>Frank Murphy<br>Robert H. Jackson<br>Wiley B. Rutledge | **Prince v. Massachusetts**<br>Rutledge (5-4)<br>Murphy, dissenting<br>Jackson, dissenting, joined by Roberts, Frankfurter<br><br>**Follett v. Town of McCormick**<br>Douglas (5/1-3)<br>Reed, concurring<br>Murphy, concurring<br>Roberts, Frankfurter, Jackson, dissenting<br><br>**United States v. Ballard**<br>Douglas (5-4)<br>Stone, dissenting, joined by Roberts, Frankfurter<br>Jackson, dissenting | Korematsu v. U.S. |

| Justices | Church-State Cases | Other Significant Cases |
|---|---|---|
| **1945–1946**<br>Harlan F. Stone, C.J.<br>Hugo L. Black<br>Stanley F. Reed<br>Felix Frankfurter<br>William O. Douglas<br>Frank Murphy<br>Robert H. Jackson<br>Wiley B. Rutledge<br>Harold H. Burton | **Marsh v. Alabama**<br>Black (5-3)<br>Frankfurter, concurring<br>Jackson, did not participate<br>Reed, dissenting, joined by Stone, Burton<br><br>**Girouard v. United States**<br>Douglas (5-3)<br>Jackson, did not participate<br>Stone, C.J., dissenting, joined by Reed, Frankfurter | |
| **1946–1947**<br>Frederick M. Vinson, C.J.<br>Hugo L. Black<br>Stanley F. Reed<br>Felix Frankfurter<br>William O. Douglas<br>Frank Murphy<br>Robert H. Jackson<br>Wiley B. Rutledge<br>Harold H. Burton | **Everson v. Board of Education**<br>Black (5-4)<br>Jackson, dissenting, joined by Frankfurter<br>Rutledge, dissenting, joined by Frankfurter, Jackson, Burton | **Adamson v. California** |
| **1947–1948**<br>Frederick M. Vinson, C.J.<br>Hugo L. Black<br>Stanley F. Reed<br>Felix Frankfurter<br>William O. Douglas<br>Frank Murphy<br>Robert H. Jackson<br>Wiley B. Rutledge<br>Harold H. Burton | **McCollum v. Board of Education**<br>Black, joined by Douglas, Murphy, Jackson, Rutledge, Burton<br>Frankfurter, separate, joined by Jackson, Rutledge, Burton<br>Jackson, concurring<br>Reed, dissenting | **Shelley v. Kraemer**<br><br>**Terminiello v. Chicago**<br>(1948–1949 term) |
| **1950–1951**<br>Frederick M. Vinson, C.J.<br>Hugo L. Black<br>Stanley F. Reed<br>Felix Frankfurter<br>William O. Douglas<br>Robert H. Jackson<br>Harold H. Burton<br>Tom C. Clark<br>Sherman Minton | **Niemotko v. State of Maryland**<br>Vinson, C.J. (7/1/1-0)<br>Black, concurs in result<br>Frankfurter, concurrence | **Feiner v. New York**<br><br>**Dennis v. United States** |
| **1951–1952**<br>Frederick M. Vinson, C.J.<br>Hugo L. Black<br>Stanley F. Reed<br>Felix Frankfurter<br>William O. Douglas<br>Robert H. Jackson<br>Harold H. Burton<br>Tom C. Clark<br>Sherman Minton | **Doremus v. Board of Education**<br>Jackson (6-3)<br>Douglas, dissenting, joined by Reed, Burton<br><br>**Zorach v. Clauson**<br>Douglas (6-3)<br>Black, dissenting<br>Frankfurter, dissenting<br>Jackson, dissenting, joined by Frankfurter | **Beauharnais v. Illinois**<br><br>**Youngstown Sheet and Tube Co. v. Sawyer** |

| *Justices* | *Church-State Cases* | *Other Significant Cases* |
|---|---|---|
| 1952–1953<br>Frederick M. Vinson, C.J.<br>Hugo L. Black<br>Stanley F. Reed<br>Felix Frankfurter<br>William O. Douglas<br>Robert H. Jackson<br>Harold H. Burton<br>Sherman Minton<br>Tom C. Clark | **Kedroff v. Saint Nicholas Cathedral**<br>Reed (8-1)<br>Frankfurter, concurring, joined by Black in part, Douglas<br>Jackson, dissenting<br><br>**Fowler v. Rhode Island**<br>Douglas (7/1/1-0)<br>Frankfurter, concurring in part<br>Jackson, concurring in the result | **Brown v. Board of Education**<br>(1953–1954 term) |
| 1957–1958<br>Earl Warren, C.J.<br>Hugo L. Black<br>Felix Frankfurter<br>William O. Douglas<br>Harold H. Burton<br>Tom C. Clark<br>John Marshall Harlan<br>William Brennan, Jr.<br>Charles E. Whittaker | **First Unitarian Church v. County of Los Angeles**<br>Brennan (6/1-1)<br>Black, concurring, joined by Douglas<br>Burton, concurring in the result<br>Clark, dissenting<br>Warren, C.J., did not participate<br>Concurrence and dissent attached to **Speiser v. Randall** (1958) | **NAACP v. Alabama**<br><br>**Speiser v. Randall** |
| 1960–1961<br>Earl Warren, C.J.<br>Hugo L. Black<br>Felix Frankfurter<br>William O. Douglas<br>Tom C. Clark<br>John Marshall Harlan<br>William Brennan, Jr.<br>Charles E. Whittaker<br>Potter Stewart | **McGowan v. Maryland**<br>Warren, C.J. (6/2-1)<br>Frankfurter, separate, joined by Harlan<br>Douglas, dissenting<br><br>**Two Guys from Harrison Allentown, Inc. v. McGinley**<br>Warren, C.J. (6/2-1)<br>Concurrence and dissent attached to **McGowan v. Maryland**<br><br>**Braunfeld v. Brown**<br>Warren, C.J., joined by Black, Clark, Whittaker<br>Frankfurter, concurring, joined by Harlan<br>Harlan, Brennan and Stewart concurring in the judgment<br>Brennan, concurring and dissenting<br>Douglas, dissenting<br>Stewart, dissenting<br><br>**Gallagher v. Crown Kosher Super Market of Massachusetts**<br>Warren, C.J. (pluralities)<br>See **Braunfeld v. Brown**<br><br>**Torcaso v. Watkins**<br>Black (7/2-0)<br>Frankfurter and Harlan concurring in the result | |
| 1961–1962<br>Earl Warren, C.J.<br>Hugo L. Black<br>Felix Frankfurter<br>William O. Douglas<br>Tom C. Clark<br>John Marshall Harlan<br>William Brennan, Jr.<br>Potter Stewart<br>Byron R. White | **Engel v. Vitale**<br>Black (6-1)<br>Douglas, concurring<br>Stewart, dissenting | **Baker v. Carr** |

| Justices | Church-State Cases | Other Significant Cases |
|---|---|---|
| **1962–1963**<br>Earl Warren, C.J.<br>Hugo L. Black<br>William O. Douglas<br>Tom C. Clark<br>John Marshall Harlan<br>William Brennan, Jr.<br>Potter Stewart<br>Byron R. White<br>Arthur Goldberg | **Abington Township School District v. Schempp**<br>Clark (8-1)<br>Douglas, concurring<br>Brennan, concurring<br>Goldberg, concurring<br>Stewart, dissenting<br><br>**Sherbert v. Verner**<br>Brennan (6/1-2)<br>Douglas, concurring<br>Stewart, concurring in the result<br>Harlan, dissenting, joined by White | Gideon v. Wainwright |
| **1964–1965**<br>Earl Warren, C.J.<br>Hugo L. Black<br>William O. Douglas<br>Tom C. Clark<br>John Marshall Harlan<br>William Brennan, Jr.<br>Potter Stewart<br>Byron R. White<br>Arthur Goldberg | **United States v. Seeger**<br>Clark (9-0)<br>Douglas, concurring | New York Times v. Sullivan<br>(1963–1964 term)<br><br>Griswold v. Connecticut<br><br>Cox. v. Louisiana |
| **1967–1968**<br>Earl Warren, C.J.<br>Hugo L. Black<br>William O. Douglas<br>John Marshall Harlan<br>William Brennan, Jr.<br>Potter Stewart<br>Byron R. White<br>Abe Fortas<br>Thurgood Marshall | **Board of Education v. Allen**<br>White (6-3)<br>Harlan, concurring<br>Douglas, dissenting<br>Fortas, dissenting<br><br>**Flast v. Cohen**<br>Warren, C.J. (8-1)<br>Douglas, concurring<br>Stewart, concurring<br>Fortas, concurring<br>Harlan, dissenting | U.S. v. O'Brien<br><br>Pickering v. Board of Education |
| **1968–1969**<br>Earl Warren, C.J.<br>Hugo L. Black<br>William O. Douglas<br>John Marshall Harlan<br>William Brennan, Jr.<br>Potter Stewart<br>Byron R. White<br>Abe Fortas<br>Thurgood Marshall | **Epperson v. Arkansas**<br>Fortas (8/1-0)<br>Black, concurring<br>Harlan, concurring<br>Stewart, concurring<br><br>**Presbyterian Church v. Hull Memorial Presbyterian Church**<br>Brennan (9-0) | Brandenburg v. Ohio<br><br>Tinker v. Des Moines Independent Community School District |
| **1969–1970**<br>Warren E. Burger, C.J.<br>Hugo L. Black<br>William O. Douglas<br>John Marshall Harlan<br>William Brennan, Jr.<br>Potter Stewart<br>Byron R. White<br>Thurgood Marshall<br>Harry A. Blackmun | **Maryland and Virginia Churches v. Sharpsburg Church**<br>Per curiam (9-0)<br><br>**Walz v. Tax Commission**<br>Burger, C.J. (8-1)<br>Harlan, concurring<br>Brennan, concurring<br>Douglas, dissenting | |

| Justices | Church-State Cases | Other Significant Cases |
|---|---|---|
| 1969–1970 (*cont.*) | **Welsh v. United States**<br>Black (4/1-3), joined by Douglas, Brennan, Marshall<br>Harlan concurring<br>Blackmun did not participate<br>White, dissenting, joined by Burger, C.J. and Stewart | |
| 1970–1971<br>Warren E. Burger, C.J.<br>Hugo L. Black<br>William O. Douglas<br>John Marshall Harlan<br>William Brennan, Jr.<br>Potter Stewart<br>Byron R. White<br>Thurgood Marshall<br>Harry A. Blackmun | **Gillette v. United States**<br>Marshall (7/1-1)<br>Douglas, dissenting<br><br>**Lemon v. Kurtman (I)**<br>Burger, C.J. (6/1/1-0)<br>Douglas, concurring, joined by Black<br>Brennan, concurring and dissenting<br>White, concurring and dissenting<br><br>**Tilton v. Richardson**<br>Burger, C.J., joined by Harlan, Stewart, Blackmun<br>Douglas, concurring in judgment, dissenting in part, joined by Black, Marshall<br>Brennan, dissenting | **New York Times Co. v. U.S.**<br><br>**Cohen v. California** |
| 1971–1972<br>Warren E. Burger, C.J.<br>William O. Douglas<br>William Brennan, Jr.<br>Potter Stewart<br>Byron R. White<br>Thurgood Marshall<br>Harry A. Blackmun<br>Lewis F. Powell, Jr.<br>William H. Rehnquist | **Cruz v. Beto**<br>Per curiam (6/1/1-1)<br>Blackmun, concurred in result<br>Burger, C.J., concurring<br>Rehnquist, dissenting<br><br>**Wisconsin v. Yoder**<br>Burger, C.J. (6-1)<br>Stewart, concurring<br>White, concurring<br>Douglas, dissenting in part | |
| 1972–1973<br>Warren E. Burger, C.J.<br>William O. Douglas<br>William Brennan, Jr.<br>Potter Stewart<br>Byron R. White<br>Thurgood Marshall<br>Harry A. Blackmun<br>Lewis F. Powell, Jr.<br>William H. Rehnquist | **Norwood v. Harrison**<br>Burger, C.J. (7/2-0)<br>Douglas and Brennan concurring in the result<br><br>**Levitt v. Committee for Public Education and Religious Liberty**<br>Burger, C.J. (5/3-1)<br>Douglas, Brennan and Marshall concurring in the judgment<br>White, dissenting<br><br>**Hunt v. McNair**<br>Powell (6-3)<br>Brennan, dissenting, joined by Douglas, Marshall<br><br>**Committee for Public Education and Religious Liberty v. Nyquist**<br>Powell (pluralities)<br>Burger, C.J., concurring in part joined by Rehnquist and dissenting in part joined by White and Rehnquist<br>White, dissenting, joined by Burger, C.J., and Rehnquist<br>Rehnquist, dissenting in part, joined by Burger, White | **Roe v. Wade**<br><br>**San Antonio Independent School District v. Rodriguez**<br><br>**Miller v. California** |

| Justices | Church-State Cases | Other Significant Cases |
|---|---|---|
| 1972–1973 (cont.) | **Sloan v. Lemon**<br>Powell (6-3)<br>Burger, C.J., dissenting, joined by White, Rehnquist<br>White dissenting, joined by Burger, C.J., Rehnquist | |
| 1973–1974<br>Warren E. Burger, C.J.<br>William O. Douglas<br>William Brennan, Jr.<br>Potter Stewart<br>Byron R. White<br>Thurgood Marshall<br>Harry A. Blackmun<br>Lewis F. Powell, Jr.<br>William H. Rehnquist | **Wheeler v. Barrera**<br>Blackman (6/1/1-1)<br>Marshall concurring in the result<br>Powell concurring<br>White concurring in the judgment<br>Douglas, dissenting | **U.S. v. Nixon** |
| 1974–1975<br>Warren E. Burger, C.J.<br>William O. Douglas<br>William Brennan, Jr.<br>Potter Stewart<br>Byron R. White<br>Thurgood Marshall<br>Harry A. Blackmun<br>Lewis F. Powell, Jr.<br>William H. Rehnquist | **Meek v. Pittenger**<br>Stewart (pluralities)<br>Brennan, concurring and dissenting, joined by Douglas, Marshall<br>Burger, C.J., concurring in part, dissenting in part<br>Rehnquist, concurring in part, dissenting in part, joined by White | |
| 1975–1976<br>Warren E. Burger, C.J.<br>William Brennan, Jr.<br>Potter Stewart<br>Byron R. White<br>Thurgood Marshall<br>Harry A. Blackmun<br>Lewis F. Powell, Jr.<br>William H. Rehnquist<br>John Paul Stevens | **Roemer v. Board of Public Works of Maryland**<br>Blackmun (3/2-4)<br>White, concurring in the judgment joined by Rehnquist<br>Brennan, dissenting, joined by Marshall<br>Stewart, dissenting<br>Stevens, dissenting<br><br>**Serbian Eastern Orthodox Diocese v. Milivojevich**<br>Brennan (6/1-2)<br>Burger, C.J. concurred in the judgment<br>White, concurring<br>Rehnquist, dissenting, joined by Stevens | **Elrod v. Burns**<br><br>**Buckley v. Valeo** |
| 1976–1977<br>Warren E. Burger, C.J.<br>William Brennan, Jr.<br>Potter Stewart<br>Byron R. White<br>Thurgood Marshall<br>Harry A. Blackmun<br>Lewis F. Powell, Jr.<br>William H. Rehnquist<br>John Paul Stevens | **Wooley v. Maynard**<br>Burger, C.J. (pluralities)<br>White dissenting in part, joined by Blackmun, Rehnquist<br>Rehnquist dissenting, joined by Blackmun<br><br>**Trans World Airlines v. Hardison**<br>White (7-2)<br>Marshall, dissenting, joined by Brennan<br><br>**Wolman v. Walter**<br>Blackmun (plurality)<br>Brennan, concurring and dissenting<br>Marshall, concurring and dissenting<br>Powell, concurring and dissenting<br>Stevens, concurring and dissenting | **National Socialist Party of America v. Village of Skokie** |

| Justices | Church-State Cases | Other Significant Cases |
|---|---|---|
| **1977–1978**<br>Warren E. Burger, C.J.<br>William Brennan, Jr.<br>Potter Stewart<br>Byron R. White<br>Thurgood Marshall<br>Harry A. Blackmun<br>Lewis F. Powell, Jr.<br>William H. Rehnquist<br>John Paul Stevens | **New York v. Cathedral Academy**<br>Stewart (6-3)<br>Burger, C.J. and Rehnquist, dissenting<br>White, dissenting<br><br>**McDaniel v. Paty**<br>Burger (4/2/1/1-0), joined by Powell, Rehnquist, Stevens<br>Brennan, concurring, joined by Marshall<br>Stewart, concurring<br>White, concurring | **Regents of University of California v. Bakke**<br><br>**FCC v. Pacifica Foundation**<br><br>**Zurcher v. Stanford Daily** |
| **1978–1979**<br>Warren E. Burger, C.J.<br>William Brennan, Jr.<br>Potter Stewart<br>Byron R. White<br>Thurgood Marshall<br>Harry A. Blackmun<br>Lewis F. Powell, Jr.<br>William H. Rehnquist<br>John Paul Stevens | **National Labor Relations Board v. Catholic Bishop of Chicago**<br>Burger, C.J. (5-4)<br>Brennan, dissenting, joined by White, Marshall, Blackmun<br><br>**Jones v. Wolf**<br>Blackmun (5-4)<br>Powell, dissenting, joined by Burger, C.J., Stewart, White | |
| **1979–1980**<br>Warren E. Burger, C.J.<br>William Brennan, Jr.<br>Potter Stewart<br>Byron R. White<br>Thurgood Marshall<br>Harry A. Blackmun<br>Lewis F. Powell, Jr.<br>William H. Rehnquist<br>John Paul Stevens | **Committee for Public Education and Religious Liberty v. Regan**<br>White (5-4)<br>Blackmun, dissenting, joined by Brennan, Marshall<br>Stevens, dissenting<br><br>**Harris v. McRae**<br>Stewart (5-4)<br>White concurring<br>Brennan, dissenting, joined by Marshall, Blackmun<br>Marshall, dissenting<br>Blackmun, dissenting<br>Stevens, dissenting | |
| **1980–1981**<br>Warren E. Burger, C.J.<br>William Brennan, Jr.<br>Potter Stewart<br>Byron R. White<br>Thurgood Marshall<br>Harry A. Blackmun<br>Lewis F. Powell, Jr.<br>William H. Rehnquist<br>John Paul Stevens | **Stone v. Graham**<br>Per curiam (5-4)<br>Rehnquist, dissenting<br>Burger, C.J., Blackmun dissent in outcome<br>Stewart dissent in judgment<br><br>**Thomas v. Review Board of Indiana Employment Security Division**<br>Burger, C.J. (7/1-1)<br>Blackmun, concurred in part and in the judgment<br>Rehnquist, dissenting<br><br>**St. Martin Evangelical Lutheran Church v. South Dakota**<br>Blackmun (8/1-0)<br>Stevens, concurring | |

| Justices | Church-State Cases | Other Significant Cases |
|---|---|---|
| 1980–1981 (*cont.*) | **Heffron v. International Society of Krishna Consciousness**<br>White (pluralities)<br>Brennan, concurring and dissenting, joined by Marshall, Stevens<br>Blackmun, concurring and dissenting | |
| 1981–1982<br>Warren E. Burger, C.J.<br>William Brennan, Jr.<br>Byron R. White<br>Thurgood Marshall<br>Harry A. Blackmun<br>Lewis F. Powell, Jr.<br>William H. Rehnquist<br>John Paul Stevens<br>Sandra Day O'Connor | **Widmar v. Vincent**<br>Powell (7/1-1)<br>Stevens, concurring<br>White, dissenting<br><br>**Valley Forge Christian College v. Americans United for Separation of Church and State**<br>Rehnquist (5-4)<br>Brennan, dissenting, joined by Marshall, Blackmun<br>Stevens, dissenting<br><br>**Treen v. Karen B.**<br>Affirmed on appeal (9-0)<br><br>**United States v. Lee**<br>Burger, C.J. (8/1-0)<br>Stevens, concurring<br><br>**Larson v. Valente**<br>Brennan (5-4)<br>Stevens, concurring<br>White, dissenting, joined by Rehnquist<br>Rehnquist, dissenting, joined by Burger, C.J., White, O'Connor | **Board of Education v. Pico** |
| 1982–1983<br>Warren E. Burger, C.J.<br>William Brennan, Jr.<br>Byron R. White<br>Thurgood Marshall<br>Harry A. Blackmun<br>Lewis F. Powell, Jr.<br>William H. Rehnquist<br>John Paul Stevens<br>Sandra Day O'Connor | **Larkin v. Grendel's Den**<br>Burger, C.J. (8-1)<br>Rehnquist, dissenting<br><br>**Bob Jones University v. United States**<br>Burger, C.J. (7/1-1)<br>Powell, concurring<br>Rehnquist, dissenting<br><br>**Mueller v. Allen**<br>Rehnquist (5-4)<br>Marshall, dissenting, joined by Brennan, Blackmun, Stevens<br><br>**Marsh v. Chambers**<br>Burger, C.J. (6-3)<br>Brennan, dissenting, joined by Marshall<br>Stevens, dissenting | **City of Akron v. Akron Center for Reproductive Health**<br><br>**Connick v. Myers**<br><br>**Regan v. Taxation with Representation**<br><br>**Perry Educ. Ass'n v. Perry Local Educ. Ass'n**<br><br>**Minnesota Star & Tribune v. Minn. Com'r of Revenue** |

| *Justices* | *Church-State Cases* | *Other Significant Cases* |
|---|---|---|
| **1983–1984**<br>Warren E. Burger, C.J.<br>William Brennan, Jr.<br>Byron R. White<br>Thurgood Marshall<br>Harry A. Blackmun<br>Lewis F. Powell, Jr.<br>William H. Rehnquist<br>John Paul Stevens<br>Sandra Day O'Connor | **Lynch v. Donnelly**<br>Burger, C.J. (5-4)<br>O'Connor, concurring<br>Brennan, dissenting, joined by Marshall, Blackmun, Stevens<br>Blackmun, dissenting, joined by Stevens | **Roberts v. U.S. Jaycees**<br><br>**Clark v. Comm. for Creative Non-Violence**<br><br>**FCC v. League of Women Voters**<br><br>**Grove City College v. Bell** |
| **1984–1985**<br>Warren E. Burger, C.J.<br>William Brennan, Jr.<br>Byron R. White<br>Thurgood Marshall<br>Harry A. Blackmun<br>Lewis F. Powell, Jr.<br>William H. Rehnquist<br>John Paul Stevens<br>Sandra Day O'Connor | **Tony and Susan Alamo Foundation v. Secretary of Labor**<br>White (9-0)<br><br>**Wallace v. Jaffree**<br>Stevens (5/1-3)<br>Powell, concurring<br>O'Connor, concurring<br>Burger, C.J., dissenting<br>White, dissenting<br>Rehnquist, dissenting<br><br>**Estate of Thornton v. Caldor**<br>Burger, C.J. (8-1)<br>O'Connor, concurring, joined by Marshall<br>Rehnquist, dissenting<br><br>**Aguilar v. Felton**<br>Brennan (5-4)<br>Powell, concurring<br>Burger, dissenting<br>Rehnquist, dissenting<br>O'Connor, dissenting, joined by Rehnquist on parts II & III<br>White, dissenting<br><br>**Grand Rapids School District v. Ball**<br>Brennan (pluralities)<br>Burger, C.J., concurring and dissenting<br>O'Connor, concurring and dissenting<br>White, dissenting<br>Rehnquist, dissenting | **City of Cleburne v. Cleburne Living Center, Inc.**<br><br>**Cornelius v. NAACP Leg. Defense & Educ. Fund** |
| **1985–1986**<br>Warren E. Burger, C.J.<br>William Brennan, Jr.<br>Byron R. White<br>Thurgood Marshall<br>Harry A. Blackmun<br>Lewis F. Powell, Jr.<br>William H. Rehnquist<br>John Paul Stevens<br>Sandra Day O'Connor | **Witters v. Washington Department of Services for the Blind**<br>Marshall (8/1-0)<br>White, concurring<br>Powell, concurring, joined by Burger, C.J., Rehnquist<br>O'Connor concurring in judgment and in part | **Bethel School District v. Fraser**<br><br>**Bowers v. Hardwick** |

| *Justices* | *Church-State Cases* | *Other Significant Cases* |
|---|---|---|
| 1985–1986 (*cont.*) | **Goldman v. Weinberger**<br>Rehnquist (5-4)<br>Stevens, concurring, joined by White, Powell<br>Brennan, dissenting, joined by Marshall<br>Blackmun, dissenting<br>O'Connor, dissenting, joined by Marshall<br><br>**Bowen v. Roy**<br>Burger, C.J. (plurality)<br>Blackmun, concurring in part<br>Stevens, concurring in part and in result<br>O'Connor, concurring and dissenting, joined by Brennan and Marshall<br>White, dissenting | |
| 1986–1987<br>William H. Rehnquist, C.J.<br>William Brennan, Jr.<br>Byron R. White<br>Thurgood Marshall<br>Harry A. Blackmun<br>Lewis F. Powell, Jr.<br>John Paul Stevens<br>Sandra Day O'Connor<br>Antonin Scalia | **Ansonia Board of Education v. Philbrook**<br>Rehnquist, C.J. (7-2)<br>Marshall concurring in part, dissenting in part<br>Stevens, concurring in part, dissenting in part<br><br>**Hobbie v. Unemployment Appeals Commission**<br>Brennan (6/1/1-1)<br>Powell, concurring<br>Stevens, concurring<br>Rehnquist, dissenting<br><br>**O'Lone v. Estate of Shabazz**<br>Rehnquist (5-4)<br>Brennan, dissenting, joined by Marshall, Blackmun, Stevens<br><br>**Edwards v. Aguillard**<br>Brennan (6/1-2)<br>Powell, concurring, joined by O'Connor<br>White, concurring<br>Scalia, dissenting, joined by Rehnquist, C.J.<br><br>**Airport Commissioners of Los Angeles v. Jews for Jesus**<br>O'Connor (9-0)<br><br>**Corporation of the Presiding Bishop of the Church of Jesus Christ of Latter-day Saints v. Amos**<br>White (5/2/1/1-0)<br>Brennan, concurring, joined by Marshall<br>Blackmun, concurring<br>O'Connor, concurring | **Turner v. Safley** |
| 1987–1988<br>William H. Rehnquist, C.J.<br>William Brennan, Jr.<br>Byron R. White<br>Thurgood Marshall<br>Harry A. Blackmun<br>John Paul Stevens<br>Sandra Day O'Connor<br>Antonin Scalia<br>Anthony Kennedy | **Lyng v. Northwest Indian Cemetery Protective Association**<br>O'Connor (5-3)<br>Brennan, dissenting, joined by Marshall, Blackmun<br>Kennedy did not participate<br><br>**Bowen v. Kendrick**<br>Rehnquist, C.J. (5-4)<br>Kennedy, concurring, joined by Scalia<br>O'Connor, concurring<br>Blackmun, dissenting, joined by Brennan, Marshall, Stevens | **Hustler Magazine v. Falwell**<br><br>**Hazelwood School District v. Kuhlmeier** |

| Justices | Church-State Cases | Other Significant Cases |
|---|---|---|
| 1988–1989<br>William H. Rehnquist, C.J.<br>William Brennan, Jr.<br>Byron R. White<br>Thurgood Marshall<br>Harry A. Blackmun<br>John Paul Stevens<br>Sandra Day O'Connor<br>Antonin Scalia<br>Anthony Kennedy | **Texas Monthly v. Bullock**<br>Brennan (3/2/1-3)<br>White, concurring<br>Blackmun, concurring, joined by O'Connor<br>Scalia, dissenting, joined by Rehnquist, C.J.,<br>Kennedy<br><br>**Frazee v. Illinois Department of Employment Security**<br>White (9-0)<br><br>**Hernandez v. Commissioner of Internal Revenue**<br>Marshall (5-2)<br>O'Connor, dissenting, joined by Scalia<br>Brennan and Kennedy did not participate<br><br>**Allegheny v. ACLU of Pittsburgh**<br>Blackmun (plurality)<br>O'Connor, concurring in part and concurring in the judgment, joined by Brennan, Stevens<br>Brennan, concurring in part and dissenting in part, joined by Marshall, Stevens<br>Stevens, concurring and dissenting, joined by Brennan, Marshall<br>Kennedy, concurring in judgment in part dissenting in part, joined by Rehnquist, C.J., White, Scalia | **Webster v. Reproductive Health Services**<br><br>**Texas v. Johnson**<br><br>**Ward v. Rock Against Racism** |
| 1989–1990<br>William H. Rehnquist, C.J.<br>William Brennan, Jr.<br>Byron R. White<br>Thurgood Marshall<br>Harry A. Blackmun<br>John Paul Stevens<br>Sandra Day O'Connor<br>Antonin Scalia<br>Anthony Kennedy | **Jimmy Swaggart Ministries v. Board of Equalization of California**<br>O'Connor (9-0)<br><br>**Employment Division, Department of Human Resources of Oregon v. Smith (II)**<br>Scalia (5/1-3)<br>O'Connor, concurring, joined by Brennan and Marshall as to parts I & II<br>Blackmun, dissenting, joined by Brennan, Marshall<br><br>**Davis v. United States**<br>O'Connor (9-0)<br><br>**Board of Education v. Mergens**<br>O'Connor (4/2/2-1)<br>Kennedy, concurring, joined by Scalia<br>Marshall, concurring, joined by Brennan<br>Stevens, dissenting | **Cruzan v. Director, Missouri Department of Health**<br><br>**Kokinda v. U.S.** |
| 1991–1992<br>William H. Rehnquist, C.J.<br>Byron R. White<br>Harry A. Blackmun<br>John Paul Stevens<br>Sandra Day O'Connor<br>Antonin Scalia<br>Anthony Kennedy<br>David H. Souter<br>Clarence Thomas | **Lee v. Weisman**<br>Kennedy (5-4)<br>Blackmun, concurring, joined by Stevens, O'Connor<br>Souter, concurring, joined by Stevens, O'Connor<br>Scalia, dissenting, joined by Rehnquist, C.J., White, Thomas<br><br>**International Society for Krishna Consciousness v. Lee**<br>Per Curiam<br>Rehnquist, C.J., dissenting, joined by White, Scalia, Thomas | **Rust v. Sullivan**<br>(1990–1991 term)<br><br>**R.A.V. v. City of St. Paul**<br><br>**Planned Parenthood v. Casey** |

| Justices | Church-State Cases | Other Significant Cases |
|---|---|---|
| **1992–1993**<br>William H. Rehnquist, C.J.<br>Byron R. White<br>Harry A. Blackmun<br>John Paul Stevens<br>Sandra Day O'Connor<br>Antonin Scalia<br>Anthony Kennedy<br>David H. Souter<br>Clarence Thomas | **Church of Scientology of California v. United States**<br>Stevens (9-0)<br><br>**Lamb's Chapel v. Center Moriches Union Free School District**<br>White (6/2/1-0)<br>Scalia, concurring, joined by Thomas<br>Kennedy, concurring in part<br><br>**Church of the Lukumi Babalu Aye v. Hialeah**<br>Kennedy (9-0)<br>Scalia, concurring in part, joined by Rehnquist, C.J.<br>Souter, concurring in part<br>Blackmun, concurring in judgment, joined by O'Connor<br><br>**Zobrest v. Catalina Foothills School District**<br>Rehnquist, C.J. (5-4)<br>Blackmun, dissenting, joined by Souter, joined in part by Stevens, O'Connor<br>O'Connor, dissenting, joined by Stevens | |
| **1993–1994**<br>William H. Rehnquist, C.J.<br>Harry A. Blackmun<br>John Paul Stevens<br>Sandra Day O'Connor<br>Antonin Scalia<br>Anthony Kennedy<br>David H. Souter<br>Clarence Thomas<br>Ruth Bader Ginsburg | **Board of Education of Kiryas Joel v. Grumet**<br>Souter (4/1/1-3)<br>Blackmun, concurring<br>Stevens, concurring, joined by Blackmun, Ginsburg<br>O'Connor, concurring in part<br>Kennedy, concurring in judgment<br>Scalia, dissenting, joined by Rehnquist, C.J., Thomas | **City of Ladue v. Gilleo**<br><br>**Madsen v. Women's Health Center** |
| **1994–1995**<br>William H. Rehnquist, C.J.<br>John Paul Stevens<br>Sandra Day O'Connor<br>Antonin Scalia<br>Anthony Kennedy<br>David H. Souter<br>Clarence Thomas<br>Ruth Bader Ginsburg<br>Stephen G. Breyer | **Rosenberger v. University of Virginia**<br>Kennedy (5-4)<br>O'Connor, concurring<br>Thomas, concurring<br>Souter, dissenting, joined by Stevens, Ginsburg, Breyer<br><br>**Capital Square Review Board v. Pinette**<br>Scalia (4/3-2), joined by Rehnquist, C.J., Kennedy, Thomas<br>Thomas, concurring<br>O'Connor, concurring in part, joined by Souter, Breyer<br>Souter, concurring in part, joined by O'Connor, Breyer<br>Stevens, dissenting<br>Ginsburg, dissenting | **Hurley v. Irish-American Gay, Lesbian and Bisexual Group**<br><br>**Virginia v. U.S.**<br>(1995–1996 term)<br><br>**Romer v. Evans**<br>(1995–1996 term) |

| Justices | Church-State Cases | Other Significant Cases |
|---|---|---|
| **1996–1997**<br>William H. Rehnquist, C.J.<br>John Paul Stevens<br>Sandra Day O'Connor<br>Antonin Scalia<br>Anthony Kennedy<br>David H. Souter<br>Clarence Thomas<br>Ruth Bader Ginsburg<br>Stephen G. Breyer | **Agostini v. Felton**<br>O'Connor (5-4)<br>Souter, dissenting, joined by Stevens, Ginsburg, Breyer<br>Ginsburg, dissenting, joined by Stevens, Souter, Breyer<br><br>**City of Boerne v. Flores**<br>Kennedy (5/1-3)<br>Stevens concurring<br>Scalia, concurring in part, joined by Stevens<br>O'Connor, dissenting, joined by Breyer in part<br>Souter, dissenting<br>Breyer, dissenting | **Washington v. Glucksberg**<br><br>**Reno v. ACLU**<br><br>**NEA v. Finley**<br>(1997–1998 term) |
| **1999–2000**<br>William H. Rehnquist, C.J.<br>John Paul Stevens<br>Sandra Day O'Connor<br>Antonin Scalia<br>Anthony Kennedy<br>David H. Souter<br>Clarence Thomas<br>Ruth Bader Ginsburg<br>Stephen G. Breyer | **Santa Fe Independent School District v. Doe**<br>Stevens (6-3)<br>Rehnquist, C.J., dissenting, joined by Scalia, Thomas<br><br>**Mitchell v. Helms**<br>Thomas (4/2-3), joined by Rehnquist, C.J., Scalia, Kennedy<br>O'Connor, concurring in judgment, joined by Breyer<br>Souter, dissenting, joined by Stevens, Ginsburg | **U.S. v. Playboy Entertainment Group**<br><br>**Boy Scouts of America v. Dale**<br><br>**Stenberg v. Carhart**<br><br>**Board of Regents v. Southworth** |
| **2000–2001**<br>William H. Rehnquist, C.J.<br>John Paul Stevens<br>Sandra Day O'Connor<br>Antonin Scalia<br>Anthony Kennedy<br>David H. Souter<br>Clarence Thomas<br>Ruth Bader Ginsburg<br>Stephen G. Breyer | **Good News Club v. Milford Central School**<br>Thomas (4/1/1/1-2)<br>Scalia, concurring<br>Breyer, concurring in part<br>Stevens, dissenting<br>Souter, dissenting with Ginsburg | **Bush v. Gore**<br><br>**Legal Services v. Velazquez** |
| **2001–2002**<br>William H. Rehnquist, C.J.<br>John Paul Stevens<br>Sandra Day O'Connor<br>Antonin Scalia<br>Anthony Kennedy<br>David H. Souter<br>Clarence Thomas<br>Ruth Bader Ginsburg<br>Stephen G. Breyer | **Watchtower Bible and Tract Society v. Village of Stratton**<br>Stevens (8-1)<br>Breyer concurring, joined by Souter, Ginsburg<br>Scalia, concurring in the judgment, joined by Thomas<br>Rehnquist, C.J., dissenting<br><br>**Zelman v. Simmons-Harris**<br>Rehnquist, C.J. (5-4)<br>O'Connor, concurring<br>Thomas, concurring<br>Stevens, dissenting<br>Souter, dissenting, joined by Stevens, Ginsburg, Breyer<br>Breyer, dissenting, joined by Stevens, Souter | **Ashcroft v. Free Speech Coalition**<br><br>**Republican Party of Minnesota v. White** |

| Justices | Church-State Cases | Other Significant Cases |
|---|---|---|
| **2003–2004**<br>William H. Rehnquist, C.J.<br>John Paul Stevens<br>Sandra Day O'Connor<br>Antonin Scalia<br>Anthony Kennedy<br>David H. Souter<br>Clarence Thomas<br>Ruth Bader Ginsburg<br>Stephen G. Breyer | **Locke v. Davey**<br>Rehnquist, C.J. (7-2)<br>Scalia, dissenting, joined by Thomas<br>Thomas, dissenting<br><br>**Elk Grove Unified School District v. Newdow**<br>Stevens (5-3)<br>Rehnquist, C.J., concurring in judgment, joined by O'Connor and in part by Thomas<br>O'Connor, concurring in judgment<br>Thomas, concurring in judgment<br>Scalia did not participate | **Lawrence v. Texas**<br>(2002–2003 term)<br><br>**Virginia v. Black**<br>(2002–2003 term)<br><br>**U.S. v. American Library Ass'n**<br>(2002–2003 term)<br><br>**Grutter/Gratz v. Bollinger**<br>(2002–2003 term) |
| **2004–2005**<br>William H. Rehnquist, C.J.<br>John Paul Stevens<br>Sandra Day O'Connor<br>Antonin Scalia<br>Anthony Kennedy<br>David H. Souter<br>Clarence Thomas<br>Ruth Bader Ginsburg<br>Stephen G. Breyer | **Cutter v. Wilkinson**<br>Ginsburg (9-0)<br>Thomas, concurring<br><br>**Van Orden v. Perry**<br>Rehnquist, C.J. (5-4)<br>Scalia, concurring<br>Thomas, concurring<br>Breyer, concurring in judgment<br>Stevens, dissenting, joined by Ginsburg<br>O'Connor, dissenting<br>Souter, dissenting, joined by Stevens, Ginsburg<br><br>**McCreary County v. ACLU of Kentucky**<br>Souter (5-4)<br>O'Connor, concurring<br>Scalia, dissenting, joined by Rehnquist, C.J., Thomas and as to parts II and III Kennedy | **Kelo v. City of New London** |
| **2005–2006**<br>John G. Roberts, C.J.<br>John Paul Stevens<br>Antonin Scalia<br>Anthony Kennedy<br>David H. Souter<br>Clarence Thomas<br>Ruth Bader Ginsburg<br>Stephen G. Breyer<br>Samuel Alito | **Gonzales v. O Centro Espirita Beneficente Uniao Do Vegetal**<br>Roberts (8-0)<br>(Alito did not participate) | **Garcetti v. Ceballos**<br><br>**Rumsfeld v. Forum for Academic and Institutional Rights** |
| **2006–2007**<br>John G. Roberts, C.J.<br>John Paul Stevens<br>Antonin Scalia<br>Anthony Kennedy<br>David H. Souter<br>Clarence Thomas<br>Ruth Bader Ginsburg<br>Stephen G. Breyer<br>Samuel Alito | **Hein v. FFRF**<br>Alito (5-4)<br>Kennedy, concurring<br>Scalia, concurring in judgment, joined by Thomas<br>Souter, dissenting, joined by Stevens, Ginsburg, Breyer | **Morse v. Frederick**<br><br>**Parents Involved v. Seattle School District**<br><br>**Gonzalez v. Carhart** |

# NOTES

## CHAPTER I

1.  *Brown v. Allen*, 344 U.S. 443, 540 (1953) (Justice Robert Jackson, concurring in the result).
2.  "Congress shall make no law respecting an establishment of religion, or prohibiting the free exercise thereof . . . ."
3.  ". . . ; but no religious Test shall ever be required as a Qualification to any Office or public Trust under the United States."
4.  *West Virginia State Board of Education v. Barnette*, 319 U.S. 624, 638 (1943).
5.  Rule 10 of the United States Supreme Court Rules.
6.  Speech by Supreme Court Associate Justice Ruth Bader Ginsburg at the annual dinner of the American Law Institute (May 19, 1994).
7.  Ginsburg speech.
8.  *Marbury v. Madison*, 5 U.S. 137, 177 (1803) ("It is emphatically the province and duty of the judicial department to say what the law is.").
9.  *Barron v. Baltimore*, 32 U.S. 243 (1833).
10. *Slaughterhouse Cases*, 83 U.S. 36 (1873).
11. *Gitlow v. New York*, 268 U.S. 652 (1925).
12. "The fundamental concept of liberty embodied in [the Fourteenth] Amendment embraces the liberties guaranteed by the First Amendment. The First Amendment declares that Congress shall make no law respecting an establishment of religion or prohibiting the free exercise thereof. The Fourteenth Amendment has rendered the legislatures of the states as incompetent as Congress to enact such laws." *Cantwell v. Connecticut*, 310 U.S. 296 (1940).
13. *Committee for Public Education and Religious Liberty v. Nyquist*, 413 U.S. 756 (1973).
14. *Zelman v. Simmons-Harris*, 536 U.S. 639 (2002).
15. *Frothingham v. Mellon*, 262 U.S. 447 (1923).
16. *Flast v. Cohen*, 392 U.S. 83, 103 (1968).

17. See *Valley Forge Christian College v. Americans United for Separation of Church and State,* 454 U.S. 464 (1982).
18. 454 U.S., 487.
19. Two excellent works on the philosophical origins of the American Revolution and Constitution are Bernard Bailyn, *The Ideological Origins of the American Revolution* (Cambridge: Belknap Press of Harvard University Press, 1967), and Gordon S. Wood, *The Creation of the American Republic, 1776–1787* (Chapel Hill: University of North Carolina Press, 1969).
20. 440 U.S. 490 (1979).

## CHAPTER 2

1. Not to mention others, such as Quakers, Mennonites, Huguenots, and Jews. But none of these groups became oppressive to minorities in the way suggested in this paragraph and described on pages twelve and thirteen.
2. The date Luther posted the famous Ninety-five Theses on the door of the Castle Church in Wittenberg, proposing a theological debate on various points of Catholic theology and church governance, particularly the theology behind and the sale of indulgences. But at that time, Luther had no intention of splitting the Catholic Church or becoming schismatic himself. That process began later (although soon).
3. Edwin S. Gaustad and Leigh E. Schmidt, *The Religious History of America*, rev. ed. (San Francisco: Harper, 2002), 68.
4. The historian of American religion Winthrop Hudson called voluntarism "the great tradition of the American churches." Winthrop S. Hudson, *The Great Tradition of the American Churches* (New York: Harper, 1953).
5. For an excellent summary of Deism, by an eighteenth century practitioner, see Thomas Paine, *The Age of Reason* (New York: Liberal Press, 1957).
6. Here Madison quoted Article XVI of the Virginia Declaration of Rights.
7. The *Memorial and Remonstrance* is quoted in full as an appendix to *Everson v. Board of Education*, 330 U.S. 1, 63-72 (1947).
8. Thomas Jefferson, *Notes on the State of Virginia*, William Peden, ed. (Chapel Hill: University of North Carolina Press, 1955), 159.
9. All quotations from Thomas Jefferson, "A Bill for Establishing Religious Freedom," from *The Papers of Thomas Jefferson*, ed. Julian P. Boyd, vol. 2 (Princeton, N.J.: Princeton University Press, 1950– ), 545-546.
10. Terry L. Jordan, *The U.S. Constitution and Fascinating Facts About It*, seventh edition (Naperville, Il.: Oak Hill Publishing, 1999), 29.
11. Isaac Kramnick and R. Laurence Moore, *The Godless Constitution: A Moral Defense of the Secular State* (New York: W. W. Norton, 2005).
12. Edwin S. Gaustad, *Proclaim Liberty Throughout the Land: A History of Church and State in America* (New York: Oxford University Press, 2003), 25-30; Kramnick and Moore, *The Godless Constitution*, 30-45.
13. Jonathan Elliot, *Debates in the Several Conventions on the Adoption of the Federal Constitution*, vol. 4, 2nd ed. (Philadelphia: J. B. Lippincott, 1907), 193.
14. Gaustad, *Proclaim Liberty Throughout the Land*, 25-30.
15. Neil H. Cogan, ed., *The Complete Bill of Rights: The Drafts, Debates, Sources, and Origins* (New York: Oxford University Press, 1997), 1-11.

16. *Wallace v. Jaffree*, 472 U.S. 38, 106 (1985) (Rehnquist, J., dissenting).

17. Steven K. Green, "Federalism and the Establishment Clause: A Reassessment," *Creighton Law Review* 38 (June 2005): 780.

18. American colonists had also expressed disfavor with the action of the British government allowing French Canadians in Quebec to retain the Catholic Church as the established religion in that province.

19. As Madison explained during the 15 August 1789 debates, "[h]e believed that the people feared one sect might obtain a pre-eminence, or two combine together, and establish a religion to which they would compel others to conform. He thought if the word 'national' was introduced, it would point the amendment directly to the object it was intended to prevent." *Annals of the Congress of the United States*, compiled from authentic materials by Joseph Gales, Sr., vol. 1 (Washington: Gales and Seaton, 1834), 731.

20. *Cutter v. Wilkinson*, 544 U.S. 709, 727-728 (2005), quoting *Elk Grove United School District v. Newdow*, 542 U.S. 1, 50 (2004) (Thomas, J., concurring).

21. Steven K. Green, "Federalism and the Establishment Clause: A Reassessment," *Creighton Law Review* 38 (June 2005): 794.

22. Douglas Laycock, "'Nonpreferential' Aid to Religion: A False Claim About Original Intent," *William and Mary Law Review* 27 (1985–1986): 917.

23. The only proposals that are arguably close to expressing concerns about protecting state arrangements with religion came from New Hampshire and Pennsylvania. New Hampshire, one of the three states with active establishments, proposed that "Congress shall make no Laws touching Religion, or to infringe the rights of Conscience," language similar to that offered later by Congressman Samuel Livingston during the House debate on the Religion Clauses. There is no legislative history of the proposal to explain whether its purpose was to protect its existing establishment from federal interference. The other "federalism" sounding proposal came from Pennsylvania, a state *without* a religious assessment, which called for an amendment to deprive the federal government of authority to "alter, abrogate, or infringe any part of the constitutions of the several states, which provide for the preservation of liberty in matters of religion," hardly a ringing endorsement of existing religious establishments. See Cogan, ed., *The Complete Bill of Rights*, 12.

24. Isaac Backus, "A History of New England (1774–75)," in *The Founders' Constitution*, Philip B. Kurland and Ralph Lerner, eds., vol. 5, First Amendment, Document 21 (Chicago, University of Chicago Press, 1987), 65.

25. Leonard W. Levy, *Judgments: Essays on American Constitutional History* (Chicago: Quadrangle Books, 1972), 175.

26. See generally 2 Elliott, *Debates*.

27. Scholars generally acknowledge that the drafters of the religion clauses were motivated in part by a desire to leave religious matters to the states. See Derek H. Davis, *Religion and the Continental Congress 1774–1789* (New York: Oxford University Press, 2000), 117-135; Laurence H. Tribe, *American Constitutional Law*, 2nd ed., § 14-3, at 1161 (Mineola, N.Y.: The Foundation Press, 1988); Douglas Laycock, "A Survey of Religious Liberty in the United States" *Ohio State Law Journal* 47 (1986): 409, 416; William Van Alstyne, "Trends in the Supreme Court: Mr. Jefferson's Crumbling Wall—A Comment on *Lynch v. Donnelly*," *Duke Law Journal* 1984 (1984): 770, 773.

28. Thomas J. Curry, *The First Freedoms: Church and State in America to the Passage for the First Amendment* (New York: Oxford University Press, 1986), 217. Accord Laycock,

"'Nonpreferential' Aid," 917. "[T]ax support for churches was deeply controversial and widely thought inconsistent with religious liberty."

29. See James Madison's *Detached Memoranda* (1832) in 5 *Founders' Constitution*, 103-104.

30. Madison's *Memorial and Remonstrance* ¶ 5.

31. See Jefferson's *Act for Establishing Religious Freedom* (1786). See also Madison's *Memorial and Remonstrance* ¶ 7: "Experience witnessseth that ecclesiastical establishments, instead of maintaining the purity and efficacy of religion, have had a contrary operation."

32. *Memorial and Remonstrance* ¶ 8.

33. *Memorial and Remonstrance* ¶ 4, quoting the Virginia Declaration of Rights, Article XVI. Establishments "degrade[ ] from the equal rank of citizens all those whose opinions in religion do not bend to the legislative authority." ¶ 9.

34. Curry, *First Freedoms*, 222.

35. *McCollum v. Board of Education*, 333 U.S. 203, 213 (1948) (opinion of Frankfurter); Michael Kammen, *A Machine That Would Go of Itself: The Constitution in American Culture* (New York: Alfred A. Knopf, 1986).

## Chapter 3

1. See, e.g., Richard H. Fallon, Jr., "How to Choose a Constitutional Theory," *California Law Review* 87 (1999): 535; Lawrence Lessig, "The Puzzling Persistence of Bellbottom Theory: What a Constitutional Theory Should Be," *Georgetown Law Journal* 85 (1997): 1837; Howard Gilman, "The Collapse of Constitutional Originalism and the Rise of the Notion of the 'Living Constitution' in the Course of American State-Building," *Studies in American Political Development* 11 (1997); William H. Rehnquist, "The Notion of a Living Constitution," *Texas Law Review* 54 (1976): 695; Michael W. McConnell, "The Importance of Humility in Judicial Review: A Comment on Ronald Dworkin's 'Moral Reading' of the Constitution," *Fordham Law Review* 65 (1997): 1269; Ronald Dworkin, *A Matter of Principle* (Cambridge: Harvard University Press, 1985); Michael J. Perry, *The Constitution in the Courts* (New York: Oxford University Press, 1994).

2. Cass R. Sunstein, *Radicals in Robes: Why Extreme Right-Wing Courts Are Wrong for America* (New York: Basic Books, 2005), 26.

3. Justice Scalia has described himself as a "faint-hearted originalist." Antonin Scalia, "Originalism: The Lesser Evil," *University of Cincinnati Law Review* 57 (1989): 849. Scalia has said that originalism, "[i]n its undiluted form, at least . . . is medicine that seems too strong to swallow." Ibid., 861. So Justice Scalia argues for a strong role for precedent, even when it is inconsistent with original meaning. And he argues for other limiting principles on the concept of originalism:

> [S]tare decisis alone is not enough to prevent originalism from being what many would consider too bitter a bill. What if some state should enact a new law providing public lashing, or branding of the right hand, as punishment for certain criminal offenses? Even if it could be demonstrated unequivocally that these were not cruel and unusual measures in 1791, and even though no prior Supreme Court decision has specifically disapproved them, I doubt whether any federal judge—even among the many who consider themselves originalists—would sustain them against an [E]ighth [A]mendment challenge. . . .

I hasten to confess that in a crunch I may prove a faint-hearted originalist. I cannot imagine myself, any more than any other federal judge, upholding a statute that imposes the punishment of flogging. Scalia, "Originalism," 861, 864.

Scalia adds: "[T]he fact that most originalists are faint-hearted and most nonoriginalists are moderate (that is, would not ascribe evolving content to such clear provisions as the requirement that the President be no less than thirty-five years of age) [explains] the fact that the sharp divergence between the two philosophies does not produce an equivalently sharp divergence in judicial opinions." Scalia, "Originalism," 862.

Based on this commentary, some have concluded that Justice Scalia is not an originalist. See, e.g., Randy E. Barnett, "Scalia's Infidelity: A Critique of 'Faint-Hearted' Originialism," *University of Cinncinati Law Review* 75 (2006): 7.

4.  *McCreary v. ACLU of Kentucky*, 545 U.S. 844 (2005).
5.  Kent Greenawalt, "Originalism and The Religion Clauses: A Response to Professor George," *Loyola Los Angeles Law Review* 32 (1998): 51, 52.
6.  Stephen Breyer, *Active Liberty: Interpreting our Democratic Constitution* (New York: Alfred A. Knopf, 2005), 3.
7.  Breyer, *Active Liberty*, 5.
8.  Breyer, *Active Liberty*, 120.
9.  Breyer, *Active Liberty*, 122.
10. Breyer, *Active Liberty*, 122-124.
11. Breyer, *Active Liberty*, 122-124.
12. Breyer, *Active Liberty*, 116.
13. Breyer, *Active Liberty*, 118.
14. Breyer, *Active Liberty*, 118-119.
15. Breyer, *Active Liberty*, 120.
16. Breyer, *Active Liberty*, 127.
17. Breyer, *Active Liberty*, 124.
18. Breyer, *Active Liberty*, 127.
19. Sunstein, *Radicals in Robes*, 38.
20. Sunstein, *Radicals in Robes*, 72.
21. Breyer, *Active Liberty*, 129.
22. Sunstein, *Radicals in Robes*, 63.
23. Sunstein, *Radicals in Robes*, 63.
24. Sunstein, *Radicals in Robes*, 65.
25. Breyer, *Active Liberty*, 5.
26. Breyer, *Active Liberty*, 6.
27. Sunstein, *Radicals in Robes*, 32.
28. Sunstein, *Radicals in Robes*, 32.
29. *Abington Township School District v. Schempp*, 374 U.S. 203, 237-242 (1963) (Brennan, concurring).
30. Robert H. Bork, "Neutral Principles and Some First Amendment Problems," *Indiana Law Journal* 47 (1971): 10.
31. Sunstein, *Radicals in Robes*, 40.
32. Jack M. Balkin, Draft of *Original Meaning and Constitutional Redemption*, 2, which may be found at http://papers.ssrn.com/sol3/papers.cfm?abstract_id=987060.
33. Balkin, Draft of *Original Meaning*, 2.

34. Michael W. McConnell, "The Origins and Historical Understanding of Free Exercise of Religion," *Harvard Law Review* 103 (1990): 1409, 1415.
35. *Everson v. Board of Education*, 330 U.S. 1, 33 (1947) (Rutledge, J., dissenting).
36. See, e.g., Robert L. Cord, *Separation of Church and State: Historical Fact and Current Fiction* (New York: Lambeth Press, 1982), 20-23; Rodney Smith, "Getting Off on the Wrong Foot and Back on Again: A Reexamination of the History of the Framing of the Religion Clauses of the First Amendment and a Critique of the *Reynolds* and *Everson* Decisions," *Wake Forest Law Review* 20 (1984): 569, 590-591.
37. *Wallace v. Jaffree*, 472 U.S. 38, 106 (1985) (Rehnquist, J., dissenting).
38. Douglas Laycock, "'Nonpreferential' Aid to Religion: A False Claim About Original Intent," *William and Mary Law Review* 27 (1985–1986): 875-923.
39. Laycock, "Nonpreferential Aid to Religion: A False Claim About Original Intent," 875, 877-879 (footnotes omitted).
40. See, e.g., Douglas Laycock, "The Underlying Unity of Separation and Neutrality," *Emory Law Journal* 46 (1997): 43. See also the section below entitled, "No-Aid Separation" v. "Evenhanded Neutrality."
41. U.S. Constitution, amend. 14, sec. 1.
42. *Cantwell v. Connecticut*, 310 U.S. 296 (1940).
43. *Everson v. Board of Education*, 330 U.S. 1, 14-15 (1947).
44. John Witte, Jr., *Religion and The American Constitutional Experiment: Essential Rights and Liberties* (Boulder, Colo.: Westview Press, 2000), 115.
45. Steven K. Green, "Federalism and The Establishment Clause: A Reassessment," *Creighton Law Review* 38 (2005): 761 (hereinafter "A Reassessment").
46. Green, "A Reassessment," 761 (footnotes omitted).
47. *Elk Grove Unified School District v. Newdow*, 542 U.S. 1, 49-51 (2004) (Thomas, J., concurring in the judgment).
48. Green, "A Reassessment," 767.
49. See Kurt T. Lash, "The Second Adoption of the Free Exercise Clause: Religious Exemptions Under the Fourteenth Amendment," *Northwestern University Law Review* 88 (1994): 1106; "The Second Adoption of the Establishment Clause: The Rise of the Nonestablishment Principle," *Arizona State Law Journal* 27 (1995): 1085.
50. Ira C. Lupu and Robert Tuttle, "The Distinctive Place of Religious Entities in Our Constitutional Order," *Villanova Law Review* 47 (2002): 37, 38-39.
51. Philip B. Kurland, "Of Church and State and the Supreme Court," *University of Chicago Law Review* 29 (1961): 1, 96.
52. See *Employment Division of Oregon v. Smith*, 494 U.S. 872 (1990).
53. See Laycock, "Underlying Unity of Separation," 43; Steven K. Green, "Of (Un)Equal Jurisprudential Pedigree: Rectifying the Imbalance Between Neutrality and Separationism," *Boston College Law Review* 43 (2002): 1111.
54. *Everson*, 330 U.S., 9.
55. Laycock, "Underlying Unity of Separation," 43, 53. Laycock refers to the theory that is here called "evenhanded neutrality" as the "nondiscrimination" theory.
56. *Mitchell v. Helms*, 530 U.S. 793, 809 (2000) (plurality opinion).
57. *Mitchell*, 530 U.S., 885. Souter further explained: "The insufficiency of evenhandedness neutrality as a stand-alone criterion of constitutional intent or effect has been clear from the beginning of our interpretative efforts, for an obvious reason. Evenhandedness in distributing a benefit approaches the equivalence of constitutionality in this area only

when the term refers to such universality of distribution that it makes no sense to think of the benefit as going to any discrete group. Conversely, when evenhandedness refers to distribution to limited groups within society, like groups of schools or schoolchildren, it does make sense to regard the benefit as aid to the recipients" (ibid., 884).

58.  *Mitchell*, 530 U.S., 828-829 (Thomas, plurality opinion).
59.  *Mitchell*, 530 U.S., 913.
60.  *Zelman v. Simmons-Harris*, 536 U.S. 639 (2002).
61.  *Police Department v. Mosley*, 408 U.S. 92 (1972).
62.  *United States v. Playboy Entertainment Group, Inc.*, 529 U.S. 803 (2000).
63.  *Widmar v. Vincent*, 454 U.S. 263 (1981).
64.  *Lamb's Chapel v. Center Moriches Union Free School District* 508 U.S. 384, 394 (1993).
65.  *Rosenberger v. Rector of the University of Virginia*, 515 U.S. 819, 831 (1995).
66.  *Wisconsin v. Yoder*, 406 U.S. 205(1972).
67.  *Sherbert v. Verner*, 374 U.S. 398 (1963).
68.  *Employment Division of Oregon v. Smith*, 494 U.S. 872 (1990).
69.  397 U.S. 664.
70.  *Church of Jesus Christ of Latter-day Saints v. Amos*, 483 U.S. 327, 335 (1987).
71.  *Cutter v. Wilkinson*, 544 U.S. 709 (2005).
72.  *Cutter*, 544 U.S., 720.
73.  *Thornton v. Caldor*, 472 U.S. 703, 709 (1985).
74.  *Cutter*, 544 U.S., 723-724.
75.  *Larsen v. Valente*, 456 U.S. 228 (1982).
76.  *Amos*, 483 U.S., 337. Religious autonomy—the right of religious communities to be largely free from governmental intrusion—is another constitutional value that clearly draws on both religion clauses. When the government steers clear of regulating clergy and their work, for example, it not only allows religion to be exercised freely, it also avoids creating excessive entanglements between religion and government, a value embodied by the Establishment Clause.
77.  *Cutter*, 544 U.S., 719.
78.  *Locke v. Davey*, 540 U.S. 712 (2004).
79.  *Locke*, 540 U.S., 725.
80.  *Cutter*, 544 U.S., 719.


## CHAPTER 4

1.  Sometimes called Hinayana Buddhism.
2.  133 U.S. 333, 342 (1890).
3.  283 U.S. 605, 633-634 (1931).
4.  367 U.S. 488, 495 (1961).
5.  367 U.S., 495, n. 11.
6.  It is interesting to note, however, that a later lower court opinion suggested that the *Torcaso* Court's references to "Ethical Culture" and "Secular Humanism" were not quite as broad as they might seem. Apparently both references were to specific organizations that had been found to be "religious for tax exemption purposes primarily because of their organizational similarity to traditional American church groups." *Malnak v. Yogi*, 592 F.2d 197, 206 (1979) (J. Adams, concurring). Ethical Culture reportedly referred to an organization that "held regular Sunday services and espoused a group of defined moral

precepts." Ibid., 206. This same court said that Secular Humanism, "however broad the term may sound, appears to be no more than a reference to the group . . . which, although non-Theist in belief, also met weekly on Sundays and functioned much like a church." Ibid.

7. 380 U.S. 163 (1965). For interesting and readable biographical sketches of Daniel Seeger and explanations of his case, see Peter Irons, *The Courage of Their Convictions* (New York: The Free Press, 1988), 153-178 and George Thomas, "Daniel Seeger: The Meaning of Pacifism," in Melvin I. Urofsky, ed., *100 Americans Making Constitutional History: A Biographical History* (Washington, D.C.: CQ Press, 2004), 182-184.

8. 40 *Statutes at Large* 76, § 4.

9. 54 *Statutes at Large* 885, 889 § 5(g).

10. 62 *Statutes at Large* 604, 612-623 § 6(j).

11. 380 U.S. 163, 166-169.

12. 380 U.S., 175 (emphasis in original).

13. 380 U.S., 176, 184.

14. 380 U.S., 185-186.

15. All citations 380 U.S., 179-183.

16. 380 U.S., 183.

17. 380 U.S., 184-185.

18. 81 *Statutes at Large* 100, 104 § (7).

19. 398 U.S. 333 (1970).

20. 398 U.S., 341.

21. 398 U.S., 339-340.

22. 398 U.S., 342-344.

23. 322 U.S. 78 (1944).

24. 322 U.S., 86-87.

25. 450 U.S. 707 (1981).

26. 450 U.S., 713-714.

27. 450 U.S., 715.

28. 450 U.S., 715-716.

29. 406 U.S. 205 (1972).

30. 406 U.S., 215-216.

31. 592 F.2d 197 (3rd Cir. 1979).

32. 592 F.2d, 200-215.

33. 592 F.2d, 207-208.

34. 592 F.2d, 208-210.

35. Kent Greenawalt, "Religion as a Concept in Constitutional Law," *California Law Review* 72 (1984): 753.

36. Greenawalt, "Religion as a Concept in Constitutional Law," 762-764 (footnotes omitted).

37. 655 F. Supp. 939 (S.D. Ala. 1987), *rev'd*, 827 F.2d 684 (11th Cir. 1987).

38. 655 F. Supp., 986.

39. 655 F. Supp., 967-968.

40. 655 F. Supp., 988.

41. 827 F.2d 684 (11th Cir. 1987).

42. For an overview and analysis of other cases in which it was alleged that the public schools were teaching secular humanism as a religion, see Ronald B. Flowers, "They Got Our Attention, Didn't They? The Tennessee and Alabama Schoolbook Cases," *Religion and Public Education* 15 (Summer 1988): 262-285.

43. John Witte, Jr. *Religion and the American Constitutional Experiment: Essential Rights and Liberties,* (Boulder, Colo.: Westview Press, 2000), 205-206. Indeed, Witte claims that this and most procedures for defining religion are used in tax exemption cases. See pages 202-215.

44. See "Churches Defined" Internal Revenue Service Web Site at http://www.irs.gov/charities/churches/article/0,,id=155746,00.html. See also Jerome Kurtz, "Difficult Definitional Problems in Tax Administration: Religion and Race," *Catholic Lawyer* 23 (1978): 301, 304; *Spiritual Outreach Society v. Commissioner*, 927 F.2d 335 (8th Cir. 1991).

45. Witte, *Religion and the American Constitutional Experiment*, 229-230 (endnotes excluded).

46. Greenawalt, "Religion as a Concept," 753.

## Chapter 5

1. Article III, section 2.
2. 262 U.S. 447 (1923)
3. 342 U.S., 397.
4. Article I, section 8, [1]: "The Congress shall have Power To lay and collect Taxes, Duties, Imposts and Excises, to pay the Debts and provide for the common Defence and general Welfare of the United States; . . ."
5. Chief Justice John Roberts, "Commencement Address at Georgetown University Law Center" (May 21, 2006) (a podcast of the address may be found at http://www.law.georgetown.edu/webcast/eventDetail.cfm?eventID=144); Hope Yen, "Roberts Seeks Greater Consensus on Court," *The Washington Post* (May 21, 2006); E. J. Dionne, "The Chief Justice Sets a Standard," *The Washington Post* (June 20, 2006).

## Chapter 6

1. Cogan, ed., *The Complete Bill of Rights*, 16, 22.
2. Thomas Jefferson, *Notes on the State of Virginia*, published in 1781, Merrill D. Peterson, ed. (New York: Library of America, Literary Classics of the United States, 1984), 285.
3. Carl H. Esbeck, "A Restatement of the Supreme Court's Law of Religious Freedom: Coherence, Conflict, or Chaos?" *Notre Dame Law Review* 70 (1995): 581, 592.
4. 98 U.S. 145 (1879).
5. Irwin Altman, "Polygamous Family Life: The Case of Contemporary Mormon Fundamentalists," *Utah Law Review* 1996 (1996): 267, 370.
6. "The exact percentage of Latter-day Saints who participated in the practice is not known, but studies suggest a maximum of from 20% to 25% of LDS adults were members of polygamous households. At its height, plural marriage probably involved only a third of the women reaching marriageable age—though among Church leadership plural marriage was the norm for a time." Daniel Bachman and Ronald K. Esplin, "Plural Marriage," in Daniel H. Ludlow, ed., *Encyclopedia of Mormonism: The History, Scripture, Doctrine, and Procedure of the Church of Jesus Christ of Latter-day Saints*, vol. 3 (New York: Macmillan Publishing Company, 1992), 1095. See generally Sarah Barringer Gordon, *The Mormon Question: Polygamy and Constitutional Conflict in Nineteenth Century America* (Chapel Hill: University of North Carolina Press, 2002).
7. 12 *Statutes at Large*, 501-502.
8. 133 U.S 333 (1890).

9.    262 U.S. 390 (1923).

10.   34 *Statutes at Large*, 596.

11.   279 U.S. 644 (1929).

12.   283 U.S. 636 (1931).

13.   283 U.S. 605 (1931).

14.   328 U.S. 61 (1946).

15.   293 U.S. 245 (1934).

16.   John E. Mulder and Marvin Comisky, "Jehovah's Witnesses Mold Constitutional Law," *The Bill of Rights Review* 2 (1942): 262. That evaluation has been echoed by later commentators. For extensive treatment of Witnesses' litigation activity and their contribution, see Merlin Owen Newton, *Armed with the Constitution: Jehovah's Witnesses in Alabama and the U.S. Supreme Court, 1939–1946* (Tuscaloosa: University of Alabama Press, 1995) and Shawn Francis Peters, *Judging Jehovah's Witnesses: Religious Persecution and the Dawn of the Rights Revolution* (Lawrence: University Press of Kansas, 2000).

17.   310 U.S. 296 (1940).

18.   249 U.S. 47 (1919).

19.   310 U.S. 586 (1940).

20.   Exodus 20:3-5.

21.   319 U.S. 624 (1943).

22.   Justices Hugo Black, William Douglas, and Frank Murphy in their dissent in *Jones v. Opelika*, 316 U.S. 584, 623-624 (1942).

23.   For more background on the pledge cases, see Richard J. Ellis, *To the Flag: The Unlikely History of the Pledge of Allegiance* (Lawrence: University Press of Kansas, 2005). See also Dan Seligman, "From *Gobitis* to *Barnette*: A Primer," *The Supreme Court Historical Society Quarterly* 27 (Number 2, 2006): 7-9, which contains statements from the Barnette sisters, who were the plaintiffs in the case that bears their name.

24.   494 U.S. 872 (1990).

25.   321 U.S. 158 (1944).

26.   321 U.S., 162.

27.   278 F. Supp. 488 (W.D. Wash. 1967), *aff'd, per curiam*, 390 U.S. 598 (1968).

28.   167 U.S. 43 (1897).

29.   162 Mass. 510, 511 (1895).

30.   319 U.S. 105 (1943).

31.   536 U.S. 150 (2002).

32.   312 U.S. 569 (1941).

33.   450 U.S. 640 (1981).

34.   505 U.S. 672 (1992).

## CHAPTER 7

1.    366 U.S. 599, 605 (1961).

2.    366 U.S., 616.

3.    See Robert H. Keller, Jr., *American Protestantism and United States Indian Policy, 1869–88* (Lincoln: University of Nebraska Press, 1983); Francis Paul Prucha, *American Indian Policy in Crisis: Christian Reformers and the Indian, 1865–1900* (Norman: University of Oklahoma Press, 1976).

## CHAPTER 8

1. *You Vang Yang v. Sturner*, 750 F. Supp. 558 (D.R.I. 1990), recalling prior opinion at 728 F. Supp. 845 (D.R.I. 1990).
2. *Minnesota v. Hershberger*, 444 N.W. 2d 282 (Minn. 1989).
3. *Minnesota v. Hershberger*, 462 N.W. 2d 393 (Minn. 1990)
4. See Douglas Laycock, "Theology Scholarship, the Pledge of Allegiance, and Religious Liberty: Avoiding the Extremes But Missing the Liberty," *Harvard Law Review* 118 (2004): 155, 211-212. Here is the list of citations that Laycock provides to these state RFRAs (n. 368):

   See Ariz. Rev. Stat. Ann. 41-1493 to -1493.02 (West 2004); Conn. Gen. Stat. Ann. 52-571b (West Supp. 2004); Fla. Stat. Ann. 761.01-.05 (West Supp. 2004); Idaho Code 73-401 to -404 (Michie Supp. 2004); 775 Ill. Comp. Stat. Ann. 35/1-99 (West 2001 & Supp. 2004); Mo. Ann. Stat. 1.302-.307 (West Supp. 2004); N.M. Stat. Ann. 28-22-1 to 28-22-5 (Michie Supp. 2000); Okla. Stat. Ann. tit. 51, 251-258 (West Supp. 2004); 71 Pa. Cons. Stat. Ann. 2401-2407 (West Supp. 2004); R.I. Gen. Laws 42-80.1-1 to -4 (1998); S.C. Code Ann. 1-32-10 to -60 (West Supp. 2003); Tex. Civ. Prac. & Rem. Code Ann. 110.001-.012 (West Supp. 2004).

5. Laycock, "Theology Scholarship," n. 369. The citation for this provision is Ala. Const. amend. 622.

## CHAPTER 9

1. William G. Ross, "*Jones v. Wolf* 443 U.S. 595 (1979)," in Paul Finkelman, ed. *Religion and American Law: An Encyclopedia* (New York: Garland Publishing, 2000), 256-257.

## CHAPTER 10

1. In 1998 the Federal Communications Commission amended its rule to conform with the broader religious exemption contained in Title VII. 47 C.F.R. § 2080 now provides: "Religious radio broadcasters may establish religious belief or affiliation as a job qualification for all station employees. However, they cannot discriminate on the basis of race, color, national origin or gender from among those who share their religious affiliation or belief. For purposes of this rule, a religious broadcaster is a licensee which is, or is closely affiliated with, a church, synagogue, or other religious entity, including a subsidiary of such an entity."
2. *Fisk v. United Methodist Children's Home*, 547 F. Supp. 286 (E.D. Va. 1982), *aff'd*, 709 F.2d 284 (4th Cir. 1983).
3. *EEOC v. Townley Engineering and Manufacturing Co.*, 859 F.2d 610 (9th Cir. 1988).
4. See *NLRB v. Kemmerer Village*, 907 F.2d 661 (7th Cir. 1990); *NLRB v. Salvation Army*, 763 F.2d 1 (1st Cir. 1985); *Volunteers of America v. NLRB*, 752 F.2d 345 (8th Cir. 1985); *Denver Post of Volunteers of America v. NLRB*, 732 F.2d 769 (10th Cir. 1984); *St. Elizabeth Community Hospital v. NLRB*, 708 F.2d 1436 (9th Cir. 1983); *Tressler Lutheran Home v. NLRB*, 677 F.2d 302 (3rd Cir. 1982); *NLRB v. St. Louis Christian Home*, 663 F.2d 60 (8th Cir. 1981).
5. See 29 U.S.C. § 203(r) and § 203(s)(5).
6. See *Dole v. Shenandoah Baptist Church*, 889 F.2d 1389, 1394-95 (4th Cir. 1990); *EEOC v. Freemont Christian School*, 781 F.2d 1362, 1367 (9th Cir. 1986).

7.  See *Gellington v. Christian Methodist Episcopal Church*, 203 F.3d 1299 (11th Cir. 2000) (barring retaliation claim by clergy); *Combs v. Central Texas Annual Conference United Methodist Church*, 173 F.3d 343 (5th Cir. 1999) (barring sex discrimination claim of female clergy applicant); *EEOC v. Catholic University*, 83 F.3d 455 (D.C. Cir. 1996) (barring sex discrimination claim of theology professor); *Young v. Northern Illinois Conference of United Methodist Church*, 21 F.3d 184 (7th Cir. 1994) (barring sex and race discrimination claim of female pastoral applicant); *Rayburn*, 772 F.2d, 1170-1171 (same).

8.  *EEOC v. Mississippi College*, 626 F.2d 477, 485 (5th Cir. 1980).

9.  *Bollard v. California Province of the Society of Jesus*, 196 F.3d 940, 946 (9th Cir. 1999) ("A church must retain unfettered freedom in its choice of ministers because ministers represent the church to the people. . . . Indeed, the ministerial relationship lies so close to the heart of the church that it would offend the Free Exercise Clause simply to require the church to articulate a religious justification for its personnel decisions"). Accord *Rayburn*, 772 F.2d, 1168 ("[a]ny attempt by government to restrict a church's free choice of its leaders thus constitutes a burden on the church's free exercise rights").

10. *EEOC v. Catholic University*, 83 F.3d, 461.


## CHAPTER 11

1.  "Thoughts Upon the Mode of Education Proper in a Republic" (Philadelphia, 1786), reprinted in Frederick Rudolph, ed., *Essays on Education in the Early Republic* (Cambridge: The Belknap Press of Harvard University Press, 1965), 10.

2.  "Bill for the More General Diffusion of Knowledge" (1779), quoted in Roy Honeywell, *The Educational Work of Thomas Jefferson* (Cambridge: Harvard University Press, 1931), 199.

3.  See Noah Feldman, "Non-Sectarianism Reconsidered," *Journal of Law and Politics* 18 (2002): 65, 66. ("Over the course of the nineteenth century, most Americans came to believe that the great purpose of separating church and state was to accommodate religious heterogeneity by keeping government in a posture that came to be called 'non-sectarian.' Non-sectarianism, it was thought, would keep the state out of bitter inter-denominational disputes, enable the flourishing of diverse voluntary, private churches, and simultaneously enable the state to take a stance in favor of broadly shared, foundational Christian values.")

4.  330 U.S. 1 (1947).

5.  330 U.S., 15-16.

6.  *The Papers of Thomas Jefferson*, vol. 2, ed. Julian P. Boyd (Princeton: Princeton University Press, 1950– ), 545-546.

7.  530 U.S. 793, 829 (2000).

8.  540 U.S. 712 (2004).

9.  Symposium: "Separation of Church and States: An Examination of State Constitutional Limits on Government Funding for Religious Institutions," *First Amendment Law Review* 2 (Winter 2003).

10. 403 U.S. 602 (1971).

11. 473 U.S. 373 (1985).

12. 521 U.S. 203 (1997).

13. 421 U.S. 349 (1975).
14. 413 U.S. 756 (1973).
15. 281 U.S. 370 (1930).
16. 281 U.S., 374-375.
17. 281 U.S., 375.
18. 310 U.S. 296 (1940).
19. William Shakespeare, *The Tempest*. Act II, scene 1, lines 253-254.
20. 392 U.S. 236 (1968).
21. 392 U.S., 238, 242.
22. 374 U.S. 203, 222 (1963).
23. 392 U.S. 236, 243-244.
24. 392 U.S., 244-248.
25. 392 U.S., 249.
26. 392 U.S., 257-258, 260.
27. 392 U.S., 252-254.
28. 392 U.S., 271, 272.
29. 413 U.S. 812 (1973).
30. 421 U.S. 349 (1975).
31. 421 U.S., 363.
32. 421 U.S., 363, 365.
33. 421 U.S., 366.
34. 421 U.S., 370-372.
35. 433 U.S. 229 (1977).
36. 433 U.S., 244.
37. 433 U.S., 247.
38. 433 U.S., 250.
39. 433 U.S., 252-255.
40. Among the courses offered were arts and crafts, home economics, Spanish, gymnastics, yearbook production, drama, newspaper, humanities, chess, model building, and nature appreciation.

## CHAPTER 12

1. Milton Freidman, *Capitalism and Freedom* (Chicago: University of Chicago Press, 1962); John E. Chubb and Terry M. Moe, *Politics, Markets & America's Schools* (Washington, D.C.: Brookings Institution, 1990).
2. 473 U.S. 402 (1985).
3. "The principle that the state should not become too closely entangled with the church in the administration of assistance is rooted in two concerns. When the state becomes enmeshed with a given denomination in matters of religious significance, the freedom of religious belief of those who are not adherents of that denomination suffers, even when the governmental purpose underlying the involvement is largely secular. In addition, the freedom of even the adherents of the denomination is limited by the government intrusion into sacred matters. '[T]he First Amendment rests upon the premise that both religion and government can best work to achieve their lofty aims if each is left free from the other within its respective sphere.'" 473 U.S., 409-410 (quoting *McCollum v. Board of Education* [1948]).

## CHAPTER 14

1. See Ronald G. Walters, *American Reformers, 1815–1860* (New York: Hill and Wang, 1978); David J. Rothman, *The Discovery of the Asylum: Social Order and Disorder in the New Republic* (Boston: Little Brown, 1971).

2. Stephen V. Monsma, "The 'Pervasively Sectarian' Standard in Theory and Practice," *Notre Dame Journal of Law, Ethics & Public Policy* 13 (1999): 321, 322 (documenting a "lively, continuing partnership between government and nonprofit service organizations, including faith-based ones"); The Aspen Institute Nonprofit Sector Research Fund, "Religion-Sponsored Social Service Providers: The Not-So-Independent Sector" (1997): 23-31, 48-50.

3. See Catholic Charities USA "1997 Annual Report," 24-25. Interestingly, that percentage has not increased but has gone down slightly since the enactment of Charitable Choice. See Catholic Charities USA "1999 Annual Report," 21 (noting that government funds account for 58 percent of Catholic Charities' total budget).

4. The Aspen Institute Nonprofit Sector Research Fund, "Religion-Sponsored Social Service Providers," 23-31, 48-50.

5. The legal and policy implications of Charitable Choice and the Faith-Based Initiative have been discussed in numerous articles and books. A good early source on the various issues raised by the law is Derek Davis and Barry Hankins, eds., *Welfare Reform & Faith-Based Organizations* (Waco, Tex.: J. M. Dawson Institute of Church-State Studies, 1999). A more recent analysis of the Faith-Based Initiative is: Ira C. Lupu and Robert W. Tuttle, "The Faith-Based Initiative and the Constitution," *DePaul Law Review* 55 (2005): 1.

6. It could be said that there are two versions of the pervasively sectarian test. One version considers a number of factors geared toward evaluating how much explicit religious practices and content pervade an entity. The *Roemer v. Board of Public Works* case from the previous chapter is one example of a case in which the Court used this multi-factor version of the pervasively sectarian test. The Charitable Choice provisions and the policies of the George W. Bush administration clearly reject this test.

   Another version of the pervasively sectarian test asks whether the institution may separate out religious activities from secular ones. Interestingly, this version of the test also was employed in the *Roemer v. Board of Public Works* case from the previous chapter, when the Court said: "*Hunt [v. McNair]* requires (1) that no state aid at all go to institutions that are so "pervasively sectarian" that secular activities cannot be separated from sectarian ones, and (2) that if secular activities can be separated out, they alone may be funded." 426 U.S., 755. The provision of the Bush executive order requiring privately funded religious activities to be separated in time or location from the government-funded program echoes this version of the pervasively sectarian test in some ways.

## CHAPTER 15

1. 521 U.S. 203 (1997).
2. 530 U.S. 793 (2000).
3. 536 U.S. 639 (2002).
4. 540 U.S. 712 (2004).
5. 330 U.S. 1 (1947).
6. 421 U.S. 349 (1975).
7. 473 U.S. 402 (1985).
8. 473 U.S. 373 (1985).

9. *Grand Rapids School District v. Ball*, 473 U.S. 373, 385 (1985).

10. *Roemer v. Board of Public Works of Maryland*, 426 U.S. 736, 747 (1976).

11. *Ball*, 473 U.S., 384.

12. Compare: "[New Jersey] cannot exclude . . . the members of any . . . faith, *because of their faith, or lack of it*, from receiving the benefits of public welfare legislation;" with "Neither a state nor the Federal Government can . . . pass laws which aid one religion, aid all religions, or prefer one religion over another." *Everson*, 330 U.S., 15-16.

13. 403 U.S. 602 (1971).

14. As used here, "divertable" means government funds or tangibles that either are not designated for express secular uses or are fungible in nature such that they can be applied toward religious rather than secular uses. See *Mitchell v. Helms*, 530 U.S. 793, 890-895 (2000) (Souter, J., dissenting).

15. 392 U.S. 236 (1968).

16. 433 U.S. 229 (1977).

17. 413 U.S. 756 (1973).

18. 463 U.S. 388 (1983).

19. *Agostini v. Felton*, 521 U.S. 203, 223 (1997).

20. Quite clearly, opposition to funding Catholic education was also a factor behind those decisions to limit government funding to public schools. See Noah Feldman, "Non-Sectarianism Reconsidered," *Journal of Law and Politics* 18 (2002): 65.

21. 175 U.S. 291 (1899).

22. This system is sometimes called "government by proxy," a term coined by political scientist Donald F. Kettl. See Donald F. Kettl, "Performance and Accountability: The Challenge of Government by Proxy for Public Administration," *The American Review of Public Administration* 18 (1988): 9-28.

23. 487 U.S. 589 (1988).

24. *Everson*, 330 U.S., 16.

25. *Walz v. Tax Commission*, 397 U.S. 664, 669 (1970) (referring to a regime of "benevolent neutrality"); *Nyquist*, 413 U.S. 756, 788 (declaring that "our cases require the State to maintain an attitude of 'neutrality,' neither 'advancing' nor 'inhibiting' religion.")

26. *Abington Township School District v. Schempp*, 374 U.S. 203, 223 (1963); *Board of Education v. Mergens*, 496 U.S. 226, 248 (1990).

27. See Frank S. Ravitch, "A Funny Thing Happened on the Way to Neutrality," *Georgia Law Review* 38 (2004): 489 ("There is no independent neutral truth or baseline to which [claims of neutrality] can be tethered."); John T. Valauri, "The Concept of Neutrality in Establishment Clause Jurisprudence," *University of Pittsburgh Law Review* 48 (1986): 83, 92 ("The conceptual complexity, formality, and ambiguity of neutrality are interrelated and mutually reinforcing. They make the concept abstract and incomplete.").

28. *Board of Education v. Allen*, 392 U.S. 236, 249 (1968) (Harlan, J., concurring).

29. *Everson*, 330 U.S., 18 (median); *Epperson v. Arkansas*, 393 U.S. 97, 103-104 (1968) (median and secular); *Tilton v. Richardson*, 403 U.S. 672, 677 (1971) (median); *Board of Education v. Allen*, 392 U.S., 245 (secular); *Meek v. Pittenger*, 421 U.S. 349, 372 (1975) (same); *Mueller v. Allen*, 463 U.S. 388, 401 (1983) (evenhanded); *Zobrest v. Catalina Foothills School District*, 509 U.S. 1, 8-9 (1993) (same). See Justice Souter's discussion in *Mitchell*, 530 U.S., 878-884.

30. See *Mueller*, 463 U.S., 398-399; *Witters v. Washington Department of Services for the Blind*, 474 U.S. 481, 490-491 (1986) (Powell, J., concurring); *Bowen v. Kendrick*, 487 U.S. 589, 608-9 (1988).

31. See *Mergens*, 496 U.S. 226; *Widmar v. Vincent*, 450 U.S. 909 (1981).

32. See *Police Department of Chicago v. Mosely*, 408 U.S. 92 (1972); *Texas v. Johnson*, 491 U.S. 397 (1989); *Simon & Schuster v. New York State Crime Victims Board*, 502 U.S. 105 (1991).

33. *Mueller*, 463 U.S. 388; *Witters*, 474 U.S. 481; *Zobrest*, 509 U.S. 1.

34. *Mueller*, 463 U.S., 398-399.

35. *Mueller*, 463 U.S., 400; *Zobrest*, 509 U.S., 12.

36. *Mueller*, 463 U.S., 402, n. 10; *Witters*, 474 U.S., 488; *Zobrest*, 509 U.S., 10.

37. *Witters*, 474 U.S., 488; *Zobrest*, 509 U.S., 12.

38. *Mueller*, 463 U.S., 399.

39. "[N]o funds traceable to the government ever find their way into sectarian schools' coffers." 509 U.S., 10.

40. *Zobrest*, 509 U.S., 12, 8.

41. *Mitchell*, 530 U.S., 809 (Thomas, J., plurality opinion).

42. "Although the presence of private choice is easier to see when aid literally passes through the hands of individuals . . . there is no reason why the Establishment Clause requires such a form." *Mitchell*, 530 U.S., 816.

    "The issue is not divertibility of aid but rather whether the aid itself has an impermissible content. Where the aid would be suitable for use in a public school, it is also suitable for use in any private school." Ibid., 822.

43. 530 U.S., 837 (O'Connor, J., concurring in the judgment). "Reduced to its essentials, the plurality's rule states that government aid to religious schools does not have the effect of advancing religion so long as the aid is offered on a neutral basis and the aid is secular in content. The plurality also rejects the distinction between direct and indirect aid, and holds that the actual diversion of secular aid by a religious school to the advancement of its religious mission is permissible." Ibid.

44. 530 U.S., 838 (O'Connor, J., concurring in the judgment).

45. According to O'Connor, the Court's earlier holdings touting the importance of neutrality "provide no precedent for the use of public funds to finance religious activities." 530 U.S., 847.

46. *Mitchell*, 530 U.S., 838 (O'Connor, J., concurring in the judgment); *Zelman*, 536 U.S., 669 (O'Connor, J., concurring).

47. Although *Zelman* relied primarily on whether the Cleveland voucher program offered "genuine and independent private choice," the decision also emphasized the program's neutrality: "[T]he Ohio program is neutral in all respects toward religion. It is part of a general and multifaceted undertaking by the State of Ohio to provide educational opportunities to the children of a failed school district. It confers educational assistance directly to a broad class of individuals defined without reference to religion." 536 U.S., 653.

48. *Witters*, 474 U.S., 488.

49. *Mitchell*, 530 U.S., 810.

50. *Zelman*, 536 U.S., 652.

51. See *Hunt v. McNair*, 413 U.S. 734, 743 (1973); *Bowen*, 487 U.S., 610.

52. 530 U.S., 828.

53. "In *Pierce [v. Society of Sisters]*, the Court affirmed the right of private schools to exist and to operate; it said nothing of any supposed right of private or parochial schools to share with public schools in state largesse, on an equal basis or otherwise. It has never been held that if private schools are not given some share of public funds allocated for education that such schools are isolated into a classification violative of the Equal Protection Clause." *Norwood v. Harrison*, 413 U.S. 455, 462 (1973).

## CHAPTER 16

1. *Edwards v. Aguillard*, 482 U.S. 578, 583-584 (1987) (citations omitted).
2. Warren Nord, *Religion and American Education: Rethinking a National Dilemma* (Chapel Hill: University of North Carolina Press, 1995), 71-74 (footnotes omitted).
3. For reading on the public reaction to the Court's school prayer decisions, see Robert S. Alley, *School Prayer: The Court, the Congress, and the First Amendment* (Buffalo, N.Y.: Prometheus Press, 1994); and Steven K. Green, "Evangelicals and the Becker Amendment: A Lesson in Church-State Moderation," *Journal of Church and State* 33 (Summer 1991): 541-567.
4. Green, "Evangelicals and the Becker Amendment," 541-567.

## CHAPTER 17

1. 998 F. Supp. 1255 (M.D. Ala. 1999). One of this book's authors served as co-counsel in *Chandler*.
2. *Chandler v. James*, 180 F.3d 1254 (11th Cir. 1999).
3. 180 F.3d, 1257 (emphasis in original).
4. 180 F.3d, 1258.
5. 180 F.3d, 1258-1259.
6. 180 F.3d, 1259-1260.
7. 180 F.3d, 1260.
8. 180 F.3d, 1263.
9. 180 F.3d, 1264.
10. 180 F.3d, 1265.
11. 180 F.3d, 1265.
12. *Chandler v. Seligman*, 230 F.3d 1313, 1316-17 (11th Cir. 2000).

## CHAPTER 18

1. Charles Haynes and Oliver Thomas, *Finding Common Ground: A Guide to Religious Liberty in Public Schools* (Nashville: First Amendment Center, 2001): 90.
2. (Nashville: First Amendment Center, 1998).
3. www.firstamendmentcenter.org
4. 68 Federal Register 9645 (February 28, 2003). These guidelines also may be found at http://www.ed.gov/policy/gen/guid/religionandschools/prayer_guidance.html.

## CHAPTER 19

1. *Board of Education v Mergens*, 496 U.S. 226, 250 (1990).

## CHAPTER 20

1. *Board of Education v. Mergens*, 496 U.S. 226, 250 (1990).
2. Martin Marty, "The Political Square, Festooned," *Sightings* (December 22. 2003) http://marty-center.uchicago.edu/sightings/archive_2003/1222.shtml.

CHAPTER 21

1. 143 U.S. 457.
2. 143 U.S., 465.
3. 143 U.S., 468.
4. 143 U.S., 470.
5. 143 U.S., 471.
6. 10 U.S.C. § 6031 (2007).
7. Lyman Beecher, *Autobiography*, ed. Barbara M. Cross, vol. 1 (Cambridge: Belknap Press of Harvard University Press, 1961), 261.
8. John Leland, *The Virginia Chronicle: With Judicious and Critical Remarks Under XXIV Heads* 43 (Prentis and Baxter 1790) microformed on Early American Imprints 1639–1800, Fiche 22616 (American Antiquarian Society).
9. Michael Perry, *Religion in Politics: Constitutional and Moral Perspectives* (Oxford University Press, 1997), 32-33 (footnotes omitted). See also Douglas Laycock, "Freedom of Speech That is Both Religious and Political," *University of California Davis Law Review* 29 (1996): 793; Michael McConnell, "Five Reasons to Reject the Claim That Religious Arguments Should be Excluded from Democratic Deliberation," *Utah Law Review* 1999 (1999): 639; Scott Idelman, "Religious Premises, Legislative Judgments, and the Establishment Clause," *Cornell Journal of Law and Public Policy* 12 (2002): 2.
10. Steven G. Gey, "When Is Religious Speech Not 'Free Speech'?" *University of Illinois Law Review* 2000 (2000): 379, 406 (footnotes omitted).
11. Kent Greenawalt, "Religious Liberty and Democratic Politics," *Kentucky Law Review* 23 (1996): 629, 639-640 (footnotes omitted).
12. Elected officials are not subject to many of the workplace rules that are imposed on unelected government employees. Further, for a legislature to enact a law restricting a governor's religious speech would implicate separation of powers concerns. Also, legislators would have a protected right to engage in religious expression based on the "Speech or Debate" clause of Article I, section 6 of the Constitution.
13. See *Garcetti v. Ceballos*, 547 U.S. 410 (2006).


CHAPTER 22

1. *Lynch v. Donnelly*, 465 U.S. 668, 687-688, 690-692 (1984) (O'Connor, J., concurring) (see chapter 17).
2. *Lynch*, 465 U.S., 687-688.
3. *County of Allegheny v. ACLU*, 492 U.S. 573, 593 (1989) (quoting *Wallace v. Jaffree*, 472 U.S. 38, 70 (1985) (O'Connor, J., concurring) (emphasis deleted and added).
4. *Grand Rapids School District v. Ball*, 473 U.S. 373, 391 (1985).
5. *Board of Education of Kiryas Joel Village School Dist. v. Grumet*, 512 U.S. 687, 697 (1994) (quoting *Abington Township School District v. Schempp*, 374 U.S. 203, 222 [1963]).
6. Herbert J. Storing, ed., *The Compete Anti-Federalist*, vol. 4 (Chicago: University of Chicago Press, 1981), 242.
7. Speech of James Iredell, July 30, 1788, reprinted in Bernard Bailyn, ed., *The Debate on the Constitution*, vol. 2 (New York: Library of America, 1993), 903.
8. See Ronald B. Flowers, *Religion in Strange Times: The 1960s and 1970s* (Macon, Ga.: Mercer University Press, 1984), 85-111.

 9.  459 U.S. 116 (1982).
10.  512 U.S. 687 (1994).

## Chapter 23

 1.  343 U.S. 306 (1952).
 2.  343 U.S., 313-315.
 3.  366 U.S. 420 (1961).
 4.  366 U.S., 431.
 5.  366 U.S., 444-445.
 6.  366 U.S., 450-451.
 7.  366 U.S., 452.
 8.  366 U.S., 453.
 9.  366 U.S., 444.
10.  479 U.S. 60 (1986).
11.  479 U.S., 68-69.
12.  479 U.S., 70-71.
13.  479 U.S., 71.
14.  479 U.S., 72-73.
15.  479 U.S., 75.

## Appendix 1

\*   Supplemental Appendix, *Everson v. Board of Education* 330 U.S. 1, 72-74 (1947).
1.   This copy of the Assessment Bill is from one of the handbills which on December 24, 1784, when the third reading of the bill was postponed, were ordered distributed to the Virginia counties by the House of Delegates. See Journal of the Virginia House of Delegates, December 24, 1784; Eckenrode, 102-103. The bill is therefore in its final form, for it never again reached the floor of the House. Eckenrode, 113.

## Appendix 3

\*   Appendix, *Everson v. Board of Education* 330 U.S. 1, 63-72 (1947).

# Selected Bibliography

## Books

### General History

Balmer, Randall, *Thy Kingdom Come, An Evangelical's Lament: How the Religious Right Distorts the Faith and Threatens America*, New York: Basic Books, 2006.

Gaustad, Edwin S., ed., *A Documentary History of Religion in America*, 2 vols., Grand Rapids, Mich.: W. B. Eerdmans, 1982.

Gaustad, Edwin S., *Dissent in American Religion*, Chicago: University of Chicago Press, 1973.

Howe, Mark DeWolf, *The Garden and the Wilderness: Religion and Government in American Constitutional History*, Chicago: University of Chicago Press, 1965.

Irons, Peter, *God On Trial: Dispatches from America's Religious Battlefields*, New York: Viking Press, 2007.

Jacoby, Susan, *Freethinkers: A History of American Secularism*, New York: Henry Holt, 2004.

Levy, Leonard W., *Blasphemy*, New York: Alfred A. Knopf, 1993.

Martin, William, *With God on Our Side: The Rise of the Religious Right in America*, New York: Broadway Books, 1996.

Marty, Martin E., *Religion and Republic: The American Circumstance*, Boston: Beacon Press, 1987.

Noll, Mark A., *One Nation Under God? Christian Faith and Political Action in America*, San Francisco: Harper & Row, 1988.

Noll, Mark A., ed., *Religion & American Politics: From the Colonial Period to the 1980s*, New York: Oxford University Press, 1990.

Stokes, Anson Phelps, *Church and State in the United States*, 3 vols., New York: Harper & Row, Pub., 1950, revised one volume edition with Leo Pfeffer, 1964.

Stout, Cushing, *The New Heavens and New Earth: Political Religion in America*, New York: Harper & Row, Pub., 1984.

Turner, James, *Without God, Without Creed: The Origins of Unbelief in America*, Baltimore: The Johns Hopkins University Press, 1985.

Urofsky, Melvin I. *Religious Freedom: Rights and Liberties under the Law*. Santa Barbara, Calif.: ABC-CLIO, 2002.

Wilson, John F. and Donald L Drakeman, eds., *Church and State in American History*, 3rd ed., Boulder, Colo.: Westview Press, 2003.

Witte, John, Jr., *Religion and the American Constitutional Experiment*, 2nd ed., Boulder, Colo.: Westview Press, 2005.

## THE COLONIAL AND FOUNDING PERIOD

Alley, Robert S., *James Madison on Religious Liberty*, Buffalo: Prometheus Books, 1985.

Brenner, Lenni, ed., *Jefferson & Madison On Separation of Church and State: Writings on Religion and Secularism*, Fort Lee, N.J.: Barracade Books, 2004.

Buckley, Thomas E., *Church and State in Revolutionary Virginia, 1776-1787*, Charlottesville: University of Virginia Press, 1977.

Butler, Jon, *Awash in a Sea of Faith: Christianizing the American People*, Cambridge: Harvard University Press, 1990. .

Curry, Thomas J., *The First Freedoms: Church and State in America to the Passage of the First Amendment*, New York: Oxford University Press, 1986.

Davis, Derek H., *Religion and the Continental Congress, 1774-1789*, New York: Oxford University Press, 2000.

Dreisbach, Daniel L., *Thomas Jefferson and the Wall of Separation between Church and State*, New York: New York University Press, 2002.

Frost, J. William, *A Perfect Freedom: Religious Liberty in Pennsylvania*, New York: Cambridge University Press, 1990.

Gaustad, Edwin S., *Faith of the Founders: Religion and the New Nation 1776-1826*, 2nd ed., Waco, Tex.: Baylor University Press, 2004.

Gunn, T. Jeremy, *A Standard for Repair: The Establishment Clause, Equality, and Natural Rights*, New York: Garland Publishing, Inc., 1992.

Kramnick, Isaac and R. Laurence Moore, *The Godless Constitution: A Moral Defense of the Secular State*, New York: W. W. Norton, 2005.

Levy, Leonard W., *The Establishment Clause: Religion and the First Amendment*, New York: Macmillan, 1986.

McGarvie, Mark Douglas, *One Nation Under Law: America's Early National Struggles to Separate Church and State*, DeKalb: Northern Illinois University Press, 2004.

McLoughlin, William G., *New England Dissent, 1630-1833: The Baptists and the Separation of Church and State*, 2 vols., Cambridge: Harvard University Press, 1971.

McLoughlin, William G., *Soul Liberty: The Baptists' Struggle in New England, 1630-1833*, Hanover, N.H.: University Press of New England, 1991.

Miller, William Lee, *The First Liberty: Religion and the American Republic*, New York: Alfred A. Knopf, 1986.

## THE NINETEENTH CENTURY

Borden, Morton, *Jews, Turks, and Infidels*, Chapel Hill: University of North Carolina Press, 1984.

Carwardine, Richard J., *Evangelicals and Politics in Antebellum America*, New Haven: Yale University Press, 1993.

Dreisbach, Daniel L., *Religion and Politics in the Early Republic*, Lexington, Ky.: University of Kentucky Press, 1996.

Firmage, Edwin Brown and Richard Collin Mangrum, *Zion in the Courts: A Legal History of the Church of Jesus Christ of Latter-day Saints, 1830-1900*, Urbana: University of Illinois Press, 1988.

Glenn, Charles Leslie, Jr., *The Myth of the Common School*, Amherst: University of Massachusetts Press, 1988.

Gordon, Sarah Barringer, *The Mormon Question: Polygamy and Constitutional Conflict in Nineteenth Century America*, Chapel Hill: University of North Carolina Press, 2002.

Hamburger, Philip, *Separation of Church and State*, Cambridge: Harvard University Press, 2002.

Handy, Robert T., *A Christian American: Protestant Hopes and Historical Realities*, 2nd ed., New York: Oxford University Press, 1984.

Handy, Robert T., *Undermined Establishment: Church-State Relations in America 1880-1920*, Princeton: Princeton University Press, 1991.

Hatch, Nathan O., *The Democratization of American Christianity*, New Haven: Yale University Press, 1989.

Jorgenson, Lloyd P., *The State and the Non-Public School 1825-1925*, Columbia, Mo.: University of Missouri Press, 1987.

McAfee, Ward M., *Religion, Race, and Reconstruction: The Public School in the Politics of the 1870s*, Albany: State University of New York Press, 1998.

Noll, Mark A., Nathan O. Hatch and George M. Marsden, *The Search for Christian America*, expanded edition, Colorado Springs: Helmers & Howard, 1989.

Nord, Warren A., *Religion and American Education: Rethinking a National Dilemma*, Chapel Hill, University of North Carolina Press, 1995.

Pratt, John Webb, *Religion, Politics, and Diversity: Church-State Themes in New York History*, Ithaca: Cornell University Press, 1967.

## RELIGION CLAUSE THEORY AND ANALYSIS

Alley, Robert S., *School Prayer: The Court, the Congress, and the First Amendment*, Buffalo: Prometheus Books, 1994.

Audi, Robert, *Religious Commitment and Secular Reason*, New York: Cambridge University Press, 2000.

Bradley, Gerard V., *Church-State Relationships in America*, New York: Greenwood Press, 1987.

Carter, Stephen L., *The Culture of Disbelief: How American Law and Politics Trivialize Religious Devotion*, New York: Basic Books, 1993.

Cord, Robert L., *Separation of Church and State: Historical Fact and Current Fiction*, Grand Rapids, Mich.: Baker Book House, 1988.

Curry, Thomas J., *Farewell to Christendom: The Future of Church and State in America*, New York: Oxford University Press, 2001.

Davis, Derek, *Original Intent: Chief Justice Rehnquist and the Course of American Church/State Relations*, Buffalo: Prometheus Books, 1991.

Davis, Derek and Barry Hankins, eds., *Welfare Reform & Faith-Based Organizations*, Waco, Tex.: J. M. Dawson Institute of Church-State Studies, 1999.

DelFattore, Joan, *The Fourth R: Conflicts over Religion in America's Public Schools*, New Haven: Yale University Press, 2004.

Eisgruber, Christopher L., and Lawrence G. Sager, *Religious Freedom and the Constitution*, Cambridge: Harvard University Press, 2007.

Epps, Garrett, *To an Unknown God: Religious Freedom on Trial*, New York: St. Martin's Press, 2001.

Evans, Bette Novit, *Interpreting the Free Exercise of Religion: The Constitution and American Pluralism*, Chapel Hill: University of North Carolina Press, 1997.

Feldman, Noah, *Divided by God: America's Church-State Problem—And What We Should Do About It*, New York: Farrar, Straus and Giroux, 2005.

Flowers, Ronald B., *That Godless Court? Supreme Court Decisions on Church-State Relationships*, 2nd ed., Louisville, Ky.: Westminster John Knox Press, 2005.

Gedicks, Frederick Mark, *The Rhetoric of Church and State: A Critical Analysis of Religion Clause Jurisprudence*, Durham: Duke University Press, 1995.

Glenn, Charles L., *The Ambiguous Embrace: Government and Faith-Based Schools and Social Agencies*, Princeton: Princeton University Press, 2000.

Greenawalt, Kent, *Does God Belong in Public Schools?*, Princeton: Princeton University Press, 2005.

Greenawalt, Kent, *Private Consciences and Public Reasons*, New York: Oxford University Press, 1995.

Greenawalt, Kent, *Religion and the Constitution*, Princeton: Princeton University Press, 2006.

Greenawalt, Kent, *Religious Convictions and Political Choice*, New York: Oxford University Press, 1988.

Hamilton, Marci A., *God vs. The Gavel: Religion and the Rule of Law*, New York: Cambridge University Press, 2005.

Neuhaus, Richard John, *The Naked Public Square: Religion and Democracy in America*, Grand Rapids, Mich.: W. B. Eerdmans, 1984.

Perry, Michael J., *Love and Power: The Role of Religion and Morality in American Politics*, New York: Oxford University Press, 1991.

Perry, Michael J., *Morality, Politics, & Law*, New York: Oxford University Press, 1988.

Perry, Michael J., *Religion and Politics: Constitutional and Moral Perspectives*, New York: Oxford University Press, 1997.

Perry, Michael J., *Under God? Religious Faith and Liberal Democracy*, New York: Cambridge University Press, 2003.

Pfeffer, God, *Caesar, and the Constitution: The Court as Referee of Church-State Confrontation*, Boston: Beacon Press, 1975.

Ravitch, Frank S., *School Prayer and Discrimination: The Civil Rights of Religious Minorities and Dissenters*, Boston: Northeastern University Press, 1999.

Ryden, David K. and Jeffrey Polet, *Sanctioning Religion? Politics, Law, and Faith-based Public Services.* Boulder, Colo.: Lynne Reinner Publishers 2005.

Smith, Steven D., *Foreordained Failure: The Quest for a Constitutional Principle of Religious Freedom*, New York: Oxford University Press, 1995.

Wills, Garry, *Under God: Religion and American Politics*, New York: Simon and Schuster, 1990.

# Articles

## Religion Clause Theory and Analysis

Berg, Thomas C., "Minority Religions and the Religion Clauses," *Washington University Law Quarterly* 82 (2004): 919-1000.

Brownstein, Alan, "Interpreting the Religion Clauses in Terms of Liberty, Equality, and Free Speech Values—A Critical Analysis of 'Neutrality Theory' and Charitable Choice," *Notre Dame Journal of Law, Ethics & Public Policy* 13 (1999): 243-284.

Brownstein, Alan, "Protecting Religious Liberty: The False Messiahs of Free Speech Doctrine and Formal Neutrality," *Journal of Law & Politics* 18 (2002): 119-213.

Choper, Jesse, "Defining 'Religion' in the First Amendment," *University of Illinois Law Review* (1982): 579-613.

Choper, Jesse H., "The Religion Clauses of the First Amendment: Resolving the Conflict," *University of Pittsburg Law Review* 41 (1980): 673-701.

Conkle, Daniel O., "The Path of American Religious Liberty: From the Original Theology to Formal Neutrality and an Uncertain Future," *Indiana Law Journal* 75 (2000): 1-36.

Esbeck, Carl H., "A Restatement of the Supreme Court's Law of Religious Freedom: Coherence, Conflict, or Chaos?" *Notre Dame Law Review* 70 (1995): 581-650.

Feldman, Noah, "The Intellectual Origins of the Establishment Clause," *New York University Law Review* 77 (2002): 346-428.

Garnett, Richard W., "Assimilation, Toleration, and the State's Interest in the Development of Religious Doctrine," *U.C.L.A. Law Review* 51 (2004): 1645-1701.

Gey, Steven G., "Why is Religion Special?: Reconsidering the Accommodation of Religion Under the Religion Clauses of the First Amendment," *University of Pittsburg Law Review* 52 (1990): 75-187.

Green, Steven K., "Of (Un)Equal Jurisprudential Pedigree: Rectifying the Imbalance Between Neutrality and Separationism," *Boston College Law Review* 43 (2002): 1111-1136.

Green, Steven K., "A 'Spacious Conception': Separationism as an Idea," *Oregon Law Review* 85 (2006): 443-480.

Greene, Abner, "The Political Balance of the Religion Clauses," *Yale Law Journal* 102 (1992): 1611-1643.

Laycock, Douglas, "Formal, Substantive, and Disaggregated Neutrality Toward Religion," *DePaul Law Review* 39 (1990): 993-1018.

Laycock, Douglas, "The Many Meanings of Separation," *University of Chicago Law Review* 70 (2003): 1667-1701.

Laycock, Douglas, "The Underlying Unity of Separation and Neutrality," *Emory Law Journal* 46 (1997): 43-74.

Lupu, Ira C., "To Control Faction and Protect Liberty: A General Theory of the Religion Clauses," *Journal of Contemporary Legal Issues* 7 (1996): 357-384.

Lupu, Ira C. and Robert Tuttle, "The Distinctive Place of Religious Entities in Our Constitutional Order," *Villanova Law Review* 47 (2002): 37-92.

Marshall, William P., "Religion as Ideas: Religion as Identity," *Journal of Contemporary Legal Issues* 7 (1996): 385-406.

Marshall, William P., "Truth and the Religion Clauses," *DePaul Law Review* 43 (1990): 243-268.

McConnell, Michael W., "The Problem of Singling Out Religion," *DePaul Law Review* 50 (Fall 2000): 1-47.

McConnell, Michael W. and Richard Posner, "An Economic Approach to Issues of Religious Freedom," *University of Chicago Law Review* 56 (1989): 1-60.

Sherry, Suzanna, "Enlightening the Religion Clauses," *Journal of Contemporary Legal Issues* 7 (1996): 473-495.

Sullivan, Kathleen M., "Religion and Liberal Democracy," *University of Chicago Law Review* 59 (1992): 195-223.

Underkuffler-Freund, Laura, "The Separation of the Religious and the Secular: A Foundational Challenge to First Amendment Theory," *William and Mary Law Review* 36 (1995): 838-988.

## General History

Eisgruber, Christopher L., "Madison's Wager: Religious Liberty in the Constitutional Order," *Northwestern University Law Review* 89 (1995): 347-410.

Esbeck, Carl H., "Dissent and Disestablishment: The Church-State Settlement in the Early Republic," *B.Y.U. Law Review* (2004): 1385-1592.

Feldman, Noah, "Non-Sectarianism Reconsidered," *Journal of Law and Politics* 18 (2002): 65-117.

Finkelman, Paul, "The Ten Commandments on the Courthouse Lawn and Elsewhere," *Fordham Law Review* 73 (2005): 1477-1520.

Green, Steven K., "'Bad History': The Lure of History in Establishment Clause Adjudication," *Notre Dame Law Review* 81 (2006): 1717-1754.

Green, Steven K., "The Blaine Amendment Reconsidered," *Journal of Legal History* 36 (1992): 38-69.

Green, Steven K., "Federalism and the Establishment Clause: A Reassessment," *Creighton University Law Review* 38 (2005): 761-797.

Green, Steven K., "The Font of Everything Just and Right? The Ten Commandments as a Source of American Law," *Journal of Law and Religion* 14 (1999-2000): 525-558.

Green, Steven K., "Justice David Josiah Brewer and the 'Christian Nation' Maxim," *Albany Law Review* 63 (1999): 427-476.

Greenawalt, Kent, "History as Ideology: Philip Hamburger's Separation of Church and State," *California Law Review* 93 (2005): 367-396.

Hamburger, Philip A., "Constitutional Right of Religious Exemption: An Historical Perspective," *George Washington Law Review* 60 (1992): 915-948.

Jeffries, John C., Jr., and James E. Ryan, "A Political History of the Establishment Clause," *Michigan Law Review* 100 (2001): 279-370.

Kurland, Philip B., "The Irrelevance of the Constitution: The Religion Clauses of the First Amendment and the Supreme Court," *Villanova Law Review* 24 (1979): 3-27.

Lash, Kurt, "The Second Adoption of the Establishment Clause: The Rise of the Non-establishment Principle, *Arizona State Law Journal* 27 (1995): 1085-1154.

Lash, Kurt, "The Second Adoption of the Free Exercise Clause: Religious Exemptions Under the Fourteenth Amendment," *Northwestern Law Review* 88 (1994): 1106-1156.

Laycock, Douglas, "'Nonpreferential' Aid to Religion: A False Claim about Original Intent," *William and Mary Law Review* 27 (1986): 875-923.

McConnell, Michael W., "The Origins and Historical Understanding of Free Exercise of Religion," *Harvard Law Review* 103 (1990): 1409-1517.

Symposium, "Separation of Church and States," *First Amendment Law Review* 2 (2003): 1-197.

## Establishment Clause

Berg, Thomas C., "Vouchers and Religious Schools: The New Constitutional Questions," *University of Cincinnati Law Review* 72 (2003): 151-221.

Blasi, Vincent, "School Vouchers and Religious Liberty: Seven Questions from Madison's Memorial and Remonstrance," Cornell Law Review 87 (2002): 783-819.

Brauer, Matthew J., Barbara Forest & Steven G. Gey, "Is It Science Yet? Intelligent Design Creationism and the Constitution," *Washington University Law Quarterly* 83 (2005): 1-149.

Brownstein, Alan, "Evaluating School Voucher Programs Through a Liberty, Equality, and Free Speech Matrix," *Connecticut Law Review* 31 (1999): 871-943.

Conkle, Daniel, "Toward a General Theory of the Establishment Clause," *Northwestern University Law Review* 82 (1988): 1113-1194.

Epstein, Steven B., "Rethinking the Constitutionality of Ceremonial Deism," *Columbia Law Review* 96 (1996): 2085-2174.

Esbeck, Carl H., "A Constitutional Case for Governmental Cooperation with Faith-Based Social Service Providers," *Emory Law Journal* 46 (1997): 1-41.

Esbeck, Carl, "The Establishment Clause as a Structural Restraint on Governmental Power," *Iowa Law Review* 84 (1998): 1-113.

Esbeck, Carl H., "Government Regulation of Religiously Based Social Services: The First Amendment Considerations," *Hastings Constitutional Law Quarterly* 19 (1992): 343-412.

Feldman, Noah, "From Liberty to Equality: The Transformation of the Establishment Clause," *California Law Review* 90 (2002): 673-731.

Garnett, Richard W., "Religion, Division, and the First Amendment," *Georgetown Law Review* 94 (2006): 1667-1723.

Gedicks, Frederick Mark, "A Two-Track Theory of the Establishment Clause," *Boston College Law Review* 43 (2002): 1071-1109.

Gey, Steven G., "Religious Coercion and the Establishment Clause," *University of Illinois Law Review* (1994): 463-534.

Gilman, Michele Estrin, "'Charitable Choice' and the Accountability Challenge: Reconciling the Need for Regulation with the First Amendment Religion Clauses," *Vanderbilt Law Review* 55 (2002): 799-888.

Green, Steven K., "Locke v. Davey and the Limits to Neutrality Theory," *Temple Law Review* 77 (2004): 913-955.

Green, Steven K., "Religious Discrimination, Public Funding, and Constitutional Values," *Hastings Constitutional Law Quarterly* 30 (2002): 1-55.

Greenawalt, Kent, "Teaching About Religion in the Public Schools," *Journal of Law and Politics,* 18 (Spring 2002): 329.

Hamilton, Marci A., "Power, the Establishment Clause, and Vouchers," *Connecticut Law Review* 31 (1999): 807-844.

Hill, B. Jesse, "Putting Religious Symbolism in Context: A Linguistic Critique of the Endorsement Test," *Michigan Law Review* 104 (2005): 491-545.

Laycock, Douglas, "'Non-coercive' Support for Religion: A False Claim About the Establishment Clause," *Valparaiso University Law Review* 26 (1991): 37-69.

Lupu, Ira C., "The Lingering Death of Separationism," *George Washington Law Review* 62 (1994): 230-279.

Lupu, Ira C., "The Problem with Accommodation," *George Washington Law Review* 60 (1992): 743-781.

Lupu, Ira C. and Robert W. Tuttle, "The Faith-Based Initiative and the Constitution," *DePaul Law Review* 55 (2005): 1-118.

Lupu, Ira C. and Robert W. Tuttle, "Historic Preservation Grants to Houses of Worship: A Case Study in the Survival of Separationism," *Boston College Law Review* 43 (2002): 1139-1176.

Macedo, Stephen, "Constituting Civil Society: School Vouchers, Religious Nonprofit Organizations, and Liberal Public Values," *Chicago-Kent Law Review* 75 (2000): 417-451.

Marshall, William P., "The Limits of Secularism: Public Religious Expression in Moments of National Crisis and Tragedy," *Notre Dame Law Review* 78 (2002): 11-33.

McConnell, Michael W., "Accommodation of Religion," *Supreme Court Review* (1985): 1-59.

McConnell, Michael W., "Coercion: The Lost Element of Establishment," *William and Mary Law Review* 27 (1986): 933-941.

McConnell, Michael W., "Establishment and Disestablishment at the Founding, Part I: Establishment of Religion," *William and Mary Law Review* 44 (2003): 2105-2208.

McConnell, Michael W., "Five Reasons to Reject the Claim That Religious Arguments Should Be Excluded from Democratic Deliberation," *Utah Law Review* (1999): 639-657.

Minow, Martha, "Choice or Commonality: Welfare and Schooling After the End of Welfare As We Knew It," *Duke Law Journal* 49 (1999): 493-558.

Minow, Martha, "Public and Private Partnerships: Accounting for the New Religion," *Harvard Law Review* 116 (2003): 1229-1270.

Ravitch, Frank S., "A Funny Thing Happened on the Way to Neutrality: Broad Principles, Formalism, and the Establishment Clause," *Georgia Law Review* 38 (2004): 489-573.

Ravitch, Frank S., "Locke v. Davey and the Lose-Lose Scenario: What Davey Could Have Said, But Didn't," *Tulsa Law Review* 40 (2004): 55-70.

Rogers, Melissa "Federal Funding and Religion-based Employment Decisions," in *Sanctioning Religion? Politics, Law, and Faith-based Public Services* (edited by David K Ryden and Jeffrey Polet, (Boulder, Colo.: Lynne Reinner Publishers 2005).

Saperstein, David, "Public Accountability and Faith-Based Organizations: A Problem Best Avoided," *Harvard Law Review* 116 (2003): 1353-1396.

Underkuffler, Laura, "'Discrimination' on the Basis of Religion: An Examination of Attempted Value Neutrality in Employment, *William and Mary Law Review* 30 (1989): 581-625.

Underkuffler, Laura, "Vouchers and Beyond: The Individual as Causative Agent in Establishment Clause Jurisprudence," *Indiana Law Journal* 75 (2000): 167-191.

Van Alstyne, William W., "What is 'an Establishment of Religion'"? *North Carolina Law Review* 65 (1987): 909-916.

Walzer, Michael, "Drawing the Line: Religion and Politics," *Utah Law Review* (1999): 619-638.

Wexler, Jay, "Darwin, Design, and Disestablishment: Teaching the Evolution Controversy in Public Schools," *Vanderbilt University Law Review* 56 (2003): 751-855.

Wexler, Jay, "Preparing for the Clothed Public Square: Teaching About Religion, Civic Education, and the Constitution," *William and Mary Law Review* 43 (2002): 1159-1263.

### Free Exercise, Religious Accommodation, and Church Autonomy

Berg, Thomas, "The Voluntary Principle and Church Autonomy: Then and Now" *B.Y.U. Law Review* (2004): 1593-1615.

Brownstein, Alan E., "Justifying Free Exercise Rights," *University of St. Thomas Law Journal* 1 (2003): 504-548.

Brownstein, Alan E., "Taking Free Exercise Rights Seriously," *Case Western Reserve Law Review* 57 (2006): 55-146.

Chopko, Mark E., "Continuing the Lord's Work and Healing His People: A Reply to Professors Lupu and Tuttle, *B.Y.U. Law Review* (2004): 1897-1920.

Garnett, Richard W., "A Quiet Faith? Taxes, Politics, and the Privatization of Religion," *Boston College Law Review* 42 (2001): 771-803.

Gedicks, Frederick Mark, "Towards a Defensible Free Exercise Doctrine," *George Washington Law Review* 68 (2000): 925-952.

Laycock, Douglas, "Religious Liberty as Liberty," *Journal of Contemporary Legal Issues* (1996): 313-356.

Laycock, Douglas, "The Remnants of Free Exercise," *Supreme Court Review* (1990): 1-68.

Laycock, Douglas, "Toward a General Theory of the Religion Clauses: The Case of Church Labor Relations and the Right to Church Autonomy," *Columbia Law Review* 81 (1981): 1373-1417.

Lupu, Ira C., "The Trouble with Accommodation," *George Washington Law Review* 60 (1992): 743-781.

Lupu, Ira C., "Where Rights Begin: The Problem of Burdens on the Free Exercise of Religion," *Harvard Law Review* 102 (1989) 933-990.

Lupu, Ira C. and Robert W. Tuttle, "Sexual Misconduct and Ecclesiastical Immunity," *B.Y.U. Law Review* (2004): 1789-1896.

Marshall, William P., "The Case Against the Constitutionally Compelled Free Exercise Exemption," *Case Western Reserve Law Review* 40 (1990): 357-412.

Marshall, William P., "In Defense of Smith and Free Exercise Revisionism," *University of Chicago Law Review* 58 (1991): 308-328.

McConnell, Michael W., "Accommodation of Religion: An Update and a Response to the Critics," *George Washington Law Review* 60 (1992): 685-742.

McConnell, Michael W., "Free Exercise Revisionism and the Smith Decision," *University of Chicago Law Review* 57 (1990): 1109-1153.

Rogers, Melissa and Alan Brownstein, "The Religious Freedom Restoration Act," in *Major Acts of Congress* (New York: Macmillan, 2003).

Smith, Steven D., "The Rise and Fall of Religious Freedom in Constitutional Discourse," *University of Pennsylvania Law Review* 140 (1991): 149-240.

Volokh, Eugene, "A Common Law Model for Religious Exemptions," *U.C.L.A. Law Review* 46 (1999): 1465-1566.

# INDEX